Register of

Qualified Huguenot Ancestors

of

The National Huguenot Society

Fifth Edition
2012

Compiled by
Jeannine Sheldon Kallal
Registrar General, 2003-2009

THE NATIONAL HUGUENOT SOCIETY, INC.

Published by The National Huguenot Society, Inc.

Library of Congress Control Number : 2012949327
ISBN #978-0-9883154-0-2

Compiled by Jeannine Sheldon Kallal
Indexed by Nancy Wright Brennan
Cover Design by Leslie Watson Tomlinson
Edited by Janice Murphy Lorenz, Esq.

Printed in the United States of America by Lightning Source

The Huguenot Cross consists of an open four-petalled Lily of France, and the petals thereby form a Maltese Cross. The four petals signify the Four Gospels. Each arm or petal, at the periphery, has two rounded points at the corners. These eight points are regarded as signifying the Eight Beatitudes. The four petals are joined together by four *fleurs-de-lis*, regarded as signifying the Mother Country of France, each of which bears a rounded point distally. The twelve rounded points described in the four petals and the four *fleurs-de-lis* signify the Twelve Apostles. A heart-shaped open space is formed between each *fleur-de-lis* and the arms of the two petals with which it is joined, suggesting the seal of the great French Reformer John Calvin. A pendant dove is suspended from the lower central petal by a ring of gold, signifying the Church under the Cross. In times of persecution, a teardrop supplanted the dove. The Languedoc Cross was discovered by Rev. Andrew Mailhet in Languedoc and dates from the 18th century.

την πίστη που μια για πάντα δοθείσα τοις αγίοις

Semel traditae sanctis fidei

Pour la foi que a été donnée aux saints une fois pour toutes

Jude.3 – "for the faith which was once for all delivered unto the saints"

FOREWORD

The *Register of Qualified Huguenot Ancestors of The National Huguenot Society, Fifth Edition 2012* identifies more than 600 Huguenot ancestors, descent from whom is proof of qualification for membership in The National Huguenot Society. The most up-to-date and comprehensive reference source for Huguenot research currently available in America, its highlights include:

- Brings each approved ancestor "to life" through a brief biographical sketch which reaches back into French and American history and culture
- Identifies two or more generations of each ancestors' descendants
- Provides a biographical sketch of descendants' lives
- Identifies related Huguenot families
- Recommends areas of further research needed to fill existing gaps in genealogical proof
- Cites to the source material from which the data was derived
- Fascinating factoids or valuable genealogical and biographical insights on every page

Listing the proven ancestors whose descendants have joined The National Huguenot Society over the years, the *Register of Qualified Huguenot Ancestors of The National Huguenot Society, Fifth Edition 2012* is more than a mere reference book; it is potentially *the* go-to source of Huguenot genealogical data available today in America. An extraordinary level of detail is presented in a readily accessible manner, and names are indexed. Genealogists, historians, potential members seeking proofs, current members seeking supplemental ancestors, researchers, and anyone else interested in French and American history and culture should consult this treasure trove of Huguenot data.

Therefore, it is with great honor and pleasure that this President General has had the honor of guiding the *Register of Qualified Huguenot Ancestors of The National Huguenot Society, Fifth Edition 2012* to publication. Our profound thanks are extended to the compiler, Jeannine Kallal, to Honorary President General Barbara MacManus, who authorized its preparation during her first administration as President General, and to our current Registrar General, Nancy Wright Brennan, who prepared the Index in such a way that researchers may easily research specific ancestors, their descendants, and potentially related families. We must also thank all of those who, since the 1995 edition, have provided The National Huguenot Society with information which clarified missing or incomplete information about potential Huguenot ancestors, and we urge you to continue assisting us in refining our data.

The National Huguenot Society celebrates the captivating story of the Huguenots and of Franco-American history and culture which began in 1520 and which continues today. We hope that the *Register of Qualified Huguenot Ancestors of The National Huguenot Society, Fifth Edition 2012*, will provide you with the information you seek, and lead you to join us in honoring Huguenots and their impact upon world history.

In Huguenot Faith From the Heart,

Janice Murphy Lorenz, Esq.
President General, 2011-2013

INTRODUCTION

You will notice a great many changes in this edition of the *Register of Qualified Huguenot Ancestors.* Of course, many new ancestors have been proven, which is good news, but several others have been dropped due to lack of proof that they were, in fact, Huguenots. The standards for verification have been tightened; the burden of proof is on the applicant when proving a new ancestor or "resurrecting" one who has been dropped. The phrase you need to keep in mind is the time frame: **10 Dec 1520 - 28 Nov 1787.** The ancestor must have been a Huguenot during that time period. The term "Huguenot" implies someone of French heritage, since the word was coined for those French citizens who resisted the efforts of their government to convert them to Catholicism. At times the link back to France can't be made but it is necessary that the ancestor be proven as being a **Huguenot**, regardless of origin. The latter begs the question, "what is a Huguenot?"

The word "Huguenot" was once a term of reproach. The French Protestants were called many names – *hérétiques (heretics)* to their bitterest enemies, *prétendants (false claimants)*, *réformistes (reformists),* or radicals. Sometimes they were lumped with other Protestants, i.e., stubborn recalcitrants! The word "Huguenot" has stymied many as to its exact derivation. Regardless of its etymology, the meaning is clear, the Huguenots were men and women who wanted a choice and they started to raise their voices c. 1520.

There are "gray" areas - families who lived in areas that are now Belgium, Holland, or Italy, but profess to being of French heritage. Some of them were in these areas for generations and their connection to France is pretty distant. There are the Walloon families who lived in Holland for generations, the Vaudois/Waldense families who lived in the Piedmont/Savoy area, much of which later became part of Italy. Some of these families were accepted years ago and that has led to the assumption that they were Huguenot, which, in some cases, is incorrect. The exact location of national boundaries was subject to change. Nowadays you know when you have crossed a border or a state line – signs tell you so, but that was not the case in earlier times.

Several entries have a new ancestor at the top of the family's entry. The parents or grandparents have been proven and the lineage increased in length which will, hopefully, open up more opportunities for membership. In several entries, where there was a marriage between Huguenot families – the second name is underlined. So you can go to the page where that 2nd family is and find additional information as well as a supplemental ancestor! There are many entries where a Huguenot name appears but the connection to the family of that name has not yet been made. Any children are listed under the entry for the husband as they bore his name. So if both parents were Huguenots and both had a listing, it has been combined to save space and avoid redundancy. A separate entry for the wife of a Huguenot is made only if information was found that gave documentation past her dates of birth and death, and/or the names of her parents, otherwise her entry is only with her husband. Also, fathers and sons have been reunited. For example, there have been separate listings for Chrétien du Bois and his son Louis (b. 1627). Louis is now back with Dad. Most of this happened because the ancestors were proven at different times and the connection was not made. Maiden names of wives are given, in parentheses, except for the Dutch women. They seemed to retain their maiden names, so they are entered differently. In many cases, there were children who died young or died without issue. They are included mainly to account for all the children. If you know that your ancestor had 12 children and only 8 are accounted for, you might wonder where the other 4 are and if they had been given any thought.

This has been a monumental job. Literally, thousands of pages of documentation were studied; previous *Registers* and *Updates* have been re-read. Special thanks are due to Grace Rice, who served as Registrar General for a term and was later the Society's Archivist. She went through the files and made lists before they were sent to me – what a help! She also "purged" the files of duplicate material. I sincerely appreciate all the time and effort that she expended on behalf of our Society. More recently, Registrar General Nancy Brennan, has been very helpful in finding additional documentation where the information the Society had was not sufficient. She also did the indexing which was a huge job. So, thank you, Nancy! Another pair of helping hands has come from Ann Woodlief, National Librarian, Huguenot Society of Manakin, who has been a great resource for those Huguenots who emigrated to Virginia. It hasn't taken quite a "village" but there have been many busy volunteers. I thank all of them for their assistance and encouragement.

Cameron Allen's articles (in *TAG*) containing French church records have provided much needed proof. The Newberry Library in Chicago has become my "home away from home."

Misspellings in the 1995 edition, particularly of place names, have been corrected and I have also tried to give the reader some context as to where some of the towns were. At times, the places no longer exist or there has been a change of name and a "guesstimate" was made. Additionally, French records were used whenever possible. In the past, they were not always used, leading to erroneous conclusions. Since the French records are a primary source, they have proven invaluable for straightening out some of the information. Happily, I am a linguist, so it was a fun project for me! I have used the French spellings, including diacritical marks, wherever possible. There are a lot of problems with the names of emigrants to a country where the language is different. Misspellings occur due to a lack of familiarity of foreign languages; attempts to spell phonetically with varying degrees of success; illiteracy on one or both sides; the immigrants were forced to accept anglicized versions of spelling and pronunciation; prejudice; some immigrants wanted to hide their origins; a desire to "fit in" their new country, etc. French is not a language which can be transcribed phonetically without knowledge of the language: too many silent letters and diacritical marks which can change the pronunciation. Accent marks affect both pronunciation and meaning. One author referred to the misspellings as "orthographical ignorance" which pretty well sums it up. In reading through all the documentation, it is clear that the documentation that was written in French was either not used or not translated correctly. One ancestor is supposed to have been in Virginia but the French records make it clear that he died in England before the events in Virginia that were attributed to him.

Events have been listed in chronological order wherever possible. Some "personal" comments have been inserted. Some of these ancestors were very interesting and it seems only right to mention that! Children are listed in the "best" order possible – birth order is often pretty much hit and miss. Names of parents, where known, have been included which, hopefully, will give the researcher some more lines to pursue. Some of the entries have gotten quite long. To save space, children have been "bunched" if not a lot is known about them. Please notice the small number to the upper right of a name. That number indicates the generation to which he/she belongs. It can be confusing but that number should help you understand who's who.

As always, corrections/comments are welcome. Some of you are going to be delighted and others will think your ancestor's entry is incorrect. Any work is only as good as the material presented. At times, the documentation was ambiguous or contradictory and the "best" available data has been used. If you have additional information that would prove or clarify a statement, please do not hesitate to send it – if it is true, that information will be published in future *Updates*. The National Huguenot Society is as anxious as any of you to obtain the most accurate information. Even with the care taken while writing this and all the proof-reading, errors will happen. Rest assured, they are not intentional. Over the years, some ancestors were dropped from the list of qualified Huguenot ancestors because there was not sufficient proof that the ancestor was a Huguenot. Some of them have been reinstated, others remain dropped and still others have since been dropped. I only included those ancestors for which the National Huguenot Society has files. Unfortunately, for several of the ancestors previously approved, there were no files. I felt I could not enter information that I was not able to read and evaluate.

Access to records is becoming somewhat easier and I encourage you to seek the best sources possible. Family histories are not always the best source unless they are properly documented. Just because someone says it's so, doesn't make it so. Very often a misstatement shows up in one book and is then repeated in following books, because the authors did not seek out the original documents. There are many examples of this. One good one seems to show that repetition is the sincerest form of flattery, combined with an ignorance of French: Isaac Chappelier had a son Étienne, b. 9 Aug 1702 – but all the family histories say he was a daughter despite the fact that the record from the French Church on Threadneedle St, London, clearly says the child was a *fils*, which is a son. Also Étienne is the French form of Stephen, which certainly sounds male!

A word about surnames. Centuries ago, there were no surnames. People identified themselves as John the tailor, John of/from London, John the Elder, John, son of John, etc. When surnames started to be used, occupations such as butcher, baker, tailor, carpenter often became surnames. John, son of John, became John Johnson. In French, Jean de Paris, simply meant "John of/from Paris" and did not imply noble lineage as some think. Many of the names of our ancestors had multiple spellings due to lack of education, mistranslation, regional differences, etc. In most cases, the word "de" follows the given name of the ancestor in the listing, per the Huguenot Society of London. Occasionally, "d'" is used because it preceded a vowel; for example, "D'Aubigné." When that name changed to Dabney, the d' was absorbed into the name.

At times, different spellings are used for the same name. A good example is the French name for Stephen. At times it is Estienne and others Étienne. Estienne is the older form. When the "s" was dropped, an accent was added to the first "e" which indicates a "missing" letter. Anthoine became Antoine (Anthony) – since the "h" was silent, there was no point! The fourth ship to Virginia was named the *Nasseau* or the *Nassau* – take your pick! Several differing points of view on that but it would seem that the first spelling is the correct one.

What is "missing?" There is no list of dropped or alleged Huguenots. If the name is not in this edition of *The Register,* he or she has been dropped due to lack of proof, inadequate documentation or documentation that was so contradictory it was impossible to determine what was true and what was not, usually due to poor source material. In a couple cases, since there was no record of descendants, an entry would have been pointless. A current list of all approved Huguenot ancestors is on the National Huguenot Society website. If you can re-establish an ancestor with new documentation, please do so. The information will be evaluated and, if accepted, the ancestor(s) will be added to that list which will be updated on a regular basis.

Please take the time to read the following pages which deal with how the entries are alphabetized and what abbreviations are used. It will facilitate finding the entry you want. In cases where there were multiple spellings of the surname, most of the entries are filed under what is believed to have been the original spelling. Also there is information re geographical entries as well as a list of important dates in the history of the Huguenots.

I wish all of you success in tracing your Huguenot roots.

En la foi,
Jeannine Sheldon Kallal
Registrar General, 2003-2009

How to use this publication:

The following rules are used for alphabetizing names, per the Huguenot Society of London:

> surnames preceded by d' or de, e.g., d'Aubigné will be listed under "A"; de Pré under "P"
> surnames preceded by des or du, e.g., Des Carrières, DuMoulin, under "D"
> surnames preceded by la or le, e.g., La Caux, Le Bas under "L"
> surnames preceded by de la, e.g., de la Chevallerie, under "L"
> surnames preceded by van, e.g. van Notten, under "N"

Abbreviations:

a	*ante*, before
BEL	Belgium (became a country in 1830; formed from Flanders)
bro/o	brother of
c	*circa*, about
ch	child/children; church
ch/o	child or children of
d/o	daughter of
ENG	England
FL	Flanders
FR	France
GER	Germany
grd/o	granddaughter of
grs/o	grandson of
HOL	Holland; actually the nation is the Netherlands; Holland is a former countship, a region in the western part of the Netherlands, where most of the Huguenots went. It was easier just to use the term HOL
HRE	Holy Roman Empire
IRE	Ireland
MM	Monthly Meeting (Quaker)
NYC	New York City
p	*post*, after
Pct	precinct
SCOT	Scotland
sis/o	sister of
s/o	son of
SWE	Sweden
SWI	Switzerland
US	United States
w/	with
wid/o	widow of

Further Explanations:

ß = GER for ss

Dit = called, also known as; second name is often an inherited nickname & after several generations it becomes the surname; sometimes refers to a place name in FR, an humorous nickname, an occupation, the name of the land or farm where the person lived

In Europe, places come and go; they are absorbed, they change names; they become parts of different countries; wars, treaties change borders; FR is no exception:

Alsace – 1639, it was captured by FR; in 1648, most of Alsace was given to FR in the Treaty of Westphalia; it was annexed in the 17th cent by Louis XIII & XIV and became a province of FR; Strasbourg, its capital, became a Protestant city in 1523; in the 19th & 20th centuries, Alsace changed hands 4 x in 75 yrs.

Angoumois – became a county in 9th century; region and former province in s.w. FR, now Charente Dépt; Angoulême is its historic capital and chief city.

Aunis – an old province/*pays*, bounded on the north by Poitou, on the west by the Atlantic and on the south and east by Saintonge; principal town Châtelaillon and later La Rochelle; now the n.w. part of Charente-Inférieure Dépt.

Flanders – orig. meant Bruges and neighborhood, but in the 8th & 9th centuries, it extended to the coast region from Calais to the Scheldt; in the middle ages, this was div. into 2 parts, one looking to Bruges, the other to Ghent; now 2 prov in BEL, West and East Flanders; the former borders the North Sea & extends from the French to the Dutch frontier, c. 40 mi, capital Bruges; E. FL lies east and n.e. of the western prov & extends n. to nr Antwerp; orig FL also contained the s. part of Zeeland and much of n.e. FR; the countships of FL and Hainaut were united c. 1191; 1322, under Louis of Nevers, FL was reduced to the status of a FR prov – much warring; the Burgundian dynasty acquired the countship and despite continuing revolts, FL never regained its independence; in 1633, it came under Spanish rule; 1648 – Philip IV, Dutch FL (n.w. portion of FL) to the United Provinces; by a succession of treaties in the mid-late 17th cent (1659, 1668, 1679), a lg. slice of the s. part of FL became FR terr. and was known as FR Flanders.

French borders – at the beginning of the 16th century the northern and eastern borders were not as they are today. The east central border was about 40 miles from the Swiss cantons and 80 miles from the Rhine. Calais, Arras, Cambrai and Lille were outside France. The provinces of Dauphiné & Provence extended into the Piedmont and Savoy in Italy.

Guienne (FR) = originally it + Gascogne formed the duchy of Aquitaine; it no longer exists, *per se*; area now referred to as Guyenne.

Hanau, GER - 25 km. e. of Frankfurt; Walloons from HOL went there at the end of 16th cent.

Hainaut – now the Hainaut Prov. of BEL & s. part of Nord Dépt. – chief cities Mons, Cambrai, Charleroi

Karlsruhe - capital of the *Land* of Baden, 33 mi s.w. of Heidelberg, 30 mi w.n.w. of Stuttgart

Lorraine – was reunited to the French crown in 1766; Lorraine was invaded by Germans in the 5th century; however, it preserved its Latin-speaking pop. except in the n.e. part of the prov. where German barbarians were established; the land was disputed bet FR and the Germanic HRE

Manakintown – church, "headquarters" in what is now Powhatan Co, VA; FR lands were in Henrico & Powhatan. Goochland Co, is across the river and when the great "land grab" began in the 1720's people went there because there wasn't enough room at Manakin.

Montbéliard – capital of an arrondisement in Dépt. of Doubs, Franche-Comté, in e. FR; it was added to Lorraine in 843 by the Treaty of Verdun; in the 11th century, capital of a countship, which formed part of the second kingdom of Burgundy & later of the German Empire, named Mömpelgard; in 1397 it passed to the house of Würtemburg till 1793; it was a Protestant enclave into 1793; in 1793 it was annexed to FR

Palatinate/*Pfalz* – Speyer was the capital; lying west of the Rhine, excluding the Saar region, 2125 sq. miles; bounded on the east by the Rhine, separated from Baden on the south Bas-Rhin Dépt. of FR, west of the Saar and parts of Prussia Rhine; on the north by Hesse

Pays de l'Alloeu – in n.e. FR, between what is now Artois and Flanders

Purysburg – settlement in SC, often written Purrysburg

Saintonge, Saintes was its chief city; up to 1789, some govt. with Angoumois; old prov. of Duchy of Aquitaine; today Charente (Charente-Maritime)

Témoingage - certificate issued by the emigré's church, proving his/her true faith

Vaudois/Waldenses – followers of Peter Waldo, a 12th century religious reformer. They were along the Durance River in Provence before the persecutions began.

Wyoming Valley, PA – roughly present day counties of Lackawanna, Luzerne & Wyoming

Important Huguenot Dates

1512	Jacques LeFèvre/Faber of Étaples pub. his *Santi Pauli Epistolae xiv… cum commentariis*, which enunciates the cardinal doctrine of reform - justification by faith; 1523, he translated the New Testament into French
31 Oct 1517	Martin Luther nailed his *95 Theses* on the door of the Castle Church at Wittenberg, Germany
10 Dec 1520	Luther publicly burned the papal bull demanding that he recant or face excommunication
1525	Jacques Pavannes, the hermit of Livry, and shortly afterwards, Louis de Berquin, were the 1st martyrs who were burned at the stake
18 Oct 1534	Placards were posted in Paris which criticized the Mass
29 Jan 1535	A General Edict was published urging extermination of heretics (Huguenots); courts of justice (*Chambres ardentes*) were formed for trials of heretics - they were abolished in 1682
16 Jul 1535	François I ended the persecution of Lutherans (the term then used for all Protestants), and allowed exiles to return with the proviso that they had 6 months in which to accept Catholicism
c. 1536	John Cauvin/Calvin wrote *Institutes of the Christian Religion.* It was 1st written in Latin, later in French
1538	King François I exhorted the *Parlements* to be more vigorous in heretic-hunting

1538	The 1st French Protestant church was founded at Strasbourg with a congregation of 1,500 refugees; John Cauvin/Calvin became its pastor
1543	The Sorbonne equipped prosecutors with a confession of the Catholic faith so that heretics could be distinguished from the faithful; censorship returned and an index of forbidden books was issued
1546	The 1st French Protestant community was founded at Meaux, which became an important Protestant center
1556	A Protestant Church was founded at Paris and, despite persecution, the reformers increased in numbers.
1558	At Poitiers, it was decided that all the Prot. Churches in FR should formulate, by common accord, a confession of faith and ecclesiastical discipline; the Synod of 1559 was convened for that purpose.
25 May 1559	First Synod of the French Reformed Church in Paris - 15 churches were represented; 2 yrs. later, 2,150 churches were represented.
1562-1580	Seven religious wars were fought.
Jan 1562	Edict issued recognizing the Huguenot Church but it said that they had to worship outside of towns and in the country, so there was a semblance of religious freedom
1 Mar 1562	Vassy Affair/Slaughter of Vassy, Champagne, where a number of Huguenots, who had assembled in a barn for worship, were killed by the de Guise faction
11 Apr 1562	Huguenot leaders & Condé signed the manifesto which stated that they were forced to take up arms against the Crown for liberty of conscience, on behalf of the persecuted saints; thus began the struggle between *La Cause* (The Cause) & *La Sainte Ligue* (the Holy League)
1 May 1562	First pilgrimage by Huguenots to North America, arr. St. John's River, FL
24 Aug 1572	St. Bathélemi/Bartholomew's Massacre – where de Coligny & all the leading Huguenots were slain; the killing of Huguenots spread from Paris to the rest of France and 1000's were killed
1 Aug 1589	Henri de Navarre became Henri IV, *de facto* King of France, but it took 10 yrs. to secure his throne; after years of struggle, he finally had to become Catholic – as he so famously said, "Paris is worth a mass"
13 Apr 1598	Edict of Nantes by Henri IV, granting religious & civil liberty to the Huguenots.
28 Oct 1628	Siege of La Rochelle ended with the surrender of last Huguenot stronghold in France
1683-1686	*Les dragonnades* – forcible conversions
18 Oct 1685	Revocation of the Edict by Louis XIV, persecutions followed; during the period following the revocation, France lost more than 400,000 of its inhabitants
28 Nov 1787	Promulgation of the Edict of Nantes; Protestants were finally able to worship without fear of retribution

France, c. 1650

A

AGÉ/AGEE/OAGE, Mathieu

b. c. 1670, nr. Nantes, FR, s/o Antoine & Judith (Chastain) Agé; Judith was the d/o Jean François & Françoise Jeanne (Reno/Regnault/Renaut, d/o Charles Renaut) Chastain

[given the dates of his marr & poss death, his assumed birth date seems a bit early]

1688 - fled FR to NETH, then to ENG or IRE

bet 1690-1701 - emigrated to VA on 1 of the 1st 5 ships

Apr/May 1705 – naturalized in Manakintown, VA

1710 - on 1st tithable list for King William Parish

m. c. 1714 VA, Ann Godwin/Gaudovin, d/o Isaac & Ann (Pleasant) Gandovin

23 Mar 1715 – issued Patent #789 - 221 acres; he had extensive land holdings; one FR tract on the James River contained 221 acres + he had 1100 acres s. of the FR territory in Powhatan Co; had 3 patents of 400, 400 and 300 acres

c. 1755- to Albemarle Co, VA – that part that became Buckingham Co. in 1761; he acquired 2 patents there – one of 1280 acres and the other of 400 acres

d. p. 1761 – a. 1773, prob. Buckingham Co, VA; some records say c. 1751, but land records belie that date; in Mar 1761 an indenture between Mathieu and his son James was recorded in Albemarle Co, VA

CHILDREN:

Anthony[2], b. c. 1719, VA; m/1, Nancy Jane Beiren/Berrin/Binn(i)on/Binyon, m/2, Christian Worley; total of **12 ch**; he d. p. 1785 VA, prob. Bedford Co, VA

Judith[2], b. c. 1720; m. Noah Austin; **no issue**

Isaac[2], b. c. 1722; m/1, Rosa Frances Beiren/Berrin/Binnon, m/2, Mary Ann Lucadou, d/o Peter Anthony & Elizabeth (X) Lucadou - **no issue**

James[2], b. c. 1724/5, nr. Five Forks, Manakintown, VA; m. 1746/7, Marie Fauré/Mary (Elizabeth ?) Ford (2 Sep 1703, VA-1821), d/o James Ford/Jacques Fauré & Ann Bondurant, grd/o Jean Pierre Bondurant and Pierre Fauré – **6 sons, 6 daus**; Rev. War soldier in the 7th VA Regt.; he d. 1820/1 nr. present Dillwyn, Buckingham Co, VA

REF: CROWE, Maude, *Descendants from First Families of VA & MD 1620-1670* (1928); AGEE, Louis N., *The Agee Register: A Genealogical Record of the Descendants of Mathieu Agee, a Huguenot Refugee to VA* (Baltimore 1982); *The Huguenot,* Publication #5 (1931); AGEE, P.M., *A Record of the Agee Family* (Independence, MO 1937); CABELL, Priscilla Harriss, *Turff & Twigg, Vol. I, The French Lands* (Richmond, 1988).

ALLAIRE, Alexandre

bp. 9 Jan 1660, La Rochelle, FR, s/o Pierre* & his 2nd wife Jeanne (Godeffroy/Godefroi) Allaire of La Rochelle; had brothers Antoine (whose son Louis emig to RI, then Boston) and Jean who m. Jeanne Bernon, sis/o Gabriel Bernon

fled FR to West Indies

m. c. 1686, prob. St. Christopher, West Indies, Jeanne Doens/Docus (b. c. 1665)

1686 - emigrated to NY, where he was one of the founders of New Rochelle in Westchester Co; was an elder in the New Rochelle FR Ch

19 Aug 1687 – naturalized

by 1693 - a permanent resident of New Rochelle; he was a cooper

d. intestate bet 2 Apr 1727-31-Jan 1735, New Rochelle, NY

CHILDREN:

Jeanne[2], b. c. 1687, prob. NYC; m. a. 2 Dec 1708, André Fresneau; she d. a. 17 Jun 1710; **no issue**

Catherine[2], b. c. 1689; m. as his 2nd wife, Pierre Barberie, s/o Jean Barberie; she d. bet 30 Oct 1760 - 25 Sep 1765; **no issue**

Susan[2], b. c. 1691; m. c. 1708, Jean Bourgnet; she d. a. 4 Jan 1709; **no issue**

Henriette[2], b. c. 1693, New Rochelle, NY

Alexander[2], b. c. 1695, d. young

Benjamin[2], b. c. 1696; m. 1729, Rachel Boice/Boyce of Antigua; **7 ch**

Pierre/ Peter[2], b. c. 1699, prob. New Rochelle; m. a. 5 Apr 1740, Marie/Mary Garland; he d. a. 14 Dec 1781; ch **Pierre**[3], **Mary**[3]

Alexander[2], b. c. 1702, New Rochelle; m/1, a. 1727, Hester/Esther Clatworthy (d. c. 1746, d/o John and Anna (Luerson) Clatworthy; m/2, 30 May 1747, Marie (Uytendaele) Lispenard (31 Dec 1711, St. Thomas-6 Jan 1805, prob. Greenburgh, NY), d/o Johannes and Maria (leBreton) Uytendaele, widow of Anthony Lispenard; Alexander d. 1782

> CHILDREN, m/1:
>
> **Catherine**[3]
>
> **Esther**[3] (bp. 28 Jun 1730, Dutch Ch, NYC)
>
> **Jean**[3]
>
> **Simon**[3]
>
> CHILDREN, m/2:
>
> **Sarah**[4], m. John Bertine, a descendant of Pierre Bertine
>
> **Peter**[3]
>
> **Uytendaele**[3]
>
> **Anthony**[3]

Philippe[2], b. 21 Aug, bp. 5 Sep 1705; d. young

Philippe[2], b. 24 Feb 1707/8, bp. 18 Apr 1708

André/Andrew[2], b. c. 1709, New Rochelle; m. Elizabeth Barberie, d/o Pierre & Susanne (Lambert) Barberie; he d. a. 29 May 1753 wp; poss. bur. in the Allaire graveyard in New Rochelle; 1 dau **Elizabeth**[3], b. posthumously

*Pierre, b. c. 1615, La Rochelle, s/o Pierre (b. c. 1590) & Jeanne (Brochelide) Allaire; m/1 a. 30 May 1639, Marie Levesque who d. by 29 Sep 1652 – 2 ch; Pierre m/2 16 Jul 1653 La Rochelle, Jeanne Godeffroy; Pierre d. 14 May 1680; Alexandre's grfa Pierre and Antoine Allaire, the grgrfa of Louis Allaire were brothers. Antoine's wife was Ester Brochelide, poss. a sister of Jeanne.

REF: BOLTON, Robert, *History of Westchester Co, NY*, Vol. 1, pp. 676-78 (NY, 1881); ALLAIRE, Violette, *Les familles Allaire et Dallaire d'Amérique* (Québec, 24 Jun 1962); FORBES, Jeanne A., *Records of the Town of New Rochelle, 1699-1828; The Huguenot Historian* (1980-82); HILL, Glenna See, "The Allaire Family of New Rochelle, France and Westchester Co, NY" serialized in *The NYGBR,* Vol. 125, #3 (Jul 1994), #4 (Oct 1994), Vol. 126, #1 an 1995), #2 (Apr 1995), #3 (Jul 1995), #4 (Oct 1995); BAIRD, Charles W., *History of the Huguenot Emigration to America*, Vol. II, pp. 139-40 (Baltimore, MD,1973); NYGBS, *Baptisms from 1639 to 1730 in the Reformed Dutch Church, NY*, edited by EVANS, Thomas Grier (NY, 1901).

ALLÉE/ALLEY/ALIÉE/ALYER/ALYEA/d'AILLY, Nicolas

b. c. 1640, surname d/Ailly

m. c. 1663, XX ,a widow surnamed Tybout/Tiebout– first name and maiden name unknown; said to have been of a noble family who disapproved of her 1st marr, also to a Huguenot

c. 1680 - left FR, went to NETH, then to ENG on the *Faith*

c. 1682 - arr in New Amsterdam; later to Hackensack, NJ

d. c. 1700, NJ

CHILDREN:

Jan/John[2], b. c. 1665, Artois Prov., FR (now in the Pas-de-Calais Dépt.); m/1, c. 1685, Susanne (Le Roux/LaRue) Hendricks (b. 9 Oct 1658, prob. Mannheim, GER-c.1708), wid/o Thomas/ Theunis Hendricke Helling, d/o Pierre & Jeanne (Guérin) LeRoux; m/2, p. 23 Sep 1709, Maritje DeGrave, wid/o of Andries Tibout and of Albert Terhuyse/Terhune, banns dated at Hackensack, NJ, not in husband's will of 1718; 22 Sep 1694, joined Dutch Ch in Hackensack; c.1706 - moved to DE, where he had purchased land, a.1687; he d. a.16 Mar 1718, wp, Kent Co, DE; will mentions sons Peter & Abraham, Johanus (*sic*), Hannah and Marry (*sic*), Jacob, Jane (wife of Simon Van Winkel), Susanna (wife of John Vangasco), Elizabeth, Rachel; surname **ALIÉE**

CHILDREN, m/1 (all b. Hackensack, surname **ALYEA**):

Jannetje/Jane[3], b. 12 Apr 1685; m/1, 18 Oct 1707, Steven Albertse Van Voorhees; m/2, 27 May 1710, Simon Jacobson Van Winkle, who d. a. 23 Jan 1752, wp, Kent Co, DE – will names wife Jane, sons **Jacob**[4], **John**[4], **Simon**[4], dau **Susannah**[4] Talbort, grson Simon Draughton; she d. p. 17 Dec 1748 (husband's will written), prob. DE

Pieter/Peter[3], b. c. 1688; m. 6 Apr 1716, Hackensack, Margrietje Albertse Van Voorhees, d/o Albert Stevense Van Voorhees & Elena Van der Schuren; Jan had willed ½ of his estate to Peter if the latter would settle in DE; Peter wished to stay in NJ and gave his portion to his bro Abraham; he d. 1760; **8 ch**

Abraham[3], b. 1690; m. Mary Raymond; his home, built 1753 at Bombay Hook (s.e. of Smyrna), is now an historical site; he d. a. 8 May 1770 wp; will names wife Mary, sons **John**[4] & **Jonathan**[4], daus **Mary**[4] Carpenter **Sabrah**[4] Tilton, son-in-law Thomas Tilton, gr son Abraham (s/o Jonathan), Abraham (s/o John), grch/o Mary Carpenter by 1st husband Henry Rothwell, grch Isaac, Abraham, Jacob, Mary – ch/o dec. son **Abraham**[4]

Johannes/John[3], b. c. 1692; m. Gertrude X; he d. a. 22 Mar 1726/7, wp, Kent Co, DE; **no issue**

Susanna[3], bp. 10 Mar 1694, Ref Ch, Hackensack; m/1, 14 Apr 1714, Andries Tibout; m/2, p. 17 Apr 1715 (date of banns), Jan Janse Van Geste; m/3, Edward Long

Jacobus/Jacob[3], bp. 12 Jun 1699, Hackensack; m. DE, XX; he d. p.16 Sep1766, wd – a. 13 Oct 1766, wp, Kent Co, DE; a minor in 1718; will mentions a wife but not by name, son **John, Jr.**[4], dau **Rebecca**[4] Killen, wife of William Killen, grdaus Elizabeth & Mary, daus/o William & Rebecca Killen

Hannah/Ann[3], b. 1702; m. 1726, DE, John Hawkins who d. a. 23 Nov 1748, wp, Kent Co, DE; will mentions wife but not by name; sons **John**[4], **Thomas**[4], **Arnal**[4], **Abraham**[4], dau **Susanna**[4] + other unnamed daus

Maritie/Mary[3], bp. 5 Nov 1704, Hackensack; m. 20 Nov 1726, William Cahoon who d. a. 11 May 1774, wp, Kent Co, DE; will names wife Mary, sons **Thomas**[4], **Charles**[4], **William**[4], **Mark**[4], daus **Elizabeth**[4], **Rachel**[4], **Jean**[4] & **Nancy**[4]; grson John Edwards

Elizabeth[3], bp. c. 1706; m. Jeunetze Alger; listed as a minor in 1718

Rachel[3], bp. c. 1708; m/1, Capt. James Tybout, d. a. 19 May 1743, adm, there was a further adm, 27 May 1746; m/2, Nicholas Van Dyke; Rachel was a minor in 1718

Rachel[2], b. c. 1670; m. Nicholas Van Dyke

NOTE: The DE branch used Allée; the NJ branch, Aliee Alyea; many of the changes in the name were the result of spellings in the church records of Hackensack and Schraalenberg, NJ

REF: Kent Co, DE Will Book D, Vol.1, John Alley's will; *The Genealogical Magazine of NJ,* Vol. 20, #2 (Apr 1946); *Alyea Family;* ALLEE, W. Arthur, *Allée/Alyer Genealogy* (Houston, 1991, 2 vol); *The Huguenot Historian,* (1982-84, NJ); KLETT, JR, *Genealogies of NJ Families,* Vol. II; de VALINGER, Leon, Jr., compiler, *Calendar of Kent County, DE, Probate Record, 1680-1800* (Dover, DE, 1944).

ALLEGRÉ(E)/ALLAIGRE, Giles (Dr.)

b. FR

3 Jul 1727- John Martin sold Patent #895, 180 acres on the s. side of the James River, for £20; Patent #896 (below) was next to it – e. of Woodmont, VA

m. 27 Jul 1730, Goochland Co, VA, Judith Cox, d/o of the county clerk (this was the 1st marr. recorded there); Judith d. p. 2 Apr 1777, wd, Albemarle Co, VA

1 of the founders of Manakintown; operated a tavern in Goochland Co, lic. 1740; later in Albemarle Co.

Jun 1737 - sold 59 acres of a 149 acre tract to William Martin, s/o John Martin (dec.), price - £50 & 60 acres to William's bro Matthew; Giles had purchased some of the acreage from John Peter & Susannah Bilbaud 4 Oct 1728 – this land was part of Patent #896 on the s. side of the James in Henrico (now Chesterfield) Co.

d. p. 28 Jul 1758 wd, Albemarle Co, VA

CHILDREN:

Judith[2], b. 18 Dec 1732; m. William Howard

stillborn boy[2], 5 a.m., 12 Mar 1735/6; miscarried due to the fact that "5 Indians entered her bedroom without permission 4 hours earlier"

Matthew[2], b. 25 Jul 1737, bp 14 Feb 1738/9, at Hanover Chapel by Patrick Henry

Giles[2]

William[2], m. XX; d. a. 2 Apr 1777; son **William**[3]

Daniel[2]

Martha/Polley[2], m. X Watson

REF: BROCK, R.A., *Huguenot Emigration to Virginia* (Baltimore, 1979); *The Huguenot Publication,* #35 (1991-93) *The Huguenot Society of the Founders of Manakin in the Colony of VA* (1996); Giles' will, Albemarle Co, VA, CABELL, Priscilla Harriss, *Turff & Twigg,* Vol. I, *The French Lands* (Richmond, VA, 1988).

AMMONET, JACOB

b. c. 1660-65, poss. Loudun, Poitou, FR, s/o Jacob & X (X) Ammonet (Jacob's bro François m. c. 1671 Paris Jeanne Crommelin, d/o Martin & Susanne (Doublet) <u>Crommelin</u> - **issue**)

1681 – emigrated to The Hague from Paris w/wife, 1 ch; became an officer in William of Orange's army which invaded England in 1688; said to have been knighted by William; also served in the French Army

m. a. 1695, FR, poss. Paris, to XX (maiden name *poss.* Aubrey, b. c. 1670 prob. FR-d. by 1714 Henrico Co, VA)

c. 1700 - to VA w/ wife, 4 ch in the *Nasseau*; in Manakintown by 1705 – one of the founders; he was awarded land on s. side of the James River by William III of England (formerly William of Orange); c. 1714, his wife had died – she is not on the *Liste Généralle*, but the list does show another ch; he purchased 2 tracts of FR land, one (#805 – 88 acres) in present Powhatan Co and the other (#912 – 186 acres) c. 5 mi down the river in present Chesterfield Co. – both of these tracts were inherited by son Andrew – Andrew sold #805 to James Harris in 1744 for £88; Andrew sold the Chesterfield tract to his bro Charles for £20 in 1734

1705 – naturalized

1707 – he was a warden in King William Parish

1726 - on tithing list; was noted as being one of a group assembled on 23 Jul 1726 in the Vestry Book of King William Parish; also on the tithing list of 1731

d. a. Feb 1732, King William Parish, Henrico Co, VA; not on tithable list p. 1731

CHILDREN:

Jacob, II,[2], b. c. 1696; d. bet 1720-23 – not on tithable lists of 1720 or 1723

André/Andrew[2], b. c. 1698, FR, chr Paris; m. c. 1728, VA, Henrico or Goochland Co., Jeanne/Jane Morriset, (c. 1702, prob. Henrico Co, VA-p. 23 Oct 1763, prob. Chesterfield Co, VA), d/o <u>Pierre & Elizabeth (Fauré) Morriset</u>; Patriotic Service during Rev. War; André d. a. 4 Feb 1764, wp, Chesterfield Co, VA; will names wife, 5 sons & 5 daus

CHILDREN:

William[3], b. c. 1728, VA, prob. Henrico Co; m. c. 1750, prob. Elizabeth Badgett (c. 1730, VA - p. 1810 census, liv. Buckingham Co, VA); he d. p. 1810 census, liv. Buckingham Co, VA

Judith[3], b. 20 Sep, bp 27 Sep 1730; m. c. 1765, John Bransford, Jr. (as his 2nd wife), s/o John & Mary (Kingsford) Bransford; **10 ch**

Jacob[3], b. 15 Jun 1732; m. Mary Ann X; d. a. 23 Sep 1771, wp; dau **Mary Ann**[4]

Jean André/John[3], b. 6 Aug 1734; m. XX; d. p. 30 Jan 1781, wd, Chesterfield Co, VA; son

> **John Jr.**[4], dau **Rebecca**[4] who m. X Russell
> **Charles**[3], b. 9 Mar 1736/7; m. XX; d. 1789; **4 daus** named in his will
> **André/Andrew**[3], liv. Chesterfield Co; m. XX; supposedly d. 1777 in Rev. War
> **Jane**[3], m. John Harris (as his 2nd wife) of King William Parish in Powhatan Co.; she d. a. 5 Feb 1779
> **Elizabeth**[3], m. 7 Dec 1778, Chesterfield Co, John Garrett/Garrott
> **Magdalene**[3], m. 5 Jun 1780, Chesterfield Co, Pleasant Thurman

Magdalene[2], b. a. 1700; m. c. 1720, Abraham Sallé (31 Oct 1700, NYC-15 Feb 1731, Henrico Co, VA), s/o

> Abraham & Olive (Perrault) Sallé(e)

Charles[2], b. c. 1700; m. Diane X

> CHILDREN:
> **Jean/John**[3], b. 29 Feb 1753; m. Bathsheba Rogers; he d. a. 1795?
> **Charles, Jr.**[3], b. 13 Oct 1758, Powhatan Co, VA; m. Phebe Hall; he d. 1833

dau?[2], b. a. 1714, prob. d. young

REF: OMOHUNDRO, Malveen H., *The Omohundro Genealogical Record* (Staunton, VA, 1950/51); *The Huguenots, Their History and Legacy* - MD State Society (1993); Records of King William Parish, Manakintown; *The Douglas Register;* André's Will, Chesterfield Co, VA; Land records, Chesterfield Co, VA; CABELL, Priscilla Harriss, *Turff & Twigg, Vol. I, The French Lands,* (Richmond, 1988); *The Huguenot,* #6, 20, 26; Wills of Elizabeth Morriset (1746) & Andrew Ammonet (1761); BROCK, R.A., *Documents Relating to the Huguenot Emigration to VA* (1966); *Publications of the Southern History Assoc.* (Washington, DC, 1899); BRANSFORD, Clifton Wood, "Jacob Ammonet, of Virginia, and a Part of His Descendants" In *Southern History Association*, Vol. 3 (1899).

ANGEVIN(E)/L'ANGEVIN, Louis

> b. 1633, La Rochelle, FR, s/o Henri & Charlotte (Guinère) Angevine; grs/o François (b. c. 1588, s/o
> > Louis) & Marie (X) Angevin, a noted glassmaker w/ a shop nr. the Hôtel-de-Ville in La Rochelle;
> > family came from Angers, in Anjou (n.e. of La Rochelle), c. 1550 and took their surname from that
> > place
> m. 1658 La Rochelle, Marguerite Chalôns, said to have been a Huguenot – needs proof
> Louis was a glassmaker in La Rochelle; his ch fled La Rochelle in1686, went to HOL & 22 Feb1689
> > arr NY; he and Marguerite did not emigrate
> d. La Rochelle, FR
> CHILDREN:
> **Zacharie/Zachariah**[2], b. c. 1664, prob. La Rochelle, FR, m/1, 1684, La Rochelle, Anastasia Baptiste
> > (c. 1666-1686, Antwerp, BEL, during flight to HOL) - had infant son who d/bur nr. Orgères-en-
> > Beauce, FR; arrived America, 22 Feb 1689, settled New Amsterdam; m/2, 15 Mar 1690, FR Ch, NYC,
> > Marie Naudin (d. p. 26 Oct 1739, wd – a. 17 Jan 1739/40, wp), d/o André and Margaret (X) Naud(a)in;
> > May 1695 - took Oath of Allegiance; 16 Dec 1695 – made a freeman; he held a series of civic offices in
> > New Rochelle, 1703-1733; Zacharie d. p. 26 Sep 1739, wd - a.17 Jan 1739/40, wp; will names sons
> > Zacharie, John, Daniel, daus Ann Moynot, Elizabeth Cottoney (Coutant), Margaret Dow, Esther Mallot,
> > gr dau Rachel Ball, son-in-law John Cottoney, son-in-law Isaac Dow, 1 of the executors; name
> > sometimes spelled ANGEUIN, ENGEUIN; he was a tailor
> > CHILDREN, m/2:
> > **Marguerite/Margaret**[3], b. 2 Jan, bp. 15 Jan 1692/3, FR Ch, NYC; m. Isaac Dow; both d.
> > > p. 1740
> > **Marie/Mary**[3], 22 Feb, bp. 24 Feb 1694/5, FR Ch, NYC; d. a. 1698
> > **Jean/John**[3], b. 11 Jan, bp. 19 Jan 1695/6, FR Ch, NYC; d. a. 1702, NYC
> > **Marie/Mary**[3], b. 15 Mar, bp. 16 Mar 1697/8, FR Ch, NYC; m. X Ball; d. prob. a. Sep 1739
> > > as she is not in her father's will but her dau is - **Rachel**[4] who m. c. 1750, Eli
> > > Pelletreau – at least **5 ch**
> > **Ester**[3], b. 21 Jan, bp. 4 Feb 1699/00, FR Ch, NYC; prob. d. a. 1702/03

Elizabeth[3], bp. 18 Jan 1701/2, FR Ch, NYC; m. John Coutant II (c. 1695-1749), s/o <u>Jean & Susanna (Gouin) Coutant</u>; Elizabeth d. p. 1740; at least **5 ch**

Zachariah[3], b. 1704, New Rochelle; m. Joanna/Johannah Mallet/Mellett (10 Mar 1710, Stratfield, CT - p. 1783), d/o <u>Jean & Johanna (Liron/Lyon) Mallett</u>; he d. p. 1760 CT; **7 ch**

Marianne/Mary Ann[3], b. c. 1706; m. Peter Moynot; d. p. 1740; **2 ch**

Daniel[3], b. c. 1708; m. Catherine X; he d. c. 1765; 1 son **Daniel Jr.**[4] who was lost at sea c. 1765

Jean/John[3], b. New Rochelle, bp. 22 Oct 1710, FR Ch, NYC; m. c. 1740, New Rochelle, Esther/Hester Palmer, d/o Obadiah & Anne (de Bonrepos) Palmer, d/o <u>Élie & Ester (X) de Bonrepos</u>; he d. p. 1770; at least **1 son**, bp. 12 Apr 1754, NYC

Ester[3], b. 2 Oct, bp. 22 Oct 1712, New Rochelle; m. David Mallet(t), s/o <u>Jean & Johanna (Liron) Mallett</u>; d. 16 Jan 1787, bur. Tashua Cemetery, Trumbull, CT

Pierre/Peter[2], b. 23 Dec 1666, La Rochelle, FR; <u>m/1</u>, Deborah Guion (c. 1668, prob. FR, d. prob. c. 1713, New Rochelle, NY) – **2 sons, 2 daus**, <u>m/2</u>, c. 1713 New Rochelle, Marguerite de Bonrepos (c. 1683-p. 1729, prob. New Rochelle), d/o <u>Élie & Ester (X) de Bonrepos</u>; Peter d. c. 1728

CHILDREN, m/1:

Pierre, II[3], b. 1697; d. young

Marie[3], b. 1699 ?

Margaret[3], b. c. 1700

Louis[3], b. 19 Feb 1702; m. Ester Sicard (1706, New Rochelle-1792, Scarsdale, NY), d/o <u>Jacques & Anne (Terrier) Sicard</u>; **3 sons, 5 daus**

CHILDREN, m/2 :

Pierre II/Peter[3] b. 15 May 1714, New Rochelle

Eli[3], b. 30 Nov 1719, New Rochelle

Esther[3], b. 1729, New Rochelle

Susanna[2], b. 1668; d. unmarr.

REF: ANGEVINE, Erma, *The Angevines in America* (1976); *Huguenot & Historical Assoc of New Rochelle* (1941); WITTMEYER, Alfred, *Register of Births, Marriages & Deaths L'Église Françoise à la Nouvelle York, 1668-1804* (1968); ANGEVINE, Clyde V., *Angevine Genealogy, 1690-1976, in America* (Endwell, NY, 1977).

ANGUENET/AGNE/ANKENY, Pierre/Peter

b. c. 1650, Pfalzburg, FR, s/o Abel & Angelica (Vinan/Vinet) Anguenot, butcher/merchant of Pfalzburg; family said to have been from Vitry-le-François in n.e. France - went to Metz (Lorraine Prov.) – to Pfalzburg/Phalsbourg-to Lixheim (n.w. of Strasbourg) - to Zweibrücken/Deux Ponts, c.1670-then to Lambsborn, Rheinland-Pfalz (n.e. of Saarbrücken and s.w. of Kaiserslautern)

a. 1673 – fled to Zweibrücken and Lambsborn from the Palatinate/*Pflaz*; 1st listed in 1673 in Zwei bracken as a carpenter and mill builder

m. a. 1674, Ottilie Trautmann, (6 May 1655, Lambsborn-21 Feb 1730, Lambsborn), d/o Georg & Anna Elisabeth (Römer) Trautmann of Vogelbach (just n. of Lambsborn); Anna Elisabeth, d/o Adam Römer, mayor of Käshofen (n.e. of Zweibrücken)

d. c. 1700/02 Lambsborn

CHILDREN:

Maria Catharina[2], <u>m/1</u>, 8 Jun 1693, Lambsborn, Nikolaus Stauch (1666, Miesau-8 Jun 1699, Bechhofen, s.w. Lambsborn), s/o Peter Stauch; <u>m/2</u>, 13 May 1700, Bechhofen, Ludwig Peter Trimm from Dutweiler

Anna Catharina[2], b. 21 Jun 1679, Zwiebrücken; m. 6 Jul 1702, Lambsborn, Friedrich Becker, a miller from Oberauerbach, s/o Philip Becker

Johannes (AGNE)[2], b. 23 Jun 1681, Lambsborn; <u>m/1</u>, 5 Feb 1709, Lambsborn, Elisabetha Sternberger (7 May 1680, Thaleischweiler-29 Jan 1712), d/o Hans & Elisabeth (Fischer) Sternberger; <u>m/2</u>, 2 Nov 1713, Lambsborn, Anna Barbara Eichaker (b. c.1690, Mörsbach); he d. 29 Oct 1758, Lambsborn

CHILDREN (2 of <u>10</u>):

Johann Jacob (AGNE)[3], b. 22 Oct 1726, Lambsborn; m. 21 Apr 1750, Anna Barbara Neumann, d/o Jacob Neumann; he d. 18 Jan 1808, Lambsborn
CHILD:
    Johann Jacob (AGNE)[4], b. 27 May 1759, Lambsborn; m. 21 Feb 1786, Lambsborn, Maria Catharina Blinn, d/o Philip Henrich Blinn
Theobald[3], b. 27 Apr 1730, Lambsborn; emigrated to US in 1753
Johann Heinrich[2], b. 23 Feb 1684, Homburg; d. c. 1698
Johann Nicolaus[2], b. 29 Apr 1685, Homburg; m. Anna Katharina Hartmann from Einöd; he was a baker at Einöd; all **6 ch** b. there; c. 1736, family emig. to U.S. on the *Harle*, arr Philadelphia
Anna Elisabeth[2], b. 29 Apr 1685, Homburg; m. 16 Jun 1711, Zweibrücken, Abraham Müller, s/o Reinhard Müller, city miller at Limbach
Anna Eva[2], b. 18 Dec 1689, Homburg
Anna Dorothea[2], b. 22 Jul 1691, Homburg; m/1, 25 Oct 1716, Contwig, Nickel Albrecht, butcher at Contwig; m/2, Friedrich Sauerbronn, s/o Friedrich Sauerbronn, from Lambrecht
Susanne[2], b. 25 Aug 1693, Homburg; m. 7 Nov 1713, Lambsborn, Peter Eichacker, s/o Peter of Mörsbach; she d. a. 1715
Johann Heinrich (AGNE)[2], b. 2 Mar 1698, Lambsborn; m. 19 Jan 1723, Anna Christina Cantor (c. 1696-bur 17 Feb 1734, Lambsborn, d/o Johannes Cantor, tanner in Saanen, Bern, SWI (n.w. Gstaad);
she m/2, Jackob Bächlein; Johann bur 25 Dec 1727, Lambsborn
CHILDREN:
Johann Theobold (AGNE)[3], b. 22 Oct 1726, bp. 16 Jan 1727, Lambsborn; emigrated with his sister Anna Magdalena to America on the *Neptune*; settled 1746, Lancaster (now Lebanon) Co, PA; m/1, Catherine X (Mary Jane Dormer/Domar is often mentioned as his wife, but this is **not** proven, Catherine's name is in baptismal recs) – **5 ch**; m/2, 1758, Margaret (Becker) Frederick, wid/o Noah Frederick* – **7 ch**; then went to Clear Spring, MD, 1762; **aka Dewalt Ankeny;** took the Oath of Allegiance in 1778; liv. in Clear Spring, Washington Co, MD; d. a. 7Apr 1781, wp, Washington Co, MD; there is a plaque at St. Paul's Ch, Clear Spring, MD, placed in memory of Dewalt, "the 1st of the name and founder of that name in America"
CHILDREN, m/1, surnamed **ANKENY**:
Christian[4], b. 25 Dec 1749; m/1, Elizabeth Shaver/Shaffer, d/o George Shaffer, she d. 1816; m/2, 1816/17, Mary Kooser; Christian d. 17 Mar 1824 Westmoreland Co, PA; **5 sons, 5 daus** all from m/1; Lt from PA in Rev War
    Peter[4], b. 6 Mar 1751; m. Rosina/Rosanna Bonnett (17 Sep 1757, PA-5 Feb 1834, dates on her gravestone, Ankeny Square Burying Ground, Somerset, Somerset Co, PA), d/o Jean/John Martin & Mary Dorothy (Bickley) Bonnet; Peter d. 23 Dec 1804, bur. Ankeny Sq. Bur. Ground; Capt, from PA, in Rev War; **10 ch** – a dau Elizabeth[5] (1782-1863) m. Michael Hugus/Hugues, s/o John & Margaretta (Shupe) Hugues
Catherine[4], b. 1753; m. c. 1775, Michael Walter (1749-1830); **6 ch**
Rebecca[4], b. 5 Jul 1755; m. George Cook; she d. 21 Jan 1832
Anna Maria[4], b. 1757; m. 6 Mar 1776, Washington Co, MD, John Chorpinning/ Corpenning; d. 1804; **10 ch**
CHILDREN, m/2:
[*John/**Johann Georg**[4], b. 27 Mar 1757; m. Magdalena Siths; d. 17 May 1810; posthumous s/o Noah Frederick (above) whom Dewalt treated as his own son; **3 ch**]
Henry[4], b. 1760; m. Susannah Jones; d. 17 May 1810; **5 ch**
David[4], b. 30 Jun 1763; m/1, Eliza Ritter; m/2, Margarethe Bird Schonnon; he d. 9 May 1838; **5 ch**
Jakob[4], m. Christine Yerion; d. 1799; **3 ch**
Margaret[4], m. John Walter;
Georg[4], m. Catherine Fiery; **1 ch**
Elizabeth[4], b. 4 Dec 1772; m. X Brading – **1 ch**
Anna Magdalena[3]

Agnes[2], b. 17 Jan 1700, Lambsborn
Peter[2], confirmed 1712 in Lambsborn

NOTE: Most of the German towns named above are within a few kilometers of Zweibrücken, which is between Saarbrücken & Kaiserslautern. One researcher theorized that the surname was originally Engken from a place in Flanders – not found. There are 2 towns called Enghein, one in FR, n. of Paris and one in Belgium, s.w. of Brussels, in what would have been Flanders at that time.

REF: Church records, Vereinigte Protestantisch-Evang. Kirche der Pfalz Lambsborn, Rheinland-Pfalz; ANGNE, Gustav, *Agne, Angne, Angene, Aukeny, Ankenen, Ankeny, Ankeney, Anguenet, etc,* (translated from the German by JENKINS, Lawrence W., Sep/Dec 1978); a genealogy translated from the German by Dr. G.W. Regenos (1974); SHULTZ, Charles R, *A Genealogy of the Descendants of Dewalt Ankeny* (1948); unidentified Ger. Records.

ARNAUD, André

b. c. 1652, La Tremblade **or** Arvert, Saintonge, FR (now in Charente-Maritime Dépt, Poitou-Charentes), s.w. of Rochefort; Arvert is a sm. town, c. 4 km s. of La Tremblade; *poss.* s/o Samuel & Anne (Moguen) Arnaud
m. Marie X (Gallihaut?)
1683 - fled FR to London, where he was naturalized; joined Huguenot Colony at Narragansett, RI, then to NYC
by 1706 - was in New Rochelle, NY, where he purchased 2 acres of land by the waterside; a *voilier* (sailmaker) and mariner
d. p. 12 Jul 1734, wd – a. 23 Jul 1735, wp, New Rochelle, NY
CHILDREN, all except for Jeanne, named in his will:
Stephen[2], m. Magdalen/Madeleine Rineurs, d/o Jacques Rineur(e)
    CHILDREN :
    Jeanne[3], b. 31 Oct, bp. 4 Nov 1722, FR Ch, NYC; m. 1744, Jacob Coutant, s/o Jean & Elizabeth (Angevine) Coutant; she d. 26 Jan 1810; **issue**
    Peter[3], m. Mary Landzine; he d. p. 30 Mar 1799
Jeanne[2], b. 25 Oct, bp. 10 Nov 1703, FR Ch, NYC; must have d. young
Marie[2], m. a. 1737, Jérémie Chardavoine, s/o Élie & Anne (Valleau) Chardavoine/Chadaine

REF: DeFOREST, L. Effingham, *Records of the French Church at Narragansett, 1686-1691* (NY); BAIRD, Charles W., *History of the Huguenot Emigration to America;* New Rochelle Chapter, NSDAR, *Old Wills of New Rochelle* (New Rochelle, 1951); WITTMEYER, Rev. Alfred V., *Registers of the Births, Marriages, & Deaths, of the Église Françoise à la Nouvelle York, 1688-1804* (Baltimore, MD, 1994).

ARNAULD/ARNAUD, Élie/Elias

Native of LaTremblade, Saintonge, FR (now in Charente-Maritime Dépt, Poitou-Charentes), s.w. of Rochefort
m. Madeline DeValau/Devallaud (d. a. 20 Feb 1730/31, wp, Prerogative Court of Canterbury, Isham 23*);
    will says she was a widow liv. in Spitalfields (section of e. London), Middlesex, ENG, and "very Ancient"; names gr son Peter, son Elias, 2 grdaus Mary Magdalen, Susanna, d/o "my late son John" and gr son Isaac Chappelier
a. Oct 1699 - fled FR to London; member FR Ch, Threadneedle St, London
d. a. 4 Feb 1725/6, wp, Prerogative Court of Canterbury, 16 Plymouth*; names wife Magdalen, ch mentioned but not by name
    * wills in French .
CHILDREN:
Anne[2], m. 28 Oct 1696, Threadneedle St. Church, London, Isaac Chappelier,
John[2], m. XX; d. by 1730
    CHILDREN:

> **Mary Magdalen**[3]
> **Susanna**[3]

Elias[2], distiller in Gosport, Southampton, England, 1730

REF: CHAPPELEAR, George W. *Families of VA – Chapplear,* Vol. II (Dayton, VA, 1932); CHAPPELEAR, Nancy, *The Chappelear Family* (Wheaton, MD); Records from the French Church on Threadneedle St.

AUBIGNÉ/AUBIGNEY/DABNEY, Théodore Agrippa d'

b. 8 Feb 1552, nr. Pons, Saintonge, FR (now in Poitou, s.w. of Cognac), s/o Jean (c. 1520-1563) & Catherine
   (L'Étange/L'Estang) d'Aubigné - Jean was the Seigneur de Brie, killed at Amboise (e. of Tours) during
   the siege of Orléans by a Catholic army; Théodore was Seigneur de Lander et la Chaillon
1568 – having rec. a good and varied education, he took up arms for Henry of Navarre, later Henri IV
m/1, 6 Jun 1583, Susanne de Lazey, d/o Ambroise de Lezai, Baron of Surimeau, & Renée de Veronet;
   she d. 1596
he became an author, propagandist and chronicler of some note; his 7 canto poem *Les tragiques* (1616)
   is considered the greatest epic poem inspired by the French religious wars of 1553-1602, a FR
   Baroque masterpiece – it is an apocalyptic allegory condemning the cruelty of war; he also wrote
   Histoire universelle (1616-18), an eyewitness history of the Huguenots during the 2nd half of the 16th
   century
m/2, 24 Apr 1623 Geneva, SWI, Renée Burlamacchi, wealthy widow of Geneva (b. c. 1568); **no issue**
d. 29 Apr 1630, nr. Geneva, where he had built a castle in Crest (now Jussy), c. 10 km s.e. Geneva; he is
   bur. in the cloister of the Cathédrale de Saint-Pierre
CHILDREN, m/1:
Louise Art(h)émise[2], b. c. 1584; m. 1610, Benjamin de Valois, sieur de Villette
Constant/Constance[2], b. 1585; m/1, 20 Oct 1608, Anne (Marchant) Courault, widow of Jean Courault,
   Baron de Châtellaillon; she was killed by Constant, 6 Feb 1619; m/2, 27 Dec 1627, Jeanne de Cardillac
   (b. 1610); he was a man of poor character with many bad habits and frequently in debt - his father
   "bailed" him out on many occasions; Constant was the Baron of Surimeau as well; he d. 31Aug 1647,
   Orange, Provence, FR, n. of Avignon (as a Protestant); he had changed his religion 10 times over the
   years
CHILDREN, m/1:
Théodulfe[3], bp. 26 Aug 1609; d. young
Agrippa Théodore[3], b. 25 Jul 1609, bp. 5 Aug 1613, La Rochelle, FR; m. XX; went to ENG, Wales,
   perhaps HOL, then to the Barbadoes, Apr 1635, on the *Alexander*; place and date of d.
   unknown
   CHILDREN:
   John[4], b. prob. FR; to VA, c. 1715-17, from Wales w/ bros Robert & Cornelius; dau
      Mary[5] m. Isaac Winston, Sr. who d. a. 6 Mar 1760, wp, Hanover Co.- **issue**
   Robert[4], from FR to Wales, then c. 1722, to Boston; m. Elizabeth X; a son **John**[5] was
      born to them in Boston, 17 Aug 1723; surname DABNEY
   Elizabeth[4], b. c. 1631; m. 10 Feb 1651/2, CT, prob. Hartford, John Savage (d. 6 Mar 1684/5) &
      Elizabeth "Dubblin/D'Aubin"; Eliz. d. 1696, Middletown, CT; **11 ch**, births of 9 of
      them, rec. Middletown, bet 1652-1678
   Cornelius[4], b. c. 1640 FR?; m. c. 1668, prob. ENG, Susanna X (she m/2, David Anderson*);
      he d. 1693/4, Hanover Co, VA; also had land in New Kent Co, VA; Susanna d. a. 5 Feb
      1724, wp, Hanover Co. (Susanna wrote her will Mar 1722 as the widow Anderson)
      CHILDREN:
      John[5], b. c. 1665; m. Sarah Jennings, d/o Peter & Catherine (Lunford) Jennings;
         John d. a. 1701, prob. Hanover Co; Sarah m/2, William Winston;
         CHILDREN (Surname **DABNEY**): **John**[6], went to sea & was never heard
         from again; **Susanna**[6], b. c. 1698, m. Francis Strother of Hanover Co, (then

Orange Co, VA, s/o Wm. Strother, Jr. & Margaret Thornton (d/o Francis & Alice (Savage) Thornton)

Cornelius, II[5], b. c. 1670; m/1, ENG, Edith X– son **George**[6] (d. p.- 1744, wd - King Wm Co?) - **issue**; m/2, Apr 1720/1, Sarah Jennings, d/o Charles Jennings, Sarah was reportedly the maid of his 1st wife; CHILDREN, m/2: **William**[6], m. Philadelphia Gwaltney; **John**[6], m. Ann Harris, d/o Robert & Mourning (Glenn) Harris-**12 ch**; **Cornelius III**[6], m. Lucy Winston, d/o Isaac Winston; **Mary Elizabeth**[6], m. Daniel Maupin, s/o Daniel & Margaret (Via) Maupin; **Fannie**[6], m. John Maupin (Daniel's bro) – **2 ch**; **Ann**[6], m. X Thompson; **Sarah**[6], m. Benjamin Brown (he d. p. 15 Apr 1762, wd); **Mary**[6], who m., as his 1st wife, Christopher Harris, bro/o Ann above; **unnamed dau**[6], who m. William Johnson; Cornelius d. p. 25 Oct 1764-a. 7 Feb 1764/5, wp, Hanover Co – in mother's will

George[5], liv & d. King William Co, VA; m. Elizabeth Anderson; CHILDREN: **William**[6], m. Anne Barrett, d/o Rev. Robert & Elizabeth (Lewis) Barrett; **George**[6]; **Susannah**[6]; **Sarah**[6]; **Judith**[6]; **Mary**[6] m. Stephen Pettus; **Elizabeth**[6], m. Mathew Anderson; Geo. Sr's wd 24 Oct 1729 – d. by 11 Apr 1734; George's will mentions a grsons George Anderson[7] & Dabney Pettus[7]

James[5], b. c. 1675, New Kent Co; m. XX; he d. p. 25 Apr 1701, King & Queen Co, VA; at least 1 son **Nelthan**[6], bp. 8 Jan 1698

Dorothy[5], m. James Trice – in mother's will

Sarah[5], b. c. 1680; m. 1705, Isaac Winston; **3 ch**

Benjamin[5], King William Co

Mary[5], b. 22 Jan 1688; m. 1704, Maj. Thomas Carr; she d. 7 Sep 1748, Caroline Co, VA; in mother's will; **5 ch**

CHILDREN, m/2:

a son[3], b. Mar 1629; drowned 1646

Charles, Chevalier[3], b. 1624; was a soldier, became a brig gen; m. Geneviève Pitre? – dau?
Françoise[4], who m. 1698, Adrien-Maurice de Noailles, the Comte d'Ayen; some accounts say Charles never marr.

Françoise[3], b.27 Nov 1635, in a prison in Niort, where her father was imprisoned as a Huguenot malcontent; her mother had Françoise bp. Catholic but later she converted to Protestantism; she m/1, c. 1651, Paul Scarron, a famous wit, who d. 1660; Françoise was able to buy the estate of Maintenon which was raised to a marquisate in 1678; m/2, 1685/6, Louis XIV as his 2nd wife; she d. 15 Apr 1719 prob. St-Cyr-l'École (nr. Versailles) where she is bur. in the choir of St. Cyr

Marie[2], b. 1586; m. 1613, Josué de Caumond, sieur d'Adde/Dadou

2 unnamed ch[2], d. p. 1597

CHILD by Jacqueline Chayer (not married)

Nathan[2], b. 1600; m/1, 1621, Claire Pelissari; m/2 1632, Anne Crespin – **4 ch**; m/3 1652, Élisabeth Hubertary; he was a doctor & d. 11 Apr 1669

NOTE: This line is complex and there are countless pieces of paper contradicting each other; the above is the best interpretation possible, given the documents provided.

REF: *The Huguenot,* #2 (1926), #29 (1979-81); CHAMBERLAYNE, Churchill Gibson, *Vestry Book and Register of St. Peter's Parish, New Kent & James City Counties, VA, 1684-1786* (Richmond, 1937); *Tyler's Quarterly,* Vol. XX; wills; HAAG, William Eugene & Emil, *La France Protestante* (Paris, 1877); DuBELLET, Louise Pecquet, *Some Prominent VA Families* (1976); DABNEY, Charles William, *The Origin of the Dabney Family of VA; Huguenot Society Founders of Manakin, VA,* Yearbook #1 (1924); VRs – Boston, Middletown; DEAN, Elaine, *Daubney Genealogy.*

AUGE/DAUGE/DOZIER, Léonard d'

b. c. 1623, Province of Berry, now located in the Cher Dépt., Centre, FR

m. c. 1660, FR, Elizabeth X, presuming she is the same Elizabeth mentioned as his wife in his will;
    Eliz. m/2, a. 1703, Nathaniel Garland of Cople Parish, Westmoreland Co, VA; Eliz. was **poss.**
    a second wife; <u>if so</u>, he m. c. 1660, FR to XX & m. c. 1680, VA to Elizabeth

1st went to Charleston, SC

by 1678 - in Westmoreland Co, VA

8 Jun 1680 – naturalized at James City/Jamestown, VA; the papers were registered 28 Jan 1734 at the request
    of son Richard and admitted 3 Feb 1734 thus allowing his heirs full & complete citizenship; his
    naturalization rec says he was b. in FR & mentions son Richard

d. a. 26 Jul 1693, adm, Westmoreland Co, VA

CHILDREN:

Richard[2], b. 1668, FR; m. a. 5 Oct 1699, Elizabeth Hudson/Hogsdon, d/o Bryan & Mary (X) Hudson;
    he d. p. 5 May 1739, wd – a. 26 Nov 1751, wp; will mentions sons Richard, Thomas, Wm; daus
    Margaret, Elizabeth, Sarah, Hannah, Martha, Mary; son in law Thomas Templeton, 2 grch;
    wife Elizabeth

    CHILDREN:

    Margaret Ann[3], m. Thomas Templeton

    Richard, Jr[3], d. p. 28 Jan 1786, wd -a. 31 May 1791, wp; d. unmarr

    Thomas[3], m. a. 1735, Sarah (Pierce)?; he d. p. 23 Feb 1770, wd -a. 29 Jun 1777, wp

    William[3], m. Molly X; he d. p. 18 Jul 1782, wd – a. 30 Jul 1782, wp; **7 ch**

    Elizabeth[3], <u>m/1</u>, Dr. Joseph Belfield (3rd wife), <u>m/2</u>, James Wilson, <u>m/3</u>, John/Jehu Glass; **ch** by each

    Sarah[3], m. William Pierce?

    Hannah[3], m. Daniel Muse

    Martha[3], m. Joseph Belfield/Bellefield, Jr., who d. 1770

    Mary[3]

Jacques/James[2], b. c. 1670, Prov. of Berry, FR; m. c. 1696, Charleston, SC, Mary Bonney (c. 1680, VA- 1712,
    Pr. Wm. Co, VA), d/o Richard Bonney (wd ,1706); 1689 - Capt. Dauge patented 1,034 acres in Norfolk
    Co, VA; was a member of the Princess Anne Co. Court, 1691-96; James d. p. 15 Apr 1719, wd-a. 2
    Sep 1719, wp, Princess Anne Co.

    CHILDREN (named in father's will):

    John[3], m. Elizabeth X; he d. p. 15 Apr 1734, wd – a. 1 May 1734, wp, Princess Anne Co, VA;
        4 ch but only the **dau**[4] who m. X Whitehurst mentioned in his will – no other ch or grch
        mentioned

    Richard[3], b. 1691 Pr. Anne Co.; m. Jane Tully, d/o Benjamin Tulle/Tully; he d. 1725 Currituck
        Co, NC; **2 sons, 1 dau**

    James[3], m. Sarah Wilson, d/o Henry & Winfred (X) Wilson; he d. 1713; **1 son**

    Macina[3] – no other info

    William[3], m. Ledey Sorey (b. a. Apr 1747), d/o Francis & Ann (X) Sorey; he d. c. 17 Mar 1752
        Princess Anne Co., VA – **5 sons**

    Mary[3], m. Peter Malbone

    Nowdina[3], m. a. 1734, Cornelius Henley (d. p. 25 Dec 1752, wd -a. 19 Jun 1753, wp, Pr. Anne Co);
    she d. p. 19 Jun 1753; 5 ch: **Cornelius II**[4], **James**[4], **Kezia**[4], m. Cason Moore, **Mary**[4], **Elizabeth**[4]

    Jacqueline[3], m. Thomas Cannon

    Peter/Pierre, Pierre/Peter[3], b. 4 Dec 1709; m. Augilloce/Angelica Grégord/Gregory (1715,
        VA-a. 1788, wp, Currituck Co, NC), d/o Luke & Sarah (Wilkie) Gregory; he d. a. 9 Nov
        1778, wp, Currituck Co, NC

        CHILDREN:

        James[4], m. Mary Malone; liv. Bute Co, NC 1772 (county abolished 1779, became
            Franklin & Warren Co., n.e. of Raleigh); another acct. says he m. Ann
            Gray, d/o Griffith & Charity (Sawyer) Gray – **6 sons, 3 daus**

Peter[4], b. 19 Dec 1739 (based on age at death, 61Y 8M 13D), Pasquotank, NC; m/1, c. 1762, prob. NC, Elizabeth Williams (b. 17 Nov 1727, NC, d. 6 May 1812, Currituck Co, NC), d/o Ludwick & Dorothy (X)Williams – **3 sons**, **3 daus**; m/2, Margaret (Sawyer) Pritchard, d/o Thomas & Margaret (X) Sawyer – **3 daus**; Peter went to Camden c. 1760; Col. of the SC Militia, 1763-1775; Peter d. 1 Sep 1801,Camden Co, NC

Willoughby[4], m. 7 Apr 1770, Millicent Munden; p. 22 Dec 1804, wd, Currituck Co, NC; **7 sons, 5 daus**

Dennis[4] – no other info

John[4], m/1 Ann Stamp – **2 sons, 2 daus**, m/2 Priscilla Hassel; he d. 1791

Tull/Tully[4], d. young, will mentions only his sibs & their ch; d. p. May 1746, wd –a. 25 Dec 1748, wp, Currituck Co, NC

Mary[4]; **Jacquelinner**[4], m. John Bray; **Angelosa**[4]; **Sarah**[4], m. Peter Sorey; **Susanna**[4], m. William Glasgow Simmons; **Rhoda**[4], m. James Etheridge, s/o John Etheridge

Frances[2], b. 1673, FR; d. p. 1713, unmarr.

Leonard II[2], b. 1680, Westmoreland Co, VA; m. bet 3 Dec 1701-4 Nov 1703, Elizabeth (Ingo) Ascough (c. 1685-a. 7 May 1748, wp), d/o John, Sr. & Mary (X) Ingo, widow of Thomas Ascough; Leonard d. a. 4 Jun 1733, Richmond Co, VA wife appt. administrator of estate

CHILDREN:

Ann[3], m. Richard Doggitt; she d. a. 1748

James Ingo[3], b. 1707; m. Elizabeth Staples; he d. a. 4 Jan 1808, wp, Warren Co, GA; **13 ch**

John[3], b. c. 1719, Richmond Co, VA; m. Isabelle/Sabella X; d. p. 19 Jan 1796 Wilkes Co, GA; **3 ch**

Leonard III[3], b. 1710, Lunenburg Co, VA; m. 30 Jan 1737, Ann Gayle (1717-1782); he d. 31 Jan 1785; **10 ch**

Mary[3], m. a. 1748, Thomas Jones

Elizabeth[3], m. a. 1748, Mark Thornton, s/o Mark & Mary (X) Thornton - **6 ch**

Sarah[3], m. George Jeter

Margaret/Peggy[3], m/1 Samuel Baker who d. 1751- **3 sons**, m/2 John Wood

Susanna[3], m. Joseph Bragg

NOTE: There appears to be some confusion over which sister mar. whom – the marriages as shown are as per Elizabeth (Ingo) Dozier's will

Thomas[2]

John[2], b. 16?2; m/1, Sarah X; m/2, 7 Jun 1736, Susannah (Jacobus) Davis, d/o Angell & Elizabeth (Clarke) Jacobus, widow of Robert Davis; John d. a. 7 Mar 1747, inv, Richmond Co, VA

NOTE: Another case of too many contradictions. Lineage needs clarification.

REF : *A Biographical History of Camden Co, NC;* VA wills; *William & Mary Quarterly,* Vol. XV; NUGENT, Nell Marion, *Cavaliers & Pioneers* (1977); *Lower Norfolk Co, VA Antiquary,* Vol. 11 Index (1899), Vol. 12 Index (1904); ROGERS, Edna, *Ancestors & Descendants of Rev. William & Mary Rogers, 1612-1950* (1952); *VA Magazine of History & Biography,* Vol. XV (1968); KING, George Harrison Sanford, *Marriages of Richmond Co, VA 1668-1853* (1964); *Transactions of the Huguenot Society of SC,* #50 (1945); Westmoreland Co, VA Records, Wills; HACKLEY, Woodford B., *VA Baptist Register,* #6 (1967); WOOD, E.B., *Baker and Wood Families of VA*; Elizabeth Dozier's will.

AUGUSTINE, Jean - see JEAN, Augustine

AYDELOT(TE)/AIDELOT, David

of Guienne Prov, FR, poss. Mauvaisin (see below) which is s. of Toulouse, now in the Haute Garonne Dépt., Midi-Pyrénées

m. Marie Schon/Sochon

28 Jun 1655 – naturalized in Westminster, ENG; he was a shoemaker

d. London, ENG

CHILDREN (bp. rec. in the FR Ch, Threadneedle St, London):

Benjamin[2], m. 6 Dec 1663, FR Ch, London, Marie Pingar, d/o <u>Jacques and Madeline (Despiné) Pingar</u> of Paris;
to America, c. 1670, settled Northampton Co, VA; 1687, to Somerset Co, MD; lived nr. Snow Hill
where he established and operated a shoe factory; d. p. 16 Jun 1703, wd - a. 3 Jun 1704, wp, Somerset
Co, MD – will mentions wife Mary, sons John, Benjamin, William, gr son James (s/o Benj), daus Mary
Blizzard, sons-in law George Blizzard, John Blizzard, Nehemiah Holland; surname at times IDOLETT,
AIDELO

    CHILDREN (all b. ENG):

    Ruben[3], bp. 15 Aug 1677 FR Ch, Threadneedle St., London; d. young

    John[3], <u>m/1</u>, Winifred X - **5 ch**; <u>m/2</u>, Mary X - **5 ch**; he d. a. 5 Jun 1759, wp, Worcester Co, MD;
will mentions wife Mary, 4 youngest ch **Caleb**[4], **Ruth**[4], **Elizabeth**[4], **Janey**[4], sons **Samuel**[4],
William[4], **John**[4], daus **Mary Lathbery/Leatherbury**[4], **Saphira McElvain**[4]

    Benjamin, Jr.[3], m. Sarah Fooks; he d. p. 21 Jan 1738, wd

    William[3], m. Eleanor X; he d. a. 4 Mar 1752 wp; **5 ch**

    Sarah[3], m. 1709, George Blizzard

    Elizabeth[3], m. Nehemiah Holland

    Mary[3], <u>m/1</u>, John Blizzard; <u>m/2</u>, Richard Lockwood

Salomon[2], bp. 28 Oct 1632

Isaac[2], bp. 22 Dec 1633; m. 30 Oct 1688, l'Église des Grecs (in Soho, a satellite of the Savoy Ch in
Westminster), Martha Bonnefous; bp rec of 1st ch **Marie**[3], says Isaac was from *Mauvaisin en Haute
Guienne*

Madelayne[2], bp. 30 Aug 1635; m. Jacob Malett; son **Étienne**[3], bp. 9 Sep 1674 FR Ch, Threadneedle St.,
London + other ch

Marie[2], bp. 11 Dec 1636

Catherine[2], bp. 17 Jul 1638

David[2], bp. 10 Jan 1641, FR Ch, Threadneedle St., London

Sara[2], bp. 11 Jul 1647, FR Ch, Threadneedle St., London

REF: AYDELOTT, George Carl, *The History of the Aydelott Family in the US* (1959); *Registers of the French Church,
Threadneedle St, London,* Vol. I (1896), Vol. II (1899); SHAW, William A., *Letters of Denization & Acts of
Naturalization: Aliens in England & Ireland, 1603-1700* (1911); Wills of Benjamin and William.

AYRAULT, Nicolas (Dr.)

nephew or brother of Pierre (below); Baird mentions that Pierre traveled with wife, son and nephew Nic(h)olas

b. c. 1656; a physician

c. 1686 - from LaRochelle to Providence, RI

m. Providence, RI, Marianne Breto(u)n (supposedly b. 1681, but 1st ch b. 1693, so prob. b. c. 1675);
she m/2, 5 Jun 1714, William Goodrich (& had 3 daus); she d. 27 Aug 1741, age 60Y(?)

1691 - to Wethersfield, CT

d. 4 Mar 1705/6, Wethersfield, CT; 8 Mar 1705/6 ,wp, will mentions wife, son Peter

CHILDREN:

Mary/Marian[2], b. 1693, Wethersfield; d. 13 Aug 1778, Wethersfield, CT, age 85Y, unmarr.

Easter/Esther[2], b. 5 Mar 1698/9 Wethersfield, CT, bp. 24 Sep 1699, FR Ch, NYC; poss. d. young

Peter[2], bp. 6 Dec 1702, Wethersfield, CT; m. 12 Nov 1744, Mary Francis; he d. 28 Oct 1779, Wethersfield, CT

    CHILDREN:

    Stephen[3], bp. 8 Aug 1743; d. 9 Aug 1745

    Marianna[3], b. 26 Sep 1745; m. 4 May 1769, Simeon Griswold

    Stephen[3], b. 22 Sep 1747

Peter[3], bp. 13 Oct 1754

Elizabeth[3], bp.3 Sep 1749; m. X Hammer; she d. 1837

Lydia[3], bp. 5 Jul 1752

Nicholas[2], b. 2 Oct 1705, Wethersfield, CT; m. 17 Apr 1730, Jane Stocking (d. Oct 1783), d/o Daniel & Jane (Mould) Stocking; he d. 29 Apr 1775, Wethersfield, CT

CHILDREN:

James[3], b. 17 Sep 1730; m. 2 Jan 1755, Abigail Kilborn, d/o Hezekiah Kilborn; **issue**

Marian[3], b. 6 May 1733; d. 26 Jan 1737/8

Daniel[3], b. 8 Dec 1735; m/1, 26 Jul 1759, Lucy Williams (d/bur 2 Oct 1781), m/2, 1 Jul 1784, Mary Balch (d. 16 Sep 1852, age 100); he d. 8 Mar 1807

Marian[3], b. 25 Feb 1737; d. 5 Sep 1741

Nicholas[3], b/d 1 May 1740

Jane[3], b. 6 Mar 1741/2; m. Ashbel Riley

Nicholas[3], b. 11 Oct 1744; d. 29 Mar 1749/50

Marian[3], b. 5 Nov 1746; d. 26 Feb 1747/8

REF: BALL, T.H., *Francis Ball's Descendants of the West Springfield Ball Family* (Crown Point, IN, 1902); BATES. John W. – Research letter (Wethersfield, CT, 7 Jul)1998; Vital Records, Wethersfield, CT; STILES, Henry R., *Gen & Biog Records of Ancient Wethersfield*; BAIRD, Charles W., *History of the Huguenot Emigration to America*; MANWARING, Charles W., *A Digest of the Early CT Probate Records,* Vol. II, Hartford District, 1700-1729; WITTMEYER, Rev. Alfred V., *Registers of the Births, Marriages, & Deaths, of the Église Françoise à la Nouvelle York, 1688-1804* (Baltimore, MD, 1994).

AYRAULT, Pierre (Dr.)

b. poss. Angers, Anjou, FR, which is at the confluence of the Loire & Marne Rivers in n.w. FR; said to have been a "native" of Angers; physician

m. Françoise X

c. 1681/85 - to Narragansett Colony, RI; called a fugitive from the Île de Ré; he suffered hardships in RI – assaults from neighbors, lack of support by the government, persecution

26 Sep 1699 - one of the petitioners asking the governor* for encouragement and assistance in maintaining a minister of the Church of England as they planned to erect a church and needed help in providing enough financing

*the governor was Samuel Cranston, his grdau Mary's fa-in-law

d. c. 4 Jan1711, Narragansett, RI

CHILD:

Daniel[2], b. 1676; m. 9 May 1703, FR Ch, NYC, Marie Robineau (28 Jun 1684-5 Jan 1729), d/o Étienne & Judith (Paré) Robineau of Poitou - Étienne/Stephen was naturalized 15 Apr 1687 in ENG with his wife and dau Mary; Daniel went to Newport, RI, where he established a business; settled Frenchtown, E. Greenwich; he d. 25 Jun 1764

CHILDREN:

Mary[3], b. 16 Feb 1704, E. Greenwich; m/1, 14 May 1721 Newport, James Cranston (29 Jul 1701, Newport-a. 3 Apr 1732, Newport), s/o Gov. Samuel & Mary (Hart) Cranston – prob. no issue; m/2, 12 Mar 1734, Newport, George Goulding; she d. 1764

Pierre/Peter[3], b. 4 Oct 1706, E. Greenwich

Daniel[3], b. 4 Oct 1705, E. Greenwich; m. Susannah Neargrass; he d. 20 Apr 1770; **2 sons, 2 daus**

Stephen[3], b. 11 Dec 1709, E. Greenwich; m. Ann Bours (2 Apr 1724, Newport-17 Dec 1754, Bristol), d/o Peter & Ann (Fairchild) Bours – **4 daus**

Elizabeth[3], b. 3 Mar 1710, E. Greenwich

Anthony[3], b. 15 Jan 1711; d. 12 Dec 1720

Elias[3], b. 13 Feb 1714

Judith[3], b. 8 Sep 1716; d. 1 Mar 1719

Frances[3], b. 22 Sep 1718, Newport; m. 26 Mar 1747, Newport, Walter Cranston (1708-25 Nov 1763, Newport), s/o Col. John & Ann Mercy(Newberry) Cranston – John was a bro of Samuel (above); she d. 2 Feb 1798 - **2 sons**

Anthony[3], b. c. 1720, Newport; d. c. 1726

Samuel[3], b. 22 Mar 1720, Newport; d. 11 Apr 1798

Susannah[3], b. 20 Jun 1723; d. 3 May 1807

Judeth[3], b. 9 Dec 1725, Newport; m. Philip Pardon Tillinghast; d. 26 Nov 1806, Wickford

REF: BAIRD, Charles W., *History of the Huguenot Emigration to America;* FOSDICK, Lucian J., *The French Blood in America* (Baltimore, 1973); DeFOREST, L. Effingham, *Records of the French Church at Narragansett, 1686-1691* – The Huguenot Society of America (NY); STILES, Henry R., *Gen & Biog Records of Ancient Wethersfield;* REAMON, G. Elmore, *The Trail of the Huguenots* (1983); WITTMEYER, Rev. Alfred V., *Registers of the Births, Marriages, & Deaths, of the Église Française à la Nouvelle York, 1688-1804* (Baltimore, MD, 1994); MASON, George Champlin , Annals of Trinity Church, Newport, RI, 1698-1821 (Newport, RI, 1890); AUSTIN, John Osgood & ANDREW, George, Genealogical Dictionary of RI.

B

BACOT, François

b. c. 1568, Tours, FR, s/o Antoine Bacot, a merchant of Sainte-Croix Parish

1583 – he was an apprentice lacemaker (*passementier*); then a merchant in Luynes, just w. of Tours

m. Marthe Daleu/Dallou (d. c. 1632)

d. 1637, Tours, FR

CHILDREN:

François II[2], merchant & *bourgeois* (citizen) of Tours who lived in the Saint-Saturnin Parish; m. 23 Jan 1629, Anne Moullu/Moullins, d/o Juanvre (?), Sieur du Bois, & Marguerite (Drouyn) Moullu, Juanvre was a squire; François d. 1632

    CHILD:

    François III[3], an apprentice silkworker in 1643

Marthe[2], m. 1632, Pierre Berthet; he m/2 28 Jan 1635, Anne DeLaboissière; Marthe d. a. 1635

Pierre I[2], b. 1597, Tours; m. 22 Feb 1637, Tours, Jeanne Moreau, d/o Esaïe and Marguerite (Corbeau) Moreau; Esaïe was a "*maître ouvrier en draps d'or, d'argent et soie*" (master worker of gold, silver and silk fabrics); Pierre was a "*maître ouvrier en soie*" (master silkworker); Pierre d. 1685; **16 ch**, b. bet. 1637-1664

    CHILDREN (all bap in the Temple of Tours):

    Pierre II[3], b. 27 Dec 1637, Tours; m. 6 Jun 1666, Jacquine Menessier/Mercier, d/o Abraham & Jacquine (Phélipeaux*) Menessier (b. 4 Apr 1649, Tours, d. 11 Aug 1709, Charleston, SC); Abraham & Pierre were master silkworkers; Pierre suffered some financial difficulties due to the Revocation & went to ENG; c. 1694, to SC – rec. land grants in1698, 1700; he d. 6 Sep 1702, Charleston, SC; **9 ch**

    *this is the spelling in the FR records of Tours; previous spelling of Selipeaux was evidently incorrect

    CHILDREN:

    Pierre III[4], **Abraham**[4], **René**[4], all b. Tours – all d. young ,Tours

    Pierre IV/Peter[4], b. 11 Nov 1671, Tours, FR; m/1, Marianne (Fleury de la Plaine) Du Gué, d/o Abraham Fleury, sieur de la Plaine & widow of Jacques DuGué; she d. a. 1716 - **no issue**; m/2, 1716, Marie Peronneau (b. 1685, SC-d. 1778, age 93Y), d/o Samuel & Jeanne (Collin) Peronneau; Peter d. Mar 1729/30, Charleston

        CHILDREN, m/2 :

        Samuel[5], b. c. 1716; m. 14 Apr 1741, Christ Church Parish, Rebecca Foissin, d/o Élie/Elias and Louise (Frisselle) Foissin; Rebecca d. p. 26 Apr 1768; he d. p. 1771; **4 ch**

        Mary[5], b. 1717; d. 1806 unmarr.

        Elizabeth[5], b.1725; m. Charles Dewar (d. p. 28 Jul 1775); she d.1789; **5 ch**

        Peter[5], b. 1728, Goose Creek; m. 11 Nov 1764, Elizabeth Harramond (6 Mar 1746/7 - 19 Sep 1799), d/o Henry & 2nd wife Elizabeth (Muncrief ,d/o Richard & X [Pomeroy] Muncrief) Harramond; he d. 7 Sep 1787 – **4 ch**

    Daniel[4], b. 30 Sep 1674, Tours, FR; went to America, then to ENG; **issue**

    David[4], b. 22 Nov 1676, Tours, m. 17 Feb 1711, Madeleine Villiers (b. 19 Nov 1678, Tours), d/o Jean & Marguerite (Maubon) Villiers; he d. 1756, Tours; **4 ch**

    Madeleine[4], b. 15 Dec 1678, Tours; d. 1706, Nantes

    François[4], b. 29 Sep 1680, Tours; d. 1691, Nantes

    Elizabeth[4], b. p.1686, SC; m. Jonas Bonhoste, prob. s/o Jonas and Catherine (Allaire) Bonhoste; dau **Elizabeth**[5]

Esaïe[3], 30 Jan 1639, Tours; m. 12 Jan 1670, Tours, Marguerite Baudouin (bp. 14 Aug 1644, Tours - a. 1 Nov 1699, London), d/o Christophe & Jeanne (Gendron) Baudouin as her 2nd husband; he d. a. 29 Jun 1684, London; **issue**

Jeanne[3] m. Hector Foucault

    Marthe[3] m. René Gilles
    Anne[3]; **François**[3]; **Paul**[3]; **Jean-Christophe**[3]; **Estienne**[3]; **Jean**[3]; **Daniel**[3]; **Françoise**[3]; **François**[3];
    Madeleine[3]; **David**[3]; **François**[3] no more info on these 12 ch

REF: *Transactions of the Huguenot Society of SC,* #77 (1972); JONES, Richard B, *Some Descendants of Pierre Bacot of Tours, France* (Wimauma, FL, 1994); ARDOUIN-WEISS, Idelette, *Les Protestants en Touraine (Les anciennes familles reformées de Tours aux XVIe et XVIIe siècles), Tome I*; BAIRD, Charles W, *History of the Huguenot Emigration to America,* Vol. I; HIRSCH, Arthur H., *The Huguenots of Colonial SC* (1928).

BADEAU, Élie

    b. c. 1670, St. Georges de Didonne, Saintonge, FR, (now Charente Maritime Dépt, in Poitou-Charentes),
        s.e. of Royan on the Gironde, s/o Pierre & Marie (Triau) Badeau fled FR, went to Bristol, ENG; listed
        in the Register of the FR Ch at Bristol, 1695-97, as a farm worker
    m. 30 Aug 1696, FR Ch, Bristol, Claud(in)e (Fumé) Blondeau, d/o Daniel & Ester (Herault) Fumé, wid/o
        François Blondeau; Élie's sister Claude m. 25 Jul 1697, FR Episcopal Ch, Bristol, Jean Magnon (son
        Élie b. 10 Oct, bp. 23 Oct 1698, FR Ch, NYC, dau Marie b. 21 Jan , bp. 4 Feb 1699/00, FR Ch, NYC)
    c. 1698 - went to NYC
    1708 - he was elected 1 of the Assessors of New Rochelle, NY; he purchased 120 acres there
    d. p. 1708 New Rochelle
    CHILDREN:
    Élie[2], b. 29 Oct, bp 6 Nov 1698, FR Ch, NYC
    Jean/John[2], b. New Rochelle; m. Madeline Parquot/Parcot, d/o Pierre & Françoise (Gendron) Parcot; he
        d. 1787, Red Mills, later Mahopac Falls, Dutchess Co, NY (now part of the town of Carmel in
        Putnam Co.); **5 ch**
        CHILD (1 of 5):
        Peter[3], b. c. 1728, m. c. 1749, Catherine Bonnefois Coutant, d/o <u>John & Jane (Renoud) Coutant</u>;
            he d. 9 Aug 1816
            CHILDREN:
            Peter[4], b. 1749 , went to Albany Co.
            Isaac[4], b. 1750, remained in Red Mills
            John[4], b. 1752, Peekskill
            Elias[4], b. 1755, Troy – soldier in Rev. War – **2 sons**
            Jacob[4], b. 1757; to Westchester Co.
            Catherine[4], b. 1759, Red Mills
            James[4], b. 1761, Green Co., nr. Catskill
            Magdaline[4], b. 1761, to Catskill
            James[4], b. 1763, Catskill
            David[4], b. 1765, d. at sea, age 22
            William[4], b. 1767 NYC
            Isaiah[4], b. 1770

REF: SEACORD, Morgan H., *Biographical Sketches & Index of the Huguenot Settlers of New Rochelle, 1687-1776*; MAYO, Ronald, *The Huguenots in Bristol*; BOYER, Carl 3rd, *Ship Passenger Lists, NY & NJ (1600-1825)* (Newhall, CA, 1978); MAYNARD, John A., *The Huguenot Church of NY* (NY, 1938), BAIRD, Charles W., *History of the Huguenot Emigration to America* , Vol. II; FOSDICK, Lucian J., *The French Blood in America* (NY, 1911); WITTMEYER, Alfred V., *Registers of the Births, Marriages & Deaths of the Église Française à la Nouvelle York*; BRINCKERHOFF, Fannie Badeau, *Genealogical & Family History of Southern NY & the Hudson River Valley* (NY, 1913).

BAILLET/BALLIET/BAILETTE, Jacob

b. c. 1641/2, Schalbach, Moselle Dépt., Lorraine, FR, n.w. of Phalsbourg, *prob.* s/o Isaac Bailliote of
    Burbach, Bas-Rhin Dépt., Alsace (s.e. of Sarre-Union)

m. a. 1670/5, Anna Fruibeau

d. 19 Feb 1706, Schalbach, bur. Rauweiler (now Rauwiller, Bas-Rhin Dépt., Alsace) – even though the
    towns are in different provinces, they are only c. 5 km. apart – Rauwiller is s.w. of Schalbach;
    he was a magistrate/ associate judge

CHILDREN (all 3 sons lived and died in FR):

Maria[2], m. 4 Sep 1690, Hornback (s.e. of Saarbrücken, 30 mi n. of Schalbach), GER, Johannes Tüller/
    Teller/Deller/Diller, a Reformed Swiss

Stefan/Steven[2], b. c. 1680; m. 26 Apr 1706, Burbach, Maria Katharina Schweitzer, d/o Nicholas Schweitzer of
    Schalbach; Stefan d. 1742
    CHILDREN, all bp. Schalbach:
    Anna Maria[3], bp. 1 May 1708; m. Jacob Allemand*
    Maria Catharina[3], bp. 17 Feb 1710; d. young
    Anna Elisabetha[3], b. 1711; m. 13 Jan 1737, Rauwiller, FR, Johannes Koch; she d. 1787
    Paulus[3], bp. 16 Aug 1716; m. c. 1749, PA, Maria Magdalena Vautrin/Wotring (bp. 16 Mar 1728),
        d/o <u>Abraham & Anna Margaretha (Mertz) Vautrin</u>; p. 1758 - in records of Egypt Reformed
        Ch, Lehigh Co, PA; naturalized 10 Apr 1759; she d. 1802; he d. 19 Mar 1777; **9 ch**
    Susanna[3], bp. 31 Aug 1721; d. young
    Susanna[3], b. 25 Aug 1722; m. 2 Jul 1742, Rauwiller, Henrich Fritz
    Maria Magdalen[3], bp.18 Jul 1723; m. Johannes Solt; emig. to Lehigh Co, PA
    Maria Catharina[3], bp. 29 Jul 1725; d. young
    Maria Catharina[3]; bp. 10 Jun 1732; m. PA, Johannes Nicholas Solt

Johan Nicholas/Hans Nickle[2], b. Nov 1680; m. 3 Dec 1707, Diedendorf, Bas-Rhin Dépt., Alsace, FR
    (s.w. of Sarre-Union), Margaretha Durand (b. 1684), d/o Mathieu Durand of Lixheim, Moselle
    Dépt., Lorraine, FR; she d. 27 Mar 1766, Schalbach; he d. 24 Jan 1745, Rauwiller; **8 ch**
    CHILD (1 of 8):
    Johan/John Nicholas[3], m. 17 Nov 1743, Schalbach, Susanna Alleman, d/o Jacob & Anna Maria
        (Balliet) Alleman(d)*; they settled in SWI, then to PA
        CHILD:
        Johannes[4], b. 1746, Schalbach; to America with parents; settled Sugarloaf, Luzerne, PA

Abraham[2], b. c. 1684; m. 22 Oct 1708, Diedendorf, Susanna Catherina Hahn, (1683-18 Dec 1777),
    d/o Jacob Hahn of Fleisheim, Moselle Dépt, Lorraine; Abraham d. 16 Apr 1766/7, Schalbach
    CHILD:
        Joseph[3], bp. 11 May 1729, Lorraine, FR; 9 Oct 1749 – arr Philadelphia; settled in Heidelburg
        Twp, Lehigh Co, PA; m. c. 1750, Maria Barbara X; he a. 16 Oct 1804 ,wp, Northampton Co,
        PA; will names wife, sons **Joseph**[4], **Jacob**[4], **Leonard**[4] & **Stephen**[4], daus **Magdalena**[4],
        Katherine[4], **Barbara**[4]; another son **Daniel**[4], b. Sept 13-d. 18 Oct
        1773

Anna[2], sponsor at baptisms in 1702, 1707; no other info

*same person

REF: BAILLIET. Stephen Clay, *The Bailliet, Bailliett, Bailiette, Balyear, Bolyard & Allied Families* (1968);
ALLEMAN, Durward B., & HENRY, Richard J.L., *The Alleman Heritage* (1997); SCHNEIDER, Magdalen, *Ancestry of
Nicholas Allemann & His Wife;* Institute of American Genealogy, *Immigrants to America before 1750;* FISHER, Charles
A., *Early Central PA Lineages*; *The Pioneer Immigrant Joseph Balliet*; BURGERT, Annette K., *18th Century Emigrants
from the Northern Alsace to America* (1992); GÖLZER, Bernd, *Ancestry of Nicholas Allemang and His Wife Magdalena
Schneider* (manuscript, 1992).

BANVARD, David

bp. 15 May 1729, Brognard, n.e. Montbéliard, FR*, Doubs Dépt, Franche-Comté, s/o Pierre & Françoise (Jean-Perin) Banvard; *Montbéliard was a principality belonging to the House of Württemburg, GER until 1793 when it was annexed to FR - it was a Protestant enclave; had sis Marie Marguerite, bp. 11 Apr 1732, Brognard

fa Pierre poss. emigrated with David as there is a Pierre Banvard, bur. 19 Aug 1754 – Nova Scotia (or he could be bro/cousin) - that information is listed on David's "page" of records - listed are Pierre, Marie Elizabeth (sister?), David, Éve

m/1, a.1752, Éve X, who d. aboard ship, bur 13 Mar 1753, age 26

17 Jul 1752 - David, a weaver, arrived at Halifax on the *Speedwell*

m/2, 20 May 1753, Halifax, Nova Scotia, Catherine Elizabeth (Lovy) Carlin who d. 12 Dec 1791, age 74; on the same marr. date, Jean Dauphiné & Marie Elizabeth Banvard also mar.

Dec 1753 – Pierre and David on the list of soldiers who were in Lunenburg, so this Pierre was a bro or cousin – father would have been a bit old for military service

d. 1770, NYC, age 41Y

CHILDREN, m/2:

David[2], bp. & d. 18 Sep 1754

Catherine Elizabeth[2], bp. 1 Aug 1755

Maria Catherine[2], bp. 29 Oct 1757

Maria Marguerite[2], bp 21 Oct 1759

Jeanne[2], bp. 20 Dec 1761

Daniel[2], b. 20 Dec, bp. 26 Dec 1767; m. 25 Dec 1791, Elizabeth Mead; he d. 2 Aug 1831, age 63 – **11 ch**

REF: Baptism Record Book, Temple of St. Suzanne, Brognard Parish, Principality of Montbéliard; Halifax, Victualing list, *Speedwell* P.R.O. Co 217/14, Folio 127; BELL, Winston, *Register of Lunenburg Settlers*; Family Bible records for Daniel & Elizabeth (Mead) Banvard - originals in A. Banvard papers (B219) MN Historical Society.

BARBERIE, Jean/John

of Guienne – formerly a region in s.w. FR, which merged with Gascogne; originally a part of Aquitaine, which the British called Guyenne

m/1, prob. FR, XX

16 Dec 1687 – asked for denization; 5 Jan 1687/8 – naturalized ENG with sons Pierre & Jean Pierre

spring 1688 - to NYC

principal founder of the FR Ch in NYC – was elder, treasurer and secretary; ch had been in existence since 1623 but did not have its own house of worship until 1688

m/2, 10 Apr 1694, FR Ch, NYC, Françoise (Brinqueman) Lambert, widow of Denis Lambert (he was bur. 29 Sep 1691 – FR Ch record, a native of Bergerac, FR); Françoise was the d/o François & Marie (Minvielle) Brinqueman – Marie was the sis/o Gabriel Minvielle, Mayor of NYC, 1684

liv NYC, but had considerable land in Westchester & Ulster Counties; he was a merchant

d. 9 Jan 1727/8, NYC, rec FR Ch, NYC; wp 20 May 1728

CHILDREN, m/1:

Pierre[2], m/1 Susanne Lambert, his stepsister; m/2 Catherine Allaire (c. 1689-a. 25 Sep 1765, wp), d/o Alexandre & Jeanne (Doens) Allaire; Catherine's will dated 30 Oct 1760, mentions bro Alexander, stepdau Elizabeth and niece Elizabeth Allaire (posthumous dau of her bro Andrew); Pierre was vestryman and elder of Trinity Ch in NY; he d. p. 8 Dec 1725, wd – a. 19 Dec 1727, wp; will mentions wife, son John, daus Frances & Elizabeth, also his father John

CHILDREN, m/1:

Susanne[3], b. 12 Feb, bp. 25 Feb 1710/11, FR Ch, NYC; not in father's will

John[3]

Frances[3]

       Elizabeth[3], b. c. 1719; m. André/Andrew Allaire, s/o <u>Alexandre & Jeanne (Doens) Allaire</u> &
            bro/o her stepmother; she d. 11 Apr 1804
Jean Pierre[2], no further info
CHILDREN, m/2:
Jean[2], b. 30 April, bp. 10 May 1696, FR Ch, NYC
Jean Pierre[2], b. 16 Jul, bp. 14 Aug 1698, FR Ch, NYC
Marie Anne[2], b. 25 Apr, bp. 14 May 1701, FR Ch, NYC

REF: HILL, Glenna See, "The Allaire Family of LaRochelle, France and Westchester Co, NY" in the *NYGBR*, Vol. 125 #3 (July 1994); BAIRD, Charles W. *History of the Huguenot Emigration to America,* Vol. II, pp. 139-40 (Baltimore, MD, 1973); WITTMEYER, Alfred, *Registers of the Births, Marriages, & Deaths of the Église Françoise à la Nouvelle York* (Baltimore, 1968); *Huguenot Ancestors Documented by the Huguenot Society of NJ.*

BARBIER, Anne – see <u>DELAUNAY</u>, Claude

BARRÉ, Pierre/Peter

    b. c. 1700, Pontgibaud, Puy-de-Dôme Dépt, Auvergne, FR, n.w. of Clermont-Ferrand, s/o Pierre & X
        (Bonnomeau) Barré
    c. 1720/22 – went to IRE; became a prosperous merchant
    m. c. 1724/5, Dublin, IRE, X Raboteau; her sister Henriette m. William LeFanu, who was of a prominent
        Huguenot family
    1758 - was an alderman in Dublin; his brother John settled estate of their father in FR (father d. c. 1739)
        - John d. in FR Sep1760 - **no issue**
    1766 – had a warehouse in Fleet St and a country house at Cullen's Wood (now Cullenswood and part of
        Dublin – it is s. of the city center)
    d. c. 1776, Dublin, IRE
    CHILDREN:
David Barr[2], b. 1725, IRE; m. c. 1749, IRE, Eleanor X (b. c. 1730, IRE); David d. IRE
        CHILD:
        Margaret[3], b. c. 1750, IRE; m. c. 1767, Capt. James Robb, Jr (b. c. 1745, Co. Down, IRE-d. c.
            1825, Jefferson Co, KY); c. 1773 they emigrated to America – landed in Philadelphia;
            liv in York Co, PA on the MD border until 1786; James served in the Rev. War; Margaret
            d. c. 1807, nr. Princeton, IN, 57 Y; **9 ch**
Isaac Barr[2], b. 1726; was the Right Honorable, member of the British Parliament; aka Col. Barré

REF: AGNEW, David C. D., *Protestant Exiles from France in the Reign of Louis XIV*; MUNCY, Alice Shawhan, *Robb Family* (Oct, 1991); ROBB, Henry (s/o James & Margaret) - letter (1854).

BARRETTE, Barbara de

    b. c. 1638, Valenciennes, FR (then Spanish NETH); had bro Peter; Isaac de Barrette of Haarlem, HOL was
        prob. her fa <u>or</u> bro – Isaac came to America c. 1656/7; surname de Barrelle on some colonial docs
    m. c. 1659, New Castle, DE, Gerret/Gerritt Van Swearingen (1636 Beemsterdam/Reensterdam, HOL* - a.
        4 Feb 1698/9 wp, St. Mary's Co.); Gerret m/2, p. 5 Oct 1676 (date of pre-nup settlement), Mary Smith
    by whom he had 5 ch; Gerret was **not** a Huguenot, he was Catholic
        *supposedly n. of Amsterdam – not found
    1660 - returned to HOL for a yr.
    24 Nov 1661- sailed from HOL on the *Pumerland Church* - passenger list shows Gerret, wife, 2 servants

a. 1664 - liv at Nieuw Amstel (now New Castle, DE) until the surrender to the British in 1664; moved to MD, settled St. Mary's Co., MD

17 Apr 1669 – Gerret, wife + 2 ch, Elizabeth & Zacharias, petitioned for naturalization in St. Mary's Co; it was granted 8 May 1669; Thomas not listed for some reason; Isaac de Barrette on the list as well

d. 1670 St. Mary's Co, MD

CHILDREN:

Elizabeth[2], b. p. 1661, Nieuw Amstel; no more known, p. 1669

Zacharias[2], b. c. 1662/3, Nieuw Amstel; m. Martha X; dau **Jane**[3] + others

Thomas[2], b. 1665, St. Mary's; m. 1687, Somerset Co, MD, Jane (Dane/Doyne/Hyde?); he d. a. 9 Mar 1710/11, wp, Prince George's Co, MD; Jane m/2, 18 Feb 1717/18, Richard Jones – she d. 1727

CHILDREN:

Thomas[3], m. Lydia Riley-**9 ch**

Van[3] m. Elizabeth Walker-**12 ch**

Samuel[3] m. Elizabeth Farmer

John[3] m. Mary Ray-**11 ch**

REF: RAY, Hope S, *Swearingens in America* (1979); The CRESAP Society, *A Van Swearingen-Cresap Register* (1940); WHYTE, Karel L., *Swearingen/Vanswearingen & Related Families* (1997); wills; naturalization papers; SWEARINGEN, H. H., *Family Register of Gerret Van Swearingen & Descendants* (1894); *Colonial Families of the U.S.*, Vol. VII.

BARRINEAU/BARRINO, Isaac

m/1, HOL?, *poss*. Rebecca van Hoose

m/2, Ferriby/Pherebe (X) Downing, widow of Renates Downing

name appears on Gaillard's list of FR Huguenots who settled on the Black River, (now) Williamsburg Dist, SC (list pub. 1848)

9 Dec 1747 - a land grant on the Santee (Craven Co.) was made to Daniel Barrineau – relationship, if any, to Isaac is not clear

by 1790 - there were only 2 Barrineaus in SC, brothers Isaac & Arthur

d. p. 24 Feb 1806, wd – a. 25 Mar 1806, wp, Williamsburg District, SC; names wife Ferriby, daus Margaret, Nancy & Leviniah, daus-in-law Margaret & Sarah, sons Jesse, Isaac & Mandwell – executors son-in-law William Liferage & son Arthur Barrineau,

CHILDREN, m/1:

Margaret[2], m. c. 1778, William Liferage/Lifrage; she d. 1806; **7 ch**

Nancy/Ann[2], m. James Hinson/Henson; dau **Ann**?

Leviniah[2], m. James Bradshaw

Arthur[2], m. Margaret Coleman, d/o Jacob & Susannah (X) Coleman; d. by 1811, Williamsburg Dist, SC; Margaret wrote will 19 Jul 1819, still alive 1820

CHILDREN:

William[3], prob. d. a. 1819 – not in mother's will

Mary K.[3], b. 1792; m/1, John Liferage, her 1st cousin, s/o William & Margaret (Barrineau) Lifrage - **2 daus**; m/2, p. 1810, 1st cousin, Levi Barrineau, s/o Isaac & Emma (X) Barrineau – **6 ch**; she d. p. 1850

Daniel[3]

Thomas[3], went to Montgomery Co, AL

Susan(nah)[3], moved to Montgomery Co, AL; died unmarr.

Margaret Hester[3], m. Williamsburg Co, SC, David Martin Staggers

George[3], b. 1798; m. Priscilla Walters, d/o Jacob Walters; 2 daus **Eleanor**[4], **Mary Jane**[4] (m. Enoch Bradshaw), 2 sons **William**[4], **Jacob C.**[4]

Jesse,[2] d. a. 12 Sep 1817, wp

Isaac, Jr.[2], m. Emma X

CHILDREN:
Isaac III[3], b. 1778; m. Mary (X) McKnight, widow (1782-1839); he d. 18 Apr 1830
Levi[3], m. 1st cousin Mary K. (Barrineau) Liferage; entry above
Hester C.[3]
Martha M.[3], m. X Graham
Julian Jane[3], m. X McKnight
Sarah Eleanor[3], m. Elijah Frink Strong
Eliza E.[3], m. X Tisdale
Manuel/Mandewell[2]
unnamed son[2], m. Sarah X; d. a. 1806

REF: WHITE, Margaret Miller, *The Huguenot Millers, A Family History; Barrineau Family History* (Manuscript); *Transactions of the Huguenot Society of SC*, #92 (1987).

BART/D'IBERT/DIBERT/LeBÈRE/DIVER, Charles Frédéric de

b. 1660; said to be from "St. Serve", FR – not found; there is a St. Sever in Gascogne, now in Landes Dépt, Aquitaine, s.w. of Mont-de-Marsan + a few other towns which "could" be his home
m. prob. FR, Magdalene Margaret (Chartier/Cartier?), b. 1661 FR-d. 1720, VA
1699 - on the 1st ship to Manakintown, VA; list just gives his name, evidently travelled alone
later went to NC; then to SC w/ Rev. Claude Philippe de Richebourg
returned from SC, settled on the VA/PA border
d. 1707, at sea
CHILDREN:
John I[2], b. 1685, FR; m. 1708, Mary Seaworth (1687-1732, killed by Indians, said to be d/o French-Canadian trader and his Shawnee wife); he d. 1732, (then) Cumberland Co, PA, killed by Indians; had 12 ch, 7 of whom were killed w/ their parents
CHILDREN: (5 of 12):
John II[3], b. 1710
David[3], b. 1713
Thomas[3] - no issue
Wilhelm[3], m/1, X Beuchler, m/2 ,X Weigner
Charles Christopher[3], b. 1719 PA, m. 1737, Eve Margaret Daubert or Nei/Ney, he d. 1757, killed by Indians, bur. Dibert Cemetery; c. 1710, John I settled in Dutch Corner, Bedford Co, PA which is c. 9 mi n. of Bedford; he was an Indian trader; the 1st white settlers in PA west of the Susquehanna River
David[2]
Henry[2]
Mary[2]

REF: The Huguenot, #25 (1971-73); WHISKER, James B., *Bedford County Archives*, Vol. 5; Proceedings of the Huguenot Society of PA (1955); BEDFORD CO. HERITAGE COMMISSION, *The Kernel of Greatness.*

BASCOM(E), Robert

b. 1 Dec, bp. 7 Dec 1499 Monthermé, Ardennes Dépt., Champagne, FR, n. of Charleville-Mezières, s/o Jean & Susanne (Barbey) Bascome; Jean was an "ardent Catholic" who d. 3 Mar 1562 at the age of 92; his wife d. p. 9 Dec 1576, wd; other children of Jean & Susanne: **Jean**, bp. 3 Nov 1500, bur 15 Apr 1504; **Suzanne**, bp 12 Jan 1504, m. 1 Mar 1521, Raimond de Mosnard; **Adelaide**, bp. 10 Jun 1505, m. 15 Oct 1526, François de Mosnard; **Guillaume**, bp 19 May 1506, d. 13 Jun 1506; **Marie,** became a nun
1520 – he was emancipated by his father

m. 12 Apr 1533, FR, Marie Dornant, d/o Joseph Anatole & Françoise (duPré) Dornant; she d. a. 1580

c. 1533 – embraced the "new faith" shortly after his marr; by doing this and emigrating, he forfeited his share of his parents' estate

c. 1537/9 - emigrated to ENG with his son Jean; wife not mentioned, may have stayed in FR w/ the younger ch

1545 – on several lists of "Strangers in London"

d. bet 1576-1580, London

CHILDREN:

Jean/John[2], bp. 11 Feb 1534, Monthermé; m. 12 Nov 1569, ENG, Margaret Barber (b. 4 Nov 1536, London), d/o William & Margaret (Martin) Barber; he d. 17 Jun 1617, ENG

    CHILDREN:

    John/Jean[3], b. 1570, ENG, m. Jane Beaumont (bp Sturminster Marshall, Dorset, 24 May 1575 - d/bur 26 Sep 1624 there), d/o Thomas Beaumont & sis/o Avis of Dorsetshire, ENG; John d/bur 6 Apr 1625

        CHILDREN:

        Elizabeth[4]

        Thomas[4], b. c. 1602, m. 13 Feb 1676, Avis X (d. 3 Feb 1676, Windsor, CT), he d. 9 May 1682, Northampton, MA, had a wd 8 Jul 1678/9, 4 ch - **Hannah**[5], **Abigail**[5], **Thomas**[5], **Hepzibah**[5]

        Boniface[4], who m. Mary X

    Thomas[3], b. 1575; m. 20 Jan 1628, Sturminster Marshall, Redigon Dilley (she m/2, 6 Feb 1637 James Mew)

    Guillaume/William[3], m. Marie Gotley

        CHILDREN:

        George[4], went to Bermuda

        Guillaume[4], went to Barbadoes

        Joseph[4], went to VA

        Phillip[4], went to Selkirkshire, Scotland

Guillaume/William[2], bp. 3 Jan 1535; m. 7 Jun 1564, Monthermé, Françoise Dudevant, d/o Jacques; returned to FR to be able to claim inheritance; he was bur 4 Jun 1579; 2 ch: **Françoise**[3], **Suzanne**[3]

Marie[2], bp. 13 Apr 1536; d. 12 Sep 1619, Monthermé, unmarr.

REF: BASCOM, Mrs. Joseph Dayton, *Bascom & Allied Families*; KUHNS, Maude Pinney, *The "Mary and John"*; HARRIS, Edward Doubleday, *Genealogical Record of Thomas Bascom & His Descendants* (1870); BARROW, Geoffrey Battiscombe, *A History of the Battiscombe & Bascom Families of England & America* (London, ENG, 1976).

BASSE, Humphrey

    NOTE: 2 lines are <u>closed</u>: Nathaniel <u>and</u> Samuel

m. a. 1588, Mary Buscier, d/o <u>Dominic & Geneviève (X) Buscier</u>

bur. 4 Jun 1616, St. Helen's, Bishopsgate, London; girdler/haberdasher/merchant nr. Mynsyng (Mincing) Lane, west of the Tower of London; wife Mary, bur. 22 Jul 1616, St. Helen's; both had wills - Prerogative Court Cant, 65 Cope, 80 Cope; H.'s will dated 13 May 1616, wp, 6 Jun 1616, names wife Mary, sons Nathaniel, Richard, Samuel, Humphrey, Luke; daus Hester, Abigail, Sarah, Mary Walthall w/o Luke, father-in-law Charles Pressy and his wife, bro Thomas, dec., bro William, Abraham Busher, John Busher, Nathaniel Busher, Jeremy Busher, etc, 65 Cope; Mary's will refers to ch but names only Nathaniel and son-in-law Luke Walthall, 80 Cope

CHILDREN (1st 11 bp St. Gabriel, Fenchurch St, London; last 7 bp St. Helen's, Bishopsgate, London):

Humphrey[2], bp. 29 Sep 1588; bur. 9 Oct 1588, London

Nathaniel[2], bp. 19 Dec 1589; Feb 1621 to VA on the *Abigail*; 1621/2, back to ENG; p. 22 Mar 1622, back to VA on the *Furtherance*; as a member of the VA Company, he was commissioned to seek colonists for VA, New England & elsewhere; he is **not** to be confused with the Capt. Nathaniel Bass who m. Mary

Jordan, **nor** was he the Nathaniel Bass, bur. 3 Jul 1655, St. Alphage, Cripplegate, London; he d. a. 30 Aug 1654, VA, adm; his estate went to his youngest bro Luke as he was the only surviving male; **NO ISSUE** – a fact attested to by his sisters

Richard[2], bp. 30 Oct 1591; d. a. 1654

Humphrey[2], bp. 7 May 1593; bur 12 Feb 1594/5, St. Gabriel

William[2], bp. 29 Oct 1594; bur 12 Feb 1594/5, St. Gabriel

Mary[2], bp. 25 Jan 1595/6; m. c. 12 Feb 1610/1 (date of lic), St. Giles in the Fields, London, Luke Walthall, who d. a.16 Dec 1617, wp, London; Mary d. a. 1654; 2 ch – **William**[3], b. 21 Feb 1613/4 – **no issue, Mary**[3], prob. d. young (not in father's will)

Hester[2], bp. 3 Jul 1597; m. 5 Sep 1616, St. Dunstan, Stepney, London, Thomas Hobson; liv. Bromley in Aug 1654

Samuel[2], bp. 20 Aug 1598; d. a. 1654; he is **NOT** the Samuel Bass who went to MA; he went to VA with his bro Nathaniel & there is no **proof** that he went to MA; according to the *NEHGS Register*, Vol. CVII (Jul 1953) Samuel Bass of MA was m. in Co. Essex to Anne Savell/Savil (b. Co. Essex); their 1st 2 ch, b. Safrron Walden, Co. Essex – it cites no information on Samuel's parentage; Robert C. Anderson in *The Great Migration Begins*, Vol. I, gives no information on that either - says Samuel was b. c. 1600-d. 30 Dec 1694, aged 94. No Samuel mentioned in the adm of Nathaniel's estate & since his younger bro Luke inherited, he must have d. a. Aug 1654, prob. VA

Humphrey[2], bp. 18 Nov 1599; d. 1623/4, Jamestown, VA

Thomas[2], b. 11 Jan, bp. 21 Feb 1601/2, London; bur 11 Jan 1602/3, St. Gabriel

Hannah[2], bur. 1 May 1605, St. Helen's

Barnaby[2], bp. 30 Jun 1605, St. Helen's; d. a. 1616 (not in father's will)

John[2], bp. 14 Dec 1606; d. a. 1616 (not in father's will)

Lydia[2], bp. 15 May 1608; bur 26 Jan 1628/9, St. Helen's

Abigail[2], bp. 14 Jan 1609; m. X Thorpe; widow liv Chissell Hampton, Oxon, Aug 1654

Luke[2], (twin) bp. 5 May 1613; d. single p. 1654

Abraham[2], (twin) bp. 5 May 1613; d. a. 1616 (not in father's will)

Sarah[2], bp. 27 Jun 1615; m. Thomas Hastler; liv. London Aug 1654

REF: BELL, Albert D., *Bass Families of the South* (Rocky Mount, NC, 1961); BANNERMAN, W. Bruce, editor, *The Parish Registers of St. Helen's, Bishopsgate, London* (London, 1904); DOWD, Lea L. & SILVESTRI, Patti L., *Early Basses in VA* (1999); Coldham, Peter Wilson, *The Complete Book of Immigrants, 1607-1660*.

BAUDOIN/BOWDOIN, Pierre

b. c. 1643, prob. LaRochelle, FR; a physician in FR and a wealthy landowner
> m. Elizabeth *Bureau* (d. 18 Aug 1720, Boston, MA, age 77Y, bur. Granary Bur. Ground), d/o Jean Bureau? – the surname is not proven - a Pierre Baudoin m. 1448, the d/o Jean Bureau, the mayor of La Rochelle - may be mixed up; the only rec. marr of a Pierre Baudoin in La Rochelle was 18 Apr 1674 to Henriette Legoux, nor are there any bap. records; was Elizabeth a 2nd wife?

fled from LaRochelle

by 1 Apr 1683 - in Dublin or Wexford (s. of Dublin), IRE
> 17 Jul 1684 – a deposition taken in Dublin stated that Pierre was a denizen of Dublin, residing in Wexford & was the owner of the ship *John of Dublin*

c. 6 May 1686 – to America on the *John of Dublin*; he is called a merchant; he was in MA by 9 Nov 1686, when he sold the ship at Salem, MA; settled 1st at Casco (Portland), MA (now ME); 3 Feb 1687, he petitioned Gov. Andross for a grant of 100 acres on Barbary Creek, Casco Bay - the petition was granted 8 Oct 1687 – the petition was written in FR; between the writing of the petition and the granting of it, he purchased some property in Falmouth (now Portland) on the corner of Spring & Emery Streets; supposedly went to Boston 16 May 1690, a day before Indians attacked Falmouth – he was definitely there by 1691

d. 8 Sep 1706, Boston, MA; bur. the Granary; 16 Jun 1704, wd- 6 Jul 1719, wp, Suffolk Co, MA; his will
    mentions wife Elizabeth, does not name ch, makes allowances for ch of dec. ch, if any

CHILDREN:

Jean/John I[2], b. 1674, LaRochelle, FR; m. Susannah (Kendall) Harmanson, d/o John & Susannah (Savage)
    Kendall of Northampton Co, VA, wid/o John Harmanson (d. a. 20 Oct 1719, wp, Northampton Co,
    VA); Jean/John d. p. 20 Feb 1716, wd - a. 6 Apr 1717, wp Northampton Co, VA - mentions Susannah
    in his will, sons Peter & John, daus Susannah & Mary; Susannah d. a. 9 May 1739 wp Northampton
    Co.; some sources say that Susannah was Susannah Stockley – doubtful - 1 of her grandsons was
    named <u>Kendall</u> Harmanson

    CHILDREN:

    Peter[3], b. c. 1700, (in father's will) <u>m/1</u>, c. 1726, VA, Adah Harmanson, half sis; <u>m/2</u>, 13 May 1733,
        Susannah (Preeson) Godwin; he d. a. 14 Jan 1746 wp; **issue**

    John II[3] (in father's will); m. Peggy X; moved to Isle of Wight Co, VA and then to NC; d. p. 11 Sep
        1786, wd – a. 4 Dec 1788, wp Isle of Wight Co, VA; will mentions sons **John III**[4], **Thomas**[4],
        Elias[4], **William**[4], wife Peggy; says that he also has 5 daus – **Mary**[4], **Hannah**[4], **Rhody**[4], **Chloy**[4]
        + **Frances**[4] -1 of the daus m. X Powell

    Susannah[3] (in father's will); m. X Satchell

    Mary[3], (in father's will); prob. d. young , no more info

    Elizabeth[3], m. X Robins (not in father's will)

James I[2], b. c. 1676/7, LaRochelle, FR; <u>m/1</u>, 18 Jul 1706, Boston, Sarah Campbell (d. 21 Dec 1713);
    <u>m/2</u>, 16 Sep 1714, Boston, Hannah Portage (d. 23 Aug 1736); <u>m/3</u>, 24 Apr 1735, Boston, Mehitable
    Lillie (2 Feb1693/4-1748), d/o Samuel & Mehitable (Frary) Lillie; James d. 5 Sep 1747, age 71 yrs,
    bur the Granary

    CHILDREN, m/1:

    James II[3], b. 5 May 1707; d. 29 Sep 1707

    Elizabeth[3], b. 27 Jun 1708 (twin); d. 12 Jul 1708

    Mary[3], b. 27 Jun 1708 (twin); m. 12 Feb 1729, Balthazor Bayard; **issue**

    John[3], b. 22 Aug 1709; d. 21 Nov 1711

    Peter[3], b. 19 May 1711; d. 1712

    William[3], b. 14 Jun 1713; m. Phoebe Murdock (d. 13 Dec 1772, Boston, bur. Granary); he d. 24 Feb
        1773, Roxbury, MA; **3 daus** (2 unmarr), 3rd dau **Sarah**[4], <u>m/1</u>, 1st cousin James Bowdoin III[4],
        s/o James II & Elizabeth (Erving) Bowdoin & grgrs/o <u>Pierre & Elizabeth (Bureau) Baudoin</u>,
        she <u>m/2</u>, Gen. Henry Dearborn, Sec. of the Navy, under Thomas Jefferson

    CHILDREN, m/2:

    Samuel[3], b. 25 Jul 1715; d. 18 Sep 1716

    Elizabeth[3], b. 25 Apr 1717; m. 26 Oct 1732, Boston, James Pitts; she d. 20 Oct 1771

    Judith[3], b. 5 Mar 1719; m. 12 Jun 1744, Boston, Thomas Flucker

    James II[3], b. 7 Aug 1726; m. 15 Sep 1748, Boston, Elizabeth Erving (d. 23 Oct 1809), d/o John Erving;
        he d. 6 Nov 1790, 64Y, bur. the Granary; James became the Gov. of MA; dau **Elizabeth**[4], m.
        1767, John Temple; son **James III**[4] (1752-1811), m. Sarah Bowdoin[4], d/o William Bowdoin
        (above) – **no issue**

Elizabeth[2], b. La Rochelle, FR; m. Thomas Robins of Chincoteague Island, Northampton Co, VA; d. p. 1747;
    issue

Mary[2], b. La Rochelle, FR; m. 22 Aug 1708, Stephen Boutineau (d. a. 22 May 1761 wp); she d. p. 1747;
    son **James**[3] m. Susannah Faneuil, d/o Benjamin & Anne (Bureau) Faneuil, grgrgrdau/o <u>Benjamin &
    Suzanne (L'Épine) Faneuil</u>

REF: MARCH, U. Bowdoin, *A Research of the Bowdoin Family in the U.S.* (1982); *New England Historic Genealogical Society Register,* Vol. 10, pp. 76077, 114; Vol. 114 (1960), pp. 243-268; SADIK, MS, *Colonial& Federal Portraits at Bowdoin College* (1966); FORBES, Allen & CADMAN, Paul F., *The Boston French* (1971);SAVAGE, J., *Gen. Dictionary of the 1st Settlers of New England,* Vol. I; Wills, John and John, Jr.; BAIRD, CW, *History of the Huguenot Emigration,* Vol. 2, p. 248 (1985); HUNTINGTON, Temple Prime, *Some Account of the Bowdoin Family* (NY, 1887); BRAULT, Gerard J., *Pierre Baudoin & the Bowdoin Coat of Arms* (1976); VR-Boston; Susannah's will.

BAUN/BANE/BAEN/BAIN/BEAUNE, Joost/Joseph de

b. c. 1642, Beaune, Côte d'Or Dépt, Bourgogne, FR; it is said that he witnessed the killing of his family & was the only member of his family to escape religious persecution

c. 1660 - went from FR to Flanders, later to Middelburg, HOL

m/1, XX; **no issue**

m/2, p. 30 Oct 1681 (date of intention), Middelburg, Elisabeth Drabbe; according to marr record, Joost was a widower from Poperinge, widowed 9 months and had no ch; Poperinge is in Flanders, 4 mi w. of Ypres/Ieper, (now) BEL, less than 2 mi n. of the French border

1683 - to America; settled Bushwick, NY, where he was town clerk

c. 1684 - to New Utrecht, NY, where he was a clerk, schoolmaster and reader in the Reformed Dutch Ch

1687 – took Oath of Allegiance in Kings Co, NY - name *Joost de baene;* record says he had been in the colony 4 yrs.

c. 1698- in New Rochelle and was 1st schoolmaster there

c. 1702 - went to Orange Co, NY, & resided at "The Pond" (aka Rockland Lake), nr. Haverstraw, now in Rockland Co

1704 - in Huguenot Colony on the Hackensack; active in affairs of the Hackensack Reformed Dutch Ch – served as elder and churchmaster

p. 1718- a. 18 Nov 1721, he d. Hackensack, NJ – his wife was called "widow of Joost" at the baptism of a grdau on 18 Nov 1721; 4 Jun 1724 Joost's wp

CHILDREN, m/2:

Jacobus/James[2], b. 9 Feb 1683, Middleburg; m/1, 12 Jan 1709, Tappan, NJ, Anatje/Anna Canniff, d/o Jeremiah & Anatje (Woelffs) Canniff of Westchester Co, NY, Anna d. 1736 - **8 ch**; m/2, Catherine X; he d. p. 1753;

Cristeyan/Christian[2], bp. 15 May 1687, 1st Reformed Dutch Ch, Brooklyn; m. 29 Jan 1709, Hackensack, Judith Demarest, d/o Samuel & Maria (Druen) Demarest (Samuel s/o David & Marie (Schier) Demarest); Christian d. c. 2 yrs later; **1 dau Christina**[3] who m. Hildebrandt Lozier & had **13 ch**

Matie/Mayke/Martha[2], bp. 4 May 1690, Reformed Dutch Ch, Brooklyn; m. 10 Nov 1705, Hackensack, David Samuel Demarest, s/o Samuel &Maria (Druen) Demarest (see above); she. d. a. 13 Feb 1761; **11 ch**

Karel/Charles[2], b. c. 1692, New Utrecht, NY; m. 14 Feb 1714, Tappan, Jane Haring (14 Apr 1698- 29 Jun 1765), d/o Peter & Margaret (Bogart) Haring; he d. 25 Aug 1765; **11 ch**

Catarina/Catherine[2], bp. 4 May 1695, 1st Reformed Dutch Ch, Brooklyn; d. young

Margrietje/Marie[2], m. Jun 1728, Theodore Romain

REF: GATES, Mary B., "The DeBaun Family in America" in the *NYGBR,* Vol. LXX (1939), Vol. LXVI (1935); SEACORD, M.H. *Biographical Sketches & Index of Huguenot Settlers of New Rochelle, 1687-1776*; WALLACE, William H., *Genealogy of the DeBaun Family* (1979), (1992); LEE, Frances B., editor, *Genealogical & Memorial History of NJ,* Vol. II (1910).

BAYARD, Nicolas

b. Grenoble, FR

m. Blandina Condé/Condi

1572 – left FR, went to HOL; very active in many of the 70 Walloon churches in HOL

a.1590 - was pastor of FR church in Antwerp, BEL; son succeeded him in that position

1599 – college professor

d. HOL

CHILD:

Lazare[2], 1591 – pastor at Antwerp; had pastorate at Zierikzee (in Zeeland, n.e. of Middelburg), 1594-1613; m. 1607, Judith Begend/Begond or DeVos, from N. Brabant Prov; he d. 1617, Antwerp
CHILDREN:

Samuel[3], b. Breda, HOL, bp. 12 Dec 1610; m. 21 Oct 1638, Anneke/Ann Stuyvesant, d/o Rev.
    Balthazar & Margaretta (Hardenstein) Stuyvesant & sis/o Gov. Peter; Sam. d. c. 1645, Alphen
    aan den Rijn, Holland (town s.e. of Leiden); 1647 – Ann left for NY w/ her 4 ch
    CHILDREN:
    Petrus[4], b. c. 1640, Alphen; m. 28 Nov 1675, Blandina Kierstede, d/o Dr. Hans &
        Sarah (Roelofs) Kierstade, grdau/o Jans & Annake (Jans) Roelofs; had land
        on the DE/ MD border but later sold it; Blandina d. 1702; Petrus d. 1699, NYC
        CHILDREN:
        Samuel[5], b. 1675, #1 Broadway, NYC; m/1, 1699, Susanna Bouc(h)elle (b. 1677), d/o
            Liège & Anna Margarette (Condé/Couda) de Boucelle; m/2, Bohemia Manor,
            Cecil Co, MD, Elizabeth Sluyter, d/o Peter Sluyter; he d. 21 Nov 1721,
            Bohemia Manor; **4 ch**
        Petrus[5], b. NYC; owned land in Ulster Co, NY; m. c. 5 Oct 1696, Rachel
            Van Bolen; had son **Richard**[6]
        Sarah[5], NYC
    Balthazar[4]
    Nicholas[4], b. c. 1644, Alphen
    Catherine[4], poss. a posthumous ch
Judith[3], m. Director-General Peter Stuyvesant (b. 1592), brother of Ann (above)
2 other sons[3]

REF: WILSON, Gen. Jas. Grant, *Colonel John Bayard (1783-1807) & the Bayard Family in America* (1885);
FORDYCE, Nannie L., *Bayard Ancestry* (1954); BULLOCH, Dr. Joseph Gaston Baillie, *A History and Genealogy
of the Families Bayard, Houstoun of GA and the Descent of the Bolton Family* (1919); BAIRD, Charles W., *History
of the Huguenot Emigration to America,* Vol. I (1973).

BAYEUX, Thomas

    b. Caen, Normandie, FR; had bro Jean/John with whom he did business in London in the 1690's – John
        d. a. 1742 as he called "deceased" in Thomas' will
m. c. 14 Jul 1703 (date of lic), Madeline Boudinot, d/o Élie and Susanne (Papin) Boudinot; she d. 3 Sep 1743
10 May 1705 - was made free of the city of NY as a merchant; he became quite wealthy
p. 1725/6 – joined Trinity Ch, an Anglican congregation, an offshoot born of a dispute with the pastor of the FR
    Ch, Louis Rou; liv. on King Street in NYC
d. c. 1742, wd, NY
    CHILDREN: (8 ch, bp. French Ch, NYC – Susanne not on list but in Thomas' will; some of the ch
    were re-bap. in the Dutch Church)
Magdelaine[2], b. 21 Jul, bp. 28 Jul 1706; m. Edward Holland (he was Mayor of NYC 1747-50)
Thomas[2], b. 5 Jul, bp. 11 Jul 1708; m. 14 Apr 1753, Mary Lispenard (b. 20 Jul 1727), d/o Anthony Lispenard
    & Elizabeth Huygens de Kleyn; his father's will left him all his "real & personal property in the
    Kingdom of France"; at least one dau **Abigail**[3] (c. 1765, NY-a. 1833, Ontario, CAN), m. 3 Jun 1790,
    NY, Elijah Vincent (24 Dec 1759-1833/35), s/o Lewis & Abigail (Fowler) Vincent
Anne[2], b. 16 Dec, bp. 24 Dec 1710; m. John Groesbeck
Marie[2], b. 5 Jul, bp. 11 Jul 1716, FR Ch, NYC; m. Rev. Richard Charlton, who d. a. 10 Oct 1777, wp,
    Richmond Co, NY – his will mentions ch/o Thomas Bayeux (presumably Thomas[2]) & Henry Bayeux
    (not sure of this connection), wife not mentioned, must have d.; **issue**
Jeanne[2], b. 20 May, bp. 31 May 1719; godmo was Susanna Bayeux – no relationship given
Élisabeth[2], b. 25 Jul, bp. 2 Aug 1721
Jean[2], b. 14 Jun, bp. 19 Jun 1723 – his uncle Jean Bayeux of London was his godfa, represented by his older
    bro Thomas (b. 1708); d. young
Marianne[2], b. 14 Jul, bp. 21 Jul 1725
Susanne[2], m. Jeremiah Schuyler

REF: BAIRD, Charles W., *History of the Huguenot Emigration to America*, Vol. II; BUTLER, Jon, *The Huguenots in America* (Harvard Press, 1983); WITTMEYER, Rev. Alfred V., *Registers of the Births, Marriages & Deaths of the "Église Françoise à la Nouvelle York from 1688 to 1804* (Baltimore, MD, 1994).

BEAU, Marie – see LeVAN, Daniel

BEAUCHAMP, Jean

bp. 3 Jun 1656, Charenton-le-Pont*, s.e. of Paris, s/o Samuel & Marie (Malherbe) Beauchamp; his father was a
   lawyer and an influential member of the Church of Paris who d. 1688, Thorpe, ENG;
*there are 2 other Charentons but this seems the most logical given his father's involvement with the Ch of
   Paris
c. 1685 - family fled to ENG
m. Marguerite Billon; she d. 8 Dec 1727, Hartford, CT, 59 yrs old; bur Center Ch
   by 1687- member of the FR Ch at Narragansett, RI; on list of parishioners who contributed yearly to
   salary of M. Carré, the minister- Jean pd. 20 sh; name is in church records up to 13 Apr 1690; may have
   gone back and forth between RI and Boston as dau Katherine was b. in Boston
c. mid-1690 - went to Boston, MA
p. 1721- to Hartford, CT
d. 14 Nov 1740, Hartford, CT, 88 yrs old; bur. Center Ch; 24 Nov 1740, wp, Hartford
CHILDREN:
Katherine[2], b. 10 Jun 1687, Boston; m. X Lataile; **issue**
Jean/John[2], b. 25 Jan, bp. 3 Feb 1689, Narragansett; went to SC – location mentioned in his father's will
Marie/Mary[2], b. 20 Jan 1690, bp. 16 Mar 1690, Narragansett; m. Dr. John Ranchon; **issue**
Mary Ann/Marian[2], b. 24 Jun 1696; m/1, Capt John Lawrence (15 Dec 1682-1719) issue, m/2, 5
   Nov 1751, 1st Ch, Hartford, Capt. John Keith (24 Jun 1696-13 Jan 1784)
Adam[2] – in father's will
Isaac[2], m. Elizabeth Lucas; **issue**
Peter[2], not in father's will
Margaret[2], b. c. 1707, m. John Michael Chenward, native of Geneva, SWI (d. 7 Apr 1735, 56 yrs, bur Center
   Ch, Hartford); Margaret d. 18 Mar 1783, 76 yrs, bur Center Ch; **issue**
Susanna[2], m. 28 Oct 1747, 1st Ch, Hartford, Allan McLean
Dau[2], m. X Shepard; not in father's will

NOTE: **not** to be confused with Jean Beauchamp/Bushong, b. 1692, m. Barbara X & went to Lancaster Co,
PA – that line was closed 1996 - no evidence that the family was either of French heritage or Huguenot

REF: DeFOREST, L. Effingham, *Records of the French Church at Narragansett, 1686-1691,* translated & edited;
BAIRD, Charles W., *History of the Huguenot Emigration to America*, Vol. II; BARBOUR, Lucius Barnes, *Families of Early Hartford, CT* (Baltimore, MD, 1977); Vital record, Boston; MANWARING, Charles William, *Early CT Probate Records*, Vol. 3, Part 1, 1737- 1742.

BEAUFORD/BEAUFORT/BUFORD, Richard

b. 1617/18 Bordeaux, FR
1 Aug 1635 - left Gravesend, ENG on the *Elizabeth* for America
m. 1640 VA, d/o Jean Vaux/Vaus – Margaret ?
1656 - in Lancaster Co, VA
d. p. 1656 Lancaster Co, VA
CHILD:

John[2], b. c. 1642; m. 11 Apr 1662, Christ Church Parish, Lancaster Co (became Middlesex Co, 1669), VA, Elizabeth Perot/Parrott (b. c. 1645), d/o Richard Sr. & Margaret (X) Perrot; John d. 18 Apr 1722, bur 20 Apr 1722, Middlesex Co, VA

CHILDREN:

Thomas[3], b. 1663, Lancaster Co, VA; m. Mary X (d. 29 Dec 1720, bur 30 Dec); **3 ch**, b. 1682-88; Thomas d. 9 Dec 1716, bur 11 Dec Middlesex Co, VA; a son **Thomas**[4], bp. 21 May 1682, Christ Ch Parish, m. Elizabeth X, liv. Christ Church Parish, Middlesex Co, VA, d. a. 7 Jul 1761 wp Middlesex Co, VA

Ambrose[3], b. 1665; m. Elizabeth X

Susannah[3], b. 1667; m. 14 Oct 1689, Thomas Guy

Elizabeth[3], b. 1669; m. William Priest

John[3], d. 18 Apr 1722

REF: BEAUFORD, William M. *Family of deBeauford in France, Holland, Germany and England;* MINTER, Marcus B., *Buford Family in America* (San Francisco, 1903); *The Huguenot,* Pub. #13 (1945-47) pub. by The Huguenot Society, Founders of Manakin; *Parish Register of Christ Church, Middlesex Co, VA, 1653-1812* (1897); BUFORD, George Washington & MINTER, Mildred Buford, *History & Genealogy of the Buford Family in America* (1924).

BEBOUT/BIBOU/BIBAU, Jan Pietersz (aka John BEBOUT, Sr)

b. 13 Jan, bp. 31 Jan 1647 (bp. Catholic), Thielt, Flanders, s/o Pieter Bebout, a devout Catholic, & his 1st wife Maria Verkindere (who d. when Jan was b.); Pieter's fa Symoen Bibau was very involved in the Protestant movement; Thielt is now Tielt in W. Flanders, BEL, 10 mi n.e. of Roulers/Roeselare

1679 - Jan sold land that he inherited from his father

early 1687 - left Aardenburg (ne of Middelburg, HOL) for New Amsterdam

m. 9 Aug 1691, Flatbush, NY, Metje/Mattie (Beekman) Van Der Hoeven (b.1657 Albany), d/o Martin Henricksen Beekman & Susanna Jans; Martin arr New Netherland in 1629; Metje had m/1 Cornelis Van Der Hoeven (bur. 10 Jan 1689) – 4 ch

11 Oct 1693 - he was put in jail in Kings Co. for "divers scandalous and abusive words spoken bye the sayde John against their majesties justices of the peace…to the contempt of their majesties authority and breache off the peace" – evidently a man of independent thought!; he was called a weaver in the record

1696 – bought a house + 42 acres in Bedford Co, LI

30 Aug 1701 - he sold his stepson Cornelis Vanderhove (*sic*) ½ of a brew house at Bedford; he was the collector of taxes in the city of Brooklyn that year

30 Aug 1705 - sold his farm at Bedford & moved to Staten Island where he ran a brewery

d. a. 27 Oct 1716, wp, Flatbush, Long Island, NY; had made his will on 28 Oct 1710 which gave his entire estate to his wife; he signed the will "Jan Bibou"; his property on Staten Island was inventoried at £26; he mentions sons Peter, Jacobus, wife Mette & her "first" ch

CHILDREN:

Marytje[2], bp. 23 Aug 1691, Brooklyn, NY; alive in 1706 – no more info

Peter[2], b. c. 1693; went to NJ; m. c. 1715, Christine Mollissen, prob. d/o John Mollissen; he served in the NJ Militia in 1715 w/ his bro Jacob; was in Piscataway by 1716; one dau **Mertien**[3], bp. 26 Oct 1715; no more info

Jacob[2], b. c. 1695; often called "Cobus"; m. 13 Feb 1717, NYC, Mary Sweem, prob. d/o Anthony Sweem; at least **2 sons, 2 daus**

Jan II/John[2], b. c. 1697, Brooklyn; m. 1720, Mary Miller (b.1700/02 NJ-d. Piscataway, NJ); he d. c. 1747 Middlesex Co, NJ; at least **2 sons**

CHILDREN:

Peter[3], b. p. 1721, Piscataway, NJ; m/1, 1 Dec 1747, Sarah Jewell – 1 son **Ebenezer**[4]; m/2, c. 1749/50, Sarah Darling – **9 ch**; he d. p. 25 Jan 1782, wd, Morris Co, NJ

John[3], b. 25 Aug 1729, Piscataway, NJ; m. Mary Thurman; he d. 21 Jun 1803 Pigeon Creek, Washington Co, PA; **5 sons, 4 daus**

REF: BERGEN, Teunis G., *Register of Early Settlers of Kings Co. (Long Island, NY)* (1881); FLICK, Alexander C., *Bebout Family History*; *Bebout Family in Flanders & North America*; HIX, Charlotte Megill, *Wills & Administrations, Richmond Co, NY, 1670-1800* (Bowie, MD, 1993).

BEC/BECK, Daniel

b. 1640/50, Abriès, old Dauphiné Prov, FR, n.e. of Château-Queyras, in the Hautes-Alpes Dépt. nr. the Italian border

m. Abriès, Catherine Martin (c. 1650, FR-d. GER)

fled FR; went to SWI; then to Hesse, GER

d. a. 1706 GER

CHILDREN:

Marie[2], b. c. 1675, Abriès; *poss.* was the Marie Bec who m. Moïse Guiremand; she was bur. 23 Mar 1713, in Berlin

Pierre[2], b. c. 1676, Abriès

Geoffroi/Cha(u)ffré[2], b. c. 1680, Abriès; m. 20 Apr 1706, Mutschelbach, Baden, GER (s.e. of Karlsruhe, n.w. of Pforzheim), Marguerite Jouvenal, (c. 1680, Val Pragela*, Le Piémont, FR-17 Jan 1743, Todenhausen, Hesse, GER (n. of Marburg, s.w. of Frankenberg); Marg. from le Villaret^ (s.e. of Briançon, Hautes-Alpes Dépt, nr. Italy), d/o Barthélemi Jouvenal; Ch. d. 24 Dec 1739 Todenhausen

CHILDREN:

Marie[3], b. 9 Mar 1708, Untermutschelbach, GER; m. 29 Apr 1732, Jean Pez; she d. 28 Apr 1761, Todenhausen

Catherine[3], b. 1709, Auerbach, GER (prob. the one n.e. of Mosbach); m. 29 Apr 1732, Jacques Vincon; she d. 1 Jun 1769, Wiesenfeld (s.w. of Frankenberg)

Catharina Susanne[3], b. 16 Oct 1710, Auerbach; m. 10 Oct 1737, Alexander Vial, s/o Jean & Susanne (Turquais) Vial; she d. 24 Mar 1786, Todenhausen; **9 ch** (4 d. young)

Jean Daniel[3], b. 1713, Mutschelbach, Baden, GER; m. Susanne Puy

Guillaume[3], b. 7 Mar 1723, Todenhausen; m/1, 17 Mar 1743, Todenhausen, Marie Sachet; m/2, 6 Jun 1746, Todenhausen, Norade Lagier (23 Dec 1724, GER-30 Oct 1784, Wiesenfeld, GER); he d. 12 Dec 1800, Wiesenfeld

CHILDREN, m/2:

Jacques[4], b. 17 Aug 1747, Todenhausen; he was a *Lehrer*, teacher

Alexandre[4], b. 23 Sep 1750, Todenhausen; m/1, 17 Dec 1771, XX; m/2, 15 Apr 1776, Ester Lagier (c. 1755, Wiesenfeld- d. p. 1808, Wiesenfeld), d/o Jaque Lagier; he d. Wiesenfeld; **4 ch**; their grgrgrsons Stephan Alexander Beck (1900-1978) and Hermann (1904-1992) emigrated to Philadelphia both sponsored by aunt Christina (Beck) Rebe who had a bro Hermann and a sis Louise Christina who also went to Philadelphia

Anna Marie[4], b. 22 Dec 1754, Todenhausen; m. 17 Jan 1778, Wiesenfeld, Jean Michel Clement; she d. 15 Jul 1718, Wiesenfeld

Jacques Guillaume[4], b. 14 Dec 1758; m. 1778, Anna Marthe Lange; he d. 1809; he was a teacher

Jean Daniel[4], b. 5 Feb 1760, Wiesenfeld

Isaac[4], b. 14 Sep 1763, Wiesenfeld

*The Val Pragela(s) is a valley between the Durance & Guisane Rivers (the Dora and the Chisone in Italy), n.e. of Briançon & s.w. of Susa, Italy – very close to the border of the 2 countries

^ this was somewhat ambiguous – either she was from le Villaret, as described, or she was from a sm. village in the Pragela

REF: VÖLKER, Karl-Hermann, *Wiesenfeld* (1988); BELION, Eugen, *The Immigration of the Families Bec in the State Hesse-Kassel, 1686-1720*; all the German vital records were written in French, verifying that the family was of French origin; picture of a Huguenot plaque in Schwabendorf, GER (se of Todenhausen) with name BEC & date 1687 on it.

BEDLO/BEDLOE/BEDLOW, Isaac

a. 1652 - from Calais, Picardie, FR, to New Amsterdam; gave his name to Bedloo's/Bedloe's Island in NY Harbor (now Liberty Island); poss. went to Batavia, Java, in the Dutch East Indies, prior to NY, as his marr record says he was from Batavia

m. 16 May 1653, NYC, Elisabeth/Lysbeth de Potter who m/2, 22 Apr 1680, Pieter DeLannoy/Delano

? 23 Jan 1662 – an Issack Bedlo, "Dutch, late of England" was naturalized in Maryland**?**

23 Dec 1667 – Capt. Robert Needham sold the island to Isaac; it remained in Isaac's estate until 1732 when it was sold for 5 shillings to NY merchants Adolphe Philipse & Henry Lane; also called Love Island; a lighthouse was there; island was used as a smallpox quarantine station and a pest house; just bef the Amer. Rev., it was to be used for Tory refugees, but the buildings were burned 2 Apr 1776; 1800 the State of NY ceded the island to the US Govt. for a fort in the shape of an 11 pt. star, called Ft. Wood, aka Star Fort; the island was chosen in 1877 as the site of the Statue of Liberty and the fort became the outline of its pedestal and the island became Liberty Island

d. a. 1680 NY

CHILDREN (all bp. rec. Reformed Dutch Ch, NYC):

Isaac[2], bp. 11 Jan 1662; m. Hermina Groenendahl; **issue**

Catalina/Catharina[2], bp. 22 May1664; m. Thomas Herdin; **issue**, incl. son **Johannes**[3], bp. 18 Aug 1689, Ref. Dutch Ch, NYC, Isaac & Elisabeth were his godparents

Pieter[2], bp 31 Jul 1667

Maria[2], bp. 3 Nov 1669; m. Claes Burger; **issue**, incl. dau **Catharina**[3], bp. 5 Oct 1684, Maria's fa or bro Isaac and sis Catharina were godparents

François[2], bp. 22 Dec 1672

REF: GANNON, Peter Steven, editor, *Huguenot Refugees in the Settling of Colonial America* (1985); BAIRD, Charles W., *Huguenot Emigration to America; Ancient Families of New Amsterdam & NY*; info on Bedloe's Island from website; INNES, J.H., *New Amsterdam & Its People* (NY, 1902); REAMON, G. Elmore, *The Trail of the Huguenots* (Baltimore, 1966); FERNOW, Bethold, *Minutes of the Orphanmasters Court of New Amsterdam, 1655-1663* (NY, 1907); *Collections of the NYG&B Society, Vol. II, Baptisms, 1639-1730, Reformed Dutch Church*, edited by EVANS, Thomas Grier (NY, 1901).

BELLANGÉE/BELLANGER/BELLINGER, Ives/Éves/Évi de

b. c. 1665-70, Poitou Prov., FR; his father was killed by Louis XIV's dragoons - his mother & her ch had to flee, 1st to ENG, then to America, bet 1682-1690

m. 10 6 mo 1697, Friends Meeting, Philadelphia, Créjanne/Christian de la Plaine (bp 21 Jan 1681 NY-

d. p. 1720), d/o Nicolas & Susanna (Cresson) de la Plaine; minutes of a Friends Mtg on 25 4th mo 1697, say that Ives produced a certificate from VA

p. 1697 - moved to Egg Harbor, NJ, p. marriage; he was a weaver

d. 2 Dec 1719, wp 10 May 1720, Little Egg Harbor; will lists all the ch but Nicholas (dec.) and Samuel, but mentions an expected child, and his wife Christian

CHILDREN:

Susannah[2], b. p. 1698

Isaac, b. p. 1698; m. twice; **4 ch**

Elizabeth[2], b. 17 4th mo 1699; m. 1720, Little Egg Harbor, Robert Smith, a Quaker; she d. 11 7th mo 1747; Robert m/2, 1749, Ann (X) Cordeary (d. 16 Nov 1763), widow of William Cordeary; **6 sons, 2 daus**, m/1

Évi/Jué[2], b. 5 or 25 Jan 1701; m. Susanna English, **7 ch**
James[2], b. 24 Jan 1703; m. 6 Nov 1727, Margery Smith (b. 28 Nov 1702/3-11 May 1790), d/o Thomas
        & Alathea (Dalton) Smith; James d. a. 18 Mar 1790, wp, Little Egg Harbor - **8 ch**
Nicholas[2], b. 2 Feb 1706; d. a. 1719
Michel/Michael[2], b. 3 Jan 1708; d. p. 1719
Joshua (Sr.)[2], b. c. 1710; m. Naomi X; he d. a. 22 Jun 1761, wp; **3 sons**, **2 daus**
Samuel[2], b. p. 1719, posthumously; m. Alice Parker, **1 ch**

REF: HINSHAW, Wm, *Encyclopedia of American Quaker Genealogy,* Vol. 2, pp. 458, 504; St. Nicholas Society, Vol. 4, p. 131; Huguenot Society of PA; NJ Archives, 1st Series, Vol. 23, p. 34 (will); Cox, J. Bellange, *Bellan-gee Family in America; The Atlantic County Historical Society*, Vol. 7, #2 (Oct 1973); *Colonial Conveyances, Provinces of East & West NJ.*

BELLEVILLE/BELVILLE, Jean/Jan/Johannes/John

b. c. 1650, St. Martin, Île de Ré, FR, *prob.* s/o Jean & Susanne (Arnaud) Belleville
28 Jul 1670 - on the membership list of the Midwout Church at Flatbush, NY; on a list 4 Nov 1670
        he is called Johannes Belleville; Jean was a weaver
m. 14 Mar 1677, Dutch Church, Staten Island, New Amsterdam, Hester Casier, (c. 1650-1710/20)
        of Sluis, Flanders, d/o Philippe & Marie (Taine) Casier
23 Dec 1685 - rec. a patent for his farm in Long Neck on Staten Island from the Governor although
        Jean had purchased it earlier from a man who had rec. a patent in 1675
7 Feb 1691/2 - purchased 160 acres on the n.w. side of Staten Island, the s. side of Fresh Kills
1698 - he donated an acre of land "unto the French Congregation" for a church bldg – this is the 1st
        recorded donation to any church on Staten Island; he and Hester may be bur. there
1701 – granted British citizenship
d. c. 1710/20 NY
CHILDREN:
Jean II[2], bp. 3 Nov 1677, Reformed Dutch Church, New Amsterdam; poss. to Albany
Philip[2], bp. 25 May 1679, Midwout Church, Flatbush; m. XX, "a Dutch wife"; d. 1736, Lackfords
        Hall, New Castle Co, DE; **3 ch**
Mary[2], b. c. 1686, Staten Island; m. Barent Sweem??
Hester[2], b. a. 1690; m. Nathaniel Britton III (b. 1687), s/o Nathaniel II & Elizabeth (Lake) Britton;
        dau **Sarah**[3], bp. 9 Apr 1732, m. Henry Lane

REF: BAIRD, Charles W., *History of the Huguenot Emigration to America,* Vol. I (1966); TAYLOR, Paul Belville, *Jean Belleville the Huguenot, his Descendants* (1973); PURPLE, Samuel S., *Records of Marriages in Reformed Dutch Church of New Amsterdam, 1639-1801.*

BELLIER, Elizabeth/Lysbeth

from Dordrecht , HOL, d/o Jean & Catherine (Herque) Bellier, prob. from Rouen, Normandie, FR
bp. 24 Jan 1615/6, Dordrecht Walloon Ch; Dordrecht is s.w. of Rotterdam
m. 16 Sep 1641, North Brabant, HOL, David Ackerman (b. 24 Jan 1615, Oss, N. Brabant, HOL - d. c.
        1662, NYC), s/o Johannes Akkerman & *prob.* Anneken Adrianse; David was a schoolmaster at Geffen
        (now Maasdonk), n.e. of 's-Hertogenbosch, N. Brabant, HOL - 's-Hertogenbosch (Duke's Wood) is
        sometimes referred to as Bois-le-Duc which is what the French called the town – c. 1794, the FR
        captured the town and made it the capital of the Lower Rhine in 1810 but left the area in 1813 when the
        Prussians drove them out
31 Aug 1662 - sailed from Amsterdam on *D'Vos* (*The Fox*) Eliz, her husband & 6 ch, ages 20, 18, 16, 12,
        8, 6; some sources say that David d. at sea but even if that is not so, he did not survive long after arr in
        NY

d. prob. Mar 1668 Harlem, NY

CHILDREN:

Anneken/Annetje/Annetie[2], b. 31 Jul 1642, Leiden, HOL; m. 28 Jun 1664, Nathaniel/Daniel Pieterszen; she d. 9 Jan 1730/1, NYC; 5 ch bap. Reformed Dutch Ch, NYC, bet. 1665-88 – **2 sons,
3 daus**; the 1st rec. says Nathaniel all the others say Daniel – either 2 husbands or a misprint –
there is an 8 yr. gap between the records, so *could* be 2 husbands, both surnamed Pieterszen

Elizabeth[2], b. 1643/4; m. 29 Jan 1668, Kier Woulters Kierson, widower of Jannetje Jans

Johannes[2], b. 21 Mar 1645; d. c. 1659

Louwerans/Laurens[2], b. 12 Jun 1650, Geffen, N. Brabant, HOL; m. 3 Aug 1679, Geertie Egberts;
he d. 3 May 1707, Little Ferry, Bergen, NJ; one dau **Lysbeth**[3], bp. 8 May 1680, and one son
Egbert[3], bp. 23 Feb 1685, both in the Reformed Dutch Ch, NYC

David[2], b. Sep 1653, Geffen, HOL; m. 13 Mar 1679/80, NYC, Hillegond Ver Planck (1 Nov 1648,
New Amsterdam, NY-17 May 1714, Hackensack, NJ), d/o Abram Isaacs Verplanck & Maria
Vigne, d/o Guleyn & Ariantje (Cuvellier) la Vigne; he d. 4 Jun 1724, Hackensack, NJ; **3 sons,
3 daus** bap. Reformed Dutch Ch, NYC – however, 2 of the ch were named Gelyn, listed here
as daus, *could* have been sons

Lodewyck[2], b. 1654, Berlicum, N. Brabant, HOL; m/1, 14 Jun 1682, Jannetie Bleyck, d/o Jacob Bleyck &
Sarah Puten – dau **Elysabeth**[3], bp. 7 Dec 1684, Old Dutch Ch, Kingston, NY, son **David**[3], b. c. 1694,
m. c. 19 May 1719, Maritie Sie, d/o Jacobus Sie & Catherine X, grgrgrd/o Nicolas Sy; m/2, 18 Apr
1699, NYC, Hillegond Bosch, d/o Albertzen Bosch & Marietje Eshuysen, dau **Marite**[3], b. 25 Feb
1699/00-d. p. 1755, son **Albartus**[3], bp. 16 Aug 1713, in the Reformed Dutch Ch, NYC; Lodewyck d. a.
1714, Philipsburg, NY

Abraham[2], b. 3 May 1656, Berlicum; m. Aeltie Van Laer, d/o Adrian Van Laer & Abigail Ver
Plancken; he d. p. 1723. Hackensack, bur. Dutch Ch on the Green; 7 ch, bap. Reformed Dutch
Ch, NYC bet 1684-93 – **3 sons, 4 daus**, 2 of whom m. sons of Cornelis Doremus

REF: *NY Marriages Previous to 1784* (Baltimore, MD, 1968); EVANS, Thomas Grier, editor, *Baptisms Reformed
Dutch Church, NY, 1639-1730* (NYC, 1901); HOES, Rosewell R., editor, *Old Dutch Ch of Kingston, Ulster Co, NY, 1660-
1809* (Baltimore, MD, 1980); BOYER, Carl 3rd, *Ship Passenger Lists to NY & NJ, 1600-1825* (Newhall, CA, 1978).

BELLUNE, Michael

poss. s/o John Bellune, the immigrant

b. c. 1735; had sibs – **Elizabeth**, m. X Brown; **Michael**; **William** -mar.- **issue**; **Sooanne**, **Mary**

m. X Boissière, who d. a. 1790, prob. before the Rev War

civil and patriotic service (SC) during Rev. War

d. a. 31 Jan 1811, NC

CHILDREN:

Elizabeth[2], b. 9 Nov 1757, Long Branch, nr. Georgetown, SC; m. X Bigelow; her will says that her paternal
grfa was an exile from FR to Carolina and that she was of "purest Huguenot descent"

Martha[2]

Daniel[2], b. 30 Mar 1766; m. a. 1783, Mary Gause (b. 14 Apr 1763), d/o William Bacot & Martha (Frink)
Gause; Daniel d. p. 3 Jul 1793, wd

CHILDREN:

Mary[3], b. 2 Feb 1738; d. p. 23 Aug 1791 (aunt's will); rec. lands from her father

William[3], b. 24 Aug 1784; prob d. young; not in aunt's will & rec. nothing from his fa

Michael[3], b. 26 Feb 1786; named in father's will and rec. property from grfa Michael; m. Elizabeth
(Hankin) Gause, d/o Dennis & Martha (Masters) Hankin, widow of X Gause; **no issue**

Sarah[3], b. 22 Dec 1787; rec. same gifts as others; m. Isaac Baker by license dated 15 Jan 1807,
Brunswick Co, SC

Elizabeth[3], b. 14 Apr 1790, rec. the same as others; m. Samuel Frink; she d. 20 Nov 1843; bur. nr. the head of the Calabash River, Brunswick Co.; **12 ch**

Martha[3], b. 16 Jul 1792

REF: *Transactions of the Huguenot Society of SC, #77,* p. 116 (1972), #81 (1976), pp. 31-46; *DAR Patriot Index,* Vol. I, p. 202.

BÉNÉZET, (Louis) Jean

s/o Étienne, grs/o Claude; Jean had brothers Antoine & Jean Baptiste (a merchant at Dunkerque); it is said that the family was originally from Carcassonne in the southern Province of Languedoc or from the Midi at Congénies, s.w. of. Nîmes (all in southern FR)

m. 16 Aug 1682, St. Quentin, Somme Dépt, Picardie, FR, Marie Madelaine Testart, d/o Dr. Pierre and Rachel (Crommelin) Testart; Marie contracted a severe cold shortly after the b. of Pierre and d. 15 days later (7 Sep 1692); Rachel Crommelin was the d/o Jean Crommelin & Rachel Tacquelet

d. 15 Aug 1710, Abbeville, Somme Dépt, Picardie, FR, of apoplexy

CHILDREN:

Jean Étienne[2], b. 22 Jun 1683, Abbeville, FR; bp 25 Jun 1683, at home; m. 29 Oct 1709, St. Eustache Ch (just n.w. of Les Halles), Paris, FR, Judith de la Méjanelle, d/o Léon & Judith (Lienrard) de la Méjanelle; Léon was a merchant of *toile* (linen); 3 Feb 1715 – the family fled to Rotterdam as Jean's goods and property had been confiscated; since emigration was illegal, it is said that he crossed the border nr. Malincourt (Nord Dépt, Nord-Pas-de-Calais), by bribing a sentry; he, wife + 2 ch arr in Rotterdam on the 15th of Feb; 22 Aug 1715 they went to ENG for 16 yrs.; arr Greenwich, ENG, on the 26th, where the family stayed for a month while Jean found a house in London; 1731 – to America and settled nr. Philadelphia, PA; he d. 1 Apr 1751, Germantown, PA; she d. 4 Sep 1767, at age 72; both are bur in the Germantown lower burying ground (Hood's)

CHILDREN:

Marie Judith Madelaine[3], b. 1 Nov 1710, St Quentin, FR, bp. 2 Nov 1710, Ch of St. Catherine; m/1, 10 Jul 1742, David Bruce of Edinburgh, SCOT; m/2, 25 Jun 1750, Dr. John Frederick Otto; she d. 27 Jan 1786, Bethlehem, PA; **no ch mentioned**

Marianne[3], b. 26 Feb, bp. 26 Feb 1712, Ch of St. Catherine; d. 12 May 1712, St. Quentin, FR; bur 13 May 1712, Ch of St. Catherine

Ant(h)oine[3], b. 31 Jan 1713, St. Quentin, bp. 1 Feb 1713, Ch. of St. Catherine; m. 13 Mar 1736, Philadelphia Friends Mtg, Joyce Marriott, d/o Samuel & Mary (X) Marriott of Burlington, NJ; he d. 3 May 1784, Philadelphia; famous humanitarian & abolitionist; **no issue**

Susanne[3], b. 25 Feb, bp. 7 Mar 1715, Walloon Ch, Rotterdam; d. 20 May 1715 Rotterdam, HOL

Marianne[3], b. 7 Jul 1716, London; bp.11 Jul 1716, L'Église de la Savoye (Savoie), on the Strand; m. 17 Sep 1742, Jacob Lischy of Switzerland, a Moravian minister; she d. York Co, PA; **1 dau**

Susanne[3], b. 22 Jul, bp. 24 Jul 1717, French Ch, Wandsworth, ENG (s.w. of London); m. 10 Jul 1742, John Christopher Pyrlaeus (b. 1713 in Vo(i)gtland, a district in s.w. corner of Saxony); she d. 8 Oct 1779, Herrnhut, Saxony, GER (sw of Gorlitz); **3 ch**

Pierre[3], b. 6 May 1719, London; bp. 10 May 1719, English Ch, Wandsworth; d. 23 May 1719 and bur. churchyard of the FR Church, Wandsworth, ENG

Jacque(s)/James[3], b. 26 Aug 1721; bp. 9 Sep 1721, Parish of Chelsea; m. 5 Jun 1747, Philadelphia, Ann Hasell; he d. 16 May 1794, Bucks Co, PA; **5 ch**

Philip(p)e[3], b. 6 Nov 1722, London; bp. 12 Nov 1722, L'Église du Quarré* on Berwick St, off Oxford St; m. 5 Jun 1766, Sarah Ayries; he d. 13 Oct 1791, Philadelphia; **2 ch**

Daniel[3], b. 26 Dec 1723, London; bp. 5 Jan 1724, L'Église du Quarré; m. 24 Apr 1745, Elizabeth North (d. 25 Apr 1797); he d. 24 Apr 1797, Philadelphia; **9 ch**

Madelaine[3], b. 15 Jan 1724/5, London; bp. 21 Jan 1724/5, L'Église du Quarré; d. 12 Jan 1726/7, bur. 14 Jan 1726/7, Poland St. Cemetery for Parish of St. James (in Soho, off Oxford St.)

Gertrude[3], 5. Mar 1726/7 London; bp. 15 Mar 1726/7 at home; d. 28 May 1728; bur. cemetery of St. Martin in the Fields (nr. Trafalgar Square)

Jean[3], b. 6 Feb 1727/8; d. 10 Feb 1727/8; bur. St. Leonard cem. in Shoreditch – junction of Shoreditch High St. and Hackney Rd.

Elizabeth[3], b.12 Jun 1730; d. 23 Dec 1730; bur cemetery of St. Leonard in Shoreditch

Pierre[2], b. 24 Jun, bp. 2 Jul 1684, Neuville (perhaps Neuville-au-Bois, s. of Abbeville); bp. rec. mentions his uncle Pierre (mother's bro), also an Isaac Testart, merchant of London, who was m. to his cousin Marie Madeleine Crommelin; Pierre d. 2 Aug, bur. 3 Aug 1686, in the Ch of St. Jacques

Jacques[2], b. 5 Oct, bp. 6 Oct 1685; m. Françoise Élisabeth Fonnereau

Jean Ja(c)ques[2], b. 21 Dec, bp. 22 Dec 1686, St. James Church, Abbeville

Cirus/Cyrus[2], b. 5 Jan 1688; bp. St. James Church, Abbeville; named after uncle Cyrus Testart

Madelaine Marguerite[2], b. 5 Mar, bp. 6 Mar 1689, in the Church of "Cath'in"; m. X de Brissac

Chilepior? Milizior?[2], son b. & bp. 12 Nov 1690; d. 2 Nov 1702 Paris

Pierre Testart[2], b. 23 Aug 1692; bp. Church of St. Catherine, named for grfa; mar. Susanne X

*This church started out as a chapel in Monmouth House on the s. side of Soho Square and the east side of Firth St; c. 1694, the congregation moved to a building on Berwick St, about 3 blks w. It was also known as L'Église du Quarré de Sohoe.

REF: COMFORT, Dr. William W., *"Anthony Benezet: Huguenot & Quaker"* in the *Proceedings of the Huguenot Society of PA*, Vol. XXIV, pp. 36-43 (1953); BENEZET, Henrietta – translation of *Memoirs Commenced Aug't 16th 1682* by Jean Bénézet and continued by his son Jean Estienne Bénézet; SMALL, Samuel Jr., *Genealogical Records of George Small, Phillip Albright, Johann Daniel Dünckel, William Geddes Latimer, Thomas Bartow, John Reid, Daniel Benezet, Jean Crommelin, Joel Richardson* (1905).

BENIN/BENNING, François/Francis

b. FR

m. prob. ENG, Anne de Bonnette of Thorigné, Deux-Sèvres, Poitou-Charentes, FR, d/o <u>Daniel & Jeanne (Courturier) de Bonnette</u>

Oct 1700 - to VA with other FR Huguenot refugees

d. a. 3 Oct 1710 Manakintown, VA; wife d. a. that date or shortly after as their son was raised by relatives

CHIILD:

Antoine/Anthony[2], c. 1705, Manakintown; m. 1726/8, Elizabeth Jouany (b. c. 1710), d/o <u>Jean & Esther (LaFuitte/Fitte) Jouany</u>; used surname BENNING; Antoine was raised in the home of his maternal uncle by marriage, <u>Pierre Dutoit/Dutois</u> (Pierre's wife Barbara and Anne Benin were sisters); he d. bet. 1761-82 Buckingham Co, VA

CHIILDREN (all b. King William Parish, Manakintown, was later Buckingham Co.):

Isaac[3], b. 8 Aug 1729

Judith[3], b. 7 Sep 1731

Joseph[3], b. 10 Feb 1733/4; d. 1807/8

Elizabeth[3], b. 17 Sep 1736; d. 20 Oct ----

Jean/John[3], b. 10 Dec (or Oct) 1737; m. 20 Jul 1775, Sarah Cobb (b. 20 Nov 1756); they went to Columbia Co, GA; he d. bet 6 Mar-17 Nov 1809; **7 ch**

James[3], b. 2 Jan 1740, Buckingham Co, VA; m. Lexington, KY, Lucy Ann Perkins (b. Jan or Nov 1749 Henrico Co, VA), d/o William & Lucy (Watkins) Perkins; he d. p. 28 Feb 1829, wd – a. Nov 1831, wp, Fayette Co, KY; will names wife Lucy, John Watkins, husband of his dec. dau **Constance**[4], sons **Anthony**[4], **William**[4], **Isaac**[4], **James**[4], **John**[4], **Perkins**[4], daus **Lucy**[4] (m. X Gray), **Judith**[4] (m. X Lewis) & 2 gr daus

REF: ROBINSON, Eva Hardin Benning, *François Benin (Francis Benning) His Descendants & Allied Families* (Independence, MO, 1981); *VA Genealogist*, Vol. 7, #4 (1963); *The Huguenot*, Vol. 29 (1979-81); James' will.

BEN(N)ET, Willem Adriaense

b. c. 1605/10, prob. HOL, s/o Adrien Benet, a Frenchman; used patronymic *Adriaense* as a surname, which would indicate Dutch origin; family used surname *Bennet* after the English occupation of the Colony by 1636 - in New Amsterdam and deeded land in Brooklyn; he and Jacques Bentyn bought 936 acres of land at Gowanus from the Keskaechquerem tribe, later known as the Canarsie Indians; this tract would later become part of Brooklyn and covered nearly all the land s. of the current 27th St.; he was a cooper

m. c. 1636/7, New Amsterdam, Mary Thomas (Badye) Verdon (c. 1605/7, HOL- p. 1697), d/o Thomas Badye & Aeltje Braconie, widow of Jacob Verdon by whom she had 2 ch; Mary m/3, p. 9 Oct 1644, Poulus Vander Beeck, surgeon, and had 6 more ch

d. bet. 9 Mar – a. 9 Sep 1644 – killed in an Indian attack in Brooklyn, New Amsterdam

surname **BENNET** was used after his death

1687- sons and grsons of Willem were recorded as having taken an Oath of Allegiance to the English Crown so were not of English origin; in the 1698 census of Brooklyn his descendants were not identified as being of English or French origin; a couple records say Willem emigrated from Helsingør, Denmark

CHILDREN: (Willemse/Willemszen was surname used sometimes by children)

Adriaen/Arie[2], b. 1636/7, Gowanus, King Co, NY; m. 3 Dec 1662, Angnietje Jans Van Dyck, (c. 1645 – p. 1711), d/o Jans Thomasze Van Dyck & Tryntje Achias Haegen; liv. New Utrecht; he d. p. 9 Feb 1704

    CHILDREN:

    Willem[3] m. Jannetje Willams – **2 ch**

    Jan/John[3] m/1, 6 Jun 1696, Fermetje Rapalje, m/2, Phebe X– total of **8 ch**

    Marytje/Maria[3], m/1, Jacob Verhulst, m/2, Jacobus Dooren – total of **5 ch**

    Catharina[3] m. 18 Dec 1685, Cornelis Rutgers Van Brunt – **2 ch**

    Isaac[3] m. Lena X – **4 ch**

    Arie[3] m. Barbertje X – **1 ch**

    Jacob[3] m. Barbara Verdon – **4ch**

    Cornelis?[3]

    Angnietje[3] m. Johannes Folkers – **1 ch**

    Abraham[3] m. Jannetje Folkers (sis/o Johannes) – **10 ch**

    Engletje[3]

    Antje

Willem/William[2], b. c. 1638/9, prob. Gowanus; m. 9 Apr 1660, Gertruyd Van Mulheym

    CHILDREN

    Willem[3], m. 15 Dec 1686, Adriaentje Vandewater – **4 ch**

    Jan[3], m/1, Arfje Hendrickson, m/2, Antje Wynants – total of **9 ch**

    Maria[3]

    prob. **Aeltje**[3]

    Heyltie[3], m Alburtus Van de Water – **1 son**

    Jacob[3], m. 9 Apr 1692, Neeltje Beekman – **7 ch**

    Gertruyd[3]

    Femmetje[3], m. Jacob Verdon – **3 ch**

Christian[2], bp. 6 Jan 1641, New Amsterdam Dutch Ch; d. young

Christian[2], bp. 30 Mar 1642, New Amsterdam Dutch Ch; prob. d. young, unmarr.

Marritje[2], bp. 9 Mar 1644, New Amsterdam Dutch Ch; m/1, c. 1664, Johannes Christoffel Schaers – **6 ch**; m/2, 25 Apr 1690, Flatbush Dutch Ch, Hendrick Thys Lanen Van Pelt – **1 ch**

NOTE: Number and names of ch. of Adriaen & Willem are not consistent in the various sources.

REF: BENNETT, Kenneth A., *William Adriaense Bennett, Descendants & Related Families* (Baltimore, 1998); LEDLEY, Wilson V., "Willem Adriaense Bennet of Brooklyn , NY, & Some of His Descendants" in the *NYGBR*, Vol. XCIII #4 (Oct 1962, pp. 193-204; BAIRD, Charles W., *History of the Huguenot Emigration to America,* Vol. 1,

p. 177; HOFF, Henry B., *Genealogies of Long Island Families*, Vol. I (Baltimore); PROVOST, Andrew J., Jr., *Early Settlers of Bushwick, Long Island, NY & Their Descendants*, Vol. 1 (Darien, CT, 1949 – unpub.); Research by Lee Crandall PARK.

BENOIT/BENOY, Pierre

    of LaRochelle, FR
    fled FR and settled in Albany, NY area
    m. 14 Dec 1696, Albany, NY, Henrikje Van Schoohoven; she was bur. 12 Oct 1729, Albany
    d. p. 1707, prob. Albany
    CHILDREN:
    Pierre[2], bp. 19 Sep 1697, Albany; m. 7 Mar 1723, Albany, NY, Anna Fort
        CHILD:
        Hendrickie[3], bp. 18 Jan 1724; m. 22 Sep 1748, Kingston, NY, John Davenport, cordwainer of
                Kingston, Ulster Co, NY; had son **Peter/Petrus**[4], bp. 23 Sep 1750
    Marie[2], bp. 30 Nov 1698, Albany
    Margarita[2], bp. 16 Aug 1702, Albany
    Geurt[2], bp. 24 Jun 1705, Albany; bur. 8 Jul 1741 (twin)
    Jacob[2], bp. 24 Jun 1705, Albany (twin)
    Martha[2], bp. 3 Aug 1707, Albany

    REF: *Dutch Settlers Society,* Vols. VIII & IX Yearbook (Albany, NY 1932-34); PEARSON, Jonathan, *Contributions for the Gen. of the Descendants of the 1ˢᵗ Settlers of Schenectady, 1662-1800* (Albany, NY, 1873); *Yearbook of the Holland Society* (1904 and 1905).

BERGERON, Jacques/James

    b. Thorigné, Poitou, France (12 mi s.e. of Niort, what is now the Deux-Sèvres Dept., Poitou-Charentes)
    m. Thorigné, Judith Péletan(t) (b. Thorigné, d. p. 14 Nov 1742, wd– a. Dec 1742, wp, Beaufort Co,
        NC); will mentions sons John, Elias, daus Judith, Jean, Margaret
        fled to Bristol, ENG; both members of FR Ch in Bristol, 1707/8; Jacques was a woolen worker
        according to church records
    1712 – in NY by this date
    p. 1719 – to VA; Judith to NC p. 1728
    d. p. 25 Dec 1727, wd-a. 12 Jun 1728, wp Northampton Co, VA (inv-10 Aug 1728); will mentions
        wife Judith & children, the latter not by name
    CHILDREN:
    Pierre[2], b. 25 Sep 1707, Bristol, ENG; not in mother's will
    Judith[2], b. 12 Oct 1708, Bristol, ENG; m. John Wilkins (b. NC or VA- d. p. 18 Jan 1774, wd ,
        Chowan Co, NC); she d. p. 1774, Chowan Co, NC
    Jeanne[2], b. 17 Feb, bp. 24 Feb 1711/2, FR Ch, NYC; m. X Barrow; she d. p. 1742
    Anne[2], b. 7 Jan, bp. 17 Jan 1713/4, FR Ch, NYC; not in mother's will
    JeanJohn[2], b. 21 Mar 1714/5, bp. 27 Mar 1715, FR Ch, NYC; d. p. 1742
    Éli/Elias[2], bp. 27 Jan 1716/7, FR Ch, NYC; d. p. 1742
    Marguerite/Margaret[2], b. 11 Mar, bp 18 Mar 1718/9, FR Ch, NYC; m. X Giddins; she d. p. 1742

    REF: BAIRD, Charles W., *History of the Huguenot Emigration to America,* Vol. 2; WITTMEYER, Alfred, *Registers of the Birth, Marriages & Deaths of the Église Françoise à la Nouvelle York;* Northampton Co, VA Wills, Deeds, #26; Judith's will from Beaufort Co; MAYO, Ronald, *The Huguenots in Bristol.*

BERNARD/BARNAR, David

b. FR

prob. m. XX, a. emigration

Jul 1700 – arr Manakintown on the *Mary Ann*

1710 – on tithable list for 1st time

1714 - on tithable list - listed with wife, 4 sons and 1 dau in VA; last one on which he was listed

d. a. 9 Feb 1715/6, inv, Henrico Co, VA

CHILDREN:

Jean/John[2], m. Anne Delpish, d/o Francis & Mary (Dupré) Delpish (Mary was the d/o Jean & Jane (X) Dupré); Jean acquired a patent for FR land in 1719 and was listed as tithable; acquired a patent for FR land, 25 Aug 1731 (patent #846 – 154 acres on the s. side of the James in Goochland, now Powhatan) located next to Delphish patents; d. a. 20 Sep 1787, wp, Powhatan Co, VA; his wife Anne was a co-patentee (with her sisters Mary, Judith) in her own right; his will lists wife, sons John, David, Francis, William, Jacob, Benjamin, daus Judith (Flournoy), Rebecca (Porter), Ann (Flournoy), Mary Ann (Harrison), Mary Magdalen (Barner)

> CHILDREN:
>
> **Judith**[3], b. 27 Oct, bp. 5 Nov 1731; m. X Flournoy; got "items" in her father's will
>
> **Rebekah**[3], b. 24 Apr 1734; m. William Porter; son **Josiah**[4], b. 10 Dec 1764; also rec. "items"
>
> **John**[3], b. 4 Apr 1736; father's will - rec. a slave girl
>
> **Anne**[3], b. 6 Oct 1738, m. X Flournoy; rec. £10 in her father's will
>
> **David**[3], b. 21 Sep 1740; father's will - rec. a slave girl
>
> **François/Francis**[3], b. 24 Jan 1742/3; father's will - rec. 5 sh
>
> **Pierre**[3], b. 17 Jul 1747
>
> **William**[3], got patent #846 per his father's will, dated 19 Jul 1786 + 3 female slaves; he and his bro Benjamin also got whatever was left after the others rec. their due
>
> **Jacob**[3] – father's will – rec. a slave woman & her son
>
> **Benjamin**[3], father's will – rec. a tract of land of 46 acres (patent #1104) + 2 male & 2 female slaves; he and his bro William got the remainder of the estate
>
> **Mary Ann**[3], m. X Harrison; rec. £10 in her father's will
>
> **Mary Magdelen**[3], m. John Barner; father's will – 2 female slaves

David, Jr.[2], m. Anne X; he d. 1735

> CHILDREN:
>
> **Marie**[3], b. 1731
>
> **David**[3], b. 1735; d. young
>
> **Magdelaine**[3], b. 1735
>
> **Ann**[3]

Anthony[2]

unnamed son[2], who d. young

unnamed dau[2]

REF: CABELL, Priscilla Harriss, *Turff & Twiggs, Vol. I, The French Lands*; GANNON, Peter Steven, editor, *Huguenot Refugees in the Settling of Colonial America* (NYC, 1985).

BERNARD, Pierre/Peter

b. FR, s/o Count Pierre Bernard; family went to ENG

m. XX

c. 1700 - to America, prob. VA

CHILD:

John[2], emigrated to America at the age of 14, without parental consent; m. Mary Abney (b. c. 1710), d/o Dannett & Mary (Lee Abney) Abney – Mary was the widow of Dannett's bro Paul; settled in Albemarle Co, VA; he d. p. 1777

CHILDREN:

John[3], b. 16 Nov 1736; m. 6 Mar 1760, Elizabeth Barnett (b. 14 Apr 1747-30 Aug 1822, Richmond),
d/o John, Jr. & Sarah (McCann) Barnett; he d. 15 Jan 1824, Milton, VA; he served in the
French & Indian Wars
CHILDREN:

Allen[4], b. 29 Jan 1763, Albemarle Co; m. 3 May 1787, Ann Mitchell, (28 Oct 1764-
1 Apr 1857); he. d. 4 Jul 1834, Nelson Co, VA

William[4], emigrated to KY

Joseph[4], remained in VA

Valentine[4], m. poss. Phoebe McCann; went to KY

Jesse B.[4], went to KY

John[4], remained in VA

Joanna[4], m. X Bragg

Elizabeth[4], moved to KY

Charlotte[4], m. 27 Dec 1796, Samuel Lyon

Mary[4], m. 24 Sep 1803, William D. Fitch

Elizabeth[3], carried away by Indians as a child

Abner[3]

Peter[3]

2 daus[3], unnamed

REF: BERNARD, Ted. B., *Bernard "Grandparents"* (unpub.); COUPER, William, "Couper Family of
Longforgan, Scotland & Norfolk, VA" in *The VA Magazine of History & Biography*, Vol. 59 (1951)
(Longforgan is nr. Dundee); MACY, E.E., *Bernard Family;* John Bernard Bible Records (NSDAR files, DC).

BERNIÈRE, Jean Antoine de/John Anthony

b. Caen, Normandie, FR, s/o Jean & Lamelett/Lancelott (X) Bernière

1685 – left FR for HOL; to ENG, later settled in Lisburn, N. IRE

3 Apr 1699 – naturalized; commissioned as ensign in Col. Brudnell's Regiment; served in IRE & Spain;
lost his left hand in the Battle of Almanza, 25 Apr 1707, during the War of Spanish Succession;
Almanza is s.e. of Gijón, León Prov.

m. Lisburn, Co. Antrim, N. IRE (s.e. of Belfast), Marie Madeleine Crommelin (14 Oct 1688-8 Jul 1715,
N. IRE, bur Lisburn Catholic graveyard), d/o (Samuel) Louis & Anne (Crommelin) Crommelin (1st
cousins); Marie Madeleine d. days aft the birth of son Louis, age 27Y; Marie supposedly bp in the Oude
Waalse Kirk, evidently in Oude, Holland (s.e. of Groningen) & b. on the date above - the plaque placed
at her grave says she d. 8 Jul 1715, age 21 – math doesn't work!; at the time of the marriage Jean was
said to have been from Alençon, Normandie, FR

d. 1729 IRE – made will giving $$ to Louis, goods and chattels to daus

CHILDREN:

Madeleine[2], m. Henry Donlevy

Mary Anne[2]

Louis Crommelin[2], b. 1715, IRE (may have been b. earlier, c. 1711); m. 1739, Elinor Marley, d/o Anthony &
Elizabeth (Morgan) Marley, sis/o Bishop George Marley; she d. 29 Aug 1759, age 47Y; Capt. Louis
had service in Canada & Senegal – he became ill in Senegal and was sent home but he d. at sea, 1762
CHILDREN:

John Anthony[3], b. 1744; m. Rostrevor, Co. Down, N. IRE, on Carlingford Lough, e. of War-
renpoint, Anne Jones; Lt. Col. John Anthony d. 1822; emig. to America – Carolinas?;
dau **Louise**[4] m. X Du Maurier, dau **Elinor**[4] + **10 others**[4]

Henry A. C[3], b. 1758; m. Elizabeth Longley, sis/o Archbishop of Canterbury; Maj. Gen.
Henry served in America and FR; d.1813, FR; had 1 son **John Henry**[4] (1801,
Rochester, Kent-1809, Verdun, FR), and 2 daus, 1 named Elinor[4]

> **Catherine**[3]
> **Elinor**[3]
> **4 others**[3]

REF: McCRADY, Louis de Bernière & BARNWELL, Mary de Bernière, *Mrs. Edward McCrady, II & Her De Bernière Family Papers* (unpub.); Huguenot Society of London, *Denization &Naturalization of Aliens in England and Ireland, 1603-1700*, Vol. XVIII (1911); BEST, E. Joyce, *The Huguenots of Lisburn, The Story of the Lost Colony* (1997).

BERNON, Gabriel

b. 6 Apr 1644, LaRochelle, FR, s/o André & Suzanne (Guillemard/Guélemard) Bernon; André was a merchant in LaRochelle who d. some yrs. before the Revocation, leaving 5 sons and 5 daus, all of majority: André, Samuel, Jean (b. 1659), Gabriel, Jacques, Esther, Jeanneton (m. Jean Allaire), Éve (m. Pierre Sanceau), Suzanne (m. Paul duPont), Marie (m. Benjamin Faneuil); Samuel & Jean became zealous Romanists, despite the fact that Samuel was m. to the d/o a Huguenot minister and Jean was the pastor of the Reformed Church of St. Just, nr. Marennes; the Bernons were a prominent and wealthy family with the name being found as early as 1191 on a list of Crusaders to the Holy Land; the family formed the nucleus of Protestantism in LaRochelle – religious services were held in their home

m/1, 23 Aug 1673, Ester LeRoy (1654-14 Jun 1710 Newport, RI), d/o François & Ester (Mocquay) LeRoy; Gabriel's father signed the marr contract, his mother Suzanne had already d.
    liv. in Canada for a time as he was engaged in extensive trade with the West Indies, the Caribbean and, especially Canada, as well as FR; 1685, since he was Protestant, he had to leave FR Québec and return to FR

13 Oct 1685— as a wealthy Huguenot, his goods were seized; a. May 1686 he was imprisoned; he became sick in prison and as it seemed he was near death, he was allowed to go home (c. 10 May 1686); it was reported to the authorities that he had died; actually he had recovered and was smuggled into Amsterdam, HOL, with the thought that his family would join him in ENG; then his wife and ch were taken to a convent where they were kept prisoners and exhorted daily to renounce Protestantism; finally Ester feigned conversion, escaped and soon rejoined her husband

1687 – denization in London

5 Jul 1688 - landed Boston, MA, on the *Dolphin*; rec. a grant of 2600+ acres in New Oxford, MA, where he built a gristmill, a sawmill, a FR church and a fort; in Boston he was a manufacturer of rosin, salt, etc; he resided in Boston and had a fellow Huguenot émigré acting as his agent in Oxford.

1697/8 - went to RI - Newport to Providence, to Wickford, back to Providence in 1719 where he lived across the street from Roger Williams and St. John's Episcopal Church which Gabriel founded

c. 1699 - he left the FR Reformed Ch and became an Episcopalian and was responsible for the building of 3 Episcopal churches in RI

m/2, c. 1712, Mary Harris (c.1688 -1 Feb 1735/6), d/o Thomas II & Elnathan (Tew) Harris; she m/2, 3 Dec 1737 Nathaniel Brown.

d. 1 Feb 1735/6, Providence, RI; wd, 16 Feb 1727/8- wp, 10 Feb 1735/6; 92 yrs. old; he was bur. beneath St. John's Episcopal Church on N. Main St.

CHILDREN m/1, b/bp. LaRochelle:

Marie/Mary[2], b. 10 Jul, bp. 18 Jul 1674; m. 24 Sep 1694, Abraham Tourtellot; she d. Gloucester, RI; **3 ch**

Gabriel[2], b. 12 Mar, bp. 17 Mar 1676; d.1706, in early manhood, in a shipwreck in Narragansett Bay; unmarr.

Esther[2], b. 22 Oct, bp. 17 Nov 1677; m. 30 May 1713, Adam Powell (d. 24 Dec 1725); she d. 20 Oct 1746, bur. Tower Hill, RI; **issue**

Suzanne[2], b. 25 Aug, bp. 29 Aug 1682; bur. 2 Nov 1683

Jacques[2], b. 19 Jun , bp. 22 Jun 1685, St. Martin, Île de Ré

Sarah[2], m. 11 Nov 1722, Benjamin Whipple (11 Nov 1688, Providence, RI-1788), s/o Benjamin & Ruth (Matthewson) Whipple; **issue**

Jeanne/Jane[2], b, 15 May 1696; m. 11 Oct 1722, Col. William Coddington of Newport as his 2nd wife; William (b. 15 Jul 1680) was the s/o Nathaniel & Susannah (Hutchinson) Coddington and grs/o Governor William Coddington; she d. 11 Oct 1722, Newport, RI; **issue**

CHILDREN m/2:

Gabriel[2], d. young

Susanne[2], b. 1716; m. 23 Aug 1734, Joseph Crawford, s/o William & Sarah (Whipple) Crawford

Mary[2], b. 1 Apr 1719, bp. 11 Jul 1721; m. Gideon Crawford, bro/o Joseph above; she d. 1 Oct 1789

Eve[2], bp. 11 Jul 1721; d. unmarr.

REF: BAIRD, Charles W. *History of the Huguenot Emigrants to America*; AUSTIN, John O. *Genealogical Dictionary of RI before 1690*; MacGUNNIGLE, Bruce C, in *Rhode Island Roots*, "Gabriel Bernon, Huguenot" (Vol. 11, #4, Dec 1985) pub. by RI Genealogical Society; MacGUNNIGLE, Bruce C. in *The Cross of Languedoc*, "Gabriel Bernon (1644-1736), Huguenot" (Aug 1985); *The Biographical Cyclopedia of Representative Men of RI* 1881); *Genealogies of RI Families*, Vol. II (1983); *The Huguenots in France & America*, Vol. II (1843).

BERRIEN, Cornelis Jansen

b. Bretagne, FR, poss. Berrien, Finistère Dépt., Bretagne, s. of Morlaix, s/o Jan Claes Berrien, grs/o Claes Berrien

a. 1668 - family had left FR, went to Alkmaar, N. HOL

c. 1668 – to America, settled Flathush, LI, NY

m., 1668/9, Long Island, NY, Jannetje Stryker, d/o Jan Stryker & Lambertje Seubering, Jan was a very influential citizen; she m/2, c. 27 Aug 1689 (date of betrothal), Samuel Edsall, as his 3rd wife

d. Dec, 1688, Newtown, LI, NY (now Elmhurst)

CHILDREN:

Jan Cornelise/John[2], m. 5 Apr 1697, Ruth Edsall, d/o his stepfather Samuel & his 2nd wife Ruth Woodhull; he d. Apr 1711; Ruth m/2, 1712, Samuel Fish; Ruth d. 28 Feb 1763; **3 sons, 3 daus**

P(i)eter Cornelise[2], b. 1672; m. 10 Aug 1706, Elizabeth Edsall (d. 6 May 1765), d/o his stepfa Samuel & (prob.) his 1st wife Jannetje Wessels; he d. 5 Apr 1737 - **7 sons, 1 dau**

 CHILD: (1 of 8):

 John[3], b. 19 Nov 1711; went to Rocky Hill, Somerset Co, NJ, m/1, 1744, Mary Leonard, d/o Capt. Samuel & Ann (X) Leonard – **no issue**, m/2, 17 Aug 1759, Margaret Eaton (1733-13 Mar 1819), d/o John & Joanna (Wardell) Eaton of Eatontown – **4 sons, 2 daus**; John d. 22 Apr 1772, Princeton, NJ – he was a merchant & a man of some prominence; Peter d. 5 Apr 1737; bur. Witherspoon St. Cem, Princeton

Jacob Cornelise[2], bp. 17 Aug 1678, Brooklyn, NY

Claus/Nicholas Cornelise[2], bp. 13 Mar 1681, Flatbush, NY; m.1st cousin Sarah Brinkerhoff, d/o Abraham Brinkerhoff & Aeltie Stryker, sis/o Nicholas' mother & widow of Jacob Rapelje – **no issue**; he d. 27 Dec 1737

Tryntie/Catherine Cornelise[2], m. 1688, Jeronimus/Jeremiah Remsen (1664-1750), s/o Rem Jansen Vanderbeck & Jannetje Rapelje

Cornelis Cornelise[2], bp. 15 Jul 1683, NY

Agnes/Angenietje[2], m. Lt. Joris Rapalje (4 Mar 1675-19 Jan 1741), s/o Daniel (**IF** this is the Daniel who m. Sarah Klock, then Joris was the grs/o Joris & Catalyntje (Trico) Rapalje – needs proof – article in the Baumeister/Plumb article says Daniel Rapalje & Sarah Klock are Joris' parents – true?); Agnes d. 13 Nov 1756, age 81

REF: KOEHLER, Albert F., *The Huguenots or the Early French in NJ*; NELSON, William, *NJ Biographical & Genealogical Notes* (1973); RIKER, J., *Annals of Newton*; BERGEN, Teunis G., *Register of Early Settlers in Kings Co.* (1881); BAUMEISTER, Margaret Kilpatrick & PLUMB, Margaret Grant, "The Berrien Family" in *Transactions of The Huguenot Society of SC,* Vol. #73 (1968).

BERTIN(E)/BERTAIN/BARTAIN/BERTON/BRETIN, dit Laronde, Pierre

of Mortagne, Saintonge Prov, FR (s.e. of Royan); now Mortagne-sur-Gironde, Charente-Maritime
Dépt, Poitou-Charentes

m. a. 1682, FR, Judith Le Roy (b. 1654), d/o <u>Gaspard & Marie (Sanceau) Le Roy</u>; she m/2, 1705,
Théophite Forche, of Marigny (prob. the one s.e. of Niort, in Poitou-Charentes)

c. 1682 – from FR to ENG, where he and his family stayed until summer 1686

settled Narragansett, RI, until 1691

to New Rochelle, NY; in church records, Pierre is said to have been a butcher

d. a. 1705, New Rochelle, NY

CHILDREN:

Pierre II[2], b. 1682, Mortagne?; m. Feb 1707, NY, Anne Borron/Barron, of Rye, ENG; d. a. 28 Feb 1732/3,
wp; a cooper; will names ch Peter, Susannah, Marie, John, Esther, Mary, Marianne – his wife had
apparently already d.

> CHILDREN:
>
> **Pierre III/Peter**[3], b. 1707; m. Catherine Sicard, d/o <u>Jacques & Anne Terrier Sicard</u>; he d. a. 26 Jun
> 1787, adm, Westchester Co, NY; **6 ch**, incl.; Susannah[4] (b. c. 1730), m. <u>Josias LeConte</u>,
> **Catherine**[4] (14 Oct 1735 New Rochelle-a. 1790) m. James Sicard, s/o <u>Jacques/James &
> Jeanne/Jane (Bonnet) Sicard - **3 sons, 6 daus**</u>
>
> **Susanne**[3], b. 15 Mar 1710; m. John Mabie, s/o Casper Pieterson & Elizabeth (Schuerman) Mabie,
> grs/o <u>Pierre Mabille</u>
>
> **Marie**[3], m. Jacques Rembert
>
> **John**[3], <u>m/1</u>, Mary Vincent, <u>m/2</u>, Dorcas (Marie) Renaud, d/o Étienne and Madeline (X) Renaud;
> **4 ch**
>
> **Esther**[3], m. Josias LeConte, s/o <u>François & Catherine (Levandier) LeConte</u>
>
> **Mary**[3]
>
> **Marianne**[3], b. 14 Oct 1727
>
> **Jeanne**[3], b. 2 Aug 1727

Judith[2], b. 28 Feb, bp. 15 Mar 1692/3, FR Ch, NYC; m. John Barheit

Susanne Madelaine[2], b. 28 Feb, bp. 15 Mar 1692/3, FR Ch, NYC; unmarr., 1730

REF: WITTMEYER, Alfred V., *Registers of the Births, Marriages & Deaths of the Église Françoise à la
Nouvelle York* (Baltimore, 1968); BAIRD, Charles W., *The Huguenot Emigration to America*; BOLTON, Robert,
History of Westchester Co, NY from its 1st Settlement to Present (1925).

BERTOLET, Jean/John

c. 1685 - family fled FR (poss. Bretagne), settled Château d'Œx, Canton Vaud, SWI (in s.w. SWI, 5 mi.
w. of Gstaad); Jean had a brother Peter who went to Oley, Berks Co, PA by 1720 & m. Elizabeth
X; Jean was a shoemaker in Bethlehem, PA, at the time of his will dated 16 Aug 1744; will
mentions a sister Mary Elizabeth, Magdalena, wife of Jacob Vetter (a turner and joiner in
Bethlehem), no other persons named.

b. c. 1687, Château d'Œx, Canton Vaud, s/o Jean (b. Picardie?)

c. 1711 – Jean went to Minfeld (then Minnefeldten), Bavarian *Pfalz*, GER, n.w. of Karlsruhe; not clear
whether other family members went there as well; said to have gone 1st to Gutenberg

m. 2 Feb 1712, Barbelroth (nr. Minfeld), Baden, GER, Susanna Harcourt, d/o <u>Jean & Judith (leSeuer) de
Harcourt</u> of Mühlhofen (a sm. town 3 mi. n. of Barbelroth, 5 mi n.w. of Minfeld); poss. spent
time in Seltz, Bas-Rhin Dépt., Alsace, FR, s.e. Wissembourg, c. 2 km. w. of GER border; Susanna
d. 1755 PA, bur. Oley, PA

29 Apr 1726 - he was issued a passport in Minfeld; went to America with wife, 5 ch & his bro Peter (m.
Elizabeth X, d. a. 3 Aug 1734, wp, Philadelphia Co. – had at least one son John, b. 2 Apr 1726, who m.
& had issue)

fall 1726 - arr and settled in Oley Valley, now Berks Co, PA; Susanna's sister Anna Maria (Harcourt)

Weimer had remarried and was living there – Anna's 2nd husband was Isaac deTurck, s/o Jacob de Turck

d. p. 4 Apr 1757, PA, when he sold his farm to son Frederick; d. later that yr., bur. nr. Oley Post Office; a a prized possession of Jean's was a Bible, printed in Geneva, in 1567, written in FR, w/ a hand-written inscription – *"Le present Bible apartien à Jean Bertolet"* – "This Bible belongs to Jean Bertolet"

CHILDREN:

Abraham[2], b. 11 Dec 1712, Minfeld, GER; m. 1735, Esther DeTurck (29 Sep 1711-17 May 1798), d/o Isaac DeTurck; Abraham d. Jul 1766, Oley, PA, bur. Bertolet Union Cemetery, Oley, PA; **3 sons, 3 daus**

Maria[2], b. 12 Jul 1715, Minfeld, GER; m. Stephen Barnett; she d. 14 Nov 1764; **3 sons, 4 daus**

Jean/John[2], b. 28 Sep 1717, Minfeld; m. Catherine Bally, d/o Peter Bally; he d. 1795; **3 sons, 10 daus**

Esther[2], b. 12 Aug 1720, Minfeld, bp. 1720, Barbelroth; m. 24 Sep 1745, Dr. George de Benneville (26 Jul 1703 London-19 Mar 1793), s/o George & Marie (Granville) de Bonneville; Esther d. 7 Mar 1795; **2 sons, 5 daus**

Susanna[2], b. 17 Nov 1724, Minfeld; m. Jacob Frey, s/o William & Anna Veronica (Merkle) Frey, grs/o Heinrich & Anna Catherine (Levering) Frey; **7 sons, 3 daus**

Frederick[2], b. winter, 1726/7, Oley, PA; m. 1750/1, Esther LeVan (b. 5 Aug 1732), d/o Abraham & Catherine (Von Weimer) Le Van; (Abraham, s/o Daniel & Marie (Beau) LeVan); Frederick d. spring, 1769; **3 sons, daus**

Peter[2], b. 1728, PA; d. 2 Sep 1744, Bethlehem, PA; bur. Moravian Cemetery; unmarr.

REF: BERTOLET, Daniel H, *A Genealogical History of the Bertolet Family, the Descendants of Jean Bertolet* (Harrisburg, PA, 1914); Jean Bertolet's Bible; notes from the Huguenot Society of PA; Peter Bertolet's will; BAIRD, Charles W., *Huguenot Emigration to America*, Vol. II, p. 77.

BERTONNEAU, Sara

b. c. 1645, Île de Ré, d/o Jacques & Élisabeth (X) Bertonneau/Bertomeau

m/1, c. 1670, Élie Jodon/Jaudon, (c.1640 - c.1684), s/o Daniel Jaudon - **2 ch**

m/2, c. 1685, Pierre Michau(d), s/o Jean & Catherine (X) Michaud of La Villedieu, Charente-Maritime Dépt, Poitou-Charentes, n.e. of St. Jean-d'Angély, then in Aunis Province; **no issue**

c. 1686 - Sara, Pierre, her 2 children and Pierre's younger brother Abraham sailed together to America; settled what became the Parish of St. James, French Santee, Craven Co, SC

1696 – family naturalized

d. p. 1696/7 SC

REF: *Transactions of the Huguenot Society of SC*, #87 (1982); *French & Swiss Protestants in Charleston* (Baltimore, 1968).

BERTRAND

(2 brothers of unknown parents)

Jean/John (Rev.)[2]

b. FR

fled FR, to ENG w/ bro Paul (below); ordained in the Church of England; went to America and settled in Old Rappahannock Co, VA (now Lancaster Co.)

m. 29 Sep 1686, London, Charlotte de Jolie, d/o Comte de Jolie

pastor, Sittingbone Parish, Richmond Co., VA, now King George Co.

d. p. 8 Dec 1700, wd – a. 10 Feb 1701, wp, Lancaster Co, VA (10 7th ber 1701 – an entry follows dated 10 Feb 1701 – letter from Charlotte asking court to prove the will even though she was unable to attend due to illness) – hard to see how "7th ber" translates to February, should be September (old style)!

CHILDREN:

William[3], m. XX; d. 1760; 1 **dau**, b. 5 Oct 1734, who m. Leroy Griffin

Mary Ann[3], b. 1690; m/1, c. 1705/10, Charles Ewell (c. 1660/65, ENG-p. 13 Jan 1721/2, ww – a. Apr 1722, wp, Lancaster Co, VA); m/2, 16 Feb 1724, William Ballendine; m/3, 25 Apr 1742, Maj. James Ball*, s/o William Ball; she d. 12 Feb 1749/50, Lancaster Co, VA; Charles Ewell was the contractor who built the 1st state capitol building at Williamsburg

CHILDREN, m/1:

Mary Ann[4], b. c. 1710; m. 11 Oct 1727, Lancaster Co, VA, Isaac White

Charles[4], b. c. 1713; m. 22 Sept 1736, Sarah Ball (b. 13 Jan 1711/12), d/o Maj. James* & Mary (née Conway, widow of John Dangerfield) Ball of Lancaster Co, VA; ch – **Jesse**[5] m. Charlotte Ewell, d/o of uncle Maj. Bertand Ewell; **James**[5], m/1, Mary Ewell, d/o of uncle Solomon Ewell, m/2, Sarah Ewell, d/o of uncle Bertrand; **Charles**[5] –no issue; **Marianne**[5], m. Dr. James Craik

Bertrand[4], b. c. 1715; m. c. 1735, Frances Kenner, prob. d/o Richard Kenner; called Major; he d. c. 1795 Prince William Co, VA; **19 ch**

Solomon[4], b. 17 May 1716/18; m. 10 Jan 1746, Eve (Ball) Taylor (b. 24 Dec 1713-18 Jan 1778), widow of Thomas Taylor, d/o Maj. James* & Mary (Conway) Ball; Solomon d. 15 Jan 1760; **5 ch**

Charlotte[4], in father's will; went to Caroline Co with sis Mary Ann White in the 1720's; m. c. 1729, Darby Gallahue/Gallahough; moved to Pr. William Co; Charlotte d. p. 1782; **7 ch**

?Frances[4], m. John Ballendine/Balantyne; not in father's will – poss. a posthumous ch; poss. ch **John**[5], **Fanny**[5]; could be a dau of m/2

CHILD, m/2:

Hannah[4], in her mother's will as was a dau named Frances – may be the Frances who m. John Ballendine or another dau Frances

*same person

Paul (Rev.)[2]

b. FR

fled with bro Jean/John (above) to ENG; ordained Church of England

m. XX; she d. p. 1766

d. Calvert Co, MD, soon aft birth of son

CHILD:

Paul[3], m. London, Mary Dearling; he d. c. 1755, Bath, ENG, where he went with his mother after the death of fa Paul

REF: HAYDEN, Horace Edwin, "A Genealogy of the Glassell Family" in the *Virginia Genealogist* (1971); HARDY, Stella Pickett, *Colonial Families of the Southern States of America* (1963); BROCK, Robert A., *Huguenot Emigration to America*; LEE, Ida J., *Abstracts Lancaster Co, VA Wills 1653-1800* (1959); PETTITT, Mary Courtright & Robert J, Sr, *Thomas M. Pettitt's Family* (1996).

BESL(E)Y, Olivier/Oliver

b. 1658, Île de Ré, FR, s/o Jacques & Diane (Fouquet) Besley; had sisters Judith and Diane; Judith m. Apr 1684, in Thairé, and Diane m. 1686, in Amsterdam; fa Jacques d. 29 Aug 1686, bur Thairé

m. prob. Thairé (town s.e. of La Rochelle), Marie Thauvet/Thevett; was a merchant and was there until at least Apr, 1684

9 Apr 1687 – naturalized London

c. 1687 – settled in Charleston, SC

by Jun 1690 – in NYC

29 May 1691 – freeman of NYC

by 1694 – to New Rochelle, NY; became a leader of the community; several municipal offices:
 supervisor, justice of the peace, capt. of the Foot Company; also very active in church affairs

1702 – back in Charleston but had returned to NY by 1705

d. intestate; son Oliver was named administrator, 21 Feb 1746, so Oliver Sr. prob. d. 1745 or
 early 1746, prob. New Rochelle

CHILDREN:

Oliver, Jr.[2], b. winter, 1687/8, Charleston, SC; m. Susan Mercier, d/o Isaac & Susannah (X) Mercier;
 he d. a. 18 Nov 1778, wp

 CHILDREN:

 James[3], m/1, 13 Oct 1743, Catharine de Forest (17 Jul 1720-1749), d/o Barent* & Catalina (Sarley) de
   Forest, she d. c. 1749; m/2, c.1749/50, Cornelia de Forest (b. 18 Dec 1728), d/o Barent* &
   Elizabeth (Ver Duyn) de Forest, his 1st wife's half-sister; James d. 28 Sep 1776 (*same person)

 Isaac[3], d. p. June 1795,, wd – a. 4 Jan 1799 wp; physician; unmarr.; will mentions sisters Mary
   & Susanna Mary, bro James

 Susanna Mary[3], m. c. 1750, Dr. John C. Goodwin; d. a. 1795; **issue**

 Mary[3], b. c. 1772; d. 25 Sep 1819, age 97; unmarr.

Thauvet/Tovat[2], b. 1691, New Rochelle, NY; m. 15 Oct 1719, Hester Vincent; d. 28 Mar 1757, NY;
 he was a silversmith

REF: *Old Wills of New Rochelle, 1784-1830*, copied by DAR; WILLITS, Georganna Klass, *Besly-Besley Notebook*, 3
Vol. (1981-85); SEACORD, Morgan H., *Biographical Sketches and Index of the Huguenot Settlers of New Rochelle, 1687-
1776*; BAIRD, Charles W., *History of the Huguenot Emigration to America*, Vol. I, p. 307.

BESSELLIEU, Mark Anthony

 from Tours, FR; s/o Philip Anthony Besselieu, a minister in the FR Protestant Ch

 m. XX

 d. a. 29 Sep 1738, inv, Charleston Co, SC

 CHILD:

 Mark Anthony, II[2], m. 8 Sep 1745, Charleston, SC, Martha Chicet/Chichet/Cheché (d. p. 28 Oct 1765), d/o X
   & Jeanne (X) Chichet; 14 Aug 1747 – naturalized in SC; Mark and Martha kept a day school in their
   home; he d/bur. 7 Apr 1765

   CHILDREN, b. Charleston, SC:

   Mark Anthony III[3], b. 9 Jul 1746; d. 10 Jul 1747

   Philip Anthony[3], b. 3 Mar 1747/48 or 31 Mar 1748; m/1, 10 Apr 1771, Charleston, SC, Susanna
     Maçon/Mason; she m/2, John Gissendanner; she d. 10 Jan 1829; Philip d/bur 9 Jan 1795;
     5 sons, 4 daus

   Lewis[3], m/1, 27 Aug 1775, Susanna Wood (d. a. 22 May 1786) – **1 son**; m/2, 19 Aug 1790,
     Elizabeth Young – **3 ch**; he d. p. 24 Nov 1792

   Mary[3], m. 24 Dec 1768, John White; d/bur 27 Aug 1769

   Susanna[3]

REF: *The Bessellieu Family Bible;* JOHNSON, Charles Owen, *The Genealogy of Several Allied Families* (New
Orleans, 1961); *Transactions of the Huguenot Society of SC*, #51 (1946); HIRSCH, Arthur Henry, *Huguenots of
Colonial SC* (1962).

BESSONET/BESSONETT/BESONETTE, Charles

 b. FR, *poss.* s/o Vicomte Claude de Bessonet, Sieur de Gaturzières (town n.e. of Meyrueis in the Lozère Dépt,
   Languedoc-Roussillon), mentioned 1598-1614 as "La France Protestante"; family said to have been
   from Die, (s.w. of Grenoble), then Dauphiné Prov., now in Drôme Dépt, Rhône-Alpes; supposedly a

father + 3 sons, Claude, Alexander and John, went to ENG and Waterford, IRE (s. IRE on the estuary of the River Slaney, the Hook Peninsula); 11 Mar 1700, a Claude Bessonet was naturalized in London and went to Waterford – was that Charles' father? Or did Charles have a son named Claude who was naturalized?

m. XX, prob. FR

c. 1685 – to America with son John; he settled in Bensalem Twp, Bucks Co, PA

1690 – purchased land in Bucks Co, PA

7 Jan 1729 – purchased 133 acres in Middleton Twp, Bucks Co

CHILD:

John[2], 1684/5, FR XX; m/1, 1720, prob. NY, Sarah Dye/Dey; m/2, p. 21 Dec 1765 (date of lic, NJ), Joyce
(X) Brelsford, wid/o Abraham Brelsford of Bristol; John d. p. 4 Mar 1774, wd – a. 26 Oct 1778,
wp; wife Joyce and all ch are named in his will but James and Margaret; Elizabeth, Mary, Sarah
are dec. – there are bequests for their ch

CHILDREN, m/1:

Elizabeth[3], b. 13 Jan 1720/1; m. c. 28 Mar 1741 (date of lic, NJ), Nicholas Larzelère (1718 NY-a. 5
Aug 1799, wp Bucks Co, PA), s/o Nicholas & Hester (Lakerman) Larzelère; she d. a. 25 May
1767, Staten Island, when Nicholas m/2, Sarah (Dupuy) Crocheron; **issue**

Mary[3], b. 7 Dec 1723; m. 10 Oct 1743, 1st Presbyterian Ch, Philadelphia, Henry L. Mitchell;
she d. 1745; **issue**

John[3], b. 21 Oct 1725; m/1, X Pennington, a Quaker; m/2, Sarah Mitchell; he became a Quaker
preacher; d. c. 1783, NYC

Sarah[3], b. 10 May 1728; m. Sep, 1748, PA, James Bodine; she prob. d. a. Mar 1774, when
her father makes provisions for her ch in his will; **issue**

James[3], b. 1730; d. at sea, a. 4 Mar 1774; **no issue**

Catherine[3], b. 7 Oct 1732; m. 29 May 1755, Old Swede's Ch, Philadelphia, Richard Goheen.
(1730-1786), s/o John & Anna (X) Goheen; she d. 10 Sep 1785; **3 sons**

Charles[3], b. 5 Oct 1734, prob. Bristol, Bucks Co, PA; m/1, c. 6 Nov 1760 (date of marr bond),
NYC, Mary Millington; m/2, 1765, Parthena Brelsford; he d. intestate 1807; 5 ch – **John**[4],
Charles[4], **James**[4], **Daniel**[4], **Mary**[4] (ch prob. all from m/2)

Anne[3], b. 28 Jan 1736; m. c. 19 Jun 1765, NJ, Thomas Butcher (c. 1735-1839)

Margaret[3], b. 18 Sep 1739; m. Mr. X Bodine?; d. a. 4 Mar 1774; **no issue**

Martha[3], b. 25 Jan 1742/3; m. 12 Oct 1763, Richard Johnson, s/o Samuel Johnson

Daniel[3], b. 25 Feb 1743; m. 31 May 1764, Sarah Johnson, d/o Samuel Johnson (above); became a
Loyalist; 1779 - left Bristol with his family & went to Nova Scotia; was a Capt in the
British Army, NJ Loyalist Volunteers; d. 1 Dec 1783, Halifax; **16 ch**

REF: STAPLETON, A. *Memorials of the Huguenots in America* (1901); BAIRD, Charles W., *History of the
Huguenot Emigration to America,* Vol. II (1885); RICHARDSON, Margaret Ellen, *Bessonett Online Research* (2006).

BEVIER, Louis

b. c. 1647, in or nr. Lille, FR

family journeyed from FR, to SWI, to the Palatinate/*Pfalz*

1664 - a family named Bevier was in Winden, GER, c. 20 mi s.w. of Speyer – may have been Louis'

m. 1673, Speyer, GER (s.e. of Heidelberg), Marie LeBlanc (b. Lille-d. 1689, New Paltz, NY)

by 1675 - settled nr. Frankenthal (e. of Mannheim and n. of Speyer); minister there wrote a certificate of
dismissal for the family on 5 Mar 1675, recommending them to their next church

Jul 1675- arr America; may have spent some time on Staten Island

29 Sep 1677 - one of the 12 original patentees of New Paltz, Ulster Co, NY; one of the founders of the New
Paltz Reformed Ch, organized 22 Jan 1683 – had a "place" in the 3rd pew

d. a. 4 Jul 1720, New Paltz, NY; 1st will dated 12 Sep 1715 – mentions 5 sons, dau Hester Hasbrouck; another wd, 2 May 1720, mentions same ch but now André is said to be *non-compos mentis* & Louis asks André's siblings to protect and care for him; wp, 4 Jul 1720, Ulster Co.

CHILDREN:

Marie[2], bp.19 Jul 1674, Speyer, GER; d. young

Jean[2], b. 29 Jan 1676, Hurley, NY; m. 14 Apr 1712, Catherine Montagne (bp. 28 Jul 1688, Kingston-1764), d/o William & Eleanora (de Hooges) de la Montagne; they res.Wawarsing, NY; he d. a. 1745; **8 ch** [several records say that Catherine's maiden name was Montanye – this is simply the result of hearing Montagne pronounced, it sounds like Montanye but it's not spelled that way!]; 2 of his daus **Elizabeth**[3] (m. cousin Isaac Bevier, s/o Samuel) & **Johannah**[3] (m. Michael Sax) were killed, along w/ their families in the 1779 attack by Tories & Hessians on the settlement at Fantinekill, nr. present day Ellenville, which is c. 5 mi. s.w. of Wawarsing; Wawarsing, s.w. of New Paltz, was destroyed in 1781 by Indians

Abraham[2], b. 20 Jan 1678, Hurley; m. c. 8 Feb 1770 (date of banns), Rachel Vernooy, d/o Cornelis C. Vernoy & Annetje Cornelis; he d. a. 23 Jul 1774, wp, Kingston; **10 ch**

Samuel[2], b. 21 Jan 1680; m/1, 1710, Magdalena Blanchan (bp. 7 Mar 1686), d/o Matthys, Jr & Margaret (Van Schoonhover) Blanchan, m/2, Esther X; he d. 1755/9; **11 ch**

André/Andries[2], b. 13 Jul 1682; d. 1768 unmarr.

Louis II[2], 6 Nov 1684; m. 6 May 1713, Elizabeth Hasbrouck, d/o Jean & Anna (Deyo) Hasbrouck; lived Marbletown, by 1715; he d. 10 Feb 1753; 1 son **Louis III**[3], b. 29 Apr 1717, m. Esther DuBois, d/o Philip DuBois of Rochester, Louis III, d. 29 Sep 1772 – **2 sons** who survived him

Esther[2], b. 16 Nov 1686; m. 7 Nov 1714, Jacob Hasbrouck, s/o Jean & Anna (Deyo) Hasbrouck

Solomon[2], b. 12 Jul 1689; d. young

REF: BEVIER, C., *Bevier Family*; LeFEVRE, Ralph, *History of New Paltz, NY and its Old Families from 1678-1820* (Baltimore, 1973); HASBROUCK, Kenneth Edward, *The Bevier Family, the Descendants of Louis Bevier* (1970); VER-STEEG, Dingman, translator/transcriber, *Records of the Reformed Dutch Ch of New Paltz, NY* (Baltimore, 1977).

BEYER/BOYER

from Gommersheim, GER, in the *Pfalz,* on the left bank of the Rhine, s.w. of Speyer; name became Boyer in America; the following are 2 sons of *Gerictsmann* (Magistrate) Johann Christoph Beyer (1646-4 Apr 1724) and his wife Kunigarde X (1648-18 Jan 1714/5)

Johann Nicolus[2], b. Jun 1677, Gommersheim, GER; m. Martia Elisabeth X; went to PA – no further info

CHILDREN:

Clara Elisabeth[3], b. 19 Sep 1726, Gommersheim; **Georg Jakob**[3], b. 12 Dec 1729, PA; **Maria Magdalena**[3], b. 1 Feb 1732, PA; **Johann Wendell**[3], b. 30 May 1734, PA; **Anna Barbara**[3], b. Jan 1739, PA; **Johann Andreas**[3], b. Dec 1681, PA; **Anna Margaretha**[3], b. Jul 1686, PA

Johann Andreas[2], b. Dec 1681, Gommersheim; m. Anna Apollonia X; arr Philadelphia, 5 Sep 1732, on the *Winter Galley,* w/ wife, 3ch

CHILDREN:

Thomas[3], b. 18 Dec 1713, Gommersheim; remained in GER

Johann Philipp[3], b. 29 Feb 1717, Gommersheim; m. Anna Elizabetha X; settled prob. in Warwick Twp., Lancaster Co. PA, then to Westmoreland Co.

CHILDREN:

unnamed dau[4]

unnamed dau[4], m. X Karns

Susan[4], m. X Heck

Elizabeth[4], m. Abraham Horner

Maria Margaret[4], b. 27 Aug 1743, bp. 18 Sep 1743, Lancaster, PA

Michael[4], b. 25 Dec 1746, Lancaster Co.; m/1, Margaret Clapper, m/2, Dorothy Wolfe Noch; he d. 9 Aug 1810, Donegal Twp, Westmoreland Co.; Rev. War service; total of **2 sons, 4 daus**

John Philip[4], b. 19 Jul 1750 Warwick Twp, Lancaster Co.; d. 1803, Donegal Twp., Westmoreland Co.

John Christopher[4], b. 21 Dec 1752, bp. 18 Feb 1753, Warwick Twp, Lancaster Co.; m. c. 1777, Mary Anna Youst (10 Jun 1756-20 Sep 1831, bur. KY); went to Westmoreland Co, c. 1790, then to Philadelphia, then to Hagerstown, MD, by 1796, to Bourbon Co, KY and in 1809, he was in Clark Co, IN; he d. 10 Feb 1832, bur. 12 Feb, Caroll Co., KY; Rev. War service.
CHILDREN:

> **Phillip**[5], b. 17 Dec 1777; m. 1802, Barbara Ann Liter (26 Apr 1783-13 Oct 1832, bur IN), d/o John & Catherine (X) Liter; he d. 3 Oct 1821, Clark Co, IN); **4 sons, 4 daus**

> **Anna Elizabeth**[5], b. 18 Dec 1779; m. Johannes Frantz/John Frank Giltner 4 Mar 1770-29 Jan 1849); she d. 18 Dec 1835; **3 sons, 4 daus**

> **John Christopher**[5], b. 17 Jan 1782; m. Mary/Polly Rowe (b. 26 Jan 1789); he d. 1835, Clark Co, IN; **5 sons, 5 daus**

> **Catherine**[5], b. 1786/7; m. Henry Liter (1768-12 Aug 1842, KY), bro/o Barbara Ann (above); **6 sons, 6 daus**

> **Abraham**[5], b. 10 Jan 1788; m. Elizabeth Deitrich Wolf; he d. 10 Jul 1869, OH; **5 sons**

> **Jacob**[5], b. 13 May 1789; m. Lucy X; liv. Boone Co, IN; **issue**

> **Mary Margaret**[5]?, b. c. 1790/92; m. Frederick Redinbow?

> **Mary Ann**[5], b. c. 1793; m. Robert Henry

> **unnamed child**, b. c. 1794/97

> **Michael**[5], b. 1 Feb 1798, KY; d. 17 Jun 1859, KY, unmarr.

> **unnamed child**[5], b. p. 1799

Eva Catherine[4], b. 1753, PA; m. Abraham Dumbauld; she d. 1837; **9 ch**

Johann Martin[3], b. 23 Jun 1720, Gommersheim

Eva Elisabeth[3], b. 27 Sep 1725, Gommersheim

REF: Ch Recs – Gommersheim Lutheran Ch; VALE, G.W., *Genealogy of the Vale, Walker, Littler & Other Related Families* (1973); GRUBER, Michael Alvin, *Boyer, Bayer, Beyer, Beier, Baire – PA Records* (National Genealogical Society Quarterly, Vol. X, 1921/2, pp. 81-84); research from Dr. John McGath

BILLEBEAU/BILBAUT/BILBO(U), Jacques

b. Saintonge Prov, FR

1681 - a Jean Bilbo fled from Port-des-Barques (at the mouth of the Charente River, w. of Rochefort - then in Saintonge) to ENG, then to n. NJ– family member?

m. XX, who d. by 1723

by 1700 - to VA on "ye First Shippe" with wife and son; settled Manakintown

1710-1717 – on tithing rolls in King William Parish

1714 – Jacques is on the *Liste Générale* w/ a wife and 1 son

23 Mar 1715 - purchased patent #896, 119:3:4 acres on the s. side of the James River in Henrico Co, VA, now in Chesterfield Co., which passed to his son by 1 Aug 1720

31 Oct 1716 - purchased patent #819, 43 acres on the s. side of the James River in Henrico Co., VA, now in Powhatan Co., which passed to his son by 1 Aug 1720

d. by 1 Aug 1720, when accounts of his estate were presented by Peter Dutoi

CHILD:

Jean Pierre[2], b. c. 1706/7, FR; m/1, Susanne X (d. 1739), m/2, c. 1740, Elizabeth X; was tithable in King William Parish in 1723; he was in possession of his father's smaller patent, #819; on the list of Manakintown residents in 1744; poss. the John Peter Bilbo whose will was proven 1751, Lunenburg Co., VA
CHILDREN, m/1:
Jacques[3], b. 30 Jun 1730; bp. 16 Aug 1730
Marie[3], b. 23 Jun 1733; m. 3 Feb 1756, Young Short; at least **1 son**
Jean/John[3], b. 26 Oct 1735; m. 16 Jun 1760, Ann Walker; **2 ch**
Elizabeth[3], b. 13 Feb 1738/9; d. 20 Mar 1738/9
CHILD, m/2:
Elizabeth[3], b. 5 Dec 1740

REF: *The Huguenot,* #5, pp. 73, 81 (1922) – The Huguenot Soc. Founders of Manakin Colony in VA; BROCK, Robert A. *Huguenot Emigrated to VA* (1979); *Vestry Book of King William Parish, VA, 1707-1750* (1988): CABELL, Priscilla Harriss, *Turff & Twigg, Vol. I, The French Lands* (Richmond, VA, 1988).

BILLIOU/BILYEU/BALLIOU/BARLOW, Thomas

of La Bassée or Wicres, (then) FR Flanders, both s.w. of Lille, now in the Pas-de Calais Dépt, Nord-Pas-de-Calais
m. Aimée X (bur. 1 Jul 1621, St. Peter's Church, Leiden, HOL)
they fled from FR; lived in Langerbrugge, E. Flanders, n. of G(h)ent (now in BEL) & in HOL
CHIILDREN:
Jean[2], b. c. 1600, FR, prob. Artois; no info on him except that Pierre[3]'s marr. rec. says that Pierre, formerly thought to have been the s/o Thomas, was the s/o Jean; the rec. said "he was sponsored by his father 'Jeanq Biljow'"; this document was found in the Leiden Archives in 1973, pub. 1986
CHILD:
Pierre/Peter[3], b. FR, bp. c. 1625, LaBassée or Wicres; m/1, 2 May 1649, Walloon Church, Leiden, HOL, Françoise DuBois (17 Jun 1622-a. 17 Jan 1695/6, NY), d/o Chrétien DuBois; 1661 – emigrated to America 9 May 1661 on the *St. Jan de Baptiste* which arr NY, 6 Aug 1661; settled on Staten Island; m/2, p. 17 Jan 1695/6, NY (date of prenup. agreement), Gerritje (Lamberts) Spiegelaer, widow of Jan Spiegelaer; 22 Aug 1663, applied for land on Staten Island; 12 Sep 1670, bought a farm in Flatbush; 5 Jun 1674, bought 26 *morgens* of plain & meadow land in Flatbush; he d. p. 11 Sep 1699, wd-a. 6 Jan 1702, wp, Staten Island; will mentions wife Gerritje, son Isaac, 2 grch (dec. son Jacob's ch), 4 sons of dau Catherine Curtis (dec.), dau Frances Larzillière Morgan, gr son Nicholas Larzillière + any ch of her 2nd husband, 7 ch of Marie Prael (dec.), daus Martha Stillwell and Chrétienne Marlet
CHILDREN, m/1:
Marie[4], bp. 3 Mar 1649/50, Leiden; m. 3 Jun 1670, Wiltwyk/Kingston, NY, Arendt Jansen Prall/Praal/Prael (1647, Naerden-1725, Staten Island), he m/2, c. 1704, Madlenor (X); she d. a. 1 Sep 1699, NY; **8 ch**
Martha[4], bp. 8 Feb 1652, Leiden; m/1, 8 Jun 1670, Lt. Thomas Stillwell (c. 1650-a. 9 May 1705, wp, Staten Island), s/o Nicholas & Ann (X) Stillwell – **3 sons, 3 daus**; m/2, p. 1718, David du Bonrepos; she d. 1736
Peter[4], b. c. 1653, Leiden
Catherine[4], b. 1654, Leiden; m. 1678, Richard Curtis; d. a. 1 Sep 1699; **5 sons**
Françoise/Frances[4], b. 1655, Leiden; m/1, Nicholas Larzelère, s/o Jacques & Maria (Grangen) Larzelère – 1son **Nicholas**[5]; m/2, 1675, John Morgan, s/o Charles Morgan; she d. p. 1 Sep 1699
unnamed ch[4], bur. 17 Jun 1656, Leiden

Chrétienne/Christina[4], b. Oct 1658, Leiden; m. 1678, Abraham Merlet, s/o Gidéon & Marie (Martin) Merlet; 3 sons - **Abraham**[5], bp. 16 May 1680, **Isaac**[5], **Jacob**[5,] **Margaret**[5,] **Frances**[5]

Isaac[4], b. at sea, bp. 10 Aug 1661, NYC; m. 2 Nov 1684, Dutch Ref. Ch, Bergen, NJ, Ida Seuberingh, d/o Jan Roel Seuberingh & Adrianna Polhemus; d. a. 22 Dec 1709, wp, Staten Island; will mentions wife Ida, 3 sons **Jacob**[5], **John**[5], **Peter**[5], daus **Francina**[5], **Ariantie**[5]; there were poss. 4 sons, 2 daus not mentioned

Jacob[4], b. 1663, Staten Island; m. c. 1683, NY, Margaret Larzelère/La Resilière, poss. d/o Jacques & Maria (Grangen) La Resilière; he d. a. 1 Sep 1699 – fa called him "deceased" in his will written on that date; at least **2 ch** – **Peter**[5], **Françoise**[5], b. c. 1685, m/1, 1709, Staten Island, Jacques Poillon, m/2, Pierre Le Co(u)nte; Margaret was not mentioned in fa-in-law's will, just her ch

?Peter[4], bp. 6 Jun 1668; m. c. 1701, Maria Breese

?John[4], b. c. 1668/70; d. young, not in father's will

Abigail[2], b. 1602, FR, prob. Artois; m. 22 Oct 1622, Leiden, John Dunham (c. 1589 ,Nottingham, ENG-2 Mar 1668, Plymouth, MA); John was a widower with 3 ch: John, b. 1616, Thomas, b. a. 1619/20, Humility, b. 1617/18, who d. young; 1630/1 family went to America & settled in MA; John m/3 Bathsheba Whiston; Abigail d. p.1669

CHILDREN:

Samuel[3], b. 1624/31; m/1, 29 Jun 1649, Martha (Beal) Fallowell, d/o John Beal, widow of William Fallowell; m/2, Sarah (X) Watson, widow; he d. Jan 1711 (80 yrs)

Abigail[3], b. 1626; m. 6 Nov 1644, Stephen Atwood; he d. Feb 1693/4

Hannah[3], b. 1630; m. 31 Oct 1651, Giles Rickards, Jr. as his 2nd wife; he d. a. 18 Dec 1702, wp

Jonathan/John[3], b. c. 1631/2; m/1, 29 Nov 1655, Plymouth, Mary De la Noye/Delano, d/o Philip & Hester (Dewsbury) Delano; she d. a. 1657; m/2, 15 Oct 1657, Plymouth , Mary Cobb (b. 24 Mar 1637 Scituate, MA), d/o Henry & Patience (Hurst) Cobb; he d. 18 Dec 1717, Martha's Vineyard, MA

Persis[3], b. c. 1628/9 or 1635; m/1, 29 Nov 1655, Benajah Pratt, he d. 17 Mar 1682; m/2, 15 Aug 1683, Jonathan Shaw; she d. p. 1701

Joseph[3], b. c. 1635/6, Plymouth; m/1, 18 Nov 1657, Mercy Morton, d/o Nathaniel & Lydia (Cooper) Morton -she d. a. Aug 1669; m/2, 20 Aug 1669, Hester Wormall, d/o Joseph Wornall of Rowley, MA; Joseph d. 1703

Benjamin[3], b. c. 1637; m. 25 Oct 1660, Mary Tilson, d/o Edmond Tilson

Daniel[3], b. c. 1639; m. 1670, Mehitable Hayward, d/o John Hayward; d. p. 1677, Plymouth

Benajah[3], b. c. 1638/40; m. 25 Oct 1660, Elizabeth Tilson, d/o Edmond Tilson; d. 24 Dec 1680, Piscataway, NJ

Anne[2], b. c. 1604, FR, prob. Artois; m. 28 May 1624 ,HOL, Nathaniel Walker

Mary[2], m. 23 Jul 1639, Stephen Foster of Rotterdam, a printer's man; betrothed 4 Jun 1639 1736, wp

?Peter/Pierre[3], bp. 6 Jun 1668, Staten Island; m. 1701, Maria Brestede, d/o Jan Jansen Brestede; he d. 1698

?John[3], b. 1670; d. infancy

REF: VAN NAME, Elmer G., *Pierre Billiou, The Walloon, Staten Island Pioneer* (unpublished); ANDERSON, Thelma C., *Workman Family History* (1962); MOORE, Sophie Dunham, *Jacob Dunham Genealogy with English & American Ancestry of Dunham Family* (1963); *TAG*, Vols. 29, (1953), 30 (1954); DEXTER, Henry M. & Morton, *The England & Holland of the Pilgrims*; Vital Records, Plymouth & Barnstable, Piscataway; Mayflower Society records.

BLANCHAN/BLANSHAN/BLANCON, Mathieu/Matthys/Matthew

b. 15 Oct 1606, Neuville-au-Cornet, Artois Prov, FR, s.e. of St. Pol-sur-Ternoise (now Pas-de-Calais Dépt., Nord-Pas-de-Calais), s/o Leonin & Isabeau (Le Roy) Blanchamp/Blanchan; had a bro Antoine who m. 12 Apr 1649, Canterbury, Martine Volque, d/o Jacques Volque– Mathieu was his best man

m. 15 Oct 1633, Armentières, Artois, FR, Ma(g)deleine [Magdalena Brissen Jorisse] Joiré, bp. 27 Oct 1611, Armentières, d/o Petrus/Pierre & Jacoba (LeBlan/c) Joiré, she d. p. 30 Apr 1688, Ulster Co, NY, prob. Hurley; Armentières is a town n.w. of Lille in the Nord region

c. 1647 - to ENG with wife & 2 daus, so it would seem that son Maximilianus had d.

p. Apr 1649 - Mathieu, wife & 2 daus went to Mannheim, GER; later to HOL

26 Apr 1660 - arr New Amsterdam on *De Vergulde Otter/The Gilded Otter* with wife, 3 daus; or he left 26/27 Apr 1660 and arr in June; he was in Esopus (Kingston), Ulster Co by December; was a distiller in Kingston, NY

26 Dec 1660 - *Mattiu Blanschan* was on the list of those rec. communion in the Reformed Protestant Dutch Ch of Kingston, NY; *Anton Crepel & Maria Blanschan, his wife* were just below Mathieu's name

d. p. 7/17 Sep 1665, ww; another will written, p. 22 Aug 1671 - a. 30 Apr 1688, wp, Ulster Co, NY; names wife and 5 ch

CHILDREN:

Catherine/Katryn[2], b. c. 1 Jan 1635/6, Artois, FR; m/1, 10 Oct 1655, Mannheim, Louis DuBois, s/o Chrétien Du Bois - **12 ch**; m/2, p. 23 Jun 1696, Jean Cottin; she d. 18 Oct 1713, Kingston; Catherine + 3 ch were captured by Indians in 1663, rescued 3 months later

Maria[2], b. 1640, Armentières, FR; m. 31 Jan 1660/1, Antoine Crispell; she d. c. 1679 - **6 ch**; Maria + 1 ch were among the captives as well

Maximilianus[2], bp. 14 Aug 1642, Armentières; prob. d. a. 1647; not in father's 1665 will

Magdelaine[2], bp. 16 May 1647, Walloon or Strangers' Ch, Canterbury, ENG; m. c. 28 Sep 1667 (date of last banns), Jan Mattys Jansen s/o Matthys Jansz Van Cuelen of Ft. Orange, NY, who d. a. 24 Nov 1724 wp, Ulster Co, NY; **10 ch**

Elizabeth[2], b. c. 1651; m/1, 27 Oct 1668, Kingston, NY, Pieter Cornelisen Louw, from Holstein, who d. Kingston, a. 4 Mar 1707/8 wp - **9 ch**; m/2, Jan Foockens Heermance; Elizabeth was also among those captured by Indians

Mathieu/Matthew[2], b. 18 Apr 1655; m. 30 Mar 1679, Margreitje Claes Van Schoonhoven; **8 ch**; Mathieu was also captured

REF: *Register of the Walloon/Strangers Church, Canterbury, England;* HEIGERD, Ruth P. editor, *Matthew Blanchan in Europe and America* (from papers of Maj. Louis DuBois) (1979); *NY Gen. & Biog. Record,* Vol. 122, #1 (Jan, 1991); ANJOU, Gustave, *Ulster Co, NY Probate Records,* Vol. I (1906); Marr. record, Mannheim; LeFEVRE, Ralph, *History of New Paltz 1678-1820* (1973); SCHOONMAKER, Marius, *History of Kingston, NY* (1888); LADELY, David, *Sleight Family Research;* MARTIN, Mary Coates, *350 Years of American Ancestors* (1979); EVANS, Thomas G, *Descendants of Anthony Crispell 1660-1950;* PARTLAN, Martha B. & DuMOND, Dorothy A., *The Reformed Protestant Church of Kingston, NY;* Church recs., Armentières.

BLANCHARD, Jean/John

m/1, a. 1688, Anna Mahoult

m/2, 30 Jun 1695, Dutch Ch, NYC, Jeanne Gautier

m/3, 27 Oct 1697, FR Ch, NYC, Susanne Rezeau (bp. 14 Oct 1674-a. 1720), d/o René and Anne (Coursier) Rezeau of Staten Island

2 Oct 1687 - Jean was a witness at a baptism at Kingston, NY – referred to as "French people"

1 Sep 1689 - took Oath of Allegiance in Ulster Co, NY

1695 - lived at New Castle on the Delaware, then part of PA

d. a. Apr 1730, Elizabethtown, NJ

CHILD, m/1:

Anna[2], bp. 7 Apr 1689, Kingston, NY; m., prob. William Dixon of Elizabethtown; Wm d. 1715; dau **Anne**[3]

CHILD, m/2:

Jeanne[2], b. 20 Jan, bp. 21 Mar 1696/7, FR Ch, NYC, sponsor Elizabeth Gautier, wife of Timothée
Archimbaud – relative?; m. 16 Dec 1725, Dirck Dey (d/bur. 11 May 1764, NY); Jeanne d/bur.
14 Aug 1756, NY; **7 ch**

CHILDREN, m/3:

Jean/John II[2], b. 2 Oct, bp. 5 Nov 1699, FR Ch, NYC - maternal grparents were sponsors; m. Marie/
Mary Jolin(e), d/o <u>André & Madeleine (Poupin) Jolin/Jaulin</u>; he d. a. 1 May 1749, wp, Elizabeth,
NJ; **4 ch**

Isaac[2], b. 14 Sep, bp. 12 Oct 1701, FR Ch, NYC; m. Jane X; d. p. 4 Apr 1727, wd – a. 16 May 1727,
wp, Elizabeth, NJ; **2 ch**

Mary[2], m. c. 1722, John Mead; **6 ch**

Peter[2], prob. b. Staten Island

Susannah[2], prob. b. Staten Island; m. John Halstead of Elizabeth, NJ; she d. c.1785

Elizabeth[2], prob. b. Staten Island; mentioned in grfa's will dated 18 Feb 1719 – no other record

REF: NELSON, William, *NJ Biographical & Genealogical Notes from the Volumes of the NJ Archives* (1973);
KOEHLER, Albert F., *The Huguenots or Early French in NJ ;* GANNON, Peter Stevens, ed., *Huguenot Refugees in the
Settling of Colonial America.*

BOBO/BAUBEAU/BEAUBEAU/BODEAU, Gabriel

name can be found in Poitou area, western FR, also in the records of the FR Ch, Threadneedle St., London

b. FR, prob.in Poitou area; went to ENG

25 Oct 1700 - Gabriel's name on a list of persons transported to VA

19 Feb 1703 - he witnessed a deed bet his wife-to-be and her 2 sons

m. by Oct 1703, Elizabeth (Spencer) White, d/o Thomas Spencer, wid/o John White; she d. p. 17
Aug 1725 (date of deed), prob. in King William Co, VA

d. apparently by 1704, VA – Gabriel not on the 1704 Quit Rent Role, just his wife

CHILD:

Spencer[2], b. c. 1703/4 VA; <u>m/1</u>, c. 1726, Jane X, who d. a. Sep 1749; <u>m/2</u>, Mary (Sparks?); he d. bet Jan 1769 -
Aug 1772

CHILDREN, m/1:

Gabriel[3], b. c. 1726; m. Elizabeth Garner, d/o Joseph Garner, Eliz. d. a. 8 Jun 1813, wp,
Prince William Co, VA; he d. p. 2 Dec 1789, wd – a. 11 Oct 1790, wp, Pr. William
Co, VA; **at least 5 ch**

Mary Elizabeth[3], b. c. 1729; m. c. 1749, John Holt; she d. 1790, Orange Co, VA; **8 ch**

Absalom[3], b. c. 1730; m. a. 1763, Amy Sims, d/o Thomas Sims, Sr.; he d. 5 Jun 1811,
Laurens Co, SC: one dau **Nancy**[4]

Sampson[3], b. c. 1735; m. Sarah/Salley Mary Simpson, d/o Joseph Green Simpson; he d. 17
April 1804, Spartanburg Co, SC; **14 ch**

Lewis[3], b. c. 1736, VA; m. c. 1757, Sarah Solomon (c. 1740, Culpeper Co,VA-1809, Union
Co, SC); he d. 1808, Union Co, SC; **11 ch**

Spencer, Jr.[3], b. c. 1739, VA; m. c. 1763, Judith/Juda Foster*; he d. c. 1800, Spartanburg, SC;
6ch [*One record says he wife was Nancy Berry based on an approved Manakintown
application – the source of that information is not known.]

REF: JOHNSON, Bryan S. *Huguenots in the Backcountry: The Bobo Family of France, VA and SC; Transactions
of the Huguenot Society of SC,* #100 (1995) – complete copy of B.S. Johnson's article; Deed, King William Co;
Gabriel's will & Elizabeth's will, Prince William Co; NEWELL, Herbert M. & Jeanie Patterson, *Bobo Cousins by
the Dozens* (1968); McCALL, Ettie T., *McCall-Tidwell & Allied Families* (1931).

BOISSEAU, Jacques/James (Rev.)

b. 1660/69, prob. Montauban, now in Tarn-et-Garonne Dépt., Midi-Pyrénées, c. 31 mi. n. of Toulouse; Montauban was a Huguenot stronghold; went ENG with bro Joseph Ehyrr Boisseau; James' father and another bro had been killed in the persecutions; given name was prob. Jacques as James is not a French name; the family was in the service of the Protestant University until the Revocation when they fled to ENG, then to VA

11 Nov 1698 – James had been accepted as a minister in ENG; signed a receipt on that date for money pd. him as an emigrant minister to the colonies

p. 11 Nov 1698 – brothers sailed for VA on separate ships; Joseph ended up in Charleston, SC and then went to St. Christopher (St. Kitt's) where he became a sugar planter; Joseph m. ENG, Mathilde H.S. De Saussure who was of Swiss descent - 1 son, 5 daus; the 2 families finally reunited c. 80 yrs. later in Prince George Co, VA – neither realized that the other bro had survived

1st parish in VA was St. Peter's Parish in New Kent Co, VA

m. c. 1700, Sarah X, who d. 1715

1705 – served another parish in Pr. George Co, prob. Martin Brandon Parish

d. bet 1705-15, prob. VA (one source says c. 1734 Manakintown –not proven)

CHILD:

James[2], vestry man of Bristol Parish in 1722; m. Mary X, perhaps a dau of Rev. Joseph Holt; Capt. James resigned the Vestry of Bristol Parish on 22 Nov 1768

CHILDREN:

Elizabeth[3], b. 20 Sep 1733

James[3], b. 22 May 1736; m. Anna (Patrick?); **7 ch**

Sarah[3], b. 3 Mar 1738

Susanna[3], b. 17 Oct 1741

John[3], b. 12 Feb 1747; m. Martha Goodwyn; **5 ch**

Benjamin[3], b. 28 Feb 1753

Molly Holt[3], 25 Sep 1756

REF: *Huguenot Society Publication*, #29 (1979-81); *Tyler's Quarterly Historical & Genealogical Magazine*, Vol. X (1929); BROCK, R. A., *Huguenot Emigration to VA* (1979); *Wm. & Mary College Quarterly*, Vol. IX (1991); WEIS, Frederick L., *The Colonial Churches & the Colonial Clergy of the Middle & Southern States* (1938); McGHAN, Judith, indexer, *Genealogies of VA Families*, Vol I (Baltimore, MD, 1981).

BOISSEAU, Jean

b. Marennes, Saintonge, FR, now in Charente-Maritime, Poitou-Charentes, s.e. of Île d'Oléron, s/o Jacques & Marie (LaCourt) Boisseau; *poss.* had sis Judith who m. David Peyre & liv. SC; David d. Craven Co, SC, a. 13 Mar 1735, wp – wife Judith, 8 ch; no connection has been made between the VA and SC Boisseaus, although it is likely

m. Marie Postel(l); she m/2 James Gignilliat, Anglican minister

on the *Liste des François et Suisses Refugiez en Caroline* (c. 1694/5)

1696 - naturalized SC

2 Feb 1698 – made a freeman of NYC; he was a cooper

d. c. 1709/10 NY, definitely a. Mar 1711

CHILD:

James[2], m/1, XX, m/2, Jane Peyre; he d. a. 23 Feb 1750/1, inv

CHILDREN, m/1:

James II[3] d. a. 11 Mar 1756, wp

René[3]

CHILDREN, m/2:

David[3], of Craven Co; d. a. 26 Mar 1759, wp; m. Mary Jerman/Gemain (1726-1791) who m/2 1759, Samuel Bonneau (1725-1788) as his 2nd wife, s/o <u>Anthony & Jeanne Elizabeth (Videau) Bonneau</u>; David's will mentions ch but not by name, bro-in-law Edward Jerman was executor
CHILDREN:
prob. **dau**[4] who became the 2nd wife of Capt. Peter Sinkler – **no issue**
James[4], was a Loyalist and rec. a commission in the British Army and afterward, a
      civil station in Nova Scotia
Samuel Peyre[3]
Charles Cantey[3]

REF: BAIRD, Charles W, *History of the Huguenot Migration to America; "Liste des François et Suisses Refugiez en Caroline…".*

BOISSEVAIN/BOISSAVI/ BOSSAVIN dit BOU(Y)SSAVY, Lucas

b. 1660, Couze-et-Saint-Front, Dordogne Dépt, Aquitaine, e. of Bergerac; s/o Lucas (d. 22 Jul 1685, Couze), grs/o Jacques
4 Dec 1687, wrote his will; said his family is in Couze, under the jurisdiction of St. Campraise (now St. Campraise-de-Lalinde, n.w. of Couze), Périgord (now Dordogne); mentions bro Jean, sis Pierette, grfa Jacques; says he is quitting the country and is abandoning his property and hopes that his friends will see that his family gets his estate which consists of a house, pastures, woods, vineyard, a chest w/ family papers, £1130 and some coins; he evidently made this will just before he left for HOL – no mention of wife or ch
16 Dec 1687 – in court in Bordeaux; said he was leaving for Geneva and was afraid that he would be detained, so he made final arrangements in case of his death, including the writing of a will. It was given to M. Pierre Marchays de Roumas ("my dearest friend on earth") who was to deliver it to Nicolas d'Arroman, Royal Notary of the City and Seneschal Dist. of Bergerac where the document was to remain until Lucas returned. The will seems to have been written in a combination of Old Dutch and FR
late 1687- evidently left for Geneva; then to Amsterdam then to Rotterdam by Sep 1700
m. 1 Sep 1700, Walloon Church, Rotterdam, Marthe Roux of Bergerac and Amsterdam; Marthe *poss.* had sis Anne who m. Jérémie Renaud, 27 May 1696, Rotterdam
went back to Amsterdam
d. 25 Apr 1705, Amsterdam; bur. 30 Apr, Leidsche Churchyard, Amsterdam
29 Dec 1727, Marthe Roux, widow of Lucas Boissevain, was listed as living in the Korte Lijdsedwstraat (Korte Leidsedwaarsstraat – located in the central part of Amsterdam by the Lijnbaansgracht Canal) with 2 ch – according to the Amsterdam Wallon Church records; 2**0** Dec 1727 is the date given as the date of her burial in the Boissevain genealogy!
CHILDREN:
Isaac[2], b. 20 Jul 1701, Amsterdam
Jérémie[2], b. 8 Oct 1702, Amsterdam; m. Marie-Charlotte du Chesne (29 Dec 1705 London-24 Dec 1779 Amsterdam), d/o Gédéon & Marie (Boissonet) du Chesne; they were managers of the Hospice Wallon/Walen Weehuis in Amsterdam (1753-61) – an orphanage as well as a home for older people; Jérémie d. 30 Jul 1762, Amsterdam; **2 ch**
Marthe Anne[2], bp. 1705, Leidsche Church, Amsterdam at 7 weeks

REF: BOISSEVAIN, Barthold Hubert, *Stamboek Der Boissevains* (in French & Dutch) (Amsterdam, 1937); translation of Lucas' will; translation of genealogical entry; information from Boissevain Family Assoc.

BONDURANT, Jean Pierre/John Peter

bp. 18 Jul 1677, Génolhac, Gard Dépt., Languedoc-Rousillon, FR, n.w. of Alès, s/o Jean Pierre & Gabrielle
(Barjon) Bondurant; the family was Huguenot but as property owners, they had to abjure and convert to
Catholicism in order to retain their property; he was orphaned young.

c. Feb 1696/7 - left FR & went to Arrau, SWI, to live w/ his maternal uncle (a Huguenot
minister) where, on 3 Oct 1697, he recanted and became a Protestant again – he was an
apothecary

1699 – with his uncle Pastor Guillaume Barjon, he went to Karlshöfen, GER, n.e. of Bremen; later to ENG

1700 - to VA on the *Peter & Anthony*

20 Sep 1700 - arr in VA; settled Manakintown, VA on the James River; he practiced medicine in Henrico Co.
(later Goochland Co.) for many years

1705 – he was granted citizenship by the Governor & House of Burgesses

he obtained 200 acres on Old Town Creek, nr. present Matoaca, across the Appomattox River from Petersburg;
sold that land 29 Dec 1708

24 Mar 1709 – bought 400 acres on the s. side of the James River in Henrico Co.

m. c. 1709, VA, Ann X; both Fauré and Tanner have been given as her surname – neither name has been
proven; it is also not clear if she was Jean Pierre's only wife

1731, 1732, 1734 – Vestryman in King William's Parish

d. p. 25 Sep 1734, wd – a. 21 Jan 1734/5, wp Goochland Co, VA; wife Ann and all ch listed in his will

bur. Birdsong Lane (Road 1217), Powhatan, Powhatan Co, VA

CHILDREN:

Jean/John[2], b. VA; m. c. 1737, Sarah Rachel (Taylor) Moseley; at least 2 sons: Rev.**Thomas**[3], m. Rhoda
Agee, **Darby**[3], m. Ruth Agee, both d/o James & Mary (Fauré /Ford) Agee; Jean d. early 1774,
Buckingham Co, VA

Pierre/Peter[2], b. VA

Joseph[2] (Dr.), b. c. 1719, Henrico Co, VA; m. 19 May 1744, Goochland Co, VA, Agnes Radford
(b. 1724), d/o John & Elizabeth (Maxey) Radford); he d. 30 Jul 1806, Buckingham Co, VA;
credited with patriotic service (VA) in Rev. War
CHILDREN (wife and all ch named in father's will):
Ann[3], b. 10 Dec 1745; m. Rev. Charles Maxey
William[3], b. c. 1747/9; m. Judith Ann Moseley
Edward[3], b. c. 1750; m. Magdalene Verile Moseley; he d. Oct 1821
Joseph, Jr.[3], b. c. 1752; m. Mary Elizabeth Davis; he d. p. 11 Aug 1827, wd – a. Sep
1827, wp Shelby Co, KY; date of death prob. 16 Aug 1827; a physician
Mary[3], b.c. 1754, m/1, Rev. Edward Maxey, m/2, Nathan Ayers; she d. 1822
Elizabeth/Betty[3], b. c. 1756; m/1, John Watkins Perkins, m/2, John Epperson
Lucy[3], b. c. 1758; m/1, X Landum, m/2, Jeffrey Davis

Anne[2], m. c. 1729?, Jacques/James Fauré/Ford, s/o Pierre & Elizabeth (Agee) Fauré

Françoise/Frances[2], m. Pierre Sallé (1708/9-1752, Cumberland Co, VA), s/o Abraham & Olive
(Perrault) Sallé; Frances d. 1777, Powhatan Co, VA – both had wills; **6 ch**

REF: Will of Dr. Joseph Bondurant; Will of John Peter Bondurant – *Goochland Co. Will Book 2*; *The Huguenot,*
Vol. 20 (1961-63), Vol. 21 (1964-66), Vol. 23 (1967-69), Vol. 25 (1971-73) – Huguenot Society Founders of Manakin in
the Colony of VA; BROCK, Robert A., *Huguenot Emigration to VA* (1962); Church Records – France & Switzerland.

BONHÔTAL, Jacques Christophe

b. 1748?, FR, s/o David & Élisabeth (Goux) Bonhôtal; a Protestant of Chenebier, FR, in the Haute-Saône,
w. of Belfort, not far from the eastern border of FR

m. 19 Feb 1776, Anne Catherine Pochard (1753-1807)

d. 1820 FR

CHILD:

Jean Georges[2], b. 10 Sep 1785; m. 9 Nov 1802, Catherine Elisabeth Perret (6 Oct 1785-1May
1871), d/o Jean Georges & Catherine (Bouteiller) Perret; he d. 29 Apr 1867
CHILD:
Jean Georges[3], b. 21 Apr 1809; m. 1 Aug 1833, Élisabeth Bourquin (8 May 1812-21 Nov
1887), d/o Pierre & Élisabeth (Maillard) Bourquin; he d. 4 Jun 1871; was mayor
of Chenebier
CHILD:
Julie[4], b. 11 Jul 1841; m. Chenebier, Auguste Golillot, (15 Nov 1842-13 Jul 1903),
s/o Michel & Marie (Marchant) Golillot; she d. 28 Sep 1928 USA

REF: *Recherches Généalogiques sur les familles protestantes des communes d'Étobon, de Chenebier et d'Échavanne,
formant anciennement la paroisse d'Étobon, comprises actuellement dans le veux paroisses d'Étobon et de Chenebier
terminées au 26 Mai 1860* – information from town and church records certified by the Mayor of Chenebier in 1971
(Records on Bonhôtal family go back to Adam, b. 1614).

BONNEAU, Jean

b. La Rochelle, FR
m. Catherine Roi
CHILD:
Antoine[2], b. 27 Jan 1647, LaRochelle, FR; m. 1678, Catherine de Bloys/DuBliss; fled LaRochelle
1685; c. 1686/90 – emigrated to the Carolinas; naturalized there; d. c. 1700, in the Carolinas
CHILDREN :
Jean Henri[3], b. LaRochelle; to SC with father
Ant(h)oine[3], b. 1680, LaRochelle; m. p. 24 Sep 1702 (date of marr contract), Jeanne
Elizabeth Videau, b.1685 (rec. 18 Nov 1685 London Church), d/o Pierre & Jeanne Elizabeth
(Mauzé) Videau of Berkley Co, VA; Antoine was liv. Charleston where he
was a cooper; held several civic offices; d. p. 20 Feb 1742, wd - a. 8 Feb 1743, wp,
Berkley Co, VA; his will mentions **5** sons: **Anthony**[4], b. 1710, SC, m. c. 1731/5,
Margaret Henriette Horry (1713—3 Apr 1761), d/o Elias & Margaret (Huger) Horry; **Henry**[4];
Peter[4]; **Samuel**[4] (1725-1788), m/1, Frances de Longuemare, m/2, 1759, Mary
(Jermain/Germain) Boisseau, wid/o Jean Boisseau – 2 daus - **Elizabeth**[5], m. Ezekial Pickens,
Floride[5], m. 1786, John Ewing Calhoun (he d. 1802)*; **Benjamin**[4] - 6 daus - **Elizabeth**[5], m.
Samuel Simons, **Catherine**[5], m. X Nicholson, **Mary**[5], m. Joshua Toomer, **Floride**[5]; **Judith**[5];
Ester[5]; no mention of his wife Jeanne who must have d. since he
left everything to his ch
*their dau **Floride**[6] (b. 1792), m. John C. Calhoun (1782-1850), Vice Pres. of the U.S.,
1825-1832 - **issue**
Jacob[3], b. a. 1695, SC; m. Jane Videau, d/o of Pierre above; 3 sons: **Anthony**[4], m. Mary
Dubois: **Jacob**[4], m. 11 Feb 1746, Mary Miller, his wd, 1765-67, **Elias**[4] (23 Nov 1717 (?)
-bur. c. 13 Jul 1773), m/1, 29 May 1734,Susannah Miller – **8 ch**, m/2, 30 Oct 1746, Mary
Darby ,who was bur 5 Sep 1770 -2 daus **Magdalene**[4] (b. 18 May 1757), m. Henry Guérin,
s/o Isaac & Martha (Mouzon) Guérin, gr s/o Louis Mouzon & **Mary**[4], bp. 12 Jul 1761
Mary[3], m. Nicholas Bochet; he d. 15 Apr 1733

REF: *Transactions of the Huguenot Society of SC,* #37 (1932) – will of Antoine Jr, #51 (1946), #79 (1974), #84 (1979);
SC Historical & Genealogical Magazine, Vol. XXV (1924), Vol. XV (1914); *SC A Guide to the Palmetto State*;
RAVANEL, Daniel, *Liste des François et Suisses* (1868, reprint 1968); *Cross of Languedoc* (Aug 1984).

BONNEL(L), Daniel

b. c. 1664, s/o Jean & Marie (Lalon) Bonnel

1687 – to SC

m. Marie Izambent; she d. a. 14 Oct 1699, adm; names husband and 2 ch; adm complete, 5 Feb 1699/00

30 Mar 1696 - naturalization petition; named as "alien born"; mentions wife; on list of FR & Swiss Protestants; Charleston, SC

d. c.1740?; prob. not d. by 14 Oct 1699, as stated previously – Daniel mentioned in the adm of Marie; another court record mentions the 2 ch John and Susannah as being the son and dau of Daniel Bonnell and Mary, his wife, deceased – believe it refers to just Mary as per later documents which mention just Maria/Mary; the will referred to is hers; this does need some clarification and it also raises the question of who raised the 2 children?

CHILDREN:

Susanne[2], b. Carolina

John[2], b.c.1697; m. Honora White; he d. 1768

    CHILDREN:

    Honora[3], b. 8 Apr 1724; m. 4 Jun 1741, John Barton

    John[3], b. 1726; m. 3 Dec 1747/8, Patience Windham; **issue**

    Susannah Mary[3], b. 11 Apr, bp. 2 Jun 1728, Christ Ch Parish; d. 3 Nov 1770

    Daniel[3], b. 8 Aug 1731; d. St. Matthews Parish, GA, later Effingham Co; Rev. War

    Hannah[3], b. 5 Jun 1737

    Elizabeth[3], b. 24 Dec 1738; d. 1748

    Anthony[3], b. 3 Mar 1740/1, bp. 19 Apr 1741 Prince Frederick Winyaw Parish; m. Mary Ann Mills (d. 22 Jan 1832); he d. 25 Apr 1809, Screven Co., GA; **issue**; Rev. War, Lt, GA

    Sarah[3], b/d 24 Aug 1744

REF : HIRSCH, Arthur Henry, *The Huguenots of Colonial SC* (1962); LEE, Hannah F., *The Huguenots in France & America* (1973); *The SC Historical & Genealogical Magazine,* Vol. 18 (1917), Vol. X (Jan 1909); NSCDXVIIC, *17th Century Ancestors*; REDDICK, James, *Family Album;* will-Anthony Bonnell; *French & Swiss Protestants, Naturalizations, 1695-6* (1968).

BONNEL(L), Thomas

m/1, XX, who d. c. 1593, ENG

    p. 1567 – fled from Hondschoote, nr. Ypres, Hainaut, FR (now Ieper, BEL); Hondschoote was in FR Flanders, s.e. of Dunkerque, today very nr. border of BEL; settled Norwich, ENG; his name is found in records of the Huguenot Society of London; Thomas appeared on a list of foreigners paying taxes; liv. in St. John's Parish in the Wymer Ward of Norwich & St. Martin at Palace Parish, also in Norwich; ch were bp in the Walloon Church in Norwich

m/2, c. 1594, Jaque Marie/Jaquemaine Bygote

1595 – Thomas was an elder or deacon of the Walloon Ch in Norwich; became mayor of Norwich

Aug 1596, London – at a *colloque* (conference)

d. a. 11 Nov 1607, wp, Norwich Consistory Court; will mentions wife Jaquelyn, sons Daniel, David, Thomas, Benjamin; grch (Daniel's ch) Daniel, Rebecca, Hester, & Abigail; gr dau Judith Marchant; grdaus Katherine & Susan (David's daus); ch of 2nd marr. not named but sons Daniel and David were to distribute £30 equally among them

CHILDREN, m/1:

Daniel[2], m. Rebecca Fenne; he was a merchant in London; bur. 26 Jul 1624, St. George, Tombland, Norwich; **4 ch** mentioned in his father's will + at least one son **Samuel**[3] who m. Rachel Sayer, d/o Thomas Sayer, a merchant in London

David[2], m. Katherine Best; he was a merchant in London; d. a. 20 Jun 1638, wp; **5 sons, at least 2 daus**

Thomas[2], not marr. by time of his father's will

Benjamin[2], b. 7 Jan 1590; 1607, he brought a letter from the Walloon Ch in Norwich to the Dutch Ch in London; he was liv. w/ his bro David in London; evidently liv abroad for a time and was well-traveled; m. XX; d. p. 17 Jul 1655

CHILD:

William[3], b. c. 1610; m. Ann Wilmot, d/o Benjamin & Ann (X)Wilmot; Ann d. a. 1 May 1654, New Haven, CT; 1 May 1654, William asked the General Court permission to return to ENG

CHILDREN:

Lydia[4], m. 10 Apr 1661, Milford, CT, Francis French, s/o William & Elizabeth (X) French; she d. 1 Apr 1708, Derby, CT; he d. 14 Feb 1690/1; **9 ch**

Benjamin[4], bp. as an adult, 23 Apr 1690, New Haven; m/1, a. Jul 1666 ,Rebecca Mallory (18 Mar 1649, New Haven-12 Mar 1691, New Haven), d./o Peter & Mary (Preston) Mallory - **10 ch**; m/2, Elizabeth (Post) Sperry (b. 22 Feb 1655, Saybrook, CT-1715), d/o John & Hester (Hyde) Post, widow of John Sperry - **2 ch**; Eliz. m/3, 19 Sep 1700, New Haven, Edmund Dorman who d. 1 May 1711; Benjamin d. c. 1696

Nathaniel[4], b. c. 1644; m. Susannah Whitehead, d/o Isaac Whitehead; **7 ch**

Mary[4], b. 4 May 1650, New Haven, CT; m. 31 Oct 1671, Eleazer Peck, s/o Henry & Joan (X) Peck; she d. 20 Jul 1724 Wallingford, CT – **9 ch**; he m/2, 31 Oct 1726 Wallingford, Elizabeth (Ford) Culver

Ebenezer[4], b. 28 Aug 1653, New Haven; d. a. May 1654, New Haven

Susan[2], b. 15 Jul 1591

Judith[2], m. 1594, John Marshall/Marchant; at least **1 dau Judith**[3]

John[2], bp. 19 Aug 1593

CHILDREN, m/2 (all bp. Walloon Ch, Norwich):

Elizabeth[2], bp. 10 Aug 1595, St. Martin at Palace or Walloon Ch, Norwich

Abraham[2], bp. 15 Apr 1599

Isaac[2], bp. 1601

Judye[2], bp. Mar 1605/6

2 unknown daus?[2]

REF: DUNCAN, Ruth C., *William Bunnell & His Descendants* (1986); GWYNN, Grace L., *Huguenot Society of London Publications*, Vol. 1, Part 2; BELLETREAU, William S. & BROWN, John H., *American Families of Historic Lineage* ; BONNELL, Bertha R., *Bonnell Family History*; VALENTINE, Carolyn Syron, *Wills, Deeds & Ways* (1925) ; CHAMIER, Adrian Charles, *Colloques et Synodes, 1581-1654*, Publication of the Huguenot Society of London (Lymington, 1890).

BONNET(T), David

b. c. 1600, *prob.* Dauphiné Province, FR

m. c. 1630/31, Marie Parandier

d. a. 10 Sep 1667, Chambons nr. Mentoulles – both places are sm. towns nr. Fenestrelle, Turin Province in the Pragela Valley; they are c. 41 mi. n.w. of Turin/Torino, ITA, c. 20 miles from the FR border of today; names of towns in the area are, for the most part, more FR than Italian; between 1536-1562 Turin was occupied by the FR, again in 1640-1706, again in1789, until 1814 when it was restored to the house of Savoy; the Pragela (in the Delfinato, the Italian Dauphiny) belonged to the former FR province of Dauphiné until 1713; FR was spoken there until the 20th century

CHILDREN (all b. Chambons):

Jehanne/Johanne[2], b. 1 Jan 1632; m. Jean Rey, s/o Guillelme Rey; dau **Jeanne**, b. 15 Oct, bp. 27 Oct 1666; Jehanne d. a. 1688

Jean[2], b. 31 Aug 1634; m. c. 1654, Madelène Rey (c. 1644-30 Apr 1706 Charlottenberg); a farmer at

Chambons; c. 1687, driven from his home because he was a Waldensian, settled GER; d. a. 30 Apr 1706); Charlottenberg is s.w. of Limburg & e. of Koblenz (**not** Charlottenburg which is w. of Berlin, now part of that city)

CHILDREN (all b. Chambons):

Jeanne[3], b. c. 1665; m. Abraham Conte (c. 1667-25 Apr 1707, Charlottenberg); she d. 14 Feb 1721, Charlottenberg

Marie[3], b. c. 1667; m. Étienne Guillelmon/Guillaumont (d. 1 Dec 1745, Charlottenberg); she d. 2 Apr 1733, Charlottenberg

Jean[3], bp. 1 Feb 1671; d. bef 1688

David[3], b. c. 1673; m. 27 Jul 1702, Holzappel (s.e. Koblenz), Suzanne Blanc (d. 17 Jan 1741, Charlottenberg); he d. bet 1732-37

CHILDREN, b. Charlottenberg:

Marie[4], b. 17 May 1703; d. 3 May 1730, Charlottenberg

Jean[4], b. 16 Sep 1705; m. Anna Dorothea Herpel from Laurenburg, a town a few km from Holzappel; he d. 16 Sep 1764 Charlottenberg

David[4], b. 23 Jun 1707, Charlottenberg; m. 16 Mar 1729, Holzappel, Marie Elizabeth Borel (9 Jun 1708, Charlottenberg-20 Aug 1792, Charlottenberg), d/o Jean Borel; he d. 1 Feb 1783, Charlottenberg – **2 daus, 6 sons**, incl. **Jean Anthoine**[5], b. 5 Mar 1737, m. 11 Jan 1757, Marie Magdalene Krieg (c.1735-13 Oct 1803), a farmer at Charlottenberg – **13 ch**, incl. son **Heinrich Carl**[6], (18 Nov 1776-12 Jul 1839), m/1, 3 Jan 1804, Catherine Wilhelmine Henneman – **3 ch**, m/2, 3 Mar 1816, Maria Elizabeth Priester/Beisasse - **10 ch**, incl son **Johann Ludwig**[7] (26 Apr 1819, Charlottenberg-c.1899, PA) who emig. 1849 to America – progenitor of the PA Bonnetts who were in Clarion and Allegheny Counties

Suzanne[4], b. 23 Jun 1707; d. 19 Jun 1738, Charlottenberg

Jean Pierre[4], b. 10 Oct 1713; d. 24 Jun 1732, Charlottenberg

Marguerite[4], b. 30 Nov 1716; m. 15 Jan 1738, Holzappel, Guillaume Toulouse (c. 1703, Chémery, Lorraine-16 Mar 1767, Charlottenberg); she d. 27 Jan 1754, Charlottenberg [Chémery is now Chémery-les-Deux, n.e. of Metz]

Madelène[3], bp. 25 Jul 1677; m. Pierre Pons; she d. 31 Dec 1707, Charlottenberg

Pierre[2], bp. 31 Aug 1638

David[2], b, 28 Nov 1643; m. 8 Jun 1679, Mentoulles, Marie Guillelmon (b. 18 Dec 1642), d/o Abraham Guillelmon ; he was a merchant; he d. Chambons – **2 daus** b. Chambons

Estienne[2], b. 2 Apr 1648

Marie[2], bp. 2 Apr 1652; d. 10 Sep 1667, Chambons

REF: *Deutsches Familienarchiv*, Vol. II (1954/55) – records from the registers of Vinay, FR (located w. of Grenoble, in the Isère Dépt, Rhône-Alpes) – records of the congregation at Mentoulles; Schaumburg immigration records – Schaumburg is a district in Lower Saxony, GER, w. & s.w. of Hannover; FR ch records from Charlottenberg; KEIFNER, Dr. Theo, *Die Waldenser* (Ötisheim-Schönenberg,1980).

BONNET(T), Jean Jacques

b. 13 Oct 1702, Friedrichstal, GER (n.e. of Dresden), s/o Daniel (1658-4 Sep 1736) & Christine (Cousine) Bonnet; Christine (c. 1661/2-Feb 1732) was Daniel's 2nd wife (1st wife was Catherine Cousine who d. a. 1682 when he m. Christine); Jean Jacques was grs/o Jean (b. 1630) who arr Baden-Durlach, from the Dauphiné, by 9 Oct 1699, (per GER Archives) in Karlsruhe

m. 19 Oct 1723, St. Évangile Ch, Friedrichstal, Anne Marie Desreux (b. 1702), d/o Abraham & Judith (Guerit) Desreux; Jean was her 2nd husband (1st husband Jean Corbeau, d. 1721, their 2 daus d. young)

27 Aug 1733- arr America on the *Elizabeth* of London; different lists him as Jacob Bonnett, age 32, or

Jaques Bonet or Jacob Bunett, farmer; on the list of women: wife Mary Bunett; ch: Suzanne Bunett, age 4,dead, Christina Bunett, age 2, dead, Margret Bunett, age 8, Johan Simon Bunett, age 0¾; he swore an Oath of Allegiance in Philadelphia on that date; settled Paoli, Chester Co, PA

d. c. 1755, PA

CHILDREN (1st 3 bp. St. Évangile Ch, Friedrichstal):

Marguerite/Margaret Catherine[2], b. 24 May , bp. 6 Jun 1725; m. Conrad Six/Sickes/Sykes; she d. 1794, Greene Co, PA – **8 sons, 4 daus**

Johann Adam Isaac/John[2], b. 22 Feb, bp. 23 Feb 1727; d. a. 1733, GER – was not w/ fam. when it travelled to America

Susanna Magdelena[2], b. 11 Jun 1729; d. 1733, on ship to America

Christine[2], b. 23 Jun 1731; d. 1733, on ship to America

Johann Martin Simon/John[2], b. 1 Apr 1733; m. 22 Apr 1755, Mary Dorothy Bickley/Biélet/Biclet; **5 ch**, incl. dau **Rosina**[3], b. 17 Sep, bp. 27 Sep 1757, Krupp Ch, Lancaster Co., PA, who m. Peter Ankeny, s/o Dewalt & Catherine (X) Ankeny; Civil Service, Rev. War; he d. p. 30 Apr 1793, wd, Bedford Co, PA, prob. 1803, Jackson Co, now WV, killed by Indians;

Elizabeth[2], b. c. 1734 PA; m. Nicholas Wetzel; she d. Jun 1805

Mary[2], b. 1735, PA; m. 1756, VA, Capt. John Wetzel; she d. Jun 1805 WV – **2 sons, 3 daus**

Lewis[2], b. Feb 1736/7, Paoli; m. 1770, PA, Anna Elizabeth Waggoner; he d. 9 Mar 1808, Wheeling, now WV – **2 sons, 3 daus**

Samuel[2], b. c, 1739, PA; m. c. 1755, PA, Mary Elizabeth Lorentz who m/2, X Mock; Patriotic Service, Rev. War; he d. a.17 Dec 1789, Monongehela country or Monongalia Co, VA – **8 sons, 4 daus**

Susannah[2], b. c. 1740, PA; m. Hezekiah Stewart; she d. Shenandoah Co, VA

REF: Records from the Evangelical Ch, Friedrichstal; STRASSBURGER, Ralph B., *PA German Pioneers* (Baltimore, 1980); STAPLETON, Rev. A., *Memorials of the Huguenots in America* (Baltimore, 1964); LECKEY, Howard L., *The Tenmile Country & Its Pioneer Families* (Knightstown, IN, 1977).

BONNET(T), Louis

b. 1630 Thorigné, Deux-Sèvres Dépt., Poitou-Charentes, FR, s.e. Niort **or** Thorigny-sur-le-Mignon, n.e. Sugèras, also in Deux-Sèvres

m. XX

prob. d. FR

CHILD:

Daniel[2], b. 1655 FR; m. Jeanne Colliver/Couturier (1662-1732), native of Meschers (-sur-Gironde), Saintonge, FR - now in Poitou-Charentes Dépt., s.e. of Royan; a Giles Courturier, *matelot* (sailor) of Meché (*sic*), s/o Giles & Suzanne (Laviger) Courturier, m. 29 Jul 1688, Bristol FR Ch, Jeanne Fumé – bro/o Jeanne???; c. 1685, left FR w/ 2 daus - family legend says they headed for the FR coast, some 45-50 mi away, with 2 small ch hidden in the panniers of a donkey and covered with vegetables; a soldier stopped them and thrust his sword into each pannier wounding one of the ch but the family was allowed to continue; to HOL; c. 1690, fled to Bristol, ENG; he was a weaver; 1693-1699 – listed as an *ouvrier en laine* (woolworker in the Register of the FR Church at Bristol, origin Thorigné, s/o Louis Bonnet, a FR Protestant of good repute & that   he had lived in Bristol for 10 yrs.; winter 1700/01 – to America (passport dated 16 Nov 1700, Bristol) w/ wife, 4 ch; he carried a certificate signed by the mayor and clerk of Bristol, stating that he was a FR Protestant & that he, his wife + 4 ch intend to settle in America; fall 1702 – purchased land in New Rochelle from Bartholomew Le Rox; 1708 – on the list of freeholders in New Rochelle; 27 Sep 1715, oath of abjuration, NY – said he was a yeoman from New Rochelle; d. New Rochelle, NY, c. 1734?

CHILDREN:

Ann[3], m. prob. ENG, François Benin; emigrated w/ husband – to VA

Barbara[3], m. ENG, Pierre Dutois/Dutoit ; emigrated w/ husband – to VA

Pierre[3], b. 2 Jun, bp. 5 Jun 1693, FR Ch, Bristol

Daniel II[3], b. 29 Jan, bp. 3 Feb 1695, FR Ch, Bristol; d. age 16

Marie[3], b. 9 May, bp. 16 May 1697, FR Ch, Bristol ; m. Jean Soulice (1695-28 Aug 1776, New Rochelle, NY), s/o Jean Soulice

Elizabeth[3], b. 2 Oct, bp. 8 Oct 1699, FR Ch, Bristol; m. James Parcot ?

Jeanne/Jane[3], b. 9 Apr 1703, New Rochelle; m. Jacques/James Sicard (1699 New Rochelle-8 Nov 1773 New Rochelle, s/o Daniel & Catherine (Woertman) Sicard; she d. 1757 New Rochelle; **issue**

Jean Jacques[3], b. 11 Dec 1709, NY, m. c. 1735,Mary Guion (1711-1769), dau/o Isaac & Marie (Malherbe) Guion

REF: BENNING, Eva H., *François Benin (Francis Benning), His Descendants & Allied Families* (1981); JONES, W. Mac, *The Douglass Register* (1966); WEISIGER, Benjamin B., III *Colonial Wills of Henrico Co, VA, 1654-1737*, Part One: CABELL, Priscilla Harriss, *Turff & Twigg, The French Lands*, Vol. 1 (Richmond, VA, 1988); The Huguenot Society of London, *Registers of the FR Ch of Bristol, Stonehouse & Plymouth,* Vol. XX (London, 1912); SEACORD, Morgan H., *Biographical Sketches & Index of the Huguenot Settlers of New Rochelle, 1687-1776*; MAYO, Ronald, *The Huguenots of Bristol*; New Rochelle Records 1669-1828; BAIRD, Charles W., *Huguenot Emigration to America*, Vol. II; BOYER, Carl, 3rd , *Ship Passenger Lists to NY & NJ, 1600-1825* (Newhall, CA, 1978).

BONNEVILLE/BENNEVILLE, Georges de

b. Rouen, FR, s/o François, a prominent Huguenot nobleman

1688 - fled FR after his château was attacked; went to ENG

m. 1697, Marie Granville (d. 26 Jul 1703, London)

d. soon aft 1703, prob. London

CHILD (9 ch in 5 yrs – 4 sets of twins in 4 yrs; only her last ch survived), 1 of 9:

George[2], b. 26 Jul 1703, London; was orphaned as a baby; he was taken under the personal care of Queen Anne of ENG & was well-educated; 1720,went to FR to preach to persecuted Huguenots – was arrested and condemned to death when a last second reprieve from King Louis XV arrived, which was the result of pressure by the British ambassador; left FR and went to GER, HOL and Flanders, preaching to the Huguenot refugees for 18 yrs.; despite being in poor health, he went to America; he arr Philadelphia, 1741; he went to Oley, at the urging of Jean Bertolet, where he was a teacher and physician; he lived in Oley Twp, 7 miles n. of Reading; 24 Feb 1745, he mar. Bertolet's dau Esther (12 Aug 1720-7 Mar 1795); 1755, he moved to Milestown, nr Philadelphia; he d. 19 Mar 1793, at his farm in Branchtown, Bristol Twp, Philadelphia Co, PA

CHILDREN:

Esther[3], b. 20 Apr 1746, Oley; m. 1764, Jacob Brown/Braun of Philadelphia; she d. 3 Feb 1833; **7 or 10 ch**

Susanna[3], b. 15 May 1748, Oley; m. 15 Oct 1771, John Keim of Reading; she d. 25 Mar 1813

Marie[3], b. 20 Aug 1751 Oley; m. 1779, John Linington; she d. 25 Mar 1813; **3 daus**

Daniel[3], b. 12 Nov 1753,, Oley; m. Elizabeth (X) Coates, widow of Dr. X Coates; he d. 4 Aug 1827

Sarah[3], b. 9 Feb 1756, prob. Branchtown; d. young

Charlotta[3], b. 13 Oct 1758, Branchtown; m. 11 Aug 1778, Philadelphia Co, PA, Dr. Jonathan Bertolet (18 Nov 1753-14 Aug 1789), her 2nd cousin, s/o John, grs/o Peter & Elizabeth (X) Bertolet; she d. 21 Apr 1826; **3 sons, 1 dau**

George[3], b. 10 Nov 1760, Bristol Twp; m. 10 May 1781, Eleanor Roberts, d/o John; he d. 17 Dec 1850; **5 ch**

REF: STAPLETON, *Memorials of the Huguenots*; KEIM, Randolph, editor, *The Keim & Allied Families*, article by Daniel M. Keim, "Brief Genealogical Gleanings Connected with the Lineage of Keim, DeBenneville, Bertolet, etc. (May, 1899), also June, 1900 edition which deals with his ministry in PA; BELL, Albert D., *The Life &Times of Dr. George de Benneville (1703-1793)* (1953); MONTGOMERY, *History of Berks Co, PA.*

BONREPOS, Alexandre de (Rev.)

he is *prob.* the father of David and Élie – both of them had a son named Alexander; Élie had a dau
    named Margaret/Marguerite; both brothers were ministers

m. Margaret X

d. St. Kitt's, W. Indies; he was a minister

CHILDREN: (not known if there were more ch than the 2 sons):

David[2], a Waldensian; liv. St. Kitt's at the time of the Revocation, according to C. W. Baird; c. 1686,
    a refugee from St. Christopher, West Indies, to Boston; was in Salem, MA; 1687- minister of the
    FR Ch in New Rochelle, NY; is called a Doctor of Divinity in 1718; 1695 - pastor of the FR Ch,
    Staten Island until 1734; 6 Feb 1696 - received letter of denization; spring 1696-1700/02 – pastor
    at New Paltz, NY; m/1, Blanche DuBois; she d. p. 13 Jun 1718, date of deed, m/2, p. 1718, Martha
    (Billou) Stillwell, d/o Pierre & Françoise (DuBois) Billiou, widow of Thomas Stillwell; she d. a.
    23 Oct 1736, wp; he d. a. 6 May 1734, wp, Richmond Co, NY; wd, 16 Jun 1733, mentions wife
    Martha, nieces Blanche Chadeu (wife/o Henry Chaden), Anna Pa(l)mer, Hester Le Count, + 3 youngest
    sons of his son Alexander, grson David; his stepson Nicholas Stillwell was 1 of the executors; wp, 6
    May 1734, Richmond Co, NY; he evidently none of his ch were alive at the
    time he wrote his will.

    CHILDREN, m/1:

    David[3], not in father's will

    John[3], not in father's will

    Alexander[3], ?

Élias/Élie[2], b. c. 1656, FR; husbandman and teacher; apparently spent some time in HOL as he owned
    property there; m/1, c. 1681/2, Esther X (1663 FR-p. 1698 NY); 1686 – to Boston; naturalization
    app; a. Nov 1687, purchased home in Salem, MA; went New Rochelle; purchased a home lot, 9
    Mar 1696; m/2, p. 1699, Jane/Jeanne X, (c. 1663?- a. 3 Apr 1719); 1710 census says she was 47
    which would make her into her 40's when daus were b. – so date may not be factual; not in Elias'
    will; 28 Jun 1705 – licensed to keep school in New Rochelle; d. a. 12 May 1719, wp, Westchester
    Co, NY; will, written 3 Apr 1719, in French, mentions only Elias II, who was to get his father's
    personal property, & Esther

    CHILDREN, m/1 (birthdates estimated from 1698 census):

    Marguerite/Margaret[3], m. 1713, Pierre/Peter Angevin (s/o Louis & Marie (X) Angevin), as his
        2nd wife - **2 sons, 1 dau**; she d. p. 1729

    Anne Marguerite[3], b. 1683; m. c. 1705, Obadiah Palmer (25 Jun 1680, Westchester,
        NY-24 Feb 1748/9 Mamaronek, NY), s/o Samuel & Mary (Drake?) Palmer; his wp, 27
        Feb 1748/9 – mentions wife & 9 ch; Anne's uncle David's will mentions his nieces
        Anna Palmer & Hester LeCount; **7 sons, 3 daus**

    Elias[3], b. 1685

    Alexander[3], b. 1687; m. XX; son **David** + **3 other sons**; evidently d. a. 16 Jun 1733 (uncle's will
        dated) as his son **David**[4] inherited part of his gr uncle's estate - the will also refers to the 3
        youngest sons of Alexander but not by name

    Hester/Esther[3], b. 1693; m. Peter LeConte; at least 1 dau **Martha**; Esther d. p. 1733

    Blanche[3], b. 1695; m. Henry Chadeu of New Rochelle; she d. p. 1733

    Marian[3], b. 1697

    Jean[3], b. 1699 (prob. ch of m/1); prob. d. young – not on 1710 census

    CHILDREN, m/2:

    Martha[3], b. 4 Feb 1704; not on 1710 census

    Mary[3], b. 1705

REF: BOLTON, Rev. Robert , *History of Westchester Co, NY*, Vol. I (NY, 1881); *NYGBR*, Vol. 59 (1928); FORBES, Jeanne A., *Records of the Town of New Rochelle, 1699-1828* (1916) – in FR w/ translation; Elias' will; article from *The Boston Transcript* , 4 Dec 1948; SEACORD, Morgan H., *Biographical Sketches & Index of the Huguenot Settlers of New Rochelle, 1687-1776* (New Rochelle, 1941); David's will; PERLEY, Sidney, *History of Salem, MA, 1671-1716,* Vol. III; BAIRD, Charles W., *History of the Huguenot Emigration to America;* LeFEVRE, Ralph, *History of New Paltz* (NY 1903).

BONTECOU, Pierre

b. FR, poss. La Rochelle

m. Marguerite Collinot

1684 – on a list of fugitives from the Île de Ré to "La Caroline" - a term used to designate N.
America; he was listed with wife, 5 ch; sailed by way of ENG

by 24 Jul 1689 - he was a merchant in NY

d. p. 1724; poss. bur. in the old Huguenot Churchyard, L'Église du Saint Esprit, NYC

CHILDREN:

Marguerite[2], b. FR; m. 16 Jul 1699, Étienne/Stephen Perdiau, a mariner, in the FR Ch, NYC;
NYC; 3 ch – **Marguerite**[3], **Étienne/Stephen**[3], **Ozée/Hosea**[3]

Peter[2], b. FR; listed as a schoolmaster in NY in 1702

Sara[2], b. FR; m. 19 Oct 1709, FR Ch, <u>Alexander Resseguie</u> of Norwalk, CT; **issue**

Daniel[2], b. 1681, LaRochelle; merchant and elder in FR Church in NYC; m. Mariane Machet, d/o
Jean; he d. p. 20 Aug 1772, wd – a. 30 Nov 1778, wp, NY; son **Daniel**[3], bp.18 Feb 1713, NY;
Daniel's will doesn't mention a wife or ch– heirs are sister Mary and nephew Timothy

Susanne[2], b. FR; d. p. 20 Sep 1724

Marie[2], b. 21 Jul 1690, NY, bp FR Ch, 24 Jul 1690; **may** have m. Francis Bassett, a friend of her bro
Daniel; Daniel's will mentions "Mary Bassett, wife of Francis"

Rachel[2] (twin), b. 21 Jul 1690, NY, bp FR Ch, 24 Jul 1690, prob. d. young

Timothée/Timothy[2], b. 17 Jun, bp 2 Jul 1693, FR Ch; c. 1715, left NY to go to France to become a
silversmith; <u>m/1</u>, in FR, Mary X (d. 5 Nov 1735, New Haven, CT); <u>m/2</u>, 29 Sep 1736, Mary
Goodrich (b. 15 Dec 1704-d. c. 1760, 56Y), d/o Col. David & Prudence (Churchill) Goodrich
of Wethersfield, CT; Timothy d. 14 Feb 1784, New Haven, CT, was bur beneath Trinity Church

CHILD, m/1

Timothy[3], b. 1723, <u>m/1</u>, 5 Nov 1747, Susanna Prout, d/o John Prout, <u>m/2</u>, p. 1755, Susan Gordon -
5 ch

CHILDREN, m/2

Peter[3], b. 1738, m. 14 Nov 1762, Susanna Thomas, d/o Jehiel & Mary (X) Thomas, Peter was a
ship captain- **9 ch**

Daniel[3], b. 1739, m. 12 Sep 1775, Rebecca (Starr) (Tyler) Rohde, widow, d/o Joseph & Sarah
(Southmayd) Starr, Daniel was a doctor– at least **1 dau**[4]

David[3], d. unmarr.; **James**[3] (1743-1760); **dau**[3], m. X Lathrop-**no issue**

REF: BAIRD, Charles W., *History of the Huguenot Emigration to America*; MORRIS, John E., *The Bontecou Genealogy.
A Record of the Descendants of Pierre Bontecou* (Hartford, CT, 1885).

BOUCHELLE, Legé de

b. c. 1633, Artois, FR

m. 1677, Düsseldorf, Anna Margaretha Conte/Couda (16 Sep 1654, Düsseldorf, GER-29 Dec 1721, Cecil
Co, MD), d/o Ansonius & Margaretha (Ules) Conte; she m/2, Petrus Sluyter; Labadist family

c. 1683- to America; settled Cecil Co

d. p. 30 May 1698, wd; mentions wife, friend Petrus Sluyter; prob. d. 1702, Cecil Co

CHILDREN:

Susanna[2], bp. 1677, Düsseldorf; m. Samuel Bayard, as his 2nd wife

Samuel[2], bp. Oct 29 1679, Düsseldorf; not in father's will

Elizabeth[2]

Magdalena[2]

Petrus[2], m. 28 Mar 1716, Mary Hezall; he d. a. 26 Jul 1736, wp, Cecil Co; at least **4 liv. ch + 1 unborn
ch** at the time that he wrote his will, 22 Aug 1735; he was a physician

REF: Records, Evangelisch Reformierte Kirche, Düsseldorf, 1663-1809; MALLERY, Charles P., *Ancient Families of Bohemia Manor* (1988); Legé's will; *Maryland Calendar of Wills.*

BOUCHER, Matthew

b. 1700, FR
m. 1734, XX
d. 1748, Loudon Co, VA, massacred by Indians
only surviving CHILD:
Peter (Sr.)[2], b. c. 1743; m. XX; in Mercer Co, KY, 1789; served in Amer. Revolution
  CHILD:
  John[3]

REF: BOUCHER, John H., Jr., *"The Bowshelder-Boucher Myth Discovered".*

BOUCHIER/BUSCIER/BUSHER, Dominic/Dominico

b. Italy, prob. of FR parents – surname is French, not Italian – perhaps from the Piedmont where
  numerous families of FR descent lived
c. 1561 - to London, ENG
m. Geneviève X, supposedly b. Rouen, FR; she m/2, license 8 Dec, m. 13 Dec 1596, Richard Deane;
  m/3, Bishopstown, Wiltshire, Charles Pressy; widow's will Prerogative Court, Canterbury, 36
  Soame, dated 3 Mar 1619/20, wp 10 Apr 1620 says she is the widow of "Dominick Buscier"
  names Nathaniel, Jeremy, Jane - Constantine's widow, Abraham's daus (he may have d.),
  John, Mary, John's wife Margaret & leaves $$ to the poor of the French Ch in London
1571- was in the Parish of St. Catherine (later **K**atherine) Coleman in London, described as having been b. in
  Italy, "Jane" his wife, b. in Rouen, and had been liv. in London for 10 yrs.; St. Catherine Coleman
  Church dates back to a. 1346, it no longer exists but was on the s. side of Fenchurch St., just e. of Mark
  Lane, n.w. of the Tower of London – church became Anglican during the reign of Henry VIII and,
  except during the reign of his dau Mary (1553-58), it remained so
"Merchant stranger" in London records, 1571, 1582, 1583, 1588
  c.1589 - on the London Subsidy Roll, "Algate Warde", "Dominike Bushere, merchant lxxx [11]" –
  presumably the numbers indicate money – *perhaps* £1 30sh 11p
d. a. 8 Dec 1596, prob. London
CHILDREN (some names from Geneviève's will, order of ch. not certain):
Nathaniel[2], m. Anne X; d. p. 1631, wd
Jeremy[2]
Jane[2], m. Sampson Hussey, Philippe Tiffield?
Constantine[2], m. Jane X
John[2], m. Margaret X
Mary[2], b. c. 1564; m. Humphrey Basse (he d. 4 Jun 1616); she d. 22 Jul 1616 & was bur St. Helen's,
  Bishopsgate, London; **17 ch**
Abraham[2], b. c. 1586; matriculated Oxford 8 Mar 1604/5, age 18

REF: *Boyd's Citizens of London*, #4054, 42873, 2112; BASS, Ivan E., *Bass Family History* (1955); PREYN, Mrs. Aleyen W., "Humprey Basse, the Huguenot & His Descendants" in the *Cross of Languedoc* (Mar, 1986); "London Subsidy Roll, 1589, from the Queen's College MS 72" in *The Publications of the Harleian Society*, Vol. CIX, CX, FOR THE YEARS MCMLVII & MCMLVIII (Leeds, England).

BOUCHILLON, Jean/John

b. c. 1744, FR

25 Dec 1763 - Jean, age 19, and his brother Joseph, age 22, were refugees from England when they left Plymouth, ENG for America on the *Friendship;* on the *"Liste des Protestants Refugiés actuellement à Plymouth pour se render en Amérique dans les possessions de sa Majesté George troisème Roy de la Grande Bretagne sous la conduite & direction de Jean Louis Gilbert Pasteur"* (22 Nov 1763), Jean is listed as a laborer and Joseph as a winegrower; 112 males and 61 females sailed for America. Two days out to sea, a great "tempest" caused the ship to be stranded on rocks, where it remained until 14 Feb 1764, they returned to Plymouth and stayed there until 22 Feb when it set sail again. They reached Charlestown, SC, on 12 Apr 1764

18 Apr 1764 - took Oath of Allegiance; Jean rec.100 acres of land, Joseph 150; they settled in New Bordeaux in the Abbeville Dist. of SC (now in McCormick Co); Joseph had a wife Marie (née Maginier/Majinnet), age 25 yrs; Marie d. and Joseph m/2, 16 Dec 1766, Elisabeth (Grégoire) Baraud, widow of Matthew Baraud

m. Mary Ann LeRoy (d/o Pierre Michel & Marie (Labrun) LeRoy from St. Python, Hainaut); she m/2, 1791, Lazarus Covin (d. 1819); Mary Ann was the last survivor of the last colony of emigrant Huguenots who settled in America; she d. 6 Nov 1839

Jean served in the Rev. War as a Lt. in the militia; Joseph was a Lt. and Capt. in the Militia

d. a. 7 Jul 1789, wp; left his brother Joseph as guardian of 3 children; will mentions sons & dau, wife

CHILDREN:

John[2], b. 1775; d. p. 30 Nov 1802, wd; poss. in 1818

Joseph James[2], 1777; m. Mar 1798, Susannah Guillebeau (15 Jan 1776-12 Sep 1814), d/o André & Mary Jane (Roquemore) Guillebeau; he d. a. 3 Jan 1803, wp; Susannah m/2, 1 Jan 1809, Francis Moragne, s/o Pierre & Cécile (Bayle) Moragne

> CHILDREN:
>
> **John**[3], b. c. 1800
>
> **Joseph Leonard**[3], b. c. 1801
>
> **Jenny**[3], b. c. May 1802

Elizabeth[2], b. 1780

REF: *Transcriptions of Wills*; *SC Historical Society Collection*, Vol. 2 (1858); *Transactions of the Huguenot Society of SC*, #42 (1937); Abbeville Dist. Court Records, Box 10, Pack 187, p. 32, Box 105, Pack 2620, p. 377; GIBERT, Anne C., *Pierre Gibert, Esq., The Devoted Huguenot* ; MOSS, Bobby Gilmer, *Roster of SC Patriots in the American Revolution* (1983); Jean's will.

BOUDIN/BAUDOIN/BODINE, Jean

b. Béthune, Artois, FR, s.w. of Lille or Cambrai, s.w. of Valenciennes (both in Pas-de-Calais); name also le Boudin, de Baudain; name of great antiquity in Cambrai

went to Saintonge Prov

m. XX – nothing known about her, evidently d. before Jean emigrated

to HOL, then ENG with his son

by 3 Nov 1677 – in NY, as he & Marie Creison (Cresson?) witnessed the baptism at the Reformed Dutch Ch in NYC, of Jan, s/o Andries Canon & Jannetje Pluck

1 Apr 1686 - he had a survey of land on Staten Island where he finally settled

d. late 1694, Staten Island, NY; a. 4 Mar 1695, adm of his estate, which was valued at £242

CHILD:

Jean[2], b. 9 May 1645, Médis (n.e. of Royan), Saintonge, FR; went to NY with his fa; m/1, 11 Jan 1669/70*, Flatbush Dutch Ch, Brooklyn, NY, Marie Crocheron, d/o Jean & Mary (X) Crocheron; Marie died & he returned to ENG; m/2, ENG, Esther Bridon, d/o François & Susanne (X) Bridon; 14 Oct 1681 – he and Esther were naturalized by royal letters-patent, Westminster; Esther's father & mother were on the same list; returned to NY by 1695; went to Charles Neck, Middlesex Co, NJ, by 1701; 12 May 1701, he purchased 80 acres on the w. side of Staten Island & he moved there; 8 May 1722 he bought another tract of 80 acres from Francis Bridon in the same place; 2 Feb 1732, Jelan & Esther Cossou, heirs of Francis Bridon, conveyed to him a dwelling house & a 10 acre tract of land, also at Charles Neck; he d. p. 7 Mar 1736, when he and Esther sold lands to Francis Coden & John Lis.

*several records say he and Marie m. 11 Jan 1680 – that is impossible as he was in ENG in 1681 – could hardly have fathered 5 ch in one year, they were not quintuplets! - that marr. date is more probably that of Jean & Esther.

CHILDREN, m/1 :

Isaac[3], m/1, Cataleyn X – **5 sons, 3 daus**; m/2, c. 1722, Jannetje X – **1 son, 2 daus**; resident of Bridgewater Twp, Somerset Co, NJ, by 26 Sep 1700, when he & his wife witnessed a baptism at the Raritan Dutch Ch; 16 Apr 1735, he was commissioner of roads for Somerset Co; he d. Jul 1752, adm.- 4 Aug 1752

Jacob[3], m/1, c. 1710, Elizabeth Lubetze – **4 sons, 3 daus**; m/2, Catherine (Bogert?); member of the Raritan Dutch Ch, 1711; 1716, he was licensed to keep an inn in Middlesex Co, NJ; he d. intestate. May 1748, Hunterdon Co, NJ; **7 ch**

Peter[3], m. Marretje X; settled Three Mile Run, Somerset Co, NJ in 1712; **3 sons, 1 dau** bp. Dutch Ch, at Three Mile Run & Somerville; *may* have been m. more than once and *may* have had more ch; d. Three Mile Run, Somerset Co, NJ

Abraham[3], m. c. 1723, Adriantje Janse; witnessed a baptism at the N. Branch (Readington) Dutch Ch in 1715; 18 Jul 1722, he purchased c. 60 acres on Ambrose Creek, nr. Piscataway, which he later sold; 24 Apr 1752, he bought a tract of land adjoining his house on the N. Branch of the Raritan; d. NJ; **4 sons, 6 daus**

Vincent[3], m. Heyltje Smith (bur. 24 May 1750); 10 Apr 1710, he & his wife witnessed a bp.; he was a mariner & in 1720, the captain of the sloop *Mary*; he d. a. 10 May 1744, wp, NY; **4 sons, 4 daus**, incl. **Judith**[4] (8 Jul 1693-16 Sep 1767), who m/1, Jacques Poillon as his 3rd wife – **issue**, m/2, Paul Mercereau

CHILDREN, m/2 :

Marianna[3], b. 5 Mar 1680/1, Rye, Sussex, ENG; m. Jean Abelin (d. a. 18 Jun 1744); 1 son **Jean**[4], bp. 7 Aug 1719

Jean/John[3], b. 23 Jan 1681/2, Rye, Sussex, ENG; d. a. 19 Jun 1724, wp; unmarr.

Eleazer[3], in brother John's will of Jan 1707

Esther[3], liv. Jan 1707

Francis[3], b. prob. ENG; m. Maria Dey, d/o James & Mary (Mulliner) Dey of Staten Island; on Staten Island at least until 1726, when he was fined for some offense against the king; he d. p. 7 Mar 1736, NJ, when he witnessed a deed; at least **3 sons**

REF: *Huguenot Ancestors Documented by the Huguenot Society of NJ*; AGNEW, David C.A., *Protestant Exiles from France in the Reign of Louis XIV* (1874); *Historical & Biographical Sketch of the Bowden, Bodine & Beaudoin Family*; SINNOTT, Mary Elizabeth, *Annals of the Sinnott, Rogers, Coffin, Corlies, Reeves, Bodine & Allied Families* (Philadelphia, 1905); BODINE, Cornelis, *History of a Branch of the Bodine Family* (Buffalo, NY, 1897) ; Vol. XVIII, Publications of the Huguenot Society of London, *Letters of Denization & Acts of Naturalization, 1603-1700,* (Lymington, 1911).

BOUDINOT, Élie/Elias

b. 1642, Marans, Aunis (old province, now Charente-Maritime Dépt, Poitou-Charentes), Marans is 11 mi. n.e. of La Rochelle, s/o Jean & Marie (Suire) Boudinot

m/1, Jeanne Baraud/Barreau (c. 1652-a. 1685)

Seigneur de Cressy – lost title and much of the property gained by the family under Henri de Navarre (later King Henri IV of FR) due to persecutions meted out by Louis XIV, Henri's grson

1685- Élie left France with his 4 children; went to London

5 Mar 1686 - naturalized in ENG w/ his 4 ch; anglicized his 1st name and those of his ch; was merchant-craftsman in London

m/2, 11 Nov 1686, London, before notary André Mucot, Susanne (Papin) d'Harriette (wid/o Benjamin d'Harriette); she was b. c. 1652 & had 2 sm. ch at time of marr to Élie – Susanne & Benjamin Harriette (Elias' will verifies the date of the marr); Susanne m/3, Jean Jacques Minvielle – had dau Françoise, b. 17 Sep, bp. 26 Sep 1703, FR Ch, NYC, sons Jacques, b. 1 Nov, bp. 11 Nov 1705, FR Ch, NYC, & David, b. 16 Aug, bp. 5 Oct 1707, FR Ch, NYC

then to poss. Antigua, definitely to Charleston, SC

1687 - arrived in NY; he helped to form the 1st Huguenot Church there - L'Église du Saint Esprit, known as the French Church; he was an elder of the ch

d. a. 26 Oct 1702, wp, NYC; written in French, mentions wife, 2 stepch, stepdau Suzanne's husband Pierre Bellin, his 1st wife whom he calls "Janice" & her son Élie, ch of m/2 - sons Jean, Benjamin, daus Madelaine, Suzanne

CHILDREN, m/1, all b. Marans:

Abraham[2], bp. 6 Nov 1677; d. Nov 1678, bur. aged 1 yr, 8 days

Pierre/Peter[2], b. 27 Feb 1674, bp. 11 Mar 1674; d. a. 1702, NYC

Élie/Elias II[2], b. 11 Nov, bp. 17 Nov 1674, Marans; m 10 Sep 1699, FR Ch, NYC, Marie Catherine Carré, d/o Louis & Prégéante (Fleuriau) Carré; issue: **Marie**[3], b. 7 Jan, bp. 12 Jan 1700/01, FR Ch, NYC, m. John Emott; **Susanne**[3], b. 19 Aug, bp. 29 Aug 1703, FR Ch, NYC, m. Pierre/Peter Vergereau; **Elias III**[3], b. 8 Jul, bp. 14 Jul 1706, FR Ch NYC, m/1, 8 Aug 1729, Susannah LeRoo, m/2, c. 1733, Catherine Williams (bp. 23 Jan 1715 Antigua-1 Nov 1765 Elizabethtown), d/o Arthur & Anna (Richardson) Williams, Elias d. 4 Jul 1770 Elizabethtown, NJ – total of **6 sons, 4 daus**; **Madeline**[3], b. 2 May, bp. 8 May 1709; **Jean**[3], b. 4 Oct 1710;
David[3], b. 15 Mar 1714; Elias II d. 1720

Jean/John[2], d. bet. 1697-1702

Marie/Mary[2], d. a. 1702

CHILDREN, m/2:

Madelaine[2], b. 1687; m. Thomas Bayeux

Susanne[2], b. 12 Jul, bp. 17 Jul 1689, FR Ch, NYC; *seems* to have m. twice: m/1, 2 Feb 1705/6, at her mother's home, rec. FR Ch, NYC, Charles D'Val/Darnall/Danvall – **no known issue***, m/2, a. 1711, David Minvielle – 6 ch, bp. FR Ch, NYC: **David**[3], b. 17 Jul, bp 22 Jul 1711, FR Ch, NYC; **Susanne**[3], b. 22 May, bp. 31 May 1713; **Paul la Coze**[3], b. 15 Nov, bp. 17 Nov 1714; **Élie**[3], b. 31 Dec, bp. 1 Jan 1716/7; **Thomas**[3], b. 16 May, bp. 3 Jun 1719; **Pierre**[3], b. 18 Mar, bp. 19 Mar 1720/1

Jean[2], b. 10 Nov, bp. 16 Nov 1692; m/1, Marie Catherine Guichenet, m/2, Magdalen (Acton) Wise; 2 ch - **son**[3], d. young, dau **Mary**[3] who m. John Litch; Jean killed May 1721 in a duel in Antigua where he had moved

Benjamin[2], b. 19 May, bp. 27 May 1694, FR Ch, NYC

***NOTE:** The Susanne Boudinot in this marr. rec. *may* not have been the d/o Élie & Susanne – no witnesses are listed to help clarify. Susanne's father had d., thus the statement that the marr was at the home of her mother. The only mention of Charles in the records of the FR Ch is the marr. record – no death record nor birth of any children. At the bap. of Susanne & David's dau Susanne, the witnesses were Benjamin d'Harriette (Susanne[2]'s half-bro) & Susanne Boudinot (prob. her mother – her niece Susanne, d/o Élie II, would have been too young). By this time her mother had m. Jean Jacques Minvielle. Jean Jacques was David's older bro, both s/o Pierre Minvielle – both were nephews of Gabriel Minvielle (c.1644, FR-Sep 1702, NY), who served as mayor of NYC in 1684. Françoise (Brinqueman) Lambert Barberie, was their cousin, gr niece of Gabriel.

REF: WITTMEYER, Alfred V., *Register of the Births, Marriages & Deaths of the Église Françoise à la Nouvelle York from 1688-1804* (1968); CLARK, Barbara Louise, *E.B., the Story of Elias Boudinot IV, His Family, His Friends and His Country* (Philadelphia, 1977); BAIRD, Charles W., *History of the Huguenot Emigration to America*; BOYD, George Adams, *Elias Boudinot, Patriot and Statesman* (NY, 1952); *The North American*, (Philadelphia, 24 Nov 1912).

BOUGRAND/BONGRAND, Louis

b. 1636, Nîmes, Languedoc Prov, FR

m/1, XX

a. 1686 - fled FR, went to St. Christopher (St. Kitts), FR West Indies

by 1686 - arr in NY where he was a merchant in NYC

19 Aug 1687 - petitioned for naturalization; cert. of naturalization dated 15 Oct 1688

21 May 1690 - purchased land at New Rochelle from Jacob Lester and sold it 3 yrs. later; reserved a plot
of 40 paces which he gave to the inhabitants for a churchyard, located at Division St. & Union
Ave. – one of the earliest public burying grounds

m/2, 8 Nov 1695, by license, Mary Van Bursum

d. p. 24 Oct 1709, ww-a. 16 Nov 1709, wp; he left £10 to the poor of the FR Ch, NYC

CHILD, m/1:

Louis[2], b. 15 Nov 1690, New Rochelle, NY; he was disinherited by his father because he went to sea, a
manner of life to which his father objected; **issue?**

REF: BAIRD, Charles W., *Huguenot Emigration to America* (Vol. II, p. 132); *Huguenot Ancestors Documented by
The Huguenot Society of NJ, Inc.*, p. 20; SEACORD, Morgan H., *Biographical Sketches & Index of the Huguenot
Settlers of New Rochelle 1687-1776* (1941).

BOULET/BULLITT, Joseph

b. a. 1650, FR, s/o Benjamin de Boulet; Benjamin, a farmer from Languedoc, fled FR, supposedly Nîmes;
Benjamin went to HOL and perhaps then to ENG

a. 6 Nov 1673 - Joseph to MD; early settler of Charles Co.

1 Jun 1683 - purchased 30 acres, Charles Co, called "Bullett's Adventure"

m. a. 12 Oct 1685, Elizabeth Brandt, d/o Capt. Randolph & Mary (X) Brandt; she d. p.12 Jan 1693, wd – a. 14
Mar 1693/4, wp; will of Randolph Bran(d)t probated 10 Feb 1698 – lands in Charles Co. to go to his
sons but if they or their male heirs are deceased, lands will go to the heirs of Joseph Bullett; Elizabeth
(Brandt) Bullitt's will leaves estate to son Joseph when he reaches 19 – "Bullitt's Folly" and dwelling
place; son Benjamin to inherit "all personalty."

d. Mar 1692/3, Charles Co, MD

CHILDREN:

Joseph[2], b. 8 Feb 1688; d. 1709

Benjamin[2], b. 28 Apr 1693, Charles Co; m/1, 1727, Elizabeth Harrison, d/o Thomas (d. 1757); m/2,
p. 1757, Sarah X Harrison; he d. p. 3 May 1766, wd-a. 27 Oct 1766, wp, Fauquier Co, VA; his will
mentions the children listed below with * & wife Sarah; refers to his & Sarah's 6 sons several times

CHILDREN (all b. Fauquier Co, VA), m/1:

*Joseph[3], b. 1728; m. Barshaba Norman; d. p. 17 Nov 1792, wd-a. 24 Dec 1792, wp, Fauquier
Co.; will mentions **dau** Susannah Redd and her sons Joseph, Permercis, **dau** Mary
Stealard (Stalliard?) and her son Joseph Bullett Stealard; **dau** Priscilla Redd & her son
Joseph Bullett Redd; wife Barshaba Norman; Philip Redd, Allen Redd & Randolph
Stalliard – prob. his 3 sons-in-law

*Thomas[3], b. 1730; as a capt in the French & Indian War, serving under Gen Washington, he
was entitled to land; d. a. 23 Feb 1778, wp, Fauquier Co.; unmarr.; will mentions bro
Joseph, sis Seth Combs, bro Cuthbert and nephew Cuthbert Combs

*Elizabeth/Seth[3] b. 1731; m. John Combs; she d. 1790; Seth <u>and</u> John Combs in her father's
will; **issue**

Benjamin[3], b. 1733; lieutenant in the "Patriot Blues" under Spotswood; d. c. 1753, killed by
Indians; unmarr.

*Cuthbert[3], b. 1740; m. c. 1760, Helen Scott (7 Jun 1739, Overwharton Par, Stafford Co, VA-
15/16 Sep 1795, Pr. William Co., VA), d/o Rev. James & Sarah (Brown) Scott; he d. 27
Aug 1791, Pr. William Co, VA; **6 ch**

CHILDREN (all b. Fauquier Co), m/2

*Elizabeth[3], unmarr., 1766; ***William**[3], surname BURDITT; ***John**[3]; ***George**[3]; ***Benoni**[3]; ***Parmanus**[3]; ***Burwell**[3]

REF: RHOADES, Nelson O, editor, *MacKenzie's Colonial Families of the United States of America*, Vol. 7 (1966); GOTT, John K., *Abstracts of Fauquier County VA Wills, Inventories and Accounts 1759-1800* (1972); KING, J. Estelle Stewart, *Abstracts of Wills, Administrations and Marriages of Fauquier County VA 1759-1800, With Cemetery Inscriptions, Rent Rolls and Other Data* (1980); GANNON, Peter S., *Huguenot Refugees in the Settling of Colonial America*; BALDWIN, Jane, *MD Calendar of Wills*, Vol. I, II, 1635-1702 (Baltimore, 1997); WULFECK, Dorothy, *Marriages of some VA Residents*.

BOULIER/BULYEA, Louis

native of Saintonge Prov, FR, now part of Charente Dépt, Poitou-Charentes; mariner

m. 23 May 1697, Old Dutch Church, Sleepy Hollow, Tarrytown, NY, Antje Konnick (b. Dergrade, HOL); she m/2, Isaac Caillaud, a wealthy Huguenot merchant, and had 3 more ch

d. p. 1712 – a. 1722; widow had son bp. 17 Jan 1722, Reformed Dutch Ch, NYC –son by Isaac Caillaud/ Calyow

CHILDREN:

Jan[2], b. 1698, Phillipsburg, NY; m. 29 Nov 1719, Helena Williams; he d. 1766

CHILDREN, all bp. Phillipsburg:

Hendrick/Henry[3], bp. 19 Apr 1720; Jul 1783, went to St. John, New Brunswick as a Loyalist; m. c. 1755, Engeltie (Storm) Yerxa; **8 ch**

Marytie[3], bp. 24 Apr 1722; m. Harman Davids; she d. a. 1750; 1 dau **Helena**[4]

Rachel[3], bp. 13 Aug 1726; m. 13 Sep 1746, Jan Orser; **6 ch**

Helena[3], bp. 27 Apr 1728; m. 13 Sep 1746, Albert Orser; she d. 1769; **5 ch**

Catharina[3], bp. 21 Aug 1731; m. Aertse/Orser Jones

Jan/John[3], bp. 25 Jun 1734; m. Rachel Davenport, d/o Samuel & Elles Davenport; son **John**[4]

Robben[3], bp 23 Apr 1737; d. a.1765

Jacob[2], bp 25 Mar 1706, Old Dutch Ch of Sleepy Hollow; m. Catharina Storm

Catharina[2], bp. 2 Nov 1712, Reformed Dutch Ch, NYC

REF: TISDALE, Florence G. Belyea & RENNIE, Marjorie A. Belyea, *The Genealogy of the Boulier-Bulyea-Belyea Family, 1670-1969* (1970); REAMAN, G. Elmore, *Trail of the Huguenots* (1966).

BOUNETHEAU/BONNETHEAU, Jean/John

1685 - from LaRochelle to Charleston, SC

m/1, Frances X; she d/bur 3 Jul 1731

m/2, 13 Sep 1731, St. Philip's Church, Angelica Gaier; she d. 24 May 1740

m/3, 1741, Mary Banbury (b. c. 1736), d/o James & Judith (Manigault) Banbury, she d. p. 1749

d. 26 May 1767, SC

CHILD, m/1:

John[2], b. 22 Mar 1729; bp. 28 Dec 1735

CHILD: m/2:

Anne[2], bur. 1738

CHILDREN, m/3:

Peter[2], b. 7 Dec 1742; bp. 4 Mar 1742/3, Charleston, SC; m/1, 28 Oct 1764, Dorchester, Ann Anderson (d. 21 Jul 1776); m/2, 14 Jan 1777, Charleston, Elizabeth Weyman (18 Jan 1765- 8 Nov 1834), d/o Edward & Rebecca (Breintnall) Weyman; Peter held many civil posts; 18 May 1781, he was sent as a prisoner to St. Augustine on the prison ship *Torbay*; Peter d. 20 Nov 1793

CHILDREN, m/1:

Ann[3], b/bp. 7 Sep 1765, Charleston

John[3], b. 17 Jun, bp. 9 Jul 1767, Charleston

Judith[3], b. 4 Jul 1771, Charleston; d. 8 May 1778

Charles[3], b. 16 Aug 1773

CHILDREN, m/2:

William Danbury[3], 24 Jan 1778; d. 10 Aug 1780

Gabriel Manigault[3], b. 27 Mar 1779; d. 31 Aug 1818, Newport

Edward Weyman[3], b. 5 Oct 1781; m/1, 1802, Martha Glen, d/o William & Martha (X) Glen, who d. 18 Feb 1849; m/2, Laura Josephine Haynes; he d. 20 Aug 1862; **7 ch**

Danbury Grimball[3], b. 21 Sep 1783; d. 28 Oct 1833

Peter[3], b. 9 Oct 1785

Robert[3], b. 14 May 1788; d. 3 Nov 1790

Eliza Bond[3], b. 27 Dec 1789

Rebecca[3], b. 3 Sep 1792; d. 8 Oct 1792 \

Thomas[3], b. 3 Sep 1792; d. 8 Sep 1792) triplets

Daniel[3], b. 3 Sep 1792; d. 3 Oct 1792) /

James[3], b. 8 Sep 1793; d. 8 Jan 1835, bur. Huguenot Ch, Charleston, next to his mother

Henry Breintnall[3], b. 4 Dec 1797; bp. 27 May 1798; m. Julia C. DuPré; he d. 31 Jan 1877; 2 sons, **Henry DuPré**[4], **Harold DuPré**[4]; tombstone in the Huguenot Church Cemetery, Charleston: "Henry Breintnal Bounetheau Dec 14 1797-Jan 31 1877 son of Peter Bounetheau and Grandson of John Bounetheau who came to Charleston from La Rochelle, France on the Revocation of the Edict of Nantes in 1685. The last two are interred beneath this Church. Un Dieu Un Roi" (*One God, One King*); Henry was a famous miniaturist

Lewison[2], bur. 4 Jan 1748

Gabriel[2], b. 6 Feb 1745/6, bp. 25 Jun 1746; d/bur. 24 May 1749

REF: HIRSCH, Arthur H, *The Huguenots of Colonial SC* (1962); *Transactions of the Huguenot Society of SC, #54* (1949); McCRADY, Edward, *The History of SC under the Proprietary Government, 1670-1719;* McCRADY, Edward, *The History of SC under the Royal Government, 1719-1776.*

BOUQUET/BOUCQUET, Jérôme

b. 1615, Walstandt, HOL; may mean Walcheren Island, sm. island where Middelburg is

m/1, 11 Aug 1641, Walloon Ch, Middelburg, Zeeland, HOL, Anna L'Agache

m/2, 16 May 1644, Middelburg, Anne Torion

went to Mannheim, GER

1663 - left Mannheim; 16 Apr 1663, Jérôme, his wife and 5 ch, ages 18, 15, 9, 6 and 3* embarked from Ripen, N. Jutland, on the *Te Bonte Koe* to New Amsterdam; went to Walloon settlements on Long Island where he was known as Jeronimus de Waal

1667 – he was the owner of a village lot in Nieuw Utrecht

d. 1709, NYC

CHILDREN, m/1:

Abraham[2], m. Tanneke Andriesse, (1652-20 Jan 1754 NYC); 15 Mar 1676, he was in Leiden; he liv. in Sluys for a while bef. emigrating; Abraham was a weaver; had **2 ch** b. Sluys, **8 ch** b. East Jersey; 26 Sep 1698, was admitted as a freeman of NY but fam. still spent time in NJ; 1705, liv. NY; he d. a. Oct 1709, wp, NY Co; surname became BOCKÉE/BOCKEE/BOKEE

Annetje[2], m. a. 1665, Anthony Duchesne (c. 1640-a. 12 May 1712, Staten Island)

CHILDREN, m/2:

Jammatje/Jeronemus[2], b. c. 1645

Francytje[2], b. 1647

Marie[2], b. 1654

*ages are a bit off and list (above) of ch is evidently not complete; seems that the ch who went w/ Jérôme were Annetje + ch of m/2

REF: Sauter, Dr. Suzanne Van H., *Some Interrelated Huguenot Families from Kings & Richmond Counties, NY* (unpublished manuscript, 1999).

BOUQUET/BOCKE(Y)/BUCKEY, Abraham

m. Elisabetha X (Hofmann?)

CHILDREN, bp. Minfeld, GER, c. 13 km. from FR border:

Sara[2], bp. 7 May 1719

Rachel[2], bp 22 Oct 1722 - emig. to America*

Maria Anna[2], bp. 9 Jul 1924

Rosina Barbara[2], bp. 20 Jan 1726; m. 8 Apr 1749, Minfeld, Hans Georg Hoffman, s/o Lorenz Hoffman – emig. to America*

Matheus[2], bp. 21 Sep 1727; m. Anna Maria Hoffman – emig. to America*; to Frederick Co, MD
   CHILDREN:
   Mathias[3]. b. 15 Apr 1759; m. Christian (Roemer) Grosch, d/o John Michael & Amilia (Hartranft) Roemer & widow of Capt. Grosch
   Margaret D.[3], m. X Danner; **issue**
   John[3], b. 25 Oct 1762; m. X Thomas?
   Catherine[3], b. 25 Jun 1772; m. Nathan England; **issue**
   Valentine[3], m. 29 Jan 1793, Charlotte Remsperger
   George[3], m. Susan Kreiger/Creager; he was a tanner who liv. Buckeystown, Frederick Co, MD
   Peter[3], b. 12 Feb 1775; m. 17 May 1796, Mary Salmon, d/o Capt. Edward Salmon; Peter d. 1848, Mary d. 20 Mar 1864; **9 ch**

Maria Johanetta[2], bp. 23 Apr? 1729

Frantz[2], bp. 11 Nov 1730

Johannes[2], bp. 31 Aug 1732

Andreas[2], bp. 1 Aug 1734

Johann Peter[2], bp. 2 Feb 1736; m. 5 Jun 1764, Minfeld (n.w. of Karlruhe), Rheinhessen-Pfalz, GER, Anna Maria Schäfer (b. 3 Feb 1744 Minfeld), d/o Christoph & Anna Appolonia (X) Schäfer; Peter, a *hufschmied* (blacksmith, farrier), went from GER to MD to Randolph Co, VA (now WV); became the owner of a hotel in Beverly, VA; 11 Mar 1775, wd, Frederick Co, MD, mentions wife Mary, "5 lawfull born children"; wp 26th (?) Mar 1775; bur w/ wife in Lutheran Ch cemetery
   CHILD:
   Peter[3], b. 1 Jan 1770, Frederick, MD; m. 22 Apr 1794 (lic 13 Apr Frederick Co), Christina Matena/ Marteny (21 Mar 1774-9 Apr 1834), d/o William; he d. 13 Mar 1850, Beverly, Randolph Co, VA
      CHILDREN, surname **BUCKEY/BOCKEY**:
      George[4], m. Elizabeth Hart, dau o Daniel Hart; **6 ch**
      William[4], moved to Sidney, OH
      John[4], moved to Knoxville, TN
      Marteny[4], unmarr.
      Eunice[4], m. X Carter
      Hannah[4], b. Dr. Squire Bosworth
      Christine[4], m. David Goff
      Mary[4], b. c. 1796; m. 29 Sep 1812, Archibald Earle (b. 1788)
      Daniel[4], m. Virginia Ball

Jacob[2], bp. 23 Apr 1739

*Matheus, Rachel, Rosina Barbara & her husband Hans Georg emig. together to America, on a document, dated 26 Feb 1762

REF: *Penna Dutchman*, Vol. I, #3 (Spring, 1957); BAUM, Dr. Fritz, *Copy of family Bible records from Minfeld;* Church records; BOSWORTH, Dr. A. S., *A History of Randolph Co, WV*; Peter[1]'s will, 1775.

BOURDEAUX/BORDEAUX, Jacques de/James

b. 1630, Grenoble, Dauphiné, FR, s/o Évrimond/Évremond & Catherine (Fresné) de Bourdeaux

m. 1670, Madeleine (Garillion/Garillond/Gaillard) Pépin, d/o Israel & Susanne (Saunier) Garillion, wid/o <u>Alexandre Pépin</u>; she m/3, SC, Pierre Le Chevalier, s/o Roland & Ester (Dallain) Le Chevalier of St. Lô, Normandie; d. soon after her husband Pierre

a.1687 - ENG; on denization list, 9 Apr 1687 – Jacques, wife, 4 daus but evidently had already gone to SC

c. 1687 - emigrated from ENG to Charleston, SC*; settled in St. Thomas Parish (on a peninsula formed by the Cooper & Wando Rivers – Daniel Island); he was a blacksmith and shoemaker; *one account says that he was a member of the Purrysburg group – <u>not so,</u> they did not come until 1732

26 Jan 1686/7 - purchased from Gov. West, eastern half of town lot #28 on the n. side of Broad St

15 Apr 1687 – made a denizen of SC

20 Oct 1692 – rec. warrant for 1 town lot; rec. another one, 24 Aug 1693, this one being for lot #160 now 106 Broad St, Charleston; he also acquired lots #161, 171, 172, 173, the entire w. side of King St., between Broad & Queen Streets; he had land in the Orange Quarter, 500 acres in Berkeley Co; the last warrant was dated 10 May 1698

c. 1695/6 – on list of those wishing naturalization in SC; liv. in the Orange Quarter of Charleston

d. a. 20 Dec 1699, SC, adm; wd, 19 Sep 1699; div. of the property, 24 Feb 1708/9 when all the ch were of age – 3 daus, 1 son alive at that time – Magdalen, Antoine, Marguerite, Judith; he was a blacksmith by trade but evidently a man of means as well - he emigrated "with means" & made a fortune in real estate

CHILDREN:

Marguerite/Margaret[2], b. Grenoble; <u>m/1</u>, Antoine Poitevin II of Maintenon, FR, s/o <u>Antoine & Gabrielle (Berou) Poitevin</u>; Antoine d. c. 1708; **1 son, 2 daus**; she <u>m/2</u>, 29 Nov 1709, <u>André de Veaux</u> as his 2nd wife

Madeleine/Magdalen[2], b. Grenoble; m. Dr. Daniel Brabant; **1 son, 1 dau**

Judith[2], b. Grenoble; m. 1706, Pierre Robert II of Basle, Switzerland, s/o <u>Pierre & Jeanne (Brayé) Robert</u>; **1 son, 2 daus**

? Jane(t)[2], b. Grenoble – a dau named Janes (*sic*) was on the denization list in ENG; could be an error or she d. young; no other info

Ant(h)oine/Anthony[2], b. c. 1688/9 SC; m. Marianne (Trézévant?, c. 1690-d. 20-Jan 1767 St. Thomas Parish, SC); he d. Charleston, SC, a. 1 Mar 1725, wp; his will mentions wife Marianna, his 4 sons, but not by name + any unborn ch; he was a joiner/ carpenter; his sons were **Anthony**[3], **James**[3] (m. Esther Savineau-**issue**), **Daniel**[3], **Israel**[3] (*prob.* the Israel, of St. Thomas Parish, who m. c, 12 Dec 1743 (date of lic.), Mary Rivers)

Israel[2], b. SC; m. XX; son **James**[3] – **no issue**

Jacques II[2], b. SC; d. a. 1699

REF: RAVENEL, Daniel, *List of French & Swiss Protestants Who Desired Naturalization* (Baltimore, 1968); *Transactions of the Huguenot Society of SC,* #79 (1974), #34 (1929), #91 (1986); SALLEY, A.S. & WEBBER, Mabel L., *Death Notices in The SC Gazette, 1732-1775* (Columbia, SC 1954); Wills of Antoine, Jacques II; MOORE, Caroline T., *Abstracts of Wills of Charleston Dist, SC, 1783-1800*; LANGLEY, Clara A. *SC Deed Abstracts*, Vol.1(Greenville,SC,1983).

BOURDIN/BURDINE, Samuel

b. 1658, Bordeaux, FR, s/o Marc & Rachel (Bouchet) Bourdin; Marc (1620-2 May 1682) supposedly from
Orléans; he and Rachel had 4 sons (François, Isaac, Marc, Samuel); Marc was a master watchmaker

1672/3 – apprenticed by his father to a master smith & jeweler

m. 2 May 1682, Begler Temple, Bordeaux, by Pastor de Sarrau, to Marthe Charneau, d/o Pierre & Rachel
(Roy) Charneau(x)/Charroneau

p. spring 1686 - no record of the family in Bordeaux– prob. fled after the Revocation; poss. went to
Alsace

CHILDREN:

Pierre[2]

Richard[2], b. c. 1685 Bordeaux; c. 1719/20, to VA, poss. from GER; m. c. 1737, Newport Parish, Isle of Wight
Co, Catherine Tanner (c. 1718- d. a. Apr 1786, wp, Culpeper Co, VA), d/o Robert Gerber/Tanner; he d.
p. 22 Jul 1761, wd-a. 15 Oct 1761, wp, Brumfield Parish, Culpeper Co. (now Madison Co.); his will
mentions his wife, all 4 sons, 2 daus; he founded the Madison Co. Hebron Lutheran Ch which was the
1st Lutheran church in the South; Richard's father-in-law Robert Tanner, aka Gerber, was a German
immigrant; his son Reginald's 2nd wife Dorothea was the d/o Christopher & Elizabeth (Oehler) Tanner,
s/o Robert and bro to Catherine, Reginald's mother

CHILDREN, used surname **BYRDINE**:

Reginall/Reginald[3], b. a. 1740 VA; m/1, Ann (Sampson?) – **6 ch**; m/2, 1780 Dorothea/Dorothy
Tanner - **1 dau**; he d. a. 5 Nov 1787, inv, Abbeville Dist, SC; only ch of age at the time of his
father Richard's death

Samuel[3], b. 29 May 1745; m. 1771, Mary Fletcher (b. 1 Jul 1754); he d. 1818/28; **4 ch**

Hannah[3], m. c. 1765, Robert V. Shotwell, s/o John & Sarah (Woodley) Shotwell, who d. p. 5 Oct
1785, wd – a. 21 Nov 1785, Culpeper Co.; Hannah d. in Monroe Co, MS; **8 ch**

Barbara[3], b. c. 1740; m. c. 1761, John Grissom/Gresham, Sr. (b. 1719-d. 1814); moved to Abbeville
Dist., SC; **6 ch**

CHILDREN:

Molly[4], m. William Poore of Pendleton Dist., SC

Hannah, m. George Poore of VA

John[4], b. 14 Mar 1761; m/1, Martha Halbert (17 Mar 1772-12 Jun 1810); m/2, Elizabeth
(Coats/Coatesworth) Watson, widow of Thomas Watson; Eliz. d. p. 29 Nov
1845, wd; issue by m/1 only; he d. 22 Jun 1835

Katy[4], m. William Keaton of Pendleton Dist, SC

Betty[4], m. John Parker of Pendleton Dist, SC

Susannah[4], b. 26 Jun 1776; m. 1 Mar 1794, Balaam Mauldin (Dec 1767-30 May 1810);
went to KY where he d.; she moved back to Pendleton Dist, SC; **issue**

Nathaniel[3], m. Ann (Lipscomb?); liv. Wilkes Co, NC, later Newberry Co, SC; d. p. 1800

John[3], b. Culpeper Co, VA, m. Elizabeth "Betty" Dicken (1755 Culpeper Co- d. p. 1810-Washington
Co, KY); he d. a. 17 Apr 1786, wp Culpeper Co, VA; said to have served in the Rev
War; **6 ch**

CHILD (1 of 6):

Susannah[4], b. 14 Jul 1775 prob. VA, d. 21 Jul 1852 nr. Fredericksburg, Washington Co,
KY m. 1 Jan 1793, Washington Co, KY, George Daniel Brengle (16 Feb 1762
Frederick Co, MD-25 Jun 1829, Washington Co, KY)

REF: CROS, Dr. Fletcher Standefer, III, *Family History* (manuscript); BURDINE, Dr. Winston E., *The Burdine Family*; YOWELL, Claude Lindsay, *A History of Madison Co, VA* (1926); Richard Burdyne's will; BURDINE, Carol Ann, "The Burdyne/Burdine Family", Part I, pub. in *Beyond Germana*, Vol. 11 #4 (Jul 1999); BROWN, James E., "Proofs of Importation of Germans Spotsylvania Co, VA 1724-1729, pub. in *Beyond Germana*, Vol. 7, #5 (Sep 1995); NORTON, Sarah Mills, *Generations Back: Norton & Related Lines* (1977); CRANE, H.M., *Compiled Information on the Dicken(s), Deakins Families of VA, KY & IN*; KINGTON, M.C., *Washington Co, KY Marriage Records, 1792-1878;* Court records, Washington Co, KY.

BOUTON, Théodore

bp. 2 Jan 1583, Metz, Lorraine, FR, s/o Bastien and Catherine (X) Bouton; fa. was a *chapelier* (a hatter) who d. by 4 Sep 1585, when Catherine remarried in Metz; had bro **Esdras** who had issue & sisters Esther, Abigail

m/1, 9 Jul 1606, Metz, Élisabeth Guillaume (bp.21 Aug 1580, Metz-d. bet 1616-1619), d/o Démange Guillaume

m/2, 28 Apr 1619, Metz, Judith Godefrin (d. 20 Feb 1658, Metz)

d. a. 28 Nov 1641, Metz, date of bur; was a *chapelier*

wp - 16 Dec 1641 – only wife Judith and dau Marie were mentioned; apparently it was an oral will, "uttered," 8 Nov 1641

CHILDREN, m/1 (all bp. Protestant Temple of Metz):

Esdras[2], bp. 29 Apr 1607

David[2], bp. 15 Feb 1609; m/1, 14 Jan 1630, Hanau, Hesse, GER, Sarah Carlie/Carlier (bp 7 Sep 1606, Hanau-d. a. 1633), d/o Philippe & Sara (X) Carlie - dau **Rachel**[3] (d. young); m/2, 4 Apr 1633, Hanau, Rachel Haseur (bp. 4 Apr 1633, Hanau), d/o Mathis & Esther (X) Haseur – **9 ch** - one son **Jacob**[3] (bp. 25 Mar 1641), m/1 Anna Maria Schneider (bur. 1 May 1687 Hanau) - **6 ch**, m /2, 3 Nov 1687, Hanau, Maria Margarete Jung (bp. 7 Mar 1661, Ostheim-bur. 11 Aug 1729, Hanau), d/o Wilhelm Jung, the Lutheran minister in Marköbel & Anna Maria (Dietz) Jung – **7 ch**, incl. **Jean Daniel**[4], b. 23 Jan, bp. 28 Jan 1691 Hanau, arr Philadelphia on the *Samuel*, 27 Aug 1739, where he d. 14 Nov 1762 – at least **4 ch**; another son **Hermann**[3], bp. 17 Sep 1643, m. 22 Oct 1674, Anna Margaretha Neegken (bp. 30 Nov 1651), d/o Johannes & Catharina (Keidten) Neegken - **7 ch**; David[2] was a merchant who was bur. 18 May 1681, Hanau; most of this branch of the family remained in the Hanau area of GER for several generations

Abraham[2], bp. 8 Dec 1619

Jacob[2], bp. 25 Dec 1611; went to Hanau; m. 14 Mar 1634, FR Prot Ch, Hanau, Hesse-Nassau, GER (s.e. of Frankfurt) Judith Colin, d/o Henry Colin

    CHILD: **Rachel**[3], bp 19 Feb 1635, Fr Prot Ch, Hanau, GER

Jean/John[2], b. 26 Mar, bp. 28 Mar 1614, Metz; m. c. 1636, CT Alice X (b. 1610, d. p. 1 Dec 1680, wd, prob. Stamford, Fairfield, CT); Alice m/2, c.1647, Matthew Marvin as his 2nd wife; John d. a. 1647 CT, *prob.* Hartford; in Boston 1635; prob. the John Bouton who arr on the *Assurance* Dec, 1635; the immigrant to America

    CHILDREN:

    John[3], b. Oct 1636; m/1, 1 Jan 1656/7, Norwalk, CT, Abigail Marvin (b. c. 1638, Hartford, d. c. 1680, Stamford), d/o Matthew & Elizabeth (X) Marvin; m/2, p. Nov 1689, Mary (X) Stevenson Allen; he d. a. 27 Jan 1706/7, wp, prob. Hartford

        CHILDREN, m/1: (recorded Norwalk, CT)

        John[4], b. 30 Sep 1659; m. Mary Hayes; he d. 2 Jan 1704/5, Danbury; **6 ch**

        Matthew[4], b. 24 Dec 1661; prob. not marr.

        Joseph[4], b. c. 1665; m. Mary Gregory; d. 1747, Norwalk; **4 ch**

        Hannah[4], b. 1663; m. James Betts

        Rachel[4], b. 15 Dec 1667; m. c. 1690, Matthias St. John/Sension; **issue**

        Abigail[4], 1 Apr 1670; m. X Smith

        Mary[4], b. 26 May 1671; m. David Waterbury

        Elizabeth[4], b. c. 1679; m. 6 Oct 1698, Edmund Waring

        CHILDREN, m/2:

        Thomas[4], **no issue**

        Richard[4], m. Mercy Platt

        Mary[4], m. Lemuel Morehouse

        Jachin[4]

    Richard[3], b. c. 1638; m. Ruth Turney (28 Jan 1643/44, Concord, MA-1666, Fairfield, CT), d/o Benjamin & Mary (X) Turney; he d. a. 21 Jun 1665, inv, Norwalk; 1 dau **Ruth**[4] who m. Moses Wheeler

    Bridget[3], b. 1642; m. p. 1655, Norwalk, Daniel Kellogg (bp. 6 Feb 1629/30 Great Leighs, Essex,

ENG-d. 1688), s/o Martin & Prudence (Bird) Kellogg, as his 2nd wife; **8 ch**

Marie[2], bp 14 Nov 1616; d. p. 16 Dec 1641

CHILDREN, m/2 (all bp. Protestant Temple of Metz):

Susanne[2], bp. 7 Feb 1620; bur. 27 Mar 1631

Jean[2], bp. 23 Feb 1622; bur. 24 Mar 1627

Susanne[2], bp. 14 Apr 1624

Judith[2], bp. 26 Oct 1625; bur. 16 Dec 1631

REF: Parish records, Protestant Temple, Metz & FR Protestant Ch in Hanau (aka Wallonischekirche), latter records in French as late as 1847; Church records from Marköbel, Totenbuch Marienkirche (in German) research by Benjamin F. Dake III of OR; JACOBUS, Donald L., *History & Genealogy of the Families of Old Fairfield*, Vol. I (1930); TAG, Vol. XI, #2 (Oct 1934), "Bouton Family of Norwalk, CT" notes by JACOBUS and JONES, William; TAG, Vol. 73, #1 (Jan 1998) "The Huguenot Ancestry of Jean/Johann Daniel Bouton of Philadelphia" by DAKE, Benjamin F. III; probate records, Norfolk, Fairfield, CT.

BO(E)YER, Alexander/Sander

b.c.1618, FR or HOL

m, XX, b. SWE; she prob. d. p. 1655

1646 - was Dutch quartermaster at Ft. Nassau

1648 - Deputy Commissioner/Commissary

1651 - transferred to Ft. Casimir, New Castle, DE

21 May 1654 – Swedes conquered Ft. Casimir, renamed it Ft. Trinity; those settlers remaining in the fort, mostly Dutch, became "the conquered Dutch" and subjects of the King of Sweden; since Boyer had a Swedish wife, he was allowed to stay at the fort; Johan Rising, Commissary & Councillor to Swedish Gov. Lt. Col. Johan Printz, & who succeeded Printz, kept a *Journal* in which he described Sander as a "malicious and hateful man"- Boyer & Printz had had many a confrontation as Printz was adamantly anti-Dutch, a term which included English and German settlers as well - Boyer tried to mediate between the 2 sides; Boyer also acted as an interpreter between the Indians and the Governor

1654-55 – sold his tobacco crop to the company store

1655 – to Manhattan for the baptisms of his sons Samuel and Peter

end of Dec 1655- returned to Ft. Trinity; the Dutch, under Peter Stuyvesant, had recaptured the fort and called it Ft. Casimir again

1656 - Stuyvesant granted Sander a lot nr. the fort

d. p. 18 Feb 1661, prob. DE

CHILDREN:

Jan[2] - 1671, he was liv. New Castle, DE, in the "Soldier's Tract," which was w. of Christiana on the n. side of Christiana Creek, extending w. to Anders the Finn's Creek - a tract of land, patented 1 Oct 1669, to 4 soldiers, incl. Jan Boyer

CHILDREN – **Elisabeth**[3], **Catherine**[3], **Helena**[3] and **Daniel**[3] (he d. 1742 Kent Co, DE)

Josine/Joseyn[2], b. c. 1649; m/1, John Marshall (d. by 1675) – **issue**, m/2, William Sample (c. 1643 ENG-a. 1 Jan 1683 New Castle, DE) - **1 ch**, m/3, X Hamilton; Joseyn d. a. 31 Mar 1696, prob. in New Castle, DE

CHILD, m/2:

Margaret[3], b. c.1676, DE; m. William Sparks, Sr. (1674, Queen Anne's Co, MD-c. 1735, Queen Anne's Co, MD); she d. a. 3 May 1729/30

Samuel[2], bp. Manhattan, 1 Dec 1655

P(i)eter[2], bp. Manhattan, 1 Dec 1655

REF: "New Sweden Settlers, 1638-1664" in *Swedish-American Genealogist*, Vol. XVIII (1998); CRAIG, Peter S., *1671 Census of the Delaware*; STAPLETON, A., *Memorials of the Huguenots in America*; JOHNSON, Amandus, *The Swedish Settlements on the Delaware, 1638-1664*, Vol. I (1911); RIKER, David M., *Genealogical & Biographical Directory to Persons in New Netherland from 1613 to 1674*; Sparks Quarterly, Vol. XLVIII #4.

BRASSEUR/BRASHIER/BRASHEAR, Robert II

b. c. 1595/98, FR; [a Benois Brasseur was chr 1595, at Bouches-du-Rhône, s/o Robert I, - Benois was
    Robert II's bro]; Bouches-du-Rhône is not a town, it is a dépt. in Provence on the Mediterranean; not
    <u>certain</u> that this is the same family as below

m. XX, prob. in FR

prob. left Fr during the 1620's; said to have emigrated, with his bros Benois/Benjamin and Thomas, to the
    Isle of Thanet, ENG, which is in the extreme n.e. corner of Co. Kent, N. Foreland area,

1 Jun 1636 - Robert renewed a promissory note in Warrisquicke/Warrosquyoake, VA (became the Isle of
    Wight Co. in 1637), so had prob. been in VA for a few yrs

24 Feb 1638 - he and Peter Rey were granted 600 acres in Upper Norfolk Co. on the Nansemond River, a
    tributary of the James

6 Oct 1640 - rec 100 acres in Upper Norfolk on the Nansemond for transportation of 2 servants

7 Oct 1640 - Thomas Pursell was mentioned as a servant to Robert Brasseur, having been transported

12 Apr 1653 – additional land was granted for a group of persons, incl. Mary, Persid/Persis, Kathe, and Bennet
    Brasseur – prob. his ch; more grants later to Ann, Benjamin Sr, Martha, Mary Sr., Robert Jr. & Susanna

1663 - Benjamin, Jr., Elizabeth & John emigrated to VA; Thomas went to VA in 1677

d. p. 4 Dec 1665, wd – a. 16 Dec 1665, wp, Calvert Co, MD; left estate to 3 men, no ch, grch mentioned;
    estate to a cousin Mary; court amended it and appointed a guardian for Robert, s/o Benjamin

CHILDREN:

(There is some confusion as to whether Robert II was the f/o or bro/o Benois; the evidence at hand
    suggests that Robert II was his father – any additional <u>proof</u> is encouraged.)

Benois(t)/Benjamin[2], b. c. 1619/20, FR; m. Marie/Mary (Richford?), who m/2, Thomas Sterling; settled
    Nansemond Co, VA by 1653, to MD, 1658, settling in Calvert Co; 4 Dec 1662, naturalized in MD as
    "late of VA and subject of the crown of France"; d. Dec 1662, Calvert Co, MD; Mary's will was
    probated, 25 May 1663, names sons Robert, Benjamin, John; daus Mary, Anne, Susanna, Martha, Eliza
    CHILDREN (birthdates/order not certain):
    Robert IV[3], b. c. 1646; m/1, XX (mother of at least 2, if not all, of 3 his ch), m/2, 1679, Mrs.
        Alice (Spriggs?) Jackson, widow of Thomas Jackson; he d. 1712, Prince Georges Co,
        MD; **issue**
    Benjamin[3], b. c. 1647, d. Feb 1676, unmarr.
    John[3], b. c. 1649; m. Anne (Dalrymple or Sterling?); d. 1696; prob. no issue as no ch mentioned
        in his will
    Mary[3], b. c. 1650; m/1, 7 May 1669, Nathaniel Robbins, m/2, c. 1688, Christopher Ellis; she d.
        23 Jan 1702, Prince Georges Co, MD
    Ann[3], b. c. 1652; m. c. 1685, prob. William Dalrymple, Jr.
    Susanna[3], b. c. 1655; m. c. 1679, prob. <u>Mareen Duvall</u>; she. d. 1692; **issue**
    Martha[3], b. c. 1658; m. 1674 Henry Kent, Jr.; **issue**
    Elizabeth[3], b. c. 1660; m/1, John Sellman - **issue**, m/2, 8 Nov 1708, Dr. William Nichols
Mary[2], b. c. 1622; d. young
John[2], b. c. 1624 FR; m/1, Mary Cocke; m/2, Mary Pitt; was his father Robert's heir & inherited land
    in Nansemond Co.; became a Quaker
Thomas[2], b. c. 1626
Persi(d)e[2], b. c. 1628; m. poss. John Cobreath
Robert III[2], b. c. 1630; m. Florence (Rey?); d. 5 Dec 1665; **no issue**
Katherine[2], b. c. 1632; poss. m. Mark Clare
Martha[2], b. c. 1636, Isle of Wight Co, VA, m/1, c. 1657, VA, Capt. William Moseley (1624-c. 1683/4);
        m/2, a. Nov 1684 ,VA, George Taylor; she d. p. 1684
        CHILDREN, m/1
    Elizabeth[3], m. c. 1689, John Hawkins, of Old Rappahannock Co, VA
    Edward[3], b. 1662; m. Elizabeth Wilson, d/o Elias Wilson, of Sittenburne Parish, Richmond Co.; **no
        issue**
    Robert[3], m. c. 1694, Martha Reeves, d/o James & Elizabeth (X) Reeves; he d. May 1707; **2 sons**
    Benjamin[3], m. c. 1689, Elizabeth (Thompson) Catlett, widow of William Catlett; he d. a. 10

Dec 1709, wp, Essex, Co, VA; **2 ch**

William[3], b. 1660; m. Hannah Hawkins, d/o Thomas Hawkins, of old Rappahannock Co, VA; Hannah d. 1695; he d. a. 10 Apr 1700,wp, Essex Co, VA; **4 ch**

Martha[3], m. William Thompson

Margaret[2], b. Sep 1642, Nansemond Co, VA; m. c. 1658, Thomas Fleming Jordan (1634-8 Dec 1699) s/o Thomas Jordan; d. 7 Dec 1708, Chuckatuck, Nansemond, VA (now in Suffolk Co, n.e. of city of Suffolk); became Quakers

CHILDREN:

Thomas[3], b. 6 Mar 1660/1; m. 6 Dec 1679, Elizabeth Burgh, d/o William Burgh, of Chuckatuck; **issue**

John[3], b. 17 Aug 1663; m. 9 Mar 1688/9, Margaret Burgh, sis/o Elizabeth (above); he d. a. 6 May 1712 wp; **issue**

James[3], b. 23 Nov 1665

Robert[3], b. 11 Jul 1668

Richard[3], b. 6 Jun 1670; m. 1706, Rebecca Rattcliff

Joseph[3], b. 8 Jul 1672

Benjamin[3], b. 18 Jul 1674

Mathew[3], b. 1 Jan 1676/7; m. 5 Sep 1699, Dorothy (Newby) Bufkin, widow of Levin Bufkin (she m/3, 17 May 1750, X Davis); he d. a. 13 Oct 1748, wp; **issue**

Samuel[3], b. 15 Apr 1679; m. 10 Dec 1703, Henrico Co, VA, Elizabeth Fleming (bp 28 Oct 168-, d. 20 Jul 1763; m/2 Thomas Raley), d/o Charles & Susanna (Tarlton) Fleming, of New Kent Co; Samuel d. a. 11 Jun 1719 ,wp; **issue**

Joshua[3], b. 31 Aug 1681; m. 1771, Elizabeth Sanbourne, d/o Daniel & Sarah (X) Sanbourne, of Isle of Wight Co; he d. p. 28 Feb 1717/8, wd; **issue**

Mary[2], b. 3 Jan 1645/6, Isle of Wight, VA, d. 1713, VA; m/1, c. 1664, James Biddlecombe, **issue**, m/2, c. 1686, Samuel Peachey, **no issue**; she d. 1713

REF: BRASHEAR, Charles & McCOY, Shirley B. - *A Brashear(s) Family History*, Vol. 1, pp. 1-15; MYRICK, Victor, *Myrick Family History* (1970), pp. 18-20; NUGENT, *Cavaliers and Pioneers,* Vol. 1, p. 41; *VA Land Patents,* Book 6, pp. 72, 346 ; BRASHEAR, Henry S,, *The Brashear-Brashears Family, 1449-1929*; GRAY, Allen, *Edward Pleasants Valentine Papers,* Vol. I; *Huguenot Society of VA*, Vol. XXVIII (1956); BACK, Troy L. & BRASHEAR, Leon, *The Brashear Story* (1962); Wm. & Mary College Magazine, Vol. II (1981), Vol. III (1982), *Genealogies of VA Families*; DORMAN, John F. & MEYER, Virginia M, editors, *Adventures of Purse & Person* (1987).

BRAY, Rachel de, see **DAVID**, Pierre

BRESSAN/BRESSAU, Anne, see **RAMBERT**, André

BRE(T)TON/BRITTON, François/Francis

b. 1660, FR

a. 17 Jun 1697 - from Picardie to lower Calais, FR, to SC

m. 1695, Elizabeth Sealy, d/o Joseph & Mary (X) Sealy; she d. 31 Mar 1724, Charlestown, SC, bur. FR Churchyard, Charleston, 1 Apr 1724

17 Jun 1697 – rec. land warrant of 200 acres

31 Sep 1709 – rec. warrant for 500 acres in Colleton Co, SC

c. 1729 - settled PeeDee Region in n.e. SC where the family liv. on the n. side of the Sampit River

d. 1731, PeeDee, SC

CHILDREN:

Philip[2], b. 1696, Pr. Geo Parish; m. Jane Goddard, d/o Francis Goddard; in the PeeDee, 1735; liv. Britton's Neck, Lee Co.; he d. 17 Jul 1749; 20 Jan 1749/50, wp, Craven Co, SC*

John/Jean[2], m. Rachel Sealey; d. 6 Feb 1729/30, Prince George's Par, Craven Co, SC; 2 Dec 1730, wp, Craven Co; mentions wife Rachel, bros Francis, Timothy, sis Hannah, Mary, mentions ch of sisters

Daniel[2], m. 26 Jan 1747/8, Pr. Frederick Parish, Elizabeth Hyrne, d/o Col. Edward Hyrne; he d. 8 Jun 1748/9; 16 Jun 1749, wp - mentions wife Elizabeth + unborn ch (**Daniel, Jr.**[3], who d. 24 Jul 1751)

Francis II[2], m. Ann Hyrne (a. 1716-1766), d/o Col. Edward Hyrne; 5 ch – **Moses**[3], **Daniel**[3], **Mary**[3], **Henry**[3], **Francis III**[3]; liv. Britton's Neck in Lee Co.; he d. 1766

Timothy[2], m. 10 Apr 1743, St. Phillip's Ch, Pr. Frederick Parish, Mary Goddard; in the PeeDee, 1729; he d. 3 Jan 1749/50, Pr. Frederick's Parish; 7 Nov 1750, wp, Craven Co, SC; 4 ch – **Mary**[3], **Philip**[3], **William**[3], **Timothy**[3]

Moses[2], m. 23 Apr 1741, Pr. Frederick Parish, Hester Jolly; in the PeeDee, 1735; he d. 1772/3; 4 ch – **Daniel Laine**[3], **Benjamin**[3], **Ann**[3], **Rebecca**[3]; he liv. Britton's Neck

Joseph[2], m/1, Sarah DuPré, d/o Josias DuPré II (s/o Josias I & Sarah (Garnier) DuPré); 2 ch – **David**[3], **Elizabeth**[3]; m/2. Ann X-7 ch – **Thomas**[3], **Philip**[3], **Timothy**[3], **John**[3], **Martha**[3], **Mary**[3], **Moses**[3], **Martin**[3], **Joseph**[3]; in the PeeDee, 1749; he liv. Pr. Frederick Parish; he d. 1773

Hannah[2], m. Pr. George Parish, William Ray; 4 ch – **John**[3], **Frances**[3], **Rachel**[3], **Anne**[3]

Mary[2], m. 18 Apr 1722, St. Philip's Par, Charles Town, SC, William Balough/Bollough; she was bur 15 Nov 1728; Wm. d. 3 Dec 1739

Elizabeth[2], m. Samuel Jenkins; she d. p. 1773; 3 ch – **James**[3], **John**[3], **Samuel**[3]

Martha[2], m. 15 May 1738, Pr. Frederick Parish, John Sinkler

Sarah[2], m. Michael Mixon; in the PeeDee, 1747, Prince Frederick Parish

*Craven Co, SC, no longer exists; it was a proprietary county from 1682 to 1769; there was no government there – it was an region covering a large area north of Berkeley to the NC border; Prince Frederick & Prince George Parishes were in Craven Co.

REF: BETHEA, Mary Belle M., *Ancestral Key to the Pee Dee*; *SC Historical & Genealogical Magazine*, Vol. XX, #2 (Apr 1919); GREGG, John M., *Early Pee Dee Settlers* (Bowie, MD, 1993); BALDWIN, Agnes L., *1st Settlers of SC, 1670-1700*; SALLEY, A.S, Jr., *Warrants for Land in SC, 1672-1711*; SALLEY, A.S., Jr., *Register of St. Philip's Parish, Charles Town SC, 1720-1758*; *SC Genealogies*, Vol. II, Articles from the *SC Historical & Genealogical Magazine*; MOORE, Caroline T, *Abstracts of the Wills of the State of SC, 1770-1760*.

BRÉVARD, Jean

b. c. 1665/75, FR

1686 - to N. IRE

m/1, aboard ship to America, X Wallace; she d. soon after

poss. as early as 1698 - to America, settled nr. Elk River, Cecil Co, MD

m/2, c. 1711, MD, Katherine (**or** poss. Mary [McKnitt] Powell, widow of Thomas Powell) McKnitt, b. 1689, MD

d. p. 10 Jan 1729, Cecil Co, MD

CHILDREN, m/2:

Adam[2], b. c. 1712; m. c. 1733, Mary McKnitt; d. p. 9 Nov 1782, wd-a. 15 Feb 1783, wp, Worcester Co, MD; will mentions wife but not by name, son **John**[3] (m. Sarah Campbell, 2 Lt, MD, in Rev. War) dau **Esther**[3] m. X Hudson, her sons Adam Brevard Hudson[4] and Benjamin Hudson[4]

John[2], b. c. 1716, MD; m. Jane/Jean McWhorter, (c.1726, IRE-25 Mar 1800, NC) sis/o Dr. Alexander McWhorter, from NJ; went to Rowan Co, NC, c. 1740 (that part that became Iredell Co.in 1788); d. 1790, Iredell Co, NC; as John was too old for military service at the time of the Rev. War, he served as the Ch. of the Committee for Safety of Rowan Co; he was commissioned a Lt. and his 8 sons all served; the county seat of Transylvania Co, NC was given the name *Brevard* in tribute to the patriotism of John and his 8 fighting sons; Patriotic Service, NC; wife Jane also had Patriotic Service, NC

CHILDREN:

Mary[3], m. c. 10 Dec 1767 (date of marr bond), Gen. William Lee Davidson (b. 1746 Lancaster Co, PA, s/o George), who was killed in the battle of Cowan's Ford, 1 Feb 1781; his will (dated 17 Dec 1780, Rowan Co) mentions wife Mary **3 sons**, **3 daus** and an unborn ch
(**a son**)

Ephraim[3], b. Charlotte, NC, c. 1750; m. X Polk, d/o Gen. Thomas Polk; d. c. 1783; was a physician; 1 dau **Martha**[4]; he d/bur, Charlotte, NC

John[3], b. 18 Feb 1751, NC; m. Dec 1783, Hannah Thompson (23 Aug 1765-1833); d. 9 Nov 1826, TN; **13 ch**; 1st Lt & Civil Service, NC

Hugh[3], b. 1748, NC; m. Jane Young; d. a. 30 Jun 1781, NC; Colonel and Patriotic Service, NC

Adam[3], b. Mar 1753; m/1, Sarah/Sally Harper, m/2, Mary Winslow; 1st member of the NC Legislature from Iredell Co; d. 2 Oct 1829; **issue by both wives – at least 2 daus**; Soldier, NC

Alexander[3], b. Apr 1755, NC; m. Rebecca Davidson (1760-1824), d/o Maj. John Davidson; d. 1 Nov 1829, NC; **8 ch**; Capt. NC

Robert[3], b. 17 Jul 1763, NC; m. Nancy X; d. 2 Jan 1847, MO; Pvt, NC

Benjamin[3], b. 1735, MD; m. Rebecca X; d. a. 27 Mar 1793, MD; Patriotic Service, MD

Nancy[3], m. Judge John Davidson; both killed by Indians at the head of the Catawba River prior to the Rev War; had at least one dau **Sarah**[4] who m. 1782, Lambert Clayton

Joseph[3], m. Rebecca Kershaw, d/o Capt. Ely Kershaw; settled Camden, SC; was an attorney, judge; **2 ch**

Jane[3], m. Ephraim Davidson, s/o Robert of Chester Co, PA and b/o Maj. John (above);

Rebecca[3], m. X Jones; moved to TN

Benjamin[2], b. c. 1717; m. Rebecca Alexander?; he d. a. 27 Mar 1793, wp, Cecil Co, MD; **6 ch**

Robert[2], b. 10 Jan 1718, Cecil Co, MD; m. 16 Apr 1744, Sarah Craig (22 Mar 1728-23 Jan 1807); went to NC; d. 20 Oct 1800, Iredell Co; Rev War soldier, NC

CHILDREN (from Robert Brevard's Bible – 2 transcriptions, some dates differ):

Joel[3], b. 20 Jun 1745, Cecil Co; d. Mar 1781, supposedly of smallpox, during Rev War service

Margaret[3], b. 1 Apr 1747, Rowan Co, NC; d. 1(?) Feb 1752

Elizabeth[3], b. 20/29 Dec 1748, Rowan Co; m. c. 1773, James Polk Reese (1739-1828); she d. 1831

Sarah[3], b. 20 Apr 1751, Rowan Co; m. c. 22 May 1772 Rowan Co. (date of bond), Alexander McLean

Margaret[3], b. 12 Jan 1754, Rowan Co; m. c. 12 Dec 1722, date of bond, Rowan Co., John Huggins; she d. 11 Sep 1790

Asenath[3], b. 26 Dec 1755, Rowan Co; m. 24 or 29 Sep 1774, James Houston; they built the 1st brick house bet the Yadkin and Catawba Rivers; she d. 13 Jun 1843

Jane[3], b. 6 Jan 1758, Rowan Co; d. Sep 1760

Lydia[3], b. 25/26 Dec 1759; d. 30 Jun 1777?

Robert[3], b. 18 Jul 1763, Rowan Co; d. 1847

Mary[3], b. 22 May 1765, Rowan Co; m. c. 21 Mar 1785, Rowan Co. (date of bond), James Huggins she d. 1812; *poss.* m/2 Benjamin Young

Jane[3], b. 9 Mar 1767, Rowan Co; m. William Tate; she d. 19 Jan 1854; *poss.* m. John Hall

Charlotte[3], b. 9 Dec 1769, Rowan Co; m. Samuel Jones

Prudence[3], b. 4/5 Jan 1772, Rowan Co; m. c.8 Apr 1784 Rowan Co. (date of bond), Enoch Poor; she d. 21 Dec 1808

Elizabeth[2], b, c. 1722; m/1, 1743 James Huggins, Jr. – **2 sons**, m/2, John Jetton (d. 27 Nov 1789) – **5 ch**; liv. in NC; she d. p. 23 Jan 1813, wd-a. Aug 1817, wp Mecklenburg Co, NC – said to have d. 2 Sep 1813, bur. Sugar Creek Presbyterian Ch, NC

Zebulon[2], b. 29 Mar 1724; m. 7 Mar 1754, Ann Templeton (Nov 1733-5 Aug 1804); went to NC; he d. 8 Mar 1798, NC; 10 ch; Soldier, NC

CHILDREN (from Zebulon Brevard's Bible):

Mary[3], b. 5 Aug 1755; m. 5 Aug 1773, Benjamin Wallace

91

David[3], b. 18 Mar 1755; d. 16 Aug ----

Elizabeth[3], b. 30 Dec 1758; m. 17 Nov 1783, William Beard

Jane[3], b. 29 May 1760 m. William Givens; she d. 1831

Sarah[3], b. 5 Jun 1762; m. William Wilson

Ann[3], b. 6 Jan 1766; m. David Edmiston

Zebulon[3], b. Feb 1769; m/1, Isabelle Edmiston; m/2, Phoebe (prob.) X Burton, widow

James[3], b. 3 Mar 1771

Rhoda[3], b. 21 Jul 1773; m. 1812, William McFee

Thomas[3], b. 25 Sep 1775; m/1, 1 Mar 1808, Sarah Sharpe Jetton (16 Jun 1788-7 May 1821) – **5 ch**; m/2, 9 May 1822, Elizabeth Troutte (b. 3 Oct 1798) – **1 son**; he d. 16 Oct 1846

(**Thomas**[2]?, b. 1726; m. Hannah Creiger; to NC – this child is mentioned in only one source)

REF: *Huguenot Ancestors Documented by the Huguenot Society of NJ*; Huguenot Society of America, *Huguenot Refugees in the Settling of Colonial America*; WHEELER, John H., *Reminiscences & Memoirs of NC* (1966); Adam Brevard's will; Robert Brevard Family Bible; Zebulon Brevard Family Bible; HAND, Robert S., *Those Members of the Brevard Family Who Descended from John/Jean Brevard...* (1991); *The Huguenot,* #14 (1947-48); CLEMENS, William M., *North & South Carolina Marriage Records* (1975); McINNESS, Robert, "The Jetton Family of Northern Mecklenberg County "in *Olde Mecklenberg Genealogical Society Quarterly*, Vol. 24, #2 (2007), pp. 6-8.

BRIAN(T), Pierre

b. c. 1580, FR, s/o Guillaume Brian; Pierre was a *tisserand* (weaver) & a *maître tisserand en toile* (master weaver of linen)

m/1, 8 Oct 1602, Sedan, FR, Marie Poupart (bp. 7 Aug 1575, Sedan-d. a. 22 Aug 1634, bur. Sedan), d/o Mathias & Jeanne (Decorby) Poupart – Mathias was a merchant in Montreuil at the time of Pierre & Marie's marr., later liv in Brù, Lorraine, FR, n.e. of Épinal; Marie's burial record says she was a native of "Etang-Gourt, nr. Conderlin" which hasn't been located – *could be* Les Étangs (n.w. of Metz) in Lorraine, there's a town nearby, called Condé-Pontigny; Montreuil – there are 30 on the current map of France – most likely are prob. Montreuil-sur-Thonnance or Montreuil-sur-Blaise, both in the Haute-Marne Dépt of Champagne; all these places are in n.e. FR

m/2, 30 Sep 1635, Élisabeth Ourlet, widow of Jérôme Vasset

d. a. 7 Feb 1641, bur. Sedan

CHILDREN, m/1:

Élisabeth[2], bp. 10 Aug 1603, Sedan

Susanne[2], bp. 12 Dec 1604, Sedan

Jeanne[2], bp. 28 Feb 1606, Sedan

Daniel[2], b. c. 1607; bur. 23 Aug 1657, Sedan; m/1, 19 Oct 1631, Sedan, Rachel Bruneau d/o Claude & Ann (Pierre) Bruneau - she d. c.1640 – **5 ch**; m/2, 8 Mar 1644, Francheval (s.e. of Sedan), Marie de Marolles, widow of Jacques Gernes- at least **3 ch**; Daniel was a *seurrier,* a locksmith or metal worker

Jacques[2], b. c. 1609, Sedan; m. 8 Dec 1637, Sedan, Susanne Gérard, d/o Jean & Jeanne (d'Orléans) Gérard, (c. 1611/12- bur. 10 Apr 1659, Sedan); he was a weaver

CHILDREN:

Daniel[3], b.10 Feb 1638, bp.19 Sep 1638, Sedan; m/1, 3 Jul 1660, Sedan, Givonne Marie Feret, widow of X du Truchot, m/2, 8 May 1686, FR Church, Mannheim, GER, Marie Roland, widow of Jean Froumi; Daniel was a weaver

Ysaac[3], bp. 27 Dec 1640, Utrecht, HOL

Jacques[3], bp. 1 Jan 1643, Utrecht; m. 20 Nov 1661, Sedan, FR, Ester Despré, d/o Jacques & Marie (Roger) Despré of Sedan

Cornelia[3], bp. 20 Apr 1651, Utrecht; m. 10 Mar 1676, Sedan, FR, Nicolas Chuno

Susanne[3], b. Utrecht; m. 31 Mar 1674/5, Sedan, FR, Abraham Soblet (1648-c.1719)

REF: *Registers of the Reformed Church* at Sedan, France (copied in French) into the *Bibliothèque Wallonne; The American Genealogist,* Vol. 78, #4, pp. 246-7; Church records from Utrecht; *Pierre Chastain,* Vol. I, Pierre Chastain Fam. Assoc, Indianapolis.

BRICOU/BRICON, Salomon

b. c. 1663, FR

fled to ENG

20 Aug 1699 - registered at the FR Church, La Tabernacle, London, as being of the village of "Censers en berry"- village is Sancerre, in the Cher Dépt, n.e. of Bourges in what was then the ancient prov. of Berry, now Centre; he was single at that time; surname Bricon

m/1, ENG, Bety X

c. Sep-Oct 1700/01 - left on *Le Nasseau* in a convoy of ships for VA; listed as traveling with his wife; surname Bricou, no ch mentioned

left VA, fairly soon after arriving; went to Staten Island

1706 – on 1st census list of Staten Island – he as a male,16-60 Y, wife Bety, 45 Y, no ch listed; surname Brickon, Bricon

m/2, 16 Feb 1712, "with license," Dutch Reformed Ch, New Amsterdam, Françoise Conelly

went to Essex Co, NJ

d. p. 1724/5, prob. NJ

CHILDREN, m/2:

Daniel[2], b. 1721; d. 26 Dec 1748, Newark, NJ (age 27); bur. Old Burial Ground, Newark, NJ

Salomon/Solomon[2], b. c. 1724/5; m. XX; d. a. 25 Jun 1791, intestate, Elizabeth, Middlesex, NJ; served in Rev. War - Pvt, NJ

 CHIILDREN, surname **BRECOUNT/BRICOUNT**, bp. St. John's Episcopal Ch, Elizabeth, NJ:

 David[3], b. 1747; bp. 23 May 1753, Elizabeth, NJ; wife unknown – Rhoda Clark?; he d. 30 Oct 1801, Woodbridge, NJ; bur. St. Georges Cem, Rahway; wp, 20 Jan 1802 – does not name wife nor ch, but does mention his sis Mary and names his bro-in-law William Connett as her heir; also names a bro-in-law Henry Williams (m. to which sis?); served in Rev. War - Pvt, Middlesex Co, Militia NJ

  CHILDREN:

  Mary[4], b. 16 Mar 1773, NJ; m. 27 Jun 1797, Mill Creek, Hamilton Co, OH Asa Hinkle (11 Apr 1778-7 Sep 1831, Auglaize Co, OH); she d. 11 Apr 1861 St. Mary's, Auglaize Co, OH

  Sarah[4], b. 1774, Somerset Co, NJ; m. 6 Jun 1793, Frederick Co, VA, Joseph Catterlin; she d. 29 Sep 1831, St. Mary's Twp, Mercer Co, OH, bur. on family farm

  David, Jr.[4], b. 22 Aug 1784, Hunterdon Co, NJ; m. Hamilton Co, OH, Lorena Lorne (17 Jul 1788-15 Jun 1878); he d. 17 Sep 1867, Butler Co, OH

 Daniel[3], b. c. 1749; chr. 23 May 1753, Elizabeth, NJ; d. c. 1802, inv, Hamilton Co, OH

 Effa[3], bp. 23 May 1753, Elizabeth, NJ

 Elizabeth[3], bp. 23 May 1753, Elizabeth, NJ

 Mary[3], b. 1759; bp 6 May 1761, Elizabeth, NJ; m. William Connett? – she must have d. a. 30 Oct 1801, as her bro's will names "bro-in-law" William Connett, as her heir

 Ruth[3], bp 6 May 1761, Elizabeth, NJ

 Salomon[3], b. 5 Aug 1763, NJ; m. 28 Sep 1785, Lydia DeCamp (1767 NJ-1851 MS); he d. 8 Sep 1799, Hamilton Co, OH, age 36Y 1M 2D – **8 ch**; Lydia m/2, 28 Sep 1802, Abraham Auter

NOTE: Records from the FR Ch, NYC: b. 25 Jul, bp. 4 Aug 1706 Pierre, s/o Nicolas Ponsin & Marie <u>Bricou</u>; b. 25 Nov, bp. 6 Dec 1713 Rebeca, d/o Benjamin Appeby & wife Françoise, godmo Marianne <u>Bricou</u>; b. 23 Nov , bp 8 Dec 1717 Jean, s/o Moïse Morin & Marianne <u>Bricou</u>. Relatives?

REF: *Proceedings of the Huguenot Society of London;* BROCK, R.A., *Huguenot Emigration to VA* (1966); STILWELL, J.E., *History & Genealogical Misc. re NY & NJ* Vol. I (1903); DICKERSON, M.S., *Salomon Bricou* (unpublished); PURPLE, Samuel S., *Records of the Reformed Dutch Church in New Amsterdam & NY (Marriages Dec 1639-Aug 1801)* (1890) ; WITTMEYER, Alfred V., *Register of l'Église Françoise à la Nouvelle York from 1668 to 1804.*

BRIQUE/BRICQUET/BRICKEY, Jean de /John

b. 1640, FR, possibly Reims <u>or</u> Artois in the present Pas-de-Calais
m. Alce/Alice X, b. c. 1640, FR; d. prob. Richmond Co, VA
c. 1680 – to America, prob. to Charles Town, SC; poss. on the *Richmond*, arr 30 Apr 1680
c. 1681 – to MD, then to VA
1690-92, 6 suits by various plaintiffs were filed against him; most were dismissed (rec. Westmoreland Co.)
d. a. 29 Oct 1718, inv., Westmoreland Co, VA
CHILDREN:
Jean/John[2], b. 1670, FR; m. Sarah X; d. 19 Dec 1732, Richmond Co, VA;
    CHILDREN (rec. N. Farnham Parish, Richmond Co, VA):
    Anne[3], b. 10 Feb 1726
    Anne[3], b. 19 Feb 1726 (could be the same dau, <u>or</u> date should be 1726/7 <u>or</u> it is a bap date of the
        1st Anne X
    Sarah[3], b. 19 Feb 1728/9
    Betty[3], b. 19 Feb 1731/2
Jarad[2], b. FR; 1 son **John**[3] who d. w/ **no issue**
Jincy[2], b. FR; m. XX
Mary[2], b. FR; m. XX
Peter[2], b. FR; m. Winifred Lucas; c 1730, settled VA
    CHILDREN;
    Jarad[3], **John**[3] (below), **Temperance**[3], **Dorcas**[3], **Winifred**[3], **Peter**[3], **Nancy**[3], **William**[3], **Elizabeth**[3],
    John[3], m/1, Mary Garner, 6 ch: **Jarad**[4], b. 10 Apr 1760, m. Amy Compton - **5 ch**; **Peter**[4], b. 10
        May 1769-d. Feb 1859, m. Nancy Smith- **no issue**; **Winifred**[4], b. 5 Jan 1772, m. John Smith -
        no issue; **Mary**[4], b. 17 Jul 1774, m. Jonas Jenkins; **John**[4], b. 20 Mar 1776, m. Jemima Caldwell
        - **2 sons**; **William**[4], b. 18 Feb 1780, m. Higail Waters - **issue**, m/2, widow Jane (X) Scott, had
        dau **Sarah**[4]; he d. 14 May 1856

REF: Brickey Family Bible (1815); BRICKEY, Raymond Luther, *The Brickey Heritage;* BRICKEY, Thomas Coke (manuscript, 1981-includes pages from previous works); BRICKEY, John, *Genealogy of the Brickey Family* (1855); BRICKEY, Lydia M. & Norville W, family history transcribed from one written by John Brickey in 1855.

BROUCARD/BROKAW/BRAGAW, Bourgeon

b. c. Mar 1645, nr. LaRochelle, FR; Mannheim recs say Mouscron, Flanders, nr. Courtrai, n.e. of Roubaix
    (Mouscron is now Moeskroen and Courtrai is Kortrijk, both in s.w. BEL) – La Rochelle and Mouscron
    are not near each other
early 1660's - fled FR, went to Mannheim, GER
m/1, 1 Dec 1663, Mannheim, Marie du May; she d. Mannheim
m/2, 18 Dec 1666, Mannheim, Catherine LeFèvre/Febre; she d. p. 1712
early 1670's - to Amsterdam, HOL
1675 – to New Amsterdam, among the earliest founders of the FR Protestant Ch in NYC; later was
    a member of the Bedford Church on Long Island
d. p. 2 Jun 1717, prob. Bushwick, LI, NY
CHILD, m/1
Marie[2], bp. 1 Feb 1665, Mannheim; d. young

CHILDREN, m/2:

Jannitze/Jeanne/Jane[2], bp. 17 Nov 1667, Mannheim; m. c. 1688, Johannes (Hans Theunis) Covert (1653/9-a. 1720), s/o Theunis Jans(en) Covert & Barbara Lucas; she d. c. 1722; **8 ch**

Marie[2], bp. 6 Apr 1670, Mannheim; m. 14 Nov 1694, NY Dutch Ch, Myndert Wiltsee, s/o Hendrick Martensen Wiltsee & Margrieje Meyers; 1 ch **Hendrick**[3]

Catherine[2], bp. 4 Jun 1672, Mannheim; d. young

Isaac[2], bp. 21 Mar 1675, Amsterdam; d. young

Isaac[2], bp. 7 Aug 1676, Brooklyn, NY; m. Hilletje Jans, prob. d/o Gysbert Jans & FytjeVan Putter; settled on LI, took surname **BRAGAW**; d. a. 14 Mar 1757, wp; **12 ch**, incl. dau **Mary**[3] who m. 11 May 1738, John Updyck

Jacob[2], b. c. 1678; went to NJ

Jan/John[2], bp. 14 Nov 1680, Flatbush; m. Sarah Teunis Van Middlesward, d/o Jan Teunis Van Middlesward & Catherine Teunis Bogart; went to NJ; he d. a. 14 Nov 1740, wp; **9 ch**

Peter[2], b. c. 1682; m. c. 1704, Judith Van Nest, d/o Peter Peterson Van Nest & Margaret (Crocheron); went to NJ; d. 16 Feb 1758; **4 ch**

Abraham[2], b. c. 1684, Bushwick; m. Maritje/Mary Davids, d/o Isaac Davids & Jannetje Maurits; he d. a. 9 Sep 1747, wp, Somerset Co, NJ; **10 ch**

Cathrina[2], bp. 14 Mar 1686, NY Dutch Church; m. c. 1704, Pieter Hoff; went to NJ; **3 ch**

REF: REYNOLDS, Cuyler, *Genealogical & Family History of Southern NY & the Hudson River Valley,* Vol. I (1914); PITTMAN, H. Minot, *The Brokaw-Bragaw Family* in NYGBR, Vol. 135 (1955); BAILEY, Rosalie Fellows, *Pre-Revolutionary Dutch Houses & Families in Northern NJ & Southern NY;* KOEHLER, Albert T., *Huguenots & Early French in NJ* (1955); FOSTER, Mrs. Elsie E., *Our Brokaw-Bragaw Heritage.*

BRO(U)SSARD, Jeanne – see GUERRI, Pierre

BROUSSE/BRUCE/BRURÈ, Jacques

b. a. 1679, FR

m. XX; must have d. a. emigration to VA

1700 – to Manakintown, on the *Mary Ann*; the list of French refugees says Brouse and 1 ch; settled Manakintown

1705 – naturalized in VA

d. p. 2 Sep 1707, Manakintown; his name appears on a list of parishioners assembled to elect a vestry on that date

CHILD:

Peter[2], b. c. 1700; he is on list of tithables in King Wm. Parish, Jul 1717; m. Mary X; he d. p. 4 Jan 1760, wd -a. Mar 1762, wp, Halifax Co, NC; used surname BRUCE; will names wife Mary, ch Peter, Ann Fountain, Elizabeth Crats, Jean, Sarah Brasswell, Alice Huett
CHILDREN:
Peter[3]
Ann[3], m. X Fountain, perhaps the John Fountain who was named a trustee of Peter Sr.'s estate
Elizabeth[3], m. X Crats
Jean[3]
Sarah[3], m. X Brasswell
Alice[3], m. X Huett

REF: BROCK, R.A., *Huguenot Emigration to VA* (1886); HOFMANN, Margaret M., *Genealogical; Abstracts of Wills, 1755-1824, Halifax Co, NC; Vestry Book, King William Parish, 1707-1750* (1988); CABELL, Priscilla H., *Turff & Twigg, The French Lands*, Vol. 1; copy of Peter's will.

BRUYÈRE/BRUÈRE, Jacques

of Chèvre, Champagne, FR (prob. what is now La Loge-aux-Chèvres, e.s.e. of Troyes); had bro Johannes

m. 29 Jun 1690, Daubhausen, Hesse, GER, Louise Douslet, also of Chèvre; Daubhausen is just n.w. of Ehringshausen, which is n.w. of Wetzlar; Greifenthal is n.w. of Daubhausen in the same area

d. a. 21 Mar 1711 – ch. called orphans on that date

CHILDREN (all bp. Daubhausen, in the FR Reformed Church):

Jean[2], bp. 8 Apr 1691

Jeanne[2], b. 12 Mar 1693, Greifenthal

Jacques[2], b. 24 Feb 1695, Greifenthal; 21 Mar 1711, he was termed an orphan of 14 yrs bound to Rip Van Dam of NY; on the Colonial Census of 1710, he is listed with sisters Jeanne, 18, & Susannah, 6, he is said to be 15; m. Susanne X; he d. a. 1744

CHILD:

Pierre/Peter[3], b. c. 1720; m. 1744, Elinor Price, d/o Edward & Mary Price, she d. 24 Oct 1784; he d. 19 Jul 1779, Allentown, NJ

CHILDREN:

Mary[4], b. 15 Apr 1745; m. X Blackwell; she d. 7 Apr 1766

Susanne[4], b. 29 Oct 1749; m. William Baker; she d. 29 Jun 1788

James[4] (surname **Brewer**), b. 9 Feb 1751, Monmouth, NJ; d. NJ; m. Sarah Horsful, d/o James & Ruth (Rogers) Horsful; he d. 2 Jul 1807; **8ch**; Capt, NJ, Rev War

Ele(a)nor[4], m. Sylvester Bills; she d. 6 Feb 1825

Pierre[2], b. 10 Aug 1697, Greifenthal

Suzanne[2], b. 25 Mar 1704, Greifenthal

REF: RICORD, F.W., *Documents of Colonial History, NJ,* Vol. XVI, 1748-55 (1891); MacWETHY, L.D., *Book of Names of Early Palatines* (1969); church records from Daubhausen, GER, written in French – church was known as L'Église Françoise de Daubhauss, a French Reformed Ch, 1685-1825; Pierre Bruyère Family Bible.

BUART, Mariane, see DUTERTRE, Louis

BUCHLE/BÜCHLI/BUEHL, Johan

b. 1670, s/o John Buehl, of the Rhine Valley, n.e. FR, nr. Strasbourg; c. 1685, family fled to GER, where his father d.

m. XX, prob. GER

d. GER

CHILD:

Johannis Conrad[2], b. 1699; m. Catherine X (1698- 21 Jan 1763, bur. St. John's Stone Cem, Harmony, PA); he and 2 sons Heinrich & Peter emigrated to America after son Conrad had settled there

CHILDREN:

Leonard[3], surname **BUCHLE**

Jacob[3], surname **BUCHLE**

Conrad[3], surname **BEIGHLEY**, b. 1737; he sailed from Stuttgart on the *Halifax* & arr Philadelphia, 22 Oct 1754, 1st of the family to emig. to America; m. 1764, Frederick Co, MD, Margaretta Wiles; he was a blacksmith, apprenticed to Margaretta's father George; 1773, moved to Bedford Co, PA; c. 1774, went to Northampton Co, PA; Conrad and son John both served in Rev. War; went to Westmoreland Co. c. 1784; Conrad d. 1824, Greensburg, PA

CHILDREN, (all m. in Westmoreland Co, PA):

John/Johannis[4], b. 1765; m. 1790, Catherine Bachmann, d/o Lt. Henry Bachmann; later went to Butler Co, PA

Susan/ Shusey[4], m. Nicholas Milliron; went to Butler Co, PA

          Henry[4], m. Catherine Milliron; went to Butler Co, PA

          Jacob[4], m. Sarah Lenhart; went to Butler Co, PA

          Elizabeth/Betsy[4], d. unmarr.

          Peter[4], m. Susan Milliron; went to Butler Co, PA

          Catherine/Cassie[4], m. Henry Baumgartner

          George[4], m. Christina Hoover; went to Butler Co, PA

          John Adam[4], b. 8 Jul 1779, Westmoreland Co.; m. c. 1805, Elizabeth Bixler who d. 2
               Nov 1871, Westmoreland Co; he d. 28 Aug 1870, Westmoreland Co.

          Mary/Polly[4]

          Daniel[4], m. Elizabeth Schreck

          William[4] , m. Annie Myers; went to Butler Co, PA c. 1800, later to OH, where he d. 1868

      Heinrich[3], surname **BUCHLE**, b. 1738

      Peter[3], surname **BUCHLE,** b. 1739

      Elizabeth[3], surname **BEIGHLEY**, b. 21 Jul 1742; d. 1 Aug 1801, bur. Zion Lutheran Cem,
          Lancaster Twp, PA

REF: SIPE, C. Hale, *History of Butler Co, PA*, Vol. 2 (1927); BEIGHLEY, Walter J., *The Beighley's Family Tree* (1972).

BUREL/BURRELL, Pierre

    b. 1669, Picardie, FR, s/o David & Jeanne (Blanchar) Burel

    m. 9 Oct 1690, Walloon or Strangers' Ch, Canterbury, ENG, Elizabeth Charoussin, d/o D'hiller & Marie
        (Aubineau) Charoussin of Poitou; *promesse* (engagement) gives names of both sets of parents, places

    d. 1729, MD

    CHILDREN:

    Jeanne Elizabeth[2], b. & bp. 12 Jul 1691, Canterbury; bp. rec. says Buret

    Marie[2] bp. 4 Sep 1692, Canterbury; bp. rec. says Buret

    Pierre[2], b. 17 Jul, bp. 21 Jul 1695, Canterbury; bp. rec. says Buret

    Francis[2]

REF: HOVENDEN, Robert, editor, *The Registers of the Wallon or Strangers' Ch in Canterbury Huguenot Society of London Quarto Series*, Vol. 5, Parts I, II,III, Book VIII, Publication of the Huguenot Society of London (Lymington, 1898); MONNETT, O. E, *Monnett Genealogy*; GANNON. Peter Steven, editor, *Huguenot Refugees in the Settling of America* (NYC, 1985).

BUTIN, Pierre

    b. 24 May 1695, Quesnoy-sur-Deûle, FR, Pas-de Calais, just n.w. of Lille, s/o Nicolas & Élisabeth
        (Tancre) Butin

    m/1, Marie Jeanne Poissonier, who d. Cadzand, Zeeland, HOL (n.w. of Oostburg) by 1730; Cadzand was
        called an island but it is not now

    m/2, 13 May 1731, Cadzand, Johanna/Jana/Jeanne Basting, d/o Josias & Martha (Zonnevylle/Zonneyville)
        Basting; she d. Cadzand

    d. 21 Apr 1762, Cadzand

    CHILDREN, prob all m/2:

    unnamed dau[2]

    Josias[2], b. 29 Dec 1747, Cadzand; stayed in Cadzand

    5 ch[2] **who d. young**

    Jannes[2], b. 31 Jan 1745, Cadzand; bp 7 Feb 1745, Walloon Ch; m/1, 6 Mar 1768, Groede, HOL (n.e. of
        Cadzand), Magdeline/Madeleine (Albert) Labyt (2 Aug 1734- 27 Nov 1780, Cadzand), d/o Pierre &
        Elizabeth (van Houte) Albert, widow of Isaac Labyt; m/2, 23 Dec 1781, Johanna Herny (8 Nov 1757-5

Sep 1817, Cazenovia, Madison Co, NY); sailed for America, 1 Apr 1797-landed NY, 27 Jun 1797; Jannes d. 14 Apr 1813, Cazenovia, bur in the orchard on his farm

CHILDREN, m/2, 1st 6, b. Cadzand:

Mariah[3], b. 4 Dec 1782; d. IN

Susanna[3], b. 23 Feb 1784; d. Hocking Co, OH

John Anthonis[3], b. 14 Dec 1786; m. spring 1810, Cazenovia, Anna Coleman (12 May 1790-23 Dec 1860, prob. Newton, Jasper Co, IA), d/o Asa & Hannah (X) Coleman; he d. 12 Jul 1867, Jasper Co, IA; **9 ch**

Johanna[3], b. 14 Jun 1788; m. Thomas van Valkenburg; she d. 30 Aug 1842, OH

Abraham[3], b. 11 Aug 1789; m. 1 Jun 1815, Cazenovia, Olive Coleman (19 May 1792, Coventry, CT-5 Jan 1855, Chillicothe, Wapello, IA – n.w. of Ottumwa); he d. 3 May 1853, Chillicothe, IA; **9 ch**

Jacob J.[3], b. 15 Dec 1791; m. Abigail; he d. 16 Feb 1814, Cazenovia, NY

Peter Isaac Josias[3], b. 3 Feb 1795, Amsterdam; m. Abigail M.(1807-18 Aug 1863); he d. 5 Apr 1852, OH

Athonis Herny[3], b. 20 Jul 1796, Amsterdam; m. Rebecca Coleman (d. 26 Sep 1890); he d. 12 Nov 1865

REF: Genealogical & Church records from FR, HOL (written in French & Dutch); Family Bibles; QUIST, Oval, *The Butins in America* (Des Moines, 1969).

C

CABANIS, Henri

b. c. 1675, Lasalle, Gard Dépt, Languedoc-Roussillon, FR, s.w. of Alès, said to be s/o Pierre & Anne
    (Soulière) Cabanis; **or** b. in/nr. Paris, poss. s/o Isaac Cabanis/Chabanas; an Isaac Chabanas &
    son were on the *Mary Ann* w/ Henri

m/1, c. 1698, FR, Marie X (d. c. 1706, VA)

c. 1698 - went to ENG

19 Apr 1700 - Henri, Marie and infant son Henri II, left from Gravesend, ENG, on the *Mary Ann;* landed
    31 Jul 1700, at the James River above Richmond, VA, and were sent to Manakin Town

bet 18 Apr-12 May 1705 – naturalized Henrico Co, VA; later to Pr. George Co

m/2, a. 1708, Magdalane Harrison, a widow w/ 1 dau named Magadalene; one source says her name was
    Mary Harrison, thus he *may not* have had a 3rd wife named Mary; wife *prob.* d/o George Harrison

1 May 1708 - claimed land in Henrico Co.

m/3, *poss.* Mary X (his will says his wife was named Mary)

he liv. in Westover Parish

d. bet 13 Jul 1719-9 Aug 1720, wp, Prince George Co, VA; mentions wife Mary, sons Henry, Matthew,
    George; fam. liv nr. Petersburg, Merchants Hope Dist.; 9 Jan 1720/1, inv; Henri was a goldsmith

CHILD, m/1:

Henri II[2], b. c. 1699, prob. ENG; m. c. 1725, Jane Allen, d/o William & Eleanor (X) Allen; he d. p. 10
    Dec 1770-a. Aug 1771, Mecklenburg Co, VA

    CHILDREN, several used surname **CAVINESS** or variations thereof; ch poss b. NC:

    Henry[3], b. 1738; m. Eleanor X; he d. 1811

    Matthew[3], b. 1740; m. Ann X; he d. 1806; **8 ch**

    William[3], b. 1741; m. Lucy Camp; he d. 1806

    Thomas[3], 1743; m. Rachel Wallace

    Richard[3], b. 1751/5; he d. 1820/30

    Amos[3], b. 1753

    Frederick[3], b. 1756/9; m. Elizabeth Kerr; he d. 1825

CHILDREN, m/2:

Matthew[2], b. 1712, VA; m. c. 1736, Hannah Clay, d/o Col. Thomas Clay; d. p. 6 Jun 1789, wd-a. 5 Aug
    1790, wp, Nottaway Co, VA

    CHILDREN:

    Ann[3], m. a. 1789 X Lumkin

    Charles[3], m. Anne X; he d. 1819, Jones Co, GA; **6 ch**

    Matthew, Jr.[3], m. Mary X; d. 1781, Amelia Co, VA; **6 ch**

    Mary[3], m. X Belcher; she d. a. 1789

    John[3], m. XX; d. p. 11 Dec 1817, wd – a. 6 Jul 1813, wp, Jones Co, GA; **issue**

    Phoebe[3], m. Francis? Belcher

    George[3], b. 1744; m/1, X Carter; m/2, c. 1780, VA, Palatea Harrison (d. 1821); he d. 1815,
    Jones Co, GA

    Henry[3], went to GA

    Elijah[3]

    Hannah[3], m. X Clark

    Elizabeth[3]

    Amy Clay[3]

George[2], b. 1714, VA; m. Grace X; he d. a. 18 May 1744, wp, Amelia Co, VA; **2 sons, 2 daus**

REF: *The Huguenot,#3, #4, #6, #11;* ANDERSON, Alloa, *Henry Cabinis, the Immigrant Infant & Some of His
Descendants,* (1971); Henry Sr.'s will, Pr. Geo Co, VA; Estate of Geo. Cabanis, Jones Co, GA; Will of John
Cabanis, Green Co, KY; Will of Matthew Cabanis, Nottaway Co, VA; *The Colonial Genealogist*, Vol. 7, #2.

CADET, François/Francis

b. c. 1655; from Niort, Poitou, FR; had bro Jacques who m. Jeanne Brauld/Brand, their 6 ch, bap. London
m. Marie Marthe LeGros (c.1662-20 Oct 1742); bur. St. Luke's Church, Old Street, Shoreditch, London
a. 1694 - to London; a *chamoiseur,* chamois or leather dresser/maker
d. 28 Dec 1712, Parish of St. Mary Magdalen, Bermondsey, Surrey, England; his will was filed in the
        Prerogative Court of Canterbury; will mentions wife and 3 sons Francis, Michael, Benjamin
CHILDREN:
Francis[2], mentioned in father's will of 1712
Michael[2], b. c. 1690, prob. FR; bp. 28 Mar 1694, FR Ch, Threadneedle St, London; to VA, 1722; m.
     Temperance Sadler (d. p. 1782); he d. 1768/9; used the surname **YOUNG**
        CHILDREN: (1st 4 ch used surname **CADET YOUNG**)
        Francis[3], b. 25 Oct 1731, Brunswick Co, VA; m. Feb 1754, Elizabeth Bennett, d/o James &
            Elizabeth (Peyton) Bennett; Eliz. d. a. 5 Feb 1799, wp, Isle of Wight Co – mentions
            sons **James**[4], **Thomas Michael**[4], **Francis**[4], **Bennett**[4], dau **Anne**[4]; he 31 Dec 1794, Isle
            of Wight Co., VA
        Thomas[3], b. 5 Jan 1732, Lunenburg (now Brunswick) Co, VA; m/1, 1744, Judith Johnston,
            d/o Robert Johnston – **7 ch**; m/2, 1772, Lucy (Ragsdale) Young, d/o John Ragsdale,
            widow of Michael Cadet Young, II, his bro
        Michael II[3], m. Lucy Ragsdale; d. a. 22 Mar 1762
        Le Gros[3], d. a. 5 Mar 1787, SC
        John[3]
        Martha[3]
Benjamin[2], mentioned in father's will of 1712
Pierre[2], bp. 1 Mar 1696, FR Ch, Threadneedle St, London; d. young
Marie[2], bp. 26 Sep 1697, FR Ch, Threadneedle St, London; d. a. 1712
Pierre[2], b. 13 Jan, bp. 23 Jan 1699, La Patente Ch, Spitalfields, London; prob. d. young

REF: *Huguenot Society of London*, Vol. XVI (Baptisms), Vols. XI, LII; *Prerogative Court of Canterbury* – François'
Will (1712); BEAUCHET-FILLEAU, *Dictionnaire Familles du Poitou*; NEALE, Gay, *Brunswick Co, History, 1720-
1925; Henrico Co, VA Deeds & Wills*; *Vestry Book, King William Parish, VA, 1707-1750* (1966); WULFECK, DF,
Marriages of Some VA Residents, 1607-1880 (1967); *Young Family Genealogical Notes*- Manuscript in the VA State
Library Archives, Richmond; *VA Historical Society Magazine,* Vol. XV; "The Search for Michael Cadet Young" by
Robert Y. Clay in *The Huguenot,* Pub. #34 (1989-91).

CALVET/CALVIT/CALVER, Jean/John (Rev.)

b. 1650-60, Lacaune, Tarn Dépt, Midi-Pyrénées, FR (n.e. of Castres), s/o Pierre & Isabeau (Pagés) Calvet
m. prob. FR, Suzanne X
22 Jan 1685 – an ordained Huguenot minister, he was expelled from his church at Saint-Rome, s.e. of
        Toulouse; went to ENG
d. c. 1711, London
CHILDREN:
Anne[2], only rec. is that she was *prob.* the Anne Cal...t (*sic*), who was a godmo to Elizabeth Sallé (b. 4 Jul
        1728), d/o Guillaume & Elizabeth (Gévaudan) Sallé
Sara[2]
Jean II[2], b. FR; m. XX; went to Manakin, VA, a. 1700; naturalized, 1705; on the *Liste Généralle*, he is
        listed with a wife, 3 sons, 2 daus; on the tithable list, 1711; rec. patent #1004 to 100 acres, 30 Apr
        1714; he d. bet 26 Dec 1718-1 Feb 1719 (date of inv), Henrico Co, VA; son Peter, as his heir, rec.
        444 acres, 100 of which were FR land;   son Anthony was a co-heir but just what he rec. is not
        clear
        CHILDREN:

       Pierre/Peter[3], b. c. 1707; m. Salome X; went to Craven Co, NC, c. 1732; naturalized, 12 Nov 1741, NC; d. p. 1752, perhaps SC; called a "lunatic"

       Antoine/Anthony[3], b. c. 1710/13, Manakintown; left for Craven Co, NC c. 1732; m. c. 1738, Mary Dean, d/o William Dean; Anthony d. a. 3 Nov 1760 – when his wife is referred to as a widow in her father's will which also mentions a William Calvit –grson; 4 sons are known: **William**[4], b. 1740, NC; m. Jane Holmes, he d. 1815/16, Adams Co, MS, **Joseph**[4], **Frederick**[4], **Thomas**[4]; Mary m/2, Daniel Higdon; she d. Feb 1807, Washington, Adams Co, MS

       Étienne/Stephen[3], b. 1714, VA; m/1, Elizabeth X, m/2, Ann Hulder; settled Craven Co, NC ; he d. c. 1767, NC

       Guillaume/William[3], d. 1744, VA

       Anne (?)[3]

       1 other dau[3]

Suzanne[2]

perhaps one other[2]

REF: STANFILL, Latayne Colvett, *Colvett Family Chronicles, the History of the Colvett Family in TN 1630-1990* (1990); CABELL, Priscilla Harris, *Turff & Twiggs, The French Lands*, Vol. I; *The Huguenot* #25 (1971-73), #27 (1975-77); *Vestry Book of King William Parish, VA 1707-1750* (1988); GIUSEPPI, M.S., *Naturalizations of Foreign Protestants in the American & West Indian Colonies* (1969).

CAMP, Laurents de/Laurens/Lourens Jansen

    b. c. 1645 FR, Picardie or Normandie, s/o Jean de Camp

    1664 - arr in New Amsterdam from HOL

    24 Aug 1675 – name on Assessment Roll of New Utrecht; was an "original" member of the Dutch Reformed Ch w/ his wife in 1677

    m. c. 1676, Elsie/Altje de Mandeville, d/o Giles Jansen de Mandeville & Altje/Elsie Hendricks

    26 Sep 1687 - took Oath of Allegiance in Kings Co, NY; moved to Staten Island shortly afterwards

    30 Dec 1701 – joined a petition of NY Protestants to be sent to King William III

    7 May 1719 – was the local pastor of the Staten Island Dutch Ch

    CHILDREN:

Joannes[2], bp 2 Apr 1677, Brooklyn, NY

Johanis[2], bp. 2 Feb 1679, Flatbush, NY; m. c. 1701, Mary Praal, d/o Pieter & Maria (Christopher) Praal, gdau/o Arendt Praal & Marie Billiou; he d. c. 1765; wd, 9 Feb 1764, wp, 28 May 1766, Essex Co, NJ; **2 sons, 4 daus**

Styntje[2], bp. 16 Jan 1681, Flatbush; called Christyntje/Christina; m. Christoffel Christopher

Hendrik/Henry[2], bp. 1682, New Utrecht, NY; m. 17 Apr 1704, Dutch Ch, NYC, Maria de Lamars; he d. a. 10 Aug 1771, wp, Middlesex Co, NJ; **9 sons, 2 daus**

Gideon[2], bp. 8 Apr 1683, Flatbush; m. Henrietta Ellis, d/o Bastian & Sarah (X) Ellis ?; **4 sons, 1 dau**

Weraichie/Maritje[2], bp. 1685, Flatbush; m. Charles Ellens – son **Johannes**[3]

Altje[2], bp. c. 1690; m. Cornelis Egmont; **4 ch**

Martha[2], bp. 23 Apr 1707, Staten Island

Christina[2], bp. 17 Apr 1711, Staten Island; m. 23 Mar 1728, David Pauer

Arent[2], b. 21 May, bp 6 Jun 1715, Staten Island

REF: MORRISON, George Austin, Jr., *DeCamp Genealogy, Laurent de Camp of New Utrecht, NY 1664 & His Descendants* (Albany, NY,1900); *NJ Register* (1956).

CANDÉE/de CANDÉ/CONDÉ, Jean/John

b. a. 1620, ENG; grs/o Jean deCandé who fled FR to ENG in 1572, after the St. Bartholomew Day Massacre; he was a friend and follower of Adm. Gaspard de Coligny who was killed during that Massacre; there are claims of relationship to the Princes of Condé - they are unfounded

m. XX

1639 – emigrated to America, settled nr. Boston, MA

a. 1650 – went to CT

d. c. 1650, Windsor, CT

CHILD:

Zaccheus/Zachariah[2], b. c. 1640; m. 5 Dec 1670, New Haven, CT, Rebecca Bristol (4 Feb 1640-New Haven-22 Sep 1739 West Haven), d/o Henry & Lydia (Brown) Bristol; he d. 1720,W. Haven, CT

CHILDREN:

Rebecca[3], b. 29 Dec 1671, New Haven; m. Thomas Painter; she d. 1 Jun 1739, West Haven

Hannah[3], b. 14 Dec 1673, New Haven; m. David Horton of Rye, NY

Zaccheus[3], b. 5 Jan 1674/5, New Haven; m. 19 Nov 1702, New Haven, Sarah Lane (d. 30 Sep 1737), d/o Isaac Lane; he d. 29 Dec 1743, Middletown, CT

CHILDREN:

Zaccheus[4], b. 6 Jun 1703 Middletown - **issue**; **Isaac**[4], b. 13 Dec 1704; **Theophilus**[4], b. 20 Dec 1706 - **issue**; **Sarah**[4], b. 3 May 1710; **Abigail**[4], b. 9 May 1714; **Mary**[4], b. 20 Aug 1716

Samuel[3], b. 24 Jul 1678, New Haven; m. 28 Apr 1703, New Haven, Abigail Pinion (c. 1680-9 Jan 1743), d/o Thomas & Mercy (X) Pinion; he d.28 Feb 1748/9, West Haven

CHILDREN:

Hannah[4], b. 1703/4, New Haven; m. 22 Apr 1724, New Haven, Nathaniel Kimberly of W. Haven, s/o Nathaniel & Hannah (Downs) Kimberly; she d. 13 Jan 1781, W. Haven

Samuel[4], b. 25 Dec 1705, New Haven; m. 1 May 1729, New Haven, Mehitabel Smith (28 Aug 1709-28 Jul 1799), d/o John & Mehitabel (Talmadge) Smith; he. d. 9 Apr 1773, W. Haven; **10 ch**

Thankful[4], b. Jun 1708, New Haven; d. 8 Sep 1725, W. Haven

Abigail[4], b. 10 Oct 1709; d. 10 Jan 1723/4, W. Haven

Gideon[4], b. c. 1711/2, W. Haven; m. 9 Mar 1740/1, New Haven, Sarah Smith (27 Aug 1718-p. 30 Jun 1757), d/o John & Mehitabel (Talmadge) Smith; he d. 28 Nov 1748, W. Haven; **3 ch**

Timothy[4], b. c. 1717; d. 11 Oct 1743

Lois[4], b. 1719; m. 20 Nov 1743, John Mix; she d. 26 Aug 1758, New Haven

Caleb[4], b. c. 1722, W. Haven; m.1743, Lois Mallory (30 Nov 1721, New Haven-1 Mar 1780, Oxford), d/o Daniel & Abigail (Trowbridge) Mallory; he d. 20 Oct 1776 Oxford, CT; **9 ch**

Mary[3], b. 18 Feb 1680, New Haven

Desire[3], b. 20 Oct 1686, New Haven

Abigail[3], b. Apr 1689, New Haven

REF: MATTHEWS, John, *Matthews' American Armoury & Blue Book*; BALDWIN, Charles Candee, *Candee Genealogy* (1882); Jacobus, Donald L., *Families of Ancient New Haven*, Vol. I-III; GANNON, Peter S., *Huguenot Refugees in the Settling of Colonial America*.

CANTINE/CANTAIN/KANTYN/QUANTIN, Moïse/Moyse/Moses

b. Royan, Saintonge, FR – now Charente Maritime Dépt, Poitou-Charentes, at the mouth of the Gironde Estuary

c. 1685 - fled from Bordeaux FR, to ENG

m/1, c. 1685/6, XX, who d. on passage to America c. 1686; **no issue**

c. 1690 - settled New Paltz, NY, where he ran a ferry at Kingston Point

m/2, 1691, New Paltz, Elizabeth (Deyo) LeFèvre, d/o <u>Chrétien Deyo</u> and widow of <u>Simon LeFèvre</u>, she d. 1690

m/3, 20 Sep 1703, Kingston, NY, Marytje (DeBois) DeWitt, widow of Bowdewyn DeWitt; **no issue**

d. 9 Sep 1744, Marbletown, Ulster, NY

CHILD, m/2:

Peter[2], bp. 21 May 1693, FR Ch, New Paltz; m. 16 Jun 1715, Elizabeth Blanchan, b. Hurley, d/o <u>Matthys & Margriet (VanSchöenhoven) Blanchan</u>; Peter used surnames **CANTEIN(E)/ KANTYN**; children used **KANTEIN/CONTEIN**; he d. 25 Oct 1769, Marbletown, NY
CHILDREN (all bp. Kingston):

Elisabeth[3], bp. 29 Jan 1716; d. young

Moses[3], b. 6 Dec 1716, bp. 13 Jan 1716/7; m. 1 Dec 1739, Maria Slegt; d. 1778; **no issue**

Margrietjen[3], b. 23 Jul, bp. 24 Aug 1718

Elisabeth[3], b. 1 Feb, bp. 21 Feb 1720; m. 8 Mar 1746, William Nottingham, Jr; she d. c. 1751

Mattheus/Matthew[3], b. 10 Mar, bp. 15 Oct 1721; <u>m/1</u>, p. 9 Dec 1744, Cathrina Nottingham, m/2, Elisabeth DuPay; he d. 21 Sep 1789

Maria[3], b. 23 Dec 1722, bp 27 Jan 1723; m. Hendricus Jansen (bp. 21 Jul 1729)

Nathaniel/Daniel[3], b. 10 Oct, bp. 25 Oct 1724; <u>m/1</u>, 30 Nov 1750, Geertje Delameter, <u>m/2</u>, 20 Jan 1756, Sara Rutsen, <u>m/3</u>, 24 Jul 1769, Dorothy Newkirt; he d. 4 Jul 1815

Catrina[3], b. 13 Mar, bp. 20 Mar 1726; m. Mar 1751, <u>Daniel LeFèvre</u> (bp. 12 Dec 1715-p. 4 Sep 1784, wd – a. 7 May 1800 ,wp); she d. 28 Feb 1799; **issue**

Abraham[3], b. 8 Dec 1727, bp 14 Jan 1727/8; m. 19 Nov 1756, Elizabeth Delameter; he d. 28 Nov 1813

Peter/Petrus[3], b. 28 Dec 1727; m. 14 Nov 1760, Magdalena LeFèvre; he d. 28 Nov 1813

Cornelia[3], b. 20 Mar, bp. 2 Apr 1732; m. 5 Dec 1767, Petru Sleght; she d. Apr 1789

Johannis/John[3], b. 20 Oct, bp. 16 Nov 1735; m. 28 Oct 1761, Mary Broadhead; he d.30 Apr 1808

REF: HUNTINGTON, Alice Cantine, *The Cantine Family: Descendants of Moses Cantine* (W. Hartford, CT 1957); LeFEVRE, Ralph, *History of New Paltz, NY and its Old Families* (1903); HOES, Roswell R., *Baptism & Marriage Registers of the Old Dutch Church of Kingston, Ulster, Co, NY, 1660-1809* (1891); ANJOU, Gustave, *Ulster Co, NY Probate Records* (1906, reprint 1996); JULIEN, Matthew Cantine, *A Preliminary Statement of the Cantine Genealogy or the Descendants in America of the Huguenot Refugee Moses Cantine* (1903).

CAQUELIN/COQUELIN/COCKLIN/GAGLIN, Sébastien I

b. 10 May 1686, s/o Nicolas Caquelin, former treasurer of L'Église au Ban-de-la-Roche; Ban-de-la-Roche was a *seigneurie* (seigniory = territory over which a lord holds jurisdiction) s.w. of Strasbourg, towns of Waldersbach, Bellefosse, Neuville-la-Roche were in it; chief town was Rothau

m. 26 Jan 1712, Waldersbach, Rhineland, Marie Barzet, d/o Christopher Barzet of Bellefosse, Alsace, (n.w. of Sélestat); she d. 15 Apr 1733, and is bur.in FR along with 3 ch who d. in infancy; Waldersbach is now in Bas-Rhin Dept, s.w. of Strasbourg; he was called a *maître cloutier,* master nailmaker or dealer, in marr. record

16 Sep 1736 – arr Philadelphia on the *Princess Augusta*; sailed from Rotterdam with his ch

c. 1751, Cocalico region, s.e. Lancaster Co, PA

CHILDREN:

Sebastian, II.[2],b. c. 1714; d. aboard ship to America, 22 yrs. old

D(i)etrich[2], b. 1716, Alsace; m. Lancaster Co, PA, X Stukey (d. 14 Jun 1772); he d. 1792; son **John**[3], b. 11 Feb 1742, m. 13 Oct 1767, Frances Bricker (17 Dec 1748-1 Oct 1804); he d. 5 Jul 1801, Cumberland Co, PA

Jean/John[2], b. 1719; m. Magdalena Eberly; naturalized 24 Sep 1760, Philadelphia; d. a. 1796, wp; **6 ch**

Marie[2], m. John Pages
Cathrina[2], m. John Disler/Jacob Ditsler, a passenger on the ship to America
Sara[2], m. David Brecht
Jean Jacques/Jacob[2], b. 20 Mar 1733; bp. Waldersbach

REF: Walderbach Church records; *COCKLYE, KACKLEY Book* (Carlisle, PA 1953); Indenture 17 May 1751, *Berks Co, PA Deed Book A-1.*

CARRÉ, Louis

b. 1659, Châtellerault (n. of Poitiers), Vienne Dépt, Poitou-Charentes, FR; *perhaps* a descendant of Jean
   Carré, a pastor (served 1618-1665) in Châtellerault
m. Prégéante/Bridget Fleuriau (c. 1659-13 Jun 1750); had bros Pierre and Daniel, sister Marquise -
   – all ch of widow Marie (X) Fleuriau
fled FR to London
25 Mar 1688 - request for denization; 5 Apr 1688, naturalized London w/ wife, daus Mary and Jane
Jun 1688 - arr NYC
May 1696 – oath of Allegiance in NYC
1713-1724 – called L'ancien (Elder) in the FR Church, NYC
d. 29 May 1744, 85Y; 14 Feb 1739, wd, codicil, 30 Aug 1743, 13/14 Apr 1748, wp
CHILDREN:
Marie Catherine[2], m. Élie Boudinot II, s/o Élie I & Jeanne (Baraud/Barreau) Boudinot - **issue**
Jane[2] – naturalized w/ parents and sis – no more info
Elizabeth[2], bp. 21 Jul 1689, FR Ch, NYC
Louis[2], bp. 1691/2, NY; m. Margaret X; d. p. 30 Nov 1732, wd, Monmouth Co, NJ; son **Louis**[3]
Pierre[2], b. 3 Dec 1693

REF: Baird, Charles W., *History of the Huguenot Emigration to America*; SEACORD, M.H., *Biographical Sketches and Index of Huguenot Settlers of New Rochelle, 1687-1776*; NJ Archives, Vol. 30, p. 86; WITTMEYER, Alfred V., *Register of the Births, Marriages & Deaths of the Église Françoise à Nouvelle York from 1688-1804* (1968); COOPER, William Durrant, *Lists of Foreign Protestants & Aliens, Residents in England 1618-1668* (Westminster, ENG, 1862).

CARRIÈRE, Jean

b. c. 1670, Normandie, FR, s/o Jean Carrière, according to the *Liste des François et Suisses refugiez en
   Caroline*
30 Apr 1680 - arr in Charles Town on the *Richmond,* as a servant boy to Capt. Jacob Guérard; was #112
   on the 1696 *Liste de habitants de Santee* seeking naturalization as an English citizen
m. c. 1697, SC, Elizabeth X (d. a. 23 Mar 1723/4)
d. p. 23 Mar 1723/4, wd – a. 28 Jan 1724/25, wp, Colleton Co, SC; was a cooper; will mentions 5 daus,
   son John; 3 youngest daus unmarr. at that time; 15 Apr 1725, estate was appraised at £207, 15 sh;
   dau Susannah served as administratrix
CHILDREN:
Elizabeth[2], b. c. 1698; m. 18 Feb 1714, St. Thomas & St. Denis Parish, Jacob Burdell
Susannah[2], (1703-29 Sep 1780), m/1, c. 1719, John Stone (d. a. Mar 1725) - dau **Mary**[3] (c. 1720-1804)
   who m/1, 29 Nov 1738, Paul Grimball (1703-1750) – 1 son **John**[4] (1747-1780) who m. 1772,
   Elizabeth Robert (1750-1818), d/o Jacques de Bourdeaux & Sarah (Jaudon) Robert, m/2, c. 1751, Capt.
   William Lawton as his 3rd wife – **1 son**[4], m/3, 15 Jan 1759, Samuell Fickling – **1 son**[4]; Susannah[2] m/2,
   c. 1740, Thomas Winborn (d. a. 23 Jan 1756, wp), - dau **Susannah**[3] , b. 1742, who m. Daniel
   Townsend – **3 sons, 2 daus**
John[2], b. 18 Nov, bp 28 Dec 1712, St. Thomas & St. Denis Parish

Deborah[2]
Martha[2]
Joanna[2]

REF: MILLER, Annie Elizabeth, *Our Family Circle* (Hilton Head Island, 1987); PEEPLES, Rev. Dr. Robert E.H., *"A Grimball Plantation Journal"* Transactions of the Huguenot Society of SC, #87, (1982), #88 (1983).

CASIER, Philippe

b. c. 1620, Calais, FR, of a family from Picardie
m. Marie Taine (b. c. 1620); she m/2, 7 Feb 1671, Jean LeRoi/Roy; she d. prob. Staten Island; Marie had
     a bro Isaac who was a burgher in New Amsterdam who m. Sarah Rezon & went to DE
c. 1635/45 – went to Martinique, French West Indies, under the auspices of the FR West India Co.
1645 – returned to Calais
c. 1650 to Sluis, Flanders
1659 – to Mannheim on the Rhine (lower Palatinate)
27 Apr 1660 – left Texel (an island in the W. Frisian Is., HOL) on the *Guilded Otter* for New Netherlands
     a farmer from Calais w/ his wife, 4 ch – aged 23, 16, 12, 3; his son-in-law David Uzille, a farmer
     from Calais w/ his wife & nursing ch
14 Mar 1662 – he is on a list of landowners having requested 24 *morgens* of land at New Harlem; early
     1662 he is listed as the original owner of lot #10, in Van Keulan's Hook, a lg. plain s. of Harlem,
     bordering on the Harlem River, originally called "Otterspoor"
20 Apr 1662 - he signed an agreement which named David DuFour a cow herder for the town of New
     Harlem; on 28 Apr, he & Lubbert Gerritsen were appt. guardians for 2 orphaned ch
2 Oct 1662 - he and Marie united w/ the ch
16 Nov 1662 - he was appt. a magistrate
11 Jan 1663 - sold his lot on Van Keulen's Hook to Jacob Eldertsen
d. Jan-Apr 1663, Harlem, Manhattan Island, New Netherlands
CHILDREN:
Philippe[2], b. 27 Jul 1636, HOL; prob. d. young
Marie[2], b. c. 1642, Martinique, FWI; m. c. 1658, Mannheim, <u>David Uzille</u>; **issue**
Jacques[2], b. 1646-55; d. p. 1673, poss. went to New Castle Co, DE
Jean/Jan[2], b. 1645/6 Martinique, FWI; <u>m/1</u>, Elizabeth Damen, d/o Jan Damen & Fytie X; <u>m/2</u>, Susannah
     LeConte, d/o Jean LeConte; he d. a. 24 Jan 1710, wp, Staten Island
Hester[2], b. c. 1656, Sluis, Flanders; m. <u>Jean/John Belville/Belleville</u> (c. 1650-1710-20); **issue**
Sarah[2], b. 1662, Harlem; m. 29 Feb 1680, Jacques Guion (as his 2nd wife), b. St. Martin, Île de Ré, a
     merchant in New Harlem, who d. 1694; she d. p. 1694; issue – **Jacques/James**[3], b. 1682, m. 1710,
     Mary Holmes (1685-1782), d/o Joseph Holmes – **issue**; **Lysbet**[3], b. 1681, who m. Pierre Drageau;
     Philip[3]; she d. 1699, Staten Island

REF: TAYLOR, Paul Belleville, *Jean Belleville, the Huguenot & His Descendants*; RIKER, James, *Revised History of Harlem* (1904, NY).

CATALIN/CATTERLIN/CASTERLINE, François

b. 1672, Rouen, FR **or** Rouans, Loire-Atlantique Dépt, Pays de la Loire, s.e. of St. Nazaire
m. XX
25 Feb 1655 – member of Huguenot Ch in Amsterdam; *témoignage* (certificate) from the Ch at Rouen
c. 1690 – emigrated
d. 12 Dec 1768, NJ?, age 96Y
CHILD:

François[2], b. 1690; m. 3 times – total of **26 ch**; d. 1796, age 106Y

    CHILDREN: **Abraham**[3], **Amariah**[3], **Jacob**[3], **Stephen**[3], **Benjamin**[3], **Samuel**[3], **Francis**[3], **Phebe**[3], **James**[3]

    Joseph[3], b. 10 Jan 1736, m/1, 16 May 1772, Susannah Lyon (d. a. 1799, Morris Co, NJ) –
        11 ch, m/2, 24 Mar 1799, Morris Co., NJ, Peninah Searing (c. 1776, Mendham, Morris,
        NJ-21 Feb 1862, Morris Co.), do William & Peninah (Burnet) Searing – **10 ch**, Joseph d.
        18 Apr 1832, Morris Co, NJ

Barneet/Bernard[2], b. HOL; m/1, *Sarah X (d. p. 25 Jul 1692), m/2, Alice X, m/3, Ann X; a. 1680, acquired land in Jamaica, LI, NY; went to Middlesex Co, NJ where he d. 8 Jun 1733, wp, Middlesex Co, NJ. *some accts don't list Sarah but she was his wife when Bernard was involved in a land transaction on 25 Jul 1692, they both signed the document

    CHILDREN, m/1:

    Jonathan[3], b. c. 1690, LI, NY; m. Sarah X

    John[3], b. c. 1692, LI, NY m. Sarah X

    CHILDREN, prob. m/2:

    Francis[3], b. c. 1700, Middlesex, Co, NJ; m. Phebe X; d. 1762, Morris Co, NJ; **6 sons, 4 daus**

    Joseph[3], b. 22 Dec 1703/4, Woodbridge, Middlesex, NJ; m. Alice X

    Nathaniel[3], b. 30 Jan 1704, Woodbridge, NJ; m. Ann X

    CHILDREN, prob. m/3

    Ann[3], b. 19 Feb 1707, Piscataway, NJ

    Mary[3], b. 30 Aug 1709 ,Piscataway, NJ

REF: DICKERSON, Melford S., M.D., *Dickerson-Willan Genealogy* (Austin, TX, 1991); Index from the Bibliothèque Wallonne, Leiden, HOL.

CAUDEBEC/CODEBEC/CUDDEBACK/KODDEBEK, Jacques/Jacob

    b. c. 1666, Caudebec-en-Caux, Normandie, FR (n.w. of Rouen); it is poss. that the surname Caudebec
        was the name of his birthplace and not his true surname – common practice among the Dutch;
        supposedly, the s/o a prosperous merchant; he was well educated

    c. 1685 - fled FR, with Pierre/Peter Guimar (a Huguenot), to ENG or HOL, later emigrated to America,
        landing in MD; later went to Deerpark, Orange Co, NY

    m. 21 Oct 1695, NYC, Margaretta Provost, d. o Benjamin Provost & Elsje Aelberts of Kingston, NY

    d. 1732, Deerpark, NY

    CHILDREN:

    Maria[2], bp. 2 Aug 1696, Kingston; m/1, 20 Aug 1716, Minisink, Orange Co, NY, Jurian Westfall
        (27 Apr 1684-c. 1731), s/o Johannes Juriaans Westphael & Marytje Cool - **4 ch**; m/2, William Cole; she
        d. c. 1796

    Benjamin[2], bp. 19 Feb 1699, Kingston; d. unmarr., c. 1779

    Elsje[2], bp. 19 Oct 1701, Kingston; m. p. 11 Jun 1717 (date of banns), Rochester, NY, Harmanus
        Van Gorden (bp. 12 Jul 1696), s/o Alberts/Gysbert Van Gorden & Rachael Rosenkrans;
        she d. c. 1780, Shippekunk/Kingston, Ulster, NY

    William[2], bp. 21 Jun 1704, Minisink; m. 8 Apr 1733, Kingston, Jacomyntjen/Jemima Elting of New
        Paltz, NY, d/o Roeloff Elting; he d. 1778, Deerpark, NY; **6 ch**

    Jacobus/Jacob[2], bp. 7 Jul 1706, NY; m. Jannettje Westbrook; went to Niagara Co, NY; **4 ch**

    James[2], bp. 7 Jul 1706 NY; m. Neeltje Decker, d/o Christopher Decker of Shippekunk/Kingston, NY;
        he d. c. 1735

    Magdalena/Eleanor[2], bp. 30 Jan 1712, Kingston; m. blacksmith Evert Hoornbeck of Rochester; she d.
        c.1782, aged 70

    Dina[2], bp. 19 Jan 1716, Minisink; m. 31 May 1738, Minisink, blacksmith Abraham Louw, s/o Tys/
        Matthys Louw & Jannetje Van Haring, grgrs/o Mattys Blanchan & Magdalena Joiré; he d. c.
        1778-88; she d. p. 1788

Abraham[2], bp. 19 Aug 1716, Minisink; m. 29 May 1751, Esther Swartwout, d/o Maj. James Swartwout
      of Peenpack; she d. 11 Apr 1798; he d. 18 Aug 1796
Naomy[2], bp. 16 Jan 1726, Rochester; m. 11 May 1757, Kingston, Lodewyck Hoornbeek, s/o Judge
      Cornelius Hoornbeck, as his 2nd wife

REF: COLLINS, H.O., *Jacques Caudebec of Orange Co, NY and Some of His Descendants* – NYGBR Vol.
27 (Jul 1896); CUDDEBACK, W.L., *Caudebec in America* (1919); Huguenot Society of America – *Huguenot
Refugees in the Settling of Colonial America* (1985); GUMAER, P.E., *History of Deerpark, in Orange Co, NY,
1690-1801* (1890); KOEHLER, Albert F., *The Huguenots or The Early French in NJ.*

CAUMONT, Pierre de (Rev.)

Rector of the church in Sainte-Marie-du-Mont in the Manche Dépt of Basse Normandie, s.w. of Utah
      Beach; said to have been a member of a noble Huguenot family who had a château in Dordogne,
      Aquitaine (s.w. FR)
Sep 1568 - fled to the Isle of Jersey; accounts say he left because of the St. Bartholomew's Day Massacre,
      but that did not occur until 1572; he became the rector of St. Peter in Jersey
CHILD:
Sara[2], m. 21 Jul 1587, Rev. Nicolas Effard, as his 2nd wife; Nicolas was the s/o Jean & Élisabeth (Perrin)
      Effard - **issue**

REF: LANDERS, John Poindexter, *Poingdeste-Poindexter, A Norman Family through the Ages, 1259-1977*
(final chapter by Robert Dawns Poindexter) (Austin, TX).

CAZENOVE, Pierre

b. 28 Aug 1670, Anduze (s.w. Alès), Languedoc, FR, s/o Charles Cazenove; had bros Charles (wife
      Madeleine - they went to HOL), Jean-Pierre (to Neuchâtel, SWI, then to HOL), sis Marie, Made-
      leine, Suzanne; Pierre, Charles, Marie & Madeleine went to Geneva; Jean-Pierre went there 20 yrs.
      later from Neuchâtel
m. c. 14 Jun 1697 (date of marr. contract), Geneva, SWI, Marie Plantamour (2 Apr 1681, Châlon-sur-Saône,
      FR-19 Feb 1740, Geneva, "of a cold and a pain in her side"); they were marr. by David Fraissinet,
      ministre réfugié
d. 21 Dec 1733, Geneva; of a severe paralytic stroke
CHILDREN:
Jean[2], b. 10 Apr 1698, Geneva; m. 4 Apr 1732, Geneva, Elizabeth Bessonet (c. 1712-a. 2 Sep 1789, wp,
      Geneva), d/o Spectable Bessonnet (minister and professor); Jean d. 6 Jul 1745, Geneva
      CHILDREN:
      Jacob[3], d. young
      Jeanne Esther[3], b. 15 Jun 1734; d. young
      Marie Charlotte[3], b. 1735; m. Jean-Pierre Eynard
      Paul[3], b. 21 Jun 1739, Geneva; m. 29 Apr 1768, Geneva, Jeanne Elizabeth Martin (c.1745, prob.
            SWI- 22 May 1798/99*, Montbrillant, nr. Geneva); *the probate record says Jeanne d. 3
            Prairial An VII which is a French Revolutionary date, = 22 May 1798/99; Paul d. 1823-
            26, Geneva
            CHILDREN:
            Jean-Antoine[4], b. 29 Jun 1770; m. 14 Jul 1795, Philadelphia, Mary Hogan, d/o Edward
                Hogan (of Tipperary, IRE) & wife Gertrude Murray (of SCOT); 2 daus - **Kitty**[5] m.
                1819, M. Odier, **Antoinette**[5] (1802-1827) m. 1819, Charles Aubert; Jean d. 1843,
                Geneva
            Antoine Charles[4], b. 8 Apr 1775, Geneva; m. 29 Jun 1797, Georgetown, DC, Anne Hogan,
                (13 Feb 1776 Baltimore, MD- 9 Jul1843, bur. Alexandria, VA), d/o Edward Hogan;

Antoine d. 16 Oct 1862, Alexandria, VA - **10 ch** (underlined), all b. Alexandria, VA: **Eliza Frances**[5], b. 5 May 1798, m. May 1816, William Collins Gardner of Newport, RI - **4 ch** (**Charles**[6], b. 17 Apr 1817, m. Maria Ridgeley Dorsey, d/o Dr. X Dorsey of Philadelphia, **Anne Eliza**[6], b. 7 Feb 1819, m. Cassius F. Lee, **Constance Tabor**[6], b. 17 Jul 1820, m. Henry Winter Davis, **William Fowler**[6], b. 27 Oct 1840, m. Harriet C. Rowland, d/o John A. Rowland of Norfolk, VA); **Paul-Charles**[5], b. 25 Nov 1799- d. 3 Jan 1801; **Charles-John**[5], b. 26 Aug 1801, m. 19 Sep 1826, Sarah Greenleaf, d/o Samuel Greenleaf of Boston – **no issue**, he d. 9 Mar 1834, Boston; **Ann Maria**[5], b. 5 Aug 1803; m. 1823, Gen. Archibald Henderson (1783-1859) - **9 ch** (**Annie Elbertina Van Ness**[6], m. H. Allen Taylor), **Elizabeth Gardner**[6], m. Edward S. Jones, **Charles Alexander**[6], **Richard Henry**[6], **Charlotte Shepard**[6], m. Eleuthère Irénée du Pont, **Octavius Cazenove**[6] + 3 others); **Ann Paulina**[5], b. 13 Apr 1806, m. 26 May 1831, Lt. Col. John Fowle, she d. 21 Apr 1891 – **3 ch** (**Paulina Adelina**[6], m. Henry Fowle Durant [b. Henry Wells Smith], other ch d. young; **Louis-Albert**[5], b. 30 Nov 1807, d. c. 1852, m/1, 1837, Frances Ansley of St. Johns, New Brunswick who d. 1847, **ch** (**Frances Anna**[6], m. Charles Minor, **Charlotte**[6], m/1, X Massie, m/2, Dr. Berryman), m/2 2 Oct 1850, Harriott Turberville Stuart , **ch** (**Eleuthera du Pont**[6] who d. young, **Charles**[6], later named Louis-Albert, Jr.); **Charlotte Busti**[5], b. 14 Jan 1812; d. 21 Apr 1836; m. c. 1836, William B. Shepard - 1 dau (**Gertrude Murray**[6)]; **Octavius-Anthony**[5], b. 27 Dec 1813; d. unmarr., 23 Apr 1841; **Harriet**[5], b. 2 May 1817, m. 11Jul 1839, Gazaway Buggs Lamar, she d. 3 May 1861, **3 ch** (**Charlotte**[6], **Gazaway DeRosselt**[6], **Harriet Cazenove**[6] (m. Frank Cazenove Jones, a cousin); **William Gardner**[5], b. 27 Oct 1819; d. 8 Aug 1877; m. 1847, Mary Elizabeth Stanard ;

Philippe-Jean[3], d. 1742

Sara[3], d. 1744

Marie[2], c. 1704; d. 21 Apr 1708

*****Henriette**[2], d. p. 15 May 1732; m. Pierre Mazel; dau **Marie**[3]

*****Philippe**[2], went to Genoa, d. p. 15 May 1732

*****Theophile**[2], went to Amsterdam; d. p. 15 May 1732

*****David**[2], d. p. 1 Mar 1740

*in father's will written 15 May 1732 and probated 25 Dec 1733

NOTE: Much of the documentation presented is in FR, citing Swiss records that are also in FR – a lot of detail.

REF: Baptismal records, Geneva; wills, Geneva; *Quatre Siècles* (Nîmes, 1908); cemetery records; *VA Magazine of History/Biography,* Vol. 78 (1970), ASKLING, John, 'editor, "Autobiographical Sketch of Anthony-Charles Cazenove; Anthony Charles' will; Joseph Downs Collection of Manuscripts & Printed Ephemera – Winterthur Library.

CAZNEAU/CASNO, Paix

a. autumn 1688 - came from Languedoc, FR, to Boston, MA; member of the French Settlement at Oxford, Worcester Co, MA

m. Boston, Margaret Germaine (12 Dec 1671, La Rochelle, FR- Apr 1749, Wrentham, MA), d/o Jean Germon/Germaine of La Tremblade, Saintonge, FR.

d. 21 Jun 1720, Boston, MA

CHILDREN :

Isaac[2], b. c. 1696, prob. Boston; m. 22 Sep 1726, Boston, Hannah Johnson, (c. 1698-8 Apr 1784), d/o Joseph & Anne (Belcher) Johnson; he d. 8 May 1774, Boston; **11 ch**

Mary[2], b. c. 1701; m. 5 Dec 1721, Wrentham, Timothy Metcalf, (2 Jul 1697-17 Sep 1767), s/o Eliazur & Meletiah (Fisher) Metcalf; Mary d. 2 Jul 1770, Wrentham; **8 ch**

Susanna[2], b. prob. Boston; m. 28 Jan 1730, Boston, Adam Dechezeau (d. 3 Sep 1738) – he was a ship captain, murdered by his crew; Susanna d. a. 13 Oct 1789; **2 ch**

Peace[2], b. c. 1707, prob. Boston; m/1, 7 Oct 1637, Boston, Mary Scutt (7 Sep 1716-2 Feb 1757), d/o James & Elizabeth (Spencer) Scutt; **10 ch**; m/2, 11 Aug 1763, Jane (Rouse) Vincent (23 Aug 1715-18 Sep 1784), d/o Jonathan & Martha (X) Rouse; both wives are bur. in the Granary Burial Ground, Boston

REF: LAINHART, Ann Smith, *Descendants of Paix Cazneau* in the NEHGR, Vol. CXLII (Apr 1988).

CHADAINE/CHAD(E)AYNE, Jean/John

b. 12 Apr 1642, Marennes, Saintonge, FR, s.w. of Rochefort, now in Charente Maritime Dépt., Poitou-Charentes; *if* that date is correct, he was the s/o Henri & Marie (Renaud) Chadeayne

m. c. 1669, Hiers, Saintonge, FR, Marie Boucherie/Bourchier, d/o Jean & Marie (Barjeau) Boucherie/Bourchier

1681/2 – with wife, 4 ch, niece Marie & mother-in-law, he fled from the village of Hiers (prob. Hiers-Brouage, s.w. of Rochefort) - Saintonge is an old prov. now in Poitou-Charentes; then to Cork, IRE

6 Jul 1682 – he was granted citizenship in Dublin, IRE

c. 1686 - to Narragansett, RI

1691 – to Staten Island, NY

1698 – a resident of New Rochelle, NY; he was a shipcarpenter, shipmaster and mariner

d. p. 27 Mar 1708, wd – a. 27 Oct 1708, wp, Richmond Co, NY; mentions wife Mary, ch John, Henry, Martha, Elizabeth & Mary, wife of Joshua Mersereau

CHILDREN (all listed in his will, except Pierre, Marie I):

Pierre[2], b. 25 Feb 1671, FR; prob. d. young

Marie I[2], b. 24 Aug 1672, FR; prob. d. young

Jean/John[2], b. 26 Apr 1674, FR; m. Judith Tillou, d/o <u>Vincent & Elizabeth (Vigneau) Tillou</u>; he d. p. 9 Oct 1742; **3 ch**

Marie II[2], b. 22 Mar 1676, FR; m. 16 Jun 1693, NY, Josué/Joshua Mercereau (1667-23 May 1756), s/o <u>Jean & Elizabeth (DuBois) Mercereau</u>, of Saintonge; **7 ch**

Marthe/Martha[2], b. c. 1677; m. Peter Rykert, s/o Matthew Rykert

Henri/Henry[2], b. 27 Jan 1678, FR; m. c. 1718/9, Blanche de Bonrepos, b. 1697/98, d/o <u>Élie & Jane (X) de Bonrepos</u>; d. p. 30 Jun 1754; **4 ch**

Élisabeth/Elizabeth[2], b. 1679, m. Henry Coutant, s/o <u>Jean & Elizabeth (Angevine) Coutant</u>

REF: HASBROUCK, K.E., editor, *The Chadeayne Family in America* (New Paltz, NY, 1984); CHADEAYNE, Leander, F., *The Chadeayne Family in America* (1984); HIX, Charlotte Megill, *Wills & Letters of Administration, Richmond Co, NY, 1670-1800* (Bowie, MN, 1993).

CHALIFOU(R)/CHALIFOUX, Paul

b. 26 Dec 1612, Périgny (town on the e. side of LaRochelle); bp. 30 Dec 1612, in the Calvinist Temple, LaRochelle, Aunis, FR, s/o Paul & Marie (Gaborit) Chalifou; Marie was the widow of X Renaud

m/1, 10 Apr 1644, Notre-Dame-de-Cogne, La Rochelle, Marie Jeannet, d/o Claude & Jeanne (Mallebault) Jeannet, of Aunis; fa was a merchant in LaRochelle

bet 1645-48 – emigrated to Québec, Canada

m/2, 28 Sep 1648, Québec, Jacquette Archambault (b. Dompierre, FR- d. 17 Dec 1700), d/o Jacques & Françoise (Tourault) Archambault; d. 17 Dec 1700, 81 Petite Auvergne, Charlesbourg (borough of the city of Québec)

d. bet 27 Dec 1678-13 Oct 1680, Notre-Dame-des-Anges, Québec; he was a *charpentier de grosses œuvres* – a carpenter who constructed the foundations of buildings

CHILDREN, m/1:

Marie[2], b. 5 Jun 1645, Notre-Dame-de-Cogne de la Rochelle; did not go to Canada

CHILDREN, m/2 (all bp.Québec):

Marie[2], b. & bp. 5 Oct 1649; m. 1662, Joachim Martin

Marguerite[2], b. 23 Apr, bp. 24 Apr 1652; m. 1665, Jean Badeau

Jeanne[2], b. Jan; bp. 22 Feb 1654; m. 1671, François Bibeau

Simone[2], bp. 18 Oct 1655; m. 1671, Julian Brosseau

Françoise[2], b. 4 Dec, bp. 16 Dec 1657; m. 1671, Jacques Nolin

Jeanne[2], b. 25 Dec, bp. 28 Sep 1659; m. 1675, Germain Langlois

Louise[2], b. & bp. 3 Sep 1661; m. 1678, Joseph Vandandaigne

Paul François[2], b. 07 May, Beauport; bp. 13 May 1663, Québec; m/1, 22 Jan 1685, Beauport, Catherine Huppé, d/o Michel & Madeleine (Roussin) Huppé – she drowned, 30 Sep 1685, Québec – **no issue**; m/2, Jeanne Philippeau (d. 27 Aug 1708, Québec) , d/o Claude & Jeanne (Énard) Philippeau – **12 ch**; m/3, 5 Apr 1711, Québec, Marie-Madeleine Brassard, d/o Jean-Baptiste & Jeanne (Quelvé) Brassard – **4 ch**; Paul François d. 29 May 1718, Québec

Marie Madeleine[2], b. 24 Mar, bp. 25 Mar 1665

Étienne[2], b. 21 Mar, bp. 23 Mar 1667; m. 11 Oct 1687, Charlesbourg, Claudine Bourbeau, d/o Simon & Françoise (Letard) Bourbeau; **no issue**

Pierre, b. 12 Dec, Beauport; bp. 18 Dec 1668; m. 17 Oct 1689, Charlesbourg, Anne Magnan, d/o Jacques & Ambroise (Doight) Magnan ; **14 ch**

Anne, b. 15 Apr, bp. 17 Apr 1670; m/1, 1686, Jean Normand; m/2, 7 Feb 1692, Beauport, Jean Delage dit La Vigueur (b. 1663), s/o Jean & Michelle (de la Mazerolle) Delage – **10 ch**; Anne d. 6 Mar 1724

Jean Baptiste, b. 9 Jan, bp. 10 Jan 1672

Claude, b. 30 Jan, bp. 31 Jan 1673

NOTE : This family prob. became Catholic once it emigrated to Québec - wouldn't have had much choice in that time period.   Records cited are those kept by Catholic priests in Québec.

REF: JETTE, René, *Dictionnaire Généalogique des familles du Québec* (Montréal, 1893); TANGUAY, L'Abbé Cyprien, *Dictionnaire Généalogique des familles Canadiennes*, Vol. IV (Montréal, 1887); LUSSIER, Mgr Irénée, *Dictionnaire National des Canadiens Français,* Vol. I.

CHAMOIS/SHUMWAY, Pierre/Peter

b. 10 Apr 1635, prob Poitou, FR; poss. St. Maixent (there are 2 in the Deux-Sèvres Dépt – St-Maixent-de-Beugné, n.e. of Fontenay-le-Comte, and St-Maixent-l'École, n.e. of Niort)

c. 1665 – from FR to Boston "on the same vessel as Peter Faneuil and the Sigourneys."

by 1675 - on the roll of the MA Colonial Soldiers; fought in King Philip's War

m. Frances R------ (d. p. 3 Apr 1714, wd – a. 2 Aug 1714 ,wp, Topsfield, MA); in her will she mentions sons Peter, Joseph, gr dau Mary Butler, dau Dorcas Butler, dau-in law Mariah

d. p. 10 Apr 1695, wd – a. 10 Jun 1695, appraisal, Topsfield, MA; will mentions wife Frances R. + ch but the latter not by name

CHILDREN:

Peter[2], b. 6 Jun 1678, Topsfield, MA; m/1, 11 Feb 1700/01, Topsfield, MA, Mariah Smith (18 Dec 1677, Topsfield, MA-17 Jan 1738/9, Oxford, MA), d/o Robert and Mary (French) Smith, m/2, 28 Feb 1740, Mary Dana; Peter d. p. 12 May 1741, wd – a. 17 Sep 1751, wp, Boxford, MA; Peter's will names 2nd wife Mary, sons Oliver, Jeremiah, David, Samuel, John, Jacob, Amos, daus Mary Barton, Hepsibah

CHILDREN, m/1

Oliver[3], bp. 10 May 1701/2, Topsfield; m. 3 Sep 1724, Oxford, Sarah Pratt (b. 18 Oct 1704, Framingham, MA); **11 ch**

Jeremiah[3], b. 9 Mar 1702/3, Boxford; bp. 21 Mar 1702/3, Topsfield; m. 13 Nov 1729, Oxford, Experience Learned (b. 24 Jul 1711, Framingham, MA), d/o Isaac & Sarah (How)

        Learned

David[3], b. 23 Dec 1705, Boxford; bp. 23 Dec 1705, Topsfield

Mary[3], b. 6 Feb 1708/9, Boxford, bp. 9 May 1709, Topsfield; m. 6 Dec 1725, Oxford, Caleb
    Barton (9 Feb 1704/5, Framingham-d. p. 1763), s/o Samuel & Hannah (Bridges) Barton;
    Mary d. 29 Aug 1747, Oxford; **5 ch**

Samuel[3], b. 6 Mar 1711, Boxford, bp. 22 Apr 1711, Topsfield; m. 19 Feb 1735/6, Oxford, Sarah
    Learned (b. 8 Jun 1718 Oxford), d/o Isaac & Sarah (How) Learned

John[3], b. 26 Jun 1713, Boxford, bp. 16 Aug 1713, Topsfield; m. 19 May 1737, Oxford, Mary
    Dana (1721-1809); John d. 15 Jan 1810, Oxford; **8 ch**

Jacob[3], b. 10 Mar 1717, Oxford; bp there; m. 14 Jan 1741/2, Sutton, MA, Martha Walker of
    Sutton; Jacob d. 15 Apr 1801, Oxford; **9 ch**

Hepsibah[3], b. 6 Apr 1720, Oxford; bp. there; m. 12 Nov 1741, Obadiah/Kosick Walker of Sutton

Amos[3], b. 31 Jan 1722, Oxford, bp. there; m. 29 May 1745, Oxford, Ruth Parker; Amos d. 2 May
    1818, Oxford

*__John__[2], b. 20 Jan 1679/80

*__Samuel__[2], b. 2 Nov 1681

Dorcas[2], b. 16 Oct 1683, Topsfield; m. 26 Nov 1711, Topsfield, Valentine Butler of Gloucester; dau
    Mary[3]

Joseph[2], b. 13 Oct 1686, Topsfield

*not mentioned in the 1714 will of their mother Frances

REF: Vital Records, Topsfield, Oxford, Boxford, MA; SHUMWAY, Asahel Adams, *Genealogy of the Shumway Family*
(1909, NYC); NEHGS Register, Vol. 84 (Oct 1930) – *The Barton Family of Oxford, MA* by Rev. Wm. E. Barton;
DANIELS, George F., *History of the Town of Oxford, MA* (Oxford, MA, 1892).

CHAP(P)ELIER/CHAPPELIÉ/CHAPPELEAR, Isaac (Dr.)

b. 1672, Uzès, Languedoc, FR (n.e. of Nîmes), s/o Rev. Louis and Simone (Rons) Chappelier

m. 28 Oct 1696, FR Ch, Threadneedle St, London, Anne Arnau(l)d, d/o <u>Élie & Magdalen (DeValau)</u>
    <u>Arnau(l)d</u>; she was b. La Tremblade, Saintonge, FR; Anne evidently d. a. 16 Oct 1730 – not in
    mother's will but her son Isaac is; prob. went to MD w/ son Isaac[2]

Isaac fled from Bagnols, (perhaps Bagnols-sur-Cèze, which is n.e. of Uzès) FR, to London p. 1685, where
    he became a surgeon; entered service on the *HMS Canterbury* as a surgeon

25 May 1702, London - naturalized

d. bet. 18 Jan 1706/7-10 May 1707, at sea, in American waters, on the *Canterbury*; p. 18 Jan 1706/7, wd-a.
    10 May 1707, wp, London, filed Prerogative Court, Canterbury, 103 Poley, which names wife
    Anne and son Isaac and unnamed ch b. while he was away

CHILDREN (births rec. FR Ch, Threadneedle St., London):

Isaac, Jr.[2], b. 16 Mar 1698, London; 24 Sep 1711, he apprenticed to Élie Arnaud (prob. his grfa) as a
    weaver; went to MD; m. Rachel Briscoe, d/o Samuel Briscoe (Rachel m/2, Edward Briscoe, a
    cousin); Isaac, d. Mar 1791, St. Mary's Co, MD; 2 sons: **Elias Arnold**[3], b. 1730/41, MD, m. Ann
    Brammell/Bramwell, d/o William Brammell, Elias Arnold d. 1796, Culpeper Co, VA – **7 ch**;
    James[3], b. MD, m. Elizabeth Dent, d/o John Dent, James d. a. 11 Oct 1808, wp, St. Mary's Co. –
    10 ch

Marienne[2], b. 25 Jan 1700, d. 1700

Marienne[2], b. 14 Jan 1701; d. a. 1706/7, London; bap. rec. says fa is an apothecary, living in Chrisping
    (Crispin) St., Stepney Parish, hamlet of Spitalfields

Arnaud[2], b. 30 Jul 1702; bp. 9 Aug 1702, London

É(s)tienne[2], bp. 11 Mar 1705; d. a. 1706/7; family now liv. East St, Stepney Parish, by Spitalfields
    Market

Louis[2], bp 23 Dec 1706; d. a. 1730, prob. no issue

REF: *Huguenot Society of London Publications,* Vol. 16; Isaac's will; CHAPPELEAR, George Warren, *Families of VA,* Vol. II – CHAPPELEAR (Dayton, VA, 1932; CHAPPELEAR, Nancy, *The Chappelear Family* (Wheaton, MD, 1963); WOOD, SR, *The Rucker Family Genealogy w/ Their Ancestors, Descendants and Connections* (Richmond, 1932); COLLEARY, Shirley, *St. Mary's Research* (Valley Lee, MD, 1981); WOOD, Sudie Rucker, *The Rucker Family Genealogy,* p. 346 ff. (Richmond,, VA, 1932); Arnold Family Assoc. of the South, Vol. 5, #4 (Summer 1975).

CHARDAVOINE, Élie

b. c. 1667-72; from Saujon, (n.e. of Royan) Saintonge (now Poitou), FR

m. 24 Aug 1692, FR Huguenot Ch, NYC, Anne Valleau (b. 7 May 1672), a native of l'Île de Ré, d/o Charles & Anne (Brigaud) Valleau; Anne (Brigaud) Valleau was bur. Dublin, IR, 25 Jun 1685; Anne (Valleau) Chardavoine had 2 half-uncles Esaïe & Étienne Valleau

26 Jul 1715 - he took the Oath of Abjuration in NYC (oath acknowledged King George of ENG as the lawful king); he was a victualler

d. c. 1736, NYC

CHILDREN:

Anne[2], b. c. 1693, New Rochelle, NY; m. c. 1714/5, Jean/John DuPuy, she d. 13 Jan 1769, Philadelphia, PA; **7 ch**, all bp Church du Saint Esprit (FR Hug. Ch), NYC; **see NOTE**

Estienne[2], bp. 16 Nov 1694, Reformed Dutch Ch, Kingston, NY

Élie/Elias II[2], b. c. 1696; m. by 16 Jun 1717, Susanne David, d/o Jean & Esther (Vincent) David; he was a petty constable in the East Ward of NYC in 1720; Susanne d. a. 10 Mar 1725, when Élie wrote his will & said his wife was deceased; he d. NYC, a. 29 Mar 1726, wp; he was a cooper
CHILDREN (bp. St. Esprit FR Hug Ch, NYC):
Élie III[3], b. 8 Dec, bp. 17 Dec 1718, Jean David was his godfather; it was prob. this Élie who, on 3 Mar 1739/40, confessed to stealing a variety of items from various places – he was sentenced to be whipped 31 lashes
Jean[3], b. 27 Apr, bp. 8 May 1720; his grfa Élie was his godfather
Susanne[3], b. 1 Jul, bp. 11 Jul 1722
Anne[3], b. 4 Aug, bp. 19 Aug 1724; her aunt Anne DuPuy was her godmother and her uncle Jérémie Chardavoine was her godfather

Jérémie[2], bp. 1 May 1698, Reformed Dutch Ch, Kingston, grmo Marie Valleau was a witness; m. a. 27 Feb 1737, Marie Arnaud, d/o André & Marie (X) Arnaud of New Rochelle, a sailmaker from La Tremblade, Saintonge & wife Marie; name also spelled Arneau, Reneau, Renoud, Renaud

Isaac[2], b. 11 Jul, bp 9 Aug 1702, FR Hug Ch, NYC; m. 18 May 1724, Reformed Dutch Ch, NYC, Anna/Hannah Caer (chr. 15 Jul 1705, Ref. Dutch Ch, NYC-Feb 1733, NYC), d/o Anthony Caer & Annetje Huyke; he d. Nov 1773; **issue**, incl. son **Anthony**[3], bp. 3 Sep 1727 Reformed Dutch Ch, NYC, witnesses were his uncle Jérémie[2] & Annetje Caer

Pierre[2], b. 14 Aug, bp 26 Aug 1705, FR Hug Ch NYC

NOTE: There is a lengthy article online that contends that Dr. Jean/John DuPuy's wife was not a Chardovaine, as previously thought. His wife was named Anne and in Charles Meredith DuPuy's book he states that she was Anne Chardovaine with no evidence to support the statement. Élie Chardovaine II's will mentions "my brother-in-law Dr. John DuPuy, executor." Dr. DuPuy, in his will, leaves a sm. bequest to "my niece Susannah Chardovaine" (d/o Élie II and the only Chardovaine mentioned in the baptismal recs of Anne's Dupuy's ch). Anne or John DuPuy served as godparents for 2 of Élie II & wife Susanne David's 4 ch. The author of this article, Gary E. Young, bases his theory on the fact that none of Anne DuPuy's children had their grandparents or Anne's brothers as sponsors/godparents – the Chardovoine siblings did. Additionally, Anne's ch did not have family names – Élie/Elias, Étienne/Stephen, Jérémie/Jeremiah, Isaac. Mr. Young feels that the Anne who m. Dr. John DuPuy was prob. Anne David, bp. 2 Oct 1687, Ref. Dutch Ch, Kingston, d/o Jean David & Esther Vincent, thus a sis/o Susanne who m. Élie Chardovaine II. Her b. in 1687 makes her a bit closer to Dr. DuPuy's age, an 8 yr. difference as opposed to 14 yrs. In that time, a brother-in-law might refer to his wife's sister's husband as a "brother-in-law." Anne Chardovaine definitely m. a Jean/John DuPuy, but he was not the Dr. Jean DuPuy who was b. 1679, d. 1744. Article is well-documented.

REF: DuPuy, Charles Meredith & DuPUY, Herbert, *The Dupuy Family. A Genealogical History* (Philadelphia, 1910); HELFFENSTEIN, Abraham Ernest, *Pierre Fauconnier & His Descendants* (Philadelphia, 1911); BOYER, Carl III, *Ship Passenger Lists, NY & NJ (1600-1825)* (Newhall, CA, 1978); WITTMEYER, Rev. Alfred V., *Registers of the Births, Marriages, & Deaths of the Église Française à la Nouvelle York* (Baltimore, 1968); BAIRD, Charles W., *History of the Huguenot Emigration to America*, Vol. II; SCOTT, Kenneth, *NYC Court Records, 1684-1760* (Washington, DC, 1982); HOES, Roswell R., *Baptismal & Marriage Records of the Old Dutch Ch, Ulster Co, NY, 1660-1809* (Baltimore, 1980).

CHASTAIN, É(s)tienne/Stephen

b. Dauphiné Province, FR (prob. Vesc*, s.w. of Grenoble); one of the old provinces, located in s.e. FR, bet Provence & Savoie (Savoy); Étienne was a physician

m/1, prob. FR, Marthe X, who d. 24 Dec 1725, VA, age 52/53; given her age at death, it seems probable that they had been married for some time; no known ch.

c. 1699 - fled FR to ENG; took Oath of Allegiance, 14 May 1699 – just his name; the Bishop of London wrote the city Chamberlain saying that "Monsieur Castyne, is going out Surgeon to ye French now departing for Virginia, he wants £20 to make up his Chest of Drugs and instruments"

1700 - to VA on the *Mary Ann*, he and his wife are on the list of passengers; 1 of 2 physicians on board

c. 1714 - Liste Générale, no issue at that time

10 Jun 1714 - was granted 280 acres; 1 of the 66 original patentees; #738 (544 acres) was his original patent, partially in the FR lands

16 Jun 1714 - he patented 138 acres

c. 1716 - patent #686 - 12 acres; #787 (c. 95 acres)

1720 - #817 -37 acres were granted to him; so, he became a substantial landowner; had 11 patents totaling 2734 acres, 509 acres of which were repatented; not all the acreage is listed here – see Priscilla Cabell's book for more detail

5 Sep 1723 - 200 acres and 219 acres "joining the land where he now lives"

m/2, c. 1726, Marthe DuPuy, d/o Bartholomew & Marie (Gardié) DuPuy; she d. p. 23 Apr 1740, wd –
a. 20 May 1740, wp, which mentions dau Marie and her bros Peter, J. James and bro-in-law John LeVillain; sons not mentioned, so they must have d. young

2 Jul 1730 - 400 acres and again 400 acres

28 Sep 1730 - 400 acres

5 Jun 1736 - he patented an amalgamation of several of the preceding tracts totaling 544 acres, 36 of which were newly granted

3 Jun 1736 - rec Patent #738 – 544 acres; this patent includes patents #686, 851, 871, 817 – 508 acres of previously patented land + 36 acres of NEW land; all patents were Chastain's except #851, which was Jean Farcy/John Farcee

29 Mar 1738 - Patent #762 – 344 acres orig. patented by William Byrd I and sold to Stephen by William Byrd II for £100; Stephen willed this to his wife + 314 acres of Patent #738

d. p. 10 Jan 1732/3, wd-a. 21 Aug 1739, wp, Goochland Co, VA; will says he was of the "place Vese* in Doffine (*sic*) in the Province of France; will mentions wife and dau Marie but does not mention his 2 sons; he left Martha his plantation + 437 acres, his dau got a plantation + 800 acres; he was still alive 29 Mar 1738, when he bought land from William Byrd II. (*Vese does not exist, has to be Vesc)

CHILDREN, m/2:

Marie Magdelaine[2], b. 23 Aug 1727, King William Parish; m/1, c. 23 Aug 1742 (date of bond), Goochland Co, James Cocke (c. 1719-1753), s/o James Powell & Martha (Herbert) Cocke; James d. Cumberland Par, Lunenburg Co, VA, wp, 3 Jul 1753 – mentions daus Martha & Elizabeth, sons James, Chastain & Stephen; m/2, 17 Jan 1754, Peter Farrar (b. 6 Jun 1730); she prob. d. Amelia Co

CHILDREN, m/1:

Chastain[3], b. 13 Nov 1743; m. Judith Archer

James Powell[3], m/1, 29 Nov 1767, Elizabeth Archer – no issue; m/2, Sep 1777, Lucy Smith;

he d. 13 Jan 1829

Stephen[3], m. Jane Segar Eggleston of Amelia Co, VA

Martha[3], m. William Cannon of Buckingham Co, VA

Elizabeth Chastain[3], m. Henry Anderson of Amelia Co, VA

CHILDREN, m/2:

John[3], b. 8 Nov 1754; m. 1 Apr 1775, Rebecca Warthen

Judith[3], b. 31 Apr 1756

Mary[3], b. 1 Dec 1757; d. 31 Jan 1758

Mary[3], b. 20 Aug 1759; d. 5 Oct 1765

Samuel[3], b. 23 Aug 1762; m. Betty Eggleston, d/o Richard & Mary (Chubb) Eggleston; he
     d. 6 Apr 1818

Rebecca[3], b. 28 Dec 1764; m. Robert Porterfield of Augusta Co, VA

Son[2], b. 3 Nov, bp. 27 Dec 1728; d. a. Jan 1732/3

Estienne[2], b. 1 Mar 1729/30, bp 12 Apr 1730; d. a. Jan 1732/3

REF: ALLEN, Cameron, "The Chastain Family of Manakintown, VA" in *TAG*, Vol. 39 (Jul 1963); BAIRD, Charles W, *Huguenot Emigrants to America*, Vol. II; BROCK, Robert A., *Documents...Relating to the Huguenot Emigration to America* (1973); CABELL, Priscilla Harriss, *Turff & Twigg, Volume One, The French Lands* (Richmond, VA, 1988).

CHASTAIN, Pierre

name was originally Chastaignier/Chateigner which evolved into Chastain in the 1300's

bp. 9 Apr 1659, Province of Berry, FR, rec. Issoudun, s/o Étienne & Jeanne (Laurent) Chastain; Issoudun is
     c.10 km. s.w. of Chârost which is considered his birthplace or area; Étienne, s/o Jacques & Jeanne
     (Audet) Chastain; Étienne was a *notaire royal*, as was his father Jacques; on 16 Aug 1682, at Bourges
     (c. 28 km. n.e. of Chârost), Étienne Chastain renounced his Protestantism – it is assumed that it was
     prompted by his desire to retain his job as *notaire royal*

m/1, 27 Jan 1687, St. Cyr Parish, Issoudun, Susanne Reynaud (b. 24 Sep 1667, bp. 6 Oct 1667, Issoudun- Feb

1700/1, Manakintown), d/o <u>Pierre & Anne (Jupille) Regnault/Renaud/Reynaud</u> of Issoudun;
     like many couples of the time, they were m. in a Catholic Ch since only those marriages were
     recognized as legal

c. 1692 - fled FR to (*poss.* 1st Yverdon) Vevey, Canton Vaud, SWI, s.e. of Lausanne, on Lake Geneva/Léman;
     his wife and 5 ch joined him by 1696; Pierre was a physician and *perruquier* (barber/wigmaker)

p. 1698- to The Hague, then to London

19 Apr 1700 – left Gravesend, ENG, on the *Mary Ann* of London, en route to VA

23 Jul 1700 - arr at the mouth of the mouth of the James River w/ wife and 5 ch; settled in Manakin;
     wife + Jean, Marie, Jeanne, Pierre Samuel, prob. Susanne

m/2, p. Feb 1700/1 – a. 10 Nov 1701, Goochland Co, VA, Anne Soblet (bp. 27 Oct 1675, Sedan, FR-3
     Apr 1723, King William Parish, Goochland Co, VA), d/o <u>Abraham & Susanne (Briant) Soblet</u>

by 10 Nov 1701 – Pierre has a wife and only 3 ch; Jean Adam survived, not clear who the other 2 were

had tract #827 (11 acres) which was in the FR territory; had tracts outside of the FR Lands

c. 1714 – list of Huguenots – Pierre has a wife 2 sons, 4 daus

1724 - patent of 379+ acres on Jones Creek

m/3, bet 19 May 1724-3 Oct 1726, Magdelaine (Verreuil) Trabue, d/o <u>Moïse & Madeleine (Prudhomme)</u>
     <u>Verreuil</u>, widow of <u>Anthony Trabue</u>; she d. p. 2 Jan 1729 ,wd – a. May 1733, wp

d. p. 3 Oct 1728, wd – a. 20 Nov 1728, wp, King William Parish, (then) Goochland Co, VA; mentions
     ch John, Peter, René, Judith, Susanna, Mary, Elizabeth, Magdalin (*sic*); owned 1154 acres
     in Goochland Co.

CHILDREN, m/1 (except for Anne & Susanne, ch. bp. Vevey, SWI; parents called "refugies" in bap.
     records):

Anne[2], bp. 23 Feb 1688, Issoudun, FR

Jean Adam/John[2], bp. 8 May 1690, Vevey, SWI; m/1, Marianne (David?) – 1 son **Jean/John**[3]; m/2, c. 1726, Charlotte Judith Amonet – **7 ch**; he d. Dec 1761, Cumberland Co, VA

Marie Susanne[2], bp. 8 Oct 169,1 Vevey, SWI; d. a. 1701, VA

Pauline Elizabeth[2], bp. 24 Aug 1694, Vevey, SWI; d. 1696-98

Pierre II[2], bp. 24 Aug 1694, Vevey, SWI; d. 1696-98

Arthuze/Aréthuse (dau)[2], bp. 4 Mar 1696, Vevey, SWI; d. 1696-98

Jeanne Françoise[2], b. 26 Feb 1697, Vevey, SWI; d. a. 1701, VA

Pierre Samuel[2], bp. 5 May 1698, Vevey, SWI; d. a. 1701, VA

Susanne[2], bp. 10 Sep 1699,Walloon Ch, The Hague, HOL; d. young

CHILDREN, m/2:

Judith[2], c. 1703, VA; m. Gille Ballew (d. 1733); had ch by common-law husband Thomas Walker; she d. bet 1765-84, Chesterfield Co, VA; she has been listed as the dau of m/1 but there is no bp. rec. for her while all the other ch were recorded so it would seem that she was the d/o of m/2; the name Judith does not appear in the Reynaud family but it does in the Soblet family – Anne's grmo's name was Judith

Susanna[2], b.c .1705, Manakin Town, VA; m. by 1730, James Robinson (d. bet 8 Oct 1745- 21 Feb 1748/9); **5 ch**

Pierre/Peter[2], b. c. 1707, Manakin Town, VA; prob. m. Mildred (Middy) Archer; d. p. 1775, prob. VA; **9/10 ch**

Mary[2], b.c. 1709, Henrico Co, VA; d. unmarr., a. 20 Nov 1728 – p. 15 Jun 1731

Elizabeth[2], b. 1711, Manakin Town, VA; m. c. 1732/3, David LeSueur as his 2nd wife; he was b. 1698, Coke Lane, Stepney Par, England, bp. 30 Jan 1704, FR Ch, Threadneedle St., London, s/o David & Catherine (Fell) LeSueur; he d. 1771/2, Cumberland Co, VA; **6 sons, 2 daus**

René[2], b. c. 1713, Manakintown, VA; m. c. 1732/3, Judith (Martain) Gevedon/Gévaudan, widow of Thomas, d/o Jean & Margaret (X) Martain; he d. p. 7 Jan - a. 6 Dec 1786,wp, Abbeville Dist, SC; **5 ch**

Janne[2], b.c. 1716, Manakin Town, VA; d. 12 Jan 1722/3

(Marie) Magdelaine[2], b.c. 1720, Manakin Town, VA; m. c. 1740, Guillaume Sallé, as his 2nd wife; she d. bet 1803-10; **8 ch**

REF: *Registers of the Reformed Church* at Sedan as copied into the *Bibliothèque Wallonne; The American Genealogist,* Vol. 39 #3, Vol. 40 #1 & #3, pp. 1-9, 138-41, Vol. 64#3 (Parish recs from Issoudun, FR & Vevey, SWI), Vol. 71#4;Vol. 75, #2, p. 103-4; *Douglas Register*; Pierre's will; *The Huguenot,* #4 (1929); Pierre Chastain Family Assoc, *Pierre Chastain & His Descendants*, Vol. I (1995) ; ALLEN, Cameron, "Pierre Chastain Revisited " in *TAG*, Vol. 14, #3 (Jul 1989); CABELL, Priscilla Harris, *Turff & Twigg, Volume One, The French Lands* (Richmond, VA, 1988) ; ALLEN, Cameron, "Susanne Regnaud/Reynault (1667-c. 1701), First Wife of Pierre[1]Chastain (1659-1728) of Manakintown, Virginia" in *TAG*, Vol. 85, #1 (Jan, 2011- pub. Nov., 2011).

CHÂTEAU/SHATTO, Jean Nichol(as)

b. c. 1715/20, Charleville, Champagne, FR (prob. the one in the Marne Dépt, Champagne-Ardenne, n.w. of Sézanne)

m. 1735-39, Maria Eva X, a Catholic; this was noted in the bap. record of her daus Anna Barbara & Catherine; the record also states that Nicholas was a Calvinist

3 Sep 1739 - arr America on the *Loyal and Judith*; took Oath of Allegiance the next day in Philadelphia; settled 1st in Germantown

c. 1744 - went to western Lancaster Co, PA, which became York Co. in 1749

d. p. 1783, prob. York Co, PA

CHILDREN:

Nicholas[2], m. XX; d. p. 24 Oct 1827, wd, Perry Co, PA; this branch of the family used SHATTO as a surname; **7 ch**

Anna Barbara[2], bp. 7 Aug 1744, nr. Germantown, PA

Catharina[2], bp. 7 Aug 1744, nr. Germantown, PA

Anna Christina Margaretha[2], called Jennie, b. 20 Nov 1745; m. 1759/60, Martin Bernheisel (19 May 1729-29 Jun 1802); she d. 20 Dec 1803, Perry Co, PA; **8 ch**

Henrich/Fridich[2], bp. 7 Aug 1744; m. 1 Apr 1766, Maria Catherine Stahl, d/o George & Anna Christina (X) Stahl; this family used the surname SCHEDDO; **4 ch**

Johannes[2], m. Catherine X; **3 ch**

Ursula[2], bp. 4 Aug 1752, Lutheran Ch, Adams Co, PA

John Anthony[2], bp. 9 Aug 1753, Lutheran Ch, Adams Co, PA

REF: CHAMBERS, *Foulke, Lupfer & Allied Families* (1952); *Proceedings of the Huguenot Society of PA,* Vol. XXVII (1955); GANNON, Peter Steven, editor, *Huguenot Refugees in the Settling of Colonial America* (1985).

CHAUDOIN/CHADOUIN, François/Francis

b. c. 1717/8, FR

m/1, a. 1754, King William Parish, VA, Sarah Weaver, d/o Samuel & XX Weaver*; she prob. d. c. 1780

by 26 Jan 1757 - Francis sold 135 acres in Chesterfield Co., that had been granted to French refugees, to John La Barrare. Francis was said to be 39, a barber, French and drafted out of the militia of the Colony to serve in the VA Regiment

m/2, prob. c. 1783, Judith X; on 21 Mar 1785, Francis & wife Judith sold some property in Goochland Co.

d. c. 1799/1800, Buckingham Co, VA

CHLDREN, m/1:

Lewis[2], b. 25 Mar 1754, Cumberland Co, VA; m. 15 Nov 1784, Kitty/Catherine/ Katurah Mims (1766-25 Oct 1821); Lewis was a minister and farmer; Rev War private from VA; he d. 4 Jan 1845, Goochland Co, VA; **9 ch**

Francis, Jr.[2], b. c. 1757, Chesterfield Co, VA; m. c. 1780, Judith (X) Hutching (c. 1760-1826), poss. widow of Lawrence Hutching; Francis was a farmer; he d. a. 1840, Green Co, KY; **5 ch**

Andrew[2], b. c. 1759, Chesterfield Co, VA; m. 20 Dec 1786, Sarah (Moore) Matthews (c. 1765-25 Dec 1850, d/o Robert & Susanna (X) Moore, widow of X Matthews; he d. 17 Nov 1845, Green Co, KY; Andrew served in the Rev War as a private from VA; **10 ch**

John (SHADDEN)[2], b. 16 Nov 1761, bp 6 Feb 1762, Chesterfield Co, VA; m. Feb 1788, Chesterfield Co, VA, Sarah Wilkinson (c. 1762-c. 1852); was a farmer; Rev War pensioner; he d. 21 Jan 1843, Franklin (now Williamson) Co, IL; **9 or 10 ch**

Jesse (SHADWIN/SHADRONE)[2], b. 18 Sep , bp Oct 1763, Chesterfield Co, VA; soldier; d. c. 1825, NC

David[2], b. 15 Feb, bp 8 Mar 1766, Chesterfield Co, VA; m. 29 Sep 1793, Buckingham Co, VA, Mary David (b. c. 1765); farmer; he d. 16 Aug 1839, Marion Co, TN; **issue**

CHILDREN, prob. m/2:

William[2], b. c. 1783; m. a. 1811, Lucy Moody, d/o John and Susannah (X) Moody; he d. c. 1835/6, Pulaski Co, KY

Reuben[2], b. c. 1785; m/1, ?Elizabeth Stewart (d. c. 1820); m/2, 19 May 1841, Matilda Hooper (b. c. 1819); he was a teacher and farmer; d. 3 Aug 1846, Dickson Co, TN; **issue**

*not d/o Samuel's 2nd wife Frances/Françoise (L'Orange) Guerrant (widow of Daniel, s/o Daniel & Marie (X) (Guerrant) Souillie (widow of Nicolas)

REF: SMITH, Gloria J. C., *Chaudoins of Virginia 1750-1900* (MD, 1995); ALLEN, Cameron, "Francis (François) Chaudoin (c. 1717/18-1799/1800) of Manakin Town and of Buckingham Co, VA An Outline of the 1st 3 Generations of His Descendants" in *The Virginia Genealogist,* Vol. 40, #2, #3 (1996), Vol. 41, #1 (1997); Will of Samuel Weaver; CABELL, Priscilla Harris, *Turff & Twigg,* Vol. One, *The French Lands* (Richmond, VA, 1988) .

CHENEAU/CHENAULT, Étienne

b. c. 1675, Languedoc Province, s.e. FR
went from Nîmes, on the eastern edge of Languedoc, to London
m. c. 1700, ENG, Mary Elizabeth Howlett
arr VA, Mar 1701, at Yorktown, on *Le Nasseau* with wife, no ch
settled Manakin Town; then to Essex Co, VA
d. p. 1741, Essex Co, VA
CHILDREN:
Howlett/Hugo[2], b. c. 1701/2, Essex Co, VA; m. XX; d. a. 20 Feb 1738, Essex Co, VA
      CHILDREN: **Stephen**[3], **John**[3], *poss* 3 other sons
Stephen, Jr.[2], b. c. 1703
John[2], b. c. 1705; m. Ann X; d. a. 17 Jun 1740, wp, Essex Co, VA
      CHILDREN: **John**[3], **Elizabeth**[3]
Mary (?), b. c. 1707; m. William Ballard
Benjamin (?), b. c. 1710; m. XX; **6 ch**
William (?), b. c. 1712; m. c. 1732, XX; d. 1780; **issue**

REF: SPARACIO, Ruth & Sam, editors, *Virginia County Court Records, Essex Co, 1735-1743*; Rogers, Charlton B., Jr., *Descendants of Estienne Chenault* (1978) CHENAULT, Belle Montgomery, *Descendants of Estienne Chenault* (1992).

CHEVRON/CHEUVRONT/CHEAUVANT, Joseph Louis

b. 2 Feb 1757, Strasbourg, Bas-Rhin Dépt., Alsace, FR, s/o François & Nicole (Fèbre) Chevron; bp.
      Catholic, denounced Catholicism and was disowned & disinherited by his family
left for ENG as a teenager
Dec 1773 - stowed away on the *Elizabeth*, bound for VA; was bound to Moses Elsworth by the ship's
      captain to pay for his passage
m/1, c. 1777, Elizabeth Elsworth (20 Mar 1759-18 Aug 1800 Harrison Co, VA), d/o Moses Elsworth
1780 – served in the VA Militia
according to Rockingham Co, VA, Deed Book #1, p. 397, he owned 62 acres of land
by c. 1790 – ordained a Methodist minister
m/2, 2 Dec 1802, Sarah Bolin (d. 1864)
d. 25 Mar 1832 nr. Good Hope, Harrison Co, VA (now WV), s.w. of Clarksburg
CHILDREN, m/1 (proven by Bible records, Methodist Historical Society, WV Wesleyan College
      Library, Buckhannon, WV):
Mary Elizabeth[2], b. 8 Dec 1777
Catharine[2], b. 29 Sep 1779
Aaron[2], b. 14 Mar 1782
Joseph[2], b. 26 Dec 1783; d. 12 Aug 1800
Priscilla[2], b. 22 Oct 1785; d. 8 Dec 1850
Moses[2], b. 30 Dec 1787; d. 1802
Simeon[2], b. 16 Mar 1790; d. 1800
Caleb[2], b. 10 Feb 1702
Amos[2], b. 23 Apr 1794; m. 11 Sep 1819 Sarah Elizabeth Joseph; he d. 12 Jan 1873
Gideon[2], b. 14 Feb 1798; d. 14 Nov 1842
James Liteford[2,] b. 25 Feb 1798; d. 1840
CHILDREN, m/2:
Thomas[2]
Enoch[2]
Casandra[2]
David[2]

REF: JUNKIN, William & Minnie, *The Henckel Genealogy, 1500-1960* (1964), pp. 207-08; Archives of the town of Strasbourg, *Registration of Baptisms, Catholic Parish, St. Laurent Cathedral, 1757*, Book N, p. 307; *My WV Pioneer Families, The Cheuvront Family* (published online); *Minutes of the Annual Conferences of the Methodist Episcopal Church for the Years 1773-1828*, Vol. I (NY, 1840), pp. 95, 96, 101, 105, 108, 223; passenger, immigration lists showing his arrival in VA, 1773-4.

CHIBAILHE/CHIVALIER/CHIVALIE, Pierre

Chibailhe is an unusual name and prob. the "product" of phonetic spelling which can result in a variety of
      forms often far from the original; possibilities are Chebelier/Chevalier/Chivalier
from Nègrepelisse, FR (n.e. of Montauban which is in the Tarn-et-Garonne Dépt, Midi-Pyrénées, s. FR)
owner of a mill at Sapiac, s.w. of. Montauban
m. 11 Oct 1579, Bernarde de Lambrail/Lombrail
d. a. 1619, FR
CHILDREN (bp. Protestant Ch, Montauban):
Ramond[2], bp. 27 Jan 1591
Jean[2], bp. 8 Aug 1593; m. 25 Jun 1617, Marie Mariette, d/o Jean Mariette; Jean[2] was a miller of grain
      in Montauban
      CHILDREN :
      Marye[3], b. 25 Apr, bp. 4 May 1625
      Anne[3], b. 8 Mar, bp. 10 Mar 1627
      Bernarde[3], b. 1 Feb, bp. 11 Feb 1629; m. 1646, Antoine Trabuc/Trabue
Guilliamette[2], b. 16 Jul, bp. 23 Jul 1595
Pierre[2], d. p. 1622
Marye[2], d. p. 1622

REF: Church & civil records, Montauban, FR; research by James Duvall Trabue of Belleville, IL.

CHIEL/DASHIELL, Jacques de

b. 1575, Lyon, FR, s/o Guillaume de Chiel; supposedly there is a Château Chiel in Lyonnais (old province
      bet the Saône and Rhône Rivers) + possessions in Ambérieu-en-Bugey, n.e. of Lyon, in l'Ain Dépt,
      Rhône-Alpes, & especially Chazay d'Azergues, n.w. of Lyon, Rhône Dépt, Rhône-Alpes
c. 1595 - emigrated to SCOT; name became Schiell
m. 16 May 1599, Edinburgh, Elizabeth Robesoune
d. c. 1625, SCOT
CHILD:
James[2], b. 1603/4, Edinburgh; m/1, 24 Nov 1631, Margaret Inglis; m/2, 17 Oct 1639, Jenet Aitkins; he d.
      c. 1645/50
      CHILD:
      James[3], b. 1634, Edinburgh; emigrated 1653, to Northumberland Co, VA; m. 1659, VA, Ann Cannon
            (1639, Yorkshire, ENG-bet 1697-1705, Wetipquin), d/o Edward & Ann (X)   Cannon;
            1663, to Wicomico section, later Somerset Co, MD; had several civil offices; he d. a. end of
            Aug 1697, wp, Wetipquin, Somerset, MD
            CHILDREN:
            James[4], b. c. 1660, Northumberland Co; m/1, Mary Waters; m/2, Isabel Mitchell; he d. a.
                14 Mar 1708/9, Somerset Co., MD
            Thomas[4], b. 23 Apr 1666, Wicomico; m. 1686, Elizabeth Mitchell (b. 27 Dec 1670, Great
                Monie), d/o George & Isabel (Higgins) Mitchell; he d. a. 17 Feb 1755/6, wp,
                Monie 100; **12 ch**
            George[4], b. 15 Sep 1669; m. Priscilla Mitchell, d/o George & Isabel (Higgins) Mitchell; he

118

d. 1733

Katherine[4], b. 15 Sep 1672; m. 1692/3, William Jones (b. 1666), s/o William & Margaret (X) Jones; she d. 1696 – not in father's will; **3 ch**

Jane[4], b. 30 Jul 1675, Wetipquin; m. 1696, John Kinder (7 Mar 1676 Wicomico-1716), s/o John & Bridget (X) Kinder; **6 ch**

Robert[4], b. 22 Sep 1677, Wetipquin; m. Sarah Haste; he d. 1718

REF: TORRENCE, Clayton, *Old Somerset on the Eastern Shore of MD* (1966); GANNON, Peter S., editor, *Huguenot Refugees in the Settling of Colonial America* (1985); *A Biographical Dictionary of the MD Legislature, 1635-1789*, Vol. 1; DASHIELL. Benjamin J., *Dashiell Family Records,* Vol I (1928).

CLARISSE, Jean/Jehan

b. Tourcoing, FR (n.e. of Lille, then Flanders), s/o Mathieu (d. a. 1600) & Jeanne (X) Clarisse (d. 6 Jan 1599/1600, Canterbury, ENG) - they also had a dau **Marie** who m. 26 Oct 1595, Canterbury, Abraham Flamen (b. in Sandwich, ENG), s/o Antoine Flamen

Clarisse family was in Canterbury by midsummer 1575

m. 20 Apr 1600, Canterbury, Sara LeConte (b. Anvers/Antwerp, now BEL-d. 30 Sep 1605 Canterbury), d/o Antoine LeConte

CHILDREN:

Samuel[2], bp. 8 Feb 1600/1, Canterbury

Catherine[2], bp. 17 Mar 1602/3, Canterbury; m. 25 Aug 1622, Canterbury, Pierre DuBois II, s/o Pierre I & Jeanne (Desmuille) DuBois; she d. 17 Sep 1633, Canterbury

REF: *NYGBR*, Vol. XCIV (1963); HOVENDEN, Robert, "The Registers of the Walloon or Strangers Church in Canterbury", Part I (Lymington, 1891), Part II (1894), Parts II, III (Lymington, 1898).

CLAUDE/CLAUD, Philippe

b. FR

20 Sep 1700 - arr Jamestown, VA, on the *Peter and Anthony*, from London; French refugee

1705 - naturalized

m. a. 1706 VA, Hannah X; she m/2, Richard Rayne

d. a. 12 Apr 1720, inv, Prince George Co, VA

CHILDREN:

Joshua[2], b. c. 1706/10; m. a. 1746, X Blake, d/o William & Mary (X) Blake; she d. a. 16 Oct 1773, Southampton Co; he d. 4 Nov 1775; wp,14 Dec 1775, Southampton Co, VA, which names his ch

CHILDREN:

William[3], b. Southampton Co; m. a. 14 Apr 1774, Charlotte Turner, d/o John Turner; she d. p. 1809, Southampton Co; he d. a. 1811, Southampton Co; **7 ch**

Phillip[3], m. Elizabeth X; he d. p. 15 Jan 1773, wd-a 10 Jun 1773, wp, Southampton Co

John[3]

Phebe[3], m. X Lundy

Elizabeth[3], m. X Mundell

Mary[3], m. X Williamson

Lidia[3], m. John Clifton

Joshua[3], d. c. 1776, Southampton Co.

Joseph[2], b. a. 1716; d. p. 14 Nov 1771 (was an appraiser of an estate on that date)

REF: DOBBINS, Anne White, *Some Descendants of Phillipe* (sic) *Claud Huguenot Immigrant to VA*; BROCK, R. A., *Documents...Relating to the Huguenot Emigration to VA* (1962); WEISIGER, Benjamin B. II, *Prince George Co, VA Wills & Deeds, 1713-1728* (1973).

CLAVELL/CLEWELL, François

b. Grenoble, Dauphiné, FR

fled from FR to Geneva, SWI, then to Baden, GER (Baden, a *Land*, in the s.w. corner of GER, just across the Rhine River from FR)

m. 1718, Auerbach, Baden, Louisa Frache (5 Dec 1695, Geneva-5 Oct 1767, Schoeneck, PA); she m/2, c. 1731, Johannes G'Fellern/Gefaeller-1 dau who d. young; m/3, a. 1750, Johannes Kuechle(y), fa/o her daus-in-law; Johannes d. c. 1756

d. 1730, Auerbach

5 Oct 1737 – Louisa, Johannes + her 2 sons sailed on the *Billender Townshead* from Amsterdam; en route, Johannes d., Louisa arr Philadelphia, a widow again

CHILDREN :

Johannes Franz/John Francis[2], b. 27 Sep 1720; m. Sep 1744, Seloma/Salome Küchleine/Kuechle (15 Jan 1728, Neureuth-18 May 1812, Nazareth, PA), sis to his bro's wife; he d. 24 Jan 1798

CHILDREN (12):

Maria Magdelena[3] (13 Jun 1745-20 Sep 1806) d. unmarr.; **Elizabeth**[3] (18 Nov 1746-16 Nov 1818), m. Leonard Koehler; **Catherine**[3] (10 Oct 1748-25 Oct 1789), m. 9 Jun 1771, Johannes Heckendorn; **John**[3] (21 Apr 1750-28 Apr 1828), m. Anna Johanna Klein; **Anna Maria**[3] (24 Jun 1752-24 Mar (1835), m. John Frederick Danke; **Francis**[3] (22 Jul 1754-4 Feb 1818), m. Anna E. E. Weinland; **Rosina**[3] (29 Sep 1757-16 Mar 1836), d. unmarr.; **Nathaniel**[3] (23 Oct 1759-25 Oct 1760); **Saloma**[3] (2 Feb 1761-10 Feb 1816), d. unmarr.; **Christina**[3] (21 Sep 1762-6 Apr 1810) d. unmarr.; **Nathaniel**[3] (25 Jan 1765-25 Jul 1814), m. Elizabeth Klein; **Julianna**[3] (16 Mar-1768-16 May 1846) d. unmarr.; **Anna Dorothea**[3] (28 Sep 1769-16 Feb 1840), m. Conrad Kreuser

George Craft[2], b. 18 Nov 1726, Auerbach; m. Oley, PA, 16 Oct 1750, Anna Maria Küchleine/Kuechle (26 Aug 1726, Neureuth-19 Mar 1809, Schoeneck, PA); he d. Schoeneck, 6 May 1793

CHILDREN (12):

Jacob[3], (21 Sep 1751-22 Jun 1824), m. 5 Dec 1775, Schoeneck, Anna Catherina Roehrig (29 Jan 1753-15 Apr 1824); **Elizabeth**[3] (16 Mar 1753-19 Sep 1833), m. George Clauss; **John**[3] (12 Sep 1754-30 Sep 1827), m. Christina Weinland; **Daniel**[3] (14 Feb 1756-29 Apr 1844), m. Susanna Klein; **George**[3] (11 Mar 1758-17 Mar 1816), m. Anna Johanna Knauss; **Joseph**[3] (3 Aug 1760-30 Jun 1832), m. Magdalena Knauss; **Abraham**[3] (9 Jan 1762-8 May 1762) d. unmarr.; **Francis**[3] (30 Mar 1763-2 Mar 1816), m. Anna Maria Leinbach; **Anna Catherine**[3] (3 Dec 1765-11 Feb 1829), m. Joseph Levering; **Saloma Maria**[3] (3 May 1767-2 Mar 1842), d. unmarr.; **Christian**[3] (2 Nov 1770-14 Aug 1847), m. Maria R. Kreider; **Abraham**[3] (11 Jul 1776-11 May 1854), m. Sarah E. Boeman

REF: Records of Moravian Churches, Bethlehem & Schoeneck, PA; CLEWELL, Lewis B, & Rev. Lewis P., *History of the Clewell Family in the USA 1737-1907* (1907).

COCHERON, Jean

b. Lille, FR

m. Mary X; his will mentions her but it is not clear if she was the mother of any of his children

d. 3 Sep 1696; wp 1696, Staten Island, NY

CHILDREN:

Nicholas[2], b. c. 1648; m. c. 1676, Anne X; he d. a. 23 Dec 1707, wp ,Staten Island

Anthony[2], d. unmarr., by 14 Dec 1697

Adrianna[2], m. 24 Oct 1677, Jacques Poillon (c. 1646-a. 14 Jun 1720, wp); she d. 1718/20; ch-

Jean[3], **Jacques**[3] who m. Françoise Billiou, *prob.* d/o Jacob Billiou & Margaret Larzelère

Katherine[2], m. 1677, Abraham Lakerman (b. 1660/61); d. Mar/Apr 1734, Staten Island

Marie[2], b. c. 1660; m. 11 Jan 1680, Jean Bodine; she d. a. 10 Feb 1702/03

Jean/John[2], b. c. 1658; m/1, 3 May 1682, Hester Lutine, d/o Walraven & Hester (Donrinees) Lutin, m/2, 28 Apr 1713/4, Mary Morgan, d/o John & Frances (Bellin) Morgan; d. a.7 Jun 1727, wp

Jannetje[2], b. c. 1660's; m. 25 Sep 1682, Gerret Klaasz Vechten; d. a. 1693

Margaret[2], m. 13 Apr 1684, Peter Van Ness; d. a. 2 May 1697

REF: MORRIS, I. K., *Memorial History of Staten Island* (1900); LENG, L.W. & DAVIS, W.T., *Staten Island and Its People,* Vol. 2, 3 (1930); CLUTE, J. J., *Old Families of Staten Island* (Baltimore, 1990); HIX, Charlotte M., *Staten Island Wills & Letters of Administration, Richmond Co, NY, 1670-1800* (Bowie, MD, 1993); *Proceedings of the Huguenot Society of America,* (1964), p. 89; HIX, Charlotte, M., "*The Crocheron Family of Staten Island:* in the *NYGBR,* Vol. 111 (Jan-Oct, 1980), Vol. 112, (Jan, 1981).

COLIGNY, Gaspard de, Comte de Châtillon, Admiral of France

b. 16 Feb 1519, Châtillon-sur-Loing, now Châtillon-Coligny, s.e. of Montargis, in the Loiret Dépt., Centre, c. 100 mi s.e. of Paris, s/o Gaspard de Coligny, maréchal de Châtillon, & Louise (de Montmorency) de Mailly, widow of Frédéric de Mailly, Baron of Conty

m/1, 16 Oct 1547, Fontainebleau, Charlotte de Laval (1530-3 Mar 1568), d/o Guy & Antoinette (de Daillon) de Laval

Gaspard participated in many battles and was one of the leaders of the Protestant movement in FR

1552 – made Admiral of France

1557 – he was imprisoned in the stronghold of l'Écluse after the loss at St. Quentin and had to pay a large ransom (50,000 *écus* or crowns, roughly 75,000 *francs*) for his release; supposedly he converted to Protestantism during his imprisonment; l'Écluse is located in the Ain Dépt, Rhône-Alpes, n.e. of Bellegarde-sur-Valerine and s.w. of Geneva, SWI

1562 – leading patron of the FR colony of Fort Caroline in Florida; FL was then a Spanish possession

1569 – sole leader of the Protestant armies

m/2, c. 1571, Jacqueline de Montbel, Comtesse d'Entremont et Launay-Gelin (1541-1588)

22 Aug 1572 – he was wounded in an assassination attempt planned by the Queen Mother Cathérine de Médici and Henri, the 3rd Duc de Guise, s/o François de Guise, who had once been Gaspard's friend but was murdered by the Huguenot Jean Poltrot de Méré; Maurevel was the name of the shooter – Gaspard lost a finger on his right hand and his left elbow was shattered

d. 24 Aug 1572 Paris – he was stabbed in his house by a servant of the Duc de Guise and his body thrown from an upper window into the street below, where his head was cut off

CHILDREN, m/1:

Henri[2], d. at 15 mo.

Gaspard[2], b. 28 Sep 1554; d. age 15

François[2], b. 28 Apr 1557; Admiral of Guienne; m. Marguerite d'Ailly de Péquigny – **4 ch**; he d. 8 Oct 1591

    CHILD (1 of 4):

    Gaspard[3], (1584-1646), marshal of France during the reign of Louis XIII

Odet[2], b. 24 Dec 1560; d. unmarr.

Louise[2], b. 1555; m/1, Charles de Téligny; m/2, William *the Silent*, Prince of Orange (1533-1584)

Renée[2], b. 1561; d. young

Charles[2], (1564-1632), brought up in a convent, restored to fam in 1577; abjured Protestantism & joined the de Guise faction; became Marquis d'Andelot; a Lt. Gen. in Champagne

CHILD, m/2 :

Béatrice/Béatrix[2], b. 1572 (posthumous); became the Comtesse d'Entremont

NOTE: In previous *Registers* there is reference to a dau Annietta who m. Jean/John Furnius Fernel – the biographies of Gaspard de Coligny do not mention her and are consistent with the fact that Gaspard had 4 sons and 3 daus – the daus named above. None of the de Coligny sons had a dau named Anniette either.

REF: *Merit Students Encyclopedia*; BERSIER, Eugene, *Coligny – The Earlier Life of the Great Huguenot* (translation, London, 1884); BESANT, Walter, *Gaspard de Coligny* (London, 1905).

COLLIN, Jean

from the Île de Ré, FR

m. 24 Feb 1643, LaRochelle, Judith Valleau, prob. d/o Nicolas & Marguerite (Plondreau) Valleau who
      m. 1623, LaRochelle

spring 1664 – Jean sailed from the Île de Ré to New Amsterdam to research that area for emigration.

CHILDREN:

Jean[2], b. 23 Jul, bp. 29 Jul 1644, Temple at St. Martin de Ré

Judith[2], b. & bp. 25 Aug 1646, La Rochelle

Paul[2], b. Île de Ré; m. Marie Germon (d. RI); fled Île de Ré in 1683 and went to Dublin, IRE; then settled in the
      Narragansett Colony in RI in 1686; went to Milford, CT c. 1691; in NY 1721

    CHILDREN:

    Paul[3], b. 25 Aug, bp. 23 Sep 1688, Narragansett, RI

    Marthe[3], b. 26 Jan, bp. 2 Mar 1690; d. 2 Mar 1690

    John[3], b. 1706; m. 29 Oct 1730, Milford, CT, Hannah Merwin (2 Nov 1709, Milford-19 Apr
      1790, Dutchess Co, NY), d/o John & Hannah (Platt) Merwin; he d. 1746 (lost at sea);
      3 sons

Pierre[2], 1696, went to SC, nr. Charleston, to settle

REF: Archives of LaRochelle; STRONG, Ruth Collin, *John Collin Stern and Branches. The Descendants of Capt. John Collin and His Wife Hannah Merwin Collin of Milford, CT* (1980); COLLINS, John Francis, *A History of Hillsdale, Columbia Co, NY* (1883); DeFOREST, L. Effingham, *Records of the French Church at Narragansett, 1686-1691,* NY Genealogical & Biographical Record, Vol. LXX, LXXI; BAIRD, Charles W., *History of the Huguenot Emigration to America*; *The Burying Place of Gov. Arnold.*

COQUEFAIRE/COCKEFAIR/COCKEVER, Alexandre

b. a. 1644, FR

1657 - arr America

1663 - settled Bushwick, LI, NY, where he bought a plantation; drum major of militia in Bushwick; appt.
    corporal , 14 Jun 1663

m/1, c. 23 Apr 1665, Judith Jans – he pd. a marriage fee of 6 guilders on that date to the Flatbush Church;
    Judith (c. 1644-a. 1684) sailed from Leiden, 12 Oct 1662

1687- took Oath of Allegiance at Bushwick; rec. says he was "foreign-born" and had been in America 30 yrs.

m/2, c. 1684, Winifred X; she d. p. 1699

    1698 - he was on the census of Kings Co, NY (Bushwick), listed as being FR w/ wife, 6 ch; on an
    assessment list of the West Ward of NYC, 15 Jul 1699

d. a. Dec 1699, transfer of property

CHILDREN, m/1:

Jan/John[2], b. 1666, Bushwick; m. Charity X (d. p. 14 Sep 1750); he d. c. Nov 1763, Jamaica, NY (d. p.
    14 Sep 1750, wd - a. 12 Dec 1763, wp, Queens Co, NY); **no known issue**

Cataline/Caroline[2], bp. 15 May 1667, Dutch Ch, Bushwick; **no known marriage or issue**

Stineche/Christina[2], b. 1668/9, Bushwick; m/1, XX, ch – **Mary**[3], m. a. 1750, Daniel Corenell, she d. p.
    1750; **Leah/Seal**[3], d. p. 1750; m/2, Thomas Farmer of Jamaica, LI, NY, a widower with 2 daus - **no
    known issue**; she d. p. 14 Sep 1750

CHILDREN, m/2 (all bp. noted were in the Reformed Dutch Ch, NYC):

Catherina/Trinche/Tryntje[2], b.1684; m/1, Willem Gerritsen (1679- ?) – 1 son **Gysbert**[3], bp. 4 Apr 1704,
    Jamaica, NY; m/2, c. 1705/6, Gideon Carstang (d. 10 Aug 1759, NYC) - 5 sons, **Jan**[3], **Isaac**[3] (bp. 2
    May 1714), **Gideon**[3] (bp. 6 May 1716, d. young), **Peter**[3] (bp. 1 Apr 1722), Gideon[3] (bp. 3 May 1724),
    & 5 daus, **Maria**[3], **Martha**[3], **Jannetje**[3] (bp. 21 Apr 1712, aunt Jannetje[2] was a witness), **Catharine**[3]
    (bp. 2 Feb 1718), **Judith**[3]; she d. 23 Jun 1759, NYC; Catherina is *prob.* the d/o Alexandre's 2nd wife

Marytje/Maria[2], b. c. 1687/8; m. c. 1709, Richard Care; 2 sons - **Johannes**[3] (bp. 23 Apr 1710), **Jan**[3] (bp. 4
    Sep 1713), 1 dau **Marytje**[3] (bp. 13 Feb 1712)

Helena/Lena[2], b. c. 1690; m. c. 1711, Cornelus Bunsen/Bulsing/Boolsan; she d. p. 14 Sep 1750; 2 daus
    Neeltje[3], **Johanna**[3]

Jannetje/Jane[2], b. 1692; m. 27 Jul 1713, Jamaica, Nicholas Lambert; she d. a. 14 Sep 1750; 2 sons **Jan/**
    John[3], **Simeon**[3], 3 daus **Stineche/Tryntje**[3], **Mary**[3], **Judith**[3]

Dara(c)k[2], b. c. 1694; moved to NJ; d. p. 1715

Sander/Alexander[2], b. c. 1696/7; m. c. 1718, Johanna Kindt; moved to Belleville, NJ; he d. p. 26 Jul 1741;
    2 sons **Alexander**[3] (bp. 1721), **Jan/Johannes**[3] (b. 6 May 1735), 3 daus **Tryntje**[3], **Elizabeth**[3],
    Judith[3]; fam. owned a tract of land nr. Third River, at Stone House Plains, Essex Co, NJ

REF: BERGEN, Teunis G., *Register of Early Settlers of Kings Co;* NYGBR, Vol. LVIII (Jul 1927), KERR, John, *"Who Was the Tryntie (Catherine) Cockever Who Married Gideon Carstang?"*; NYGBR, Vol. XIV (Oct, 1883), *"List of Early Immigrants to New Netherland"*; Tax Lists and Census Records; NYGBR (1987), *"Genealogy of Long Island Families"*.

COQUIEL, Jehan de, dit le Mercier, Seigneur d'Aischaval

(Jehan de Coquiel dit le Mercier)

b. 1530, Tournai, FR (now BEL), s/o Renaud & Antoinette (Thérissart, Dame d'Aischaval) de Coquiel,
    both b. Tournai; family can be traced back to the 1200's in the Tournai area

c. 1550, m. Peronne de la Hoüe of Ypres (now Ieper, BEL) who d. a. 18 Oct 1579

1568 - went to London; the term *"le mercier"* prob. refers to Jehan's occupation – merchant; eventually
    mercier became the family name

d. ENG

CHILD:

Jean/Jan[2], b. c. 1559, Tournai, Hainaut, now BEL; m. 18 Oct 1579, Southampton, ENG, Jeanne/Janne Le
    Clerc (b. Valenciennes, Hainaut, now Nord, Pas-de- Calais Dépt, FR -d. 28 Mar 1620/1, ENG),
    d/o Arnould & Jeanne (Lippenson) Le Clerc; he d. 3 Jan 1625/6, prob. ENG; called Jean Le
    MERCIER DIT COQUIEL

    CHILDREN, surname **MERCER**:

    Jane[3], b. 3 Jun 1581; m. Pierre/Peter Pryaulx, a merchant of Southampton who d. a. 31 Dec 1644,
        wp; **7 ch**

    Marie/Mary[3], bp. 1 Sep 1582; m. Martin Vander Bist, merchant of La Rochelle; d. a. 3 Nov
        1631, wp; **no issue**

    Elizabeth[3], b. 9 Jun 1586; m/1, X Stroad (d. by 1608), m/2, X Blanchard; **issue**

    Judith[3], bp. 30 May 1587; m. X Johnson (d. 1650-51); **2 daus**

    Pierre/Peter[3], bp. 29 Aug 1588; d. p. 1667; dau **Hester**[4] who m. Thomas Cary; son **Thomas**[4]

    Philippe[3], bp. 14 Dec 1589; d. young

    Hester/Esther[3], bp. 23 May 1591; d. young

    Philippe[3], bp. 3 Mar 1593

    Samuel[3], bp. 4 Sep 1594; d. a. 1650

    Anne[3], bp. 2 Jul 1600; m. Peter Houblon; d. a. 1661

    Daniel[3], bp. 24 Jul 1601; m. Sarah (X) Houblon, widow; d. a. 6 Sep 1650, wp; he was a dyer of
        St. Olave, Southwark; **3 ch**

    Hester/Esther[3], bp. 1 Aug 1602, Huguenot Ch, Southampton; m. Nathaniel Batcheller (1590,
        ENG-c. 1630/45, prob. ENG), s/o Stephen & Ann (X) Bachiler; she d. a. 1650; **5 ch**;
        their son Nathaniel[4] went to New England where name became Batchelder – he m. 3
        times, had **17 ch**

    Francis[3], minister at Godmanstone, Dorset, ENG (n. of Dorchester); m. widow Katherine (X)
        Browne; he d. p. 31 Jan 1668 wp; **5 ch**

    Paul[3], unmarr. merchant of Southampton; d. a. 9 Sep 1661, wp

REF: GODFRAY, Humphrey Marett, *Registre des Baptesmes Mariages et Morts et Jeusnes de l'Église Wallonne et des Isle de Jersey, Guernsey, Serq, Origny, etc. Etablié à Southampton par Patente du roy Édouard Six[e] et de la Reine*

Elizabeth (Lymington, 1890); PIERCE, Frederick Clifton, *Batchelder, Batcheller Genealogy* (Chicago, 1898); WEIS, Frederick Lewis, *Sir William Phips, Governor-General of New England* (1963); ANDERSON, Robert Charles, *The Great Migration Begins*, Vol. I (Boston, 1995); "Genealogical Gleanings in England" in the *NEHG Register*, Vol. XLVII (Boston, Oct 1893).

COQUILLET, François

b. c. 1665, FR
m. Silvie Sicard, d/o <u>Ambroise Sicard</u>
by 1701- in New Rochelle; a blacksmith
1715 – sold his property & moved to Mamaroneck, Westchester Co, NY, until 1729 when he went to Tappan, Rockland Co, NY
d. c. 1733, prob. Tappan
CHILDREN:
Sylvie[2], m. Abraham Mabille/Mabie (bp. 18 Nov 1705 NYC), s/o Caspar (bp 15 Feb 1660 NYC) & Elizabeth (Schuerman) Mabille/Mabie who m. 14 Dec 1687, Dutch Ch, NYC, & grs/o <u>Pierre Mabille</u>; bap. of ch Trinity Ch, New Rochelle
François[2]???

REF: SEACORD, Morgan H., *Biographical Sketches and Index of the Huguenot Settlers of New Rochelle, 1687-1776* (New Rochelle, 1941), pp. 17, 37; FRISBEE, Edward S., *The Frisbee-Frisbie Genealogy* (Albany, 1919); FROST, Josephine C., *Ancestors of Evelyn Wood Keller, Wife of Willard Underhill Taylor* (1939).

CORLIEZ, Antoine

b. 12 Jun 1568, Noyon, Oise Dépt. Picardie, FR, n.e. of Compiègne; bp. 3 Feb 1568/9, Noyon, s/o Antoine & Henriette (Auger) Corliez
1587- apprenticed to Jean DuBois, a goldsmith of Rotterdam, HOL
1593- went to London where he is listed as a merchant goldsmith of Billingsgate Ward
m/1, 1605, Noyon, Marie DuBois (c. 1585, Noyon-c. 1615, Noyon)
1609 - returned to FR
m/2, 2 Apr 1617, Noyon, Marguerite Baudoin/Beaudoine (c. 1590, Noyon-c. 1650, Noyon)
d. 3 Sep 1650, Noyon
CHILD, m/1:
Marie[2], b. 3 Dec 1609, Noyon; d. c. 1680, London
CHILDREN, m/2:
George[2], b. 8 Jan 1617/8; emig. 1639, to Newbury, MA; m. 26 Oct 1645, Haverhill, MA, Joanna Davis; 18 Oct 1686, wd; he d. 19 Oct 1686, Haverhill; used surnames of **CORLIES, CORLISS**
    CHILDREN, b. Haverhill:
    Mary[3], b. 8 Sep 1646, m. 23 Jan 1665/6, William Neff; **John**[3], b. 4 Mar 1647/8, m. 17 Dec 1684, Mary Wilford; **Joanna**[3], b. 28 Apr 1650, m. 29 Dec 1669, Joseph Hutchins; **Martha**[3], b. 2 Jan 1652/3, m. 1 Dec 1674, Samuel Ladd; **Deborah**[3], b. 6 Jun 1655, m. 20 Jan 1679/80, Thomas Eastman; **Ann**[3], b. 8 Nov 1657, m. 1 Nov 1677, John Robie; **Huldah**[3], b. 18 Nov 1661, m. 5 Nov 1679, Samuel Kingbury; **Sarah**[3], b. 23 Feb 1663/4, m. 24 Nov 1686, Joseph Ayer
Jean[2], b. 11 Feb 1618/9 Noyon; emigrated to ENG, then to IRE a. 1648; m. 1648, Elizabeth Synnott (c. 1628-c. 1700), d/o James Synnott; resided Durgan St., Dublin
    CHILDREN, b. Dublin:
    Nicholas[3], b. 16 Nov 1650; m. 4 Aug 1675, Mary Kinney; he'd. c. 1720, Dublin
    Jane[3], b. 11 Sep 1651; m. Michael Erikson of Jönköping, SWE; she d. c. 1720, Jönköping
    William[3], b. 19 Aug 1652; m. 14 May 1679, Sophia Shay; d. c. 1720, Dublin
    George[3], b. 7 Feb 1653/4; emig. a. 1680, Shrewsbury, NJ; was a Quaker; <u>m/1</u>, 10 Dec 1680, Exercise Shattuck (12 Nov 1656, Boston-14 Nov 1695, Shrewsbury), d/o William & Hannah Shatuck;

m/2, 23 Nov 1699, Deborah Hance (1 May 1675, Shrewsbury-3 Apr 1757,Shrewsbury), d/o
John & Elizabeth (Hanson) Hance; he d. 10 Sep 1715, Shrewsbury; 25 Aug 1715, wd-23 Nov
1715,wp – names wife Deborah, ch John, William, Elizabeth, Mary, Benjamin, Timothy,
Deborah, Dinah, George, Joseph, an expected ch, 5 ch of dec. dau Hannah who are named;
used surnames **Corleis, Curlies, Curlis(s)**; Geo. was a cordwainer/shoemaker
CHILDREN, m/1:
John[4], b. 11 Mar 1681/2; m. 2 Feb 1707/8, Naomi Edwards (c. 1689-1756), d/o Abiah
& Elizabeth (X) Edwards; he d. a. 28 May 1750; **5 ch**
Hannah[4], b. 25 Oct 1684; m. 18 Jan 1702/3, Henry Allen; she d. 15 Mar 1712/3; **5 ch**
Elizabeth[4], b. 1 Jul 1687; m. 26 Jan 1703/4, William Brinley, Jr.; she d. a. 19 Sep
1739
William, b. 15 Jul 1689; m/1, c. 1715, Jerusha West, d/o John & Jane (Wing) West;
m/2, 13 Jan 1730/1, Sarah Wing; he d. a. 10 Apr 1754, inv
Mary[4], b. 31 Mar 1691/2; m. 1716, Jonathan Allen; she d. c. 1748
George[4], b. 19 Oct 1694; m. 1726, Sarah West; he d. c. 1789
CHILDREN, m/2:
Thomas[4], b. 3 Nov 1700; d. 23 Jan 1700/1
Deborah[4], b. 11 Apr 1702; m. 12 Dec 1727, Walter Herbert III; she d. 3 Apr 1757
Joseph[4], b. 14 Mar 1704/5; m. 1730, Margaret Woodmansee; he d. 26 Mar 1784
Benjamin[4], b. 31 Aug 1707; m. 24 Mar 1731/2, Mary Jackson; he d. 11 Oct 1739
Timothy[4], b. 10 Apr 1710; d. 23 Mar 1732/3; unmarr.
Dinah[4], b. 17 Dec 1712; m. 19 Dec 1734, Britton White; she d. 1798
Jacob[4], b. 14 Oct 1715; m. 22 Dec 1737, Sarah White; he d. 8 Dec 1767
Nicol[2], b. 7 Sep 162?, Noyon; m. Josephine Budd; liv. London
Louis[2], b. 14 Aug 1622, Noyon; m. Marie Dudevant; liv. FR

REF: SMITH, Barbara C., *George Corlies & Some of His Descendants, A Quaker Family of Monmouth Co, NJ*;
NELSON, William, *Documents Relating to the Colonial History of the State of NJ, Wills, Vol. 1 -1670-1730* (1901); Vital
Records, Haverhill, MA; SALTER, Edwin, *A History of Monmouth & Ocean Counties* (1890); STILWELL, John E.,
Unrecorded Wills & Inventories, Monmouth Co, NJ (1975).

CORTELYOU/CORTELJOU, Ja(c)ques

b. c. 1625, Utrecht, HOL; bp. at the Walloon Church there, s/o Jacques & Elsken (Hendricks) Cortelyou;
Jacques, Sr. was a Walloon who had fled FR
1643 – attended the Univ. of Utrecht; he studied philosophy; spoke Latin and French, he was a mathematician,
had knowledge of several sciences and some knowledge of medicine; "a man of many parts"
p. 26 Apr 1652 - to America to serve as a tutor to the sons of Cornelis van Werckhoven, *schepen* (city father) of
Amsterdam, who went to New Netherland to establish 2 colonies; Jacques was also a land surveyor and
helped his patron during his inspection trips
m. c. 1655/6, New Amsterdam, Neeltje Van Duyn, d/o Cornelius Gerrit Van Duyn & Macktelje Huyken;
she d. a. Dec 1695
23 Jan 1657 – became surveyor general for the colony; he laid out, surveyed & divided land for 50 acre
lots in New Utrecht with a lot for himself at Najack (now Ft. Hamilton on the tip of Brooklyn,
just s. of the Verrazano-Narrows Bridge)
Sep 1687- swore allegiance to England
d. a. 24 Jul 1693, when an agreement was reached re the settlement of Jacques' estate by his ch – all ch
but Cornelis & William are named; mentions orphan ch **Annetje**[3], d/o Cornelis[2]
CHILDREN:
unnamed ch[2], b/d 1657, 1st ch b. New Utrecht
Jaques[2], b. 1660; m/1, 4 Oct 1685, Marretje Hendricks Smack (d. 7 Apr 1705), d/o Hendrick Matthyse
Smack/Smock & Geertje Harmens Coerten– **8 ch**; m/2, 10 Jan 1706, Altie Boerman (d. 1732)

– **7 ch**; he d. 3 May 1731

Cornelis[2], b. c. 1662; m. Neeltje Volckers, prob. d/o Volkert Dircks & Neeltje Cornelissen; he d. a. Sep 1692; **1 dau**; Neeltje m/2, 1692, Johannes Van der Grift

Pieter[2], b. c. 1664/5; m. c. 1691/2, Deborah/Diewertje DeWitt; he d. 10 Apr 1757; **10 ch**

Helena[2], b. c. 1666?; m/1, 19 Sep 1683, New Utrecht, Nicholas Rutgersz Van Brunt – **1 ch**; m/2, 12 Apr 1685, New Utrecht, Denyse Teunissen (widower of Elizabeth Polhemus) – **7 ch**; m/3, Hendrick Henrickse Hafte – **2 ch**; she d. p. 1726

Maria[2], b. c. 1669?; m. 1697, Willem Willemse Barkelo/Barkald – **5 ch**

Willem/William[2], b. c. 1671?; d. a. 1693; **no issue**

REF: CORTELYOU, John Van Zandt, *The Cortelyou Genealogy* (1942); BAILEY, Rosalie F., *Pre-Revolutionary Dutch Houses & Families;* BERGEN, Teunis G., *Register of the Early Settlers of Kings Co, Long Island, NY* (1881); Huguenot Society of America, *Huguenot Refugees in the Settling of Colonial America*; DILLIARD, Maud Esther, *Old Dutch Houses of Brooklyn* (1945).

COSSART/COZART, Jacques

b. 1595, FR, poss. Picardie or Normandie

by 1607- family was in Liège, Liège Prov. (now BEL) – a Walloon center

m. c. 1630, Rachel(le) Gelton of Liège

went to Amsterdam, then to Leiden; he was a merchant

d. p. 1639

CHILDREN:

Rachelle[2], bp 24 Jun 1632, Amsterdam, HOL

poss. 2 sons[2] – "family tradition" says they emigrated to America; one remained and the other returned to Europe with the intent of renouncing his Huguenot faith in order to reclaim the family fortune; there was a Jan Cossart, a wealthy merchant of NYC, who d. there c. 1700, also a Dr. George/Joris Cossart who was said to have returned to Europe on a ship that was lost at sea; any relationship to Jacques is currently conjecture

Jacques[2], bp. 29 May 1639, Leiden; m. 14 Aug 1656, Frankenthal, Bavaria, GER, in the *Pfalz*, Lea/Lydia Willems/Villeman; 14 Oct 1662, sailed from Amsterdam on the *Pumerlander Kerck* to New Amsterdam; 1 Apr 1663, joined Dutch Reformed Ch in New Amsterdam; Jacques was a mill owner; his home was on lower Broadway, at Whitehall & Marketfield Streets where the NY Produce Exchange Bldg was built in 1883; c. 1673, moved to Bushwick (now in Brooklyn) where he farmed and d. 1685; Lydia prob. d. a. 1698

CHILDREN:

Lea[3], bp. 31 May 1657, Walloon Ch of Frankenthal; prob. d. young in NY

Rachel[3], bp. 11 Nov 1658, Walloon Ch of Frankenthal; prob. d. young in GER

Susanne[3], bp. 3 Feb 1661, Walloon Ch of Frankenthal; prob. d. young in NY

Jannetje[3], b. 1665, NYC; bp. 28 Nov 1665, Dutch Ch, NY; m. 10 Jan 1668, Jacobus Goelet (bp. 1 Apr 1668, NYC, s/o Francis Goelet from LaRochelle-d. a. 21 May 1736, adm, NY); she d. 1736; **10 ch**

Jacques[3], b. 1668, NYC ; bp. 11 Apr 1668, Dutch Ch, NY; m. 1696, Ann Maria Springsteen, d/o Johannes Caspers Springsteen; he d. 1731, Brooklyn; **10 ch**; surname evolved to CASHOW, KERSHAW, etc

David[3], bp. 18 Jun 1671, NYC; m. 11 Oct 1696, Styntje Joris Van Horne, d/o Joris Janses Van Horne & Maria Rutgers; he was a stone mason, builder/contractor; he d. c. 1740, Bound Brook, Somerset, NJ; **11 ch**; surname CASSAT, etc

Anthony[3], b. 14 Nov 1673, NY, bp. 19 Nov 1673, Manhattan; m/1, 2 Aug 1696, Elizabeth Tymensen Valentine, d/o Jan Tymensen Valentine of Schenectady – **6 ch**; m/2, Judith X – **2 ch**; he d. Bound Brook, NJ; surname CASAD, COZAD, etc.

REF: BUCK, Dee Ann Shipp, *The Robert MacKay, Sr. Family History*, Vol. 23, *A Tabulated History of the Family of Jacques Cossart, Jr. & Lea Villeman*; Records from the Walloon Ch in Leiden ; COSSAIRT, Joseph A., *Cossart Family* (1933); BAIRD, Charles W., *Huguenot Emigration to America*; RIKER, James, *Revised History of Harlem* (1904); BERGEN, Teunis G., *Register of the Early Settlers of Kings Co, LI* (1881).

COTHONNEAU/CUTTINO, Jérémie

b. c. 1645, La Rochelle, FR, s/o Germain & Élisabeth (Nombret) Cothonneau

m. La Rochelle, Marye/Marie Billon

c. 1687 - to SC; he was a cooper

10 Mar 1697 - granted citizenship

d. p. Mar 1697, prob. SC

CHILDREN:

Germain[2], b. La Rochelle, FR; d. 1699; **no issue**

Pierre[2], b. La Rochelle, FR; in Berkeley Co, SC as early as 1697; m. XX; d. a. 5 Apr 1746, inv, Georgetown, SC

    CHILDREN (used surname **Cuttino**):

    Jacob[3]

    Peter[3], d. a. 10 Jun 1766, adm, Georgetown, SC; at least 1 dau (Elizabeth?) who m. X Dunnom

    Jeremiah[3], m. 10 Oct 1744, Ann Judith Bossard (b. 19 Dec 1725-16 Mar 1803), d/o Henry Bossard; he d. c. 1761; he was a gunsmith

        CHILD:

        William[4], b. 30 Nov 1747; m. c. 1770/1, Mary Elizabeth Coon; he d. 11 Sep 1806, Georgetown, bur. old Baptist Cemetery

            CHILDREN:

            Sarah[5]

            Elizabeth[5], b. 14 Sep 1773; m. 5 May 1795, Savage Smith (30 Jul 1766-7 Apr 1817); she d. 9 Nov 1827 – **10 ch**

            Mary[5], b. 1774; m/1, Thomas Hutchinson (1771-1801) – **daus**, m/2, Richard Chackelford; she d. 8 Nov 1811

            Ann Judith[5], d. 16 Mar 1805

            Peter[5], b. 14 Jul 1786; m. Elizabeth Mary/Eliza Gaillard (1786-1859) – **5 ch**; he d. 22 Apr 1833

            David William[5], b. 1789; m. 1814, Susan Parnice Park, d/o Dr. Thomas & Mary (Botsford) Park – **2 ch**; he d. 3 Apr 1820

            Henry[5], (1794-27 Jan 1856) bur. old Baptist Cem

            Thomas I[5], d. young

            Thomas II[5], d. young

            Benjamin Thomas[5] b. 21 Oct 1797, Georgetown; m. 1827, Elizabeth Ingraham Spooner (1803-1881) – **6 ch**; he d. 1 Nov 1852

Ester Marthe[2], b. SC

REF: CUTTINO, G. P., *History of the Cuttino Family* (1982); CUTTINO, G. P., "Further Notes on the History of the Cuttino Family 1687-1932" in *Transactions of the Huguenot Society of SC*, #65 (1960), #45 (1940) & #92 (1987); *"Liste des François et Suisses* - French & Swiss Protestants who settled in Charleston on the Santee & at the Orange Quarter in Carolina (1968).

COUILLANDEAU, Pierre

b. La Tremblade, Saintonge, FR; s/o Pierre & Marie (Fougeraut) Couillandeau of La Tremblade

m. FR, Susanne X; she evidently d. in FR as she is not listed with him as a refugee

he arr in SC with his mother who was described as the widow of Moïse Brigaud; Marie was m. 4 times and evidently Moïse was her 4th husband; her name and the name of her son with the name of his father appear on the "*Liste*" cited below; father d. in FR

1689 – naturalized in SC

1705/6 - founded the Huguenot town of Jamestown, SC

CHILDREN:

Pierrot[2], m. Susanne X

Susanne[2], b. c. 1668, La Tremblade; m/1, c. 1688, Isaac DuBose, s/o Louis & Anne DuBose; she m/2, 1733, Bentley Cooke; she d. c. 1740, SC

REF: "*Liste des François et Suisses*" - French & Swiss Protestants who settled in Charleston on the Santee & at the Orange Quarter in Carolina (1968); MacDOWELL, Dorothy Kelly, *DuBose Genealogy* (1972); KONOPA, Leola Wilson, "The Isaac DuBose Family of SC" in *Transactions of the Huguenot Society of SC*, Vol. #77, 78 (1992, 1993).

COU(S)TANT, Jean I

b. c.1658, FR, *poss.* Arville – not sure which one – one in Centre another in the Île de France

c. 1689 - to NY

1692 – in NYC

m.. c. 1695, Susanna Gouin (15 Dec 1675, FR-20 May 1719, NY), d/o Abraham & Jeanne (Guion) Guion

1696 - settled in New Rochelle, NY

6 Feb 1695/6 - denization granted

May 1696, NYC - signed Oath of Allegiance

d. p. 27 Mar 1713-a. 1 Mar 1715, NY

CHILDREN (4 of 8?):

Jean II[2], b. 1695; m. Elizabeth Angevine (bp. 18 Jan 1700/1-1749), d/o Zacharie & Marie (Naudin) Angevine; he d. 1747/9, New Rochelle, NY

> CHILDREN (4 of ?) :

> **Guillaume/William**[3], b. 27 Jan 1725; m. Ester X

> **Henry**[3], b. 1727; m. c. 1749, Elizabeth Chadeayne, d/o Jean & Marie (Boucherie) Chadeayne; **6 sons, 3 daus** Henry d. 12 Jul 1803

> **Elizabeth**[3], b. 19 Mar 1729; m. 1748, Daniel Gerow/Giraud III, s/o Daniel II & Catherine (Sicard) Giraud; she d. Feb 1816; **5 sons, 7 daus**

> **?Zacharie**[3], m. Catherine Hatock

> > **Isaac**[2], b. 23 Sep 1697, NY; m. 2 Feb 1717, Catherine Bonnefoy (16 Nov 1699-18 Oct 1776), d/o David Bonnefoy; Isaac d. 1747?; **2 sons, 4 daus**, incl: **Catherine**[4], b. 1726; m. 1748, Peter Badeau – **3 sons, 2 daus**

> > **Jacob**[3], b. 30 Nov 1721, New Rochelle; m. Jeanne Renaud/Arnaud (31 Oct 1722-26 Jan 1810) – dau **Jeanne/Jane**[4] (13 Mar 1745-1 Sep 1794), m. Israel Sicard/Seacord (1748-2 Nov 1819), s/o Jean/Jacques & Jeanne/Jane (Bonnet) Sicard; son **Jacob**[4], b. 1744, m. 24 Sep 17, Phoebe Liggett - **7 sons, 7 daus**, he d. 1824, Ulster Co, NY; dau **Madeleine**[4], bp. FR Ch, New Rochelle; Jacob[3], d. 14 Nov 1794, New Rochelle; wp, 30 Sep 1795 – names wife Jane, son David, daus Jane (wife of Israel "Seguar" = Seacord, Magdalen (wife of John Bailey), grson William Henry Pinckney (son of dau Hester, now wife of Caleb Russell); he was a chairmaker

Susanne[2], b. 21 Feb 1700; bp 10 Apr 1700, FR Ch, NYC

Marie[2], bp. 1 Jan 1701/2, FR Ch, NYC

Daniel[2], b. 1703

REF: SEACORD, Morgan H., *Biographical Sketches & Index of the Huguenot Settlers of New Rochelle 1687-1776* (1941); BOLTON, Robert, *A History of the County of Westchester, from its First Settlement to the Present Date* (NY, 1848); WITTMEYER, Alfred V., *Register of l'Église Françoise à la Nouvelle York from 1668 to 1804*; New Rochelle Chapter, NSDAR, *Old Wills of New Rochelle, NY* (1950-51).

CRESSON, Pierre

b. c. 1609/10, Mesnil (prob. now Mesnil-Domqueur, n.e. Abbeville) Picardie, FR, s/o Pierre & Élisabet Vuilesme) Cresson; previously the town was given as Menil but this was prob. an incorrect spelling – Mesnil-Domqueur is located exactly where the records say "Menil" was

m. 15 Jun 1639, Sedan, FR, Rachel Claussé/Clossé (11 Feb 1617/8, Picardie or Delft-c. 1692, Staten Island, NY), d/o Pierre & Jeanne (Famélart) Claussé; marr. record says Pierre Cresson was a *serger* (a serge maker/weaver) & Pierre Claussé was a *maçon* (mason, bricklayer); both Rachel and Pierre were liv. in Sedan; a Jacques Cresson was m. Sedan, 2 Dec 1640, to Élisabeth Hufron – poss. a bro/o Pierre; when Pierre was in Sluis, there were 2 Cressons there – Nicolas and Venant

1640 - in Leiden, HOL

1657 - sailed from Amsterdam; 1st to Nieuw Amstel/New Castle, DE

1658 – went to Manhattan at the urging of Gov. Stuyvesant; then went back to HOL

25 Apr 1669 – arr NY on the *Beaver*

settled Harlem, later Staten Island, NY

15 Mar 1673 – Pierre and Rachel made joint will

d. p. 3 Aug 1681, Staten Island

CHILDREN:

Susannah[2], b. Ryswyck, HOL; m. 1 Sep 1658, New Amsterdam, Nicolas de La Plaine (b. 1592 Bressuire, Poitou, FR-1696 NY); she d. NY; **3 daus**, incl. **Marie**[3], c. 14 Nov 1668, m. c. 27 Jun 1692, Jean Le Chevalier - **11 ch**

Jacques[2], bp. 12 Mar 1640, Sedan; m. 1 Sep 1663, Marie Reynard; he d. 1 Aug 1684, NY; she d. Philadelphia, 10 8mo 1710; **9 ch**

Christina[2], b. c. 1650/2, Sluis, Flanders; m/1, 26 Apr 1665, Jean Letelier (d. 4 Sep 1671 New Utrecht, LI, NY), m/2, c. 1673, Jan Gerrits de Haes/Haas/Garrison (bp. 14 Oct 1646 New Amsterdam- 1708/9 NJ), s/o Gerrit Jansen van Oldenburg & Clara Matthys (aka de Mof)

Rachel[2], b. c. 1656, Delft, HOL; m/1, David Demarest, Jr., s/o David & Marie (Sohier) Demarest; m/2, Jean/Jan Durié, s/o Pierre & Marguerite (Charoy) Durié; m/3, Roelof Vanderlinde

Joshua[2], bp. 8 Jun 1658; m. Alche/Olive Gerritsen; liv. Staten Island; he d. a. 1690

Élie/Elias/Elizacus[2], bp. 17 Dec 1662; liv. Richmond Co, NY

REF: VAN NAME, Elmer G., *Pierre Cresson the Huguenot of Staten Island, PA & NJ* (1968); *The Genealogical Register*, Vol. I (1913), MERVINE, William M., editor; Records from the Société de l'Histoire du Protestantisme Français, Paris; RIKER, James, *Revised History of Harlem* (1904).

CRISPEL(L)/CRÉPEL, Antoine

b. 1635, St. Guin, Artois, FR, now Sainghin-en-Weppes, in the Nord Dépt., Pas-de-Calais, s.w. of Lille; m/1, 31 Jan 1660, FR Reformed Ch, Mannheim, GER, Marie Blanchan, d/o Matthieu & Madeleine Joiré Blanchan

27 Apr 1660 - sailed on *The Gilded Otter*, arr c. 7 Dec 1660, Wiltwyck

May 1661 - was allotted #12 of the "new lots" at Esopus but settled at Hurley (the New Village)

17 Jun 1666 - was granted a parcel of land nr. the New Village; 1670 was granted 16 acres in Hurley

7 Jun 1663 - Wiltwyck, his wife and dau Mary were captured by Indians but were later rescued; referred to as the "Massacre at Wiltwyck"

he was one of the 12 original Patentees of New Paltz but he never lived there

m/2, c. 1680, NY, Petronella DuMond/LeMan; she d. a. 6 Nov 1707

d. p. 6 Nov 1707, wd – a. 10 Jan 1708, wp, Ulster Co; will, written in Dutch, mentions deceased son Pieter and Pieter's ch, son Jan, daus Maria M., Jannetie, Elizabeth, Sara; son-in-law Huybert Suylandt; references to inheritances from Mattys Blanchan, his deceased father-in-law

CHILDREN, m/1 (bap. Reformed Dutch Church):

Maria Magdalene[2], bp. 12 Feb 1662, RDC, Kingston, NY; m. a. 1681, Mattys Cornelis Sleght, s/o Cornelis Barentsen Sleght & Tryntje Tysen Bos; **9 ch**

Pieter[2], bp. 21 Dec 1664; m. c. 1689, Neeltje Gerritsen Newkirk (d. p. 1727), d/o Gerrit Cornelissen & Hendrickje (Paulus) <u>or</u> Chieltje (Slecht) Van Nieukerk; he d.1696 - **3 ch**; Neeltje m/2, 18 Feb 1697, Johannes Schepmoes

Lysbet[2], bp. 3 Oct 1666; d. young

Lysbet[2], bp. 15 Oct 1668; m. Elias Ulin/Ean; **5 ch**

Sara[2], bp. 18 Jun 1671; m. a. 1696, Huybert Suylandt of Hurley; **5 ch**

Jan[2], bp. 21 Jul 1674; m. 25 May 1701, RDC, Kingston, Geertje Jans Roosa (bp. Kingston 7 Jan 1683), d/o Jan Roosa & Hillegond Willemsz Van Buren; **9 ch**

CHILDREN, m/2:

Jannetie[2], bp. 4 Jun 1682; d. young

Jean[2], bp. 12 Oct 1684; d. young

Jannetie[2], bp. 7 Feb 1686; m. p. 30 Dec 1704 (banns RDC), Kingston, Nicolas Hoffman, s/o Martinus Hoffman & Emerentje DeWitt; **9 ch**

REF: HASBROUCK, Kenneth E., *The Crispell Family in America* (1976); NYGBR, Vol,. XXI (1890), EVANS, Thomas G., *"The Crispell Family of Ulster Co, NY"*; ANJOU, Gustave, *Ulster Co, NY Probate Records* (1906); HOES, Roswell R., *Baptismal & Marriages of the Old Dutch Church of Kingston, Ulster Co, NY 1660-1809* (1980).

CROCHERON, Jean

b. c. 1610/15, FR, poss. Nantes

c. 1645, m. Marie X (b. FR-d. p. 1696, Staten Island)

a. 1670 - left FR for America, arr with a group of French Vaudois (Waldenses); settled Staten Island, NY; supposedly of a prosperous family, he converted everything into cash and was smuggled out of Marseilles in a hogshead

1670 - he had title to land at Long Neck, now New Springville; erected his homestead c. 1 mile from what is now the location of the Asbury Church

d. p. 13 Dec 1695, wd- a. 3 Sep 1696, wp; inv, 17 Dec 1696 and again, 9 Jan 1696/7, Staten Island; will mentions wife Mary, sons Nicholas, Anthony, other ch mentioned but not by name

CHILDREN (all prob. b. Flanders):

Nicholas[2], b. 1648, Zele, E. Flanders; m. c. 1676, Anne X; he d. p. 10 Feb 1702/3, wd-a. 24 Jul 1707, wp; **no issue**

Anthony[2], d. unmarr., by 14 Dec 1697; bro Nicholas deeded land left to Anthony by father Jean to bro John

Adrianna[2], m. 24 Oct 1677, Flatbush, Capt. Jacques Poillon (c. 1646-1720); she d. p. 14 Jun 1720, probate of Jacques' will; 4 ch: **Marie**[3], (bp. 27 Apr 1679 Flatbush-d. a. 1 Nov 1718), m/1, Thomas Stillwell (d. 1703), s/o Capt. Thomas & Martha (<u>Billiou</u>) Stillwell, m/2, Valentine <u>du Chesne</u>; **Jean Crocheron**[3], b. c. 1680, Brooklyn, m. Sarah Lake, d. a. 7 Dec 1724, wp – **2 sons, 2 daus**; **Jacques**[3] (1681, Flatbush-5 Mar 1732, Staten Island), m/1, Katherine X, m/2,1709, Staten Island, Françoise Billiou (c. 1685-1714), prob. d/o Jacob & Margaret (Larzelère) <u>Billiou</u>, m/3, Judith Bodine, d/o Vincent, grdau/o <u>Jean & Marie (Crocheron) Bodine</u> – total of **4 sons, 5 daus**; **Catherine**[3], b.1684, m. Samuel Osborne - **issue**

Katherine[2], m. c. 1677, Abraham Lakerman (c. 1660/1-Mar/Apr 1734), s/o Louis & Anne (de Sanchoy) Lakerman; she a. 1733 – **3 sons, 5 daus**

Marie[2], b. c. 1660; m. 11 Jan 1680, Midwout, <u>Jean Bodine</u>; she d. a. 10 Feb 1702/3; **7 ch**

John[2], b. 1658; m/1, 3 May 1682, Flatbush, Hester Lutines, d/o Walraven & Hester (Donrinees) Lutin – **4 ch**; m/2, 28 Apr 1713/4, Mary Morgan, d/o John & Frances (Bellin) Morgan – **1 ch;** he d. p. 6 Aug 1725, wd-a. 7 Jun 1727, wp; Mary m/2, a. 3 Jun 1730, Benjamin Ayres

Jannetje[2], m. 25 Sep 1682, Staten Island, Gerret Klaasz Vechten, s/o Claes Nicholas Arentse & Lammetie (X) Van Lechten; she d. a. 20 Mar 1693 – date of Gerret's 2nd marr to Magdelana Jans, widow of Jan Homs; 1 dau **Lummetje**[3] who m. her 1st cousin Abraham Lakerman; another ch was prob. of Gerret's 2nd marr

Margaret[2], m. c. 13 Apr 1684, Staten Island (date of betrothal), Peter Van Ness, s/o Pieter & Judith (Rapalje) Van Ness, d/o <u>Joris Jansen & Catalyntje (Trico) Rapalje</u>; d. a. 2 May 1697; **3 ch** incl a dau **Judith**[3] who m. Peter Brokaw, s/o <u>Bourgeon & Catherine (LeFèvre) Broucard</u> and a son **Peter**[3] who m. Magdalena duBois, d/o <u>Louis & Catherine (Blanchan) du Bois</u>

REF: *NYGBR*, Vol. 111, #1 (Jan 1980), #2 (Apr 1980), #3 (Jul 1980), #4 (Oct 1980), Vol. 112, #1 (Jan 1981) HIX, Charlotte M., *"The Crocheron Family of Staten Island"*; *Huguenot Ancestors Represented in the Membership of the Huguenot Society of NJ* (1965); HIX, Charlotte M., *Staten Island Wills & Letters of Administration Richmond Co, NY 1670-1800* wills of John (1695), John (1725), Nicholas (1702/3).

CROCKETAGNÉ/CROCKETT, Antoine Desasure/Desasurre Perronette de

b. 10 Jul 1643, Montauban, FR, s/o Gabriel Gustave de Crocketagné

1664 - awarded a commission by Louis XIV & was appt. an agent for wine and salt for the King's Household Troops

m. 1669, Louise de Saix (b. 10 Jul 1643, FR)

he converted to Protestantism through the preaching of James Fontaine & the influence of employer Matthew Maury; was banished by Louis XIV; Antoine was a commercial agent for the Maurys and Fontaines

1672 - fled to s. IRE, where the name became **CROCKETT**

CHILDREN:

Gabriel Gustave[2], b. 12 Oct 1672, nr. Bordeaux; poss. the progenitor of a Scottish branch of Crocketts; **issue**

James[2], b. 20 Nov 1674, Bantry Bay, IRE; m. Martha Montgomery, d/o Thomas Montgomery, an Irishman serving in the English navy; some of his descendants came to America; **issue**

Joseph Louis[2], b. 9 Jan 1676, IRE; m. Sarah Stewart/Stuart of Donegal, N. IRE; went to New Rochelle, NY, in 1708; then to PA and, in 1717, to VA; **10 ch**; ancestor of Davy Crockett

Robert Watkins[2], b. 18 Jul 1678, Kenmore Parish, IRE (in Bantry Bay, co. Cork); m. Rachel Watkins, a 3rd cousin; emigrated to VA; **5 ch**

Louise Desaix[2], b. 20 Feb 1682, Kenmore Parish, IRE

Mary Frances[2], b. 20 Sep 1683, Kenmore Parish, IRE

Sarah Elizabeth[2], b. 13 Apr 1685, Kenmore Parish, IRE

REF: *Collections of the Huguenot Society of America*, #7, #24; FRENCH, Janie P. C. & ARMSTRONG, Zella, *Notable Southern Families, The Crockett Family & Connecting Lines*, Vol. V.

CROMMELIN, Daniel

b. 28 Feb 1647, s/o Jean Crommelin/Crommelinck & Rachel Tacquelet; Jean was a rich manufacturer of St. Quentin, Picardie, FR; Daniel was the 13th of 15 ch; there is a *Place Crommelin* in St. Quentin

Daniel went to Paris and entered into business

m. 28 Oct 1674, St. Quentin, at Lehaucourt*, Anne Testart, d/o Pierre Testart & his 1st wife Catherine Bossu; she d. 1702/3, NYC; her father m. as his 2nd wife Rachel Crommelin, sis/o her husband Daniel

c. 1680 - he engaged in trade in S. America but lost everything & returned to Europe, penniless

c. 1680-92 - he spent time in ENG

c. 1692 - he went with his elder son Charles and 2 nephews to Jamaica, where his nephews d. of a fever a few days after their arrival; Daniel and his son left for NY and were soon joined by his wife and younger son Isaac

17 May 1696 – wife Anne was a sponsor at a baptism in the FR Church, NY

18 Jun 1698 – made a freeman in NYC

a. 1716 – Daniel was part owner of the Wawayanda patent in Orange Co; in 1716 he established a settlement called "Greucourt" which was commonly called the "Grey Court House" was nr. Chester, NY; it was later an inn; name is said to have been derived from "Gricourt" which is a small FR town 4 mi n.w. of St. Quentin; Daniel's mother Rachel's father Guillaume Tacquelet was the feudal lord of Gricourt

d. 1725, bur. Trinity Ch, NYC

CHILDREN:

Charles[2], b. 1 Jan 1676, Charenton, FR; m. 6 Nov 1706, Dutch Ref Ch, NYC, Anna Sinclair (b. 31 Jan, bp. 1 Feb 1691 Ref. Dutch Ch, NYC), d/o Robert & Maria/Marritie (Duyckinck) Sinclair/Sinclaer; he d. 9 May 1740, NY, bur. Trinity Ch, NYC

CHILDREN, ch with an asterisk were bp. Reformed Dutch Ch, NYC:

*   ***Daniel**[3], b. 11 Nov, bp. 19 Dec 1707 – grfa Daniel & grmo Maria Duyckinck were witnesses; went to HOL 1724; became a *poorter* (freeman) of Amsterdam in 1727; m. 30 Oct 1736, Amsterdam, Marie Le Plastier (11 Oct 1711 Amsterdam-30 Mar 1777 Amsterdam), d/o Daniel & Judith (Congnard) Le Plastier; Daniel became a prosperous merchant – his firm *Daniel Crommelin & Sons* made large loans to America after the Amer. Revolution; he d. 18 Jan 1788, Amsterdam; 10 ch, **5** of whom survived infancy; a dau **Judith**[4], b. 16 Sep 1739, m. 26 Apr 1761, her American cousin Samuel Verplanck (19 Sep 1739 NYC-c. 1820), s/o Gulian Verplanck and Marie Crommelin (d/o Charles[2]); Judith, d. 17 Sep 1803, NY, age 64 – 1 son **Daniel**[5], 1dau who d. young
*   ***Marie Anne**[3], bp. 11 Sep 1709; d. Nov 1710
*   ***Marie**[3], b. 11 Jul, bp. 20 Jul 1711; m. Guillaume/Gulian Verplanck; son **Samuel**[4] m. Judith Crommelin[4]
*   ***Anne**[3], b. 6 Jul, bp 11 Jul 1714; d. 27 Jan 1715
*   **Elisabeth**[3], b. 6 Nov, bp. 20 Nov 1715, FR Ch, NYC; m. 8 May 1748, Trinity Church, NY, Gabriel Ludlow as his 2nd wife; Gabriel was the s/o Gabriel & Sarah (Hanmer) Ludlow; 4 ch – **Daniel**[4], **Robert Crommelin**[4] (m. Elizabeth Conklin) + **2 daus**[4] who m. X Lewis & X Dashwood
*   **Robert**[3], b. 13 Feb, bp. 16 Feb 1717/8 FR Ch, NYC
*   ***Anne**[3], b. 16 Dec, bp. 25 Dec 1719
*   ***Charles**[3], b. 22 Aug, bp. 29 Aug 1722

Isaac[2], b. 23 Feb 1682, St. Quentin, bp. 15 Mar 1682, Lehaucourt; d. 1702/3 NYC

NOTE: Lehaucourt is a commune c. 10 km. n. of St. Quentin. There was a Calvinist temple there. It is located in the *arrondissement* (division) of the *département* of St. Quentin.

REF: BAIRD, Charles W., *History of Huguenot Emigration to America*; NYGBR, Vol. VIII (1877) – wills of Robert & Maria Sinclair; NYGBR, Vol. XXIII (1892) – gen. of Duyckinck Fam.; WITTMEYER, Alfred, *Registers of the Births, Marriages, and Deaths of the Église Françoise à la Nouvelle York, 1688-1804* (1886); FOWLER, Robert L., *Our Predecessors & Their Descendants* (1883); EVANS, Thomas Grier, editor, *Collections of the NYGBS – Baptisms from 1639 to 1730 Reformed Dutch Ch, NYC,* Vol. II (NY, 1901).

CUVELLIER, Adrienne, see la VIGNE, Guleyn de

D

DAMOUV(R)EL/DAMOURVILLE/DeMOURVELL, Samuel

b. c. 1672, FR; called Dr. Samuel; evidently he was doctor in FR but it is presumed that due to his poor
command of English, he was a cooper in VA

c. 1690 to VA

m. 6 Jul 1692, Hannah (Cox?) Lamkin, *poss.* the d/o Vincent Cox of Westmoreland Co, VA & widow
of George Lamkin whom she m/1, c. 1667; she d. a. 25 Sep 1744, wp, Westmoreland Co ; her
will mentions son Peter Lamkin*, grdau Hannah Demovell (*sic*), grdau Mary Middleton, grdaus
Hannah & Sarah Armistead, gr dau Jane More*, grdau Hannah Hartley*, grsons James & Samuel
Lamkin*, grdau Hannah Brown*, grdau Magdalen Jackson, dau Elizabeth Middleton, grdau
Magdeleine Claughton*, son-in-law Benjamin Middleton, John Armistead (no relationship
mentioned) *desc. from her 1ˢᵗ marr.- Hannah Hartley & Magdeleine Claughton are *prob.*
members of the Lamkin family

Samuel Tucker brought suit against him because the 12 hogsheads that he had Samuel make
were "faulty and leaky" and all the cider he had stored in them was lost – Tucker won

24 Apr 1712 - naturalized in VA; states that Samuel is "a natural born subject of the ffrench King";
naturalization record shows name as Damouvel

25 Nov 1717 - rec a patent from Lady Fairfax for a tract of land (404 acres) on Pohick Creek in Stafford Co
(became Fairfax Co, 1742)

d. a. 8 Aug 1723, wp, Westmoreland Co, VA; will says name is Damourvel; mentions wife Hannah.
son Samuel, daus Magdaline, wife of Jeremiah Rust & Elizabeth, wife of William Harrison;
Samuel² got 200 acres of land in Stafford Co., 6 slaves, all his father's surgical instruments, his
books, medicines + all his carpenter & cooper tools; Madeleine rec. 100 acres in Stafford Co.;
Elizabeth got 140 acres in Stafford Co.; wife Hannah – 2 slaves, 2 horses, 2 beds and furniture

CHILDREN:

Samuel Lewis², b. c. 1698; m. Rose (Neale) Bonum, d/o Richard & Dorcas (Spence) Neale, widow Philpot
Bonum; he d. 1735/6, Westmoreland Co, VA; **3 ch**; Rose m/3, Francis Aubrey, Jr.

Magdaline², b. c. 1700; m/1, a. 28 Nov 1721, Jeremiah Rust (1690-7 Aug 1731; wp, 29 Sep 1731
Westmoreland Co.), s/o Samuel & Martha (X) Rust; ch – (named in Jeremiah's will) **Peter³**,
Matthew³, **John³**, **George³**, **Samuel³**, **William³**, **Jeremiah³**, m. Frances (X) Minor, **Matthew³**,
Benjamin³, **Hannah³**, m. Thomas Boggess, **Martha³**, **Ann³**, m. X Harrison; m/2, p. 28 Nov 1731,
Christopher Dominick Jackson, ch – **Julius³**, **Thaddeus³**, m. Elizabeth Fleming, **Christopher
Maccabeus³**; Magdaline d. p. 11 Aug 1766 ,wd, Cople Parish, Westmoreland Co, VA

Elizabeth², b. c. 1703; m/1, a. 1723, William Harrison - **issue**, m/2, p. 1723, Benjamin Middleton s/o John
Middleton – **issue**

?Hannah², *if* Samuel & Hannah had a dau Hannah, she must have d. young – no further info

REF: Naturalization record from HENING, Wm. Walter, *Statutes at Large,* Vol. IV; HELLIGO, Martha S.,
George Mason...& Related Lines of Demourvell, etc.; will of Vincent Cox; Samuel's will; WILKINS, Harold
E. & MATTHEWS, Barbara J., "The Legatees of Hannah (Cox) (Lamkin) Demouvel/Demonville, 8 Sept. 1744,
Westmoreland Co. VA" in *Virginia Genealogist,* Vol. 43, #2, 3 (1999).

DANDONNEAU, Jacques

m. 3 Mar 1613, Calvinist Temple, La Rochelle, FR, Isabella Fain

no evidence that Jacques or Isabella left FR nor is it known if they had more children

CHILD:

Pierre² (dit La Jeunesse), b. 28 Oct 1624, Nieul-sur-Mer, Aunis, FR (n.e. of La Rochelle); bp. 28 Oct
1624 Calvinist Temple, LaRochelle; m. 16 Jan 1653, Ameau (Trois Rivières), Françoise Jobin (1634
FR-6 Jul 1702 Champlain, CAN), d/o Jacques & Marguerite (Roy) Jobin; he d. bet. 27 Sep 1690-11 Jan
1695 St-Luc-de-Vincennes Champlain, Québec, Canada; like most of the emigrés to Québec, this

family became Catholic; all the records cited are from Catholic ch records – family apparently Catholic once Pierre arr from FR

CHILDREN (all b. Trois Rivières, Québec):

Louis[3], bp. 9 Apr 1654; m. 8 Oct 1684, Jeanne-Marguerite LeNoir, d/o Jean & Jeanne (Jacob) LeNoir; **6 ch**

Jeanne[3], bp. 20 Jul 1655; m. 1670 Jacques Babie

Marguerite[3], b. 10 Jan, bp. 11 Jan 1657; d. 1666

Élisabeth[3], b. 8 Apr, bp. 12 Apr 1658; d. 1666

Marguerite[3], b/bp. 20 Jun 1659; m. 15 Nov 1672, Jacques Brisset, s/o Jacques & Jeanne (Fétis) Brisset ; she d. 22 Mar 1740; **14 ch**

Marie-Renée[3], b. 1661; m. 1679, Adrien Neveu

Étiennette[3], b/bp. 28 Dec 1662; m. 1678, Pierre Mercereau

Françoise-Pétronille[3], b. 3 Jan, bp. 4 Jan 1665; m. 1682, Jean Desrosiers

Marie-Louise[3], b. c. 1665; m. 1688, Joseph Aubuchon

Jacques[3], b. 1670; m. 11 Jan 1695, Catherine Duteau, d/o Charles & Jeanne (Rivaud) Duteau; **11 ch**

Françoise-Marguerite[3], b/bp. 29 Sep 1677; d. 7 Oct 1709, Québec

REF: JETTÉ, René, *Dictionnaire Généalogique des familles du Québec* (Montréal, 1983).

DAVANT/DAVAN, Jean/John

b. FR, *prob.* s/o Jean & Marie (Hardilly) Davant; fa Jean was a *faiseur de toille peinte* (worker, maker of painted cloth, poss. chintz), who also had son Isaac, bp. 21 Sep 1701, Ch of Leicester Fields, m. 30 May 1725 Ch of Leicester Fields - Elizabeth Dorselle - **4 ch**, bp. Ch at Rider Court; a dau Julie, bp. Nov 1708, Ch at Rider Court; there is also a Louis Davant there - prob. the bro/o Jean/John; Louis was godfather to 2 of bro Isaac's ch; Jean/John & Louis were prob. b. in FR, the 2 younger ch, Isaac and Julie, in London

m/1, XX, who d. a. 1730

went from FR to London where there are many references to the family in the records of the Huguenot churches there – Ch on Threadneedle St, Ch of Leicester Fields, Ch at Rider Court (which was sort of an annex to the Leicester Fields Ch and the congregation was mostly Davants) & St. Jean Ch in Spitalfields. The earliest rec of the family is in the Ch on Threadneedle – Isaac & Jeanne Duvant were godparents to Pierre LeSage, s/o Pierre & Anne LeSage, 15 Feb 1691

m/2, a. Feb 1731, prob. ENG, Hester/Esther Long, who d. 26 Feb 1733/4, Tybee, Chatham, GA

John was one of the 11 "Foreign Protestants" who were part of Oglethorpe's settlers to GA; he was a cabinet maker; there was also a Lewis Davant (a shoemaker) and his wife Elizabeth on the same ship – Lewis d. 19 Sep 1733 and Elizabeth d. 11 Jan 1734/5 – a Louis Davant and Elizabeth Séguin were godparents to his son Jean, b. 1731 – relationship not known

20 Jun 1733 – left ENG – said to have sailed the 15th but didn't for some reason; arr GA 29 Aug 1733

d. Sep 1733 Tybee, GA

CHILD, m/1:

Jean/John[2], b. ENG; 2 Apr 1734, he rec. the grant at Abercorn, GA (c. 15 mi. n. of Savannah) which would have been his father's; 25 Dec 1739, he was on Edisto Island, SC where he was paid £30 by the Colony to be a Lookout; he was called a carpenter of Edisto Island when he purchased a plantation of 150 acres in 1740 for £2000 from Isabella (X) Watson, widow of Joseph Watson, whom he m. 11 Apr 1740, St. Philip's Ch, Charleston, SC; he d. Oct 1768 Port Royal, Beaufort, SC; an inventory was taken, 10 Jan 1769

CHILDREN:

John[3], b. c. 1741, Edisto Island, Berkeley, SC; m/1, XX – dau **Sarah** who m. 6 Apr 1786, John Grimball as his 4th wife, she d. 8 Feb 1788 – **no issue**, m/2, Ann X, who d. 1786

Isaac[3], b. c. 1743; m. Tabitha Williams; son **Isaac**[4], b. 18 Mar 1772; Isaac, Sr. d. a. 18 Jun 1772

James[3], b. 9 Sep 1744 Edisto Island; m/1, 30 Jan 1769, Lydia Page (12 Jan 1751-20 Apr 1795) – **4 sons, 4 daus**, m/2, 19 Mar 1797, Elizabeth (X) White, widow of Charles White; she d. c. 1821, Savannah, GA – **no issue**; he d. 31 Jan 1803, Savannah, GA

Mary[3], b. c. 1748, Edisto Island; m. 26 Apr 1764, Thomas Tailler/Taylor of Lady's Island, SC; **4 sons**

Charles[3], b. c. 1750, Edisto Island; m. c. Jun 1776, Elizabeth (Fendin) Bland (b. 28 Oct 1751) , widow of Richard Bland; she m/3, Christian Rankin; Charles d. Dec 1781, Hilton Head Island, SC

CHILD, m/2:

Jean/John[2], b. 23 Feb, bp. 15 Mar 1731, Ch at Rider Court, London

REF: *A List of Early Settlers of GA* (GPC, Baltimore 1983); *Transactions of the Huguenot Society of SC*, #74 (1969), HANAHAN, Hardin Davant, "Davant Family History", Appendix I – "The Davant Family in London, England"; Publication of the Huguenot Society of London, Vol. XXX, *Rider Ct. records, 1700-1738.*

DAVID(S)

(brothers of unknown parents – according to Baird, quoting from *La France Protestante*, "one of the best families of La Rochelle, a family not less distinguished by reason of the positions which its members have filled, than eminent for the services it had rendered." 1572 – Jean David, *pair de corps de ville* (evidently some sort of town "official"), was appt. w/ 2 others, to go to ENG for the purpose of soliciting the help of Queen Elizabeth, and of hastening Montgomery's departure with the promised fleet for the relief of the besieged city; 1628, Jacques David, who had twice been mayor of La Rochelle, was sent w/Philippe Vincent upon a similar embassy to Charles II, & succeeded in influencing the king to sign a treaty with the Protestants – ancestors of Jean and Josué, their father was *prob.* Jean)

Jean[2], b. c. 1645, FR, of La Rochelle

21 Oct 1681 – *prob.* the Jean David on the list of témoignages in the FR Ch, Threadneedle St, London

a Huguenot refugee from a seaboard province of western FR who emigrated to nr. Montréal, Québec, Canada

for 20+ yrs, Jean traveled and lived w/ the Indians along the Mohawk & Hudson Rivers; he negotiated for the release of the captives after the attack on Kingston by the Esopus Indians

m. Ester/Hester Vincent; she had brothers Jean & François

was in the Narragansett settlement w/ his bro for a while

c. summer 1687, went to Kingston, NY

1689 – took Oath of Allegiance in Ulster Co, NY

by Oct 1692 in NYC

5 Oct 1707 – Hester Vincent, w/o Jean David, was godmother at bap. of Hester Peltrau, NYC

d. a. 1709, Newtown, LI, NY

CHILDREN:

Jean II[3], m. Louise Streing, d/o Daniel & Charlotte (LeMaître) Streing; ch – **Jean**[4], b. 23 Dec, bp. 25 Dec 1702 FR Ch, NYC, grpar were his godparents, **Daniel**[4], b. 1 Dec, bp. 10 Dec 1704 FR Ch, NYC

Marguerite/Margaret[3], m/1, c. 1688/9, Pierre Montras/Montross – **Margriet**[4], b. 25 Jun 1691, bp. 12 Nov 1993*, Old Dutch Ch, Kingston, **Angelique**[4], b. 6 Nov, bp. 12 Nov 1693, Old Dutch Ch, Kingston, **Hendrick**[4] – Pierre d. c. 1703, Margaret returned to Kingston; m/2, Richard Reyster *Margriet was not bap. when an infant as her parents were Catholic at that time, according to the ch. rec.; they must have converted

Madeleine[3], m. 29 Jun 1701, FR Ch, NYC, Jean Faget, *ouvrier en laine* (woolworker), from Mirambeau, Saintonge as his 2nd wife, Jean was s/o Jean Faget; he became victualer in NYC, was made a freeman, 26 May 1699, one of the *"chefs de famille"* in the FR Ch, 1704; Mirambeau, now in Charente-Maritime Dépt., Poitou-Charentes, s.w. of Jonzac

Angelica[3], b. c. 1685, Laval, Québec, Canada; m. 10 Oct 1708, Tarrytown, NY, Paul Ruton

Anne[3], bp. 2 Oct 1687, Dutch Ch, Kingston, NY – her baptismal rec. says her parents were "French people"; m. c. 1712, Dr. Jean DuPuy (1679-1744)

Daniel[3], b. 2 Apr , bp. 22 Apr 1694, French Ch, NYC; his parents were also his godparents

Carel[3]

Ezachiel/Ezéchiel[3,] b. 3 Jul, bp. 5 Jul 1696 FR Ch , NYC

Susanne[3], b. 6 Nov, bp. 19 Nov 1699 FR Ch, NYC – bap. rec. says mother was Madeleine, must be an error – Madeleine Vincent was her godmo, "Live/Luie" Vincent her godfa; m. c. 1717, Élie Chardavoine

Josué[2], b. FR, of La Rochelle

    m. FR, Marie Scramverier

    20 Nov 1681 – témoignage, FR Ch, Threadneedle St, London, he and Marie

    by 1686 - early settler at Narragansett, RI; shown on map as having property on the great river running to the east and into the woods and nr. the great road that runs bet. the home lots to the great plain & to the way to Boston; one lot for David Senior and one next to it for David Junior; by 1691, in New Amsterdam

    c. 1691 – to NYC

    CHILD:

    Josué[3], b. FR; m. 23 Sep 1687, FR Ch, Narragansett, Marie Audebert

        CHILDREN:

        Josué[4], b. 27 Aug, bp 2 Sep 1688, FR Ch, Narragansett; d. young

        Josué[4], (twin) b. 15 Aug, bp 16 Aug 1691, FR Ch, NYC; d. young

        Pierre[4], (twin) b. 15 Aug, bp. 16 Aug 1691, FR Ch, NYC

        Daniel[4], b. 12 Mar, bp. 19 Mar 1692/3, FR Ch, NYC; m. XX; had son **John**[4], b. 20 Jun 1721, m. c. 11 Jan 1746 (date of banns), Elizabeth Wyngaart (7 Aug 1726-9 May 1806 Albany), d/o Johannes Wyngaart & Maritje Huysen; John[4] served in the Rev. War and d. 26 Jun 1794, Albany; **7 ch**

        Jean[4], b. 13 Jul, bp 21 Jul 1695, FR Ch, NYC; bap. rec. states that Josué & Marie Traverrier (*sic*) David are his godparents

        Marie[4], b. 22 Sep, bp. 27 Sep 1697, FR Ch, NYC

        Josué[4], b. 6 Jan, bp. 28 Jan 1699/00, FR Ch, NYC; names of parents not given but Anne Audebert was godmo, prob. mo/o or sis/o Marie (Audebert) David

        Jacques[4], b. 30 Jan, bp. 7 Mar 1702/3, FR Ch, NYC

        Anne[4], b. 20 Feb, bp 10 Mar 1705/6, FR Ch, NYC

REF: BAIRD, Charles W., *History of the Huguenot Emigration to America*; POTTER, Elisha R., *Memoir Concerning the French Settlements and French Settlers in the Colony of RI* (1968); TAYLOR, John W.& Eva Mills Lee, *Montross: A Family History*; WITTMEYER, Alfred V., *Registers of the Births, Marriages, & Deaths of the Église Française à la Nouvelle York* (1886) ; NYGBS, *Baptisms from 1639 to 1730 Reformed Dutch Ch, NY* (NY, 1901); MINET, William & Susan, *Libre des Témoignages de l'Église de Threadneedle Street, 1669-1789*- Publication of the Huguenot Society of London, Vol. XXI (London, 1909) ; GANNON, Peter S., editor, *Huguenot Refugees in the Settling of Colonial America*; DeFOREST, L. Effingham, *Records of the French Church at Narragansett, 1686-1691*; MINET, William & Susan, *Libre des Témoignages de l'Église de Threadneedle Street, 1669-1789*- Publication of the Huguenot Society of London, Vol. XXI (London, 1909).

DAVID

(brothers of unknown parents)

Pierre[2], of Bolbec, Haute-Normandie, FR, n.e. of Le Havre

    m. Rachel Debrey/DeBray

    emigrated to ENG

    d. p. 1710

CHILDREN:

Pierre[3], b. 1685, Bolbec, FR; 24 Jun 1702 in London – rec. says he was 17 yrs. old, b. Bolbec, s/o
Pierre; m. 22 Jan 1710, Threadneedle St. Church, Spitalfields, London, ENG, Anne Dutertre, d/o Louis
    & Mariane (Buart) Dutertre; Anne of Orléans, FR, d. a. Nov 1750, wp, Cumberland Co, VA; 22
    Oct 1710 - in the bp. record of his son Pierre, he is called a Grenadier of the Queen & that the
    family lived in St. Martin Parish; by 1714 - in VA; 2 Mar 1715 - awarded 88 acres in
    Henrico Co, VA; 23 Mar 1715- settled Manakintown, VA; d. p. 28 May 1729, wd - a. 18 Aug
    1730, wp, Goochland Co, VA; inv, 17 Nov 1730

CHILDREN:

Pierre/Peter[4], b. 8 Oct, bp. 22 Oct 1710, La Patente Ch, Spitalfields, London; his godfa was
    his uncle Abraham David and grmo Marianne Duterte was his god mo; he did not go
    to VA w/ parents but was in VA by 1732; m. a.1738, Elizabeth Morriset (1Mar 1721,
    King William Par., Goochland Co, VA-p. 25 Nov 1785, liv. Henry Co, VA), d/o Pierre
    & Elizabeth (Fauré) Morriset; he d. a. 25 Nov 1785, wp, Henry Co, VA; **10 ch** are
    mentioned in Pierre's will

CHILDREN:

Anne[5], b. 15 Jan 1737/8; in father's will

Peter[5], b. 1 Jul 1747; m/1, Elizabeth White, d/o Henry White -**3 ch**, m/2, 8 Nov
    1793, Elizabeth Hale **4 ch**; poss one unproven dau Nancy; d. intestate bet
    1832-40, Madison Co, GA; in father's will

Isaac[5], b. 30 May 1756; m/1, c.1775, Mildred/Nilly White (1 Jan 1755-a. 14 Oct
    1798), d/o Henry & Celia (Page) White, sis/o Elizabeth above-**10 ch**, m/2,
    14 Oct 1798, Susannah (X) Vaughan, widow of James Vaughan; in
    father's will; he d. 11 Apr 1840, Madison Co, GA

Abraham[5], b. 1 Jul 1763; m. 15 Dec 1803, Franklin Co, VA, Rachel Edmond – **6
    ch**; in father's will

Jude[5], in father's will, no further record

Elizabeth[5], in father's will

Mary[5], in father's will

Jeney[5], m. X Raby; in father's will

Magdalene[5], in father's will

Phebe[5], in father's will

Esaye[4], bp. 3 Sep 1711, La Patente, London; fam. living Wille St, Stepney; d. a. 18 Oct 1750

Isaac[4], heir to 400 acres in father's will; d. a. 20 Apr 1742, unmarr.

Maryan[4], b. c. 1716, VA; m/1, William Burton (d. a. Nov 1749 wp Cumberland Co, VA) - his
    will mentions wife Maryan, dau **Ann**[3], m/2, c. 1751, Stephen Easley, s/o John & Mary
    (Benskin) Easley – **issue**

Anne[4], b. 10 May, bp. 23 Dec 1722, VA; m. 1745, Daniel Easley, s/o William & Mary (Pyrant)
    Easley?; she d. a. 1765, when Daniel m/2, Elizabeth Echols, d/o William; **5 ch?**

Abraham[2], b. Bolbec, FR

went to ENG w/ his bro Pierre[2]

m. XX

CHILD:

Pierre[3], called the Pierre/Peter the Younger to distinguish him from his1st cousin Pierre[3] above; b. a.
    1701, Bolbec, FR; was in ENG with his father; by 1717, he joined his uncle Pierre[2] in
    Manakin, VA; m/1, VA, Rachel Morell, d/o Louis Morell – she had sisters Elizabeth (m. David
    LeSueur) & Susanna (m. X Moss); c. 1731 – returned to ENG; Rachel d. bet. 1739-44;
    emigrated to Charleston, SC; m/2, 6 May 1744, SC, Ann (X) Keating, a widow; he d. 29 Mar
    1754, SC, bur. Charleston

CHILDREN, m/1:

Abraham[4], in father's will

Pierre[4], bp. 16 Jan 1732/33, London; not in father's will

Henriette[4], bp. 16 Dec 1733/34, London; not in father's will
Rachel[4], bp. 7 Dec 1735, London; in father's will
Marie[4], bp. 28 Jan 1739, London; not in father's will
Judith[4], in father's will

REF: *The Huguenot* #14 (1947/49), #26 (1973/75), #32 (1985/87); CABELL, Priscilla Harriss, *Turff & Twigg, Vol. I -The French Lands* (Richmond, VA, 1988); *The David Journal*, pub. by Pierre David Family Assn., Vol. 1 (Jan/Jul 1983); Pierre's will; *Huguenot Publication*, #32, #26; BROCK, Robert A., *Huguenot Emigration to VA* (1962); REEVES, LeRoy, *Ancestral Sketches*; TRIMBLE, David B., *Stroud & Stubblefield of VA; The David Journal*, pub. by Pierre David Family Assn., Vol. 1, #3 (Jul 1983); *Huguenot Publication,#32*.

DELANO/De la NOYE, Marie Louisa

b. c. 1710, Aix-la-Chapelle (Aachen, GER), d/o Carlo Delano(e), a FR Protestant draper; Aachen suffered greatly during the religious wars & was twice put under the ban of the Empire for Protestantism; it is n.e. of Liège, BEL, s.w. of Köln/Cologne, GER, about equidistant from the borders of both BEL & HOL

m. 5 Oct 1729, at Hainaut, Flanders, Michael Christopher Spears/Speyers (8 Jul 1709, Arnsburg, Westphalia, GER-1772, Hagerstown, MD); Michael prob. the s/o Peter Abram and Margaret Graefenreid Henlopin) Spears

went to New Rochelle, NY, where a bro/o Maria Louisa was living; Henry, a bro/o Michael's went w/them

c. 1750 -Michael & Henry were visiting in VA; Benjamin Burden, Agent for Lord Fairfax, Proprietor of the Northern Neck, persuaded the bros to settle in VA; they returned to NY for their families & settled nr. Rockingham, VA, called the Valley of VA=Shenandoah Valley

prob. c. 1731/2 - to VA

d. PA or MD

CHILD (1 of 5-3 sons, 2 daus):

George Frederick[2], b. 6 May 1731 Aix-la-Chapelle, m. c. 1754, Christenah Hardwin, in Augusta (now Rockingham) Co, VA; Geo. began buying & selling land in VA & became a landowner of some note; later he started buying land in Lincoln Co, KY; served in the Rev. War; fam. liv on Linville Creek, just n. of Harrisonburg, nr. present town of Edom; he d. p. 14 Oct 1796, wd-a. Nov 1803, wp, Rockingham Co, VA – will names wife and all ch but Daniel; Christenah d. p. 1810 Rockingham Co, VA; **or** both d. Lincoln Co, KY

CHILDREN:

Elizabeth[3], b. 5 Dec 1755; m/1, c. 1778, John Carpenter; m/2, 30 Sep 1791, Asher Morrison; she d. 26 Oct 1832

Jacob[3], b. 7 Feb 1757, VA; m/1, 3 Jun 1781, Lincoln Co, KY, Elizabeth Neely who d. young – **2 sons, 1 dau**; m/2, 17 Dec 1791, Abigail Huston, d/o Archibald & Mary (Stephenson) Huston – **6 sons, 3 daus**; Rev. War service; he d. 1818

Catherine[3], b. 6 Sep 1760; m/1, c. 1777, John C. Frye; m/2, 9 Mar 1785, Adam Carpenter; she d. 1 Apr 1848

George F.[3], b. 11 Aug 1764, VA; m. 24 Feb 1785, Lincoln Co, KY, Mary Neeley (20 Aug 1761, nr. Charleston, SC-26 Jan 1852, Clary's Grove, Menard Co, IL), d/o William Neely; went to Green Co, KY; he d. Apr 1838, Clary's Grove; Rev. War service; **5 sons, 3 daus**

Mary Agnes[3], b. c. 1766; m. 23 Mar 1783, Christopher Rife; she d. 25 Mar 1852

Hannah[3], b. 14 Mar 1769; m. 1 Oct 1793, Jonathan Newman; she d. 8 Jan 1835

John[3], b. 14 Apr 1771, VA; m. 30 Aug 1793, Margaret Chrisman (1777-13 Nov 1855), d/o Capt. George & Hannah (McDowell) Chrisman; went to Lincoln Co, KY, then to Fayette Co., the part that later became Jessamine Co.; he d. 14 Jan 1866, Danville, KY; **6 son, 2 daus**

Daniel[3], b. c. 1773; m. 26 Feb 1801, Barbara Bowyess

Sarah[3], b. c. 1774; m. 2 Oct 1792, John Rader

David[3], b. c. 1777, unmarr.

REF: SPEARS, Joseph F. *The Spears Saga* (1982), pp. 14 ff; pp. 56 ff; PA Archives, Second Series, Vol. 14, p. 711; DAR Patriot Index, Vol. III (Baltimore, MD, 2003).

DELANO/deLANNOY/de la Noye, Jan/Jean

b. c. 1570, s/o Gysbert (de) Lano; at his betrothal said to be "of Tourcoing" a town n.e. of Lille in the
  Nord region; Gysbert converted to Protestantism c. 1555

c. 1585 - went to Leiden, HOL

m. c.13 Jan 1596 (date of betrothal), Walloon Church, Leiden, Holland, Marie Mahieu (sister to Hester
  Mahieu who m. Francis Cooke), d/o <u>Jacques & Jeanne (X) Mahieu</u>; Mahieu family prob. from Lille;
  Marie m/2, Robert Manoo, she d. 1650

d.1604, Leiden, HOL

CHILDREN:

Isaïe/Isaiah[2], bp. 26 Mar 1599, Leiden

Jeanne[2], bp. 18 Mar 1601, Walloon Ch, Leiden

Philippe/Philip[2], b. 1602, Leiden, HOL, bp 6 Nov (or 7 Dec) 1603, Walloon Ch, Leiden; to Plymouth, MA
  1621 on the *Fortune*; <u>m/1</u>, 19 Dec 1634, Plymouth, MA, Hester Dewsbury (d. a. 1653 prob. Duxbury,
  MA); <u>m/2</u>, a. 17 Jan 1653/4, Bridgewater, Mary (Pontus) Glass (c. 1625-d. p. 5 Jul 1682), d/o William
  and Wybra (Hanson) Pontus, widow of James Glass; he d. p. 22 Aug 1681 (memorandum) - a. 4 Mar
  1681/2 (inventory), prob. Duxbury, MA

CHILDREN, m/1:

Mary[3], b. c. 1635; m. 29 Nov 1655, Jonathan Dunham (m/2 15 Oct 1657, Mary Cobb); she d.
  c. 1656/7; **no issue**

Hester/Esther[3], b. c. 1638; <u>m/1</u>, Samuel Sampson, <u>m/2</u>, 1678, John Soule; she d. 12 Sep 1733

Philip[3], b. c. 1640/1; m. c. 1686, Elizabeth Clark, d/o William & Martha (Nash) Clark; **3 sons**; he
  d. 1708

Thomas[3], b. 21 Mar 1642, Duxbury, MA; m. a. 30 Oct 1667, Duxbury, MA, Rebecca Alden
  (c.1643, Duxbury, MA- p. 12 Jun 1696, Duxbury), d/o John and Priscilla (Mullins) Alden;
  he d. a. 22 Apr 1723, wp, Duxbury, MA; **9 ch**

John[3], b. c. 1644; m. c. 1679, Mary Weston, d/o Edmund Weston; he d. p. 1680

Jane[3], b. c. 1646; d. p. 1681, unmarr.

Jonathan[3], b. c. 1647/8; m. 28 Feb 1677/8, Mercy Warren, d/o Nathaniel & Sarah (Walker)
  Warren; h e d. a. 6 Mar 1721, wp, Dartmouth, MA; **13 ch**

CHILDREN, m/2:

Rebecca[3], b. c . 1657; m. 28 Dec 1686, John Churchill (m/2 Hannah Bartlett & d. 1723); she
  d. 6 Apr 1709, Duxbury; **5 ch**

Samuel[3], b. 1659; m. a. 1679/82, Duxbury, Elizabeth Standish, d/o Alexander & Sarah (Alden)
  Standish; he d. 1728; **9 ch**

REF: Leiden Church Records (*Gemeetelijke Archiefdienst,* 1975); NEHGS *Register*, Vol. 14, 55; ANDERSON, RC, *The Great Migration Begins,* Vol. I, III; *Genealogies of Mayflower Families*, Vol. I, III (1985); WARREN, Rev. Thomas, *History & Genealogy of the Warren Family* (1902); SKEHAN, Arlene M., "The Parentage of Philippe de la Noye" in *Plymouth Colony Genealogical Helper* ; DELANO, Major Joel Andrew, *Genealogical History & Alliances of the American House of Delano, 1621-1899* (1899); WINSOR, Justin, *History of the Town of Duxbury, MA* (1849).

DELATRE/DeLATRE/DELAUTRE/DELAUTER, David

b. c. 1655 La Bassée, FR, s.e. of Lille, then FR Flanders; was taken to GER where he was bp. in
  Oggersheim (w. of Mannheim) at about 3 mo. of age

m/1, XX – evidently no issue

m/2, Margaretha X, bur. 16 Apr 1701

m/3, 22 May 1701, Anna Maria Reipel(in) (c. 1671-13 Nov 1735, Schifferstadt), d/o Jacob Reipel, the
 mayor of Friesenheim (just w. of Mannheim)

d. 14 Jan 1726, nr. Schifferstadt (s.w. of Mannheim); bur 16 Jan 1726, Grobschifferstadt; rec in
 Schifferstadt church states that he fled persecution in FR

CHILDREN, m/2:

David[2], chr 1700, Schifferstadt; m/1, 22 Sep 1718, Anna Elisabetha Geringer, d/o Jacob & Susanna (Glatt)
 Geringer; emig. from Edenkoben, GER (s.w. of Mannheim); arr 2 Oct 1741, Philadelphia, on the *St.
 Andrew*; purchased MD land warrants in Mar 1743; naturalized Frederick Co, MD, 8 May 1749; m/2, a.
 1749, MD, Anna Barbara (Kelli) Hess, (29 Sep 1707, Hagsfeld, GER [n.e. Karlsruhe] -23 Sep 1783,
 Frederick, MD), d/o Johannes Georg Kelli, widow of Jacob Hess; David d. a. 18 Feb 1767, wp,
 Frederick Co, MD; the assumption is made that this David was the s/o David b. 1655

CHILDREN, m/1:

George William[3], b. 1719 (named the eldest son in father's will but inherited only 1 shilling); had
  son **George**[4] who went to Edgefield Dist, SC, m. 1783, Charlotte/Charity Pace, d/o Capt.
  Drury Pace, d. a. 13 Dec 1830, wp – sons **George**[5], **Solomon**[5], **Absalom**[5], daus **Rebecca
  Taylor**[5], **Eleanor Thurmond**[5], **Abigail Lloyd**[5], named in his will

Johann Nicholaus[3], chr 19 Nov 1724, Schifferstadt

Johann Jacob[3], b. c. 1726-28; rec. warrant to patent land, Jan 1749; m. c. 1752, MD, Elisabetha X;
  naturalized 10 Apr 1762 liv. Anne Arundel Co, MD; 7 ch: **Anna Barbara**[4], b. 28 Dec 1753;
  David[4], b. 15 Apr 1754, m/1, 28 Apr 1775, Catherine Trautmaenin – **10 ch**, m/2, 19 Sep 1815,
  Elizabeth (Kline) Harshman, wid/o Jacob Harshman, David d. 19 Jan 1862; **Heinrich/ Henry**[4],
  bp. 16 May 1758; **Anna Maria**[4], bp. 6 Jun 1767; **Jacob**[4], b. a. 1768, m. Catherine Mahn;
  Charlotte[4,] **Catherine**[4]; Jacob d. bet 1773-75; Elisabetha. m/2, 7 Mar 1775, Frederick, MD,
  Jacob Zimmerman

Christina[3], chr 21 Feb 1728, Schifferstadt

Johann Heinrich[3], chr 1 Apr 1731, Schifferstadt

Maria Catharina[3], chr 30 Mar 1738, Schifferstadt

Philip Lorenz[3], chr 17 Feb 1740, Schifferstadt; in MD church records, 1754; fought in the French
  & Indian Wars

Madelina[3], m. Matthias Silver (named in father's will, rec. £5)

CHILDREN, m/2:

Johannes[3], b. 6 Aug 1749, Frederick, MD (named in father's will – rec. land)

Catharina[3] (in father's will – to share 2/3 of father's estate w/ Johannes & Barbara, mother Anna
  Barbara rec. the other third)

Barbara[3] (in father's will)

Margaretha[2], chr 25 Jul 1700

CHILDREN, m/3 (all chr Schifferstadt, no other information):

Judith[2], chr 9 Apr 1703; **Johann Jacob**[2], chr 1705; **Anna Maria**[2], chr 2 Jan 1707; **Maria Elisabeth**[2], chr 14
Nov 1708; **Maria Catharina**[2], chr 2 Nov 1710; **Anthoni**[2], chr 6 Jul 1713; **Marie Jeanne**[2], chr 8 Mar 1716

REF: KIMMEL, Helmut, editor, *Hugenotten in der Pfalz* (Braunschweig, GER, 1973); church records, Schifferstadt;
WEISER, Frederick Sheely, *Records of Marriages & Burials in the Monocacy Church in Frederick Co, MD & in the
Evangelical Lutheran Congregations in the City of Frederick, MD, 1743-1811*; WEISER, Frederick S. *Maryland
German Church Records, Baptismal Records 1742-1770*, Vol. 3, *1746-1789*, Vol. 5; ANDERSEN, Patricia A., *Frederick
Co, MD Land Records, 1761-63*; David's will, dated 30 Apr 1757, probated 18 Feb 1767 Frederick Co;
FRY, Pauline G. DeLauter, *DeLauter Families in America* (Elgin, IL, 1982).

DELAUNAY, Claude

s/o Louis Delaunay (1546-1568), *médecin ordinaire*, "common" doctor in La Rochelle

m. 21 Mar 1580, Temple Calviniste de LaRochelle, FR, Anne Barbier

CHILD:

Louis[2], m. LaRochelle, Marguerite Cazalede; Louis was also a *médecin ordinaire* in La Rochelle

CHILDREN:

Anne[3], b. 10 Jul, bp. 20 Jul 1635, Calvinist Temple, LaRochelle, FR; a. 1661, to Québec, CAN; m. 23 Oct 1661, Québec, Pierre Mailloux dit Desmoulins (1631, Brie, FR-bur 11 Jun 1699, Québec), s/o Jacques & Suzanne (Arnaud) Mailloux dit Desmoulins of St-Pierre Parish of Brie-sous-Matha (n.e. of Saintes); surname also given as Maillou des Moulins; she d. 12 Dec 1700, Québec

CHILDREN (rec., Catholic churches):

Joseph[4], b. 25 Apr, Beauport, bp. 29 Apr 1663; m/1, 10 Sep 1685, Suzanne Richard (c.1669-c. 23 Mar 1690, Québec), d/o Jacques & Louise (DesPrez) Richard of Courçon (s.w. of Niort) - **2 daus**, m/2, 7 Aug 1690, Louise Achon – **1 son, 5 daus**; Joseph was a *maçon* (mason, bricklayer), *tailleur de pierres*, (stone cutter) and architect; he d. 26 Dec 1702, prob. Québec

Noël[4], b. 29 Mar, bp. 16 May 1666, Québec; m. 7 Nov 1690, Beauport, Louise (Marcoux) Gagné, widow of Joachim Gagné; 1724, capt. in the militia; **9 ch**

Jean-Baptiste[4], b. 20 Sep 1668, Québec; m/1, 7 Feb 1695, Québec, Louise Philippeau, (bur 24 Dec 1702, Québec), d/o Claude & Jeanne (Énard) Philippeau - **no issue**; m/2, 2 Jul 1703, Québec, Marguerite Caron (d. 30 Apr 1719, Québec), d/o Vital & Marguerite (Gagnon) Caron - **13 ch**; m/3, 31 Oct 1720, Québec, Marie-Catherine Amiot, d/o Charles & Rosalie (Duquet) Amiot - **no issue**; Jacques was a mason, architect and the King's contractor

Anne[4], b. 29 Nov, bp. 30 Nov 1670, Québec; m/1, 22 Nov 1688, Jean DuBois, m/2, 10 Jan 1711, Noël Levasseur

Marie[4], b. 7 Jun, bp. 8 Jun 1673, Ste-Famille; d. 31 May/bur 1 Jun 1676, Québec

Jeanne[4], b. 9 Jul 1674 ; m. 1694, Nicolas Colombe

Pierre[4], b. 12 Jan, bp. 20 Feb 1676, Ste-Famille; m/1, 9 Jun 1701, Québec, Anne LeFebvre, d/o Thomas & Geneviève (Pelletier) LeFebvre; Anne was bur 27 Jan 1703, Québec -**1 dau**; m/2, 24 Nov 1704, Québec, Marie-Charlotte Moreau (d. 27 Apr 1717 Québec), d/o Pierre & Marie-Madeleine (Lemire) Moreau – **8 ch**; m/3, 2 Oct 1717, Québec, Angélique Trépanier, d/o Charles & Marguerit (Jacquereau) Trépanier; **9 ch**; he d. 30 May 1750

Marie[4], b/bp. 30 Jul 1679, Québec; d/bur 1 Aug 1679

Jeanne[2] m. Jean Lespinasse

REF: JETTÉ, René, *Dictionnaire généalogique des familles du Québec* (Montréal, 1983); TANGUAY, L'Abbé Cyprien, *Dictionnaire généalogique des familles canadiennes*, Vol. I (Baltimore, 1967), Vol. VII (Montréal, 1890); LUSSIER, Monseigneur Irénée, *Dictionnaire national des canadiens français, 1608-1760*, Vol. I, II (Montréal).

DELPISH, Francis

b. 1663, FR
to Manakintown on the 4th ship
m. Mary Dupré, d/o John & Mary (X) Dupré; she m/2, by 1737, Charles Pain - **issue**; m/3, John Whitehead
d. 1724 VA, age 61Y
[1755 patent issued to his 3 daus as he was "long deceased"]
CHILDREN:

Marie/Mary[2], alive 27 Nov 1755, unmarr.

Judith[2], alive 27 Nov 1755, unmarr.

Anne[2], m. John Bernard, s/o David Bernard; John d. King William Parish, Powhatan Co, VA p. 1755
CHILDREN:

Judith[3], b. 27 Oct, bp. 5 Nov 1731

Rebekah[3], b. 24 Apr 1734

John[3], b. 4 Apr 1736

Anne[3], b. 6 Oct 1738
David[3], 21 Sep 17??
Francis[3], b. 24 Jan 1742/3
Pierre[3], b. 14 Jul 1747
Peter[2], d. bet 1741-51

REF: CABELL, Priscilla Harriss, *Turff & Twiggs*, Vol. I *"The French Lands"* (Richmond, VA, 1988).

DEMARÊTS/DEMAREST/des MARÊTS/des MAREST, David

b. 1620, Beauchamps (s.w. of Abbeville), Picardie, FR, s/o Jean & Marguerite (de Herville) des Marêts

m. 29 Jul 1643, FR Ch, Middelburg, Walcheren Island, Zeeland, HOL, Marie Sohier of Nieppe, Hainaut, d/o François & Marguerite/Margrieta (X) Sohier; various dates have been given as the marr. date – ch. recs. say that banns were announced 4 and 19 Jul 1643 with the marr. on the 29th; Marie d. c. 1667/8; Nieppe is 13 mi. e. of Hazebrouck, Nord Dépt., Nord-Pas-de-Calais

c. 1651 – went to Mannheim, GER

16 Apr 1662 - arr New Amsterdam on the *Bontekoe* (Spotted Cow); David settled on Staten Island

1664 - was a magistrate; delegate to the Provincial Assembly of New Netherland

1665 - went to New Harlem

1666 - rec a grant of land loc. on the East River on what is now 125th St; became an overseer & constable

1673 - the Dutch retook New Amsterdam; he was appt one of 4 magistrates who were to administer the affairs of the village

1677 - went to live on the Hackensack River in NJ; several of his ch went there too

d. a. 16 Oct 1693, Kinderkamack, NJ (heirs made a division of his property on this date; wd, 26 Oct 1689, wp, 30 Jul 1697)

CHILDREN:

Jean[2], bp. 14 Apr 1645, Middelburg; m/1, 9 Sep 1668, NY, Jacomina de Ruine (b. Hainaut), d/o Simon Druine & Magdalena Van Derstraaten – **11 ch**; m/2, 23 Mar 1692, Marretje (van Winckle) Slot, d/o Jacob Wallings Van Winckell & Trientje Jacobs, widow of Peter Jansen Slot; m/3, 20 Dec 1702, NY, Magdalena (Laurens) Tullier, widow of Jean Tullier; d. a. 10 Nov 1719, wp, Trenton, NJ

Marie[2], bp. 21 Oct 1646, Middelburg; d. young

David[2], bp. 22 Jun 1649, Middelburg; d. in infancy

David[2], b. 20 Dec 1651, Mannheim; m. 4 Apr 1675, NY, Rachel Cresson (b. c. 1656, Delft), d/o Pierre & Rachel (Claussé) Cresson; he d. Aug 1691 – **10 ch**; Rachel m/2, Jan Durié, s/o Pierre & Marguerite (Charoy) Durié, m/3, 25 Apr 1702, Hackensack, Roeloff Vander Linde/Vanderlinda

Samuel[2], b. 5 Aug 1656; m. 11 Aug 1678, Bergen, NJ, Marie de Ruine (b. 1 Jan 1662, New Harlem, sis/o Jacomina above); he d. a. 19 Oct 1728, wp; **11 ch**

Marie[2], b. 27 Mar 1659, Mannheim; d. young

Marie[2], b. 17 May 1662, Mannheim; d. young, NY

Daniel[2], bp. 7 Jul 1666; d. 8 Jan 1672, NY – was run over by a horse and cart

REF: DEMAREST, Voorhis D., *The Demarest Family,* Vol. I (1964); DEMAREST, Mary A. & William H.S., *The Demarest Family* (New Brunswick, NJ, 1938); *Proceedings of the Huguenot Society of America* (2 Jun 1884-20 Apr 1888); DEMAREST, David D., *The Huguenots on the Hackensack* (New Brunswick, 1886); ch recs – Middelburg.

DEMÉRÉ/DEMÉRAY, Louis

b. 1580, prob. Poitiers, FR; Tours records state that the family was originally from Poitiers; had a sis Catherine who m/2 Pierre Daniau, a merchant in Tours, she d. 1641; poss. the surname was originally one of origin, i.e., of/from the town of Méré/Mairé which is on the Creuse River just n.e. of Châtellerault, Poitou

m. Suzanne Masson

d. 4 Oct 1641, Poitiers; he was a merchant in Poitiers, liv. in Nôtre-Dame-la-Petite Paroisse/Parish
CHILD:

Louis II[2], b. c. 1618, Poitiers; m/1, 11 Jun 1641, Tours, Françoise Aubry, d/o Jean & Françoise (Sibot)
    Aubry of Tours; Jean was a merchant in Tours, Louis apprenticed with him after his marr;
    Tours records say that Louis was "one of the reformed ones" who had to construct a shed nr. the
    Temple de la Butte in order to shelter his horses; a. 1665, went to Moncrabeau, Guienne, (now
    Aquitaine), s.w. of Agen; later to Nérac, n.w. of Moncrabeau and s.w. of Agen; m/2, 22 Jul 1665,
    Annette LaMude of Moncrabeau (she m/2, 4 Jun 1673, Peter Cayran; she d. a. 28 Jun 1710, wp)
    CHILDREN, m/1:
    Françoise[3], b. 10 Apr 1642, Tours; m. 3 Sep 1661, Jean Vidar, a silkworker; she d. 23 Sep 1697,
        St-Saturnin Parish, Tours
    Louis III[3], b. 9 Jul 1643, Tours; m. 29 Oct 1673, Élisabeth Norieux, d/o Noé & Françoise (Villamoine)
        Norieux; Louis and Noé were both master silkworkers; Louis left Tours after
        the Revocation, went to Amsterdam and then to London where he & his wife affiliated with the
        FR Ch on Threadneedle St; **5 ch**, incl. **Louis IV**[4] (b. 1675)
    Marguerite[3], b. 24 Aug 1645, Tours
    Jean[3], b. 23 Feb 1648, Tours; listed in the records from Tours but not in SC article cited below
    Jacob[3], b. 19 Nov 1651, Tours; 1677, he affiliated with the FR Ch, Threadneedle St, London
    Samuel[3], not in Tours records but is in SC article
    CHILD, m/2:
    Isaac[3], b. 1666, Nérac; m. 3 Nov 1698, Nérac, Marie La Chapelle; d. 11 Apr 1739, bur. Nérac;
        was a successful merchant; his family used surname **DEMERÉ**, dropping the 1st accent
        CHILDREN, all emigrated to ENG:
        Raymond[4] b. 17 Jul 1702, Nérac; 25 Aug 1737, purchased his commission as a Lt. in the
            British Army; left ENG, arr GA, 8 May 1738, where he distinguished himself in battles
            against the Spanish; became a Capt; he was engaged in numerous forays on the
            frontier; 4 Aug 1757, he relinquished command of Ft. Loudoun to his bro Paul; he
            became a prosperous sea island planter; d. 21 Apr 1766, St. Simons Island, GA (nr.
            Brunswick, GA); had son **Raymond** (1752-1829), who remained loyal to the
            British during the Rev. at great personal cost; returned to St. Simons and became
            1 of the 1st planters of sea island cotton – **issue**
        Margaret[4]
        Catherine[4]
        Paul[4], in the British Army; ret to ENG, 1753, to rec. commission as Capt on 26 Jun 1754;
            by Mar 1754, he was ordered to report to VA; d. c. 10 Aug 1760, killed after the
            surrender of Ft. Loudoun, on the SC frontier (now in TN); the fort was in the
            Appalachian Mts. nr. Vonore, TN, close to the NC border; it was built by SC which
            hoped to enlist the aid of the Cherokees against the French in the French & Indian
            Wars but it ended with Indians killing most of the inhabitants of the fort; 1 son
            Raymond[5] (1750?-1791), was a Major in the American Rev.

REF: ARDOUN-WEISS, Idelette, *Les Protestants en Touraine (Les anciennes familles réformées de Tours aux XVIe et XVIIe siècles)*,Tome II; DEMERE, Patrick M., "The Huguenot Redcoat Captains Raymond & Paul Deméré"- *Transactions of the Huguenot Society of SC*, #102 (1997).

DEPPE/DEPP, Pierre

    b. by 1698, FR
    [bet 1710-1711 there are entries in the Vestry Book of King William Parish for a Jean Dep(e) – *poss.* Pierre's
        father *or* a family member]
    c. 1714 - on list of French Protestant families settled on the James River – single, no ch
    m. p. 1714, Jane Lester

1714-32 - taxed at Manakintown, VA (1710-11, a Jean Dep on the list of tithables in King William Par – not on 1712 list) – *may* have been Pierre's father); must have been over 16 to be on the list

3 Jun 1727 - sold 46 acres (patent #780) to Jacob Capon for £10

Jun 1744 - on a list of King William Parish

20 May 1735 - he sold 100 acres to John Peter Panitour/Pankey; a. 3 Feb 1737, he sold him 76 acres (patent #823); he witnessed John's will, 6 Oct 1749

17 May 1737 - he was an executor of Gideon Chambon II

2 Apr 1774 - wd, Cumberland Co, VA; mentions Jane Lester of Chesterfield Co – he wills her his estate if she "lives with me during my natural life & takes care of my body & estate"

d. a. 22 Jul 1776, wp, Cumberland Co

CHILD:

Peter II[2], m. Susannah X; d. p. 13 Mar 1807, wd, Powhatan Co, VA; will mentions wife Susannah, 5 ch, 4 grdaus*: dau Ann Howard, son John, dau Elenor Johnston, son William, grsons Peter & John (sons of Wm), grdau Marshell Johnston, gr dau Nancy (dau of Wm), son Thomas; *actually he later mentions 4 <u>grandchildren</u> (2 grsons, 2 grdaus), not 4 granddaus

CHILDREN:

Ann[3], m. James Howard of Chesterfield Co, VA

John[3]

Thomas[3]

Elenor[3], m. William Johnston; **issue**

William[3], went from Powhatan Co, VA to Barren Co, KY; son **Peter**[4] m. 31 Mar 1817, Mary H. Courts, went to Warren Co, KY – **6 sons, 3 daus**

REF: *Huguenot Society* #6, #7 (1933); Pierre's will; Peter II's Will; FIFE, Robert H. & R.L. Maury, "Vestry Books of King William Parish" *VA Magazine of History & Biography* Vol. 12, 13; JONES, W. Mac, *The Douglas Register* (Richmond, VA, 1928); BROCK, R.A. *Huguenot Emigration to VA*, pp. 75, 113 (1966); CABELL, Priscilla Harriss, *Turff & Twigg, Vol. I, The French Lands* (Richmond, VA, 1988).

DEPLANCQUE/DES PLANQ/DELPLANQUE, Guillaume

b. c. 1550, FR

m. a. 1575, Vincentine/Sentyne Carlier; she d. p. 17 Sep 1600, prob. Amsterdam

p. 1579 - went from Lille, FR to Amsterdam

d. p. 20 Sep 1603, prob. Amsterdam

CHILDREN (all b. Lille/Rijssel, FR Flanders):

Anne[2], b. c. 1575; m. 30 Aug 1596, Walloon Ch, Amsterdam, Jacques du Fau

Jacques[2], b. c. 1576, Lille, FR; m. 17 Sep 1600, Walloon Ch, Amsterdam, Sara Fauconnier, d/o <u>Pierre & Margariete (DuPont) Fauconnier</u> - marr. intention dated 26 Aug 1600, Amsterdam; he d. by Apr 1617 (widow marr 14 Apr 1618, Nicholas Agache, stating that she had been a widow for 1 yr); Jacques was a *bourassier*, a boratworker – borat was a kind of worsted yarn made from combed wool or a silk/wool mixture used for clothing, especially stockings, in French, *bourasse*

CHILDREN:

Sara[3], b. c. 1614/5, Amsterdam; <u>m/1</u>, 23 Mar 1636, <u>Pieter Montfoor/Montfoort</u>

Marie[3], bp. 1616, Walloon Ch, Amsterdam

Josse[2], b. c. 1579; m. 17 Oct 1603, Walloon Ch, Amsterdam, Maria Hasbroucq/Haesbroug from Antwerp (c. 1583-a. 27 Jun 1626), d/o Christophe/Christoffel Hasbroucq/Haesbroug; he d. a. 27 Jun 1626; at least 1 dau **Rachelle**[3] who m. c. 27 Jun 1626 (date of int.), Jean del Pierre; Josse was a boratworker

NOTE: Surname had several spellings; *Deplancque* is the one most frequently used

REF: MACY, Harry, Jr., "Sara (DePlanck) Monfort" in *NY Genealogical & Biographical Record*, Vol. 122 #3 (Jul 1991); marriage intention, Amsterdam.

DES BRISAY/DU BRISAY/DE BRISÉ, Théophile de la Cour

b. c. 1671 - may have been as early as 1662 – one acct. says he was 105 when he d.!; prob. not b. in FR, but was certainly the son or grson of French Huguenots; *perhaps* grs/o Jacques de Brisay, a Huguenot refugee, who fled from FR to HOL and d. there in 1625

1689 - commissioned as an officer in the army, so earlier b. date is probable

c. 1689 - left HOL and went to ENG

m. 13 Dec 1692, Savoy Temple, London, Madelaine Boisrond de St. Léger, d/o Samuel Boisrond de St. Léger

14 Aug 1698 - at Ostend, on a "Liste of what Protestants past Review before Major General Ramsay, in the 3 French Regiments of Foot"; was a captain; his unit was disbanded, 1699

d. prob. 15 Jul 1717, Dublin, IRE, bur. Huguenot Cemetery, Merion Row, St. Stephen's Green

CHILDREN:

Magdalaine Marie de la Cour[2], b. 1693; m. (as his 2nd or 3rd wife) Brig. General Solomon Blosset de Loches (c. 1648-21 Oct 1721), s/o Paul de Blosset; **no known issue**

Samuel Théophile/Theophilus de la Cour[2], b. 1694, Thurles, Co. Tipperary, IRE (n.e. of Limerick on the Suir River); m. 1718, FR Ch, Dublin, Magdelaine Vergèze d'Aubussargues (c.-1703-13 Dec 1788, bur Nonconformist FR Ch, Dublin), d/o Capt. Jacques Vergèze d'Aubussargues; Theo. became a capt in the British Army, stationed in IRE; d. 5 Jul 1772, Dublin, bur. Boileau tomb, Merrion St. Cemetery; aka just Theophilus

CHILDREN (9 of 10), most of whom stayed in IRE and ENG:

Lt. Col. **Paul**[3]; Rev. **Henry**[3]; Capt. **Theophilus**[3]; Lt. Col. **James**[3]; General **Jasper**[3]-issue

Bonne[3], m/1, Randal Adams – **1 dau**, m/2, Robert Thorpe – **6 ch**

Elizabeth[3] m. George L'Estrange, **no known issue**

Madeleine Elizabeth[3], b. c. 1720; m. 6 Aug 1741, Simon Boileau de Castelnau (10 Oct 1717, Southampton, ENG-15 Jul 1767, Dublin), s/o Charles & Marie Madeleine (Collot d'Escury) Boileau; she d. 12 Jan 1786; **17 ch**

Thomas de la Cour[3], b. c. 1732/3, prob. Thurles; m. c. 1753, Ellen Landers/Landen (1736, Thurles-19 Oct 1819, Prince Edward Island); he d. 25 Sep 1818, Charlottetown, Pr. Ed. Island, Canada; served as Lt. Gov of the province; **16 ch** incl. son **Theophilus**[4] who was the 1st Protestant minister on PEI

REF: LART, Charles E., *Huguenot Pedigrees*, Vol. II; LOWE, Donald W., *The Descendants of Captain Théophile Desbrisay*; REAMAN, G. Elmore, *The Trail of the Huguenots*.

DES COU(X)/DECOU/DECOW, Leuren

b. c. 1615 FR, poss. Arvert, Saintonge (now Charente-Maritime Dépt, Poitou-Charentes), s. of La Tremblade; this area is full of salt marshes; in the same area is a town called Coux, s.e. of Arvert; the family emigrated to Hatfield Chase area on the Isle of Axholme (area in n.w. Lincolnshire, e. of Scunthorpe) which was then a large marshy tract c. 18 mi x 5 mi, c. 47,000 acres; in 1627, Charles I hired Cornelius Vermuyden, a Dutchman, to make the land fit for tillage; this led to a lg. number of Flemish workmen settling the area much to the displeasure of the English citizens there

m. Jacquemine X, who d. 1664, Tudworth, Yorkshire, ENG

c. 1630 fled from 25 mi s. of La Rochelle, to Sandtoft, Lincs, ENG, where there was a colony of Huguenots; family started to attend Quaker meetings

1655 Leuren signed a petition which stated that the signers had worshiped in the ch for 20 yrs; Sandtoft is w. of Scunthorpe

bur. 17 Jan 1663, Fishlake, Yorks, ENG; c. 8 mi n.w. of Sandtoft

CHILDREN:

Isaac[2], b. Tudworth, Yorks, ENG; m/1, 12d 3m 1667, Settle Monthly Meeting, Yorkshire, Susanna Ashton (c. 1640, of Ealand, just n.e. of Sandtoft- 21 Oct 1679 Drax Abbey, n. of Thorne), bur. Summer-croft, Yorks, ENG; m/2, 24d 6m 1680, ENG, Rebecca Whitten; sailed w/ sons Jacob & Isaac from Hull, 8

Mar 1686, on the *Shields* of Stockton, arr New Castle, DE, 5 Jun 1686; purchased 2500 acres in Bucks Co, PA, called "The DeCou Tract"; he d. 13 Feb (12 m) 1686/7, New Castle, DE
CHILDREN, m/1:
Jacob[3], b. 2d 7m 1668, Thorne, Yorks (e. of Fishlake); m. 21 Dec 1699, Elizabeth (Powell) Newbold, d/o Robert & Prudence Powell, widow of James Newbold – Eliz was the 1st English ch b. Burlington Co, NJ; he d. 12m 1735, Mansfield, NJ; **8/9 ch**
John[3], b. 25d 9m 1670, Thorne; d. 31d 10m 1721, ENG
Isaac[3], b. 6d 10m 1673, Thorne; m/1, 27d 9m 1695, Rachel Newby; m/2, 25d 2m 1705, Anne Davenport; m/3, 3m 1742, Martha (Newberry) Davenport Allen; he d. 1755 Burlington Co, NJ
Elizabeth[3], b. 25d 8m 1675; m. 5d 4m 1695, Richard Dell
Emanuel[3], b. 19d 5m 1678; he d. 27d 10m 1681, Drax, Yorkshire
CHILD, m/2:
Susanna[3], b. 16 Apr 1682; m. Ambrose Field; d. Chesterfield, NJ
Susanne[2], m. 1669, ENG Estienne Le Conte who d. by 1674
Abraham[2], m. a. 1674, Sarah X (d. 1707); he remained in ENG; ch: **Daniel**[3], **Elizabeth**[3], **Hannah**[3], **John**[3], **Mary**[3], **Sarah**[3]
Jacob[2], m. 10d 1m 1677, MM, ENG, Hannah Marshall; to America, 1686, w/ bro Isaac; d. 7 Feb 1688, New Castle, DE;
CHILDREN:
Isaac[3], d. 1686, ENG
Hannah[3], m. Thomas England
Abraham[3], d. 1700

NOTE: The English towns named are s. of the Dutch River and e. of the River Trent & Scunthorpe; Tudworth apparently no longer exists but it would have been s.e. of Fishlake. Summercroft also gone but said to have been in the area of Long Drax, n. of Thorne. Some towns in Yorkshire, some in Lincolnshire.

REF: OWEN, E.A., *Pioneer Sketches of Long Point Settlement* (Toronto, 1898); de COU, Frances B., *Descendants & Ancestors of George de Cou & Margaret Haskell Daniels de Cou* (W. Hartford, CT 1970); DeCou, S. Ella & John A., *The Genealogy of the DeCou Family* (Moorestown, NJ, 1910).

DES MEAUX/DISMUKES, Guillaume/William

b. 1672 FR, s/o Guillaume & Sara (Evynard) Des Meaux
went to ENG
1695- to VA; settled Mattapony, n. end of King & Queen Co which became part of Caroline Co, 1727
m. c. 1696, Elizabeth Thornton (b. c. 1675), poss. d/o Francis Thornton of Essex & Caroline Co, VA
d. 1770, Caroline Co, VA
CHILDREN:
James[2], b. c. 1698, King & Queen Co; m. c. 1720/25, Ruth X (d. p. Aug 1793); he d. a. Oct 1770, wp, Caroline Co.
CHILDREN (as named in will):
James[3] – m. XX; dau **Elizabeth**[4] (c. 1755-1831) who m/1, c. 1773, John Johnston (c. 1752-a. 9 Feb 1786, wp) - **3 ch**; **Benjamin**[4], **Lucy**[4] who m. X Almond
William[3]
Mary[3], m. James Yarbrough
Sarah[3], m. Henry Yarbrough
Reuben[3], m. c. 1785, Margaret (X) Collins, widow of Thomas Collins
Millie[3]
Ann[3]
William[2], b. c. 1700, King & Queen Co; m. a. 1725, Mary Ellis; he d. 1769, Caroline Co

CHILDREN:

Evynard[3]

Elisha[3], b. c. 1725/30; m/1, XX– **2 ch**, m/2, c. 1760, Ann Thompson – **9 ch**; he d. c. 1816

John[3], m/2, Elizabeth/Betsy X; he d. a. 27 Apr 1802, Halifax Co, VA; **4 ch**

James[3]

William[3], m. Frances X; he d. 1778

Mary[3], b. 1733 m. Samuel Walden, Sr.

Anna[3], m. Richard Wilson

REF: *The Huguenot*, #27 (1975-77); HOPKINS, William L., *Caroline Co, VA Court Records 1742-1833 & Marriages, 1787-1810* (Richmond 1990).

DESPINÉ, David

b. c. 1595, Rouen, FR

m. XX

CHILD :

Ma(g)deleine[2], b. c. 1620, Paris; m.23 Jun 1639, FR Ch, Threadneedle St., London, Jacques Pingar (b. 1615, Paris)

CHILDREN:

Marie[3], bp. 28 Mar 1641, London, FR Ch, Threadneedle St.; m. Benjamin Aydelot, s/o David & Marie (Sochon) Aydelot; **4 sons, 3 daus   m. 6 Dec 1663**

Ma(g)deleine[3], bp. 28 Mar 1641, London, FR Ch, Threadneedle St.; this is a separate entry from that of Marie- twin ? ch b. earlier, bp. the same day ? Record does name mother – Magdelaine Despiné was a witness

Jacques[3], bp. 5 Nov 1642, London, FR Ch, Threadneedle St.

REF: MOENS, William John Charles, *The Registers of the FR Ch, Threadneedle St., London,* Vol. 13 – Registre II, 1636-[7] to 1645; (Lymington, ENG, 1899).

DES PREZ/DU PREZ/DU PRÉ, Hércule/Hercules

b. 1645, Courtrai, FR Flanders, now Kortrijk, BEL, just across the border n.e. of Tourcoing, FR

m. c. 1669/70, Cécilia d'Athis (1650-c.1720) who had bro Nicolas

1688/9 from Vlissingen (on Walcheren Island, Zeeland), HOL on the *De Schelde* to Cape Town, S. Africa; family was referred to as "Walloon Refugees" in HOL and S. Africa; S. Afr record says he came with his wife & 5 ch and they were French "*vluchtelings*" refugees; farmed at De Zoete Inval., Paarl; they were limited as to how much luggage they could take; 2 items were included: a FR Bible and a certificate of their church membership; the latter stated that "the pastor & elders of the Walloon Ch of Vlissingen cert. that Hercules des Prez and his wife have confessed the Reformed faith openly, have lived amongst us with increasing devotion, that they attended church services and that they partook in the Sacrament of Holy Communion…"- it was signed 11 Feb 1688

d. 22 Nov 1696, S. Africa

CHILDREN:

Elizabeth[2], b. 1670, Courtrai; m. 25 Jul 1688, Pieter Janz Van Marseveen from the Netherlands

Hercules[2], b. 1672; m/1, Marie LeFèvre (1651-12 May 1712) from Marck (e. of Calais) or Calais, Picardie, FR, d/o David & Elizabeth (LeBleu) LeFèvre; m/2, Cornelia Villion/Viljeon (bp. 13 Oct 1686, Stellenbosch-1758), d/o François & Cornelia (Campenar) Villion; he d. 9 May 1721, Drakenstein, Western Cape Prov., S. Africa

Marie-Jeanne[2], b. 1675, Béthune, Pas-de-Calais, FR, s.w. of Lille; m. Jacques Therond (1668-2 Dec 1739 Drakenstein) from Nîmes, Languedoc, FR; she d. 1763

François-Jean[2], b. 4 Jul 1677, Courtrai; m. Marie Cordier, d/o Louis & Françoise (Martinet) Cordier

Jacquemine[2], b. c. 1679; m. Abraham Vivier from Le Perche area (Orne Dépt, Basse-Normandie), FR; she d.1715

Philippe[2], b. 1681, Artois, FR; m. Elisabeth Prévo(s)t (1683, Marck, FR-18 Jan 1750, Tulbagh), d/o Charles & Marie (LeFèvre) Prévo(s)t; he d. 21 May 1721, Tulbagh; **12 ch**; Marck is in the Pas-de-Calais Dépt, Nord-Pas-de-Calais, e. of Calais; Tulbagh is in W. Cape Prov., S. Africa, in the Witzenberg municipal region, n.e. of Cape Town

REF: Genealogical info from Die Hugenote-Gedenkmuseum (Hug. Memorial Museum), Franschhoek, S. Africa; ROSENTHAL, Eric, *South African Surnames* (Cape Town, 1965); du PREEZ, M.H.C., *More about the Origin & Arrival of Our Ancestors*; de VILLIERS, Christoffel Coetzee, *Geslacht-Register der Oude Kaapsche Familien* (Kaapstad, 1894).

DEVANTIER/DEVANTIÉ, Pierre

b. 1637, La Gorgue, FR c. 17 mi w. of Lille, in what was called *Pays de l'Allœu* – the word today is *alleu* meaning "freehold"; the *Pays* was a small Huguenot enclave, the capital of the area was Laventie which is s.e. of La Gorgue in what was FR Flanders then and the Pas-de-Calais Dépt. of FR today

m. Marie Labauve (1641 Calais-1 Oct 1715 Woddow)

fled FR with wife & 7 ch from Lille in FR Flanders to Friesenheim in the *Pfalz* and then to the Uckermark which is bet. Berlin and Stettin; Uckermark is an historical region in n.e. GER, divided now bet the Uckermark Dist of Bradenburg & the Uecker-Randow Dist of Mecklenburg-Vorpommen; the traditional capital is Prenzlau, which is s.w. of Stettin

d. Dec 1692 Woddow (s.w. of Stettin); he was a farmer

CHILDREN:

Abraham[2], m. 12 Jul 1692, Bergholz in the Uckermark (n.w. of Woddow), Marguerite Gombert of Stein-weiler in S. *Pfalz* s.e. of Landau, d/o Jacques & Margaret (Salomé) Gombert; farmer in Friesenheim (west bank of the Rhine, just w. of Mannheim); 1693 in Prenzlau, then in Battin in the Uckermark (c. 70 km n.e. of Leipzig); son **Pierre**[3] bp May 1693 Prenzlau - **others**

Pierre[2], b. c. 1662; m/1, Jan 1695, Elisabeth Desmarets, d/o Adrian & Susanne (Collier/Collié) Desmarets, Eliz. d. 24 Feb 1704, m/2, Nov 1706, Judith Desjardins, d/o Jean & Jeanne (Deluran) Desjardins; he d. 7 Feb 1741, Bagemühl; farmer in Bagemühl, just s. of Woddow in the Uckermark

CHILDREN, m/1:

Pierre[3], b. 21 Jan 1696; **Isaac**[3], b. 22 Nov 1698; **Jacob**[3], b. 12 Aug 1701 m. M. Bray

CHILDREN, m/2:

Judith[3], b. 15 Feb 1707, m. Abraham Humberdroz;

Jehan[3], b. 14 Nov 1708

David[3], b. 12 Mar 1710, m. 3 times

Marie[3], b. 8 Feb 1712

Ester[3], b. 13 Mar 1714

Jacques[3], b. 26 May 1718, Bagemühl, m/1, 11 Dec 1748, Esther Tancré – **4 ch**, m/2, 18 Oct 1756, Anne Tancré – **4 ch**, both wives d/o Abraham & Chrétienne (Gombert) Tancré

Abraham[3], b. 13 Jul 1720, d. young

Elizabeth[3], b. 14 Jun 1721

Abraham[3], b. 22 Feb 1725 m. Charl. Desmaret

Suzanne[3], b. 11 Feb 1730, m. Isaac Noé

Jacob[2], m. 1697, Marie Coppet, d/o Oliver & Marie (Scabelle) Coppet; farmer in Woddow, from Friesenheim in the *Pfalz*; **9 ch**

Isaac[2], b. c. 1666; m. 1706, Catherine Destouché, (1678, Flamersheim/Flomershein , *Pfalz*, s.w. Frankenthal-23 Jan 1745, Woddow); farmer in Woddow; he d. 17 Mar 1753, Woddow

Jeanne[2], m. 1692, Jacques Leclercq/LeClercq

REF: Information from a genealogist for the German Huguenot Society; Records French Reformed Church, Battin Prenzlau; BERINGUIER, Richard, *The Brandenburg – Colony List of 1699* (Berlin, 1888); BERINGUIER, Richard, *The Family Trees of the Members of the French Colony in Berlin* (Berlin,1887).

DEYO/DEYOE/DE JOUX, Chrétien/Christian

(many possible spellings)
b. c. 1610, FR, poss. s/o Pierre du Joue
m. c. 1642, Jeanne Verbeau/Wibau
c. 1675 – from Mannheim, GER to NY
eldest of the Patentees of New Paltz, NY
d. p. 1 Feb 1686/7, wd, Ulster Co, NY
CHILDREN:
Anna[2], b, 1644; m. Jean Hasbrouck; she d. 5 May 1694, New Paltz
Pierre[2], b. 1646/50, prob. St. Pol, Artois, FR; m. c. 1672, Mutterstadt (6 mi s.w. of Mannheim), Agatha
    Nichol
    CHILDREN:
    Abraham[3], b. 16 Oct 1676; m. 23 Nov 1702, Kingston, Elsie Clearwater, d/o Teunis Jacobsz
        Clearwater & Marretje Hansen; he d. Oct 1725; **3 ch**
    Mary[3], bp. 20 Apr 1679; m. Jacob Clearwater (b.1663, HOL), s/o Teunis Jacobsz Clearwater
        & Marretje Hansen; settled 4000 acre patent in Shawangunk; **1 son**
    Christian[3], bp. 17 Apr 1681, Kingston; m 21 Feb 1701/2, Kingston, Maria de Graff, d/o Moses &
        Hester (LeMaître) LeConte de Graaf; **7 ch**
    Pierre[3], bp. 14 Oct 1683, d. p. 1755 unmarr.
    Margaret[3], b. 14 Oct 1683; prob. d. young
    Madeline[3], b. 17 Apr 1687; prob. d. young
    Hendricus[3], bp. 12 Oct 1690; m. 31 Dec 1715, Kingston, Margaret VanBommel (bp. 23 Apr 1693-
        21 Feb 1747), d/o Peter & Deborah (Davids) Van Bommel; **10 ch**
Marie[2], b. 1653, Mutterstadt; m. 17 Nov 1675, Abraham Hasbrouck; she d. 27 Mar 1741, New Paltz
Elizabeth[2], b. c. 1655 Mutterstadt; m/1, 1678, Hurley, Simon LeFèvre, m/2, 1691, Moses Cantine
Margaret[2], b. c. 1662; m. 6 Mar 1681, Abraham DuBois, s/o Louis & Catherine (Blanchan) Du Bois;
    their dau **Leah**[3], m. Philip Ferrée, s/o Daniel & Marie (de la Warenbuer) Ferrée

REF: HASBROUCK, Kenneth E. & HEIDGARD, Ruth P., *The Deyo (Deyoe) Family* (New Paltz, 1958, rev.
& enlarged, 1980); HASBROUCK, Kenneth E., *The Hasbrouck Family in America*, Vol. I (New Paltz, 1961);
BAIRD, Charles W., *The Story of the Huguenot Emigration to America* Vol. 1; RIDER, R.G., *"The Deyo Family
In France and New Paltz, Ulster Co, NY"* in *The American Genealogist*, Vol. 49, #1 (Jan 1973); VAN WAGENEN,
Gerrit H., *"Early Settlers of Ulster Co, Abraham & Jean Hasbrouck"* in *NY Gen & Biog Record*, Vol. 17 (Oct 1886).

DILL(I)ER, Caspar Élias

b. 25 Jun 1696, Alsace; s/o Huguenot refugees who then went to HOL where Caspar learned to make
    wooden shoes; supposedly a descendant, poss. a son or grson of Jean Dillier, a Huguenot author,
    minister, who went to HOL; original name said to be Deller
c. 1709-1714 - went to ENG
m/1, c. 1721/2, ENG, Anna Barbara Pratter/Pretter (c.1703-a. 1766)
c. 1722 - went to the Palatinate
17 Aug 1733 – arr Philadelphia on the *Samuel* w/ wife and 4 ch – Philip Adam (10), Hans Martin (8),
    Rosina (4), Christina (2)
m/2, 14 Apr 1766, Eva Magdalena Meyer
d. 1787 (25 Nov 1786?), Lebanon Co, PA, bur. Hill Evangelical Lutheran Ch – gravestone gives b.
    date, says he was 91 Y 5 mo at death
CHILDREN:
Philip Adam[2], b. 8 Mar 1723. nr. Heidelburg; m. 7 May 1745, Mary Magdalena Ellmaker (9 Aug 1727-4
    Dec 1807), d/o Leonard Ellmaker; he d. 8 Sep 1777, New Holland, PA; **8 ch**
Jean/Hans Martin[2], b. c. 1725; had sons **Adam**[3], **John**[3] + prob. other ch
Rosina[2], b. c. 1729; m. 1747, John Adam Deininger (23 Apr 1722 GER-16 Feb 1803 PA), s/o Leonard &

Margaret (X) Deininger; **8 ch**

Christina[2], b. c. 1731; m. XX

Margaret[2], b. 1734, PA; m. 21 Feb 1749, New Holland, Lancaster Co, PA, Michael Keinadt/Keiner (29 Jan 1720, Winterlingen, GER-7 Nov 1796, Augusta Co, VA), s/o Conrad Keinadt; she d. 18 Nov 1813, VA, 79Y; **13 ch**; surname also KOINER

Casper[2], b. 23 Sep 1744, PA; m/1, Julianna Lang, d/o Urban & Christian (X) Lang; m/2, Margaret X; he d. a. 24 Nov 1796, wp, Cumberland Co, PA; number of ch per wife, not known; 7 sons – **Caspar**[3], **Martin**[3], **John**[3], **David**[3], **Benjamin**[3], **George**[3], **Solomon**[3]; 5 daus – **Elizabeth**[3] m. Abraham Pollinger, **Catharine**[3] m. George Carle, **Magdalene/Molly**[3] m. George Fosler, **Juliana**[3] m. Abraham Righter, **Christina**[3]

Mary Magdalena[2], m. 24 Nov 1757, Sebastian Nagel

Juliana[2], m. 24 Nov 1757, John Nicholas Brechbiel/Breckbill

Eleanor[2], m. 14 Nov 1758, Johann Schwenckhard Imboden

1 other dau[2] – she and sis Christina m. men named Sensabach, Croft or Sweiger – not clear which one

NOTE: There was <u>much</u> conflicting information re this line. Above is the best estimate of what really happened!

REF: RINGWALT, J.F., *The Diller Family* (Nov 1877); *A Historical Sketch of Michael Keinadt & Margaret Diller, His Wife* (Staunton, VA 1893); STAPLETON, Rev. A., *Memorials of the Huguenots in America* (Carlisle, PA 1901); LONG, William G., *History of the Long Family* (Huntington, WV, 1930); *The Pennsylvania-German*, Vol. XI, #9 (Sep 1910).

DOREMUS, Cornelius

prob. b. c. 1650, Middelburg (or Breskens), HOL, s/o Hendrik D'Oremus

family orig. from FR; thought is that the surname was originally de Rheims, implying the they were from the town of R(h)eims

m. 12 May 1675, Reformed Ch in Middelburg, HOL, Jannetje Joris *Van Elsland* = of Elsland, b. Groede d/o Joris Matthyssen & Hubrechtje Jans; ship list says she b. Stapleholm, nr. Friedrichstadt, Schleswig-Holstein, GER

bet Sep 1684-Apr 1687 - to NJ; settled Acquackanonk – now the Passaic/Paterson area Jannetje was on the membership list of the Reformed Dutch Ch in NY, 2 Sep 1685

1708 – Cornelis purchased 150 acres of farmland in Wesel, NJ, now Paterson; 1711 he purchased 350 acres on Wesel Mountain

d. p. 28 Jan 1714/5 wd-a. 8 Feb 1714/5, wp, Essex Co, NJ; supposedly written while he was on his deathbed

CHILDREN:

Thomas[2], bp. 24 Mar 1676, Middelburg; d. young – said to have d. on trip to America, bur. at sea; 3 of his grandparents were witnesses at his baptism

Maijke[2], bp. 17 Nov 1677, Middelburg; d. young, prob. HOL

Janneke[2], bp. 3 Jan 1680, Middelburg; d. young, prob. HOL

Cornelis[2], bp. 3 Feb 1682, Middelburg; m. 12 Aug 1710, Bergen, NJ, Rachel Pieterse(n) (b. 14 Sep 1682 Bergen), d/o Pieter Hessels & Lysbeth Gerrits; he d. p. 1756; **6 ch**

Johannes[2], bp. 7 Sep 1684, Middelburg; m. p. 19 Aug 1709, Hackensack, Lysbeth/Elisabeth A. Ackerman (bp.19 May 1684 Bergen-p. 5 Jul 1754), d/o Abraham Davidse Ackerman & Aeltje Van Laer, grd/o David Ackerman & <u>Élisabeth Bellier</u>; he a. 7 Feb 1758, wp, NJ; **6 ch**

Thomas[2], bp. 11 Apr 1687, Bergen, NJ; m. Anneke Abramse Ackerman (sis/o Elisabeth above & a <u>Bellier</u> descendant)

Jannetje[2], bp. 4 Jun 1691, Bergen; m. c. 22 Oct 1715 (banns), Hackensack, Frans Oudtwater (bp. 14 Oct 1688), s/o Thomas Franzen Oudewater & Tryntje Jans Van Breestede; he d. a. 1726; **3 ch** surnamed OUTWATER

Joris[2], b. Acquackanonk; m. c. 16 Mar 1717 (banns) Hackensack, Marretie Berdan (b. 1694 N. Amersfoort, LI, NY), d/o Jan Baerdan/Berdan & Eve Sicklen; he d. p. 25 Mar 1733 - **5 ch**; she m/2, 6 Dec 1733, Jacob Tisort/Tietsoort

Hendrick[2], bp. 26 May 1695; m. 14 Apr 1716, Annatie Essels/Hesselse, prob. d/o Hessel Pieterse & Elisabeth Claes; **7 ch**

REF: NELSON, William, *Genealogy of the Doremus Family in America* (Patterson, NJ 1897); KOEHLER, Sara M., compiler, *Huguenot Ancestors Represented in the Membership of the Huguenot Society of NJ* (1965); BOYER, Carl, 3rd, *Ship Passenger Lists, NY &NJ, 1600-1825;* Schermerhorn, Richard Jr., "Representative Pioneer Settlers of New Netherlands" in *NYGBR*, #65 (1934).

DOUAY/DUEY/DUY, Jacques de

b. 1552, St. Python, Nord Dépt, Pas-de-Calais, FR, n.e. of Cambrai, s/o Adrien & Jehanne (Telier) Douay
m/1, c. 1571, St. Python, Paquette/Pasques Bantegnie
m/2, c. 1580, St. Python, Philipotte Deudon (1555-p. 18 Dec 1608)
d. p. 1610-a. 3 Nov 1611, St. Python; he was a merchant
CHILD, m/1:
Amand[2], b. 1572; m. Antoinette Le Mesureur; d. 1624; **2 ch**
CHILDREN, m/2:
Thomas[2], b. c. 1580-90, St. Python; m/1, c. 1612, St. Python or Liège, where Thomas worked, Jeanne Lespineu – 1 son (below), Jeanne, bur 22 Dec 1615, Hanau, m/2, 27 Sep 1620, Breda, HOL, Marguerite Ferri - 1 dau **Catherine**[3]; he d. c. 1636, Hanau, GER; he was a weaver of serge wool
  CHILD, m/1:
  Thomas[3], b. c. 1615; m/1, 30 Nov 1636, Amsterdam, Eva Jeanne Foquan – **no issue**; m/2, c. 1648, Amsterdam, Sabina X - **4 sons**, the eldest **Nicholas**[4] (1657-Oct 1738) m. Angelica Frantz – their son **Johan Conrad**[5] (1689-1766) was the immigrant to Bucks Co, PA; Johan Conrad m/1, Anna Margaretha Boehm – **7 ch**, m/2, Anna Marie Reiss – **no issue**
Simonne[2], b. 1583; m. 12 Dec 1608, Anthoine Bijeu; she d. 1650
Pierre[2], b. c. 1585; m. Marguerite LeClercq; he d. c. 1620; 1 dau **Claudine**[3]

REF: Records from the Municipal Archives of St. Python; records from Kriegsfeld, *Pfalz,* GER Evangelical Lutheran Church; Walloon Church records; STROUD, Steve, *Duy Family Genealogy.*

DRAGAUD/DRAGOO, Pierre

b. c. 1639, St. Nazaire-sur-Charente, Saintonge, FR, s.w. of Rochefort; poss. had bro Jean
m. Jeanne Garnier/Garnié/Garnée
was in the French Navy; evidently deserted or was dismissed for religious reasons
c. 1681-85 - went to ENG; poss. joined British Navy
d. p. Nov 1699; he was a saltmaker and mariner; marr. rec of son Jean says fa dec. but Pierre was at son Pierre's wedding in Nov; evidently the family thought he was lost at sea in Aug
CHILDREN:
Pierre II[2], b. 1669, nr. Moïse (now Moëze, s.e. of St. Nazaire-sur-Charente), Saintonge, FR; m. 12 Nov 1699, FR Ch, Bristol, ENG, Elizabeth Tavaud, d/o Pierre & Marie (Goubeilla) Tavaud; liv. on Staten Island, NY; he d. a. 3 Apr 1712, adm, Staten Island; wool worker
  CHILDREN:
  Jean/John[3], b. 1700/1, prob. Staten Island; d. p. census, 1706/7; no further info
  Marie/Mary[3], b. Staten Island; m. Jan/Feb 1726, Teunis Van Pelt (bur. 5 Dec 1774, NY, 25 Mar 1775, wp, Richmond Co, NY), s/o Anthony Teunissen Van Pelt & Magdalena Joosten; she d. p. 1738; **issue**
  Pierre/Peter III[3], b. c. 1707, Staten Island; m. 1727, Elizabeth/Lysbeth Guyon/Guion (b. 9 Apr

1701, Staten Island), d/o Jacques II & Anne (Vigneau/Vincent) Guion; Jacques II was the s/o Jacques I & Sarah (Casier) Guion, grs/o Philippe & Marie (Taine) Casier; 2 known ch – **Peter IV**[4] m. Mary X – **9 ch, Margrietza**[4] who m. 1759, Samuel Littler; both ch went to Frederick Co, VA, 1753, but Peter[4] d. in w. PA on the way; Peter III d. p. 1753

Jean/John[2], b. St. Froult, n.w. of Moëze; m. 26 Aug 1699, FR Ch, Bristol, Susanne Morrye, d/o Jacques & Jeanne (Blondel) Morrye (Jacques d. & Jeanne m/2 Daniel Jaudon); he was a member & elder of the FR Ch in NYC; saltmaker & mariner; he & Susanne were godparents to Jean Harden, s/o Jacques & Abijah (Bouquet) Harden, 12 Jan 1728/9 in FR Ch NYC; poss. returned to ENG p. 1735

poss. a dau[2]

REF: BAIRD, Charles W., *History of the Huguenot Emigration to America*; HIX, Charlotte M., *Staten Island Wills & Letters of Administration, Richmond Co, NY, 1670-1800* (1993); LART, Charles E., *Registers of the French Churches of Bristol, Stonehouse & Plymouth*, Vol. XX (1912); DUNCAN. Alice Y., *History of Dragoo, Speer, Duncan, Woodside Families* (1972); Dragoo Family Assoc.

DuBOIS, Chrétien

b. 1597; of Wicres/LaBassée, Artois, FR, c. 10 mi s.w. of Lille; poss. s/o Wallerand & Madeleine (de Croix) du Bois **or** Jean (b. c. 1563), who had a bro Pierre who m. Jeanne (see below), **or** Charles Maximillien des Fiennes & Henrietta de Reignier de Boisleau

m. c. 1620, Cornelia X

d. c. 1628/29 – d. suddenly; Cornelia m/2 Chrétien's older bro Jean - son **Martin**[2], b. 1630; they joined the Protestant Ch at Middleburg, GER, 2 Mar 1646

CHILDREN:

Françoise[2], b. 17 Jun 1622, bp. 18 Jun 1622, Wicres; m. 20 Apr 1649, Leiden, HOL, Pierre Billiou; she d. a. 17 Jan 1695, prob. NY; **5 ch**

Anne[2], bp. 30 Nov 1625, Wicres, France; in Leiden in 1643

Louis[2], b. 27 Oct, bp. 13 Nov 1626, Lille, FR; m. 10 Oct 1655, FR Ch, Mannheim, Catherine Blanchan, d/o Matthew & Magdaleine (Joiré) Blanchan; left Mannheim for America, c. 1660; 1st went to New Amsterdam, then to Esopus where in 1663 his wife & 3 ch were captured by Indians & later rescued; fam. settled New Paltz, NY; he d. p. 22 Feb 1695/6, ww - a. 26 Mar 1696, wp, Kingston, Ulster Co, NY; another will written, 27 Mar 1694, proven, Ulster Co, NY, 23 Jun 1696; he was a merchant; Catherine m/2 Jean Cottin, she d. p. 23 Jul 1712, wd-a. 10 Dec 1713, wp, Ulster Co, NY

CHILDREN:

Abraham[3], b. 26 Dec 1657, Mannheim ; m. 6 Mar 1681, Kingston, NY, Margaret Deyo, d/o Chrétien & Jeanne (Verbeau) Deyo; he d. 7 Oct 1731, New Paltz, NY

CHILDREN :

Benjamin[4], res. Catskill

Sarah[4], b. 18 May 1682, bp. 20 Jun 1682; m. 13 Jun 1703, Roelof Elting (bp. 27 Oct 1678-1745/7), s/o Jan Elting & Jacomyntie Slecht; **7 ch**

Abraham[4], bp. 17 Apr 1685; m. 12 Oct 1717, New Paltz, NY, Maria La Resiliere/Larzalere (bp. 12 Jun 1681), d/o Jacques & Marie (Grangen) La Esiliere/Larzalere; settled Somerset, NJ; **9 ch**

Leya/Leah[4], bp. 16 Oct 1687; m. Philip Ferrée, s/o Daniel & Marie (de la Warenbuer) Ferrée; settled Lancaster Co, PA where her father had a patent of 1000 acres

Mary[4], bp. 13 Oct 1689; d. young

Rachel[4], bp. 13 Oct 1689; m. 6 Apr 1713, cousin Isaac du Bois, s/o Solomon du Bois; settled Peskoine Creek, PA

Catherin[4], bp. 21 May 1693; m. 24 Oct 1728, William Donnelson; settled Lancaster Co, PA

Noah[4], bp. 18 Feb 1699

Joel[4], bp. 20 Jun 1703; d. 1734; **no issue**

Isaac[3], b. 1659 Mannheim; m. 1 Jun 1683, Maria Hasbrouck, d/o Jean & Anna (Deyo) Hasbrouck;

he d. 28 Jun 1690, age 31 yrs.; **2 sons**

Jacob[3], b. 1661, bp. 9 Oct 1661, Kingston, NY; m/1, 8 Mar 1689, Lysbeth Varnoye, d/o Cornelis
Cornelissen Vernoye & Annatje Cornelis Van Der Cuyl – **1 dau**, m/2, 1691/2, Gerretje
Gerritsen Van Nieuwkirk, d/o Gerit Cornelissen Van Nieuwkirk & Chieltie Gerrits - **8
ch**; he d. Jun 1745, age 84 yrs.

Sara[3], b. 14 Sep 1664, Kingston, NY; m. 12 Dec 1682, Joost Jansen Van Metern, s/o Jan Joosten
Van Metern & Maeyken Hendicksen; she d. 1726, Salem Co, NJ; **9 ch**

David[3], b. 13 Mar 1667, Kingston, NY; m. 8 Mar 1689, Cornelia Vernoye, sister of Lysbeth
(above) d. p. 1729, prob. Rochester, NY; **6 ch**

Salomon[3], bp. 3 Feb 1669, Dutch Ref Ch, NYC; m. c. 1692, Tryntje Gerritsen Focken, d/o Gerrit
Cornelissen Focken & Jacomyntje Cornelise Slecht; d. 2 Feb 1759, New Paltz, NY; he d. a. 15
Feb 1759, wp, Ulster Co, NY; **7 ch**

Rebecca[3], bp. 18 Jun 1671; d. young

Rachel[3], bp. 18 Apr 1675; d. young

Louis[3], b. 1677, Hurley, NY; m. 19 Jan 1701, Rachel Hasbrouck, d/o <u>Abraham & Maria (Deyo)
Hasbrouck</u>; he d. 1749; **7 ch**

Mattheus[3], b. 3 Jan 1679, Hurley, NY; m. 17 Jan 1697, Sara Matthyseen Van Keuren, d/o Matthys
Matthyssen Van Keuren & Taatje De Witt; he d. 1748, Dutchess Co, NY; **12 ch**

Magdalen[3], bp. 12 May 1680, NY; m. Peter Van Ness, grs/of Jean & Marie (X) Crocheron

Jacques[2], bp. 27 Oct 1628, Lille, FR; m. 25 Apr 1643, Walloon Church, Leiden, Pierronne Bentyn;
d. a. 1677, Kingston, NY; from GER to Leyden, to Kingston, NY 1675; **8 ch**

REF: ANJOU, GUSTAVE, *Ulster Co, NY Probate Records,* Vol. I (NY, 1906); HEIDGERD, William, *The American
Descendants of Chrétien DuBois of Wicres, France,* Parts 1-20 (1968-1984); LeFEVRE, Ralph, *History of New Paltz, NY
and Its Old Families* (1909); BAIRD, Charles W., *Huguenot Emigration to America* (Baltimore, 1985); NOURSE, Eva
Miller, *The Miller-du Bois Family* (1928); HOES, Roswell Randall, *Baptismal & Marriage Registers of the Old Dutch
Church of Kingston, NY* (Baltimore, 1980).

DuBOIS, Jacques/James

b. Marennes, Saintonge, FR, s.w. of Rochefort
m. FR, prob. Marennes, Blanche Sauzeau
fled to HOL, then to the West Indies
by 1685 - in NYC
d. 1688, NY
CHILD:

Blanche[2], b. a. 1685, Marennes, Saintonge, FR; m. a. 2 Jun 1708, René Het; they liv. "in the
Vly" – now 216 Pearl St.; she d. 31 Jan 1739/40, bur. Trinity Churchyard, NYC; he d. a. 8
Nov 1768, wp, NYC; René's will stated that his burial be decently performed "after the manner
of the French Protestants in the City of New York"; he was a merchant; Pearl St. is just w.
of the present Manhattan Bridge and s. of I-278 in Brooklyn; René was very prob. a Huguenot
but since nothing is known of his antecedents, he is listed with his wife, rather than a separate
listing as was done in the past; he and his wife were godparents to Estienne Mesnard (bp. 21 Sep
1717, FR Ch, NYC) s/o Daniel & Élisabeth (Vincent) Mesnard & to René Bueau (b. 3 Jul, bp. 17
Jul 1726, FR Ch, NYC), s/o Daniel & Ester (Gaillard) Bueau
CHILDREN:

Sarah[3], b. 25 May, bp. 2 Jun 1708, FR Ch, NYC; m. Capt. William Smith; Sarah d. a. 1 Apr 1754,
as her father referred to her as deceased in his will written on that date
CHILDREN:

Blanche[4], m. Jedediah Chapman of Orangetown, Essex, NJ; had 2 surviving ch:
Robert Hett[5] & **William Smith**[5]

Sarah[4], prob. d. unmarr.

Marie/Mary[3], b. 24 May, bp. 20 Jun 1710, FR Ch, NYC; m. p. 10 May 1730, William Smith, Esq. (1696, ENG-23 Nov 1769, bur. Presbyterian Ch cem. on Wall St, NYC), a lawyer – on that date, his future in-laws gave him a house and lot located at what is now 179 Pearl St; later liv. on the s.e. corner of Broadway & Exchange Pl. (just s. of Wall St., in the Financial District, Manhattan); in his will René mentions that Mary and William had sons and daus but does not name anyone but Joshua Het Smith

CHILDREN (2 of ?):

Joshua Het[4] liv. in the "Treason House" in Rockland Co, NY; it was owned by his bro Thomas but he was liv. there in 1780 when Gen. Benedict Arnold & Maj. John André were hatching their plot – Joshua became a dupe of the 2 conspirators

Thomas[4]

REF: BAIRD, Charles W., *History of the Huguenot Emigration to America,* Vol. II; *NY Wills,* Vol. XIV, pp. 54-57; will of René Het, dated 1 Apr 1754 in *NYC Wills, 1766-1771*, p. 428.

Du BOIS, Louis

b. c. 1668 (age 40 in 1706/8)
a. Aug 1696 - to NY, moved to Staten Island
m. p. 28 Aug 1696 (date of license), Ester/Hester Grasset, d/o Auguste & Marie (Pelé) Grasset
1706 or 1708 – on census roll – 40 yrs. old, wife, 3 ch-Louis, Charles & Margaret
1715 - on Militia Rolls on Staten Island
d. a. 19 Mar 1717/8 NY; he was a blacksmith
CHILDREN:

Louis[2], b. 21 May, bp. 23 May 1697, FR Ch, NYC; m/1, a. 19 Mar 1717/8, Martha X; m/2, c. 9 Feb 1736 (date of bond), Catherine/Trynje Van Dyck, d/o Cornelius Rutgersz, widow of Jacob Van Dyck; he d. a. 1 Oct 1745, wp, Richmond Co, NY – names wife & **8 ch**; he was a blacksmith

Auguste[2], b. 20 May, bp. 28 May 1699, FR Ch, NYC; d. a. 1706

Charles[2], b. c. 1701; m. Agnes X; d. a. 24 May 1750, Amwell, Hunterdon Co, NJ; weaver; **no known issue**

Margaret[2], b. c. 1703, Staten Island; m. a. 1731, Jean Grandin (a boatman, d. a. 22 Dec 1764, wp); she d. p. 2 Feb 1749/50; **issue**

Mary[2], b. c. 1709; m. Isaac Prall (bp. 25 Jul 1710-27 Jan 1774); she d. p. 15 Aug 1770; **issue**

REF: THOMPSON, Neil D., "Auguste Grasset of La Rochelle, London, & NY" in *National Genealogical Society Quarterly,* Vol. 66 #1 (Mar 1978); *Register of Ancestors of the Huguenot Society of NJ*; WITTMEYER, Alfred, *Église Françoise à la Nouvelle York* ; HIX, Charlotte, M., *Staten Island Wills & Letters of Administration Richmond Co, NY, 1670-1800.*

DuBOIS, Pierre I

poss. uncle of Chrétien DuBois
m. Jeanne Desmuille/Desmullie/Desmulle of Herseaux, who m/2, c. 2 Jun 1644 (date of marr contract), Eleazer Des Jong/De Jonque, widower, of Sandwich, ENG
liv. Herseaux, FR Flanders, now BEL, n.e. of Lille, s. of Courtrai/Kortrijk
d. bet Feb 1623/4-Oct 1625
CHILDREN (all b. Herseaux):

Jacques[2], b. c. 1595; m/1, 19 May or 17 Aug 1620, Canterbury, Jeanne Capon, d/o Nicolas & Anne (X) Capon; m/2, c. 4 Sep 1628 (date of contract), Canterbury, Elizabeth Laignel/Laigneil, d/o Jean Laignel; he d. 12 Jun 1638, Canterbury
CHILDREN, m/1 (all b. Canterbury):
Jeanne[3], b. 1 Jul 1621; **Judith**[3], b. 27 Jul 1623; **Jeanne**[3], b. 25 Feb 1624 , m. 15 May 1646, Philip

Houze Michelsz

CHILDREN, m/2 (all b. Canterbury):

Jacques[3], b. 13 Feb 1624, m. 10 Feb 1654, Marie de Harlie; **Jean**[3], b. 11 Mar 1631; **Jacob**[3], b. 20 Nov 1634, m. 10 Apr 1658, Lea LeQueux; **Élisabeth**[3], b. 21 May 1637, m. 1 Apr 1659, Jean Pateu-Jeanz

Jean[2], b. c. 1597; m. 22 Oct 1620, Canterbury, Jeanne de la Marlière, d/o Jacques de la Malière

Laurent/Laurens[2], b. c. 1599; m. 14 Feb 1630, Canterbury, Marie Capon, d/o Nicolas & Anne (X) Capon; dau **Anne**[3], b. 13 Mar 1631, Canterbury

Pierre II[2], b. 17 Mar 1601/2; m/1, 25 Aug 1622, Canterbury, Catherine Clarisse (bp. 17 Mar 1602/3, Canterbury-17 Sep 1633, Canterbury), d/o Jean & Sara (LeConte) Clarisse (Sara, d/o Antoine LeConte); m/2, (contract dated 31 Oct 1633) 24 Nov 1633, Canterbury, Marie Poachin/Pouchin, d/o Jacob Poachin/Pouchin

CHILDREN, m/1:

Michel[3] (dau), bp 13 Jul 1624, Canterbury

Esther[3], bp. 9 Oct 1625, Canterbury; m/1, 24 Apr 1652, FR Walloon Ch, Amsterdam, Claude Le Maître, as his 3rd wife; m/2, 6 Nov 1687, Jan Tribout

Abraham[3], bp. 14 Oct 1627, Canterbury; **Marie**[3], b. 22 Nov 1629, Canterbury; **Judith**[3], bp. 16 Sep 1632, Canterbury – alive on 31 Oct 1633

CHILDREN, m/2:

Pierre[3], b. 3 Nov 1634; **Isaac**[3], b. 6 Mar 1636; **Jacob**[3], b. 8 Apr 1638; **Pierre**[3], b. 6 Oct 1639; **Jacques**[3], b. 7 Feb 1641; **Marye**[3], b. 22 Jan 1643; **Elisabeth**[3], b. 28 Feb 1644, Amsterdam, HOL

George[2], b. c. 1603; m. c. 24 Dec 1628 (date of contract), Canterbury, Marie Gignon, d/o Jean Gignon; dau **Rachel**[3], b. 18 Jul 1639, Canterbury

Abraham[2], b. c. 1605; m. Susanne X; ch – **Eleazer**[3], b. 29 Nov 1635-d. 8 Jun 1639; **Abraham**[3], b. 29 Jan 1637; **Pierre**[3], b. 16 Sep 1638; **Jeanne**[3], b. 8 Mar 1648

REF: MURPHY, Matthew H., *"Pierre DuBois Supplement"* to *The European Ancestry of Chretien Du Bois of Wicres, France, 1597-1628, with Royal Descent* (1987, rev. 1990, 1994, 1995, Claverach, NY); PITMAN, Minot, *"Esther DuBois, Second Wife of Claude LeMaitre"* in the *NY Genealogical & Biographical Record* Vol. XCIV, #3 (July 1963); Walloon Ch records, Canterbury; PITMAN, H. Minot, "Esther DuBois, 2nd Wife of Claude LeMaitre" in *NYGBR*, Vol. XCIV (1963).

Du BOSC/Du BOSE, Louis

b. c. 1620, Normandie, FR, *prob.* s/o Pierre & Françoise (Olivier/Olliver de Lienville) Du Bosc

m. 1650/55, Anne X of Dieppe, Normandie, FR; she m/2, a. 1682, Richard LeGrand

d. a. 1682

CHILD:

Isaac[2], b. c. 1660/5, Dieppe; m. c. 1688, Suzanne Couillandeau, d/o Pierre & Suzanne (X) Couillandeau, from la Tremblade, Saintonge; settled Jamestown, SC, on the Santee, c. 1686, where he purchased lot #12; naturalized, 1689; he d. SC, p. 19 Jun 1714, wd; in his will he mentions wife, 8 ch; he d. bet 1714-1721, when Suzannne purchased land as a "widow"; Suzanne m/2, c. 1733, Bentley Cooke; she d. c. 1740; 12 Jun 1742, division of her estate – the ch participating in that division – Isaac, Elizabeth Whilden, Daniel, Stephen, John, Andrew, Peter

CHILDREN (order, dates of birth are uncertain):

Antoine[3], d. a. 12 Jun 1742; **no known issue**

Isaac[3], b. c. 1693; m/1, a. 1728, Madelaine Rembert (b. p. 1697), d/o André & Anna (Bressau) Rambert – **1 son, 1 dau**; m/2, Hester Elizabeth (Gourdin) Bean, d/o Louis Gourdin*, widow of John Bean, she d. a. 1 Aug 1763, wp – **3 sons, 2 daus**; he d. p. 12 Jun 1742, wd-a. 17 Sep 1742, wp, Craven Co, SC – mentions wife Hester, sons **Isaac**[4] (m/1), **Jonathan**[4], **Joshua**[4], **Jeptha**[4], daus **Susannah**[4], **Beersheba**[4] & **Esther**[4], eldest dau **Madelaine**[4] (m/1) evidently dec.

Elizabeth[3], b. 1695; m. c. 1721, Jonathan Whilden (d. a. 21 Mar 1736, wp), s/o John Whilden; she
d. p. 12 Jun 1742, Christ Church Par, SC; **4 sons, 2 daus**

Daniel[3], b. 1697; m. a. 4 Mar 1736, Anne Rembert, d/o Pierre & Jeanne (X) Rembert, grdau/o
<u>André & Anna (Bressan) Rambert</u>; liv. St. James Parish; he d. a. 9. Jun 1755, inv; 1 dau
Anne[4] who m. 1759, Daniel Jaudon, s/o <u>Daniel & Elizabeth (Videau) Jaudon</u>

John[3], b. 1694/1700; <u>m/1</u>, 1727, Susannah Lemonier, d/o James/Jacques Lemonier – **1 dau**; <u>m/2</u>,
Mary Whilden, d/o John Whilden – **4 sons, 5 daus**; he d. 1778

Stephen[3], b. c. 1702/3; <u>m/1</u>, Lydia X (d. c. 1739) – **1 son**; <u>m/2</u>, Elizabeth X – **2 sons, 1 dau;** settled
on the s. side of Lynch's Creek what later became Cartersville, SC; he d. p. 1770

Peter[3], b. c. 1705, SC; m. c. 1725/28, Madelaine/Magdelene X, a grdau/o <u>André & Anna
(Bressan) Rambert</u> – *prob.* was the d/o Marguerite Rembert & <u>Pierre Guerri</u> who had a
a dau named Madeleine – André Rambert's will names a grdau Madeleine, wife of
Pierre DuBose; liv. Christ Church Parish, later was in Pr. Frederick Parish on the Black
River; he d. p. 1756, SC; **3 sons, 1 dau**

Andrew[3], b. c. 1710/12; m. c. 1730/35, Berkeley Co, SC, Elizabeth Sinclair, poss. d/o George
Sinclair; Andrew went to Lynch's Creek in what is now Darlington Co; he d. c. 1787;
3 sons, 2 daus

[*Louis Gourdin, the emigrant, came from Artois, FR, s/oValentine & Marie (Piedenon) Gourdin. Per the
mural tablets in the Huguenot Church, Charleston, SC, he was a Huguenot.]

REF: Issac, Jr.'s will; deed from Susanna DuBose Cook to son Isaac to gifted sibs Elizabeth Whilden, Daniel,
Stephen, John, Andrew, Peter, dated 12 Jun 1742; MacDOWELL, Dorothy Kelly, *DuBose Genealogy* (1972, 1975);
DuBOSE, Samuel & PORCHER, Frederick A. *A Contribution to the History of the Huguenots of SC* (1887); HIRSCH,
Arthur Henry, *The Huguenots of Colonial SC* (1928); KONOPA, Leola Wilson, "The Isaac DuBose Family of SC" in
Transactions of the Huguenot Society of SC, Vol. #77 (1972), #78 (1973).

Du BOURDIEU, Pierre

Gouverneur of the château de Bergerac, Dordogne Dépt, Aquitaine, FR, under Henri IV; family can be
traced back to the Crusades

CHILDREN:

Pierre[2], Gov., l'Île Bouchard; m. Michelle Maulevault

CHILDREN:

Pierre[3], m. Marie le Fèvre; he was an artist; **4 ch**

Olivier[3], b. 1616; <u>m/1</u>, Marguerite de Gennes – **no issue**; <u>m/2</u>, Marie de Gennes; he was a minister;
also the Gouverneur du château de l'Île de Bouchard

CHILDREN, m/2:

Jean[4]

Samuel[4], bp. 25 Mar 1650, Vitré, Bretagne, FR, n.w. of Laval; <u>m/1</u>, 25 Dec 1681, Vitré,
Rachel Le Moyne (bp. 11 Mar 1654-d. 1 Jan 1683, Vitré), d/o Pierre & Marguerite
(X) LeMoyne; 1685, emig. to SC, <u>m/2</u>, Judith DuGué/Dugué, <u>m/3</u>, Louise
Thoury ? – prob. Fleury

CHILD, m/1:

Pierre[5], bp. 10 Sep 1682, Bretagne

CHILD, m/2:

*Samuel[5], b. Carolina

CHILD, m/3:

*Louis-Philippe[3], b. Carolina

*Samuel & Louis-Philippe could be reversed

Olivier[4]

Elizabeth[4], m. Louis de Gaillardy; **4 ch**

Isaac[4]

Ester[4], m. Louis Fleury, cousin; **4 ch**

Mathieu[4]

Renée[4]

Pierre[4], stayed in FR; m. Catherine de Moucheron; **11 ch**

Charlotte[3], m. Rev. Pierre Fleury; son Rev. **Louis**[4] m. cousin Ester[4] (above)

Isaac[2], b. c. 1597, Bergerac; m/1, c. 1620, X LeValet/LaValade; 1629, studied at Montauban; was a minister at the Huguenot Church in Bergerac, m/2, 1641, Bergerac, Marie de Costebadie, d/o Rev. Jean de Costebadie; 1650-1682 – minister of *"Le Grand Temple"* at Montpellier, Languedoc, said to have been the most beautiful Protestant sanctuary in Europe at the time; m/3, 1660, Jeanne de Poytevin - **no issue**; 1681, fled to ENG, when the ch at Montpellier was destroyed & he was banished by the *Parlement de Toulouse* because he continued to give communion to ex-Catholics; he was the pastor of the FR Church of the Savoy, London; he went to London with son Jean/John and gr son; d. c. end of 1699, London

CHILDREN, m/1:

(Lord) **James**[3], m. d/o Count de La Valade; she fled FR, c.1684, with infant son **Jean Armand**[4] (b. Montpellier), went to London - James was killed by Catholics, 1684; Jean Armand became a minister at the FR Church of the Savoy, 1701, m. Charlotte Massey, Countess d'Esponage; chaplain to the Duke of Devonshire; Jean Armand d. c. 1726, – their son **Saumerez**[5], b. 1 Sep 1717, London, m. Mary Thompson & was the progenitor of the Irish branch of the family; Saumerez was also a minister

Andrée LeValet[3], b. c. 1622; m/1, Jean Vachan, m/2, Jean Boybellaud/Boisebeleau - **issue**

CHILDREN, m/2:

Isaac[3], m. Isabeau Deytet

Jean de Bourdieu[3], b. c. 1642/3; he was in the seminary at Puylaurens in 1665 (Tarn Dépt, Midi-Pyrénées, w. of Toulouse), left and went to Geneva where he m. 1666, Margaret Voysine; he d. 1720, bur Savoy FR Ch, next to his father; 3 sons all of whom were ministers in ENG, 3 other sons + 4 daus, 2 of whom were still in Montpellier at the time of Jean's will; Jean was also a minister at the Savoy FR Ch in 1685; was a resident of St. Martins-in-the-Fields Parish at death; **10 ch**

Armand[3], b. Montpellier; m. Isabeau Delpreuch

Jean[2], Consul of Algiers

REF: DuBourdieu, Rev. William J., *Baby on Her Back, A History of the Huguenot Family DuBourdieu* (Lake Forest, IL, 1967) with a later ms. by his son Richard; LART, Charles E., *Huguenot Pedigrees*, Vol. I (Baltimore, 1973); AGNEW, Rev. David C.A., *Protestant Exiles from France in the Reign of Louis XIV* (London, 1874); *Publications of The Huguenot Society of London*, Vol. XXVI, "Registers of the Churches of the Savoy, Spring Gardens & Les Grecs" (Manchester, 1922).

DuBREUIL/DUBRIL/DIBRELL, Christophe/Christoffe/Christopher

b. c. 1680, Lagny-sur-Marne, e. of Paris

c. 1700 - fled to VA; settled on the James River; he was a physician/surgeon

m. c. 1727, Marianne Dutoit, (1706, FR-a. 1745, VA d/o Pierre & Barbara (de Bonnette) Dutoit; she m/2, John Lucadoo, m/3 John Goss

d. a. 15 May 1728, Manakin, VA

CHILD (posthumous):

Jean Antoine[2], b. 15 May, bp 1 Aug 1728, Manakin; m/1, 1756, Elizabeth Lee of Urbanna, York Co, VA (1734-1770), d/o Thomas Lee, m/2, p. 1777, Magdaline Burton (d. 1806) – **no issue**; changed his name to **DIBRELL**; fifer + patriotic service, Rev. War; d. May 1799, VA

CHILDREN, m/1:

Charles[3], b. 24 Oct 1757, Buckingham Co, VA; m/1, 1776, Martha Burton – **8 ch**; m/2, c. 1801, Lucy Patterson – **4 ch**; ensign in Rev. War; 1782, moved to Silver Creek, KY; d. 16 Jul 1840

Lee Ann/Leanna[3], b. c. 1759; m. 1777, Buckingham Co, VA, *Michael Jones

Judith[3], b. 15 Sep 1761; m. c. 1780, Buckingham Co, VA, *David Patteson, Jr.; she d. 26 Nov 1844, Buckingham Co, VA

* info given earlier re Leanna & Judith was incorrect – the husbands listed were for daus of their bro Charles)

Anthony[3], b. 24 May 1763, Buckingham Co, VA; m. Nov 1790, Wilmuth Watson, d/o James Watson of Amherst Co, VA – **13 ch**; Pvt, Rev. War; he d. 22 Jun 1816, Buckingham Co, VA

REF: *The Huguenot,* Publication #9 (1937-39), #23 (1967-69); McALLISTER, John M. & TANDY, Lura B., *Genealogies of the Lewis & Kindred Families* (Columbia, MO, 1906); *DAR Patriot Index* (2003); BROCK, R.A., *Huguenot Emigration to VA* (Baltimore, 1979); LEE, Edmund J., *Lee of VA, 1642-1892* (Philadelphia, 1895).

DuCHEMIN/DISHMAN, Samuel

may have had a bro Isaac who m. Martha X & d. 1699 – no known issue

a. 1693- emigrated to VA from FR via ENG; was 1st in Manakintown, later settled in Westmoreland Co; naturalized in VA under the name Dishman

m. Cornelia X (d. 1730)

1 Nov 1701 – bill of sale for 200 acres of land recorded Richmond Co, VA

27 Feb 1705 - Westmoreland Co, Samuel appeared in court to swear he had the right to claim lands

1711 – he rec. a patent for land on the Occoquan River, then in Stafford Co

16 Jun 1714 – he was granted a patent for 816 acres in Essex Co

d. a. 31 May 1727, wp, Westmoreland Co, VA

CHILDREN:

John[2], b. c. 1700; m. Frances Sanford, d/o Capt. Richard & Susannah (Franklin) Sanford; he d. a. 27 Nov 1739, wp, Westmoreland Co; Frances m/3, 1742, Robert Harrison; 2 sons **Samuel**[3], **John**[3]

Elizabeth[2], b. c. 1702; m. c. 1727, Original Brown (d.1757); she d. 1771, Westmoreland Co.

Anne[2], b. c. 1704; m. 1729, Thomas Grigsby (d. 1745, Stafford Co, VA)

Peter[2], b. c. 1706; m. Sarah X; d. intestate, Essex Co., c. 1763; **6 ch**

David[2], b. 1707/8; m/1, Ruth Clark, d/o James & Susanna Clark; m/2, Sarah Weedon, d/o John Weedon (d. 1740); he d. 1794, wp, Essex Co – **8 ch**

Mary[2], b. 1710; m. X Rutherford (d. 1771)

James[2], b. c. 1712; m. Mary Weedon, d/o John Weedon (d. 1740) – **6 ch**; was living in King George Co on 13 Jun 1796, age about 84, when he gave a deposition re a case in Essex Co; d. 1800, King George Co.

REF: Wills of Samuel & John, Richard Sanford; OAKLEY, HARRIS, Nancy L. Edwards, *Genealogy of the Samuel Dishman Family* (1987); John Weedon's will/estate; *The Huguenot,* Publication #6 (1933); DOWLING, Edwin Joseph, *The Dishmans in America* (n. p., not dated).

DuCHESNE, Anthony

b. c. 1640

c. 1663 - emigrated to New Amsterdam by way of HOL

m. a. 1665/6, Annetje Boquet, d/o Jérôme & Anne (Torion) Boquet

1667 – bought a lot in New Utrecht

29 May 1671 – bought a farm from Abram de Toict for 1600 *guilders*

by 26 Sep 1687 – took Oath of Allegiance

d. a. 12 May 1712, wp, Staten Island, Richmond Co, NY; will mentions wife, sons Michael, Jerome, Valentine, daus Anna Golders, Jannetje Mangels, Magdalena Claason, Fransentie Egberts

CHILDREN:

Jerome[2], b. c. 1666; m/1, Catherine Canon (b. 30 Aug 1700), m/2, Margaret X; he d. c. 1736, DE

Francytje[2], b. c. 1671; m. Egbert Egbartsz; at least 1 son **Isaac**[3], bp. 10 Apr 1720, Port Richmond, NY

Jannetje[2], b. c. 1675; m/1, c. 1695, Peter Janse Roll (c. 1670-1712/3) – **1 son, 6 daus**, m/2, c. 1715,
Teunis Egbert – **1 son**; family also used the name Mangels

Magdalena/Mary[2], bp. 27 Jul 1679, New Utrecht, NY; m. Jan Claason Van Spare; at least 1 dau
Francynatje[3], bp. 8 Jun 1717, Port Richmond, NY

Valentine[2], b. c. 1681; m. p. 1703, Marie Poillon (1679-a. 1 Nov 1718), d/o Jacques & Adrianna (Crocheron)
Poillon, as her 2nd husband; he d. 1735, New Castle, DE; at least 1 dau **Ann**[3]?

Gerret[2], b. c. 1684; m. Anna X; d. p. 1738, DE

Anna[2], m. Abraham Golders

Michael[2], m. c. 1710, Susanne Van der Hoven, prob. d/o Cornelis Van der Hoven & Matye Beekman; d. p.
1739, DE; at least **3 sons**

REF: SAUTER, Dr. Suzanne Van H., *Some Interrelated Huguenot Families from Kings Co and Richmond Co, NY* (ms, 1999).

DuFOUR/DuFUR/DEVOOR, David

b. c. 1620/25 Mons, Hainaut, FR (now BEL)
m/1, FR, Marie Boulon/Boulen/Boulyn (d. c. 1655/7)
fled to Sedan, then to Amsterdam; referred to as a Walloon; he became a drayman in Amsterdam.
m/2, 10 Jul 1657, Amsterdam, Jannetje Frans/Jeanne Frances (c. 1625-p. 1699) from Quiévrain, s.w. of
Mons
c. 1657 - to New Amsterdam with 2nd wife and sm. son; was an original proprietor of New Harlem
d. p. 14 Sep 1671, wd – a. 1 May 1699, Turtle Bay, Manhattan, NY
CHILD. m/1:
Jean/Jan (DuFour)[2], b. c. 1651, prob. Sedan; m/1, 1676, Jannetje/Jeanne Jans van Isselsteyn (c. 1656,
Leiden-p. May 1701), d/o Jan Willems & Willimtje (Jans) Van Isselsteyn; m/2, Mary Van Woglum,
d/o Capt. Peter Van Woglum of Albany; he d. p. 24 Jul 1717, wd – a. 13 Apr 1724, wp, Essex Co,
NJ/NY; **12 ch**, m/1
CHILDREN, m/2:
Joris (Bevoor)[2], bp. 7 Jul 1658, Reformed Dutch Ch, NYC; d. a. 1671 (not in father's will)
David (Devoor)[2], b. 1659, New Harlem; m. 1689, Elizabeth Jansen; he d. NYC; son **David**[3] (b. 1693) m.
Jannetie de la Montagne, d/o Abram & Rebecca (Van Huyse) de la Montagne, grdau/o Jean
& Marie (Vermilye) de la Montagne
Peter/Pieter (Devoor)[2], bp. 15 Oct 1662, NY; in father's will but nothing p. 1699
Teunis/Anthony (Devoor)[2], b. c. 1664, NYC; d. 31 Aug 1668, shot & killed by drunken soldier
Andiaen (Devoor)[2], bp. 28 Jan 1665, NYC; prob. d. a. 1671 (not in father's will)
Glaude (Devoor)[2], b. c. 1667; d. p. 23 Feb 1676 or 87; in father's will, but nothing p. 1699

REF: MANN, Betty M., *The Devore/De Vore Families 1500-1992* (Lansing, MI, 1992); RIKER, James, *Harlem, Its Origin and Early Annals* (NY, 1881); FERRIS, Esmond DeForest, *Parallels to the Diagonal* (Placentia, CA, 2001); NYGB Society, *Records of the Dutch Reformed Ch, NYC* (NYC 1901).

DUFOUR(S)/DuFOUR/DeFORD, Jean

b. 14 Jul, bp. 10 Nov 1566, s/o Jean Dufour, seigneur of Guînes, & Susanne Charpentier; paternal
grparents Jehan & Matilde (Beaudoin) Dufour; Guînes is in Pas-de-Calais Dépt., s. of Calais
m/1, c. 31 Jun 1579, Noyelles, Émilie Duprat, d/o Pierre & Émilie (X) Duprat; there are 11 towns named
Noyelles, 9 of which are in Calais, so exact location is unclear, none is very near Guînes; however,
Émilie's brother was *seigneur de Croiset* (prob. Croisette), which is s.e. of Noyelles-lès-Humières,
Pas-de-Calais, & e. of St.-Pol-sur-Ternoise; Jean is called "Jean de Douvres" in the marr. record –

that is now Douvres-la-Délivrande, n. of Caen; he was an *écuyer*(squire), rec. says *escuyer* = esquire

m/2, 19 Nov 1594, Aurélie (Hocart) Monpensier, widow of Richard Monpensier; marr. rec. calls Jean a *rentier* which indicates a man of independent means, property; their marr. contract was to serve as their wills

d. 4 Jul 1622, Noyelles

CHILDREN, m/1:

Théodore[2], bp. 17 May 1580; m. 4 Jun 1607, Marie Robin of Courtrai – **2 sons**; c. 1621, went to London with the intent to go to VA; he was a draper; record in ENG says he was a member of a group of Walloons; Théodore went to VA, accompanied by his sister Marie, her husband & ch

Marie[2], bp. 9 Mar 1581; m. 11 Nov 1600, Jerôme LeRoy, a clothweaver; went to VA; she d. a. 4 Jul 1622; **4 ch**

Claud[2], bp. 2 Feb 1583; m. 1 Dec 1611, Catherine Gazeau, d/o Jean Gazeau; emigrated to London by Sep 1628; he was a silkweaver

Jean[2], b. 9 Mar 1586; d. young

Pierre I[2], bp. 10 Jun 1589; m. 18 Jan 1611, Guînes, Anne Fayen, d/o Abraham Fayen; 29 Dec 1670, Pierre made provisions for his ch – the number of grch are as he stated at the time, there could have been others; he d. 14 Aug 1671

CHILDREN (bap Protestant Ch, Boulogne-sur-Mer, Pas-de-Calais Dépt., on n.w. coast of FR):

Pierre II[3], bp 11 Feb 1612; m. 4 Apr 1633, Anne de Cottigny; he d. 14 Aug 1672; **7 sons, 1 dau**

Abraham[3], bp 3 Apr 1616; m. 2 Jun 1639, Marie de Fontaine; **2 sons, 1 dau**

Richard[3], b. 7 Jul 1617; went to America, no further record

Marie[3], bp. 1 Nov 1619; m. 23 Jun 1669, Pierre de Fayen; **2 sons, 1 dau**

Joseph[3], bp. 1 Nov 1619; Aug 1640, transported to America by Ralph Bean of MD

William[3], b. 19 Oct 1620; 1641 transported to America; carpenter, assemblyman in Kent Co, MD; m. XX; son **Joseph**[4], prob. others; he d. 1648

Jacques, bp 5 Aug 1621; m. Marie Clinquement; **1 son, 1 dau**

Sara, bp 10 Dec 1622; d. 31 Aug 1672, St. Pierre (de Brouck?)

Jean[3], bp 4 Nov 1623; m/1, 11 May 1649, Anne Fournier – **6 sons**; m/2, 11 Nov 1668, Marie de Zebry – **2 daus**; he d. 1 May 1679, Guînes

Isaac[3], bp 7 May 1625; no further info

Émilie[2], bp. 4 May 1590; m. 16 Jun 1614, Nicolas Bertin of Guînes

CHILDREN, m/2:

Joseph[2], b. 12 Sep 1604

Aurélie[2], b. 7 Oct 1605

Émilie[2]

Félix[2]

Délie Corneille[2], not clear if Corneille is her marr. name; she is called that as early as 1622; her b. date is not known

Hyacinthe[2]

NOTE: Guînes, after 13 Apr 1598 (Edict of Nantes), was a center for Protestantism. By Nov 1622, the only 2 safe places for Huguenots were Montauban and La Rochelle. As a result, the emigration began in force.

REF: Marriage, baptismal records from FR; Pierre I's will; Land Records from MD.

DUGUÉ, Jacques

b. FR

m/1, Judith Soupzmain

m/2, Élizabet Dupuy, ch. on the *Liste* said to be ch of Jacques & Élizabet

bet. 1681-86 – left FR, went to SC

CHILDREN, b. Buzançais, Berry, FR, now in Indre Dépt, Centre (n.w. Châteauroux)

Pierre[2]

Isaac[2]

Elizabeth[2]

Jacques/James[2], m. (Damaris) Marianne Fleury, d/o <u>Abraham Fleury</u>

REF: "Liste des François et Suisse Refugiez en Caroline qui souhaittent d'être naturalizés Anglois" in *Transactions of the Huguenot Society of SC.*

DuHAMEL, Isaac

b. FR

a surgeon in the French army who left FR, a. the Revocation

8 Mar 1681/2 - made a citizen of England.

d. in ENG

CHILD:

Peter[2], b. FR; naturalized in ENG, 15 Apr 1687; studied medicine, later came to America; m. Rachel X
>   (b. prob. in MD-d. p. 25 Apr 1755, wd, Queen Anne Co.) her will mentions sons James, John, dau Ann[3]; he d. c. 1750, Queen Anne Co., MD

>   CHILDREN:

>   **James**[3], <u>m/1</u>, Araminta Offley, <u>m/2</u>, Ann (X) Morgan, widow; of Queen Anne Co; he d. p. 4 Jun 1789, wd, Queen Anne Co – mentions sons John, Benjamin, Robert, Samuel, dau Anne

>>   CHILDREN, m/1:

>>   **Benjamin**[4], m. Margaret Wilcox, d/o Daniel Wilcox

>>   **John**[4], b. 1762, Queen Anne Co; <u>m/1</u>, 15 Dec 1785, Ann Brodaway; <u>m/2</u>, Ann Hackett; d. 5 May 1818, Queen Anne Co; was a surgeon there for many years

>>>   CHILDREN, m/1:

>>>   **William**[5], m. Mary Pleasanton; **issue**

>>>   **James**[5], b. 4 Nov 1795, Queen Anne Co; m. 10 Jan 1819, Martha (Seth) O'Bryan (1757-Queen Anne Co-1815), d/o William C. Seth; he d. 14 Jul 1869, Baltimore; served in the Militia in the War of 1812; he was a merchant in Baltimore; **4 ch**

>>>   CHILDREN, m/2:

>>>   **Rachel**[5], m. James Price Richardson as his 2nd wife

>>>   **Alfred**[5], m. Margaret Clayton; **issue**

>>   **Samuel**[4]

>>   **Anne**[4]

>   **John**[3], b. c. 1729-32; m. 26 Feb 1759, Damsel Wilcox, d/o Daniel Wilcox; he d. 26 May 1818, Queen Anne Co; **issue**

>   **Ann**[3]

>   **Jane**[3], d. a. 25 Apr 1755 – not in mother's will

REF: SHAW, William A. (editor), *Letters of Denization and Acts of Naturalization, 1603-1700,* Huguenot Society of London (Lymington, 1911) THOMPSON, Laura Jones, *Jones, Richardson, DuHamel and Allied Families of MD*; *American Ancestry*, Vol. IX (1894), p. 66.

DUMAS, Jérôme/Jeremiah

b. 1681, *prob.* Antraigues-sur-Volane in the Ardèche Dépt. of Rhône-Alpes region just n.e. of Languedoc; Saint-Fort-sur-Gironde, Saintonge, has been suggested as his birthplace, but no <u>proof</u>; s/o Jérémie & Susanna (Fauré) Dumas??; the 2 places are on opposite sides of FR

Jul 1700 – arr VA, on the *Mary Ann*; listed as a refugee

m. 1701/2, Unity Smith

1703 - in St. Peter's Parish, New Kent Co, VA

d. a. Nov 1734, date of inv, Goochland Co, VA

CHILDREN:

Mathen[2], (dau) bp. 10 Oct 1703, St. Peter's Parish; prob. d. young

Benjamin[2], b. 1705, New Kent Co, VA; <u>m/1</u>, c. 1725, Frances Clark (c. 1706 VA-1752 NC), <u>m/2</u>, Anson Co, NC, Martha McClendon (a. 1755-1766) – **no issue**; he d. p. 1763, Anson Co, NC
>   CHILDREN, m/1:
>   **Benjamin**[3], b. c. 1728; <u>m/1</u>, Jamima McLendon -**10 ch**, <u>m/2</u>, Ruth Serdow – **issue**; he d. 1796
>   **David**[3], b. 1730; m. Sarah Moorman (b. 1738); he d. c. 1803
>   **Sarah**[3], b. c. 1730; m. Edmund Fleming Lilly; she d. a. 1760, Anson Co, NC
>   **Jeremiah**[3], b. c. 1735; d. c. 1760; **no issue**
>   **Frances**[3], b. 1740; m. 1758, Francis Smith; she d. c. 1766

Jeremiah[2], b. c. 1707; d. p. 1744, when he was liv in Louisa Co, VA, on land belonging to his father

Sarah[2], b. c. 1709; m. 27 Jun 1737, Benjamin Harris, a Quaker, s/o William & Temperance (Overton) Harris, who d. a. 13 Mar 1762, Hanover Co, VA; she d. a.7 Sep 1780, wp, Hanover Co; **issue**

Temperance[2], b. c. 1711; <u>m/1</u>, Robert Yancey (d. 1745), <u>m/2</u>, Prewid Hix/Hicks of Louisa Co, VA

REF: BROCK, R.A., *Huguenot Emigration to VA*; WILSON, John H., *Descendants of David Dickerson Dumas* (Ft. Worth, TX, 1978); DAVIS, Virginia L. Hutcheson, *Tidewater VA Families: Generations Beyond* (Baltimore); MICHELIN *Atlas of France*; *The Huguenot*, #29 (1979-81); *The VA Genealogist*, Vol. 22, #1 (Jan-Mar 1978).

DUMAS/DeMOS(S), Louis II

family poss. from Montpelier, FR

b. c. 1688 - HOL, s/o Count Louis DeMoss who fled Paris, FR Oct 1685, & went to HOL where he d.; Louis had a bro Charles who went to America with him but he was killed by Indians soon after they arr

1700 - went from HOL to America – exact place unclear – SC & VA have been mentioned, no definitive proof; said to have one of those who were to settle in the Northern Neck of VA; that settlement was not successful and some of those families were invited to go to MD; Louis went to Baltimore Co, MD; to VA. a. 6 Nov 1735

m. prob. MD, Catherine X, said to be a dau of VA planter

d. p. 17 Jun 1743, wd-a. 9 Mar 1743/4, wp, Frederick, Co, VA; will says he is of Opequon in Orange Co, VA, names son-in-law James Crabtree & his ch by dau Catherine, sons Lewis, Peter, William, Thomas, James, Charles, John; wife Catherine; used surname Demos for the ch but signs the will Lois (*sic*) Dumas; Opequon is the name of a river – tributary of the Potomac

CHILDREN:

Catherine[2], m. James Crabtree (16 Feb 1716, Baltimore Co, MD-1784, Washington Co, MD), s/o William & Jane (X) Crabtree; she d. p. 1784; **4 sons**

Louis/Lewis III[2], bp. 1 Nov 1715, St. John's Parish, Joppa, Harford Co, MD; m. 1 Jan 1743, Baltimore Co, MD, Margaret Ramsey; went to Washington Co, PA, then Hampshire Co, now WV; d. a. 6 Jul 1749; **issue**

William[2], bp. 22 Sep 1716, St. John's Parish; m. Rachel X; son **William**[3]

John[2], bp. 9 Aug 1718, St. John's Parish; m. 1 Jan 1743, St. John's Parish Susan(nah) Ramsey; he d. by 1801; son **John**[3] who had **issue**

Peter[2], bp. 9 Aug 1718

Jane[2], b. c. 1720; m. p. 1743, Pater Sagathy

Pine/Ping[2], b. 25 Oct 1723; d. a. 1743 (a dau - not in father's will); name could be Price, record unclear

Thomas[2], b. 5 Sep 1726; unmar. in 1790 census

James[2], b. 8 Sep 1728; m. 1748, Phebe X, a Quaker, liv. NC; both d. a. 10 Nov 1775

Charles[2], b. 1730; bp. 2 Nov 1731; m/1, 1751, Fannie X (d. a. 1765); m/2, 1765, Rebecca Throckmorton
(b.1742/3); he d. a. 9 Jun 1786, wp, Berkeley Co, VA; **11 ch**

NOTE: Caughron history seems to have mixed up Louis II and III – the few extant facts seem to indicate the above lineage. It is not clear if there was another Louis in the line

REF: KING, J. Estelle Stewart, *Abstracts of Wills, Inventories, & Administrations Accounts of Frederick Co, VA* (1961); Records from St. John's Parish, Harford Co, MD; HORNBY, JoAnn Robertson, *DeMoss Family History* (Wichita, KS, 1997/98); CAUGHRON, Edith S. DeMoss (Neodesha, KS, 1952) & *Sequel to the DeMoss Family in America* (1967); STAPLETON, Rev. A., *Memorials of the Huguenots in America* (Carlisle, PA, 1901).

DuMAY, Étienne

b. c. 1680, FR

c. 1680-88 - to SC, emig. as a child; settled on the Santee River

m. c. 1714, Jane/Jeanne Elizabeth Guerry (c. 1695, Carolina- 3 Jun 1767, St. James Parish, Santee, SC),
d/o Pierre & Jeanne (Broussard) Guerry; her will, dated 10 Feb 1758, mentions grson Stephen + any other ch b. later to her son Peter

d. a. 4 Feb 1734/5, wp, Charleston Co, SC (Will Book 3, p. 168)

CHILD (only ch mentioned in father's will):

Peter[2], prob. their only son, b. c. 1715, St. James Parish, SC; m/1, a. 1734, prob. Damaris Chauvin, d/o Isaac Chauvin whose will (1734) mentions dau Damaris and grson Peter DuMay, her son; m/2, c. 1757, Martha X; he d. 6 Feb 1766

CHILDREN, m/1:

Peter[3], b. c. 1734, St. James Parish; d. a. 1758

Stephen[3], b. 15 Jul 1748, St. James Parish; m. c. 1786, Nova Scotia, Bethia Chapman (b. 7 Feb 1753, Waterford, CT); Stephen was a Loyalist during the Rev. War; d. 16 Dec 1826, bur. New London, CT; **issue**

CHILDREN, m/2:

Mary Jane[3], b. 23/25 Apr, bp 25 Jun 1758; d. & bur. 22 Aug 1764

Joseph[3], b. 14 Oct, bp. 7 Dec 1760

Elizabeth Martha[3]

(Mercy & Jean – illegitimate daus/o Martha)

REF: WILSON, Ida De May, *The DeMay, Quinlin & Jorgensen Families* (St. Helena, CA, Jan 1986); *SC Historical & Genealogical Magazine*, Vol. XVII (Baltimore, 1916).

DUMONT, ?Jean?

CHILDREN:

Margaret[2], m. Pierre Noë; to New Amsterdam in 1663, with husband & sis Elizabeth on the *Spotted Cow*; settled in Woodbridge & Elizabethtown, NJ

Elizabeth[2], emig. 1663 with sis Margaret; later m. Meynard Journeay

Wallerand[2], b. 1640 Coomen, Flanders now Comines/Komen, in the Nord Dépt., n.w. of Lille
he was a cadet (*adelborst*) in a company of soldiers sent by the Dutch West Indies Co. to NY
1657 sailed from Amsterdam on either the *Draetvat* 2 Apr 1657 **or** the *Jan Baptist* 23 Dec 1657 –
prob. the latter as it carried soldiers for Gov. Stuyvesant and Wallerand named one of his

      sons Jan Baptist

c. 1660 - settled at Esopus (now Kingston), NY

m. 13 Jan 1664, Esopus, NY, Grietje/Margaret Hendricks, widow of Jan Aertson/Arentsen; her dau
      by Jan m. Hendrick Kip; Margaret d. c. 1728

influential man – *schepen* (magistrate), member of Military Council, church deacon

d. bet 25 Jul 1713, wd– 13 Sep 1713,wp, Kingston

CHILDREN:

Margaret[3], bp. 28 Dec 1664, Kingston, NY; m. a. 18 Oct 1682 (bp 1st ch), William Loveredge; settled
      Perth Amboy, NJ

Walran[3], bp. 13 Nov 1667, Kingston, NY; m. 24 Mar 1688, Catrina Terbosch of NY; liv Ulster
      Co., NY

Jan Baptist[3], m. a. 18 Nov 1694 (bp dau), Neeltje Cornelus Van Vegten; some descendants to
      Greene Co, NY, later to w. NY, MI & WI

Jannetje[3], m. c. 1697, Michael van Vegten; moved to Somerset Co, NJ, a. 1700

Francyntie[3], bp 21 Jul 1674, Kingston, NY; m. Frederick Clute/Cloet; settled Schenectady

Peter[3], b. 20 Apr 1679, Kingston, NY; m/1, 25 Dec 1700, Femmetje/Fannie Teunise Van
      Middleswart (d. 25 Dec 1706), d/o Ian Teunissen – 2 sons **John**[4], **Abraham**[4]; m/2, 23 Feb
      1707, Catelyntje Rapalyea (d. 30 Jan 1709), d/o Jeronimus Jorise Rapalie – 1 dau
      Catelyntje[4]; m/3, 16 Nov 1711, Janetie Vechten/Veghte, d/o Hendrick Claesen Vechten –
      6 ch; Peter settled NJ, c. 1700

REF: SMITH, Anne, *"Early History of the Dumond Family"* in *Old Ulster,* Vol. 4 (1908); MESSLER, Abraham, *Centennial History of Somerset Co, NJ* (Somerville, NJ, 1878); McPIKE, Eugene F., *Tales of Our Forefathers* (Albany, NY, 1898); McPIKE, Eugene F., "Dumont & Allied Families" in the *NY Gen. & Biog. Record,* Vol. 29 (Apr 1898).

DuPEUX/DuPOUX/DuPUS/DuPEE, Élie

b. 1635, Port-des-Barques, Saintonge, FR, w. of Rochefort; he was a *matelot*, sailor

m. c. 1660, FR, Mary X

10 Sep 1681 - arr in ENG w/ wife & 3 ch, from Soubise, a town s.w. of Rochefort; rec says sons were 7
      and 2, dau was 6; a sister and 2 sisters-in-law were also with Élie; however, a denization list dated
      14 Oct 1681, mentions 4 ch; Jean is said to be 18 yrs old and a seaman

21 Mar 1682 - naturalized in London – he, Mary + 4 ch

1687 - to Boston, MA

1691 – to Huguenot Colony in New Oxford, MA

1696 – back in Boston

d. c. 1700, Boston, MA

CHILDREN:

Elias[2], b. 1662; d. 1725, Boston

Jean/John[2], b. c. 1663; m. c. 1687, XX; became an elder in the FR Ch in Boston; he was a distiller; d. 7
      Jun 1743, bur. FR Ch, Boston, wp 9 Jun 1743, Boston; will mentions ch **John**[3], m. 7 May 1713,
      Boston, Naomi Walde(r)n (b. 10 Aug 1691, Salem), d/o John & Dorcas [Rice] Waldern) - **issue**;
      Daniel[3], m. 1 May 1710 Boston, Lydia Rider (d. 11 Oct 1721, Boston, 34 Y) - **issue; Charles**[3],
      m/1, 30 Jun 1712, Boston, Elizabeth Smith, m/2? 6 Jan 1733, Boston, Mary Pollard, he d. 17 Feb
      1743/4, Boston, 53 Y; **Isaac**[3], m. 4 Jun 1730, Boston, Sarah Bromfield, d/o Edward Bromfield, he
      d. 26 Jun 1766, Boston, 74 Y – called Capt. Isaac, she d. 3 Jun 1773, Boston, 83 Y; **Elias**[3], m. 2 Jul
      1735, Boston, Mary Goodridge - **issue**

Mary[2], b. 1664; d. 13 Oct 1732, Boston

Susanna[2], b. 1666; d. c. 1735, Boston

REF: BAIRD, Charles W., *History of the Huguenot Emigration to America*; *Publications of the Huguenot Society of London*, Vol. XVIII (1911); VR – Boston, Salem; DANIELS, George F., *The Huguenots in the Nipmuck Country or Oxford Prior to 1713* (Boston, 1880); John's will; GANNON, Peter Steven, editor, *Huguenot Refugees in the Settling of Colonial America* ; HANDS, A.P. & SCOULOUDI, Irene, *French Protestant Refugees Relieved Through the Threadneedle Street Church, London*, Vol. XLIX (Huguenot Soc. of London; London, 1971); FORBES, Allan & CADMAN, Paul, F., *Boston and Some Noted Emigrés* (Boston, 1938).

DuPONT, Jehan

b. 1538, FR, prob. Bretagne

had 2 brothers: **Charles** (1529-1614) who m/1, Guillemette Brière, d/o Robert II & Jehanne (Guerry) Brière, m/2, Marie Dagorne – **issue**; **Pierre** (1540/2-1614) m/1, XX – **issue**, m/2, Jehanne Le Gaigneur - **issue**

c. 1556- left the Catholic Ch and converted to the Reformed or Huguenot Ch

m/1, c. 1564, Guillemine Brière (1536-1581), d/o Robert II & Jehanne (Guerry) Brière

1566 - was in Rouen

m/2, Löyse des Hommets (1552-1608)

d. 14 Aug 1604, Rouen, 66 yrs. old

CHILDREN, m/1:

[7 sons, 3 daus – 4 of the sons & 2 daus d. in infancy or early childhood]

Jonas[2], b.1566; m. Anne de Lestre; ancestor of the Dutch and English branches of the DuPont family; he d. 1602

Marie[2] m. Thomas Vivien

Abraham[2] , b. 1572, ancestor of the Delaware & SC branches; m/1, 1600, Rouen, Marie Auber (d. 1626) - **no issue**, m/2, 10 Feb 1627, Marie Cossart (5 Jul 1597-2 Dec 1648), d/o Jacques & Marguerite (Toustain) Cossart; lived on the s.e. corner of la rue des Bons Enfants & la rue Écuyère in Rouen, nr. the Seine; he d. 1640

CHILDREN, m/2:

Jean[3], b. 1631; m/1, Marie DuBuse/Busc (bp. 1632) – **2 sons, 4 daus** (3 of whom d. unmarr.), m/2, Jeanne Tranchepain; he d. 1710

CHILDREN, m/1:

Abraham[4], b. 3 Dec 1658, Rouen; m. 3 Jun 1697, Anne Faucheraud (c, 1678, Porte de Barques, Saintonge- 29 Aug 1756, SC), d/o Charles & Anne (Vignaud) Faucheraud; went to London, 1681, and was naturalized, 15 Apr 1693; by 1695, he was in SC; d. 1731

CHILDREN:

Abraham[5] b. 5 Mar 1699; m. Jane Elizabeth DuPré (b. 12 Oct 1709), d/o Cornelius & Jeanne (Brabant) DuPré, who was the d/o Daniel & Magdalen (de Bordeaux) Brabant; he d. a. 6 Feb 1761, wp, Charleston, SC; will names ch **Cornelius**[6], **Josiah**[6], **John**[6], **Gideon**[6], **Jane**[6], also had son **Charles**[6]

Mary Anne/Marie[5], b. 1701; m. c. 1721, Richard Singleton (d. a. 8 Mar 1735, Wp); she d. 1774; **issue**

Esther[5], b. 1707; m.1733, Peter Rodolph (de) May(1708-1763), s/o John Rodolph & Mary Elizabeth (de Guignilliat) de May who was the d/o Jean François & Suzanne (LeSerrurier), who was the d/o Jacques & Elizabeth (Léger) Le Serrurier) de Guignilliat; **issue**

Ann[5], b. 1709; m. Daniel Dean

Gideon[5] , b. 2 Oct 1712; m. 1741, Anne Goodbee (23 Jan 1723-10 Apr 1781); he d. 27 Dec 1785 - **issue**

Alexander[5], b. 1718; m. 28 Sep 1745, Anne Guerry, d/o Peter & Marguerite (Rembert) Guerry; was a wealthy physician; he d. 1751; 3 **daus**

Jean[4], m. 14 Jun 1693, Rouen, Marie de la Porte (1674-1759), d/o Pierre & Marie (Le Sauvage) de la Porte of Montivilliers, n.w. of Rouen; had **8 sons, 3 daus**,

2 of the sons and one dau d. in infancy; son **Samuel**[5] (1708-1775), m. 1737,
Anne Alexandrine de Montchanin (1720-1758); their son **Pierre Samuel duPont de
Nemours**[6] (1739-1817) came to America in 1800 – was the progenitor of the DE
branch

Esther[4] m. Jacques Peyrolet; **12 ch**

Jehan[2] (1576-1645) – m/1, Judith Auber, m/2, Jehanne Langlois; **11 ch**, 4 were sons of whom 3 d. in
infancy or were unmarr.; 4th son m. twice, had 2 sons both of whom d. in infancy

CHILDREN, m/2:

Judith[2], m. Guillaume Le Faulx; daus **Rachel**[3], **Anne**[3]

Eustace[2], b. 1584; m. Marie Le Vasseur; **6 ch**, 2 of them sons both of whom d. without issue; he d. 1639

Marie[2], m. Salomon de Verton; dau **Marie**[3]

DuPONT, Pierre S., *Genealogy of the DuPont Family, 1739-1942* (Wilmington, DE, 1943); DuPONT, Henry A., *The
Early Generations of the DuPont & Allied Families* (NY, 1923); BAIRD, Charles W., *History of the Huguenot
Emigration to America,* Vol. II; *Transactions of the Huguenot Society of SC*, #76 (Charleston, 1971).

DuPRÉ(E)/DuPRAY

(3 brothers of unknown parents)

Thomas[2], b. c. 1675, FR; family *poss.* from Paris, Île de France
1700/01 – arr Henrico Co, VA on the *Mary Ann*
12 May 1705 – was naturalized as a FR Huguenot of Manakin
m. a. 7 Dec 1710, Margaret Easley, d/o Robert & Ann (Parker) Easley; she m/2, James Watson
d. a. 5 Oct 1725, Henrico Co, VA
CHILD:
Thomas[3], b. c. 1711/13; m. c. 1731, Susannah X (d. p. 1802); he d. p. 10 May 1784, wd-a. 9 Feb 1786,
wp, Lunenburg Co, VA
CHILDREN:
Lewis[4], b. 1732, Goochland Co, VA; m/1, XX; m/2, Amy Willingham, m/3, Median
Atkinson; he d. 1799, Laurens Co, SC
Joseph[4], b. c. 1736, prob. Goochland Co; m. a. 1758, Mary X; he d. p. 18 Mar 1814, wd-a.
21 Apr 1818, wp, Lunenburg Co; ch – **William**[5], **Nancy**[5]
Elizabeth[4], m. c. 1774, Thomas Whitlock
Margaret[4], m. David Stokes, Sr. (d. a. 1784); she d. p. 1802.
Mary[4], m. a. 1763, William Brizendine (c. 1743-1822)

Jean[2], b. c. 1677, prob. FR; on 1714 list of FR Protestants in King William Parish, Henrico Co – listed w/ 1
wife, 1 dau; m/1, Mary X, m/2, Jane X (d. p. 1738); he d. a. 6 Jan 1734/5, wp, Henrico Co, VA – will
mentions dau Mary Delpish, wife of Francis, wife Jane, brother Lewis, dau Jane Leuro (*sic*), gr sons
Peter & Moses Furkerin (Fourqueran)
CHILDREN, m/1:
Mary[3], m/1, Francis Delpish – **issue**, m/2, by early 1734, Charles Pain - **issue**
Jane[3], m/1, Jean Fourqueran – **issue**, m/2, p. 1 Aug 1720 (date of inv of Jean's estate) – a. 4 May
1724, Moses Liverau as his 2nd wife, she presented both Jean's and Moses' accounts of
their estates on that date

Louis/Lewis[2], b. c. 1680-90, prob. FR; Apr 1700, to VA from London; naturalized, 1705; m. c. 1708,
Lurana (Ellesby?);1720 - was in the Isle of Wight Co, VA; he d. p. 12 Jul 1748, Brunswick Co,
VA
CHILDREN:
John[3], b. c. 1710. Isle of Wight Co; m. c. 1730, Lucy Little, d/o Robert Little; he d. bet 26 Apr
1798-20 Apr 1799; **issue**

Louis/Lewis[3], b. c. 1715; m. Hannah Reid (1724-c. 1798); **issue**

James[3], b. c. 1720, VA; m. c. 1753, Mary Donaldson, d/o Benjamin Chapman Donaldson; he d. c.
      1780, Pitt or Edgecombe Co, NC; **issue**

?Thomas[3]

?Haley[3], m/1 Susannah Garris, m/2 Keziah Marmen

REF: LANGLEY, Emimae Pritchard, *The DuPré Trail*, Vol. I (1965), Vol. II (1966); BAIRD, Charles, *Huguenot Emigration to America;* Jean's will; *People of Purpose*, Vol. 2; MANNING, W. H., Jr. & Edna Anderson, *Our Kin* (Augusta, GA, 1958); BELL, Landon C., *Lunenburg Co. Wills, 1746-1825*; De MARCE, Virginia Easley, *U.S. Easley Lines Prior to 1800* (1968); BROCK, R.A., *Huguenot Emigration to VA*; CABELL, Priscilla Harriss, *Turff and Twigg,* Vol. 1, *The French Lands* (Richmond, VA, 1988).

DuPRÉ, Josias

b. c. 1640, FR, s/o Samuel DuPré (d. a. 1695)

m. c. 1660-65, FR, Martha X (Simons?)

c. 1685 - fled FR; went to ENG

c. 1686 - to SC

1697 – Josias & sons Cornelius and Josias became citizens

20 Jan 1702 – was granted land in the Orange Quarter

bur. 7 Jul 1712, St. Thomas & St. Denis Parish, SC

CHILDREN (order not certain, may be more ch.):

Martha[2], m. a. 1 Jul 1695, Francis Blanchard

Mary Esther[2], m. 1692, Benjamin Simons (d. 18 Aug 1717); she d. 15 Apr 1737; Benjamin had
      been informally adopted by the Du Pré family when they were in ENG; Martha DuPré was
      said to have been his aunt – not clear if Benjamin was the s/o a bro or sis/o Martha; **issue**

Josias II[2], b. c. 1670; m. 17 Jul 1702, Sarah Garnier, d/o <u>Daniel & Elizabeth (Fanton) Garnier</u> of the
      Île de Ré; he was a justice of the peace for Berkeley Co in 1721, a vestryman of Prince
      Frederick's Parish in 1731, "enquirer & collector of taxes: for parish of St. Denis in 1715 &
      1716; he d. c. 1747, wp, SC; **6 ch**

James[2], 1699; liv. in Europe

Cornelius[2], m. 20 Nov 1708, Jeanne Brabant, d/o Daniel & <u>Magdalen (de Bordeaux)</u> Brabant, d/o
      <u>Jacques & Madeleine (Garillon) de Bourdeaux</u>; Jeanne d. a. 12 Mar 1749/50, inv, Charleston;
      7 ch – dau **Mary Magdelen**[3] m. James Gignilliat, s/o <u>Jean François & Susanne (Le Serrurier)</u>
      <u>Gignilliat</u>, dau **Jeanne Elizabeth**[3], m. Abraham DuPont, dau **Elizabeth**[3], m. cousin Paul Porcher,
      s/o <u>Isaac II & Rachel (DuPré) Porcher</u>, dau **Martha**[3], m. cousin Isaac Porcher, s/o <u>Isaac II &</u>
      <u>Rachel (DuPré) Porcher</u>

Rachel[2], m. 1712, Isaac Porcher II, s/o <u>Isaac I & Claude (de Cherigny) Porcher</u>; **issue**

Sarah[2], m. John Alston- **1 dau**

REF: McIVER, Petrona Royall, "Josias & Martha DuPré & Some of Their Descendants" in *The SC Historical Magazine*, Vol. 71 (1970); *Transactions of the Huguenot Society of SC*, #89 (1984); CLUTE, Robert F. *The Annals & Parish Register of St. Thomas & St. Denis Parish in SC, from 1680 to 1884* (Charleston, 1884); LANGLEY, Enimae Pritchard, *The DuPré Trail* (1965).

DuPUY, André

b. prob. from Marennes, now in the Rhône Dépt, Rhône-Alpes

m. 14 Jul 1705, Jeanne (Archambaud) Gouin, widow of Abraham Gouin of NY

1715 - was with group of Huguenot settlers in Charleston , SC

d. a. 11 Oct 1722, wp, Charleston; will in FR

CHILDREN:

Jane[2], b. 28 Jun 1705, NY; bp. FR Church, NYC; m. c. 1722/23, Samuel Grasset (1702, Staten Island, NY-May 1733, Charleston), grs/o <u>Auguste & Marie (Pelé) Grasset</u>; she was bur. Aug1735, St. Philip's Churchyard, Charleston, SC; **issue**

Andrew[2], silversmith in Charleston; bur. St. Philip's, 22 Sep 1743; **no issue**

Hester[2], m. William Brown

Marianne[2], m. Joseph Maybank

REF; THOMPSON, Neil D., "Auguste Grasset of La Rochelle, London & NYC" in *National Geographic Quarterly*, Vol. 66, #1 (March 1978). *Transactions of the Huguenot Society of SC*, #13, pp. 17-19, "Will of Andre Dupuy in French & English".

DuPUY, Bartholomé/Barthélémy/Bartholomew

b. 1650-3, prob. St. Jean de Maruéjols, Languedoc (now called St-Jean-de-Maruéjols-et-Avéjan), n.e. of Alès, in the Gard Dépt. of Languedoc-Rousillon; another poss. birthplace is Uzès, n.e. of Nîmes in the same département; the baptismal records of Amsterdam and Magdeburg say that Barthélémy and his wife Marie were from St. Jean de Maruéjols and/or Uzès; *poss.* s/o Jean & Anne (St. Heyer) DuPuy

m. c. 1685, prob FR, Marie Gardié/Gardier who prob. d. a. 1742; he did **NOT** m. Comtesse Susanne LaVillon/Villain *nor* is there <u>proof</u> that he served in Louis XIV's army

fled Languedoc, went to Amsterdam

c. 1691- to Magdeburg, Saxony, GER (s.w. of Berlin)

1699 - to ENG

c. 1702/3 to VA – wife + 4ch ; petitioned for naturalization, 21 Apr 1704, it was granted 12 May 1705

d. p. 7 Mar 1742/3, wd – a. 17 May 1743, wp, Goochland Co, VA; will mentions sons Peter, John James, grson John Bartholomew (s/o John James), son-in-law John Levilain, Jr.

CHILDREN:

Jeanne[2], bp. 21 Jul 1689, Amsterdam; prob. d. young

Antoine[2], bp. 30 Aug 1691, Magdeburg, GER; bur. there 16 May 1694

Catherine[2], bp. 18 Apr 1693, Magdeburg; bur. there 28/29 May 1694

Pierre/Peter[2], bp. 25 Mar 1695, Magdeburg; m. c. 1722, King William's Parish, Manakin, Henrico Co, VA, Judith LeFèvre, d/o <u>Isaac & Magdelaine (Parenteau) LeFèvre</u>; Judith (c. 1702- p. 15 Sep 1783, wd– a. 22 Sep 1785, inv, Nottoway Parish, Amelia Co, VA); he d. p. 29 Jul 1773, wd – a. 25 Sep 1777, wp, Amelia Co, VA; **11 ch**

Jean-Pierre[2], b. c. 1697; d. p. 16 Jun 1714 (perhaps c. 1719)

Marthe[2], b. c. 1699; m. c. 1726/7, King William's Parish, <u>Étienne/Stephen Chastain</u>; she d. p. 23 Apr 1740, wd– a. May 1740, wp; **2 ch**

Jean-Jacques/John James[2], b. c. 1701, prob. ENG; m. c. 1728, Susanne LeVil(l)ain (b. 1710 VA), d/o <u>Jean-Jacques & Olympe (X) LeVil(l)ain</u> of Tessy-sur-Vire (se of St. Lô), Normandie; d. p. 9 Feb 1775, wd – a. 27 Feb 1775, wp, Cumberland Co, VA; **8 ch**

Philippa[2], b. c. 1703 VA; m. c. 1730, King William's Parish, Goochland Co*, VA, Jean-Pierre/John LeVil(l)ain, Jr. (c1707/8 VA-Feb 1768), s/o <u>Jean-Jacques & Olympe (X) LeVil(l)ain</u>; d. c. 1738; **4 ch**, 3 d. in infancy, 1 dau **Elizabeth**[3]. *Goochland formed from Henrico Co in 1728

REF: ALLEN, Cameron, *The Origin of Barthelemy Dupuy of Manakintown, VA and His Wife; The American Genealogist,* Vol. 74, #1 (Jan 1999); DUPUY, Rev. Benjamin Hunter, *The Huguenot Bartholomew Dupuy and His Descendants* (1908); BROCK, Robert A., *Huguenot Emigration to VA* (1973); HARPER, Lillie DuPuy Van Culin, Editor, *Colonial Men and Times; VA Historical Collections,* Vol. 5; Wills; **CAUTION:** except for Cameron Allen's article, many references have much incorrect information – some are cited here because they do have some useful facts.

DuPUY/ DuPUI(S)/DePEW
(2 brothers of unknown parents)
Nicolas/Nicolaes[2]

b. c. 1635; said to be from Artois, FR but poss b. Paris which he left in 1651 and went to HOL – poss. via Artois

m. Catharina Renard/de Vos; both names are used in the Dutch Ch, NYC baptismal records – *reynard* = fox in FR and *vos* – fox in Dutch; 1st name also Cathlyna, Cathryntie; surname also Reynarts

Oct 1662 - sailed in the *Purmerland Church* to New Amsterdam w/ wife and 3 ch, aged 6, 5, 2; on the list of immigrants to NY, Oct, 1662, he is listed as being from Artois; member of Dutch Ch, NYC, later transferred to the FR Ch

1st settled on *Herren Graft*/Broad St (Lower Manhattan, now in the Financial District, crosses Beaver St - mentioned below)

19 Mar 1663 - granted a plantation on Staten Island

Oct 1664 - swore allegiance to ENG

1667 - purchased land on Prince St.

by 1677 - in New Utrecht on Long Island

by 1682 - in Bergen, NJ

1685 - he says he lives in NYC; liv. Beaver St, 1686 (Beaver St. is in Lower Manhattan, in what is now the Financial District)

d. a. 15 Sep 1691, wp, NY; will was written in Dutch; Catharina, d. a. 13 Jul 1705 - letters of administration granted to son John

CHILDREN:

John[3], b. c. 1655; m/1, Elizabeth (Sweem) Tysen, d/o Barent Sweem, m/2, c. 1677, NY, Dutch Ch, Petronella/Petroneltje Sweem, sis/o Elizabeth; d. a. 14 Jun 1732, wp, Richmond Co, NY; total of **10 ch**

Moses[3], b. c. 1657; m/1, c. 1680, Maria Wyncoop (1660, Ft. Orange/Albany-c. 1724), d/o Cornelius & Maria (Langedyck) Wyncoop – **11 ch**, all bp Dutch Ch, Kingston – poss. one more son, b. 1705, but not in bap records; 1 Sep 1689, Moses on list of inhabitants of Ulster Co who took Oath of Allegiance; m/2, 17 Oct 1724, Kingston Dutch Ch, Pieternelletjen/Peternelje De Pree, widow of Marinus Van Aaken – **no issue**; Moses was a freeholder in Rochester, Ulster Co, 1728; alive 1 Dec 1748, poss. d. 1754

prob. Nicolas[3], b. c. 1660, prob. d. young

Joseph[3], bp. 5 Feb 1663, Reformed Dutch Ch, NYC; d. young

Aaron[3], bp. 30 Nov 1664, Reformed Dutch Ch, NYC; in father's will; no further record

Magdalena[3], bp. 16 Feb 1667, Reformed Dutch Ch, NYC; not in father's will; no further record

Susanna[3], bp. 7 Apr 1669, Reformed Dutch Ch, NYC; m/1, a. 1700 Obadias Winter, m/2, c. 1704 John Pamerton

Nicholaes/Nicholas[3], bp 11 Jul 1670, Reformed Dutch Ch, NYC; was in Kingston, NY in 1690; in father's will; no further record

Paulus[3], bp. 11 Aug 1675, Reformed Dutch Ch, NYC; prob. d. young

François[2]

bro of Nicolas (above), prob. younger

fled from Calais, FR, according to info given in marriage banns

by 14 Mar 1661 - in Breuckelen (Brooklyn), NY – name on a petition

m/1, 26 Sep 1661, Dutch Church, New Amsterdam, Geertje Willems from Amsterdam; banns 1st published 26 Aug 1661; Geertje, poss. d/o Willem Jacobse Van Boerum of Flatbush

21 Dec 1680 - granted 80 acres on the s. side of Fresh Kill, Staten Island; 4 Apr 1685, a grant at Smoking Point

m/2, 1687/89, Annie Elsten

d. p. 1702, prob. Tarrytown

CHILDREN, m/1:

169

     Willem[3], b. c. 1663, Bushwick; m. 10 Aug 1688, Kightwanck/Kichtewang, Manor of Cortlandt, Elizabeth White from Barbados

     Jannetje/Jane[3], b. Flatbush; m. c. 1693, Kellan MaKorry/Cory/Quorry; **4 ch** bp. NYC & Tarrytown

     Grietje/Margaret[3], bp. 1 Oct 1671, Reformed Dutch Ch, NYC; m. 1698, Jan Ward of Haverstraw; **3 ch**, bp. Tappan

     Jean/John, bp. 20 May 1674, Reformed Dutch Ch, NYC; m. 16 Apr 1701, Tappan, Jannetje Wiltsie (bp 7 Jan 1663, Kingston, NY), d/o Hendrick Martensen Wiltse, widow of Myndert Hendrickse Hogencamp; **7 ch**; he d. p. 1722, Orange Co, NY

     Marie?, bp. 14 Feb 1677, Reformed Dutch Ch, NYC (name not given in bap record); m. c. 1702, Abraham Lent

     Sara, bp. 23 Feb 1679, Flatbush; m. Apr, 1704, Tappan, Herman Hendrickse Blauvelt

     Geertje, bp. 18 Sep 1681, Flatbush

     Nicholas, bp 17 Oct 1686, Reformed Dutch Ch, NYC; m. Barbara X

     CHILD, m/2:

     Mary, bp. 3 Mar 1689, Reformed Dutch Ch, NYC

REF: CONKLING, Frank J., *"Family of DuPuis, DuPuy, Depew"* in the *NY Gen. & Biog. Record,* Vol. 32 (Apr/Jul 1901); PURPLE, Edwin E., *Contributions to the History of the Kip Family of NY & NJ* (NY, 1877); BAIRD, Charles W., *History of the Huguenot Emigration to America,* Vol. I (NY); PURPLE, Samuel S., *Records of the Reformed Dutch Church in New Amsterdam, & NY* (NY, 1890); *Colonial & Revolutionary Lineages of America,* pub. by The American Historical Company (NY, 1939); HOFF, Wannetta R., *History of the DePui Family, Nicholas DePui French Huguenot Refugee in America* (1939); HEIDGARD, Ruth P. & SMITH, Jean M., *DePuy Family History,* Vol. I (Port Ewen, NY, 1994; HOES, Roswell Randall, *Baptismal & Marriage Registers of the Old Dutch Ch, Kingston* (NY, 1891).

DuPUY, Jean/John

     b. 1679, FR

     1682 - to ENG, with fa Jean, lord of Villefranche; rec. his medical training in ENG

     a. 1709 - to Jamaica

     m. c. 1712, Port Royal, Jamaica, Anne David (bp. 2 Oct 1687, Ref. Dutch Ch, Kingston, NY), d/o <u>Jean & Esther (Vincent) David</u>; her sis Susanne m. Élie Chardovaine II*

          *see entry for Chardovaine which explains the change in the lineage

     p. 11 Mar 1713 - to NYC

     4 Feb 1714 - purchased a home on King (now Pine) Street from John David – *prob*. Anne's father

     28 Jun 1715 - freeman of NY

     d. 16 Jun 1744, NYC, bur. churchyard of Trinity Episcopal Ch on Broadway

     CHILDREN:

Hester[3], b. 1713, prob. Port Royal, Jamaica; m. John Moschel/Marshall; in father's will; d. p. 1753

Jane/Jeanne[3], bp. 15 Feb 1715, FR Hug Ch; m. Peter David, a goldsmith; d. 1 Oct 1752 ,Philadelphia; in father's will

John[3], b. 20 Oct 1717; m. Frances Elliston; d. 21 Jul 1745; in father's will; surgeon; **issue**

Daniel[3], b. 30 Apr, bp 10 May 1719, NYC; m. 6 Sep 1746, Philadelphia Eleanor (Cox)Dylander (1719 Philadelphia-16 Mar 1805 Philadelphia), d/o Peter & Margaret (Dalbo) Cox, widow of Rev. John Dylander; Daniel d. 30 Aug 1807, Philadelphia; in father's will; gold and silversmith; **issue**

Thomas[3], b. 2 Sep, bp 11 Sep 1720, FR Hug Ch; said to have been lost at sea with his bro Paul – they were being sent to Europe to be educated

Francis[3], b. 20 Oct, bp 8 Nov 1721, FR Hug Ch; d. 1750, at sea; in father's will; a physician

Paul[3], b. 8 Jul, bp 17 Jul 1723, FR Hug Ch; lost at sea

Isabel[3], b. 26 Aug, bp 6 Sep 1727, FR Hug Ch; d. young

REF: DuPUY, Charles M., *The Dupuy Family, A Genealogical History* (Philadelphia, 1910); WITTMEYER,

Rev. Alfred V., *Registers of the Births, Marriages, & Deaths of the Église Françoise à la Nouvelle York* (Baltimore, 1968); *PA Marriages Prior to 1790* (Baltimore, 1968).

DURAND, François Josèphe/Francis Joseph

b. 1735-40, Besançon, FR, then in Bourgogne, abt 30 mi. w. of SWI; supposedly lineage goes back to Charles Emmanuel Durand, ennobled by the King of Spain during the time that Burgundy belonged to Spain; Charles Emmanuel is thought to have been Francis' grfa, his fa prob. Charles; the family said to be strongly Catholic which may have been the reason for his emigration

c. 1755/7- emigrated abt age 16; 1st to West Indies, then Norwalk, CT

m. 22 Dec 1762, New Canaan, CT, Patience Weed

he served as a private from NY in the Rev. War

d. Jun 1817/18, Charlotte, VT

CHILDREN:

Joseph Francis[2], b. 1765; m. Elizabeth Arnold; settled Elizabethtown, NY, c. 1794; d. 10 Apr 1843; **9 ch**; served as a private from NY in the Rev. War

Alexandre[2], b. 25 Feb 1767, Norwalk, CT; m. c. 1787, Norwalk, Elizabeth Whalley (20 Oct 1768-23 Feb 1839); he d. 1 Feb 1836, Charlotte, VT; **11 ch**

Simeon[2], b. 21 Oct 1768, Norwalk, CT; m. c. 1791, VT Elizabeth Cable (d. 1866, Amherst, OH); to OH, 1817; hc d. 25 May 1831, Henrietta, OH

Merari[2], b. 19 Jul 1770; m. VT/Elizabethtown, NY, Susannah Grey; **6 ch**

Eleazor[2]

Anna[2], b. 1772; unmarr.

Charlotte[2], b. 11 May 1777; m. VT/CT, Charles Pardo

Mary/Polly[2], b. 22 Oct 1779; m/1, X Lewis – **8 ch**, m/2, John Sherman (7 Jun 1754/7-13 Oct 1831, Moriah, NY) – **3 ch**; she d. 29 Jan 1856, Moriah, Essex, NY

REF: *Durand History*; SNOW, Helen F., *The John Durand Family Huguenots: A Transcript* (12 Apr 1963); DURAND, Celia C., *Genealogical Register of the Family of Francis Joseph Durand* (Oberlin, OH, 1925); HEWITT, Frances Bailey, *Genealogy of the Durand, Whalley, Barnes & Yale Families* (Chicago, IL 1912); BROWN, George Levi, *Pleasant Valley A History of Elizabethtown, NY* (1905).

DURAND, Jean/John

b. 26 Dec 1664, bp. 18 Jan 1665, La Rochelle, FR; prob. s/o Je(h)an & Anne (Moran(d)/Meraud/Moraud) Durand; poss. had bro Joseph, sis Marie

fled FR to ENG - accompanied by his uncle Noah and 2 cousins George and Louis who were sons of his uncle Charles

1684 - naturalized ENG; he was a doctor, surgeon

went to SC - was there a yr; went to NY, liv in New Rochelle for a few months and then went to CT, 1st to East Haven; he was the only member of his father's family to emigrate to America

c. 1696 - went to Milford, CT

10 Sep 1698 NY - rec. a license to marry Elizabeth Bryan (19 Apr 1680, Milford, CT-d. p. 20 Jun 1757), d/o Richard & Mary (Wilmot) Bryan

1699 - moved to Derby CT

1709 - served as a surgeon of a CT regiment during the expedition against Canada

d. 29 Mar 1727, Derby, CT; bur Colonial Cem.

CHILDREN (all b. Derby, CT):

John[2], b. 10 Nov 1700; m/1, 5 Nov 1730, Sarah Lum (24 Nov 1701-2 Jun 1747, Oxford, CT), d/o Jonathan & Sarah (Riggs) Lum - **6 ch**; m/2, 2 Jun 1748, Oxford, Sarah Chatfield (4 Nov 1722-23 Nov 1787, Oxford), d/o John & Elizabeth (Johnson) Chatfield – **7 ch**; he d. 8 Mar 1773, Derby, CT

Andrew[2], b. 17 Dec 1702; m. 1729, Jane Andrew (bp 16 Apr 1699, Milford-15 Feb 1778, Milford), d/o
   Rev. Samuel & Abigail (Treat) Andrew; he d. 28 Oct 1791, Milford; **5 ch**
Elizabeth[2], b. 19 Jul 1705; d. in infancy
Noah[2], b. 27 Aug 1707; m/1, 9 Nov 1732, Abigail Riggs; m/2, Damaris (Wooster) Hawkins, widow of
   Ebenezer Hawkins
Joseph[2], b. 20 Dec 1709; m. 25 Apr 1734, Ann Tomlinson (d. 14 Feb 1778, age 65), d/o Isaac & Patience
   (X) Tomlinson; he d. 6 Aug 1792
Samuel[2], b. 7 Jul 1713; m/1, Hannah X; m/2, Mary X; he d. 17 May 1785
Abigail[2], b. 2 Jun 1716; m. Abner Johnson, s/o Jeremiah Johnson
Elizabeth[2], b. 6 Feb 1718; m. Joseph Johnson; she d. 1784
Mary[2], b. 4 Mar 1721; m. Samuel Johnson
Ebenezer[2], 7 Dec 1724; m/1, Hannah Johnson; m/2, Hannah White

NOTE: Despite the common sources, no tie has been made between François Josèphe and Jean/John;
La Rochelle and Besançon are on opposite sides of FR.

REF: DURAND, Samuel , *Durand Genealogy; Durand History*; SNOW, Helen F., *The John Durand Family Huguenots: A Transcript* (12 Apr 1963); DURAND, Celia C., *Genealogical Register of the Family of Francis Joseph Durand* (Oberlin, OH, 1925); ABBOTT, Susan Woodruff, *Families of Early Milford, CT* (Baltimore, 1979).

DURIER/DURIÉ/DURÉE/DURYEA, Pierre

   b. by 1630, FR, perhaps s/o Jean Durier
   m. Marguerite Charoy
   fled FR
   by 1654 – a resident of HOL
   he was not a member of the Walloon Ch nor did he own property in Utrecht; outside of the bp. records
      of his 3 ch, there are no other records; 9 Dec 1663 at Yzendyke, Jan Durié, s/o Jan & Marie (Le
      Grand) Durié was bp with Daniel Durié & Marguerite Soies as sponsors – relatives?
   CHILDREN (all bp. Walloon Church, Utrecht):
   Jean/Jan[2], bp. 12 Nov 1654; m/1, prob. Jeanne (Hersulier or Gautier?) who d. c. 1691, m/2, 1692, Rachel
      Cresson, widow of David Demarest, Jr; settled in Bergen Co, NJ by Jul 1686; member of the FR Ch; he
      d. p. 10 Jun 1698, wd-a. 2 Sep 1698, Perth Amboy, NJ
      CHILDREN, m/1 (**all** children bp. French Church, Bergen Co, NJ)
      Jeanne/Janeken[3], b. c. 1688; m/1, 3 Apr 1708, Hackensack, Epke Banta, s/o Cornelius & Jeanne
         (DePré) Banta – **5 ch**; m/2, 28 Jul 1730, Hackensack, Thomas Frans Outwater, widower of
         Tryntje Breestede and Matje Pieterse – he d. 1753
      Pierre/Pieter[3], b. c. 1690; m. 21 Jul 1711, Hackensack, Judith (Demarest) Debaun (b. c. 1690), d/o
         Samuel & Maria (DeRuine) Demarest, widow of Christian Debaun; he d. a. 1767; **8 ch**
      CHILDREN, m/2:
      Marguerite[3], b. c. 1693; m. 6 Dec 1712, Hackensack, John Zabriskie (c. 1682-a. 21 Jan 1766, wp),
         s/o Albert & Machtelt (Vanderlinda) Zabriskie, widower of Elizabeth Romeyn; **10 ch**
      Jean[3], b. 1695; m/1, 30 Aug 1718 Hackensack, Angenitie Bogert (b. 1 Sep 1700, Hackensack), d/o
         John & Maria (Bertholf) Bogert -**12 ch**; m/2, 25 May 1751, Margaret Van Horn, d/o Jacques &
         Wybrech (Hendrickse) Laroe, widow of Christian Cornelius Van Horn; he d. 7 May 1773
   Catherine[2], bp. 26 May 1656
   Jeanne[2], bp. 3 Aug 1662

REF: DURIE, Howard I., *The Durie Family: Jean Durier of the Huguenot Colony in Bergen Co, NJ* (Pomona, NY, 1985).

DURRETT(E), François/Francis Parrain de

b. Bourges, Berry, FR, s/o Paul Parrain & Antonia (X) de Duret
he was a Benedictine priest of the congregation of St. Maur
1699 – converted to Protestantism and took refuge in ENG where he took on the function of pastor of
      the FR churches in Chelsea and Crispin St.; became the chaplain in Macartney's Regiment, then that of
      Lord Cobham; he was a minister on the Isle of Guernsey after his return from the Spanish campaign; he
      was elevated to the rank of dean but congregation did not want a "foreigner" in charge; he went to
      London to plead his case but he became ill and d. at the home of his dau; author of many works, several
      of which caused controversy in the church
m. XX
25 Feb 1702/3 - naturalized ENG; no mention of wife or ch being nat. on that date; record gives
      Francis' place of birth, names of parents
1711-16 - La Tremblade, Chaplain to Royal Dragoons
1714 - at the Chelsea & (Lect.) Savoy Ch; named on a list of Huguenot Clergy
1718 - wrote a book <u>A Treatise Concerning the Abuse of Confessions of Faith</u>; written in French but
      translated into English; the Bishop of London suggested that the attack was instigated "by
      Rome" and that Durette should not be allowed to preach in the Leicester Fields Ch; 9 mo. later,
      Durette signed the Thirty-nine Articles and the interdict was lifted but the Leicester Fields Ch
      did not agree and said that the scandal had upset the parishioners too much
d. Aug 1727, Canterbury, ENG, at his dau's home
CHILD:
unnamed dau, no info; prob. remained in ENG; issue????

NOTE: Despite previous attempts to link François to the VA Durretts, that connection has **not been proven**. The Francis Durrett who went to VA was <u>not</u> his son. There was a Paul Duerrat in Manakintown in 1710, 1711. Again <u>no proof</u> that he was Paul Parrain de Duret, the father of François above. Much speculation, <u>no proof</u>.

REF: D'AMAT, Roman, *Dictionnaire de Biographie Française*, #LXIX (Paris, 1969) p. 758; *Proceedings of the Huguenot Society of London*, Vol. XI, #2 (London, 1916), Vol. XIII, #6 (London, 1929); *Publications of the Huguenot Society of London*, Vol. XXVII (Manchester, 1923).

DURRETT, Richard

b. 7 Jan 1712 FR; *poss..* had bro Robert who m. Elizabeth Goodloe & d. a. 1 Jul 7 1765, wp
m. 6 Mar 1741/2, Sarah Marshall (b. 20 May 1721), d/o Wm. & Elizabeth (Williams) Marshall
d. p. 28 Jul 1767, wd - a. 4 Jul 1768, wp, Spotsylvania Co, VA
CHILDREN (all ch in father's will, except Mildred and Benjamin who are mentioned in Orphan Court
      record):
Mildred[2], b. c. 1750, VA; m. a. 7 May 1770, Aquilla Johnson, Jr (he d. a. 13 Jun 1821, wp, Fayette
      Co, KY); she d. 1821, Lexington, KY; **3 daus, 1 son**
William[2], b. 24 Nov 1748; m/1, 1770, Abigail Terrell (6 Dec 1751-a. 1790, Caroline Co), d/o Henry &
      Sarah (Woodson) Terrell, m/2, 2 Jan 1790, Sarah (X) Conner, widow of Francis Conner*; she d.
      1816, Caroline Co., he d. 25 Jan 1804, Caroline Co, VA; **5 sons, 3 daus**; 1768, named guardian for
      his bros/sis and was one of the executors of his father's estate; Captain & Patriotic Service, VA,
      Rev. War
Ann/Nancy[2]
Mary[2], poss. m. c. 1777, John Vivian (1756-1832 Cole Co, MO); liv. Clark Co, KY, bef MO
Richard[2], m. a. 21 Dec 1775, Elizabeth X (d. p. 1824); d. 1823/4, Mason Co, KY; a Methodist minister;
      1 son, 5 daus
Marshall[2], b. c. 1760; m/1, c. 1783, X Conner*, d/o William & Frances (Williams) Conner – **2 sons, 1
      dau**, m/2, 8 Feb 1800, Amherst Co., Dorothy (Digges) Woodroof, d/o John Digges, widow of
      Wiatt Woodroof

James[2], b. 20 Apr 1762; <u>m/1</u>, X Conner*, d/o William & Frances (Williams) Conner – **1 dau**, <u>m/2.</u> X
Lindsay, d/o Daniel & Catherine (Goodloe) Lindsay – **1 son, 2 daus**, <u>m/3</u>, 18 Nov 1804, Amherst
Co, VA, Nancy Digges (17 Dec 1769-15 Jan 1853, Albemarle Co.), d/o John Digges – **2 sons, 2
daus**; he d. 20 Jan 1822, Albemarle Co, VA; Pvt, VA, Rev. War
*all ch of William & Frances (Williams) Conner

Sarah/Sally[2], b. c. 1765; poss. m. c. 1785, Marshall Yates who d, 17 May 1796 – c. **6 sons, 2 daus**

Benjamin[2], poss. b. c. 1767; evidently d. a. 21 Dec 1775 as he is not named in the division of his father's
real estate but he is not named in his father's will either – may have been a posthumous child

NOTE: Since this Richard was in VA before the others, not sure if there is a connection to the other
Durretts.

REF: BLAYDES, Mary Douglas, *More than Skin Deep or Spotsylvania Ancestors of Maxey Lee Blaydes & Some of
Their Connections* (not dated, not pub.); HARTER, Mrs. Bert, "Durrett Family" in *The VA Genealogist*, Vol. 15, #2
(Apr/Jun, 1971), #3 (Jul-Sep, 1971); BROCKMAN, William Everett, *Orange County VA Families*, Vol. II (1959).

DURYÉE/DURYEA/DuRIEU/DURIE, Joost/George

b. c. 1637, Picardie, FR, s/o Simon & Adrienne (Rau/Roul) DuRieu; Joost had bro Jacques, sis Marie,
Elizabeth, Françoise; his fa Simon m. 2 more times
m/1, prob. FR, XX
fled FR to Mannheim, GER
m/2, 28 Feb 1672, FR Protestant Ch, Mannheim, GER, Magdeleine LeFèvre, d/o Antoine & Antoinette
(Vilain) Le Fèvre
c. 1675- to NY w/ wife, 2 sons, his mother* – went to New Utrecht, LI; later settled Bushwick by 1683; a
memorial window inscription in the Huguenot Ch, Staten Island, reads, "Jost Durie came to Bushwick,
LI, about 1670." (date obviously wrong!) *prob. mother-in-law as fa m/2, 14 Mar
1677, and is said to have been a "widower"
1698 - census of Brooklyn – listed as Joost Duré, Senior, French – 1 man, 1 woman, 6 ch, 2 slaves
m/3, Cornelia (Monfoort) Schomp, (bp. 3 May 1719- d. a. 31 May 1771), d/o Peter Monfoort & Margaret Haft,
widow of Joost Schomp
d. a. 9 Jun 1727, Bushwick, LI, NY
CHILDREN, m/1:
Joost/Justin[2], b. c. 1660; <u>m/1</u>, 17 Apr 1681, Magdalena/Helena/Lena Verschuer (bp 23 Apr 1682,
Midwoud [Flatbush] Dutch Ch), d/o Wouter Gysbertsen Verschuer & Dorothea Jochems (Caljer) –
5ch, <u>m/2</u>, Rebecca Folkerts?, poss d/o Volkert/Folkert Dircksen & Annetje Philips – **1 son**; he d.
p. 17 Jun 1727, wd
Peter[2], b. c. 1663; m. Agnietje Nicque
Cornelius[2], b. 1668 ; liv. Flatbush, 1729
CHILDREN, m/2 :
Magdeleine[2], b. 11 Nov 1672, Mannheim; believed to have d. young
Elizabeth[2], b. 28 Sep 1674, Mannheim; believed to have d. young
Jacques/Jean[2], b. 6 Jun, bp. 13 Jul 1679, Dutch Ch, Flatbush, LI, NY
Antoinette[2], bp. 11 Dec 1681, Dutch Ch, Brooklyn, NY; m. Abraham L'Écuyer/Laquer, s/o <u>Jean L'Écuyer
& Rachel Dirckse</u>; **issue**
Abraham[2], b. 1683/85; m. Elizabeth Polhemus (bp. 5 Nov 1693, Brooklyn), d/o Theodorus Polhemus &
Aertje Bogaert; was farmer in Brooklyn; d. a. 28 Feb 1764 wp; **9 ch**
Jacob[2], bp. 21 Nov 1686, Dutch Ch, Brooklyn; m. Catrina Polhemus; he d. 1758
Magdalena[2], bp. 19 Oct 1687, Dutch Ch, NY; <u>m/1</u>, Jan Okie, <u>m/2</u> , X Van Nuyse
Philip[2], b. c. 1689; m. 14 Dec 1714, Belje Corvets/Goverts
Charles[2], b. 15 Oct 1690; <u>m/1</u>, Cornelia Schenck, <u>m/2</u>, 9 Jun 1743, Maria Roberson; d. 3 Jul 1773
Simon[2], bp. 26 Nov 1693, Dutch Ch, Brooklyn; m. 20 May 1717, Annetje Sprung

REF: *Duryee Genealogy*; BERGEN, T.G., *Early Settlers of Kings Co, NY*; RIKER, James, *The Annals of Newtown in Queens Co, NY* (NY, 1852); JOHNSON, Rhes D., *Our Durya and Tucker Lines*; STOUTENBURGH, Henry A., *A Documentary History of the Dutch Congregation of Oyster Bay* (1903); MACY, Henry Jr., "The Vershuer Family of Buckwick: Its Roots in the Netherlands & Descendants through Comegys, Fyn, Duryea, Covert, & Simonson" in *The NYGBR*, Vol. 124, #4 (Oct 1993), Vol. 125, #1 (Jan 1994) #2 (Apr 1994) #3 (Jul 1994); MACY, Harry, Jr., "New Light on the Origins of Joost Duryea" in the *NYGBR*, Vol. 121 #1 (Jan 1990).

DuSAUCHOY/DISOWAY/du (de) SOISON, Marc

b. 1626 FR, prob. a town along the Somme River, which runs s.e. from Abbeville in Picardie

c. 1655 - to New Amsterdam, Flatbush, from HOL, prob. Leiden; then went back to Europe

2 Apr 1657 - sailed from Amsterdam to return to New Amsterdam on the *Draetvat* (the *Wire Cask*) to settle; he was a *peigneur de laine,* a wool-carder/comber, in Europe, but a miller and farmer in NY; on the passenger list his name was given as "Marcus de Chousoy", sailing w/ his wife, 2 workmen, 2 boys (no relationship, if any, given), no mention of ch

m. c. 1657, Elisabeth Rossignol/Lysbeth Rosiljon (Dutch sometimes used *Nachtigaal* as her surname, which means "nightingale" as does *rossignol*)

10 Apr 1661 - transferred ch membership to Brooklyn from New Amsterdam

c. 3 Jan 1664 - moved to Harlem

c. 15 Mar 1667 - went to Fordham (now part of NYC)

7 Jun1683 – he and his wife joined the FR Ch in NYC by letter from the Dutch Ch in New Amsterdam; moved to Staten Island

d. p. 1 Oct 1706-prob. a. 27 Nov 1708, as his son Marcus had succeeded to his lands by then

CHILDREN:

Madeleine/Magdaleentie[2], bp. 20 Jan 1658, Reformed Dutch Ch, NYC; m. 5 Mar 1671, Reformed Dutch Ch, NYC, Martin Hardwyn/Hardin; **5 ch**

Marcus[2], bp. 21 Mar 1659, Reformed Dutch Ch, NYC; m. Jannetie X; liv. Staten Island; he d. p. 23 Dec 1713, wd-a. 27 Jan 1714, wp; **9 ch**

Janneties[2], b. 17 Dec 1662; m. Conrad Hendricks Boch of Harlem

Jean, bp. 25 Oct 1665, Reformed Dutch Ch, NYC

Maria[2], bp. 13 Oct 1669, Reformed Dutch Ch, NYC

REF: RIKER, James, *Harlem: Its Origins & Early Annals* (Upper Saddle River, NJ); HOLTZCLAW, B. C., *Ancestry & Descendants of the Nassau-Siegen Immigrants to VA, 1714-1750*, Germanna Record, #5 (Harrisonburg, VA); O'CALLAGHAN, Edmund Bailey, *Lists of the Inhabitants of Colonial NY* (Baltimore, 1979); NYG&B Society, *Records of the Reformed Dutch Church* (NY, 1901).

DuTOI(S)/DuTOY/DuTOIT, Pierre/Peter

b. 7 May 1671, Moudon, Vaud Canton, SWI, n.e. of Lausanne and c. 20 mi. e. of FR border, s/o Pierre & Marie (Frossard [de Saugy]) DuToit

m. c. 1705, ENG, Barbara de Bonnet(te), (b. c. 1686, FR-d. p. 1726 Goochland Co, VA), d/o Daniel & Jeanne (Courturier/Couterrie/Coliver) DeBonnet

1699 – to Manakintown from Bristol, ENG

1714 - patent for 400 acres on "a Great Branch" of Manakintown Creek which became known as "Dutoy's Creek" – not in the FR lands; a second patent was part of the 5000 acres donated to the French refugees & was less than ½ mile downriver from the mouth of Upper Manakin Creek; this patent, #808, was the plantation on which he lived; on the list of French Protestant refugees with wife + 2 daus

d. p. 2 May 1726, wd-a. 3 Oct 1726, wp, King William Parish, Henrico Co, VA; will mentions wife Barbara, daus Elizabeth and Maryan, son Isaac, nephew Anthony Benin (s/o Ann [de Bonnet] Benin, his wife Barbara's sis) and sis-in-law Jeanne Sobrish*; wife was the executrix

*prob. the wife of Gaspard Sobriche

CHILDREN:

Elizabeth[2], b. c. 1705, VA; m. c. 1730, Capt. Thomas Porter (c. 1685-a. 27 Apr 1767, wp, Cumberland Co,
  VA), s/o Thomas & Mary (Kemp) Porter; she d. 1772; both mentioned in Isaac's will
  CHILDREN:
  Anne[3], m. Charles Sampson
  Elizabeth Barbara[3], b. 16 Mar 1732; m. Daniel Branch; in uncle Isaac's will as his niece
  Dutoy[3], b. 17 Feb 1738; in uncle Isaac's will of 1750, but underage, named nephew
  John[3], Captain; liv & d. in Cumberland Co, VA; in Isaac's will as his nephew
Mary Ann[2], b. c. 1706, VA; m/1, c. 1727, Christoffe DuBreuil (d. 1728), m/2, bet 11 Apr-28 Sep 1732,
  John Lucadou/Loucado/Lookadoe (d. a. 16 Aug 1737), s/o Jean Lucadou, m/3, 1738, James
  Goss/Goff (c. 1715-9 Oct 1788, ENG); in bro Isaac's will which states that she was his sister and
  gives married name of Goss; James served a corporal in the Rev. War; she d. c. 1794, Goochland Co.
  CHILD, prob. m/1:
  William[3], b. c. 1737, Goochland Co, VA
  CHILDREN, m/2:
  Elizabeth[3], b. 25 Oct 1738, Goochland Co; d. p. Oct 1794
  Sara Bonne[3], b. 3 Aug 1740, Goochland Co
  David[3], b. c. 1741, Goochland Co; m. Elizabeth Goss (b. c. 1742)
  Benjamin[3], b. 2 Oct 1742, Manakintown; m. 14 Apr 1764, Elizabeth Hamilton (12 May 1743-
    3 May 1815); d. 11 Nov 1813, Elbert Co, GA; **12 ch**
Isaac[2], prob. b. p. 1714, VA; d. p. 26 Nov 1750, wd-a. Mar 1752, wp, Cumberland Co; his nephew Dutoy
  Porter was to receive the 400 acres originally granted to his grfa Pierre when he was of age; Isaac
  evidently did not marry

REF: *The Huguenot*, #6 (1933); GANNON, Peter Steven, editor, *Huguenot Refugees in the Settling of Colonial
America* (NYC); CABELL, Priscilla Harriss, *Turff & Twigg*, Vol. I, *The French Lands* (Richmond, VA, 1988);
CLARK, Henry William, *A Genealogy of the Goss Family* (Montgomery, AL, 1905); PITTMAN, Mrs. H.D. &
WALKER, Mrs. R.K., editors, *Americans of Gentle Birth*, Vol. I (Baltimore, 1970); JONES, W. Mac, *The Douglas
Register* (Richmond, VA, 1928).

DUTERTRE, Louis

of Orléans, FR; Dutertre families were in Touraine, province next to Orléanais, c. 1573-1680, but no
  connection has been made to Louis
m. FR, Marianne Buart, prob. b. Orléans, FR; her parents are not known
by 1710 - living in Parish of St. Giles, Soho, London
d. prob. London, ENG
CHILD:
Anne, b. Orléans; m. 22 Jun 1710, FR Ch, Threadneedle St, London, Pierre David, s/o Pierre &
  Anne (DeBray) David of Bolbec, Haute-Normandie

REF: MINET & MINET, for the Huguenot Society of London, *Livres de Témoignages de l'Église de Threadneedle
Street, 1669-1789* (1909); MINET & WALLNER, for the Huguenot Society of London, *Registers of the Church La
Patente in Spitalfields* (1848); MINET for the Huguenot Society of London, *Registers of the Churches of La Patente de
Soho, Wheeler St, Swanfields & Hoxton* (1956).

DuTRIEU(X)/DeTRUYE/TRUAX, Philippe I

b. bet 18 Jul-14 Aug 1586? certainly by 1588, Roubaix, FR, n.e. of Lille; 22 Apr 1601, a Jaquemyne,
  widow of Philippe du Trieu, was rec. into the Walloon Ch at Leiden by letter from Norwich, ENG
  – parents of Philippe?
m/1, c. 11 Apr 1615 (date of betrothal), Amsterdam, Jacquemine Noiret, d/o Arnould & Barbe (du Chesne)

Noiret; Philippe 27, Jacquemine 22 yrs old (prob. b. Lille, 1593); 2 Apr 1616, Amsterdam, a Jaspar/Gaspard du Trieu (b. 1590, Robaix) m. Jeanne Noiret (18 yrs, b. Lille) – brother and sister to Philippe and Jacquemine?

15 Aug 1617- he and Jacquemine became members of the Walloon Ch in Leiden by letter from Amsterdam

31 Dec 1617 - he and Jacquemine received into ch of Amsterdam by letter from Leiden

m/2, Aug 1621, Susanna du Chesne, according to betrothal record, "of" Sedan; Philippe was liv in the Runtstreat in Leiden at the time of the betrothal, 17 Jul 1621, 34 yrs old, Susanna 20 and an "orphan" with a cousin named Jean Pinson, liv. Bisschopstreate; Susanna *poss.* bp. 30 Jun 1602, Sedan, d/o Pierre & Anne (Fabri) du Chesne

25 Mar 1622 - Susanne de Chesne, wife of Philippe de Trieu, rec. into membership in the Walloon Ch in Amsterdam by letter from Ch in Middelburg, HOL

9 Mar 1624- rec. his certificate from the church in Leiden to go *pour Westinde* - New Amsterdam; sailed on the *New Netherland* from Amsterdam, arr May or Jun, 1624

erected a house on *Bever Graft* – Beaver St., one of the 1st, if not the 1st, house on that street

by 1638 - had land known as "Smit's Vly" which later became part of Fulton Market

apparently a bit contentious as there were several lawsuits over the years, many of which went against Philippe

d. a. 8 Sep 1653, New Amsterdam – Susanne called a widow on that date; he was a worsted dyer in HOL; also said to have been a dresser of plush or mock velvet; Susanna d. p. 23 Oct 1654

CHILDREN, m/1:

Philippe₂, bp 3 Jan 1616, Amsterdam; d. young

Marie², bp. 5 Apr 1617, Leiden; had dau (acknowledged in 1642) by Pieter Wolfertsen; m/1, c. 1640, Cornelius Volckertsen– **4 ch,** used name Vilen/Viele; m/2, c. 20 Feb 1650 (date of banns), Jan Peeck – **4 ch**; she d. p. 28 Feb 1670/1

Philippe II/Philip², bp 10 Feb 1619, Amsterdam; m. XX; he d. a. 8 Sep 1653, NY, poss. murdered by Indians along w/ his father; liv. Albany; **7 ch**

Madeleine², bp 9 Feb 1620, Amsterdam; d. young

CHILDREN, m/2:

Sara², b. New Netherland; m. c. 9 Jun 1641 (date of banns), Isaac de Forest, s/o Jesse & Marie (du Cloux) de Forest; **14 ch**

Susanna², b. New Netherland; m. c. 31 Jul 1644 (date of banns), Evert Jansen Wendell (1615, Embden, E. Friesland-1709, Albany) of Beverwyck – **8 ch**; Susanna d. c. 1660 [Evert m/2, Maritje Abrahamse, d/o Abraham Pieter Van Deursen, widow of Thomas Janse Mingael, m/3, Ariaantje X]

Rachel², b. New Amsterdam; m/1, c. 30 Sep 1656 (date of banns), Hendrick van Bommel – **8 ch**; m/2, 8 Aug 1677, Dirk Jansen de Groot – **3 ch**

Abraham², prob. b. New Amsterdam; a skipper on the Hudson River; m. XX - 1 dau **Maria**³

Rebecca², b. prob. New Amsterdam; m. Simon Symonse Groot; **10 ch**

*****Isaac**², b. 21 Apr 1642, New Amsterdam; m. Maria Brouwer, d/o William Brouwer – **9 ch**

*****Jacob**², bp. 7 Dec 1645, New Amsterdam; m. Lysbeth Post of NY, prob. d/o Lodewyck & Agnietje (Bonen) Post – **9 ch**

*NOTE: It is *possible* that these 2 sons were sons of Philippe II

REF: SANDERS, John, *Early History of Schenectady* (Albany, NY, 1879); VIELE, Kathlyne Knickerbacker, "Philippe Dutrieux" in the *NYGBR*, Vol. XLV (Jan 1914); RANDOLPH, Howard S.F., editor, "The House of Truax" in the *NYGBR*, Vol. LVII (Jul 1926, Oct 1926), Vol. LVIII (Jan 1927); PEARSON, Jonathan, *Genealogies of the 1st Settlers of Schenectady* (1976); SMITH, Barbara Carver, *The Truax/Truex Family of Monmouth & Ocean Co. of NJ, 1675-1690, Descendants of Philippe DuTrieux.*

DuVAL/DUVAL, Daniel

b. c. 1675 FR, Normandie?

p. 1685 - went to ENG

8 Dec 1700 - sailed from Blackwall in London on the *Le Nasseau* – no mention of wife, ch, relatives but some sources say he m. in FR

5 Mar 1701 – arr York River, VA; settled Ware Parish, Gloucester Co, VA; an architect and joiner

prob. m. soon after arr in VA; the name Philadelphia DuBois, d/o Jean & Marie (Deyaget) DuBois has been mentioned – not proven

settled on a tract of land on the s. side of the James River, c. 20 mi. above Richmond

by 24 Jun 1704 – he was in York Co. & took on an apprentice who wanted to learn the trade of architect and joiner

CHILDREN:

William[2], b. c. 1704; m. XX – **4 sons, 4 daus**; he d. 1784, Petsworth Parish, Gloucester Co

Daniel[2], b. c. 1706; m. 29 Dec 1732, Abbington Parish, Gloucester Co, Mary Thompson (bp 4 Apr 1714), d/o Henry & Susanna (X) Thompson - at least **4 sons**; he d. a. 13 Mar 1777, wp, Caroline Co, VA

Benjamin[2], b. c. 1708; m. Ann Kay, prob. d/o Robert Kay of Caroline Co – **4 sons, 4 daus**; he d. 1770, Henrico Co, VA

Samuel[2], b. 1714; m. Lucy Claiborne, d/o William Claiborne IV; he d. a. 1 Mar1784, wp, Henrico Co, VA; **5 sons, 3 daus**

Mary/Polly[2], m. X Amos of Surrey Co; had dau **Elizabeth**[3]

REF: GRABOWSKII, Bessie Berry, *The DuVal Family of VA 1701*(Richmond, VA, 1931); BUCHANAN, Margaret Gwin, *DuVals of KY from VA, 1704-1935* (Lynchburg, VA); THACKER, Jack H., in *The Longhunter*, Vol. IX, #2 (Summer 1988, pub. by the KY Gen. Soc.), "Correcting the Genealogy of Samuel DuVal, Jr.".

DuVAL, DUVAL(L), Marin/Mareen

b. c. 1625/32, supposedly Laval, FR (s.e. of Vitré), then in Normandie, s/o Thomas & Nicola (Stagard) Duvall; said to have sailed to America from Nantes, Bretagne, FR, s.w. of Laval, on the Loire River

28 Aug 1650 - said to have arr in MD on that date – however, no record

served an indentureship with John Covell; became a freeholder c. 1657

m/1, c. 1658, XX - poss. named Mary; **may** have m. earlier in FR in which case this would have been wife #2 but there is no real evidence of that

25 Jul 1659 – asked for the 50 acres of land due him for his indentureship

22 Jan 1659/60 - 1st land patented to him by Lord Cecilius Baltimore, 100 acres on the w. side of the South River in Anne Arundel Co, which he called "Laval"; he was a planter, carpenter and merchant

1664 – patented the land called "Middle Plantation" by the Lord Proprietary (Cecilius Baltimore); over the years he purchased many more acres

m/2, c. 1673/4, Susannah X (b. c. 1652), *poss.* d/o Benois & Marie Brasseur/Brashear

1683 – he was a member of the Provincial Commission which laid out town sites and ports of entry

m/3, c. 1693, Mary X (who m/2, 1695, Col. Henry Ridgely, m/3, p. 1711, Rev. Jacob Henderson, Rector of Queen Ann's Parish, Pr. George Co, MD); she d. 19 Jan 1735/6

d. 5 Aug 1694, Middle Plantation, MD, on n. side of US 50, e. of MD 424 & Rossback Rd in Davidsonville

13 Aug 1694, wp, Anne Arundel Co; names wife Mary, sons Lewis, Mareen (both), Benjamin, John, Samuel, daus Eliza(beth), Catherine, Mary, Johanna, sons-in-law Robert Tyler, John Roberts

CHILDREN, m/1:

John[2], b. c. 1660; m. Elizabeth Jones, d/o William Jones, Sr; bur. 20 Apr 1711, All Hallows Ch; **7 sons, 4 daus**

Mareen (the Elder)[2], b. 1662; m. 1685/6, Frances Stockett, d/o Thomas & Mary (Wells) Stockett; d. a. 22 Aug 1735; **1 son**

Lewis[2], m. 6 Mar 1699, Martha Ridgely, d/o Robert & Martha (X) Ridgely of St. Inigoes, St. Mary's Co,

MD; went to SC; he d. 1724, SC; **4 daus**

Samuel[2], b. 1667; m. 18 Jun 1697, Elizabeth (Ijams) Clark, d/o William & Elizabeth (Cheney) Ijams, widow of Capt. Daniel Clark; he d. a. 24 Mar 1741, wp, Pr. Georges Co; **6 daus**

Eleanor[2], not in father's will; sources say she m. John Roberts, but, according to her father's will, John's wife was her sister Elizabeth; poss that Eleanor was John's 1st wife and her sister Elizabeth was his 2nd **or** father got the names wrong! Elizabeth was not yet 16 at the time that the will was written (2 Aug 1694) and the will mentions that she will get her portion when she reaches 16 or the day of her marriage, whichever comes 1st, neither of which had apparently happened yet; no legitimate issue

CHILDREN, m/2, all minors in father's will, i.e., sons were not 18, daus not 16:

Susannah, b. c. 1677; m. a. 1694, Robert Tyler (6 Jan 1671-1738), s/o Robert & Joan (X) Tyler; she d. 12 May 1716; **3 sons, 5 daus**; not in father's will by name but mentions her husband Robert Tyler

Mareen (the Younger), b. c. 1680; m. 21 Oct 1701, Elizabeth Jacob (d. Feb 1752), d/o Capt. John Jacob; he d. a. 9 Jun 1741, wp, Pr. George's Co; **7 sons, 4 daus**

Catherine, m. 22 Oct 1700, William Orrick (1680-1720) of Anne Arundel Co, s/o James & Mary (Slade) Orrick; she d. 1703; **1 son**, who d. young

Elizabeth, m. John Roberts?; he is named as her husband in her father's will; Abraham Clarke has been said to have been her husband - given what is mentioned above re sister Eleanor, that is possible; if Abraham was her husband, **2 sons, 1 dau**

Mary, m. 5 Feb 1701, Rev. Henry Hall, Rector St. James Parish, Anne Arundel Co.; **6 sons, 3 daus**

Johanna, b. c. 1685; m. 12 Aug 1703, Richard Poole of MD; she d. 1712; **2 sons**

Benjamin, b. 1692; m. 1713, Sophia Griffith (27 Apr 1691-19 Apr 1730), d/o William & Sarah (Maccubin) Griffith; he d. c. 1774 ; **4 sons, 2 dau**

NOTE: Birth order of children is not absolute nor is the number of ch per wife.

REF: HARDY, Stella Pickett, *Colonial Families of the Southern States of America* (Baltimore, 1968); SPENCER, Richard Henry, *Genealogical & Memorial Encyclopedia of the State of MD*; *MD Calendar of Wills,* Vol. II (abstracts); Mareen's will – complete copy of the original will; CLARK, Raymond B, Jr, indexer, *Genealogies of VA Families*, Vol. III (Baltimore, 1981); NEWMAN, Harry Wright, *Mareen Duvall of Middle Plantation* (Baltimore, 1984 reprint).

E

EDDENS/ED(D)INS/EDDINGS, John

m. XX

6 Dec 1726 - witnessed a deed in Spotsylvania Co between his son William & William McConnico

1744 - he is listed as a Huguenot refugee liv. in King William Parish

CHILD:

William[2], m. a. 1715, Rebecca X; liv St. George Parish, Spotsylvania Co, 1726-1730; 1732-34 – liv. St. Marks Parish, Spotsylvania Co; Rebecca d. p. 6 Aug 1754, he d. a. 6 Aug 1754, prob. Lunenburg Co, VA; 6 Aug 1754, wp, Lunenburg Co; besides the ch listed below, he mentions a dau-in-law Anne – not sure who she "belongs" to

> CHILDREN (in his will dated 2 Feb 1754, surnamed EDDINGS):
>
> **Theophelus**[3], b. c. 1715, Spotsylvania Co, VA; m. a. 1735, Elizabeth X; 6 Jan 1730, witnessed a deed in Spotsylvania Co between his father and Duncan Bohannan; 4 Jun 1734, he is liv. St. Mark's Parish, Spotsylvania Co., according to a deed; d. c. 1784, Abbeville Dist, SC - **issue**
>
> **Jacob**[3]
>
> **Benjamin**[3]
>
> **Isaac**[3], not m. in 1754
>
> **Mary**[3]
>
> **John**[3]
>
> **Joseph**[3]
>
> **Abraham**[3]
>
> **William**[3]
>
> **Elizabeth**[3]
>
> **Rebecca**[3]

REF: CROZIER, William Armstrong, *Spotsylvania County Records, 1721-1800* (Baltimore, 1955); BROCK, R.A., *Huguenot Emigration to VA; The Huguenot* #29 (1979-81) , #30 (1981-83) (William's will).

EFFARD, Nicolas

b. FR, prob. Normandie, s/o Jean/John & Élisabeth (Perrin) Effard, d/o Edmund Perrin of Jersey, seigneur of Rozel Manor; Jean/John, Jurat R.C. (Judge of the Royal Court) was from Guernsey

Sep 1568 - fled to the Isle of Jersey from Normandie where he had been a Rector at Ste-Marie-du-Mont; he was educated at Elizabeth College in Guernsey as listed in the register of the Walloon Church in Southampton, 6 Apr1572.

m/1, Marie leDuc, d/o Rev. Nicolas leDuc, rector of St. Jean in Jersey

25 Mar 1587 – installed as rector of St. Saviour's Church in Jersey

m/2, 21 Jul 1587, Sara de Caumont, d/o Rev. Pierre de Caumont, rector of St. Peter in Jersey

d. 27 Apr 1638, bur. 29 Apr 1638, St. Saviour Cemetery, Jersey

CHILDREN, m/2:

Martha[2], b. 1589

Sara[2], b. 1590

Jean[2], b. 1593

Judith[2], b. 1595

Elizabeth[2], b. 1597; m. 14 Dec 1614, St. Saviour's Ch, Thomas Poindexter (bp. 11 Aug 1581, St. Saviour's Church, Jersey), s/o Édouard & Marguerite (Messervy) Poingdestre; Marguerite was the d/o Clément & Catherine (Lemprière) Messervy; Thomas d. 1669

> CHILDREN:
>
> **Philip**[3], bp. 11 Feb 1621; BA degree, Oxford 1641; d. 1665
>
> **Jacob**[3], bp. 2 May 1624

Rachel[3]

George[3], b. 23 Dec 1627; m. a. 1657, Susannah (Nicholls?); 1657, emigrated to VA, during the
Cromwellian Revolt, settled in York, Co; his cousin Peter Effard and uncle John Poindexter
went with him; Susannah d. 1693, he d. 1690

Susanna[2], b. 1600

Marie[2], b. 1602

Nicholas, Jr.[2], b. 1605; 27 Jun 1639, returned from Turkey where he was employed to redeem
captives and to deliver his bro Peter from slavery

Pierre/Peter[2], b. 1606; went to VA, c. 1655

Jeanne[2], b. 1607

REF : LANDERS, John Poindexter, *Poingdeste-Poindexter, A Norman Family through the Ages, 1259-1977*
(final chapter by Robert Dawns Poindexter) (Austin, TX); TURK, Marion G., *The Quiet Adventurers in N. America.*

ESLE/ES(E)LY/d'ESLEY/EASLEY, Robert

b. c. 1655, ENG; family was of French origin - left FR after St. Bartholomew Massacre & went to ENG;
some of the family went to SWI, where they were silk merchants - surname ISLYN; it is said
that some of the family later went back to FR from SWI

c. 1676 - to VA and was granted lands in the allotment made to the French refugees

m. p. 1 Oct 1679, VA (Jamestown?), Ann Parker (a. 1658, prob. VA- a. Jan 1720, wp, Henrico Co, VA),
d/o William & Ann (Well) Parker

by 1680 - prob. by 11 Oct 1679 - in Henrico Co.

d. p. 17 Dec 1711, wd - a. 3 Mar 1711/12, wp, Henrico Co, VA; wife and all ch named

CHILDREN:

John[2], b. 1680-88, Henrico Co, VA; m. c. 1711, prob. Henrico Co, VA Mary Benskin (b. c. 1691,
prob. Henrico Co), d/o Jeremiah & Elizabeth (X) Benskin(e)

CHILDREN:

Stephen[3], b. 1715/6; m. c. 1751, Mary Ann (David) Burton (1716-1815, Sullivan Co, TN), d/o
Peter & Anne (Dutertre) David, widow of Pierre David; he d. 1803

CHILDREN:

Sarah[4], b. 1 Dec 1752, **Robert**[4], b. 25 Nov 1754, **Thomas**[4], b. 23 Nov 1765, **Daniel**[4], b.
4 Dec 1759, **Stephen**[4], b. 16 May 1763, **Peter**[4], b. 15 Oct 1765

Daniel[3], b. c. 1720; m. 1745, Ann David (10 May 1722-c. 1764); he d. a. 19 Jan 1786, Halifax
Co, VA; **issue**

Warham[3], b. 1721/28, prob. Henrico Co, VA; m. 1751/54, VA, Ann Woodson (1736 VA-
a. Oct 1801, wp, Patrick Co, VA), d/o John & Mary (Miller) Woodson; he d. p. 12 Aug
1790, wd, Henry Co, VA; will mentions wife "Nanney", sons John, Miller, Daniel, Joseph,
Worham, William, daus Susanah Francey (Frances), Judah; wife and son Miller, executors;
Miller was **Miller Woodson Easley**[4] (c. 1756, Cumberland Co, VA-19 Aug 1834, Grainger
Co, TN) who m. 2 Aug 1782, Henry Co, VA, Mary Lyon, d/o James & Christian (Harmon)
Lyon of Henry Co. – **9 ch**; **Judith** (Judah)[4] m. X Gaines

William[3], m. XX; liv. Dinwiddie Co, VA; at least 1 ch – **Benskin**[4] who m. & had **issue**

Robert[3]

Warham[2], b. c. 1685/7; m. Sarah Barnes (c. 1680-1734/5); he d. c. 1747

Margaret[2], b. 1686/92; m/1, Thomas DuPré (b. c. 1679), m/2, James Watson

Elizabeth[2], b. 1690/5

William[2], b. 1690/5

Robert[2], b. 1702/6-1736

REF: Grainger Co, TN *Heritage Book*; JOHNSON, K.E. *Our Easley Ancestors and Their Relatives*; EASLEY, J.
D. *300 Years of Easley Genealogy*; Huguenot Publication #5 (1931); REEVES, *Ancestral Sketches*; Manakintown Records; MANNING, W.H. Jr. *Our Kin*; DeMARCE, Virginia Easley. *Easley Lines Primarily to Year 1850*

(Jul 1981 reprint, unpub.); *The VA Genealogist,* Vol. 2 (1958); SUTHERD, Calvin E., *A Compilation of Gaines Family Data with Special Emphasis on the Lineage of William & Isabella (Pendleton) Gaines* (Ft. Lauderdale, FL, Aug 1972).

EYMAR/AYMAR(D)/AIMA, Jean

said to be from Dauphiné Prov.

supposedly fled FR as a child w/ his parents thru GER to ENG; Jean to Nassau, then to NY

m. Françoise Belon (d. p. 27 Oct 1765)

by 1731- in NYC (bp. rec FR Ch, NYC); was an elder and doorkeeper for the FR Ch in NYC

owned vineyards

26 Feb 1746 - purchased home and land on Nassau St.

d. 1755 NYC; 31 Mar 1749, wd; will mentions wife, sons John, Daniel, James, daus Judith,   wife
    of Daniel Hutcheson, mariner, Magdalen, Lucretia, Charlott (*sic*), Mary, Jean

CHILDREN (named in father's will):

Judith[2], m/1, 1739, NYC, Daniel Hutcheson/Hutchinson – **issue**, incl. dau **Elizabeth**[3], b. 7 Jun, bp. 14
    Jun 1741, FR Ch, NYC, her grandparents, Jean & Françoise were her godparents; m/2, 2 Jul 1759,
    NY, James Alexander

Madeleine[2], m. 1749, NYC, François Magny (bp. 6 Apr 1707, NY), s/o Jacques & Anne (Vincent)
    Magny/Many; **issue**, incl. dau **Françoise**[3], b. 8 Jul, bp. 14 Aug 1750 FR Ch, NYC

Lucrèce[2], m/1, NYC, Gérard Jamain; m/2, 14 Jan 1759, NYC, Pierre Magny, **issue**

Jean[2], b. 1728; m/1, Elizabeth Dobbs – **4 ch**, m/2, 16 May 1762, FR Ch, NYC, Jeanne Raveau (19 Dec, bp.
    26 Dec 1742, FR Ch, NYC-30 Aug 1823, NY), d/o Daniel & Marie (Raven) Raveau – **11 ch**; he d.
    4 Sep 1796, NY; accord. to marr. rec. Jean was a *tonelier* – prob. means *tonnelier*, a cooper

Charlotte[2], m. 27 Oct 1765, at home of Pierre Magny, Jeune - rec. FR Ch, NYC John Moffit; d. 1780, NY;
    issue

Marie[2], b. 18 Nov, bp. 28 Nov 1731, FR Ch, NYC; m. 3 Feb 1755, FR Ch, NYC, Pierre Rougeon; she d.
    1767, NY; **issue   James de Lancey, Lt. Gov, NY**

Daniel[2], b. 17 Nov, bp. 28 Nov 1733, FR Ch, NYC; m. 24 Sep 1756 Anna Magdelene Magny (18 Nov 1738,
    NY-May 177?, NY), d/o François Magny/Many & Annatje Kip; he d. 25 Jun 1815, NYC, bur. St.
    Esprit Churchyard; **12 ch**

Jean Jacques[2], b. 2 Aug, bp. 13 Aug 1735, FR Ch, NYC; m/1, 6 Mar 1760, Margaret Brown – **4 ch**; m/2,
    25 Sep 1774, Mary Mann – **2 ch**; he d. May/Jun 1797, NY

Jeanne[2], b. 7 Aug, bp. 15 1739, NYC, sis Judith was her godmother; m. 3 Feb 1756, FR Ch, NYC, Dennis
    Wortman, marr. rec. says he was a *charpentier de Navire* – a ship's carpenter

REF: AYMAR, Benjamin, "Aymar of NY" in *Proceedings of the Huguenot Society of America*), Vol. III, Part 2
(NY, 1903); WITTMEYER, Alfred V., *Registers of the L'Église Françoise à Nouvelle York* (Baltimore, 1968).

F

FAIN, Isabella – see <u>DANDONNEAU</u>, Jacques

FAISON/FAYSON, Henri von Doverage/Henryk van Doveracke

fam. originally from Gascogne, FR, went to GER, c. 1572; perhaps went back to FR, but they did
end up in HOL; the appendage of von Doverage/van Doveracke refers to a place – Douveria* in
Normandie, n. of Caen, w. of the mouth of the Seine; by 1733 the family just used Faison
[*now Douvres-la-Délivrande, Calvados Dépt, Basse-Normandie – Douveria is also the name that
the FR call Dover, ENG]

prob. b. c. 1620-25

1640-48 - in Sedan, FR; name in register of the Huguenot Ch there

m/1, c. 1650, Rebecca Plouvier (c. 1630-10 May 1671); Rebecca's parents were evidently Pierre/Peter &
Françoise (X) Plouvier, who appear in land transactions between the families in VA; [Pierre &
Françoise also had a son Pierre II, bp. 5 Dec 1647, Walloon Ch, Canterbury, ENG; Pierre was a doctor;
Françoise d. p. 12 Jan 1666 & Pierre m/2, Elizabeth Booth; he d. a. 25 Feb 1677/8, wp York Co, VA]

a. 1652 - to York Co, VA from HOL. w/ other FR Huguenots

1666 – rec. a grant of land in York Co, VA

24 Sep 1672 - one of 40 Huguenots naturalized New Pocosin (Poquoson) Parish, York Co, VA

m/2, Katherine X

d. 7 May 1693, York Co, VA; he was a cooper; he refers to himself as "Hendrick fforson" in his will (wd,
26 Feb 1693); will names wife, sons James & Henry, grsons Henry Clarke & James

CHILDREN, m/1 (all b/bp Charles Parish, York Co, VA):

Elizabeth[2], b. 18 Feb 1652, York Co; m/1, John Clarke – **1 son, 1 dau**, m/2, prob. John Morris – **1 dau**

Henry[2], b. 14 Feb 1656/7, York Co.; m. 1679, Anne Hickle; he d. 9 Dec 1697, York Co.

    CHILDREN:

    James[3], b. 2 Dec 1680, York Co; m. Mary Love (20 Oct 1680-12 Apr 1734), d/o Elias & Sarah
        (X) Love; he d. c. 1746/47, Northampton Co, VA

        CHILDREN :

        Elizabeth[4], b. 4 Mar 1704/5, York Co; d. 11 Apr 1705

        James[4], b. 30 Aug 1706, York Co; m. Frances (Dixon?); he d. 13 Apr 1773 – **4 sons**

        Elias[4], b. 20 Jan 1709/10, York Co.; d. 13 Mar 1753, York Co.

        Sarah[4], b. 15 Mar 1718/9, York Co., bp. 19 Apr 1719

        Elizabeth[4], b. 9 Feb, bp. Mar 1721/22; d. 17 Sep 1731

        ?Henry[4]

    Elizabeth[3], bp. 17 Jun 1683, York Co; d. 11 Apr 1705 unmarr.

    Rebecca[3], 6 Jan 1688/9, York Co.

    Ann[3], b. 29 Mar 1692, York Co.

    Henry[3], b. 26 Apr 1695, York Co.; m. Elizabeth X; d. 13 Mar 1735/6, York Co.; **2 sons, 3 daus**

?James[2], b. 2 Dec 1660; one source names this son, but others do not – majority of sources say that
Henry[1] had only 2 ch – Elizabeth & Henry; **needs proof**

REF: BOONE, Minnie Speer, *Our Family Heritage* (NY, 1956) ; WILLIAMS, Robert Murphy, *Williams & Murphy
Records & Related Families* (Raleigh, 1949) ; HILL, John Sprunt, *History of Henry & His Wife Diana Griffin,
Progenitors of the Family of, NC & Genealogy of Family in NC & Other Southern States* (manuscript) ; research by F. L.
MORRIS; "Fayson Family" in *Tyler's Quarterly Magazine*, Vol. VI (1925); HOVENDEN, Robert, editor, *The Registers of
the Walloon or Strangers' Church in Canterbury, Part I* (Lymington, 1891).

FANEUIL, Benjamin

b. 1593, La Rochelle, FR
m. 29 May 1615, Suzanne de l'Espine/l'Épine
d. 19 Dec 1677, La Rochelle, FR; he was a merchant
CHILD:
Pierre[2], b. 2 Aug 1618; m. 9 Dec 1640, Marie Cousseau; family said to have a coat of arms
    CHILDREN:
    Benjamin[3], b. 16 Mar 1645, FR; m. Marie Bernon, d/o <u>André & Suzanne (Guillemard) Bernon</u>;
        1st settled nr. New Rochelle, NY; owned a large farm on North Ave. in New Rochelle; also had
        a financial interest in the Huguenot settlement at Oxford, MA, but after the end of the Oxford
        settlement, he went to NY; 1699 Benjamin was given the freedom of NYC where he was one of
        its principal merchants; he d. 31 Mar 1719, bur. n. side of Trinity Ch, NYC
        CHILDREN:
        Suzanne[4]; **Marie**[4]; **Pierre**[4]; **Marie**[4]; **Esther**[4]; **Jeanne Catherine**[4]; **Jean**[4], d. young
    Pierre[3], m. 10 Jul 1666, Marie DuPont; his 3 sons went to America and were on a list of FR refugees
        admitted to the Bay Colony, 1 Feb 1691; he was a merchant in La Rochelle; he d. 22
        Feb 1688, FR; 2 sons went to America supplied with money and jewels
        CHILDREN:
    Benjamin[4], b. 5 Jul 1668; m. 28 Jul 1699, Anne Bureau, d/o François & Anne (X) Bureau
        of Niort, Poitou, FR; 1st settled nr. New Rochelle; 1699, he was given the freedom of
        the city of NY; he was a principal merchant of NYC; he d. 31Mar 1719 NYC, age 60Y
        8M, bur. Trinity Ch, NYC; **11 ch**, 4 of whom d. young
        CHILDREN (7 of 11, all bp. FR Ch, NYC):
    Peter[5], b. 20 Jun, bp. 15 Jul 1700; went to liv w/ uncle Andrew (below) p. 1719;
        he erected Faneuil Hall as a market place & presented it to the city of
        Boston in 1742; he d. 3 Mar, bur. 10 Mar 1742/3, Granary; d. unmarr
    Benjamin[5], b. 29 Dec 1701, bp. 11 Jan 1701/2; went to liv w/ uncle Andrew
        (below) p. 1719; m. c. 1729, Mary Cutler, prob. d/o Dr. Timothy Cutler, which
        displeased his uncle who cut him out of his will; liv. corner of Washington &
        Summer St., Boston, later in Brighton; was completely blind for the last 20 yrs
        of his life; liv. to be 84 Y; d. 2 Oct 1785, bur Granary; wife d. 13 May 1777,
        bur. Granary; 2 sons left Boston at beg. of Rev War - **Peter**[6] to CAN,
        Benjamin[6] to CAN, then ENG, where he d. 1785, at Bristol, dau **Mary**[6] stayed
        and m. 13 Oct 1754, Boston, George Bethune - **issue**
    François/Francis[5], b. 21 Aug, bp. 19 Sep 1703
    Marie/Mary[5], b. 16 Apr, bp 26 Apr 1708; m. 6 Aug 1725, Boston, Gillam Phillips
        (d. 17 Oct 1770, bur. Granary); she d. by 22 Jun 1778, bur. Granary
    Anne[5], b. 19 Oct, bp 1 Nov 1710; m. 9 May 1739, Boston, Rev. Addington Daven-
        port, Rector Trinity Ch, Boston; he d. 8 Sep 1746, she d. 15 Nov 1744, both in
        Boston
    Susanne[5], b. 14 Mar, bp 22 Mar 1712/3; m. 30 Aug 1738, Boston, James Boutin-
        eau, a Boston lawyer; they liv. on Milk St, nr. the Old South Meeting House;
        she d. 1785
    Marianne/Mary Ann[5], b. 6 Apr, bp 17 Apr 1715; m. 15 May 1742, Boston, John
        Jones who d. 1767, Roxbury; she was a Loyalist, liv for some time in Windsor,
        Nova Scotia
    Jean/John[4], b. 1670; he was a mariner; ret. to FR, d. 24 Jun 1737, La Rochelle
    André/Andrew[4], settled in Boston, by 1691; made a large fortune as a merchant; m. Mary
        Catherine X, a woman whom he mar in HOL (she d. 16 Jul 1724, Boston); **no issue**
        reached majority; adopted his nephews Peter[5] and Benjamin[5]; he offered to make
        Benjamin[5] his heir *only* if Benjamin remained single, but Benjamin mar. and his
        brother Peter[5] became the heir; Andrew was the richest man in MA, he liv. at the corner

of Somerset & Beacon St., nr. the Old Granary Burying Ground; he d. 13 Feb 1737/8
and is bur. on the s. side of the Commons in the Granary

Suzanne[4], remained in La Rochelle, FR; m. 14 Jul 1683, Abraham de la Croix/Delacroix

Jeanne/Jane[4], m. Pierre Cossart; went to IRE

REF: BAIRD, Charles W., *Huguenot Emigration to America*; STARK, James H., *The Loyalists of MA & the Other Side of the American Revolution* (Boston, 1910); FOSDICK, Lucien F., *The French Blood in America* (NY. 1911); BROWN, Abram English, *Faneuil Hall & Faneuil Hall Market* (Boston, 1900); WEISSE, Mrs. John A., *A History of the Bethune Family* (NYC, 1884); "Data Relative to the Faneuil Family" in the *NYGBR* (Vol. 47) – FR recs from La Rochelle; VR, cemetery recs – Boston; WITTMEYER, Alfred V., *Registers of L'Église Françoise à Nouvelle York* (Baltimore, 1968).

FARCY/FARCI/FARCEE/FORSEE, Jean/John

m. prob. Susannah X

1680's-1690's - minister in Mouchamps, Poitou, FR, n.e. of La Roche-sur-Yon, & in London

Jul 1700 – sailed to VA on the *Mary Ann*, the 1st ship to carry FR refugees to Manakintown

12 May 1705, VA - naturalized

1707 - member of King William Parish; served as vestryman, 1707-30 Dec 1715

1710 – on 1st tithable list; 1717 was the last one he was on – no servants and no sons age 16 or older

1714 - on the *Liste Généralle* of FR refugees with wife and 3 sons (3rd son unknown, prob. d. young)

31 Oct 1716 - patentee for patent #851, 40 acres on the s. side of the James River in Henrico Co (now
Powhatan) – part of the 1st 5000 acres granted to the FR refugees – it was willed to his
son Stephen, c. 1719

d. p. 19 Dec 1718, wd, VA

CHILDREN:

Jean-François[2], he and his bro lived in Estienne Chastain's house after their father d.; Chastain is said to
have been a *kinsman*; m. c. 1727, Susanne X; ch: **Pierre**[3], b. 10 Feb 1728, **Marie**[3], b. 10 Feb, bp.
21 Mar 1728/9 (they may have been twins, records unclear); he d. a. 30 Jun 1731

Estienne/Stephen I[2], b. c. 1709/10; m. c. 1731, Marie Perrow (b. 1710) d/o Charles Perrault/ Perrow; he d.
p. 8 Nov 1772, wd-a. 22 Nov 1773, wp, Cumberland Co.; will mentions wife but not by name,
sons Stephen John, Francis (not yet of age), Charles, William, daus Elizabeth, "Maryann Maxi,"
Ann Martin, Jane "Briant," Judith Price; executors were wife, Stephen and Francis
CHILDREN:
John[3], b. 1732; d. p. 28 Aug 1766, wd-a. 27 Oct 1766, wp; **no issue**
Mariane[3], b. 9 Sep 1734; m. 19 Jan 1758, Manakintown, John Maxey
Anne[3], b. 7 Mar 1736/7; m. 9 Dec 1765, Manakintown, Austin Martin; **issue**; she was named for
maternal aunt Anne (Perrow) Epperson
Jane[3], b. 29 Aug 1739; m. James Bryant, Jr., s/o Jacques & Elizabeth (LeFèvre) Brian; Elizabeth
was the d/o Isaac & Madeleine (Parenteau) LeFèvre
Elizabeth[3], b. 25 Nov 1741
Judith[3], b. 19 Oct 1744; m. X Price
Estienne/Stephen II[3], b. 2 Nov 1750; m. Frances Bryant, d/o Jacques & Clare (X) Brian; he d.
p. 3 Jan-a. 18 Sep 1799
Francis[3], b. c. 1752
Charles[3]
William[3]

Judith[2], m. a. 20 Aug 1728, Joseph Bingley

REF: CABELL, Priscilla Harriss, *Turff & Twigg*, Vol. I (Richmond, VA); BOCKSTRUCK, Lloyd D., "Naturaliza-tions & Denizations in Colonial VA" in *National Genealogical Society Quarterly*, Vol. 73, #2 (Jun 1985); BROCK, R.A., *Huguenot Emigration to VA*; JONES, W. Mac, *The Douglas Register* (Richmond, VA, 1928); wills of Stephen, Austin Martin; *The VA Genealogist*.

FAUCONNIER, Pierre

m. c. 1575, Margariete DuPont; she m/2, 7 Apr 1590, Walloon Ch, Amsterdam, David Goris, a laceworker from Antwerp, age 30; she d. p. 1600

d. c. 1585, poss. Amsterdam or Antwerp (Anvers)

CHILDREN:

Anne[2], b. c. 1575; 30 Mar 1593, received in Walloon Ch, Amsterdam

Matthieu[2], b. c. 1577; m. 12 Sep 1599, Walloon Ch, Amsterdam, Beatris Berdule, from Antwerp, age 26, d/o Jacob Berdule

Sara[2], b. 1579; m/1, Jacques Deplancque - **issue**; m/2, Nicolas Agache

REF: MACY, Harry, Jr., "Sara (DePlanck) Monfort" in *The NYGBR*, Vol. 11, #3 (Jul 1991).

FAUCONNIER, Pierre II

b.1659, Tours, FR, s/o Pierre I & Anne (de la Forcade) Fauconnier*; Pierre I was a *maître orfèvre* (master gold/silversmith) who later lived in Angoulême & d. a. 1684

m. 16 Apr 1680, Temple of Tours, Madeleine Pasquereau (b. 1665, Tours-d. Hackensack, NJ), d/o Pierre & Madeleine (Houssaye) Pasquereau*; she d. bet. 15 Jan 1734-10 Apr 1745, prob. Hackensack

1681 - fled FR to ENG where Pierre was a *marchand avisé* (a shrewd or prudent merchant)

24 Mar 1684/5 -he and Madeleine were on a list of those FR refugees who wished to be free denizens under James II – for some reason Louis and Madeleine Pasquereau's ch were listed with them; on the Patent Roll, it lists just Peter and Magdalen, w/ Louis and his wife Magdalen listed with their 3 sons

4 Apr 1685- he and Madeleine were naturalized ENG along with Louis Pasquereau (bro of Madeleine) & his wife Madeleine Chardon of Tours & their ch Louis II, Peter, Isaac; Louis I, prob. d. in London & his widow Madeleine m/2, Philippe Gendron – their dau Mary Magdelen Gendron m. Samuel Prioleau 17 May 1685 – Pierre's témoignage at the FR Ch, Threadneedle St., London; témoignage was from Angoulême - témoignage was a cert from the ch from which the refugee came

3 May 1702, arr NYC w/ wife, 4 ch; 1st mention of the name in the FR Ch, NYC, was on 21 Nov 1703, bap of Anne, d/o Henry & Marianne (Grasset) de Money, Madeleine was her godmo; in NY, he was a member of the FR Ch, private secretary to the governor of NY, later he was the super-intendant, receiver general (tax collector) for the state of NY; later settled NJ

10 Dec 1702 – Pierre & Madeleine were wanting a patent on Staten Island

d. a. 27 May 1747, Hackensack, Bergen, NJ

CHILDREN:

(Most of the descendants used surname **FALCONER**.)

Théodore/Theodorus[2], bp. 19 Feb 1681, Threadneedle St. Ch; d. unmarr. bet 1716-21, Martinique, West Indies

André[2], b. ENG; d. unmarr.

Susanne Madeleine[2], bp. 13 May 1685, FR Ch, Threadneedle St, London; m. c. 1712, Peter Valleau (b. 1663, FR-c.1738, NJ), s/o Esaïe/Isaiah & Suzanne (Descard) Valleau; prob. Peter's 2nd or 3rd wife; **6 ch**; some recs. say just Madeleine, others Susanne Madeleine

Pierre[2], (twin), bp. 24 Jun 1686, FR Ch, Threadneedle St., London; m/1, XX – 1 son **William**[3], m/2, Dec 1746 Trinity Ch, NYC, Phoebe Purdy, d/o Seth & Phoebe (Ketchum) Purdy of Rye, NY – 1 son **John**[3]

Étienne[2], (twin), bp. 24 Jun 1686, FR Ch, Threadneedle St, London; d. young

Étienne[2], bp. 20 Apr 1689, FR Ch, Threadneedle St, London; d. young

Jeanne Élisabeth[2], b. NY; m/1,12 Aug 1725, Christ Ch, Philadelphia, Robert Asseton, m/2, 8 Apr 1729, Christ Ch, Philadelphia, Rev. Dr. Archibald Cummings, m/3, 11 Apr 1748, Christ Ch, Philadelphia, Rev. Robert Jenney – **no issue** from any of her marr.

Anne Madeleine[2], b. NY; m/1, Dr. John Kearsley of Philadelphia, m/2, Theophilus Caille

*****NOTE:** Parents were previously given as Jean & Madeleine (de la Touche) Fauconnier as per the Helffenstein bio but records from Tours give the parents listed above. Also a correction was made re Madeleine Pasquereau's parentage for the same reason. Since both were from Tours, those records are a primary source. The only Pasquereau descendants of this family are through dau Madeleine.

REF: CENTRE GÉNÉALOGIQUE en TOURAINE, *Les Protestants en Touraine*, Vol. III; HELFFENSTEIN, Abraham E., *Pierre Fauconnier & His Descendants* (Philadelphia, 1911); HUGUENOT SOCIETY OF LONDON, *Register of the French Ch of Threadneedle St, London*, Vol. I, II, III; DURIE, Howard I., *Some Lesser-Known Huguenots on the Hackensack* (1971); MINET, William & Susan, *Témoignages de l'Église de Threadneedle Street, 1699-1789* – Publications of the Huguenot Society of London (London, 1909) Vol. XXI; MINET, William & Susan, *Libre des Témoignages de l'Église de Threadneedle Street, 1669-1789*- Publication of the Huguenot Society of London, Vol. XXI (London, 1909) ; PERRIN, Anna Falconer & MEEKER, Mary Falconer Perrin, *Allied Families of Purdy, Fauconnier, Archer, Perrin* (NYC, 1911).

FAURÉ, Daniel Isaac

prob. b. c. 1650/55; of Auvergne, FR

m. Anne Tibault, who emigrated to VA as the "*veuve* (widow) Fauré," with 4 ch – 2 sons – Daniel & Jean, 2 daus – Elizabeth and ?, called "infants" which meant they were all under 21; arr 23 Jul 1700, at the mouth of the James River; settled Manakintown

d. c. 1699/00, prob. London, just bef he was to leave for Jamestown on the *Mary Ann*

CHILDREN:

Daniel[2], b. c. 1673/4, FR; m/1, prob. FR, XX – **2 ch**; m/2, VA, Elizabeth (X) Hudson, widow; naturalized 12 May 1705 as Daniel **Ford**; Mar 1715, rec. a patent of 296 acres in the lands surveyed for the FR refugees in Henrico Co, VA; 28 Aug 1718, he was a vestryman in King William Parish; he d. a. 1735 CHILDREN, m/1:

  Jean/John[3], b. c. 1694; m. c. 1738, Mary (Scott) Martain, d/o Walter & Ursula (Goode) Scott, widow of John Martain; she d. p. 18 Jun 1771, wd, Chesterfield Co, VA; he d. a. Jul 1748, wp, Henrico Co, VA; 1 son **John**[4], 2 daus **Elizabeth**[4] (m. John Cox), **Mary**[4] (m. William Scruggs)

  Daniel[3], b. c. 1695

Pierre[2], b. c. 1674/5, FR; m/1, FR, Elizabeth Agé; arr VA 4 Mar 1701, on the *Nasseau* w/ wife, 1 son; said to have come from St. Sévère, Berry (not found – prob. Sancerre, Cher Dépt, Centre – loc. where Berry used to be); naturalized 12 May 1705, as Pierre **Ford**; rec. 150 acres of land in Henrico Co, 1 Jun 1709; m/2, VA c. 1719, Judith Goodwin, d/o Isaac & Ann (Pleasant) Goodwin; she d. a. 29 Apr 1744, when Pierre/ Peter's will was written as she is not mentioned; he d. a. 16 Apr 1745, wp, Goochland Co, VA CHILDREN, m/1:

  Jean/John[3], b. c. 1697; d. a. 24 Sep 1753, wp, Cumberland Co, VA, no wife/ch named in his will

  Daniel[3], b. c. 1701; d. p. 1755; no known wife or heirs

  Peter[3], b. 1706; m/1, XX – **1 ch**; m/2, 1742, Cumberland Co, VA, Marie Gauwin – **13 ch**; he d. 1 Jan 1780, Bourbon Co, KY; surname Fore/Foree

  Jacques/James[3], b. 1708, VA, m. c. 1728/9, Anne Bondurant, d/o Jean Pierre & Ann (X) Bondurant; d. c. 1810, VA; **9 ch**, all bap. King William Parish

CHILDREN, m/2:

  Judith[3], b 3 Sep 1723; not yet 21 in father's will of 1744; m. bet 1744-53, John Leake; family went to Rockingham Co, NC, founded a town called Leaksville which merged with 2 other towns and is now Eden, NC

  Mary[3], b. p. 1723, as not yet 21 in father's will of 1744; m. bet 1744-53, William Fuqua, s/o William & Elizabeth (X) Fuqua

  Joseph[3], b. 31 May, bp 16 Jul 1729, King William Parish; d. a. 1744, not in father's will

Jean/John[2], m. Anne Ren(n)o/Regnault, d/o Stephen Ren(n)o; he d. p. 21 Aug 1733, prob. c. 1748, Henrico Co; **issue**

Elizabeth[2], b. FR; m. Feb/Nov 1701, Pierre Morriset; she d. p. 17 Dec 1745, wd, Henrico Co, VA

poss. another dau

REF: SOUTHWORTH, Mary Ford, *Fauré Foard-Ford,* Part I (n.d., n.p.); BROCK, Robert A., *Huguenot Emigration to VA* (Baltimore, 1973); GARRETT, Hester Elizabeth, *A Book of Garretts, 1600-1960* (Lansing, MI, 1963); *The Huguenot,* #7 (1933-35); JONES, W. Mac, *The Douglas Register* (Baltimore, 1977); RICHARDSON, Flora E. Fopre, *The Huguenot Family of Foure & Allied Families* (1943); various wills.

FAYSSOUX/FOISSEAU, Daniel

    b. FR

    c. 1737 - prob. arr America as one needed to have been a resident for a minimum of 7 yrs to be
        naturalized - a law passed in 1740

    m. Frances X; she m/2, 6 Dec 1746, James Hunter of Charlestown, SC; she d. 9 Dec 1768

    18 Oct 1744 - Charleston, SC, naturalized as a British citizen; his naturalization cert. states that he was
        a faithful Calvinist; he was a member of the Charleston FR Ch, as the minister of his ch confirmed, as
        well as the fact that Daniel had recently taken communion; he was a baker by trade

    d. a. Mar 1745, evaluation of his estate

    CHILDREN:

    Mary Ann[2], b. 1743; m/1, John Dodd, a gunsmith of Charleston, who d. 7 Aug 1770 – 1 ch **Rhody**[3],
        m/2, 10 Apr 1774, John Hall (d. 1780), m/3, 11 Jan 1787, Capt. Jacob Schrieber; she d. 24
        Jul 1806

    Peter[2], b. 1745; m/1, 6 Feb 1772, Sarah Wilson, d/o Algernon Wilson, she d. Aug 1776 – **1 dau**,
        m/2, 20 May 1777, Ann (Smith) Johnston, d/o William Smith, wid/o William Johnston – **7 ch**, she
        d. 11 Mar 1810; he d. 1 Feb 1795; 1766-69 - he studied in Edinburgh, SCOT, to become a doctor –
        wrote a thesis in classical Latin, entitled *De Tetano* (*Concerning Lockjaw*); he was a good friend of
        Dr. Benjamin Rush of Philadelphia; Rev. War service

REF: HUGUENOT SOCIETY OF MD, *The Huguenots* (1993); DAVIDSON, Chalmers B., *The Life of Dr. Peter Fayssux of Charleston, SC* (1950); *Publications of the Huguenot Society of London,* Vol. XXIV (Manchester, ENG, 1921).

FERET/FERRÉ/FERRY, Christophle/Christophe

    b. c. 1530/40

    m. XX

    liv Tourcoing, Nord, FR, n.e. of Lille, nr. the border of what is now BEL

    CHILDREN:

    Pierre[2], b. c. 1560, Tourcoing, Nord, FR; m. Tourcoing Marguerite Poilet/Pellet, d/o Arnold; c. 1581 –
        emigrated to Canterbury, ENG; he d. 24 Oct 1601, prob. Canterbury

        CHILDREN:

        Marie[3], bp. 17 Dec 1581, Canterbury

        Pierre[3], b. c. 1585, Canterbury; m/1, 18 Nov 1610, Canterbury, Marie Daucet (b. 1589, Monnaie (?),
        Indre-et-Loire, FR, d. a. 1628 Canterbury), d/o Pierre Dausey; m/2, 16 Sep 1628, Jeanne (Snellart)
        Bara, widow of Giles Bara; he d. p. 1646

            CHILDREN, m/1: (all bp. Canterbury)

            Marie[4], bp. 17 Dec 1581

            Jean/John[4], bp. 19 Dec 1613, St. Alphage (Walloon) Ch, Canterbury; m. 21 Sep 1634,
                Threadneedle St. Church, London, Catherine Lodisoir/Laudesoir (b. 1617, Rumegies,
                Nord, FR); he d. c. 1659/60, London; **7 ch** incl Charles (below)

                CHILD: **Charles**[5], bp. 23 Apr 1636, Canterbury; m. 29 Mar 1661, Springfield, MA,
            Sarah Harmon (b. 24 Jun 1644/5, Springfield, d. 31 Oct 1740, Springfield), d/o John and
            Elizabeth (X) Harmon; he d. 3 Jul 1699, Springfield, MA – the emigrant to America; **10 ch**

            Sara[4], bp. 17 Nov 1616; d. a. 1623

            Marguerite[4], bp. 17 Jun 1618; m. 28 Jan 1637/8, Simon Daigneau, widower, native of

LeBourg, Hainaut, (now) BEL, c. 2.6 km. w. of Tournai; she d. 31 Jan 1652/3

Pierre[4], bp. Sep 1619 ; d. a. 1628

Jacques[4], bp. 10 Nov 1622 ; d. 6 May 1647

Marie[4], bp. 7 Jun 1625; m. 29 Sep 1644, Salmon Descamps; d. 5 May 1645

CHILDREN, m/2:

Jeanne[4], bp. 26 Feb 1632; m. 26 Sep 1654, Jean DeLespau, s/o Salomon, native of Canterbury

Samuel[4], bp. 1 Jan 1635/6

Marguerite[4], bp. 3 Sep 1637

Pierre[4], bp. 25 Jul 1639; m. 25 Oct 1663/66, Susanne DeHausey. d/o Hery De Hausey

Vincent[3], b. c. 1589, Canterbury; m. 26 Dec 1614, Martine Hache, d/o Pontue Hache of Hainaut; he d. 1649

Christophe[3], b. c. 1592, Canterbury; m. 29 Jun or 19 Jul 1618, Sarah Acar/Acart, d/o Philippe of Canterbury; he d. 12 Sep 1623

Elizabeth[3], b. c. 1594, Canterbury; m. 1 Jun 1617, Jean de Monceau

Jean[2], d. p.. 29 Aug 1620, wd, Canterbury

Nicolas[2], emigrated to ENG

Antoine[2], emigrated to ENG

REF: FERRY, Edward M., *The Charles Ferry Family in America* (Northampton, MA, 1978); BURT, Henry M., *The 1st Century of the History of Springfield,* Vol. II (Springfield, MA, 1899); STOTT, Clifford L., *Vital Records, Springfield, MA to 1850* (CD-NEHGS).

FERNEL/FERNALD, François Junius (Rev.)

b. 3 Mar 1533, Bourges, FR, s/o Jean & Magdalene (Luillier) Fernel; Magdalene, d/o Jean Luillier (26 Apr 1497, Clermont, FR?-1558), who was a famous author of medical works and a physician at the   court of King Henri II of FR; it has been said that Jean was the s/o King Charles VIII – that is not true – Charles d. 7 Apr 1498 with no living descendants

studied at Geneva; was minister of the Walloon Ch in Antwerp; was chaplain to the Prince of Orange; translated the Bible and wrote 64 books

m/1, XX (Marie de Riant?)

m/2, 2 Apr 1555, Maria Commeni (10 Oct 1532-29 Mar 1571), d/o John Amos & Marie (X) Commennus

m/3, Rebecca Tremellius,d/o Emanuel & Rachel (X) Tremellius

m/4, Elizabeth Fenelon, d/o Marquis Bertrand Fenelon

d. 10 Sep 1602, at sea, supposedly off coast of Sulawesi, Indonesia (aka Celebes Is., Greater Sunda Islands)

CHILDREN, m/2:

Jean[2], b. 15 Mar 1556, Heidelberg; m/1, 4 Jan 1571, Josephine Vigne, d/o Marguerine de Vigne, m/2, c.   1573, XX (1 Apr 1550?-23 May 1623?), his 2nd wife was **not** Annietta d/o Gaspard de Coligny (see Coligny entry), her name *may* have been Annietta, her surname *may* have been de Coligny but she was not the dau/o Admiral Gaspard nor of any of his sons; son William was by a 2nd marr. but the name of mother is not proven; Jean he was killed by the Jesuits, 25 Aug 1575

CHILD, m/2:

William[3], b. 12 Jun, Castle of Heidelberg, bp. 16 Jun 1575, Church of the Holy Ghost, Baden; used surname FERNALD; m. 16 May 1594, his cousin Elizabeth[4] A(r)mand (3 Apr 1571-1 Oct 1648), d/o Commander Girard & Elizabeth (Washington) A(r)mand - fought against the Spanish Armada & was knighted by 8 Oct 1597; Wm. d. 8 Apr 1669, Bristol, ENG; surname **FERNALD**

CHILDREN:

Renald/Reginald[4], b. 6 Jul 1595, Bristol, ENG; m. 1 Jan 1619, Joanna Warburton   (1 (Feb 1603-10 May 1660), d/o Sir John & Mary (X) Warburton; went to NH & ME; to Portsmouth, c. 1631 as the surgeon on a naval ship; he d. bet. 17 May-7 Oct 1656,

Doctor's/Pierce Island, NH (in the Piscataqua River, just s. of Portsmouth Naval Shipyard); a physician and surgeon

CHILDREN:

Thomas[5], m. Temperance X – **10 ch**

Elizabeth[5], **no issue**

Mary[5], m. John Partridge – **8 ch**

Sarah[5], m/1 Allen Lyde – **2 ch**, m/2 Richard Waterhouse – **6 ch**

John[5], m. Mary Spinney – **6 ch**

Samuel[5], m. Hannah Spinney – **5 ch**

William[5], m. Elizabeth Langdon – **13 ch**

Thomas[4], b. 13 Aug 1597

Henry[4], b. 5 Dec 1599

William[4], b. 30 Dec 1600, Eastwich; prob. to Cambridge and ,by Aug 1668, to Charlestown, MA; d. 19 Mar 1673

Robert[4], b. 20 Mar 1604; m. Anna Cotton, d/o Robert Bruce Cotton, went to VA, 1630, on the *King Philip*; their ch **John**[5] and **Temperance**[5] went w/ them

John[4], b. 9 Apr 1607

Edward[4], b. 4 Oct 1611; m. Mary X

Strong/Strongue[4], b. 16 Nov 1614; m. Aellone X; 1643, admitted to ch of Boston; son **Joseph**[5], b. 5 Aug 1648; d. 10 Sep 1730, Paris, FR

Joseph[4]

Maria[2], b. 10 Jun 1559; m. Capt. John Smith; she d. 1596

Ann[2], b. 20 Nov 1560; m. Samuel Washington; she d. 1621; their grdau **Elizabeth**[4] m. William Fernald, above

Francis[2], b. 1563; d. 1603

CHILDREN, m/3 **or** m/4:

Magdalen[2]

Margaret[2]

Nicholas[2], surname **FERNALIUS**

Joannen[2], surname **FILLELEN**

Otto[2], surname **FENNE**

Tobias[2], surname **FENNEL**

Henriette Catherine[2], surname **FERNELL**

Alexander[2], surname **FURNAS**

Daniel[2], surname **FURNIEU**

Peter[2], surname became **FANUEIL**

Francis[2], surname **FANIS**

Bertrand[2], surname **FERNELION**

Thomas[2], surname **FURNIVAL**

Joanna[2], surname **FURNIVAL**

Josse/Justus[2], surname **VONDEL/FONDEL**

NOTE: There was a Fernald Island, aka Dennett's Island, opposite Portsmouth & part of Kittery, ME; it later became part of Seavey Island when the government needed more land for the Portsmouth Naval Shipyard

REF: FERNALD, Charles Augustus, *Genealogy of the Ancient Fernald Families* (1909); CRANE, Ellery Bicknell, editor, *Genealogical& Personal Memoirs of Worcester Co, MA*, Vol. IV (1907); NOYES, Sibyl, LIBBY, Charles T., & DAVIS, Walter G., *The Genealogical Dictionary of Maine & New Hampshire* (Baltimore, 1972); *Merit Students Encyclopedia*; *Encyclopedia Americana*, Vol. 7; STACKPOLE, Marie A., *Old Kittery & Her Families* (1981); CUTTER, William Richard, *Encyclopedia of Biography; Merit Students Encyclopedia*; FERNALD, Charles Augustus, *Genealogy of the Ancient Fernald Families* (1909); *Encyclopedia Americana,* Vol. 7; STACKPOLE, Marie A., *Old Kittery & Her Families* (1981); CUTTER, William Richard, *Encyclopedia of Biography.*

FERNEY/FERNAY/FORNEY/FARNEY (Pierre, Chevalier de?)

It is unproven tradition that this family descended from Pierre who was of the nobility, a
comte (count), the owner of the Château de Ferney; according to *Huguenot Memoirs* of the FR Prot. Ch,
Charleston – fam. was orig called de Ferney but aft being in Alsace where there was a German influence, it
became Forney. Thus, the father of Jacob is **not** proven – he does name his 2nd son Peter, which *may have*
significance

b. FR; name Ferney from an estate in the l'Ain Dépt of Rhône-Alpes, 5 mi. n.w. of Geneva; now called
   Ferney-Voltaire, as the French author Voltaire bought the property, c.1758; it is right on the
   border between FR and SWI; there is a town called Fernex c. 3 mi. s.w. of Geneva in Geneva
   Canton

c. 1685- went to Alsace, FR, on the Rhine River – some of the family went to SWI and to the Palatinate,
   mainly s.w. of Mannheim; have **no** lists w/ the names of his ch; Jacob is said to have had a Hug.
   father who went from to Alsace and d. c. 1725, doesn't necessarily make that father Pierre

d. c. 1725, perhaps GER

CHILD:

Jacob[2], b. 1721, Alsace, FR; went to Amsterdam, c. 1735; arr 3 Sep 1739, Philadelphia, on the *Friendship*
   from HOL; went back to GER; arr 23 Sep 1752, America on the *Saint Andrew*; m. c. 1752,
   Philadelphia, Maria Bergner/Bergman (d. 1810, Lincoln Co, NC) who was Swiss; 1754, moved to
   Anson Co (then Tyron, then Lincoln Co), NC; he d. a. spring, 1806, wp ,Lincoln Co, NC; he & Maria
   are bur. nr. the Old Dutch Meeting House in Catawba Springs Twp.
   CHILDREN, (used surname **FORNEY**):
   Jacob[3], b. 6 Nov 1754; m. Mary Corpening; he d. 7 Nov 1840; **11 ch**
   Peter[3], b. 21 Apr 1756, Lincoln Co; m. 27 Feb 1783, Nancy Abernathy; d. 1 Feb 1834, NC; Peter
        was a General in the Rev War and was a member of Congress
   Abram[3], m. Rachel Gabriel
   Catherine[3], m/1, Abram Earhardt, m/2, Robert Rosamond
   Elizabeth[3], b. c. 1761; m. John Young
   Christina[3], b. 1762; m. 27 May 1780/2, David Abernathy (1759-1838), bro of Nancy above; d.
        1842 Giles Co, TN; **9 ch**
   Eve[3], m. Robertson/Robison Goodwin
   Susannah/Susan[3], m. 1784, John Abernathy (b. 1761); **12 ch**

REF: HOWARD, Nell H. & QUINN, Bessie W., *Moragnes in America & Related Families*; GRIFFIN, Clarence W.,
History of Old Tyron & Rutherford Co, NC, 1730-1936 (1937); CRAWFORD, William W., *Forney Forever*; Jacob
II's will, dated 28 Jul 1804, probated Lincoln Co, NC; *The Huguenot*, #14 (1947-49); WHEELER, John Hill, *Historical
Sketches of NC, 1584-1851* (1974); CRAWFORD, Lee Forney, *William Webb Crawford ...& Family Sketches,
Genealogies* Vol. XXV (1954); LeFEVRE, George Newton, compiler, *The PA LeFevres* (Strasburg, PA, 1952).

FERRÉE/ Fier(r)e, Daniel (Fuehre/ Führe in GER)

b. c. 1650; family said to be of Torchamp, Orne Dépt, Basse-Normandie, s.w. of Domfront

m. 1669/75, FR, Marie de la Warenbuer/Warembur (1653, Rhine [prob. means Alsace], FR-Jan 1716, bur.
   Ferrée/Carpenter graveyard, s. of Paradise in Lancaster Co, PA)

c. 1685 - fled FR to Strasbourg, p. the Revocation, then to Bavaria; a wealthy silk manufacturer/merchant

10 Mar 1708 - pd. for permission to emigrate to PA, via HOL; papers signed Billigheim (now Billigheim-
   Ingenheim, s.e. of Landau); certificate said for Daniel Firre (*sic*) and his fam., so Daniel was
   still alive on this date; was in HOL only a short time, if at all

d. early 1708, Landau, Bavaria, 18 mi. n.w. of Karlsruhe, or Steinweiler (sm. town s. of Landau), in the
   Pfalz

by summer, 1708 - family was in ENG where they stayed c. 6 mo; "family history" says that Marie met personally with William Penn who then introduced her to Queen Anne; however, it is not clear if the entire family was in ENG at the same time; Daniel & his family, Isaac LeFèvre & his family were granted letters of denization on 25 Aug 1708, thus giving them the right to own land in America

c. Oct 1708 - widow + 6 ch (Daniel, his wife, son; Catherine, her husband, son; John 24, Philip 23, Jane 22, & Mary) sailed to NY on the *Globe*, arr 1 Jan 1709; 1st went up the Hudson River to New Paltz or Esopus (now Kingston)

10 Aug 1709 - the letters of denization were entered in the Office of the Secretary of the Prov. of NY

c. 1712 - granted 2000 acres by patent by Martin Kendig in Strasburg, Lancaster Co, PA; Marie then had the patent granted in Philadelphia, 12 Sep 1712, to sons Daniel & Isaac – cost was £150; they were the only white people there; Marie founded the Huguenot Colony, Pequea Valley, PA

CHILDREN:

Daniel II^2, b. 1676/7; m. c. 1700, Steinweiler, Anna Maria Leininger (b. 1678); he obtained a certificate from the Reformed Walloon Ch of Pelican, Steinweiler, for him and his family attesting to the fact that the family was of the "pure Reformed religion" and were faithful members of the church; d. a. 9 Aug 1762, adm

CHILDREN:

Andrew^3, bp 28 Sep 1701, Steinweiler; m. Mary Reed; he d. 20 Dec 1735, Lancaster Co., PA; **4 sons, 1 dau**; dau **Lydia**^{4} (1731-1778) m. c. 1751, cousin Samuel^3 LeFèvre (28 Jun 1719, PA-4 May 1789, PA), s/o Isaac & Catherine (Ferrée)^2 LeFèvre

John^3, b. 2 Feb, bp. 8 Feb 1702/3, Rohrbach (sm. town bet Landau & Steinweiler); m. c. 1725, Lancaster Co., PA, Barbara Stautenberger; d. 1735; **4 sons, 1dau**

Daniel III^3, b. 1706; m. 1 May 1739, Lancaster Co., PA, Mary Carpenter, d/o Henry & Salome (Rufenu) Carpenter; became a Quaker; he d. a. 4 Sep 1750, wp, Lancaster Co., PA; **3 sons, 5 daus**

Elizabeth^3, b. 1710; m/1, c. 1728, 1st cousin Abraham LeFèvre (9 Apr 1706-20 Nov 1735, Lancaster Co.), s/o Isaac & Catherine (Ferrée)^2 LeFèvre – at least **2 sons**; m/2, c. 1736, Christian Kemp, s/o John & Anna (Fouerfauch) Kaempf – **2 sons, 3 daus**

Joseph^3, b. 1712, Lancaster Co., PA; m. c. 1729, Sarah Delaplaine, d/o James & Elizabeth (Shoemaker) Delaplaine; d. p. 1789; **1 son**

Isaac^3, b. c. 1715; m/1, Elisabeth^3 Ferrée, his 1st cousin, d/o Philip^2 & Leah (DuBois) Ferrée – **4 sons, 2 daus**; m/2, Susan Green – **2 sons, 5 daus**; Susan m/2, Joel Ferrée^3 (below); Isaac d. a. 2 Feb 1782, Lancaster Co., PA

Catherine^2, b. 26 Mar 1679; m. c. 1704, Bavaria, Isaac LeFèvre (26 Mar 1669, FR-1 Oct 1751, PA)s/o Abraham & XX(Antoinette Jerian?) LeFèvre; son **Abraham**^{3}, m. cousin Elizabeth Ferrée^3, d/o Daniel II^2 & Anna Marie (Leininger) Ferrée, son **Samuel**^{3}, m. cousin Lydia^4 Ferrée, d/o Andrew^3 & Mary (Reed) Ferrée **4 sons, 2 daus**

Jane^2, b. c. 1682?; m. Richard Davis; she d. a. 26 Oct 1754, wp, Belmont, PA; **no known issue**

Marie/Mary^2, b. c. 1683; m. 30 Jun 1715, Wilmington, DE, Thomas Faulkner (d. 28 May 1752, Bucks Co, PA); she d. a. 1745; **1 son, 4 daus**

Philip^2, b. 1686/7, Steinweiler; m. 2 Jun 1713, 1st Dutch Ch, Kingston, NY, Leah DuBois (16 Aug 1687, bp. 10 Oct 1687-12 Sep 1758, PA), d/o Abraham & Margaret (Deyo) DuBois (s/o Louis & Catherine (Blanchan) DuBois); he d. 19 May 1753, Lancaster Co., PA

CHILDREN:

Abraham^3, b. Aug, 1715; m. 1738, Elizabeth Elting/Eltinge (b. 30 Aug 1717, Esopus); d. 7 Mar 1775, PA; **2 sons, 4 daus**

Magdalena^3, b. c. 1713; m. 24 Nov 1749, Lancaster, PA, William Buffington; she d. c. 1778, VA; **5 sons, 2 daus**

Elisabeth^3, b. 1718; m/1, 1738, her 1st cousin, Isaac Ferrée^3; s/o Daniel^2 & Anna Maria (Leininger) Ferrée; she d. 27 May 1752, Lancaster Co., PA; **4 sons**, incl. **Jacob**^{4} who m. Rachel Ferrée^4, d/o Joel^3 & Mary (Copeland) Ferrée & **2 daus**; m/2, X Ellemaker

Isaac^3, b. 1725; m. Elizabeth Forbush; he d. 1759 Rowan Co, NC, poss. scalped by Indians; **1 son, 3 daus**; surname **FREE**

Jacob^3, b. 1728; m. Barbara? Susannah? Carpenter (1738-1775), d/o Emmanuel & Catherine

        (Lein) Carpenter; Jacob d. 5 May 1782, Gettysburg, PA; **4 sons, 4 daus**

    Philip[3], b. 24 Mar 1729/30, bp 1 Apr 1711; m. Ann Copeland (18 Mar 1735-1807); he d. 24 Apr
        1796, Lancaster, PA; **6 sons, 4 daus**

    Joel[3], b. 19 May 1730, Lancaster Co, PA; m/1, Mary Copeland; m/2, 5 Nov 1759, Jane Johnston;
        m/3, Susan (Green) Ferrée, widow of Isaac[3] Ferrée (above); m/4, Sallie (X) Davis, widow;
        he d. 19 Jun 1801, Pittsburgh, PA; **issue** from only m/1- his dau **Rachel**[4] (1753-1782) m.
        Jacob Ferrée[4], s/o Isaac[3] & Elisabeth[3] (Ferrée) Ferrée

    Leah[3], m. Peter Baker (b. 1710, GER); **5ch**

John[2], b. c. 1694; m/1, a. 1720, Mary Musgrave, d/o John & Mary (Hastings) Musgrave – **4 sons, 5 daus**;
    m/2, 4mo 10d 1736, Darby, Chester Co., PA, Ruth Buffington, d/o Thomas & Ruth (Cope)
    Buffington – **1 son, 2 daus**; became a Quaker; he d. a. 8 Apr 1773, Lancaster, PA

NOTE: This was a challenge! Different lists, different #s of ch, countless intermarriages w/ cousins.
Above seems to be the best conclusion – dates are uncertain, except where a complete date is given.

REF: DELONG, Irwin Hoch, "Inscriptions on the Tombstones in Carpenter's Graveyard, Lancaster Co, PA" in the
in the *National Genealogical Society Quarterly*, Vol 14, #3 (Sep 1925); *Proceedings of the Huguenot Society of PA*,
William, *The American Descendants of Chrétien DuBois of Wicres , FR*, Part 2 (New Paltz, NY, 1969); ROWLEY, Homer
King & Ruth McCammons, *Rowley-King & Allied Families* (Sun City, AZ, 1980) – contains transcript of Philip's will;
Will abstract from Lancaster Co, PA; "Madame Mary Ferrée & the Huguenots of Lancaster Co." – paper read before the
Lancaster Co Historical Society (1917).

FLEURY, Abraham, Sieur de la Plaine

    b. Tours, FR, s/o Charles & Madeleine (Soupzmain/Soubmain) Fleury; bro **Isaac** b. Tours
    Abraham went to ENG
    m. prob. FR, XX
    17 Dec 1679 - sailed on the *Richmond*, 1st to the Barbardoes
    30 Apr 1680 - arr SC; Isaac arr a. 2 Feb 1685; on the *Liste* as 'Abraham Fleury, De la Plaine, né à
        Tours, fils de Charles Fleury, et de Madeleine Soupzmain . Marianne Flery, sa fille, veuve
        du défunct Jacques Dugué, et du dit Marianne Fleury, née en Caroline
    w/ the Petit-Guérard Colony
    m. Marianne X
    9 Sep 1696 – 2 grants, 1for 500 acres in Berkeley Co., SC, another for 160 acres; he sold the latter grant
    15 Sep 1705 – granted 330 acres on Goose Creek, St. James Parish which were next to his 500 acre grant
    2 Aug 1721 – wd; willed his land to his bro Isaac; if he was dec., then to his granddau Marianne
        Fitch, wife of Tobias Fitch
    d. p. 1721, SC
    CHILD:
    (Damaris) Marianne[2], b. Paris; m/1, Jacques d'Augé/Dugué II (d. by 17 Jan 1695/6), m/2, Pierre Bacot –
        no issue
        CHILD, m/1:
        Marianne[3], b. SC, m. Tobias Fitch – **Stephen**[3], **Mary**[3]

REF: List of French & Swiss refugees at Caroline, p. 64; Records from the FR Hug Ch of the Parish of St.
James, Goose Creek in the *Transactions of the Huguenot Society of SC*, Vol. 16 (1909).

FLOURNEY/FLOURNOY, Laurent

    b. c. 1523, prob. Magneux près Vassy, Champagne, FR; just n.w .of Magneux, is a town called Flornoy in
        the Haute-Marne Dépt.; names of parents unknown – had 3 sibs: **Claude**, **Nicolas**, unnamed **sister**
        – all mar. and had issue

p. 1562 – left Champagne after the massacre at Vassy (Wassy); went to Lyon, FR

m. a. 1567, prob. Lyon, Gabrielle Mellin (c. 1532, prob. Lyon, FR-1 Feb 1601, Geneva, SWI), d/o Antoine Mellin; Laurent was Gabrielle's 3rd husband.

by 1572- to Geneva; he was a merchant jeweler, a lapidary (according to death rec.); he is listed among the goldsmiths and jewelers of 16th century Geneva; liv. on La Rue de Orfèvres – Goldsmith/ Silversmith St.

d. 8 Dec 1593, Geneva

CHILDREN:

Gédéon[2], b. 29 Jul 1567, Lyon; m/1, 5 Aug 1595, Geneva, Marie de Cross, d/o André & Jeanne (Ferra) de Cross - she d. 4 Aug 1619, m/2, 2 Jan 1620, Geneva, Marie Gando, d/o Sibois & Barthelémie (Morel) Gando; he d. 26 Feb 1650, Geneva; father of a total of **16 ch**

Jean[2], b. 21 May, bp. 26 May 1574, St. Pierre, Geneva; m/1, 15 Feb 1597, Geneva, Françoise Mussard (3 Jun 1579, Geneva-3 Nov 1618, Geneva), d/o Simon & Anne (Le Grand) Mussard, m/2, 21 Sep 1619, Geneva, Susanna (Guincestre) Puerari (widow) (15 Jun 1586, Geneva-8 May 1658, Geneva), d/o Jean & Marie (de St. Amour) Guincestre; he, like his father was a merchant lapidary & liv. on La Rue de Orfèvres for a while; he d. 3 Jun 1657, La Cité area of Geneva

CHILDREN, m/1:

Jean[3], b. 19 Mar, bp. 26 Mar 1598, Ch. of the Madeleine, Geneva; he d. 16 Aug 1599, of smallpox

Jean[3], b. 30 Oct, bp. 4 Nov 1599, Ch. of the Madeleine, Geneva; m. c. 1624, Judith Payari, d/o Étienne & Hortense (Puerari) Payari; he d. a. 16 Apr 1673 when Judith d. in Geneva

Esther[3], b. 22 Dec, bp. 28 1600, Ch. of the Madeleine, Geneva; she d. 17 Oct 1601, Geneva

Marie[3], b. 13 Aug, bp. 26 Aug 1602, Ch. of the Madeleine, Geneva; m.. 13 Mar 1625, Ch. of St. Pierre, Geneva, Jean Henri Esther, a clockmaker, b. Schweinsberg, Duchy of Hesse (s.e. of Marburg); s/o Jean & Elizabeth (Ehbrurzen) Esther; she d. 31 Dec 1668, Geneva

Jeanne[3], b. 23 Feb, bp. 4 Mar 1604, Ch. of the Madeleine, Geneva; m. 13 Mar 1625, Ch. of St. Pierre, Geneva, Étienne Gando, a goldsmith; she d. 14 Apr 1681, Geneva

Mie[3], b. 11 Feb, bp. 16 Feb 1606, Ch. of St. Gervais, Geneva; m. c. 1628, Laurent Légare, a gold-smith, of Chaumont in *Bassigny* (there are 5 towns called Chaumont and 11 more with Chaumont in their names – impossible to decide which one); she d. 13 Jul 1629, Geneva

Jacques[3], b. 19 Jul, bp. 28 Jul 1608, Ch. of St. Gervais, Geneva; m/1, 1 4 Feb 1638, Ch. of St. Pierre, Geneva, Élisabeth Boussens (c. 1620- d. 24 June 1644, Plainpalais, 24 Y), d/o Amblard & Élisabeth (Le Noir) Boussens, m/2, 9 Feb 1645, Ch. of the Madeleine, Geneva, Giuditta/Judith Puerari (bp. 8 Apr 1624, Geneva), d/o Daniel & Jeanne (Marcet) Puerari - (her mother-in-law's niece); he d. 19 Mar 1675, Geneva; he was a linendraper, merchant jeweler, goldsmith

CHILDREN, m/1:

Michel[4], 8 Dec, bp. 9 Dec 1638, Ch. of St. Pierre, Geneva; he d. 29 Jan 1639, Geneva

Jean[4], b. 21 Dec 1640, Geneva; bp. Ch. of the Madeleine; he d. 25 Mar 1642, Geneva

Élisabeth[4], 7 Mar, bp. 12 Mar 1642/3, Ch. of St. Pierre, Geneva; m. 6 Feb 1659, Geneva, Antoine Marcet, a merchant, s/o Jean Marcet; she d. 13 Jul 1714, Geneva

CHILDREN, m/2:

Jeanne[4], b. 27 Nov, bp. 30 Nov 1645, Ch. of St. Pierre, Geneva; m. 18 Sep 1670, Ch. of St. Gervais, Geneva, Pierre Archimbaud, a goldsmith, s/o Jean Archimbaud; she d. 14 Nov 1688, Geneva; Pierre m/2, 15 Jun 1690, Susanne DeLuc, d/o Antoine DeLuc

Sara[4], b. 3 Jun, bp. 8 Jun 1647, Ch. of the Madeleine, Geneva; she d. 14 Jan 1648

Délie[4], b. 31 Oct, bp. 9 Nov 1648, Ch. of St. Pierre, Geneva; perhaps m. X Goy – dau **Jacqueline**[5], who d. late 1701

Jeanne-Marie[4], 3 May, bp. 11 May 1651, Ch. of St. Pierre, Geneva; d. 29 Aug 1724, Geneva; perhaps m. Jacques Cartier

Élisabeth[4], b. 26 Aug or Sep 1653, Geneva; bp. Ch. of the Madeleine; poss. m. Michel Barrilliet

Anne-Gabrielle[4], b. 3 Dec, bp. 7 Dec 1665, Ch. of the Madeleine, Geneva; m. Jean
Thomegeux/Thomegay, a clockmaker; she d. 17 Dec 1687, Geneva

Jacques[4], b. 15 Sep, bp. 20 Sep 1657, Ch. of St. Pierre, Geneva; m. 21 Apr 1683, Ch. of
St. Gervais, Geneva, Julie Eyraud (16 Aug 1664-16 Aug 1756), d/o Gaspard &
Rachel (Legris) Eyraud; he d. 22 Feb 1725, Geneva , he was a lapidary, jeweler,
goldsmith – worked in Paris for a time

CHILDREN:

Rachel[5], b. 7 Apr, bp. 1o Apr 1685, Ch. of St. Gervais, Geneva

Jean Jacques/John James[5], b. 17 Nov , bp. 10 Dec 1686, Ch of the Madeleine,
Geneva; 1 Oct 1713, received by the Church in Amsterdam; stayed there for a
few years w/ his cousin Daniel Flournoy then went to VA, c. 1717; m. 23 Jun
1720, Goochland Co, VA, Elizabeth (Williams) Jones (b. 25 Dec 1695,
Williamsburg, VA); he d. Henrico Co, VA, 23 Mar 1740; **issue**

Marie[5], b. 1 May, bp. 6 May 1689, Ch. of St. Gervais, Geneva; d. 16 Aug 1689

Julie[5], b. 9 Jul, bp. 14 Jul 1690, Ch. of St. Gervais, Geneva; she d. 14 Feb 1691

Gédéon[5], b. 2 Dec 1691, Geneva; m. Jeanne Françoise Comparet (b. 4 Feb 1690),
d/o Jean-Antoine & Sarah (Mallet) Comparet

Julie[5], b. 7 Oct, bp. & Oct 1692, Ch. of St. Gervais, Geneva; d. 14 Oct 1692
unnamed **son**[5], b. & d. 5 Aug 1693

David[5], b. 8 Nov, bp. 12 Nov 1698, Ch. of St. Gervais, Geneva; d. 2 Jul 1745,
unmarr.

Julie[5], b. 29 Nov, bp. 30 Nov 1699, Ch. of St. Gervais, Geneva; d. 30 Nov 1699

Jacques[5], b. 2 Feb, bp. 2 Feb 1703, Ch. of St. Gervais, Geneva; d. soon after

Esaïe[4], b. 13 Jan 1659/60, Geneva; m. Amsterdam, HOL, Christine Eggens; he d. 23 Jul
1714, Ceylon

Jacob[4], b. 5 Jan 1662/3, Geneva; m/1, 24 Feb 1684/5, Geneva, Marthe Morel (3 Jun 1663,
Geneva- d. Berlin, GER), d/o Louis & Marguerite (Forel) Morel; m/2, XX; m/3, 9
Dec 1703, VA, Madeline/Magdaleine (Prodham/Prudhomme) widow Moïse
Verreuil (24 Jan 1658, Den Haag (The Hague), HOL-d. VA); to VA on the *Peter
and Anthony* 1700, settled Manakintown; he d. 22 Feb 1724/5, Henrico Co, VA

CHILDREN, m/1:

Magdalene[5], b. c. 1685; m/1, 1699, HOL, Sir Anthony Trabue - d. 28 Jan 1724,
VA; m/2 Pierre Chastain; she d. 1731

Francis[5], b. 31 Jan 1686/7; m/1, Mary Baugh, b. c. 1687; m/2, c. 1733, VA, Mary
Gibson; he d. a. 5 Mar 1773, wp, Chesterfield Co, VA

Jacques[5], b. 14 Dec 1688, GER; he d. 1740, VA, unmarr.

Marie[5], b. 3 Jun 1690, Geneva; she d. young

Jeanne-Marie[5], b. 18 Jan 1693; she d. 1700, London

Jeanne-Françoise[5], b. 28 Mar 1695, Berlin; m. Robert Ashurst; she d 1717, VA

Henry[4], b. 19 Aug 1666, Geneva

Marguerite[3], b. 8 Sep, bp. 17 Sep 1611, Ch. of St. Gervais, Geneva; m. 11 Dec 1631, Italian Ch.,
Geneva, Frédéric Canadelle/Fedirigo Canadelo, s/o Moïse Canadel; he was a surgeon &
d. 20 May 1695, Geneva - **no ch**

André[3], b. 17 Nov, bp. 28 Nov 1613, Ch. of St. Gervais, Geneva; he d. 9 Jan 1614, Geneva,
smothered by his wet nurse!

Françoise[3], b. 23 Nov, bp. 23 Nov 1614, Geneva; she d. 20 Feb 1617

Judith[3], b. 3 Jan 1617, Geneva; m. Simon Honnie of Hanau

Gabriel[3], b. 10 Oct, bp. 13 Oct 1618, Ch. of St. Gervais, Geneva; he d. 15 Oct 1618, Geneva

CHILDREN, m/2:

Élisabeth[3], b. 7 Oct, 10 Oct 1620, Ch. of St. Pierre, Geneva; m. 25 Jun 1643, Ch. of St. Pierre,
François Sabourin, a master surgeon, s/o Pierre Sabourin of St. Maixent, Poitou, FR; she
d. 4 Dec 1670, Geneva

Susanna[3], (twin) b. 10 Mar, bp. 11 Oct 1622, Ch. of St. Pierre, Geneva; she d. 16 Mar 1622, Geneva

Anne[3], (twin) b. 10 Mar, bp. 11 Oct 1622, Ch. of St. Pierre, Geneva; she d. 16 Mar 1622, Geneva

unnamed infant[3], stillborn, 4 Dec 1623

Esaïe[3], b. 18 Jan, bp. 27 Jan 1625, Ch. of St. Pierre, Geneva; m. 14 Sep 1661, Amsterdam, Gurtruydt LeStevenon; he d. 10 Nov 1699, Amsterdam; he was a merchant jeweler

REF: RATHBONE, Bettye S. *Some of the Ancestors of Francis Flournoy, Sr. of Chesterfield Co, VA* (Austin, TX); FLOURNOY, Gédéon (b. 1691, s/o Jacques, bro of the immigrant to VA Jean Jacques) *Flournoy Genealogy* (1732-1759) - mss. on file in Bibliothèque Wallonne, Leiden; GEISENDORF, Paul-Frédéric, *Livre des Habitants de Genève* (1963); GALIFFE, Jacques-Augustin & J.B.G., *Notices Généalogiques sur les Familles Genevoises, depuis les premiers temps jusqu'à nos jours* (1836); Church Records, Geneva, Switzerland; FLOURNOY, E. M., *Gibson Flournoy and Related Families* (1972).

FONVIELLE/FONVEILLE /FONVILLE, Jean/John

b. 16 Apr 1679, Lorraine, FR, s/o Jean & Marguerite (Nouvel) Fonvielle of Mazères, Ariège Dépt, Midi-Pyrénées; Jean I (b. 1641, Mazères , m. 19 May 1667, Mazères); Jean I was a successful merchant in Mazères where he d.; **2 sons, 2 daus**

fled to ENG w/ his mo & sibs

m/1, 27 Jun 1699, by license, Hungerford Market Huguenot Ch, London (later Castle St. Church; Hungerford Market was razed in 1860 to make way for Charing Cross Station), Françoise L'Amy, aged 32, liv. in St. Giles in the Fields Parish as was Jean; Françoise prob. d. c. 1709

Jul 1700 - arr VA on the *Mary Ann*

1707-Mar 1718 - member of 1st Vestry of King William Parish

1710 – on the tithing list

1714 - was listed with a wife and son on the *Liste Généralle*

31 Oct 1716 - rec. Patent #916 for 168 acres on the s. side of the James River in Henrico (now Powhatan) Co, which he sold a. 1719 to William Timson

1717 - last mentioned on the tithing list in King Wm. Parish; went to Craven Co, NC

m/2, by 1714, Anne Graves

a. 21 Sep 1719 - his tract was transferred to William Timson

m/3, c. 1730, Craven Co., Jane/Jeanne X, who survived him; she m/2, by Sep 1741, William Windham

d. 1741, Newbern (now New Bern), Craven Co, NC; his will mentions sons John, Peter, David, Isaac & his wife (but not by name)

CHILDREN, m/1:

John[2], b. c. 1701/2, VA; m/1, 1729, Elizabeth Brice, d/o William & Ann (X) Brousse/Brice; m/2, Mary (Hatch ?); he d. a. 27 Jan 1773, wp, Craven Co; Mary d. p. 1773

CHILDREN, m/1, all b. Craven Co and all in father's will:

John[3], b. a. Mar 1730; m/1, XX; m/2, Sarah (Turner) Graves, widow of Thomas Graves; ch by 1st wife only - **3 or 4 ch**

William Brice[3], b. a. Dec 1733; m. a. 1760, Hannah Graves, stepdau of his bro John; he d. a. 1780; **7 ch**

Francis Marion[3], b. a. 1738; m. Sarah (Bright, d/o Simon Bright ?); d. 1798, Craven Co; **8 ch**

Mary[3], b. c. 1738; m. a. 1773, Lemuel Hatch, Sr; d. p. 1776; 9 ch

Frederick[3], b. c. 1740; m. Mary X who m/2, William Green; he d. 1785, Craven Co; dau **Elizabeth**[4] (in grfather's will) + **5 other ch**

CHILDREN, m/2, all b. Craven Co and all in father's will:

NOTE: some sources say only Esther was ch of m/2 **or** that Elizabeth, Jeremiah and Esther are ch of m/2 – it is not clear and there is a " break" bet Frederick and Stephen; the only fact is that they are all John[2]'s ch.

Stephen[3], b. 1743; m. Lucy Kibble, d/o Abraham Kibble; d. 1775, Onslow Co, NC; **3 ch**

Elizabeth[3], b. 1745; m. a. 1773, John Hatch; lived Onslow Co; 1 known ch **Elizabeth**[4]

Jeremiah[3], b. 1748; m/1, Elizabeth Rhodes, d/o Henry Rhodes; m/2, Mary Johnston, d/o Jacob
      Johnston; he d. 1823, prob. Maury Co, TN; **at least 8 ch**
Esther[3], b. c. 1750
Cornelius[2], a. 1705, Manakintown; d. 1730, Craven Co, NC
Thomas[2], b. c. 1708, Manakintown; d. a. 19 Dec 1738, Craven Co, NC
CHILDREN, m/2 :
Anne[2], c. 1716
Priscilla[2], c. 1718
CHILDREN, m/3:
Peter[2], b. c. 1733; d. young, shortly p. 1742, Craven Co.
David[2], b. 1736; m. Ann X; d. c. 1770, wd; prob. no issue
Isaac[2], b. c. 1739; m. Sarah Fields, d/o Samuel Fields of Onslow Co; d. 1780, Charleston, SC; served Rev.
      War; at least son **David**[3], dau **Elizabeth**[3]

REF: JONES, W. Mac, *The Douglas Register* (Baltimore, 1973); CABELL, Priscilla Harriss, *Turff & Twigg, Vol.
1 The French Lands* (Richmond, VA); *NC Wills* – John Fonvielle's complete will – 1773, Craven Co; research by
Judith W. Hanson of Orem, UT and by Ariminta "Minnie" Stewart Rogers of Chattanooga, TN; BROCK, Robert A.,
Huguenot Emigration to VA(Baltimore, 1966).

FORÊT/FOREST, Jean/Jehan de

b. c. 1548, Avesnes, Hainaut, FR Flanders (now Avesnes-sur-Helpe, Nord Dépt. s. of Maubeuge), s/o
      Melchoir II & Catherine (du Fosset) de Forêt; Catherine – wd, 1572, she d. c. 1579
m. c. 1575, Avesnes, Anne Maillard (b. Felleries, FR, n.e. of Avesnes-sur-Helpe -d. 21 Apr 1640,
      Amsterdam)
1st in the family to become a Protestant; a merchant draper
d. c. 1606, Vosmeer, NETH, nr. Bergen or 1620, Avesnes
CHILDREN:
Jean[2]
Jesse[2], b. c. 1576, Avesnes; a merchant in Sedan, FR in 1601, prob. selling woolen cloth; m. 23 Sep 1601,
      Sedan, Marie du Cloux, d/o Nicaise & Marie (Aubertin) du Cloux, a merchant in Sedan; she had sis
      Magdeleine who m. David de Lambremont; 1607 – Jesse was a merchant in Montcornet, Picardie, n.e.
      Lacon; 1608 – still in Picardie and now a merchant-dyer; 1615, on Leiden Walloon Register; Jesse and
      Gérard were dyers; Jesse was a master artisan and was licensed "to dye serges and camlets in colors" –
      a tribute to his skill; he lived in a home nr. the Walloon Ch in the *Gasthuys Vierendeel* (Almshouse
      Quarter); his parents were also liv. in Leiden; 1621 - he wrote Sir Dudley Carleton, the ENG
      ambassador at the Hague, to ask if the King of ENG would permit 50-60 Walloon families, all FR and
      of the Reformed Religion, to settle in VA, to aid them with an armed vessel to make the voyage,
      guarantee them protection, grant them land to cultivate, allow them to form a town; on 11 Aug 1621,
      they rec. permission, sort of; the Virginia Company's conditions were different from what the Walloons
      had asked and they decided to stay put; autumn 1622, he registered for poll tax: a dyer with a wife and
      5 ch, maid servant Magariete Du Can, liv. on Breedestraat within the Almshouse Quarter; 1623, led an
      unsuccessful expedition of 10 men to select a site in the New World for colonization; the West Indies
      Co. would not permit families to go but allowed Jesse + 10 other men to go; embarked from
      Amsterdam, 1 Jul 1623, on *The Pigeon*, headed for the Amazon; d. 22 Oct 1624, off the coast of
      tropical America, Guiana Colony, nr. the Oyapock/Oiapoque River, which is the border bet FR Guiana
      and the state of Ampará, Brazil; p. 1624, his widow and ch went to New Netherland but she & some of
      the ch returned to HOL
CHILDREN:
Marie[3], bp. 7 Jul 1602, Sedan; prob. d. young
Jean[3], bp. 22 Jul 1604, Sedan; m. 9 Mar/6 Apr 1633, Leiden, Marie Vermeulen; he d. 6 Apr 1668,
      Leiden

Henry/Hendrick[3], bp. 7 Mar 1606, Sedan; m. 1 Jul 1636, Amsterdam, Gertrude Bornstra, d/o Wybrant-Andres Bornstra; with wife & bro Isaac left the Texel (an island in the W. Frisian Is., HOL) for New Amsterdam, 1 Oct 1636, in the *Rensselaerswyck*; sis Rachel/husb were to go as well but came the following spring; he arr 4 Mar 1637; went to Fort Orange; Henry chose the flats of Muscoota to settle – rec 100 *morgen* = 200 acres from Wouter Van Twiller, the Director General of New Netherland, in Muscoota (name means flat place) – area n. of today's 59th St – became Nieuw Haarlem, then just Harlem in 1664; d. 26 Jul 1637, *prob*. VA; bro Jean appeared in court to petition the division of Hendrick's property – widow Geertruyt van Bornstra mentioned, but no ch, there were prob. no ch; widow m. NY, Andries Hudde

Elizabeth[3], bp. 1 Nov 1607, Sedan; prob. d. young

David[3], bp. 11 Dec 1608 Sedan; went to New Amsterdam, 1659, but returned to HOL 1665; **issue**

Rachel[3], bp. 1609, prob. Leiden; m. 12 Dec 1626, Jean/Johannes de la Montagne

Anne[3], b. c. 1611; prob. d. young

Nicaise[3], b. c. 1613 ; prob. d. young

Jesse[3], bp. 1 Mar 1615, Leiden; m. c. 1634; d. 1639 - **3 ch**

Isaac[3], bp. 10 Jul 1616, Leiden; emigrated to New Amsterdam, 1636; m. 9 Jun 1641, NYC, Sarah duTrieux, d/o Philippe & Susanna (du Chesne) du Trieux; Sarah d. 9 Nov 1692; he d. bet 25 Jul – 26 Sep 1674, New Amsterdam; he was a tobacco planter, brewer; Great Burgher and *schepen*; surname became **DeFREEST**

CHILDREN: **Jesse**[4], b. 1642; **Susannah**[4], b. 1645, m. Peter de Riemer; **Gerrit**[4], b. 1647; **Marie**[4]; **Michael**[4], b.1649; **John**[4], b.1650, m. 8 Jun 1673, Susannah Verlet – only **1 dau** survived, John was a chirurgeon; **Philip**[4], b. 1652, m. 5 Jan 1676, Tryntie Kip – **9 ch**, he was a cooper; **Isaac**[4], b. 1655, m. 4 Sep 1681 Elizabeth/ /Lysbet Vanderspiegel – **5 ch**, he was a baker; **Hendrick**[4], b. 1675, m. 5 Jun 1682, Fiammetia/Phebe van Flaesbeek, he was a glazier – **7 ch**; **David**[4], bp 1660; **David**[4], bp. 1663; **Maria**[4], b. 1666, m/1, Bernard Darby, m/2, Isaac de Reimer, s/o Peter de Reimer; **David**[4], b. 1669, m. 1696, Martha Blagge, he was a glazier -**10 ch**

Israel[3], bp. 7 Oct 1617; d. young

Philippe[3], bp. 13 Sep 1620; d. young

Michel/Melchior[2], b. c. 1577; m. Marie Gobert; **issue**

Gérard[2], b. c. 1583, Avesnes; m. 12 Aug 1611, Leiden, Hester de la Grange, d/o Crispin & Agnes (X) de la Grange; 6 Oct 1617, purchased right of citizenship in Leiden; he was a dyer & merchant; d. Aug 1654, leaving an estate of 15,325 florins

(Probable) CHILDREN:

Dau[3], m. Johannes Panhuysen, a director of the Dutch West India Co.

Crispin[3], b. 9 Dec 1612; 1st banns 7 Jun 1636, m. 1 Jul 1636, Amsterdam, Margareta Bornstra, d/o Wybrant-Andresz Bornstra, sis/o Gertrude (wife of cousin Hendrick); planned to leave that fall for New Netherland but, for some reason, did not, stayed in Leiden; he did **NOT** have a son Michel who went to Port Royal, Nova Scotia; Canadian records clearly state that that Michel de Forest was the s/o Henri & Marie (X) de Forest of Avesnes who m. 1635- no known connection to the other de Forests in this entry; more recently, DNA testing has failed to establish a connection between the Acadian & NY Forests; **issue**

?Henri[2], b. c. 1584, Avesnes; d. c. 1654, Leiden, 71 yrs; dyer of beautiful fabrics

Jeanne[2], m. X Cartier of Colombier, FR

Anne[2], m. 24 Jan 1607, Amsterdam, Jean Le Fèvre

REF: RIKER, James, *History of Harlem*; DeFOREST, J.W., *The DeForests of Avesnes* (New Haven, CT, 1900); *Proceedings of the PA Huguenot Society*, Vol. XXIV (1953); DeForest, Mrs. Robert W., *A Walloon Family in America*, Vol. I (Boston, NY 1914); BERGERON, Adrien, *Le Grand Arrangement des Acadiens au Québec* (Montréal, CAN, 1981); INNES, J.H., *New Amsterdam & Its People* (1902); DuLONG, John P., "The Origins of the Acadian Michel Forest" (17 May 2008) – http://habitant.org/forest/index.htm - extensive research, documented.

FORTINEUX, Jonas

a. 1654, Fortineux family left FR and went to the Palatinate/*Pfalz*

b. c. 1654, Lambrecht, GER, s. e. Kaiserlautern

c/ 1665 – to Otterberg, *Pfalz*, GER, n. of Kaiserlautern

c. 1674, m. Otterberg, Sara Menton (c. 1647, Otterberg, GER-12 Dec 1715, Otterberg); had **5 sons** (2
      d. young) & **2 daus**

1689 – family went to Holzappel, s.e. of Koblenz

1695 – back to Otterberg

d. bet. 1702-09

CHILD (3 of 7, all bap. in the FR Reformed Ch, Otterberg):

Jean Henri[2], b. 2 Apr, bp. 7 Apr 1675, Otterberg, Rheinland-Pflaz; confirmed 16/17 Apr 1691, Holzappel;
    m/1, 9 Feb 1703, Renarde/Renata Spo(h)n of Gundersweiler (c. 9 km. n.e. Otterberg); bur. 14 Sep
    1710, Otterberg, m/2, 14 Apr 1711, Otterberg, Marie Louys, d/o Philippe Louys; she d. 1/7 Jul
    1753; he d. 5 Nov, bur 9 Nov 1715, Otterberg

    CHILDREN, m/1:

    Jean Henry[3], b. 15 Jan 1704, Otterberg; prob. d. young

    Marie Rosine[3], b. 4 Dec 1705, Otterberg; prob. d. young

    Jean Henry[3], b. 22 Sep, bp Sep 25 1708, Otterberg; arr Philadelphia, 29 Aug 1730, on the *Thistle
        of Glasgow* from Rotterdam via Dover or Cowes, ENG; m. c. 1735, (Mary) Catherine/
        Charity Berger, d/o Andreas Berger (she d. p. 27 Jan 1794, wd, Frederick Co, MD); bet.
        1737-42, other family members emigrated, most settled MD and PA; d. a. 12 Jul 1753
        (date of obit), Frederick Co, MD – prob. bet 1-7 Jul, killed by lightning; surname became
        FORTNEY

        CHILDREN (all, except in David, in mother's will):

        Susanna (Catherine) Catarina[4], b. Oct 1737, bp 7 Jun 1738, Monocacy, MD, m. 2 Oct
            1765, Frederick GER Reformed Ch, Lewis Hoff; **3 ch**

        (John) Hendrick/Henry[4], b. 31 Dec 1739, Pr. George Co (now Frederick Co), MD; bp 21
            Sep 1740, Monocacy; m/1, Anne Elizabeth Hathaway – **2 ch**; m/2, bet 1786-1796,
            Frederick Co. Anna Barbara (X) Pickenpaugh, widow of Peter Pickenpaugh; she d.
            p. 8 Aug 1805; he d. p. 1808, Monongalia Co, VA (now WV)

        Charity (called **Charlotte**)[4], b. 15 Oct 1741, Frederick, MD; m,1764, Gottlieb (Michael or
            Barnabas) Lauffer, aka Henry Runner (1738-14 Jul 1784) - **8 ch**; Gottlieb changed
            his name when he emigrated; she d. 28 Nov 1825, bur. Mt. Zion Lutheran Ch,
            Feagaville, MD (s.w. of Frederick, MD)

        David[4], b. 1744/47; d. 17 Jan 1787, Fredericksburg, VA, frozen to death, age 40

        Christina[4], b. c. 1748; m. X Galman

        Daniel[4], b. c. 1752, Frederick, MD; m. Barbara Pickenpaugh, d/o Peter & Anna Barbara
            (X) Pickenpaugh & stepdau of his bro Hendrick; he d. 15 Feb 1818, Monongalia
            (now Preston Co, WV) VA; **4 sons, 6 daus**

        Peter[4], b. Mar/Apr 1754, Frederick, MD; m. 8 Oct 1775, Frederick, MD, Anna Elizabeth
            Hohn, d/o Casper & Christina (Porth) Hohn; **4 sons, 4 daus**; he d. p. 1814

    CHILDREN, m/2:

    Marie Margarite[3], b. 1715

    Marie Rosine[3], b. 1716

Jonas Peter[2], b. 11 Sep 1677, Otterberg; m. 15 Sep 1701 Susanne Rosina "Rosa" Spohn (b. 18 Apr 1685,
    Katzenbach); went to PA; **6 sons, 4 daus**

Jean Jacob[2], b. 17 Oct, bp. 18 Oct 1690, Otterberg; m/1, 7 May 1771, Alsenborn, Maria Elisabeth
    Weckman (Jan 1695-31 Mar 1728 – **3 sons, 2 daus**; m/2, 7 Sep 1728 Waldfischbach, Maria
    Elisabeth Glas – **1 son, 1 dau**; m/3, 15 Jun 1732, Otterberg, Maria Susanne Le Soigue; m/4,
    15 Jan 1739, Rohrbach, Maria Elisabeth Culmann; he d. a. 27 Jun 1751; 2 of his sons went to
    America

REF: Records of the French Reformed Church at Otterberg, Rheinland-Pfalz; *An Abbreviated Genealogy Delineating the First 5 Generations of the Families Whose Progenitors were Jonas Fotineux-Sara Menton of Otterberg, the Palatinate* (1986); Fortney-Fortna Genealogy Family, Inc., *The Fortineaux-Fortinet Family (Fortney, Fortna, Fordney, Furtney) in America* (Marceline, MO, 1989).

FOUACE/FOUASSE, Gabriel

b. Caen, Normandie, FR; a Jean & Jeanne (X) Fouace of Caen – témoignage, 16 Oct 1698, Threadneedle St Ch, London – connection?; a Charles & a Stephen Foüace (a clerk) were on the denization list of 9 Apr 1687, Whitehall

p. 1685 – left FR

4 Feb 1711 – naturalized London; of St. Anne's Parish, Soho (Shaftesbury Ave & Wardour Street, n.e. of Piccadilly Circus)

m. 13 Oct 1720, St. Paul, Covent Garden, London, ENG, Sarah Burton, d/o Joseph Burton; St. Paul's is on Bedford St., n. of the Strand, often referred to now as the Actors' Ch. as it is in the theater district and several famous actors have been members there

1740 - was director of the French Protestant Hospital in London

he was a magistrate of the City of Westminster

bur. 15 Aug 1753, St. Paul, Covent Garden, London ENG

CHILD:

Sarah[2], chr. 2 Sep 1735, St. Paul's; m. 30 Sep 1753, ENG, John Nourse (19 Jul 1731, Weston-under-Penyard, Herefordshire, ENG-10 Oct 1784, Annapolis, MD), s/o John & Eliza (Gregory) Nourse; **21 ch** - 18 named + 3 unnamed, b. bet 1754-1778; last ch b. in London in 1768, next ch b. VA, 1770; Sarah d. 7 Sep 1784, Annapolis

REF: *A Supplement to Dr. W.A. Shaw's Letters of Denization & Acts of Naturalization* – Publication of the Huguenot Society of London, Vol. XXXV (Frome, 1932), Quarto Series; MARMOY, Charles F.A., *The French Protestant Hospital: Extracts from the Archives of "La Providence" Relating to Inmates & Applications for Admission 1718- 1957 and to Recipients of & Applications for the Coqueau Charity 1745-1901*, Vol. I – Publication of the Huguenot Society of London, Vol. LII (1975) Quarto Series; LYLE, Maria Catherine Nourse, *James Nourse and His Descendants* (Lexington, KY, 1897); SMITH, Raymond, *Records of the Royal Bounty and Connected Funds, The Burn Donation & the Savoy Church in the Huguenot Library, University College, London* – Publication of the Huguenot Society, of London, Vol. LI (1974), Quarto Series; WILLIS, H.J., *Registers of the Aske's Hospital Hoxton (Shoreditch), London.*

FOUCHÉ(E)/FOUSHEE, Jacques/James

a. 1690/92 - poss. in VA

m/1, Mary X, who d. 8 Oct 1724; **may** have been m. a. arr VA

Jun 1699 – deed from James Foushee, then liv at "Long Neck" nr. Totoskey Creek in Richmond Co, VA

6 Feb 1711/2 – Patent of Naturalization, Richmond Co, VA – states "James Foushee a naturall Borne subject of the French King haveing settled and Inhabited for severall yeares in the County of Richmond in this Colony…."; patent admitted to record, 8 Mar 1711/2

1719 -liv Lancaster Co, VA – pd. tithables on 3 persons

m/2, Ruth X, who d. p. 11 Jan 1731/2, wd – a. 9 Feb 1731/2, wp, Lancaster Co, VA; she may have been m. before as her will names a lot of people, incl. a sister Mary Hart; **no issue w/ James**

d. p. 4 Sep 1729, wd – a. 11 Feb 1729/30, wp, Lancaster Co, VA – mentions wife, son John, daus Charlotte, Susanna Bertrand

CHILDREN, m/1:

Charlotte[2], b. 5 Jun 1692; m. Daniel Tebbs of Westmoreland Co, VA (Daniel in Ruth's will)

Susannah[2], b. 12 Dec 1695; m. Nov 1713, William Bertrand; d. p. 1731 (both in Ruth's will)

John[2], b. Sep 1697; m/1, c. 1718, Elizabeth Dawson, d/o John & Sarah (X) Dawson, m/2, Winifred Williams, d/o Mrs. Winifred Williams – **6 ch, m/3**, c. 1766, Sarah Ann (Garlington) Hack, d/o Christopher &

Elizabeth (Conway) Garlington, widow of Peter Spencer Hack -**no issue**; he d. a. Nov 1769, Halifax Co, VA (John in stepmother Ruth's will); John was a man of some importance in VA – held many municipal offices, perhaps had some legal training; his will mentions wife Sarah Ann, son **William**[3], dau **Charlotte**[3] Neilson + others

CHILDREN, m/1:

Mary[3], b. 19 Aug 1719; m. c. 1736, John Lewis III (c. 1714, Northumberland Co, VA-13 Jan 1746, Northumberland Co), s/o John II & Elizabeth (Christopher) Lewis – **issue**

Elizabeth[3] (b. 1720/25), m. Capt. Bushrod Fauntleroy, s/o Griffin & Ann (X) Bushrod Fauntleroy – **4 sons, 2 daus**;

NOTE: No <u>known</u> connection bet this ancestor and the next entry; there is a claim that the 2 were branches of the same family but no <u>proof</u> was given.

REF: FLEET, Beverly, *Virginia Colonial Abstracts,* Vol. I, p. 299 (Baltimore, 1988); PORTER, Mrs. W. A., "Foushee" in *The Huguenot*, #11 (1941-43); LEE, Ida J., *Abstracts Lancaster Co, VA Wills 1653-1800* (Baltimore, 1973); LONG, Daniel Reid, Jr., *John Lewis "The Lost Pioneer, 1690-1970"* (1971); GANNON, Peter Steven, editor, *Huguenot Refugees in the Settling of Colonial America* (NYC).

FOUCHÉ (E)/FAUCHÉ/FOUSHEE, Jean/John

b. FR, *poss.* Midi-Pyrénées Dépt, nr. Foix, n. of Spain
30 Jul 1700 - to VA on the *Mary Ann*?; some say he arr by 1685; settled Richmond Co
prob. m/1, Elizabeth Spoe (d. p. 1716) – her name was on a deed, 1716
m/2, Meelin Donnaman/Downmann, d/o William Donnmann
d. p. 4 Nov 1733, wd, Orange Co, VA; will mentions wife Meelin, son John and "all my children"

CHILDREN, m/1:

John[2], b. Richmond Co, VA; m. Aphia Thornton; liv. Cedar Run in Culpeper Co, VA; d. p. 15 Apr 1777, wd– a. 21 Jun 1779, wp, Culpeper Co; will lists wife Apphia (*sic*), ch Nancy, John, George, Benjamin, Thornton, Charles, Joseph, William, Elijah, Daniel, Jeminah, Hannah, Tureman (son-in-law John?), Elizabeth

CHILDREN:

John[3], m. 5 Oct 1788, Culpeper Co, Sally Crutcher

Thornton[3], b. c. 1756, VA; m/1, Rose Hobbs, m/2, 28 Jul 1791, Orange Co, VA, Nancy Graves; he d. p. 15 Feb 1830 VA (c. 1832)

George[3], b. c. 1753; m/1, Esther Allen; m/2, 1819, Susan Foushee

Charles[3], m. Lucy Crutcher; d. a. 1825

Joseph[3], m. Eleanor Stafford

William[3], b. 26 Oct 1749, VA; m. Susan C; d. 21 Aug 1824, VA

Elijah[3], m. Ann Stewart; d. c. 1837

Daniel[3], b. 1775; m. 1796, Elizabeth Slaughter (b. c. 1776-d. Nelson Co, KY), d/o Francis & Sarah (Coleman) Slaughter; he d. p. 18 Feb 1824, wd, Nelson Co, KY; **7 ch**

Nancy Ann[3], b. c. 1752, m/1, John Tureman; m/2, p. 1787 Daniel Farmer; she d. 1826; **issue**, both mar.

Jeminah[3], b. c. 1766

Hannah[3], b. c. 1768

Elizabeth[3], b. c. 1769; m. 24 Nov 1789, Thomas Dawson

Benjamin[3]

CHILDREN, prob. m/2:

Charles[2], d. c. 1757

Joseph[2]

Nathaniel[2], b. Nov 1733, bro John was appt his guardian when their father d; d. 1810, SC, Upcountry

REF: McCLURE, Paul, *The Cash Family Record* (1976); correspondence w/ Tom Wortham (31 Dec 1996), Col. Roger Babson Foushee of Durham, NC (23 Dec 2000); *Wortham Genealogy & History.*

FOUNTAINE, Nicolas (alias WICART)

b. c. 1638/40, FR

24 Feb 1661/2, naturalized as Nicholas Fountaigne of Wicart; 13 Jul 1665, MD, a record lists him as a subject of the crown of FR & shows that he was in VA before arr in MD & that he had a patent of denization for MD

m/1, Grace X

1665 – rec. 300 acres from Lord Baltimore, known as "Fountaine's Lott" – "payment" for transporting settlers to MD

1671 – rec. 50 more acres called "Normandie"; later he added 600 acres

m/2, Joanna X, who m/2, John Brown

d. a. 1 Oct 1708, wp, Somerset Co, MD; will gives son Mercy 100 acres called New France, which was to go to grson William & his heirs when Mercy d.; sons Nicholas and Stephen rec. Fountain's Lott, Normandy, Peake, Rumly, heifers to be divided equally; wife Joanna gets house & plantation, a third part of other goods and moveables, the other 2/3s to be div. between his 3 sons and dau Dennis Lane; wife Joanna was to be executrix

in documents surname is consistently Fountaine/Fountain

CHILDREN, m/1:

Dennis (Denise?)[2], b. 1663/4; m. George Lane

Mercy/Marcy[2], b. 1667; m. 14 Sep 1686, Somerset Co, MD, Mary Bosman (b. 15 Mar 1670, Manokin, Somerset, MD), d/o John & Blandina (Risdon) Bosman; he d. a. 6 Apr 1727, wp, Somerset Co, MD; **12 ch**; his will mentions wife Mary, sons **Mercy**[3], **Andrew**[3], **Samuel**[3], dau **Prudence**[3]

CHILDREN, prob. m/2:

Nicholas[2], b. c. 1692; m. Mary X (d. a. 20 Mar 1771, wp, Somerset Co, MD); d. a. 10 Feb 1743/4, wp, Somerset Co, MD; **7 ch** – sons **Mercy**[3], **William**[3], **John**[3], **Collier**[3], daus **Anne**[3], **Mary**[3], **Bridget**[3]; Mary's will mentions only dau Bridget Tull, son William

Stephen[2]

REF: *The Huguenot*, publication #29 (1979-81); TORRENCE, Clayton, *Old Somerset on the Eastern Shore of MD*; Records from the MD State Archives; wills of Nicolas, Mercy, Mary, Nicholas.

FOUQUET/FUQUA(Y), Guillaume

b. c. 1667

fled FR, prob. to ENG

c. 1685- arr VA; called Gill or Gilly

m. c. 1687 - Jane Eyre (b. c. 1671), d/o Joseph & Margaret (Humphreys) Eyre, grd/o William Humphreys

d. p. 1 Aug 1698, Henrico Co, VA, when he was paid 505# of tobacco by the estate of Sarah Cocke, the widow of William Cocke (tobacco was an accepted means of exchange since "hard money" was almost non-existent at that time in VA)

CHILDREN, used surname FUQUA:

William[2], b. c. 1688, Charles City Co, VA; m. c. 1720/23, Elizabeth X (d. a. 17 Feb 1780, wp, Charlotte Co, VA); he d. a. 3 Mar 1761, wp, Lunenburg Co, VA; **7 ch**, incl. son **William**[3] (c. 1723-1774) m. Marie Fauré/Mary Ford (1729-1779) d/o Pierre/Peter & Judith (Goodwin) Fauré/Ford

Joseph[2], b. c. 1690/93, Charles City Co; m. c. 1720/24, Anna Sampson, d/o Francis & Bridget (X) Sampson (d. a. 19 Mar 1744, wp, Goochland Co); he d. a. 22 Sep 1788, adm, Cumberland Co, VA; **9 ch**

Giles[2], b. Charles City Co; m. c. 1724, Elizabeth X (d. p. 22 Nov 1760); he d. a. 5 Jun 1771, wp, Charles City Co; **8 ch**

Ralph[2], b. Charles City Co; m. c. 1734, Priscilla Owen, (1702, Henrico Co-p. 1779, Russell, Bedford Co), d/o Thomas & Elizabeth (Brooks) Owen (he d. a. May 1774, wp, Henrico Co); he d. a. 24 Jul 1770 wp Bedford Co, VA; **12 ch**

REF: Irwin, Alya Dean (Smith), *Fuqua-A Fight for Freedom* (Houston, 1974); UNDERHILL, Patsy Louise Crox, *A History & Lineage of the Baldwin, Crox, Eldridge & McClary & Allied Families* (not dated); William Humphreys' will; LINDSAY, Joyce H., compiler, *Marriages of Henrico Co, VA, 1680-1808* ; Thomas Owen's will.

FOURQUERAN/FORQUERAN(D)/FORCURON, Jean/John

b. c. 1666, Castelmoron-sur-Lot, Guienne, FR, n.w. of Agen (now in Lot-et-Garonne Dépt, Aquitaine)

9 Sep 1688 - he was in the "Reconnaissances of L'Église Françoise de la Savoye", London; gives place of origin, age - 22 yrs old

m/1, prob. ENG, Elizabeth X; she d. p. 1700, VA

4 Feb 1700 – he and his wife on the list of the passengers on *Le Nasseau* sailing to VA

m/2, c. 1708, VA, Jeanne/Jane Dupré (she d. p. 1736), d/o John & Mary (X) DuPré; she m/2, a. 4 May 1724, Moses Livereau (d. 1724); John DuPré names Peter & Moses (below) as his grandsons in his will, 13 Nov 1734

1 May 1708 – Jean certified that he was eligible for 250 acres of land for the importation of 5 persons – himself, his 1st wife Elizabeth, his 2nd wife Jeanne, James Duero & (Olimp?) Duero, his in-laws

1710-1719 - on tithables lists of King William Parish

1714 – on *Liste Générale de Tous les François Protestants Refugiés* in King William Parish – he, wife & 2 sons

31 Oct 1716 - received patent #902, 170 acres on the s side of the James River in the lands surveyed for the French Refugees in the part of Henrico Co. that became Chesterfield Co; son Moses got this land at d. of father, then it passed to Moses' son John who sold it to James Harris on 7 Apr 1758 for £65

d. a. 6 Jun 1720, wp, Henrico Co, VA; will written in French; 1 Aug 1720 – inv. presented, 4 May 1724 - accts of his estate presented by widow Jane "Livero"

CHILDREN, m/2:

Moses[2], b. 1710/11; m. Susanne X; he d. a. 6 Sep 1751, adm, Henrico/Chesterfield Co, VA

    CHILDREN, b. Manakintown:

    Jean/John[3], b. 15 Mar 1735/6; m. Judith X; d. a. 14 Oct 1797, adm, Chesterfield Co, VA; 6 sons **Peter**[4], **James**[4], **Samuel**[4], **Bartlett**[4], **William**[4], **John**[4], 4 daus **Martha**[4] (m. John Newby – issue), **Sarah**[4], **Mary**[4], **Nancy**[4]

    Janne[3], b. 24 Sep 1737

    Elizabeth[3], b. 7 Oct 1739; m. c. 16 Dec 1759 (date of mar. bond), Manakintown, David Stanford

Peter[2], m. a. 7 Oct 1739, Joyce X; liv. Bedford Co, VA; d. a. Jun 1798, wp, Bourbon Co, KY; will mentions wife Joyce, 2 sons, dau, 2 grsons, 1 grdau (children of dau Betty); Joyce d. p. 1784

    CHILDREN:

    John[3], m. Feb 1772, Mary Guthry

    Peter[3], m. Grace Hall

    Elizabeth/Betty[3], b. c. 1745; m/1, Edward Mastin – **Peter**[4], **James**[4], **Jenny**[4] (m. Pleasant Branch); m/2, Caleb Hall

REF: BROCK, R.A., *Huguenot Emigration to VA* (Richmond, VA, 1886); *Publications of The Huguenot Society of London*, Vol. XXII (London, 1914); CABELL, Priscilla Harriss, *Turff & Twigg, Vol. I, The French Lands*, (Richmond, VA, 1988); *Henrico Co, VA Court Orders* (1707-1709, p. 34), "Proof of Importations"; *Vestry Book of King William Parish, VA, 1707-1750* ; WEISIGER, Benjamin B. III, *Colonial Wills of Henrico Co, VA, 1654-1737*, Part 1.

FRANTZ, Paulus/Paul

b. c. 1687, prob. Schalbach, Lorraine, FR; he was a wheelwright

m. 8 Nov 1718, Lutheran Ch, Neusaarwerden (now Sarre-Union), Alsace, FR, Anna Maria Herter of Schalbach, d/o Johann Bartholomaus Herter, also a wheelwright

30 Aug 1737 - arr in Philadelphia on the *Samuel*

d. p. 3 Dec 1763, wd - a. 13 Oct 1766, wp, Lower Saucon Twp, Northampton Co, PA

CHILDREN:

Johann Paulus/Paul Jr.[2], b. Schalbach, bp. 4 Jun 1733, Reformed Church at Rauweiler/Rauwiller, Alsace, FR*; m. c. 1755, prob. PA, Anna Maria Schall (bur. 14 Aug 1783, Indian Creek Ch); he was bur. 1 Feb 1796, Indian Creek Ch, Telford, Montgomery Co, PA; 11 ch

CHILDREN (1st 5 listed in records of the Lower Saucon Reformed Ch):

Nicholas[3], b. 25 Jan 1756; m. a. 1793, prob. PA, Christina X; he d. 13 Feb 1843, Trumbauersville, Bucks, PA

CHILD:

John K[4], b. 14 Mar 1799, Hilltown, Bucks, PA; m. 24 Feb 1835, Bedminster Twp, Bucks, PA, Catherine Ziegenfuss (17 Jul 1814, Bedminster Twp-28 Mar 1898), d/o Adam & Catherine (X) Ziegenfuss; John d. 17 Apr 1874 - both bur. St. James Lutheran Ch, Chalfont, Bucks, PA

John George[3], b. 10 Feb 1758

Michael[3], b. 7 May 1760

John[3], b. 1 Apr 1764

Paulus[3], b. 17 Apr 1762; m. 28 Jan 1790, Maria Dames

Sarah[3] m. Benjamin Starkey

Additional children listed in 1796 petition: **Jacob**[3]; **Philip**[3]; **Nancy**[3]; **Tobias**[3]; **Elizabeth**[3]

Johann Jacob[2], b. 11 Mar 1736, Rauweiler church record

Susanna[2], m. X Artman (in father's will)

Catarina[2], m. X Slought (in father's will)

Madland[2], m. X Dornblesser (in father's will)

Mary[2], m. X Hartzell (in father's will)

Barbary[2], m. X Grove (in father's will)

Nicholas[2], named in father's will

Ludwig[2] – named in father's will

*The two towns, Schalbach and Rauweiler, are only about 5 km. apart (c. 3 miles) but in different provinces. The line between Alsace and Lorraine is less than 1 km. east of Rauweiler. According to 18th century maps, the two towns were in the same provinces then as now.

REF: Church records: Neusaarwerden & Rauwiller, FR, Lower Saucon Twp, PA, Telford, PA, Bedminster Twp, Bucks, PA, Chalfont, PA; BURGERT, A.K., *Eighteenth Century Emigrants from the Alsace to America*; Administration of J. Paulus' estate; STRASSBURGER, R.B., *Pennsylvania German Pioneers*, Vol. I; *Gemeindeblatt des Reformierten Confiftoriums Straßburg*, Vol. I, #2, April 1925 - publication of the Reformed Consistory of Strassburg (Strasbourg) - tells the history of the Huguenot Church at Rauweiler/Rauwiller.

FREER/FRÈRE, Hugo/Hugues

a native of "Harley en Boulonois" (from marr. rec., Mannheim), now Herly in Pas-de-Calais Dépt, Nord-Pas-de-Calais, FR, s.e. Boulogne; went to the Palatinate/*Pfalz*

m/1, 2 Oct 1660, FR Ch, Mannheim, GER, Marie de la Haye (b. "Douaye"- d. 1666); he is called *Hugues Frère* in marr. record, which gives birthplaces for both; Marie and her 2 daus d. in the plague that wiped out over ½ the congregation of the church in 7 mo; "Douaye" is prob. Douai, now in Nord Dépt, Nord Pas-de-Calais, w. Valenciennes

m/2, 22 Jan 1667, Jannetje/Jeanine/Jeanne Wibau, a native of Bruyelle, s.e. of Tournai, d/o Toussaint Wibau, widow of Simon Flocquet; she d. 8 Dec 1693, New Paltz

a. 1679 – to NY; one of the patentees at New Paltz, NY

1683 - 1st deacon of the FR Ch in New Paltz; became an elder of the church in 1690

d. p. 4 Jan 1697/8, wd, New Paltz; will written in FR; son Hugo was executor of his will; will names
       Hugo, Jacob, Jean/John, Sara, Marie

CHILDREN, m/1:

Marie[2], b. 13 Sep, bp. 22 Sep 1661, Mannheim; d. young, GER

Sara[2], b. 22 Jan, bp. 31 Jan 1664, Mannheim; d. young, GER

Hugues/Hugo[2], b. 1 Jul, bp 2 Jul 1666, Mannheim; m. 7 Jun 1690, New Paltz, <u>Maria Anne LeRoy</u> (b. 7
       May 1673, Québec), d/o Siméon & Claude (Deschâlets) LeRoy; had 2 wills, last one dated 15 Jan
       1727/8, written in Dutch, which names ch **Hugo**[3], **Isaac**[3], **Simon**[3], **Jonas**[3], **Maria**[3], **Sarah**[3],
       Hester[3], **Catrina**[3], **Blandina**[3], **Rachel**[3], **Jannetie**[3], **Rebecca**[3], **Elizabeth**[3] – there were **15 ch** -
       Johannes & Benjamin must have d. young, as they are not in the will; he d. p. 29 Jun 1732 (date of
       indenture), New Paltz

CHILDREN, m/2:

Abraham[2], b. 11 Jan, bp., 19 Jan 1668, Mannheim; prob. d. young

Abraham[2], b. 11 Jun, bp., 16 Jun 1670, Mannheim; m. 28 Apr 1694, New Paltz, Aagien/Aeche Willem
       Tietsorte/Titsoort (b. 1674, Schenectady), d/o Willem Titsoort & Neeltje Swart; **16 ch**

Isaac[2], b. 1 Feb, bp. 9 Feb 1672, Mannheim; d. 9 Aug 1690

Marie/Mary[2], b. 1676, Hurley; m. 12 Oct 1697, Kingston, NY Louis Viele, s/o Pieter Cornelison Viele &
       Jacomyntje Swart; liv. Schenectady; **8 ch**

Jacob[2], bp. 9 Jun 1679, Kingston; m. Sep 1705, Antje Van Weyen (bp. 5 Sep 1686, Marbletown), d/o
       Hendrick Van Weyen & Annatjie Hoogland Gerrits; liv. Kingston; **13 ch**

Joseph[2], b. 1680

Jean/John[2], bp. 16 Apr 1682, Marbletown; m. Kingston, Rebecca Wagener/Van Wagenen (b. 11 Apr ,
       bp. 12 Apr 1685, Kingston), d/o Jacob Van Wagenen & Sarah Pels; prob. d. Wagondale; **8 ch**

Sara[2], b. 1688; m. 1708, Teunis Clausen Vander Volgen, s/o Claus Lourens Vander Volgen & Maritie
       Swart of Schagticoke; **8 ch**

REF : HEIGERD, Ruth P., *The Freer Family, the Descendants of Hugo Freer, Patentee of New Paltz, NY* (New Paltz, 1968); LeFEVRE, Ralph, *History of New Paltz and its Old Families* (Baltimore, 1923); MORRISON, George A., "The Freer Family of New Paltz, NY" in the *NY Gen. & Biog. Record,* Vol. 33, 34 (1902/03) ; records from the FR Ch in Mannheim, GER; VIELE, Kathlyne Knickerbocker, compiler, *Viele, 1659-1909, 250 Yrs. with a Dutch Family of NY* (NY, 1909).

FRESNEAU, André

b. c. 1675, La Rochelle, FR, s/o Jean; a family Bible (printed Geneva, SWI, 1587) was in the Fresneau
       Family by 1590 when it was given by Philip P. Fresneau to his only son Jacques on 3 Jan 1590;
       the entries continue to Philip Morin Freneau who d. 18 Dec 1832

André prob. went to ENG 1st

c. 1705 - arr Boston

he went to Simsbury, CT, where copper was being mined; he shipped a load of copper to London but the
       ship was captured by a FR cruiser and he ended up with nothing; the copper mine became New-
       gate Prison, the 1st state prison in CT, and is now a tourist site called "Copper Hill"

by spring 1707 - he was in NYC; he was in the shipping business and acted as an agent of the "Royal West
       India Co. of FR" in association w/ Étienne Delancey, Auguste Jay, Benjamin Faneuil, René Het &
       others

m/1, a. 2 Dec 1708, NY, Jeanne Allaire (c. 1687-a. 17 Jun 1710), d/o <u>Alexandre & Jeanne (Doens/Docus)</u>
       <u>Allaire</u>; **no issue**

by 1709 – an elder in the church in NY

m/2, 17 Jun 1710, NYC, Marie Morin, d/o <u>Pierre & Marie (Jamain) Morin</u>

22 Aug 1710 – made freemen in NY; acquired land in the East Division in New Rochelle same year

4 Aug 1714 – on a jury, NYC

d. a. 16 Aug 1725, wp; bur. Trinity Churchyard, NYC

CHILDREN, m/2 (all bp. French Ch, NYC):

André[2], b. 24 Jul, bp. 29 Jul 1711; d. unmarr.

Marie[2], b. 4 Feb, bp. 8 Feb 1712/3; d. 1738 unmarr.

Marguerite[2], b. 8 Oct, bp. 9 Oct 1715; d. 1728

Pierre[2], b. 11 Jan, bp. 19 Jan 1717/8; m. Agnes (3 Apr 1727-18 Aug 1817), prob. d/o David Watson who
> had *poss.* m. a d/o Alex Napier; Agnes m/2, Major Thomas Kearney; liv. Mt. Pleasant, NJ; Pierre
> went to Monmouth Co, NJ, to start a wine business – purchased almost 1000 acres in northern NJ;
> he d. 1767 & is bur. Trinity Ch, next to his father; 5 ch, incl. **Philip Morin**[3], b. 2 Jan 1752, NY, m.
> Eleanor Forman & d. 18 Dec 1832, NJ, at the age of 80Y 11M 13D – **4 daus**[4] – he is the Philip
> Freneau called the "Poet of the Revolution"; <u>NOTE</u>: name now Freneau (no "s")

Thomas Louis, b. 5 Mar, bp. 8 Mar 1718/9

François, b. 2 Jul, bp. 24 Jul 1720; m. Helen Provoost

REF: AUSTIN, Mary Stanislas, *Philip Freneau, Poet of the Revolution* (NY, 1901); SEACORD, Morgan H., *Biographical Sketches & Index of Huguenot Settlers of New Rochelle, 1687-1776* (New Rochelle, NY, 1941); WITTMEYER, Alfred V., *Registers of the Births, Marriages, & Deaths of the Église Françoise à Nouvelle York*; HORNOR, William S., *This Old Monmouth of Ours* (Freehold, NJ, 1932); BOYER, Carl,3rd, *Ship Passenger Lists NY & NJ (1600-1825)* (Newhall, CA, 1978).

FREY, Heinrich

> b. c. 1652, Altheim, Alsace, FR, on the Bickenalbe River, <u>now</u> in GER, s.w. of Zweibrücken & a few km.
>> n.w. of Ormersviller, which is in the Moselle Dépt., Lorraine, FR; *poss.* s/o Jacob & Anna
>> (Hirtzeller) Frey

> 1675 - emigrated to NY; said to have been the 1st German Huguenot settler in America

> a. 1680 - arr Philadelphia; he was a turner (one who formed articles, such as dishes or tools, with a lathe)

> 12 Oct 1685- arr Germantown, PA, as the servant of Gerhard Hendricks

> m. 26 Apr 1692, Mennonite Meeting House, Germantown, PA, Anna Catherine Levering (b. Mar 1676,
>> Mülheim-an-der-Ruhr, s.w. of Essen), d/o Wigard & Magdalena (Boker) Levering; lived lot #18,
>> corner of Walnut Lane & Germantown Rd.

> 1692 - settled Roxborough, Philadelphia Co, PA, where he purchased 100 acres; lived there until 1713
>> when he moved to Towamencin Twp., Montgomery Co, PA

> d. 1734 (aged 81 yrs.); bur. Frey Cemetery, Frederick Twp, Montgomery Co, PA where there is a large
>> stone marker

CHLDREN:

Jacob[2], b. 1694; m. Margaret X; he d. c. 1757, Hanover Twp, PA

William[2], b. c.1695; m. Anna Veronica Markle; he d. 15 Jun 1763, bur. Bertolet Cem., Frederick Twp,
> Montgomery Co, PA; his son **Jacob**[3] m. Susanna Bertolet, d/o <u>Jean & Susanna (Harcourt) Bertolet</u>

Henry[2], b. 1698; m. Christina Tunnis; he d. p. 1763

Abraham[2], b. c. 1700; m. XX; d. Chester Co, PA

John[2], b. 1703; m. Maria Keisler/Keyser; d. 23 Oct 1766, bur. Franconia Mennonite Cem, Montgomery
> Co, PA

George[2], b. 1705; d. 1750

Benjamin[2], b. 1707; m. Christina Anne X; liv. Cedar Creek, VA; d. a. 6 Nov 1753, wp, Frederick Co, VA;
> will mentions his wife, **7 sons, 2 daus**

Rebecca[2], d. unmarr.

Elizabeth[2], b. 1717; m. c. 1732, Dr. Johannes Muller; she d. 1758

Amelia Elizabeth[2], b. 1 Jul 1719; m. 2/10 Jun 1737, Frederick Leinback

REF: LEVERING, Col. John, *Levering Family History & Genealogy* (1897); *Historical Sketches of Montgomery Co, PA*, Vol. IV (1910); HUMPHREY, John T., *Early Families of Northampton Co, PA*, Vol. I (1991) ; FRY, Sarah Elizabeth, *Heinrich Frey's History* ; JONES, Horatio Gates, *The Levering Family* (1893) .

G

GABEAU, Anthony

b. 1756, nr. Eymet, Aquitaine, FR, s.w. Bergerac, s/o Pierre Antoine Gabeau of Bordeaux

Apr 1764 – arr. SC, from Plymouth, ENG; had left FR with Huguenot minister Rev. Jean Louis Gilbert; went 1st to Abbeville Settlement/New Bordeaux; settled Charleston w/ his mother, p. death of his father

c. 1774 - joined Rev. War; Sgt in the "The True Blues"

m. 23 Sep 1778, St. Philip's Parish, Charleston, SC, Elizabeth Brinkley Henley (Jun 1755-6 Jun 1841), grd/o Thomas Henley of Co. Middlesex, ENG

d. 11 Feb 1829, Charleston, SC, aged 71

CHILDREN, b. SC :

James[2], b. 1780; d. 15 Jun 1820, aged 40Y 11M, bur. Huguenot Ch Yard, Charleston

Elizabeth[2], d. 30 May/6 Jun 1841

Anthony[2], b. c. 1784; d. 30 Mar 1823, age 39; bur. Huguenot Ch Yard, Charleston

Samuel[2]

John[2]

Mary Hannah[2], b. 1795; m. 1 Sep 1808, Charleston, John Hancock Willis, a Charleston merchant; she d. 19 Apr 1864

Simon[2]

Benjamin[2]

Daniel[2], b. 1793; m. and had ch; d. 6 Dec 1821, age 28Y 6M 11D, bur. Huguenot Ch Yard, Charleston

Susannah[2], b. 4 Sep 1796; m. X Evans; she d. Dec 1845

REF: FISCHER, David, compiler, *Transactions of the Huguenot Society of SC*; *The SC Magazine of Ancestral Research*, Vol. V, #3 (Summer, 1977); HOLCOMB, Brent H., compiler, *Marriage & Death Notices from the (Charleston)Times, 1800-1821*(Baltimore, 1979); Death records, Charleston ; SMITH, D.E. Huger & SALLEY, A.S., Jr., editors, *Register of St. Philip's Parish, 1754-1810* (Charleston, SC, 1927) ; List of the Names of the Abbeville Settlement in *Transactions of the Huguenot Society of SC*, #5 (Charleston, 1897); *Transactions of the Huguenot Society of SC*, #75 (Charleston, 1970), #88 (1983), #89 (1984).

GACHET/GASHET, Henri/Henry

b. c. 1675, FR (date based on age stated in will)

1695/97 - to America w/ bro David from La Rochelle; Henri settled Dighton, MA; they were boat builders; David went to Raynham, Bristol, MA, & used the surname GUSHEE – he m. 12 Jun 1705, Taunton, Alice Godfrey (b. 20 Aug 1680), d/o Richard & Mary (Richmond) Godfrey; Henri's surname became **GAISHET, GASHET, GASHITT, GASHEL**, his sons used **GASSETT**

m. 2 Sep 1697, Taunton, Bristol, MA, Sarah Haskins/Hoskins (b. 31 Aug 1679, Taunton), *poss.* d/o William & Sarah (Caswell) Haskins/Hoskins; Sarah said to have been a native of ENG but no proof

d. p. 8 Mar 1737/8, wd-a. 18 Apr 1738, wp, Bristol Co, MA; called a "yeoman" in his will

CHILDREN (listed in Henry's will):

Daniel[2], m. Hannah Walker; liv. Hopkinton, MA - 3 sons bp. there bet 29 Mar 1747-26 Jul 1750; **12 ch**

Sarah[2], m. X Pitts

Abigail[2], m. X Jones

Mercy[2], m. X Perry, bro/o John, who m. Elizabeth Gachet

Hannah[2], m. c. 1728, Jasiel Smith (b. c. 1700), s/o Samuel & Hester/Ester (Caswell) Smith; she d. c. 1755/57, 12 days p. d. of husband, who was a blacksmith; **10 ch**

Martha[2], m. 24 May 1733, Taunton, Robert Crossman; she d. 2 Oct 1762, Taunton, he d. 6 Jul 1799, Taunton; **issue**

Elizabeth[2], m. 15 Jun 1732, Swansea, Bristol, MA, John Perry (d. 8 Nov 1777, Taunton, aged 72); **issue**

Susannah[2], m. 7 Nov 1738, Taunton, Ephraim Tisdale; he prob. d. 8 Dec 1778, Taunton; **issue**

Isaac[2], d. aged 18/19

REF: CARVER, Fred E. & Margaret, *Genealogy of the Rev. Eleazer Carver Family* (1971) ; VR – Taunton, Swansea; "Genealogy of Henri Gachet" in *NEHG Register*, Vol. I (Boston, 1847); extract from a sermon given by Rev. George L. Thompson of Dighton on 23 Sep 1928, printed by the Old Colony Historical Society in Taunton.

GAILLARD, Jean/Jehan

bp. 29 Nov 1592, Reformed Ch, Montpellier, Languedoc, FR, 8th ch of Jean & Anne (Gervaise) Gaillard; fa was a *chaussetier* (hosier)

m. Montpellier, Marie Vincens, prob. d/o Joachim Vincens

d. 13 Nov 1663, Montpellier

CHILDREN:

Joachim[2], b. 19 Jul, bp. 20 Jul 1625, Montpellier; m. 24 Feb 1663/4, Montpellier, Esther Paparel, d/o Jean & Catherine (Bollioud) Paparel of Lyon, France; to SC, a. 10 Oct 1687, settled nr. Charleston; naturalized, 1696, Santee, SC; marr. record says Esther's fa was Jean, other "records" say André;

he d. 1711; in Montpellier, he was called a *"receveur des gabelles"* - receiver or collector of the salt taxes

CHILDREN:

Simond[3], b. 1664; d. Jul 1669

Bartholomew[3], b. a. 1667; m. Elizabeth X (m/2, 26 Mar 1718/19, Jonathan Skrine); he d. p. 15 Jul 1718, wd, SC

CHILDREN:

Frederick[4], b. a. 1705; m. a. 18 Jul 1736, Elizabeth Guerry (who m/2 Henry Varnor, m/3 Isaac Rembert, Sr.); he a.1741; **no issue**

Theodore[4], b. 1710; m/1, a. 4 Mar 1735, Elizabeth Serré, d/o Noë & Catherine (Challion) Serré – **6 ch**; m/2, Lydia Peyre (1720-1785), d/o David & Judith (Boisseau) Peyre – **3 ch**; he d. a. 7 Jul 1781, wp

Hélène/Eleanor[4], unmarr.

Alcimus[4], b. a. 1716; m/1, Sarah Belin, d/o James & Sarah (Torquet) Belin – **2 ch**; m/2, 28 Jul 1744, Elizabeth Gendron, d/o John & Elizabeth (Mazyck) Gendron – **1 ch** (she m/2 Joseph Palmer); he d. 1759

Tacitus[4], b. a. 1718; m. a. Jun 1744, Anna LeGrand (d. p. 1763), d/o Isaac & Anne (Bruneau) Le Grand, d/o Henry & Marianne (X) Bruneau – Anne was the adopted dau/o Jacques LeGrand de Lomboy & wife Ann François; 1778/9, to LA or MS; **6 ch**

Jean/John[3], b. a. 1669, Montpellier; m/1, c. 1699, Susanne (LeSerrurier) Giguilliat, d/o James & Elizabeth (Léger) LeSerrurier, widow of Jean François Gignilliat – poss **4 ch**, definitely a dau **Susanne**[4]; m/2, Mary Esther Page (who m/2, James Kinloch); he d. 19 Feb 1716/7

CHILDREN, m/1:

Susanne[4], b. c. 1700; m. Feb 1716, James Nicholson Mayrant (d. 1727); she d. p. 16 Sep 1735, wd; **issue**

John[4]

Esther[4], m. James Crokatt, s/o Charles Crokatt of Edinburgh, SCOT; **issue**

Elizabeth[4]

Pierre/Pierre[3], b. Montpellier; d. c. 1710; **no issue**

Jean[2], bp. 1 Nov 1627, Montpellier

Marie[2], bp. 17 Dec 1633; m. 30 Jan 1676, Jean Bonneterre

Pierre[2], bp. 30 Nov 1639, Montpellier; a merchant of drugs & chemicals, m. 31 Jan 1666, Montpellier, Isabeau Imbert, d/o Isaac & Isabeau (Carquet) Imbert; some confusion here, one source says Jean bap. on that date, but the marriage record clearly states **Pierre**, s/o Jean & Marie

Marguerite[2], m. 20 Jun 1666, Claude Perdiguer

REF: MACDOWELL, Dorothy K., *Gaillard Genealogy, Descendants of Joachim Gaillard & Esther Paparel* (Aiken, SC, 1974); "Early Generations of the Gaillard Family" in the *Transactions of the Huguenot Society of SC*, #44 (1939); WEBBER, Mabel L., "Gaillard Notes" in the *SC Historical & Gen. Magazine*, Vol. 39 (1938); Correspondance from the Bibliothèque de la Ville et du Musée Fabre, Montpellier, FR + ch records, French Reformed Ch in Montpellier; *SC Genealogies,* Vol. II (Spartanburg, 1983).

GAILLARD/GAYLORD, Nic(h)olas II

b. FR, poss. Normandie, s/o Nicolas Galiard I, who was naturalized 16 Apr 1537, London, "from the
   dominion of the King of France"
m. Johan/Joan X (who m/2, Giles Alvin/Alvyn); she d. a. 17 Aug 1572, wp, bur. Pitminster, ENG, which
   is s.w. of Taunton
16 Apr 1540 - naturalized ENG "from dominion of the King of France"
d. a. 8 Apr 1546, wp, bur. Pitminster, Somerset, ENG
CHILDREN, surnamed **GAYLARD**:
Hugh[2], bp. 1546; m. poss. Alice X (bur. 17 Feb 1628/9, Pitminster); he was bur. 21 Oct 1614, Pitminster
   CHILDREN (all bp. Pitminster):
   Catherine[3], bp. 26 Sep 1576
   Elizabeth[3], bp. 30 Apr 1581; m. 13 Aug 1617, Tobias Barrett
   George[3], bp. 20 Sep 1583; m/1, Margery X (bur. 11 Feb 1628/29) m/2, Elizabeth X; he d. a. 1 Jun
      1667, wp; total of **7 ch**
   Edmund[3], m. 16 May 1615, Joan Crosse (bur. 12 Jul 1649); bur. 10 Nov 1661, wp, 18 Apr 1663; **5
      ch**
   Richard[3], bp. 1 Apr 1591; m/1, 22 Apr 1616, Mary Pococke (?) (bur. 12 May 1616/7), m/2, 24   Sep
      1617, Martha Bennett (bur. 10 Oct 1648); he was bur. 26 Mar 1656; **11 ch**
   Alice/Alis[3], bp. 10 May 1594; m. 27 Apr 1615, Richard Trott/Treat (bp. 28 Aug 1584 Pitminster-
      a. 3 Mar 1669/70, wp, Wethersfield, CT); emigrated to America; Alice d. a. 3 Mar 1670, CT,
      prob. Wethersfield; Richard was the Gov. of CT: **10 ch**
Christopher[2], m. 19 Nov 1575, Elizabeth Pase/Pare (bur. 21 Nov 1625); he was bur. 6 Mar 1660/01
   CHILDREN:
   John[3], bp. 7 Sep 1578; m. XX; bur. 4 Apr 1641; at least 1 dau **Antis**[4] (bp. 28 Jan 1604/5)
   Alice[3], bp. 4 Mar 1579/80; bur. 23 Sep 1591
   William[3], bp. 20 Jun 1582
   Mary[3], bp. 30 May 1585
   Luce[3], bp. 2 Feb 1588/9; m. 25 Oct 1614, Edward Mead/Meare of Dinicott – not found, could
      mean Dinnington, s.e. of Pitminster
   Joan/Jane[3], bp. 14 Mar 1590/1; m. 8 Sep 1614, Richard Scadding of Pitminster
William[2], m. X Manley; d. a. 1572; at least 2 daus **Mary**[3], **Elizabeth**[3] (minors in 1572)
Elizabeth[2], m. 9 Nov 1572, John Bullpaine, poss. her 2nd husband; said to have m. Hugh Luddon
John[2], b. a. 1546; m. 15 Jun 1572, Jane Wallin (bur. 5 Jun 1589); he was bur. 26 May 1607,
      Drayton, ENG, n.e. of Pitminster
   CHILDREN:
   Agnes[3], bp. 5 Dec 1574
   John[3], bp. 6 Oct 1577
   Joan[3], bp. 16 Oct 1579
   William[3], bp. 11 Mar 1582; m/1, 11 Jun 1617, Long Sutton, Somerset, Jane Ashwood, m/2, Mary
      Walter; **9 ch**; said to have gone to America on the *Mary and John* with his bro John who
      returned to ENG, 1630; Wm. went to Windsor, CT, where he d 20 Jul 1673, age 88; wife d. 20
      Jun 1657; 5 ch b. ENG
Ede/Edith[2], bp. 19 May 1588; m. 8 Apr 1619, John Sealy
Mary[2]
Edmund[2], m. 22 Nov 1574, Margaret Langham/Langhorn (bur. 14 Jun 1610); Edmund bur. 9 Jun 1614

CHILDREN:
Joan[3], d. young
Joan[3], bp. 28 Nov 1576
Valentine[3], bp. 7 Mar 1577/78
Honor[3], bp. 8 Nov 1579; m. 15 Jun 1616, Bartholomew Gidding
Robert[3], bp. 14 Nov 1580; bur. 21 Jul 1590

REF: GAYLORD, Benjamin H., *"The English Ancestry of Deacon William Gaylord, New Light & Observations"* in *The American Genealogist,* Vol. 58, #4 (Oct 1982); *"Clues from English Archives Contributory to American Genealogy"* in the *NY Gen. & Biog. Record,* Vol. 16 (1910); *Letters of Denization & Acts of Naturalization for Aliens in England, 1509-1603,* in the *Publication of the Huguenot Society of London,* Vol. 8 (1893); Ch. records, Pitminster.

GA(I)NEAU/GENEAU/GANO, Étienne

b. c. 1630. FR, father *poss.* the Étienne Gaineau who d. 1658, La Rochelle, aged 68; the latter was said to have been from the village Puilboreau, just n.e. of La Rochelle; a Marie Geneau bur. La Rochelle, 13 Jun 1682, aged 72 – *poss.* his mother

m. 16 Mar 1653, La Rochelle, FR, Lydie Mestereau; they leased a house on Rue Les Cloustiers in La Rochelle; signed lease Étienne Gayneau; he was a merchant & *poêlier* (stovemaker)

fled La Rochelle, FR; sailed 9 May 1661, from Amsterdam in *De Bever* which arr at Manhattan on 29 Jul 1661 - listed as *Estiene Genejoy,* from Rochelle, wife + 3 ch - 7, 3, ½ yrs old; he was often called *Étienne Rochelle* in early records

29 Apr 1662 - purchased property in New Amsterdam

15 Jul 1670 - bought house and lot on Broadway; 22 Apr 1672, he and Lydia bought another on *Bever Graft*

1675- in Harlem; by 1676, on Staten Island where he was granted 80 acres of land "near the commons"

d. bet. 1680-1709, Staten Island, NY; both Étienne & Lydia were liv. in 1680 in Richmond Co, (Staten Island), NY

CHILDREN:
Stephen, Jr.[2], bp. 29 May 1654, La Rochelle; m. a. 21 Apr 1680, Susannah V(e)sleton, d/o Francis V(e)sleton I, of Staten Island; **13 ch**; at least 4 are known to have marr.:
    Daniel[3], b. 1681; m. Sarah Britton, d/o Nathaniel Britton; liv. Hopewell, NJ, 1763; **8 ch**
    James[3], m/1, Eleanor (Fouke?); m/2, Jane Owen; m/3, Mary O'Rouk; **issue**
    Francis[3], b. 1686; m. Judith (X) Bernard, widow of Samuel or Thomas Bernard of New Rochelle; they settled there
    Louis[3], m. Anna Cisneau, had dau **Susanna**[4], bp. 20 Apr 1729, Port Richmond, Staten Island
Louis[2], d. 1658, La Rochelle, FR
Lidie Marie[2], bp. 6 Jan 1658, La Rochelle; m. X de Boer?
Marie Madeleine/Mary[2], bp. 17 Oct 1660, Amsterdam
Sarah[2], bp. 4 Feb 1663, Reformed Dutch Ch, NYC; m. c. 1687, Jean Mambru/Membru/Manbrut/Membrut; 5 sons – **Étienne**[3], b. 20 Oct, bp. 14 Nov 1688, d. young ; **Élie**[3], b. 15 Aug, bp. 16 Aug 1691 m. Susanne X – **issue**; **Étienne**[3], (twin) b. 22 Jan, bp. 28 Jan 1693/4 ; **Ezéchiel**[3], b. 16 Dec, bp. 27 Dec 1696 ; **François**[3], b. 20 Aug, bp. 1 Sep 1700; 2 daus - **Lidie**[3], (twin) b. 22 Jan, bp. 28 Jan 1693/4; **Sarra**[3], b. 13 Sep, bp. 3 Oct 1703- all ch bap. FR Ch, NYC

NOTE: In the *Denman Family History* by Mrs. H. N. Harris, reference is made to a Francis Gerneaux who has been misidentified as Étienne; Francis had a son Jeremiah & a dau Mary who m. John Denman; John Denman's will mentions wife Mary and bro-in-law Jeremiah Gannugh (*sic*) of Flushing; John and Mary Denman's 1st ch (of 7ch) was b. 1700 when Mary Gano, d/o Étienne, would have been 40.

REF: FURNAM, Consuelo, "Identity of Susannah, wife of Stephen Gano, Jr. of Staten Island" in *The American Genealogist*, Vol. XIX, #1 (Jul 1942); LEMASTER, Howard M., *Gano Family, USA* (Carlinville, IL, 1970); BANTA, Theodore M., *Year Book of the Holland Society of NY, 1902*; RIKER, James, *Harlem, Its Origins & Early Annals* (NY, 1881); CHANCE, F. Gano, *Chance & Allied Families* (NY, 1949); info from Archives, La Rochelle, FR; WITTMEYER, Alfred V., *Registers of the Births, Marriages, & Deaths of the Église Françoise à Nouvelle York*.

GALLAUDET, Pierre Elisée

b. Mauzé, in the old province of Aunis, FR, now Mauzé-sur-le-Mignon, Deux-Sèvres Dépt, Poitou-Charentes, n.e. of Rochefort; s/o Joshua & Margaret (Prioleau) Gallaudet; Margaret was the d/o Élisée Prioleau, minister of Exoudun (1649-1663), n.e. of Niort

m. Jane X

by 1711 - to New Rochelle, NY

1726 - bought land in New Rochelle

d. p. 1 Mar 1732 NY; he was a doctor

CHILDREN:

Peter[2], colonel in Rev. War

Elisha[2], m/1, c. 1755, Jeane DuBois, m/2, 24 Nov 1770, Naemoe Reade (?)

Jean[?], b. 3 Jul, bp. 17 Aug 1720

Susanna[2], b. 2 Sep 1721, bp. 1 Jan 1721/2

Hester[2], m. 1756, Reuben Oliver, 1st ch bp. New Rochelle; **issue**

Thomas[2], b. 1724/25, New Rochelle; m. 1753, Catherine Edgar (1725-bur. Dec 1774, Woodbridge, NJ); he d. c. 1772/74, NYC, age 48; **issue**

Leah[2], m. 7 Feb 1759, Joshua T. de St. Croix

Paul[2], m. 21 Jan 1765, Anna Hazard

David[2], m. 7 May 1776, Rebecca Banks

REF: HAYDEN, Horace E., "The Gallaudets of New Rochelle, NY" in the *NY Gen. & Biog. Record*, Vol. 19 (Jul 1888); BAIRD, Charles W., *History of the Huguenot Emigration to America*, Vol. I.

GARCELON, Pierre

b. 1685, Clermont, FR; there are 19 Clermonts in FR, in various forms; one source says that the family was from Auvergne, if so, his birthplace is Clermont-Ferrand

educated for the priesthood but converted; later became rector of St. Pierre duBois Protestant Episcopal Church, Isle of Guernsey, 1739-1772

m/1, Jeanne Bedat, a native of the Charterons Dist of Bordeaux (n.e. part of the city, on the left bank of the Garonne River), d/o Jean & Petronille (Léger) Bedat; she d. c. Mar 1742 (dau Louise outlived her mother by 5Y 4½ M, according to Pierre)

m/2, Annie Carey

said to have had 11 ch but James[2] (below) was his only son, according to his monument in the Garcelon Cemetery, Lewiston, ME, located on River Road

d. 16 Sep 1772, Guernsey

CHILDREN, m/1:

Louise[2], b. 4 Feb 1735/6; d. 25 Jul 1747, Guernsey, aged 11Y 5M 21D

James[2], b. 4 Apr 1739, Guernsey; m. 29 Feb 1760, Gloucester, MA, Deliverance Annis (7 Nov 1735, Gloucester-16 Nov 1828, Lewiston), d/o Curmac & Mary (Chase) Annis – Curmac was from Enniskillen, on Loch Erne in N.IRE; James left Guernsey for ENG for schooling; 1752, to America as a cabin boy; he was apprenticed to Capt. Daniel Gibbs at Gloucester; 1773, went to Falmouth (n. of Portland), ME and liv. there until the night bef the British Commander Mowatt burned that town; family went to Harriseeket (now Freeport), to Lewiston Falls in 1776, where their last ch was born; he established the 1st ferry across the Androscoggin River c. 1778; he d. 13 Nov 1813, Lewiston, ME; he was a mariner.

CHILDREN (1st 5 ch all b. in Gloucester, MA):

James[3], bp. 6 Sep 1761; m/1, Elizabeth Dyer, m/2, Jeannette Pettingill; he d. 28 Dec 1851, Lewiston

William[3], b. 2 Jul 1763; m. 2 Mar 1784, Maria Harris; he d. 20 Jan 1851, Lewiston

Peter[3], bp. 14 Jul 1765; m. Katherine Millbanks; he d. 19 Jun 1827, Lewiston

Daniel[3], b. 5 Feb 1768; m. Polly Parker; he d. 15 Nov 1798, Lewiston

Mark[3], b. 22 1771; m/1, 10 Oct 1792 Hannah Ames, m/2, Mrs. Elizabeth Field; he d. 27 Dec 1830, Lewiston

Lucy[3], b. 27 Sep 1773, Falmouth; m. 19 Jan 1792, Ezra Ames; d. 4 Mar 1851

Sally[3], b. 27 Jun 1776, Lewiston, ME; m. Robert Moody; d. 4 Sep 1776

REF: deGARIS, Marie, *The Story of St. Pierre duBois Church Guernsey;* Vital Records, Gloucester, MA; JORDAN, Eloise, "Garcelon Cemetery" in the Lewiston, ME *Journal* (11 Jan 1947); *Maine Families in 1790* Vol. 1 (ME Gen. Society).

GARNIER, Daniel

b. Île de Ré, FR, s/o Daniel & Marie (Chevallier) Garnier

m. Elizabeth Fanton

1685 - left FR for SC w/ wife, 6 ch & his sis-in-law Rachel Fanton

on the *Liste des François et Suisses* who settled in Charleston originally

1696 - listed as an inhabitant of Santee, SC; he was a merchant

CHILDREN (all b. Île de Ré):

Étienne/Stephen[2]

Elizabeth[2], m. c. 23 Aug 1692 (date of marr bond) SC, Daniel Horry, *prob.* bro/o Élias Horry; he d. a. 1696

CHILDREN, b. SC:

Elizabeth Mary[3], m. 8 Aug 1713, St. Thomas & St. Denis Parish, SC, Charles Lewis

Lidie[3]

Mary[3], m. 28 Aug 1714, St. Thomas & St. Denis Parish, SC, John Laroche

Rachel[2]

Marguerite[2]

Anne[2]

REF: GREGG, John M., *Early PeeDee Settlers,* Part One (Bowie, MD, 1993); BAIRD, Charles W., *History of the Huguenot Emigration to America* (Baltimore, MD); *Transactions of the Huguenot Society of SC;* SMALLWOOD, Grahame Thomas, Jr., *French Refugees in SC.*

GARNIER, Isaac

b. prob. Île de Ré, FR; relationship to Daniel, above, if any, is not known

a. 1692 - fled LaRochelle to ENG

1692 – member of the FR Ch, NYC; witness at a wedding there, 27 Apr 1692

m. a. Mar 1692/3, Elizabeth Doublet, d/o Jean & Marie (X) Doublet

1695 – made a freeman of NYC; he was a cordwainer

d. p. 7 Jul 1727, wd, NYC

CHILDREN (all bap. French Ch, NYC):

Elizabeth[2], b. 19 Mar, bp. 20 Mar 1692/3

Isaac[2], b. 13 Jun, bp. 20 Jun 1694; d. young

Marie[2], b. 13 Sep, bp. 22 Sep 1695

François[2], b. 3 Jan, bp. 9 Jan 1697/8; m. Anna Sicard, d/o <u>Jacques & Anne (Terrier) Sicard</u>; 1st of family to New Rochelle; went to Mamaroneck in 1721; 1729, to Rockland Co, NY, purchasing lot #6 in Conklin's Range in the Kakiat Patent, Town of Ramapo; joined the Dutch Ch at Tappan; this family later used surname **GURNEE**

Susanne[2], b. 4 May, bp. 15 May 1700; d. young

Isaac[2], b. 23 Aug, bp. 8 Sep 1702; m. Marie Machfiedt/Machfet/Manswell/Maxwell (all names appear in various baptismal records)

> CHILDREN (all bap. French Ch, NYC):
> **Elizabeth**[3], b. 5 Feb, bp. 8 Feb 1737/8
> **Anne**[3], b. 19 Jul, bp. 25 Jul 1739
> **Susanne**[3], b. 5 Mar, bp. 18 Mar 1741
> **Isaac**[3], b. 12 Jan, bp. 19 Jan 1743; m. Elizabeth Fletcher, had son **Isaac** b. 9 Feb, bp. 13 Mar 1774 French Ch, NYC
> **Louis**[3], b. 24 Oct, bp. 26 Oct 1748

Jean[2], b. 7 Aug, bp. 8 Aug 1705

Susanne[2], b. 14 Jun, bp. 23 Jun 1714

REF: HERMAN, Clayton J., *The Book of Joyce June Herman* (Rochester, NY, 1934); WITTMEYER, Alfred V., *Register of the Births, Marriages & Deaths of the Église Française à la Nouvelle York, 1688-1804* (Baltimore, 1968); SEACORD, Morgan H., *Biographical Sketches & Index of the Huguenot Settlers of New Rochelle, 1687-1776* (New Rochelle, NY, 1961); BAIRD, Charles W., *History of the Huguenot Emigration to America* (Baltimore, 1990); "The Marriage Bond of Daniel Horry & Elizabeth Garnier in *Transactions of the Huguenot Society of SC*, Vol. 32 (1927).

GAR(R)ARD, Pierre/Peter

b. c. 1660, FR

c. 1685 - to ENG with 2 young sons, one *perhaps* named Anthony

8 May 1687 - naturalized ENG

2 sons[2], one b. c. 1686, m. c. 1711; one b. c. 1688, m. c. 1714

apparently Pierre/Peter & his 2 sons remained in ENG; his grsons emigrated

> CHILDREN of 1 unnamed son[2]:
> **William**[3], b. c. 1715, ENG; in Stafford Co, VA, by 14 Apr 1781, when he was a lieutenant in the Stafford Co. Militia; <u>m/1</u>,Mary Lewis, <u>m/2</u>, Mary Naughty, <u>m/3</u>, p. 1760, Elizabeth Moss; he d. a. 12 Feb 1787, wp, Stafford Co; will mentions wife Elizabeth & his 4 younger ch; gives some sm. items to James, Mary Anne, grdau Elizabeth Mountjoy
> CHILDREN, m/1:
> **Daniel**[4], b. 1736
> **James**[4], b. 14 Jan 1749, Stafford Co; m. 20 Dec 1769, Elizabeth Mountjoy; served as a colonel in the VA Militia in the Rev. War; 1783, went to Bourbon Co, KY; became the 2nd governor of KY; he d. 19 Jan 1822
> **Mary Anne**[4], b. 1753; m. Col. John Montjoy; **issue**
> CHILDREN, m/2 (*prob.* all 4):
> **William**[4] – inherited father's land in KY; named as executor of father's will
> **Henry**[4]
> **Robert**[4]
> **Eleanor**[4], m. & had **issue**
> **J. (poss. Gerard)**[3]
> CHILDREN of the other son (Anthony?)[2]:
> **Robert**[3], b. c. 1720, ENG; to VA; d. NC or SC; **issue**
> **John**[3], b. c. 1725, ENG, went w/ bros to VA, then to SC, GA; settled Wilkes Co, GA; <u>m/1</u>, c. 1758, Mary Bolt of SC who d. c. 1805, <u>m/2</u>, Elizabeth X; moved to Jones Co, GA c. 1805; he d. Mar 1807, GA; **issue**

        Jacob[3], b. c. 1730, ENG; to VA c. 1750 w/bros; liv. Stafford Co, VA, later went to NC; he was killed in the Rev. War along with 2 sons; **issue**

REF: KNIGHT, Lucien L., *Georgia's Bicentennial Memories & Memories,* Vol. 3 (Atlanta, 1920); des COGNETS, Anna Russell, *Governor Garrard of KY, His Descendants & Relatives* (1898, 1962); *The Huguenot,* Pub. #18 (1957/59).

GARRIGUES, Jacques

m. Elizabeth de Barthes

was a judge in Nages in the Parish of Castres, n.e. of Mazamet, owner of noble estates of la Devéze, la Grifouléde, Naujac & Montégut, then all in Languedoc; believed in the Reformation but gave his consent to have his ch. raised as Catholics; his consent was forced as he was threatened with the loss of properties & prerogatives of a noble; his decision drove his wife into exile in the Netherlands

1632 - Elizabeth Garrigues, Jacques' wife, was accepted into the Walloon Reformed Ch in The Hague

he d. 1649/52, FR

CHILDREN:

Jean[2], called Jean de Garrigues-la Devéze; m. Marie de Franchimont; he was a Protestant minister, liv. Périgord, FR; Périgord is a former province in FR, now in the Dordogne Dépt, Aquitaine; 1685, went to The Hague/den Haag; family became members of the FR Reformed Ch in The Hague; 31 Aug 1685, Marie renounced her "Calvinist heresies" – she identified herself as the "widow of Jean Garrigue"; he d. 28 Sep 1682, NETH

CHILDREN:

Rachel[3], m. Preacher X Mathurin; **3 ch**

François[3], b. FR; m. The Hague, Marguerite deQuenet/Duguenois; to West Indies 1713/14, then to Philadelphia, PA; d. Philadelphia; **3 ch, line extinct**

Mathurin[3], b. 1679 Languedoc, FR; m. 28 May 1702, at The Hague, Suzanna Roche(t) (bur. 30 Sep 1746, Christ Episcopal Ch, Philadelphia); 1712/3, to the West Indies then to Philadelphia, bur. 6 Sep 1726, Christ Episcopal Ch, 5th & Arch St., Philadelphia

CHILDREN:

Margaret Jeanne[4], b. 1 Jan 1702/3

François Philippe[4], bp. 29 Oct 1704, Rotterdam; m/1, Ann X– **7 ch**, m/2, 1 Jan 1747, Mary Knowles – 1 son **Francis**[5]; bur. 3 Feb or 16 Mar 1783, Christ Ch, Philadelphia

Pierre[4], b. 1709; m. Sarah X – 4 daus **Mary**[5], **Sarah**[5], **Susanna**[5], **Hannah**[5]; bur. 6 Jul 1746

Matthew[4], b. 1712, St. Kitts, W. Indies; served in British Army at Albany, 1746-47; was a cooper; moved to SC; **issue**

Isaac[4], b. 1715, Philadelphia; m/1, 1732, Philadelphia MM, Christian Boradgate – **Isaac**[5], **Sarah**[5], m/2, Sarah Powell – **Elizabeth**[5], m. 12 Feb 1766, William Smith – **7 ch**

Jacob[4], b. 1716, Philadelphia; m. Sarah X (1720-18 Jul 1777); served in Rev. War; at least **8 ch -** 4 of his sons were in the Rev. War; d. 12 May 1798, Rockaway, Morris Co, NJ, bur. Morristown

Samuel[4], b. 12 Feb 1718

John[4], b. 1720

Abraham[4], b. 1722

Pierre[3], member of Reformed Ch, Amsterdam, 26 Jan 1739; departed for London; d. with **no issue**

Moyse[2], liv. Mazamet, Languedoc, now in Tarn Dépt, Midi Pyrénées, n.e. of Carcassonne; m. Justine Wacher; he was a goldsmith; 1685, to Brandenburg (Old Prussia – a margraviate & electorate, which later become the kingdom of Prussia); he d. 8 Oct 1715

Pierre[2], m/1, Esther Raynal, m/2, Isabeau Martel; liv. Mazamet; c. 1700, went to the Duchy of Orange where he d. c. 1713/4; his widow & 3 youngest ch moved to Magdeburg to be with Jacques[3]

CHILD, m/1:

Jacques[3], b. 1677, Mazamet; went with his uncle Moyse to Brandenburg & he was apprenticed to become a goldsmith; m. 18 Oct 1707, Marguerite Nicolas (1686-Sep 1726), from Grenoble, d/o Jean Nicolas, a doctor and lawyer; 28 Oct 1707, rec. citizenship in the FR colony; he inherited his uncle's business & house in Magdeburg; became mayor of Magdeburg and a prominent citizen; he d. 1730; they had **14 ch**, half of whom d. young

CHILDREN :

Moyse[4], b. 9 Sep 1708, Magdeburg; took over his father's business; m. 1731, Wilhemine-Henriette Serres (c. 1711-Aug 1795), d/o FR refugees Guillaume & Marie (Barabon) Serres, Calvinists who liv. in Berlin; became a leading citizen; he d. 1 Feb 1750 - **9 ch**, incl: his eldest son **Guillaume**[5] took over the business and he d. Apr 1763; bro **Antoine-Henri**[5] (30 Dec 1747-1826) took over the business when Guillaume d., he went to Halle on the River Saale & joined the FR congregation at Mortizburg, m. 7 Jun 1781, Magdeburg, Marie-Henriette-Suzanne du Vigneau (d. 26 Jan 1838, Copenhagen), d/o Prussian Councilor of Warfare & "demesne" Jean-Isaac du Vigneau - **9 ch**, incl. **Jean-Antoine-Henri**[6] (18 Jul 1782-5 Aug 1857), Portuguese General Consul at Copenhagen who m. 3 Apr 1814, Maria Dorothea (Nanette) Palmié (6 May 1796-24 Jan 1854), **Jacques-Louis**[6] (19 Jan 1789-8 Oct 1854), Danish Consul General at Havana, Cuba, who m. 9 Dec 1818, Cécile Olivia Duntzfelt (9 Nov 1798-9 May 1863) - issue, **Charles-George-Ferdinand**[6] (27 Sep 1791-31 May 1853), merchant at Dresden who m. Eugénie Messmer (15 Nov 1804-15 Nov 1877)

Justine-Élisabeth[4], b. 1710-d. young 1712; **Antoine**[4], d. young, 1712; **Jean-Frédéric**[4], d. young 1713; **Étienne**[4], b. c. 1714-d. 1719; **Marie**[4], b. 22 Aug 1715, m. in Berlin, Pastor August Friedrich Wilhelm Sack; **Jacques**[4], b. Aug 1716, jeweler & goldsmith, d. Jun 1742; **Anne**[4], d. young, 1718; **Jean-Claude**[4], b. 1719- d. 1720; **Jeanne**[4], b. 1720-d. 1721; **Justine-Marguerite**[4], 28 Jul 1721, m. Isaac Abraham Schwartz; **Charlotte- Frédéric**[4], b. 2 May 1723, m/1, 1740, Privy Councilor Jean Frédéric Manzelius, m/2, 1754, Colony Director & FR Judge in Magdeburg, Jean-Daniel Kessler, she d. 22 Mar 1804; **Dauphine**[4], b. 1724-d. 1728; **Marthe**[4], b. 1726-d. 1728

CHILDREN, m/2 :

Judith[3], b. 1688; went to Magdeburg with her uncle Moyse, c. 1703; m. 8 Mar 1707, Magdeburg, Antoine Marconnier

Jean[3], b. 1689, Mazamet

Moyse[3], b. 1695, Mazamet

Marthe[3], b. 1700, Mazamet; m. 6 May 1724, Isaac Pages from Berlin; she d. 6 Aug 1741, Prenzlau

Elizabeth[2]

REF: GARRIGUES, C. H. N., *Our Garrigues Ancestors* (updated & compiled by Patricia Wright Strati, translated by Corinna Mannel Meraldi) (Baltimore, 1992) – sources include Walloon Archives in Leiden, Henri Tollin's *History of FR Colonies of Magdeburg,* info from German Huguenots Assoc., Halle Parish records, family records & letters ; GARRIGUES, Edmund, *A Genealogy of Matthew & Suzanna Garrigues & Their Descendants* (Massillon, OH, 1938); STONE, Wilbur F., *History of Colorado* (J.P. Clark Pub. Co, 1918).

GARRISON, Isaac

b. 1685 Montauban, Gascogne, now in Tarn-et-Garonne Dépt, Midi-Pyrénées, FR, s/o Isaac & Catherine (de Romagnac) Garrison who went to ENG, c. 1688

m. Jeanne Raganar/Regeinor

19 Mar 1705/6 – naturalized NY, as subjects of Queen Anne of ENG – rec. says he was from Montauban, names parents and that he professed the Protestant religion; he was a sea captain & merchant

CHILDREN :

Isaac[2], b. c. 1710; family moved from NY & NJ to PA,VA & then to NC

    Joseph[3]

Moses[3]

James?[3]

Isaac[3], b. 6 Jan 1732, PA; m/1, XX, m/2, Martha X; a frontiersman & soldier in the Rev War, served 2nd PA Regt; d. 1836, Greene Co, MO, DAR credits him with PS, NC; **issue**

David?[3]

Beverly/Bavil[2], b. c. 1712; m 4 Dec 1737, Fishkills, Dutchess Co, NY, Catherine Springsteen

    CHILD:

    Isaac[3], b. 1738 NY; m. Elizabeth Couvert; Lt, Rev. War d. 1816 NY; son **Oliver**[4], (1778 NY-1840-45 NY), m. Catherine Schuler Kingsland –this line leads to the St. Louis Garrisons

REF: BAIRD, Charles W., *Huguenot Emigration to America* (Baltimore, 1985) ; Naturalization certificate issued by English Parliament & filed in NY, 1705; Isaac Garrison Family Assoc, *The Family of Isaac Garrison, 1732-1836* (1980); SCOTT, Kenneth & STRYKER-RODDA, Kenn, *Denizations, Naturalizations & Oaths of Allegiance in Colonial NY* (Baltimore, 1975).

GASTINEAU, Pierre

b. FR

m. c. 1660, Lusignan, Poitou, FR, s.w. of Poitiers, Elizabeth Herbert/Herbaire

to ENG, where he settled in Spitalfields in the borough of Stepney, London

1682 – received aid from the Threadneedle St. Ch; FR churches in ENG helped the FR refugees as many of them arr. with next to nothing; in 1681, King Charles II ordered an appeal be made to all parish churches for assistance – the Threadneedle St. Ch was in charge of distributing the funds

d. by 1692; a stocking maker

CHILDREN (all ch b. and bp., Lusignan):

Magdeleine[2], bp. 4 Dec 1661

Elizabeth[2], bp. 24 Jan 1664

Matharin[2], bp. 23 Jul 1666; m. 8 Nov 1692, Spitalfields, Jeanne Chaboussant, d/o Jean & Catherine (Bellet) Chaboussant; Matharin was a weaver, admitted as a "foreign master" to the trade in 1663; naturalized, 1709; liv. on Pearl St., n. of Pruson St, Wapping; 17 ch – only 9 named in his will; d. Dec, 1748, Spitalfields, bur. 1 Jan 1749, Christ Ch, Spitalfields

    CHILDREN (2 of 17):

    Matharin[3], chr. 16 Jul 1701, La Patente FR Hug. Ch, Brown's Lane, Spitalfields; prob. to America as an indentured servant; 1730, he was in Somerset Co, MD, in the household of Joseph Cottman; d. 1765, Somerset Co, MD

    George Lewis[3], chr. 20 Feb 1715, La Patente FR Hug. Ch; 1739, in America; served as a soldier in Col. William Gooch's Regiment of Foot during the "Cartagena Expedition" & was discharged 12 Oct 1741; he was a schoolmaster in Somerset Co, MD, owned a 100 acre plantation called "Chance"; m. Mary X; d. a. 4 Oct 1768, wp, Somerset Co, MD – mentions wife Mary, ch **Job**[4] (m. Elizabeth Nutterwell – **issue**), **Jane**[4] Russel (wife of John Russell), **Tabitha**[4] Mezzick (wife of Nehemiah Messick), **Elizabeth**[4], **Mary**[4]

Jean[2], m. Louise Chaboussant, sis/o Jeanne (above); d. 1750; **issue**

Pierre[2], bp. 13 Feb 1669

Marie[2], bp. 21 Mar 1670

Louis Salomon[2], bp. 21 Jan 1673

Marguerite[2], bp. 14 Jan 1676

Olivier[2], bp. 5 Jun 1680

REF: GASTINEAU, Loyd D., *Our Gastineau Family* (Mt. Vernon, IA, 1994) ; *Transactions of the Huguenot Society of SC*, #38 (Charleston, 1933); George Lewis Gastineau's will; CLARK, Murtie June, *Colonial Soldiers of the South, 1732-1774* (Baltimore, 1986) ; Records from La Patente French Huguenot Ch.

GASTON, Jean

b. c. 1600, FR; *supposedly* a descendant of Gaston IX de Foix, Duc de Nemours (1489-1512) , s/o
Jean/Gion (desc. of the Counts de Foix) de Foix & Marie d'Orléans (1457-1493), sis/o King
Louis XII - **not proven**; the possible lineage between the Counts of Foix and Jean Gaston is
underlined; Jean[1] is the earliest <u>certain</u> ancestor of the Gaston family in America; at least 8 of his
grsons emigrated - Hugh, Joseph, John, James – to NJ, Joseph, William – to PA, John to CT &
Alexander to MA

c. 1640 - fled FR, went to SCOT as a refugee

m. c. 1641/2, SCOT, XX, 1st name *poss.* Agnes

d. p. 1650, SCOT, poss. at Melrose Roxburghshire, s. e. of Galashiels

CHILDREN (4 of ? -3 went to Co. Antrim, N. IRE a. 1668):

William[2], b. c. 1642, SCOT; m. XX; liv. at Carnlough, nr. Ballymena, Co. Antrim, N. IRE, Ballymena is n. of
the town of Antrim; he d. N. IRE; his grch emigrated to America

CHILD:

unnamed son[3]

CHILDREN:

Alexander[4], b. 5 Feb 1702; m. XX; d. IRE; 3 sons, 1 dau; son **Joseph**[5] & dau **Jane**[5] (m.
Thomas Walker) went to SC; son **Matthew**[5] said to have arr. in Charleston,
SC, aged 19, a. 22 Dec 1767 w/ sis Jane, he went to NC, m. Ann Simonton, then to
GA where he d. c. 1779, Greene Co; son **Robert**[5] – no more info

Hugh[4], of NJ; m. XX; ch - **Joseph**[5] of NJ, **Joseph**[5] of PA, **William**[5] of PA, **John**[5] of NJ,
James[5] of NJ, **John**[5] of CT

Jean/John[2], b. 1645, SCOT, m. XX; in Magheragall, N. IRE by 1669, d. there (c. 3 mi e. of Lisburn)

CHILDREN:

William[3], b. c.1685, Carnlough; m. Mary/Olivet Lem(m)on (d. a. 23 Dec 1762); he d. 1755, intestate,
prob. Mount Bethel Twp (n. of Easton), Northampton Co, PA; settlement of his estate names
eldest son John, widow (since dec.) 5 ch – John, William, Hugh, Jennet, James Wm, Hugh,
Jennet above 14 yrs, James under 14 - Orphan's Ct, 23 Dec 1762, Easton, Northampton, PA; at
issue were 192 acres, appraised at £180 - £160 to son William, the 2nd son (the eldest, John,
having refused), was to see that his sibs rec. their proper share – suit names 4 other ch John,
Hugh, Jennet and James

CHILDREN:

John[4], b. 4 Apr 1703 <u>or</u> 1710, m. c. 1738,IRE, Esther Waugh (1715-1789); emigrated to PA;
c. 1751-2 to Chester District, SC, settling on Fishing Creek; he was a surveyor &
Justice of the Peace in Craven (later Chester) Co.; he d. 1782, Chester Co. - **12 ch**;
Fishing Creek is c. 4-5 mi. n. of Great Falls; his home, on the s. side of the creek, was
burned during the Amer. Rev. by Lt. Col. Banastare Tarleton; all 9 of his sons served in
the War, 4 died

Elizabeth[4], m. John Knox; settled Chester Co, SC; **5 ch**

Hugh[4], a Presbyterian minister and author; m. Mary Thomson, d/o Rev. James Thomson; emig. to America; d. 20 Oct 1766 at house of bro John, shortly after he
arr; **8 ch**

Mary[4], m. James McClure, called Capt. and Justice; emigrated to Chester Co, SC; he d.
1771, wp, Charleston, SC; Mary d. c. 1802, wp, Chester Co.; **7 ch**

Robert[4], b. c. 1720 N. IRE; m. Margaret Logan (?); a. 10 Jul 1757, emig. to Lancaster
Co, SC; 1767, moved to Lynch's Creek, Lancaster Co, SC, 28 mi n. of Camden, 2
mi e. of Hanging Rock; he d. 9 May 1787; at least **6 ch**

Jennet/Janet/Jinny[4], b. 1726; m. Charles Strong (d. 1783), emig. to Chester Co, SC; she
d. 1801, bur. Gladney Cem., Lebanon, Fairfield, Co., SC; **5 ch**

William[4], m. Jane Harbison, sis/o James Harbison, d. p. his 40th birthday, drowned at
Kell's Ford, Chester Co, SC; patriotic service, Rev. War; **2 ch**

Martha[4], m. Alexander Rosborough; emig. to SC; **5 ch**

Alexander[4], physician, emigrated; 1765, settled in New Bern, NC; m. 1775, Margaret

Sharpe; he was killed by British and Tories, 20 Aug 1781, in New Bern; **2 ch**

Hugh[3], b. 1687, Co. Antrim, N. IRE; m. 1718, IRE, Jennett (Kirkpatrick?, 1698-1 Aug 1777); he was in Mount Bethel Twp, Bucks (now Northampton) Co, PA, by 10 Feb 1746, in Bedminster Twp, NJ, bet 1750-60; he d. 23 Dec 1772, Bedminster Twp, Somerset Co, NJ - both bur. Lamington Cemetery; 5 ch – **William**[4], b. c. 1718/9, purchased land in Bethel Twp., 20 Feb 1751 (same day as fa Hugh), he was killed by Indians, Dec 1755, leaving a widow & 5 ch; **Joseph**[4]; **James**[4] & **John**[4] of NJ; **Margaret**[4] m. 8 Nov 1750, William Moffat

unnamed son[3], **James?** Co. Antrim, IRE; m. XX – son **John**[4], who d. IRE, leaving **1 dau**[5]

Joseph[3], b. 1700, N. IRE; prob. came through port of Perth Amboy, NJ, c. 1720; m. Margaret X (Linn?, 1705-31 Aug 1795, aged 90Y, Hardwick Twp, Sussex Co, NJ); liv Bernards Twp, Somerset Co, NJ, where he d. a. 11 Apr 1777, inv; his will names wife Margaret, dec.; son **John**[4]'s (10 Nov 1730-3 Oct 1776) **5 ch**, m/1, 27 Jun 1758, Elizabeth Ker (4 Apr 1738-6 May 1765), m/2, Sarah Ogden – he had civil and patriotic service in Rev. War; son **Robert**[4], m. Rosanna Cooper – he was a Lt. Col in the Rev War, also credited with patriotic service; son **Joseph**[4], m. Margaret Linn ; dau **Martha**[4], m. X Patterson; dau **Margaret**[4], m. Andrew Kirkpatrick (b. c. 1722, Watties Neach, SCOT), s/o William & Catherine (X) Kirkpatrick; dau **Purcilla**[4], m. Daniel McCain; 3 gsons who were s/o David Chambers, widower of dau **Ann**[4;] several other grch – not clear whose ch they were

John[3], b. 1703/4 Ballymena, Co. Antrim, N. IRE, n.w. of Belfast; emig. 1726; m. 1735, Janet Thompson (1711, SCOT-3 Nov 1806, Killingly, CT), d/o Rev. Alexander & Mary (X) Thompson; he d. 29 Mar 1783, Voluntown, CT; emigrated to America bet 1725-30, w/ bro Alexander; landed Marblehead, MA, went to Voluntown; 3 ch – **Margaret**[4], b. 1738 (twin), m. James Dixon, **Alexander**[4], b. 1738 (twin), **John**[4], (1750-1805) m. Ruth Miller, he d. 29 May 1783, Voluntown, CT

Alexander[3], b. 1707, Ballymena, N. IRE; emigrated to America bet 1725-30; m. 29 Sep 1743, Voluntown, CT, Mary Wilson (c. 1717- 30 Jul 1804); he d. 24 Aug 1783, Richmond, Berkshire Co, MA; **6 sons, 4 daus**

Alexander[2], b. c. 1648, SCOT; went to Co. Antrim; d. IRE; some of his descendants *may* have gone to Canada

?Hugh[2], b. SCOT; no more info

NOTE: John of CT and Alexander of MA *may* have landed at Philadelphia with brothers Hugh & Joseph and perhaps other brothers; Joseph and William of PA, John and James of NJ *may be* sons of Hugh. Family uses the same names generation after generation. Much contradictory documentation. Foix, during the Middle Ages, was the capital of the Counts of Foix. It was in s.w. FR bordering on the Pyrenees. The House of Foix eventually was merged w/ the House of Bourbon when Henri of Navarre became King of FR in 1589, and the lands became part of the FR royal domain. Nemours was given to Charles III, King of Navarre, in 1404. His dau Béatrix then brought the duchy to her husband, Jacques de Bourbon. In 1505, it reverted to the FR Crown. In 1507, Louis XII gave it to his nephew Gaston de Foix (1489-1512), s/o Jean de Foix & Marie d' Orléans (Louis XII's sister). It passed through several families until it was sold to Louis XIV who gave it to his bro Philippe, Duc d'Orléans, whose descendants held it until the FR Revolution. Another of those entries with much conflicting information.

REF: MACKENZIE, George N., *Colonial Families of the USA*, Vol. III (Baltimore, 1966), pp. 174-75; PERRY, Max, *American Descendants of John "Jean" Gaston* (Greenville, SC 1989); GEE, Mary Gaston, *The Ancestry & Descendants of Amzi Williford Gaston II of Spartanburg Co, SC* (1944); HANNA, Charles A., *Ohio Valley Genealogies* (Baltimore, 1972); McPHERSON, Lewin Dwinell, *The Gaston Family* (not dated); BOYER, Carl, 3rd, *Ship Passenger Lists, NY & NJ, 1600-1825* (Newhall, CA, 1978); HOLCOMB, Brent H. & PARKER, Elmer O., *Early Records of Fishing Creek Presbyterian Ch, Chester Co, SC, 1799-1859* (Bowie, MD, 1991); DAVIDSON, Chalmers Gaston, *Gaston of Chester* (Davidson, NC, 1956).

GAURY/GUERRI/GOREE/GORY, Jean/John

b. c. 1645, poss. Soubise, Charente-Maritime Dépt, Poitou-Charentes, FR, s.w. of Rochefort*

m. Mary Rue, b. c. 1655/60

may have gone 1st to HOL; definitely was in ENG at least for a while

31 Jul 1700, arr Jamestown, "In ye first Shippe", the *Mary Ann,* with a wife + 1 ch; son Pierre[2] was on
the same ship; they went up the river to Manakin, VA

d. a. 1 Jun 1709, wp, Henrico Co; will states that he was a FR refugee and inhabitant of Manakin; names
wife Mary Rue Gory, eldest son Peter, son Claud (*sic*) in will dated 20 Mar 1708/9; Mary was to get
plantation, 80 acres and all his other estate of goods and chattels during her natural life; son Peter was
to get 1 shilling; Claude was to get the entire estate upon the death of his mother

CHILDREN (only 2 are known, may have been others who remained in FR or ENG; surname **GORY**):

> **Pierre/Peter**[2], b. c. 1675, FR; m. XX; emigrated w/ parents; did not rec. much from his father
> but that may have been because he had rec. his portion earlier; had **at least one ch**,
> b. FR, as a ch of Pierre's is on the list of the ship's passengers; he d. c. 1720

> **Claude/Glaude**[2], b. c. 1696, FR (said to have been 16 in 1712 but prob. b. earlier); by 1714, had a
> wife Jeanne X; 31 Oct 1716, patented (#824) 50 acres on the s. side of the James River, then in
> Henrico Co., now in Powhatan Co; alive on 12 Feb 1735, when he sold his land; prob. d. bet
> 1736-38

> CHILDREN (at least 2 sons):

> **Daniel**[3], (1725 VA-8 Mar 1810 Newberry Dist., SC) m. Elizabeth Britton/Brittain, d/o
> William & Mary (Owen) Britton

> **Jean**[3], b. 21 May 1727

*****NOTE:** Jean/John was NOT the s/o Pierre & Jeanne (Broussard) Guerri as has been stated in some
sources. See the entry for Pierre. He was b. in Poitou but did not go to VA, he went to Ireland then to SC.
He had a son Jean, but he was b. in SC. *If* there were any family connection, it was **not** as father and son.
On the *Liste générale*, 1714, there are 2 children listed as orphans – Isaac and Jean Gorry – not known if
there is a connection to the above family.

REF: DOUGLAS, Rev. William, *The Douglas Register* (Richmond, VA, 1928), CABELL, Priscilla Harriss, *Turff &
Twigg*, Vol. I; BROCK, Robert A., *Huguenot Emigration to VA* (Baltimore, 1979); John Gory, Sr.'s will (dated 20 Mar
1708/9); William Brittain's will (dated) 22 Jul 1764.

GEROULD, see JERAULD

GÉVAUDAN/GIVAUDAN, Antoine

b. prob. from Gévaudan, a commune in the canton of Barrême, e. of Barrême & c. 35 km. s.e. of Digne-les
Bains, Alpes-de-Haute Dépt, Provence

20 Sep 1700 - arr Manakintown on the *Peter & Anthony,* from London

m. p. 1 Dec 1700, XX

1710 – on 1st Tithable Lists, King William Parish, Goochland Co, VA

1714 – *Liste générale* – lists Antoine, wife, 1 son, 1 dau

23 Mar 1715 - granted 128 acres in King Wm. Parish, the lands distributed to the French refugees; patent #684

25 Aug 1718 - 1st elected Vestryman King Wm. Parish;

16 Apr 1723 - elected Church Warden for a year

4 Mar 1725/6 – patented another 200 acres on Jones Creek

14 May 1726 – he rendered an acct. of his administration as church warden – last reference to him as alive; not
on tithable list of 1726

d. p. 14 May 1726, Goochland Co, VA

CHILDREN:

Thomas[2], b. c. 1702; m. 1728/29, Judith Martin, d/o <u>Jean Martain</u> (she m/2, c. 1731/32, <u>René Chastain</u>); Thomas d. 1730/31, King Wm. Parish, Goochland Co, VA

    CHILD:

    Jean/John[3], b. 1 Mar 1729/30, bp. 12 Apr 1730, King William Parish; m. Magdalene, *poss.* Chastain, d/o Pierre & Mildred (Archer) Chastain, grdau/o <u>Pierre & Anna (Soblet) Chastain</u>; he d. c. 1780, Buckingham Co, VA

    CHILDREN:

    Ann[4], b. c. 1750; m. 1774, Buckingham Co, VA, Joseph Foree (31 May 1744, VA-1835, Shelby Co, KY); she d.1823, Shelby Co, KY; **2 sons**, **3 daus**

    John[4], b. 1756, Albemarle Co, VA; m. c. 31 Jan 1785 (date of bond), Mary Mims (b. 18 Jun 1766, Goochland Co), d/o Shadrach & Elizabeth (Woodson) Mims; he d. 17 Apr /May 1835, Henry Co, KY

    Joseph[4], b. c. 1767, Buckingham Co, VA; <u>m/1</u>. Judith Carter, <u>m/2</u>, Elizabeth X; by 1800, to Shelby Co, KY; he d. 1830

    Thomas[4], b. 1770; in Buckingham Co, VA in the 1790's; m. c. 1794, Leah Hendrick (1772-1884), d/o Ezekial Hendrick; he d. c. 1818; **issue**

Elizabeth[2], b. c. 1710; m. a. 4 Feb 1727, Guillaume Sallé (b. c. 1705), s/o <u>Abraham & Olive (Perrault) Sallé</u>; she d. p. 27 Jul 1739 - **issue**; Guillaume m/2, Magdelene Chastain, d/o <u>Pierre & Anne (Soblet) Chastain</u> (issue)

NOTE: No marr record has been found but land records bet Thomas and the Sallés would lead to the conclusion that the 1st wife of Guillaume was Elizabeth Gévaudan + the fact that Thomas was Elizabeth's eldest child's godfather and Guillaume served as Thomas' only son's godfather

REF: ALLEN, Cameron, *"Antoine Gévaudan of Manakin Town and His Immediate Descendants"* in the *Genealogies of VA Families,* Vol. III – also in *The VA Magazine of History & Biography*, Vol. 73, #1 (Jan 1965); CABELL, Priscilla H., *Turff & Twig, Volume I, The French Lands*; BROCK, Robert A., *Huguenot Emigration to VA*; "Vestry Book of King William Parish" in *The Virginia Magazine of History & Biography*, Vol. XII (June, 1905).

GHISELIN, César

    b. c. 1670, *poss.* s/o Nicholas Ghislein, a gold & silversmith, naturalized London, 1681/2; Nicholas had bros Jean & William; the latter was a diamond cutter who had a son César

    fled from Rouen, FR, to ENG

    29 Sep 1698 - naturalized in London

    a. 4 Dec 1701 - to Philadelphia where he worked as a silversmith

    c. 1715- settled in Annapolis, MD

    m. Katherine Reverday (d. 29 Apr 1726, rec. St. Anne's Ch, Annapolis), d/o Pierre Reverday, who was a Huguenot from Niort, Poitou, naturalized London, 1684, to NY, 1687, to New Castle, DE, 1693

    d. 13 Feb 1733/4, Philadelphia, bur Christ Ch

    9 Mar 1733/4, wp, Philadelphia – names sons Nicholas & William, daus Hannah, Septima & Mary Catherine and bro-in-law George Shead

CHILDREN:

Nicholas[2]

William[2], m. Naomi Lusby; d. 11 Mar 1743, Annapolis; at least 2 sons **Reverdy**[3], **William**[3]

Hannah[2]

Septima[2]

Mary Catherine[2], m. X Rutter

REF: PLEASANTS, J. Hall & SILL, Howard, *Maryland Silversmiths, 1715-1830* (Baltimore, MD, 1930); *Publications of the Huguenot Society of London*, Vol. 18, p. 292; AGNEW, Rev. David C.A., *Protestant Exiles from France in the Reign of Louis XIV* (London, 1874)

GIBERT, Pierre/Peter

b. 1755, Lunas, Hérault Dept., Languedoc, FR, n. of Béziers, s/o Pierre & Marie (Mizel) Gibert; Marie was from St-Jean-du-Gard, Gard Dépt., Languedoc, s.w. of Alès; he was a nephew of Rev. Jean Louis Gibert, head (along w/ Rev. Pierre Boutiton) of the Huguenot settlement in New Bordeaux, SC, 1764; this settlement was in Upper SC (Old 96 Dist) – it no longer exists, its location was s.w. of the town of McCormick at junction of State Rd 33-7 & Huguenot Pwy in the Sumter National Forest

c. 1770 - went to London where he liv. w/ his uncle Rev. Étienne Gibert in the Soho Dist., City of Westminster; went to school there & stayed for c. 2 yrs.

1772 - went to SC

1773 - was in New Bordeaux when his uncle Jean Louis d. & Pierre had to take charge of the settlement; Pierre was not a minister, he was a teacher

m. SC, Ysabeau/Elizabeth Bienaime (d. 20 Aug 1818), d/o Peter & Anne (Beraud) Bienaime; Elizabeth, aged 4, & her widowed mother were part of the original group of colonists who emig. w/ Jean Louis Gibert; the Bienaime & Beraud families were from Guienne Province, FR

was a lieutenant in the American Revolution – was an ardent Patriot; he and his wife ran a private school called the "French & Grammar School"; rep. Abbeville Dist. in the General Assembly of SC

d. 11 Jun 1815, SC, prob. at his plantation on Mill Creek in what is now McCormick Co; he had become a man of means, with over 1000 acres of land

CHILDREN:

Peter[2], b. 14 Jan 1776; lawyer; d. unmarr., c. 1812, New Orleans of yellow fever; bur. LA

Stephen[2], b. 27 Feb 1778; m. 4 Jun 1804, Sarah B. Pettigrew; he d. 1822

John Louis[2], b. 5 Dec 1779; m. 16 May 1810, Jennie Moragne; he d. 9 Jan 1825

Clement[2], b. 4 Jul 1782; d. unmarr., 1815

Lucy[2], b. 5 Apr 1785; m. 29 Jul 1818, Benjamin Kennedy; d. 19 Dec 1864

Mary[2], b. 26 Dec 1779; m. John Wright; she d. 1852

Joseph Bienaime[2], b. 24 Jan 1790; m. 24 Jan 1815, Jane Terry, d/o Capt. Jeremiah Stephen & Susanna (Carothers) Terry; Jane m/2, Alexander Hunter; she d. 19 Jun 1859; Joseph was a doctor who d. 18 Sep 1826; **6 ch**

Elijah[2], b. 21 Feb 1792; d. unmarr., 1823

Harriet[2], b. 8 May 1794; m. 9 Jul 1817, Rev. Joseph Hillhouse; she d. 21 Nov 1868

Elizabeth[2], b. 22 Jun 1796; m. 8 Mar 1815, Stephen Lee; she d. 1840

Susan[2], b. 9 Mar 1790; m. c. 1821, Rev. David Humphreys; she d. 1824

REF: GIBERT, Anne Caroline, "A Short Sketch of Peter Gibert of New Bordeaux" in *Transactions of the Huguenot Society of SC*, #66 (1961); Bible records from the John Houston & Elizabeth Drucilla Gibert Bible; HILLHOUSE, Albert M., *Pierre Gibert, French Huguenot, His Background & Descendants* (Danville, KY).

GIGNILLIAT, Abraham

b. 24 Oct 1622, Vevey, SWI, s/o Gaspard & Stephe (Seigneux) Gignilliat; Vevey is on Lac Léman/Lake Geneva, s.e. of Lausanne; family was in Avenches, SWI (in Vaud Canton, s.w. of Bern), a French-speaking area, where they lived for several generations

m. 19 Nov 1643, Vevey, Marie de Ville (bp. 15 Feb 1621, Vevey), d/o Georges & Claudia Antoinia (de Roveréaz) de Ville

d. a. 15 Feb 1657

CHILDREN:

Étienne[2], b. 20 Oct 1644, Vevey

Benjamin[2], b. 25 Apr 1646, Vevey

Jean Louis[2], b. 3 Apr 1648, Vevey; m. Judith d'Yeverdon; Jean was a councillor & bailiff's assessor in
    Vevey

Madeleine[2], b. 13 Jun 1650

Jean François[2], b. 17 May 1652, Vevey; m. Susanne le Ser(r)urier

Judith[2], b. 28 Jan 1655, Vevey

REF: BOND, Christy Hawes & edited by Williams, Alicia Crane, *Gateway Families* (Boston, MA, 1994) which
references the Archives de la ville de Vevey; KENAN, Robert Gignilliat, *History of the Gignilliat Family of
Switzerland & SC* (Easley, SC, 1977).

GILLET(T)/GYLLET, William (Rev.)

Rev. Jacques de Gylett fled to SCOT, p. St. Bartholomew Day's Massacre, where fam. resided 57 yrs –
    he was prob fa/o or grfa/o Rev. William; another source says Jonathan and Nathan (below) were
    sons of Huguenot parents who had fled their home nr. Burge (*sic*), FR (not found, poss Bourg, of
    which there are several, or a misspelling of Bergerac); to SCOT in 1572

family believed to have come originally from Bergerac, Guienne, FR, now in Dordogne Dépt, Aquitaine

4 Feb 1609/10 - was rector of Chaffcombe, Co. Somerset, ENG (sm. town s.e. of Taunton) where he served
    until his death

d. a. 2 Apr 1641, inv, Chaffcombe; 16 Apr 1641, wp, Archdeaconry Court, Taunton; will mentions bro
    Richard, daus Habiah & Mary, sons Nathan, William, Jeremiah, Thomas, no wife mentioned

CHILDREN:

Jonathan[2], b. c. 1600, SCOT (?); went to America, 1630, on the *Mary & John*; returned to ENG, m. 29 Mar
    1634, Colyton, Devon, ENG (sm. town s.w. of Axminster), Mary Dolbere/Dolbiar (bp. 7 Jun 1607,
    Colyton - d. 5 Jan 1685/6, Windsor, CT), d/o Rawkey & Mary (Michell) Dolbere of Cadhayne (sm.
    town in Colyton Parish); Jun 1634, returned to America, 1st to Dorchester, MA, c. 1639, to Windsor,
    CT; he d. 23 Aug 1677, Windsor, CT

    CHILDREN:

    Jonathan[3], b. c. Dec 1634, MA; m/1, 23 Apr 1661, Mary Kelsey (d. 18 Apr 1676), d/o William
        Kelsey – **4 ch**, m/2, 14 Dec 1676, Miriam Dibble (Feb 1644/5-18 Apr 1687), d/o Thomas
        Dibble – **5 ch**; d. 27 Feb 1697, Windsor

    Cornelius[3], m. a. 1658, Priscilla Kelsey (d. 7 Jan 1722/3, Windsor), sis/o Mary Kelsey (above); he
        d. 26 Jun 1711, Windsor; **9 ch**

    Mary[3], (*poss.* Cornelius' twin) m. Peter Brown of Windsor; **14 ch**

    Anna/Hannah[3], b. 29 Dec 1639, Windsor; m. 29 Oct 1663, Samuel Filley (24 Sep 1643, Windsor-
        4 Jan 1711/2, Windsor), s/o William & Margaret (X) Filley; Anna d. 18 Nov 1711,
        Windsor; **11 ch**

    Joseph[3], bp 25 Jul 1641; m. 24 Nov 1663, Elizabeth Hawks, d/o John & Eliza (X) Hawks of
        Haddam; Joseph killed 18 Sep 1675, Battle Creek, during King Philip's War; **7 ch**; she
        m/2, 16 Dec 1680, Nathaniel Dickinson

    Samuel[3], b. 2 Jan 1642/3; m. 23 Sep 1668, Hannah Dickinson, d/o John & Frances (Foote) Dickin-
        son; he was killed 9 May 1676, Hatfield, MA, in "battle with the Indians"; she m/2, 15
        May 1677, Stephen Jennings

    John[3], b. 5 Oct 1644, Windsor; m. 8 Jul 1669, Windsor, Mary Barber (bp. 12 Oct 1651, Windsor-
        31 Dec 1725, Suffield), d/o Thomas & Jane (Coggin) Barber – **6 ch**; moved to Simsbury, CT,
        where he Nov 1682; Mary m/2, Capt. George Norton of Suffield

    Abigail[3], bp. 28 Jun 1646; d. 1649

    Jeremiah[3], b. 20 Feb 1646/7; m. 16 Oct 1685, Deborah Bartlett (d. 29 Sep 1753); he d. 1 Mar 1692; **3**
        ch; Deborah m/2, 23 Apr 1694, Samuel Adams

    Josiah[3], bp. 14 Jul 1650, Windsor; m. 30 Jun 1676, Joanna Taintor (29 Apr 1657, Branford, CT-

23 Jan 1735, Colchester), d/o Michael & Elizabeth (Rose) Taintor; 1702, went to Colchester, CT; he d. 29 Oct 1736; **11 ch**

Mary[2]; **William**[2]; **Thomas**[2]

Nathan[2], 1630-went to MA w/ bro Jonathan

Jeremiah[2], prob. went to New England as well, believed to have returned to ENG

Habiah/Abiah[2]

Silas/Elias[2], b. c. 1612 (20 when he entered Oxford Univ. 7 May 1632) - B.A. Oxford, 7 Jun 1632, M.A., 23 Apr 1635

REF: ALDRIDGE, Bertha Bortle Beal, compiler, *Gillette Families* (Victor, NY, 1955); CODDINGTON, John Insley, "Jonathan Gillett of Dorchester, MA, and Windsor, CT, and Mary Dolbere or Dolbiar, His Wife" in *The American Genealogist*, Vol. XV #4 (Apr 1939); THOMAS, Wilma Gillet, *The Joseph Gillet/Gillett/Gillette Family of CT, OH & KS* (Chicago, 1970): PRIEST, Alice Lucinda, "The Brothers Jonathan & Nathan Gillet & Some of Their Descendants" in *NEHG Register* (Vol. 100, Oct 1946).

GINDRAT, Abraham

bp. 1713, s/o Pierre & Eve (Droz) Gindrat

1732 - to SC, from Bern Canton, SWI; settled Purysburg, Beaufort Dist (now Jasper Co), SC; Purysburg was settled, c. 1731/2, by 600 poor Swiss Protestants; it was named after Jean Pierre de Pury of Neuchâtel, SWI; it was on the banks of the Savannah River, n.w. of current Hardeeville, n. of Savannah, GA; the settlement was abandoned about a century later

16 Sep 1738 - Abraham rec. a grant of 50 acres; record gives surname of Jindra; may actually have been awarded the land at an earlier date

m. a. 1739, Susanne Marguerite Tallet, d/o Abraham Tallet

liv. St. Peter's Parish, Beaufort Dist, SC

9 Feb 1759 - an indenture bet Abraham Gindra & wife and Stephen Vanguer (Vegneur) & his wife Mary Ann (Mary Ann/Marianne Tallet, was the sis/o Susanne (Tallet) Gindrat)

d. a. 4 Jun 1767, wp, Charleston, SC; will (dated 7 Feb 1760) mentions wife, sons Daniel Henry, Abraham Henry, Louis, daus Catherine, Mary Magdalena, Marguerite

CHILDREN:

Daniel Henry[2], b. c. 1739, Purysburg; m/1, Mary May, m/2, Dorcas (Stafford) Williams, d/o William Stafford, widow of X Williams; Rev. War service; called Henry; he d. Jan/Feb 1801, Bryan Co, GA

CHILDREN:

Abraham[3], b. 1764, Purysburg; m. 17 Mar 1803, Barbara Clark; he d. 1811, Bryan Co, GA

Mary[3], b. c. 1767; m. GA, Dr. X St. Mark of GA

Susan[3], b. c. 177-; m. GA, X Morel

John[3], b. 29 May 1777, Purysburg; m/1, a. 1804, Margaret X (d. 1808), m/2, Sarah Stallings; he d. a. 24 Jan 1812, wp, Columbia Co, GA

Rhoda[3], b. 177- ; m. X Gilliland; d. a. 7 Dec 1818, adm

Dorcas[3], b. 178-; m. X Washburn as his 2nd wife

Henrietta[3], b. 178-; m. X Clark

3 other ch[3], d. in infancy

Abraham Henry[2], b. c. 1741, Purysburg; served in Rev. War; d. a. 21 Jun 1785, prob. unmarr.

Louis[2], b. c. 1746, alive in 1767

Catherine[2], alive in 1767

Mary Magdalena[2], alive in 1767

Marguerite[2], alive in 1767

REF: DAVIS, Harry Alexander, *The Gindrat Family, A Supplement to Some Huguenot Families of SC & GA* (Washington, DC, 1933); *Transactions of the Huguenot Society of SC*, #38 (1933); *Will Book II, Charleston Co, SC*, p. 57.

GIRARDEAU, Jean

b. c. 1665, Talmont (now Talmont-sur-Gironde), Poitou, s.e. of Royan, in Charente-Maritime Dépt, Poitou-Charentes, s/o Pierre & Catherine (Lareine) Girardeau

c. 1686 - emigrated from FR to Charleston, SC area, via ENG

1695 - on list of FR & Swiss Protestants in Charleston desiring naturalization

m. a. 1703, Ann LeSade, d/o Pierre & Ann (Gornier) LeSade of Normandie, FR (she m/2, 18 Jun 1723, Andrew Deveaux – no issue); she d. Jan 1729/30, bur. St. Andrew's Parish, Berkeley Co, SC

he lived on or nr. the Ashley, Winyah & Pon Pon Rivers

bur. 28 Feb 1720/1, St. Andrew Ch cem., Berkeley Co; at the time of his death, he owned dwelling house + 210 acres in St. Andrews Par, Berkeley Co, 450 elsewhere in Berkeley Co, 500 acres in Craven Co. on the Winyah & 1510 acres in Colleton Co. His will was proven 28 Apr 1721 - mentions wife Ann, sons Peter, John, Richard, James and Isaac

CHILDREN:

Peter[2], b. c. 1705, Berkeley Co, SC; m/1, 19 Dec 1730, Elizabeth Bohun (d. 1737/46) – **4 ch**; moved to St. Bartholomew's Par, Colleton Co. by 1737; m/2, 19 Mar 1746, Elizabeth Heap(e) – poss 1 son; he d. a. 13 Jan 1757, inv

John[2], b. c. 1708, Berkeley Co; m. c. 1730, Jerusa Rantowle; d. a. 8 Dec 1747, inv, Colleton Co; d. intestate, **no issue**

Richard[2], b. c. 1712, Berkeley Co; m. c. 1738, Priscilla X (d. 27 Mar 1778, GA); he d. 25 Apr 1766, Liberty Co, GA; **5 ch**

James[2], b. 1715, Berkeley Co; m. 1740, Mary Postell (d. a. 1752); he d. a. 7 Jan 1757, wp, SC; **3 ch**

Isaac[2], b. 1718-21, bp 25 Feb 1720/21, St. Andrews Parish, SC; m. c. 1750, Ann [prob. Chamberlain, d/o Job & Sarah (Norman) Chamberlain]; went to Liberty Co, GA in 1755; d. 14 Apr 1773; **4 ch**; this is the son from whom all those who are descendants of Jean Girardeau, surnamed Girardeau, in the US today, descend as the other lines died out or were female lines

REF: WEBBER, Mabel L., *"Register of Andrew's Parish, Berkeley Co, SC; The SC Historical & Genealogical Magazine,* Vol. 12 (Oct 1911)*;* STACY, Rev. James, *The Published Records of Midway Congregational Church,* Vol. 1; RAVENEL, Daniel, *French and Swiss Protestants settled in Charleston, on the Santee & the Orange Quarter in Carolina who desire Naturalization 1695/96,* Baltimore (1968); CROWE, Ronald Girardeau & GIRARDEAU, Elizabeth Lee, "The Girardeau Family of the US" in *Transactions of the Huguenot Society of SC* #91 (1986), #94 (1989), #95 (1990), #96 (1991).

GIRARDIN, Jean Henri

b. FR

c. 1696 - to SC; settled Purysburg, the Huguenot settlement on the Savannah River, where he rec. 250 acres - 100 for himself, 50 for his wife, 50 for each of 2 ch

m. 1697, SC, Mary Préduin

d. SC

CHILDREN:

Henry[2], b. c. 1700; m. Marguerite X (b. c. 1700); 17 Mar 1735, rec. 50 acres in (then) Granville Co. which became part of the Beaufort Dist in 1798

CHILDREN:

David[3], b. c. 1725; served in the Southern Regt. of Granville Co – on muster roll of 1756

Henry[3], b. c. 1728

Anne[3], b. c. 1730

Louis[2], m. Christine Moyenden (said to have been a "rich Dutch widow"); liv. Beech Island, Aiken, SC, s.e. of Augusta, GA

REF: GANNON, Peter Steven, *Huguenot Refugees in the Settling of Colonial America*; HIRSCH, Arthur Henry,

The Huguenots of Colonial SC; "SC Land Grants to Huguenots, 1674-1765" in *Transactions of the Huguenot Society of SC,* Vol. 88 (1983); "The Huguenots of the Old Beaufort District" by George C. Rogers, Jr. in *Transactions of the Huguenot Society of SC,* #85 (1980).

GIRAUD/GEROW, Daniel

b. c. 1664/5, FR; prob. Poitou or Saintonge

from LaRochelle, FR; prob. to ENG 1st

c. 1688 - to NY

m. Jeanne X; given that Daniel[2] was b. 1697, Daniel[1] prob. m. in NY to a woman younger than he

19 Jul 1699 - was godfather to Jean Roy's dau in the FR Ch – 1st mention of his name in NY

11 Mar 1699/00 - naturalized by Royal Letters Patent at Westminster – apparently returned to ENG for
    to take Oath of Allegiance

1701 –named town assessor of New Rochelle, NY; 1st of many town offices

d. a. 10 Aug 1757, NYC, when his will was read; had left New Rochelle p. 1743

CHILDREN:

Daniel[2], b. 1697, NY; m. 1724, Catherine Sicord (10 Oct 1704-p. 11 May 1771, North Castle, Westchester, NY), d/o Daniel & Catherine (Woertman) Sicord, grd/o <u>Ambroise Sicard</u>; he held many town offices in New Rochelle; c. 1745, moved to Cortlandt Manor; he d. bet Jul 1756-10 Aug 1757; this family started using surname GEROW

    CHILDREN:

    Daniel[3], b. 26 Mar, bp. 28 Mar 1725, New Rochelle; m. 1747/8, Elizabeth Coutant (19 Mar 1729?-1816),d/o <u>Jean & Elizabeth (Angevine) Coutant</u>; settled Westchester Co, NY; d. a/ 7 Mar 1791, inv., New Marlboro/ Plattekill, Ulster, NY; **12 ch**

    Jeanne[3], b. 19 Feb, bp. 17 Mar 1729, New Rochelle; m. 1748/9, Major Richard Garrison (15 Apr 1727, Philips Manor, NY-1803, Plattekill), served in Rev. War; **6 ch**

    Marie[3], b. 27 Jan, bp 5 Mar 1731/2, New Rochelle; m. Joshua Purdy (1732, Rye, NY-28 Mar 1825); Marie d. 1 Jun 1778; both bur. Sparta Cem. nr. Ossining, NY; **4 ch**

    André[3], b. 27 Aug, bp. 22 Sep 1734, New Rochelle; m. Anne Wicks; a. 1769 to Cortlandt Manor; fought with the British during the Rev War; d. a. 14 Dec 1809, wp, New Rochelle; will names wife and all **11 ch**

    Benjamin[3], b. 1739; m. Catherine Sicard, d/o <u>Jacques/James & Jeanne/Jane (Bonnet) Sicard</u> (Jacques s/o Daniel & Catherine (Woertman) <u>Sicord</u>, Jeanne d/o Daniel & Jeanne (Couturier) <u>Bonnet</u>)

    Isaac[3], b. 11 Sep 1742, New Rochelle; bp. 20 Feb 1743; m. Charity X; liv. North Castle, NY; he was a Loyalist & served w/ the British during the Rev War; he was bur 28 Jul 1778, Trinity Churchyard, NYC; **6 ch**

André/Andrew[2], b. 1699, NY; m. Jan 1720/1, Anne Burger (d. a. 6 Apr 1784, wp); liv Fishkill, NY; d. a. 14 Jan 1774, wp, NYC; his will mentioned only wife Anne, gr dau Ann Martin; wife's will named son André, ch of son Pierre, ch of son Daniel, dau Catherine, Mary E., Anne; he was a cordwainer; retained surname **GIRAUD**

    CHILDREN:

    Jeanne[3], b. 1721; d. young

    Pierre/Peter[3], b. 8 Oct, bp. Oct 16 1722, NYC; m. May 1748, Dutch Reformed Ch, NYC Anne Williams/Annetje Willemse (1729-1827), d/o Frederick Willemse & Marytje Waldron; liv. NYC; 6 ch of whom **Peter**[4], **Mary**[4], **Frederick**[4] were named in grmo's will

    Daniel[3], b. 28 Sep, bp. 4 Oct 1724, NYC; m. Mary X; liv NYC; d. 1753/4, NYC; his 2 ch **Mary**[4], **William**[4] were named in grmo's will

    André[3], b. 1726; d. young

    Comfort[3], b. 18 Nov, bp. 20 Nov 1728, NYC; d. a. 1765

    Catherine[3], b. 1 Mar, bp. 4 Mar 1731, NYC; m. 19 Jul 1750, John Ferris

    Jeanne[3], b. 19 Jul , bp 22 Jul 1733, NYC; d. a. 1765

        Marie Elizabeth[3], b. 25 Aug, bp. 31 Aug 1735, NYC; <u>m/1</u>, 12 Aug 1758, John Martin – **1 dau**, <u>m/2</u>, John Shaw; she d. bet 1784-86

        André/Andrew[3], b. 24 Feb, bp. 1 Mar 1737/8, NYC; m. 14 Jul 1763, Elizabeth Henderson; d. p. 6 Apr 1784; **2 ch**

        Anne/Annie[3], b. 22 Apr, bp. 23 Apr 1740; m. 24 Apr 1758, John Tomlinson

Benjamin[2], b. 1707, New Rochelle; m. 29 Jan 1726, Annetje Kuiper (bp. 30 Jun 1698), d/o Jan Claessen Kuiper & Trinitie Stratmaker; resided NJ & southern NY; d. p. 28 Aug 1769; surname **GEROW**
CHILDREN:

        Maria[3], m. Jean/John Secor/Sicor, Sicard, s/o <u>Jacques & Anne (Terrier) Sicard</u>; liv. Rockland Co, NY; **6 ch**

        Tryntie[3], b. 10 Jun, bp. 11 Jun 1728; m. Johannis De Vries; **7 ch**

        Daniel[3], b. 15 Nov, bp. 6 Dec 1730; m. 10 Oct 1751, Elizabeth House (b. 22 Mar 1731), d/o Reinhard House & Anna X; he d. a. 19 Oct 1822; **9 ch**

        Jannetie[3], b. 30 Jul, bp. 19 Aug 1733; m. Matthew Stiel; **2 ch**

        Lea[3], b. 21 Jun, bp. 13 Jul 1736, Tappan, NY

        Benjamin[3], b. 3 Mar, bp 8 Apr 1739, Tappan; m. Catherine Sicard (18 Dec 1733-Jan 1791), d/o <u>Jacques & Jane (Bonnet) Sicard</u>; liv. Cortlandt Manor & Fishkill; he d. c. 1820, Kortright, Delaware Co, NY; **8 ch**

REF: Gerow Family Assoc, *The Giraud-Gerow Family in America 1st 4 Generations in America* (New Paltz, NY, 1981), Vol. 1,2; New Rochelle Chapter, NSDAR, *Old Wills of New Rochelle, 1784-1830* (1951); REYNOLDS, Cuyler, *New York & Hudson River Valley*, Vol. II; WITTMEYER, Alfred V., *Registers of the Births, Marriages, & Deaths of the Église Française à la Nouvelle York, 1688-1804* (Baltimore, 1968).

GIRAULT, Jean/John

b. 24 Feb, bp 9 Mar 1755, Threadneedle St. FR Ch, London, s/o Jean & Perinne (X) Gir(e)ault who were in London by 26 Jul 1752, when they were listed in the Threadneedle St. Ch as having testified to their Protestantism

a. 1771 - to America; he witnessed a baptism in the Fr Ch, NYC, on Aug 1771; served as a clerk in an importing house

1777 – in Illinois Country as a trader

served w/ George Rogers Clark during the Rev. War, as a translator; was a Captain serving from VA (IL "belonged" to VA at the time)

p. 1783 - officially discharged from the army; went to Natchez & New Orleans where he continued as a trader

m. 1 May 1788, Natchez Dist, MS, Mary Spain (2 Feb 1766, Amelia Co, VA-18 Oct 1825, Jefferson Co, MS)

d. 28 May 1813, Bayou St. John, LA (the Bayou St. John area in the FR Quarter in New Orleans?)
CHILDREN:

Helen Perina[2], b. 3 Feb 1789, at "The Retreat," the family plantation, on St. Catherine Creek, presumably the area s of Natchez; <u>m/1</u>, 26 Jun 1806, James Andrews, <u>m/2</u>, 19 Jun 1814, Charles Beatty Green

Francis Spain[2], b. 23 Oct 1790, at "The Retreat"; m. 27 Mar 1818, Jane M. Kemp, d/o Col. James Kemp of Natchez

John Ruffin[2], b. 6 May 1792, at "The Retreat"; m. 1818/19, Anna Eliza Moore; he d. c. 29 Dec 1829

James Augustus[2], b. 6 Aug 1793, at "The Retreat"; <u>m/1</u>, Mary Jane Crosier, <u>m/2</u> Susan Dunbar

Perina[2], b. 13 May 1795, at "The Retreat"; d. 29 Jul 1798

Mary[2], b. 10 Jul 1796; d. 31 May 1797

Ann Mary[2], b. 15 Oct 1797, at "Bellevue" nr. Natchez, a farm belonging to her parents; m. 14 Aug 1816, "Bellevue," Dr. George Heriot Hunter; she d. 22 Jun 1819, New Orleans; 1 dau **Mary**[3]

Isaac Farrar[2], b. 17 Jul 1799, at "Villa Gayoso" on Coles Creek (n. of Natchez); d. Aug 1823; another record gives his name as Benjamin Farrar

Clara Scott[2], b. 1 Sep 1802, at "Recess" her parents' plantation on Coles Creek; she d. 1836
Martha Cordelia[2], b. 17 Dec 1804, at "Bellevue"; m/1, Julius C. McConnell, m/2, Matthew Atchinson
unnamed dau[2], b. 7 Apr 1807; d. 11 Apr 1807
Thomas Richard[2], b. 1 Oct 1808
George Rogers Clark[2], b. 13 Apr 1813; m/1, Henrietta McCaleb, m/2, Emily Jane (Stowers) Lobdell; he
      d. 15 Apr 1857; **issue**

REF: MINET, William & Susan, editors, *The Publications of the Huguenot Society of London*, Vol. XXI – *Livre des Temoignages de l'Église de Threadneedle Street, 1669-1789* (London, 1909); notes from Chuck Stuck citing several sources (1992), including the Draper Papers; Girault Family Bible; Historical Records of IL, VA Series; ROWLAND, Dunbar, *Encyclopedia of MS History* (Madison, WI, 1907); "George Rogers Clark Papers, 1771-81"; Collections of the IL State Historical Library; *Territorial Papers of the US*, Vol. 5; *The Territory of MS, 1798-1817*, Vol. VIII.

GO(U)DON, Jacob

    b. c. 1575/80, poss. Tournai, FR
    1599/1600 - arr ENG; "alien resident"; a shoemaker
    m. Marie de Moulin
    1601 - liv. Holywell St. (old street that ran parallel to the Strand in London where used clothing and "indecent"
        prints and volumes were sold, later it became more respectable)
    15 Oct 1635 - "return of strangers in the metropolis" – Jacob Godowne, "slemaker" resident 35 yrs, wife
        + 4 ch; liv St. Botolph's, Bishopgate Ward
    d. p. 1621
    CHILDREN (bap. FR Ch, Threadneedle St, London):
Rachel[2], bp. 5 Oct 1600
Ester[2], bp. 4 Nov 1604
Jan[2], bp. 4 Jan 1607; prob. m. 2 Dec 1627, St. Dunstan, Stepney, Susan Turville
    CHILDREN:
    Peter[3], **Samuel**[3], **Abraham**[3], **Gabriel**[3]
Caterynne/Catherine[2], bp. 20 Dec 1608; m. 15 Apr 1628 Fr Ch, Threadneedle St., Pierre Pacque
Elisabeth[2], bp. 21 Jul 1611
Abraham[2], bp. 11 Aug 1616; m. 27 Sep 1640, St. Dunstan, Elizabeth Duffield (bp. 20 Sep 1620, St.
    Dunstan, Stepney), prob. d/o William & Priscilla (Farnsead) Duffield; he was bur. 11 Apr 1653, St.
    Botolph without Bishopgate Ch, London; he was a weaver on Wentworth St., Whitechapel
    CHILDREN, surnamed **GODOWNE**:
    Elizabeth[3], bp. 28 Jun 1641, St. Botolph without Aldgate; d. young
    Mary[3], bp. 26 Aug 1642, St. Dunstan's; m. 29 Mar 1671, Westbury Friends Mtg, John Carlile-
        7 ch
    Jacob[3], bp. 18 Oct 1646, St. Botolph Bishopgate; d. young
    Jacob[3], bp. 31 Mar 1650, St. Botolph Bishopgate
    Joseph[3], bp. 16 Mar 1651, St. Botolph Bishopgate
    Elizabeth[3], bp. 20 Feb 1653, St. Botolph Bishopgate
    Abraham[3], m. 1668 Jan Tomkins; d. Bishopgate
Isaac[2], bp. 28 Aug 1621; poss. m. Judith X

REF: "Registers of the French Ch, Threadneedle St. London, Vol. I, in *Publications of the Huguenot Society of London*, Vol. IX, (1896); "Aliens in London" in *Publications of the Huguenot Society of London*, Vol. X, Part III (1907); baptismal, marr. records St. Dunstan's; baptismal, burial records St. Botolph.

GOLILLOT, Antoine

b. FR?
m. Rose Élisabeth Potot
d. FR?
CHILD:
Michel[2], b. 1797/99; m. Marie Marchant (22 Jul 1802-17 Dec 1888), d/o Jean-Claude & Marie (Dubois) Marchant; he d. 9 Dec 1849
CHILD:
Auguste[3], b. 22 Sep 1842?; m. Chenebier, Haute-Saône Dépt., Franche-Comté, FR, n.w. of Belfort), Julie Bonhôtal (11 Jul 1841-28 Sep 1928, USA), d/o Jean George & Elizabeth (Bourguin) Bonhôtal, grgrdau/o <u>Jacques Christophe & Anne Catherine (Pochard) Bonhôtal</u>; he d. 13 Jul 1903

REF: Genealogical research by Mayor of Chenebier, FR (1971).

GOURY/GORY/GAURY/GARRY, Jean

b. from Sepvret, Deux-Sèvres Dépt, Poitou-Charentes, FR, s.e. of Niort, s/o Peter?
m. Mary Rue (d. c. 1712)
1700 - listed as inhabitant of King William Parish, wife + 1 ch; arr in the 1st ship, the *Mary Ann*
d. a. 1 Jun 1709, wp, Henrico Co, VA; will states that he was a FR refugee and inhabitant of Manakintown; also says he is the owner of 80 acres in Manakintown and Henrico Co which he wills to his wife "Mary Rue Gory", one shilling to eldest son Peter, land after mother Mary's death to son Claude; Mary and Claude named executors; his wd, 20 May 1708/9
CHILDREN:
Peter[2]
Claude[2], b. c. 1696 (at least 16 by 1712, when he was listed as a tithable); m. by 1714; 31 Oct 1716, rec patent for 50 acres on the s. side of the James River
Isaac[2], orphan on 1712 list
John[2], orphan on 1712 list

REF: CABELL, Priscilla Harriss, *Turff & Twigg, Vol 1, the French Lands* (Richmond, VA); BROCK, R. A., *Huguenot Emigration to VA* (Baltimore, 1979); GANNON, Peter Steven, *Huguenot Refugees in the Settling of Colonial America* (NYC).

GOSSELIN/GORSLINE, Jacob II

b. c. 1600 Dieppe, Seine-Maritime Dépt, Haute-Normandie, FR, s/o Jacob I
bet 1609-12 - family fled HOL; went to Amsterdam, joined L'Église Wallonne d'Amsterdam
m. a. 1622, prob. Amsterdam, Marthe Chauvel, b. Dieppe
said to have d. 1681, Dutch West Indies
CHILDREN (ch all bp in the Walloon Ch):
unnamed son[2], b. 1622, Amsterdam; d. 4 Nov 1623, Amsterdam
Jan[2], b. 1624, bp. 2 Feb 1624, Amsterdam; d. 5 Mar 1624, Amsterdam
Jacob III[2], bp. 31 Mar 1627, Dutch Reformed Ch, Amsterdam; m. 1 Apr 1655, FR Ch, Threadneedle St, London, Sarra/Sarah Gooris, d/o Solomon/Samuel Gooris of London; he was naturalized 29 Dec 1660; Jacob d. c. 1672/6, London
CHILDREN (9 ch b., most d. in infancy, bp. FR Ch, Threadneedle St, London):
Marie[3], bp. 8 Jun 1656, d. 1676; **Jean**[3], bp. 12 Sep 1658; **Sarah**[3], bp. 19 Feb 1660
Jacob IV[3], bp. 24 Nov 1661, London, d. young; **Guillaume**[3] & **Philippe**[3], bp. 17 Jan 1664; **Claude**[3], bp. 9 Apr 1665; **Guillaume**[3], b. 4 Aug 1667

Jacob IV[3], bp. 20 Aug 1669, London; returned to FR to learn to be a weaver; early 1680's, m. at Charenton, FR, a suburb of Paris, Judith L'esveilée/L'esveille; 1684, they went to ENG and joined the FR Ch in Threadneedle St., London – témoignage from Charenton, 11 Jan 1684 – Jacob called a *ouvrier en soye* (silkworker); Jacob was a weaver until 1699, when they moved to Canterbury; not long after that, the family was in NY and members of the FR Ch in NYC; he purchased a farm in Newton, LI, NY, where he d. 1722; name became **GORSALINE/ GORSLINE**

CHILDREN:

Marie Madeleine[4], bp. 26 Oct 1690, FR Ch, Threadneedle St, London; must have d. young

James[4], b. 1691, London

?John[4], b. 169<u>3</u>, London; m. Apr 1727, Newton, NY, Rebecca X; he d. p. 1763, Newton; at least **5 ch** (3sons, 2 daus), bp. Newtown Presbyterian Ch; a **Jacob** bp. 30 Mar 169<u>3</u>, London - same person?

Samuel[4], b. 1695, London; m. 12 Oct 1738, Judith Wood; d. 23 Dec 1738, Newton, LI, NY

Jacob[4], bp. 7 Nov 1697, London; d. p. 1 May 1733, Newton, LI, NY

Mary/Mary Madeleine[4], bp. 4 Mar 1699, Canterbury, ENG; m. 24 Dec 1729, Newton, John Reeder (d. 1750, Newton); she d. 30 Jan 1739, Newton, NY; **2 sons, 1 dau**

Josse/Joseph[4], b. 7 Oct, Newtown, bp. 9 Nov 1701, FR Ch, NYC; also a weaver; <u>m/1</u>, c. 1720, Elizabeth Alburtis/Albertus, d/o Samuel & Elizabeth (Scudder) Albertus- **8 sons, 3 daus**, <u>m/2</u>, 21 Dec 1761, Martha Smith – **2 sons**; he d. 20 Nov 1772; he was also a weaver; was town constable for 9 yrs., owned a farm

Judith[4], b. 24 Jun, Newtown, bp. 5 Sep 1703, FR Ch, NYC; m. Thomas Fairly (d. 2 Dec 1749, Newton); she d. p. 2 Apr 1750, prob. Newton, LI, NY

Étienne[2], b. 1630, bp 27 Feb 1630; d. London, p. 1684

REF: REAMAN, G. Elmore, *The Trail of the Huguenots* (Baltimore, 1986); RIKER, James, Jr., *The Annals of Newton, in Queens Co, NY* (NY, 1852); BAIRD, Charles W., *History of the Huguenot Emigration to America*, Vol. II; WITTMEYER, Alfred V., *Registers of the Births, Marriages, and Deaths of the Église Françoise à la Nouvelle York* (Baltimore, 1968).

GOSSET, Jean

b. 26 Jul 1618, St. Sauveur, Normandie, FR (now St. Sauveur-le-Vicomte, Manche Dépt, Basse-Normandie), s. of Cherbourg-Octeville; name originally Goussé; said to have been a noble family

m. FR, XX

1685 -to Isle of Jersey, ENG

d. 1712, Manor House of Bagot, Isle of Jersey; bur. St. Saviours Ch, nr. St. Helier

CHILDREN:

John[2], b. 26 Jun 1649, St. Sauveur; m. a. 1699, Isle of Jersey, Susan D'Allain (b. Cerisy, now Cerisy-la Salle, Manche Dépt, Basse-Normandie-d. Isle of Jersey); John d. 9 May 1730, Isle of Jersey

CHILDREN, surname becomes GOSSETT:

John[3], b. 1699; to the Cumberland Valley, PA, 1734/5 (now Franklin & Cumberland Co.); 13 Jun 1735, he obtained license for 300 acres on the w. side of the Susquehanna River, which included the 200 acres on the s.e. branch of the Conegochege, where he had already settled; prob. was unmarr. when he emigrated; had ch, but details are not clear – names of ch include: **Peter**[4], m. Eve X, **John**[4], served in FR & Indian Wars in VA, **Mary**[4], m. Rev. Morgan Morgan, **William**[4], m. Nancy X, **Matthias**[4], m. Mary X (Littler?)

Abraham[3], b. 1701; m. Jane White; d. 1785; <u>only</u> son to remain on Isle of Jersey; **3 daus**

Jacob[3], b. 1703; d. 1788, Hempstead Parish, London; bur. London

Peter[3], b. 11 Mar 1705; m. Catherine du Four (May 1705, Normandie-p. 1765, Chester Co, PA);

went to PA bet 1750-60; wife Catherine was warranted land in 1765 & was listed as a taxpayer, so it would seem that Peter was d. despite 1 account that he d. 29 Sep 1796, Chester Coe ; 5 ch – **John**[4], m. Martha Groom, pvt., VA Continental Line, Rev. War, d. 1818 (desc. went to VA, SC), **Matthew**[4], **Jane**[4], m. c. 1750, Jersey, Abraham D'Allain, **Esther**[4], **Mary**[4]

    Gideon[3], b. 1707; m. Ann X (c. 1706-26 Mar 1761, age 56,bur. Old Marylebone Cem., London); he d. 6 Aug 1783, bur. Old Marylebone Cem., London

    Isaac[3], b. 1713; m. X Bosquet; he d. 28 Nov 1799, bur Old Marylebone Cem., London; an artist & modeler of portraits in wax; 1 son, the Rev. Dr. **Isaac**[4] (1744-16 Dec 1812, London), m. Catherine Hill – **issue**; he was also bur. Old Marylebone Cem.; Isaac [3] may have had daus

Matthew[2], b. 1683; in London, 1709, when he was naturalized; m. Jane Esther/Ester (d.28 May 1748, age 73); he d. Mar 1744, bur. Old Marylebone Cem., Paddington St., London – all the family burials listed above were in his tomb; he was an artist, a modeler of portraits in wax; liv. in Horton House, Wraysbury, London; **no issue**

Abraham[2], b. c. 1685; in London, 1709, when he was naturalized

NOTE: **If** the birth dates of Matthew & Abraham are correct, they suggest a _second_ wife. Gossett Genealogy does not identify the wife of Jean[1] nor does it address the gap between the 1st son and the younger ones.

REF: NEWCOMER, Evangeline Gossett, _Family of Gossett_; BURKE, _The Landed Gentry_; AGNEW, D.C.A., _Protestant Exiles from London_.

GRASSET, Auguste

b. 18 Jan 1645, LaRochelle, FR, s/o Pierre & Élisabeth (Coustardeur) Grasset; bp. Huguenot _Temple de la ville neuve_, 5 Feb 1645; Pierre & Élisabeth m. there 7 Dec 1642, they d. a. 1672

m. 27 Jan 1672, Marie Pelé, d/o Pierre & Marie (Gautier) Pelé; her parents d. bef 1672; marriage rec. says Auguste was a merchant

fled FR, went to London; rec. charity from the FR Ch of Threadneedle St; he was a schoolmaster who taught mathematics and astronomy

8 Mar 1681/2 – letter of denization, with many other Huguenots

21 Oct 1681 – became members of the FR Ch of Threadneedle St

p. 4 Mar 1682/3 - to NY, after rec a final grant from the FR Ch to go to "New England"

a. 25 Mar 1688/9 - was in NYC; served in some public offices

d. 7 Apr 1712, NYC; he was murdered during an abortive slave rising

16 Apr 1712 - Gov Hunter issued letters of administration to Louis Dubois, Joseph Oldfield, Henry de Money, his sons-in-law; there was no will

CHILDREN:

Jacques[2], b. 21 Sep, bp. 23 Sep 1672, LaRochelle; d. 4 Oct 1672, LaRochelle

Ester[2], b. 6 Nov 1673, LaRochelle; m. c. 28 Aug 1696 (date of lic.), Louis DuBois; she d. p. 17 Apr 1731, Staten Island; **5 ch**

Marthe[2], b. 1 Oct 1675, LaRochelle; m. a. 28 May 1699, Joseph Oldfield, s/o John & Sara (X) Oldfield, who d. a. 24 Nov 1742, wp; she d. a. Joseph, prob. Goshen, Orange, NY; **6 ch**

Samuel[2], b. 14 Sep 1676, LaRochelle; m. Martha Poupin; a. 1721, to SC; bur. 25 May 1729, St. Philip's Parish, Charleston, SC

    CHILDREN:

    Auguste[3], b. 15 Mar 1698/9, Staten Island

    Ester/Hester[3], b. 2 Apr 1700, Staten Island; m. 1715/6, Jean Samuel Laurens; bur. 3 Apr 1742, Charleston, SC

    Samuel[3], b. c. 1702, Staten Island; m. Jane Dupuy (28 Jun 1705, NYC-bur Aug 1735, Charleston, SC), d/o André & Jeanne (Archambaud) DuPuy; **5 ch**

André[3], b. 26 Mar 1794

Marianne[2], b. 31 Oct 1678, LaRochelle; m. 30 Apr 1701, <u>Henry de Money</u>; d. a. 29 Jan 1755, Elizabeth, Essex Co, NY; **9 ch**

son[2], perhaps **Auguste**, b. Jan 1681, London; bur 2/3 Nov 1681, London – rec. a grant from the Threadneedle St Ch for the burial; also rec. a grant for the bur of ch, 26/27 Oct 1681

Auguste[2], bp. 4 Mar 1682/3, London; perhaps d. young

REF: THOMPSON, Neil D., "Auguste Grasset, of LaRochelle, London, & NY" in *National Genealogical Society Quarterly*, Vol. 66 #1 (Mar 1978); *Register of Ancestors of the Huguenot Society of NJ* (1975).

GUENON/GENON/GENUNG, Jean/Jan

b. a. 1645, said to have been b. Saintonge, FR, nr. LaRochelle, but it is more likely that he was b. in Leiden, prob. of FR parents

2 Apr 1657 - sailed on the *Draetvat* from Amsterdam w/ Marcus de Sauchoy; arr New Amsterdam; settled Flushing, LI, NY

m. 13 Aug 1662, at the Director General's farm, on Manhattan Island, n. of the wall, s. of the New Harlem settlement, on the East River (rec. Bruekelen Ref. Dutch Ch, NY) Margreta/Grietie Sneden (b., prob. Amsterdam, HOL- d. a. 4 Mar 1727, wp, Flushing), d/o Jan Sneden & Grietje Jans; her wd, 21 Feb 1721/2, names sons John & Jeremiah, daus Hannah Hedger & Susanna Loureer + 2 grdaus

d. a. 21 May 1714, wp, Flushing, NY; wd, 24 Nov 1703, which mentions sons John, Jeremiah, wife Margaret, with Margaret named sole executrix

CHILDREN (all bp. Dutch Reformed Ch, Jamaica, NY):

Hannah/Annetje[2], bp. 26 Apr 1664; m. Joseph Hedger; d. a. 1767; **issue**

Grietje[2], bp. 1 Nov 1665; m. John Field?; d. a. 1721/2 (not in mother's will); **no known issue**

Susanna[2], bp. 26 May 1667; m. X Loverser/Louereer/Lowery; **adopted ch**

John/Jan[2], bp. 31 Jan 1669; d. prob. 1767/8; liv. with parents, 1698, apparently unmarr.; said to have been a cripple who later liv w/ his bro Jeremiah

Jeremias[2], bp. 9 Apr 1671; m. c. 1690, Martha (Denman?); d. a. 20 Jun 1748,Westchester Co, NY; **issue**

Saertje[2], bp. 18 Mar 1674; d. a. 1721/2 (not in mother's will); prob. d. unmarr.

REF: RIKER, James, *History of Harlem*; Records of DR Ch, Jamaica, NY – LDS film; GENUNG, Mary Josephine, & NICHOLS, Leon Nelson, *Genung-Ganong-Ganung Genealogy* (Brooklyn, NY, 1906).

GUÉRARD/GUÉRRARD, Jacques/Jacob

b. 1640, Normandie, FR; said to have been Seigneur de Boscheon du Bourg

moved to London

m. XX, in FR or ENG

Mar 1679 - he, Sir Thomas Dolmans & M. René Petit, his Majesty's agent in Rouen, petitioned the King of ENG for the transportation of several FR Protestant families to Carolina; Petit & Guérard asked for 2 royal frigates + £2000 – May 1679, Charles II ordered the ships and money be made available; a list was requested with the names of the prospective colonists, it was submitted & the deal was finalized, 29 Oct 1679; 2 ships were fitted to transport the families; the 1st contingent (45 people) boarded the *Richmond* and set sail for Charles Town/Charleston, SC 17 Dec 1679 - he rec. a grant by the Lord Proprietors for 4000 acres in SC; a warrant dated 16 Nov 1680, was issued to Jacob for a manor of four thousand acres in *"some convenient place not yett laid out or marked to be laid out for any other person or use and if it happen upon any navigable River or river capable to be made soe you are to allow onely the fifth part of the depth thereof by the water side and a Certificate fully specifying the bounds & scittuacon thereof you returne to use with all convenient speed"*

Jan 1680 - the frigate *Richmond* arr Charles Town, SC; Jacob led the 1st contingent of settlers and poss. founded a settlement w. of CharlesTown on Wisboo Creek, a tributary of the Cooper River, later known as French Quarter Creek; the settlement came to be called the Orange Quarter; the record shows that Jacob came with a wife, 4 sons, 2 daus, 1 dau-in-law, 3 servants

d. 1703, Carolinas

CHILDREN (according to the passenger list of the *Richmond*, there were 3 other ch, their names are not known):

Isaac[2], 4 May 1682, apprenticed himself to Maurice Mathews, the Surveyor General

Pierre Jacques/Peter Jacob[2], m. Hannah X (d. 1736); he d. p. 1703; he was an inventor – one invention was the "Pendulum Engine" which husked rice; dau **Margaret**[3] had d. in London – **no further issue**

Jean[2], m. Martha X; he d. 1714

CHILDREN:

David[3], d. unmarr.

John[3], b. SC; m/1, 19 Feb 1735, Elizabeth Hill (d. 7 Jun 1744), d/o Charles Hill – **5 sons**, **1 dau**; m/2, 1745, Marianne Godin (b. 8 Nov 1728), d/o Benjamin Godin – **4 sons**, **1 dau**; his executors disposed of more than 5000 acres after his death

Benjamin[3], d. unmarr.

Martha[3], m. 8 Jun 1725, Rev. Alexander Garden (1685 SCOT-1756), commissary of the Bishop of London, for the Carolinas & GA; **issue**

3 unnamed ch[2]

REF: GUERARD, George C., *Memoirs of the Guerard Family* (Tampa, FL, 1931, not pub.); FRIEDLANDER, Amy Ellen, *Carolina Huguenots, A Study in Cultural Pluralism in the Low County, 1679-1768*; *Warrants for Lands in SC, 1672-1711*; HIRSCH, *Huguenots of Colonial SC.*

GUÉRIN/GUÉRRANT, Daniel

b. 5 Jan 1663, St. Nazaire, Saintonge, FR, prob. now St. Nazaire-sur-Charente, w. of Rochefort, in the Charente-Maritime Dépt, Poitou-Charentes

m. Marie X

was in ENG for while bef emigration to VA

1700 - to VA, on the *Nasseau* w/ wife and 4 ch; since the *Nasseau* came up the Rappahannock River, family prob. went to the Northern Neck or Middle Neck region 1st; his grant was outside the 10,000 acre French lands and he was not on a tithable list in Manakin until 1715

d. p. 18 Jun 1730, VA

CHILDREN:

Pierre/Peter[2], prob. b. ENG; m. c. 1732, Magdeleine Trabue, d/o Anthony & Magdeleine (X) Trabue; he was a major in the colonial wars; d. a. 25 Jun 1750, wp, Cumberland Co, VA; will names all 7 ch + wife

CHILDREN:

John[3], b. 17 Jul 1733, Manakintown; m. Elizabeth Porter; he d. 1823; **issue**

Esther[3], b. 2 Oct 1735, Manakintown, VA; m. 1753, John Bartholomew Dupuy (1723-1791), s/o Jean Jacques/John James & Susanne (LeVillian) Dupuy; she d. 1760/64

Peter, Jr.[3], b. 17 Oct 1737; m. c. 1760, Mary Perreault/Perrow (d. a. Jul 1817), grd/o Charles Perreault; he d. 1819, Montgomery Co, KY; left a will dated, 20 Jul 1817 – names 9 living ch + 2 grch, ch of deceased son William; **10 ch**

Magdelaine[3], b. 31 Aug 1740; m. 23 Sep 1756, Manakintown, Robert Moseley (1732-1802); she d. 19 Mar 1820

Jane[3], m. 11 May 1758, Manakintown, Jacques Brian/James Bryant, Jr.

Judith[3], b. 17 Sep 1745, Manakintown; m. George Smith

Daniel[3], b. 23 Apr 1747; m. 19 Jul 1770, Manakintown, Mary Porter

Jean/John[2], prob. b. ENG; was a lieutenant; son **John**[3] was a pvt in Rev. War; **issue**

Daniel[2], prob. b. ENG; m. Françoise L'Orange (b. c. 1700), d/o Jean Velas & Françoise (X) L'Orange;

he d. a. 17 Aug 1731, inv, Goochland Co, VA – **3 ch**; she m/2, a. fall 1734, <u>Nicolas Souillié</u> who d. summer, 1735, m/3, a. Aug 1738, Samuel Weaver whose wp, 1799, Cumberland Co, VA

Jane[2], prob. b. ENG; no further info

REF: *The Huguenot,* #5 (1931); BROCK, R.A., *Huguenot Emigration to VA* (Baltimore, 1973); JONES, W. Mac, *The Douglas Register* (Richmond, VA, 1928); "Notes from Douglas Register of Records of Goochland Parish" in the *William & Mary College Quarterly*, Vol. II.

GUÉRIN, Pierre

m. Jeanne Billebeau/Billebaud

CHILDREN (birth order not certain; Mathurin, Francis, Peter, definitely bros; Thomas & Vincent *may* be; **see** note below):

Vincent[2], b. St. Nazaire, Saintonge, FR; m. 12 Jul 1703, Parish of St. Denis, SC, Judith Gerin; fled FR & arr Charleston, SC, c. 1688/90

CHILDREN:

Isaac[3], b. 19 Apr 1704; m. 15 Apr 1730, St. Thomas & St. Denis Parish, SC, Martha Mouzon, d/o <u>Louis Mouzon</u>

CHILDREN[4]:

Isaac, Jr.[4]; **Lewis**[4], 1733- 735; **Henry**[4], b. 14 Mar 1736, m. 5 Oct 1760, Magdalene Bonneau, d/o <u>Jacob & Jane (Videau) Bonneau</u>, he d. Apr 1772; **Samuel**[4], bp. 1737, m. 3 Mar 1774, Frances Dochett ; **Esther**[4], m/1, 11 Dec 1760, James Dubois, m/2, <u>John Vincent Guérin</u>, her cousin; **Robert**[4] ,b. 21 Jun 1738, m. Sarah Sanders, he was bur. 12 Jul 1759

Susannah Elizabeth[3], b. 18 Sep 1706; m. 3 Jul 1729, Robert How

John[3], b. 25 Feb 1709/10; m. 20 May 1740, Elizabeth Roberta Johnson; he d. 30 Oct 1756

CHILDREN[4]:

John Vincent[4], bp. 15 Jan 1744, SC, m. 10 Aug 1773, <u>Esther (Guérin) Dubois</u>, his cousin, he d. p. 27 Dec 1792, wd – a. 13 Mar 1793, wp; **Robert**[4], bp. 19 May 1756, SC; **Elizabeth**[4], bp. 28 Feb 1747, m. 22 Feb 1759, Thomas Singletary, she was bur. 5 Oct 1772; **Mary Johnson**[4], bp. 19 Aug 1753, d. p. 22 Jan 1780, wd – a. 11 Aug 1784, wp

Judith[3], b. 20 Feb 1711/12

Marian[3], b. 7 Aug 1714; m. 6 Dec 1733, Abraham Roulain

Peter[3], b. 27 Mar 1717; m/1, 4 Jan 1749/50 Mary Ann Norman, m/2, Margaret X; he d. 12 Apr 1765

CHILDREN:

Martha[4], bp. 24 Nov 1751, m. 5 Jan 1772, Paul Jaudon; **Peter**[4], bp. 18 Apr 1756, d. 28 Jan 1792; **Susannah Isabella**[4], bp. 20 Sep 1761; **James Bileau**[4], bp. 28 Oct 1764

Andrew[3], bp. 13 Dec 1720; m. 26 Dec 1758, Elizabeth McMurtry; d. 18 Dec 1768

François/Francis[2], m. Anne Arriné; d. a. 2 Apr 1730, wp; **no issue**

Pierre/Peter[2], b. St. Nazaire, Saintonge; m. Charlotte X; d. 22 May 1722, SC; fled FR, arr Charleston, SC c. 1688/90; 3 ch: **James**[3], **Frances**[3], **Charlotte**[3]

Thomas[2], b. St. Nazaire, Saintonge; m. XX; d. 1724/25, Whippany, Hanover Twp, Essex Co, NJ; fled FR; Charleston, SC, c. 1688/90; to Essex Co., c. 1713/14; he was a blacksmith; had a French *Bible*

CHILDREN:

Thomas[3], b. 1713, SC; m. c. 1733, Jane (Whitehead?); d. 12 Jun 1790, Morristown, NJ;

CHILDREN: **Moses**[4] (1734-1815); **Joshua**[4] (1737-1808); **Levi**[4], b. 1740; **Epemetus**[4] (1742- 1820); **Joseph**[4] (1748- 1828); **Nathan**[4] (1750-1819); **Mehetible**[4] (1751-1778?); **Vincent**[4] (1756-1828), m. Azubah Brown; **Sarah**[4]; **Jemima**[4], b. 1760; **Susannah**[4]

Joseph[3]

Mathurin I[2], b. c. 1669, St Nazaire, Saintonge; fled FR, arr Charleston, SC, a. 1688 – recorded on St. Julian's list of Swiss and French refugees; m/1, Marie Nicholas, d/o Andre & Françoise (Dunot) Nicholas, a native of La Chaume, Poitou, m/2, 18 May 1708, Susannah (Bouquet) Dessenex, d/o

François Bouquet, widow of Peter Dessenex; Mathurin d. a. 1732, Charleston, SC; Susannah m/3, Mathurin Boigard
CHILDREN, m/2:
Mary/Manon[3], b. 1709, SC; d. 16 Jul 1772, SC, unmarr.
Mathurin II[3], b. 30 Sep 1710, Charleston, SC; m/1, Elizabeth Sandiford, who d. 6 Feb 1770,
    m/2, 7 Jan 1774, Mary Peacock; he d. 3 Nov 1780, Charleston, SC
    CHILDREN, m/1:
    Mathurin III[4], d. 13 Dec 1792, unmarr.; **Francis**[4], b. 1743, Charleston, m. 31 Dec 1782, St
    Andrews Parish, SC, Agnes Bush, he d. 1809; **William**[4], m. 24 Nov 1763, Mary Elliott (d. 20
    Jan 1768), he d. 20 Jun 1768; **James**[4], d. a. 3 Oct 1774, Charleston, SC; **Frances**[4], m. 3 May
    1759, Thomas Stone; **Elizabeth**[4], m. David Cruger, she d. p. 1772; **Susannah**[4], b. 1757, m. 26
    Jan 1785, Charleston, SC, Joseph Gibbs, she d. 1840; **Thomas**[4], d. c. 2 Oct 1777; **John**[4] (?)
Frances[3], m. 20 Jan 1725/6, St. Philip's Ch, SC, William Elliott; she d. 18 Dec 1752, SC

NOTE: Francis' will proves that Peter and Mathurin were his bros; Peter, Thomas, Francis & Vincent appear to have acted as a family group where business & legal transactions were concerned but Francis' will mentioned only the families of Peter and Mathurin, both of whom were deceased by then. Given the fact that this Guérin family and that of Daniel (above) and an Étienne who went to NY in 1705 all came from St. Nazaire, there is prob. a family connection but what it is exactly is not known. Proof needed.

REF: STRAWN, Ann W., "Guerin Family" in the *Transactions of the Huguenot Society of SC*, #90 (1985); BAIRD, Charles W., *History of the Huguenot Emigration to America* (Baltimore, 1966); CLUTE, Robert F. *The Annals and Parish Register of St. Thomas & St. Denis Parish in SC from 1680-1884* (1884, reprinted 1989); BURNS, Martha B., "Vincent Guerin of St. Thomas and St. Denis [SC] in the *Transactions of the Huguenot Society of SC*, #69 (1964); RICE, Denise Guerin, *Guerin Genealogy Manuscript* (1996); RICE, Denise Guerin, *Guerin Family & Allied Lines* (1998); Mathurin II's will; EAKIN, Anita V., *Mathurin Guérin's Children.*

GUERRI/GUERRY, Pierre

    b. c. 1645, FR, Sepvret, Poitou, now in Deux-Sèvres Dépt, Poitou-Charentes, s.e. of Niort, s/o Jacques &
        Anne (X) Guerri
    m. FR, Jeanne Broussard, d/o Louis & Judith (Broussard?) Broussard, also of Sepvret; record says Seuvret
        – no such place
    from Poitou to Dublin, IRE to SC
    1696 - naturalized, prob. SC
    d. Georgetown, SC
    CHILDREN:
François[2], b. Dublin
Jean[2], b. SC
Pierre II[2], b. SC ; m. Marguerite Rembert, d/o André & Anne (Bressau) Rembert; he d. a. 5 Apr 1737, wp,
    St. James Parish, Santee, SC; will names wife, sons Elisha, Andrew & Peter, does not name 5 daus
    CHILDREN:
    Anne[3], m. 28 Sep 1745/6, Alexander duPont, s/o Abraham & Anne (Faucheraud) du Pont; **Madeleine**[3];
    Elizabeth[3]; **Margaret**[3]; **Elisha**[3], m. cousin Jeanne/Jane Guerri, d/o Jean-Jacques & Jeanne
    Rembert) Guerri - 6 ch; **André**[3], m. Anne X; **Peter**[3], m/1, Mary Ann LeGrand, d/o Isaac, grdau/o Isaac
    & Élisabeth (Dieu) LeGrand of Caen, Normandie, FR - 6 ch; **Lydia**[3]
Jean-Jacques[2], b. SC; m/1, Jeanne Rembert, d/o André & Anne (Bressau) Rembert, m/2, Esther X; he d. a
    4 Feb 1734/5, wp, Charleston Co, SC
    CHILDREN, m/1: **John**[3], m. XX – **1 son, 1 dau** ; **James**[3], (1717-1782), m. 1738, Mary Jane
        Rembert (1720-1786), *poss.* d/o James & Jeanne (Rembert) Guerri – at least **3 sons, 1
        dau**; **Jane**[3], d. c. 1758
    CHILDREN, m/2: **Esther**[3], m. 1744, John Perdiau; **Stephen**[3], m. 9 Sep 1769, Mary Sanders who

m/2, 3 May 1774, Jonah Roberts, Stephen d. 1772; **Mary**[3]

Jeanne Elizabeth[2], b. c. 1702, SC; m. Étienne Dumay

REF: "Liste des françois et suisses réfugiez en Caroline qui souhaittent d'être naturalizés anglois (1696)" in the *Transactions of the Huguenot Society of SC* #76 (1971); RAVENEL, Daniel, *French & Swiss Protestants settled in Charleston, the Santee & the Orange Quarter in Carolina who desire Naturalization, 1695/96* (1968) ; WILSON, Rv. Robert, "The Pedigree Tables of Guerry, Rembert, Michau, DuPont & Cromwell" in *Transactions of the Huguenot Society of SC*, #75 (1970). SIMMONS, Agatha Aimar, *Abstracts of the Wills of the State of SC, 1670-1670*, Vol. I.

GU(E)TILIUS/GUTELIUS, Jean Pierre/Johann Peter/John Peter

b. 1708, FR, s/o Adam Frederick Gutilius, a FR Army surgeon

said to have been a physician to the Queen of FR who banished him for marrying "outside his station"; given his age at the b. of his son John Peter (57), it would seem possible that he was m/1 in FR and that Anna Maria was his 2nd wife whom he mar. in PA; there is a 15 yr. gap between his arrival in PA and the birth of his son John Peter who is reportedly his eldest son

arr Philadelphia on the *Nancy* from Rotterdam, via Cowes; name is Johann Peter Gutelius on the ship's passenger list; the ship's list give only the names of the male passengers

31 Aug 1750 – took Oath of Allegiance in Philadelphia

m. Anna Maria Deitzler (said to have been of Dutch descent)

d. 29 Sep 1773, Manheim, Lancaster, PA; both he & Anna Maria are bur. in the cem. of the Reformed Ch in Manheim

CHILDREN (known, poss. others):

John Peter[2], b. 1765

Frederick Adam[2], b. 26 Dec 1766, Manheim; m. 31 Aug 1790, Anna Catherine Bistel (2 Apr 1773-11 May 1828, age 65Y 1M 9D); went to Mifflinburg, c. 1800, where they liv. on the n.e. corner of 5th & Green St.; he was a blacksmith & surveyor, held several civic offices; he d. 30 May 1839, Mifflinburg, Union, PA (age 72Y 5M 4D); he and his wife are bur. in the old cem. of the Reformed Ch in Mifflinburg; **11 sons, 4 daus**

Mary[2], b. c. 1768; m. 1785, Joseph Ultz (1762-1808)

REF: Manuscript Collection of the Huguenot Society of PA; *Reformed Church Messenger* (5 Dec 1918) – no citation as to its origin; GUTELIUS, John Peter, *History of the Gutelius Family* (1916); GUTELIUS, Will Buckles, *History of the Gutelius Family* (Bluffton, IN, 1915); STRASSBURGER, Ralph Beaver, *PA German Pioneers*, Vol. I (Baltimore, 1966); STRASSBURGER, Ralph Beaver, *PA German Pioneers*, *Facsimile Signatures Volume* (Springfield, VA, 1992).

GUIBERT, François/Franz

of Brizay, Indre et Loire Dépt, Centre, FR, n.w. Châtellerault

m. Margaret Nicholas

CHILD :

Franz[2], b. 1775; m. Catherine Salome (X) Süss (1767-1836), widow of Bartholomew Süss

CHILD:

Johann George[3], b. 1797, Alsace; m/1, XX, m/2, 1824, Maria Magdelene Sommer (1800-1870), d/o Philip & Maria Margaret (Wolf) Sommer - their dau **Anna Maria Catherine**[4], b. 16 Apr 1836, Frœschwiller, Bas-Rhin Dépt, Alsace, s.w. of Wissembourg, m. 25 Jan 1854, Pittsburgh, PA, Adam Bert of Rohrbach, Hesse, GER; Johann d. 1847, New Brighton, Beaver, PA

REF: Family Records - Frœschwiller, Alsace.

GUIBERT/GUYBERT, Josué/Joshua

b. Rennes, Bretagne, FR, s.w. Le Mont-Saint-Michel; some have interpreted "Rheines" (below) as Reims, however, Reims was never in "high Brittany"

by 1667 - immigrated as "a free adult" from FR; resided "Lukeland," Chaptico 100, St. Mary's Co, MD

m/1, prob. MD, Elizabeth Barber, poss. d/o Luke Barber

1678 – petitioned assembly of MD for naturalization; states that he was b. in the city of "Rheines in high Brittany in the Kingdom of France"

m/2, p. 1693, Elizabeth (Gerard) Blakiston, d/o Thomas Gerard (1608-1673), widow of Ralph Rymer & Nehemiah Blakiston (d. 1693); she d. a. 17 Sep 1717, wp, St. Mary's Co

d. a. 16 May 1713, wp, St. Mary's Co; he was a planter, attorney, merchant; served in the Lower House, St. Mary's Co (1708-1711), was also a justice in St. Mary's Co (1694-1708)

CHILDREN, prob. all m/1 (1st 6 ch in father's will; last 2* in Elizabeth's will of 1717, but not in Joshua's - they are either Elizabeth's daus by one of her earlier marr, **or** they were minor ch in 1713):

Thomas[2]

Matthew[2]

Joshua[2]

Mary[2], m. X Mason; **issue**

Elizabeth[2], m. Thomas Turner

Anne[2], m/1, John Blackston/Blakiston, her stepbro, s/o Nehemiah (above)- **issue** ; m/2, William Phippard; she d. p. 7 Jan 1738/9, wd

[*Susanna, m. X Attoway, *Rebecka, m. X Walters; one interesting "quirk" of Elizabeth's will is her repeated insistence that her heirs be Protestant]

REF: NEWMAN, Harry Wright, *To Maryland from Overseas* (Baltimore, 1985); COTTON, Jane Baldwin & HENRY, Roberta Bolling, editors & compilers, *The MD Calendar of Wills*, Vol. IV (Baltimore, 1968); PAPENFUSE, Edward C., DAY, Alan F., JORDAN, David W. & STIVERSON, Gregory A., *A Biographical Dictionary of the MD Legislature, 1635-1789* (Baltimore); wills of Joshua, Elizabeth, dau Ann, St. Mary's Co, MD.

GUIGNARD, Gabriel

b. 12 Dec 1708, Île d'Oléron, nr. La Rochelle, FR; had a sister Anna who m. X Jafford, they had son John

c. 1735 - to SC

m/1, XX (d. a. 10 Nov 1746); had son who also d.; both bur. Charleston, SC;

m/2, 10 Nov 1746, Christ Ch Parish, Charleston, SC, Frances de Liesseline (1730-1773), d/o Jean & Magdelen (Bruneau) de Liesseline

d. a. 30 Sep 1757, wp, Charleston, SC; he was a cooper and merchant; had a lot of property, slaves & cash when he d.; bur. FR Huguenot churchyard in Charleston next to 1st wife and son; liv Colleton Square; wanted his ch to be educated in the "French tongue" and to attend the FR Protestant Ch in Charleston

CHILDREN, m/2:

John Gabriel[2], b. c. 1751; m. Elizabeth Sanders (c. 1764-1 Sep 1814), d/o James & Sarah (Slann) Sanders; he d. 9 Jan 1822, Columbia, SC

Anna Magdalen/Nancy[2], b. 7 Feb 1750; m. 13/21 Oct 1768, Charleston, SC, William Richardson (31 Jul 1743, Charleston-13/17 Feb 1786, bur. Bloom Hill family cem), s/o Edward & Elizabeth (X) Richardson; she d. 23 May 1810

   CHILD:

   William Guignard[3], b. 16 Apr 1773; m/1, 26 Feb 1798, Harriet Ann Everleigh, d/o Thomas & Ann (Simmons) Everleigh - **4 ch**, m/2, 5 Mar 1809, Emma Cooper Buford, d/o William & Frances June Buford - **12 ch**; he d. 8 Sep 1849, Clermont Co, SC, bur. Bloom Hill

Frances[2] m. George Joor

Margaret[2] m. Peter Horry; **no issue**

REF: *Registers, St. Philips and St. Patrick Churches*; *Transactions of the Huguenot Society of SC,* Vol. LV, pp. 46-7, Vol. 75, pp. 80-1 (1970), Vol. 79 (1974); *Family Bible*; *SC Hist. & Gen. Magazine,* Vol. XX, Baltimore (1919), p. 61 & Vol. XXXVIII (1937), p. 51; BAILEY, N.L., editor, *Biographical Directory of SC Senate,* Vol. II, Columbia (1986), p. 1373; SALLEY, A.S., Jr., *Marriage Notices in the SC & American General Gazette, 1766-1781,* Columbia (1914), p. 11; LANGLEY, C.A., *SC Deed Abstracts, 1719-1772,* Vol. II; CHILDS, Arney R., editor, *Planters & Business Men The Guignard Family of SC, 1795-1930* (Columbia, SC, 1957); MOORE, Caroline T., *Abstracts of the Wills of the State of SC, 1740-1760.*

GUILLET, Jacques

[there is some conflicting data on the lineage but the following is *prob.* correct; ch of Jacques are in church records and re the info on the ch of James Louis, sources agree]

b. c. 1693, Blain, Bretagne, FR, s/o Jacques Louis Guillet; Blain, n.w. of Nantes, now in Loire-Atlantique Dépt, Pays de la Loire

fled FR to Isle of Jersey & became a member of St. Helier Parish

m. 16 Nov 1713, St. Saviour, Isle of Jersey, Marie LeTellier

d. prob. Isle of Jersey

CHILDREN (all 7 ch bap. St. Helier Parish):

Jacques[2], bp. 24 Oct 1714,

Marie Ann[2], bp. 25 Aug 1717

Elizabeth[2], bp. 28 Feb 1719

Thomas[2], bp. 11 Mar 1721

James Louis[2], bp. 26 Jan 1725/6; m. Mary (X) Westaway; he was bur. 17 Apr 1793, St. Helier

 CHILDREN:

  James Charles[3], **Mary Ann**[3], **Daniel**[3], **Sally Ann**[3] (d. young), **George**[3] - nothing more,

  Elizabeth[3], b. c. 1765, m. 19 Feb 1787, Westminster Abbey, Joshua Gabourel – **issue**;

  Charles Willliam[3], b. c. 1772, m. 1796, Marie Thoreau (bp 12 Feb 1772-6 May 1810), d/o Jean & Marie Anne (Tantin) Thoreau; he d. 12 Dec 1809 – **issue**, Marie was the 2nd cousin, once removed, of Henry David Thoreau, the celebrated American author (1817-1862)

Jean[2], bp. 25 Dec 1728

Moyes[2], bp. 1729

REF: REAMON, B. Elmore, *Trails of the Huguenots* (Baltimore, 1966); GUILLET, Edwin C., *The Guillet-Thoreau Genealogy* (Toronto, CAN, 1971); *The Thoreau Society Bulletin,* #148 (Summer, 1979).

GUIMAR/GUYMARD, Pierre

b. 1666, Moëze, Saintonge, s.w. of Rochefort (now in the Charente-Maritime Dépt, Poitou-Charentes), s/o Pierre & Anne (d'Amour) Guimar/Gumaer

c. 1686 - from FR to ENG; then to MD, with letter from Reformed Ch – emigrated with Jacques Caudebec; the only work they could find to do was sorting and combing flax which didn't pay well so they decided to go to New Amsterdam (Manhattan); went up the Hudson to Esopus/Kingston; then to New Paltz

m. 18 Apr 1692, New Paltz, NY, Hester Hasbrouck, d/o Jean & Anna (Deyo) Hasbrouck

d. a. 4 Oct 1732, wp, Albany, NY

CHILDREN:

Anna[2], b. 20 Mar 1693; m. (Maj.) James Jacobsen Swartout

Hester[2], b. 5 May 1697; m. Samuel Swartout

Rachel[2], b. 8 Feb 1700

Mary[2], b. 8 Dec 1702; m. Jan Elting; **issue**

Elizabeth[2]

Pierre[2], b. 15 Nov 1708; m. Charity Dewitt (1710-12 Nov 1766); **issue**

REF: LeFEVRE, Ralph, *History of New Paltz, NY, & its Old Families from 1678-1820* (Albany, 1903); GUMAER, Harry T., *A Minisink Fragment* (1981).

GUINÈRE, Louis

1628 – Louis & François Angevine were sent by Guiton, the LaRochelle leader, to speak to Cardinal Richelieu; they were told that King Louis XIII would be merciful with the people of La Rochelle but that the king would set the terms; the siege continued and thousands d. of hunger. Before the siege, which began in 1627, there were 27,000 inhabitants of LaRochelle, by 28 Oct 1628, when it ended, only 5000 had survived.

CHILD:

Charlotte[2] m. Henri Angevine, s/o François & Marie (X) Angevine; the 3 ch of their son **Louis**[3] were the emigrants to America

REF: Angevine, Erma, *In America – the Angevines* (Washington, DC, 1976, not pub.).

GUION, Louis II

b. 1654, LaRochelle, FR, s/o Louis Guion I, an *écuyer* (squire, equerry, riding master, but also one who carries the shield (*écu*) of a knight)

m. T(h)omasa Forestier/Forestière of Saintonge (b. 1656); erroneously called Mary on the 1710 census

c. 1681 - left FR for ENG; later to America

c. 1687 - settled New Rochelle, NY

1690/1 - purchased property in New Rochelle nr. the Episcopal Ch; 8 Oct 1725, he conveyed it to son Aman

6 Feb 1695/6 - rec. letters of denization from King William of ENG; signed the Oath of Allegiance, May 1696; letters said to be for Louis and his son; since Louis III was too young, Louis I must have emigrated with his son Louis II, thus adding to the confusion!

d. a. 23 Nov 1732, wp; he was a blacksmith; his will mentions wife Tomaza, sons Lewis, Jr, Isaac and Aman – no mention of Susannah; will dated, 8 Oct 1725 and he is said to have d. "some short time thereafter"

CHILDREN:

Isaac[2], b. 1685, ENG; m. 25 Aug 1710, Marie Malherbe, d/o Nicolas Malherbe; he d. p. 9 Feb 1769, wd-a. 7 May 1783, wp; **7 or 8 ch**

Susannah[2], b. 1685, ENG; nothing more known

Louis III[2], b. 1686, at sea; m. 1712, Dinah deVeaux, d/o Frederick DeVeaux, she m/2, Tobias Cochelin; Louis d. 1731; **6 daus, 2 sons**

Aman/Louis Amon[2], b. 1691, New Rochelle; m/1, Margaret Suire – **1 son**, m/2, Elizabeth Samson – **2 daus, 3 sons** ; he d. a. 7 Jun 1760, wp

NOTE: There were other Guions in NY but no connection has been made – Jacques/James on Staten Island by 1675; Louis Guion from Mauzé, a sm. village nr. LaRochelle, who m. Marie Morin & had son Louis, bp. 21 Aug 1694, FR Ch, Glasshouse St, London – family later went to New Rochelle; Deborah Guion who m. Pierre/Peter Angevine – had son Louis, b. 19 Feb 1702

REF: GUION, J. Marshall IV, *Descendants of Louis Guion, Huguenot of LaRochelle, FR & New Rochelle, Westchester Co, Province of NY* (Olean, NY, 1976) ; BOLTON, Robert Jr., *History of the County of Westchester Co*, Vol. I (NY,1848); SETH, Natalie M., compiler, *The Guion Family* (White Plains, NY, 1956, unpub.).

GUIT(T)EAU/GUITAUT/GUYTEAU, François I

b. bet.1617-25, FR, s/o Moïse & wife #2 Philippe (Bellin) de Guitaut; she was bur. 20 Nov 1676, La
    Mothe-Saint-Héray, aged 59; Moïse (b. 1584) was a Huguenot soldier who served in Henri IV's
    army, was a Capt. in the Royal Guard; protected Anne of Austria, mother of King Louis XIV,
    whom he aided in her flight to St. Germain, Jan 1649/50

m. c. 10 Jul 1651 (date marr. contract was signed at La Mothe), Suzanne (Levèsque) Baugier, d/o Louis &
    Catherine (Fraigneau) Levèsque, wid/o Jean Baugier; Suzanne d. p. 3 Jun 1714, prob. at Poitiers

François was the Court Physician supposedly up to c. 1680

d. p. 9 Jul 1662, wd, La Mothe-Saint-Héray, n.e. of Niort, now in Deux Sèvres Dépt, Poitou-Charentes;
    since son Josué was bp. 1677, he d. long after his will was written; said to have gone to HOL
    with his family, so may have d. there

CHILDREN:

Philippe[2], bp. 26 Apr 1654, La Mothe Saint-Héray; m. Samuel Marchand, physician of Saint-Jean-
    d'Angély, s.e. of Saintes, now in the Charente-Maritime Dépt, Poitou-Charentes; in FR, Philippe
    means both Philip and Philippa, in the case of her mother and herself, it means Philippa

François II[2], b. c. 1660, Paris; m. c. 1685/6, Marthe Guidon, d/o Olivier Guidon, seigneur of Chaumes &
    Palluau; in HOL, by 17 Aug 1687 – member of the Walloon Ch; left for London, 3 May 1699;
    1710, naturalized London, which is the last official record; said to have been liv ENG in 1723 but *may*
    have been alive as late as 18 Feb 1742/3

    CHILDREN:

    Louis-Olivier[3], bp. 2 Apr 1687, Couhé, s.w. of Poitiers, now Vienne Dépt, Poitou-Charentes; m.
        11 Oct 1718, La Mothe, Susanne Servant; he d. bet 12 Dec 1741, wd-7 Sep 1744, wp,
        Canterbury, ENG

    child[3], bur. Westerkerk, Amsterdam, 10 Dec 1689; fam. liv. Lauriergracht; ch. was on Prisengracht
        in the neighborhood (today the Anne Frank House is 1 block n. of the ch.); *gracht*=canal

    François/Francis III[3], b. c. 1690; to America by 1710; m. 23 Feb 1714, Wallingford, CT, Mary
        Tyler (1 Sep 1695, Wallingford-11 Aug 1774, Woodbury), d/o William & Mary (Lathrop)
        Tyler; he d. 2 Sep 1760, Woodbury CT; he was a physician

        CHILDREN (1st 7 b. Wallingford, others b. Woodbury):

        Theophilus[4], b. 22 Nov 1716; d. 12 Dec 1716, Wallingford

        Joshua[4], b. 2 Jan 1718; m/1, 3 Jul 1745, Woodbury, CT, Esther Judd, m/2, 7 Jan 1747/8,
            Woodbury, Jerusha Judson, m/3, 20 Jan 1775, Woodbury, Anna Northrup

        Mary[4], b. 19 Aug 1720; m. 8 Apr 1742, Lebanon, CT, David Lyman, as his 3rd wife; she d.
            1803, prob. Bethlehem, CT; **issue**

        Martha[4], b. 17 Apr 1723; d. 19 Jul 1725, Wallingford

        Ebenezer[4], 28 Nov 1725; not in father's will

        Ruth[4], b. 21 Apr 1728; m. 28 Nov 1758, Litchfield, CT, Robert Waugh

        Sarah[4], b. 8 Sep 1730; m. 14 Apr 1763, Woodbury, CT, Thomas Doolittle

        Phebe[4], b. 16 Nov 1732; m. 19 Jan 1768, Canaan, CT, James Stephens

        Francis IV[4], b. 12 Aug 1736; m/1, 10 Jan 1765, Middletown, CT, Anna Macky, m/2, 4
            Sep 1781, New Ashford, MA, "the widow Wheeler"

        Ephraim[4], b. 22 Jun 1738; m. 21 Oct 1762, Norfolk, CT, Phebe Humphrey (10 May 1745-
            27 Feb 1828), d/o Michael Humphrey; he was a physician; he d. 21 Apr 1816,
            Norfolk, CT; **issue**

    Marc[3], bp. Waals Hervormde Kerk, Amsterdam, 7 Jun 1691 – church is s.e. of the Westerkerk in
        The Walenpleintje (a square) off Oude Hoogstraat (a street); the name of the ch means
        Reformed Walloon Ch; a child, prob. Marc, bur. 9 Jul 1694, Waals Hervormde Kerk,

    François Théophile/Francis Theophilus[3], bp. Waals Hervormde Kerk, Amsterdam, 29 Aug 1694;
        m. 9 Aug 1743, Spring Garden, London, Marie St. Paul, of Chelsea; he d. p. 12 Feb 1763, wd-
        a. 7 Nov 1764, wp, Canterbury; **3 ch**, bap Threadneedle St, London

Moïse-Louis[2], seigneur of Parandeau; by 1693, held the fiefdom of Perjaudière; lived Loubigné, s.e. of
    Saintes, now in Deux Sèvres Dépt, Poitou-Charentes

[?François Théophile[2], b. c. 1673; m. c. 23 Jan 1699, Amsterdam (date of marr int) Alida de Lange, 18 yrs old of the Cape of Good Hope, both liv. on the Anjeliersgracht; he was a surgeon]*

Josué/Joshua[2], bp. 2 Feb 1677, La Mothe; immigrated to Amsterdam and London with brother François; m/1, 1728, Anne Lambert who d. a few yrs. later; m/2, 12 Oct 1732, St. Martin Ongars, (Josué called a *lecteur* of Bruns (Brown's) Lane, Spitalfields) Marthe Voyer ,who d. p. 21 Jan 1769, wd Christ Church, Middlesex - a. 13 Feb 1769, wp, Prerogative Ct of Canterbury; Joshua d. p. 26 May 1756, wd-a. 11 Jan 1757, wp.

Susanne[2], prob. in HOL by 7 Jul 1688; witness at bap of nephew Marc in 1691Amsterdam

*This record of an intent to marry was in the church records from Amsterdam; given the date of birth, name + the fact that he was a surgeon, leads to the *possibility* that he was another s/o François II.

REF: *The American Genealogist,* Vol. 319 #3, pp. 164-176; SHAW, William A., "Letters of Denization & Acts of Naturalization for Aliens in ENG & IRE 1701-1800" in *Huguenot Society of London Quarto Series,* Vol. 27 (1923); Vital Records – Wallingford & Woodbury, CT; JACOBUS, Donald Lines, *Families of Ancient New Haven*; *Genealogy of the Guiteau Family* (not pub, dated) – includes items from *Life & Times of Louis XIV* by P. R. JAMES (London, 1891); bap records, Walloon Ch, Amsterdam (in French).

GUSTIN, Jean/John - see JEAN, Augustine

H

HARCOURT/HARAUCOURT/HERANCOURT/HÉRAUCOURT, Jean de

b. 1658, FR
m. Judith le Seure/Feure (1660-30 Oct 1726, Mühlhofen, GER)
a. 1690, he and his family went to Mühlhofen (n.w. Karlsruhe) in the Rheinpfalz; 1 dau remained in FR
d. 18 Sep 1740, Mühlhofen, GER
CHILDREN:
Tochter[2] (dau) – GER ch rec says she remained in FR, so must have been the 1st ch born; could mean
    that she d. in FR
Paul[2], b. 1692; m. Susanne Erné (1704-11 Aug 1762, Mühlhofen); he d. 15 Jan 1766, Mühlhofen
Anna Marie[2], m/1, X Wiemer; m/2, Isaac de Türk, s/o Johannes & Hester (Kip) de Turk
Pierre/Peter[2], b. 5 Aug, bp. 12 Aug 1696, FR Ch, Mannheim; m. 4 May 1727, Christine Jourlis, d/o
    Jakob Jourlis; **6 ch**
Susanne[2], m. 2 Feb 1712, Barbelroth, GER, Jean Bertolet
Esther[2], b. Barbelroth; m. Mühlhofen, Johan Jakob Steiner

REF: HERAUCOURT, Will, PhD, *Genealogie auf wissenshaftlicher Grundlage der Familien Haraucourt Herancourt-Héraucourt* (Marburg, 1964); BERTOLET, Daniel H, *A Genealogical History of the Bertolet Family, the Descendants of Jean Bertolet* (1914).

HARDIN/HARDOUIN/HARDEWYN, Martin

said to have been b. in Rouen, FR; fam. said to have come to NY, by 1626, w/ the Dutch East India
    Co. – no proof of that –seems too early; name may be Flemish, not French, thus Dutch, but
    could be a result of living in Holland for a time; Martin's parents unknown
1671 - in Fordham, NY
m. 5 Mar 1671, Dutch Reformed Ch, NYC, Madeleine du Sauchoy (bap. 20 Jan 1658*), d/o Marc(us) &
    Elizabeth (Rossingnol) du Sauchoy; both parties liv. in Fordham; Madeleine/Magdaleen
    admitted to membership in that church, 2 Mar 1676; *doubtful that she was 13 at the time
    of her marr. – she was prob. not an infant at the time of the bap.
by 7 Feb 1680 - to Staten Island when Martin was the plaintiff vs. Clas Smith for debt and on the
    same day, defendant in suit by Andros Canon for debt
5 Apr 1684 - he had a survey done for 103 acres on the w. side of Staten Island, which adjoined
    property owned by his father-in-law
1696 – he bought property in NJ; death dates for Martin and Madeleine have not been found; there
    was a Martin Hardin who, on 26 Dec 1719, made an inventory of Samuel Hunt's estate in
    Hunterdon Co, NJ; could have moved to NJ, or this reference *could* be a 6th ch, as suggested
    below
CHILDREN:
Abraham[2], chr. 15 May 1673 (twin), Dutch Ch , NYC
Isaac[2], chr. 15 May 1673 (twin), Dutch Ch, NYC
Elizabeth/Lysbeth[2], chr. 19 Feb 1676, Reformed Dutch Ch, NYC
Jacob[2], chr. 13 Mar 1678, Reformed Dutch Ch, NYC
Marcus/Mark[2], chr. 26 Mar 1681, Staten Island
prob. **Martin**[2], m/1, Hannah Hunt, 4 Jan 1714, Philadelphia, PA, m/2, Catherine X; he d. p. 10 Jun 1764, wd,
Hunterdon Co, NJ; **5 ch**

NOTE: The lineage of this family has been mixed up. Apparently the immigrant was not Mark[2], which has
been suggested previously. There is, of course, a *possibility* that the Mark Hardin who was in VA, was the son
of Martin and Madeleine – again, no absolute proof of that statement. Mark Hardin of VA did not name his ch

after the NY Hardins, with the possible exceptions of Martin, Elizabeth. The Mark Hardin in VA was said to have been a Huguenot, b. 1680 in FR – again, no PROOF.

REF: HOLTZCLAW, B.C., *Ancestry & Descendants of the Nassau-Siegen Immigrants to VA, 1714-1750*, pp. 315 ff; WULFECK, Dorothy F., *Hardin & Harding of VA & KY; The Huguenot* #13, (1945/47); JETER, Donald C., "Hardin Family" in *Marshall Co. Historical Quarterly*, Vol. 14 (Fall 1983); RIKER, James, *Revised History of Harlem* (NY, 1904); Records Reformed Dutch Ch, NYC.

HASBROUCQ/HASBROUCK, Jean

m. Esther X
CHILDREN:
Jean[2], b. c. 1643, nr. Calais, FR; merchant who went to Mannheim, c. 1666/7; m. Mannheim, Anna Deyo (1644-5 May 1694), d/o Chrétien & Jeanne (Verbeau) Deyo; dismissal letter from Mannheim Ch dated 27 Mar 1672; 15 Jul 1701, denization in NY; he d. a. 14 Aug 1714, wp, Ulster Co, NY
  CHILDREN:
  Maria[3], b. 8 Jan 1664, Mutterstadt, s.w. of Mannheim; m. 1 Jun 1683, Kingston, Isaac DuBois (1659/60-Jun 1690), s/o Louis & Catherine (Blanchan) DuBois; she d. 26 Nov 1709; **5 ch**
  Anna[3], b. 30 Sep 1666, Otterberg, GER, n.e. of Kaiserlautern & w. of Mannheim; d. young
  Hester, b. 12 Nov 1668, Mannheim; m. 18 Apr 1692, New Paltz, Peter Gumaer/Guimar of Minisink, s/o Pierre & Anne (d'Amour) Guimar; she d. 15 May 1712, bur. Guimar Cem., nr. Cuddebackville; **6 ch**
  Abraham[3], b. 27 Aug 1677, bp. 31 Mar 1678, Kingston, NY; p. 1691, went to ENG, did not return
  Isaac[3], b. 15 Jan 1680, bp. 17 Apr 1680 rec. Brooklyn; marched w/ Capt. Wessel TenBrouck's Company on the invasion of Canada, 1711; never returned; but sis Eliz.'s diary says he d. 9 Oct 1709
  Elizabeth/Lysbet[3], b. 25 Feb 1685, bp. 4 Apr 1685; m. 2 Jun 1713, Louis Bevier, s/o Louis & Marie (Le Blanc) Bevier , d. 10 Jun 1760
  Jacob[3], bp. 15 Apr 1688; m. 14 Dec 1717, Hester Bevier, d/o Louis Bevier, s/o Louis & Marie (Le Blanc) Bevier; d.c.1761 **6 ch**
Andries[2]
Elizabeth[2], m. Pierre Haayar
Peter[2], m. Barbara X; they appear in Mannheim recs., 1673
Abraham[2], b. c. 1650, nr Calais, FR; m. 17 Nov 1675, Maria Deyo, d/o Chrétien & Jeanne (Verbeau) Deyo; he d. 7 Mar 1717, Maria d. 27 Mar 1741; he was the patentee; supposedly served in the English army; 1685 – commissioned lieutenant, 1689 captain of foot in "Ye Paltz"; appt. justice at Hurley
  CHILDREN:
  Rachel[3], bp. 12 May1680, Reformed Dutch Ch, NYC; d. young
  Anna[3], bp. 9 Oct 1682; d. young
  Joseph[3], b. 28 Jan 1684, bp 23 Oct 1684 ; m. 27 Oct 1706, Elsje Schoonmaker (bp. 13 Dec 1685-27 Jul 1764), d/o Joachim & Petronella (Sleght) Schoonmaker; he d. 28 Jan 1723
  Salomon[3], b. 6 Oct 1686, bp. 17 Oct 1686; m. 7 Apr 1721, New Paltz, Sara VanWagenen (b.1 Dec 1701), d/o Jacob Aertsen & Sara (Pels) Van Wagnen; **8 ch**
  Jonas[3], b. 14 Oct 1691; d. young
  Daniel[3], b. 23 Jun 1692, bp 3 Jun 1694; m. 2 Apr 1734, Wyntje Deyo (24 Jan 1708-30 Oct 1787), d/o Abraham & Elsie (Clearwater) Deyo; he d. 5 Jan 1759 ; **9 ch**
  Benjamin[3], bp. 3 May 1696; m. 13 Jan 1737, Jannetje DeLange
  Rachel[3], bp. 12 May 1696 ; m. 19 Jan 1701, Louis DuBois, (1677-1749), s/o Louis & Catherine (Blanchan) DuBois

REF: VAN WAGENEN, Gerrit H., "Early Settlers of Ulster County" in *NYG&B Record,* Vol. 7 (Oct 1886): HASBROUCK, Kenneth E., *The Hasbrouck Family in America* (New Paltz, 1961); HASBROUCK, Kenneth E. & HEIDGERD, Ruth P., *The Deyo (Deyoe) Family* (New Paltz, 1958).

HAUSER, Martin I

b. 11 Nov 1696, Reichenweier, Alsace, FR, 8 km. n.w. of Colmar, now called Riquewihr, s/o Hans Georg & Susanna (Burckhardt) Hauser; bp Lutheran

1721 - m. Maria Margaretha Schaefer, b. 4 Nov 1702, Lampertsloch, Alsace, s.w. of Wissembourg, d/o Johann Michel & Maria Barbara (Geiger) Schaefer; she d. NC, Jan, 1775

[FR influence & increased presence in the area led to religious strife and there was the burden of double taxation as both the French and the rulers of Württemberg-Montbéliard demanded money]

c. 1726 - fam. left Alsace, went to Rotterdam, HOL, where he worked as a carpenter, work he did in US

summer 1727 - emigrated on the English ship *Molly*, landing in Deal, E. Kent, ENG, and then across the Atlantic

30 Sep 1727 – arr. Philadelphia; Margaretha found her mother Barbara living in Conshohocken, Montgomery Co, n.w. of Philadelphia; they stayed there for 2 yrs

c. 1734 - crossed the Susquehanna to the Conowago River, s.w. of York, where they stayed 6 yrs

1744 - moved to MD where Martin began farming; went to NC w/ sons Georg & Michael along with wife, Martin Jr, Georg Peter, Daniel

d.12 Jun 1761, nr. Bethania, Forsyth, NC, n.w. of Winston-Salem; his will was dated, 23 May 1761 & written in German, names wife, son Peter, son George; says that other ch who has already rec money should have that sum subtracted from his/her inheritance upon the death of their mother

CHILDREN:

Martin II[2], b. c. 1724; 1727, bur at sea

Johann Georg/Hans[2], b. 8 Feb 1730, PA; 1751, went to Carolina, returning to MD, Nov 1752; m/1, Jul, 1753 Anna Margaretha Ellrod (b. 7 Jul 1736), m/2, Barbara Diez; he, bro Michael and fa Martin went to the Yadkin Valley in NC; he d. 28 Feb 1801; **issue**

Michael[2], b. 1731, Berkiana River, PA, 30 mi n.w. of Philadelphia; went to Carolina with Hans & returned to MD; m. Anna Cunigunda Fiscus (b. 4 Apr 1734); he d. 24 Apr 1789, Bethania, NC; **issue**

Martin (twin)[2], b. 16 Oct 1733, Skippack Twp; left NC to return to w. PA; m. Susanna Maria Kessler (b. 2 Jul 1735); he d. 9 Nov 1794, Bethania, NC, so must have returned to NC

Jacob (twin)[2], b. 16 Oct 1733, Skippack Twp; remained in PA until 1759; m. Eleonore/Lenora Margaretha Fiscus; he d. 20 Jan 1806, Hope, Union, NC

unnamed dau[2], b. c. 1735 PA m. Dieter/Peter Danner

Georg Peter[2], b. 30 May 1740, Conowago, n.w. of Hanover, PA; m. Maria Elizabeth Spönhauer (b. 26 Feb 1746); he d. 31 Mar 1802, Bethania, NC

Daniel[2], b. 11 Mar 1744, Conowago, n.w. of Hanover; m. Elizabeth M(e)yer (b. 25 Feb 1741); he d. 1812, Bethlehem, PA

REF: HAUSER, Kenneth John, Jr., *Alsatian-American Family Hauser* (Winston-Salem, NC, 1977).

HENNO(T)/HENNE/de HENNE/EN(N)O, Jean/John

Collard Henno[1] of Mons, Hainault in1463; had son Jacques[2] who m. X Pesquier, d/o Nicolas Pesquier, Bailiff of Gand (Ghent); had son Jean[3] who m. Isabelle Jeanne Caille, d/o Toussaint & Josine (Pellerin) Cail; had son Jacques[4] who m. Jeanne Doyé > Jacques was a lieutenant of the guard formed by the Huguenot citizens of Valenciennes to resist the Spanish; after the capture of the town, Jacques fled to ENG c. 1598 – his lands were confiscated and he was declared an outlaw with "price on his head"

b. FR, s/o Jacques[4] & Jeanne (Doyé) de Henne; Jeanne d/o Antoine, Bailiff & Receiver of Gommegnies & Rose (Dugardin) Doyé who was the d/o Alard & Jeanne (Roger) Dugardin; Gommegnies is s.e.

of Valenciennes
m. 1582, Catelaine Joué
d. prob. London, ENG
CHILD:

Jacques/James[2], bp. 21 Aug 1625, Threadneedle St. Church, London, ENG; to America, c. 1646/8, settled Windsor, CT; m/1, 12 Apr 1646, Threadneedle St. Ch, Anna Gronbal – 2 ch who d. young, m/2, 18 Aug 1648, Windsor, CT, Anna Bidwell (d. 7 Oct 1657)*; m/3, 5 Aug 1658, Elizabeth (X) Holcomb (d. 7 Oct 1679), widow of Timothy Holcomb; m/4, 29 Apr 1680, Hester (Williams) Eggleston (d. 10 Jul 1720), widow of James Eggleston; James rec. a grant called "Massacoe" which was in Simsbury; James was a barber; James d. 11 Jul 1682
  *Anna is called the widow of, or the d/o, Richard Bidwell who had dau Anna b. 22 Oct 1634 which would make her not quite 14 at the time of the marr to Jacques so it would seem that Anna was Richard's dau not widow
  CHILDREN, m/2: Surname was **ENO**, by 1700

Sarah[3], b. 15 Jun 1649, Windsor, CT; m/1, 11 Apr 1667, Benajah Holcomb; m/2, Samuel Phelps; she d. Apr 1732; **3 ch**

James[3], b. 20 Oct 1651, Windsor, CT; soldier in the Indian wars; m. 26 Dec 1678, Abigail Bissell, (6 Jul 1661-19 Apr 1728), d/o Samuel & Abigail (Holcombe) Bissell; he d. 16 Jul 1714, Windsor, CT; **5 sons, 4 daus**

John[3], b. 2 Dec 1654; m. 10 May 1681, Mary Dibble, d/o Eben & Mary (Wakefield) Dibble; he d. 6 Jul 1714; liv Simsbury; **4 ch**

REF: ENO, Henry Lane, *The Eno Family NY Branch* (1920); RICHARDSON, Douglas S., *The Eno & Enos in America* (1973); *The Publications of the Huguenot Society of London,* Vol. XIII (1899); BASSETTE, Buell B., *One Bassett Family in America* (New Britain, CT, 1926).

HET, René, see DuBOIS, Jacques/James

HORRY/HORRŸ, Jean

b. c. 1640, Charenton, FR, what is now Charenton-le-Pont, Val-de-Marne Dépt., Île de France
m. a. 1653, Madeleine DuFrêne
he was an Elder in the FR Reformed Ch in Paris; he was a wine merchant
d. p. 1686; he d. a martyr in prison, prob. in Paris
CHILDREN:

Claudius[2], b. c. 1659, Vitrey, in Haute-Saône, prob. what is now Vitrey-sur-Mance, Haute-Saône Dépt, Franche-Comté, s.e. of Langres; m. a. 1680, FR, Amata Gaulthier

Élie/Élias I[2], b. 1664, Paris, FR; c. 1690, emigrated to SC; m. 17 Aug 1704, Santee, Margaret Huger (21 Feb 1677/8, LaRochelle, FR-1730), d/o Daniel & Margaret (Perdriau) Huger; he d. 25 Sep 1736, bur. FR Ch, Charleston, SC; wp, 29 Sep 1736 – names Daniel Huger, sons Daniel & Elias as executors, sons Daniel, Elias, John, Peter, daus Margaret Henrietta, Magdalen
  CHILDREN:

Daniel[3], b. 1705, SC; m/1, 1737, Sarah Bettison (d. 1742) – **2 sons**, m/2, 12 Jan 1743, Santee, SC, Sarah Ford–**no issue**; he d. 11 Sep 1763

Elias II[3], b. 24 Dec 1707, Santee Parish, SC; m. Margaret Lynch (Nov 1711-19 Feb 1785), d/o Jonathan & Susannah Margaret (Schulf) Lynch; he served in the Rev. War as a colonel w/ Gen. Francis "Swamp Fox" Marion, a fellow Huguenot; he d. 18 Dec 1783, Echaw, SC, bur. St James Santee "Echaw" burying ground
  CHILDREN:
  Richard Alexander[4], b. 1741; m. Rebeckah X; d. p. 1768; **1 ch**

           Elias III[4], b. 22 Mar 1745; m. 15 Nov 1770, Charleston, SC, Elizabeth Branford (15 Nov
               1752-17 Jun 1785), d/o William S. & Elizabeth (Savage) Branford, sis/o Ann/
               Nancy (below); he d. 11 Feb 1785; **1 son, 1 dau**
           Thomas[4], b. 13 Jun 1748; m. Ann/Nancy Branford (30 Nov 1754-12 May 1817), sis/o
               Elizabeth (above); he d. 5 Jan 1820; **4 ch**
           James[4], b. 1756; d. 15 Jan 1773; **no issue**
        John[3], b. 1709, SC; m/1, 10 Aug 1740, Anne Roberts (d. 1759), d/o Capt. Peter & Mary (Lynch)
           Roberts-**issue**, m/2, 5 Jul 1759, Anne (X) Royer, widow of John Royer; he d. 10 Apr 1770,
           Craven Co, SC, bur St. James Santee
        Peter[3], b. 1711, SC; m. 23 Jun 1737, St. Philips Ch, Charleston, SC, Martha Romsey; he d. 8 Mar
           1739, Charleston, bur. Charleston; **1 dau who d. young**
        Margaret Henrietta[3], b. 1713, Georgetown, SC; m. 1735, Anthony Bonneau, s/o Antoine &
           Jeanne Elizabeth (Videau) Bonneau; she d. 3 Apr 1761, St. Thomas Parish, SC, he d.
           1757, Berkeley Co, SC; **at least 4 ch**
        Magdalen[3], b. 1715, Georgetown, SC; m. 22 Sep 1743, Georgetown, Paul Trapier (1716-24 Oct
           1793), s/o Paul & Elizabeth (DuGue) Trapier; she d. 27 Jul 1767, Prince George "Winyaw",
           SC; **2 ch**
?Daniel[2], m. c. 23 Aug 1692, Elizabeth Garnier, d/o Daniel & Elizabeth Garnier

REF: de SAUSSURE, Charlton, *Low Country Carolina Genealogies* (Greenville, SC, 1997); HORRY, William, *The Ancestry of Adam Jeffrey Horry* (1961, unpub); *Transactions of the Huguenot Society of SC,* Vol. 5, Chart #72 (1967); "The Marriage Bond of Daniel Horry & Elizabeth Garnier in the *Transactions of the Huguenot Society of SC,* Vol. 32 (1927); "Wills of the SC Huguenots" in *Transactions of the Huguenot Society of SC,* Vol. 32 (1927).

HOTTEL/HODEL/HOED(E)L/HODDLE/HUDDLE, Jean/Johannes/John

b. c. 1700, prob. SWI, of a Palatinate family who had supposedly fled FR to SWI; some descendants
     went to HOL and GER
m/1, prob. GER, Elisabetha X (8 Sep 1686-22 Dec 1726), bur. Alsheim bei Gronau, Rhineland-Pfalz, s.w.
     of Mannheim; her children all b. and baptized there
m/2, 23 Jun 1728, Meckenheim, GER, Maria Margaretha (Steph) Rhinewald (b. c. 1702, LaBlansch, Bern,
     SWI), d/o Johannes Steph, widow of Casper Rhinewald; their son Johann Heinrich Rhinewald
     (bp. 31Jan 1725) is prob. the Heinrich Hottel listed on the passenger list of the *Pennsylvania*
11 Sep 1732 - arr Philadelphia on the *Pennsylvania*, arr w/ wife + 5 ch (all under 16) from Rotterdam;
     settled in northern Bucks Co.
1745-1750 - moved to Shenandoah Valley, VA; ch Anna, George and Charles went w/ him
d. a. 5 Nov 1760, wp, Frederick Co, VA; will mentions wife Margaret, eldest son Charles, youngest
     son George (named to be executor along w/ bro-in-law George Keller); stepson Henry not
     named – stayed in PA, poss. rec. his portion before his parents moved to VA
CHILDREN, m/1:
Anna Barbara/ Anna[2], b. 5 Dec, bp. 10 Dec 1713; m. George Keller (b. 15 Mar 1719, prob. nr
     Zweibrücken, Bavaria, in the *Pfalz*) ; Children: **George**[3], **Anna**[3], **John**[3], **Elizabeth**[3], **Margaret**[3],
     Mary[3], **Jacob**[3], **Henry**[3], **Barbara**[3]
Johann Carl/Charles[2], b. c. 25 Oct, bp. 2 Nov 1718; m. Barbara X; was in Augusta Co, VA, 1748/9 ;
     settled on a farm in Toms Brook, Shenandoah Co; d. a. 12 Sep 1814, wp, Woodstock, Shenandoah, VA;
     will mentions 5sons: **John**[3], **Jacob**[3], **Joseph**[3], **Solomon**[3], **Daniel**[3], dau **Magdalene**[3] who all rec. land
     and cash; daus **Barbara**[3], **Mary**[3], **Elizabeth**[3], **Anna**[3], **Susannah**[3] rec. cash
Joahnn Georg/George[2], b. c. 4 Apr, bp. 12 Apr 1722
Catharina Elizabetha[2], b. c. 17 Nov, bp. 25 Nov 1725; prob. d. young – not on passenger list of
     the *Pennsylvania*

REF: HUDDLE, Rev. W.D. & Lulu May, *History of the Descendants of John Hottel* (Strasbourg, VA, 1930 & Toms

Brook, VA, 1992); *History of Virginia,* Vol. IV, (1924); Records from the Kirchenbuch Alsheim Bei Gronau, a Reformed ch in Alsheim.

HOUD(E)LETTE, Charles Étienne

b. 1707, FR
m/1, Marie Gallois, d/o Comte X Gallois
1748 - fled to GER
m/2, c. 1749, Susanne Margaret McRae
1750 - to Boston; then to Dresden, ME
d. 27 Oct 1784, Dresden, Lincoln Co, ME
CHILDREN, m/1:
Marthe[2], m. Charles Jean Pochard
Lucy[2], m. Francis Rittal
Mary[2], m. 11 Aug 1767, Philip Mayer
Louis[2], b. 8 Sep 1746, FR; m. 31 Jan 1770, Mary Cavalier, d/o Louis Cavalier; 10 ch – **Louis**[3], m. Joanna Kendall, **Sally**[3], m. George Goodwin, **Charles**[3], m. Susanna Reed, **James**[3], m. Lucy Stilphen, **George**[3], m. Mary Theobald, **Philip**[3], m. Hannah Blair, **Mary**[3], m. Seth Currier, **Francis**[3], m. Nancy Theobald, **Lucy**[3], m. Nathan Call, **Elizabeth**[3], m. Benjamin Branch
CHILDREN, m/2:
Jane, b. 8 May 1750; m. X Brown
Mary, b. 28 May 1755, Boston; m. 25 Nov 1773, George Mayer
Dorothy, b. 10 Sep 1757; m. 1783, Abram Page
Anne Catherine, b. 10 Jun 1760; m. Aaron Bickford

REF: HOUDLETTE, Edith Laura, *The Houdlette Family, 1707-1909* (Boston, 1909); ALLEN, Charles Edwin, *History of Dresden, ME* (1931); ALLEN, Charles Edwin, *Some Huguenot& & Other Early Settlers of the Kennebec in the Present Town of Dresden* (1892).

HOUPELEINE/(VAN) OBLINUS, Juste/Joost

b. 1640, HOL or Flanders, s/o Joost & Martina (X) Oblinus; family escaped Flanders, went to HOL, then to Mannheim, GER
m. 1661, Maria Sammis, according to a family record
1663 – from HOL or ENG to New Haarlem where his parents bought a lot on Van Keulen's Hook (large plain just s. of the town of Harlem) on 8 Nov 1663, from the heirs of Philip Casier; parents soon returned to Europe where apparently all of their other ch still lived
12 Jun 1666 - he was appt an overseer; 28 Jan 1675, was sworn in as a commissioner for Harlem; Joost became a very prominent member and major benefactor of the community
d. 1706, NY
CHILDREN:
Peter[2], b. 1662, Mannheim, GER; m/1, 8 Jun 1685, Cornelia Waldron, d/o Resolved Waldron, m/2, 1715, Agnietie Brett (d. 1743); he was a weaver
John[2], b. 1664; d. 1717, unmarr.
Maria[2], b. 1668; m/1, 5 Apr 1692, Thomas Tourneur, m/2, X Aldrich
Hendrick[2], b. 1672; m. 28 Aug 1692, Jannetie Tibout; he d. 1745; **issue**
Josyntie/Jossynthea[2], b. 1678; m/1, 29 May 1702, Teunis Corssen – son **Teunis**[3], m/2, 16 Jan 1707, Isaac Vermilye, s/o Johannes Vermilye & Aeltie Waldron - **issue**
Josina[2], bp 21 Aug 1678; d. young, unmarr.

REF: TOLER, Henry Pennington, *New Harlem Register, A Genealogy of the Descendants of the 23 Original Patentees of the Town of New Harlem, Containing proofs of Birth, Baptism and Marriage from the*

Year 1630; TOLER, William & NUTTING, Harmon DePau, *New Harlem Past and Present* (NY, 1903); RIKER, James, *Revised History of Harlem* (NY, 1904).

HUBERT, Benjamin B.

b. FR, s/o Eldred Hubert, who was b. 1667 & m. in Alsace-Lorraine, FR

a. 1745 - to VA

m. 1748, Mary (X) Williams, widow of Paul Williams of Frederick Co, VA

1774 - on Committee of Safety in Caroline Co, VA

30 Aug 1777, VA - took Oath of Allegiance

to Caswell Co, NC

c. 1785/6 - from NC to Warren Co, GA (then a part of Wilkes Co)

d. a. 25 Apr 1794, wp, Warren Co, GA; will mentions wife Mary, youngest son David, 3 daus Fanny Runnels, Poly (*sic*) Rutherford and Hester Runnels, sons William, Matthew, Gabriel, gr son Hubert Runnels (s/o Fanny), stepson Jacob Williams; John Rutherford, sons Matthew and David were executors

CHILDREN:

William[2], b. 15 Feb 1749; m. Esther X; **issue**

Fanny[2], b. 1 Nov 1754; m. 1771, Capt. Dudley Runnels (c. 1750-c.1798); **issue**

Matthew[2], b. 22 Feb 1757, VA; m. 1775, NC, Martha Wallace (b. IRE-d. 31 Aug 1835, Warren Co, GA), d/o Robert Wallace; Matthew d. 29 Nov 1812, Warren Co, GA; **issue**

Mary/Polly[2], b. 16 May 1759; m. Col. John Rutherford of Newberry Dist, SC; moved to Warren Co, GA, then to Washington Co, GA; **issue**

Hester[2], b. 19 Nov 1762, NC; m. c. 1779, Col. Harmon Runnels; moved to TX; **issue**

Gabriel[2], b. 22 Feb 1769, NC; m. 1790 Elizabeth (Betsey) Bonner, b. 13 Jun 1767; he d. c. 1812, Clarke Co, GA; **issue**

David[2], b. 15 Jun 1771, NC; m. GA; c. 1815, moved to MS

REF: HUBERT, Sarah Donelson, *Genealogy of the family of Benjamin B. Hubert, A Huguenot*(Atlanta, GA, 1879); WALLACE, Camille Shield, *Genealogy of the Family of Benjamin B. Hubert A Huguenot* (a reprint of the previous work with additions – Ft Worth, TX, 1984); *The Huguenot* #13, #19 (1959-61).

HUGER, Jean

b. c. 1618, Loudun, Touraine (now in Vienne Dépt, Poitou-Charentes), FR c. 45 mi s.w. Tours, s/o Daniel & Marie (Bichet) Huger; bp in Reformed Ch, Loudon

m. FR, Anne Rufin/Rassin (she d. Oct 1661/2), d/o Antoine & Marie (Rou)Rassin/Rufin, merchant druggist of Loudun; *Liste* says Rassin but Daniel[2]'s "family record" says Rufin

d. Oct 1667, aged 49 Y; he was a royal notary

CHILDREN:

Daniel I[2], b. 1 Apr 1651, Loudon, FR, bp. Reformed Ch in Loudon; m. May 1677, LaRochelle, FR, Margaret/Marguerite Perdrian/Perdriau (1652, La Rochelle-1717, Santee, SC), d/o Orie & Margaret (Gourvin) Perdrian; he, his wife & 2 ch left l'Île de Ré – he was called a *marchand* (merchant) in the record; 8 Mar 1682, naturalized in ENG; to SC, c. 1683/5; he d. 24 Dec 1711, "Wambaw" Santee, Craven Co, SC, bur. Wambaw Plantation
CHILDREN:
Margaret/Marguerite[3], b. 21 Feb 1677/8, LaRochelle; m. 17 Aug 1704, SC, <u>Élias Horry</u>; she d. 1730

Magdalen/Madeleine[3], b. SC; d. aged 18Y; bur. FR Ch, Charleston, SC, unmarr.

10 other ch, all of whom d. young

Daniel II[3], b. 16 Mar 1688/9, Craven Co, SC; <u>m/1</u>, 25 Jan 1709/10, Elizabeth Gendron (d. 23

May 1740), d/o Philip & Magdalen (X) Gendron – **no issue**, m/2, 14 May 1741, Mary Cordes
(d. 30 Dec 1746, p. giving b. to 4th son), d/o Isaac & Eleanor (X) Cordes – **4 sons**, m/3, 4 Dec
1747 Lydia Johnson (d. 5 Sep 1748), d/o Robert & Mary (X) Johnson – **1 son** (b. 31 Aug 1748
& d. 4 hrs. old), m/4, 19 Oct 1749, Ann LeJau (d. 6 Dec 1754), d/o Francis & Mary (Ashby)
LeJau – **2 sons, 2 daus**, 1 of whom d. at birth; he d. 8 Dec 1754, Limerick Plantation, on the
Cooper River, Berkeley Co, SC (nr. Charleston)

Jean[2], m. 1681, X Bonavas, d/o Jean Bonavas, a "merchant in iron" in Loudun
Marie[2], d. young, a few months after her father's death
Anne[2], unmarr. when bro Daniel left FR
Magdaleine[2], d. young, a few months after her father's death

REF: HUGER, Dr. Wm. H., "Huger Family Records," in *Transactions of the Huguenot Society of SC* #72 (1967) –
translation of Daniel I's family record which he wrote in French; handwritten pedigree, unsigned, undated;
HORRY, William, *The Ancestors of Adam Jeffrey Horry* (unpub., 1961); DeSaussure, Charlton, *Low Country Carolina
Genealogies* (Greenville, SC, 1997); RAVENEL, Daniel, editor, *Liste des françois et suisses* (Charleston,
1868); WELLS, T. Tileston, *The Hugers of SC* (NY, 1931).

HUGUENIN/HUGENIN/HUGENOR/HUGONY, David

b. 1672, LeLocle, SWI, in the Jura Mts, s.e. of Besançon, FR; his grgrfa Othenin Huguenin fled FR
m/1, 1693, Jeanne Marguerite Huguenin (relation?)
m/2, 11 Dec 1717, Susanne Jacot (b. 1685), d/o Daniel Jacot
1732 – to SC, from SWI; settled Purysburg, SC
22 Dec 1732 – took Oath of Allegiance
1735 - granted grant; rec. another grant in 1738
d. p. 1738, prob. Beaufort, SC
CHILDREN, m/1:
Anne Marie[2], b. 14 Jan 169-
Jeanne Marie[2], b. 29 Apr 1700
David[2], b. 16 Aug 1703; d. 1723
Susanne[2], b. 170-; m. Jacques Montaudon
Jean Jacques[2], b. 17--
CHILDREN, m/2:
Daniel[2], bp. 12 Mar 1718, LeLocle; c. 1743, moved to NY or NJ, later to Albany, NY; m/1, Jane Willis -
8 known ch; m/2, c. 1786, XX – *prob.* **1 son**[3]
Jeanne Marguerite[2], bp. 27 Dec 1720; m. p. 1743, François Gabriel Revout/Ravot; she + 3 bros
were granted 200 acres jointly in 1743; she d. c. 1752
Abraham[2], bp. 14 Feb 1723, LeLocle; went to NY, p. 1743; m. 1748, Christina Von Valkenburgh (bp. 10
Nov 1728, NY-p. 1800); he d. 1768, Kinderhook, Columbia, NY – **5 ch**
David[2], bp. 28 Oct 1724; to GA, early 1750's; m/1, a. 1758, Marie Bourquin (d. May 1771), d/o Henri
François Bourquin – **4 ch**, m/2 1772, Sarah Kennoy of Barnwell Dist, SC
Rose Marie[2], bp. 18 Dec 1729; d. 1731, SWI

REF: DAVIS, Harry Alexander, *Some Huguenot Families of SC & GA* (Washington, DC, 1937); *SC Historical &
Genealogical Magazine,* Vol. 10, p. 208; NYGB Society.

HUGUES/HUGUS, Jacques/Jacob

b. Abriès, then in Dauphiné, now in Hautes-Alpes Dépt, Provence-Alpes-Côte d'Azur, FR, s.e. of Briançon,
close to the border of FR & Italy; ancestral home said to be Montbardon, a sm. town s.w. of
Château-Queyras; just n.w. of Montbardon is the *Serre d'Hugues*
m. Isabeau Bellon (bur. 4 Dec 1706, Schöneberg, Hesse, GER, n.w. of Kassel); passed through Zurich on 4

Nov 1700 w/ 3 ch, through Frankfurt on 24 Nov 1700 & settled in Schöneberg

fled the Queyras Region of FR to SWI; went through Schaffhausen, SWI (n. cen SWI on border w/ GER), & Frankfurt, GER, to Hofgeismar

by Dec,1686 - in Hofgeismar w/ wife & 2 ch; arr in Hofgeismar w/ the Bridgade Pragelas; he rec. support in Jan,1687; a little later, in Grebenstein (n.w. of Kassel); nothing further

d. a. Nov 1700, when Isabeau was called a widow

CHILDREN:

Suzanne[2], went to Frankfurt, 4 Nov 1686, w/ her blind bro Pierre, with the intent of going to Kassel to search for her parents and bro Guillaume; 5 Nov 1700, she was registered in Zurich, 24 Nov 1700, in Frankfurt, traveled to Schöneberg where she m. 3 Apr 1707, Jean Bellon, s/o François Bellon

David[2], b. c. 1687; d. 31 Mar 1707, Schöneberg, age 20 Y

Pierre[2], last mentioned in Frankfurt on 4 Nov 1686

Guillaume[2], b. c. 1674, Abriès; went to Schöneberg w/ his mother; merchant there; m/1, 1709, Marie Boulnois, widow of X Hanot, m/2, Philippine Barbe Julion (d. 1759); he was in Karlshafen in 1735; he was a ch warden of the FR Parish in Hofgeismar; he d. c. 1750, Hofgeismar, c. 76 Y

CHILDREN, m/2:

William[3], b. 1740; went with bro John to America; said to have served in the Rev. War

Jean/John[3], b. 11 Jul, bp. 14 Jul 1741, FR Ch, Hofgeismar; to US, c. 1761; m. Margaretta Shupe; served in the Rev. War as a private, also credited with patriotic service; he d. Oct, 1806, Unity Twp, Westmoreland Co, PA; bur. Union Cemetery, Trauger, PA

CHILDREN:

Sarah[4], m. Christian Lawfer/Laffer/Lauffer; she d. 1802; **2 sons, 4 daus**

Jacob[4], b. 9 Jun 1768, Bucks Co, PA; m. Catherine Flick (1770, Northampton Co, PA- 9 Jun 1850, Tuscarawas Co, OH); he d. 28 Jan 1835, Greensburg, PA; **4 sons, 9 daus**

John J.[4], b. 1771; m. Eleanore Philippina X (1772-1849); he d. 1843; **1 son, 3 daus**

Magdalena[4], b. 17 Sep, bp. 10 Oct 1773, Bucks Co, PA; m. Frederick Mechling; she d. a. 10 Oct 1810

Michael[4], b. 16 Jan 1775; m. 31 May 1801, Elizabeth J. Ankeny (1782-1863), d/o Peter & Rosanna (Bonnet) Ankeny; he d. 25 Nov 1825, Somerset, PA; **5 sons, 6 daus**

Henry[4], b. 1779; m. Elizabeth Swartz (1783-1853); he d. 1848; **5 sons, 5 daus**

Catherine Margaretta[4], b. 1781; m. Jacob Bott; **1 son, 4 daus**

Peter[4], b. 1783; m. Barbara Yeager (1781-1831); he d. 1826; **3 sons, 6 daus**

Paul[4], b. 1785; m. Susanna Swartz (b. 1790) – sis/o Elizabeth above; he d. 1868; **6 sons, 4 daus**

Wilhelm/William[4], b. 1789; m. Elizabeth X; he d. 20 Oct 1822 "on the Susquehanna River"; **1 dau?**

NOTE: The area nr. Hesse-Kassel was a FR "colony" inhabited by FR Huguenots who had fled FR after the Revocation.

REF: Ch records from Franzosisches Kirckenbach Hofgeismar, written in French; BELLON, Eugen, *Scattered to all the Winds (1685-1720)* (fully annotated, English translation, West Lafayette, IN, 1983); BELLON, Eugen, *The Immigration of the Hugues Families (Huegues) into the Municipality of Hofgeismar (Hessen) 1686-1700*; ch records from the Tohickon Reformed Ch, Bucks Co, PA; RICHARD, Didier, *Queyras Pays du Viso* (maps).

HULINGUES/HULINGS, Jean Paul Frederick, Marquis de

b. Béarn Prov, FR (formerly a sm. prov. in s.w. FR, now in the Basse-Pyrénées area), poss. Oloron-Ste-Marie, nr. the Spanish border

m. c. 1572, Dieppe, FR, Isabelle du Portal, a native of Toulouse, and a lady in waiting to Queen Catherine de Medici; couple fled Paris at the time of the St. Bartholomew's Day Massacre; left FR heading for ENG but a storm at sea carried them to the coast of Denmark and they proceeded to Göteborg, SWE, where they stayed; Jean had been a companion of Henri of Navarre (later Henri IV, King of FR), & attached to the FR court

CHILD:

son[2], whose name is unknown

> CHILD:

> **Lars/Laurens**[3] (surname **HULING**); to DE w/ Swedish emigrants a. 1640

>> CHILDREN (had at least 3 sons):

>> **Laurens II**[4], m. Katherine X; he d. p. 25 Aug 1700, wd, Gloucester Co, NJ; had son **Laurens III**[5] who d. a. 4 Jun 1748, wp – names sons **Laurens IV**[5], **Michael**[5], **Abraham**[5], **Israel**[5], **Joseph**[5], **Marcus**[5], dau **Dinah**[5]; names bro Michael[4] of Philadelphia, an executor of his will

>> **Marcus I**[4], b. c. 1640/5; m/1, XX; m/2, Brigitta Danielsson; m/3, Christina X, a widow; d. Gloucester Co, NJ, 4 May 1689; 2 known sons:

>>> **Laurens**[5], b. c. 1672, m. Catharine Laican/Lycon, d/o Michael & Helena (Lom) Laican; Laurens d. Waterford Twp, Gloucester Co, NJ, a. 1 Mar 1701, wp

>>> **Marcus II**[5], b. c. 1684/7, m. Margaret Jones, d/o Mouns Jones – went to Molatton on the Schuylkill River where Douglassville, Berks Co, PA is located, Marcus II d. there, 1757 – **5 ch**

>> **Michael**[4], executor of bro Laurens II's will

REF: Col. Dames of America Archives, *Ancestral Records & Portraits*, Vol. II (Baltimore 1969); *Proceedings of the Huguenot Society of PA*, Vol. XXVII (Philadelphia, 1955); STAPLETON, Rev. A. *Memorials of the Huguenots*; CRAIG, Peter S., *The Colonial Hulings Descendants of Marcus Laurence, Holstein* (Washington, DC 1990); CRAIG, Peter S., *The 1693 Census of the Swedes on the Delaware* (Winter Park, FL 1993).

HUMBERT, Noël

b. 5 Aug 1609, Nancy, Lorraine, FR, s/o Nicolas & Judith (X) Humbert
m/1, 5 Oct 1638, Rue St. Jacques, Nancy, Marie Vosqun/Vosguin, d/o Noël Vosqun
m/2, 13 Apr 1650, Messaline Benoit
d. 6 May 1670, prob. FR

CHILD, m/1:

Jacques[2], b. 11 May 1641, Nancy; m. 7 Jul 1664, Eleanore Charpentier, d/o Antoine & Marguerite (Dijon) Charpentier; Marguerite was the d/o Joseph Dijon

> CHILDREN:

> **Antoine**[3], b. 13 Apr 1665, Nancy; fled FR, 1685 to FR Colony at Frauenberg (s.w. of Bonn), GER; then to Marburg, Hessen (n. of Frankfurt), then to Mainz, GER (s.w. of Frankfurt); later to Kelsterbach (s.w. of Frankfurt), founded Neuen (New) Kelsterbach; m. 1686, Marie Brideau, d/o Samuel Brideau; Marie d. 1724, Berlin; Antoine d. 7 Sep 1710 or 1719, Kelsterbach; he was a furrier

>> CHILDREN:

>> **Antoine/Anthony**[4], b. 4 Aug 1690, Kelsterbach; m. 22 Jun 1726, Barbara Ditmar

>>> CHILDREN (all emigrated to America, 1750-67):

>>> **Wilhelm**[5], b. 9 Mar 1727; m. Magdaline Weisbach; immigrated from Rotterdam on the *Osgood*, arr Philadelphia, 29 Sep 1750 – 1st of the Humberts to sail to America

>>> **Frederick**[5], b. 20 Jan 1728, Kelsterbach; m/1, Margaret X, m/2, 3 Jun 1750, Susanna Hetzel, d/o William Hetzel; emigrated on the *Janet* on List 99, 7 Oct 1751; he d. 16 Apr 1818, Ayr Twp, Bedford, PA **or** nr. Dayton, OH, on the 10th!; m/2 - **13 ch**

>>> **Philip Jacob**[5], b. 19 Nov 1728; emigrated on the *Janet*, arr 7 Oct 1751; rec. a

Deed, 7 Mar 1768, in Frederick Co, MD; later bought lg. farm called "Braden's Lott" and "Beatty's Venture"; **issue**

Johannes George[5], b. 19 May 1730; emigrated on the *Brothers* from Rotterdam, arr Philadelphia, 30 Sep 1754

Peter[5], b. 11 Jan 1731, Kelsterbach; m/1, 4 Nov 1759, Margaret Konig, d/o Abraham Konig/Koneg, m/2, 23 Apr 1778, Rebecca Bunn; emigrated on the *Richmond*, 5 Oct 1763

Adam[5], b. 17 Oct 1733; m. Elizabeth Emerson; emigrated on the *Hamilton* from from Rotterdam, arr Philadelphia, 6 Oct 1767; taught school and was a carpenter; d. 1783

Charles[4], b. & d. 3 May 1692

Jean[4], b. & d. 19 Apr 1695

Charlotte[4], b. 21 Jan 1696; m. Jean Chapell

Charles[4], b. 27 Mar 1697, Kelsterbach; d. 1729, Berlin

Joseph[3], b. 4 Jan 1667; m. Anne Charles; **issue**; ancestor of the Humberts of Tonnay in Saintonge- today there are 2 – Tonnay-Charente, just e. of Rochefort and Tonnay-Boutonne, e. of Tonnay-Charente; both towns are in Charente-Maritime Dépt., Poitou-Charentes

REF: PYATT, Leslie James, *The Pyatt Family 892-2000 (One Branch)* (Ft. Worth, TX, 2001); MONLUX, Frances Mackin, *The Humbert Family History* (Ames, IA, 1983); KAMINKOW, Jack & Marion, *A List of Emigrants from England to America 1718-1759* (Baltimore, 1966).

J

JACQUEMIN(E)/JACOB, Abraham

b. c. 1590, Alsace/Lorraine region, FR

1623-1629 - resided in Bouquenom, an old medieval town on the right bank of the Sarre River, later called Bockenheim; 16 Jun 1794, Bockenheim was joined with Neusaarwerden, a town on the left bank, to form the city of Sarre-Union, located Bas-Rhin, Alsace Dépt

m. Johanna X (c. 1592-5 Mar 1665, Zweibrücken)

d. 9 Jan 1668, Zweibrücken, GER (e. of Saarbrücken)

CHILDREN (surnamed **JACOB**):

Hans Christoffel[2], b. c. 1617, Zwiebrücken; m. 14 Dec 1641, Zwiebrücken, Elizabeth Mueller/Müller (1616, Bockenheim-1676, Zwiebrücken), d/o Tobias Müller; he d. 21 Jan 1706, Zwiebrücken

CHILDREN:

Abraham[3], b. 29 Oct 1642, Zweibrücken

Anna Catharina[3], b. 19 Aug 1644, Zweibrücken

Agnes[3], b. 23 Sep 1645, Zweibrücken

Johanna[3], b. 31 Jan 1649, Zweibrücken; m. 15 Nov 1670, Zweibrücken, Johannes Krafft

Veronica[3], c. 1655; confirmed 1671, Zweibrücken

Hans Wolff[3], b. c. 1658; m. 13 Apr 1675, Niederauerbach, Catharina Elisabeth Weidtmann, d/o Andreas Weidtmann; he d. 12 Mar 1730, Niederauerbach, sm. town n.e .of Zweibrücken

CHILD:

Anna Catharina Margaretha[4], b. 14 Nov 1703, Niederauerbach; m. 2 Nov 1728, Johann Andreas Sumwald; d. 1743/49, York Co, PA; emigrated to America, 1737, settled in PA

Anna[2], b. 2 Jan 1623, Bockenheim

Abraham[2], b. Pentacost, 1624; m/1, 19 Apr 1654, Zweibrücken, Catharine Margaretha Lauff, d/o Christoph Lauff – **5 ch**, m/2, 1684, Zweibrücken, Maria Margaretha Paul, widow of Nickel Trautmann, she d. 1722, Zweibrücken; he d. 14 Nov 1717, Zweibrücken

Susanna[2], b. 22 Apr 1628, Bockenheim; m. Jun 1651, Zwiebrücken, Georg Jacob Paus

REF: *Huguenotten im Zweibrucker Land* (1987); Records of Zwiebrücken Reformed Ch; THODE, Ernest, *Genealogical Gazetteer of Alsace-Lorraine* (Indianapolis, 1986).

JA(C)QUES/JACK, Jacobus/Jean

b. 4 Oct 1528, Utrecht, HOL [*poss.* s/o Roger, a trader in Utrecht who d. in London *or* Jacob & Sara (Van Haestrecht) Jaques]; Jacob was a merchant in Utrecht

m. 19 Dec 1549, Hesdin, Artois, FR, Corinne Bloedel/Bloedil (1532, Hesdin-p. 1609, Le Chesne), d/o Guillaume & Jeanne (Beauprez) Bloedel; Hesdin was then in Artois, now Nord-Pas-de-Calais Dépt.

d. 4 Apr 1609, Le Chesne, now in Ardennes Dépt, Champagne-Ardenne, FR, s.e. of Charleville-Mézières; there were several other "choices," but given the location of the marriage, this Le Chesne seemed to be the best choice, also given its proximity to Charleville-Mézières

CHILD (of 6 ch):

Jean[2], bp 3 Aug 1551, Le Chesne; m. 3 Jun 1590, Marguerite de Ronde (1555-14 Aug 1644); he d. 19 May 1643, Le Chesne

CHILD (said to be only son of 7 ch):

Guillaume[3], bp 7 Feb 1592; m. 4 Apr 1627, Marguerite de Gasque; he was a jeweler & goldsmith; Guillaume was *rentier* (person of property) in Nouzon, where he d.; Marguerite m/2, Jean Charpentier of Nouzon; Nouzon is now Nouzonville just n. of Charleville-Mézières

CHILD (one of 11 ch):

Guillaume[4], bp 16 Sep 1633, Le Chesne; m. 4 Aug 1654, as her 3rd husband Jeanne Daniel, d/o Antoine Daniel, widow of Jean Breman **&** Henri de Ronde; 1672, emigrated to SCOT, settled Edinburgh; he d. a. 6 May 1713, Edinburgh; Jeanne d. 1714, Toulouse, FR

CHILDREN:

Jacob[5], bp. 19 May 1655, Le Chesne; m/1, 17 Apr 1678, Edinburgh, Nancy Farqhar (4 Aug 1657-14 Nov 1699 Edinburgh), d/o Alexander & Margaret (Leitsche) Farquhar, m/2, 4 Aug 1701,Madelaine Dornand, d/o Jacques Dornand; a. 4 Aug 1709, he was in Letterkenny, Co Donegal; he. d. p. 1709, prob. Letterkenny, Co Donegal, IRE; **issue** by both wives – 6 sons by Nancy, 3 daus by Madeline; 1 son **Patrick**[6] (3 Dec 1678- 30 Jan 1726, Chester Co, PA) m. Ellen/Elizabeth Jarvis – **issue**

Thomas[5], b. 3 Aug 1657, Le Chesne; m/1, 1693 Mary M'Ghie, of Balmaghie, m/2, 3 May 1696, Nancy McMillan; family left Edinburgh, went to Londonderry, IRE; **issue**

Margaret[5], bp. 5 Sep 1663, Nouzon; m. 4 May 1687, Daniel McFarland

NOTE: Le Chesne, has been written Chesney, Chesnay, etc. It has been placed in the Nord Dépt & Eure-et-Loire in Centre Dépt. The latter is Le Chesnay on the outskirts of Paris, e. of Versailles. It would seem that the best fit is Le Chesne in Champagne. It is near the other towns where the family was such as Nouzon. But this is still something that <u>needs</u> more proof. Marguerite de Gasque (wife of Guillaume[3]) is said to have d. in Prendemmis-no such town has been located

REF: WILLIAMSON, Mary Frances, *History of the Rogers Family 1643-1950* (DAR, 1958-59); *The Jack (Jacques, James) Family* (no author cited, apparently unpub).

JANVIER/JAUVIER/JANUARY, Thomas

b. 8 May 1669, LaFlotte, Île de Ré, FR, s.e. of Saint-Martin-de-Ré; bp. 12 May 1669, Protestant Ch, Saint-Martin-de-Ré, s/o Thomas and Suzanne (Mousnier) Janvier; his father was a merchant & the s/o Philippe Janvier I & Marie Annonier

23 Jun 1686 - arr in Philadelphia on the *Desire* from Plymouth, ENG, as an indentured servant to Francis Rawles; he was a carpenter

m. c. 1692, New Castle Co, DE, Sarah Jourdain, d/o Dr. John & Mary (Tayne) Jourdain, & step d/o William Crosse (d. a. 31 Jan 1697/8, wp, New Castle Co, DE – Thomas Janvier was executor); Sarah d. p. 11 Nov 1775, wd; marr was definitely a. 28 May 1695, when a deed was recorded for Thomas Janvier and his wife; the deed names her stepfa William Crosse, her "late" mother Mary, widow of John Jourdain; the deed was between them & John & Elizabeth Bisk – Elizabeth was the sis/o Issac Tayne/Tine and of Sarah's mo Mary Jourdain; William Crosse and Isaac Tayne were naturalized in New Castle on 21 Feb 1682/3

21 Feb 1694/5- naturalized "Province of Pennsilvania Country of New Castle" (now DE)

15 Aug 1707 – one of the founders of the Presbyterian Ch in New Castle; he and Sarah sold a 27' X 30' lot for £12 for the purpose of erecting the church; one of the purchasers was Roeloff De Haes, father-in-law of 2 of his ch

d. a. 27 Mar 1728, wp, New Castle Co, DE

CHILDREN:

Mary[2], b. 1693, DE; m. Joseph Hill – **no known issue**; he m/2, Mary Jacquet

Thomas II[2], b. 1695, New Castle, DE; m. Susannah X, New Castle, DE; he d. c. 1760/1, Philadelphia, PA; **issue**

Isaac[2], b. 1697, DE; m. 16 Apr 1734, Rebecca Welch, d/o John Welch of Christiana Bridge; he d. 1742; **issue**

Philip[2], b. 1699, DE; m/1, Anna Kettle?- **issue**, m/2, Mary Silsbe, d/o Samuel Silsbe – **5 ch**; he d. 1752

Francis[2], b. 1705, New Castle, DE; m/1, Elizabeth (Calvert) Anderson, d/o John Calvert – at least **1 son**, m/2, Sarah De Haes, d/o Roeloff & Sarah Williamsen (Neering) de Haes – **5 ch**; he d. 25 Dec 1751,

DE

John[2], b. c. 1703, DE ; m. Mary de Haes, sis/o Sarah above; he d. 1781; **4 ch**

Sarah[2], b. 1706, DE; she d. 16 Aug 1785, DE, unmarr.

Benjamin[2], b. 1708, DE; m. Ann X; he d. 31 Aug 1799, Philadelphia, PA

Susannah[2], b. 1712, DE; m. XX; she d. c. 1786, Philadelphia, PA

REF: KINKEAD, Clara Janvier, *The Kinkeads of Delaware as Pioneers in Minnesota 1856-1868* (Wilmington, DE, 1949); SUBLETTE, Donald J. & SMITH, Elizabeth Bond, *Thomas Janvier of New Castle, DE 1669-1728* (hand written, not pub.); SHEPPARD, Walter Lee, Jr., compiler & editor, *Passengers & Ships Prior to 1684* (Baltimore, 1970); baptismal record from Saint-Martin-de-Ré Protestant Ch; BRYANT, Carol & GARRETT, Carol J., *New Castle County, DE Land Records* (Westminster, MD, 1998); Colonial Society of PA, *Records of the Court of New Castle on Delaware,* Vol. II (Meadville, PA, 1935); *A Calendar of Delaware Wills* (Baltimore, MD); Research by Roger Henry of Seattle, WA.

JARNAT/JARNETTE, Jean de

b. c. 1680, FR, poss. province of Poitou

c. 1699/1700 - to VA prob. from LaRochelle; said to have on the 4th ship bringing Huguenots to VA

17 Mar 1702 - petitioned for naturalization in Prince Edward Co, VA

m. c. 1702/03, Gloucester Co, VA, Mary Mumford **(**c. 1683, Gloucester Co, VA - a. 19 Aug 1765, wp, Prince Edward Co, VA), d/o Edward and Mary (Watkins) Mumford

18 Apr 1705 - petition for naturalization granted

d. p. 1720, prob. Gloucester Co, VA

CHILDREN:

Elias[2], bp. 20 Aug 1704, Abingdon Parish, Gloucester Co, VA; m. a. 1728, Elizabeth X; lived in that area of Amelia Co which became Pr. Edward Co; d. p. 9 Aug 1768, ww - a. 18 Jul 1769, wp, Prince Edward Co, VA

CHILDREN:

Ann Rebecca/Annaka[3] - d. unmarr., p. 26 Nov 1804, wd-a. 27 Jan 1806, wp, Halifax Co, VA

Elias[3], m. Sarah (Hall?); he d. Halifax Co, 1784 – **6 ch**; Sarah m/2, Israel Pickens and d. 23 Feb 1814, SC - death rec Rocky River Meetinghouse Baptist Church (Abbeville Co)

Marymiah[3] m. 7 Jan 1765, Farmville, VA, James Hinds

John Thomas[3], m. Millasant Hall; John Thomas d. p. 11 Apr 1788, ww - a. 20 Apr 1789, Prince Edward Co, VA; **10 ch**

Thomas[3], m. Nancy X; resident of Halifax Co, VA until 3 Dec 1788 - no further record in VA; went to Henry Co, KY; d. p. 1818; **7 ch**

Mary[3], b. c. 1728, prob. Amelia Co, VA; m. a. 8 Sep 1761, VA, prob. Prince Edward Co., Thomas Palmer (12 Oct 1725, Richmond Co, VA-a. 16 Jul 1804, Union Co, SC), Thomas s/o Robert & Martha Palmer; she d. a. 10 Aug 1768, Prince Edward Co, VA

John[2], bp. 4 Nov 1706, Abingdon Parish

Mary[2], bp. 5 Feb 1708, Abingdon Parish

Elizabeth[2], b. 1709; m. 1735, Edward McGehee, s/o Thomas & Ann (Bastrop) McGehee of King William Co, VA, Edward d. c. 1771 (will), Cumberland Co, VA which lists **10 ch**; Eliz. d. p. 1783

Daniel[2], bp. 24 Jan 1713, Abingdon Parish; m. VA, Martha Ford (d. p. 3 Jan 1780, ww - a. 16 Mar 1782, Wp, Prince Edward Co, VA); he p. 11 Sep 1754, ww - a. Sep 1755, wp, appraisal, Dec 1755; **8 ch**

Joseph[2], bp. 3 Feb 1716, Abingdon Parish; m. Mary Pemberton; d. p. 10 Mar 1763, prob. Caroline Co, VA; **7 ch**

Ellenor[2], b. 5 Sep 1720, bp. 20 Nov, Abingdon Parish; m/1, 30 Oct 1737, Jacob McGehee (1707-6 Dec 1783), s/o Thomas & Ann (Bastrop) McGehee of King William Co, VA; Eleanor d. 14 Jun 1775, Prince Edward Co, VA – **12 ch**; Jacob m/2, Ann X – no ch; his will dated, 8 May 1781, wp, 4 Mar 1784, Prince Edward Co, VA

REF: FROST, E.C. & M., *DeJarnette & Allied Families in America*; *Abingdon Parish Register*; Manakintown

Records; Deeds, Prince Edward Co & Halifax Co, VA, Union Co, SC; *Genealogies of VA Families* (Wm & Mary Quarterly), Vol. II; *Genealogies of VA Families* (from Wm & Mary Quarterly Historical Magazine), Vol. II (1982).

JAUDON/JODON/JEUDON, Daniel

b. c. 1615 Soubise (s.w. of Rochefort), Charente Maritime Dépt, Poitou-Charentes, then Saintonge Prov, s/o François (b. c. 1590) & Marie (Roy) Jaudon; Daniel had bro Pierre who m. c. 2 Sep 1643 (date of marr contract); no more info

CHILD:

Élie/Elias[2], b. c. 1640, Île de Ré or Soubise; m. c. 1670, Sara Bertonneau (b. c. 1645, Île de Ré), d/o Jacques & Élisabeth (X) Bertonneau; Sara m/2, c. 1685, Pierre Michau(d) and they sailed for SC 1686; Élie d. c. 1684, Île de Ré; Sara, Pierre, Esther, Daniel were naturalized 1696, SC

CHILDREN:

Esther[3], b. c. 1672, Île de Ré, FR; m. c. 1685, FR, Abraham Michau(d) (c. 1670, Poitou, FR- c. 1730, SC), bro of Esther's stepfa Pierre; settled Craven Co, SC; 3 daus – **Jeanne**[4], m. Moïse Carion, **Esther**[4], **Charlotte**[4]; Esther[3] d. c. 1698, SC; Abraham m/2, c. 1700, Madeleine Rembert – 1 dau **Madeleine**[4] who m. Nicholas LeNud

Daniel[3], b. c. 1683, Île de Ré, FR; m. 1708/9, Elizabeth Videau (d. p. 12 Apr 1743, wd); d. a. 10 Apr 1739, inv, SC; 10 ch - **Daniel**[4] m. 31 May 1759, St. James Santee Parish, Anne DuBose, d/o Daniel & Anne[4] (Rembert) DuBose (m. at bride's uncle Isaac[3] Rembert's house w/ Isaac Rembert and Paul Jaudon as witnesses), **Susannah Elizabeth**[4], **Noah**[4], **Elias**[4], **Matthew**[4], **Sarah**[4], **Esther**[4], **Paul**[4], **David**[4], **Elisha**[4]

REF: *French & Swiss Protestants in Charleston* (Baltimore, 1968); MILLER, Annie Elizabeth, *Our Family Circle* (Linden, TN, 1975); PEEPLES, Robert E.H. & PINCKNEY, Sarah Nicholas, "Jaudon of Carolina" in *Transactions of the Huguenot Society of SC*, #87 (Charleston, 1982); BAIRD, Charles W., *Huguenot Emigration to America.*

JEAN, Augustine (aka Jean AUGUSTINE/Jean/John GUSTIN)

b/bp. 9 Jan 1647, Le Tocq, Isle of Jersey; bp. St. Ouen's Parish, s/o Edmond & Esther (le Rossignol) Jean; Esther was the d/o Jean LeRossignol

Spring, 1675 - to America

1675/6 - served in King Philip's War and rec. a grant of land in Falmouth (now Portland), ME, for his service; about this time his name started to get transposed, his surname became his 1st name and his 1st name got shortened

m. 10 Jan 1677, Marlborough, MA, Elizabeth Browne (b. 26 Mar 1657, Cambridge, MA), d/o John & Esther (Makepeace) Browne

1690 - left Falmouth due to Indian attacks, went to Lynn, MA

returned to Portland where he ended up owning what is now the entire business district

d. 3 Jul 1719, Portland, ME; signed his will *John AUGustin*

CHILDREN:

Mary[2], b. 1678; m/1, Richard Ward, m/2, John Bushnell (she is listed in *The Quiet Adventurers*, not in the *Compendium)*

Sarah[2], b. 1679, Falmouth, ME; m/1, Jonathan Bly; **8 ch**

Samuel[2], b. 1681, Falmouth, ME; m. Abigail X; d. 1777; **6 ch**

William[2], b. c. 1687; m. Abigail Thayer; d. young

Elizabeth[2], b. c. 1688; m. 12 Aug 1708, Boston, James Lowle/Towle; moved to Frankford, Sussex, NJ

John[2], b. 5 Nov 1691, Lynn, MA; m. Mary X (d. 3 Dec 1762); he d. 15 Oct 1777, Sussex Co, NJ; **12 ch**

Abigail[2], b. 9 Dec 1693, Lynn, MA; m. Thomas Fuller

Ebenezer[2], b. 4 Oct 1696, Lynn, MA; moved to Phippsburg, ME

Thomas[2], b. 5 Mar 1698/9, Lynn, MA; m. 1722, Sarah Holmes; resided Colchester, CT; he d. 1765; **3 sons**

David[2], b. 6 Feb 1702, Lynn, MA

REF: BAIRD, Charles W., *Huguenot Emigration to America* (Baltimore, 1991); *The Quiet Adventures in America* (Cleveland, OH, 1975), 2nd in a series of family genealogies, Jersey & Scottish ancestry; WEAVER, Gustine Courson, *The Gustine Compendium* (Cincinnati,1929); Vital records Lynn, MA.

JERAULD, Jacques/James

b. c. 1664?, Languedoc, FR, to a family of successful silk manufacturers; Jacques was a physician, said
    to have been 36 yrs old at time of his marr but this birthdate seems early as he would have been 96
    when he d. – b. prob. closer to 1675; he was supposedly 73 when he d. which would make his
    date of b. 1687 and thus 13 when he marr.! Also supposedly 22 Y when he arr in MA but since
    the date of his arrival is unknown…..
m. 1700, Boston, MA, Martha Dupuis/Dupee (c. 1684*-25 Mar 1763, Medfield, MA); *said to have been
    b. on a ship en route to America and that Jacques was also on that ship and that he delivered her
    – nice story, not proven!
d. 25 Oct 1760, Medfield, MA, said to have been 73 yrs old; 15 Sep 1759, wd, names wife Martha, grsons
    James, Dutee (sons of his son James), sons James, Gamaliel, Stephen, Dutee, daus Mary Spaulding,
    Hannah, Susanna, grdau Ruth (d/o son James)
CHILDREN:
James[2], m. c. 1731/2, Ruth Stevens (b. c. 1711/13), d/o Ensign Thomas & Ruth (Hall) Stevens; he d. 11
    Aug 1747, Plainfield, MA; **7 ch**
Martha[2], d. 23 Sep 1733, Medfield
Gamaliel[2], b. 23 Sep 1718, Medfield; m/1, 25 Dec 1741, Rebecca Lawrence (d. 12 Jan 1751) – **2 sons, 3**
    daus, m/2, 11 Oct 1751, Jerusha Mann (d. Nov 1762) – **5 sons, 2 daus**, m/3, 10 Aug 1763, Mrs. Mary
    Everett (d. 4 Jan 1810); he d. 18 Oct 1795, Wrentham, MA
Stephen[2], b. 29 Nov 1720, Medfield; m. XX; d. 22 Jan 1785, Sturbridge, MA; surname GEROULD
Dutees (Dupee?)[2], b. 5 Mar 1722/3, Medfield; m. 26 Apr 1744, Freelove Gorton (9 May 1722 ,Warwick,
    RI-31 Oct 1803); he was a physician who settled in E. Greenwich, RI; d. 13 Jul 1813, Warwick, RI;
    10 ch
Mary[2], b. 8 Jul 1725, Medfield; m. 7 Sep 1744, Plainfield, CT, Azariah Spaulding (19 Jan 1724-
    Plainfield- Mar 1795, Plainfield), s/o Phillip & Ann (Cleveland) Spaulding; she d. 2 Oct 1769
    CHILDREN, b. Plainfield, CT:
    Molly[3], b. 21 Jul 1745, m. 13 Jun 1764, Plainfield, CT, Aaron Wheeler; **Magdalen**[3], 18 Jun 1747- 2
    Dec 1768; **Martha**[3], b. 22 Mar 1749, m. Moses Wheeler*; **Rufus**[3], 16 May 1751- 26 Jul 1772, unmarr;
    Susannah[3], b. 20 Sep 1753, m. Peter Kendall, as his 2nd wife; **Hannah**[3], 21 Jun 1755-1 Jul 1808
    Royalton, VT, m. Abraham Waterman (9 May 1756-30 Dec 1842), s/o Abraham & Anna
    (Brown) Waterman*; **Zilpha**[3], b. 23 Nov 1757, m. Spencer Cole; **Daniel**[3], b. 13 Dec 1759- d. 31 Dec
    1798; **Hesther**[3], b. 20 Apr 1762- d. 15 Jun 1768; **Charles**[3], b. 12 Mar 1764- d. 4 Oct 1791; **Molle**[3], b. 5
    Mar 1767- d. 27 May 1790, unmarr.
    *one account says Martha m. Abraham Waterman but Waterman family history says it was
    Hannah
Johanna/Hannah[2], b. 2 Nov 1728, Medfield; d. unmarr
Susanna[2], b. 6 Nov 1730, Medfield; d. 16 Sep 1770, prob. unmarr

REF: GEROULD, Samuel Lankton, *The Genealogy of the Family of Gamaliel Gerould* (Bristol, NH, 1885); American
Historical Society, *New England Families, Rhode Island Edition* (NY, 1925); Vital Records, Medfield MA & Plainfield,
CT; GORTON, Thomas Arthur, *Samuel Gorton of RI and His Descendants* , Vol. I, II combined (Baltimore, 1985);
HAYWARD, Kendall P., "Gerauld (Jerauld) Family Notes" in *TAG*, Vol. 28, #1 (Jan 1952).

JOIRÉ, Magdalen – see BLANCHAN, Mattys

JOLIN(E)/JAULIN, André

b. Saint Palais, Saintonge, FR; today it is Saint-Palais-sur-Mer, on the Gironde River, in Charente-Maritime Dépt, Poitou-Charentes Région

fled FR to Bristol, ENG

by 6 Aug 1686 - he was in NYC

m/1,Madeleine Poupin/Pepin

15 Apr 1693 - denization NYC; naturalized 15 Apr 1693

m/2, Mary Trotter (22 Jan 1654, Newbury, MA-a. 18 Jun 1741, prob. NJ)

went from NY to Elizabeth, NJ where he skippered the sloop *Woodbridge* which made trips bet. Perth Amboy, NJ, and Philadelphia

d. a. 13 Feb 1741/2, wp, Essex Co, NJ; liv. Elizabeth, Essex, NJ; will names wife Mary, ch John (Jean) & Mary, grch Andrew, Ann, Mary - ch of Mary & Jean Blanchard

CHILDREN, m/1:

Jean[2], b. 3 Mar, bp. 7 Mar 1693/4, FR Ch, NYC; "Capt. Jean"

Anne Madelaine[2], b. 10 Mar, bp. 8 Apr 1696, FR Ch, NYC; not in father's will

David[2], bp 12 Feb 1698/9, FR Ch, NYC; not in father's will

?André[2], bp not in FR Ch records; prob. d. by 1741, not in father's will

Jeanne[2], b. 19 Jul, bp 23 Jul 1701, FR Ch, NYC; not in father's will

CHILD, m/2 :

Marie/Mary[2], m. Jean Blanchard, Jr; **4 ch**

REF: Wittmeyer, Alfred V., *Registers of the Births, Marriages, & Deaths of the Église Françoise à la Nouvelle York* (NY,1896); *Huguenot Ancestors of the Huguenot Society of NJ;* JOLINE, *André Jolin & His Descendants;* BAIRD, Charles W., *History of the Huguenot Emigration to America*, Vol. II (1973); *Huguenot or Early French in NJ.*

JOUANY/JOANNIS/JONES, Jean/John

b. c. 1680, FR

a. 1700, m. Esther LaFuitte, d/o François & Joanne (X) LaFuitte/LaFite/LaFête; Esther d. p. Sep 1731; she *may* have been his 2nd wife and Elizabeth her only ch

23 Jul 1700 - emigrated on the *Mary Ann* from ENG with wife and 2 ch; arr at the mouth of the James James River on 12 Aug 1700; ch apparently did not survive the trip

25 Apr 1702 - one of the 1st Manakintown French to acquire land of his own – 77 acres in Henrico Co; started using the name John Jones

1705 – naturalized

1714 – resided Manakintown; on the tithing list of King William Parish

d. p. 3 Oct 1726, when he witnessed a will – a. 3 Oct 1728, when his bro-in-law Tobias LaFuitte's will was written

CHILDREN:

2 ch[2], b. prob. ENG; d. c. 1700 – *poss.* 2 sons **Jean**[3] & **Isaac**[3]

Hester/Esther[2], c. 1705, VA; m. c. 1725, William Lansdon/Langsdon who d. a. 24 Mar 1743, appraisal; she d. a. 19 Dec1793, wp, Powhatan Co, VA; **5 ch**; she inherited her father's land in St. James Parish

Elizabeth[2], c. 1710 VA; m. a. 1728, Antoine Benin(g) (c. 1705-bet 1761-82), s/o François & Anne (de Bonnette) Benin; **6 ch**; she inherited her father's land in King William Parish

REF: *VA Genealogist,* Vol. 7, #4 (Oct-Dec, 1963) ; Renfro Genealogy & Allied Families.

JOÜET/JOUETT/JEWETT, Daniel II

b. c, 1660/5, St. Martin, Île de Ré, FR, s/o Daniel I & Élisabeth (X) Joüet

m. c. 1680, FR, Marie Coursier, d/o Jehan & Anne (Perrot[e]au) Coursier; she d. a. 25 Nov 1732, wp, Elizabethtown, NJ

c. 1685/6 - emigrated to Plymouth, ENG

summer 1686 - sailed to Boston then to RI, settled 1st in Rochester, then to Narragansett

c. 1689 - to NY

fall 1695 - to Charleston, SC, where Marie's parents had emigrated; he, Marie, Daniel, Pierre, Marie Elizabeth and Anne were naturalized c. 1695/6

1711 - to Elizabethtown, NJ

d. p. 7 Jun 1711, wd-a. 13 Oct 1721, wp, Trenton, NJ; d. Elizabethtown, NJ; he was a sailmaker in SC

CHILDREN:

Daniel III[2], b. c. 1681/2, Île de Ré, FR; m. Mary X; d. a. 21 Mar 1750, wp, Elizabeth, NJ

Pierre/Peter[2], b. c. 1683, Île de Ré, FR; m. c. 1701, XX; by 1710, went to VA; he d. 18 Dec 1743, Albemarle Co, VA or Elizabethtown, NJ; **issue**

Marie/Mary[2], b. 1686, Plymouth, ENG; m. William Dixon (1680-a. 10 Oct 1715, wp, Elizabeth, NJ) as his 2nd wife; she d. 1713, Elizabeth, NJ

Ézéchiel[2], bp. 2 Apr 1689, FR Ch, NYC; d. a. 1696 – not w/ fam in SC nor in father's will

Jean[2], bp. 28 Oct 1691, FR Ch, NYC; d. a. 1696 – not w/ fam in SC nor in father's will

Élizabeth[2], bp. 28 Dec 1692, FR Ch, NYC; m. Absalom Ladnor

Anne[2], b. 2 May, bp. 5 May 1695, FR Ch, NYC; d. a. 1711 – not in father's will

REF: FROST, Michael D., "Origins of the Jouet (Jouett) Family of the Île de Ré, near La Rochelle, France" (extracts – not clear if it was based on a book or an article); WITTMEYER, Alfred V., *Register of the Église Françoise à Nouvelle York, 1688-1804*; BAIRD, Charles W., *History of the Huguenot Emigration to America; NJ Colonial Documents – Calendar of Wills*; *"Liste de François et Suisses".... Settled in Charleston, on the Santee and at the Orange Quarter in Carolina Who Desired Naturalization* (Baltimore, 1968); CORONA, Joanne Cullom Moore, "Some History & Genealogy of the Jouett Family" in *The Huguenot*, #32 (1985-87).

JOURNÉE/JOURNEAY, Meynard/Moilliart/Meyndert/Malliard

b. c. 1630/40, Mardyck, Flanders, now in Nord, Nord-Pas-de-Calais Dépt., s.w. of Dunkerque

went to Mannheim, GER

16 Apr 1663 - arr in NY on *De Bonte Koe/* the *Spotted Cow*; liv. Brooklyn

9 Apr 1664 - he joined the church in Brooklyn with a certificate from Mannheim

m. 2 Jun 1664, Brooklyn, Elizabeth Dumont, sis/o Margaret (Dumont) Nöe & Wallerand Dumont

to Harlem; he was an overseer, 29 Oct 1675

c. 1677 - to Staten Island

d. 30 Jan 1678, Staten Island, NY; 8 Jul 1678 – new executors named, Richmond Co, NY – names wife Elizabeth & ch (but not by name); Elizabeth was m. again by that date

CHILD (there were daus but names are unknown, poss. another son):

John[2], b. 1666; 1700, purchased land on Staten Island; m. 8 Jan 1703, Elizabeth Deyo (d. a. 8 Dec 1827, St. Charles Co, MO, inv); he d. a. 4 Dec 1738, wp

    CHILDREN:

    John[3], b. 1704/6

    James[3], b. c. 1707; d. a. 28 Feb 1784, Middlesex Co, NJ; liv. Perth Amboy; **issue**

    Peter[3], b. c. 1710, NY; m. 31 Oct 1735, Shrewsbury, NJ, Audrey Osbourne; he d. p. 22 May 1760, Wd, NJ; 7 ch – **John**[4], **Catherine**[4], **James**[4], **Elizabeth**[4], **Audrey**[4], **Joseph**[4], **Ann**[4]

REF: HUTCHINSON, Elmer T., *NJ Colonial Document*, Vol. VI (Trenton, NJ, 1939); HONEYMAN, A. Van Doren, *NJ Colonial Documents,* Vol. IV (Somerville, NJ, 1928; Monmouth Co, NJ Deed Book A, pp. 276-77; LENG, Charles W., *Staten Island & Its People*, Vol. II (NY, 1930); BAIRD, Charles W. , *History of the Huguenot Emigration to America*, Vol. I (Baltimore, 1973); *Genealogy of the Journey Family*(1970, not pub.); RIKER, James,

Revised History of Harlem (City of New York); HIX, Charlote Megill, *Wills & Administrations, Richmond Co, NY, 1670-1800* (Bowie, MD, 1993).

JOUY/JOUIS/JUE/SCHUI/SCHWE/SHUEY, Daniel

b. c. 1679, FR, s/o Daniel Jouy who was bur. 4 Nov 1724, Dannstadt, at the age of 89

Daniel referred to as a "refugee" in the Parish Records of the Reformed Ch at Dannstadt, GER (s.w. of Mannheim); said to have been from Grigy (s.e. of Metz, Moselle, Lorraine), FR

m. 24 Jan 1702, Reformed Ch at Oggersheim, GER (w. of Mannheim), Judith L'Avenant; she m/2, 20 Feb 1738/9, widower John Jacob Becker; she d. 1746

d. 22 Aug 1738, Dannstadt, aged 59

CHILDREN (births in ch records, Oggersheim, Rheinland-Pfalz) :

Susanne[2], d. 10 May 1703, Oggersheim

*(David/)Daniel[2], b. 9 Apr 1703, Oggersheim; m. 16 Oct 1725, Dannstadt, Maria Martha Schilling; 18 Sep 1732, arr Philadelphia, on the *Johnson*; settled Lancaster Co, PA (in that part that is now Lebanon Co); he d. a. 21 May 1777,wp, Lancaster Co, PA

CHILDREN (bap recs. from Reformed Ch, Dannstadt):

Ludwig Heinrich/Lewis Henry Shuey[3], b. 12, bp. 15 Oct 1726; m. c. 1746, Elizabeth X (20 Apr 1726-20 Feb 1792); he d. 25 Feb 1775, 48Y 4M 13 D, Lancaster Co, PA; both bur. Klopp Church graveyard; **8 ch**

Anna Margaretha[3], bp. 15 Feb 1729; m. Nicholas Pontius (1728-1794); **issue**

Johannes[3], bp. 24 Nov 1730; d. 28 Nov 1730

Peter[3], m. XX; **issue**

Daniel[3]

Martin[3]

John[3]

Elizabeth[3], m. Henry Moser; **issue**

Catherine[3], m. Jacob Giger

Barbara[3], m. George Freesers

Maria Magdalena[2], b. 25 Apr 1706

Salomon[2], b. 22, bp 25 Sep 1707; d. 13 Apr 1733, unmarr.

Charles[2], b. 9 , bp 12 Nov 1709

David[2], b. 4, bp. 7 Dec 1710

Abraham[2], bp. 5 Nov 1713

Johann Peter[2], 8 Mar 1722

*ch record says name was David but as he was the 1st son and as a son David was b. 7 yrs later, that seems unlikely

REF: YODER, Don, *Rhineland Emigrants* (Baltimore, 1981); YODER, Don, editor, *Rhineland Emigrants list of German Settlers in Colonial America* (Baltimore, 1985); SHUEY, D.B., *History of the Shuey Family in America from 1732 to 1876* (Lancaster, PA, 1876); SHUEY, D.B., *History of the Shuey Family in America from 1732 to 1919* (Galion, OH, 1919); Records from the Ludwigshafen-Oggersheim Ch; PONTIUS, Harry, *The Descendants of David Jouy~Shuey* (Mar, 1998).

JUIN(G)/JUNE, George

b. Cherveux, Poitou, FR, now Cherveux le Goguelais, n.e. of Niort, s/o René & Judithe (Pié) Juin; prob. had bros Jean, René, Louis, sis Elizabeth who m. Philippe Normand – all liv. in the Orange Quarter; there was a Jean Juin in NY & CT – some say it is doubtful that this family had any connection to the SC Juins, but some think he was George's bro who went from SC to NY by 1709 – definitely <u>not</u> George's son Jean[2]

m. Suzanne le Riche (bp. 9 Sep 1677, London, ENG), d/o Jean & Anne (Ferment) le Riche; fam. on list
    of "Foreign Protestants for Carolina in 1679" as part of the Guérard Contingent

1696 - on St. Julien list of Huguenots to SC along with bros René and Louis

26 Sep 1697 - he had a warrant for 100 acres in the Orange Quarter (Berkeley Co.); rec. the grant 17 Aug
    1700; Louis Juin had a warrant for 200acres, 30 Oct 1696, rec. the grant, 12 Dec 1696

d. p. 1702

CHILD:

Jean/John I[2], b. a. 1702, SC; m. 5 Mar 1718/9, St. Thomas & St. Denis Parish, Ann(a) Howard; he d. a. 26
    Aug 1743, wp, Craven Co, SC

    CHILDREN (order uncertain, as named in father's will):

    John II[3], b. 18 Apr 1721; m/1, XX; m/2, 28 Dec 1743, Lucretia/Lucy Kennel; he d. a. 2 Feb
        1770, wp, Craven Co; his will names sons **John III**[4], b. 13 Nov 1744, m. Charlotte
        Gourdin, d/o Theodore Gourdin, John d. c. 1803 – **issue**; **Peter**[4], m. Tabitha [Johnson?],
        he d. a. 3 Jun 1768, wp, Craven Co. – **issue**; **Solomon**[4], m. 30 May 1727, St. Thomas & St.
        Denis Parish, Anna Stanley, d/o Edward Stanley, Solomon d. a. 6 Aug 1767, wp, Craven
        Co - **issue**; daus **Catherine**[4], m. Samuel Newman; **Frances**[4], **Lydia**[4], **Susanna**[4], **unnamed**
        ch[4]

    Anna[3], b. 1723/4

    Susanna[3], b. 1726

    Elizabeth[3], b. 1739

    George II[3], d. p. 2 May 1747, deed, Berkeley Co, SC, to nephew Solomon June

    Stephen[3], *poss.* the Stephen June who m. Lydia (Guerri) Steele, d/o Pierre & Marguerite
        (Rembert) Guerri, as her 2nd husband

    Edward[3]; **Nancy**[3]

REF: CLUTE, Robert F., *The Annals & Parish Registers of St. Thomas & St. Denis Parish in SC from 1680 to 1884* (Charleston, 1884); BAIRD, Charles W., *History of the Huguenot Emigration to America,* Vol. II (Baltimore, 1966); Juin Family research by Anne C. Gibert of Columbia, SC (1979); MOORE, Caroline T., *Abstracts of the Wills of the State of SC 1740-1760 & 1760-1784*; Craven Co, SC wills; "The Petit-Gerard Colony" in the *SC Historical Genealogical Magazine*, Vol. 43 (Charleston, 1942); BOYER, Carl ,3rd, *Ship Passenger Lists, NY & NJ (1600-1825)*, (Newhall, CA, 1978).

K

KIEF(F)ER, Johan Jacob

b. 6 May 1717, Gœrsdorf, Alsace, FR, s.w. of Wissembourg, s/o Johann Melchoir & Catharina (Schnepp) Kiefer

m/1, 1742, Gœrsdorf, Dorothee Hoffmann, d/o Peter Hoffmann from Lobsann, Alsace, n.e. of Gœrsdorf; she d. c. 1751

to America, settled in what is now Lebanon Co, PA

m/2, Catherine Altman

d. Aug 1804, Lebanon Co, PA; bur Bindnagle Ch, on Gravel Hill Rd, Palmyra, Lebanon Co, PA

CHILDREN, m/1:

Hans Georg[2], b. 1745

Andres/Andrew[2], b. 1750/1; m. 27 Oct 1767, Lebanon Co, PA, Mary Elizabeth Bickel; he d. 16 Jan 1828, Hanover Twp, Lebanon Co, PA; 25 Jan 1828, wp, Lebanon Co; used surname **KEEFER**; will names sons **George**[3], **Frederich**[3], **Andrew**[3], **Jacob**[3], **John**[3], daus **Elizabeth**[3] (wife of John Baumgardner), **Eve**[3] (m. Casper Dasher), **Catherine**[3] (m. Philip Johannes), **Sarah**[3]; Frederich & John Baumgardner, executors

REF: Andrew's will; Report of Mme. Jean Peres of Strasbourg, researcher (1973) – records from Preuschdorf (town located bet Gœrsdorf & Lobsann); EGLES, *Notes & Queries*, 3rd Series, Vol. 2.

KYPE/KIP, Ruloff de

b. 1544 FR, s/o Ruloff de Kype - a Catholic from Bretagne, who left FR for HOL, p. massacre at Vassay, Champagne (1562), he later returned to FR where he d. 13 Mar 1569 – he had 3 sons, only Ruloff had issue

remained in HOL, became a Protestant; settled in Amsterdam; surname becomes KYPE

m. XX

d. 1596, HOL

CHILD:

Hendrick[2], b. 1576; m. Margaret de Marneil; was active in the "Company of Foreign Countries" which was an assoc. formed to obtain access to the Indies which resulted in the discovery of the mouth of the (now) Hudson River and ultimately the settlement of NY by the Dutch; there is no evidence that he emigrated; the emigrant was Hendrick Hendrickszen[3], (Hendrick s/o Hendrick); had Hendrick [2] been the emigrant, according to Dutch nomenclature, he would have been called Hendrick Ruloffszen

CHILDREN:

unnamed dau[3] m. Bloemert Sandert; Bloemert, called Hendrick's bro-in-law, "assisted" Hendrick when he appeared before the "commissioners of marriage matters"

Hendrick Hendickszen[3], b. 1600, Niewenhuys (prob. in Groningen); 1615 moved to Servetsteech in Amsterdam; he was tailor; m. p. 20 Apr 1624, Amsterdam (date of betrothal/request to proclaim banns), Tryntje Lubberts of Swoll (prob. Zwolle in Overijssel), an orphan liv. Angelierstraat in Amsterdam, b. c. 1599; bet. 1637-43, to New Amsterdam w/wife & 5 ch; 28 Apr 1643, rec. patent for lot east of the fort, on present day Bridge St nr. Whitehall (lower Manhattan) where he erected his house and shop; he became one of the leading men of New Amsterdam and a *Great Burgher*; last mention of wife Tryntje was c. 1657; he d. p. 1665; the surname became **KIP**

CHIILDREN (1st 2 bap. New Church, next 4 at the Old Church, Amsterdam):

Abraham[4], bp. 6 May 1625; d. young or remained in HOL – not in NY records

Isaac Hendickszen[4], bp. 10 Jan 1627; m/1, 8 Feb 1653, Catalyntje Hendrick Snyers/ Snyder/de Suyers – **issue**, m/2, 26 Sep 1675, New Harlem, Maria (Vermilye), widow of Jean de la Montagne – **no issue**; he d. a. 6 Oct 1686

Beertjen/Baertje[4], bp. 8 Mar 1629; m. 17 Jan 1649, New Amsterdam, Jan Janszen/Jan

Janszen Van St. Obyn/Jan Wanshaer; **issue**

Jacob Hendrickszen[4], b. 16 May, bp. 25 May 1631; m. 8 Mar 1654, Maria de la Montagne, d/o Jean & Rachel (de Forêt) de la Montagne; he d. 24 Dec 1690, New Amsterdam; Maria d. 25 Aug 1711; **5 ch**

Hendrick Hendrickszen[4], bp. 14 Aug 1633; m. Anna de Sille, d/o Nicasius & Cornelia (Muelmans) de Sille; d. 1670, Flatbush, NY

Tryntje[4], bp. 8 Jun 1636; m. 10 Aug 1659, New Amsterdam, Abraham Janszen Van der Heul; **7 ch**

Femmetje[4], prob. bp 19 Apr 1643, NY; no info past 13 Jul 1667, when she was a sponsor at a baptism

REF: KIP, Frederic Ellsworth & HAWLEY, Margarita Lansing, *History of the Kip Family in America* (1928); NYGBR, Vol. VIII (Apr 1877) – lineage errors; PURPLE, Edwin R., *Contributions to the History of the Kip Family* (NY, 1877) – lineage errors from NYGBR repeated, but has other info.

L

la BARRE, Abraham de

b. 1654, Metz, FR

m. Marie Jeanne Charlé (b. Flanders-d. 24 Jul 1728, Strasburg)

d. 13 Jan 1699, Strasburg, Prussia, GER (n.w. of Stettin); he was a singer, poet, precentor, or lay clerk - he was called a *chantre* which can mean all of those!

CHILD:

François[2], b. 23 Jul 1698, Strasburg; m. 26 Feb 1721, Strasburg, Elizabeth Challié (27 Feb 1697, Strasburg-23 Jul 1780, Strasburg), d/o Michel & Anne (Tavernier) Challié; he d. 7 May 1767, Strasburg; he was a master tailor and brewer

CHILD:

François[3], b. 2 Aug 1738, Strasburg; m. 3 Nov 1759, Strasburg, Elizabeth Perrin (16 Aug 1739, Strasburg-14 Jun 1816, Strasburg), d/o Abraham & Marie (LeJeune) Perrin; he d. 3 Mar 1820, Strasburg; he was a butcher

CHILD:

Abraham[4], b. 2 Apr 1769, Strasburg; m. 7 May 1790 ,Strasburg, Marie Defrenne (13 Feb 1774, Strasburg-25 Nov 1855, Strasburg), d/o Abraham & Esther (Rebour) Defrenne; he was a brewer

CHILD:

Johann Carl[5], b. 22 Nov 1796, Strasburg; m. 21 Mar 1833, Strasburg, Marie Dorothie Christine Anna de Latre (b. 15 May 1809, Strasburg), d/o Jean & Christine Marie (Bentz) de Latre; he d. 12 Jan 1852, Strasburg ; he was a laborer; 7 ch b. Strasburg, one of whom emig. to America:

Ferdinand Louis[6], b. 26 Dec 1833, m. Anna Maria Stuteck (1831, SWI-1910, ND); he d. 1936, Elizabeth, ND – had gone 1st to IN then ND

NOTE: There were undoubtedly more children in each generation but the chart submitted by the Hug. Soc. of Germany just followed the line shown above

REF: *Deutscher Hugenotten-Verein E.V.* (Hug. Soc. of Germany, Hannover) – records are in French.

LABORIE, Jacques/James (Rev.)

b. Cardaillac, Guienne, FR, n.w. of Figeac, Lot Dépt, Midi-Pyrénées; had a bro Anthony, a surgeon, who was in Guilford, CT in the early 1700's

12 Mar 1688 - completed study of theology at the Academy of Geneva; 30 Oct 1688, was ordained at Zurich

c. 1689 - went to ENG, where he officiated in the FR churches of London; obtained a license from the Bishop of London for teaching grammar and catechizing the parish of Stepney

m/1, Jeanne Resseguire/Ressiguier/Resseguie

c. 1698/9 - to America where he was the minister in the FR colony at New Oxford, MA, and was a missionary to the Indians in that area

15 Oct 1704-25 Aug 1706 - was minister of the FR Ch, NYC; he then engaged in the practice of medicine & surgery

c. 1708/9 - to Stratford, CT

Aug 1710 - went on the Port Royal Expedition as a *chirurgeon*; chaplain on the transport brigantine *Mary*

m/2, a. 12 Apr 1711, Mary Burr, d/o Nathaniel & Sarah (Ward) Burr

May 1714 - a Lieutenant in the Fairfield Co. Troop

d. a. 4 May 1731, wp, Fairfield, CT; mentions wife Mary, sons James, John, daus Anne, Jeanne, Mary,

grson John; to his son James he left *"all my Instruments of chirurgery and all my French writings"*
CHILDREN, m/1:

Susanne[2], b. a. 1698, prob. ENG; was with her parents when they arr Oxford, MA; must have d. young

James[2], b. 1692, ENG; m. 29 Aug 1716, Stratford, CT, Abigail Blackleach, d/o Richard & Abigail
(Hudson) Blackleach; he was a doctor; d. 26 Dec 1739, age 48 yrs.; **8 ch**

John[2], evidently "lost" to his family – father's will mentions son John *"if he Comes again"*

Ann[2], m/1, 18 Jan 1721/2, Stratford, Samuel Whitney, m/2, 23 Jul 1759, Greenfield, CT, Benjamin Banks

Jeanne[2], b. 5 Mar, bp. 10 Mar 1705/6, FR Ch NYC (called Jane in bp rec)

CHILD, *probably* m/2:

Mary[2]

REF: BAIRD, Charles W., *History of the Huguenot Emigration to America,* Vol. II; ORCUTT, Rev. Samuel, *A History of the Old Town of Stratford and the City of Bridgeport CT*, Part II (1886); JACOBUS, Donald Lines, editor, *History & Genealogy of the Families of Old Fairfield*, Vol. I (Fairfield, CT, 1930); James' wd 7 Mar 1730.

la CALMES, Marquis de

b. c. 1675, FR, of Huguenot parents who fled to England, c. 1686; many of that surname lived in
Languedoc

5 Jan 1687 – denization in ENG

m. ENG, Isabella Elliche, said to have been b. in FR

1695-1700 - to VA with Marquis' bro **William**; Wm. then went to SC

1705 - rec. land warrant of 711 acres in Stafford Co.

d. a. 1741, Stafford Co, VA

CHILD:

Marquis (II)[2], b. c. 1705, Stafford Co, VA; m. 1725, Winnifred Waller (c. 1709-6 Oct 1751), d/o William
& Elizabeth (X) Waller; among 1st settlers of the valley of VA, on the Shenandoah River s. of
Harper's Ferry (now Clarke Co., VA); he d. 10 May 1755

CHILDREN:

Marquis (III)[3], b. 1726; m. Elizabeth Combs (d. 1804); he d. a. 2 Apr 1794, wp, Frederick Co,
VA; **no issue**

William Waller[3], b. 18 Jan 1727/8; m. Lucy Neville (18 Jan 1732-20 May 1789), d/o George &
Mary (Gibbs) Neville; he d. early 1774; **6 sons, 2 daus** (Mrs. Benson, Mrs. Catlett)

Isabella[3], b. c. 1727, VA; m. Aug 1746, William Richardson, a Quaker, b.1712, s/o Joseph &
Sarah (Thomas) Richardson; she d. 10 Jun 1796; **9 ch**

Elizabeth[3], b. c. 1732; m. Robert Catlett

Ann[3], b. Jan 1738; m/1, Peter Catlett, m/2, Capt. William Helm; she d. 22 Jun 18090

REF: BLAKEMORE, Maurice Neville, *Blakemore Family & Allied Lines* (1961); BUCK, Walter H., *A Short Sketch of the Calmes Family*(reprinted from the Clark Co. Historical proceedings); WAYLAND, John W., *History of Shenandoah Co, VA* (1927); Frederick Co, Will Book 4; Stafford Co, VA Northern Neck Land Grants, Liber 3; *The Huguenot*, #13 (1945-47).

la CHAIR, Jan de/CHAIRS, Jean/John

b. 1625, Rouen, FR

m. 1658, Dame Elizabeth Adee (c. 1630, FR-4 Jun 1730, Queen Anne's Co, MD)

1662 – to New Netherland from Amsterdam on the *Fox*

1666 – settled in Somerset Co, MD

d. c. 1690, Queen Anne's Co, MD

CHILD:

John[2], b. c. 1668, Somerset Co, MD; m. 1698, Kent Co, MD, Catherine Collins (1670, Queen Anne's

Co.-p. 14 Jan 1728, Queen Anne's Co), d/o Thomas Collins; he d. p. 16 Sep 1717-a. 5 Jun 1718, wp, Queen Anne's Co, MD

CHILDREN:

John[3], **James**[3], **Hannah**[3] (m. X Ellis), **Benjamin**[3], **Nathaniel**[3], **Thomas**[3] – all named in John's will

Joseph[3], b. 1692, Talbot Co, MD; m. 1713, Queen Anne's Co., Rebecca X (d. p. 3 Nov 1750, Queen Anne's Co)

REF: *Maryland Archives, 1ˢᵗ Parishers of Province of MD,* Vol. 23; John Chair's will; CHURARD, Silbert, *History of NY,* Vol. III; HART, E., *Heraldic Families & Huguenots' Pedigrees Register* (1928).

la CHAUMETTE, Arnoul/Arnell de; SHUMATE/SHUMWAY, Arnoul

b. FR, s/o Daniel de la Chaumette

1685 - liv in the Lower Parish, along Pagan Creek, Isle of Wight Co, VA

m/1, XX, who d. a. 1694

m/2, 1694, Anne (Whitley) Williams, widow of John Williams

d. a. 9 Feb 1698, wp

CHILDREN, m/1:

Alice[2], m. James Davis (d. 1741); c. 1700, moved to Stratton Major Parish, King & Queen Co; acted as guardians for her bro Moses who was "abnormal"

Moise/Moses[2], d. c. 20 Oct 1749

Jane[2]

Sarah[2]

Margery[2]

Frances[2]

REF: Von STAUFFENBERG, Theodor-Friedrich, *The Shumate Family. A Genealogy* (Washington, DC, 1964).

la CHAUMETTE, Jean de; SHUMATE/SHUMWAY, John

b. c. 1660, Rochechouart, FR, w. of Limoges, now in Haute-Vienne Dépt., Limousin; de la Chaumettes were in Rochechouart by 1260; Jean <u>possibly</u> s/o Daniel, an attorney, & Marie Aucouturier; Daniel is said to have m/2 Geneviève Fourgéaud, d/o Joseph Fourgéaud – no issue; it is thought that he and 2 brothers Pierre & Daniel escaped with Pastor Clovis Palasy to ENG in 1681; a Pierre de la Chaumette, b. 5 Apr 1664, m. Anne Palasy, d/o Clovis – this family *may* have emig. to NJ

c. Sep-Nov 1687 - to London – his name is on King James II Bounty Papers, a record of the Royal Treasury monies provided for deserving Huguenot refugees; obviously Jean did not leave ENG until later

m/1, c. 1690, XX; **no issue** (there is no info on this marr. – may have been earlier, may have m. in FR)

m/2, 29 Sep 1695, Threadneedle St. Church, London Elizabeth (Bourgeois) Bouvet, a native of Paris, widow of Henri Bouvet; she d. a. 1715, Martinique, during an epidemic

c. 1708 - went to Martinique, FR West Indies

c. 1718 - went to the Isle of Wight, VA, where his bro Arnoul lived; found that his bro had d.; Arnoul/ Arnell is **not** on the list of Daniel de la Chaumette's children bap. in Rochechouart, but has been listed as one of his ch. in references

a. 1722 - to Elk Run, Stafford Co, VA, with his 3 sons and bought a tavern; on 1723 Rent Rolls of Stafford Co – purchased land from William Allen, 9 Oct 1723, in Overton Parish, Stafford Co; grew tobacco

d. c. 1728 – supposedly killed by a highwayman who tried to rob him

CHILDREN, m/2:

Antoine[2], b. a. 1705; remained in Martinique; was there in 1725

John, Jr.[2], b. c. 1707/8; m. Judith Bailey; he d. a. 25 Oct 1784, wp, Fauquier Co, VA; 10 ch – **Thomas**[3], m. Elizabeth X, went to KY - **issue**; **Bailey**[3], m/1, Mary Dodson, m/2, Mary Jones; **William**[3]; **Richard**[3]; **John III**[3], m/1, Winifred Oxford, d/o Roger & Margaret (Strother) Oxford – **6 ch**, m/2, Susanna Crump, d/o Benjamin & Mary Barbour (Price)   Crump - **6 ch**; **Joshua**[3], **Daniel**[3], **James**[3], **Lettice**[3], **Jemima**[3], m. John Winn (order of birth not certain, all ch b. bet 1728-1746 – all but Richard in John II's will)

Samuel[2], b. c. 1710, m. c. 1730, Stafford Co, Lucy Blackwell/Blackley, d/o Samuel & Mary Downing Hudnall Blackwell; moved to SC, a. 1740; he d. a. 1790; Lucy d. bet 1790-1800; 8 ch – **Samuel**[3], b. c. 1735, prob. d. a. 1810 census; **Blackwell/ Blackley**[3], b. c. 1737 – was in Anderson Co, TN in 1805; **Moses**[3], b. c. 1739, 1810 in Chesterfield Co, **John**[3], b. c. 1745, m. Elizabeth X, prob. liv SC; + **4 daus**

Daniel[2], b. c. 1712; d. 1784, inv, Prince William Co, VA; m/1, c. 1736, poss. Elizabeth Taliaferro, d/o John & Sarah (Smith) Taliaferro, 2 ch - **Deveril**[3], **Winifred**[3], b. 1739, m. George Adams; m/2, 1 Feb 1757, Frederick, MD, Mary Elizabeth Hoffmann, d/o John & Barbara Hoffman of MD, 7 ch – **Benjamin**[3], m. Minnie Gregory, **Mark Hardin**[3], m. Deborah de Marques, **John**[3], m. Margaret Snap, **Thomas**[3] – **8 ch**, **Lydia**[3], m. Joseph George, **Anne**[3], m. Davis Holden, **Susanna**[3], m. John Wyatt: m/3, Tabitha Dodson, d/o Abraham & Barbara (Russell) Dodson, 7 ch - **Mary**[3], m. Martin Parker, **Lewis**[3], m. Mary Chadwell - **10 ch**, **Strother**[3], m. Annie McDavid– **9 ch**, **Daniel II**[3], m. Jane McDavid, **Margaret/ Peggy**[3], m. Harris Whitecotton, **Nancy**[3], m. Edward Kenny/Kinney, **Charlotte**[3], m. Peter Conway

> **NOTE:** Some sources say that it was Daniel's son Daniel II who m. Tabitha Dodson; Daniel I's will names Tabitha as executrix; with so many sons, it is doubtful that he would have named a dau-in-law as his executrix, so she was prob. his third wife.

prob. one or two more ch, names unknown

REF: STRONG, Jeanne Waters (Los Altos, CA, 1984), *Our Shoemaker Roots*; Von STAUFFENBERG, T. Friedrich, *The Huguenot Familly of de la Chaumette;* RILEY, Robert S., *History of the Shumate Family* (Utica, KY, 1992); WILLIAMS, Mrs. Sherman, compiler, *The Dodson (Dotson) Family of N. Farnham Parish, Richmond Co, VA*, Vol. 1; Vonn STAUFFENBERG, Theodor-Friedrich, *The Shumate Family A Genealogy* (Washington, DC, 1964).

La CHAUMETTE, Pierre de; DeLASHMUTT

b. 1661? FR – *may* have been the same Pierre bp. 13 Apr 1661, Rochechouart, s/o Daniel and Marie (Aucouturier) de la Chaumette

left FR, differing accounts place him in Alsace or Basle, SWI

p. 1664 - to America via ENG;

a. 1698 - was called for jury duty in Gloucester Co, NJ, so must have been there for a while; he did not appear and was considered "delinquent;" family says he didn't appear because he had returned to ENG to be married

m. ENG, Anna/Susanna X (d. 22 Jan 1734)

May 1700 - sailed from Cowes, ENG, to NJ – record reported but not found

1 Dec 1701 - Peter de la Chaumette, yeoman of Gloucester Co, was given a deed by Andrew Robeson, executor of Samuel Robeson, for 100 acres on the n. side of the Barclay River

d. bet 1725-1740, NJ

CHILDREN:

Anna[2], b. c. 1703; surname **LaSHAMET**

John[2], b. c. 1705; surname **DeLASHMUTT/DeLASHMET**; may have gone to MD with bro Elias; m. Sarah Nelson, d/o John, Sr. & Jane (X) Nelson, of Point of Rocks, Frederick MD; John lived in MD, c. 15-20 yrs

Mary[2], b. c. 1705-07; surname **DeLASMUTT**

Catherine[2], b. c. 1706-10; surname **DeLASHMOTT**

Peter II[2], b. c. 1705-10; surname **LAGAMET**

Elias[2], b. c. 1710-15; surname **LASHAMAST/DeLASHMUTT**, m. c. 1735-39, Elizabeth Nelson (she d. 1785/6, Frederick Co, MD), d/o John, Sr. & Jane (X) Nelson, sis/o Sarah (above); Elias d. bet 23 Feb-15 Apr 1778, wp, Frederick Co, MD; his will names sons **Elias**[3], **Basil**[3] (m/1, Mary Ankrum, m/2, Mary Jacobs), **Lindsay**[3], daus **Rachel**[3] (m. X Lemaster), **Ann**[3] (m. X Warfield), **Elizabeth**[3] (m. Edward Boteler) + several grch

REF: CLOSE, Virgil D., *The DeLashmutt Story* (Baltimore, 1994); NELSON, William, editor, *Documents Relating to the Colonial History of the State of NJ*, 1st Series, Vol. XXI (Patterson, NJ, 1899).

la CHAUMETTE, Pierre de; CHAMOIS, Pierre; SHUMWAY, Peter

may be of the same family as Jean & Pierre above, but not proven, *possibly* a cousin; some think that this Peter's original surname was **CHAMOIS** and not de la Chaumette; also he was from a different area of FR

b. 10 Apr 1635, FR, perhaps St. Maixent l'École, Deux Sèvres, Poitou-Charentes, n.e. of Niort; parents *might* have been Jacob & Marie (Lenain) Le Chamois

bet 1660-75 - to America

1675 - on the roll of MA colonial soldiers; fought in Narragansett War in RI

m. c. 1675, prob. Topsfield, Frances R. (Peter refers to her as "Frances R." in his will; some have said she was Frances Gould, d/o Zaccheus & Phebe (Deacon) Gould, but there is **no proof** of that - her name does <u>not</u> appear in the lists of Zaccheus' ch; Frances b. c. 1656-d. a 2 Aug 1714, wp, Essex Co, prob. d. Topsfield

to Oxford, MA

d. a. 10 Jun 1695, inv, Topsfield; Jul 1696 wp, Essex Co.

CHILDREN:

Peter[2], b. 6 Jun 1678, Topsfield, MA; m/1, 11 Feb 1700/1, Topsfield, Maria Smith of Boxford, MA (18 Dec 1677-17 Jan 1738/9, Oxford); m/2, 28 Feb 1739/40, Oxford, Mary (Wood) Dana (b. 17 Mar 1689/90, Concord), d/o Isaac & Elizabeth (Merriam) Wood, widow of Joseph Dana; went from Topsfield, MA to Oxford, c. 1714; he d. a. 17 Sep 1751, wp, Worcester Co, d. prob. Oxford

CHILDREN, m/1:

Oliver[3], b. 8 Jun 1701, Boxford, bp. 10 May 1702, Topsfield; m. 3 Sep 1724, Oxford, Sarah Pratt; he d. 21 Oct 1801, prob. Oxford

Jeremiah[3], b. 9 Mar 1702/3, Boxford, bp. 21 Mar 1702/3, Topsfield; m. 13 Nov 1729, Oxford, Experience Learned (b. 24 Jul 1711, Framingham), d/o Isaac & Sarah (How) Learned; he d. prob. Sturbridge, MA

David[3], b. 15 or 16 Dec 1705, Boxford, bp. 23 Dec 1705, Topsfield; m/1, 20 May 1736, Brimfield, Esther Hoar; m/2, 20 Sep 1751, Sturbridge, Alice Ainsworth; he d. 10 May 1796, Sturbridge, MA

Mary[3], b. 6 Feb 1707/8, Boxford, bp. May 1708, Topsfield; m. 6 Dec 1725, Oxford, Caleb Barton; note: birth rec Boxford says 6 Feb 1708/9 but bp. rec in Topsfield says May 1708!

Samuel[3], b. 6 Mar 1711, Boxford, bp. 22 Apr 1711, Topsfield; m. 19 Feb 1735/6, Oxford, Sarah Learned (8 Jun 1718, Oxford-26 Dec 1809, Sturbridge), d/o Isaac & Sarah (How) Learned; he d. 2 Sep 1800, Sturbridge

John[3], b. 26 Jun 1713, Boxford, bp. 16 Aug 1713, Topsfield; m. 19 May 1737, Oxford, Mary Dana (b. c. 1721- d. 1809, Oxford); he d. 13 Jan 1810, Oxford

Jacob[3], b. 10 Mar 1717, Oxford; m. 14 Jan 1741, Sutton, Martha Walker; he d. 15 Apr 1801, Oxford

Hepzibah[3], b. 6 Apr 1720, Oxford; m. 12 Nov 1741, Oxford, Obadiah Walker (8 Jun 1721, Marlborough-29 Aug 1810, Croydon, NH), s/o Obadiah & Hannah (Learned) Walker; she d. 1820, Croydon

Amos[3], b. 31 Jan 1722, Oxford; m. 29 May 1745, Oxford, Ruth Parker who d. 3 Oct 1792, Oxford; he d. 2 May 1818, Oxford

John[2], b. 20 Jan 1679/80, Topsfield

Samuel[2], b. 2 Nov 1681, Topsfield; d. intestate a. 16 May 1715, adm; prob. unmarr.

Dorcas[2], b. 16 Oct 1683, Topsfield; m/1, 26 Nov 1711, Topsfield Valentine Butler of Gloucester; m/2, 1 Jun 1719, Henry Whittingham

Joseph[2], b. 13 Oct 1686, Topsfield; d. p. 16 Apr 1715 wd, Topsfield; sister Dorcas was his heir; he was prob. unmarr.

REF: SHUMWAY, Asahel Adams, *Genealogy of the Shumway Family* (NY, 1909); DANA, Elizabeth Ellery, *The Dana Family in America* (Cambridge, MA, 1956); Vital Records – Boxford, Brimfield, Framingham, Oxford, Sturbridge, Topsfield.

LACY/LACEY/DELA(N)CY, Thomas

b. c. 1650, ENG; family *said to be* from the town of Lassy in Calvados Dépt., n.e. of Vire, now in Basse-Normandie; name *poss.* DeLacy; *poss.* s/o William Lacy

a. 1682 - arr VA - his name appeared on a list of people transported to VA

m. c. 1682 VA, prob. Hanover Co., Phoebe Rice (b. c. 1660), poss. d/o Thomas Rice

1704 – on Rent Rolls then; he was listed as one of the Huguenot settlers in Manakintown

d. - bur. Hanover Co.

CHILD:

Thomas II[2], b. c. 1684, VA; m. c. 1704/5, Ann Burnley, d/o Thomas Burnley

CHILDREN:

Stephen[3], b. c. 1705, King & Queen Co; m/1, XX; m/2, 1738, Sarah (X) Johnson, a widow (d. p. 1778); he owned 400 acres on branches of Owens Creek in Goochland Co, nr. Gum Spring; liv. in Hanover Co for many yrs before moving back to Goochland; he d. a. 20 Jul 1772, wp, Goochland Co, VA; will mentions wife Sarah, sons Thomas, Charles, Benjamin, Jesse, Matthew, Elijah, Johnson, daus Mary Anderson, Sarah Farrar, Lucy.

CHILDREN, m/1:

Thomas[4], m. Kessiah Griffith, d. p. 1 Oct 1793, wd, Anson Co, NC

Charles[4], m. 28 Jul 1774, Lousia Co, VA, Elizabeth Hudson - **8 ch**, Rev. War service

Jesse[4], m. 6 Sep 1774, Louisa Co, VA, Mary Johnson

Matthew[4], 8 Apr 1772, m. Susanna Rutherford; Rev. War service

Benjamin[4], b. 1755, VA, m. 25 Oct 1774, Goochland Co, VA, Judith Christian (d. 1820, bur. Charlottesville, VA), d/o Charles Christian, Jr.; he served in the Rev. War; he d. fall, 1826 bur. Charlottesville – **4 sons, 2 daus**

Mary[4], m. X Anderson

Sarah[4], m. 3 Dec 1758, Hanover Co, VA, Perrin Farres/Farrar/Ferrar, s/o William & Sarah (X) Farrar – **2 sons, 5 daus**

CHILDREN, m/2:

Elijah[4], m. 26 Nov 1787, Louisa Co, VA, Frankie Holland (b. 8 Apr 1766), went to KY, then to IN – **3 sons, 3 daus**; Rev. War service

Johnson[4], a. 2 Jun 1788, m. Frances X

Lucy[4], d. p. 1810, unmarr

Thomas III[3], b. c. 1707/08; m. XX; **4 sons, 2 daus**

William[3], b. 26 Feb 1713, King & Queen Co; m. Elizabeth Rice (1715-1770), d/o James & Elizabeth (House) Rice; he d. 28 Feb 1775; 5 sons, 3 daus, incl: **Henry**[4], **Drury**[4], **Noah**[4], **Agnes**[4], **Keziah**[4]

Nathaniel[3], b. c. 1715, VA; m. Marie Bootle; he d. 1781

Phoebe[3], m. Thomas Godsey, Jr.; **1 son, 1 dau**

Elkanah[3], b. c. 1720/30; m. Mary Brown; he d. 1777; **4 sons**

Elliott[3], b. c. 1725; m. c. 1760 Lois (?) Brown; he and his sons Elliott, Nathaniel all served in the Rev. War – Elliott[3] (d. 20 Nov 1777) and son Elliott[4] d. during the War; **5 sons, 3 daus**

NOTE: There was a William Lasie/Lacy (b. 1607 ENG) who emigrated to VA in 1624 on the *Southampton* who had a son Wm. II who purchased land in New Kent Co., VA. Wm. II had a son Thomas. There is no proof that this is the same Thomas who liv. in Manakintown. It is said that 3 Lacy brothers were in Manakintown in 1700 – the name does not appear on Gov. Nicholson's list of those arr on the *Mary Ann*, 23 Mar 1699/00, nor is the name in the <u>Vestry Book of King William Parish, 1707-1750</u>. R. A. Brock mentions the surname Lacy but with no further information, no dates, no Christian names.

REF: LANDIN, Mary Collins, *The Collins & Travis Families & Their Allies*; LANDOLL, Dorothy Lacey, *Family Reunion* (Cullman, AL, 1987); *The Huguenot*, #11 (1941-43) #23(1967-69); BROCK, R.A., *Documents Relating to the Huguenot Emigration to VA*; HOLMES, Alvahn, *Some Farrar's Island Descendants* (1979).

LADOU(E)/LADOUX/LADUE, Pierre

b. 1662, FR

m. FR, Martha Anneraud (1673-a. 22 Jan 1714/5, wp); her will, written in FR, mentions sons Daniel, Pierre, Étienne/Stephen, Ambroise, daus Elizabeth, Magdelen, Judith, Jeanne, Marie

11 Mar 1697 - he purchased 50 acres of land in New Rochelle from Marie Guespin, widow of Josias LeVillain

31 Jan 1698 – took Oath of Allegiance in New Rochelle, NY

held several town offices

d. a. 22 Jan 1714/5, wp, New Rochelle; will, in FR, mentions son Daniel, wife; he is said to have d. a. 28 Apr 1713 – his will was dated, 27 Mar 1713; his and his wife's wills were both recorded on the same date

CHILDREN:

Elizabeth/Betty[2], b. c. 1693

Daniel[2], b. c. 1694; m. 1718, Mary Canby (1695-1775, Mt. Pleasant), d/o James Canby of Westchester Co, NY; d. 15 Nov 1772, age 78 yrs.; bur. New Rochelle Cemetery; he was a weaver; at least **3 sons**

Magdalaine[2], b. c. 1697

Judith[2], b. c. 1700

Peter[2], b. c. 1702

Étienne/Stephen[2], b. c. 1703

Martha[2], b. 18 Jan, bp. 30 Jan 1703/4, FR Ch, New Rochelle; not in mother's will

Ambrose/Andrew[2], b. 10 Aug, bp 30 Aug 1705

Jeanne/Jane[2], b. c. 1708; m. 17 Feb 1724/5, Simsbury, CT, John Hill (d. 1 Aug 1771, Simsbury); she d. 2 Nov 1732, Simsbury; **issue**

Marie/Mary[2], b. c. 1710; d. 14 Nov 1732, Simsbury

REF: RIDEOUT, Mrs. Grant, *Ancestors & Descendants of Sarah Eleanor Ladue* (Chicago, 1930); SEACORD, Morgan H., *Biographical Sketches & Index of the Huguenot Settlers of New Rochelle, 1687-1776* (New Rochelle, NY, 1941); LADUE, Pomeroy, *Pierre Ladoue, 1662-1713, Huguenot New Rochelle, NY* (Detroit, MI, 1932, n.p.); Vital Records, Simsbury, CT.

LAFITTE, Peter

b. 1670, FR

c. 1685/7 - fled FR w/ his parents, went to SWI

m. Mary X (d. a. 6 Aug 1737, date of burial)

1732 - to SC; settled in Purysburg

3 Feb 1737 – 2 grants of land, 1 for 150 and another for 400 acres in Purysburg

d. c. 1739, SC

CHILD:

Peter[2], b. c. 1703/5, SWI; m. 1728/9, Mary Verdier (d. 1752), d/o André & Jane (X) Verdier; he d. a. May 1763
    CHILDREN:
    Jane[3], b. 1730; m. a. 1752, Charles Blundy
    Peter[3], b. 1732, SC; m. c. 1760/1, Mary Montague, d/o Col. Samuel Montague; he & Mary d. a.
        1787 Savannah, GA, & are bur in the old cemetery of Christ Ch; **3 ch**
    David[3], in father's will; no further record

REF: TROSDAL, Mrs. Einar Storm, *The Broyles, Laffitte & Boyd Relatives & Ancestors of Montague Lafitte Boyd, Jr., MD* (Savannah, GA, n.d.).

La FON, Nicholas

    m. Elizabeth Streshly; she m/2, 1765, John Reynolds
    d. a. 20 Mar 1749, Tappahannock, VA; inv. dated, 10 May 1750
    CHILDREN:
    Hannah[2], m/1, Robert Seayres, m/2, James Martin
    Richard[2], d. young
    Elizabeth[2], b. c. 1740; m/1, 1773, Capt. Joseph Bohannan, m/2, 1825, John Bohannon of KY; she d. c.
        1828

REF: *The Huguenot Publication*, #35 (1991-93).

la FONTAINE, Jean de (Sieur de la Fontaine)

    b. 1500, Maine Prov (former prov. s. of Normandie, n. of Anjou); his father Gilles procured a place for him
in the household of King François I – what was called *"L'Ordonnance du Roi"*; during that time, he
married, fathered 4 sons, and was commissioned as an officer in the king's forces
    m. XX
    1535 converted to Protestantism; he and his father were both converts
    was a soldier during the reigns of François I, Henri II, François II & Charles IX
    1561 – resigned his court position; retired to live on his estates in Maine; the Edict of Pacification, granted 17
        Jan 1561/2, gave limited tolerance to Protestants, made him think that he would be safe in his home; on
        the contrary, it only provoked the extremists to violence
    d. 1563 – he, his pregnant wife and faithful valet were killed in their home by a gang from Le Mans;
        the eldest son (18 yrs) was prob. killed as well as he was never heard from again; 3 younger sons
        escaped to La Rochelle
    CHILDREN:
    son[2], b. prob. 1545; killed 1563
    Jacques/James I[2], b. 1548/9, Genouillé FR (prob. the one now in Charente-Maritime Dépt, Poitou-
        Charentes, n.e. of Rochefort, although there is another one not very far away in the Vienne Dépt,
        Poitou- Charentes, s.w. of Poitiers); m/1, XX; fled to La Rochelle; became a *cordonnier*
        (shoemaker), then a merchant; d. 1633, leaving an estate of 9,000 *livres*; by 1st wife he had 3 ch
        who survived to adult hood; m/2, XX – this wife tried to poison him, she was sent to prison and
        was hanged, no issue
        CHILDREN, m/1, surname **FONTAINE**:
        dau[3], m. X Bouquet; **issue**
        dau[3], m. X Reau/Réaud, Rochelle merchant; **2 sons**
        Jacques II[3], b. 1603; became a minister, was at Vaux & Royan; m/1, 1628, London, Elizabeth
            Thompson (d. 1640/1), m/2, 1641, Marie Chaillon, from Pons, Saintonge, who d. 1670; they
            purchased an estate at Genouillé + the adjacent manor of Jaffé; he d. 1666
            CHILDREN, m/1:

Jane[4], b. 1628 ; m. X L'Hommeau, a wealthy man of unfortunate habits; remained in FR; she ran a school to support her family; **5 ch**

Judith[4], b. 1630; m. X Guiennot; widowed, she & her daus escaped to ENG following imprisonment; they supported themselves by doing needlework in London; **4 ch**

James[4], b. 1633; he was educated for the ministry; d. a. 1658; his widow was imprisoned and later banished from FR; she went to ENG; had **3 sons**, one of whom became a Protestant minister in GER

Elizabeth[4], b. 1636; m. Rev. Isaac Sautreau, pastor at Saujon, Saintonge; went to Dublin; decided to go to America; Eliz., her husband + 5 ch d. in a shipwreck nr. Boston harbor

Peter[4], b. 1638; minister appointed to the church at Vaux (prob. now Vaux-sur-Mer, Charente-Maritime Dépt, Poitou-Charentes, n. of Royan); was confined at the Île de Oléron; had at least **2 daus**; went to London; dau **Esther**[4] m. John Arnauld, grs/o his aunt X Bouquet[3]

Francis[4], b. 1640; went to the college at Saumaur with bro Peter; d. young

CHILDREN, m/2:

Susanne[4], b. 1643; m. Étienne Gachot, grs/o Rev. Merlin of La Rochelle; Stephen was also a minister in Saintonge and Aunis; remained in FR; **2 daus**

Peter[4], m. 1646; m. X Oissard; remained in FR; **5 ch**

Marie/Mary[4], b. 1648; m. Rev. Peter Forestier, pastor in Angoumois; escaped to ENG w/ 2 ch; had **5 ch**, including **Janette**[5] who went to ENG with uncle Jacques (III)

Anne[4], b. 1651; m. Léon Tescard, Sieur des Meslars; went to Plymouth, ENG; descendants settled Amsterdam

Jacques/James III[4], b. 7 Apr 1658, Genouillé; studied for the ministry, rec. an M.A. from the College of Guienne; was imprisoned for his religious meetings; abandoned his estates & sailed from Tremblade with his fiancée Anne, her sister Élisabeth, niece Janette, arr ENG, 1 Dec 1685; m. 24 Feb 1685/6, Barnstaple, ENG, Anne Élisabeth Boursiquot, d/o Aaron & Jeanne (Guillot) Boursiquot of Taillebourg, Saintonge; they went to Taunton, ENG, where he rec. Holy Orders, 10 Jun 1688; went to Cork, IRE, arr 24 Dec 1694; he established a fishing business and was justice of the peace; waged "war" against Irish smugglers and French privateers; then moved to Dublin, c. 1708, where he established a school; he d. a. 27 May 1728, wp; he & Anne Elizabeth (d. 29 Jan 1720/1) are bur in the Huguenot Cem, in Merrion Row, n.e. corner of St. Stephen's Green, Dublin; he wrote an extensive family history, in French, for all his children

CHILDREN:

James[5], b. 10 Oct 1686, Barnstaple; m/1, 1711, Cork, Lucretia Desjarrie, who d. c. 1735 King Wm. Co, VA - **6 ch**; arr Yorktown, VA, Oct 1717; m/2, c. 1737/8, Elizabeth Harcum – **3 ch**; he d. 1745/6, Northumberland Co, VA

Aaron[5], b. 1688, Taunton; d. 1699, Cork, of tuberculosis

Mary Anne[5], b. 12 Apr 1690, Taunton; m. 20 Oct 1716, Dublin, Matthew Maury of Castelmaurou, Gascogne (n.e. of Toulouse), s/o Abram & Marie (Feauguereau) Maury; they went to VA, Sep 1719; she d. 30 Dec 1755, Charles City Co, VA; Matthew d. 1752, King Wm Co, VA; **3 ch**

Peter[5], b. 1 Dec 1691, Taunton; m/1, 29 Mar 1714, Elizabeth Forreau (c. 1700-c. 1722) – **2 ch**; rec. a B.A. from the Univ. of Dublin, spring, 1715; a minister; he arr VA, Oct,1715; m/2, c. 1740, Sarah Wade, d/o Joseph Wade – **6 ch**; he d. p. 30 Jun 1757, wd (probably Jul, 1757), Westover Parish (Charles City), VA

John[5], b. 28 Apr 1693, Taunton; sailed to VA, 1710; ensign in the British army who went on an expedition in search of a passage across the Blue Ridge in 1716; m. 1728, London, Mary Magdalen Sabatier (bur. 25 Aug 1781, Newchurch), d/o John Sabatier, a silk weaver - **9 ch**; John had been a watchmaker and then became a silk weaver as well; 1748 went to s. Wales; bur. 26 Nov 1767, Newchurch, Carmarthen Co, Wales

Moses[5], b. 15 Oct 1694, Taunton; rec. a B.A., 1716, M.A., 1717, from the Univ. of Dublin; studied law but became an engraver; bur. 19 Feb 1766, New-church); d. unmarr. – **no issue**

Francis[5], b. 16 Sep 1697, Cork; a minister – rec. a B.A. summer, 1716 & a M.A. from Trinity College, Dublin, summer, 1719; m/1, 4 Jan 1721, London, in the FR chapel of St. James, Marie Glenisson, d/o of John Glenisson, she d. 1733; arr VA, May, 1721; **4 ch, m/2**, c. 1735, Susanna (Brush) Barbour, widow – **2 ch**; prof. of Oriental languages at Wm. & Mary; he d. Yorkhampton Parish (York), VA, a. 19 Mar 1749, wp, York Co.; Susannah d. a. 21 Jul 1760, adm, York Co, VA

Elizabeth[5], b. 3 Aug 1701, Bearhaven (Castletown Berehaven, on Bantry Bay, Co. Cork); m. 31 Oct 1729, St. Martin Orgars, London, Daniel Torin (b. c. 1707, Wandsworth-bur. 1 Jun 1767, Wandsworth); she d. c. 1764; **3 ch**

Abraham[2], b. c. 1551; fled with bro Jean to LaRochelle; issue - a dau who m. X Brousseaux

son[2], b. c. 1554; fled to LaRochelle with his brothers

REF: RESSINGER, Dianne W., editor, *Memoirs of the Rev. Jaques Fontaine 1658-1728* (1992); CARPENTER, J.S., "Fontaine & Connected Families" in *VA Magazine of History & Biography*, Vol. XXII (1914); FONTAINE, Winston Francis, compiler, *From Rags to Respectability, The History of the Fontaine Family & Kinfolks* (Mobile, 1987); TYLER, Lyon G., *Encyclopedia of VA Biography*, Vol. I, II; KINKEAD, June Mefford, *Our Kentucky Pioneer Ancestry* (Baltimore, 1992); FONTAINE, Rev. Peter, *Memoirs of a Huguenot Family,* translated by Ann Maury, originally pub.1852; BROCK, R.A., *Documents Relating to the Huguenot Emigration to VA* (VA Hist Soc, 1886); WEST, Sue Crabtree, compiler, *The Maury Family Tree* (Birmingham, AL, 1971, 1979, 1983).

La FORCE, René

rec. 900 acres in Henrico Co, VA

m. Sarah X (d. a. 18 Jan 1757, wp, St. James Parish, Goochland Co, VA); her will mentions ch René, Sarah Hardain, Judith (*poss.* a posthumous ch as she is not mentioned in René's will); Sarah evidently did not remarry as her will is signed by an x with the words *Sarah Laforse* written in)

d. a. 17 Sep 1728, wp, St. James Parish, Goochland Co, VA; his will mentions wife Sarah & 3 ch - René, Sarah, Rachel; he was a physician

CHILDREN:

René[2], m. by early 1756, Agnes Moseby; owned land in Goochland & Henrico Co. as well as 900 acres in what is now Powhatan Co but owned no land in the FR territory

CHILDREN (recorded in the *Douglas Register*):

Robert[3], b. 27 Aug 1756, VA

Ann[3], b. 14 Aug 1758, VA

Agnes[3], b. 10 Nov 1760, VA

Judith[3], b. 8 Sep 1765, VA

Monsire[3], b. 21 Jul 1768, VA

Sarah[2], m. William Hardain/Harding (d. p. 7 Jan 1766, wd, Goochland Co), s/o Thomas & Mary (Giles) Harding; son **Giles**[3] (15 Jun 1749-a. 7 May 1810), m/1, 30 Jan 1773, Louisa Co, VA, Amidia/Amy Morris, m/2, 31 Jul 1804, Davidson Co, TN, Martha Donnelly, d/o James & Isabel (X) Donnelly; William also had sons **Thomas**[3], **William**[3] who were in his will; Sarah d. a. Feb 1797, wp, Goochland Co

Rachel[2], prob. d. young as she is not mentioned in her mother's will, *unless* Rachel and Judith are the same person

Judith[2], m. 13 Oct 1757, Robert Burton; dau **Mary**[3] (6 Feb 1763, Buckingham Co, VA-1845), m. 5 May 1785, as his 3rd wife Thomas Fearn (24 Oct 1745-4 Oct 1805), s/o John & Leeanna (Lee) Fearn - **issue**; Robert d. a. Feb 1778 (estate) Orange Co, NC

REF: CABELL, Priscilla H., *Turff & Twigg, The French Lands,* Vol. I (Richmond, VA 1988); JONES, W. Mac, *The Douglas Register* (Baltimore 1966); Goochland Co. Will Book I, p. 37 - Will of Rene LaForce, 1728 - Will Book 7, Will of Sarah LaForce, 1757; WILLS, Ridley II, *The History of Belle Meade* (Nashville, 1991).

La FORGE/LeFORTE/LAFORT/LaFORD (alias Liberté), Jean/Johannes/Jan/John

b. *poss.* nr. or in Lyon, FR; said to have liv. in "La Forge-Nocey," Poitou – not found, but there are 2 towns in Poitou, one named Forges, w. of Surgères, and Les Forges, n.e. of Niort & s.w. of Poitiers, which is the general vicinity cited; apparently "La Forge" was applied to Huguenots who came from a meeting place in southern France and the phrase "*la forge*" was used as a password and also was given as their surname when asked their name by outsiders

m/1, a. 1650, FR, XX (d. a. 1652)

went to HOL, then to NY; *may* have emigrated to NY via Canada

1652 - to New Amsterdam w/ son Adriean; settled on Staten Island

7 Oct 1663 - joined Dutch Ch, NYC

settled Canastagione (now Clifton Park in Saratoga Co,) on n. bank of the Mohawk River, c. 5 mi. above Half Moon, across the river from Niskayuna

m/2, c. 1678, prob. NY, Marguerite/Margriet Rinckhout, d/o Jan Rinckhout & Eva Jurriaens

d. p. 3 Nov 1706, wd - a. 3 Oct 1707, wp, Albany Co, NY; liv. Nistagogone (Albany Co.); **all** his ch were named in his will

CHILD, m/1

Adriean I/Abraham[2], b. c. 1650/1, FR, poss. nr. Lyon; signed Oath of Allegiance in Bushwyck, NY, 26-30 Sep 1687, states that he has been "in the country" for 15Y, prob. refers to when he arr in NYC; m. Jannetje/Jane Loije/Lozier (bp. 4 Jun 1662, Brooklyn), d/o Jans Corneliszen Losee/Lozier

CHILDREN:

Charles[3], b. c. 1678/9; **issue**

John[3], b. 1680, Bushwyck; m. Frances Marlett (1682-1754), d/o Abraham & Christina (Billiou) Marlett (Christina was d/o Pierre & Françoise (DuBois) Billiou); settled Piscataway, NJ, c. 1710; he d. a. 1751; **5 ch**

Nicholas[3], b. c. 1681/82, Bushwyck; m. Geertje (Lubberts?); d. a. 3 Mar 1767, wp, Richmond Co, NY; will does not mention wife or ch but nephews (sons of bro Charles, Daniel & sister Mary); **3 ch**, bp. Jamaica, NY, who must have d. young since they are not in his will

Catherine[3], b. c. 1684; m. Michael deGrae

Marie/Mary[3], bp. 1685, Albany Co, NY

Aeltje[3], bp. 1685, Albany Co, NY

Peter[3], bp. 11 Oct 1689; m. Hester X; moved to Yonkers, NY, c. 1730; **7 ch**

David[3], b. c. 1691; d. p. 2 Nov 1718; **issue**

Jane[3], m. Johannes Swin/Sweem

Adrian II[3], b. c. 1691; settled Staten, Richmond Co, NY, in 1714; m. 15 Jan 1715/6, Albany, Anna Barber Clute, d/o Frederic Clute/Cloet & Francyntje Dumont; Francyntje, d/o Wallerand Dumont & Margaret Hendricks; he d. p. 1 Nov 1777, wd - a. 31 Dec 1777, wp, Richmond Co, NY; **5 sons, 1 dau** named in his will

CHILDREN, m/2:

Johannes/John[2], m. Rebecca Van Antwerpen (bp. 25 Dec 1692, Albany), d/o Daniel Janse Van Antwerpen & Maria Groot, d/o Symon Symonse Groot; he was a soldier; in Piscataway, by 1715; **10 ch**

Daniel[2], bp. 11 Sep 1687, Albany; m. Sara Reyly of NY; son **Johannes** bp. 1 Apr 1750

Nicolaas[2], bp. 15 Apr 1693, Kingston, NY; m. 11 Feb 1720, Maritje Van Antwerpen (bp. 3 Jan 1695, Schenectady), d/o Daniel Janse Van Antwerpen & Maria Groot; **7 ch**

Jacob[2], m/1, 14 Jan 1726, Sara de Wandelier, m/2, Maritje Oosterhout; d. 17 May 1760

Isaac[2], bp. 3 Sep 1690, Albany; m/1, 7 Sep 1729, Jacomyntje/Joan Viele, d/o Lewis Viele – **4 ch**, m/2, 7 Jul 1751 Sara Viele – **3 ch**

Maria/Mary[2], m. Johannes/John Vedder
Annatje/Anna[2], bp. 5 Apr 1702

REF: MONNETTE, Ora E., *First Settlers of Ye Plantations of Piscataway and Woodbridge, Olde East NJ, 1664-1714* (LA, CA, 1935); HIX, Charlotte M., *Staten Island Wills & Letters of Administration, Richmond Co, NY, 1670-1800;* MACKENZIE, Grenville C., *Families of the Colonial Town of Phillipsburgh* (Tarrytown, NY, 1976); FORT, Jerome H., *Genealogy of the Fort Family in NY State* (1924); PEARSON, Jonathan, *Genealogies of the First Settlers of the Ancient County of Albany* ; PEARSON, Jonathan, *Contributions for the Genealogies of the Descendants of the First Settlers of Patent & City of Schenectady, 1662-1800* (Baltimore, 1982); SCHUYLER, George W., *Colonial NY Philip Schuyler & His Family* (NY, 1885); REAMAN, G. Elmore, *Trail of the Huguenots* (1966); SCOTT, Kenneth & STRYKER-RODDA, Kenn, *Denizations, Naturalizations & Oaths of Allegiance in Colonial NY* (Baltimore, 1975).

La GRANGE, Jean/John (Omie) de

it is said that 3 brothers (natives of Normandie) came to NY from Amsterdam, c. 1656 – 2 have
        been identified: Joost (m. Margaretta – their son Arnoldus went to MD) and Jean/John/Omie
b. c. 1625, FR
went to Amsterdam, HOL
1656 to America, settled New Amsterdam
c. 1664 m. Annatie DeVries, d/o Johanns & Margarieta (Costers) De Vries; she was b. 1650, HOL, d. 1735,
        NY
a. Aug 1666 – to Ft. Orange (Albany)
d. 26 Apr 1731, age c. 106, bur. Normans Kill, Albany Co, NY; master tailor, owned a saw mill and
        considerable property
CHILDREN:
Johannes[2], b. c. 1664; m. 28 Sep 1697, NYC, Eytje Roosevelt/Croesvert (bur 26 May 1746, Albany); he d.
        6 May 1748, Bergen, NJ; **6 ch**
Jellis[2], b. 1667; m. 1690, Jannetje Adrianse Molenaar (bp. 5 Apr 1672) d/o Joost Arriansen Molenear &
        Elizabeth Crom; he d. Jan 1710, Albany; **5 ch**
Omie[2], b. c. 1672; m. 28 Mar 1697, Albany, Elsie Van Loon (d. a. 18 Jun 1753, wp), d/o John Van Loon;
        he d. p. 22 Jan 1724/5, wd; **no issue**; Elsie m/2, Jun 1727, Barent Egbert Metselaer
Annetje[2], b. c. 1675; m. 19 May 1700, Kingston, Ari Molenaar (7 Sep 1676, Kingston-1761, Somerset Co,
        NJ), s/o Joost Arriansen Molenear & Elizabeth Crom; she d. p. 22 Dec 1757, wd-a. 22 Jul 1761, wp,
        Somerset Co, NJ; **no issue**
Isaac[2], bp. 28 Apr 1686, Albany Reformed Ch; m. 6 Apr 1722, Marytje Burgaart (bp. 27 Feb 1698), d/o
        Coenraadt Hendrickse Burgaart & Geezie Hendrickse VaWie; he d. a. 26 Sep 1767, wp; **9 ch**
Christiana[2], bp. 10 Oct 1688, Albany Reformed Ch; m. John Lansing
Jacobus[2], bp. 23 Apr 1692, Albany Reformed Ch; m. 24 Oct 1717, Dutch Ch, Schenectady, NY, Engeltie
        Veeder (b. 27 Oct 1700, Schenectady), d/o Johannas Veeder & Susanna Wemple; he d. 9 Aug 1765,
        Normans Kill; **10 ch**

NOTE: there is much contradictory information on this line; the above seems to be the best "solution."

REF: REYNOLDS, Cuyler, *Hudson & Mohawk Valleys*, Vol. III (1911); PEARSON, Jonathan, *Early Records of the City and County of Albany & Colony of Rensselaerswyck, 1656-1675* (Albany, 1869); HAMBURGER, Elizabeth M. Ellis, *Descendants of Omie de la Grange & Wife Annetje de Vries*; LEONARD, Vreeland Y., "The La Grange Family" in *Dutch Settlers Society of Albany Yearbook*, Vol. XXIV; BENNETT, Allison, *Times Remembered.*

la HUNTÉ/DILLAHUNT(Y), Daniel de

b. FR, supposedly s/o a FR nobleman; family left FR at the time of the Revocation

went 1st to HOL, then to Dublin, IRE

c. 1715, Daniel to MD

m. Mary (O'Hare?) who d. a. 2 Dec 1746 (not mentioned in Daniel's will)

d. p. 2 Dec 1746, wd-a. 10 Aug 1748, wp, Kent Co, MD

CHILDREN (as named in Daniel's will; also mentioned a Mary Greene – relationship, if any, not given, & a grdau **Ann**[3]):

Edmond[2]

John[2], b. 8 Dec 1728, Havre-de-Grace, MD; m. 4 Jun 1747, Hannah Neal (30 Mar 1732, MD-5 May 1816, TN), a Quaker & d/o Francis & Anna (Farrell) Neal of Baltimore; went to VA, then to Craven (now Jones) Co, NC; he was a Baptist minister; Patriotic Service, Rev. War, NC; he d. 9 Feb 1816, Davidson, TN – he & his wife are bur. in the Dillahunty Cemetery nr. Bellevue, TN, s.w. of Nashville; surname became **DILLAHUNT(Y)**

> CHILDREN:
> **Samuel**[3], **Daniel**[3], **William**[3]
> **John**[3] (sometimes called John Silas) m. Rachel (Baker/Baber?); **issue**
> **Thomas**[3], m. Sarah Becton; **issue**
> **Rachel**[3], m. Col. Joseph E. Johnson
> **Mary Ann**[3], m. George West; **issue**
> **Hannah**[3], m. X Quilling
> **Ann(a)**[3], m. John Colvett II

?Mary[2] – called Mary Neal in will – *may not* have been a dau but some other relation – not clear from will or she *may* have been the Mary Greene cited above – needs proof

Abraham[2]

Isaac[2]

REF: STANFILL, Latayne Colvett, *Colvett Family Chronicles, The History of the Colvett Family of TN, 1630-1990* (Glendale, CA, 1991); GREER, Addie Lee Oliver, "Sketch of the Daniel De La Hunté Family" in *Family Histories*, Vol. I (TN DAR); NSDAR Ancestor database.

LAMAR/LAMORE/LEMAR

(2 brothers of unknown parents; by 1697, the name was **LAMAR**)

Pierre/Peter[2]

> b. FR; went 1st to VA
>
> 17 Nov 1663, naturalized; records identify him as a "subject of the crown of France"
>
> m. c. 1665, MD, Frances X
>
> d. a. 31 Mar 1694, wp, Calvert Co, MD; he left extensive property; will mentions wife Frances, 3 daus, grson Peter O'Neill
>
> CHILDREN:
>
> **Ann**[3], m. Peter O'Neill; **issue**
>
> **Mary**[3], under 16 & unmarr. on 9 Oct 1693, when father wrote his will
>
> **Margaret**[3], under 16 & unmarr. on 9 Oct 1693, when father wrote his will

Thomas[2]

> b. FR; one source says he was from Wicres, Flanders – not proven; he went 1st to VA
>
> may have been in MD as early as 1659; record of a survey done 20 Aug 1659, was made for "Thomas Laymour"
>
> 17 Nov 1663 - naturalized; records identify him as a "subject of the crown of France"; liv in Calvert Co. then – the part where he lived became part of Pr. Georges Co. in 1696
>
> m/1, a. 24 Nov 1665, Mary X

m/2, Anna (Pottinger?)

d. a. 29 May 1714, wp, Prince Georges Co, MD; prosperous and held important positions; will mentions only his wife Ann and 2 sons Thomas and John

CHILD, m/1:

Thomas[3], b. c. 1670; m. Martha (Blanford/Beven or Urqhuhart); d. a. 31 Jan 1748, wp, Prince Georges Co, MD

CHILDREN:

Robert[4], m. Sarah Wilson, sis/o Joseph (below), he d. a. 1771, SC – **issue**

Samuel[4], m. a. 1753, went to SC

Alexander[4] – **issue**

John[4], m. Rachel – **issue**

James[4], m. Valinda Osborn - **no known issue**

unnamed dau[4], m. William Williams

Mary[4], m. Clementius Davis, went to SC/GA

Thomas[4], m. Eleanor, went to SC

Elizabeth[4], b. 26 Oct 1722, m. 18 Jun 1747, Joseph Wilson, bro/o Sarah (above) - **issue**

CHILD, m/2:

John[3], b. 1690; m. 21 Jan 1714, Susanna Tylor, d/o Robert & Mary (X) Tylor; went to SC, later to GA; d. a. 1 Nov 1758, wp

CHILDREN:

Thomas[4], m. Mary Hill

John[4], m. Sarah Marshall, he d. 1756 – **issue**

Robert[4], m. Sarah Hall, he d. 1815

Susanna[4], m. Alexander Magruder – **issue**

Ann[4], m. Dr. John Briscoe;

Mary[4]; **Elizabeth**[4]; **Mareen**[4]; **Richard**[4]; **Priscilla**[4]

Rachel[4], m. William Harding

REF: LeMAR, Harold Dihel, *History of the Lamar or Lemar Family in America* (Omaha, NE, 1941); LAMAR, William Harmong, "Thomas Lamar of the Province of MD, and a Part of his Descendants" in *Southern History History* publication Vol. I (Washington, DC, 1897); AUSTIN, Jeannette Holland, compiler, *GA Bible Records* Baltimore, 1985).

La MARE, François de (DELAMAR/LAMAR)

b. FR

c. 1663 - fled FR, to America; was in that part of VA which became a colony called Albemarle, soon after became known as Carolina

c. 1692/3 - to Pasquotank Pct, NC

1 Jan 1694 - rec. a grant for 125 acres in Pasquotank Co. along with Isaac Delamar (brother? nephew?)

m/1, a. 10 Oct 1694, Susannah (X) Travis, wid/o Daniel Travis

c. 1702 - naturalization petition in Albemarle Co, NC; in a statement made to the General Court of NC, as part of his application for citizenship, Francis said that he was a Frenchman by birth and a Protestant who was forced to flee FR because of his religion; further states that he has been in NC for 11 yrs; this statement is repeated in several documents but the date is uncertain – prob. when he petitioned for naturalization

m/2, a. 29 Mar 1703, Ann (Mayo) Pope Scarborough, d/o Edward Mayo, Sr, widow of Richard Pope **&** X Scarborough, she m/4, John Jennings; she d. a. 2 May 1720, wp, Pasquotank Co, NC

1706-1712 – served as a justice in Pasquotank Co.

he is thought to have been an attorney; was a church warden and member of the NC House of Commons

d. a. 28 Jul 1713; wife Ann appt. administratix of his estate; he poss. d. during Indian wars

CHILD, m/1:

Francis II[2], b. c. 1695/1700; m. Susannah X; settled 1st in Bath Co; d. a. Mar 1741/2, wp, Beaufort Co, NC

CHILDREN:

Francis III[3], b. 1730/34; m/1, Oct 1759, Mariam Barclift, d/o William & Ann (Durant) Barclift –
issue, incl dau **Sarah**[4] (m. 1784, Thomas Clayton), son **Francis IV**[4] (b. c. 1759, m/1,
Elizabeth Dawson), m/2, 19 Jan 1788 Hasty (X) Nelson, widow; he d. a. Jul 1799, wp,
Craven Co, NC; Capt, Rev. War;

Thomas[3], b. c. 1730; m/1, X Carraway, a sis/o William, poss. Sarah, m/2, Ann X(she m. a. Mar 1790,
X Thomas); Rev. War; he d. a. 1787, wp, Craven Co, NC; he was a carpenter

CHILDREN, m/1:

Francis[4], b. c. 1760, m/1, c. 5 Dec 1782 (date of bond), his cousin Elizabeth Dawson, d/o
Francis & Elizabeth (Bryan) Dawson, m/2, 11 Nov 1806, Elizabeth (Brooks)
Morris, d/o Joseph Brooks and widow of John Morris

CHILDREN, m/2:

Ann[4]

Smith[4] (m. 7 Oct 1800, Craven Co, NC, Sally Shine)

John[4]

Stephen[4] (m. 29 Jun 1805, Craven Co. ,Mary (X) Carney, widow)

Mary[4]

Sarah[4]

Rhesa[4] m. Thomas Sparrow

(Francis was most prob. s/o 1st mar.; others *prob.* Ann's ch although there could have
been another wife bef Ann)

?Susannah[3], b. 6 Dec 1720; m. c. 1741, James Willis (10 Feb 1717-9 Dec 1798) she d. 1 Oct
1793; **issue**

CHILDREN, m/2:

Stephen[2], d. unmarr., p. 2 Oct 1732 ,wd-a. 1 Nov 1732, wp, Albemarle Co

Isaac[2], d. a. 15 Jul 1730, intestate & unmarr.

Anne[2], m/1, Joseph Stockley/Stoakley (d. a. 3 Jan 1729/30), m/2, X Dawson, m/3, 10 Jan 1733/4, Pasquotank Co., William Bryan, s/o Edward & prob. Christiana (X) Bryan, who d. a. Jun 1747, wp, Craven
Co; she d. a. 9 Mar 1773, wp, Craven Co

CHILDREN, m/1:

Mary[3], m. X Cook; **Isaac**[3]; **Joseph**[3]

CHILDREN, m/3:

William[3], b. 29 Sep 1734, Pasquotank Co; d. 1746, Craven Co.?

Elizabeth[3], b. 6 Mar 1735/6, Pasquotank Co; m. Francis Dawson; she d. 1773, Craven Co; **issue**

Lewis[3]

John[3], m. 1774, Elizabeth Oliver, d/o John & Mary (Shine) Oliver; d. p. 19 Jan 1781, wd; **issue**

Anne[3]

Jesse[3], b. 3 Jan 1744, Craven Co; m. Mary Carney (1757-1793); Lt, Rev War; d. 15 Jan 1794, New
Bern, NC

REF: *Albemarle Co, NC Court Records; Pasquotank Co, NC Deed Book A, Deed Book K; General Court
Minutes, 1695-1712; NC Council Minutes, Will & Inventories Book 1; Craven Co NC Deed Book, 1729-1741;*
SMALLWOOD, Marilu Burch, *Burch, Harrell & Allied Families,* Vol. II (1968), Vol. III (1976); DELAMAR,
Marybelle, *Delamar, Some Descendants of Francis Delamare*; GRIMES, J. Bryan, *NC Wills & Inventories.*

LAMBERT, Daniel

native of Saint-Palais, Saintonge, FR; currently there are 5 towns named Saint-Palais in the area that
was once Saintonge; the Saint-Palais in Gironde, Aquitaine Dépt, s.w. of Jonzac, seems likely
by 1687 - to Narragansett, RI
by 1691- to NY – godparents to Daniel Coudret, 7 Jun 1691
May 1696 - Oath of Allegiance, NYC
m. 8 Nov 1691, FR Ch, NYC, Marie Tébaux from Niort, Poitou (now in Charente-Maritime Dépt., Poitou-

Charentes) or Saint-Palais

by 1708 - in New Rochelle

d. p. 1717

CHILD:

Frances[2], b. 17 Apr 1692; m. 9 Dec 1713, NYC, Col. John Moore (1686, SC-1749, NYC), s/o John
& Rebecca (Axtell) Moore of Philadelphia; she d. 21 Mar 1782, NYC, age 90 yrs, bur. Trinity
Churchyard, NYC

    CHILDREN (18 ch, 11 of whom either d. young or d. unmarr.): Surname Moore

    Frances[3], b. 1715, m. Samuel Bayard, she d. 1895; **issue**

    Rebecca[3], b. 1717, unmarr; **John**[3], b. 1719, d. unmarr., 1749; **Susanna I**[3], b. 1720, d. young

    Peter I[3], (twin), b. 1721, d. young; **Thomas I**[3], (twin) b. 1721, d. young

    Peter II[3], (twin), b. 1722; **Thomas II**[3], (twin), b. 1722, d. young

    Richard[3], b. 1724

    Susanna II[3]

    Daniel I[3], (twin), b. 1727, d. young

    Lambert[3], (twin), b. 1727

    Daniel II[3], b. 1728, d. young; **Daniel III**[3], b. 1729, d. unmarr., 1789; **William**[3], b. 1730, unmarr.

    Charles[3]

    Stephen[3]

    Anne[3], b. 1738, d. unmarr., c. 1826

REF: HALL, David Moore, *Six Centuries of the Moores of Frawley, Berks, ENG & Their Descendants* (Richmond, VA, 1904); Records from Trinity Ch, NYC; SEACORD, Morgan H., *Biographical Sketches & Index of the Huguenot Settlers of New Rochelle 1687-1776* (New Rochelle, 1941); BAIRD, Charles W., *History of the Huguenot Emigration to America*, Vol. II (NY); WITTMEYER, Alfred V., *Registers of the Births, Marriages, & Deaths of the Église Française à la Nouvelle York* (Baltimore, 1968).

La MONTA(I)GNE, Jean Mousnier de/Johannes

b. c. 1595, Saintes, Saintonge, FR; *mousnier* or *monier* = miller and *de la Montagne*, the mountainous
region of Bourgogne/Burgundy from which the family came (east central FR)

1619 - fled to HOL to attend Univ. of Leiden to study medicine; enrolled as "Johannes Monerius Mon-
tanus"; given his age, he must have studied elsewhere 1st and prob. had a degree; in 1626, he boarded
in the home of Marie de Forêt/Forest, his future mo-in-law

1623/4 - went with future fa-in-law to Guiana where the latter d.

m/1, 12 Dec 1626, Leiden, HOL, Rachel de Forêt/Forest, d/o <u>Jesse & Marie (du Cloux) de Forêt/Forest</u>;
she d. 1643

25 Sep 1636 - sailed to New Amsterdam on the *Rensselaerswyck*; most of the Huguenot families who
were in HOL for any length of time became more Dutch than French; Jean became Johannes and that is
his name in the records in America; Riker and Baird say he was on *The Fortune* in 1636

m/2, 18 Oct 1647, Old Dutch Ch, NY, Angenietie Gillis Ten Waert, d/o Gillis Ten Waert & Barbara
Shut, widow of Arent Corssen Stam & sis/o Margaretta/Grietje Ten Waert who m. <u>David
Provost</u>

d. c. 1670, Kingston, Ulster, NY

CHILDREN, m/1:

Jolant[2], b. 1627, Leiden; d. young, Leiden

Jesse[2], b. 1629, Tobago, W. Indies; 1637, went to New Amsterdam; d. p. 1647, prob. at Fort Amsterdam

Jean/Jan/John[2], b. 1632, Leiden; <u>m/1</u>, 14 Mar 1655, Slooterdyk, a town nr. Amsterdam, Peternella
Pikes/Pyckes (1634-c. 1662), d/o Jan Pikes – **3 sons**, <u>m/2</u>, 10 Jun 1663, Maria Vermilye, d/o
<u>Isaac & Jacomina (Jacobs) Vermeille/Vermilye</u> –**5 ch**; he d. p. 13 May 1672, wd, New Harlem, NY;
she m/2, 26 Sep 1675, New Harlem, Isaac Kip ; she was bur. 23 Nov 1689, New Harlem

Rachel[2], b. 1634, Leiden; m. 1657, Dr. Gysbert Van Imbroech as his 2nd wife; they went to Wiltwyck; he

d. 29 Aug 1665, she d. 4 Oct 1664; 3 ch - **Elizabeth**[3] m. John Peeck – **8 ch**; **Johannes**[3], m/1, Margaret Van Schaick – **1 dau**, m/2, Catherine Sandford – **6 ch**; **Gysbert**[3] m. Jannetie Mesier – **9 ch**

Maria, b.25 Jan 1637, on a ship off Madeira; m. 8 Mar 1654, New Amsterdam, Jacob Hendrickszen Kip (16 May 1631, Amsterdam-24 Dec 1690, New Amsterdam), s/o Hendrick Hendrickszen Kip & Tryntje Lubberts; she d. 25 Aug 1711, NYC; **5 ch**

Willem/William, bp. 22 Apr 1641, New Amsterdam; m. c. 19 May 1673 (date of banns), Kingston, NY Elenora de Hooges (b. 15 Aug 1655, Rensselaer, NY), d/o Anthony de Hooges & Eva Albertson Bradt; he d. 9 Feb 1689/90, prob, Mombaccus, NY; he was a wine dealer; lived Esopus, then Mombaccus, both in Ulster Co., NY; **3 sons, 5 daus**; she m/2, 1692, Cornelis de Duyster

CHILDREN, m/2:

Gillis, b. 1650; d. young

Jesse, b. 1653; d. young

REF: STEWART, Lois Dodge, *The Ancestors & Descendants of James Montaney (1799-1857) of Oppenheim, Fulton Co, NY* (Baltimore, 1982); EARLE, Isacc Newton, *History & Genealogy of the Earles of Secaucus* (Marquette, MI); RIKER, James, *Revised History of Harlem* (NY, 1904).

LaMOTTE/LAMOTT, Jean Henri/Johannes Heinrich

b. 1705, FR; Provence?

1749 - emigrated on the *Phoenix*; went to MD

m. X Bolinger, a widow, b. in SWI

c. 1754 - to Hanover, York Co, PA

d. p. Mar 1803, wd, Baltimore Co, MD; bur. Joseph Bollinger farm, Lineboro, Carroll Co, MD, which is just s. of the York Co, PA line

CHILDREN:

Henry[2], b. 1751; m. Barbara Hupman, d/o Jacob & Anna Barbara (X) Hupman; went from Havre de Grace, MD to Hampstead, MD, c. 1798; d. p. 5 Jan 1798, wd, Harford Co, MD; d. May, 1798; **10 ch**

Daniel[2], b. 10 May 1753; m/1, Oct, 1778, Elizabeth Forney, d/o Philip & Elizabeth (Sherz) Forney – **2 ch**, m/2, Mary Ann Evans; he d. 2 May 1812 Baltimore Co, MD

John Henry[2], b. 1755; m. Hannah Forney, sis/of Elizabeth (above); he d. 1794, Baltimore Co, MD; **1 son**

Francis[2], b. 1758; m. Christina Roth; d. 1814, York Co, PA; **5 ch**

Abram[2]

REF: BATEMAN, Thomas H., *DuPont & Allied Families, A Genealogical Study* (NY, 1965); LAUX, James B., *The Huguenot Elemant in PA*; *Proceedings of the Huguenot Society of America,* Vol. III, Part I (1894/5); BOLINGER, John of Pinney Pt, MD furnished a copy of *A Lamott Family History.*

L'AMOUREUX/LAMOUREUX, André

b. c. 1660, Meschers-sur-Gironde, Saintonge, FR, now in Charente-Maritime Dépt, Poitou-Charentes s.e. of Royan on the Gironde, s/o André Lamoureux; Meschers then called Méché

m. Suzanne LeTour/Latour; she d. p. 29 May 1720

fled FR to ENG w/ wife, 2 ch

1689-95 - resided at Bristol; he was a shipmaster & pilot, *m^e de navaire devant à Méché*

22 Jun 1694 – took out denization papers for himself, his wife, 2 ch Elizabeth & Judith in anticipation of his emigration; last record of him in ENG, 25 Mar 1695, when he witnessed the marr. of 2 friends

by May 1700 - in NY; members of FR Ch, by 13 Jan 1702/3, when André was a witness at the marr of Daniel Beau/Bueau & Ester Gaillard - their dau Ester, b. 25 Dec 1703, bp. 1 Jan 1703/4, FR Ch, NYC– Daniel Gaillard & Suzanne Lamoureux were godparents

d. p. 4 May 1706, prob. New Rochelle, NY
CHILDREN:
Elizabeth[2], b. c. 1685, FR; m. 1700, Gerret Dusjean; she d. Dec 1708, NYC
Jacques[2], b. 1687, FR; bur. 19 Mar 1689/90, Bristol
Judith[2], b. 12 Dec, bp. 16 Dec 1689, FR Ch, Bristol; m. Pierre Chaperon; **issue**
Daniel[2], b. 24 Dec 1693, bp. 7 Jan 1694, FR Ch, Bristol; d. young
Daniel[2], b. 29 Nov, bp. 1 Dec 1695, FR Ch Bristol; m/1, 28 Jun 1719, NYC, Jeanne Massé (b. 22 May, bp.
    5 Jul 1696, FR Ch, NYC-d. c. 1739), d/o Pierre & Elizabeth (Mersereau) Massé; m/2, 9 Jun 1744,
    Aaltje (Storm) Bancker/Bankert, d/o Gregory Storm, widow of Frederick Bankert; Daniel went
    to New Rochelle, to New Bedford, then to what is now Putnam Co, NY; he was a cordwainer, a
    bootmaker; d. Phillipstown, Putnam, NY
    CHILDREN, m/1:
    Daniel[3], b. 18 May, bp. 29 May 1720, FR Ch, NYC; gr mo Suzanne was godmother
    André/Andrew[3], b. 10 Jan 1722, NYC; m. 30 Jan 1743, Elizabeth Covert (2 Aug 1722-8 Nov1798),
        d/o Isaac Covert; liv. Shrub Oak (now part of Yorktown), NY; d. 8 Nov 1809, Yorktown,
        Westchester Co, NY; **9 ch**
    Jean/John[3], b. 31 Dec 1723, NYC; m/1, 1745, Philipstown, Dutchess Co, NY, Charity Davenport,
        d/o Thomas & Elizabeth (Leggett) Davenport; m/2, Rombout, Dutchess Co. Elizabeth Tice; he
        d. Monroe, Orange Co, NY, 1809; **8 ch**
    Pierre/Peter[3], b. 3 Sep 1728, New Rochelle; m. 30 Oct 1748, Phoebe Wood; he d. Mar 1821,
        Southfield, Orange Co, NY; **10 ch**
    Elizabeth[3], b. 8 Dec 1728
    Jacques/James[3], b. 12 Feb 1731; m. Hannah (Clements?); he d. 1815, Westerloo, Albany Co, NY
    Isaac[3], b. 15 Nov 1732; m. Hannah Conklin, d/o Timothy & Mary (Tompkins) Conklin; he d.
        1817, Pleasant Valley, Dutchess Co, NY; **12 ch**
    Susanne[3], b. 26 Dec 1736, prob. Bedford, NY
    Josué/Joshua[3], b. 9 Jan 1739, prob. Philipstown; m. Elizabeth Ogden; went to nr. Scarborough,
        Canada; **7 ch**

NOTE: Some references infer that the Catherine Lamoreux who m. Daniel Jandein, was the d/o André &
Suzanne, yet she is not mentioned in the ch records. Given that she had a son bp. 1701, she would have been b.
c. 1680-85 but she is not mentioned in the Bristol records either. There may be a family connection but it is not
known.

REF: L'AMOUREUX, Harold Dane, editor, *The Lamoureux Record, A Study of the Lamoureux Family in America*, #2
(Apr 1939) taken from *The Lamoureux Record*, #1 (Oct 1919) by A. J. Lamoureux; LART, Charles Edmund,
Registers of the French Churches of Bristol, Stonehouse, Plymouth, & Thorpe-le-Soken (London, 1912); *Yesteryears*
Vol. 7 #26 , found in Orange Co. Genealogical Society Library, Goshen, NY; WITTMEYER, Alfred V., *Registers of the
Births, Marriages, & Deaths, of the "Église Française à Nouvelle York" from 1688 to 1804* (Baltimore, 1968).

LANCY/LANCEY/DELANCEY, Étienne de/Stephen

    b. 24 Oct 1663, Caen, Normandie, FR, s/o Jacques & Marguerite (Bertrand) DeLancy; the family was
        of the minor FR nobility; despite being Huguenot, the family served the French Crown as
        administrators & bureaucrats for over 200 yrs.
    fled Caen, to Rotterdam, HOL – said to have had a portion of the family jewels sewn in his clothing; later
        to ENG
    3 Mar 1686 - naturalized in ENG
    6 Jun 1686 - arr NYC; 7 Jul 1686, rec. letters of denization from Gov. Dongan
    9 Sep 1687 – took the Oath of Allegiance to the British Crown & became Stephen Delancey
    14 Nov 1688 - he was a *diacre* (deacon) of the FR Huguenot Ch, NYC
    he sold his portion of the family jewels for £300 British and became a merchant; he became one of the most

successful merchants in the colony

m. 23 Jan 1699/00, Anne Van Cortlandt, d/o Stephanus Van Cortlandt & Gertruj Van Schuyler (Stephanus/ Stephen was the 1st native-born mayor of NYC & Gertruj/Gertrude was the sis/o Pieter Schuyler, a colonial governor of NY and mayor of Albany); the couple liv. at 54 Pearl St. & Broadway in NYC – land given to Anne by her father as a wedding gift – in 1762, the house was sold at auction to Samuel Fraunces who converted it into the *Queen Charlotte Tavern*, now known as *Fraunces Tavern*

he was an alderman for several yrs., member of the NY Provincial Assembly & the Governor's Council; he presented the city w/ its 1st town clock and its 1st fire engine

1730's – built a lg. mansion on Broadway, by Trinity Church; that was demolished in 1792 – the Boreil Building was later on that site

d. 18 Nov 1741, NYC, leaving an estate in excess of £100,000 British (c. $18,000,000 today)

CHILDREN (all bp. l'Église Françoise, NYC, except Susannah):

Étienne/Stephen[2], b. 28 Aug, bp. 8 Sep 1700; d. young

Jacques/James[2], b. 5 Apr, bp. 12 May 1702; d. young

Jacques/James[2], b. 27 Nov, bp. 19 Dec 1703; m. Anne Heathcote – **8 ch**; he became Chief Justice of the Supreme Court of NY & Lt. Gov.; he d. 1760

Pierre/Peter[2], b. 26 Aug, bp. 23 Sep 1705; m. Elizabeth Colden – **6 or 7 ch**; he was a merchant – had a lg. mill in what is now the Bronx; he served in the NY Provincial Assembly for many yrs.; he d. 1770

Susannah[2], b. 1707; m. Admiral Sir Peter Warren & had **3 ch**; she d. 1771

Anne[2], b. 14 Nov, bp. 25 Nov 1711; d. young

Étienne/Stephen[2], b. 1 Feb, bp. 7 Feb 1713/4; d. 1741, unmarr.

Jean/John[2], b. 11 Jul, bp. 5 Aug 1716; d. 1745 unmarr.

Olivier/Oliver[2], b. 16 Sep, bp. 8 Oct 1718; m. a. 14 Jun 1749, Phila Frank(s)* – **7 ch**; he was also a merchant; he was an alderman in NYC & a member of the NY Assembly; served as a Brigadier General in the British Army dur. the Rev. War; his house was plundered & confiscated and he left for ENG in 1783, where he d. 27 Oct 1785, Beverly, Yorkshire; he is bur. in Beverly Minster *they were godparents to Phila Joncourt, d/o Pierre de Joncourt & Jeanne Couillete on that date & were called husband & wife

Anne[2], 23 Apr, bp. 23 May 1723; m. Jul 1742, John Watts (5 Apr 1715-Aug 1789), s/o Robert & Maria (Nicoll) Watts; John was a prominent businessman; **5 sons**, **5 daus**; Anne & John left for ENG, 4 May 1775, on the *Charlotte*; Anne d. 3 Jul 1776, ENG

REF: WITTMEYER, Alfred V., *Registers of the Births, Marriages, & Deaths, of the "Église Françoise à Nouvelle York" from 1688 to 1804* (Baltimore, 1968); BAIRD, Charles W., *History of the Huguenot Emigration to America;* JACKSON, Kenneth T., *The Encyclopedia of New York City* (Yale Univ. Press, 1995); *Appleton's Cyclopedia of American Biography* (1900); STORY, D.A., *The de Lanceys: Romance of a Great Family* (Toronto, 1931); RIVES, George Lockhart, *Genealogical Notes* (NY, 1914).

LANDON/LANGDON, Jacques Morin de

family *poss.* from s. of Nemours, Seine-et-Marne Dépt, Île-de-France, s. of Fontainebleau; there is a Château Landon c. 15 km s. of Nemours; the Vienne Dépt., Poitou-Charentes, s.w. of Tours, has also been mentioned as well as nr. Dole, s. of Mt. Roland, in the Dura Dépt., Franche-Comté, s.w. of Besançon; others say it is a noble Norman family (1200-1500); s/o Jacques

m. FR, X le Duc; went to ENG

d. ENG

CHILDREN:

Jacques Nathaniel[2]

George(s)[2], Herefordshire, ENG; m/1 ENG, XX; to America, c. 1640; in Wethersfield, CT; m/2, Hannah (X) Haynes, wid/o Edmund Haynes of Springfield; he moved to Springfield, then to Northampton where he was 1 of the early settlers; he d. 29 Dec 1676, Northampton, MA

CHILDREN, m/1:

Jean/John[3], b. 1619, ENG d. 1689, Farmington, CT

    CHILDREN:

    John[4]

    Samuel[4], b. 1652/3; m. 1 Dec 1676, Elizabeth (Copley) Turner, wid/o Praisever Turner; he d.
        11 Aug 1683; **3 sons**

    Joseph[4], bp. 18 Mar 1659; m. Oct, 1683, Susannah Root, d/o <u>John</u> & Mary (Kilborne)
        <u>Root</u> - **issue**

    Elizabeth[4]

    Nathaniel[4], b. Farmington, CT; d. 9 Mar 1718, LI, NY

  Deliverance[3], <u>m/1</u>, Thomas Hanchet, <u>m/2</u>, 14 Dec 1686, Jonathan Burt of Springfield; she d.
    1718, Suffield?

  unnamed ch[3], m. X Corbee/Corbin of Haddam, CT

  Hannah[3], m. 4 Feb 1652, Springfield, Nathaniel Pritchett

CHILD, m/2:

  Ester/Hester[3] b. 22 Aug 1649, Springfield, m. 20 Apr 1675, John Hannum

Daniel[2], m. Anne X; fled FR to ENG w/ wife & ch; to Herefordshire? (nr. Wales); said to have rec. a
soldier's grant of land in Bristol, RI

CHILDREN (there were other ch, but names are not known, supposedly at least 5 sons):

Nathan[3], b. 1664; m. in America, Hannah (Bishop?) (1666-26 Jan 1701/2), poss. d/o Stephen
    & Tabitha (Wilkinson) Bishop; p. 1680 settled Southold, Suffolk Co, LI, NY; he d. 9
    Mar 1718, age 54; both bur. Southold; ropemaker, cordwainer

CHILDREN:

  Nathan[4], 14 Sep 1696, Southold; m. 19 Sep 1723, Southold, Prudence Osmon; **issue**

  Samuel[4], b. 20 May 1699, Southold; m. 26 May 1720 (?), Southold, Bethia Tuthill (12
    Dec 1703-30 Aug 1761, 58Y); he d. 21 Jan 1782, both bur. Southold; at least **1
    son**

  Elizabeth[4], b. 12 Jun 1700, Southold; d. 28 Apr 1707/8

  prob. **Hannah**[4], m. John Vail; **issue**

James[3]*, b. 29 Mar 1685 Bristol, RI; <u>m/1</u>, May 1707, Southold, Mary Vail (d. 28 Aug 1722),
    d/o John & Grace (Braddick/Burgess) Vail, <u>m/2</u>, 12 Jun 1723, Southold, Mary
    (Brown) Wilmot, a widow, (d. 13 Dec 1753, Southold); he d. 19 Sep 1738, Litchfield

CHILDREN, m/1, b. Southhold, LI, NY:

Mary[4], b. 26 Nov 1707

Joseph[4], b. 18 Dec 1708; m. 14 Nov 1734, Southold Margaret Hallock; he d. 8 Oct
    1773; **issue**

James[4], b. 5 Aug 1711; from Litchfield to Salisbury, CT where he m. Sarah
    Bishop, d/o Samuel & Abigail (Wetmore) Bishop; **12 ch**

Daniel[4], b 7 Jan 1713/4; <u>m/1,</u> X Fiske, Brooklyn, <u>m/2</u>, 22 May 1736, Litchfield,
    Martha Youngs, d/o Rev. John Youngs; Daniel & Martha + Daniel's bros
    James, David & John went to Litchfield, CT, c. 1740; he was a staunch
    Episcopalian who often read the service and sermon; he d. 11 Jul 1790,
    Litchfield, & is bur W. Burying Ground, Litchfield; **8 ch**

Rachel[4], b. 12 Oct 1716; m. 9 Oct 1735, Southold, Samuel Moore

David[4], b. 8 Jul 1718; to Litchfield, then to Salisbury

John[4], b. 21 Jul 1720; from Litchfield – a John Langdon m. 5 Nov 1741, Litchfield, Katherine
    White – *poss.* this John; to Salisbury, CT

Lydia[4], b. 1722

CHILDREN, m/2:

Ann[4]

Nathan[4]

Daniel[3], tried for piracy in New Bristol, RI or Boston, MA; pardoned after spending a few months in jail; he served in King Philip's War under Capt. Samuel Mosely (10 Dec 1675), Major Thomas Savage (24 Apr 1676), Capt. Isaac Johnson (27 Aug 1675), Capt. James Oliver (29 Feb 1675/6), served in the garrison at Mendon (14 Sep 1675); m. XX; his son **Benjamin**[3] was a grantee of Narragansett Twp, now Bedford, part of Merrimac & Manchester, NH); he d. 1693?; said to have had a total of **7 ch** - wife *poss.* Ann Lobdell

*****NOTE:** James is often called the s/o Nathan[3] with a b. date of a. 1698 and that he m. Mary Vaile in 1717. The marr. date is 1707. It seems that James liv. w/ Nathan after the d. of his father thus the erroneous conclusion.

REF: MIRES, Maynard H., "LANDON: A Huguenot Tale" in *The Colonial Genealogist,* Vol. VII, #4 (1975); LANDON, James Orville, *Landon Genealogy,* Part II (1928); HOFF, Henry B., *Long Island Source Records, from The NY Genealogical & Biographical Record* (Baltimore, 1987); Vital Records, Southold, NY; Litchfield, CT; VAIL, Henry H., *Genealogy of Some of the Vail Family Descended from Jeremiah Vail* (NY, 1902); BODGE, George M., *Soldiers in King Philip's War* (Boston, 1906); *NEHGS Register*, Vol. 53 (1899); ROBBINS, William A., "Salmon Records, 1698-1811" in the *NYGBR* (Vol. 49, 1918); TRUMBULL, James Russell, *History of Northampton*, Vol. 3, Part 1 (1898).

LANG, Peter

b. c. 1649, Flanders

m. Anna Barbara Sturm (bp. 3 Aug 1656, Schifferstadt-13 Jul 1719, Klein Schifferstadt), d/o Philip & Anna Maria (Ruester) Sturm; **6 ch**, according to Anna Barbara's death rec., but only Veronika has been identified

d. 25 Jan 1719, Klein Schifferstadt, s.w. Heidelberg, in the *Pfalz*, c. 6 mi. n.w. of Speyer/Spires

CHILD:

Anna Veronika[2], b. 1690; m. 10 Jan 1713, Johann Michel Thomas (b. 1688), s/o Christian & Anna Margaretha (X) Thomas; to America, arr 19 Jun 1730, Philadelphia, on the *Thistle of Glasgow* from Rotterdam; they had **11 ch**, bp. Klein Schifferstadt; son Christian (16 yrs.) emigrated w/ his parents but women and ch were not listed; a Johannes & Valentine Thomas were naturalized in MD, 17 Apr 1759, prob. sons of Michael & Veronica; 1742-46, family went to Frederick Co, MD

CHILDREN (all bap., Klein Schifferstadt – 2 others d. young): surname THOMAS

Christian[3], b. 1 Jan, bp 3 Jan 1714; m. 1745, Magdalena X; **issue**

Philipp Henrich[3], b. 12 Sep, bp 15 Sep 1715; **issue**

Maria Catharina[3], b. 2 Feb, bp 8 Feb 1718; d. 7 May 1724 – one source says she emigrated to America but German rec. say she d; instead of *Maria* Catharina, must have been *Anna* Catharina who emigrated

Hans Michel[3], b. 3 Oct, bp 8 Oct 1719; m. 1744, Barbara X; liv that part of Frederick Co that is now Washington Co; bur old Reformed Ch burying grounds outside Boonsboro; **issue**

Gabriel[3], b. 9 Jun, bp 12 Jun 1721; m. 1744, Anna Margaret X; d. 18 Jan 1794, bur. nr. Adamstown, MD; **issue**

Johann Valentin[3], b. 28 Sep, bp 30 Sep 1724; m. 1751, Margaret X; d. 27 Aug 1796, bur. nr. Adamstown; **issue**

Anna Catharina[3], b. 29 May, bp 2 Jun 1726

Johannes[3] (twin), b. 20 Jun, bp 21 Jun 1728; m. 1753, Catherine X; **issue**

Christoph[3] (twin), b. 2 Oct, bp 10 Oct 1729; m. 13 Dec 1756, Mary Weisz; **issue**

REF: JOHNSON, Arta F., *Kinfolk in Germany-Kinfolk in Maryland* (Columbus, OH, np); THOMAS, George Leicester, *Genealogy of the Thomas Family* (1951-54).

LANGEL, Jacques/James

m. Anne Allegné

1764 - emigrated as an adult w/ the last group of FR Huguenots to New Bordeaux, SC, in what is now McCormick Co

25 Mar 1764 - he and Anne each rec. 35 (£s? $?)– a fund for new settlers

18 Apr 1764 - rec. a grant of 300 acres – the exact amount allotted to a man w/ wife + 3 ch; 1 ch must have d. soon after as only 2 daus are known; took the Oath of Allegiance and swore to the truth of their petitions for Land and Bounty

CHILDREN:

Susannah[2], b. 8 Jan 1758; m. 6 Nov 1771, Peter Elijah Bellot (10 Oct 1744/5-p. 1800?), s/o John & Lydia (Gogul) Bellot; she d. p. 1792, bur. s.e. of Willington, SC; **issue**

Elizabeth[2], b. 25 Sep 1766, Bordeaux, SC; m. c. 1801, John Champion Hayes (11 Jun 1783-7 Jun 1847); she d. 28 Dec 1831, Bordeaux, SC; John Hayes may have been a 2nd husband – source unclear; **issue**

REF: KINNEY, Shirley F., compiler, *Langel Genealogy* (Rome, GA, 1985, unpub); REVILL, Janie, *A Compilation of the Original Lists of Protestant Immigrants to SC 1763-1773* (Baltimore, 1968); JONES, Jack Moreland & WARREN, Mary Bondurant, *SC Immigrants 1760 to 1770* (n.d.).

LANGILLE, Daniel

m. Françoise Perrenot

CHILDREN:

Daniel[2], b. 1686, FR; m. 2 Dec 1711, Dampierre-Outre-les-Bois, FR, Anne Brand; town is now called Dampierre-les-Bois located in Doubs Dépt, Franche-Comté, s.e. of Montbéliard, nr. the Swiss border

CHILDREN:

Anne[3], b. 18 Dec 1712, Dampierre-les-Bois

David[3], b. 19 Jan 1715, Dampierre-les-Bois; m/1, XX, m/2, Marie Catherine X, a widow with son Jacques/James; she d. 30 Sep 1752, Halifax, bur. St. Paul's Cemetery; 1751 – members of the Protestant Ch in & around Montbéliard, due to renewed attacks on their ch, accepted a British offer to settle in the New World; 6 Jun 1752, sailed for Halifax, NS, on the *Sally*; David is listed as a farmer from Dampierre-Outre-les-Bois, aged 34, w/ wife Marie Catherine, son John James, aged 16, stepson James, half-bro Matthew; arr 14 weeks later; 1st settled Lunenburg; m/3, 24 Dec 1753, St. John's Ch, Lunenburg, NS, Marie Catherine Bezanson; 1771, moved to n. shore of NS, settling on the Des Barres Grant at Tatamagouche (n. of Truro on the Northumberland Strait); d. Jul 1804, Tatamagouche, NS

CHILD, m/1:

Jean Jacques/John James[4], b. c. 1736, Dampierre-les-Bois; went to Lunenburg w/ his fa; m. 4 May 1763, Éve Leau, d/o George & Éve (X) Leau/Lowe; went to Tatamagouche, in 1771 & settled on the French River; he d. 1794; **5 sons, 2 daus**

CHILDREN, m/2:

James[4], b. c. 1735/40, FR; m. Jane X; liv. at Brule Point, NS, on the North Shore, e. of Tatamagouche, & is poss. bur. in an old cemetery there; **3 sons, 1 dau**

Margaretta[4], b. 16 Sep 1752, Halifax, NS; d. on the 23rd, her mother dying a week later; she was bur. next to her mother in St. Paul's Cemetery, Halifax

CHILDREN, m/3 – 1st 10 b. Lunenburg, last 2 in Tatamagouche:

John Nicholas[4], bp. 28 Jun 1755; went to U.S.

Catherine[4], bp. 24 May 1757

Marie Magdalena[4], bp. 4 Oct 1758; m. 24 Dec 1778, Samuel Fisher of Stewiacke (s.w. of Truro), s/o William & Eleanor (Archibald) Fisher; **3 sons, 5 daus**

> **Marie Elizabeth**[4], bp. 22 May 1760; m. 1784, as his 3rd wife, George Tattrie (1732-1827); **3 sons, 7 daus**
> **John Frederick**[4], bp. 2 Nov 1761
> **Marie Catherine**[4], bp. 6 Jan 1764
> **Margaret**[4], bp. 7 Nov 1765; m. Peter Hind of River John; **10 ch**
> **Catherine Margaret**[4], bp. 25 Sep 1767; d. 1854
> **Susanne Catherine**[4], bp. 15 Oct 1769
> **John David**[4], bp. 17 Aug 1771; m. Catherine Louisa Perrin (b. 2 Mar 1782), d/o Christopher & Marie Catherine (Dauphiné) Perrin; he was known as "Big Miller"; **5 sons, 6 daus**
> **John George**[4], b. 1773; m. Marie Catherin Perrin (27 Dec 1789-1849), d/o Christopher & Marie Catherine (Dauphiné) Perrin; he d. 1864; **4 sons, 6 daus**
> **Lewis**[4]

Léonard[3], b. 20 Nov 1718, Dampierre-les-Bois; d. 2 Apr 1721, Dampierre-les-Bois
Mathieu/Matthew[3], b. 1726, Dampierre-les-Bois; prob. the Matthew who arr on the *Betty*, farmer aged 26; the *Betty* loaded, 16 May 1752, in Rotterdam and arr Halifax 9 weeks, 5 days later; Matthew emig. alone and was *perhaps* a half-brother although ch rec says he was the s/o Daniel & Anne; m. 20 Feb 1758, Lunenburg, Susan Catherine Menago; **5 ch**

David[2], b. 1700, Dampierre-les-Bois; m. Catherine Bout(h)enot, who d. 12 Jan 1750, Dampierre-les-Bois; d. 13 May 1765 Dampierre-les-Bois
CHILDREN:
David[3], b. 21, bp 29 Jun 1721; emigrated to NS on the *Betty*, 1752; settled Lunenburg; carpenter/joiner; wife Catherine X d. 23 Mar 1753; nothing more is known – said to have d. on an expedition against the Indians
Léopold Frédéric[3], b. 26, bp. 27 Jun 1728; m/1, 11 May 1751, Dampierre-les-Bois, Marguerite Sandoz (29 Dec 1730 Dampierre-les-Bois-26 May 1775 Lunenburg), d/o Jacques & Marie Madeleine (Amez) Sandoz; he was a carpenter/joiner; emigrated to NS on the *Betty*, 1752 w/ his wife, baby, bro and cousin Matthew (above); he m. 2 more times; bur. 27 Sep 1817, Lunenburg; **issue**, incl. **John George**[4], bp. 21 Jun 1756 ,Lunenburg, m. 27 Feb 1776, Anna Catherine Keyser (bp. 24 Oct 1758, Lunenburg-19 Nov 1814, Blandford, NS), he d. p. 1812
Catherine-Elizabeth[3], b. c. 1731; m. Benôit Peugeot
Jacques[3], b. 1738; m. 31 Jan 1769, Dampierre-les-Bois, Anne-Judith (Hauser) Pechin, widow X Pechin (d. 15 Sep 1788, Dampierre-les-Bois); he d. 23 Jan 1798, Dampierre-les-Bois
Françoise[3], m. Abraham Parrot; she d. 9 Feb 1777, Dampierre-les-Bois
Frederick[3], b. 25 Oct 1745; d. 4 Jun 1752, Dampierre-les-Bois

REF: Church records, Dampierre-les-Bois; Passenger List, *Betty*, 1752; LANGILLE, Stewart C., *A History & Genealogy of the South Shore Langilles of Nova Scotia* (Bridgewater, NS, 1977); BYERS, G., "The North Shore Langilles of Nova Scotia" in *The Nova Scotia Historical Quarterly*, Vol. 7, #3 (Sep 1977); PUNCH, Terry M., *Langille, the European Roots* (unpub., not dated); BELL, Dr. Winthrop, *The Foreign Protestants & the Settlement of NS* (1961).

LANIER, Nicolas
b. c. 1530/40, Rouen, FR
1559/60 - he was a musician to the Court of Henri II; Nicolas was the founder of a family of musicians, artists, statesmen & poets
1561- to London to be a musician to the English Court
m/1, a. 1565, to XX
1571- "Return of Aliens," London, his entry says "no church"
m/2, m. 13 Feb 1571, All Hallows Barking, Lucretia Bassano (24 Sep 1556-bur. 4 Jan 1634, St. Alphage, Greenwich, ENG), d/o Anthony Bassano
d. a. Jul 1612, wp, London

CHILDREN, m/1:

Innocent[2], b. c. 1555; d. early 1625, unmarr.

Ellen[2], prob. bp. 1565, Parish of St. Olave; m. Alphonse Ferrabosco (bur. 11 Mar 1627/8); she was bur. 3 Aug 1638; **6 ch**

Alphonse[2], b. a. 1563; m. 18 Oct 1592, Amelia Bassano (bur. 3 Apr 1645), d/o Baptista & Margaret (Johnson) Bassano; he d. Nov 1613; **2 ch**, although the son *may* have been fathered by another

John[2], b. 1565 ENG; m. 17 Oct 1585, Holy Minories, Frances Galliardello (bp. 4 Nov 1566), d/o Mark Anthony & Margerie (Giardella) Galliardello of Venice; he was bur. 5 Dec 1616, Camberwell Ch in Co. Surrey; wd, 2 Nov 1616, names **4 sons, 3 daus**; his grson **Mark**[4], b. 1617, was in VA, a. 1638

CHILDREN, m/2:

Clement[2], b, c, 1585; m. Mar 1628, Hannah Collet (bur. 22 Dec 1653, E. Greenwich); he was bur. 6 Nov 1661, E. Greenwich, ENG; will mentions **11 ch**; his son **John**[3] b. Oct 1631, emigrated to VA

Jerome[2], m/1, 20 Dec 1610, Phrisdiswith Grafton (bur. 30 Nov 1625) – **4ch**; m/2, 10 Jan 1627, Elizabeth Williford (bur. 20 Nov 1661) – **8 ch**; he was bur. 1 Dec 1659

Frances[2], b. c. 1572; m. 4 Feb 1618, St. Margarets, Lee, Co. Kent, Thomas Foxe (d. a. 1633); she d. a. 1633

Andrea[2], b. c. 1605; m. Joyce Perry; he was bur. 2 Nov 1660; **9 ch**

Katherine[2], m. Daniel Farrand (d. 1651); she d. a. 2 Sep 1660

Mary[2], bur. 13 Oct 1676, unmarr.

REF: INGERSOLL, Louise, *Lanier, A Genealogy of the Family Who Came to VA & the French Ancestors in London* (1965); SAWYER, Mamie Chambers, *The Lanier Family of France, England, VA & Duplin Co, NC* (1972); THOMPSON, Margaret Drody, *Elizabeth Jane Lanier, Her Ancestors, 1540-1982*; KAUFMAN, Mary Arnold, *Martin-Arnold & Allied Families* (1995); LASOKI, David, *The Bassanos-in England, 1531-1665*; SADIE, Stanley, *New Grove Dictionary of Music & Musicians*; *Proceedings of the Huguenot Society of London,* Vol. VII (1905).

LANOIS/LANNOY/LAUNOY/La NOY/DELANO, Gysbert/Gilbert de

b. 1545 Tourcoing, Normandie, FR (n.e. of Lille), supposedly a disinherited s/o Jean (who d. 25 May 1560) & Jeanne (de Ligne, Dame de Barbançon) de Lannoy; b. Roman Catholic; the family was Norman and Flemish

c. 1556 – converted to Protestantism which caused rift with his father

m. c. 1569, Jeanne/Sjan X

d. p. 13 Jan 1596; c. 1599?

CHILDREN:

Jean/Jan[2], b. c. 1570, prob. Tourcoing; m. c. 13 Jan 1596 (betrothal date), Leiden, HOL, Marie le Mahieu of Lille/Brabant; Marie was the sis/o Hester Mahieu who m. Francis Cooke; he d. 1604, Leiden, HOL; she m/2, c.18 Feb 1605 (betrothal), Robert Mannoo, a woolcomber from Namur (another source say she m. 1605, Jean Pesyn/Pesin, but the Mannoo marr is in the Leiden records) - **no issue**; Marie was the d/o Jacques & Jeanne (X) Mahieu; she d. 1650

CHILDREN:

Esaie/Isaiah[3], bp. 26 Mar 1599, Walloon Ch, Tournai (e. of Lille), Flanders

Jenne[3], bp. 18 Mar 1601, Leiden

Philippe/Philip[3], b. 1602, bp. 6 Dec 1603, Walloon Ch, Leiden; 1621, to Plymouth, MA, on the *Fortune*; m/1, 19 Dec 1634, Hester Dewsbury, m/2, 1657, Mary (Pontus) Glass, d/o William & Wybra (Hanson) Pontus, widow of James Glass; he d. a. 4 Mar 1681/2, inv, Bridgewater, MA; surname **DELANO**

CHILDREN, m/1:

Mary[4], b. c. 1635; m. 29 Nov 1655, Plymouth, Jonathan Dunham, s/o John & Abigail (Barlow) Dunham?; she d.1656/7; not in father's will of 22 Aug 1681; **no known issue**

Philip[4], b. c. 1637; m. c. 1670, Elizabeth Sampson, d/o Abraham & Esther? (Nash) Sampon; he
  d. Dec 1708, Plymouth; **5 ch**

Esther[4], b. c. 1641; not in father's will of 22 Aug 1681

Thomas[4], b. 21 Mar 1642, Duxbury, MA; m. a. 30 Oct 1667, Duxbury, Rebecca
  Alden (c. 1643, Duxbury-a. 13 Jun 1688, Duxbury), d/o John & Priscilla
  (Mullins) Alden; he d. c. 13 Apr 1723, Duxbury; **9 ch**

John[4], b. c. 1644; m. c. 1679, Mary Weston, d/o Edmund & Jane (Delano?)
  Weston; **6 ch**

Jonathan[4], b. c. 1648; m. 28 Feb 1677/8, Mercy Warren, d/o Nathaniel & Sarah
  (Walker) Warren; he d. 28 Dec 1720, Dartmouth, MA; **13 ch**

CHILDREN, m/2:

Jane[4], b. c. 1657; prob. d. a. 1682 – not in settlement of father's estate

Samuel[4], b. c. 1659; m. a. 1679, Elizabeth Standish, d/o Alexander & Sarah (Alden)
  Standish; he d. 1728; **9 ch**

Rebecca[4], b. c. 1661; m. 28 Dec 1686, Plymouth, John Churchill, s/o John & Hannah
  (Pontus*) Churchill; she d. 6 Apr 1709, Plymouth; **6 ch**
  *sis/o Mary Pontus [Glass Delano] who m. 2nd Philip Delano above

prob. **Marie**[2], **Antoinette**[2], **Margriete**[2] m/1, Olivier la Pla, m/2, Jan de Rousseau

Jacques[2], m. May 1601, Walloon Ch, Courtrai (n.c. of Lille), Flanders, XX, a woman from
  Courtrai; they escaped to Leiden

CHILD:

Henri Martin[3], went to Haarlem, HOL and mar.

CHILD:

Abraham[3], b. 1623, who emig to New Netherland c. 1651, with wife Maritie Lubberts &
  sons Abraham and Pieter; family liv on Stone (Canal) St; Abraham was a tapster
  by trade and a burgomaster of the city in 1653; he d. a. 1662; Maritie m/2, 1663,
  Frederick Gysbertszen

CHILDREN:

Abraham[4], b. 1647, Haarlem; m. 11 Jan 1681, Cornelia Toll, widow of Evert
  Duycking; lived on Beaver St; he d. 1702; **6 ch**

Pieter/Peter[4], b. a. 1651; m/1, 22 Apr 1680, Elizabeth de Potter, widow of Isaac
  Bedlow – **no known issue**; liv. on the Strand, m/2, 1696, Maria Edsall –
  1 dau **Maria** (bp. 21 Feb 1697) who m. Walter de Graw/Graau

Maria[4], bp. 1652; m. 1681, Peter Gruendyck

Catalyntje[4], bp. 1655; m/1, 1680, Isaac Van Velck; m/2, 1697, Abraham Kip

Cornelia[4], bp. 7 Nov 1657, Reformed Dutch Ch, NYC; m. 1687, Engelbert Lott

REF: MACKENZIE, Grenville. *Families of the Colonial Town of Phillipsburgh* (Tarrytown, NY 1976); DELANO,
Joel A., *The Genealogical History & Alliances of the American House of Delano 1621-1899* (NY 1899); BANGS,
Jeremy D., "The Pilgrims & Some Other English in Leiden Records" in *NEHGR*, Vol. CXLIII (Jul 1989); JONES, Ellen
M. & HONEA, Barbara M., *Yankee Stock* (Decorah, IA 1992).

La PIERRE, Jean de/John (Rev.)

b. 1679-81 FR, s/o Charles de La Pierre*, a minister, from Lasalle, Gard Dépt., Languedoc-Roussillon,
  s.w. of Alès, in the Cévennes Valley; family went to ENG, c. 1700, where Charles (by Nov 1701)
  became the minister of the FR Chapel of Spring Gardens called "Ye Little Savoye"; Charles' wife had
  d. in FR, as a Huguenot martyr; Charles m/2, another FR refugee, Magdeleine LeNoir, who
  was godmother to Jean's dau Jeanne bp. 1706 (Charles was her godfather)

1701 - went to IRE; 8 Aug 1701, entered Trinity College, Dublin, 22 yrs old; 5 Feb 1705/6, rec. A.B.

m. Susanne X

May 1707 - he was authorized to practice as a schoolmaster in Dublin

1 Dec 1707 - made a deacon St. Paul's Cathedral

23 Feb 1707/8 – he was ordained, at the Bishop of London's Palace at Fulham

c. 1708 - went to SC; served the Parishes of St. Thomas (English) & St. Denis (French), on the Cooper River, Orange Quarter, (Berkeley), 1708-1728; also served in the French Protestant Ch in Charleston in 1728

1728 - was sent to Cape Fear (New Hanover), NC; 1st Anglican minister in NC; founded St. Philip's Episcopal Ch in Brunswick and St. James' Episcopal Ch in Wilmington

1734 - to New Bern (now Wilmington New River Section, NC); established several other parishes in NC

d. p. Jan 1755 NC, prob. Craven Co.

CHILDREN:

Jeanne[2], bp. Feb 1706, Parish of St. James, London – grfa Charles La Pierre was her godfather; m. Andrew Mansfield; **issue**

Martha[2], b. SC; m. 1736, Benjamin Fordham; Martha d. p. 1754; Benjamin m/2, Alice X who d. c. 1784; Benjamin's will dated, 10 Jul 1777, wp, c. 1785 – only ch mentioned was Benjamin
    CHILDREN:
        Benjamin, Jr.[3], b. 27 Nov 1743, Craven Co, NC; m. Mary (Blackshear?); liv. on the Trent River in Jones Co, NC; Rev. War service; d. p. 26 Oct 1810; **12 ch**
        Abraham[3], d. a. 1784; **dau Annie**[4]
        Martha[3], m. Jacob Koonce, s/o George Koonce (1704-1778) from the Palatinate; **issue**

2 other ch[2], who prob. d. young

NOTE: *Charles' 1st wife was Jeanne Roque. There is a birth record from Lasalle for a Jean b. 2 Feb 1681, s/o Charles & Jeanne. It is very probable that this is the Jean/John who was the John ordained Dec 1707. When he entered Trinity College the record says he was 22 yrs. of age, thus b. c. 1679; however, the date of 1681 would have made him 20 which seems more reasonable for one starting college. Also, John had a dau named Jeanne with a godfather named Charles LaPierre.

REF: WEIS, Rev. Frederick Lewis, *The Colonial Clergy in VA, NC & SC* (Boston, 1955); WOOD, Lillian Fordham, *Compilation of Descendants of Colonial Ancestors* (New Bern, NC 1944, np), also a later version; WOOD, Lillian F., "The Reverend John LaPierre" in *The Historical Magazine of the Protestant Episcopal Church*, Vol. XL, #4 (1971); *Colonial Records of NC*; SPARROW, W. Keats, "The Sweet Irony of John LaPierre, Huguenot" in *The Cross of Languedoc* (Aug, 1982).

La PLAINE, Nicolas de

b. 1592, Bressuire, Poitou, or La Rochelle, c. 1593; poss. s/o Jacques de la Plaine, of the Seigneurie de la Grand Pleine nr. Bressuire; **NOTE**: this b. date seems *very early* considering dates of marr and births of ch – could be a generation missing; *very probable* that this is the father (who remained in FR) of the immigrant; given that, the immigrant Nicolas/Nicolaes was prob. b. c. 1633; Nicolas's father-in-law Pierre Cresson was b. 1609/10

c. 1646 - emigrated to ENG (poss. went to HOL a. going to ENG)

a. 1649 - left ENG, went to New Amsterdam

13 Apr 1657 – took Oath of Allegiance

14 Apr 1657 – made a small *Burgher* which gave him the right to trade and to hold minor offices; he was a tobacco twister by trade

m. 1 Sep 1658, Dutch Ch, New Amsterdam, Susanna Cresson, d/o Pierre & Rachel (Claussé) Cresson; Susanna, b. Ryswyck, HOL – now Rijswijk, a suburb of The Hague

21 Oct 1664 – took Oath of Loyalty to Great Britain

1674 – on a list of property owners in New Amsterdam – had $3000, a house on the w. side of Broad St., between Wall and Beaver

d. 1696-1712, New Amsterdam or Philadelphia

CHILDREN: (bap. records for all but James found in records of the Dutch Church, New Amsterdam)

James[2], b. 1660; m. 28 Aug 1692, Hannah Cock (b. 1669), d/o James & Sarah (X) Cock of Long Island; James became a Quaker; he d. 12 Apr 1750, Germantown, PA; **7 ch**

Elisabeth[2], bp. 6 Aug 1662; m. 12 6 mo 1686, NYC, Casper Hoodt; she d. 14 Aug 1699, Germantown, PA; **4 ch**

Nicholas[2], bp. 1 Oct 1664

Jean[2], bp. 7 Dec 1666

Marie[2], bp. 14 Nov 1668; m. 27 Jun 1692, NY, Jean Le Chevalier; **1 dau**[3]

Susanna[2], bp. 31 Dec 1670; m. c. 27 8 mo 1693, Friends Mtg, Philadelphia, Arnold Cassel from Kresheim/Kreigsheim, in the Palatinate; she d. Germantown, PA; their dau **Elizabeth**[3] m. Samuel Boone

Judith[2], bp. 22 Dec 1672; m. 1691, Friends Mtg, Philadelphia, Thomas Griffith

Rachel[2], bp. 27 Jan 1674/5

Carel[2], bp. 23 Mar 1677

Isaac[2], bp. 15 Jan 1679

Créjanne/Christiana[2], bp. 22 Jan 1681; m. 1697, Friends Mtg, Philadelphia, Ives Bellangée; went to Egg Harbor, NJ; **8 ch**

REF: GIBBS, Ethel Price, *Family History-Delaplaine*; STAPLETON, Rev. A., *Memorials of the Huguenots in America* (Carlisle, PA, 1901); minutes from Philadelphia MM; *Proceedings of the Huguenot Society of PA*, Vol XXVII (1955), XXIX (1957); *Huguenot Ancestors Represented in the Membership of the Huguenot Society of NJ* (1945); *NYGBR*, 6:87, p. 150; Baptismal & Marriage Records from Dutch Ch, NYC.

LARDENT/LARDANT/LARDAN(S), Jacques I

b. 25 May 1655/6, Dieppe, FR, s/o Jacques & Marie (Poullard) Lardan; a family of weavers
m. Luneray, Seine-Maritime Dépt., Haute-Normandie, FR (c. 10 km. s.w. of Dieppe), Marthe Moreau
1685 - to NYC
c. 1687- to Charleston, SC; Jacques was a joyner/carpenter
1694 - purchased Lot #224 (later #43) in Charleston; on Church St. today next to the French Ch property
a. 1696 - applied for citizenship; it was granted Mar 1696
d. a. 16 Mar 1697/98, adm
CHILD:
Jacques II[2], b. 1692, SC; purchased 200 acres, 24 Aug 1720 on Edisto Island, on Palmeters/Parmetiers Creek (now Store Creek) and 100 more acres on 1 Jun 1738; m. 2 Jul 1736, Mary (Wilkins) Odingsell, d/o William & Elizabeth (Woodward) Wilkins, previously m. to Charles Odingsell – the marr ended in either divorce or annulment; he d. 23 Jan 1741, Edisto Island, SC
CHILD (only known ch):
Martha[3], b. 17 Aug 1737, Charleston; m. 24 Nov 1754, James Reid; she d. 23 Oct 1755; **no issue**

NOTE: To prove any lineage from this family it would have to be through another child of Jacques & Marie (Poullard) Lardent; Jacques & Marthe Moreau had only one child Jacques, who had only one known child Martha, who had no issue.

REF: LARDENT, Charles L., "The Huguenot Family of Lardent: The Saga of a Quest" in *Transactions of the Huguenot Society of SC*, Vol. 102 (1997).

LaRESILIÈRE, Jacques/Jacob

b. c. 1640/5, *poss.* Artois, FR, *prob.* s/o Nicolas LaResilière
m/1, FR, XX
a. 1667 - to America; settled Flatbush, LI, NY, where he was member of the Flatbush Dutch Ch
m/2, 1667/8, Dutch Ch, Flatbush, Maria/Marie Gremjon/Grangen/Grançon/Granson (c. 1640- a 15 Feb

1693/94, inv)

c. 1677 - transferred by letter to the FR Congregation, prob. on Staten Island

4 Mar 1679/80 - purchased 2 tracts of land in "New Lotts" section of Flatbush; 7 May 1682, purchased lots 13 & 14 in Flatbush; there were other purchases in Flatbush

20 Feb1685/6 - pd. £200 for a house and lot on Staten Island, s. of Freshkill; his last real estate deal was 8-12 Jul 1686, recorded 16 Nov 1686 – this deed was the last reference to Jacob alive

d. a. 6 Mar 1687 (adm to son Nicholas), Richmond Co; wife called his "relict" in deed dated 22 Mar 1688/89

CHILD, m/1:

Nicholas[2], b. a. Mar 1666; m. Françoise Billiou, d/o Pierre & François (DuBois) Billiou; Françoise m/2, c. 1697, John Morgan – 2 sons,1 dau; Nicholas d. a. 1697

CHILDREN:

Nicholas[3], b. c. 1695; m. by 1722, Hester Lakerman (d. 1734) ,d/o Abraham & Catherine (Crocheron) Lakerman*; he d. a. 1 Apr 1766, wp, Staten Island; **2 sons**, **4 daus**; said to have m/2, a. 1739, XX – son **Benjamin**[4], dau **Elizabeth**[4]

* Abraham, s/o Louis & Maria (Wouters/Walters) Lakerman, Catherine d/o Jean & Marie (X) Crocheron

Marya/Marie[3], b. c. 1698/99; m. 12 Oct 1717, New Paltz, NY, Abraham DuBois (b. 17 Apr 1685, New Paltz, NY), s/o Abraham & Margaret (Deyo) DuBois**; d. date given for both is 3 Mar 1758, Somerset Co, NJ; **2 sons**, **7 daus**

**Abraham was s/o Louis & Catherine (Blanchan) DuBois; Margaret was d/o Chrétien & Jeanne (Verbeau) Deyo

CHILDREN, m/2:

?Margaret[2], b. c. 1670; m/1, Jacob Billiou (b. 1663, Staten Island), s/o Pierre & François (DuBois) Billiou, m/2 c. 1702, Pierre LeConte who d. a. 10 Apr 1704, wp, Richmond Co, NY which mentions wife Margaret and his 3 sons; Margaret d. a. 13 May 1736, wp - a Nicholas Larzelère was a witness when her will was written, 19 Sep 1734 – prob. her nephew; some of this is speculation – a Margaret Larzelère did m. Jacob Billiou – it seems feasible that bro & sis m. sis & bro, several sources say Margaret was the d/o Jacques & Marie – **needs proof, in either case**

Magdalen[2], bp. 5 Jan 1679, Dutch Ch, Amersfoort (now Brooklyn; was called Nieuw Amersfoort by the Dutch, named after the Dutch city, Amersfoort; also called "Flatlands")

Mary/Marij/Maria[2], bp. 12 Jun 1681, Dutch Ch, Breukelen; m. c. 1710/11, William Swaim/Sweem, as his 2nd wife; **4 sons**

poss. **?Anthony**[2], b. c. 1676, **?Catherine**[2], b. c. 1683, Flatbush, **?James**[2], b. c. 1685, **?Peter**[2], b. c. 1687 **?Michael**, d. 1717, intestate, Salem Co, NJ – again, **proof needed**

REF: GANNON, Peter Steven, editor, *Huguenot Refugees in the Settling of Colonial America* (NYC); STAPLETON, Rev. A, *Memorials of the Huguenots in America* (Baltimore, 1964); MULLANE, Joseph F., SWAIM, Lloyd B., JOHNSON, Mary Decker, *The Swaim-Tysen Family of Staten Island, NY, NJ & Southern States* (1987 Supplement); BLOOM, Jeanne Larzalere, material from the Huguenot Society of America (1998); HIX, Charlotte Megill, *Staten Island Wills & Letters of Administration, 1670-1800* (Bowie, MD, 1993); BARDSLEY, Elda S., "The Early Larzeleres" in the *NYGBR*, Vol. 122, #4 (Oct 1991).

LATANÉ, Pierre (Rev.)

from Nérac, FR, Lot-et-Garonne Dépt., Aquitaine, s.e. Marmande

by 23 Mar 1610 - student at Franeker, Friesland, HOL, e. of Harlingen; he was a minister at churches in Bria (sic) (prob. was Brias in Pas-de-Calais), Moncaret, Mussidan (both in Aquitaine, w. of Bordeaux)

m. Susanna de Barrau, d/o Sieur de Fournir

CHILDREN:

Joseph[2], m. Anna de Brugière, d/o Isaac de Brugière; he d. Gueldre – prob. means La Gueldre which refers to Gelderland, a province in eastern HOL; he was a Doctor of both Civil and Canon Law, a judge of Mussidan and 15 neighboring districts

CHILDREN, 9 b., 4 d. young:

Pierre[3], b, 2 Feb 1658, Mussidan, Dordogne Dépt., Aquitaine, n.w. Bergerac; m. 1 Apr 1694, Margaret Steindam, d/o Abraham Steindam, Doctor of Theology & Philosophy; he d. 16 Jul 1726, Frisia, HOL – coastal area, along the Wadden Zee, aka German Bight on the n. coast; prominent professor of medicine and botany, physician to the House of Orange & Nassau; 3 daus - only **Anna**[4] survived to adulthood, she m. Dominick Balck

Isaac[3], b. Mussidan; a minister; d. Heusden, Gueldre, now on the border of Gelderland and N. Brabant, n.w .of Hertogenbosch

Joseph[3], captain in the army; became his parents' principal heir

Susanna[3], m. Peter Desrivières

Henri[2], most likely a Protestant minister & the one "detained" in his effort to depart FR during the "Hostilities"; imprisoned in the Château Trompette at Bordeaux where he spent the remainder of his life

CHILDREN:

Henry[3], fled to London where he lived & d. p. 1724; **no issue**

Lewis[3], b. 1672, Jouan, Guienne, FR, now in Lot Dépt, Midi-Pyrénées, s.w. of Fumel; Oct, 1685 fled FR to ENG; 24 Nov 1691, matriculated Queen's College, Oxford; 22 Sep 1700, London, ordained in the Ch of England, as a deacon, 18 Oct 1700, as a priest; arr VA, 5 Mar 1701, on the *Mary Ann*; settled S. Farnham Parish, Essex Co, VA, as rector 1701-32; m/1, XX, m/2, Phebe (Slaughter?) Peachey, widow of William Peachey – she d. 10 Jan 1710/1, m/3, 11 Jun 1716, VA, Mary Deane; liv. at "Langlee" on the Rappahannock, 13 mi above Tappahannock; he d. 1732

> CHILDREN, prob. m/2:
>
> **Charlotte**[4], b. 28 Dec ----; m. c. 1723, Abraham Montague (bp. 28 Sep 1710, Middlesex Co, VA-d. Jun or Jul, 1740, Essex Co, VA), s/o William Montague; she d. a. 22 Jul 1747, wp; **issue**
>
> **Phebe**[4], b. Sep ----
>
> **Susanna**[4], b. Feb ----
>
> **Henry**[4], b. 28 Jan ----; was sent to ENG for school; d. of smallpox, 1721
>
> **William**[4], b. 11 Dec ----; was sent to ENG for school; d. of smallpox, 1721
>
> **Henrietta**[4], b. Dec ----; m. William Jones; 1 dau **Susanna**[5] m. William Jones
>
> CHILDREN, m/3:
>
> **Catherine**[4], b. 9 Sep 1717; d. in infancy
>
> **Lewis**[4], b. 4 Sep 1720; d. by 1724
>
> **John**[4], b. 11 Oct 1722; m. Mary Allen; d. 1773; one surviving son **William**[5] had **issue**
>
> **Maryanne/Marian**[4], b. 26 Feb 1724/5; m. Dr. John Clements; **issue**

REF: STANFILL, Latayne Colvett, *Colvett Family Chronicles, The History of the Colvett Family of TN 1630-1990* (Glendale, CA, 1991), p. 458; LATANÉ, Lucy Temple, *Parson Latané 1672-1932* (Charlottesville, VA, 1936); *The VA Magazine of History & Biography*, Vol. 8, #1 (Jul 1900), p. 58; *The Huguenot*, Pub. #10 (1939/41); WEIS, Rev. Frederick Lewis, *The Colonial Clergy of VA, NC & SC* (Boston, 1955); MONTAGUE, George William, *History & Genealogy of Peter Montague* (Amherst, MA, 1899).

La TOUR/LaTÜR/LATTURE, Thomas

b. c. 1655, prob. s/o Nicklai

m. Anna Maria Catherine X

c. 1700 - family moved from Blieskastel (w. of Zweibrücken) to Haßloch (11 mi w. of Speyer); Böhl & Haßloch were on the w. side of the Rhine, part of FR, at the time; family story is that Herman[2] & his sons Jacob & George returned from a hunting trip to find their family and servants slain & possessions destroyed – they fled up the Rhine to Rotterdam

d. 1734, Haßloch, *Pfalz*, GER

CHILDREN:

JohannesThomas[2], b. 1696, Blieskastel; m. Maria Elisabetha Bitaniers; **2 sons**

Johannes Hermannus/Herman[2], m/1, Anna Elisabeth Fongallon; arr Philadelphia, 15 Sep 1749, on the
Phoenix from Rotterdam via Cowes, Isle of Man, with passengers from the Palatinate; Herman on
passenger list w/ son Jacob, son George Michael not listed as he was too young, no wife listed so Anna
Elisabeth must have d. a. Herman left GER; m/2, 26 Feb 1750, Warwick Twp, Lancaster Co, PA,
Catherine Barbara Spicler; he d. a. 20 Jan 1774, wp, Mount Joy, Lancaster, PA; will mentions wife
Catherine, ch George, Herman, Susanna & Elisabeth; surname became **LATTURE**

CHILDREN, m/1:

Nicklaus[3], b. 1726; d. 1729, Haßloch

Jacob[3], b. 1730 Böhl or Haßloch; d. America

George Michael[3], b. 1732, Haßloch; d. 1733, Haßloch

George Michael[3], b. 1736, Haßloch; d. p. 1797, Sullivan Co, TN

CHILDREN, m/2:

Susanna Margaretha[3], b. 7 Jul 1751; m. 1770, Jacob Eckert/A(c)kard; went to VA, then TN, nr.
Paperville (s.e. of Bristol); she d. c. 1813, Sullivan Co, TN; he d. 27 Sep 1826; **4 sons, 3 daus**

Elisabeth[3], m. David Hilden; evidently stayed in PA but there seems to have been a family schism
as Herman left Elisabeth 5 shillings (although she had rec. some land previously) saying
that the couple had treated him "very ill"

Harmon/Herman[3], b. Apr 1756, Lancaster Co; m/1, a. 1785, XX – **1 son, dau**, m/2, a. 1793,
Agnes Boles – **4 sons, 4 daus**; 5 of his 10 ch did **not** marry – **Elizabeth**[4], **Susannah**[4],
James[4], **Thomas**[4], **Nancy**[4]; to VA, c. 1783; bought 238 acres, 16 Jun 1792, in Washington
Co, VA, on the s. fork of the Holston River; to TN, c. 1800, where he settled in Reedy
Creek Valley Silvicola, TN (nr. Kingsport); Herman was Pvt in the Lancaster Co Militia
during the Rev. War; he d. 18 Nov 1833, Sullivan Co, TN, bur. Blountville, TN

Elisabetha[2], b. 1703, Haßloch; m. X Blume

Anna Margaretha[2], b. 1706 Haßloch

Georgius Michael[2], b. 1708 Haßloch; m. Anna Maria Backar; **2 sons, 2 daus**

REF: OVERBAY, Paul L., *Lattures in America 1749-1979* (self-pub, 1978); brochure from the Latture/Akard Reunion, 26 Aug 1932; land record Washington Co, VA; Herman[2]'s will; Rev. War records, Herman[3].

La TOURETTE/LaTOURRETTE/LATOURETTE, Jean

b. c. 1651, Osse-en-Aspe, s. of Oloron-Ste.-Marie, then in Béarn Province, FR, in the former Basses-Pyrénées
area, nr. border w/ Spain, now in Pyrénées Atlantiques Dépt, Aquitaine, s/o David LaTourette, notary in
Osse-en-Aspe; s/o David (1625-1697) & Magdeleine (X) (1630-1696) LaTourette; his fa was a *notaire*
an *ancient* of the Protestant Temple, a prominent man; had sibs Jacob (c. 1650-1711) and Marie (c.
1661-1731); Jacob remained in Osse as did Marie but a grson of Marie's d. 1778 at the confluence of
the Mississippi and Arkansas Rivers – he was the progenitor of the Laclede family of St. Louis

1685 – left Osse as a *cadet* (an unmarr. younger son); was in Frankfurt, GER in Nov of that yr.

24 Apr 1686 - in Rotterdam with other Huguenot refugees; said to be unmarr.

Jun 1686-Aug 1687 – in London, where he sought aid from the Huguenot Ch there; still unmarr.

by 18 Aug 1687 – he & his good friend Rev. Pierre Peiret, had left London & had sailed to America on the
Robert; arr NYC by 10 Nov 1687

m. 16 Jul 1693, St. Esprit Ch, NYC, Marie Mercereau (1670-c.1733), d/o Jean & Elizabeth
(DuBois) Mercereau; there was thought that this marriage ceremony was to "confirm" a marriage
that had taken place in FR (c. 1684), which was no longer valid as Huguenots were denied civil
rights; this theory has been disproven

1695 - NY petitioned for citizenship; he was a carpenter

1697 - had a house in the South Ward of NYC, 1699 he was in the West Ward

c. 1698 - went to Fresh Kills, Staten Island, Richmond Co. where he rec. a deed for a half acre for a church

for the French people – he lived c. 200 yards s. of the ch
1715 - he was Assessor; 1723 Warden of St. Andrew's Ch; 1725 a Judge by Special Sessions Court
d. c. 17 Jul 1725, Fresh Kills, Staten Island, NY
CHILDREN:
Marie/Mary[2], b. 23 Sep, bp. 16 Dec1693, FR Ch, NYC; m. Samuel Broome; she d. 1770/3; **issue**
Jean/John[2], b. 6 Oct, bp. 20 Oct 1695, St. Esprit Ch, NYC; m. c. 1725, Marie Mercereau, d/o Josué &
    Marie (Chadaine) Mercereau, his 1st cousin; he d. a. 1794, wp, Mariners Harbor, Staten Island
    CHILDREN:
    David[3], b. 1726
    Mary[3], b. 1728; unmarr.
    Peter[3], b. 1730; m. 1756, Abigail Mercereau, d/o Josué & Abigail (Broome) Mercereau
    Henricus[3], b. 1731; d. young
    John[3], b. 1734; m. 1757, Susanna Christopher; d. 1784
    Elizabeth[3], b. 1686; m. 1755, Nicolas Backer
    Paul[3], b. 1738; m. 1760, Sarah Merrill
Pierre/Peter[2], b. 22 Nov, bp. 28 Nov 1697, St. Esprit Ch; m. 1st cousin Marianne Mercereau, d/o Daniel &
    Susanna (Doucinet) Mercereau; d. 1754, Staten Island
    CHILDREN (all bp. Dutch Ch, Port Richmond, NY):
    Peter[3], b. 1726; m. Cliffy Patmore; d. 1808
    Daniel[3], b. 1728; d. 1827, unmarr.
    (David)[3], b. 1730; m. Catrina Lane
    (James)[3], b. 1730
    Marie Susanne[3], b. 1734; d. 1820, unmarr.
    Elizabeth[3], b. 1735; m. X Johnson
David[2], b. 28 Dec 1699. Staten Is, bp. 7 Jan 1699/00, St. Esprit; m. 1730, Catherine Poillon, d/o Jacques &
    Catherine (LeConte) Poillon
    CHILDREN:
    Fanny[3], b. 1731; m. Jonathan Lewis
    Jacques/James[3], bp. 19 Mar 1731/2, Reformed Dutch Ch, Port Richmond, NY; m. Elizabeth
        Lewis; he d. 1785
    David[3], b. 1739; m/1, Elizabeth Morgan, m/2, Mary Simonson
    Marie[3], bp. 1 Sep 1734, Reformed Dutch Ch, Port Richmond, NY
    Cathrin[3], b. 1738; m. 1766, Stephen Bedell
Susanne[2], b. c. 1702; m. Jan Van Pelt
Esther[2], b. 1704; m. a. 1728, Paul Mercereau; she d. 19 Jan 1781; **issue**
Henry[2], b. c. 1708, Staten Island; m/1, Susanne Perlier, d/o Jean & Anne (Rezeau) Perlier, m/2, 28 Sep
    1764, Sarah (Lane) Wood, widow of Stephen Wood – she d. 1806; he d. 1794; he was called
    "The Weaver"
    CHILDREN, m/1:
    Susanne[3], b. 1743; m. 1764, Peter Cole; d. 1812
    Henry[3], b. 1745
    John[3], b. 1749; m/1, 1775, Elizabeth Bond of Manchester, ENG – **7 ch**, m/2, 1800, Ruth (Black-
        Ford) Mollison, widow of Gilbert Mollison; he d. 1813
    Ann[3], b. 1751; m/1, Abraham Cannon, m/2, 1780, William DeGroot; d. 1843
    Peter[3], b. 1754; m. 1782, Elizabeth Androvette; d. 1831
James[2], b. 1710, Staten Island; d. 1738, Staten Island, unmarr.

NOTE: Béarn is a former FR "frontier" province in s.w. FR; its southern border is the Pyrenees & Spain

REF: LATOURETTE, Lyman E., *Latourette Annals in America* (1954); DRIGGS, Lawrence LaTourette, "The Family" in *The Huguenot*, Vol. III, #3 (Apr 1933), Vol. IV, #1 (Jan/Mar 1934), #2 (Apr/Sep 1934), #3 (Oct/Dec 1934); LIPPE, Raymond Wills, "References & Sources"; CADIER, Alfred, *Histoire de l'Église Réformée de la Vallée d'Aspe*; research by John LaTourette, Ph.D.

La VERDURE, Pierre

b. FR

m. c. 1630/1, ENG, Priscilla Melanson/Mellison (c. 1595, ENG-1691/2, MA); she m/2, 8 Apr 1680, Capt. William Wright, of Dorchester, MA; she d. 9 Jan 1689/90, aged 92 yrs.

spring 1657- from ENG to Nova Scotia on the *Satisfaction* w/ Sir Thomas Temple

c. 1667- left Canada to go to Boston to escape "from the wrath of his Countrymen Papists, at Johns fort & thereabouts"; he lost his property and was forced to live in extreme poverty, his son John was his sole support

d. a. 3 May 1677, poss. Boston; widow petitioned the MA General Court on that date for reimbursement to pay her landlord the money that he had posted for her son John who had fled; she identified herself as English and her late husband as "a Frenchman and Protestant that came under this government for shelter from the wrath of his countrymen Papists"

CHILDREN, 1st 2 sons evidently used their mother's surname: **MELANSON**

Pierre[2] Melanson, Sieur de la Verdure, b. 1632/3, ENG; m. c. 1664/5, Port Royal, Marie Marguerite Muis d'Entremont, d/o Philippe & Madeleine (Hélie) Mius d'Entremont; both he and his bro Charles abjured & embraced Catholicism

  CHILDREN:

  Marie[3] b. 1664, Port Royal; prob. d. young

  Marguerite[3], b. 1666, Port Royal; prob. d. young

  Marie Anne[3], b. 1668, Port Royal; m/1, c. 1686, Jacques de la Tour, m/2, c. 1700, Alexandre Robichaud; she d. 14 May 1751

  Cécile[3], b. 1670, Port Royal; m/1, c. 1684, Abraham Boudrot, m/2, c. 1686, Alexandre Boudrot, m/3, c. 1699, Jean Antoine Belliveau

  Françoise[3], b. c. 1672; m. c. 1698, Jean Sire

  Isabelle[3], b. c. 1673, Port Royal; m. c. 1689, Michel Bourg

  Charles[3], b. c. 1675, Port Royal; m. c. 1701, Marie Anne Bourg; he d. 7 Jan 1758

  Madeleine[3], b. c. 1677, Port Royal; m. c. 1695, Jean Belliveau

  Marie[3], b. c. 1679, Port Royal; m. c. 1699, Charles Belliveau

  Pierre[3], b. c. 1685 (twin), Port Royal; m. 7 Nov 1712, Marie Anne Granger

  Ambroise[3], b. c. 1685 (twin), Port Royal; m/1, 10 Nov 1705, Françoise Bourg, m/2, Marguerite Combeau

  Claude[3], b. c. 1688, Port Royal; m. 22 Jan 1714, Marguerite Babineau

  Jean[3], b. c. 1690, Port Royal; m. 22 Jan 1714, Madeleine Petitot dit St. Seine

  Marguerite[3], b. 1693, Port Royal; m. 22 Jan 1714, Jan Baptiste Landry

Charles[2] Melanson dit la Verdure, b. 1643, ENG; m. c. 1663, Port Royal, Acadia, Marie Dugas (1648, Acadia- 9 Jul 1737), d/o Abraham & Marguerite Louise (Doucet) Dugas; **issue**

John la Verdure, b. ENG; m. Sarah X; he was a seaman; he was in Boston and Maine; **5ch**

REF: HANNAY, James, *The History of Acadia, from its First Discovery to its Surrender to England* (St. John, New Brunswick, 1879); Petition of widow Priscilla from Suffolk Co. files, Vol. 18, Case1592 Dec 1-10; D'Entremont, Rev. Clarence J., "Du Nouveau sur les Melanson" in *La Société Historique Acadienne*, Vol. III, #8, #9 (Moncton, NB, Jul, Aug, Sep, 1970 & Oct, Nov, Dec, 1970); D'Entremont, Rev. Clarence J., "Les Melanson d'Acadie sont français de père et anglais de mère" in *La Société Historique Acadienne*, Vol. IV, #10 (Moncton, NB, Jul, Aug, Sep 1973) – articles reprinted in English in the *French Canadian & Acadian Genealogical Review*, Vol. II, #4 (winter, 1969), Vol. VI, #1 (spring, 1978).

la VERGNE, Nicolas de

b. 1697/1702, FR; said to have been a cousin of General La Fayette's mother

c. 1720- arr America, on a FR man-of-war; called the "little French doctor; was 1st in Westchester Co., NY; in Poughkeepsie, NY, by 27 May 1749

m/1, 11 Feb 1737/8, Frances Warner of CT (c. 1718-8 Mar 1748/9), d/o Dr. Benjamin Warner

m/2, c. 1750, Charlotte Pct, Mary Husted of Stamford, CT (c. 1732-d. Troy, NY), d/o Ebenezer & Sarah

(Holmes) Husted

1761 – took Oath of Allegiance

1738 - was a justice of the peace; also a probate judge for Dutchess Co.

d. a. 8 Apr 1782, wp, Dutchess Co, NY; bur. Washington Hollow Cem.

CHILDREN, m/1:

Louis[2], b. 5 Nov 1739; m. 8 May 1759, Rachel Greene; he d. 15 Jun 1805, Amenia, NY; **7 ch**

Benjamin[2], b. 18 Aug 1742; m. c. 1770, Anna Baldwin (26 Sep 1752-26 Feb 1792), d/o Isaac & Susannah Baldwin; he d. 25 Jan 1830, Washington Hollow, NY; served in the Rev. War in the Dutchess Co. Militia; he was a doctor; **12 ch**

Frances[2], b. 25 Apr 1748; m. c. 1766, Timothy Greene (Rachel's bro); d. 13 Mar 1819, Coxsackie, NY (some accounts say she was b. 1740, others say her mother d. shortly after her birth); **10 ch**

CHILDREN, m/2:

Giles[2], b. 1750, Washington, NY; m. Rachel Greene; d. 1850, Amenia, NY

Mary[2], b. 1754, Washington, NY; m. Samuel Mosher

Joseph[2], b. 1756; m. 8 Sep 1774, Sarah Gillett; d. Canada

Sarah[2], b. 1758; m. Jeremiah Howland; d. Saratoga Co, NY

Elizabeth[2], b. 6 Sep 1760; m. 5 Sep 1783, James Baremore; d. 23 Dec 1858

Nicholas[2], b. 9 Nov 1761; m. Sarah Mosher; d. 1839, Esperance, NY; **9 ch**

James Henry[2], b. 1763; m. Anna Case; d. 1838, Greenwich, NY

Hannah[2], b. 7 Apr 1766; m. 18 May 1784, Silas Bullis; d. 16 Mar 1852, Stanford, NY

Susanna[2], b. 17 Dec 1769; m. ? Green; d. 11 Feb 1847

Walter[2], d. 16 Nov 1819, nr. Savannah, GA

Ebenezer[2], b. 20 Oct 1776; m. Ruth Green; d. 28 Aug 1852, Newark, NJ

REF: SMITH, James, *History of Duchess Co, NY* (1882); 2 undated, manuscripts – no author given; records from Poughkeepsie, NY; GREENE, H.L., *Family of* Greene; GARVEN, Dorothy, *The Dillivins* (1979); HASBROUCH, *History of Dutchess Co, NY; Records of Christ Episcopal Church*, Poughkeepsie, NY.

la VIGNE, Étienne de/ LeVINESS, Stephen

b. c . 1638 Royan, (now Charente-Maritime, Poitou-Charentes) Saintonge, FR, on the Gironde, s.w. Saujon

m. Elizabeth (**not** Isabelle) X – Étienne & Elizabeth were godparents to Isabeau Fougère, 28 Mar 1691, FR Ch, NYC

1686 - one of the settlers at Narragansett, RI

a. Mar 1691 - went to NYC, became a member of the FR Ch

6 Feb 1696 - rec. letter of denization in New Rochelle, NY

d. p. Feb 1696, prob. New Rochelle

CHILD:

Stephen[2], b. Royan; m. Maria Boulier who m/2, Jacob Parker; Stephen d. a. 1702, NY

    CHILD:

    Amos[3], b. NY; m. Mary X; a. 1723, liv. Phillipsburg where he had a leasehold of 286 acres by the Saw Mill River; **6 ch**; at least 1 of his grson's used surname LeViness

REF: ROCHE, O.J.A., *The Days of the Upright* (NYC); LeViness Genealogy from Ardsley, NY Historical Society; *NY Genealogical & Biographical Record*, Vol. 100; SEACORD, Morgan H., *Biographical Sketches & Index of the Huguenot Settlers of New Rochelle, 1687-1776) (1941)*; DeFOREST, L. Effingham, *Records of the French Church at Narragansett, RI, 1686-1691;* WITTMEYER, Rev. Alfred V., *Registers of the Births, Marriages & Deaths of the Église Françoise à la Nouvelle York, 1688-1804;*LeVINESS, Osmund W. & Claudia S., *LeViness Family Genealogy* (1969).

la VIGNE, Guleyn/Guillaume de/ VIGNÉ, Ghislain

b. 1590, prob. Valenciennes, s/o Jean de la Vigne who was b. Valenciennes, then part of Hainaut; family thought to have been from Cambrai, s.w. of Valenciennes; Jean fled to HOL, c. 1585, where he was a Walloon minister in Amsterdam until 1622

a.1610, m. Adrienne/Ariantje Cuvellier/Cuvilje, d/o Jean; she m/2, 30 Apr 1632, Jan Jantzen Damen, a prosperous neighbor – **no issue**; she d. a. 25 Nov 1655, perhaps May, 1655

Sep 1618 - they were in Leiden according to Walloon Ch. recs. so could **not** have emigrated in 1613 on the 1st Dutch ship, the *Tiger,* to New Amsterdam as has been said in some sources, incl. Baird; a dau Rachel was bp. in Leiden, 2 Sep 1618, and her parents were received into membership there in Oct, 1618– doubtful that the family would have gone back to HOL from NY for that; Guleyn & Adrienne are mentioned in Leiden ch. recs. as late as 19 Mar 1623 with several other baptisms listed

1624 - emigrated on the *Eendracht* or the *Nieuw Nederland/New Netherland* w/ 3 daus; the *Eendracht* sailed from Amsterdam, 25 Jan 1624, and the *Nieuw Nederland,* c. 30 Mar 1624

he had a farm below what is now Wall St., east of Broadway, or, as it was then called, *Breede Weg*

d. a. 30 Apr 1632, estate settled, New Amsterdam

CHILDREN:

Maria[2], b. c. 1610; m/1, Jan Roos of Haarlem, HOL, who was killed by Indians, m/2, c. 1630, Abraham Isaaczen Ver Planck; she d. 1670/1, he d. c. 1690/1

   CHILD, m/1:surnamed **ROOS**

   Gerrit Janses Roos[3], m/1, Aeltje Lamberts-**3 ch**, m/2, c. 5 Sep 1659 (date of banns), Tryntje Arents; he d. a. 1704

   CHILDREN, m/2:sutnamed **VER PLANCK**

   Abigail[3], m. c. 1660, Adrian Van Laer (bp. 17 Jan 1634, Amsterdam-c. 1702, Albany), s/o Gerrit Stoffelsen Van Laer & Barbara Adriaens; she d. 1st and he remarr.

   Catalyna[3], m. 13 Oct 1657, David Pieterse Schuyler of Beverwyck; she d. 8 Oct 1708, he d. 9 Feb 1690; **7 ch**

   Guleyn[3], b. 1 Jan 1637; m. Jun 1668, NYC, Hendrickje Wessels (b. 23 Sep 1644), d/o Metje Wessels; he d. 23 Apr 1684, NYC - **8 ch**; Hendrickje m/2, Jacobus Kip

   Isaac[3], bp. 26 Jun 1641, New Amsterdam; d. young

   Susanna[3], bp. 25 May 1642; m/1, 4 Dec 1660, Marten Van Woert - **1 son**, m/2, 20 Apr 1669, John Gurlandt (d. 1674) - **2 sons**, m/3, 1679, Daniel Brown (d. 1695)

   Jacomyntje[3], bp. 6 Jul 1644; prob. d. young

   Ariaentje[3], bp. 2 Dec 1646; m. 4 Dec 1660 (?), Melgert Wynantse Van der Poel, s/o Wynant & Tryntje (Melgers) Van der Poel; she d. a. 1692, when Melgert m. Elizabeth W. Tellor; **8 ch**

   Hillegond[3], bp. 1 Nov 1648; m. Albany, David Ackerman of Hackensack, NJ, s/o David Ackerman & Elizabeth Bellier

   Isaac[3], bp. 26 Feb 1651; m. Albany, Abigail Uyten Bogart; he d. c. 1729; **9 ch**

Kristyn/Christina[2], b. c. 1612; m. c. 1630, Dirck Volkertszen (c. 1595, NOR-c. 1680); she d. p. 21 Feb 1663-a. 24 Apr 1677, Bushwick, NY; **8 ch**

   CHILDREN, surnamed **DIRCKS/DIRCKSEN**:

   Grietje/Margaret[3], b. 1632, New Amsterdam; m/1, 1649, Jan Harmensen Schut from Lubeck, m/2,1652, Jan Nagel from Limburg – **3 ch**, m/3, 11 Mar 1658, New Amsterdam, Barent Gerritszen (b. c 1630, Zwol, Overyssel, N. HOL-d. c. 1708, Bushwyck, NY) as his 2nd wife

   ? Christina[3], b. 1633

   Magdalena[3], b. c. 1636; m/1, 1652, Cornelis Hendricksen from Dort who was killed by Indians, 15 Sep 1655, m/2,1657, Harmen Hendricksen Rosecrans from Bergen

   Sara[3], b. c. 1638

   Rachel[3], bp. 8 Sep 1641; m. 1663, Jan Escuyer/Jean L'Esquier from Paris

   Volkert[3], bp. 15 Nov 1643, Dutch Ch, New Amsterdam; m. 1655, Bushwyck, LI, Annetje Phillipse Langelan, d/o Phillip Langelan; he d. 1701/2; **issue**

   Jacob[3], b. c. 1646; d. unmarr.

   Artiantje[3], bp. 21 Aug 1650

Jannetje[3], bp. 7 Dec 1653
? Philip[3]
? Nicholas[3]
Rachel[2], bp. 2 Sep 1618, Wallon Ch, Leiden; prob. d. young
Abraham & Sara[2], bp. 26 Sep 1619 Walloon Ch, Leiden; prob. d. young
Abraham[2], bp. 26 Dec 1621, Walloon Ch, Leiden; prob. d. young
Rachel[2], bp. 19 Mar 1623,Walloon Ch, Leiden; m. a. 1638, Cornelius Van Tienhoven from Utrecht, who d. 1658; she d. 1663; **5 ch**
Jan/Jean/John[2], b. 1624, NY; m/1, Emmentje Goosens Van der Sluys, widow – **no issue**, m/2, 15 Feb 1682, Breuklen, Weiske Huyten/Wit Wytes, widow of Andries Andrieszen; Jan d. 21 Jan 1689; said to have been the 1st white male child b. in New Amsterdam, obviously not given date of arrival, but he *may* have been the 1st white male ch to survive

REF: ABBOTT, John Howard, *Book of the Courtright Family*; *NYGBR,* Vol. XXIV (1893),Vol. XC (Jan 1959), pp. 2-5 (Jul, 1959), pp. 164-65; *NYG&B Newsletter* (Winter 1999) "375th Anniversary of the *Eendracht & Nieuw Nederland* by MACY, Harry, Jr.; ROLLINS, Sarah Finch Maiden, *The Maiden Family of VA & Allied Families* (Wolfe City, TX, 1991); PARSONS, N. Vincent & Margaret P., editors *Sebring Collections The Genealogy & History of the Family, Compiled by Walter Wilson Sebring & John Cletus Sebring, 1908-1965* (1975); *New Netherland Connections*, Vol. 3, #1 (Jan-Mar 1998), "The Pedigree of Cornelia Roos, an Ancestor of Franklin D. Roosevelt" by KOENIG, Dorothy A & NIEUWENHUIS, Pim; *National Genealogical Society Quarterly,* "Ariaentje Cuvilje, Matriarch of New Amsterdam".

Le BARON, François/Francis

b. 1668, FR
said to have been aboard a FR privateer that had been outfitted at Bordeaux; ship wrecked in Buzzards Bay (w. coast of Cape Cod) & the survivors were sent to Boston as prisoners; Francis, the ship's surgeon, remained in Plymouth as he was sick; while there he performed an operation that saved a woman's life; the grateful inhabitants petitioned the Lt. Gov. to allow Francis to remain in Plymouth as a free man; the petition was granted as long as Francis agreed to stay in Plymouth
m. 6 Sep 1695, Plymouth, Mary Wilder (7 Apr 1668-25 Sep 1737), d/o Edward & Elizabeth (Eames) Wilder of Hingham; she m/2, 10 Dec 1707, Return Waite (1678, Boston-1751, Plymouth)
d. 8 Aug 1704, Plymouth, MA; 22 Sep 1704,wp – mentions wife Mary, ch James, Lazarus, Francis
CHILDREN:
James[2], b. 23 May 1696, Plymouth; m. 28 Jun 1717, Rochester, Martha Benson (b. 5 Mar 1703, Rochester)*, d/o John & Elizabeth (Briggs) Benson; he was a farmer in Middleboro; he d. 10 May 1744; she m/2, 15 May 1745, William Parker; *b. & marr. of Martha in Rochester
vital records, seems she m. at 14!
CHILDREN:
James[3], b. 22 Dec 1721; d. 16 Sep 1725
John[3], b. 2 Apr 1724; m. 23 Feb 1748, Mary Richmond of Middleboro (she d. 23 Mar 1791); he d. 1 Aug 1801; **8 ch**
James[3], b. 10 Dec 1726, Middleboro; m. 4 Feb 1746/7, Hannah Turner of Rochester (30 Jun 1729, Middleboro-3 Aug 1807, Middleboro), d/o Japhet & Elizabeth (Morse) Turner; he d. 3 Oct 1780, Middleboro; **11 ch**
Joshua[3], b. 10 Oct 1729; m. 20 Nov 1761, Grace Bush of Sheffield (27 Feb 1744-20 Dec 1819); he d. 9 Mar 1806; **11 ch**
Martha[3], b. 9 Apr 1732; d. young
Francis[3], b. 20 Dec 1734; d. 8 Jul 1761
Mary[3], b. 9 Aug 1737; m. 4 Jan 1756, Plympton, Abiel Shurtleff (11 Mar 1733-6 Jan 1826), s/o David & Bethia (Lucas) Shurtleff; liv. Carver, MA; she d. 12 May 1816; **9 ch**
David[3], b. 27 Apr 1740; m. 20 Nov 1764, Martha Chatfield (18 Jun 1746, Killingworth, CT-22 Jan 1820, Benson, VT), d/o Cornelius & Martha (Kelsey) Chatfield; David was a Pvt from CT in the Rev. War; d. 1 Feb 1819, Benson, VT; **11 ch**

Lydia[3], b. 26 Jan 1743; d. p. 21 Jul 1757

Lazarus[2], b. 26 Dec 1698, Plymouth; m/1, 16 May 1720, Plymouth, Lydia Bartlett (1 Jan 1697/8, Plymouth-19 May 1742, Plymouth), d/o Joseph & Lydia (Griswold) Bartlett, m/2, 2 May 1743, Lydia (Bradford) Cushman (23 Dec 1719-28 Oct 1756), d/o David & Elizabeth (Finney) Bradford, widow/o Elkanah Cushman; he d. 3 Sep 1773, Middleboro (inv, 25 Oct 1773)

CHILDREN, m/1:

Lazarus[3], b. 7 May 1721, Plymouth; m/1, 10 Nov 1748, Barbados, West Indies, Margaret Newsome - issue, m/2, 14 Oct 1756, Plymouth, Mary (Thomas) Lothrop, widow of Ansel Lothrop; she d. 23 Apr 1792, age 73Y; Lazarus was a physician who d. 15 Nov 1784, Plymouth

Joseph[3], b. 1722, m. Sarah Leonard

Lydia[3], b. 1724, m. Nathaniel Goodwin

Mary[3], b. 1731, m. 22 Mar 1750/1, Dr. William Bradford, s/o Samuel & Sarah (Gray) Bradford

Hannah[3], b. 1734, m. Benjamin Goodwin

Theresa[3], 1736-1738

Bartlett[3], b. 1739, m/1, Mary Esdell, m/2, Lydia Sargent

CHILDREN, m/2:

Isaac[3], b. 25 Jan 1744, m. 1 Dec 1774, Martha Howland (b. 22 Dec 1739), d/o Consider & Ruth (Bryant) Howland

Elizabeth[3], b, 1 Jan 1745/6, m. 1762, Rev. Ammi Ruhamah Robbins of CT

Lemuel[3], b. 1747, m. Elizabeth Allen

Francis[3], 1749-1773;

William[3], b. 1751, m. Sarah Churchill

Priscilla[3], b. 1753, m. Abraham Hammett, s/o Abraham & Lucy (Howland, sis/o Martha above) Hammett

Margaret[3], 1755-1756

Francis[2], b. 13 Jun 1701, Plymouth; m. 23 Nov 1721, Plymouth, Sarah Bartlett (b. 24 Mar 1702/3), d/o Joseph & Lydia (Griswold) Bartlett; he d. 6 Aug 1731; **2 sons, 4 daus**

NOTE: There has been some discussion as to whether Francis was Roman Catholic. It is believed that he was one of the Huguenots on the ship that ended up in Buzzards Bay. He was buried in a Huguenot burial ground, thus unconsecrated ground for a Catholic. It would seem that he was a Huguenot. His descend-ants certainly married into many of the prominent Protestant families in MA.

REF: *Mayflower Quarterly* (June, 2006); *Mayflower Families* – William Bradford, Edward Doty, John Howland, Richard Warren; BAIRD, Charles W., *Huguenot Emigration to America* Vol. II; VRs – Middleboro, Plymouth, Rochester; LeBARON, Allen, *A LeBaron Migration Story: Landmarks & Lives* (Logan, UT, 1999 – self pub).

Le BOITEUX/BOYTEAUX/BOYTEULX, Gabriel

b. c. 1664/5, La Rochelle, FR

1685 – fled FR w/ bros Pierre & Paul

1687 – in NY

5 Jan 1688 - naturalized as a ship owner; made freeman of the city; one of the Elders of the FR Ch

m/1, 17 Apr 1689, FR Ch, NYC, Marquise Fleuriau (bur. 11 Oct 1693, Trinity Churchyard, NYC)

m/2, a. 1695, Dutch Ch, NY Agnes Constance LeBrun, b. Island of Guadaloupe, d/o Moïse LeBrun; she was naturalized, 1689, NY; she m/2, Rudolph Sebring

1702 - bought 200 acres in Middlesex Co, NJ

by 20 Mar 1728 - he was in Piscataway, NJ, where he wrote his will

d. a. 10 Apr 1734, wp; he was a prominent merchant; his will mentions only his wife, son Paul, daus Catherine & Mary

CHILDREN, m/1:

Marie[2], b. 28 Apr, bp. 14 May 1690, FR Ch, NYC; m. Rev. Louis Rau; she d. 1712/3

Elizabeth[2], b. 26 Sep, bp. 27 Sep 1691, FR Ch, NYC; perhaps m. X Parrain
Marquise[2], b. 16 Feb, bp. 26 Feb 1692/3, FR Ch, NYC
CHILDREN, m/2:
Suzanne[2], b. 25 Aug, bp 12 Sep 1696, NYC
Jeanne[2], b. 4 Apr, bp. 10 Apr 1698, NYC
Paul[2], b. 19 Nov, bp. 22 Nov 1699, NYC; m/1, 1719, Elizabeth Smock – **6 ch**, m/2, 9 Nov 1749, Elizabeth
    Henry
Peter[2], bp. 23 Mar 1703, NJ; m. c. 1730, Jemyme Bries; **issue**
Jantien[2], bp. 1 Aug 1704, NJ
Benjamin[2], bp. Apr 1709, NJ
Catherine[2], b. c. 1710/14, NJ; m. Daniel Sebring (2 Jul 1682, Midwout/Flatbush, NY-a. 19 Nov 1763, wp,
    Hunterdon Co, NJ) s/o Jan Roeloffsen Sebring & Adrianna Polhemus; she may have m. again
Mary[2], bp. 18 May 1715, NJ
Gabriel[2], bp. 3 Mar 1728, NJ

REF: Gabriel's will; WITTMEYER, Alfred V., *Registers of the Births, Marriages & Deaths of the Église
Françoise à la Nouvelle York* (Baltimore, 1968); SEACORD, Morgan H., *Biographical Sketches & Index of the Huguenot
Settlers of New Rochelle 1687-1776* (New Rochelle, 1941); BAIRD, Charles W., *History of the Huguenot Emigration to
America* (Baltimore, 1973).

Le CHEVALLIER/CHEVALIER, Jean/John

s/o Jean & Jeanne (de Creguy) Chevallier, prob. of St. Lô, Normandie, FR
m. Jane X
15 Apr 1687 – naturalized ENG with wife and ch
no evidence that he left ENG
CHILDREN:
Jean/John[2], emig. to America; m. c. 27 Jun 1692 (date of lic), Old Dutch Ch, NY, Marie de la Plaine, d/o
    Nicolas & Susanna (Cresson) de la Plaine; he d. 1720, NYC
    CHILDREN:
    Marie[3], b. 6 Jun, bp. 7 Jul 1693, FR Ch, NYC
    Susanne[3], b. 11 Mar, bp. 3 Apr 1695, FR Ch, NYC; m. John Roome
    Ester[3], b. 18 Feb, bp 28 Feb 1696/7, FR Ch, NYC
    Élisabeth[3], b. 26 Aug, bp. 30 Aug 1703, FR Ch, NYC
    Jeanne[3], bp. 7 Mar 1704/5, FR Ch, NYC
    Rachel[3], b. 16 Feb, bp 22 Feb 1707/8, FR Ch; m/1, Francis Bowes – **issue**, m/2, John Sayre, Sr. as
        his 2nd wife (her dau **Mary**[4] m. a son of John Sayre, Sr.)
Daniel[2]
Peter[2], emig. to America; m/1 Belitje Claerhout, m/2, 3 Apr 1697, Old Dutch Ch, NY, Cornelia Bosch;
    Peter in the Dutch ch recs called Pieter Cavelier
    CHILDREN, m/1 (bap. FR Ch, NYC):
    Catherine[3], bp. 17 Dec 1693
    Peter[3], bp. 1 Jan 1695
    CHILDREN, m/2 (bap. Reformed Dutch Ch, NYC):
    Johannes[3], bp. 24 Jul 1698
    Henricus[3], bp. 21 Feb 1699/00
    Helena[3], bp. 15 Apr 1702
Elizabeth[2]
Judith[2]

REF: Baird, Charles W., *Huguenot Emigration to America*, Vol. II; WITTMEYER, Rev. Alfred V, *Registers of the Église
Françoise à la Nouvelle York, 1688-1804* ; STAPLETON, Rev. A., *Memorials of the Huguenots in America; Proceedings*

of the Huguenot Society of PA, Vol. XXV (1954); GANNON, Peter Steven, editor, *Huguenot Refugees in the Settling of Colonial America* (NYC); *Records of the Reformed Dutch Ch, NYC – Baptisms 1639-1703* Vol. II (1901, NYC).

Le CLERC, Jeanne - see <u>COQUIEL</u>, Jehan de

Le COMPTE, Anthony

b. Picardie, FR

went to ENG and is said to have served in the British Army for 11 yrs.

a. 1655 - went to MD, settled 1st Calvert Co; 7 Feb 1655, he waived his right to 200 acres of land, due him, to Ishamel Wright

1658/9 - he was a patentee of a 75 acre freehold in Calvert Co, known as "Compton"

1659 - rec. patent for 700 acres in Horne Bay in Dorchester Co.; the land was surveyed 13 Aug 1659, for 800 acres, and named " St. Anthonia" or "Antonine"; it was located on the s. side of the Choptank River bet. Castle Haven Pt. and Horn Pt.; Horne Bay was later called "Lecompte Bay" or "Monsieur's Bay" and the creek on the w. side of the Bay is known as "Lecompte Creek" or "Monsieur's Creek"

c. 1659 - returned to FR, where he met his future wife; they went to London to marry

m. 11 Jun 1661, St. Helen's Parish, Bishopsgate, London, Ester Doatloan/Dottando of Dieppe, FR (she m/2, p. 1674, Mark Cordea; she d. p. 1680); marr. rec says Anthony was of the parish of "Macke neere Callis" in FR – *poss.* Machy or Machiel, towns next to each other in Somme, Picardie Dépt, n. of Abbeville & s. of Calais

by 2 Mar 1662/3 - he was back in MD with Ester

22 Feb 1664 - Patent of Denization granted by General Assembly of MD for Anthony, Ester, ch

6 May 1669-71 – he was a Justice of Dorchester Co.

d. a. 25 Oct 1673, wp, Dorchester Co, MD; mentions wife, all 4 sons, dau Hester

CHILDREN (all b. Dorchester Co, MD):

John[2], b. 1662; m. Ann Winsmore, d/o Dr. Robert Winsmore; he d. a. 6 Jun 1705, wp, Dorchester Co.; **7 ch**

Moses[2], m. Mary Skinner (b. 1667-d. p. 1741), d/o Thomas Skinner; he d. a. 15 Mar 1720/1, wp, Dorchester Co.; **11 ch**

Philip[2], d. c. 1705; d. unmarr.

Anthony[2], m. Margaret Beckwith; d. a. 6 Jun 1705, wp, Dorchester Co.; **3 ch**

Esther/Hester[2], m/1, Henry Fox, m/2, c. 1695, William Skinner

Katherine[2], m/1, James Collins, m/2, Thomas Bruff

REF: CULVER, Francis B., "LeCompte Family" in the *Maryland Historical Magazine*, Vol. XII (Baltimore, 1917); MOWBRAY, Calvin & Mary, *Settlers of Dorchester Co, & Their Lands*: JONES, Elias, *History of Dorchester Co, MD* (Baltimore, 1902), *New Revised History of Dorchester Co, MD* (Cambridge, MD, 1966); PAPENFUSE, Edward C., DAY, Alan F., JORDAN, David W. & STIVERSON, Gregory A., *A Biographical Dictionary of the MD Legislature, 1635-1789*, Vol. 2 (Baltimore).

Le COMTE, Michel

27 Feb 1643 - Michel, his wife + 4 ch were members of the Huguenot Ch at Middelburg, Zeeland, HOL

CHILDREN (1st 4, b. Couture, Picardie, FR, according to Middelburg Ch records; Couture is now in Pas-de-Calais, n.e. of Béthune); not certain that all 7 ch were from 1 marriage:

Jacques[2], m/1, 8 Nov 1644, Middelburg, Susanne Massu, m/2, 11 Sep 1652, Middelburg, Marie Petry

Marguerite[2], m/1, 10 May 1650, Middelburg, Philippe Matton, who d., she m/2, 20 Dec 1659, Middelburg, Abraham van Burge

Élisabeth[2], m. 11 Mar 1659, Middelburg, Nöe Carmière

Marie[2], m. 28 Nov 1660, Middelburg, Olivier du Gaure

Jean[2], b. c. 1640, Picardie, FR; m. 12 Dec 1660, Middelburg, Marie Laurens; went to Mannheim, poss to
    ENG; 1674, to America on the *Diamond*; he d. 24 May 1675, NYC
    CHILDREN:
    Moses[3], bp. 13 Mar 1661; m/1, Maria Le Blanck – son **Samuel**[4], bp. 12 May 1680, NY; m/2, c.
        1683/4, Hester LeMaître/LeMaistre, d/o <u>Claude & Hester/Ester (DuBois) Le Maître/Delamater</u>;
        he d. p. Jan 1720/1, prob. Kingston, NY; **9 ch**; name became DeGRAAF which is Dutch for Le
        Comte (the count) – variations are **DeGRAFF/DeGROFF**
        CHILDREN, m/2:
        Maria[4], bp. 19 Jul 1685, Kingston; m. 21 Feb1701/2, Christian Deyo, s/o <u>Pierre & Agatha</u>
            <u>(Nichol) Deyo</u>
        Jan[4], bp. 6 Mar 1687, Kingston; moved to Dutchess Co., by 1712; m. Maria Pekok/
            Peacock, d/o Robert & Elizabeth (Denis) Pekok/Peacock; he d. a. 5 May 1736; **9**
            ch
        Esther[4], bp. 23 Dec 1686, Kingston
        Susanna[4], bp. 7 Jan 1691, NYC; m. Gideon VerVeeler
        Abraham[4], bp. 9 Jun 1695, Kingston; went to Dutchess Co; m. Elizabeth Palmatier; **6 ch**
        Margaret[4], bp. 3 Oct 1697, Kingston; m. Theunis Terpenning
        Boudewyn[4], bp. 17 Dec 1699, Kingston; m. 19 Apr 1722, Rebecca Consalis-Duk (bp. 21
            Sep 1701, Kingston), d/o Manuel & Marytje (Davids) Consalis-Duk of Marble-
            town; d. c. 1771; **issue**
        Jannetje[4], bp. 26 Apr 1702, Kingston; m. Jul 1720, Abraham Freer (b. 31 Oct 1697, Kingston),
            s/o <u>Abram Freer</u> & Aeche Willems; she d. a. 26 Jan 1735/6; **3 daus, 1 son**
        Rachel[4], b. c. 1704; m. Dirck Terpenning
    Marie[3], (twin) bp. 3 Jun 1663; d. young, a. 1675
    Jacqueline[3], (twin) bp. 3 Jun 1663; d. young, a. 1675

Charles[2], m/1, 1 Jan 1661, Middelburg, Jenne Liart who d., m/2, 3 Jun 1668, Middelburg, Marie Maupin

prob. Michel[2]

REF: DeGROFF, Ralph L., *DeGroff*; RIKER, James, *History of Harlem*; letter from H. Boeke, Conservator, Bibliothèque Wallonne, Leiden; WEBER, Carol Harris, *LeComte/DeGraff* (manuscript, Wayne, NJ, 1992); Church Records,
Kingston, NY.

Le CONSEILLE(R)/de CONCHILIER/CONSELYE(A)/CONSELJE, Jean/Jan/John

    b. Normandie, FR; "an adherent of the Reformed religion"
    fled FR, went to Amsterdam then to Leiden, HOL
    Oct 1662 – he, his wife + 5 ch were members of the Pumerland Ch; he was called Jan de Conchilier
    18 Feb 1662/3 - arr NY on *de Pumerlander Kerck* which had left Amsterdam, 12 Oct 1662
    1 Apr 1663 - joined Reformed Dutch Ch of New Amsterdam; went to Bushwyck
    26-30 Sep 1687 – took Oath of Allegiance; liv. Boswijck/Bushwyck; said he'd been in NY for 25 yrs.;
        this *could* have been his son Jean/Jan II – not clear, as Jean I's date of death is not proven and
        no age is listed
    c. 1689 - said to have d. in Bushwick; there is a Conselyea St. in Bushwick – e. of I-278, n. of
        Metropolitan Ave. – becomes Maspeth Ave. – currently considered to be in the Williamsburg area
    CHILDREN (2 of 5):
    Jean/Jan II[2], b. c. 1650; m. c. 1676, Frytje/Phebe Shut(t), (bp. 23 Apr 1651, NY Dutch Ch), d/o Sgt. Jan
        Hermanse Shut(t) & Margaret/Grietje Dirckse, d/o Dirck Volckerszen & <u>Christina de la Vigne</u>; he
        d. c. 1689, Bushwick
        CHILDREN (all baptisms in Dutch Ch, NYC):
        Lysbet[3], bp. 21 May 1677, NY; m. Jacobus Looyse/Luce, s/o Cornelis Loyse; **dau Maria**[4], bp. 21
            Mar 1710, Jamaica Dutch Ch

John[3], b. 1679; m. XX; **4ch**

Magaret/Grietje[3], m/1, 03 Aug 1698, Johannes Van Tilburg (as his 2nd wife), 2 ch – **Jan**[4], bp. 11 Mar 1702, **Catherina**[4], bp 5 Sep 1703; m/2, 23 Feb 1707, Nicholas/Claes Janse Bogert (he d. spring, 1727),10 ch – **Cornelia**[4], bp. 28 Dec 1707-d.young, **Belitje**[4], bp. 5 Dec 1708-d. young, **Cornelia**[4], bp. 2 Apr 1710, **Johannes**[4], bp. 9 Sep 1711 (aunt Annetje was a witness), **Margrietje**[4], bp. 8 Mar 1713, **Elizabeth**[4], bp. 19 Sep 1714, **Belitje**[4], bp. 13 Jun 1716, **Anneke**[4], bp. 20 Apr 1718 (gr mo Frytje, witness), **Cornelia**[4], bp. 2 Apr 1720, **Petrus**[4], bp. Sep 1720, m. Marie Roome

Barbara[3], b. c. 1683

Annaken/Annetje[3], bp. 27 Jun 1686; m. a. 1710, George Willis – at least **Elizabeth**[4], bp. 6 Jul 1712

Pieter/Peter[3], bp. 25 Nov 1688 Dutch Ch, Brooklyn; m/1, c. 1712, Abigail DuPuy*, m/2, c. 1719, Sarah Miller (her bro David was mentioned in Peter's will – Sarah & David prob. ch of William & Geertie (X) Molenaer/Miller); served in the Kings Co. Militia, 1715; Peter d. bet 10 Feb 1768, wd-11 Jan 1770, wp

*said to have been the d/o Nicholas DuPuy as he & his family were on *de Pumerlander Kerck* w/ the Conseille family, but Nicholas did not have a dau Abigail - *poss*. dau of William de Pue

CHILDREN, m/1

Antje[4], b. c. 1713; m. Gabriel Sprong(h)/Sprungh, *poss*. s/o Gabriel Janse Sprong & Geertruy Dirckse

Sarah[4], bp. 23 Oct 1717

CHILDREN, m/2(all named in his will):

John[4], b. c. 1720; m. 8 Jun 1746, Janike Van Cats/Cott; he d. Feb 1749/50, Oyster Bay, LI, NY; son **Peter**[4], bp. 8 Jun 1747, NY Dutch Ch, m. c. 21 Apr 1770 (date of license) Antonette Lequier/Antaletta LaQuir – d/o Isaac Lequier & Anetje Cortelyou (who m. 29 Mar 1710/1, Bushwyck) – rec. says *Consely*, he d. a. 20 Oct 1789, wp, she d. a. 14 Apr 1718, wp; dau **Deborah**[4] who m. John Skillman; Peter named in grfa's will

Barent[4],b. c. 1722; m. c. 22 Dec 1763 (date of license), Catherine Woortman, d/o Teunis Woortman - rec. says Barent *Consely*

Arie[4], bp. 1724; m/1, 4 Nov 1751, Cornelia Molenaer – **1 dau**, m/2, c. 14 Feb 1758 (date of license), Hannah Fine – rec. says *Aray Counsalye*; he d. p. 10 Feb 1768

Elizabeth[4], b. c. 1725; m. 28 Jun 1743, Ref. Dutch Ch, Flatbush, Jacob Bennet; **2 sons, 2 daus**

Barbara/Barratje[4], b. c. 1726; m. her cousin Tunis **or** Johannes Van Cott; she d. p. 22 Jul 1768; **issue**

Sarah[4], c. 1728 NY; m. 4 Aug 1750, Dutch Ch, NY, Abraham Vanderwoort; **4 sons**

Petrus[4], b. c. 1730; m. 29 Aug 1750, Sarah Miller, d/o Willem Miller & Gertruyt (X) Springsteen, widow of Caspar Springsteen (d. 12 Jun 1740), 2 sons bp. Flatbush Dutch Ch - **Jan**[5], bp. 29 Sep 1751, **Willem**[5], bp. 17 Jun 1753

Andries[4], b. c. 1732; m. 3 Mar 1759, Mercy Fine; **2 sons**

John[4], b. c. 1734; m/1, XX, m/2, 28 May 1781, Rachel Carr (d. 1785) when he made his will which mentions son **John**[5] who m. 18 Mar 1792, Phebe Williams, dau **Mary**[5]; marr. rec. say John's dau *Sarah* (misprint?) m. 22 Jul 1792, Jacob Bennett – Mary was the only dau listed – apparently all ch from m/1; he d. a. 29 Nov 1785, wp

William[4], b. c. 1736; m/1, Phoebe Duryea, d/o Peter & Deborah (Blake) Duryea, m/2, 19 Jun 1773, Mercy/Mary Skillman, d/o Joseph & Sarah (Meserole) Skillman

poss. **Pieter**[2], a Pieter and wife Annetje Concelye (*sic*) were witnesses at the 1717 baptism of Sarah[4] above; since Jean II had a son Peter, it would seem logical that Peter was a family name.

REF: Research by STRYKER-RODDA, Harriet; BAIRD, Charles W., *Huguenot Emigration to America*, Vol. I (Baltimore, 1966); BOYER, Carl 3rd , *Ship Passenger Lists, NY & NJ, 1600-1825* (Newhall, CA, 1978); EVANS, Thomas Grier, editor, *Collections of the NYGB Society, Baptisms 1639-1730 in the Reformed Dutch Church, NY* (NY, 1901); VAN COTT, Mrs. Annie Anderson, *The Female Ancestors of Losee Van Cott in America & Europe*

(Salt Lake City, UT, 1937 – unpub.); PROVOST, Andrew J., Jr., *Early Settlers of Bushwick, LI, NY & Their Descendants*, Vol. II (Darien, CT, 1953 – unpub.); KELLY, Arthur C.M., *Flatbush Dutch Church Marriages & Baptisms, 1677-1757* (Rhinebeck, NY, 1997).

Le CONTE, François

     b. 1666, Pont-l'Évêque, (now in Calvados, Basse-Normandie) Normandie, FR, s.e. of Deauville, s/o
          François & Marie (Amon) Le Conte

     1693- to NY; was a Catholic but made a public abjuration of his faith, 7 May 1693, in the FR Ch, NYC

     m. 31 May 1693, FR Ch, Catherine (Lavandier) Marchand, d/o Josias & Ann (Dufour) Lavandier, widow
          of Daniel Marchand; Catherine was from Caen, Normandie

     by Jul 1694 - purchased tract of land in New Rochelle from Guillaume LeConte (from Rouen, *poss.* a
          relation)

     17 Apr 1695 - rec. letter of denization; 18 Apr 1695, was a freeman of NYC

     May 1696 - NYC, signed Oath of Allegiance

     1696 - recorded as an innkeeper on Beaver St. in NYC; was also a victualer

     c. 1701 - opened an inn in New Rochelle; held several civic offices

     d. p. 1724/5, NY

     CHILDREN:

François[2], b., 2 Mar, bp. 4 Mar 1693/4, FR Ch, NYC; prob. d. a. 1710

Josias I [2], b. 20 Feb, bp. 21 Feb 1696/7, FR Ch, NYC; m/1, Huldah Kobel, m/2, c. 1725, New Rochelle,
     Esther Bertine, d/o Pierre & Anne (Borron) Bertine; he d. c. 1745, New Rochelle

     CHILD, m/1:

     Catherine[3], b. c. 1720; m. Isaac Sicard (1715-1759), s/o Jacques & Anne (Terrier) Sicard; she d. p.
          1771; **5 ch**

     CHILDREN, m/2:

     Anne[3], b. 6 Dec, bp. 25 Dec 1726

     Josias II[3], b. c. 1728; m/1, Susanna Bertine, d/o Peter & Catherine (Sicard) Bertine – **3 ch; m/2**, 29
          Oct 1762, Susanna Soulice, d/o John & Mary (X) Soulice – **2 ch; m/3**, Mary Angevine (31
          Dec 1735-9 Jan 1841), d/o John Angevine – **no issue**; he d. 1803

     Judith[3], b. 18 Dec 1729, bp. 25 Jan 1729/30

     Francis[3], b. 14 Feb, bp 7 Apr 1732; m. Judith X; **5 sons, 6 daus**; he d. 20 Feb 1824 New Rochelle

Madeleine[2], b. 15 Mar, bp. 20 Mar 1697/8, FR Ch, NYC; poss. d. by 1710

REF: KNAPP, Lorenzo H., "Notes on the LeConte Families of New Rochelle, NY" in *The Quarterly Bulletin* pub. by the Westchester Co, NY Historical Society; WITTMEYER, Rev. Alfred V., *Registers of the Births, Marriages, and Deaths of the Église Française à la Nouvelle York* (Baltimore, 1968); SEACORD, Morgan H., *Biographical Sketches & Index of the Huguenot Settlers of New Rochelle, 1687-1776* (New Rochelle, 1941).

Le COMTE/Le CONTE, Guillaume

     b. 6 Mar 1659, Rouen, Normandie, FR

     c. 1685, left FR, poss. went to HOL then to ENG, as an officer in William of Orange's army

     c. 1689 – to NY to manage Jacques Lâty/Lâtys' property

     21 Jan 1690 - admitted to the privileges of NY; Elder of the FR Ch, 1691

     p. 1691 - went to New Rochelle where his wife had inherited a lot of property from her father

     m/1, c. 1692, St. Kitts, West Indies, Anne Martha Lâty, d/o Jacques Lâty/Lâtys, sis/o Catherine who m/1,
          Bartholomew Mercier & m/2, David Bonnefoy; Anne Martha d. c. 1701

     m/2, 16 Feb 1701, West Indies, Marguerite de Valleau, d/o Pierre Joyeulx of Martinique

     m/3, 17 May 1703, New Rochelle, Margaret/Marguerite Mahault (c. 1668-15 Sep 1720, NYC)

     15 Feb 1710/11, NYC, Guillaume and Margaret d. yellow fever; his will was proven, 2 Mar 1710/11

     CHILDREN, m/1:

HesterEsther[2], b. c. 1693; m. Ezekiel Bonyot/Boignyot, a mariner of NYC; 4 ch: **Marianne**[3], **Esther**[3], **Ezekiel**[3], **Marie**[3]

Guillaume/Willam[2], b. c. 1694, prob. New Rochelle; m/1, Marianne Mercier (d. c. 1727), d/o Isaac & Susanne (X) Mercier; m/2, p. 1727, Susanne Mercier, Marianne's sis; he was a merchant who held many civic offices; d. a. 13 Dec 1758, wp; will mentions dau Anne, 2 grsons William & Richard Bayley, dau Susanne & her husband William Bayley, dau Mary Anne, wife of John Boyd, dau Anne LeConte

CHILDREN, m/1:

Anne[3], b. 14 Oct, bp. 30 Oct 1723 FR Ch, NYC; m. 14 Apr 1764, Peter Flandreau; 1 son **Adam**[4]

Susanne[3], b. 5 Feb, bp. 8 Feb 1726/7, FR Ch, NYC; m/1, William Bayley – sons **Richard**[4], **William**[4], m/2, John Guerineau - son **John Peter**[4]

CHILD, m/2:

Marianne[3], m. John Boyd – Susanne *prob.* her mother, William *may* have had a 3rd wife; date of Susanne's death is not known, evidently d. by 9 Oct 1758, when Wm. wrote his will

CHILD, m/2:

William[2], b. 3 Dec 1702

CHILD, m/3:

Pierre[2], b. 25 Jul, bp. 10 Dec 1704, NYC; by 1734, settled Monmouth Co, NJ where he was a physician; m/1, 18 Mar 1733, Margaret Pintard (d. 30 Jan 17360), d/o Antoine & Catherine (Stelle) Pintard – **no issue**, m/2, 29 Jan 1737, Valeria Eaton (17 Mar 1715, Shrewsbury, NJ-1788, Orange, NJ), d/o John & Joanna (Wardell) Eaton of Eatontown, NJ; he d. 29 Jan 1768, was bur. Matawan, NJ

CHILDREN, m/2:

William[3], b. 20 Mar, bp 12 Apr 1738; m. 6 May 1782, Elizabeth Lawrence; he d. 4 Nov 1788, Savannah, GA; **no issue**

John Eaton[3], b. 2 Sep 1739

Margaret(ta)[3], b. 11 Jul , bp. 24 Nov 1741; m. Rev. Jedediah Chapman (27 Sep 1741-22 May 1813); she d. 4 Nov 1788; **3 ch**

Thomas[3], b. 23 Jun, bp. 26 Jul 1747; d. 27 Sep 1770; **no issue**

Peter[3], b. 13 Apr, bp. 19 May 1751; d. 23 Nov 1776, GA; **no issue**

Esther[2]

REF: ARMES, William Dallam , editor, *The Autobiography of Joseph LeConte* (NYC, 1903); KNAPP, Lorenzo H., "Notes on the LeConte Families of New Rochelle, NY" in *The Quarterly Bulletin of the Westchester Co. Historical Society*, Vol. 19, #3 &4 (Jul-Oct,1943); WICKES, Stephen, *History of Medicine in NJ* (Newark, NJ, 1879); BAIRD, Charles W., *History of the Huguenot Emigration to America,* Vol. II (Baltimore, 1966).

L'ÉCUYER/L'ESCUYER/L'ESQUIER/LEQU(I)ER, Jean/Jan

b. c. 1635, Paris, FR, prob. s/o Jean or Guillaume L'Écuyer; surname means "squire" poss. signifying a profession, which later became a surname

19 Jun 1658 - arr New Amsterdam, on *DeBruynvis (Brownfish)* – listed as Jan LeQuie from Paris

by 1660 - settled Esopus (Kingston), NY – member of the militia there in 1660, when on Mar 16th, he was enrolled in Ensign Dirck Schmitt's Co. at Esopus

moved to Bushwyck where he petitioned for land, which he rec. 28 Feb 1663; he owned c. 20 *morgens* (40 acres) further north in Newton; became a member of the militia in Bushwick, called *Jan Parys* (John Paris)

m. 11 Nov 1663, New Amsterdam Dutch Reformed Ch, Rachel Dircks (bp. 9 Sep 1641, New Amsterdam Dutch Ch-d. p. 13 Dec 1705), d/o Dirck Volckertszen & Christina de la Vigne; she prob. outlived her husband

3 Apr 1664 – rec. permission to have a mill erected on Mespath Kill (Newton Creek)

1 Oct 1664 - named a magistrate at Bushwick, and elected *schepen* the same yr.

1676 - on assessment roll of Bostwyck/Bushwick; had 28 *morgens* of land

his 1st property of c. 40 acres was on the upper waters of Nespat Kill (Newtown Creek), just s. of what is now Meeker Ave. & Kosciusko Bridge

1686 – he was listed as Ensign "Jan Lequie" on the rolls of Capt. Joost Kockhuyt's foot company of Bushwick

1687 – took Oath of Allegiance, Bushwick

1698 – census Bushwick - 3 men, 2 women, 1 ch

1706 – owned 133 acres; operated a tidal grist mill; surname variously given as Lequea, Laquer, Lescuier, Lequere, Liequie, Leurst, Luquer

d. a. 8 Sep 1713, wp, Bushwick, LI, NY; his will dated 13 Sep 1705, names wife Rachel, eldest son Johannes + other ch Mary, Rachel, Peter, Abraham, Isaac, William

CHILDREN:

Christina[2], bp 14 Dec 1664, NY Dutch Ch; prob. d. a. 1705 – not in father's will

Catherine[2], b. 30 May 1666; m. Augustine Hicks Lawrence; not in father's will

Jan/Johannes[2], b. 31 May 1666, Bushwick; m/1, 1696, prob. Hannah Close (12 Mar 1672-Dec 1728), d/o Thomas & Sarah (X) Close of Greenwich, CT – prob. a son **Gerardus**[3] + 2 more **sons, 2 daus;** *poss.* m/2, Maria X or Cornelia Titis; he d. c. 1735

Maria/Mary[2], b. c. 1668, Bushwick; m. 22 Sep or 11 Oct 1693, Jan/John Se(a)venhoven from Rochelle; **1 son, 1 dau?**

Nicholas[2], b. 27 Apr 1669; m. Sara Middaugh - 1 son **Nicholas**[3]; not in father's will

Guilliam/William[2], bp. 22 Sep 1670, Brooklyn Dutch Ch; m. Catrijntje X; 1 son **John**[3], bp. 7 Aug 1705, m/1, Jannetje X – **issue**, m/2, Elizabeth X; maybe 2 more ch; not in father's will but had rec. £225 from him a. 1705; he d. p. 1754

Ragel/Rachel[2], bp. 14 Dec 1679, Brooklyn Dutch Ch; m. 17 Nov 1694, David Sprong of Flushing (d. 15 May 1739); **3 sons, 4 daus**

Pieter[2], b. c. 1681; m. Annetje de Hart (bp. 6 Jul 1687), d/o Simon Aertszen & Geertie Cornelis; **2 daus**

Abraham[2], b. a. 1685; m. Antoinette Duryea (bp. 11 Dec 1681), d/o Joost & Madeline (Le Fèvre) Duryea; he d. p. 1755; **5 ch**

Isaac[2], b. c. 1685; m. 29 Mar 1711, Flatbush, Anetje Cortelyou (bp. 9 Sep 1698), d/o Cornelis Cortelyou & Neeltje Volkerse - **John**[3], b. c. 1712, m. Janetje Van Cott - their dau **Antonette**[4] m. c. 21 Apr 1770, Peter Conselyea (c. 1747-a. 20 Oct 1789); **Annetje**[3] bp. 14 Oct 1730, Harlingen DRC

REF: BANTA, Theodore M., *Year Book of the Holland Society of NY* (1902); *Collections of the NY Genealogical & Biographical Society, Marriages from 1639 to 1801 in the Reformed Dutch Ch, NY*, Vol. 1 (NY, 1890); BERGEN, Teunis G., *Register of the Early Settlers of Long Island, NY* (Cottonport, 1973); PROVOST, Andrew J., Jr., *LeQuier A Very Early Family at Boswick……* (New Rochelle, NY, Jun 1955); PROVOST, Andrew J., Jr., compiler, *Early Settlers of Bushwick, LI, NY & Their Descendants*, Vol. 3 (New Rochelle, NY, 1955, rev. 1960).

L'ÉGARÉ/LÉGARÉ, François

b. c. 1636, FR; he was a jeweler

m/1, Anne Lançois (d. c. 1686)

1681- fled Lyon, FR, went to ENG; family legend says Solomon was away at college when his family left FR; he went to Geneva, SWI, and then joined his family in Bristol, ENG

16 Nov 1681- François requested denization for himself, wife, 3 sons; 4 Dec 1681, a warrant of denization was entered

8 Mar 1682/3 – the family was naturalized

1686 - François and fam. on the roll of Narragansett settlers

m/2, by 1689, Elizabeth Kirtland (d. Nov 1710)

1 Feb 1691- François & 2 sons were admitted to Colony of MA; had been in Boston since 1687

m/3, Ann X (d. 1722)

d. 30 Dec 1711, Braintree, MA, age 75 Y; his will dated 3 Feb 1710/1, mentions son Solomon liv. in SC but leaves him only 20 shillings as Solomon m. against his father's will and consent & had " deserted his father's service "

CHILDREN, m/1:

François Solomon[2], b. 1673/4, FR; m/1, 1690/93, ENG, poss. Bristol, Sarah X, an English woman (d. 12 Feb1712); 1696 - in Charleston, SC; was known as a silversmith in Charleston; was granted 280 acres in Berkeley Co on 12 Feb 1701; m/2, p. 12 Feb 1712, Keltie (X) Carter (d. 2 Oct 1714), widow of Capt. Zebulon Carter; m/3, Ann (X) Jones (d. Jul, 1736), widow of Thomas Jones; he d. 8 May 1760, leaving an estate appraised at over £18,000; his will written 20 Jan 1756, lists sons Solomon, Daniel, Thomas, dau Mary Ellis, dau Hannah & her 4 daus & was proven 9 Jan 1761
   CHILDREN, m/1:
   Solomon[3], b. 17 Sep 1693, Boston, MA; prob. d. young
   Sarah[3], b. 18 Jul, bp. 28 Jul 1695, Boston; m. Thomas Barksdale; **issue**
   Mary[3], b. c. m/1, Timothy Bellamy - **issue**, m/2, X Ellis; d. a. 1797, SC, age 81
   Solomon[3], b. 1703; m. Mary/Amy (Stock ?); d. a. 22 Nov 1774 (date of obit), SC; he was a tanner & currier; **6 ch**
   Daniel[3], b. 1711; m/1, 21 Jul 1730 Mary Hall, m/2, 4 Mar 1783, Frances Thomas; d. 1791, SC; **issue**
   CHILD, m/2 **?**:
   Hannah[3], m/1, John Miller (d. 1751) – **4 daus**; m/2, XX
   CHILDREN, m/3:
   Thomas[3], b. 1715; m/1, Eleanor Jour, m/2, Mrs. Mary (X) Seabrook; d. 1778
   John[3], m. Akra X; **issue**
   NOTE: one account says Solomon[2] had 9 ch but can only account for 8; also the lists of which children were b. of which wife vary; 3 other daus are listed, not accounted for above – Mrs. X Holmes, Mrs. X Perroneau, Mrs. X Everleigh
Daniel James[2], d. a. 1689
Stephen John[2], not in father's will; prob. d. young
CHILD, m/2:
Daniel[2], b. 1689

REF: SMITH, Linda D., *Gare L'Egaré Some Descendants of the Legarés of SC;* BURTON, E. Milby, *SC Silversmiths, 1690-1860* (Charleston, SC, May 1942) ; *Publications of the Huguenot Society of London,* Vol. XVIII (1911) ; BAIRD, Charles W., *History of the Huguenot Emigration to America*, Vol. I (Baltimore, 1966) ; "Early Generations of the Legaré Family in SC" in *Transactions of the Huguenot Society of SC*, #46 (Charleston, 1941) & #54 (Charleston, 1949) & #71 (Charleston, 1966).

LeFEBRE, Isaac

   b. FR
   m/1, Jannetje Bonderick (b. 1666)
   1683 - to Bushwyck, LI
   m/2, 23 Jun 1689, Wyntje Korten, d/o Myndert Korten of New Utrecht, LI, NY
   d. p. 1689, prob. NY
   CHILD, m/2:
   Myndert[2], bp. 16 Mar 1690, Flatbush, LI; m. 2 Nov 1714, NY, Catherine Van Blarcom; moved to Monmouth Co, NJ
      CHILDREN:
      Abraham[3], bp. 9 Oct 1726, Dutch Reformed Ch, New Brunswick, NJ
      Maria[3], bp. 5 Jan 1729, Dutch Reformed Ch, New Brunswick, NJ

REF: KOEHLER, Sara Morton, *Huguenot Ancestors Represented in the Membership of the Huguenot Society of NJ,* (3rd edition, 1965); Records of the Dutch Reformed Ch, New Brunswick, NJ.

LeFÈVRE

(3 brothers of unknown parents; father *poss.* André, b. 1604)

Abraham[2], b. 1632; massacred, 16 Oct 1685 w/ his wife, 3 sons, 3 daus

    CHILD:

    Isaac[3], b. 26 Mar 1669, Château-Chinon, in the Valley of the Yonne River, Nièvre Dépt, Bourgogne, FR, n.e. of Nevers; 16 Oct 1685 – his family gone, he escaped w/ his life and the family *Bible* (printed in Geneva, 1608), which was concealed in a loaf of bread & is now in the Lancaster Co., PA Historical Society; fled FR to Bavaria, GER; m. c. 1704, Bavaria, Catherine Ferrée/Fuehre, d/o <u>Daniel & Marie (de la Warenbuer) Ferrée</u>; went to NETH & ENG, before arr in America; 31 Dec 1708 – arr. NY on the *Globe* w/ wife, son Abraham + in-laws; went to Esopus/Kingston, NY; 10 Sep 1712 - he & his bro-in-law Daniel Ferrée were granted 2000 acres in what was then Chester Co, PA, now Lancaster Co; d. 1 Oct 1751, Strasburg Twp., Lancaster Co PA

    CHILDREN:

    Abraham[4], b. 9 Apr 1706, FR; m. c. 1728, Elizabeth Ferrée, d/o <u>Daniel & Anna Maria (Leininger) Ferrée Ferrée</u>; he d. c. 20 Nov 1735; **2 sons**

    Philip[3], b. 16 Mar 1710, Kingston, NY; m. c. 1730, Mary Herr, d/o Christian Herr; he d. Sep 1761; he was a gunsmith and blacksmith; **8 ch**

    Daniel[3], b. 29 Mar 1713; m. c. 1736, Mary Catherine Kerr; **8 ch**

    Mary[3], b. 24 Aug 1715; m. 20 Mar 1738, Dr. David Deshler of Wilmington, DE (b. 1711, ENG-d. 1792); d. 25 Feb 1774

    Esther[3], b. 3 May 1717; m. Daniel Harmon; d. a. 1751

    Samuel[3], b. 28 Jun 1719; m. c. 1751, Lydia Ferrée, <u>Daniel & Anna Maria (Leininger) Ferrée</u>; he d. 4 May 1789; he was a miller; **8 ch**

André[2], b. 1636; he and bro Simon emigrated to the *Pfalz*; then to NY, where he d., unmarr.

Simon[2], b. c. 1640, FR, poss. Lorraine; s/o *prob.* André; emigrated with his bro André, from FR to the Palatinate; a. Apr 1665 - in Kingston, NY, when he & André joined the ch; liv. in Hurley; m. c. 1676, Hurley, NY, Elizabeth/Lysbet Deyo, d/o <u>Chrétien & Jeanne (Verbeau) Deyo</u>; Lysbet, m/2, 23 May 1693, <u>Moses Cantine</u>; 26 May 1677 – Simon, Andrew + 10 other Huguenots bought a lg. tract of land, c. 40,000 acres, from the Esopus Indians; the tract extended from the Shawangunk Mts. to the Hudson River and became the New Paltz Tract and the town of New Paltz was founded; 29 Sep 1677, Gov. Edmund Andros granted a royal patent for the land; 1 Sep 1687 - Simon took the Oath of Allegiance; bought land in the New Paltz Tract/Patent; by 1713 his ch. owned 6000 acres in that tract; d. a. 1 Aug 1689, prob. New Paltz, NY

CHILDREN:

Abraham[3], bp. 11 Apr 1679, Kingston; d. a. 1690

Andries[3], bp. 11 May 1679* Kingston, NY; m/1, Cornelia Blanshan, d/o <u>Mattys/Matthew Blanshan & Margrietje Claasse Van Schoonhoven</u>; m/2,? Diana Deyo? – only 1 source mentions a 2nd wife; he d. a. May 1793; *not found in Kingston Ch records but the record for Abraham was – date from a family history

    CHILDREN, m/1:

    Simon[4], bp. 11 Sep 1709; m. 24 Jun 1735, Petronella Hasbrouck (bp. 25 Dec 1710-p. 1774), d/o <u>Joseph Hasbrouck & Elsje Schoonmaker</u>; he d. 7 Sep1743; **2 sons, 2 daus**

    Matheus/Matthew[4], b. 10 Apr, bp. 10 Nov 1710, Kingston; m. 7 Jun 1737, Margaret Bevier (b. 30 Jun 1717), d/o <u>Samuel & Magdalene (Blanshan) Bevier</u>; **6 sons, 6 daus**

    Élisabeth[4], b. 8 Sep , bp. 28 Sep 1712, Kingston; m. 25 Aug 1732, Jonathan DuBois (bp. 31 Dec 1710-27 Jul 1746), s/o <u>Louis & Rachel (Hasbrouck) DuBois</u>; she d. 22 Sep 1749; **issue**

Margrietje/Margaret[4], bp. 13 Mar 1714/5, Kingston; m. 10 Jun 1739, Coenrad Vernooy (bp. 16 Oct 1715), s/o Cornelis Vernooy & Sarah Ten Broeck; **4 sons, 2 daus**

Zara/Sarah[4], bp. 3 Feb 1717; m. 10 Jun 1739, Samuel Bevier (9 Jun 1715-20 Jan 1764), s/o Abraham & Rachel (Vernooy) Bevier; **issue**

Maritjen/Marie[4], bp. 1 Mar 1718/9; m. her 1st cousin Nathaniel[3] LeFèvre, s/o Jan & Catherine (Blanshan) LeFèvre; **3 sons, 2 daus**

Catrina/Catherine[4], bp. 2 Apr 1721, Kingston; m. 7 Oct 1742, 1st cousin Simon[4] DuBois (bp. 28 Jun 1717-1799), s/o Daniel & (Mary LeFèvre) DuBois

Magdalene[4], bp. 11 Oct 1724, Kingston; m. 2 Sep 1747, Johannes Bevier (bp. 9 Sep -27 Oct 1795), s/o Samuel & Magdalene (Blanshan) Bevier; **issue**

Rachel[4], bp. 23 Jun 1728, Kingston; m. 9 Aug 1747, Johannes Bevier (bp. 29 Apr 1724-1797), s/o Abraham & Rachel (Vernooy) Bevier; she d. a. 1764; **issue**

Isaac[3], b. 5 Aug, bp 21 Oct 1683; m/1, Catrina Freer – son **Philip**[3], b. 1 Apr 1711, m/2, 16 May 1718, Marit/Maritjen Freer (b. 5 May, bp. 31 May 1696), sis/o Catrina, daus/o Hugo & Marie (Le Roy) Freer; res. Bontecoe; he d. 31 Oct 1752

CHILDREN:

Isaac[4], bp. 25 Dec 1718; d. young

Petrus/Peter[4], b. 27 Dec 1720, bp. 19 Feb 1720/1; m. 2 Jan 1760, Elizabeth Vernooy (bp. 3 Sep 1733-4 Jun 1807); Rev. War service; he d. 25 Oct 1806; **6 sons, 4 daus**

Johannes[4], b. 10 Oct , bp. 18 Nov 1722; m. 20 May 1751, Sarah Vernooy (bp. 6 Feb 1732-20 Apr 1753); he d. 27 Jun 1771; **1 son, 1 dau**

Daniel[4], b. 8 Nov, bp. 12 Dec 1725, Kingston; m. 1 Mar 1751, Catrina Cantine (b. 13 Mar, bp. 20 Mar 1726-28 Feb 1799), d/o Peter & Elizabeth (Blanchan) Cantine, grdau/o Moïse & Elizabeth (Deyo) Cantine - **3 sons, 3 daus**; he d. 10 Feb 1800 (wd, 4 Sep 1784-wp, 7 May 1800)

Simon[4], bp. 10 Nov 1728, Kingston; d. young

Mary[4], b. 2 Mar, bp. 26 Mar 1732, Kingston; m. 12 Apr 1751, Johannes Hardenbergh, s/o Johannes & Maria (DuBois) Hardenbergh; **issue**

Simon[4], b. 17 Dec, bp. 25 Dec 1738, Kingston

Jan/John[3], bp. 28 Oct 1685; m. 20 Nov 1712, Catherine Blanshan, d/o Mattys Blanjean/Matthew Blanshan & Margrietje Claasse Van Schoonhoven; res. New Paltz Plains; he d. 27 May 1744

CHILDREN:

Margaret [4], bp. 20 Dec 1713, Kingston; d. young

Abraham[4], bp. 25 Mar 1716, Kingston; m. 1742, Maria Bevier (5 Oct 17--- 3 Mar 1795), d/o Samuel & Magdelene (Blanshan) Bevier; he d. 3 Jan 1792; **6 sons, 4 daus**

Elisabeth[4], bp. 2 Oct 1717 New Paltz; d. a. 1744

Nathaniel[4], bp. 2 Nov 1718, Kingston; m. 1st cousin Marie LeFèvre, d/o Andries & Cornelia (Blanshan) LeFèvre; **3 sons, 2 daus**

Andries/Andrew[4], b. 25 Feb, bp. 18 Mar 1721/2, Kingston; m. p. 20 Oct 1745 (date of banns), Rachel DuBois (1 Mar 1727-7 May 1781), d/o Nathaniel & Gertrude (Bruyn) DuBois; he d. 25 May 1812; **2 sons, 6 daus**

Margaret[4], bp. 9 Feb 1724, Kingston; m/1, 6 Dec 1744, Kingston, Jacob Hoffman, m/2, Abner Richards; **5 sons, 4 daus**, not certain by which husband

Mary/Maritje[3], bp 13 Oct 1689; m. 18 Jun 1713, Daniel du Bois (bp. 28 Apr 1684-21 Apr 1752), s/o Isaac & Maria (Hasbrouck) du Bois; res. New Paltz Village; she d. a. 1720; **2 sons, 1 dau**; son **Simon**[4] m. cousin Catrina/Catherine[4] LeFèvre, d/o Andries & Cornelia (Blanchan) LeFèvre

NOTE: There are several **LeFèvre/LeFebre** families and sorting them out isn't always easy! Peter went to New Amsterdam, 1653; brothers Andrew & Simon (b. c. 1640) were in Esopus/Kingston a. 1665, Simon later had extensive property in New Paltz; Hippolytus in Salem, NJ, by 1676; Isaac (b. 1669), nephew/o Andrew and Simon, went to Esopus, c. 1712, to PA; John, b. 1752, s/o John, went to New Rochelle; Isaac

(b. 1667), went to VA; another Isaac went to LI, NY, 1683, had son Myndert. Aside from the stated relationship between Abraham, Andrew, Simon and Isaac, no other connections have been made.

REF: LeFEVRE, Ralph, *History of New Paltz, NY & Its Old Families*, (2nd edition, Baltimore, 1973); LeFevre Family Assoc., compiled by Donald L. Wright, *The New Paltz LeFevres* ; Church records, Kingston; LeFEVRE, Franklin D. & George Newton, co-compilers, *The Pennsylvania LeFevres* (Strasburg, PA, 1952, 3rd edition, 1979); STAPLETON, Rev. A., *Memorials of the Huguenots in America* (Carlisle, PA, 1901); RUPP, I. Daniel, *History of Lancaster County* (Spartanburg, SC, 1984); LeFEVRE, Franklin D. & Paul S., *Historical Tour of the PA Huguenot LeFevre and Ferree Families* (PA, 1994).

Le FÈVRE, Isaac

20 Sep 1700 - arr Jamestown, VA, on the *Peter & Anthony*

m. a. 10 Nov 1701, VA, Madeline Parenteau (d. a. 6 Jun 1720, wp, which names only 3 daus; her bro Isaac was named administrator)

1710-17 - was on the tithing lists of King William Parish

1714- on the *Liste Généralle de Tous les Francois Protestants Réfugies*, he is listed w/ a wife, 1 son, 3 daus

31 Oct 1716 -patented 68 acres on the s. side of the James River, in Henrico Co, although it seems he owned that land a. that date

d. bet 1717-19, VA; no will has been found

CHILDREN:

Judith[2], b. c. 1702; m. bet 1720-23, Pierre Dupuy, s/o Bartholomew & Marie (Gardier) Dupuy; she d. a. 22 Sep 1785, inv, Nottoway Parish, Amelia Co, VA; **4 sons, 6 daus**

Magdelaine[2], b. c. 1706; d. 1724, unmarr.

unnamed son[2], liv. 1714, not in mother's will dated 19 Apr 1720

Elizabeth[2], b. c. 1712; m. by 16 May 1732, Jacques Brian, s/o Jacques Brian; d. bet Jul 1740-44 King William's Parish, Goochland Co, VA; **2 sons, 2 daus**

NOTE: Previously a son Abraham, b. 1713, has been listed. Given the documentation available there is absolutely **no** *proof* that Isaac & Madeline had a son Abraham. The National Librarian at the Huguenot Society of Manakin in VA & Priscilla Harriss Cabell, author of *Twigg & Turff*, a recognized source for information on the French refugees in Manakintown, have no information on a son named Abraham. Since the "unnamed" son has not been named and nothing more is known of him, it is impossible to assume that he was Abraham. The fact that the "unnamed son" was not in his mother's will of 1720, would suggest that he had d. Hard to believe that she would "forget" her only son. He would have been a minor, but certainly, provisions would have been made. Therefore, until that line can be proven, Abraham LeFèvre, as a s/o Isaac above, will not be an acceptable Huguenot ancestor.

REF: ALLEN, Cameron, "Isaac Lefebre (Lefevre) of Manakin Town & His Immediate Descendants" in the *VA Magazine of History & Biography* (1966); CABELL, Priscilla Harris, *Turff & Twigg,* Vol I (Richmond, VA, 1988).

LÉGER, Jacques

b. St. Quentin, FR, prob. the one in Aisne, Picardie

m. Elizabeth Bossu; 1681- she is listed in St. Quentin as a widow of "Jaques Lege Chirugien"; 1683, she was fined for being a Protestant; 29 Jul 1688, she presented her témoignage at the Threadneedle St. Ch in London

d. by 1681, prob. St. Quentin; he was a *chirurgien* (surgeon)

CHILDREN:

Elizabeth[2], b. FR; m. Jacques LeSeurrier

Pierre[2], b. FR; m/1, Marie X (d. p. 1709, SC), m/2, Elizabeth X; c. 1680, went to ENG, where he was a refugee receiving relief from the Threadneedle St. Ch, May 1682 – it was said that he was going to HOL and that he was a "drugget maker" – drugget is a coarse cloth; 1709, went to America; rec. land in Craven Co, SC; d. SC
CHILDREN, m/1:
Sara[3], bp. 29 Apr 1694, Threadneedle St. Ch., London
Peter[3], b. c. 1700; m. 31 Oct 1730, Mary Evans; d. a. 15 Jan 1762, wp; will mentions wife & ch
    Elizabeth[4] (m/1, George Crofts – **4 ch**, m/2, Capt. Henry Lenud), **Peter**[4], **Love**[4] who m. John
    Ward & their 2 sons **John Peter**[5] & **William**[5]

REF: SYMONDS, F.C., "Leger, Lenud, Theus Campbell Families" in *William & Mary Quarterly*, Vol. XIV, #4 (Oct 1934); SYMONDS, Rev. Francis Campbell, *The Descendants of 4 Members of the 1st Colony of VA in 1609* (1964); info from the Huguenot Society of London.

LEGEREAU, Eugénie, see STELLE, Poncet

Le GRAND, Pierre

b. c. 1662, Normandie, FR
[c. 1685 - left Bohain, now Bohain-en-Vermandois, Aisne, Picardie, FR, n.e. St. Quentin] This location needs proof.– however, this area would have been very close to the Normandie region at that time]
left FR - 1st went HOL, then ENG
m. Judith Vreil/Vryl (c. 1670-1719) who m/2,, a. 1716, VA, Moses Levereau
Sep 1700 - arr Jamestown, on the *Peter & Anthony*; settled Manakintown; list of passenger shows Pierre,
    wife + 5 ch (1 of the ch, b. HOL, must have already d.)
4 Feb1700/1 - listed as having a wife + 6 ch
d. a. 1710, Henrico Co, VA
CHILDREN:
Anne[2], bp. 13 Apr 1687, The Hague, HOL; prob. d. young
Jacques/James[2], bp. 20 Jun 1688, The Hague; m. Elizabeth X; he d. a. 3 Sep 1716, wp, Henrico Co, VA; no ch
    mentioned in will, names his wife and bro John; says that he was "late of La Haye (The Hague) in
    HOL" & was in King William Parish, 20 Aug 1716; his land split evenly bet John and Elizabeth
Isaac[2], bp. 9 Nov 1690, The Hague; prob. d. young
Daniel[2], bp. 20 Dec 1691, The Hague; d. bef his 16th bday
Jean/John[2], bp. 5 Dec 1694, The Hague; m. c. 1721, Catherine Fleming (c. 1701-p. 1731); he d. a. 18 May
    1731, intestate; Peter LeGrand, Sr. was appt. guardian for Jane and Judith
    CHILDREN:
    Jane Magdalene[3], b. c. 1722
    Judith[3], b. c. 1724
    Elizabeth[3], b. 25 Jul, bp. 19 Oct 1729; prob. d. young as a guardian was not appt. for her
Jean Pierre/John Peter[2], bp. 2 Jun 1697, The Hague; m. c. 1720, Jane Magdalen Michaux (b. 24 Oct
    1697, bp. 3 Jan 1697/8,* HOL-c. 1750), d/o Abraham & Susanne (Rochet) Michaux; he d. a. 19 Jul
    1737, wp, Goochland Co, VA; will names his son Abraham, Richard & Susanna Cardwell, son John
    *some differences in various sources
    CHILDREN:
    John[3], b. c. 1722; m. c. 1754, Elizabeth Chandler (c. 1736-p. 1786), d/o William & Judith (X)
        Chandler; he d. a. 1 Jun 1784, Halifax Co, VA; **7 ch**; she m/2, 20 Oct 1786, Halifax Co.,
        Josiah Walker Cathiel
    Abraham[3], b. c. 1724, Goochland Co, VA; m. c. 1752, Agatha/Agnes Nichols (c. 1732-a. 29 Dec
        1803), d/o John & Mary (X) Nichols; he d. a. 15 Sep 1800, Pittsylvania Co, VA, intestate; **9 ch**

Susanna[3], b. c. 1726; m/1, Richard Cardwell (5 Apr 1719-8 Mar 1780)– **issue**, m/2, William
    Owen (1776-1856), s/o Col. Brackett & Elizabeth (McGehee) Owen; she d. 30 May 1813

Peter[3], b. 1728; m/1, Mary Woodson, m/2, Lucy Nash, d. o Col. John Nash, Sr.; d. Jan 1813,
    Fayette Co, KY

Alexander[3], b. 25 Dec 1732; m. 23 Nov 1757, Lucy Walker (15 Dec 1742-15 Oct 1825), d/o
    William & Judith (Baker) Walker; he d. 25 Jan 1822, Pr. Edward Co, VA; **5 ch**

James[3], b. c. 1734; m. 1763, Elizabeth Wade, d/o Robert Wade or d/o Hampton & Jane (Ellis)
    Wade; he d. 15 Jul 1800, Montgomery Co, NC; **9 ch**

REF: *The Huguenot,* Publication #24 (1969-71), pp. 139 ff. #29 (1979-81), p. 113; Baptismal records from
The Hague; BROCK, R. A., *Huguenot Emigration to VA* (Baltimore, 1979); CABELL, Priscilla Harris, *Turff & Twigg,*
Vol. I (Richmond, VA, 1988); LeGRAND, Louis Everett, *Pierre LeGrand in VA 1700* (Baltimore, 1995).

Le/La GROVE/Le GROU, Nicholas

b. c. 1645, FR, of Huguenot parents; some sources say b. 1654, but if that were so, he would have been very
    young to emigrated to MA on his own as there is no documentation that he emigrated w/ his parents
family settled Isle of Jersey
a. 1668 - to Salem/Beverly, MA; he signed a petition in Oct 1668, so must have been of age
m. 16 May 1671, Essex Co, MA, Hannah Sallows (b. 9 Sep 1654), d/o Robert & Freeborn (Woolfe)
    Sallows; she d. 1718, Beverly, MA
8 Mar 1682 - naturalized as a FR Protestant by Royal Letters Patent, Westminster, ENG; he was a seaman
d. a. 11 Feb 1702/3, Beverly
CHILDREN:
Susannah[2], b. 8 May , bp. 29 Sep 1672, Beverly, MA; m. 16 Jul 1694, Benjamin Patch (d. 1730);
    she d. 2 Nov 1733; **8 ch**
Nicholas[2], bp. 19 Apr 1674, Beverly; d. bet 11 Sep 1726-22 Jan 1728; **no issue**
Hannah[2], bp. 10 Sep 1676 ,Beverly; m. 12 Apr 1698, Robert Moulton, s/o Robert & Mary (Cook)
    Moulton; she d. p. 1756; **issue**
Peter[2], bp. 14 Sep 1679, Beverly; m/1, 26 Jan 1702/3, Hannah Winter, d/o Edward & Deborah (Golt)
    Winter of Salem – **2 ch,** m/2, 1708, Abigail X who d. bet. 17 Nov 1717-16 Mar 1718 – **4 ch**;
    m/3, 7 Jan 1718/9, Hannah (Woodbury) Stone (28 Mar 1680-Jan, 1747), d/o William & Hannah
    (Haskell) Woodbury & widow of David or Daniel Stone who had d. 20 Jan 1713 – **4 ch**; m/4, 8 Oct
    1747, widow Mary (X) Maxfield/Maxwell who d. bet Apr & Dec 1764; he was a mariner
John[2], b. 24 Sep 1681, Beverly; aka **LAGRO**
Freeborn[2], b. 11 Feb 1683, Beverly; aka **LARGOE**; liv. 7 Feb 1703/4

REF: AGNEW, Rev. David C.A., *Protestant Exiles from FR* (London, 1874); TURK, Marion G., *The Quitet Adventurers in America;* GROVES, William T., *A History & Genealogy of the Groves Family in America* (Ann Arbor, MI,
1915); Vital records, Salem., Beverly.

Le JAU, François/Francis (Rev.)

b. c. 1665 Angers, Maine-et-Loire, Pays de la Loire, FR, n.e. of Nantes
c. 1685- to ENG
graduate of Trinity College, Dublin, IRE; 1693, earned M.A. , 1696, a B.D.; ordained Ch of ENG; 1700,
    rec. a D.D.; he was named a canon in St. Paul's Cathedral, which was a great honor, but decided to go
    to the West Indies for his health
    m/1, 13 Apr 1691, Dublin, Jeanne Antoinette/Jane Antonia Huguenin (c. 1672-25 Dec 1700, St.
    Christopher, West Indies), bur. Churchyard of Christ Church, Nicola Town Parish
m/2, 30 Dec 1701, Westminster, Elizabeth Harrison (d. 18 Sep 1729, bur. St. John's Churchyard, SC)
18 Oct 1706 - arr Charleston as a missionary for the Society of the Propagation of the Gospel

d. 10 or 17 Sep 1717; bur. under the communion table in St. James Ch, Goose Creek, SC (n. of Charleston)

CHILDREN, m/1:

Francis Thomas[2], b. 1 Oct 1692, Dublin; d. 14 Jul 1693, bur. FR Churchyard, Dublin

Dorothy[2], b. 24 Dec 1693; d. 30 Dec 1693, bur. St. Andrew's (Round Church) Parish Churchyard, Dublin

Francis[2], b. 25 Aug 1695, Dublin, bp. the next week, St. Bride's Parish; m. Mary Ashby, d/o John Ashby ; was a planter in St. John's Parish, Berkeley Co, SC; d. a. 1 Dec 1758, wp; son **Francis**[3], d. age 34, unmarr; dau **Ann**[3], m. Daniel Huger, s/o Daniel & Marguerite (Perdriau) Huger, as his 4th wife – **3 ch**, only 1 of whom, Francis[4] marr & had ch; dau **Mary**[3], m/1, Richard Downes – sons d. young, 1 dau Elizabeth[4] m. Rev. Thomas Frost & had ch, m/2, John Parry

Catherine[2], b. 23 Apr 1697, Dublin; bp. St. Peter's Parish

CHILDREN, m/2:

Elizabeth[2], b. 14 Sep 1703, on the *Cumberland*, Bay Bulls, Newfoundland, s. of St. John's, on the coast; bp. the next week; m. Thomas Ashby, s/o John Ashby

George[2], b. 21 Jul 1705, St. Bartholomew Parish; d. 31 Aug 1706, London, bur. St. Sephulchre's Church-yard, London

REF: "Some Descendants of the Reverend Francis LeJau " *Huguenot Society of SC*, Vol. 34 (1929); KLINGBERG, Frank J., editor, *The Carolina Chronicle of Dr. Francis LeJau, 1706-1717* (CA, 1956).

Le MAÎTRE/Le MASTER, Abraham

b. c. 1638/9, Derval Parish, Diocese of Nantes, FR, s/o Jean & Sarah (X) Le Maître; Abraham and Claude below are *prob.* related but that has not been proven; Derval is in Loire Atlantique Dépt, Pays de la Loire, as is Nantes – Derval is n. of Nantes; *however,* Abraham swore on 27 Jun 1720, Charles Co, MD, that he was born in " the Old Jerseys in the Parish of St. Maries" which means St. Mary's Parish on the Isle of Jersey, off the coast of Normandie, FR

a. 1668 - to MD

m. prob Elizabeth X (d. c. 1727)

1700 - settled Charles Co. where he patented LeMaster's Delight, Betty's Delight + a number of other tracts

d. 6 Dec 1722, Charles Co, MD; 20 Dec 1722, wp; will mentions wife (prob. Eliz.), sons Richard, John Isaac, daus Sarah, Mary, Ann

CHILDREN:

Sarah[2], b. c. 1660; m. John Tennison poss. as his 2nd wife –it was his dau Christian who m/1, John Cooksey – **issue, &** m/2, John LeMaster (below) which would mean that she was the dau of John and a 1st wife, thus no issue w/ Sarah

Mary[2], b. c. 1663; m. Robert Barron (d. a. 1 Oct 1717, wp)

Richard[2], b. c. 1670 m. Martha Dennis (d. 1713/23); he d. p. 1735, prob. Charles Co, MD; he was a carpenter; **6 sons, 1 dau**

Issac[2], b. c. 1677; prob. m. XX; d. c. 1740, Charles Co, MD

Anne[2], b. 24 Apr 1681; m. Stephen Nöe; she is simply *Ann* in father's will while her 2 sisters were listed by their married names but the will does say she can dwell on some of her father's land & have a milk cow" during her husband's absence"

John[2], b. 1682 ; m/1, XX – **1 dau Eleanor**[3] who m. Cleoborn Semmes; m/2, stepniece Christian (Tennison) Cooksey, d/o John & X Tennison, widow John Cooksey; he d. c. 1748; 3 sons, 1 dau in his will but sons named Cooksey, dau Priscilla Barron so are the ch of Christian & 1st husband John Cooksey

REF: *Maryland Genealogical Bulletin*, Vol. 8, #32 (Oct, 1937); LEMASTER, Howard Marshall & HERBERGER, Margaret, *LeMasters, USA 1639-1965* (1965) ; GANNON, Peter Steven, editor, *Huguenot Refugees in the Settling of Colonial America* (NYC).

Le MAÎTRE/ Le MAISTRE/ DELAMATER, Claude/Glaude

b. c. 1613, Richebourg, Artois, FR, in present day Nord Dépt., then in Walloon Flanders (said to be 50 in 1663); s/o Guillaume le Maistre/Maître

m/1, p. 29 Oct 1638 (date of mar. contract), Canterbury, ENG, Louise Quennell. d/o Anthoine Quennell & Marguerite le Maistre (not clear if le Maistre was her maiden name or the name of her current husband); Louise d. c. 1646/7, prob. Leiden, HOL

m/2, 19 May 1648, Middelburg, HOL; (15 Apr 1648, date of int., Leiden) Jeanne de Lannoy, widow of Jean de Clercq; Jeanne prob. d. a. 15 Oct 1651

1652 - a widower liv in the *Looiersdwarsstraat* (Tanners' cross-street), Amsterdam; grosgrain worker

m/3, 24 Apr 1652, FR Walloon Ch, Amsterdam, HOL (6 Apr 1652, date of int), Esther/Hester Du Bois, bp. 9 Oct 1625, Canterbury, ENG, d/o Pierre & Catherine (Clarisse) Du Bois; she m/2, 6 Nov 1687, Jan Tibout; she d. 1710

by Mar 1653 - to New Amsterdam

c. 1653 - in Flatbush; worked as a carpenter

31 Jul 1662 - sold Flatbush property and went to Harlem where he had a garden lot on the Great Way aka Church Lane, w. of the Harlem River, bet. 2nd and 3rd Avenues

15 Apr 1670 - Claude & Hester made a joint will

d. c. 1683, Harlem, NY

CHILDREN, m/1:

Susanne[2], bp. 28 Feb 1640/1, Walloon Ch, Canterbury, ENG; d. 29 Mar 1642, Canterbury

Mary[2], bp. 11 May 1643, Walloon Ch, Canterbury, ENG; d. 10 Sep 1643, Canterbury

Abraham[2], bp. 6 May 1646, Walloon Ch, Leiden, HOL; no further info

CHILDREN, m/3, all b. Flatbush:

Johannes/Jan[2], bp. 9 Mar 1653; m. 11 Aug 1678, NYC, Ruth Waldron, d/o Resolved Waldron; he d. New Harlem, p. 25 Oct 1702, wd-a. 9 Sep 1703, wp; **9 ch**; Ruth m/2, 1703, Henry Bogert of Marbletown; she d. 1707, New Harlem

Abraham[2], b. 1656; m/1, 18 Jun 1682, Kingston, NY, Celeste/Selitje Vernoy, bp. 22 Mar 1665, Kingston, d/o Cornelius Vernoy; **4 ch**; m/2, c. 1693, Elsje Tappan, d/o Jurian Tappan, widow of Hillebrant Lechier; he d. 20 Nov 1734; **6 ch**

Isaac[2], b. c. 1658; m. 3 Dec 1681, Albany, Cornelia Evertse Van Ness; **9 ch**

Susanna[2], b. c. 1660; m. 24 Feb 1673, Arent Harmanse Bussing; **3 ch**

Esther/Hester[2], b. 1662; m. Moses La Comte/Le Count/de Graaf of Kingston, NY; **4 ch**

Jacobus[2], b. 1665; m. 23 Sep 1688, Kingston, Geertje Ysselsteyn (b. 1666), d/o Martin Cornelisz Ysselsteyn/Esselsteyn of Claverack; he d. 1741; **10 ch**

REF: RIKER, James, *Harlem, Its Origins & Early Annals* (NY,1881) (NY,1904); RIKER, David M., *Genealogical & Biographical Directory to Persons in New Netherland, 1613-1674*, Vol. 1 (1999); *NYGBR*, "New Light on the European Origins of the Delamater & Du Bois Families" by Douglas Richardson, Vol. 124, #1 (Jan 1993), #4 (Oct 1993); RIKER, James, *History of Harlem, Its Origins*; DELAMATER, Philip D., *Connecting with Our Past: A Genealogy of Descendants of Claude Le Maître*, Vol I (2002).

Le MERCIER, Jean, dit Coquiel – see COQUIEL de

Le MOINE/Le MOYNE, Moïse/Moses

b. c. 1650, *poss.* from Normandie

m. c. 1680, Jeanne Drommeau

c. 1687 – to America; 1 of the 1st settlers at Narragansett, RI

d. c. 1720, East Greenwich, RI

CHILDREN:

Moyse[2], bp. 3 Oct 1686, Threadneedle St. Ch, London; d. c. 1750, E. Greenwich, RI

Françoise[2], bp. 4 Mar 1687/8, FR Ch, Narragansett, RI; d. c. 1750, E. Greenwich, RI

Peter[2], bp. 29 Sep 1689, FR Ch, Narragansett; m/1, 6 May 1714, Mary Tillinghast (1694-24 Feb 1726/7). d/o Pardon & Mary (Keech) Tillinghast; m/2, 14 Feb 1728/9, Mercy Tillinghast (1704-1761), sis/o Mary; **total of 8 ch**; he was an Ensign in the 1st Regt. of the Militia in Aug 1722, by Aug 1747, he was a Colonel; he d. 9 Sep 1754, Providence, RI; surname **MAWNEY**

Mary[2], b. c. 1699, E. Greenwich, RI; m. 8 May 1718, John Smith; d. c. 1760, NY

NOTE: Name later was corrupted to MONEY, MAWNEY.

REF: BEAMAN, Alden G., editor, *RI Genealogical Register*, Vol. 11 (Princeton, MA, 1988); BAIRD, Charles W., *History of the Huguenot Emigration to America*, Vol. I; DeFOREST, L. Effingham, *Records of the FR Ch at Narragansett, 1686-1691*(NYC); ARNOLD, James N., *Vital Records of RI, 1636-1850* (Providence, RI, 1891).

Le PLAT/LEPPLA, Daniel

b. 1600?, FR

m. XX

he and wife said to be "of Sedan" (Ardennes Dépt, Champagne-Ardenne), FR

1668, FR Ch, Otterberg, GER, were godparents to Jean Hubert; they liv at Heiligenmoschel, n. of Otterberg (n. of Kaiserlautern) in the *Pfalz*

CHILD:

Jean Jacques Henri/Johann Jacob Heinrich[2], in Heiligenmoschel, by 1697; m/1, c. 1665/70, Countess X von Fölkling, d/o Johann Hermann von Fölkling, m/2, Anna Margarete X (d. 14 Feb 1732, Heiligenmoschel)

CHILD, m/1:

Jacob[2]

CHILDREN, m/2:

Jean/Johan Daniel[2], originator of the "miller" branch of the family; b. 11 Dec 1678, Heiligenmoschel, d. 27 Jun 1746, Heiligenmoschel; m. Anna Katharina X (c.1689-22 Oct 1752)

CHILD:

Anna Katherine[3], b. 1728, m. 17 Jan 1754, Heiligenmoschel, Philipp Lutz - **issue**

Jean Pierre[2], originator of the "farmer" branch centered in Heiligenmoschel; b. 23 Oct 1681, prob. Heiligenmoschel; m. Anna Barbara X (c. 1681-25 Aug 1749, Heiligenmoschel); he d. 23 Aug 1746

CHILD:

Johann/Hans Georg[3], b. c. 1722, Heiligenmoschel, m. Anna Maria Fender (c. 1737, Roth [n.w. of Kaiserlautern]- 3 Jun 1797, Heiligenmoschel), he d. 22 May 1796 - **issue**

REF: GROH, Raymond Philip, Jr., *The Heritage of the Humboldt Parkway Grohs* (Mount Clemens, MI, Jul 1982, unpub.); German research by Wilhelm Beuleke, Roland Paul & Sigfried Gauch.

Le ROUX/La RUE/LAREW

(*prob.* 2 bros of unknown parents)

Antoine[2], b. c. 1610, FR, prob. Calais area

m/1, Jeanne Joquen?

m/2, 6 May 1655, FR Reformed Ch, Mannheim, GER, Marie (Jery) Fremeau, widow of Jean Fremeau of Armentières, FR; the phrase "widower of La Leu in the Low Country" *may* refer to his 1st wife's surname or his origin; in 1665 he was listed as being of the Pays de l'Alloeu which was in the area of Valenciennes, FR, then in Artois, now Nord Dépt, Pas de Calais

m/3, 7 May 1665, Mannheim, Catherine (Olivier) Rénard, widow of Richard Rénard; she m/2, 19 Mar 1667, François de France

d. bet 1665-67, Mannheim, prob. during the outbreak of plague which decimated the population of Mannheim during those 2 yrs.

CHILDREN, m/l:

Abraham[3]; b. c. 1637; m. 6 Dec 1658, FR Reformed Ch, Mannheim, Jeanne (Du Four) Fremor/Fremeau/Fourmeau, d/o Jean Du Four, widow of Isaac Fremor; Abraham d. c. 1666, Mannheim, during "The Black Death"; she m/2, 17 Apr 1667, Louis de France

CHILDREN:

Jeanne[4], b. 19 Oct, bp. 28 Oct 1660, Mannheim

Abraham[4], b. 1 Mar, bp. 6 Mar 1664, Mannheim; to America on the *de Trouw*, which arr NY, 1678; m/1, c. 1687, Magdalen Gille/Usillie, d/o David & Marie (Casier) Usillie, m/2, c. 1690, Alche/Olive (Gerritsen) Cresson, widow of Joshua Cresson (1658-a. 1690), s/o Pierre & Rachel (Clausée) Cresson; liv. Staten Island, NY; d. a. 14 Jun 1712, adm, Hunterdon Co, NJ

CHILD, m/1 (descendants settled VA, KY):

Peter[5], bp. 25 Mar 1688, Dutch Ch, Kingston, NY; m. Elizabeth Cresson (d/o his stepmo, grd/o Pierre & Rachel (Clausée) Cresson; went to Bucks Co, PA; he d. a. 7 May 1783, wp, Frederick Co, VA; 5 ch – **Abraham**[6], **Isaac**[6], b. 1712, NJ, m. Phebe Carman, went to Frederick Co, VA (had **10 ch**[7]), **Jacob**[6], **Elizabeth**[6], m. X Pierceson, **Anna**[6], m. X Suber

CHILDREN, m/2 (descendants settled, PA, OH, IN, MI):

Abraham[5], b. 1693; m. Harmekie X; d. a. 15 Feb 1749, wp, Hopewell Twp, NJ; **7 ch**

Daniel[5], b. 1697; m. Ann Praul; d. 1 Feb 1795, Middletown Twp, Bucks Co, PA; **5 ch**

David[5], d. a. 18 Feb 1732, adm, Hopewell Twp, NJ

Isaac[5], m. 6 Oct 1743, Abington, PA, Rebeckah Vansant, d/o Jacobus Vansant; he d. c. 1760, Bensalem, PA; **4 ch**

Pierre[2], "of Calais", according to marr. rec. of son Pierre[2]; Pierre[1] was *prob.* bro/o Antoine[1]; there is a definite family connection; Pierre's wife poss. Jannetje X

CHILD:

Pierre[3], m. 23 Jan 1656, FR Ch, Mannheim, GER, Jehanne Guering/Jeanne Guérin of Artois; Pierre, w/ wife & ch went to America w/ *cousin* Abraham[3]; Pierre d. during the voyage; son Jacques must have come earlier

CHILDREN:

Jacques[4], b. 2 Dec, bp. 7 Dec 1656, Mannheim; 25 Aug 1673, took the Oath of Allegiance in New Harlem; 7 Nov 1673, was appt. one of the soldiers to serve on the night watch in New Harlem; 1677, he was a member of the Reformed Dutch Ch in NY; c. 1678, went w/ David Demarest to NJ, where they established a FR colony on what was called the "The French Patent", nr. Hackensack, NJ; 1680, to Bergen, NJ; helped found the FR Ch at the new FR settlement in Hackensack; m. 2 Jan 1681, Bergen Dutch Reformed Ch of Hackensack ,Wybregh Hendricks (bp. 15 Dec 1662, NYC), d/o Hendrick Teunisz Helling & Grietie Samuels; 5 Apr 1696, he presented a letter to the Dutch Ref. Ch of Hackensack where his 6 youngest ch were bap.; he d. a. 2 Sep 1730, wp; he left a lg. estate, incl 600 acres in Ramapo, NJ; in his will he calls himself a yeoman and uses the name James **LAROE**; will names wife, sons Hendrick, Samuel, Abraham, grdau Elizabeth, daus Jannecke, Mary, Ann, Margrit; ch of daus Susanna & Angenietie

CHILDREN:

Jannetie[5], b. Bergen; m. 27 Feb 1703, Hackensack, Lucas Kierstede; she d. p.

1721; **no issue**

Pieter[5], m. 23 Sep 1710, Hackensack, Luyda Remeyn; he d. a. 19 Sep 1714; dau **Elizabeth**[5]

Antie[5], b. Hackensack; m. 12 Aug 1710, Hackensack, Andries Van Norden as his 2nd wife

Maria[5], b. Hackensack; m. 17 Apr 1714, Albert Cornel

Margaret[5], in father's will, 1728; no further record

Hendrick[5], m. 13 Nov 1715, Tappan, NJ, Marritie Lammerse Smidt, d/o Lambert Andreaesen Smidt; he d. Ramapo, a. 13 Jun 1760, wp; at least **2 sons**

Samuel[5], b. 7 Mar, bp. 5 Apr 1695, Hackensack; m. 16 May 1719, Tappan, Catrynt je Smidt; he d. a. 9 Oct 1761, wp

Rachel[5], bp. 10 Mar 1698, Hackensack; not in father's will,1728; prob. d. young

Angentie[5], bp. 12 Jun 1699, Hackensack; m. 24 May 1718, Hackensack, Isaac Van Deusen, Jr.; she d. a. 14 Dec 1723, when Isaac m/2; **2 ch**

Susanna[5], bp. 11 May 1701, Hackensack; m. 19 Apr 1718, Hackensack, Willem Albertse; at least **3 ch**

Abraham[5], bp. 18 Mar 1705; m. 10 Dec 1736, Annetje Berdan (bp. 1 Jun 1718, Hackensack)

Johannes[5], bp. 4 Jul 1708; not in father's will of 1728; prob. d. young

Susanne[4], b. 9 Oct, bp. 17 Oct 1658, Mannheim; m/1, 20 May 1683, Bergen Dutch Ref Ch, Thomas Hendricks, m/2, c. 1685, Jan Allée, s/o Nicolas Allée

Marie[4], b. 11 Aug, bp. 24 Aug 1662, Mannheim

Anne[4], b. 17 Aug, bp. 21 Aug 1664, Mannheim

poss. **David**[4]

REF: Church Records, Mannheim, GER; McClure, Daniel E., Jr. *Two Centuries in Elizabethtown & Hardin Co, KY* (1979); MATHER, Otis M., *Six Generations of LaRues & Allied Families* (Hodgenville, KY, 1921); HOES, Roswell Randall, *Baptismal & Marriage Registers of the Old Dutch Ch of Kingston, NY* (NY, 1891); *History of Bucks Co, PA;* LAREW, Dr. Karl, *Garret Larew, Civil War Soldier (1975);* POLLER, Oskar, *Zur Geschichte der Stadt Ludwigshafen am Rhein, Friesenheimer Bürgerbuch die Einwohner von Friesenheim, 1584-1814;* CAMPINE, E.M., *Jacques Le Roux The French Huguenot & Some of His Descendants Le Roux, LaRoe, LaRue* (Minneapolis, 1939); *Records of the Reformed Dutch Churches of Hackensack & Schraalenburgh, NJ,* Part I (1891); NELSON, William, *Documents Relating to the Colonial History of the State of NJ,* Vol. XXII – *Marriage Records, 1665-1800* (Patterson, NJ, 1900) & Vol. XXIII – *Calendar of NJ Wills, 1670-1730,* Vol. 1 (Patterson, NJ, 1901); "Records of the Reformed Dutch Ch in NY" in *NYGBR,* Vol. VI (NYC, 1875).

Le ROY, Ant(h)oine

b. c. 1535, prob. Poitiers, e. of La Rochelle; family established there for centuries
a judge & man of prominence
d. FR
CHILD:
?Jacques[2] m. Renée Le Mercier
    CHILD:
    François[3], m. 1 Dec 1577, La Rochelle, Marie Fauguion; d. p. 18 Oct 1614, when he was a sponsor at his grson David's baptism
    CHILDREN(bp. La Rochelle):
    François[4], bp. 1578; m. a. 24 Mar 1606, Marie Gratel/Grutel; *procureur* (public attorney); son **Francois**[5], bp. 24 Mar 1606, La Rochelle
    Jacques[4], bp. 28 Nov 1579; **Esther**[4], bp. 1580; **Louis**[4], bp. 1 Apr 1583; **Siméon**[4], bp. 25 Feb 1587; **Jean**[4], bp. 2 Mar 1588-d. a. 1639; **Ezekiel**[4], bp. 18 Mar 1590
    David[4], bp. 10 Jul 1585; m. a. 25 Feb 1611, Esther Thomas (c. 1592-26 Apr 1668, La Rochelle); he was a lawyer in *Parlement* of La Rochelle; he d. a. 11 Jan 1619

CHILDREN:

François[5], b/bp. 25 Feb 1611, La Rochelle; m. c. 26 Apr 1639 (date of contract), La Rochelle, Esther Mocquay, d/o Élie & Marie (de la Coste) Mocquay; he d. 25 Feb 1675; **3 sons, 4 daus**, incl. **Esther**[6] (b. 9 Sep, bp. 10 Nov 1652, La Rochelle - d. 14 Jun 1710, Newport, RI) who m. 20 Sep 1673, La Rochelle, Gabriel Bernon (5 Apr 1644, La Rochelle-1 Feb 1735/6, Providence, RI), s/o André & Suzanne (Guillemard) Bernon

David[4], b/bp. 28 Oct 1614, La Rochelle; m. XX; d. 13 June 1660, La Rochelle

Étienne[4], b/bp. 10 Nov 1615, La Rochelle; m. XX; d. p. 8 Sep 1677

Gaspard[4], b. 26 Dec 1617, bp. 2 Jan 1617/8, La Rochelle, FR; m. 26 Apr 1648, La Rochelle, Marie Sanceau (b. 1625-p. 25 Sep 1680), d/o Pierre & Marie (Cholet) Sanceau – her bro Pierre m. Eve Bernon; he d. p. 17 May 1679; **8 ch** – at least 2 daus went to America

CHILDREN:

Marie[5], b. 12 Jun, bp. 20 Jun 1649, La Rochelle; m. 19 Jun 1670, La Rochelle, Jean DuBois/DuBroix; she abjured the Protestant faith 15 Oct 1685, La Rochelle

Marie Magdeleine[5], b. 19 Jun, bp. 26 Jun 1650, La Rochelle; she abjured 15 Oct Oct 1685, La Rochelle; she was rec. in Rotterdam from the English Ch in Amsterdam, 22 Feb 1705, so seems to have reverted to Protestantism

Ester[5], b. 20 Sep, bp. 10 Oct 1651, La Rochelle; d. 16 Feb 1653, La Rochelle

Gaspard[5], b. 6 May, bp. 23 May 1653; d. 17 May 1656, La Rochelle

Judith[5], b. 12 Oct, bp. 20 Oct 1654, La Rochelle; m. c. 1681, Pierre Bertine; prob. d. p. 1705, La Rochelle

?Guernarie[5], m. c. 1688, Jean du Brois, emig. 1693

Pierre[5], b. 22 Sep, bp. 29 Sep 1655, La Rochelle, m. c. 27 Apr 1678, La Rochelle

(date of contract), Marie Van Sevenhoven (bp. 27 Apr 1658, La Rochelle - a. 15 Dec 1723), d/o Theodore van Sevenhoven & Anne Guisbert; fam. emigrated to HOL; Pierre d. p. 18 Aug 1723

CHILDREN:

Gaspard[6]; **Théodore**[6]; **Marianne**[6]; **Henriette**[6], **Madeleine**[6], **Catherine**[6], **Henri**[6]

Daniel[6], b. 26 Aug 1691, La Rochelle, FR, m. 11 Nov 1722, HOL, Ingenatia Van den Bergh (1697-20 Jan,1764) of Rotterdam; c. 1750, to NY w/ wife & son **Jacob**[7], dau **Maria Anna**[7] b. NY

Isaac[6], **Benjamin**[6]

Amatheur[5], b. 25 Feb, bp. 11 Mar 1657, La Rochelle; m. 17 Jan 1677, Marie Papin (c. 1660-7 Dec 1678), d/o Georges & Marie (Brunet) Papin; Amatheur was a capt. of infantry at Ft. Royal on Martinique in 1678; dau **Marie**[6], b. 8 Oct, bp. 13 Nov 1678, m. 11 Apr 1674, Jean Cochon DuPuy, she d. a. 1718

Gaspard[5], bp. 30 May 1660, La Rochelle; m. Ann X who must have stayed in HOL; he d. 18 Nov 1772, NY

CHILDREN:

Maria Ann[5], b. 16 Aug 1723; m. 15 Jul 1753, J.H. Chabanel; d. 10 Apr 1786; **no issue**

Jacob[5], b.20 Feb 1727, Rotterdam; 22 Jan 1746, made a confession of faith & joined Walloon Ch of Amsterdam; m/1, 13 Dec 1753, NYC, Cornelia Rutgers (bp. 31 Oct 1736-11 Jul 1765), m/2, 31 May 1766, Catherine Rutgers, sis/o Cornelia, both d/o Herman Rutgers III; he d. 3 Jan 1793; he was a leading merchant, a man of wealth and a prominent citizen

CHILDREN, m/1

Elizabeth[6], b. 6 Sep 1754-d. 11 Aug 1755

Daniel[6], b. 12 Dec 1755-d. 20 Oct 1756

Ingenatia[6], b. 28 Nov 1756-d. 4 Oct 1757

Herman[6], b. 16 Jan 1758; m. 19 Oct 1786, Hannah Cornell (c. 1760-25 Dec 1818); he d. 13 Mar 1841; **12 ch**

Maria Ann[6], b. 23, bp. 31 Jan 1759; m. 11 May 1777, John Livingston (11 Mar 1749, NYC-22 Oct 1822, Oakhill, Columbia, NY), s/o Robert Livingston; she d. 7 Apr 1795; **7 sons, 1 dau**

Daniel[6], b. 4 Nov 1761; d. 19 Sep 1791, unmarr.

Jacob[6], b. 19 Nov 1763; m. 26 Jan 1792, Martha Banyer (19 Jan 1769-10 Oct 1829); he d. 13 Feb 1815; **no male issue**

CHILDREN, m/2:

Elizabeth[6], b. 17 Mar 1767; m. 5 Feb 1793, Julian McEvers; she d. 12 Aug, 1820

Robert[6], b. 6 Feb 1768; m. 9 Feb 1794, Catherine Cuyler (5 Feb 1771- 1 Mar 1869); he d. 7 Feb 1845; at least **1 son**

Jacques[3], b. 11 Jan 1619, La Rochelle

NOTE: Not all members of this family were Protestants. François[2], Jacob[3], François[3], Esther[4], Gaspard[3], Judith[4], Jacques[3] were; no known connection to other Le Roy families; the abjurations in 1685 were prob. due to the fact that the *dragonnades* were doing their "work" + the Revocation

REF: Records from a FR manuscript in the Huguenot Society of America Library, NYC; BAIRD, Charles W., *Huguenot Emigration to America*, Vol. I (Baltimore, 1966); DuBIN, Alexander, editor, *LeRoy Family & Collateral Lines* (Philadelphia, 1941); LeROY, Edward A., *Genealogical Chart & History of the LeRoy Family* (June 1933); STEWARD, Scott Campbell & LeROY, Newbold III, *The LeRoy Family in America, 1753-2003* (Boston, MA, Laconia, NH, 2003).

Le ROY, Pierre Michel

b. 28 Feb 1723, prob. St. Python, s. of Valenciennes, now Nord Dépt, Nord-Pas-Calais; then in what is now Hainaut Prov. of Belgium; s/o Adrien & Marie Joseph (Blass) LeRoy

m. Feb 1744, St. Python, Marie Michelle LeBrun of St. Python, d/o Jean Philippe & Marie Anne (Druart) LeBrun

c. 1761- to Amsterdam; he was a *mulquinier*, an old term of commerce – one who makes fine linens

30 Aug 1761 - London, he filed a *témoignage* (testimonial) in the Threadneedle St. Ch which said the family came from Amsterdam; Marie prob. d. in London

1768 - sailed to Halifax, Nova Scotia, w/ his ch, but ill winds sent the ship s to Charleston, SC

c. 1768 - settled in New Bordeaux Settlement, SC, w. of McCormick, SC; Pierre/Peter Michel King (LeRoy= le roi which means the king), is on SC list, showing that he owned 200 acres in Hillsborough Twp, on the Savannah River; 8 Jul 1768, Peter Michel LeRoy petitioned for a town and vineyard lot in Hillsborough Twp. – 4 ½ acres, lots #96, 61

d. p. 19 Nov 1776. SC, when he witnessed a will

CHILDREN:

child[2], b. 28 Nov 1745, St. Python

Veronique[2], b. 16 Jan 1747, St. Python; d. 20 Jan 1747, St. Python

Pierre Antoine[2], b. 14 Jan 1758, St. Python; d. 4 Dec 1752, St. Python

Charles Louis[2], b. 2 May 1750 St. Python

Jean Philippe[2], b. 29 Apr 1752, St. Python; d. 1 Dec 1752, St. Python

Pierre/Philippe I[2], b. 13 Oct 1754, Pas-de-Calais Prov, FR, bp. 16 Oct 1754, Ch at St. Python; served in the American Revolution during which he was captured by the British twice; called Philip King in 3rd SC Regiment, enlisting 17 Jun 1777; m. 5 Feb 1785, Elizabeth David (10 Aug 1767, New Bordeaux, SC-19

Jan 1835, New Bordeaux); he d. 1 Feb 1829, New Bordeaux, SC; bur. LeRoy Family Cemetery, n.e. of Willington, SC, now in the Sumter National Forest, s.e. of Mt. Carmel

CHILDREN:

Peter Charles[3], b. 9 Dec 1786; m. c. 1819, X Beattie; d. 27 Jun 1827; **2ch**

John[3], b. 30 Oct 1788; m. Nov 1720, Susan Bellot; serv. in the War of 1812; d. 29 Feb 1872; **3 ch**

Susan Anne[3], b. 11 Jan 1791; d. 21 Nov 1807

Mary[3], b. 1 Mar 1793; m. 16 Mar 1819, James Hemphill; went to AL; no further record

Philip II[3], b. 11 May 1795; m/1, 14 Jan 1819, Abbeville Co., SC, Martha Hutchinson – **5 ch**, m/2, 11 Feb 1852, Anne Guillabeau (3 Jul 1810-22 Oct 1860), d/o Pierre & Mary Jane (Bellot) Guillebeau – **no issue**, m/3, Elizabeth Dean – **2 ch**; he d. 18 Mar 1869, Mt. Carmel, SC

Elizabeth[3], b. 23 Oct 1797; m/1, 23 Feb 1819, John Louis Brock – **1 son**, m/2, Elijah LeGard – **no issue**

Isaac[3], b. 25 Dec 1799; m. 20 May 1824, Susanna Langel Britt; d. 14 Jan 1848; **3 ch**

Charles Louis[3], b. 3 Apr 1803; m. XX of whom he family disapproved; went West, no further record

Jeanne[3], b. 11 Mar 1805; d. 2 Sep 1808

Jonathan[3], b. 30 Nov 1807; d. 24 Aug 1814

Marie Anne[2], b. 31 Jul, bp. 1 Aug 1756, St. Python; m/1, 1773, SC, Jean Bouchillon (1744, FR-7 Jul 1778, SC), s/o Capt. Joseph & Marie (Majinett) Bouchillon – **4 sons** (son **Joseph James**[3], m. Susannah Guillebeau, d/o André & Mary Jane (Roquemore) Bouchillon – **2 sons, 1 dau Susannah**, m/2, 1809, Francis Moragne; Marie Anne, m/2, c. 1791, as his 2nd wife, Lazarus Covin, s/o Lazare Couvain - 4 ch - **Elizabeth**[3], **Susan**[3], **Mary Anne**[3], **Louis**[3]; Marie Anne d. 6 Nov 1839, Bordeaux, SC

NOTE: The Guillebeau family was FR Huguenot, liv. Bordeaux settlement in SC.

REF: LeROY, Lansing Burrows, Sr., "LEROY Ancestry-Historical & Genealogical" in *Transactions of the Huguenot Society of* SC, #49 (Charleston, 1944); LeROY, Lansing Burrows, *The LeRoys of New Bordeaux, SC* (an update, 1941, unpub.); PIKE, Mary Upshaw, compiler, "LeRoy Genealogy" in *Transactions of the Huguenot Society of SC*, #89 (Charleston, 1984); GIBERT, Anne C., *Pierre Gibert, Esq., The Devoted Huguenot*; Huguenot Society of London, *Livre Des Témoignages de L'Église de Threadneedle Street 1667-1789,* Vol. 21, transcribed & edited by MINET, William & Susan (1911).

Le ROY, Siméon

Siméon & his wife were NOT Protestant; 2 of their ch listed below m. Protestants and can claim Huguenot lineage **through their spouses**

b. c. 1640, s/o Richard & Gilette (Jacquet) Le Roy of Créances Parish, Coutances, Normandie, FR

1668 - to Québec, single

m. 3 Sep 1668, Nôtre Dame de Québec Catholic Ch, Claude Des Châlets, d/o François & Jacquette (Chevallereau) d'Eschâlets of Fontenay-le-Comte, Vendée Dépt, Pays de la Loire, n.w. Niort; she d. Feb 1708, Kingston, NY, sometimes called Blandina

Oct 1688 - rec. lands in Charlesbourg on the St. Charles River, nr. Québec, where they stayed until 1679

13 Dec 1676 - bought lot in Québec City

Jul 1679- in Montréal

28 Nov 1681 – bur. of dau **Marie**[2], last record of family in Montréal

p. Nov 1681 - to NY w/7 ch, all bap in Catholic Ch, Québec Province; 1 son **Jean**[2] remained in Canada & had **issue**

1686/7-1710 - resident of Kingston, NY

1689 – he and his son **Olivier**[2] did not appear to take the Oath of Allegiance; the Oath contained abjuration of all Catholic doctrines, thus their non-appearance would seem to imply that they were still Catholic

d. c. 1710, NY

CHILDREN (4 of 11 ch; only 6 of the 11 left issue):

Marie Anne[2], b. 7 May, bp. 11 May 1673; m. 7 Jun 1690, New Paltz, NY, Hugo Freer, Jr.. s/o Hugo &

Marie (Haye) Freer; her uncle Jean Giron (m. Magdeleine Des Châlets, her mother Claude's sis), in a letter congratulating her on her marr, commented that he would be have been happier had she marr in "our" religion; so Marie Anne *prob.* converted at the time of her marriage; **issue**

Leonard Treny[2], b. 15 Sep, bp 18 Sep 1674; m. 28 Sep 1703, Kingston, Maria Oeycke Usille, d/o <u>David & Marie (Casier) Usille</u>; known as Jonar/Jonas **LARAWAY** in NY; **issue**

François/Frans[2], b. NY; m. c. 1705, Celetje/Celia Damen, d/o Jan Cornelissen Damen & Sophia Martens

Sara[2], b. NY; m. a. 1706, Johannes Van Pelt of Staten Island

NOTE: There has been much discussion as to whether or not Siméon or Claude ever converted – such a conversion is possible, but <u>not proven</u>. Some of their ch served as officers in Protestant churches. The information re Siméon is offered only as background. The 2 youngest ch. (Frans & Sara) m. into Dutch families & had **issue**. They themselves were prob. Protestant but descendants of these families <u>need to supply documentation</u> to that effect.

REF: "The Life & Family of Simeon Le Roy" in the *NYGBR*, Vol. 64 (Jan, 1933).

LESESNE (Le SENS ?), Isaac

b. c. 1674 FR, *poss.* Caen
by 1690's - in SC, in St. Thomas & St. Denis Parish
owned 238 acres on Daniel Island, at the junction of the Wando & Cooper Rivers, s.e. of Charleston
m/1, 1701, Elizabeth Trézévant (d. 10 Jul 1721)
m/2, 30 Aug 1722, Frances Netherton
d. 1 Oct 1736, Daniel Island, Berkeley Co, SC; he was a cooper, planter
CHILDREN, m/1: (all bap St. Thomas & St. Denis Parish)
Isaac II[2], b. 5 Sep 1709; m. Elizabeth Walker (d. 28 Jul 1775); he d. 18 Mar 1772
  CHILDREN:
  Sarah[3], b. 27 Aug 1743; m. 26 Dec 1760, William S. Parker (d. 1782/3); she d. 29 Oct 1809; **3ch**
  Isaac Walker[3], b. 2 Feb 1745; m. 28 Nov 1766, Hannah Noarth of Philadelphia, d/o Capt. William Noarth; **1 dau**; he d. 1792?
  Ann[3], b. 14 Feb 1749; m. 27 Mar 1769, Thomas Walter (1740-1789); she d. a. 1779, when Thomas m/2 Ann Peyre, m/3 1780, Dorothy Cooper
  Elizabeth[3], b. 1751; m. 4 Nov 1774, M. Thomas Broughton
  Daniel[3], b. 31 Dec 1752; d. 25 Mar 1772
  Thomas[3], b. 1754; m. 2 Jan 1786, Elizabeth Boyd, d/o Capt. Robert Boyd; served in Rev. War; Thomas d. 6 May 1792
  William[3], bp. 1763; d. 16 Aug 1764
  Juliana[3], bp. 1772; d. 1780
Henry James[2], b, 16 Nov 1711; m. 21 Dec 1741, Sarah Walker (3 Apr 1728, New Providence, Nassau-19 Jan 1798, Charleston, SC); he d. 26 Nov 1752
  CHILDREN:
  James[3], b. 1746; d. 2 Dec 1776
  John[3], b. 1749; capt. in the Rev. War; m. 2 Jul 1778, Charleston, Mary Frederick, d/o Jeremiah Frederick; John d. 2 Feb 1792; 1 son who had **no issue**
  Elizabeth[3], b. 29 Jan 1744; <u>m/1</u>, 14 Jun 1761, Joseph Scott – **1 son** who d. 1772, <u>m/2</u>, 14 Dec 1769, Barnard Beekman (d. 21 Jul 1797) – **1 son** who d. 17 Feb 1797; she d. 21 Feb 1815
  Susannah[3], b. 6 Oct 1747; <u>m/1</u>, 14 Dec 1769, Robert Hawie, <u>m/2</u>, Dec 1777, Thomas Cochran – **2 sons**
  Anne[3], m. 10 Apr 1777, Capt. John Hart McCall; **1 son**
Esther/Hester[2], b. 28 Jan 1714/5, <u>m/1</u>, George Threadcraft (prob. d. c. 1742), <u>m/2</u>, John Cuthbert
  CHILDREN, m/1:
  George, Jr.[3]

Jammie[3]

Sarah[3], m. 1 Jan 1756, Lachlan MacIntosh; **8 ch**

Sarah[2], b. 4 Sep 1716, prob. d. young (not in father's will)

Daniel[2], b. 27 Jan 1718/9; m. 22 Jan 1756, Mary Simons (1740-15 May 1791), d/o Benjamin & Ann
    (Keating) Simons; Daniel d. 30 Nov 1782; **12 ch**

CHILDREN, m/2:

Francis[2], b. 17 Feb 1726/7, Charleston, SC; m. Mary McDonald (1725-1789), d/o Daniel and Mary
    (Lewis) McDonald; he d. 24 Apr 1767, Williamsburg Co, SC (wd, 24 Aug 1767-wp, 13 Feb 1768,
    Williamsburg Co)

    CHILDREN:

    Francis II[3], m. 28 Jun 1813, Christiana Cantey d/o Samuel & Martha (Brown) Cantey; capt. in the
        Rev. War; Francis was a minister; **1 dau**

    Mary[3]

    Martha[3], m. Adam McDonald

    James Henry[3]

    Charles Frederick[3], b. 1759, he was a minister; m. 1786, Binkey McDonald (a 1st cousin), d/o James
        & Susannah (Lee) McDonald; he served in the Rev. War as a Pvt & 2nd Lt. of Horse in the
        Militia; she d. c. 1832, Williamsburg Co, SC; he d. 1821, Williamsburg Co, SC; **2 sons**

John[2], b. c. 1729; m. Elizabeth X; went to Georgetown, SC; he d. 2 Feb 1771; prob. **3 sons**

Peter George[2], b. 2 Nov 1731; m. prob. Mary X; went to Georgetown, SC; d. p. 1791; **3 ch**

REF: PIERSON, Mary Jane McMichael, *Our Southern Heritage,* Book Two (1999); OWINGS, Nettie Smith & Marvin
Alpheus, "Lesesne Genealogy" in *Transactions of the Huguenot Society of SC,* #84 (Charleston, SC 1979); CLUTE, R.F.,
The Annals & Parish Register of St. Thomas & St. Denis Parish, 1680-1884 (Baltimore 1974); BAIRD, C.W., *History of
Huguenot Emigration to America;* LESESNE, H.H.,III, *The Lesesne Family from 1699-2000;* BODDIE, W.W., *History of
Williamsburg* (Columbia, SC, 1923); *The Huguenot Society of America* (1884).

Le SER(R)URIER, Jacques/James

b. c. 1635, St. Quentin, Picardie, FR, s/o Jacques & Marie (Le Compte) Le Serurier; both d. London;
    called *Count*

m. Elizabeth Léger of Picardie, FR; she returned to London, p. 1706, where she liv. in St. Ann's Parish,
    Westminster; she d. a. 1 Jul 1725, wp, London; in her will she left money to the charity house in Soho
    for the poor FR refugees, her servant Hester Valle, grdau Susanne de Gignilliat, her dau Susanne's ch.
    by J.F. Gignilliat & her dau by Jean Gaillard, ch. of grdau Mary Elizabeth, her son Henry, dau
    Catherine, dau Damaris, dau Marianne & her ch.

one of the Chefs de Famille of the Church of St. Quentin; a wealthy merchant of London & Carolina

a. 1683 - arr Carolina

d. a. 4 Oct 1706, wp, SC

CHILDREN:

Susanne[2], m/1, a. 1690, Jean François Gignilliat (17 May 1652, Vevey, SWI-a. 20 Nov 1699, wp),
    s/o Abraham & Marie (de Ville) Gignilliat, m/2, Jean Gaillard, s/o Joachim & Esther (Peperel/
    Paparel) Gaillard – **4 ch**; Jean François emigrated to SC, a. Jan 1689; was granted 3000 acres but soon
    afterwards rec. or bought many more acres; Jean François' will was written in FR, proven 20 Nov 1699;
    he left an estate valued at over £1123

    CHILDREN, m/1, b. SC:

    Marie Elizabeth/Mary[3], b. c. 1690; m/1, Rodolphus May-**issue**, m/2, a. 1721 (William Adams?)

    Henri/Henry[3], b. c. 1692; m. c. 1718, Esther Marion, d/o Benjamin & Judith (Baluet) Marion;
        bur. FR churchyard Feb 1742; **10 ch**

    Pierre/Peter[3], b. c. 1694; m. prob. on St. Kitts, W. Indies, Susanna de la Coussaye, d/o Philippe

Brouard de la Coussaye of St. Kitts – **2 ch**; Pierre, orphaned, went to live w/ his uncle James Smith[2] on St. Kitts by 3 Jan 1711; by 1718, he was a prospective grantee of land there; Pierre bur. 22 Jan 1733/4, St. Ann Sandy Point Parish, St. Kitts; Susanna m/2, 13 Jun 1735

Abraham[3], b. c. 1696; liv. Feb 1708; m. X Smith

Susanne[3], b. c. 1697; liv. unmarr., Jun 1725

François/Francis[3], b. c. 1698; liv. Feb 1708

John[3] (twin), b. posthumously, c. 1700; m. Mary Magdalen DuPré, d/o <u>Cornelius & Jeanne (Brabant) DuPré</u>; he d. 25 Mar 1750; **7 ch**

James[3] (twin), b. posthumously, c. 1700

CHILDREN, m/2:

John[3]

Susanne[3], m. James Nicholas/Nicholson Mayrant; **3 ch**

Esther[3], b. 1702

Elizabeth[3], b. 1704

Catherine[2], b. c. 1677; m. Henry LeNoble who d. by 1721

Damaris Elizabeth[2], m. <u>Pierre de St. Julian</u>; she was liv. 1721, but widowed

Marianne[2], b. 1675; m. a. Oct 1693, Isaac Mazyck; d. 1723

Jacques/James[2], b. St. Quentin, FR; naturalized ENG, 1 Jun 1685; in father's will, not in his mother's; changed his surname to **SMITH**

Pierre[2], not named in parents' wills; changed his name to **SMITH**

REF : *Transactions of the Huguenot Society of SC,* Vol. 64 (1959); KENAN, Robert G. *History of the Gignilliat Family of Switzerland & SC* (Easley, SC, 1977); BOND, Christy Hawes, edited by WILLIAMS, Alicia Crane, *Gateway Families* (Boston, MA, 1994).

L'ESPENARD/LISPENARD, Antoine

b. c. 1610, FR

*1669 left La Rochelle, FR with his wife – Abeltje or another wife?

1670 - settled Albany, NY, where he gave permission to the bakery of Jan Rinckhout to bake for both Christians & Indians; later went to New Rochelle

m. 20 Sep 1671, Abeltje de Forge, date according to a family diary, although accounts say Abeltje came w/ him from FR to NY* which would mean they m. earlier; in any case she was much younger than Antoine & the mother of all his ch b. in NY

3 Apr 1685, wd, New Rochelle, NY; mentions wife Abeltje, ch David, Anthony, Johannes, Cornelia, Margarita, Abigail; this was his 1st will; he had started being the special messenger bet Gov. Thomas Dongan of NY & Marquis Jacques-René de Brisay de Denonville, Governor of Canada – perhaps realized the danger and wanted to protect his family if he failed to return home

p. 16 Nov 1686 - was sent to Canada to confer with the Governor re a treaty that was broken by the FR; during that trip he learned of plans to burn Albany; he imparted this info to Col. Peter Schuyler who led an expedition against the FR which resulted in a victory for the NY troops

1689 - he purchased a home on Brewer St in NYC (now in Soho area)

1691- in New Rochelle; he was granted land where he built a gristmill on the east side of the Neck (later known as Davenport's Neck); built a stone house there that was used during the Rev. War as a hospital for the British & was still standing in 1903

d. a. 29 Jul 1696, wp (his 2nd will, dated, 1 Jul 1696) he was 86 at the time of his death; 2nd will names son Anthony, daus Margaret & Abigail (neither of them of age), indicates that Johannes and Cornelia are deceased; he was a baker

1st Tues, Nov 1697, NYC – 4 Negro & Indian slaves were indicted for stealing Jasper Nessepolt's sloop, one of them, Peroe, belonged to the "widow Lepinar"

CHILDREN:

Margarita[2], b. 2 Oct 1672, Albany; a family diary says that Margaret d. soon after birth

Johannes[2], b. c. 1675, Albany; he d. a. 1 Jul 1696

Cornelia[2], b. Albany; d. a. 1 Jul 1696

David[2], b. Albany; m. Elizabeth X; d. 1697; had 1 son **John**[3]

Anthony[2], bp. 31 Oct 1683, Dutch Ch, Albany; d. young

Abeltje/Abigail[2], bp. 21 Sep 1684, prob. Albany

Anthony[2], b. c. 2 Apr 1685; m. bet 2-7 Nov 1705, Dutch Ch, NYC, Elizabeth Huygens de Klyne/de Kleyn (bp. 29 Mar 1688), d/o Leonard Huygens de Klyne; name on Dutch recs – *Lippenar*; he was in New Rochelle by 1709 when he purchased property on " the Neck"- he erected mills & a dam there; held several civil offices in New Rochelle; he d. a. 3 Jan 1759, wp, New Rochelle; **9 ch**, incl. dau **Mary**[3], b. 20 Jul 1727, m/1, William Rodman, m/2, 14 Apr 1753, Thomas Bayeux, s/o Thomas & Sara (Cuyler) Bayeux

Margarita[2], since Antoine named an underage dau Margaret in his 2nd will, then he had a 2nd dau named Margaret and the 1st Margaret did d. in infancy as she would have been c. 24 yrs. old in 1696

REF: "Antoine L'Espenard, the French Huguenot", *NYGBR*, Vol. 24 (Jul 1893); FROST, Josephine C., *Ancestors of Henry Rogers Winthrop & His Wife Alice Woodward Babcock* (1927); SEACORD, Morgan H., *Biographical Sketches & Index of the Huguenot Settlers of New Rochelle* (1941); PEARSON, Jonathan, *Genealogies of the 1st Settlers of Albany* (Baltimore, 1984); SCOTT, Kenneth, *NYC Court Records, 1684-1760* (Washington, DC, 1982).

L'ESTRANGE – see STREING

Le SUEUR, David

b. c. 1666/7, poss. Canteleux, Pas-de-Calais Dépt, Nord-Pas-de-Calais, FR, n. of Amiens, s/o Pierre & Esther (Buire) Le Sueur

fled FR, went to ENG; was a weaver there a. 1692

m. 30 Jun 1700, St. Dunstan's, Stepney, London, Katherine Fell

d. 19 Jan 1745/6, St. Leonard's, Shoreditch, London, age 79 Y

CHILDREN (all bap. FR Ch, Threadneedle St, London) :

Esther[2], bp. 6 Jul 1701

David[2], bp. 24 Jan 1702/3; prob. d. young

David[2], bp. 30 Jan 1703/4; c. 1724, in Manakintown; is on the tithable lists of 1724, 1725, 1726, in the household of Pierre David, "signor"; m/1, c. 1727/8, Elizabeth Morell, m/2, c. 1732, Elizabeth Chastain, d/o Pierre & Anne (Soblet) Chastain; d. a. 24 Feb 1772, wp, Cumberland Co, VA

CHILD, m/1:

Elizabeth[3], b. 9 Nov 1728, King William Par; d. young

CHILDREN, m/2:

David[3], b. 25 Nov 1733; d. young

Catherine[3], b. 12 Nov 1735; m. Robert Thompson

David[3], b. 4 Oct 1738; d. a. 26 Jun 1769, wp, Cumberland Co, VA; **no issue**

Jacques/James[3], b. 25 Dec 1740; m. Susanna X; **2 ch**

Chastain[3], b. 24 Dec 1744; settled Buckingham Co; m. Anne Perrow; he d. 1818; **3 ch**

Samuel[3], b. 15 Oct 1747; m. Martha Brian/Bryant, d/o Jacques Brian; liv. Buckingham Co.; **8 ch**

Peter[3] (twin), b. 23 Oct 1750; liv. Buckingham Co; m/1, XX – **5 ch**, m/2, Susan Williams – **1 ch**

John[3] (twin), b. 23 Oct 1750; prob. d. a. May 1769

Elizabeth[3], b. c. 1753; m. p. 20/28 Feb 1774 (date of bond), Samuel Short who d. a. 30 Sep 1782, appraisal; **3 sons**

Fell[3], b. c. 1755; m. Mary X ; d. prob. Bedford Co; **3 ch**

Martell[3], b. 6 Mar 1758; m. 10 Jun 1781, Chesterfield Co., VA, Elizabeth Bacon; **9 ch**

Marie[2], bp. 25 Dec 1705

Marie Anne[2], bp. 19 Oct 1707
Catherine[2], bp. 21 Aug 1709
Jacques/James[2], bp. 29 Oct 1710
Samuel[2], bp. 16 Nov 1718

REF: ALLEN, Cameron, "David LeSueur (1703/4-1771/2) of Manakin Town, VA" in *The American Genealogist*, Vol. 71, # 1(Jan 1996); ALLEN, Cameron, "The Chastain Families of Manakin Town in VA" in *The American Genealogist*, Vol. 40; ALLEN, Cameron, "David LeSueur (1703/4-1771/2) of Manakin Town, VA" in the *VA Genealogist*, Vol. 43, #1 (Jan-Mar 1999); NSDAR, *Abstracts of Wills of Cumberland Co, VA, Will Book I, 1749-1792*.

Le SUEUR/LECHIER/LOZIER

(bro/sis of unknown parents)

François[2]

b. 1625 Challe-Mesnil (now Colmesnil), Seine-Maritime Dépt, Haute-Normandie, FR, 3 mi. s. of Dieppe; family had been clothmakers in Rouen for a century before his birth; had a bro **Eustache**[2] who remained in FR where he was a painter and, in 1648, a member of the FR Academy

1657 - to Flatbush, LI, NY; poss. in St. Kitts, West Indies, prior to arr. in NY

m. 12 Jul 1659, Dutch Ch, New Amsterdam, Jannatie Hildebrand, d/o Hildebrand Pietersen; she m/2, Antoine Tilba/D'Elba – **1 ch**

1661 - to Harlem

1663 - to Esopus

d. bet 1669-71; he was a civil engineer

CHILDREN:

Jannatie[3], b. 1660; m/1, c. 1675, Harlem, Jan Jansen Postmael/Post, m/2, Thomas Ennis, bro/o William, who m. his cousin Cornelia[3]

Hildebrand[3], b. 1663, Esopus; m. 1688, Elsie Tappan, d/o Julien Tappan; he d. soon after the marr – dau **Jannatie**, b. 1689, m. William Elting; Elsie m/2, Abraham Delamater

John[3], bp. 1665, Esopus; m. 1686, NY, Rachel Smedes; at least **3 ch**

Jacob[3], bp. 26 Sep 1665, Esopus

Nicholas[3], b. Esopus, bp. 10 Jun 1668, New Amsterdam; m/1, 8 May 1691, New Amsterdam, Tryntie Slote, d/o Peter Slote, she d. 1707/8, he m/2, 26 Jan 1709, prob. Hackensack, Antie Banta, d/o Dirck Epse Banta; moved to Hackensack p. 1st marr; d. a. 8 Apr 1761, wp, Bergen Co, NJ; surname **LOZIER**; **18/20 ch**, 1st 8 prob. m/1

Jeanne/Jannetie[2]

left FR w/ her bro François; arr. New Amsterdam in 1657

m. 1668, Old Dutch Church, Kingston, Ulster Co, NY, Cornelis Arentsen Viervant (b. Lexmont, Utrecht, NETH -d. 1675, Fordham, NY)

CHILD:

Cornelia[3], m/1, William Ennis; liv. Kingston, NY – **8 ch**; m/2, Lambert Brink

REF: KOEHLER, A.F., *The Huguenots or the Early French in NJ*; RIKER, J., *History of Harlem*; RIKER, J., *The Revised History of Harlem*; "LeSueur-Lozier Lineage of Dr. Samuel Outwater" in *NYGBR*, Vol. LV (NYC, 1924); SAXBE, William B., Jr, "Four Fathers for William Ennis of Kingston" in *NYGBR*, Vol. 129, #4 (NYC, Oct 1998).

Le VAN, Daniel

bp. c.1672, Picardie, FR
m. c. 1697, Picardie, Marie Beau
fled FR to NETH; affiliated with Amsterdam Refugee Church of the Walloons
d. prob. in Amsterdam
CHILDREN:

Abraham[2], b. 20 Sep 1698, Amsterdam; arr. 9 Jan 1729, Philadelphia, PA, on the *Mary Galby;* m. Catherine Weimar (b. FR-d. 29 Sep 1768), d/o <u>Anne Marie (Harcourt) DeTurck Weimar</u>; d. 21 Apr 1779, Oley, Berks, PA; **7 ch**

Isaac[2], b. c. 1700; 9 Jan 1729, arr. Philadelphia, on the *Mary Galby;* m. Mary Margaret X (d. a. 1786); he d. 1783, Reading, PA**; 6 ch**

Jacob[2], b. c. 1703; arr. 9 Jan 1729, Philadelphia, on the *Mary Galby*; m. Mary X (d. 1785); he d. 1768, Eagle Point, Maxatawny Twp, Berks Co, PA; **7 ch**

Joseph[2], b. 1705; d. 1729, at sea, en route to America with his bros Abraham & Isaac

Daniel[2], m/1, XX – **3 ch**, m/2, Susanna Siegfried (d. 1778), d/o Johannes & Elizabeth (X) Siegfried –**12** or **13 ch**; 21 Sep 1727, arr. America on the *William & Sarah*; d. a. 5 Jul 1777 wp, Maxatawny Twp, Berks Co, PA

Anna Elisabeth[2], 1727, to America from ENG, settled in PA; m. 1733, Maxatawny, Berks, PA, Sebastian Zimmerman; she d. 9 May 1782; **10 ch**

NOTE: Accounts differ re the arrival in PA of the brothers – some say Abraham, Isaac & Jacob sailed in 1715 and Daniel in 1727. Record found for Daniel only.

REF: COON, Warren Patten, *Genealogical Records of the LeVan Family* (1927); STAPLETON, Rev. A., *Memorials of the Huguenots in America*; SPICER, Florence LeVan, *History & Genealogy of 1 Branch of the LeVan Family* (Eugene, OR, 1977); FREEZE, John Gosse, *A History of Columbia Co, PA* (1888).

Le VILLIAN, Jean II

b. Tessy-sur-Vire, Manche Dépt, Basse-Normandie, s.e. of St. Lô, s/o Jean LeVillian I
m. Olympe X; d. a. Apr 1730
1700 - arr Manakintown in the 2nd group of refugees; arr w/ his wife
1710-1723 – the sole tithable in his household
23 Mar 1715 – Patent #685 – 200 acres, on s. side of the James River, Henrico Co. (now Powhatan) – willed to son John Peter
1722 – landholder list shows him with 200 acres in King William Parish; 1727 list shows the same
1721 – rec. patent #685 for 200 acres, in FR lands; also held patents #803 for 170 acres in FR lands, adjoining #685, 2 more of 400 acres each, s. of the FR lands in Chesterfield Co.
1723 – tithable list – Jean + 1 negro servant François
1724 – tithable list -3 – Jean, son, François
1726 – tithable list - Jean, son, François + Maria (a negress)
1730 – listed with a 2nd son Antoine on the tithable list
29 Sep 1730 – patent #803, 170 acres, on the s. side of the James in Goochland Co, (now Powhatan) – willed to son Anthony
18 Apr 1730 – wd; says he's from "Jessy" in lower Normandy, FR; wife not mentioned, prob. d.; sons John Peter and Anthony; JP to rec. ½ of the plantation (200 acres) + 3 negroes; Anthony to rec. plantation that his fa purchased from Thomas Randolph, 200 acres + 3 negroes; daus Susannah Dupuy – 2 negroes, goddau – Olimpe Dupuy – 4 guineas; 10 sh to the poor of the parish; to his 3 ch – 2 plantations in Henrico Co., on the n. side of the Appomattox River, 400 acres each; to son Anthony 9 pistoles, etc.; wp, 17 Jun 1746 - entire holding of 1170 acres was intact and allocated to his 2 ch
1731 – last time he was on the tithable list; prob. dec

CHILDREN:

Jean/John, Jr./John Peter[2], m. Philippa DuPuy, d/o <u>Bartholomew & Marie (Gardié) DuPuy</u>; he went to
    Cumberland Co.; d. p. 28 Jan 1765, wd-a. 22 Feb 1768, wp
    CHILDREN:
    Mary[3], b. 2 Oct 1731
    Susanne[3], b. 28 May 1735
    Jean[3], b. 12 Oct 1735
    Elizabeth[3], b. 28 Nov 1737; m. 28 Nov 1753, Matthew Woodson - **8 sons, 2/3 daus**; she rec.
        Patent #685 from her father JP
    Samuel[3]? – Brock lists him but without a date or record
Antoine[2], m. Elizabeth X; inherited 200 acres, 9 Spanish pistoles, 1 moidore, 5 guineas; dau **Mary**[3], m. a.
    31 Aug 1764, Jesse Saunders – **issue**; Anthony d. a. 13 Mar 1750, inv; widow m/2, a. 20 Mar 1751,
    X Young, m/3, c. 1753, Joseph Starkey
Susanne[2], m. c. 1728, Jean Jacques/John James DuPuy, s/o <u>Bartholomew & Marie (Gardié) DuPuy</u>, **3 sons**,
    5 daus, incl. **Olimpe/Olymphia**[3], who inherited 4 guineas from her grfa, m. 1744, Jean Jacques/
    Jacob Trabue, s/o <u>Antoine & Magdeleine (Verreuil) Trabue</u> – **5 sons, 3 daus**; Olymphia, d. KY, 93
    yrs. old

REF: *The Huguenot*, #25 (1971-73; BROCK, R.A., *Huguenot Emigration to VA* (Baltimore, 1966); CABELL,
Priscilla Harriss, *Turff & Twigg*, Volume I, *The French Lands* (Richmond, VA, 1988).

L'HOMMEDIEU, Benjamin

    b. 1657, La Rochelle, FR, s/o Pierre (d. a. 1665) & Martha (Peron) L'Hommedieu; they had 2
        other sons Pierre & Osée (Hosea); Benjamin was an officer in the FR Army
    Martha & her ch left FR – went to London, ENG; Osée became a goldsmith in London, 1702, & prob.
        did not emigrate to America; Pierre & his mother went to America; Pierre d. a. 30 Mar 1692,
        wp, Kingston, NY – his will mentions his mother
    1 Feb 1686 - Benj. arr Newport, RI, w/ his stepbro John Bourchard; appear to have come via St. Kitts,
        West Indies; they took a boat to NY
    10 Mar 1686 – NY, letters of denization w/ liberty to trade & traffic "as an Englishman"; he became a
        merchant
    went to New Rochelle, NY; later to Southold, LI, NY (at the e. end of LI)
    27 Sep 1687 - he and John were naturalized NY; John was naturalized as Jean L'Hommedieu
    m. 1694, Patience Sylvester (1 Nov 1664-2 Nov 1719) , d/o Nathaniel & Grissell (Brinley) Sylvester of
        Shelter Island
    d. 4 Jan 1748/9, Shelter Island (e. of Southold) <u>or</u> Southold, Suffolk Co, NY
CHILDREN:
Benjamin[2], b. 3 Dec 1694; m/1, 1717, Mary Conklin, m/2, 1 Jul 1731, Martha Bourne; he d. 17 Sep 1755,
    bur. Clinton, CT
Hosea[2], b. 16 Apr 1697; m. 11 Feb 1719, Freelove Howell (d. 26 May 1769), d/o Joseph & Lydia (Stocking)
    Howell; d. 6 Nov 1752, Shelter Island; **8 ch**
Peter[2], b. 19 Aug 1699; m. Sarah Corwin
Grissell[2], b. 20 Apr 1701; m. Samuel Hudson (d. 17 Oct 1781), s/o Jonathan & Sarah (X) Hudson; she d.
    16 Oct 1776; **9 ch**
Sylvester[2], b. 7 Jan 1703; m/1, Elizabeth Moore, m/2, 1737, Elizabeth Booth (1704/5-6 Nov 1798); he d. 9
    Mar 1788, Southold, LI, NY; **5 ch**, prob. from m/2
Susannah[2], b. 14 Dec 1704; m. 22 Feb 1722/3, Jonathan Tuthill (1692/3-8 Feb 1741), s/o Henry & Bethia
    (Horton) Tuthill; she d. 16 May 1743; **1 son, 1 dau**
John[2], b. 11 Jan 1707, Southold; m. 22 Feb 1726/7, Mary Hudson, sis/o Samuel above; d. 25 Jan 1777,
    Southold; **5 ch**

REF: L'HOMMEDIEU, William A. & Patia H., *L'Hommedieu Index,* Vol. 1, 11, Port Washington, NY (1942); MOORE, C. B., " Biography of Ezra L'Hommedieu " in *The NYGBR*, Vol. II, #1 (Jan, 1871); Tombstone Inscriptions, Oakland Cem, Sag Harbor, LI; MATHER, Frederick Gregory, *The Refugees of 1776 from Long Island to CT* (Albany, 1913); WHITTEMORE, Henry, *The Founders & Builders of the Oranges* (Newark, NJ, 1896); BAIRD, Charles W., *History of the Huguenot Emigration to America, Vol. I* (NYC).

LILLARD, Jean

b. c. 1668, nr. Nantes, FR, s/o Moïse & Lilli (Balssa) Lillard/Lillart; Moïse was the s/o Jasper & X (Isaacs) Lillard; his father was the owner of a vineyard, liv. on the Loire River, nr. Angers, FR, & operated a line of boats on the river; Jasper was a Huguenot – had at least 5 sons, Moïse being the 3rd son; Moïse was also a Huguenot & owned a small vineyard nr. his parents; his wife Lilli was a great aunt of author Honoré de Balzac, who "adjusted" his surname

c. 1685- fled FR from nr. Nantes to VA w/ younger bro Benjamin who drowned in the James River; 1st settled nr. Richmond

m/1, 1700, Mildred Jones (d. c. 1720)

m/2, Martha (X) Littlejohn (d. 1734 Prince William Co, VA)

d. a. 8 Mar 1734, inv, Prince William Co, VA

CHILD, m/1:

Benjamin[2], b. c. 1700/1, VA; m. 1724, Elizabeth Lightfoot, d/o William Lightfoot; served in the FR & Indian Wars at Fort Duquesne w/ the VA troops under Geo. Washington; also fought in Lord Dunsmore's War under Col. William Fleming; later was at Fort Pitt under Cresap; Elizabeth was related to the Lee family of VA; he d. Culpeper Co, VA

CHILDREN:

James[3], b. c. 1725; m. Keziah Bradley, a 2nd cousin of James Madison; he was a Rev. War soldier; liv. in that part of Culpeper Co. which became Madison Co.; **5 sons, 2 daus**

Thomas[3], b. c. 1726; m. Anne X (d. a. 22 May 1827, wp, Culpeper Co); he was a Sgt, Rev. War; d. 22 Nov 1814; **3 sons**

William[3], m. Anne X, called Nancy; he d. a. 25 Jul 1793, wp, Madison Co.; **issue**

Nancy[3], m. X Garrett; dau **Rachel**[4] m. 1st cousin John Lillard, s/o of uncle Thomas

Moses[3], m. & moved to NC; **5 sons, 1 dau**

Elizabeth[3], m. Lawrence Bradley, bro/o Keziah above; **1 son**

Sarah/Sally[3], m. Capt. Augustine Bradley, bro/o Keziah; **1 son, 3 daus**

unnamed son[3] m. Molly Field

John[3], b. 3 Nov 1737; m/1, 22 Dec 1758, Susanna Ball (1738-1782), d/o Samuel & Anne (Taylor) Ball & cousin of Geo. Washington; 1782, fam went to Lincoln District of VA, now Ft. Harrod/Harrodsburg, Mercer Co, KY – **8 sons, 5 daus**; m/2, Anne (Moore) Thomas, d/o Col. Francis Moore, widow of Capt. Robert Thomas; Capt, Rev. War; d. a. Aug 1801, wp, Mercer Co.; inv. dated 27 Aug 1801; dau Mary/Polly[4] m. cousin Augustine Bradley, s/o Lawrence & Elizabeth (Lillard) Bradley as his 2nd wife

CHILD, m/2:

Sarah[2] no further info

REF: LILLARD, Jacques Ephraim Stout, *Lillard A Family of Colonial VA, 1415 to 1928* (Richmond, VA, 1928); LILLARD, David Hicks, Jr., *Lillard: A Family of Colonial VA*, 2nd Edition, Vol. I, II (Greenville, SC, 1991).

LOACH, Michael de

b. c. 1645, FR; name poss. originally De Loche, de Logue, Deloge, Des Loges; supposedly from "Maglans", FR – not found but there is a town called Magland, s.e. of Cluses, in the Haute Savoie

a. 1663 - went to Bristol, ENG

14 Aug 1663 - Michael on a list of servants bound from Bristol to VA; he was to be "bound" to Charles

Taplady of VA for 4 yrs.

m. a. 9 Aug 1671, Isle of Wight Co, VA, Jane Griffith (c. 1650-c. 1719), d/o Ro(w)land Griffith

9 Aug 1671 - Roland gifted Michael and Jane with all of his estate, c. 765 acres in Blackwater, with the condition that they not sell it

d. c. 1698, or later

CHILDREN:

Michael[2], b. c. 1671; m. c. 1696, Mary X (d. a. 1 Jan 1756, inv); he d. 1727; 2 sons **Thomas**[3], **Michael**[3] - both had **issue**

William[2], b. 1678; m. c. 1701, Eleanor Collins (c. 1683-a. 26 Sep 1750, wp, Brunswick Co, VA), d/o John and Eleanor (Oliver) Collins; William d. a. 3 Mar 1747, wp, Brunswick Co, VA; son **Francis**[3] (m. Charlotte X), dau **Martha**[3] (m. Harmon Hill), dau **Ann**[3] (m. William Hill), son **William**[3] (c. 1702-p. 1765, m. c. 1725, Judith Wall, d/o Richard & Lucy Wall); all had known **issue**

Thomas[2], had 3 sons **Samuel**[3], **Thomas**[3], **William**[3]

REF: BODDIE, John Bennett, *Historical Southern Families*, Vol. II (Baltimore, 1970); DeLOACH, Harry R., *DeLoach Families, 1630-1980* (Reidsville, GA, 1981); COLDHAM, Peter Wilson, *The Bristol Registers of Servants Sent to Foreign Plantations, 1654-1686* (Baltimore, 1988); HARGREAVE-MAWDSLEY, R., *Bristol and America, A Record of the First Settlers in the Colonies of North America, 1654-1685* (Baltimore).

L'OBEL/LOBEL, Mathias/Mathieu de

b. 1538, Lille, FR, s/o Jean de l'Obel, a lawyer

attended the Univ. of Montpellier where he graduated with a degree in medicine; also attended the Univ. of Louvain; he was a physician, a botanist of great renown and an author; well-traveled

c. 1569 - went to London

1574 - to Antwerp, then Delft, where he become physician to William the Silent (1533-1584), Count of Nassau & Prince of Orange

1584 - back to London; later became James I's (reigned 1603-1625) physician and botanist; lived in Highgate, a suburb of London

m. a. 1599, XX, said to have been English

1599 - he was living in the Parish of St. Dionysius, Backchurch

d. 3 Mar 1616, in St. Michael's Parish, Cornhill, bur 10 May 1616, Chancel of St. Dionis

CHILDREN (all b. a. 1599; listed in a Lay Subsidy Roll of 1599):

Faldoe[2]

Katherine[2]

Mary[2], m. a. 1599, Louis Le Myre; had son **Mathyas**[3], bp. FR Ch, 6 Apr 1600, his grfa Mathyas was a witness; not on the 1590 list, so prob. m. a. 1599

Louise/Lucy[2], m. 16 Dec 1605, FR Ch, Threadneedle St, London, Jacques Coole/Coel (James Cole) native of Anvers/Antwerp; mar. rec says that "Louye" was the d/o "Mestre Matias de Lobel, a native also of Anvers"

Anne[2]

Mathias had a grson **Mathias Bouchaeous**[3] – not clear by which of his ch

NOTE: There is **no** proof that Mathias had a dau Mary who m. James Cole & went to MA. There is no record in ENG of such a marriage. R.C. Anderson in *The Great Migration Begins*, Vol. I, states that James Cole was from Barnstaple, Devon, ENG, m. there, 1 May 1625, Mary Tibbes and she d. p. 7 Mar 1659/60 – he & Mary were the emigrants to Plymouth.

REF: MORREN, Édouard, *Mathias de L'Obel, Sa Vie et Ses Oeuvres, 1538-1616* (Liège, FR, 1875); "English Background of Three N.E. Families" in the *NEGHR* (Oct 1961); letter from the Huguenot Society of London naming children of Mathias; marr. rec. FR Church, Threadneedle St.

LOGÉ/ LOGIER, Pierre/Peter

b. 1641, *Pays Bas du Sud*, Flandre, aka Le Pays de L'Alloeu, now the area bet Béthune & Armentières, Nord-Pas-de-Calais region; had bro **Jean**[1] who had a son **Pierre**[2] who m. Maria Magdalena Hauck, d/o Barthel Hauck, who was originally from Steinweiler

m. Catherine de Safre (c. 1633, Pays de L'Alloeu-14 Jan 1713, Bergholz, Prussia)

fled the Pays de l'Alloeu, FR; 1664, was in Steinweiler in the *Pfalz*; one of 21 families to settle there at that time – his was family #17; Elector Karl Ludwig of Billigheim granted a concession by which immigrants from s.w. of Lille, then in Flanders, were allowed to settle in Billigheim and villages under its jurisdiction which included Steinweiler; the colony was under the governmental control of Heidelberg; it received the designation "L'Alloeu Nouveau"

p. 1685 - to Bergholz, Prussia; members of a Huguenot settlement; they rebuilt the town and the Huguenot Ch, which had been almost obliterated by the 30 Years War (1616-1648)

d. a. 1703, Bergholz, w. of Szczecin/Stettin

CHILD:

Charles[2], b. c. 1667, Steinweiler; m/1, Susanne DeVinage, m/2, 11 Nov 1707, Bergholz, Maria Detouche (c. 1684, Grossenzeit?-6 Dec 1760, Bergholz), d/o Jean & Louise (Vaquier) Detouche; d. he 28 Mar 1727, Bergholz; surname **LOGET/LOGÉ**

CHILD:

Charles Antoine[3], b. 13 Mar 1713, Bergholz; m. 19 Oct 1731, Bergholz, Elizabeth Desombre (c. 1713,Schmölln*-27 Dec 1763, Bergholz), d/o Jean & Magdeleine (Parent) Desombre; he d. 14 Apr 1770, Bergholz; surname **LOGÉ/LOGER/LOGET/LOGEZ**

CHILD:

Jacques[4], b. 5 Aug 1734, Berholz; m. 7 Jun 1764, Bergholz, Marie (Sy) Senéchar (20 May 1727 Bagemühl*-d. 25 Feb 1806, Bergholz), d/o Pierre & Jeanne (Dujardin) Sy, widow of David Senéchar; he d. 10 May 1783, Bergholz; surname **LOGÉ/ LOGER/LOGET**

CHILD:

Jacques[5], b. 8 Oct 1768, Bergholz; m. 29 Oct 1794, Bergholz, Marie Paul (22 Sep 1777, Bergholz-22 Sep 1841), d/o Abraham & Judith (Hurtienne) Paul; he d. 22 Sep 1841; surname **LOGÉ**

CHILD:

Pierre[6], b. 9 Apr 1810; m. 5 Nov 1837, Christine Louise Wulff (b. c. 1813), d/o Friedrich & Sophie (Ziethen) Wulff; family sailed on the *Stephanie*, arr America 1844; d. 25 Sep 1890, Bergholz, Niagara Co, NY; **4 ch**, incl. **August Ferdinand**[7] (b. c. 1840), **Wilhemine Christine**[7] (b. c. 1841)

*__NOTE:__ towns in Prussia, bet. Prenzlau & Stettin

REF: KIMMEL, Helmut, *Hugenotten in der Pfalz* (Braunschweig, GER, 1973) + correspondence from him; CAMANN, Eugene W., *Uprooted from Prussia Transplanted in America* (Buffalo, NY, 1991); vital records from the Consistorium der Franzosischen Kirche in Berlin for 6 generations.

L'ORANGE, Jean Velas

b. c. 1675, FR

1682 - fled St. Sauveur Parish, La Rochelle, went to ENG

m. a. 1700, Françoise X, who d. a. 9 Apr 1740

1700 - to Manakintown, VA on the *Nasseau* accompanied by a wife, 1 ch

1707 - was a vestryman

1710 - on the 1st tithable list; again in 1711

12 May 1705 – naturalized, VA

d. bet 1711-14 VA – not on the *"Liste Généralle"* of 1714; Françoise is listed as a widow

1716 - widow rec. 2 patents for FR Lands in Henrico Co. in his right; one patent #822 (59 acres) was in the present county of Powhatan and the other #909 (133 acres) in present Chesterfield Co.; she appears in the Vestry Book until 1719

CHILD:

Françoise[2], m/1, a. 1714, Daniel Guérrant – **3 ch**; m/2, c. 1733, Nicolas Souillié – **1 dau**; m/3, p. 1737, Samuel Weaver - son **Daniel**[3], b. 6 May 1739, m. Sarah Dunham; Françoise d. p. 28 Aug 1769

REF: Cabell, Priscilla Harriss, *Turff & Twigg*, Vol. I, *The French Lands* (Richmond, VA, 1988); *The VA Genealogist,* Vol. 40, #2,3 (1996);l BROCK, R.A., *Huguenot Emigration to VA*; Samuel Weaver's will dated 16 Dec 1763, proven 28 Aug 1769 Cumberland Co, VA.

LORENTZ/LAURENTS, Johannes/Jean

b. 1661/6, La Rochelle, FR **or** b. GER of FR parents; name often spelled Lowrence/Lowrance

m. 13 Feb 1691, Bellheim, *Pfalz*, GER, e. of Landau, to Anna Margaretha Heiliger (1671, Oberlustadt, [n.e. of Landau], GER- p. 12 Jul 1745, prob. Somerset Co, NJ), d/o Jois Heiliger

c. 1708/9 - went to London

Aug 1710 – arr. NY on the *Medford*

a. 1716 - in Somerset Co, NJ, nr. Peapack

d. p. 12 Jul 1745, wd - a. 3 Dec 1745, wp, Peapack, Somerset Co, NJ; he was a miller

CHILDREN:

Ablonia/Anna Apollonia[2], bp. 12 Dec 1692; m. John Eveland; she prob. d. a. Jul 1745 – not in her father's will

Anaelizabeth/ Anna Elisabetha/Anna Lys/Anna Elizabeth[2], bp. 1 Mar 1695; m. Bernardus Kellerrr/ Bernhard Kötter

Madlen/Magdalena[2], bp. 28 Jan 1698; m. Johannes Mohr/Moore

Barwer/Anna Barbara[2], bp. 5 Sep 1700; m. Jacob Beshearer/Bescherer

*****Susanna**[2], bp. 22 Apr 1704; d. a. 1708, in the *Pfalz*

*****Anna Margaretha**[2], bp. 22 Apr 1704; d. bet 1708-10

*****Johann Jacob**[2], b. 23 Aug 1707; d. in the *Pfalz*

Alexander[2], b. 1708, bp. 16 Aug 1710, aboard ship from HOL to NY; m. c. 1730/32, prob. Somerset Co, NJ, Maria/Mary Iffandt/Evelan(d) (c. 1718, NJ-p. 1760, Rowan Co, NC); he was killed by Indians, a. 20 Oct 1760, Rowan Co, NC; **8 ch**

Daniel[2], b. 13 Dec 1713; m. Elizabeth Drake, d/o Abraham & Deliverence (Wooden) Drake; **10 ch**

Johannes Peter[2], bp. 15 Feb 1716; m/1, NJ, Mary Perkins (1716-1760) – **10 ch**, m/2, Annie Nichols, d/o Joshua Nichols – **7 ch**; he d. 23 Apr 1781, Rowan Co, NC

NOTE: There are discrepancies between the family Bible and church records - church records are cited where available.

*These ch were not in family Bible but records say that Johannes and Anna had 10 ch-4 sons, 6 daus

REF: *Early Germans of NJ, Their History, Churches & Genealogies*, pp. 439, 442; RUPP - *Lists*, p. 444; *NJ Abstracts of Wills,* Vol. 2, p. 320: Lorentz Family Bible records; JONES, Henry Z., Jr. - *The Palatine Families of NY: A Study of German Immigrants Who Arrived in Colonial NY in 1710* (1985, University City, CA), pp. 569-70; *The Heritage of Rowan Co., NC,* ed. by PETRUCELLI, Katherine S., Vol. 1 (1991), p. 449; SHERRILL, William A. *Captain William Sherrill, Son of Adam & Elizabeth & Some of His Descendants* (1979); *Documents Relating to the Colonial History of the State of NJ: Calendar of NJ Wills, Administrations, etc., 1730-1750* ed. by HONEYMAN, A. Van Doren, Vol. II (1918), p. 308; *The Heritage of Catawba Co, NC* ed. by FULBRIGHT, Lucille M., Vol. I (1986), p. 319.

LOUIS/LEWIS, Guillaume/William

b. FR, said to be of Castres in the Tarn Dépt, Midi-Pyrénées, e. of Toulouse; s/o Jean Louis

Guillaume & his 2 bros Samuel & Jean/John left FR – all went to ENG; Samuel went to Wales then to Portugal, no further info; John (1678-1770) stayed in ENG for a while – joined the ENG Army, became a Field Marshal, he was a lawyer, bought an estate in Wales & had **3 sons** who were also lawyers: William[2] – went to VA (Middlesex Co.?), another son was in London - went to VA after his bro and settled on the Rappahannock, the other son was in Wales

William went to N. IRE

m. N. IRE, Mary McClelland

d. IRE

CHILDREN:

William[2], settled in IRE

Andrew[2], left FR, went to Wales, to IRE, where he m. Mary Calhoun, to America, settling in VA

    CHILDREN:

    John[3], b, 1678, Donegal, IRE; m. 1715/6, Margaret Lynn (1693-1775), d/o William Lynn, the Laird of Loch Lynn in SCOT & wife Margaret Patton; from N. IRE to VA, c. 1731; he was the 1st white settler in Augusta Co, VA where in 1732, he built Ft. Lewis; he was a Colonel in the Militia, a Justice, a high sheriff; he d. 1 Feb 1762; his will (presented 18 Nov 1762, Augusta Co.) names wife Margaret, son William, grson **John**[5] (s/o Andrew[4]), dau Margaret Crow, son Charles, sons Thomas, Andrew

        CHILDREN:

        Samuel[4], b. 1716, IRE; Capt in the war bet the English & French colonists along with bros Andrew, William & Charles; also defended Greenbrier Co. & the border settlements from the Indians; d. unmarr., prob. a. 28 Nov 1761 - not in his father's will

        Thomas[4], b. 27 Aug 1718, Donegal, IRE; m. 26 Jan 1749, Jane Strother (1732, Stafford Co-19 Sep 1820, Lynnwood), d/o William Strother; a man of learning, member of the VA House of Burgesses & of the VA Convention of 1776; d. 31 Jan 1790, Lynnwood, nr. Port Republic, Rockingham Co, VA; **5 sons, 8 daus**

        Andrew[4], b. 1720, IRE; m. 1749, Elizabeth Anne Givens, d/o Samuel & Sarah (Cathey) Givens; was a General, called "the Hero of the Point" (Pt. Pleasant – at the junction of the Great Kanawha & Ohio Rivers, on the OH/WV border, n.e. of Huntington, WV) – there is a statue of him in Capitol Square, Richmond; he liv. in Botetourt Co in a home called "Richfield", nr. Salem, VA; d. Sep 1781, Bedford Co, VA, c. 22 mi from his home, of a fever while on a journey home; wp, 14 Feb 1782, Botetourt Co; wills mentions wife (no name) & 5 sons, 3 grsons, dau, bros Thomas & William, sis Margaret; had **5 sons, 1 dau**

        William[4], b. c. 1724, IRE; went to school in Philadelphia, became a doctor; m. 8 Apr 1754, Ann Montgomery (1 Sep 1737-Jul 1808) of Delaware; was a colonel in the Rev. War; d. Nov 1812, at the Brick House, nr. Sweet Springs, VA (now WV); **issue**

        Margaret[4], b. 1726, IRE; m/1, a. 7 Mar 1758, William Long (d. 5 May 1760) – **1 son**, m/2, c. Apr 1761, Augusta Co., William Crow (b. c. 1726, SCOT) – **3 sons, 2 daus**

        Anne[4], b. 1728, IRE; m. 1752, Michael Finley, Jr. (23 Feb 1718, Armagh Co, IRE-19 Jun 1785, Hamilton Bann Twp, York Co, PA –now in Adams Co), s/o Michael & Ann (O'Neill) Finley; not in her father's will; d. York Co, (now Adams Co.), PA

        Charles[4], b. 11 Mar 1736, Augusta Co, VA; m. 19 Jun 1762, Sarah Murray; he was a colonel at the Battle of the Point where he d. 10 Oct 1774

        Alice[4], m. X Madison

    Samuel[3], b. 1680; **no issue**

NOTE: The early history of this family is a bit questionable, dates, etc. The lineage, particularly starting with John[3], s/o Andrew & Mary (Calhoun) Lewis, grs/o William Lewis/Guillaume Louis, has enough documentation. A couple sources name a 4th brother (of Guillaume/William) Robert who d. in Gloucester Co, VA – that connection needs to be proven.

REF: BELLET, Louise Pecquet du, *Some Prominent VA Families*; KIRKWOOD, Alberta Carson, *They Came to KY* (Baltimore, 1976); PEYTON, John Lewis, *History of Augusta Co, VA, 2nd Edition* (Bridgewater, VA, 1953), FRAZIER, Irvin, COWELL, Mark W., Jr. & FISHER, Lewis P., *The Family of John Lewis, Pioneer* (San Antonio, TX, 1985).

LUCADOU/LOUCADO/LUCKADO/LOOKADOO, Jean/John

23 Jul 1700 - he and his wife arr James City, VA on the *Mary Ann*

12 May 1705 - naturalized in VA

1710 - on the tithable list

d. a. 1714; he d. before he could finalize his claims for land to which he was entitled; wife must have
   d. by this date as well as their sons were then called "orphans"

CHILDREN (must have been b. in VA as they are not mentioned in the ship's list):

Jean[2], listed as an orphan in 1714; m. bet Apr-Sep 1732, Maryann Dutoi, d/o Pierre & Barbara (de
   Bonnette/Bonnet) Dutois; he d. a. 16 Aug 1737; Maryann m/2, James Goff/ Goss

Pierre Antoine/Peter Anthony[2], listed as an orphan in 1714; m. Elizabeth Thomas (who d. p. 15
   Apr 1790, Powhatan Co.); he owned 294 acres of land – a land grant from King George II of ENG, 19
   Jun 1738; d. a. 25 Jul 1768, wp, Cumberland Co, VA; will mentions wife Elizabeth, sons Peter, Isaac,
   daus Mary Ann Agee, Elizabeth Lunny, Rebecca Thomas, Judith

CHILDREN:

Isaac[3]

Peter[3], m. a. 16 Jul 1756, Rebecca Thomas, d/o David Thomas

Marianne/Mary Ann[3], m. Isaac Agee, s/o Mathieu & Judith (Chastain) Agé/Agee

Elizabeth[3], chr. 27 Sep 1736, King Wm. Parish, Goochland Co; m. X Lunny

Rebecca[3], m. 1 Sep 1762, St. James Parish, Goochland, Thomas Thomas

Judith[3], unmarr. According to father's will

Jean/John[3], b/chr. 27 Sep 1738; m. 24 Jan 1762, St. James Parish, Goochland, Susannah Spalden;
   he d. 1767

   CHILDREN:

   Isaac[4], m. 3 Oct 1785, Powhatan Co., Sally Noell; **issue**

   James[4], b. 1762; m. 24 Apr 1799, Albemarle Co., VA, Hannah Mabry; c. 1800, went to
      Rutherford Co, NC; at least **6 sons**

   William[4], m. 7 Feb 1786, Keziah Lacey

   John[4], m. 16 Nov 1786, Powhatan Co., Mary Taylor

Guillaume/William[3], chr. King Wm. Parish, Goochland, 2 Apr 1743

REF: BOYER, Carl 3rd, *Ship Passenger Lists, the South (1538-1825)*; GRIFFIN, Carolyn Leigh Lucado, *Lucadou, Lookadoo, Luckado & Lucado Family History* (Jan, 1986); GRIFFIN, Carolyn Leigh Lucado, *Supplement to the Lucadou, Lookadoo, Luckado & Lucado Family History* (2nd edition, Jul 1987); CABELL, Priscilla Harriss, *Turff & Twigg, Vol. I, The French Lands* (Richmond, VA, 1988); TEPPER, *New World Immigrants*, Vol. I; *The Huguenot*, Vol. 6, pp. 82-86; Saline Co., AR History & Heritage Society, Vol. 10, #3 (Sep 1995).

M

MABILLE de NEVI/MABIE, Pierre

had estates in Anjou, FR; said to be from Neuvy, now Neuvy-en-Mauges, 15 mi. s.w. of Angers, now in the
Maine-et-Loire Dépt, Pays de la Loire

m. FR, XX

said to have served in de Coligny's Army

p. 24 Aug 1572 - (St. Bartholomew's Day Massacre) escaped to Naarden, N. HOL, on the Zuider Zee, s.e.
of Amsterdam

CHILD:

Casper[2], prob. b. c. 1575, HOL; Casper is the Dutch equivalent of Gaspard, so may have been named
after Admiral Gaspard de Coligny; called "The Sergeant" – he was in the military service of HOL
during the 30 Yrs. War; went to New Amsterdam, c. 1650; 12 Feb 1652 - last record of him in NY

CHILD:

Pieter[3], aka Pieter van Aerden/Pieter Casparre Mabie Van Naarden; b. 1600, HOL; Pieter was on a list
of Frenchmen at Leiden who, in Jul 1621, petitioned to be sent to America – he signed his
name Pierre Gaspard; arr NY, 1623, on the *New Netherland*; he was an official of the West
India Company and bought furs from the Indians; 1626, he was liv. at "The Ferry" (Brooklyn);
said to have m/1, XX, & had ch a. 1639; by 1645 he was in Manhattan; m/2, c. 1651, NY,
Aechtje/Agatha Jans Van Naerden, d/o John Van Naerden/Norden, widow of Abraham
Williamzen (she d. p. 26 Dec 1689); liv. on the w. side of Broad St.; he was made an excise
commissioner and was a small burgher; he d. c. 1664

CHILDREN, m1:

Sara[4], m/1, Jan Jansen Schepmoes – **8 ch**, m/2, 7 Oct 1656, William Couck from ENG

Pieter[4], m. XX; 2 sons, surnamed MABIE

Elizabeth[4]

CHILDREN, m/2 (all bp in the Dutch Ch, New Amsterdam):

Marritje/Martha[4], bp. 12 Sep 1652; m. 8 Apr 1671, Jan Peters Bant

Jan/John[4], bp. 4 Oct 1654; m. c. 1684, Anna Pieterse Borsboom, d/o Pieter Jacobse Borsboom;
d. 8 Apr 1725, Schenectady, NY; he was a surveyor; **9 ch**

Engeltie/Angelica[4], bp. 6 Sep 1656; m. 20 Nov 1675, Esopus, NY, Jan Jansen Mol;
5 sons, 5 daus

Metje/Mary[4], bp. 14 Apr 1658; m. FR Ch, Jan Pero/Pierrot, native of Soubise, Saintonge,
FR, who fled from FR to ENG in 1681, to NY in 1685; **3 sons, 2 daus**

Casper Pieterson[4], bp. 15 Feb 1660, NY; m. 14 Dec 1687, Dutch Ch, NYC, Elizabeth
Schuerman, d/o Frederick Schuerman; moved to Harlem, 1700, to New Rochelle,
1708, to Bergen Co, NJ; d. Bergen Co, NJ; he used surname MABILLE; **7 sons,
4 daus** (3 of 11) -**Abraham**[5] m. Silvia Coquillet, d/o Francis & Silvia (Sicard)
Coquillet; **Simon**[5], m. Marie Landrin, d/o Guillaume & Marie (Sicard) Landrine;
Johannes/John[5], m. Susanna Bertine, d/o Pierre/Peter Bertine

Tryntie/Catherine[4], bp. 17 Dec 1662, NY; m. 1 Aug 1683, Hans Hendricks Spier of
Bergen, NJ; **issue**

REF: "The Founders of the Beck & Mabie Families in America" in *The NYGBR*, Vol. XXXVIII (Apr 1907);
MUTRIE, R. Robert, *6000 NY Ancestors: A Compendium of Mabie Research* (Simcoe, Ontario, CAN, 1986);
SEACORD, Morgan H., *Biographical Sketches & Index of the Huguenot Settlers of New Rochelle 1687-1776*
(New Rochelle, 1941); VAN NORDEN, Theodore Langdon, *The Van Norden Family* (1923).

MAÇON/MACON, Gideon

b. c. 1637/48, FR; Saône has been thought to be the area where he lived; there is a town called Mâcon in the
Saône-et Loire Dépt., Bourgogne; there is a town called Saône in the Doubs Dépt, Franche-Comté, e. of

Besançon; his parentage is <u>not</u> proven; there are several theories, most of which involve noble lineage; the proposed names of the various sets of parents are not repeated in the names of Gidéon's children nor in those of his grandchildren which would seem to indicate that the suggested lineage is suspect; surname <u>may</u> have had diacritical marks, Mâcon or Maçon naturalized in ENG; had to have been naturalized in ENG in order to go to VA as only subjects of the English Crown and supporters of the Established Ch were allowed to go there at that time

c. 1670 - to VA

1671-81 – an attorney in York Co, VA

1673 – he was a sub-sheriff, New Kent Co, VA

1677 – was an Indian interpreter & secretary to Sir William Berkeley, Governor of VA

1680 - settled New Kent Co

m. c. 1680/1 - New Kent Co, VA, Martha Woodward, d/o William Woodward; she m/2, 14 May 1702, Nathaniel West – 1 dau; m/3, 1727, William Biggers – no issue

1693 – he was a Burgess & again in 1696-97, 1698, 1699, 1700-02; he was a large landowner, w/ many slaves; his estate was called "The Island" or Macon's Island in New Kent Co. on the Pamunkey River; he had a plantation nearby on the s. side of that river, "Mount Prospect" – in James City Co.; he was a prominent citizen, a proficient lawyer, and leader; was made Commander-in-Chief of the Military Forces of New Kent Co, acquired title of Colonel; vestryman of Bruton Parish Ch., Williamsburg

d. a. 4 Mar 1702, New Kent Co., VA , bur. family cem. on Macon's Island; his will was dated, 10 Oct 1700, left £200 to each of his 4 daus (the names of 2 of them are unknown), his wife named executrix

CHILDREN, bp. St. Peter's Parish, New Kent Co:

Gideon[2], b. 20, bp 22 Jun 1682, St. Peter's Parish, VA; alive 28 Apr 1704, *prob.* d. unmarr.

Ann(e)[2], b. 15 Dec 1684, bp. 2 Feb 1684/5, St. Peters Parish, New Kent Co, VA; m. 7 Nov 1705, VA, Charles Massie (1678, ENG or St. Peter's Parish, New Kent Co, VA-p. 1736, Goochland Co, VA), s/o Peter Massie – **11 ch**; were members of the Black Creek MM bet 1722-27; she d. p. 1729

CHILDREN, b. St. Peter's Parish:

Anne[3] bp. 20 Apr 1707

Elizabeth[3], b. 5 Nov 1709, St. Peter Parish, New Kent Co, VA; m. c. 1735, prob. Goochland Co, VA, John Moss (c. 1707 VA-a. 19 Dec 1785, wp, VA); she d. p. 1785, prob. Goochland Co, VA; **9 ch**

Gideon[3], b. 17 Dec 1710

Charles[3], b. 13 Oct 1712; m. XX; d. 1755; **issue**

?[Thomas[3], b. 1715/25; m. Susannah Holland; he d. 1756; **issue** - *found in only one ref. not in list of Massie ch]*

Gordon[3], b. 17 Dec 1716

Peter[3], b. 4 May 1718; m. Ann X

David[3], b. 3 Sep 1721; m. Ann Holland

Mary[3], b. 23 Dec 1723

James[3], b. 16 Oct 1725

Nathaniel[3], 2 Aug 1727; <u>m/1</u>, Elizabeth Watkins, <u>m/2</u>, Ann Clark

Cecilia[3], b. 3 Oct 1729

Quaker records mention a *sister* Sarah – could be a sister-in-law

29 Aug 1751 - in the *Virginia Gazette* – advertisement for the sale of 440 acres on Black Creek in New Kent Co; purchaser was to apply to Thomas Massie of Goochland Co. or to Gideon Massie of New Kent Co.; Charles Massie[2] had bro Thomas who had a son Thomas b. 2 Aug 1716 who had a son Thomas; Charles himself had a son Thomas who d. 1756; the Massies liv next door to G. Macon

Martha[2], b. 1687; m. 31 Jan 1703, Orlando Jones (31 Dec 1681-12 Jun 1719), s/o Rowland Jones, Rector of Bruton Parish Ch; Orlando m/2 Mary Williams; Martha d. 4 May 1716; 2 ch – **Frances**[3] (m. John Dandridge & was the m/o Martha (Dandridge) Custis Washington), **Lane**[3]

dau[2], prob. **Mary**[3], b. c.1690, a dau of Gidéon's named Mary is in the will of Anne Macon, widow, of St. Bodolph's Aldgate, London, dated 7 Sep 1699, proven 3 Aug 1700; either this dau or the one b. c. 1698, was *prob.* named Mary

William[2], b. 11/12 Nov 1693 New Kent Co; m. 24 Sep 1719, Mary Hartwell (18 Jun 1703-19 Nov 1770), d/o William Hartwell; he d. 1 Nov 1773; he was the heir to his father's estate, became a very prominent man; **11 ch**

John[2], b. 17 Dec 1695, St. Peters Parish, New Kent Co; m. a. 1 May 1714, Anne Hunt (d. 25 Feb 1724/5, bur. St. Peter's Episcopal Ch, Putneys Mill, New Kent Co.), d/o William III & Tabitha (Underwood) Hunt – **6 ch?**; not proven that he m/2 Sally Woodson – **4 ch**; he d. p. 1 Mar 1752, bur. St. Peter's

unnamed dau[2], b. c. 1698

James[2], b. 28 Oct 1701, New Kent Co.; m. c. 1740, Elizabeth (Moore) Lyde/Lloyd as her 2nd husband, d/o Augustine Moore of King William Co; d. a. 15 Dec 1768; **2 daus**

NOTE: In the 2004 *Update* the husband of Anne Macon was corrected to Charles Massie, not James Christian. The correction was made without all the documents in the Macon file but Charles still appears to be Anne's husband even with all the documents on hand. Naming patterns seem to favor Charles Massie. The fact that Anne and her husband Charles were members of the Black Creek MM led to the "closer." That information was given in another source and led to looking at Hinshaw. Anne & Charles Massey are listed as members of the Black Creek MM in 1722 & their son Charles, Jr.[3] is also listed as a member of the same MM in 1734, as well as his sister Cecilia[3]. The Black Creek MM was part of the Henrico MM. It would be helpful if future applicants of this line would supply wills.

REF: MACON, Alethea Jane, *Gideon Macon of VA & Some of His Descendants* (1956), revised by Jarvis WOOD (1979); HARRIS, Malcolm Hart, *Old New Kent Co – Some Accounts of the Planters and Places in New Kent Co*, Vol. I (1977); *Parish Register of St. Peter's , New Kent Co, VA, 1680-1787* (1966); JOHNSON, John Michael, *The Heritage* (1974); VA Historical Society, *VA Magazine*, Vol. XXXII (1968); *The Huguenot*, #14 (1947-49), #22 (1965-67); *Tyler Quarterly Magazine*, Vol. 6, p. 118; *The Vestry book of St. Peter's*; MASSEY, F.A., *Massey Genealogy Addendum;* Gideon Macon's will; BENTLEY, Elizabeth Petty, indexer, *Genealogies of VA Families*, Vol. III (Baltimore, 1982) – Macon Family Bible records; HINSHAW, William Wade, *Encyclopedia of American Quaker Genealogy*, Vol. VI (Baltimore, 1973); Cem. recs. – St. Peters, New Kent Co, VA.

MAGNE /MANJE/ MAINJE, Jean/Jan/John

b. c. 1600 Calais, FR

m. FR, Marthe/Martha Chambert of Nieuwkerke, Flanders (n.w. Lille, FR); she m/2, 10 Jul 1644, as his 2nd wife, Pieter van der Linde; she d. c. 1655

went to Amsterdam, NETH, they were part of the Walloon community there

bet 1624-41 - to New Amsterdam; *perhaps* on Long Island by 1638

11 Sep 1642 - rec. twenty *morgens* of land on Long Island; a *morgen* = c. 2.1 acres

d. c. 11 Mar 1644, Stamford, CT, in a battle w/ the Indians during "Governor Kieft's War"*; made a testamentary disposition of his property as he lay wounded in Stamford – the declaration was made on 11 Mar and his son-in-law signed for Judith's share of his estate on 31 Mar 1644
*Kieft's War or Wappinger War,1643-45 - the settlers of New Netherland vs. the Lenape (Delaware) Indians; "Wappinger" refers to the Wappani Indians who were an Algonquin tribe as were the Lenape; there was an attack on an Indian encampment n. of Stamford which is evidently where Jean was mortally wounded. Willem Kieft was the Governor of New Netherland.

CHILD:

Judith Janse[2], b. Amsterdam; m. 24 Aug 1642, Dutch Ch, New Amsterdam, Pietro Caesare Alberti, bp. 20 Jun 1608, Isola di Malamocco (strip of land bet. Venice, Italy [which is on the Laguna Veneto] and the Golfo di Venezia), s/o prob. Andrea & Veronica (X) Alberti; he arr New Amsterdam 2 Jun 1635 on the *King David (de Coninck David)* & was the 1st Italian to settle permanently in New Netherland, prob. in the whole of N. America; he liv in the Wall St. area and later in the Ft. Greene area of Brooklyn; they both d. a. 9 Nov 1655, Manhattan

CHILDREN, surnamed ALBERTUS, ALBURTIS, BURTIS:

Jan/John[3], bp. 30 Aug 1643, Ref. Dutch Ch, NYC; m. c. 1666, Elizabeth Scudder; he d. Apr 1691,

Newtown; **4 ch**

Marles/Martha?[3], bp. 7 May 1645, Ref. Dutch Ch, NYC; she d. bet 1655-1691; **no issue**

Aert/Arthur[3], bp. 14 Apr 1645; m. Elizabeth Way; he d. 1692, Hempstead, LI, NY

Marritje/Marie/ Mary[3], bp. 27 Jun 1649; m. John Pietersen Bandt

Francyntje[3], bp. 2 Apr 1651; d. a. 1654

William[3], bp. 31 Mar 1652, Ref. Dutch Ch, NYC; m. Mehitable X; he d. in the 1730's

Francyntje[3], bp. 3 May 1654; m. John Allen/Alewyn

REF: ROLLINS, Sarah Finch Maiden, *The Maiden Family of VA & Allied Families 1623-1991* (Houston, TX, 1991); CALLAGHAN, E.B., editor, *Calendar of Historical Manuscripts* (1866); "Records of the Reformed Dutch Ch in NY" in the *NYGBR*, Vol. V (NYC, Apr 1874); BOEER, Louis P., "Pre-American Notes on Old New Netherland Settlers" in *The Genealogical Magazine of NJ* #1 (Jul 1925)

MAGNY/MAN(N)Y

(prob. bros/o unknown parents)

Jean/John[2], b. Meschers-sur-Gironde, Charente Maritime Dépt, Poitou-Charentes FR, on the Gironde
River, s.e. of Royan

was in Jamaica for a while, involved in the West Indies trade

15 Apr 1693 - rec. letters of denization

m. a. 1696, Jeanne Machet/Jane Manchet, d/o Jean & Jeanne (Thomas) Machet (Jean was a ship
carpenter from Bordeaux who d. a. 10 Nov 1699); other Machet ch, **Marianne, Jean** (not in
mother's will dated 6 Feb 1705/6) & **Pierre/Peter**; Jeanne (Thomas) Machet d. a. 22 Jun 1708,
wp; Jeanne (Machet) Magny m/2, 7 Feb 1710, Élie Pelletreau (had son Benjamin, bp. 23 May
1714, FR Ch, NYC); Élie d. c. 1728, she d. a. 22 Jun 1708, wp

by 1696 - in NYC; liv. in the East Ward; assoc. w/ FR Ch in NYC; taxpayer in NYC, 1696-99

1699 - left NYC; prob. went to New Rochelle by 1702/3

d. a. 7 Mar 1702/3, inv, New Rochelle, NY; name is on the Huguenot Monument in New Rochelle;
ship captain, mariner

CHILDREN (all bap. FR Ch, NYC):

Elizabeth[3], b. 6 Dec, bp. 13 Dec 1696; *perhaps* m. 1st cousin Jacques/James Maney, s/o Jacques[2]

Jean/John[3], b. 31 Aug, bp. 28 Sep 1698; m. 23 Jan 1728/9, Ann Wines; poss. went to the West
Indies w/ bro Jacques and half bro Benjamin

CHILDREN:

(John) Wines[4], b. 1730; **issue**

Barnabas[4], b. 1735; m. c. 1760, Anne (Nancy) Everitt (c. 1746-10 Oct 1822), d/o Robert
& Esther (Butterfield) Everitt; he d. c. 1815; **11 ch**

James[4], b. c. 1738; m. Sarah X; dau **Lois**[5], b. 7 Jul, bp. 17 Aug 1775, Goshen, NY

Gabriel[4], b. 11 Mar 1740; m/1, 9 Mar 1766, Mary Horton – son **John**[5], m/2, 4 Feb 1770,
Mary Merritt (18 Mar 1746-9 Mar 1828) – **7 ch**; he d. 28 May 1808

Jacques/James[3], b. 5 Oct, bp. 12 Oct 1700; d. p. 1738, when he was liv. in the S. Ward of NYC;
poss. went to West Indies w/ Jean and half bro Benjamin; poss. d. unmar.

poss. **Jeanne Magdeleine**[3], bp. 11 Apr 1703 (bap. record not found in FR Ch)

Jacques/James[2], b. FR

m. c. 1700, Anne Vincent (surname given as *Finsang* in Dutch records), b. c. 1682, d/o Jean &
Susanne (Nuquerque/Newkirk) Vincent

CHILDREN:

Jacques/James[3], b. 23 Sep, bp. 30 Sep 1705 FR Ch, NYC; *poss.* went to VA

François/Francis[3], bp. 6 Apr 1707 NY Dutch Ch (name listed as *Frausoa*, later *Fransoa*); m.
Mary Miranda; they had a son **Francis**[4] who m. Madeleine Eymar, d/o <u>Jean & Françoise
(Belon) Aymar/Eymar</u>- they had son **Vincent**[5], b. 30 Nov, bp. 9 Dec 1753 FR Ch, NYC

NOTE: There was another Francis, b. 18, bp. 19 Aug 1711 FR Ch, s/o of Jérémie & Marguerite (Vincent) Magny; he m. Annatje Kip; Jérémie rec. denization in London 22 Jun 1694; he was a mariner; had at least 3other ch – Jeremias, bp. 30 Apr 1707 Dutch Ch, NY, Anna Magdalena, bp. 29 May 1709 Dutch Ch, NY & a 2nd Jeremias. Obviously, there was a relationship w/ Jean[2] and Jacques[2], but the documentation on hand is not sufficient to state what it was. Francis Magny & Annatje Kip had a dau Anna Magdalena, b. 18 Nov 1738, who m. 24 Sep 1756 Daniel Aymar/Eymar, s/o <u>Jean & Françoise (Belon) Aymar/Eymar.</u>

REF: Schoonmaker, Kenneth B., *Many Families Named Magny, Manee, Maney, Manney, Manny & Many* , Vol. 1 (New Paltz, NY, 1986) & Vol. 2 (New Paltz, NY 1989); WITTMEYER, Alfred V., *Registers of the Births, Marriages, & Deaths of the Église Françoise à Nouvelle York* (Baltimore, 1968); NYGB Society, *Baptismal Records, Reformed Dutch Ch, NYC* (Upper Saddle River, NJ, 1968); SEACORD, Morgan H., *Biographical Sketches & Index of the Huguenot Settlers of New Rochelle* (New Rochelle, NY, 1941).

MAHIEU, Jacques

m/1, XX

m/2, Jeanne X

Walloon family from area around Lille, FR, parts of which are now in BEL; 1st to ENG

10 Jun 1590 he & his wife (unnamed) were rec. into communion in the Leiden Walloon Ch w/ letters of transfer from the Walloon Ch in London, dated 30 Apr 1590

prob. d. Leiden, HOL

CHILD, m/1:

Jeanne/Jenne[2], "from Armentières" *prob.* d/o Jacques by a previous marr; <u>m/1</u>, Nicola Cordonne, <u>m/2</u>, p. 4 May1602 (date of betrothal) Jan de la Roche of Reims; in the *NEHGR* #143, she was described as being accompanied to her 2nd marr by her *stepmother* Jenne Mathieu & her *stepsister* Antonette Mahieu

CHILDREN, m/2:

Marie[2], <u>m/1</u>, 1602, <u>Jan de Lannoy</u>, <u>m/2</u>, p. 18 Feb 1605 (date of betrothal), Leiden, Robert Manoo

Françoise[2], "from Bondu" (Bondues, by Lille), m. 10 Jun 1611, Leiden, Daniel Cricket, a woolcomber from Sandwich, ENG

Hester[2], b. c. 1584, prob. Canterbury, ENG; she, her mother & sis Jeanne went to Leiden; 1 Jun 1603, admitted to the FR Reformed Ch/Walloon Ch in Leiden; m. c. 30 Jul 1603, Leiden, Francis Cooke (1582/3- 7 Apr 1663 Plymouth, MA), a woolcomber from ENG; 8 Aug 1606, went to Norwich, ENG, ret. to Leiden by 1 Jan 1608, with at least 1 trip back to Leiden bet those dates for the bap. of son John; 1608 the fam. liv on the Levendaal, a canal on the s.e. side of Leiden; 1621. Francis & John sailed on the *Speedwell* from Delfshaven to ENG then to New England on the *Mayflower*; Hester & 3 ch came on the *Anne* in 1623; she d. bet 8 Jun 1666-18 Dec 1675 Plymouth, MA

CHILDREN:

Jane[3], c. 1604, HOL; m. p. 22 May 1627, Plymouth, Experience Mitchell; she d. a. 1650; only **2 ch proven to be Jane's** – **Elizabeth**[4], (c. 1628-1681-84), m/ John Washburn II.– **issue**; **Thomas**[4], (c. 1631-1683/4-1687) - **issue**

John[2], bp. bet 1 Jan-31 Mar 1607, Leiden m. 28 Mar 1634, Plymouth, Sarah Warren, d/o Richard & Elizabeth (X) Warren; he d. 23 Nov 1695, Dartmouth, MA; **5 ch**

unnamed ch[3], bur. 20 May 1608, Leiden

Elizabeth[3], bp. 26 Dec 1611, Leiden; no more info, prob. d. a. 22 May 1627; may have been the 3rd, unnamed ch who came on the *Anne*

Jacob[3], b. c. 1618 HOL; <u>m/1</u>, p. 10 Jun 1646 (date of contract), Plymouth, Damaris Hopkins, d/o Stephen Hopkins – **7 ch**, <u>m/2</u>,18 Nov 1669, Plymouth, Elizabeth (Lettice) Shurtleff, d/o Thomas Lettice, widow of William Shurtleff – **1 dau**; he d. a. 18/28 Dec 1675, Plymouth, inv

Hester[3], b. c. 1624, Plymouth; m. 21 Nov 1644, Plymouth, Richard Wright (c. 1608-9 Jun 1691); she d. bet 21 May 1669-7 Dec 1675; **6 ch**

Mary[3], b. bet Mar 1626-22 May 1627, Plymouth; m. 26 Dec 1645, Plymouth, John Thompson

(1616/7-16 Jun 1696, Middleboro, MA); she d. 21 Mar 1714, Middleboro; **12 ch**
Antoinette/Antonette[2], "from Houpelyne" (Houplines, by Armentières); <u>m/1</u>, Guillaume de Sint Merty,
<u>m/2</u>, 15 May 1605, Leiden, Guillaume de Renquyre, a woolcomber from St. Thomas

NOTE: Despite the fact that the Cooke family has been written about in countless books, not everyone seems to be able to agree on the birth dates, and, in some cases, the birth order of the Cooke children. Despite those differences, the names above are correct as are the names of their spouses.

REF: ANDERSON, Robert C., *The Great Migration Begins*, Vol. I (Boston, 1995); ROSER, Susan E., *Mayflower Marriages* (Baltimore, 1990); *The Mayflower Descendant*, Vol. II (Boston, 1900), Vol. VII (Boston, 1905); BOW-MAN, George E., "The Mayflower Marriage Records at Leyden & Amsterdam" in *The Mayflower Descendant*, , Vol. XXII (Boston, 1920); HARRISON, Walter James, "New Light on Francis Cooke, His Wife Hester Mahieu & Their Son John" in *The Mayflower Descendant*, Vol. XXVII, #4 (Boston, Oct 1925) – church records from Leiden; BANGS, Jeremy Dupertuis, "The Pilgrims & Other English in Leiden Records: Some New Pilgrim Documents" in the *NEHGR*, Vol. CXLIII (Boston, Jul 1989); WOOD, Ralph V., Jr., *Francis Cooke of the Mayflower* (Camden, ME, 1996).

MAILLIET/MAILHET/MELLETT(E)/MELET, Pierre

b. FR, poss. s/o Jean & Elizabeth (LeClerc) Mailliet
c. 1695/6 to SC, settled Charleston
m. XX
d. SC, prob. Charleston
CHILDREN:
Peter[2], b. 1705 Charleston, SC; d. p. 19 Jul 1763, wd - a. 22 Jun 1764, wp, Craven Co, SC; m. Mary
(Snipes) Perriman, d/o Thomas Snipes, widow of John Perriman, who prob. d. a. 19 Jul 1763,
as she is not named in Peter's will; his will mentions son Peter, daus Martha, Sarah, Mary,
gr dau Anne Howze/Houze, poss. d/o Sarah or Mary
CHILDREN:
Peter[3], b. 1730-35, <u>m/1</u>, Mary Brunson; <u>m/2</u>, Margaret (Haynsworth) Greening; d. p. 7 Sep 1799,
wd-a. 1800, wp, Claremont Co, SC; his will mentions sons John, Richard, James, daus
Margaret & Ann, 2 unnamed daus (may have referred to Margaret & Ann as they were
named earlier in the document), dau Rebecca Barden, sis Martha; Rev. War service with
General Francis Marion (the "Swamp Fox")
CHILDREN, m/1:
Peter[4], b. 1750, d. 1785; poss. m. Lydia Lee
John[4], b. c. 1755, d. intestate, Sumter Co., SC a. 6 Jan 1807; m. Rachel (prob. Haynsworth)
who d. a. 3 Jan 1830, wp, Sumter Co, SC; 1 son **Milton J.**[5], b. c. 1794, m. Rebecca A.
Spann - **issue**
Rebecca[4], m. a. 7 Sep 1799, X Barden
CHILDREN, m/2:
Richard[4]
James[4], m. Huldah Wilder d/o Capt. Spencer & Sarah (Yopp) Wilder; **2 sons**, **3 daus**
Margaret[4], referred as just Margaret, no marr. name
Ann[4] – referred as just Ann, no marr. name
Martha[3], alive in 1799; prob. d. unmarr.
Sarah[3], m. a. 19 Jul 1763, Daniel Brunson
Mary[3], m. Richard Wells
Gideon[2]

REF: NICHOLS, C. *Historical Sketches of Sumter Co: Its Birth & Growth,* Sumter, SC 1975; *The SC Historical & Genealogical Magazine, #XXXIV,* Baltimore; GREGORIE, AK, *History of Sumter Co, SC;* HIRSCH, AH, *The Huguenots of Colonial SC; Wills* - Peter and Peter, Jr., John.

MALBON, Daniel

b. FR, prob. Montbéliard
m. FR, Marguerite/Margaret Humbert
fled to GER
1751/2 - to Boston, MA on the *Priscilla* from Rotterdam
said to have gone to Halifax, Nova Scotia, for a short time
1753 - to Frankfort, now Dresden, ME, where he rec. a grant; was also called Pownalborough
d. Dresden, ME
CHILDREN:

Betsy/Elizabeth[2], b. FR; m. Pownalborough, Peter Pochard, also on the *Priscilla*; she d. a. 1827; Peter aka Pierre Emanuel Pochard (bp 9 Oct 1742, Chenebier, Haute-Saône Dépt, Franche-Comté, n.w. of Belfort- d. a. 14 Jan 1828, wp, Lincoln Co, ME), s/o Jean & Jeanne (Mounier) Pochard; **8 ch**

James[2], b. 14 Mar 1740, FR; m. Sally X, who d. 8 Mar 1815, Skowhegan; he stated that he was an adherent of the Ch of England; went to Canada dur. the Revolution; a. 1790, had a land grant in Wesserunsett Settlement; owned a mill and a lot of land; he d. 20 Apr 1808, Skowhagen; both bur. Malbon Cemetery

CHILDREN, b. Pownalborough:

Daniel[3], b. 1775; d. 30 Apr 1827, unmarr.
Nathaniel[3], b. 1777; m. Polly Fogg, d/o Samuel & Ruth (Lane) Fogg; he d. 3 Jun 1847; **6 ch**
Polly[3], b. 9 Dec 1770; m. Stephen Hilton; **9 ch**
Nancy[3], m. Trueworthy Smith, s/o Bailey Smith; **2 ch**
James[3], b. 1782; m. Mar 1811, Betsy Fogg, sis/o Polly above; he d. 25 Jul 1847; **8 ch**
Betsy[3], m. William Flanders; **10 ch**
Peter[3], b. 18 May 1787; m. Sarah Smith, d/o Biley Smith; served in the War of 1812; d. 15 Mar 1862, Skowhegan; **7 ch**
Joanna[3], m. X Jenkins
Sally[3], m. Reuben Homsted; **2 ch**
Rachel[3], m. Joseph Horn; **4 ch**
Lucy[3], a minor when her father d.; no further info

REF: GRAY, Ruth, editor, *Maine Families in 1790*, Vol. III (Camden, ME); *Malbon Genealogy, Descendants of* Daniel *Malbon French Huguenot of Dresden, ME (author not given, not dated)* – info from Allen's *History of Dresden, ME,* Vital records, Skowhegan, Malbon Family Bible.

MALLETT(E), David

b. FR; called "David Mallette of La Saille" – there is a town called Saillé in the Loire Atlantique Dépt, Pays de la Loire, located in the Marais Salants (saltmarshes) n.w. of La Baule; there is also a town called Lasalle in the Gard Dépt, Languedoc-Roussillon, s.e. of Alès – pretty much opposite sides of FR

m. FR, XX
served in the army of King Louis XIV as did his 5 sons, Jean[2] being his 3rd son; was in the commissary of the 4th Division
c. 1687 - he & 4 sons escaped to ENG after the Revocation; a 5th son had been broken on the wheel in FR; one son was a physician in Yorkshire, one son went to GER; Jean[2] & the other son went to America;
d. 1691-96, ENG
CHILD (1 of 5):

Jean/John[2], b. c. 1644, prob. Bolbec, Seine-Maritime Dépt, Haute-Normandie, FR, n.e. Le Havre; said to have escaped from FR w/ his broadaxe & *Bible*; m. XX, prob. FR; said to have returned to FR where he rescued his wife and ch; *may* have remar. in MA but no confirmation - a John Mallet m. 26 Aug 1712, Boston, Ann(e) Mico – the father or the son? Or neither? Needs proof; 1696, to

Boston, MA w/ 6 ch; no mention of a wife; 1702, purchased land in Somerville, MA, where he built a homestead and a mill; moved there w/ his son Andrew and daus Mary & Elizabeth; he d. 31 Jan 1722/3, Charlestown, MA, 78 Y; his will was dated 30 Aug 1720, wp, 19 Feb 1722/3 - will mentions sons John, Matthew, Lewis, Andrew, daus (unnamed) rec. legacies, no wife mentioned; called a shipwright; surname **MALLET/MALLET**; according to his grson Peter, Jean bought land in on the Santee River, SC, also bought land in Boston where he settled; he bought land in New Rochelle for himself but exchanged it for land at Fairfield, CT, where he liv. by 1710

CHILDREN (order based on marr. dates):

Jean/John[3], b. 1673, Rochefort, FR; went to America - said to have emigrated with a brother & a nephew Peter; he went to SC; he m/1, in ENG or SC, XX, who d. there along with 2 of his sons; he bought land on the Santee River; his nephew stayed there; Jean went to Boston w/ his remaining ch who d. in the North, established his bro in Boston; he went to New Rochelle, NY, & then to Fairfield, CT; he was evidently a man of means – said to have been a shipbuilder; m/2, 21 Jan 1703, Boston, Joanna Lirion (1663-16 Sep 1764, Stratfield, CT*), sis/o Lewis Liron**) – she was said to have been a servant who had accompanied him from FR; he d. 28 Sep 1745, Stratfield, CT, 72 yrs, wp, Fairfield, 8 Oct 1745 – will names eldest son David, sons John, Lewis, Peter, dau Joanna Angevine & wife; both are bur. Stratfield (Pequonnock) Burying Ground; Tashua is now a neighborhood in Trumbull; Stratfield was part of Fairfield & is now part of Bridgeport – all in Fairfield Co, within a few miles of each other

*tombstone says she was 101 yrs. of age at d. – may be an exaggeration – she would have been c. 49 when Peter was b. – not impossible, but …..;

 ** separate listing for him has been eliminated – he had no issue

CHILDREN (all b. Fairfield, bp. Stratfield, CT):

David[4], b. 10 Jan 1701; m. Esther Angevine (d. 16 Jan 1787, Trumbull, CT); he d. 22 Aug 1777, Tashua/Trumbull

  CHILDREN:

  John[5], b. 28 Oct 1731; m. 25 Sep 1754, Rebecca Porter

  Joseph[5], m. 4 Feb 1768, Trumbull, Jerusha Middlebrook; **3 sons, 2 daus**

  David[5], b. 15 Nov, bp. 23 Nov 1735; m/1, Rhoda French, d/o Gamakill French, m/2, Bethia Bennett, d/o Gideon Bennett, m/3 , Polly (Young) Williams

  Esther[5], b. 1 Jan 1745; m/1, 26 Jan 1761, John Wheeler (who d. 1801), m/2, David Summers; she d. 9 May 1818, Trumbull

  Hannah[4], m. Seth Porter

Lewis[4], b. 14 Aug 1708; m. Eunice Newton, d/o Ezekial & Abigail (Briscoe) Newton; he d. 7 Sep 1790

  CHILDREN:

  Lewis[5], b. 10 Mar 1734; m. Mary Merwin (10 Mar 1734-27 May 1802), d/o Miles & Mary (Trowbridge) Merwin; he d. 1 Apr 1804; **3 ch**

  Eunice[5], bp. 9 Nov 1735; m. Nathan Baldwin (bp. 24 Dec 1721-9 May 1804), s/o Nathan & Elizabeth (Rogers) Baldwin; she d. 1824

  Avis[5], bp. 10 Apr 1737; m. 2 Feb 1764, Major David Baldwin (bp. 1 Mar 1723/4-4 May 1784), s/o Nathan & Elizabeth (Rogers) Baldwin; she d. 26 Jan 1813; **1 son, 1 dau**

Joanna[4], b. 10 Mar 1709/10, bp. 29 Oct 1710; m. Zachariah Angevine; her wp, 9 Oct 1764, Fairfield, CT – names sons John, Peter, David; **3 sons, 4 daus**

Peter[4], b. 31 Mar 1710/11; m. Mary Booth, d/o Ebenezer & Mary (Clark) Booth; he d. 10 Jan 1760, smallpox; descendants went to Fayetteville, NC; **6 sons, 3 daus**; 1 of the sons was Colonel Peter[5] (14 May 1744-2 Feb 1805) who lived w/ his grandparents for many years – said that his grandma Joanna spoke only FR

John[4], b. 16 Oct 1712; m/1, Sarah French (c. 1717-5 Dec 1742 Stratfield), d/o Samuel & Abigail (Hubbell) French - **2 sons, 4 daus**, m/2, Martha X – **4 daus, 2 sons**; d. a. 4 Jul 1776, wp, Fairfield Co, CT

Matthew[3], m/1, 25 Jan 1703/4, Cambridge, Abigail Linn, m/2, 9 Jul 1729, Charlestown, Ruth

Chamberlain of Malden; **issue**

Mary[3], m. 4 Apr 1709, Charlestown, Daniel Blodgett of Woburn

Andrew[3], m. 7 Jul 1715, Charlestown, Martha Morris of Cambridge; he d. 1744, Charlestown, MA; he was a miller; **8 ch**

Elizabeth[3], m. 4 Jan 1718/9, Boston, Daniel Viaux

Louis/Lewis[3], m. a. 23 Nov 1721 (birth of son Lewis, Charlestown), Margaret Fosdick, who was called a widow on 19 Nov 1757, when she rec. Thanksgiving money; at least 4 ch – **1 son, 3 daus**

NOTE: Many lists ignore Jean[2] & go straight to Jean/John[3]. The wills tell the story.

REF: WYMAN, Thomas, *Genealogies & Estates of Charleston, MA, 1629*-1818; BAIRD, Charles W., *History of the Huguenot Emigration to America*, Vol. II (Baltimore, 1966); SINNETT, Rev. Charles N., *The Mallet Family of MA, ME* (1923); Vital Records - Boston, Cambridge, Charlestown; MALLETT, Anna S., John Mallet, The Huguenot and His Descendants, 1694-1894 (Harrisburg, PA, 1895); JACOBUS, Donald Lines, *History& Genealogy of the Families of Old Fairfield*. Vol. I; ABBOTT, Susan Woodruff, *Families of Early Milford*, CT; CLEAVER, Mrs. Robert, *The History of the Town of Catherine, Schuyler Co, NY*.

MALLET(T)/MALET/MALLOTT/MALLE, Étienne/Stephen

b. Bordeaux, *poss.* s/o Jacob & Madeleine (Aidolet) Malet

bp. 9 Sep 1674, Threadneedle St. Ch, London, ENG

m. Marie X (d. p. 1714)

Jul 1700 – arr. VA on the *Mary Ann*; settled Manakintown

12 May 1705 – naturalized, VA

d. a. 2 Jul 1712, wp, Henrico Co, VA; it was written in FR, states that he was from Bordeaux, Guienne, FR; names ch Étienne, Marie, Susanne

CHILDREN:

Etienne/Stephen[2], b. 1706/7; m. a. 4 Jul 1728 VA, Olive Magdeleine Sallé, d/o Abraham & Olive (Perrault) Sallé; 31 Oct 1716 he received patent #779 of 125 acres on the s. side of the James River in Henrico (now Powhatan) Co that was originally owned by his father; 1750, moved to Lunenburg Co, VA, the part that later became Mecklenburg Co.; Olive d. c. 1762; he d. p. 4 Aug 1769

CHILDREN, all b. King Williams Parish:

Marie[3], b. 8 Mar, bp. 20 May 1730

Étienne/Stephen[3], b. 29 Nov 1731; m. Rachel X; **4 sons**

Guillaume/William[3], b. 28 Jan 1733/4; m. Lunenburg Co., Rachel Baker, d/o William Baker; she d. c. 1792; he d. by 1789; **issue**

Judith[3], b. 2 Sep 1736; m. John Clark; went to SC c. 1767

Ester[3], b. 27 Nov 1738; had illegitimate son **Thomas** Mellett[4], b. 1759, NC

Elizabeth[3], b. 20 Jan 1740/1

Marie Magdeleine[3], b. 10 Nov 1742

Marie[2], d. a. 19 May 1741, unmarr

Susanne[2] m. Tobias Lafeit/Lafitte; she d. 15 Dec 1722; dau **Ester**[3]

REF: BODDIE, John Bennett, *Historical Southern Families,* Vol. I; CABELL, Priscilla Harriss, *Turff & Twigg*, Vol. I, *The French Lands*, (Richmond, VA, 1988); WEISIGER, Benjamin B., compiler, *Colonial Wills of Henrico Co, VA 1654-1737*, Part One; baptismal records, Manakintown; BROCK, R.A., *Huguenot Emigration to VA* (Baltimore, 1962); JONES, W. Mac, *The Douglas Register* (Richmond, VA, 1928).

MANDEVILLE, Giles Jansen/Yellis de

b. 1625, Normandie, FR - Rouen?, s/o Jan who d. 1657, Garderen, HOL

m. a.1648, Guilderland, HOL, Elsie Hendricks

12 Feb 1659 - to New Amsterdam on the *De Trouw* (the Faith) from Garderen, HOL (now part of Barneveld, s.e. of Amsterdam) w/ wife + 4 ch, ages 1½, 5, 6, 9 – passage for all was 90 guilders; became a farmer in Flatbush, LI and Manhattan

had a grant of land on the Hudson extending from Ganzevoort St. upwards & incl the present Abington Sq., which was then the family burying ground, i.e., Greenwich Village - from below 14th St. to 21st St., from the Hudson to Warren Rd

d. p. 15 Sep 1696, wd – a. 22 May 1701, wp, NY

CHILDREN:

Hendricks[2], b. c. 1649/50, HOL; m/1, 18 Jul 1680, Annetje Pieterse Scholl – **4 ch**, m/2, 21 Apr 1699, New Amsterdam, Elizabeth Jansen Berry – **3 ch**; he d. 1712, Mountain View, NJ

Tyntje/Catherine[2], b. c. 1652/3, HOL; m. Cornelis Jansen de Seeu, aka Van der Veer, from Alkmar, HOL; **9 ch**

Jan[2], b. c. 1655

William[2], b. c. 1656, HOL; m. Elizabeth X; he d. a. 30 Oct 1679

Aeltje/Elsie[2], m. 1676, Laurens Jansen de Camp; liv. Staten Island; **7 ch**

Gerretje[2], m/1, John Muthel, m/2, Pieter Meet

David[2], b. Flatbush; named in father's will

Greitie[2], m. John Meet

REF: MORRISON, George A., Jr., *DeCamp Genealogy* (Albany 1900); PIERSON, David L., *History of the Oranges*, Vol. 4; WHITTEMORE, Henry, *Founders & Builders of the Oranges* (Newark, NJ 1896); *NJ Register* (1956); WOODWARD, Weltha B. *A Genealogical Record of the Mandeville Family* (Waterloo, NY 1962).

MANEVAL, Pierre

b. c, 1665, Embrun, "Bas" Dauphiné, FR, s.w. of Briançon, now in Hautes-Alpes Dépt, Provence-Alpes-Côte d'Azur; Waldense family

m. c. 1696, FR, X Rabeau, b. c. 1675, FR; GER record says she was Isabeau Bouchon

1698 - fled FR, poss. to the Piedmont then to Lausanne, SWI w/ wife + 1 ch

1699 - to Brugg, SWI w/ wife + 2 ch, then to Dürrmenz & Schmie (where he had a house & 1 cow); Dürrmenz & Schmie are in Württemberg, GER; Dürrmenz is c. 10 km. n.e. of Pforzheim, Schmie is c. 3 km. n. of Dürrmenz

1707 - he went nr. Neu-Isenburg, s. of Frankfurt, w/ wife + 3ch; Neu-Isenburg was founded 1699 as a town of exiles by Huguenots

1719 – no further records of him

CHILDREN:

Charles Daniel[2], b. c. 1697, FR; m. Dürrmenz, Catherine Centurier (1688-18 Sep 1762), d/o Antoine Centurier; he d. 1757

CHILDREN:

Isaac[3], b. 1725

Lucrèce[3] m. Christophel Pichler

Jean[3]

Mathieu[2], b. c. 1699, prob. SWI

Judit[2], b. 1701, GER

Jérémie[2], b. c. 1704, Dürrmenz; m. 30 Jan 1725, Madeleine Arnaud/Arnaux (16 Sep 1772-14 Feb 1792), d/o Moïse Arnaud of Dürrmenz; he d. 29 Mar 1773, Schmie

CHILDREN, all b. Dürrmenz:

Pierre[3], b. 19 Aug 1725; d. 20 Apr 1796

Jean[3], b. 1727

      Charles Daniel[3], b. 1728 m. 16 Nov 1762, Marie Madeleine Cheinel (b. 27 Aug 1742), d/o Pierre & Marie (Latour) Cheinel - **8 ch**, incl. son **Jeremi**[4] (b. Mar 1765), who went to America in 1819 w/ his wife Marie Susanne Pastre (d/o Pierre & Madeleine [Perrot] Postre) (they m. m. 14 Feb 1792, Grossvillars, GER, n.e. of Pforzeim), & 7 of his 9 ch (**5 sons, 4 daus**); at least one son is said to have remained in GER, while another emigrated later

      Suzanne[3], b. 13 Jan 1729

      Marie Madeleine[3], b. 1730

      Isaac[3], b. 1731

      Salomon[3], b. 1 Nov 1735

      unnamed[3]

Elisabet/Isabeau[2], b. 1704; m. a. 1722, Étienne/Stephen Ozias (d. c. 1752), s/o <u>Antoine & Isabeau (Lormeiasse) Ozias</u> of Nîmes, FR; Elizabeth went to America in 1753 with sons **John**[3], **Peter**[3], dau **Catherine**[3]; she d. soon after their arrival; **9 ch**

REF: *Stammfolge, Maneval*, German records; BELLON, Eugen, *Geschichsblätter des Deutschen Hugenotten-Verreins e. V. Vertrieben, verweht, verwurzelt. Die französisch-reformierten Einwanderer in Dürrmenz 1699-1735* (1987); MANEVAL, Francis H., *Genealogical Helps for Blockhouse Ares,* Vol. 1 (1976); MANEVAL, Willis E., *The Maneval Family* (1929, unpublished); MANEVAL,Willis E., *Historical & Genealogical Records of the Maneval, Miller & Wilson Families* (Columbia, MO, 1954, unpublished).

MANIGAULT/MANIGAUD, Pierre

      b. c. 1664/5 La Rochelle, FR, s/o Gabriel and Marie (Dubartet) Manigault; had a brother **Gabriel**[1] who also emigrated to SC & rec. a warrant on 28 Jun 1695, for land on the Santee n.e. of Charleston; later he & Peter purchased 300 acres upstream at Echa Creek; Gabriel never m. and d. spring 1704

      c. 1685 - fled FR, went to London, ENG

      by early 1695- had settled in Charleston, SC area; 22 Jun 1696, rec. a warrant for 100 acres on the Santee

      m/1, c. 1699, Judith (Giton) Royer,(b. La Voulte, Languedoc, FR) widow of Noë Royer, whom she m. in SC & by whom she had 3 ch; Judith d. 1711, 46Y

      m/2, 1713, Ann Reason (d. 1727); **no issue**

      d. 8 Dec 1729, Charleston, SC, bur. French Churchyard

      CHILDREN, m/1:

Judith[2], b. 8 Jan 1701/2, Charleston, bp. in French Ch; <u>m/1</u>, 1717, James Banbury (d. 1732) – **issue**, <u>m/2</u>, Thomas Witter; she d. 5 Sep 1778

Gabriel[2], b. 21 Apr 1704, Charleston, bp. in French Ch; m. 29 Apr 1730, Ann Ashby, d/o John & Constantia (Broughton) Ashby; she d. Apr 1782; he d. 5 Jun 1781, Charleston; he was a wealthy merchant & planter; Patriotic Service, Rev. War

      CHILD: **Peter**[3], b. 10 Oct 1731; studied law in ENG and stayed in Europe for a few years, returning in 1754; m. 8 Jun 1755, Elizabeth Wragg, d/o Joseph Wragg; had **7 ch**, 3 dying young - 2 sons, 2 daus survived; Peter d. 12 Nov 1773, London

      CHILDREN:

      Gabriel[4], b. 17 Mar 1758, SC; m. Mary Izard; he d. 4 Nov 1809, PA; Rev. War – Pvt, SC

      Joseph[4], b. 19 Oct 1763, SC, <u>m/1</u>, Charlotte Drayton, <u>m/2</u>, Henrietta Middleton; he d. 5 Jun 1843; Rev. War - Sol, SC??

REF: CROUSE, Maurice Alfred, *The Manigault Family of SC 1685-1783* (Ph.D. dissertation, Northwestern University, Jun 1964); pages from what appears to be a biographical publication which discusses several members of the Manigault family, incl. the early generations.

MANNEVILLE, Jean de/MANVILLE, John

b. Picardie, FR

went to ENG

1675 - supposedly went to NY as a soldier in King Philip's War but name is not found on lists of
soldiers

m. a. 1683, ENG, XX

CHILD:

John[2], b. 1683; to America, settled Woodbury, CT; he was a tailor; d. CT

    CHILD: Surname **MANVILL, MANVEL, MANVIEL**

    Nicholas[3], b. 1710 ENG; m. 1735/6, Mary/Molly Murray, prob. d/o Daniel & Mary (Sperry)
Murray (b. 19 Nov 1716, New Haven); he d. 17 Mar 1751, Woodbury; 6 May 1751,
wp, Woodbury – names wife Marah, John, mentions other ch without name; 3 Apr 1751,
inv, names the 7 ch; Molly m/2, Joseph? Tuttle – 1 dau Sarah, she m/3, X Titus – 2 sons,
2 daus; Nicholas and Molly liv in Quassapaug, bet Woodbury and Middlebury

    CHILDREN:

    John[4], bp. 5 Sep 1736, Woodbury; m. 8 Feb 1759, Oxford, CT, Elizabeth Weed (b. 11 Dec
1736, Waterbury, CT), d/o John & Alice (Clark) Weed; **8 ch**; liv on father's property

    Mary[4], b. 30 Mar 1737, Woodbury; m. 25 Mar 1756, Obadiah Wheeler; **10 ch**

    Nicholas[4], b. 28 Jul 1738, Woodbury; m. 21 Aug 1760, Lurana Rose; moved to Susquehanna
Co – not heard from afterwards – said to have been on the run with 2 Indians after him
– left behind a wife and 3 ch; settled Wyoming Valley, Luzerne
Co., PA; **4 ch**

    Daniel[4], bp. 8 Jun 1740, Woodbury; m. 11 Feb 1765, Hannah Sherman; **2 ch**; Rev. War -
Pvt, VT; he d. c. 1785, NY

    James[4], bp. 16 Oct 1743, Woodbury; m. Elizabeth/Betty Judson (bp. 10 Jan 1747/8), d/o
Nathan & Damaris (Sherman) Judson; liv. Derby, CT; **6 ch**

    David[4], bp. 12 Apr 1747, Woodbury; m/1, 26 Aug 1768, Susanna Hill (1753-24 Oct 1796,
Watertown), d/o Jonathan & Elizabeth (Perry) Hill; liv Watertown, CT; **10 or 11
ch**; m/2, 3 Oct 1798, Huntington, Beulah Patterson (1773-1844), d/o Samuel &
Hannah (Hubbell) Patterson; he d. 1 Apr 1839, Watertown; Rev. War – Cpl, CT;
his fa-in-law Jonathan Hill was a Pvt, CT, in Rev. War

    Adrian[4], bp. 26 Feb 1748/9 Woodbury; liv. Fredericksborough, Ballston, NY; **3 ch**

REF: MANVILLE, Stewart R., *The Manville Families in America*; JOHNSON, Andrew, "The Manville Family
of New England & NY State" in *Yesteryears*, Vol. 20 #77 (Aurora, NY 1976); JACOBUS, Donald L., "Manville of
Woodbury, CT" in *TAG*, Vol. 22 (Jul 1945); CT Church Records, Woodbury, 1st Congregational Ch.

MARCHAND, Henri

b. prob. Caen, Normandie, FR

1685 - to NY w/ his 13 yr old son; left son w/ friends; apparently left sufficient funds for his son as
Henri II was able to become an owner of a lot of property

Henri returned to FR to bring the rest of the family to America – no more info

CHILD:

Henri II[2], b. c. 1672, FR; m. a. 1698, Newtown (now Elmhurst), LI, NY, Ann X; to NJ, c. 1700; he d. 20
Sep 1738, Maidenhead, NJ; 25 Oct 1738, inv; he was a weaver; surname **MERSHON**

    CHILDREN:

    Henry[3], b. c. 1698, Newtown; m/1, p. 20 Jan 1728 (date of marr bond), Mary Yard (bp. 21 Feb
1707, Philadelphia), d/o William & Mary (X) Yard **3 sons**, m/2, p. 11 Dec 1739 (date of marr
bond), Ann Major (d. a. 1 Apr 1763) – **1 son**; he d. a. 4 Mar 1777, wp

    Mary[3], b. c. 1702, Maidenhead; m. 26 Aug 1723, Hunterdon Co, NJ, Thomas Houghton (b. 1700);
9 ch

Andrew[3], bp. 6 Aug 1706, Dutch Reformed Ch, Raritan, NJ; m. c. 1730, Francina Anderson; he d. p. 7 May 1793, Hunterdon Co, NJ; **10 ch**

Peter[3], b. 1707, Maidenhead, NJ; m/1, 1731, Elizabeth X – **4 ch**, m/2, c. 1741/2, Jane Van Cleve – **2 ch**; he d. 1747, Maidenhead

Ann[3], b. c. 1709, Maidenhead; m. Andrew Smith; d. p. 16 Oct 1784, Maidenhead

Thomas[3], b. 1710, Maidenhead; m. 1743/4, Maidenhead, Susannah Stockton; he d. 1790, bur. Princeton, NJ

Rebeckah[3], b. 10 Mar 1711/2, Maidenhead; m. 29 Oct 1729, Princeton, Nathaniel FitzRandolph of Princeton (b. 11 Nov 1703), s/o Benjamin & Sarah (Dennis) FitzRandolph; she d. 12 Mar 1784, Princeton; **14 ch**

Elizabeth[3], bp. 22 Jun 1714, Maidenhead; m. 15 Jun 1738, Princeton, Joseph Green; she d. 12 Mar 1784; **4 ch**

Sarah[3], in father's will of 1738; no more info

Houghton[3], b. c. 1718, Maidenhead; m. XX; d. a. 13 Jul 1798, wp, Princeton; **6 ch**

REF: RANDOLPH, Oris H.F., *Edward Fitz Randolph Branch Lines* (1976, not pub.); MERSHON, Grace Lucile Olmstead, *Our Pioneers East & West of the Mississippi* (1953, 1957); MERSHON, Grace Lucile Olmstead, *My Folks*, 1946, orig. written by MERSHON, Oliver Francis, chapters 13, 14, 15 (Rahway, NJ, 1946).

MARCHAND, Jacob

s/o Jean Marchand of Sonvilier, Bern Canton, SWI, a Huguenot who had fled FR; *may* have been from Montbéliard, Doubs Dépt, Franche-Comté, which is c. 25 mi (as the crow flies!) n.w. of Sonvilier; Sonvilier is c. 7 mi. from FR & 2 km. s.w. of St. Imier, SWI; the area surrounding Sonvilier is a region where many French people emigrated during the religious wars in FR and it is an area where French is spoken

m. Marie Eve Pettremond, d/o Daniel Pettremond of Sonvilier

d. Mar 1768, SWI, at a "great age"

CHILDREN, bap. Ch of St. Imier, Erguël, nr. Sonvilier; all that remains of Erguël are the ruins of the castle, located bet St. Imier & Sonvilier; it was once an ancient seigniory (a feudal jurisdiction):

Jehan[2], b. Dec 1703; m. Barbelet L. (d. 1770/88)

Jacob[2], b. Nov 1705; d. 1773

Adam[2], b. Jul 1707; he d. a. May 1746; had son **David**[3]

David[2], b. May 1709; m. Sonvilier, Judith Marie (Jacob) Gentle, widow of Isaac Perrot Gentle, d/o David Jacob of Le Locle, SWI; both trained as doctors; 1753, were in Dampierre, s.w. of Besançon, in the Jura Dépt, Franche-Comté, where they kept a school, sanitarium and inn; to America from Rotterdam on the *Nancy*; arr. Philadelphia, 14 Sep 1754; settled Lancaster Co, PA; he d. a. 17 Aug 1761, wp, Hagerstown, MD; Judith m/3, John Davis and she d. c. 1789

  David[3], b, 4 May, bp. 8 May 1746, Sonvilier; m. 1766, Elizabeth Kemerer (1744-14 Jun 1817), d/o Ludwick Kemerer; Rev. War -Capt, PA; d. 22 Jul 1809, Westmoreland Co, PA
  CHILDREN (info taken from David[3]'s Bible):
  Catherine[4], b. 3 Mar 1767
  Elizabeth[4], b. 5 Nov 1768
  Susanna[4], b. b. 13 Oct 1770
  Judith[4], b. 12 Jan 1772
  Daniel[4], b. 8 Dec 1773
  Esther[4], b. 23 Aug 1775
  David[4], b. 10 Dec 1776
  Lewis[4], b. 23 Jun 1782
  Frederick[3], b. 1748

Marie Marguerite[2], b. Oct 1713; m. Jacob P.

Susanna[2], b. Jun 1717

Marie Magdeleine[2], b. Aug 1719
Abraham[2], b. Oct 1722

REF: MARCHAND, Louis, *History of the Marchand Family* (1906); JORDAN, John W., *History of Westmoreland Co, PA*, Vol. III (1906); ch records, St. Imier, SWI.

MARIE/MARYE, Jacques/James (Rev.)

b. 7 Jun 1692, Bertreville Parish, Saint-Ouen, FR*, s/o Jacques & Susanna (Morisse) Marie; family said
    to have a been a wealthy & titled one
studied for the priesthood at a Jesuit College, the Collège de Bourbon at Rouen, where he received the
    tonsure, 16 Mar 1714; was nominated a Deacon, 25 Mar 1717; however, he began protesting the
    treatment of the Huguenots; he renounced his family and faith and fled to ENG
1726 - in ENG where he was licensed (not ordained) to officiate in the Anglican Ch; his family demanded
    his return to FR and the Catholic Ch; he refused & all communication ceased; he changed the
    spelling of his surname, changed his 1st name and became James Marye; studied for the
    Protestant ministry
m/1, Oct 1728, Stepney, London, Laetitia Maria Anne Staige (d. bet Feb 1738/9-Oct 1739), dau/o Rev.
    William Staige
early 1730 - left ENG for VA where he rec. 133 acres in Manakintown; he officiated at a baptism, 20 May
    1730, there
1731-35 served in King William's Parish
Oct 1735 - called to St. George's Ch in Fredericksburg, VA, where he served until his death; he also taught
    school in Fredericksburg, one of his pupils was George Washington
m/2, 17 Oct 1739, Elinor Purcell Dunn - **no issue**
26 Apr 1743 - naturalized Williamsburg, VA; recorded 1 Jun 1743 & his certificate was issued; he began
    to purchase what would eventually amount to 1900 acres in Spotsylvania Co.
d. 26 Jan 1768, Spotsylvania Co, VA; his wp, 4 Jul 1768, Spotsylvania Co., mentions sons James, Peter,
    grdaus Lucy & Susanna Marshall, dau Lucy Marshall, grch James & Laetitia Heath, dau Susanna
    Heath; Rev. James Marye was bur. on his farm "Fayetteville", c. 8 mi. from Fredericksburg
CHILDREN, m/1:
Lucy Mary[2], b. 10 Oct, bp 12 Oct 1729, London, ENG; m/1, 16 Mar 1747, Rev. Mungo Marshall of
    Orange Co, VA who d. 1758/9 – **4 ch**, m/2, Dr. James S. Marsden who d. a. 9 Aug 1777 – **no
    issue**; Lucy d. p. Oct 1780; bur. in KY
James[2], b. 8 Sep 1731, Goochland Co, VA; 27 Dec 1755, ordained an Anglican priest; m/1, 29 Apr 1761,
    Sarah Vaulx (d. c. 1767/70), d/o Robert & Sarah (Elliott) Vaulx – **3 daus, 1 son**, m/2, 20 Jan 1770,
    Mary Kenner (d. 7 Oct 1770) – **no issue**, m/3, Elizabeth Osborne (Neale) Grayson (d. 22 Mar 1831),
    d/o Christopher & Ann (Osborne) Neale, widow of Benjamin Grayson – **3 daus**; James d. 4 Oct 1780,
    Fredericksburg, VA, Rector of St. George's Ch, bur. on the Marye farm "Fayetteville"
William C.[2], b. 6 Apr 1733, Goochland Co, VA; schooled in Edinburgh, SCOT, as a doctor; d. Gravesend,
    ENG, just prior to his return to VA; unmarr.
Susanna[2], b. 17 Jun 1735, prob. Goochland Co, VA; m. a. 4 Sep 1761, Dr. Henry Heath; **1 son, 1 dau**
Peter[2], b. 20 Feb 1739, Spotsylvania Co, VA; m. 6 Dec 1773, Eleanor C. Green, d/o Col. William & Anne
    (Coleman) Green; he was a graduate of William & Mary College; member of the House of Burgesses,
    1769, from Spotsylvania Co; he d. 15 Oct 1810; **2 sons, 3 or 4 daus**

NOTE: Pinpointing the correct St. Ouen is impossible – there are 38 in FR, incl. 8 in Haute-Normandie
& 8 in Basse-Normandie; there are 4 nr. Rouen – St.-Ouen-de-Thouberville, St.-Ouen-du-Tilleul, St.-Ouen-
de-Pontcheuil, & St.-Ouen-des-Champs, all w. or s.w. of Rouen; there is a town named Bertreville in the
Seine-Maritime Dépt, Haute-Normandie - a town named St. Ouen-le-Mauger due east of it c. 29 km.; not clear
if the term Bertreville Parish refers also to the town of Bertreville. The only certain thing is that the

St. Ouen from which Jacques Marie came, was in Normandie. R. A. Brock credits James[2] with a 1st wife Letitia Courtney – 1 son, 1 dau – not found anywhere else; he also says that Jacques & family went to VA c. Sep 1729 & that Lucy Mary was b. at sea – not so, she was bp. in London prior to the journey to VA.

REF: DORMAN, John Frederick, editor, *The Virginia Genealogist,* Vol. 15 (1971); WORTHINGTON, Grayson Marye Ray, Sr., "The Rev. James Marye, Sr." in *The Huguenot Publication,* #35 (1991-93); EBERHAR, Edith Whitcraft & ROBERTSON, Adaline Marye, *The Maryes of VA 1730-1985* (Baltimore, 1985).

MARIN/MARINE/MAREEN, Milleson de

b. 1634, Île de France, the region around Paris, s/o Alexandre & X (Milleson) Marin; his father d. in London & had at least 2 other sons Jacob & Alexander; the latter Alexander was *prob.* the Alexander Mareen who settled St. Mary's in 1669; family appears in the records of Canterbury & Threadneedle St., London; the surname Milleson is also in the Threadneedle St. records

1655 - to Somerset Co, MD; had plantation on Secretary Creek; said to have been among the 1st white settlers on the Eastern Shore

m. c. 1662, Lavina/Lovea/Lovey Major, d/o Thomas Major of Accomack Co, VA

1663 - sold his land and went to DE

d. 1679, Sussex Co, DE

CHILDREN:

Jonathan[2], b. c. 1665; m. 1689, Kezia(h) X; he d. May 1736, Dorchester Co, MD; he was a Quaker; **7 ch**

William[2], b. c. 1667; d. 28 Feb 1716, unmarr.

Charles[2], b. 1669; d. p. 1717

James[2], b. 1671; d. a. 28 Feb 1748, wp

Alexander[2], b. 1673; d. young

Thomas[2], b. 1675; m. Mary X; d. 1749

John[2], b. 1677; d. p. 1716

Major[2], b. 1679/80

REF: JONES, Elias, *History of Dorchester Co, MD*; PARRAN, Alice Norris, *Register of MD Heraldric Families, 1634-1935* (1935); MacKENZIE, George Norbury, *Colonial Families of the USA*, Vol. VII (1966).

MARINER, Jean/John

b. 1644, FR

m/1, FR, Elizabeth X

20 Jul 1688 - recorded at Boston, MA, Letters Patent of Denization – John Marin, clerk or preacher, Elizabeth his wife and 2 daus

m/2, Rachel X; she d. 24 Oct 1723, Gloucester, Essex, MA, c. 76Y; after John d., she was granted c. 3 acres above Fresh Water Cove

1708 - at age 64 he appeared in Gloucester with son John

22 Jun 1708 - was granted c. 6 acres of ground on the Cape Side in Gloucester & c. 12 acres on the Chebacco Side; he drew lot #64 in the 25 Jan 1709 drawing; 22 Feb 1715, the Proprietors voted to give him money or land equivalent to 1 thatch lot

d. 21 Dec 1717, Gloucester, MA, age c. 73Y

CHILDREN, m/1:

John[2], b. c. 1680/85, FR; evidently he did not emigrate w/ his parents & sisters; 1st mention of him was in 1706 in Gloucester; m/1, 1 Apr 1708, Gloucester, Sarah Sawyer (1683-26 Aug 1724, Gloucester), d/o James & Sarah (Bray) Sawyer, m/2, 16 Feb 1724/5, Ipswich, Essex, MA, Mary Cobb, m/3, 15 Nov 1737, Falmouth, ME, Martha Turner; he was a mariner; he was a successful man – left an estate valued at over £2486; d. a. 28 Mar 1749, inv; prob. he and his son John were both lost at sea in 1748

CHILDREN, m/1:

Sarah[3], b. 7 Jan 1709, Gloucester; m. 26 Oct 1727, Gloucester, David Elwell (10 Mar 1678/9-c. 1751), s/o Isaac & Mehitabel (Millet) Elwell; **3 ch**, b. Gloucester, may been others

Elizabeth[3], b. 20 Oct 1712, Gloucester; m. Samuel Staples (b. 12 Mar 1707/8, Kittery, ME), s/o James & Mary (Tetherly) Staples; at least **1 son**

John[3], b. 21 Jun 1716, Gloucester; m. p. 19 Jun 1737 (date of int.), Sarah Roberts (b. 11 Apr 1720, Gloucester), d/o Ebenezer & Sarah (Elwell) Roberts; he d. a. 5 Oct 1748, inv; he was a mariner; **4 ch**

Joseph[3], b. 29 Aug 1719, Gloucester; m. p. 28 Jun 1741 (date of int), Abigail Hanscom; he d. 20 Jul 1811, Cape Elizabeth, ME; he was an innkeeper; **6 ch**

Rachel[3], b. 19 Aug 1724, Gloucester; m. 27 Jan 1743, Samuel Fogg (1 Jun 1716-30 Oct 1798 Scarborough), s/o Daniel & Anna (Hanscom) Fogg; she d. 24 Mar 1768, Scarborough; **10 ch**

CHILDREN, m/2:

Mary[3], b. 17 Jan 1726/7, Gloucester; m. p. 11 Nov 1744, Falmouth (date of int), James Dyer (b. 12 Jan 1721, Truro, MA), s/o Henry & Anna (Small) Dyer

Hannah[3], bp. Sep 1730, Falmouth; m. 8 Apr 1749, Falmouth, Micah Dyer (b. 8 Mar 1728, Truro), s/o Jonathan & Susanna (Brown) Dyer

CHILDREN, m/3:

Susanna[3], under 14 yrs. of age in 1752

Benjamin[3], under 14 yrs. of age in 1752

Martha[2], not found after the 1688 Letters Patent; poss. d. young

Susanna[2], m. 1 Nov 1700, John Dolliver (b. 2 Sep 1671), s/o Samuel & Mary (Elwell) Dolliver; she d. 28 Feb 1705/6, Gloucester, MA

CHILDREN:

John[3], b. 24 Aug 1702, Gloucester; drowned 15 Mar 1716/7, Rowley

Susanna[3], b. 26 Nov 1704, Gloucester; m. Dec 1728, Gloucester, Thomas Varrel of Ipswich; by 1747, they were in Falmouth, ME; **4 ch** b. Gloucester, may have been others b. Falmouth

REF: UNDERHILL, Lora Altin Woodbury, *Descendants of Edward Small of New England,* Vol. III (Boston, 1934); Town Records & Vital Records, Gloucester, MA.

MARION, Benjamin

b. Chaume, Poitou, FR, now La Chaume, Vendée Dépt, Pays de la Loire, on the Atlantic coast w. of Les Sables-d'Olonne, s/o Jean & Perrine (Boutignon) Marion

m/1, FR, Judith Baluet

1689 - expelled from La Rochelle

1690 - fled to SC w/ wife; settled St. James Parish, Goose Creek, Berkeley Co., on a tract of land believed to have been part of the northern portion of "The Elms"; the original grant was 100 acres at the head of Goose Creek, called "Yeaman's Creek", dated 14 Mar 1704; purchased more land over time

17 May 1694-27 Sep 1695 – naturalized during this time

m/2, SC, Mary X

d. a. 2 May 1735, wp, Goose Creek Parish, Berkeley Co, SC

CHILDREN, m/1:

Esther[2], b. bet 1690/95, SC; m. Henry Gignilliat, s/o Jean François & <u>Susanne (le Serrurier) de Gignilliat</u>; **6 ch**

Gabriel[2], b. c. 1693, SC; m. 1711/16, Esther Cordes, his 1st cousin, d/o Dr. Anthony & Esther Madeline (Baluet) Cordes – Esther was his mother's sister; he d. bet 1747-51; **6 ch**, incl. **Francis**[3], b. c. 1732, Winyah, SC, nr. Georgetown, SC, was a general in the Rev. War, nicknamed "the Swamp Fox",

m. Apr 1786, SC, cousin Mary Esther Videau (17 Sep 1737-26 Jul 1816 SC), d/o Joseph Henry & Ann (Cordes) Videau, Francis d. 27 Feb 1795, St. John's Parish, SC – **no issue**; a descendant of Francis' sister **Esther**[3] was Julia Ward Howe, who wrote "The Battle Hymn of the Republic"

Benjamin[2], b. bet 1690/95, SC; m. Elizabeth Cater, d/o William Cater; he d. a. 12 Mar 1778, wp; **9 ch**
CHILDREN, m/2:
John[2], m. Frances X; d. a. 5 Mar 1739, wp; **1 son, 3 daus**
Paul[2], m. Elizabeth Peronneau, d/o Samuel & Jeanne (Collin) Peronneau; d. a. 27 Jan 1737/8, wp
    CHILDREN: **Paul**[3]; **Peter**[3]
Peter[2], m. XX; d. a. 19 Nov 1795, inv; n**o issue**
James[2], m. May X; **3 sons**
Mary[2]
Anne[2]
Elizabeth[2]
Judith[2]

REF: "The Marion Family" in *Transactions of the Huguenot Society of SC,* Vol. 21 (1915); RAVENEL, Daniel, *French & Swiss Protestants settled in Charleston, on the Santee & at the Orange Quarter in Carolina Who Desired Naturalization, 1695/6* (Baltimore, 1968).

MARLITT/MERLET/MALOTT

(2 sons of unknown parents)

Gédéon/Gidéon[2] b. c. 1624, prob. Roucy, Champagne, FR, n.w. of Reims, now in Aisne, Picardie Dépt, just outside the border of the Champagne-Ardenne Dépt.; parents *poss.* Josias & Jeanne (Robb) Marlet
    Dec 1643 - to Leiden
    m. 21 Aug 1644, Walloon Church, Leiden, HOL, Marguerite Marie Martijn/Martin, from Limburg,
        BEL (1622-bef 1683)
    p. 26 Jul 1648 - to Mannheim, GER
    c. 1658 - back to Leiden
    12 Oct 1662 - landed in New Amsterdam on the *De Purmerlander Kerck*; passenger list – Gideon w/
        wife 4 ch ages 4, 6, 8, 15
    d. a. 20 Mar 1684, Staten Island, NY, or poss. Feb 1683, Piscataway, NJ
    CHILDREN:
    Josias/Josué /Joseph[3], b. 17 Sep 1644; d. 1715; **no known issue**
    Marie[3], b. 11 Nov 1646; d. a. 1662
    Esechias[3], bp. 26 Jul 1648; d. a. 1662
    Paulas/Paul[3], b. 1654 ; m. Lysbet Burwick; 1 dau **Jannetje/Janneken**[4], bp. 18 May 1679,
        Flatbush
    Abraham[3], bp. 7 Feb 1656, Mannheim; m. 1677, Chrétienne/Christina Billiou, d/o Pierre &
        Françoise (DuBois) Billiou
        CHILDREN:
        Isaac[4]
        Jacob[4]
        Margaret[4], bp. 31 Mar 1678
        Abraham[4], bp. 16 May 1680, New Utrecht, NY
        Frances[4], b. 1682; m. John LaForge/LaFort, s/o Adriean/Abraham LaForge & Jane Lozier
    Jean Pierre/John Peter(son)[3], b. 18 Apr, bp. 2 May 1658, Mannheim; m/1, c. 1690, NY, Marie
        Bellemain (1660-1699, Piscataway, NJ), m/2 Mary (X) Jehou, widow; he d. p. 30 Jan 1702/3,
        wd – a. 18 Apr 1704, wp, Piscataway, Middlesex Co, NJ; surname **MELOT**
        CHILDREN, m/1:
        Marie[4], b. 1691 m. Stephen Hooper
        Hannah[4], b. 1691

Jean Pierre/Peter[4], b. 1692

*Theodores[4], b. 27 Jan 1693, NY; m/1, c. 1719, NJ, Catherine Maple, d/o Benjamin &
Elizabeth (Lee) Maple, m/2, 2 Mar 1727, Catherine Delashmutt (c. 1707-a. 18 Jan
1771), d/o Pierre de la Chaumette; he d. a. 19 Mar 1750/1, wp, Frederick Co, MD; will
names wife, sons Peter, Benjamin, John, daus Elizabeth, Catherine, Mary, mentions a
Theodotius Malot but does not call him son (poss. s/o his son Peter)
CHILDREN, m/1, surname **MELLOTT**:
Peter[5], m. Sarah Tracy
John[5], m. Sarah Stillwell
CHILDREN, m/2, surname **MALLOT**, birth order not certain:
Peter[5], b. 1728 MD; m/1, Sarah X, m/2, Rachel X; 1754 - leased 106 acres in
Dorchester Co, MD; d. a. 23 May 1806, wp Washington Co, MD; **10 ch**
Elizabeth[5], m. X Dawson
Catherine[5], m. X Crossley
Benjamin[5], b. 1734, Frederick Co, MD; m. Eloise X; d. 18 Sep 1815, Washington
Co, MD; **7 ch**
Mary[5], in father's will , no info
Joseph[5], b. 1745; m. Sarah X; **6 ch**
Ruth[5], b. 1751?; m. 1779 Henry Wald
Madeline[4], b. 26 Feb 1697/8
Anne[3], b. c. 1666, drowned age 15 in East River

Paul[2], m. 20 Feb 1654, Mannheim, GER, Elizabeth Moreau
CHILDREN:
Gédéon[3]; **Nöe**[3]; **Henry**[3]; **Jeanne**[3]

NOTE: *Theodores/Theodorus was a separate entry in 1995. Said entry stated that he went to Manakintown in
1700 – not so. The Malot who was in Manakintown briefly was Théophile Mallott w/ his wife. Priscilla Harriss
Cabell in *Turff & Twigg*, says Théophile was actually Étienne/Stephen Mallet who came from Bordeaux & the
3 orphans listed on the 1714 *Liste Générale*, Estienne, Suzanne, Marie were his ch; in 1995 the Society did not
have the church records from Europe which clarified some of the lineage.

REF: Theodores Malot's Will; Monograph from Fulton Co, PA Historical Society; John Peterson Mellat's Will;
Purmerland Church records; HORTON, M.J., *Descendants of John & Sarah (Stilwell) Mellott of Fulton Co, PA* (1996);
Records, Walloon Church, Leiden; Records French Huguenot Church, Mannheim; CLOSE, Virgil D., compiler, *The 1st 4
Generations Descended from Pierre de la Chaumette* (1984); LOOMIS, Margaret White, *Malott Family Genealogy*
(1941); BOYER, Carl 3rd, *Ship Passenger Lists NY & NJ (1600-1825)* (Newhall, CA, 1978).

MARLOT, Jean

b. c. 1677
6 Oct 1700 – arr. Manakintown, on the 2nd ship, *Peter & Anthony*; according the passenger list, he was
not w/ any family members
m. prob. VA, Ann (Pasteur?); she m/2, Timothy Sullivan; she d. a. Nov 1742, wp
1704 - was in the employ of William Byrd of Westover, Charles City Co, prob. as his secretary
1705 - he was in Williamsburg where he was licensed to keep an ordinary
1708 - purchased a tavern which was eventually run by his son-in-law James Shields and called Shields Tavern;
the original tavern disappeared a. the Civil War; 1954, Colonial Williamsburg reconstructed a tavern on
the original site of John Marlot's tavern – it is called Shields Tavern, on E. Duke of Gloucester St.
d. a. 16 Dec 1717, wp, York Co, VA; he d. as a result of an attack by one Francis Sharpe
CHILDREN:
Edith[2], m. 1717, Samuel Cobb(s) (1698-1757) of Amelia Co, VA, s/o William & Mary (X) Cobbs;

Samuel ran an ordinary in Williamsburg; d. a. 28 Jul 1757, wp, Amelia Co; she d. a. 2 Jul 1761, wp; **2 sons, 6 daus**

Anne[2], m/1, James Inglis (d. a. 1737) – **1 dau**, m/2, James Shields (1700- 1750), s/o Mingo & Anne (Bray) Shields, as his 2nd wife – **1 son, 2 daus***, m/3, 11 Jun 1751, Henry Wetherburn, keeper of the Raleigh Tavern in Williamsburg, who d. a. 15 Dec 1760, wp – **no issue**

*one dau **Anne**[3] (b. 31 Jul 1742) m. Robert Booth Armistead, their dau **Mary Marot Armistead**[4], m. John Tyler III – they were the parents of President John Tyler (1790-1862)

Rachel[2], m. Richard Booker, s/o Edward & Mary (Goode) Booker of Amelia Co, VA; Richard was a Colonel in the Amelia Co. Militia; he d. 1760; **5 sons, 1 dau**? (accounts vary!)

REF: MACKENZIE, George Norbury, *Colonial Families of the United States of America*, Vol. II (Baltimore); BROCK, Robert A., *Documents Relating to the Huguenot Emigration to VA* (Baltimore, 1962); *Genealogies of VA Families, from Tyler's Quarterly Historical & Genealogical Magazine,* Vol. I (Baltimore, 1981), Vol. II (Baltimore, 1982); *William & Mary College Quarterly Historical Magazine*, Vol. V (NY. 1966); wills – York Co, VA & Amelia Co, VA.

MARR, John

b. 1660/65, FR

c. 1688 - arr, VA, prob. went to Northumberland Co.

m/1, by 1688, VA, XX (d. by 1727)

1695-96 - on tithing lists in Lancaster Co, VA

1700 - in Stafford Co; referred to as a "Frenchman" in a 1702 Northumberland Co. deed

1720 - his land was now in Hanover Parish, King George Co.

m/2, by 1729, Elizabeth (Fishback) Rector, d/o Philip & Elizabeth (Heimback) Fishback, widow of John Jacob Rector – **no known issue**

d. a. 28 May 1744, wp, Prince William Co, VA; will names wife Elizabeth, sons Daniel & Christopher

CHILDREN:

John[2], b. 1691; d. a. 24 Jul 1716; **no issue**

Christopher[2], m. Abigail X; d. a. 21 Mar 1780, wp, Pittsylvania Co, VA; **issue**

Daniel[2], b. by 1693; m. Anne X; he d. p. 25 Jun 1753, wd, Prince William Co, VA; son **John**[3] **& others**

Mary[2], m/1, Thomas Kingcart, Jr. (d. a. 22 Sep 1716, Richmond Co, VA) – dau **Martha**[3] who m/1, John McBee, m/2, Dr. William Kirns; Mary[2] m/2, c. 1717, John Bradford - **issue**

unnamed dau [2], m. X Hardin; **issue**

poss. a 3rd dau who m. X Nettle; had dau **Mary**[3]

REF: HIDEN, M.W., "John Marr of Stafford Co." in *Genealogies of VA Families*, Vol. II (Baltimore, 1998).

MARTAIN/MARTIN, Jean/John

1700 - to VA on the *Peter & Anthony*, the 2nd ship of French refugees; settled Manakintown

Feb 1700/01 - on the miller's list for those who were to receive Indian meal at Falling Creek mill

m. by 1 Nov 1703, Margaret X (poss. d/o James & Margaret (Coop) LeCaze); she m/2, John Four/Fore; she d. p. 1744

1710-13 - on the tithing lists, no mention of a family

1714 - on the *Liste Générale*, King William's Parish, he had a wife 3 sons & 1 dau

held more FR patents of anyone – 5 totaling 1298 acres, issued between 1715-19

d. p. 12 Mar 1736, wd – a. 15 May 1739, St. James Parish, Goochland Co, VA

CHILDREN (all but John listed in Jean's will):

Jacques/James[2], m. by 1727, Janne X; at least **3 sons**

John[2], m. Mary X (poss. d/o Moses Forcuron); d. by Mar 1736; at least **1 son**

Pierre/Peter[2], m. Mary Ann Rapine, d/o Anthony & Margaret (X) Rapine; at least **3 sons**

Judith[2], m/1, c. 1728/29, Thomas Gévaudan - **1ch; m/2**, c. 1732/3, René Chastain – **5 ch**
Jane[2], unmarr. 12 Mar 1736, when father wrote his will

REF: WITHERSPOON, Martinette V., *My Ancestors; A Brief Account of the Ancestry of Lister Witherspoon & his wife Martinette Viley* (1922); CABELL, Priscilla H., *Turff & Twigg,* Vol. I *The French Lands* (Richmond, 1988).

MARTIAU, Nicolas

      b. 1591, Île de Ré, FR
      1611- to HOL
      by 11 May 1615 - in London where he was Richard Toche's godfather at his bap in the FR Hug. Ch. on Threadneedle St.
      1619 - given power of attorney by Lord Henry Hastings, 5th Earl of Huntingdon; became Hastings' agent in the VA Company
      naturalized in ENG
      11 May 1620 - sailed to VA on the *Francis Bonaventure*; arr. Aug in Jamestown
      1622 - commanded a company of men searching the forest for Indians after the March massacre along the James River; called Capt. Martiau
      23 Mar 1623 - he gave testimony to the Council & General Court of Colonial VA; elected to the House of Burgesses from the district of Keskyache/Cheesecake in the bounds of Elizabeth City
      m/1, 1624/5, Jane (X) Berkeley, widow of Lt. Edward Berkeley; she d. a. 1640*
      1630 - family moved to Chiskiack on the York River; 1632, he was Burgess for Kiskyake & the Island of Kent
      1633 - Burgess from Kiskyake (Yorktown)
      1635 - leader in a planter revolt against Sir John Harvey, Royal Governor
      m/2, 1645, Sybilla (X) Felgate, widow of Capt. Roger Felgate*
      m/3, 1646, Isabella (X), widow of George Beech*
      24 Sep 1655 – last appearance in Court, had served for 32 yrs.
      d. p. 1 Mar 1656/57, wd – a. 24 Apr 1657, wp, Yorktown, VA; will mentions daus Elizabeth Reade, Mary Sca(r)sbrooke, Sarah Fuller; had become a significant landowner
CHILDREN:
Elizabeth[2], b. 12 Dec 1625, Elizabeth City Co, VA; m. 1641, Col. George Reade, s/o Robert & Lady Mildred (Windebank) Reade; she d. 1686, Yorktown; their dau **Mildred**[3] m. Col. Augustine Washington, George Washington being their grgrson; **11 other ch**
Nicolas[2], b. 1627; d. c. 1636
Mary[2], b. c. 1629/0; m. Col. John Searsbrook/Scarbrook, leader in Bacon's Rebellion; d. a. 1657; **issue**
Sarah[2], b. 1631; m. Capt. William Fuller, later Gov. of MD; **issue**

****NOTE:** There is some thought that he was m. once before Jane – not proven; also there is a suggestion that Sybilla and Isabella were the same person, a widow of both Roger Felgate & George Beech before m. Nicolas. While interesting, it is a moot point as his only known ch were by Jane.

REF: JESTER, Annie L., *Adventures of Purse & Person, 1607-1625* (1956 & 1987 revision by MEYER & DORMAN, & DORMAN's 4th Edition); Nicolas Martiau Descendant Assoc.*, Membership Manual & National Register*; York Co. – Nicolas' will; SMITH, Jonathan Kennon, *Captain Nicolas Martiau 1591-1657* (unpub., not dated); STOUDT, John Baer, *Nicolas Martiau The Adventurous Huguenot, The Military Engineer & The Earliest American Ancestor of George Washington* (Norristown, PA, 1932).

MARTILINE/MARTLING, Jean/Johannes

his family fled southeastern FR; prob. 1st went to the NETH, then to St. Eustatius, Dutch W. Indies;
     Waldensians
b. c. 1650, Dutch West Indies
m. 20 Jan 1675, Dutch Ch, NYC, Aeltje Jans
1677 - to Staten Island, NY, where he rec. a land grant of 94 acres at Karl's Neck, a FR hamlet
d. Staten Island
CHILDREN:
Barent[2], m. 1702, Deliante Van Namen, d/o Jochem Engelbert Van Namen & Elizabeth Evert Pels
Peter[2], m. Jannetje/Jane Heereman; **issue**
Abraham[2], b. 5 Sep 1693, Staten Island; 1714, went to Philipsburg; m. 16 Apr 1715, Old Dutch Ch of
     Sleepy Hollow, Rachel DeVeaux, d/o Abraham & Mynno (Yerkes) DeVeaux/De Voe; d. 22 Aug
     1761 (67 y 7 m 17 d); he was a blacksmith; years later, Washington Irving claimed that he laid the
     scene for "The Legend of Sleepy Hollow" in Abraham's home which Abraham had built for his
     bride Rachel on the King's Highway in the Manor of Philipsburg
     CHILDREN:
     Hendrick[3], bp. 5 Sep 1724; m. Hester Conklin
     Johannis[3], bp. 1717; m. Elizabeth Brown
     Abraham[3], b. c. 1719; m. 17 Mar 1739, Tarrytown, Janitie Ackerman, d/o David Ackerman &
          Maritie Sie – David, grson/o David Ackerman & <u>Elizabeth Bellier</u>, Maritie, grgrgrdau/o
          <u>Nicolas Sy</u>; Rev. War soldier; d.16 Jun 1786, bur. Old Dutch Burying Ground of Sleepy
          Hollow; Janitie also bur. there - she d. 23 Aug 1782, age 59 Y; **8 ch**
     Adaline[3], bp. 1724; m. Daniel Devoe
     Myno[3], bp. 1721; m. Caspar Conklin
     Barent[3], bp. 1731; m. Adaline Yerkes
     Peter[3], bp. 1734; m. Catherine Storm
     Daniel[3], b. c. 1737; m. 5 Feb 1758, Maria Von Wart/Work (bp 1737-15 Mar 1791), d/o John Von
          Wart & Mary Wilsea; Rev. War soldier, he was a Lt, then Captain; he d. 14 Jun1788, age 51 Y;
          both bur. Old Dutch Burying Ground of Sleepy Hollow; **5 ch**
     Isaac[3], b. 1741; m/1, Elizabeth Hek, m/2, Antjie Cox; was a Captain; he d. 26 May 1779
Isaac[2], m. Anna Van Namen, sis/o Deliante (above); **issue**
2 daus[2]

REF: DAVIS, Norman, *Westchester Patriarchs* (Bowie, MD, 1988); CLUTE, J.J., *Old Families of Staten Island*;
RIKER, James, *Revised History of Harlem (City of NY) its Origins & Early Annals*; HISTORY RESEARCH SOC.
of THE TAPPAN ZEE, *The Old Dutch Burying Ground of Sleepy Hollow* (1926); YONKERS HISTORICAL &
LIBRARY ASSOC., *First Record Book of the "Old Dutch Church of Sleepy Hollow"* (1901); HUGUENOT SOCIETY
OF NJ, Glenna See Hill, compiler, *Huguenot Ancestors Documented by the Huguenot Society of NJ, Inc.* (1975).

MATHENAY/METTENEYE/MATHENY, Jean/John

family said to have come from the Jura Dépt, Franche-Comté Région, then in Bourgogne (Burgundy),
     the original name being <u>de Mathenay</u>, a *seigneurie* there, in the area of Arbois – town of Mathenay
     c. 8 km n.w. of Arbois; the named prob. changed to Metteneye while in Flanders – more of a
     Dutch spelling
b. c. 1542, Flanders, s/o Richard Metteneye & his1[st] wife, whom he m. in Flanders where she prob. d.,
     they were members of a Flemish Huguenot Ch there; Richard was in London by 28 May 1550,
     when Jean was bap. & where he m/2, 29 Jul 1550, Christ Ch, Newgate St., London, Margaret
     Veelham
bp. 28 May 1550, Christ Ch, Newgate St., London, opposite St. Paul's Cathedral
m. 1568, Katheryne X (b. c. 1545, Bourgogne, FR); c. 1568, moved to Bishopsgate, St. Botolph Parish,
     London, nr. intersection of London Wall and Bishopsgate St.

CHILD:

Charles[2], b. c. 1569, St. Botolph Parish, London

> CHILD: **William**[3], b. c. 1600, Canterbury, Co. Kent, ENG; m. Elizabeth X; settled Canterbury; went to Bossenden, nr. Dunkirk (e. of Canterbury) on Faversham Rd., 5 mi from Canterbury, a. 1640
>
> CHILDREN:
>
>> **Daniel**[4], b. c. 1638, ENG; emigrated to America, settled Surry Co, VA; a. 1663, to Charles Co, MD, where he bought 300 acres; 5 Aug 1664, bought a plantation called "Wentworth Woodhouse" from Thomas Wentworth whose dau Sarah Wentworth (1648-1700) he m. c. 1665, MD; bought more land & established his home at Mattawoman which he patented under the name "Mathena's Folly; 1681 he was 1 of the leaders in a Protestant uprising against the Catholics in MD; when the uprising failed, he moved across the river to Stafford Co, VA, where on 6 Mar 1683, he bought a plantation "The Hope" on Aquia Creek in Overwharton Parish; d. 19 Oct 1689, Stafford Co, VA; **1 son, 3 daus** – 2 of the daus, d. young
>>
>> **William**[4], bp. 28 Nov 1640, St. Paul's, Canterbury
>>
>> **Michael**[4], c. 1642; he went with his bro Daniel to VA, 1st to Surry or Isle of Wight Co

REF: STEADMAN, Joseph Earle, *The DesLoges Family* (1981); MATHENA, Raleigh L., Jr., *Matheny Genealogy* (unpub, 1942?); MATHENY, William Blake, *Genealogical Notes Concerning the Matheny-Methany Family of VA* (1955); CUMBERLAND CO. HISTORICAL & GENEALOGICAL SOCIETIES OF IL, *Cumberland Co. History* (not dated).

MAUPIN, GABRIEL

> b. c. 1666/7 FR, *poss.* nr. Abbeville, then Ponthieu District, Normandie, at the mouth of the Somme River, now Somme Dépt, Picardie; surname Maupin common there for centuries; however, marr. record says he was from Gargau, i.e., Gargeau, now Jargeau, which is in the Loiret Dépt, Centre, s.e. of Orléans where a Daniel Maupin was bp. in 1628, so *poss.* father of Gabriel who named his 2nd son Daniel – 1st son said to have been named for Claude Brousson, his godfather and a great Huguenot minister who was martyred, 4 Nov 1698
>
> by 3 Nov 1688- in HOL, where he was received by the Amsterdam Ch., Oct, 1688, & again, Feb,1688/9, for "confession of faith"
>
> m. 2 Sep 1691, Walloon Ch, Amsterdam, Mary Hersent (b. Gueures, Seine-Maritime Dépt, Haute-Normandie, bp. 15 Sep 1664, Temple of Luneray, both towns s.w. of Dieppe), d/o Louis & Marie (Pillon) Hersent/Erssen; she was 25, liv. in the Hartenstraat, parents deceased; he was 25, a tailor liv. in the Bethaniënstraat at the time of his marr., parents deceased; a cousin Louis Le Gendre was a witness at the marr.; Mary m/2, 1724, Thomas Creas; she d. 1748.
>
> 1700 -arr Manakintown, VA on the ship *Nasseau*, w/ wife & 3 ch
>
> 18 Apr 1705 – naturalized, Williamsburg
>
> c. 1708 - settled Williamsburg, VA; applied for his headrights of 250 acres of land in Henrico Co, VA, 1 Jun 1709 (headright = 50 acres for each person in the emigrant family)
>
> d. a. 30 Apr 1720, wp, Williamsburg, VA; will mentions wife, sons Daniel & Gabriel, dau Mary

CHILDREN:

Magdeleine[2], bp. 22 Jun 1692, Walloon Church, Amsterdam, HOL; living,1709

Claude[2], bp. 4 Apr 1694, Walloon Church, Amsterdam, HOL, godfa Claude Brousson & his mother Jeanne; prob. d. young

Marie/Mary[2], bp. 6 Apr 1698, Walloon Church, Amsterdam, HOL; living Sep 1719, unmarr.

Sara Catherine[2], bp. 6 Apr 1698, Walloon Church, Amsterdam, HOL; prob. d. young

Daniel[2], b. 25 Mar 1700, Amsterdam, HOL, d. 20 Oct 1788, Albemarle Co, VA; m. 1719, Margaret Via (bp. 3 Aug 1701, St. Peter's Parish, Hanover Co, VA-d.1789), d/o Amer Via; **10 ch** 2 of his sons mar. d/o Cornelius D'Aubigne/Dabney (John[3] m. Frances, Daniel[3] m. Elizabeth)

Gabriel[2], b. c. 1705 VA, d. p. 22 Apr 1742, wd; <u>m/1</u>, Judith Pasteur, d/o <u>Jean & Mary(Blouet)</u>
    <u>Pasteur</u>, she d. 9 Nov 1737, Burton Parish, VA; <u>m/2</u>, Mary (X) Saunders, widow of Robert Saunders.

NOTE: Gabriel Maupin was <u>not</u> of the nobility <u>nor</u> did he marry into it. The claims of nobility have not been <u>proven</u>. Nor was he a general or even an officer in the army. A letter to the *VA Magazine* in 1901, responded to previously printed "facts". The person who had supplied said "facts" was not identified in the magazine but it was clear that he did not have any documentation to prove his statements.

REF: MAUPIN, Florence Mary - *Notes on the Maupin Family, Including: French Maupins, Immediate Family of Gabrielle, Gabriel Branch (*Typescript); SHAFFETT, Dorothy Maupin - *The Story of Gabriel & Marie Maupin: Huguenot Refugees to VA in 1700* (1994, Baltimore); Records, Walloon Church, Amsterdam, Holland; *"The Maupin Family"* in the *VA Historical Magazine* Vol. 8 (1901); *the Huguenot Society Founders of Manakintown, VA Year Book #1 (1924).*

MAURY, Matthew

    b. 18 Sep 1686, Castel Maurou, Gascogne, n.e. of Toulouse, now Haute-Garonne Dépt, Midi-Pyrénées,
        s/o Abram & Marie (Feaugerrau/Feauguereau) Maury
    c. 1714 - fled FR, went to Dublin, IRE
    m. 20 Oct 1716, Dublin, Mary Anne Fontaine (2 Apr 1690, Taunton, ENG-10 Dec 1755, Charles City,
        VA), d/o Rev. <u>James & Anne Élisabeth (Boursiquot) Fontaine</u>
    c. 1717 - to America
    returned to IRE for wife, son, 13 servants
    autumn 1719 – arr. VA
    d. 1752, King William Co, VA
    CHILDREN:
    James[2], b. 8 Apr 1718, Dublin; m. 11 Nov 1743, Mary Walker; he was a minister; d. 9 Jun 1769; **13 ch**
    Mary[2], b, 1728; m. Daniel Claiborne; **4 ch**
    Abraham[2], b. 12 Mar 1731; m. 2 Nov 1759, Lunenburg Co, VA, Susanna Poindexter (1745/6, Fluvanna
        Co, VA-22 Jan 1801, Franklin, TN), d/o Phillip & Elizabeth (X) Poindexter; d. 22 Jan 1784,
        Cumberland Parish, Lunenburg Co.
        CHILDREN:
        Matthew[3], b. 6 Jul 1760; bp. Nottaway Par, Amelia Co.; m. 1 Dec 1780, Frances/Euphany Tabb;
            he was a Rev. War soldier; he d. 25 Sep 1783, of wounds rec. in the Battle of Guilford
            Court House, on 15 Mar 1781; 13 Nov 1783, wp Lunenburg Co.
        Elizabeth[3], b. 16 Mar 1762; bp. Cumberland Par, Lunenburg Co.; m. William Dowsing
        Susanna[3], b. 24 Jun 1764; bp. Cumberland Par; m. Joel Parrish
        Abraham[3], b. 17 Feb 1766; bp. Cumberland Par; m. 21 Feb 1793, Amelia Co., Martha Branch
            Worsham
        Mary Anne[3], b. 27 Mar 1768, bp. Cumberland Par; m. 2 Jun 1783, Metcalfe de Graffenried
            (c. 1760-1803, nr. Franklin, TN), s/o Tscharner & Sara (Rust) Lowry de Graffenried; she
            d. 1801, Town Creek, Lawrence Co, AL; at least **6 ch**
        Philip Poindexter[3], b. 9/10 Oct 1770; bp. Cumberland Par; m. 15 Dec 1793, Elizabeth Ann
            Cunningham
        Martha[3], b. 10/17 Jun 1772; bp. Cumberland Par; m. Chapman White
        James[3], b. 1774; bp. Cumberland Par

REF: BROCK, R.A., *Documents Chiefly Unpublished Relating to the Huguenot Emigration to VA* (Richmond, VA, 1886); WEST, Sue Crabtree, *The Maury Family Tree* (Birmingham, AL, 1979, 1983) – contains entries from Maury Family Bibles.

MAUZÉ/MOZÉ/MAUZY, Michel/Michael

b. c. 1650, FR; there is the village of Mauzé-sur-le-Mignon, then in Aunis, now in Deux-Sèvres Dépt, Poitou-Charentes, c. 20 mi. n.e. of La Rochelle, where there is a medieval Mauzé castle – *poss.* the home of Michel; several Mauzé families came from the La Rochelle area

m. prob. FR, XX; no mention of a wife in ENG records, she must have d. in FR

16 Dec 1687 - naturalized with ch at Whitehall, London, ENG

d., prob. ENG

CHILDREN:

Michael[2]

John[2], b. 11 Dec 1676, La Rochelle?, FR; m/1, c. 1692, London, ENG, Elizabeth Connyers, d/o Dr. William Connyers – **3 sons, 2 daus**?; he went from FR to ENG; 1685, to Charleston, SC, 1700; in VA, by 13 Dec 1711, when he witnessed a will; c. 1714, to the Northern Neck of VA, Stafford Co.; m/2, c. 1712, VA, Mary (Crosby) Mountjoy (1676- a. 14 Dec 1756 ,wp, Stafford Co), d/o George Crosby, widow of Capt. Edward Mountjoy – **1 son, 1 dau** (she m/3, 1723, widower Joseph Waugh); John he d. 6 Jun 1718, Fauquier Co., VA; it seems as if John[2] was the only one of his siblings to emigrate to America

CHILDREN m/1:

    John[3], b. c. 1696, ENG; m. 1721, his cousin Hester Connyers (b. c. 1700, London), d/o Henry Connyers (John[3]'s mother's bro, s/o Dr. William Connyers; **4 sons, 3 daus**

    George[3], b. c. 1698; d. 10 Jan 1754, Overwharton Parish, Stafford Co, VA

    Margaret[3], b. 1702, VA; m. 21 Sep 1721, Major Peter Hedgman; she d. 16 Jan 1754, age 52, bur. nr. Brooke, Stafford Co, VA; **11 ch**

CHILDREN m/2:

    Peter[3], b. 1713, Stafford Co, VA; m. 9 Feb 1735, Elizabeth Sumner, d/o Joseph Sumner; he d. a. 11 Jun 1751, wp, Stafford Co; **5 ch**

    Elizabeth[3], b. c. 1714; m/1, William Markham (d. c. 1734 Pr. William Co, VA), s/o Lewis Markham – 1 son **John** (1732, Pr. William Co.-a. 13 Feb 1804, wp, Stafford Co.) who m/1, spring 1763, Alice Miller (c. 1739-1775) , d/o Simon Miller – **2 sons, 3 daus**, m/2, XX – **2 daus**, m/3, Apr 1781, Stafford Co., Jane/Jenny Waller (b. 28 Jul 1746), d/o George & Elizabeth (Allen) Waller – **3 sons, 1 dau**, Elizabeth m/2, c. 1740, Thomas Conway- **7-8 ch**, incl. 7 sons who fought in the Rev. War + 1 dau?; she d. a. 1784

Peter[2]
Isabel[2]

REF: MAUZY, Armand Jean, "The Mauzey-Mauzy Family" in the *Virginia Magazine of History & Biography,* Vol. 58 (Richmond, VA, 1950); MAUZY, Armand Jean, "On to Glory" in the *Transactions of the Huguenot Society of SC*, Vol. 82 (1977); MAUZY, Richard, *The Mauzy & Kissling Families* (1911); BLAKEMORE, Maurice Neville, *The Blakemore Family & Allied Lines*; KING, George Harrison Sanford, *"Copies of Extant Wills from Counties Whose Records Have Been Destroyed"* in Genealogies of VA Families in Tyler's Quarterly, Vol. IV.

MERCEREAU/MERSEREAU, Jean

b. c. 1638, Saintonge, FR, s/o General Josué Mercereau

m. Elizabeth DuBois (b. c. 1642, FR- d. p. 16 Aug 1693, Staten Island, NY); she & their ch went to ENG, c. 1685, then sailed for Philadelphia but due to a storm, the ship went to NYC, by 1689; her name appears on the marr. record of her son Daniel, 16 Aug 1693

studied law; was a saddler; captain in the Army, said to have been the commanding officer at Rochefort, s. of La Rochelle

d. a. 1685, FR, Moïse, Saintonge -town not found, prob. Moëze, now in Charente-Maritime Dépt, Poitou-Charentes; s.w. of Rochefort

CHILDREN:

Josué/Joshua[2], b. 6 Jan 1658, FR; went to ENG; to NY, p. 1685; m. 16 Jun 1693, FR Ch, NYC, Marie

Chadaine, d/o <u>Jean & Marie (Boucherie/Bourchier) Chadeayne</u>; settled on Staten Island; he d. 23 May 1756, NY

CHILDREN (prob. others):

Marie[3], b. 16 May, bp. 19 May 1695, FR Ch, NYC; m. 1st cousin John LaTourette, s/o <u>Jean & Marie (Mercereau) La Tourette</u>

Josué/Joshua[3], b. 18 May, bp. 5 Jul 1696, FR Ch, NYC; m. 21 Oct 1727, Mary Corsen (21 Oct 1704-8 Jul 1763), d/o Jacob Corsen of Staten Island; he d. 9 Aug 1769, Staten Is.; **7-10 ch**

Paul[3], m. Judith (Bodine) Pouillon (d. 16 Sep 1767, 74y 2m 8d), d/o <u>Vincent & Heyltje (Smith) Bodine</u>, widow of Jacques Poillon; he d. a. 10 Dec 1777, wp; he was a shipwright; no ch mentioned in his will

David[3], m/1, prob. Ann Granger – **4 ch**, m/2, 26 Sep 1768, Elizabeth Perine – **6 ch**

Elizabeth[3] m. 1st cousin **Jean**[3]Mercereau, s/o <u>Daniel & Susanne Marie (Doucinet) Mercereau</u>

Elizabeth[2], b. c. 1660, FR; m. 29 Apr 1693, Pierre Massé; **issue**

Jean[2], b. c. 1662, FR; prob. d. young as no further info

Daniel[2], b. c. 1665; m. 16 Aug 1693, FR Ch, NYC, Susanne Marie Doucinet (from "la rosselle" – La Rochelle?); he was a tailor

CHILDREN:

Daniel[3], b. 10 Aug, bp. 18 Aug 1695, FR Ch, NYC

Susanne Marie[3], b. 8 Jul, bp. 18 Jul 1697, FR Ch, NYC

Marianne[3], b. 31 Oct, bp. 5 Nov 1699, FR Ch, NYC; m. 1st cousin Pierre La Tourette, s/o <u>Jean & Marie (Mercereau) La Tourette</u>

Jean[3], m. 1st cousin **Elizabeth**[3] Mercereau, d/o <u>Josué & Marie (Chadaine) Mercereau</u>

Paul[2], b. 1 Jan, chr 8 Jan 1668; said to have remained in ENG

Marie[2], b. 6 Nov, chr 9 Nov 1670, FR; went to ENG; to NY, p. 1685; m. 6 Jul 1693, FR Ch, NYC, <u>Jean LaTourette</u>; liv. Schenectady & was there at the time of the massacre of 1690 – her husband & children were slain & she was scalped and left for dead but recovered; went to live w/her bro Joshua; she d. c. 1733

Marthe/Martha[2], m. NY, X Chadaine/Chadeayne

REF: MERSEREAU, Henry Lawrence, "Mersereau Family Genealogy" in the *NYGBR*, Vol. XXVII (1896); CUTTER, William Richard, *Genealogical & Family History of Central NY*, Vol. I (NY, 1912); BAIRD, Charles W., *History of the Huguenot Emigration to America*, Vol. I (Baltimore, 1973); WITTMEYER, Alfred V., *Registers of the Births, Marriages, & Deaths of the Église Françoise à la Nouvelle York* (NY, 1886); CLUTE, J.J., *Annals of Staten Island* (NY, 1877).

MERKEL/MERKLEN/MARKLE, Pierre/Peter

b. 17 Aug 1640, Metz, Moselle Dépt, Lorraine, FR, s/o Pierre & Sophia Maria (Beaudoin) Merkel; Sophia Maria was the d/o Jacques Beaudoin

21 Feb 1672 - requested that his father grant him the homestead at Colmar (a few mi s. of Strasbourg) as was about to marry & needed a home

m. 24 Feb 1672, Metz, Magdalen Coehorn, d/o Christian Coehorn

d. ?

CHILDREN:

Hans[2], b. 23 May 1673; **no issue**

Christian[2], b. 11 Sep 1675; d. young

Johan Christian[2], b. 19 Jul 1678, Metz; m/1, Amsterdam, Jemima Weurtz (1680-1770), m/2, Catherine Bruckner, m/3, Eva Kelchner; 1st to America, c. 1703; left Jemima in PA, went back to GER & m. Catherine; back to PA, c. 1718/9, settled Salem Springs, Berks Co, PA where he purchased 1500 acres; he was a coachmaker; on his land he built a wagonmaker's shop, a blacksmith shop & a gristmill; took Oath of Allegiance, 10 Apr 1742; he d. a. 22 May 1766, wp

CHILDREN, m/2:

Anna Catharina[3], b. 14 May 1715, Lambsheim, GER (w. of Mannheim); m. 8 Apr 1733, Rev. Johann Casper Stoever (21 Dec 1701-13 May 1779); she d. 7 Oct 1795; **11 ch**

Maria Apollonia[3], b. 1718, prob. GER; m. 13 Jul 1737, Johann Jacob Hill (10 Mar 1716-20 Aug 1776); **6 sons, 3 daus**

Peter[3], b. 13 Apr 1721, PA; m. 11 Nov 1750, Catherine Grim (30 Apr 1726-31 Jul 1803), d/o Johan Egidius & Anna Catharina (X) Grim; he d. 25 Jul 1785; **issue**

Anna Maria[3], b. 1729, PA; m. 10 Dec 1745, Johann Frederick Kramer

Anna Helena[3], b. 21 Feb 1725, PA; m. 3 Dec 1750, Peter Biehlen (21 Mar 1726-20 Feb 1802); she d. 18 Mar 1803

Francianna[3], b. 1727 PA; m. 16 Apr 1745, Michael Rugh/Ruch (1723-1820); d. 1809

Christian[3], b. 28 Aug 1728, PA; m. 14 Nov 1758, Juliana Guerst (21 Mar 1734-13 Dec 1803); he d. 15 Feb 1814

George[3], b. 29 Jul 1729, PA; m. 18 Dec 1750, Anna Christina Hill; he d. 15 Feb 1779

Casper/Gaspard[3], b. 16 Sep 1730, PA; m/1, 1 Apr 1755, Elizabeth Grim, sis of Catherine (above) who d. Westmoreland Co, PA – **3 sons, 6 daus** + 2 others, m/2, 1776, Berks Co., Maria/Mary Roadarmel/Rothermel (1756-1832) – **6 sons, 5 daus**; he d. 15 Sep 1819, Berks Co, PA

Jacob[2], b. 2 Sep 1679; m. a. 11 Sep 1728, Maria Rhode; emigrated to America, 11 Sep 1728; **issue**

George[2], b. 19 Sep 1680; m. Margaret Schneider; he d. 1767, Greenwich Twp, Berk Co, PA; **no issue**

John[2], b. 1685

NOTE: The documentation for this ancestor is very contradictory. The above seems to be the best interpretation possible.

REF: ELLIOTT, Ella Zerbey, *Blue Book of Schuylkill County* (Pottsville, PA, 1916); LONG, William Gabriel, comp. & ed, *History of the Grim Family of PA & its Associated Families* (1934); MEISNER, Joseph A., comp. & ed., *Rothermel Families in America* (1989); MERKEL, Norton W., *The Merkel, Merkle, Markle, Markel Freündschaft* (unpub., not dated).

MERTZ, Anna Margaretha – see VAUTRIN, Abraham

MESUROL(L)E/MESUROLL/MESEROLL, Jean

b. 1633, Calais, FR

m. 19 Jun 1660, Mannheim, GER, Jeanne Cretin/Carten (b. Ringlet, Flanders, not found); she m/2, a. 1704, Charel de Nison (d. c. 1707)

16 Apr 1663 - to New Netherland on the *Spotted Cow*

28 Oct 1663 - admitted to Brooklyn Reformed Dutch Ch. by letter from the Mannheim Ch.

liv. New Utrecht, Flatbush & Bushwick

1667 – bought land in Bushwick

d. 1695, NY

CHILD:

Jean II[2], b. 4 Aug, bp. 11 Aug 1661, Mannheim, GER; m. 11 Nov 1682, Marritye Tennis Couvers; d. a. 16 Dec 1712, wp

CHILDREN:

John[3], bp. 2 Sep 1683, Amersfoort, NY (now a section of Brooklyn); m. Lysbeth/Elizabeth Praa (bp. 13 May 1691), d/o Pieter Praa & Maria Hay; he d. 1756, Bushwick; **4 ch**

Cornelius[3], m. 3 Oct 1711, Janetye Horns

Margaret[3], m. X Durje

Deborah[3], m. X Cotts

Jane[3], bp. 29 Apr 1696; m. 11 Nov 1712, Joris/George Elsworth

REF: MESEROLL, David B., Jr., *One Meserolla Genealogy, 319 Years & 12 Generations in America* (not pub., 1982).

METTETAL, Jean Georges

b. c. 1728, Étupes, Doubs Dépt, Franche-Comté, FR, s.e. of Montbéliard
m. c. 1749, Étupes, Suzanne Catherine Mauvau, b. Étupes
d. a. 28 Oct 1785, prob. Étupes
CHILD:
Jean Christophe[2], b. c. 1750, Étupes; m. 17 Sep 1771, Temple of Étupes, Catherine Perrenon (b.
    Belverne, Haute-Sâone Dépt, Franche-Comté, FR, w. of Belfort), d/o François & Françoise
    (Pourchot) Perrenon; he was a carpenter
    CHILD:
    Pierre Christophe[3], b. 28 Oct 1785, Étupes, FR; m. Marie Françoise Doriot (b. 16 Dec 1785,
        Étupes), d/o Jean Nicolas & Jeanne (Ponssot) Doriot - **8 ch;** he went to America, 1847/8
        w/ son **David**[4] (1827, Étupes-1902, Philadelphia) & 2 of David's sons, **Peter**[5] & **Frédéric**[5],
        both b. Étupes; Pierre[3] d. 19 Sep 1854, Philadelphia, PA. Marie returned to FR & is bur. in
        Étupes; Pierre & Marie also had a dau **Louise**[4], b. 1 Nov 1818, who m. 10 Sep 1839, Étupes,
        David Bouthenot
Pierre Christophe[2]
prob. **Catherine Marguerite**[2], m. Jacques Maillard

NOTE: According to Archives of Étupes, name has been Matetaul, Metetaul, Mathetaux, Matteta and dates back to 1431 in a town called Glay, s.e. of Montbéliard. The cited Mettetal genealogy, has copies of the original vital records from Étupes written in French.

REF: KUSTER, Della Mettetal & METTETAL, Hazel, *Genealogical Record of the Mettetal Family, 1728-1965* (unpub., c. 1965).

MELYN, Cornielle/Cornelis

bp. 17 Sep 1600, St. Walburga's Ch, Antwerp, s/o André & his 2nd wife Marie (Ghuedinx-Botens) Melyn;
    she d. Oct 1606); André d. Nov 1606; Cornelis' half-bro Abraham (b. 1581) became his guardian
1610 - apprenticed to a tailor
by 1627 - in Antwerp/Anvers, a Walloon refugee, where he was listed as a *seemtouwer,* leather dresser
m. p. 22 Apr 1627, Amsterdam, Janneken Adriens (b. c. 1600, Myerdt, prob. N. Brabant, HOL)
12 May 1638 - sailed from Texel (an island in the W. Frisian Is., HOL) for New Netherlands on the *Hep*
    Waren van Noorwagen
Arr. 4 Aug 1638 - New Amsterdam; shortly after arr., he went to Newfoundland where he & his shipmates
    caught 12,000 codfish and went to FR where they sold the ship and the fish
returned to New Netherland and applied for Patroonship of Staten island
p. 1641 - on Staten Island w/ wife & ch with a patroonship; patentee of the Staten Island Colony
made many trips back & forth to Europe bet 1638-1660
1643-45 - was president of the "Council of Eight Men"
18 Jun 1647 - Gov. Kieft brought charges against Cornelis of *lèse-majesté* (high treason), saying he didn't
    represent the people; Cornelis disputed the charge but, on 25 Jul 1647, he was found guilty,
    sentenced to banishment for 7 yrs., and fined 300 guilders; his case was appealed at the Hague &
    Cornelis was allowed return to NY
1655 - involved with Director Kieft's War; was a captive of the Indians, along with 50 others for 31 days
    until 1440 guilders were raised for ransom for Cornelis, his wife, son Isaac and son-in-law
    Claes Paradijs; left Staten Island as their property had been destroyed and went to Manhattan
1656 - to New Haven, CT; he had problem w/ Peter Stuyvesant's administration so decided to side w/ the

British

7 Apr 1657 - New Haven , took Oath of Allegiance to the British

Dec 1658 - sailed to the NETH, where he surrendered his Patroonship of Staten Island to the West India Co. for 1500 guilders

d. p. 13 Mar 1662/3, New Haven, CT; Janneken d. c. 20 yrs. later

CHILDREN:

Cornelia[2], bp. 27 Feb 1628, Amsterdam; m/1, p. 30 Jun 1647, Amsterdam, Jacob Loper – **2 ch**, m/2, p. 7 Apr 1653 (date of banns), Jacob Schellinger – **6 ch**; she d. 25 Feb 1716/7

Johannes[2], bp. 17 Apr 1629, Amsterdam; d. poss 27 Sep 1647 in the wreck of the *Princess*

Cornelis[2], bp. 6 Sep 1630, Amsterdam; d. a. 11 Oct 1633

Cornelis[2], bp. 11 Oct 1633, Amsterdam; d. Sep 1655, Staten Island, NY Indian massacre

Abraham[2], bp 27 May 163,5 Amsterdam; no more info

Mariken[2], bp. 29 Mar 1637, Amsterdam; m/1, p. 18 Jun 1655 (date of banns), Claes Allertsen Paradijs – **2 ch**, m/2, 26 Aug 1664, Matthias Hatfield – **6 ch**; she d. 1694/99

Isaac[2], bp. 21 Nov 1638, NY; d. a. 22 Jul 1646

Jacob[2], bp. 17 Apr 1640; m. 1662, Hannah Hubbard (bur. 15 Nov 1717, Boston, MA); he d. 13 Dec 1706, Boston; **5 ch**

Susanna[2], bp. 14 Jun 1643, NY Dutch Ch; m. 25 Aug 1664, New Haven, CT, John Winans (d. Dec 1694); d. 1687/93; **9 ch**

Magdalen[2], bp. 3 Mar 1645; no more info

Isaac[2], bp. 22 Jul 1646, NY Dutch Ch.; m/1, Dorothea Samson – **2 ch**, m/2, Temperance Loverage – **4 ch**; d. 18 May 1693

REF: GANNON, Peter Steven, *Huguenot Refugees in the Settling of Colonial America* (NYC, 1985); *The Melyn Family in Holland & America* (no author named, no date); BURTON, Paul Gibson, "The Antwerp Ancestry of Cornelis Melyn" in the *NYGBR* (Apr, 1936), "Cornelis Melyn, Patroon of Staten Island & Some of His Descendants" in the *NYGBR* (Jan, Jul, & Oct, 1937).

MICHAU/MICHAUD, Jean

from La Villedieu, now in Charente-Maritime Dépt, Poitou-Charentes, n.e. of St.-Jean-d'Angély, then in Aunis Province

m. Catherine X

CHILDREN:

Pierre[2], b. FR; m. Sara (Bertonneau) Jaudon (c. 1645, FR-p. 22 Dec 1709, SC), d/o Jacques & Élisabeth (X) Bertonneau, widow of Élie Jaudon/Jodon, c. 1686 to SC; settled St. James Parish, French Santee, Craven Co; naturalized 1696; d. a. 26 May 1706; **no issue**

Abraham I[2], b. c. 1670, Poitou, FR; m/1 c. 1685, FR, Esther Jaudon, bro Pierre's stepdau; 1686, to SC; settled Craven Co., naturalized, 1696/7; m/2, c/1699, SC, Madeleine (X) Courège*, widow of François Courège; she had at least 3 Courège ch: Manassah, Madeleine who m. Nicholas LeNud II (3 ch), Charlotte (below); he d. p. 8 Mar 1705- prob. a. bro Pierre's death

CHILDREN, m/1:

Abraham II[3], b. c. 1696, SC; m/1, c. 1719, Charlotte Courège (c. 1695-c. 1729), d/o François & Madeleine (X) Courège; m/2, c. 1731, Lydia X; he d. a 16 Jan 1767, wp, Craven Co; his will mentions eldest son Abraham, sons Peter, Daniel, Paul, William, wife Lydia, heirs of daus Julian, Lydia, Hester; his will deposes well over 3500 acres; he was a planter, Echau/ Echaw Plantation, Berkeley Co, on the Santee c. 12 mi. from McClellansville which was granted in 1773 to Oliver Cromwell & Louis Dutarque

CHILDREN, m/1:

Julienne[4], b. 18 Jan 1721/2, bp 22 Apr 1722, Pr. Frederick Winyaw Par; m/1, XX, m/2, X Perry; d. a 2 Jul 1765 (father's will says she's dead); **issue**

Abraham III[4], b. 20 Nov 1723, bp. 21 Mar 1723/4, Pr. Frederick Winyaw Par; m. Sarah X; d. p. 13 Aug 1776, wd

Peter[4], b. 6 Mar 1724/5, bp. 3 May 1725, Pr. Frederick Winyaw Par; m. 26 Jan 1758, Charleston, Constant (X) Sutton, widow – dau **Charlotte**[5], b. 17 Apr, bp. 27 May 1759, Charleston; he d. a. 19 Jun 1772, adm SC; Constant m/3, 11 Jul 1775, Percival Pawley (7 Mar 1724-1 Jan 1787); Peter d. a. 19 Jun 1772, adm, SC

CHILDREN, m/2:

Daniel[4], b. 1733; m. 6 Apr 1756, Mary Jennings

Noah[4], b. 1735; not in father's will, prob. d. a. Aug 1776

Paul[4], b. 1736; in father's will

Lydia[4], b. 1738; m. X Claig; d. a. 2 Jul 1765 (father's will says she's dead); **issue**

William[4], in father's will – ch of m/2?

Hester[4], b. 17 Jan 1743/4, bp. 12 Apr 1744, Pr. Frederick Winyaw Par; m. Oliver Cromwell

Jeanne[3], b. SC; Moïse Carion II

Hester/Esther[3], b. SC; m. Jean Jacques Guerri as his 2nd wife; **issue**

Charlotte[3], b. c. 1695, SC

Daniel[3], b. c. 1706

CHILDREN, m/2:

Paul[3]

William[3]

*Madeleine m/3 André Rembert

REF: HIRSCH, Arthur H., *The Huguenots of Colonial SC*; *Transactions of the Huguenot Society of SC*, #44 (1944) – Abraham[3]'s will, Craven Co, dated 2 Jul 1765; GOURDINI, Virginia, "The Mysterious "Madeleine Rembert'" in the *Transactions of the Huguenot Society of SC*, #88 (1983), also #28 (1923) – will of Madeleine Rembert, dated 4 Feb 1734, Craven Co. also #49 (1944) will of Abraham, dated 2 Jul 1765; *Liste des François et Suisses settled in Charleston on the Santee & at the Orange Quarter in Carolina Who Desired Naturalization* (Baltimore, 1968); *The Register Book for the Parish Prince Frederick Winyaw* (Baltimore, MD, 1916); SMITH, D.E. & SALLEY, A.B., *Register of St. Philip's Parish 1754-1810* (Charleston, 1927).

MICH(E)AUX/MISSHEUX, Abraham

b. 23 Feb 1672, Sedan, FR, s/o Jacob & Anne (Severin/Sauvin) Michaux

to Amsterdam; he was a tinsmith, according to marr. record; member of the FR Ch, 28 Jan 1691

m. 13 Jul 1692, FR Ch, Amsterdam, Susanne Rochet (b. Jul 1674, Sedan-a. 18 Dec 1744, wp, VA), *prob.* d/o Isaac & Jeanne (Dufray) Rochet

8 May 1701 - to ENG; became members of the Huguenot Ch of Threadneedle St, London, 20 Aug 1702

to VA, 1st to Stafford Co

a. 1705- to King William Parish, Henrico Co.; 2 Nov 1705, rec. patent for 574 acres on the s side of the James River which he sold in 1707 – later survey showed that the acreage was almost twice that much

12 May 1705- naturalized, VA

1710, 1711- on tithing lists

27 Jan 1713 - rec. patent #704 for 850 acres on the s. side of the James; patent #828 for 230 acres in Henrico Co., 23 Mar 1715 – patent #828 was in the French Lands

1714 - on list w/ wife, 4 sons, 6 daus

d. a. 5 Aug 1717, wp, Henrico Co. VA, which names (in order) – sons Jacob, John, Abraham, wife Susanne, 3 oldest daus Anne, Jane Magdalin, Susanne, dau Olive Judi, 3 young daus Elizabeth, Ann Madalin, Esther Mary

Susanne's will, 17 Dec 1744, wp, Goochland Co., VA, names only son John Paul

CHILDREN (1st 6 ch bp. Walloon Ch, Amsterdam):

Anne/Nannie[2], bp. 7 May 1693; d. p. 13 May 1717, unmarr.

Jeanne/Jane Magdalin[2], bp. 24 Oct 1694; m. c. 1720, Jean Pierre/John Peter Le Grand, s/o Pierre & Judith (Vreil) Le Grand – headrights/deeds prove that; **6 ch**

Jacob[2], bp. 11 Dec 1695; m. a. 1726, Judith Woodson, d/o Richard & Ann (Smith) Woodson; d. 15 Jan 1745, Goochland Co., VA; **4 ch**; Judith m/2, Littleberry Mosby, Sr., of Cumberland & Powhatan Co.

Jean/John[2], bp. 3 Jan 1697; m. Sarah X
Susanne[2], bp. 13 Apr 1698; m. a. 20 May 1727, John Quinn of Henrico Co, VA – at least **2 ch**
***Isaac**[2], bp. 28 Jun 1699; d. a. 1714, Henrico Co, VA
***Jacques/James**[2], bp. 15 Aug 1700; poss. m. X Tompkins & d. Jan/Feb 1771
Abraham[2], b. c. 1704; killed by Indians, 28 Nov 1747, Lunenburg Co., VA; unmarr.
Olive Judith/Judi[2], b. c. 1706, Henrico Co, VA; m. Anthony Morgan, a Quaker
John Paul[2], b. 17 Mar 1708, Henrico Co, VA; m. Judith Wilmore?; **no known issue**
Elizabeth[2], b. c. 1710, Henrico Co, VA; m. Sanborn Woodson? or m. 7 Mar 1725, Daniel Croom?
Ann Madelin/Agnes[2], b. c. 1710/1; m. Richard Woodson, s/o Richard & Ann (Smith) Woodson; **2 ch**
Esther Mary[2], b. c. 1712/3; m. Alexander Cunningham; **10 ch**

***NOTE:** Names on some lists, not on others, but in Amsterdam bap. records

REF: Abraham Michaux's will, dated 13 May 1717; Susanne's will, dated 22 Mar 1740;EGGLESTON, J.D., "The Huguenot Abraham Michaux & His Descendants" in *Genealogies of VA Families from the VA Magazine of History & Biography*, Vol. IV (Baltimore, 1981); JESTER, Annie Lash, *Adventurers of Purse & Person VA 1607-1625 (1964);* CABELL, Priscilla Harriss, *Turff & Twigg,* Vol. 1 *The French Lands* (Richmond, VA, 1988); Vital Records from the *Centre Généalogique de l'Eydoux,* Montauban-sur-l'Ouvèze (Drôme Dépt, Rhône-Alpes, se Nyons); *The Huguenot,* #24 (1969-71); *The VA Magazine of History & Biography,* Vols. XLIV, XLV (Richmond, VA, 1936, 1937).

MICHEL, Francis Louis/Franz Ludwig

b. 29 Jul 1675, Bern, SWI, s/o David & Ursula (Fels) Michel, a Swiss Huguenot family; family name was Michel von Schwertschwendi; David was Lord of Ralligen, served on the Great Council of Bern, prefect of Gottstatt; a family of position and influence; Franz was well-educated
a. 1700 - served in the FR Army
1701-04, 1707-08 - to America twice to explore for colonization of Swiss & FR religious refugees
m. c. 1707, Bern, Anna Barbara Lerber/Herbert, d/o Franz Ludwig Lerber
d. 1720 Bern
CHILD:
Christoph/Christopher[2], b. 4 Apr 1708; m. a. 25 Nov 1735, Anna Catherina X; to America on the *Snow Good Hope,* from Hamburg, via Cowes, ENG, arr 29 Sep 1753, Philadelphia & took Oath of Allegiance 1 Oct 1753; c. 1754, to Frederick Co, MD where he bought 250 acres bet. Middletown & Sharpsburg; he attended Reformed Churches in PA & MD; he d. 14 Aug 1783, Washington Co, MD, bur. old Mt. Moriah Reformed Ch Cemetery, Sharpsburg; surname became **MICHAEL**
CHILDREN:
Petter[3], b. 27 Nov 1735, SWI; m. 28 Feb 1764, Frederick Co, MD, Dorothea Schmitt (15 Apr 1746-16 Feb 1820); he d. 12 Apr 1808, bur. Middletown, MD; **7 ch**
Anna Barbara[3], b. 21 Aug 1741; d. 23 Feb 1783, bur. Sharpsburg, MD
George[3]
Ludwig[3], b. c. 1745; naturalized Elizabeth Twp, Lancaster Co, PA; m. Catherine X; d. 1805, MD
Christopher[3], b. 7 Oct 1749
Anna Maria[3], b. 3 Aug 1752

REF: WEISGERBER, Virginia Edna, extensive research, primary docs; "The Journey of Francis Louis Michel" in the *VA Historical Magazine,* Vol. XXIV, #1 (Jan, 1916); *Historische Biographisches Lexikon der Schweiz,* V (Neuenburg, aka Neuchâtel, SWI, 1929).

MICHELET, Jacques

b. 1550, Metz, Lorraine, FR
m/1, Suzanne Joly (d. 1590)

1579 - he was a *receveur*, taxation officer; 1587 - was promoted to *commissaire du trésorier royal* (asst. to the royal treasurer); 1593 *commissaire de l'extraordinaire des guerres* (superior of one or more army units)

m/2, 28 Jul 1591, Suzanne Viriat

4 Dec 1604 - purchased land from Jacquemin Petre in Vallières (which one?) but continued to liv in Metz

d. 1610, Metz, FR

CHILDREN, m/1:

Jacques[2]

Suzanne[2]

Pierre[2]

Paul[2], bp. 16 Jan 1585, Metz; m. 12 May 1613, Anne Pillon, d/o Josué Pillon

    CHILDREN:

        Paul[3], bp. 6 Sep 1617, Metz; m. c. 1647, Vang Parish, NOR, Karen Michelsdatter (1614, Vang Parish-1665, Furnes, NOR); 1644 ,a lieut; 1657, was a major in the Oppland regt; fatally wounded at the Battle of Borge Ch., d. 20 Mar 1660 Smaalenene (s.w. Trøgstad, which is s.e. Oslo), NOR

        CHILD:

        Hans[2], b. 1650, Freberg (n.e. Oslo), Furnes (now Ringsaker, n. of Oslo), NOR; m/2, Jul 1696, Christianla (Oslo), NOR, Bartha Brandt (14 Jan 1677, Eidsvoll [n.e. Oslo], NOR-11 Jul 1727 Rodenes [s.e. Oslo], NOR); he was a Captain; he d. 9 Mar 1716, at the Battle at Høland Church

        CHILD:

        Christian Frederick[3], b. 5 Mar 1697, Helsjo (sm. lake), Høland, NOR; m. 30 Jul 1737, Hersaeter*, Trøgstad, NOR, Johanne Christiane Augusta Holst (21 Feb 1718, Hersaeter-21 Nov 1788, Trøgstad); he was a soldier; he d. 30 Jan 1769, Hersaeter

        *not found, may have a different name now, or town has "disappeared," or the spelling is incorrect

        CHILD:

        Johan Wilhelm[4], b. 13 Nov 1753, Nordresaeter, NOR; m. 25 Mar 1790, Laerdal (n.e. Bergen), NOR Sophie Amalie Tuxen (11 Aug 1769, Bergen, NOR-6 Mar 1848, Hersaeter); he d. 27 Feb 1805, Moland, Fyresdal (in Telemark Co), NOR

        CHILD (1 of 6):

        Jakob Post[5], b. 20 Jul 1796, Fyresdal, NOR; m. 6 Jul 1843, Fåberg Oppland Ch, Vardal, NOR, Gregine Oldsdatter (7 Nov 1812 Gjøvik (s. Ringsaker), NOR-5 Mar 1879 Coon Prairie, Vernon Co, WI); emigrated to US, 1851,on the *Incognito*; he d. 19 Nov 1866, Coon Prairie, WI; son **Carl/Charles Jules**[5]

    Jacques/Jacob[3], b. 1619, Metz; fled FR, arr. NOR, Apr 1644 w bro Pau; 1645 capt. in the Akershus National Infantry Regt.; m. Anne Christensdatter Mule (d. 1698); 1675, liv. Hedmark, Vang Parish; d. by 1678 Vang, NOR

    CHILDREN:

    Hans[3], **John**[3], **Madeline**[3], **Peter**[3]

CHILDREN, m/2:

Rachel[2]

Michel[2]

REF: FINNE-GRØNN, S. H., *Slegten Michelet Genealogisk- Personalhistoriske Meddelelser* (Christiania,1919); ROLAND, Hjalmar R., *Coon Prairie Book* (Minneapolis, 1927); *Militaerbiografier II*; MARVIK, Steiner, *Fyresdal Gards-og ættesoge* (Fyresdal Kommune, 1992).

MICHELET, Louis (Rev.)

b. 17 Dec 1675 prob. Metz, Lorraine, FR; a merchant, later a Protestant pastor

m. 1697, Susan Mangeot (b. 26 Jun 1674, Metz-d. by 1715)

1697 - fled w/ wife from Metz, FR, to Zweibrücken/Deux Ponts where he served as minster of the FR Ch. there

ret. to Metz where the last 4 ch. were b.; no indication that any of the ch., other than Jean Jacques, emigrated to America

d. 27 Feb 1750, Zweibrücken

CHILDREN:

Jean Jacques/John Jacob[2], b. 1697, Zweibrücken; left 6 May 1733, Rotterdam on the *Hope*, 28 Aug 1733, arr. Philadelphia; went 1st to Oley, Berks Co, then to Whitehall; m. PA, Elizabeth Barbara Burk-halter, d/o Ulrich Burkhalter of Whitehall Twp; surname became **MICKLEY**; settled Lehigh Co, PA; d. 18 Aug 1769; **7 ch**

Louis[2], b. 1705; 1720, went to Berlin, GER; m. & had **issue**

Pierre[2]

Barbé[2]

Marie[2]

NOTE: Given the name Michelet and the common "home town" of Metz, Louis & Jacques may have had a family connection but it is not known nor proven.

REF: ROBERTS, Charles R., STOUDT, John B., KRICK, Thomas H., DIETRICH, William J., *History of Lehigh Co, PA*, Vol. III (Allentown, PA, 1914); MICKLEY, Minnie E., *The Genealogy of the Mickley Family of America* (Mickleys, PA, 1893); STAPLETON, Rev. A., *Memorials of the Huguenots in America* (Carlisle, PA, 1901).

MICOU, Paul

b. c. 1667/8, FR

c. 1685 - from Nantes, FR to ENG

by 1693 - to VA, to nr. the Rappahannock River – Port Micou; c. 1600 acres with 6 mi. of river frontage, later became 2000 acres; location today nr. Loretto, Essex Co, VA – Loretto is s.e. of the Fort A.P. Hill Military Res.

m. VA, Margaret prob. Cammock, b. VA, d/o Warwick & Margaret (Williams?) Thatcher Cammock (her 1st husband was Sylvester Thatcher); Margaret Cammock's will dated 24 Mar 1709, refers to her dau "Margaret Micou" and Paul Micou is 1 of the executors of her estate; Margaret Micou's wp, Essex Co., 17 Mar 1740/1 – names sons Paul, Henry, daus Judith, Margaret, Mary Fry, grdau Clara (dau of son John)

1700-1720 - serv as Justice of the Peace in Essex Co, VA (he was educated to be a lawyer)

d. 23 May 1736, Essex Co, VA; bur. Vauter's Churchyard, St. Anne's Parish; he was a physician, merchant & justice; wp, 16 Nov 1736 – names wife, sons Paul, John, James, Henry, daus Mary Hill, Margaret Fauntleroy, Judith, 2 grch (Eliz.'s ch)

CHILDREN:

Paul[2], d. a. 16 Nov 1742, wp – names bros John, James, Henry, sis Margaret, Judith, Mary, nephew Paul (son of John); unmarr.

John[2], Justice of the Peace, 1731-35 m. Catherine Walker, d/o James Walker; he d. 1754; **9 ch**

James[2], alive, 1736; no more info

Henry[2], alive, 1736; no more info

Mary[2], m/1, Col. Leonard Hill (d. 1734) – **2 sons**, m/2, Col. Joshua Fry – **5 ch**; she d. 20 Aug 1772

Margaret[2], m. a. Jun 1718, Moore Fauntleroy (1679-d. a. 3 Mar 1739 wp), s/o William & Katherine (Griffin) Fauntleroy; she d. 1742; **8 ch**

Judith[2], b, c, 1724. m. p. 1740/1, Lunsford Lewis/Lomax

Elizabeth[2], m. James Scott who d. a. 4 Jun 1718, wp; she d. a. 1736; **2 ch**

unnamed dau[2], m. Rev. Mr. Waddell, "the blind Preacher"

NOTE: There has been much discussion re the identity of Margaret (X) Micou's parents. An entry in a Will Book from Richmond Co, says that Margaret Cammock, d/o Margaret Cammock, m. Paul Micou; several other legal transactions would seem to support this conclusion. Margaret could have been the d/o of Sylvester but he d. 1667 – prob. too early for him to have been her father. If her dau Judith was b. in 1724, that would make her mo Margaret c. 57, if Sylvester had been her father. Paul's wife was definitely NOT Margaret LeRoy/Roy.

REF: GREEN, Raleigh Travers, *Genealogical & Historical Notes on Culpeper Co, VA* (Baltimore, not dated); MICOU, Rev. Paul, "Paul Micou, Huguenot Physician, & His Descendants" in the *VA Historical Magazine,* Vol. XLVI, #4 (Oct 1938); FRYE, George W., *Colonel Joshua Fry of VA* (Cincinnati, OH, 1966); RLAND, Elizabeth Hawes, "Paul Micou, Chyrurgeon" in the *William & Mary Quarterly* (Apr, 1936).

MIL/MILT/MILL/MILLE, Isaac Anthonis de

b. 1584, St. Liéven, FR Flanders, 1 of 9 ch. of Anthonis Laurensz & Grietgen (Pieters/Plovier) DeMil; Grietgen was the d/o Pieter Plovier of Menen, BEL, just over the FR border, n.w. of Tourcoing [Sint-Lievens-Houkem, Sint-Lievens-Esse, both s.e. of G(h)ent in present-day E. Flanders, BEL; S-L-E is s.e. of S-L-H (named after an Irish monk who evangelized Flanders in the 7th cent)]; Mennonite family
m. a. 24 Mar 1633, XX
d. p. 25 Nov 1650,HOL; was "a dean of bakers" in Haarlem, HOL
CHILD:
Anthony[2], b. 1625 Haarlem, HOL; m. 19 Sep 1653, Dutch Reformed Ch, Haarlem, Elisabeth van der Liphorst (b. 1628), d/o Pieter Lucaszoon Van der Liphorst & Maria Van Brugh/Brugge; went to America from HOL on the *Gilded Beaver* in May 1658, arr. 17 Jul 1658, New Amsterdam; he was elected 17 Aug 1673, to be *schout* (sheriff) of NYC; she d. p. 28 Aug 1678; he d. a. 10 Sep 1689, NYC (inv, 10 Oct 1689, wp, 10 Dec 1689); will mentions deceased wife Elisabeth, ch Isaac, Mary, Anne, Peter and Sarah; he was the 1st Chief Magistrate after restoration of authority of the States General
CHILDREN:
Maria[3], b. c. 1654, Amsterdam; bp. 11 Jul 1655; m.4 Nov 1674, Flatbush, Bowen/Boudewyn Loen, a soldier from Edam, HOL
Anna[3], b. Amsterdam; bp 21 Aug 1657, Reformed Dutch Ch, Haarlem; m. 17 Nov 1677, NYC, Hendrick Vanderburgh (bp. 18 Apr 1655, NYC), s/o Lucas Dirckszen Vanderburgh & Annetie Cornelis
Isaac[3], b. New Amsterdam; bp. 7 Dec 1659; m. 17 Dec 1684, New Amsterdam Reformed Dutch Ch., Sarah Joost Van Sassyar/van Sise, d/o Joost Carelszen van Sise/Sysen & Stynje Jans
Pieter/Petrus[3], bp. 12 Oct 1661, New Amsterdam; m. 4 Aug 1687, Maria Van der Heul (bp. 19 Nov 1664, NYC-1759, Stamford, CT), d/o Abraham Janszen Van der Heul & <u>Trintje Hendricks (Kip)</u>: progenitor of the Stamford branch of the family which used the name DeMilt; he was a baker; he d. 10 Sep 1722, Stamford; 10 ch, 3 of whom d. young, 3 did not reach maturity, the remaining 4 – **Peter**[4], **Anthony**[4], **Mary**[4], **Hannah**[4] mar. & had **issue**
Sarah[3], bp. 30 Dec 1663, New Amsterdam; m. 20 Oct 1686, Isaac Kip (bp. 15 Jan 1662, New Amsterdam Reformed Dutch Ch.), s/o <u>Isaac Kip & Catalina de Suyers/Hendricks Snyder</u>
Anthony[3], bp. 14 Mar 1666, NY Reformed Dutch Ch.; d. a. 24 May 1689 – not in father's will

REF: STAPLEY, Issa M. R. Teeples, *DeMille Family History & Genealogy* (1953); SCHUTTE, Otto, "Origins of the DeMilt/DeMill(e)Family of New Amsterdam" in *NYGBR,* Vol. 133, #4 (Oct 2002); deBOER, Louis P., *The deMil Family in Europe & America.*

MONEY/MONYE, Henri de

b. c. 1676, Bordeaux, FR, according to marriage record

m. 30 Apr 1701, Dutch Ch, NYC, Marianne Grasset, d/o Auguste & Marie (Pélé) Grasset; Auguste
Grasset was godfa to grch Susanne & Jean

liv Staten Island for some time but ch. bp., NYC; 1706/8 census shows him, wife + 5 ch. on Staten Island

c. 1720's - moved to Elizabeth (then Elizabethtown), NJ

d. Elizabeth, NJ, p. 29 Jan 1755, wd – a. 5 Feb 1755, wp, Essex Co, NJ; he was a tailor; 2 sons, 4 daus
mentioned in will; for some reason he is called "Dennis" in Gannon's book

CHILDREN, all b. Staten Island :

Susanne[2], b. 6 Jan, bp.11 Jan 1701/2, FR Ch, NYC; unmarr. in 1755

Albert[2], b. c. 1702; in 1706/8 census but prob. d. young

Anne[2], b. 15 Nov, bp. 21 Nov 1703, FR Ch, NYC; m. X Wood

Peter[2], b. c. 1704; in census of 1706/8; prob. d. young

Jean/John[2], b. 20 Nov, bp. 25 Nov 1705, FR Ch, NYC; in census of 1706/8; prob. d. young – not in
father's will

Ester[2], b. 1706/7; m. X Freeman

Maria/Mary[2], bp. 7 Nov 1708, NY Dutch Ch, NYC; m. Joseph Frasey/Frazee, an executor of her father's
will; prob. **issue**

Henry[2], b. 1711; m. Phebe X; bur. 11 Dec 1777, Westfield, Essex, NJ; **issue**

Auguste/Augustus[2], b. 11 May, bp. 24 May 1719, FR Ch, NYC; m. poss. Mary X; prob. **issue**

REF: *NJ Archives 1st Series*, Vol. 32 - Henri's will; WITTMEYER, Alfred V., *Register of the Église Françoise à la
Nouvelle York, 1688-1804* ; GANNON, Peter S., editor, *Huguenot Refugees in the Settling of Colonial America*;
THOMPSON, Neal D., "Auguste Grasset of La Rochelle, London & NYC" in *National Genealogical Society
Quarterly,* Vol. 66 #1 (Mar 1978); HONEYMAN, A. Van Doren, editor, *Documents Relating to the Colonial
History of the State of NJ* (Somerville, NJ, 1924); NYGBS, *Baptisms from 1639 to 1730 in the Reformed Dutch
Church, NY* (NY, 1901).

MON(T)FORT/MON(T)FOORT, Jean/Jan

Jean/Jan was a *passementier*, laceworker

m. Jacqueline Moreau

25 Jan 1624 - sailed from Amsterdam on the *Eendracht*; had a certificate (attestation) from the Walloon Ch of
Amsterdam

bet 1630-36 - ret to Amsterdam

by 17 Mar1639 - back in New Netherland; acquired farms at the Wallabout nr. Brooklyn as well as
property on Manhattan Island

CHILD:

Pierre/Pieter/Peter[2], b, c, 1616, Valenciennes, FR; according to marr. int (1636) he was from
Valenciennes, then part of HOL under Spanish rule; m. 23 Mar 1636, FR (Walloon) Ch,
Amsterdam, Sara de Planck (b. c. 1615, Amsterdam), d/o Jacques & Sara (Fauconnier) des
Plancque; Pierre & Sara sailed with his parents back to New Netherland; he d. 4 Jan 1661; Sara
m/2, 1 Jan 1663, Lambert Janszen Bosch from Ootmarsum, Overijssel, HOL; she d. p. 23 Jul
1664

CHILDREN:

Jannetje[3], bp 8 May 1646; m. 12 Feb 1665, Willem Gerritse van Couwenhoven
(b. 1636, Flatlands-c. 1728) as his 2nd wife; **11 ch**

Jan/John[3], bp. 23 Feb 1648; m/1, Geertje Pieters who d. c. 3 Jun 1686, m/2, p. 17
May 1687 (date of betrothal), Ida Joris Brinckerhoff, d/o Abraham Jorise
Brinckerhoff; he d. 1737; **7 ch**, m/2

Pieter[3], bp. 21 Jul 1652; m. c. 1676, Marretje/Maria Pieters Luyster; **10 ch**

Sara[3], bp. 2 Apr 1656; m. Claes Pieterse Wyckoff, s/o Pieter Claesen Wyckoff &

Grietje Van Ness; **7 ch**

NOTE: A dau Maria[3] has at times been suggested; supposedly b. in HOL & left there by her parents. Family was back in NY by 1639; Maria (b. 1638) would have been an infant– hard to believe! Maria does not appear in a deed of 1701 where Pieter[2] listed his ch. Maria & her family came to NY, 1662. William J. Hoffman, a highly respected Dutch-American genealogist, has convincingly disproven this claim.

REF: MACY, Harry, Jr., "Sara (DePlanck) Monfort" in *The NYGBR*, vol. 11, #3 (Jul 1991); HOFF, Henry B., *Genealogies of Long Island Families*, Vol. I, II (Baltimore, 1987); SISSER, Fred III, *The Monfoort Family of NY & NJ* (Somerville, NJ, 1969).

MONNET, Pierre

b. c. 1640/5, Poitou, FR, *prob.* s/o Pierre & Susanne (Chastain?) Monnet
m. Catherine Pillot (bp. 30 Apr 1665), *prob.* d/o Israel & Jeanne (Goudry) Pillot
25 Mar 1688 ENG – naturalized
d. 1715, ENG; his will asked the he be buried according to "our Holy Reformed Protestant Religion"
CHILDREN:
Isaac[2], b. c. 1670, Poitiers, FR; m. c. 1700, Elizabeth Williams (d. 1751, Annapolis, MD), d/o William & Sarah (X) Williams; naturalized, 1688, London; may have gone to NY w/ bro Pierre then to Calvert Co, MD by 1700; he d. 1740's
    CHILDREN (may have been more than 10):
    Ann[3], b. 4 Apr 1700; m. 27 Jan 1718, William Turner
    William[3], b. 21 May 1702; m. Elizabeth Kent; d. c. 1776, Calvert Co, MD; at least **11 ch**;
        1 of his sons, James, used the surname **MONEY/MOONEY**
    Abraham[3], b. 28 Aug 1706; no more info
    Elizabeth[3], b. 20 May 1709; no more info
    Isaac[3], b. c. 1711; no more info
    Mary[3], b. c. 1713; liv. 1748
    Aaron[3], b. 1715; liv. 1748
    John[3], m. X Hance
    Pierre[3] no info
    Sarah[3], m. X Mackall
Robert[2], emigrated to Cecil Co, MD; m. 4 Oct 1706, Cecil Co, MD, Margaret Darrell
Thomas[2]
Abraham[2]
William[2]
Pierre[2], bp. 25 Nov 1683, Threadneedle St. Ch, London; emig. to NY, settled Staten Island, c. 1700; m.
    Mary X; d. a. 8 Apr 1712, wp, NY Co., NY; **4 sons**
Catherine[2]
Susanne[2], bp. 8 Feb 1684/5, Threadneedle St. Ch; d. young
Jean[2], bp. 25 Apr 1686, Threadneedle St. Ch; d. young
Susanne[2], bp. 4 Sep 1687, Threadneedle St. Ch
Jean[2], bp. 24 Nov 1688, Threadneedle St. Ch

REF: MONNETTE, Orra Eugene, *Monnet Family Genealogy* (Los Angeles, CA, 1911); MONEY, Harold S., *James Money, KY Pioneer* (Utica, KY, 1983).

MORAGNE, Pierre

b. 16 Nov 1740, on the Dordogne, in the Parish of St. Avide du Tizac, FR, s/o Pierre & Marie (Paris) Moragne; St. Avide is now St. Avit-du-Tizac, n. of Ste.-Foy-la-Grande, e. of Bordeaux; educated in Paris

m/1, c. 1761, FR, XX; in his diary which gives an account of his journey, he speaks only of himself & does not mention a wife but one phrase re his time in Plymouth "we have undergone much trouble, which is too bitter to speak of here" – may refer to the loss of his wife

30 Jul 1763 - he left his father's house, made his way to Royan on the coast, where he sailed for Plymouth, ENG, on 9 Aug 1763, & arr. there on 25 Aug

25 Jan 1764 - sailed to America from Plymouth, ENG, with a group of 212 Huguenots led by Rev. Jean Louis Gibert who acted as agent for the colony & negotiated w/ the British for a ship & provisions; for a variety of reasons, the ship returned to Plymouth & the group set out again on 22 Feb; the list of passengers names only him, no wife &, apparently, no children

12 Apr 1764 – arr. at Charleston where the group remained for 6 mo. then settled in the Abbeville District, SC, on the Savannah River, c. 40 mi. n. of Augusta, GA, where they laid out the village of New Bordeaux, c. 3 ½ mi from the Savannah River

18 Apr 1764 – took Oath of Allegiance & was presented with 100 acres of land; eventually owned 384 acres

m/2, 16 Jul 1765, New Bordeaux, SC, Cécile Bayle (1741, FR-a. 1806, SC), d/o Jean & Marie (Seyral) Bayle

d. 1807, Abbeville Dist, SC

CHILDREN, m/2 (unless indicated, all SC events were in the Abbeville Dist):

Pierre II[2], b. 1766, SC; m. Susannah David; he d. May 1813, New Bordeaux, SC; **5 ch**

Francis[2], b. 30 Jul 1770, SC; m. 1 Jun 1809, Susannah (Guillebeau) Bouchillon (15 Jan 1776, SC-12 Sep 1814, SC), d/o André & Mary Jane (Roquemore) Guillebeau, wid/o Joseph James Bouchillon (d. 1803), s/o Jean & Mary Ann (LeRoy) Bouchillon; he d. 1 Mar 1818, SC

John[2], b. 1772, SC; m. 15 Jun 1809, Catherine Read Williams (8 Aug 1792, NC-8 Aug 1871, Gadsden, AL); he d. 22 Jun 1842, AL

Isaac[2], b. 4 Jul 1774, SC; m. 11 Sep 1814, Margaret Blanton Caine (11 Sep 1799, SC-29 Oct 1852, SC); he d. 18 Mar 1830, SC

Marie[2], b. 31 Mar 1776, SC; m. 18 Mar 1802, Peter Bayard Roger (24 Jun 1775, Mecklenburg Co, NC Feb 1839); she d. 18 Jan 1810, SC

REF: HOWARD, Nell H. & QUINN, Bessie W., *Moragnes in America & Related Families* (Birmingham, AL, 1971); MORAGNE, Mary E., *The Neglected Thread,* edited by Delle Mullen Craven; REVILL, Janie, *A Compilation of the Original Lists of Prostestant Immigrants to SC, 1763-1773* (Baltimore, 1968); *Transactions of the Huguenot Society of SC*, #68 (Charleston, 1963).

MORIN, Pierre

b. La Rochelle, FR, s/o Pierre & Marie (Jamain) Morin; father was a merchant

m. 12 Jun 1692, FR Ch., NYC, Marie Jamain, d/o Étienne & Marie (Billard) Jamain, both from La Rochelle and both deceased by this date (Marie was bur. 15 May 1689 [rec. FR Ch., NYC]); Étienne was a merchant

a. 1736 - Pierre d; he was a *brasier* (one who works in brass)

a. 1736 - Marie/Mary purchased land in New Rochelle, NY, which she offered for sale in 1748, 1749

c. 1761, Marie/Mary d.

CHILDREN (all bp. French Ch, NYC):

Marie, b. 28 Mar, bp. 2 Apr 1693; m. André Fresneau

Marguerite, b. 30 Jul, bp. 12 Aug 1694

Pierre, b. 29 Feb, bp. 8 Mar 1695/6

Estienne, b. 20 Dec , bp. 1 Jan 1697/8

Judith, b. 13 Apr, bp. 20 Apr 1701
Marie Anne, b. 1 Oct, bp. 17 Oct 1703
Pierre, b. 24 Feb, bp. 10 Mar 1705/6

REF: WITTMEYER, Alfred V., *Registers of the Births, Marriages, & Deaths of the Église Françoise à Nouvelle York* (Baltimore, 1968); BOYER, Carl 3rd, *Ship Passenger Lists, NY & NJ (1600-1825)* (Newhall, CA, 1978); SEA-CORD, Morgan H., *Biographical Sketches & Index of the Huguenot Settlers of New Rochelle, 1687-1776* (New Rochelle, NY, 1941).

MORRISET(TE), Pierre/Peter

31 Jul 1700 – arr. Manakintown, VA on the *Mary Ann*; on a list of FR refugees from SWI, via Rotterdam
m. bet Feb-10 Nov 1701, Henrico Co, VA, Elizabeth Fauré, d/o <u>Daniel & Anne (Tibault) Fauré</u>; she d. a. 2
     Mar 1750, wp, Chesterfield Co, VA
12 May 1705 - naturalized
1715 - rec.129:1:35 acres in Henrico Co. on the s. side of the James River (now Chesterfield Co.)
d. a. 17 May 1734, inv, Henrico Co.
CHILDREN:
Jeanne/Jane[2], b. a. 1714; m. Andrew Ammonet, s/o <u>Jacob Ammonet</u> of Paris, FR
John[2], b. a. 1714; m. p. Jun 1744, Elizabeth Blankenship?; d. p. 5 May 1782, wd, Chesterfield Co, VA
    CHILDREN:
    Judith[3], m. 25 Mar 1758, Manakintown, John Gordon of St. James Northam Parish, Goochland
        Co.
    Mary[3], m. William? Goode
    Daniel Fauré[3], m. Martha X; d. p. 21 Nov 1806, wd, Chesterfield Co.
    David[3], m. Jane Baker, d/o Thomas; he d. p. 31 Aug 1793, wd, she d. a. 13 Jul 1807, wp - both
        wills in Chesterfield Co; at least **3 sons, 3 daus**
    Margaret[3], not of age in May, 1782
    William[3], not of age in May, 1782; m. 1783, Ann Farrar
Katherine[2], b. a. 1714; m. X Taboy
    CHILD:
    Elizabeth[3]
Elizabeth[2], b. 1 Mar, bp. 22 Mar 1721/2, Manakintown; m. a. 1738, Pierre David, s/o <u>Pierre & Anne
    (Dutertre) David</u>; he d. 1785, Henrico Co.

REF: *The Huguenot,* #27 (1975-77), #29 (1984); CABELL, Priscilla Harriss, *Turff & Twigg*, Vol. 1(Richmond, 1988); BROCK, R.A., *Huguenot Emigration to America*; WEISIGER, Benjamin B., III, *Colonial Wills of Henrico Co, VA*, Part 1 (1654-1737, Part 2 (1737-1781); Elizabeth's will dated 17 Dec 1746; John's will dated 5 May 1782.

MOSER/MOSIER/MUSSER, Samuel

b. c. 1680, s/o Hans Moser
m. 14 May 1714, Bischwiller, Catherine Weiss, d/o Hans Michael Weiss; Bischwiller, n.e. of Strasbourg,
    Bas-Rhin Dépt, Alsace, FR; formerly called Bischweiler in the Duchy of Zweibrücken
d. 22 Feb 1755, Bischwiller, age 75; he was a farmer
CHILDREN:
Samuel[2], b. 31 Mar 1715, Bischwiller, FR; <u>m/1</u>, Catharina François, d. o Jean François, <u>m/2</u>, Salome King;
    owned land in Springettsbury Manor in York Twp, York Co, PA; he d. a. 3 Jul 1796, wp
    CHILDREN, m/1:
    Maria Esther[3], b. 18 Sep 1746, Bischwiller; m. 1766, York Co, PA, Adam King/Kern
    Anna Maria[3]
    Johann Peter[3]

Johann Michael[3]
CHILDREN, m/2:
Samuel[3], b. 1750 Adams (now) Co, PA; served in 6th Co, 3rd Battalion, York Co. Militia, Rev. War;
    m/1, Eva Geiselman, d/o Michael & Margaret (X) Geiselman – **1 dau**, m/2, Margaret X –
    no issue, m/3, Barbara X – **2 sons**; Barbara d. 1834, age 73, he d. 1816
Maria Elizabeth[3], m. 1797, York, PA, Christian Landis
Johann/Hans Michael[2], b. 11 Jun 1717, Bischwiller; m. 16 Jan 1741, Bischwiller, Eva Maria Elsasser (11
    Sep 1717-27 Jun 1807), d/o Melchoir Elsasser, she is bur. Old Lutheran Ch Cemetery, Springfield Twp,
    Mahoning Co, OH – inscription on her gravestone says "A Huguenot Pioneer"; he prob. d. 1789, York
    Co, PA – 1790 census lists a "widow Mosser" in York Twp; she went to OH in 1801; Johann Michael
    Moser & E.M. Elsasser were on a list of emigrants from Bischweiler that said the people on the list
    emigrated bet 1760-64; although it appears that they may have arr in PA c. 1749/50, perhaps on the
    Lydia; last church records for this family in Bischwiller are dated 1749
    CHILDREN (8 of 11):
Hans Michael[3], b. 26 Aug 1742, Bischwiller; m. Mary Anna Shaffer; went to Beaver Co, PA;
    d. 1811; **5 ch**
Hans Peter[3], b. 26 Apr 1744, Bischwiller; m. Margaret Wortman; d. 26 Nov 1808; **5 or 6 ch**
Samuel[3], b. 16 Feb 1746, Bischwiller; m/1, Elizabeth X – **2 sons**, m/2, Anna Maria X – **5ch**; he
    d. 1811/18
Abraham[3], b. 2 Jul 1748; m. Mary X (who *may* not have been his only wife); he d. p. 14 Jan
    1822, wd, Tuscarawas Co, OH – will names daus **Mary**[4] Taylor, **Elizabeth**[4] Hormish, **Eve**[4] Good &
    her dau Mary Stout; gr dau Susanna Blosser, 3 sons-in-law John Taylor, Christly Hormish, Jacob
    Good; wp, Jan Term, 1822; he is said have been b. on ship to America but dates don't support that –
    births of siblings Samuel and Anna Maria are rec. Bischwiller
Anna Maria[3], bp. 2 Nov 1749, Bischwiller
John[3], b. c. 1750; m. Catherine X; to Washington Co, PA; he d. 1826; **5 ch**
John Jacob[3]. b. 9 Feb 1756; m. Catherine X; **1 dau**
Daniel[3], b. 4 Apr 1759; m. Margaret X; to Columbiana Co, OH; he d. 15 Dec 1817; **3 sons**
Aron[2], father Samuel d. at his house in Bischwiller
Johann Peter[2], b. 16 Jul 1724, Bischwiller; m. Anna Maria Laub; at least **4 sons**, b. Bischwiller
Anna Maria[2], b. 21 Sep 1729, Bischwiller

REF: Parish Recs, Bischwiller Protestant Reformed Ch; *National Genealogical Society Quarterly*, Vol. 59 (1971) –
list from book *Geschichte von Bischweiler* (Strasburg, 1826) by CULMANN, Friedrich Wilhelm; Abraham's will,
dated 14 Jan 1822; FARLEY, Belmont, manuscript; PECKER, Charles, *The People of the Marsh, from the Rhine
Valley to PA*, Vol. 1, #6 (May-Jun 1973).

MOULIN/des MOULINS/MULLEN, Abraham

b. c. 1630, Paris, FR
m. Madeleine Chupret (c. 1640, FR-p. 1706, London); bet 1685-87, fled FR to London where she was
    listed as a widow w/ 4 ch; she m/2, Benjamin Godde; family liv in London Parish of St. Giles, for some
    yrs. on West St. (s.e. of Cambridge Circus, e. of Charing Cross Rd.)
d. a. 1687, prob. FR
CHILDREN:
Paul[2], b. Paris; m. 18 Sep 1698, London, Jeanne de la Ruelle, d/o Guillaume & Rachel (Loret) de la Ruelle;
    he was an *ébénist*, cabinet-maker
Abraham[2], b. c. 1678/80, Paris; m. 27 Dec 1699, L'Église Français des Grecs, London, Rachel Broret; to
    America on the *Mary Ann* which arr 12 Aug 1700, James City; went to Manakintown; by 8 Apr 1707,
    was in Perquimans Co, NC (county on Albemarle Sound); he liv on the n. side of Beaver Cove Swamp;
    he d. p. 17 Mar 1744, Perquimans Co.; he was a *faiseur de savon*, maker of soap
    CHILDREN:

Abraham[3], m. a. 1743, Eleanor Ming(e); d. 25 Nov 1762, Perquimans Co.

Isaac[3], m. Elizabeth Sutton; d. a. Oct 1743, wp; **issue**

Jacob[3], b. c. 1700, VA; m. Sarah Nicholson, d/o Nathaniel Nicholson; d. a. Nov/Dec 1757/8, wp

Jean[2], an *avocat,* lawyer

Marie[2], m. L'Église Français des Grecs, London, George Orvin, a lawyer

REF: WAITS, Rev. Emmett Moore, "Mullen" in *The Huguenot,* #27 (1975-77); LAMBETH, Mary Weeks, *Memories & Records of E. NC* (not dated); CABELL, Priscilla Harriss, *Turff & Twigg,* Vol. I, *The French Lands*; WINSLOW, Mrs. Watson, *History of Perquimans County* (1990).

MOULINARS, Jean Josèphe Brumeau de (Rev.)

b. Châtellerault, Poitou, FR, s.w. of Tours, s/o Jean Brumeau, Sieur de Moulinars, a minister there, 1683

c. 1683 - family fled to HOL where Jean was ordained as a minister in the Reformed Ch by the Walloon Synod

by 1710 - to NYC

12 Nov 1718 - 1st mention of him as *"ministre"* of NY FR Ch.

m. prob. NY, Judith Marie, who prob. d. a. death of Jean Joseph

1722-26 – travelled to New Rochelle quarterly as part of his duty as pastor of the NY FR Ch.

2 Jul 1726 - last entry as *"pasteur"* of NY FR Ch.

1726 - went to New Rochelle and was pastor of the dissenting or Calvinist congregation

d. p. 1 Oct 1741, wd-p. 13 Oct 1741,wp, New Rochelle

CHILDREN:

Susanne Hélène Moulinars[2], bp. 11 Feb 1718/9, FR Ch, NYC

Jean Moulinars[2], b. 13, bp. 14 Feb 1721/2, FR Ch, NYC

REF: LIÈVRE, *Histoire des Protestants du Poitou,* Vol. 3; NJ Huguenot Society, *Ancestor Register*; *Collections of the Huguenot Society of America,* Vol. I, pp. 149, 164; SEACORD, Morgan H., *Biographical Sketches & Index of the Huguenot Settlers of New Rochelle, 1687-1776*; BOYER, Carl 3rd, *Ship Passenger Lists, NY & NJ (1600-1825) (Newhall, CA, 1978)*; WITTMEYER, Alfred V., *Registers of the Births, Marriages, & Deaths of the Église Françoise à la Nouvelle York* (Baltimore, 1968).

MOUNIER, Pierre

bp. 17 Jul 1645, Île de Ré, FR, s/o Louis & Elizabeth (Martineaux) Mounier

m. Louise Robinet, d/o Louis Robinet

fled FR to ENG

15 Apr 1687 – naturalized, ENG

19 Dec 1679 - sailed to SC on the *Margaret*; arr Oyster Pt, SC, 30 Apr 1680

CHILDREN:

Sarah[2], m. SC, Jacques Benoit II as his 2nd wife; Jacques was b. Poitou, s/o Jacques & Gabrielle (Mercier) Benoit; **issue**

Moïse/Moses[2], m. Mary X (d. p. 1751); to SC, 1687; he d. 4 Oct 1740, Orange Quarter, Berkeley Co, SC; both *poss.* bur. in the Cemetery of the FR Ch. at St. Denis; he was a planter and mariner

CHILDREN, surnamed **MILLER**

Susannah[3], m. 29 May 1734, Elias Bonneau (c. 1717-bur. 13 Jul 1773), s/o Jacob & Jane (Videau) Bonneau; she d. a. 1746

Mary[3], m. 11 Feb 1746, Jacob Bonneau (d. 1765, wp, Berkeley Co), s/o Jacob & Jane (Videau) Bonneau; she d. a. 1765

Moses[3], m. 1747, Ann Jeffords, d/o John & Margaret (X) Jeffords; he d. 1792, Berkeley Co.

Magdalene[3], b. Orange Quarter, SC; m. 1 Jun 1749, John Jeffords, s/o John & Margaret (X) Jeffords

William[3], m. 13 Sep 1763, St. Thomas Parish, SC, Renée Brown (she d. a. Apr 1798, wp); he d. 31 Dec 1778, Charleston

Samuel[3], m. Martha X; d. a. 17 Nov 1758, wp, Charleston, SC

Jacob[3], m. 12 Apr 1748, Odelia Houscausen

Étienne/Stephen[2], m. Marie X (Foissen?); 1731, was a member of the FR Ch in Charleston; d. a. 19 Jan 1749, wp, Charleston, SC; he was a merchant; will names wife , 2 sons, son-in-law, gr son Stephen Dunbar, nephew Moses, niece Madeleine; this will establishes that Moses was Stephen's brother, thus a son of Pierre & Louise

CHILDREN:

Étienne/Stephen[3], bp. 9 Jan 1724/5, St. Philip's Parish, Charleston, SC; m. 19 Jun 1746, SC, Martha Dutarque; **issue**

John[3],

unnamed dau[3], m. Goutier Dunbar; **issue**

NOTE: Meunier = miller, surname may have been Meunier rather than Mounier. Although records in La Rochelle say Mounier. Seems that Pierre & Louise sailed w/ only 1 ch, so sons were either b. in SC or sailed separately.

REF: WHITE, Margaret Miller, *The Huguenot Millers, A Family History* (Fulton, MS, 1986); BAIRD, Charles W., *History of the Huguenot Emigration to America*; Étienne's will; HIRSCH, Arthur Henry, *The Huguenots of Colonial SC*; GAY, Frances L., "The Mounier Family" in *Transactions of the Huguenot Society of SC*, #101 (Charleston, 1996); CLUTE, Robert F., *The Annals & Parish Register of St. Thomas & St. Denis Parish, SC 1680-1884* (Baltimore).

MOUTON/MUTTON, Jean/John

b. c. 1620, FR

c. 1643- settled in VA

m. XX, who is not mentioned in his will

8 Mar 1663/4 – denization, Northumberland Co, VA - identifies him as FR & that he embraces the "true Protestant Religion"

20 Sep 1671 – naturalized James City

d. a. Mar 1680, wp, Northumberland Co, VA; mentions that he wants his body bur. according to the Church of England; will names son John, daus Sarah, Elizabeth, son-in-law John Lewis; says he has 3 ch; Frances is not mentioned, perhaps she had already rec. her portion at her marr

CHILDREN:

Frances[2], m/1, a. 1678, John Lewis (d. by 1694), m/2, John Nickless; she d. c. 1713

Elizabeth[2], in father's will, 1678

Sarah[2], in father's will, 1678; m. Alexander Cummings (b. 10 Dec 1677, St. Stephen's Par, Northumberland Co), s/o William Cummings

John[2], b. c. 1654; m. Sarah X; in father's will, 1678; a. 16 Jul 1707, Northumberland Co.; **issue**, surname **MATOON**

REF: SPARACIO, Ruth & Sam, *Northumberland Co, VA Order Book Abstracts, 1661-1665* (1995); HENING, William Waller, *The Statutes at Large Being a Collection of all the Laws of VA*, Vol. II (NY, 1823); John's will, Dated 26 Nov 1678.

MOUZON, Louis/Lewis

said to have come from Mouzon, Ardennes Dépt, Champagne-Ardenne, FR s.e. of Sedan

m. XX

c. 1685 - poss. arr Charleston, SC; not on St. Julien's list, but on Gaillard's

owned 1195 acres in Berkeley Co, SC

d. a. 16 Jan 1756, wp, Berkeley Co, SC

CHILDREN:

Louis/Lewis[2], m/1, Ann Dutarque (24 Mar 1710-c. 1729/30), d/o Lewis Dutarque; m/2 17 Oct 1731, Mrs. Ann (X) Duberdeaux (*prob.* Marianne/Marianna, widow of Antoine DeBourdeaux); Louis he was a planter in Berkeley Co, d. a. 16 Dec 1748, wp

    CHILDREN, m/1:

    Louis/Lewis[3], b. 1725/30; m. 13 Jun 1750, Susannah Elizabeth Bochet, d/o Nicolas & Marianne (Videau) Bochet, Mariane was d/o Pierre & Jeanne Elizabeth (Mauzé Videau; he d. a. 24 Jan 1744, date of bur., St. James Santee; wp, 25 Feb 1744

        CHILDREN: **Elizabeth**[4]; **Lewis**[4;] **James**[4], bp. 9 Jan 1765; **Peter**[4,], b. 1755/6; **Mary**[4]; **Samuel**[4], b. 9 Nov 1765; **Ann**[4], bp. 2 Jan 1769; **Henry**[4]

    James[3], b. a. 1729/30

    CHILDREN, m/2:

    Peter[3], b. p. 17 Oct 1731-a. 1745; m. Judith X; planter, St. James, Santee; he d. a. 29 Aug 1787, wp

        CHILDREN: **Peter**[4], b. 6 Aug 1758, bur. 16 Aug 1758; **Judith**[4], b. 15 Apr 1762; m. 22 Feb 1783, Isaac Lesesne; **Eleona**[4], b. 15 Apr, bp. 5 May 1762, m. 23 Oct 1783, Georgetown, Joseph Wragg (1754-1808), s/o Samuel & Judith (Rothmahler) Wragg – **4 ch**; **Peter**[4], b. 18 Sep 1764, bp. 20 Sep 1764, bur. 3 Oct 1764; **Susanna**[4], b. 6 Aug 17--, bp. 9 Nov 17--

    Samuel[3], b. p. 17 Oct 1731-a. 1745; m. 17 May 1770, St. James, Santee, Anne Maynard

        CHILD (prob. others):

        Charles[4], b. 4 Jan 1771; m. Esther Susanna McClellan (Mar 1776-21 Jun 1809); d. 7 Sep 1856; **5 ch**

    Henry[3], b. p. 17 Oct 1731-a. 1745; d. a. 17 Apr 1777, inv; no wife or ch. recorded

    Elizabeth[3], b. 1731/45; m. 19 Dec 1751(?), Peter Sinkler/Sinclair (1725-1782), s/o James & Jane (Guerard) Sinclair; she d. a. 17 Oct 1775; at least **2 sons, 2 daus**; 1 dau **Elizabeth**[4] (b. 1766) m. Samuel DuBose (1758-1784)

    Ann[3], b. 1731/45; m/1, Josias Blake DuPré, s/o Josias Garnier & Ann (Blake?) DuPré – **9 ch** she m/2, 20 Aug 1769, Daniel Sinkler

    Isaac Anthony[3], b. p. 1745, when his father's will was written – not in will

Henry[2], m. c. 1737, Ann X (d. 6 Jan 1791, age 57); a planter in Berkeley Co; d. a. 9 Feb 1749/50, wp, SC

    CHILDREN: **Ann**[3], b. 19 Sep 1738; **Esther**[3], b. 20 Nov 1739; **Henry II**[3], b. 18 May 1741, m. 10 Jan 1769, Susanna Taylor (1 Dec 1752-6 Aug 1817), d. o Samuel & Ann (Plowden) Taylor, Henry II was educated in FR, was a surveyor & civil engineer, he drew the 1st map of NC & SC pub. in London, then Paris, was a captain in Rev War – **6 sons, 4 daus**, d. 25 Aug 1807; **Sarah Jane**[3], b. 11 Jan 1744; **Susanna Elizabeth**[3], b. 21 Sep 1746; **Mary Ann**[3], b. 11 Sep 1748; **Susannah Mary**[3], b. 20 Feb 1750

Martha Esther[2], m. 15 Apr 1730, Isaac Guérin (10 Apr 1704-a. 1757, wp), s/o Vincent & Judith (X) Guérin

    CHILDREN: **Isaac**[3], b. 5 Mar 1731; **Lewis**[3], b. 5 Mar 1733-d. 19 Feb 1735; **Henry**[3], b. 14 Mar 1736, m. 5 Dec 1760, Magdalene Bonneau (b. 18 May 1757, d/o Jacob & Jane [Videau] Bonneau), gr dau o/ Pierre & Jeanne (Mauzé) Videau, he d. 1772 – **3 ch**; **Robert**[3], b. 21 Jun 1738, m. 12 Jul 1759, Sarah Sanders, he was bur. 8 Apr 1776 – **2 daus**; **Samuel**[3], m. 3 Mar 1774, Frances Bochett – **2 ch**; **Esther**[3], m. 11 Dec 1760, James DuBois

REF: HASELL, Annie B., "Some Generations of the Louis Mouzon Family" in *Transactions of the Huguenot Society of SC*, #70 (1965); FITZSIMONS, Mabel Trott, "Some Descendants of Henry Mouzon Map Maker & Surveyor" in *Transactions of the Huguenot Society of SC*, #69 (1964).

N

NAUDIN/NAUDAIN, André

b. c. 1641, Saint-Maixent, Poitou, FR; prob. St-Maixent-l'École, Deux-Sèvres, Poitou-Charentes, n.e. of
Niort; said to have gone to La Tremblade

m/1, FR, poss. Marguerite/Margaret X

8 Mar 1681/2 - letters patent of denization for him & 3 ch

30 Jul 1682 - was a member of the Threadneedle St. FR Ch, London; he was a linen weaver w/ a wife,
3 ch; rec. grants of assistance from the ch

30 Jan 1683/4 - rec. more money as he had a 4th ch; one of the ch must have d. later – no info on a 4th ch

12 Oct 1684 – he was suspended from communion until he repaid the grants

by 5 Mar 1690/1- in NYC

22 Nov 1694 - purchased home lot in New Rochelle – 200 acres from Gabriel Le Boylteux; served in
several town offices

6 Feb 1695/6 - rec. letters of denization for himself & 2 sons

c. Jan 1698 - signed oath of allegiance

1698 NY census - he was listed as being 57 yrs old, wife Margaret, 52, with 1 son

m/2, by 1710, Mary X

m/3, by 1713, Ann X

d. a. 1 Jun 1720

CHILDREN (prob. m/1):

Marie[2], b. c. 1668, FR; m.5 Mar 1690/1, FR Ch, NYC, <u>Zacharie Angevin</u> as his 2nd wife

André II[2], b. c. 1677, FR; m. 10 Jun 1705, FR Ch, New Rochelle, Susanna DeVaux (bp. 1 Jul 1682, Dutch
Ch, NYC-a. 30 Nov 1762, wp, Yonkers), d/o <u>Frédéric & Esther (Tourneur) DeVaux</u>; he d. a. 27
May 1761, Yonkers

CHILDREN (all b. New Rochelle, surname **NODINE**):

Ann[3], b. 1706/7; no more info

Andrew[3], b. 29 Mar 1708; m. c. 1735, Elizabeth X; d. 9 Apr 1802, Milford, Litchfield, CT; **6 ch**

Judith[3], b. c. 1710; m. Cornelius Jacobs; **issue**

Elizabeth[3], b. 17 Aug , bp. 21 Sep 1712; m. Israel Pinckney

Lewis[3], b. 5 Jan 1714/5, Stamford, CT; m. 9 Feb 1737/8 ,Mary Farrel; d. a. 1761; **1 dau**

Peter[3], b. c. 1720; m. by 1741, Mary Brown/Braun; d 8 Mar 1811, Westchester Co, NY; **8 ch**

Louis[2], he is mentioned as André's son when he rec. a letter of denization; no further info

REF: SEACORD, Morgan H., *Biographical Sketches & Index of the Huguenot Settlers of New Rochelle, 1687-1776;*
ALTOMARE, Adele M., "The Naudin/Nodine Family" in *The Genealogist,* Vol. 4, #2 (NYC, 1983); WATERS,
George L., *Naudin (Nodine), Tourneur, DeVaux & Allied Families* (Lincoln, NE, not pub.); STRYKER-RODDA,
Kenn, *Denizations, Naturalizations & Oaths of Allegiance in Colonial NY (Baltimore, 1975).*

NAUD(A)IN, Élias/Élie

b. 1655, FR

m. 1676, Jael Arnaud; she m/2, 18 Mar 1689, Narragansett, RI, Jacob Ratier – they had son **Jacob**, bp.
Narragansett

1681- fled to ENG

17 Mar 1681- London, ENG, rec. letters patent for naturalization

5 Nov 1681 - accepted as a member of the FR Ch.; a seaman, said to be from La Tremblade, FR

8 Mar 1682 - London he, his wife, 3 ch were naturalized

d. p. 26 Apr 1685, ENG, prob. London

1688 - widow emigrated to America, w/ her was André Arnaud from La Tremblade, prob. her brother; 1st to Narragansett, RI; the family then went to NYC, where Jael & Jacob Ratier & Arnauld Naudain were naturalized, 8 May 1697, & where Jacob d; Jael went then to New Castle Co, DE; Jael d. c. 1720/21, DE

CHILDREN:

Arnauld[2], b. 1677; prob. d. 1702

Mary[2], b. 1679

Élias[2], b. 1681, La Tremblade; m/1, Susanna André/Andrew, m/2, 21 Jul 1715, Lydia/Alida LeRoux, d/o Peter & Alida (Vryman) LeRoux in 1st Presbyterian Ch, Philadelphia; m/3, Mary (X) Stone, widow of Thomas Stone; settled in DE, p. 1715 d. p. 3 Nov 1749, wd – a. 6 Dec 1749, wp, New Castle, DE; **8 ch** by 2nd wife

Françoise[2], bp. 6 Sep 1682, FR Ch, Threadneedle St, London; d. young

Françoise[2], bp. 7 Feb 1686, FR Ch, Threadneedle St, London

NOTE: André Naudain (above entry), among the 1st settlers of New Rochelle, *may* have been the bro/o Élias. They were in London at the same time, both from La Tremblade, Poitou; Andre Naudin was rec. by the FR Ch, 30 Jul 1682, says he had a cert from St. Maixent du Poitou

REF: BAIRD, Charles, *History of the Huguenot Emigration to America,* Vol. II; BENNETT, Ruth, *Naudain Family of Delaware* (1941); NAUDAIN, Warner Woodward, *Descendants of Elias Naudain, The Huguenot Beginning 1655* (1988).

NEUFVILLE, Sébastien de

b. 1545 Anvers, FR (now Antwerp, BEL), s/o Robert Neufville of Anvers; was involved in the Flemish cloth trade; had bro Robert who arr Frankfurt in 1575; Sébastien arr there, 1580

m. 30 Sep 1577, Anna Cock von Opeynen (3 Mar 1549-25 May 1615, Frankfurt); name is Cochx on her grave stone

started a "branch" of the cloth trade in Frankfurt & extended the business to include silk, jewels, and metals which greatly increased the family's wealth; liv. in very high style; many of the family stayed in Frankfurt for generations – kept the name "Neufville," sometimes preceded by "de" and sometimes by "von," as shown by the gravestones in Frankfurt's main cemetery where generations of the family are buried; a website re this family and the cemetery goes on for pages from 1609 into the 1900's

26 Jul 1580 - became a citizen of Frankfurt, GER; called Bürger

d. 3 Mar 1609, Frankfurt; he and Anna are both bur. in the main cemetery in Frankfurt

CHILD:

Sébastien[2], b. 14 Sep 1581, Frankfurt; was involved with the Flemish cloth trade; m. 13 Nov 1607, Catherine Mertens; there was a Johann Mertens involved w/ the de Neufvilles' banking business, poss. fa or bro/o Catherine; Sébastien d. 24 Nov 1634, Frankfurt

CHILDREN:

Abraham[3], b. 1617; d. 1665

Peter[3], b. 1623; was a banker in Frankfurt; d. 1691

David[3], b. 1623; m. Anna Margaretha Neef; was a banker in Frankfurt; d. 1684; at least a dau **Anna Maria**[4] (1672-1709), m. Peter de Cherf, son **Jacob**[4] (1680-1730)

REF: de NEUFVILLE, A.C., *Histoire Généalogique de la Maison de Neufville* (Amsterdam, 1809) ; church recs, Peterskirchhof, Frankfurt ; cem. recs, Frankfurt.

NEUPARZ, Georg/Jörg

b. c. 1578

m/1, Jun 1605, Anna Mauhr, d/o Nickel & Barbara (X) Mauhr; she d. 9 Jan 1623, Offwiller m/2, 1623, Ottillia X, widow of Hans Plosch

d. 21 Nov 1633, Offwiller, Bas-Rhin Dept, Alsace, FR, e. of Sarre-Union, n.w. of Strasbourg; he was a blacksmith

CHILDREN, m/1:

Dorothea[2], d. 20 May 1613

Andreas[2], bp. 1609; d. young

Margaret[2], bp. 6 Nov 1614

Hans Michael[2], b. 27 Apr 1617, Offwiller; m. 6 Oct 1650, Ottilia (Junt) Maur, widow of Diebolt Maur; she d. 9 Feb 1657, he d. Offwiller; **3 ch**

CHILDREN, m/2:

George[2], bp. 1 Feb 1624

Peter[2], bp. 9 Jul 1626

Andreas[2], bp. 25 Nov 1630

REF: Records of the Evangelisch Kirche of Offwiller, Canton Niederbronn, Bas-Rhin, FR.

NICOLA, Jean/John

b. c. 1650 FR, prob. old province of Aunis, s/o Daniel & Susan (Malengin) Nicola

m. c. 1680, X du Cloisy

from La Rochelle, FR, to ENG, where he rec. a commission in the British Army

liv in the Huguenot settlements of Portarlington & Dublin, IRE

d. a. 1763, IRE

CHILD:

Charles[2], b. c. 1685; m. c. 1715, Charlotte DeVignoles; an officer in the British Army in IRE; d. IRE

  CHILD:

  Louis/Lewis[3], b. 1717, Dublin; m/1, 1740, IRE, Christina D'oyle (d. 1759), m/2, Apr 1760, Jane Bishop (d. 20 Feb 1797, Philadelphia); was a major in the British Army; emigrated to America, arr. 29 Aug 1766, Philadelphia; he opened a sm. dry goods shop & a circulating library; moved to Allentown, then to Easton, then back to Philadelphia; Colonel, Rev. War; later a Brigadier General; d. 9 Aug 1807, bur. Old Presbyterian Meeting House Cemetery, Alexandria, VA; seems to have used surname **NICOLA & NICHOLAS**

  CHILD, m/1:

  John[4], b. c. 1741, the survivor of a set of twin boys & the only ch of this marr to live beyond infancy

  CHILDREN, m/2

  Charlotte[4], b. 9 Feb 1761, IRE; m/1, 1 Mar 1781, Dr. Matthew Maus, m/2, Dr. William Cozens; she d. 1830/1, DC; **issue**, both marr.

  Lewis[4], he is named in his father's will, no other info

  Margaret[4], b. 1 Mar 1764, IRE; m. X Bigham; **2 daus**

  Jane[4], b. 4 or 28 Feb 1765, Kinsale IRE; m. 17 Jun 1782, Lt. Talmadge Hall (24 Jan 1754, New Fairfield, CT-1793), s/o Elnathan & Hannah (Bishop) Hall; she d. 1795; **2 sons, 2 daus**

  Mary[4], b. 14 Apr 1766, IRE; m. 9 Jun 1785, Capt. Thomas Nash; **issue**

  Ann[4], b. 1770/1, Northampton Co, PA; m. 19 Jul 1790, John Fisher; she d. 6 Jan 1793; **1 dau**

  Sarah[4], b. 15 Nov 1779, Philadelphia; m. 22 Dec 1796, Philadelphia, Jacob Webb; **1 son**

REF: BELL, Whitfield J., Jr., *Colonel Lewis Nicola, Advocate of Monarchy, 1782* (Philadelphia, 1983); *The PA Magazine of History & Biography*, Vol. IV (Philadelphia, 1880); BILLON, Frederic L., *Annals of St. Louis in Its Territorial Days from 1804 to 1821* (NYC, 1888); WEVILL, George, *Pedigree of the Nicholas Family* (1879, not pub.); Lewis'[3] will, dated 26 Jan 1807.

NOÉ/NOË/NOUE/NIU/NEVE/NUEE, Pierre

b. early 1600's, Walslant, FR – Walloon country, prob. now in BEL; another source says Pays de
        Vaud, which is the area around Lausanne, SWI

m. c. 1650, Walslant, <u>Margaret Dumont</u> (d. 1709, NJ)

16 Apr 1663 - arr New Netherland on *De Bonte Koe/The Spotted Cow*

d. a. 28 Apr 1710, wp, Elizabeth, NJ; wd, 16 Dec 1709, Elizabethtown, NJ which mentions wife, son John
        & his wife Damaris, his dau Mary & her husband John

CHILDREN:

Jean/John[2], b. 1662, FR; m. 2 Dec 1694, FR Ch, NYC, Elizabeth Damaris Girard d/o Isaac Girard; d. a. 30
        Dec 1751, wp, Middlesex Co, NJ

    CHILDREN:

    Marguerite/Margaret[3], bp. 22 Sep 1695, Huguenot Ch, NYC; m. X Always

    Peter[3], b. 1697; m. Sarah X (1703-1750); he d. 10 Jul 1756; both bur. Woodbridge, NJ; **4 sons**

    Isaac[3], b. 1700; m. Sarah Marsh (1710-1777), d/o John Marsh; he d. 2 Apr 1777, bur. Presbyterian
        Ch, Rahway, NJ; **4 ch**

    Daniel[3], b. c. 1702; m. Sarah (Hodeson?)

    John[3], m. Hannah Force

    Damaris[3], m. John Marsh (d. 1802, Middlesex Co, NJ)

    Magdalene[3], m. X Tooker

Mary[2], b. 18 Oct 1653; m. NYC, Jean/John Trembly, s/o Jean Jacques Tremble of Poitou; settled Elizabeth, NJ,
        where John d. a. 22 Oct 1754, wp

    CHILDREN:

    Peter[3], b. c. 1690

    John[3]

    Mary[3]

    Margaret[3]

    Ann/Hannah[3], b. 7 Jun 1679; m. 24 Sep 1698, Philip Cox, as his 3rd wife

    Elizabeth (Rachel)[3], m. c. 1739, Joseph Runyon *prob.* the s/o Thomas[2], s/o <u>Vincent & Ann</u>
        <u>(Boutcher) Rongnion/Runyon</u> – needs proof

    Sarah[3], b. 1715

REF: LITTLE, John, *Family Records & Genealogies of the First Settlers of Passaic Valley* (1852); COLES &
STEINWAY, *Huguenot & Walloons who Settled in the State of NY*; HATFIELD, Edwin F., *History of Elizabeth,
NJ, Including the Early History of Union Co* 9NY, 1868); MONNETTE, Orra E., *First Settlers of Ye Plantations
of Piscatawa and Woodbridge Olde East New Jersey 1664-1714* (Los Angeles, 1935); McPIKE, Eugene F., "Dumont
& Allied Families" in the *NYGBR*, Vol. 29 (Apr, 1898).

NOËL, JACOB

b. c. 1599 Sedan, Ardennes, France, s/o Pierre and Elizabeth (DeNault) Noël

m. 14 Jan 1621, Leiden Dutch Reformed Ch, HOL, Tryntgen Cornelis, d/o Cornelis

CHILDREN (all bp in Dutch Reformed Ch, Leiden):

Cornelis[2], bp. 11 Apr 1622; d. 19 Jun 1622

Cornelis[2], bp. 8 Nov 1623; emigrated to Old Rappahannock and Essex Counties, VA; m. c. 1664,
        Elizabeth Page, d/o Thomas Page; naturalized 27 Apr 1686; he d. a.10 Jun 1699, wp, Essex Co, VA

    CHILDREN:

    Daniel[3], b. c. 1665, Essex Co, VA; m. Elizabeth Elliott

    Mary[3], b. c. 1669, Essex Co, VA; m. Thomas Cloutsome

    Margaret[3], b. c. 1671, Essex Co, VA; m. Edmond Connalee

    Cornelius[3], b. c. 1675, Essex Co, VA; m. Sarah Stallard

    Elizabeth[3], b. c. 1678, Essex Co, VA; m. John Ridgaile

    James[3], b. c. 1680, Essex Co, VA; m. Elizabeth Evans, d/o Reese & Elizabeth (X) Evans; he d. a.

21 Apr 1741, wp; **14 ch**

Siburgh[2], (son) bp. 8 Aug 1627; d. 28 Oct 1627

Boudewyn[2], (son) bp. 22 Apr 1629

Jan/John[2], bp. 1 Feb 1632; m. 1658, Lydia Perkins, d/o Nicholas & Mary (X) Perkins; d. VA

REF: Cornelis' Will; Hooglandsche Kerk (Church) records, Leiden; NOEL, Mary Roberts & Weeks, Jennie Noel, *Emigrant Cornelius Noel from Holland to VA & His Descendants in America* (Salt Lake City, UT, 1977, 1978), Vols. 1, 4.

O

OGIER, Pierre

b. 1655, Sigournais, Bas Poitou, now Vendée Dépt, Pays de la Loire, s.w. of Cholet

m. 1678, Jeanne Bernardin (1658-1738, ENG) of Moncoutant, Poitou, s.w. of Bressuire

p. 1685 - to ENG; 9 ch went 1st, parents joined them later, so must have had family or friends there as most of the ch. were under age

d. 1697, prob. ENG

CHILDREN:

Moïse[2], b. 1678; d. Poitou, FR

Pierre[2], b. 14 Dec 1680; m. 1710, Catherine Rabaud (1680-1744, London); he d. 5 Dec 1740, London
   CHILDREN:
   Pierre[3], b. 1711; m. Elizabeth Gastineau (1710-1800); he d. 23 Dec 1775, London
   Jeanne[3], b. 1713; m. Abraham Julian; d. 12 May 1791, Twickenham, ENG, s.w. of London; **no issue**
   François[3], b. 1714; alive 1744 (mother's will)
   Thomas Abraham[3], b. 1716; m. Madeleine Bernard (1720-1779); d. 1770, Blackheath – the one s.c. of London?
   Françoise Catherine[3], b. 1718; m. Isaac Merzeau (1704, Exeter-1743, Deptford, ENG); d. 1 Dec 1782, London; Exeter is in Devonshire; there is a Deptford, s.e. of London and one in Wiltshire
   Marie Renée[3], b. 1719; d. 1745
   Jean[3], b.1723; m. Martha Clavelle (b. 1725); **no issue**
   Louis[3], b. 16 Jul 1726, Moncoutant, FR; m. 15 Jul 1751, St. John's, Hackney, London ,Catherine Creuzé (b. London-17 Jul 1808, Clapton, ENG), d/o Francis & Elizabeth (X) Creuzé; he d. 8 Oct 1780, Ashley River, St. Andrew's Parish, SC; **2 sons**; the Clapton, in the London Borough of Hackney, now called Upper Clapton??
   Louise Perrine[3], b. 1729; m. Samuel Courtald (b. London-d. 1765); she d. 12 Dec 1807, Clapton, ENG

Daniel[2], b, 1683; m. Mousse Fernand of Auvergne Prov., FR – located in central FR, in the Massif Central, area of Clermont-Ferrand

Louise[2], b. 1689; m/1, 27 Mar 1714, Charles Dubé, s/o Francis & Marie (Barbey) Dubé/Dubois, m/2, 1717, Pierre Margot (he d. 1747)

Pierre Abraham[2], b. 1690; m. 1717, Esther DuBois (1689-1766, Clapton); d. 1757, Clapton, ENG; at least 1 son **Abraham**[3], b. 12 Sep 1717, London who m/1, Marthe Turquand (1723-1763), d/o René Turquand, m/2, Mary Gasherie (d. c. 1770), m/3, Charlotte Gauvain (1711-1800)

Jean[2], m. 1719, Louise Françoise Maillard

André[2], m. 25 Dec 1722, Marianne Hanrot, d/o Jonas & Marianne (Bocquet/Boquet) Hanrot; Marie d. 1739

Elizabeth[2], b. 1697; m/1, François Grellier – **no issue**, m/2, 1729, François Paul Andeer (1698-1768) – **3 daus**; she d. 1768, London

Jeanne[2], m. Pierre Paillet; at least 1 son **Pierre**[3], b. 1724, dau **Jeanne**[3], b. 8 Sep 1728; Jeanne[2] d. 1759

Marie[2], m. 19 Dec 1708, London , Pierre Ravenel; at least 1 son **Abraham**[3], b. 3 Oct 1709

REF: "Genealogical Notes" in *Transactions of the Huguenot Society of SC*, #77 (1972); BAYLISS, Mary, "Corrections to Genealogical Notes" in *Transactions of the Huguenot Society of SC*, #101 (1996).

ORANGE, Louis

m. Mary X

1700 - emigrated to VA on the *Mary Ann* w/ wife, 1 ch

d. a. 7 Apr 1735, wp, Henrico Co, VA
CHILDREN:
Lewis[2], m. Keziah X; d. p. 26 Mar 1792, prob. Cumberland Co, VA; **issue**
Peter[2], m. Ann X
John[2], m. Judith X
Judith[2], m. X Ligon
Elizabeth[2], m. X Willis
Magdalin[2], m. X Atkins
Mary[2], m. X Turner

REF: Louis' will dated 24 Aug 1734; des COGNETS, Louis, *English Duplicates of Lost VA Records*; O'BRIEN, Bayne Palmer, *Orange Family of Henrico, Cumberland & Amelia* (1977, not pub.).

ORLÉANS, Jean d'

b. FR

m. Antoinette de Hole; she is definitely the m/o Judit but *poss.* not of the other ch; Judit is the only ch for whom there is a baptismal record; marr. recs of Ester, Marie, Judit mention Jean as their father but do not mention their mother, who may have d. by then

CHILDREN:

Jacques[2], b. c. 1570, m. 17 Mar 1591, Sedan, FR, Elizabeth Perin; Eliz. m/2, 18 Jan 1604, Sedan, Gérard Bouchet, s/o Antoine Bouchet; she was bur. 23 Mar 1637, Sedan; Jacques was a surgeon; he d. c. 1595/6

    CHILDREN:

    Janne/Jeanne[3], bp. 26 Dec 1591, Sedan; m. Jean Gérard (c. 1580/90-a.1637)

    Suzanne[3], bp. 1 Aug 1593; m/1, Denis Bonviver, m/2, 2 Feb 1631, at Givonne (town, n.e. of Sedan, Ardennes Dépt., Champagne-Ardenne), Pierre Bauda

    Jacques[3], bp. 23 Jun 1596, Sedan; m. Marie Sauvage; he was an *arquebusier* (gunmaker); **8 ch**

Anne[2], b. c. 1572; m. 28 Feb 1593, Sedan, Éloi Vigreux, a *passementier*, (lacemaker and/or seller of of lace); she was bur. 2 Nov 1622; **6 ch**

Ester[2], b. c. 1573/4; m/1, 5 May 1591, Sedan, Collignion de Thelin, a soldier; m/2, Jean de Blaine, a merchant; she was bur. 26 Jul 1660, Sedan

Marie[2], b. c. 1578 ; m. Oct 1600, Sedan, Adouin de Stonne; **3 ch**

Judit[2], bp. 3 Jan 1580; m/1, 29 May 1605, Sedan, Thevenin Robinet, s/o Jean Robinet; he was bur. 9 Jun 1632, 48 Y, native of Sedan, a merchant of leathers and/or textiles – at least **4 ch**; m/2, 1633, Sedan, Jérémie Baujot, merchant who m. 30 Dec 1640 Barbe Antoine, widow of Jean Guillardit; Judit was bur. 21 Dec 1639, Sedan

REF: ALLEN, Cameron, "Ancestral Table of Susanne Brian, Wife of Abraham Soblet" – records in the article are from the *Registers of the Reformed Church,* Sedan, France copied into the *Bibliothèque Wallonne,* as well as church records from the Walloon Church in Utrecht - *The American Genealogist,* Vol. 78, #4 (Oct, 2003), pp. 249-52.

OZIAS, Antoine

Protestant tailor from Vivarais District of Languedoc, France, now in Ardèche Dépt, Rhône-Alpes, s.e. FR, s. of Lyon; name was prob. **AUZIAS** originally, with stress on 1st syllable; a Vaudois family, later Waldense

m. Isabeau Lormeiasse of Nîmes, Languedoc

p. 1685 - fled to Savoy

by 1701- in SWI

by 1702 - the family was in Dürrmenz, Württemberg, GER, n.w. of Stuttgart, where there was a Waldense community; he liv. on Waldense Strasse by 1752, d. GER

CHILDREN:

Étienne/Stephen[2]: b. Languedoc, FR; m. a. 1722, Elizabeth Maneval, d/o <u>Pierre Maneval</u> of Embrun, FR, Hautes-Alpes Dépt, Provence-Alpes-Côte d'Azur; he d. c. 1752; they had **9 ch**; Elizabeth emigrated to America, p. 18 Apr 1753 (when she sold her house in Dürrmenz) w/sons John, Peter, dau Catherine Lucrèce; arr on the *Lydia*, 15 Sep 1753; the mother listed as a widow in 1755, per St. Michaels Lutheran Ch, Philadelphia

CHILDREN:

Henry/Heinrich[3], b. 1723; m. Catherine Elizabeth Schardt; in Philadelphia, a. 1750; **2 ch**

Jeanne Marie[3], b. & bp. 8 Aug 1725, Dürrmenz; m. as his 2nd wife Mathieu Morel; couple rec. permission to emigrate to PA; **3 ch**

Madeleine[3], b. 23 Mar 1728; m. Jaques Collums; liv. Erfurt, GER

Charles Daniel[3], b. 24 Aug 1729; m. Elizabeth Latour (d. 4 Jul 1759, Dürrmenz); **issue**

Antoine[3], b. 25 Feb 1731; d. young

Lucresse/Lucrèce[3], b. 12 Aug 1734; d. young

Pierre/Peter[3], b. 2 Jul 1738; m. 1760, Magdalena/Mary Hergert (1741-1795); he became a wealthy merchant in Philadelphia; d. 1824; **5 ch**

Catherine Lucrèce[3], b. 21 Aug 1740

Jean/John[3], b. 1742/3, prob. Ludwigsburg, GER; farmed in Berks Co, PA; m. c. 1767, Elizabeth Fall (1738-2 Jan 1826), d/o Dietrich & Anna Margaretha (X) Fall/Fahl; went to Guilford Co, NC, c. 1770, to Preble Co, OH, c. 1803; d. 9 Aug 1825, Preble Co, OH; **9 ch**

Jeanne[2], chr 21 Jun 1701, FR Ch, Bern, SWI

REF: ROHRER, Albert Lawrence, *History of the Ozio, Osius, Ozias Families* (1943); STAPLETON, Rev. A., *Memorials of the Huguenots in America* (Baltimore, 1969).

P

PAISANT/PAYSANT, Louis Philippe

b. c. 1698, St. Pierre area of Caen, Basse-Normandie, FR, s/o Antoine and Suzanne (Lecocq) Paisant;
Antoine was a silk merchant in Caen as was Louis Philippe

m/1, 9 Aug 1723, Anne Marguerite LaMasson (d. Caen 23 Dec 1737)

m/2, 20 Jan 1738/9, St. Helier, Isle of Jersey, Marie Anne Noget/Nazette (c. 1717, Caen-1796, Falmouth,
Nova Scotia, CAN)

16 May 1738 - on list of Denizations at Hampton Court

1753 - settled in Nova Scotia

d. 8 May 1756, Covey Island, Nova Scotia, CAN – an island in Mahone Bay, nr. Lunenburg; he was
murdered by Indians, his wife & ch were captured & taken to Québec where she was imprisoned by the
British,1759; she was granted land by the Crown at Falmouth Twp, 1761; Falmouth is on
the Avon River w. of Windsor

CHILDREN, m/1:

Suzanne[2], b. c. 1724, FR; was enrolled in a convent,1734; removed by her fa, 1738; went to Isle of Jersey

unnamed son (Jacques?)[2], b. a. 1737, FR; sent away from FR as a child, *poss.* to ENG

Anne[2], bp. 2 Apr 1737, FR

CHILDREN, m/2:

Marie[2], bp. 9 Nov 1740, St. Helier; bur. 10 Apr 1746, St. Helier

Jean Louis[2], bp. 25 Nov 1741, St. Helier; bur. 17 Oct 1744, St. Helier

Anne[2], bp. 15 Apr 1743, St. Helier; bur. 10 Apr 1746, St. Helier

Philippe/Philip[2], bp. 26 Nov 1746, St. Helier; m. Martha Hood; served Rev. War, MA

Marie/Mary[2], b. 23 Jan, bp. 3 Feb 1747/8, St. Helier; m. c. 1763/4, Falmouth Twp, Halifax, Nova Scotia ,
Jean-Jacques/John James Juhan (bp. 2 Apr 1736, Yverdon, Vaud Canton, SWI [s. end of Lac
Neuchâtel]-d. bet 1787-1804), s/o Jean-Marc & Suzanne-Marguerite (Guesler) Juhan; family went to
Boston, 1768, to Charleston, SC, 1772-73, then to the Island of Hispaniola where she d. a. 4 Dec 1804;
Jean-Jacques was in Philadelphia p. Rev. War w/ 3 ch, so perhaps Marie had already d.; **5 ch**

Jean/John[2], bp. 27 Oct 1749, St. Helier; m. 1774, Falmouth, NS, Mary Aline (1753-1 Jan 1835), d/o
William & Rebecca (Clark) Aline; d. 10 Apr 1834, Liverpool, Nova Scotia; minister; **8 ch**

Louis[2], bp. 3 Jul 1751, St. Helier; m. 1760, Grace Davison (10 Jul 1754, Preston, CT-25 Sep 1829, Falmouth,
NS), d/o John & Sarah (Babcock) Davison; d. 30 Nov 1845, Falmouth, Nova Scotia; **8 ch**

Lisette[2], bp. 1756, Québec City, CAN; m. George Jess; d. 1819, Scots Bay, Nova Scotia; **7 ch**

REF: PAYZANT, Marion M., *The Payzant and Allied Jess and Juhan Families in N. America* (Wollaston, MA,
1970) ; DUNCANSON, John Victor, *Newport, Nova Scotia A Rhode Island Township* (Belleville, ONT, 1985);
Church recs, Parish of St. Helier, Isle of Jersey/

PANETIER/PANETIÉ/PANIT(O)UR/PANKEY, Jean/John

b. c. 1665, Soubise, Saintonge, FR, s.w. of Rochefort, now in Charente-Maritime Dépt, Poitou-Charentes

8 Mar 1682 - naturalized ENG as a *fugitif de Soubise*

1700 - emigrated to VA from ENG, arr on the *Mary Ann* Jul 1700

12 May 1705 – naturalized, VA

m. c. 1710, prob. Manakintown, VA Angell X who m/2, p. 1717, Peter Depp

1714 – *Liste Généralle*, Jean is recorded w/ wife & 1 son

31 Oct 1716 - rec. patent #823 for 76 acres on the s. side of the James River in Henrico (now Powhatan)
Co.; his son John sold this land to Peter Depp a. 1727

d. Jul 1717, Manakintown, VA; 19 Oct 1717, inv. of his estate, valued at £14 16 sh 6 p, recorded 4 Nov
1717

CHILDREN:

Étienne/Stephen[2], b. c. 1711, Manakintown, VA; m/1, c. 1735, Judith X; m/2, 1785, Elizabeth Kelshaw, d/o John Kelshaw, who m/2, 1 Feb 1792, William Lankford; Stephen d. a. 8 Jan 1789, wp, Lucys Springs, Chesterfield Co, VA
CHILDREN, m/1:
John[3], b. c. 1736; m. Keziah Chambers; he d. 1810, Tower Hill, Buckingham (now Appomattox), Co, VA, nr. town of Appomattox; **8 sons, 1 dau**
Samuel[3], b. c. 1738; m/1, c. 1759, Henrico Co., VA, Betsy Kinsey Binford, d/o Thomas & Elizabeth (X) Binford – **2 sons, 3 daus**, m/2, c. 1775, Chesterfield Co, VA Martha Burton, d/o John Burton; he d. Aug 1807, nr. Manakintown, VA; **2 sons, 1 dau**
Mary Ann[3], b. c. 1740; m. c. 1760, Edward Branch, s/o Matthew Branch, Sr; she d. c. 1821, nr. Hannah Springs, Chesterfield Co, VA; **3 sons, 3 daus**
Stephen[3], b. c. 1742; m. c. 1765, Mary Watkins, d/o Thomas Watkins; he d. Mar 1791, Lucy Springs, VA; **2 sons, 10 daus**
dau[3], b. c. 1744; m. X Wade; she d. a. 1788
CHILDREN, m/2:
Elizabeth[3], b. 24 Sep 1786, Lucy Springs, VA; m/1, 1813, Chesterfield Co, VA, Jeremiah Hancock (d. 5 Jan 1825) – **4 son, 1 dau**, m/2, 9 Jan 1832, Chesterfield, Co, VA, Martin Adkins; she d. 19 Apr 1871, nr. Hannah Springs, VA
Sarah[3], b. 24 Sep 1786, Lucy Springs, VA (twin of Eliz.); m. 11 Aug 1813, Lucy Springs, Carter Moody (c. 1778, Essex Co, VA-Mar 1834, Lucy Springs); she d. Nov 1837– **4 sons, 3 daus**
Loring Young[3], b. 16 Apr 1788, Lucy Springs; m. 6 Nov 1817. Buckingham Co, VA. Eliza Rebecca Bolling Branch (20 Jan 1797, Buckingham Co-13 Mar 1881 - she m/2, 1842, James Austin; Loring d. 25 May 1833, Manchester (now S. Richmond), VA; **2 sons, 3 daus**
Jean Pierre/John Peter[2], b. c. 1713/4, Manakintown, VA; 1st on the tithable list in 1732; m. c. 1737, Dorothy X (d. 2 Oct 1772, Lunenburg Co, VA); he d. Jun 1750, nr. Manakintown; 25 Jun 1750, wp, Cumberland Co
CHILDREN:
Edward[3], b. c. 1739; d. c. 1755, Manakintown, unmarr.
John[3], b. c. 1741; m/1, 8 Oct 1766, Halifax Co, VA, Betty Powell (d. c. 1779), d/o William & Mary (X) Powell – **6 sons, 1 dau**, m/2, a. 1791, Ann X – **2 sons, 2 daus**, he d. Apr 1804, Sumner Co, TN
Stephen[3], b. c. 1743; m. c. 1766, prob. Cumberland Co, VA, Mary Ann Smith, d/o James & Caroline Mathilda (X) Smith; he d. p. 17 May 1825, prob. Marion Co, TN – prob. **8 sons, 3 daus**
Elizabeth[3], b. c. 1745, m. 23 Sep 1762, Benjamin Huddleston (c. 1733-c. 1808); she d. p. 1778, Cumberland Co, VA; prob. **5 sons, 3 daus**
Dorothy[3], b. 1750, d. p. 1805, prob. Halifax Co, VA; unmarr.

NOTE: Research of Soubise ch. records for the period of 1654-75, found 4 Jean Panetiers. It is not possible to determine which, if any, is the Jean Panetier who emigrated to VA. The names of the parents in those records are not repeated in the children of this Jean.

REF : PANKEY, George Edward, *John Pankey of Manakin Town, VA & His Descendants*, Vol. I (1969), Vol. II (1972); PANKEY, William Russell, *the Pankey Family of VA 1635-1968* (Richmond, VA, 1968); *Early Manakin Town Records*; CABELL, Priscilla Harriss, *Turff & Twigg*, Vol. I (Richmond, 1988).

PARMENTIER, Pierre/Peter

b. c. 1630 FR, perhaps Courtrai, then in Flanders (now BEL); **or** 3 Aug 1627 Condé-sur-l'Escaut, Nord Dépt, Nord-Pas-de-Calais, s/o Jean & Jeanne (Fouré) Parmentier? Condé-sur-l'Escaut is n.e. of Valenciennes, very close to the current border between FR & BEL

m. FR, Antoinette Terrin, b. c. 1635, FR
to Mannheim, GER
16 Apr 1663 – arr. NY w/ Jan Louwe Bogert & a group of refugees from Mannheim on the *Spotted Cow*
23 Sep 1663 – received into Brooklyn Ch with a certificate from Mannheim
liv. in Bedford, LI, NY, part of present-day Brooklyn; had a gristmill there; then went to Harlem, then
  to Kingston
d. c. 1701, Kingston, Ulster, NY
CHILD:
Michael Pieterse[2], b. c. 1653/4 FR; m. c. 1679, Neeltje Janse Damen, d/o Jan Corneliszen Damen &
  Sophia Martense; the Damen family once owned the Wall St. section of Manhattan, which became the
  most valuable real estate in the world in the 20th century; Michael was a magistrate in 1679, 1681 and a
  Lt. in the Foot Guard; had a mill in Bushwyck which he sold in 1695 and he sold his house in 1699,
  going to Kingston; he d. p. 1724
  CHILDREN:
  Pieter Michaelse[3], bp. 13 Jun 1680, New Utrecht; m/1, 18 Oct 1702, Kingston, Sara Van Kleeck
    (c. 1682-1713/4), d/o Baltus Van Kleeck & Tryntje Buys – **6 ch**, m/2, p. 21 Nov 1714 (date of
    banns), Kingston, Helena Van de Bogart (b. c. 1694/5), d/o Myndert Van de Bogart & Helena
    Schermerhorn – **7 ch**; he prob. d. Poughkeepsie
  Jan Michaelse[3], bp. 19 Mar 1682, New Utrecht, NY
  Antointette[3], bp. 27 Jul 1684, New Utrecht, NY; m. Barent Van Kleeck
  Michael[3], b. 1687; m. Maria Tietsoort; **9 ch**
  Neelje[3], bp. 20 Oct 1689, Brooklyn; m. Myndert Van de Bogart
  Sophia[3], b. 1691/2; m. Hendrich Pels; **6 ch**
  Damen Michaelse[3], bp. 21 Jan 1694, Brooklyn; m. Helena Tiertsoort; **11 ch**
  Lysbet[3], bp. 16 Jul 1699, Brooklyn; m. Abraham DeGraff; **5 ch**
  Joanna[3], bp. 5 Jul 1702, Kingston, NY; m. Frans Van de Bogart; **3 ch**

REF: *NY Historical Manuscripts: Dutch, Old 1st Dutch Reformed Ch of Brooklyn, NY, 1600-1752*; HOES, Roswell Randall, *Baptismal & Marriage Registers of the Old Dutch Ch of Kingston*, (NY, 1891); GLAZIER, Prentiss, *Palmatier-Parmentier Family* (unpub., Apr 1976); BAIRD, Charles W., *History of the Huguenot Emigration to America*, Vol. I (Baltimore, 1966), RIKER, James, *Revised History of Harlem*; BOYER, Carl, 3rd, *Ship Passenger Lists, NJ & NY, 1600-1825* (Newhall, CA, 1978).

PASTEUR, Charles

b. FR; *poss.* related to Jean (below)
1699 - to Manakintown, VA on the *Nasseau* w/ wife; they were on list of *Genevois* who emigrated to VA –
  so evidently spent time in Geneva, SWI
CHILD:
James[2], m. Jane X; 1754 – he was a lecturer in Norfolk Parish, VA
  CHILDREN:
  Charles[3], m. 1761 Susanna Roe
    CHILD:
    Charles[4], m. Martha X; d. a. Feb 1794 wp, Halifax Co, NC; will names wife, daus
      Martha Jane[5], **Mary Gilmour**[5], **Annie Mckinnie**[5], **Sarah Elizabeth**[5], sons
      Francis[5], **John James**[5]
  John[3]

REF: *The Huguenot*, #3 (1927), #4 (1929); BROCK, R.A., *Huguenot Emigration to VA* (Baltimore, 1979)

PASTEUR, Jean

b. FR; went to Geneva, SWI; he was a physician

1699 - to Manakin Colony as a FR Huguenot from Geneva, single; on the list next to Charles
Pasteur, poss. relationship; settled Williamsburg, was a surgeon, barber & wigmaker
Maker

12 May 1705 – naturalized, VA

m/1 Mary Blouet(t) (d. 25 Mar 1727)

m/2 Martha Harris

d. a. 16 Nov 1741, wp

CHILDREN, m/1:

?**William**[2], m. Elizabeth Stith, d/o William Stith; prob. the William Pasteur who, in 1752, was an
apprentice to Dr. George Gilmer (a surgeon, physician, apothecary in Williamsburg); he
d. 1795

    CHILDREN:

    William[3], b. 1760

    Blouvet[3]

?**Martha**[2]

?**Anne**[2], m. Samuel Cobbs

Mary[2], b. 1706; m. a. 1741, Mark Crosby

Magdalene[2], b. c. 1708; m. Samuel Crosby (1705-a. 16 May 1743, wp, York Co, VA), s/o John
& Sara (X) Crosby; **4 ch**

Lucretia[2], m. Matthew Shields

Judith[2], m. Gabriel Maupin, s/o Gabriel & Marie (Hersent) Maupin; Judith d. 9 Nov 1737, Bruton
Parish, VA

John II d. 2 Jun 1727

James Blouvet[2], m. Mary X; prob. the James Pasteur who was a minister, "lecturer"- Norfolk
Parish, Norfolk Co, 1754

    CHILD:

    William[3], b. 1768

CHILD, m/2:

John[2], b. p. 1729; m. Honour Wilson; Capt., privateer in Rev. War; d. 22 Aug 1794, Smithfield,
VA; 2 Dec 1794. wp, Isle of Wight Co, VA names sons Charles, Solomon, daus Polly,
Elizabeth

    CHILDREN:

    Mary/Polly[3], b. 1780-d. 1837 m. Joseph Bridger Hodsden

    Elizabeth[3], **Charles**[3], **Solomon W.**[3]

REF: BROCK, R.A. *Huguenot Emigration to VA* (Baltimore, 1979); *The Huguenot*, Vol. 3 (1927), #4 (1929) –
John's will, 1794; *Tyler's Quarterly Magazine*; *William & Mary College Quarterly*; WULFECK, D., *Marriages of
Some VA Residents, 1607-1800.*

PEGUES, Claudius

b. 1719, ENG. s/o Claudius & XX (his Swiss wife, *poss.* X Zwilt/Gwilt) Pegues, who fled to ENG to
escape persecution; family history says that the Pegues family was from the south of FR, nr. Rodez,
Aveyron Dépt, Midi-Pyrénées, n.e. of Montauban

4 Nov 1736 - arr Charleston on the *Charles*

m. 18 Sep 1749, Charleston, SC, Henrietta Butler (b. 19 Oct 1725, Prince Frederick Winyaw Parish), d/o
Christopher & Abigail (X) Butler; she d. 29 Jun 1758, Cheraw Dist., SC

bet 1755-58 - he went to Georgetown, then to the Cheraw Dist, SC, & settled not far from the NC line

owned a lot of land, was active in business & public affairs, 1768, elected to the Royal Assembly from
Marlboro Co; served in 1775, 1776, in the 1st and 2nd Provincial Congresses, then the 1st General

Assembly of SC
d. 22 Jan 1790, SC
CHILDREN:
William[2], b. 16 May 1750, Georgetown; m/1, Elizabeth (Murphy?) – dau **Harriet**[3] (15 Aug 1770 Chesterfield Co, SC-10 Jan 1758) m. 10 Jan 1788, SC, William Powe (22 Oct 1766, SC-d. Wayne Co, MS) – **3 sons, 2 daus**; m/2, Sarah Gardiner
Claudius[2], b. 4 Aug 1752 Georgetown; d. young
Claudius[2], b. 9 Apr 1755 Georgetown; m. Marcy/Marcia Saunders (10 Sep 1751-3 Nov 1813), d/o George & Hannah (Gibson) Saunders; he d. 23 Nov 179x, poss. 1792; **issue**
Henriette[2], b. 22 Jun 1758 Cheraw; d. young

REF: CLARK, Chovine Richardson, "The Rev. Wesley Leatherwood Pegues" in *Transactions of the Huguenot Society of SC*, #86 (1981); *Transactions of the Huguenot Society of SC*, #75 (1970); HALL, William B., "The Marriage License of Claudius Pegues (1719-1790)" in *The SC Historical & Genealogical Magazine,* Vol. XXXVIII (Baltimore, 1937); GREGG, Right Rev. Alexander, *History of the Old Cheraws* (Columbia, SC, 1925).

PEIRET/PEYRET, Pierre (Rev.)

b. 1644, Pontacq, FR, s.e. of Pau, Pyrénées-Atlantiques Dépt, Aquitaine
m. Osse-en-Aspe, FR, s. of Oloron-Ste-Marie, Marguerite de Grenier la Tour, des Verriers de Gabre
c. 1685 - fled Foix, FR (former province in s. FR bordering on the Pyrenees & Spain); went to ENG
1686/7- arr. NYC on the *Robert*; served as minister of the FR Ch in NYC until his death
1703- census of NYC – Peter Pieret, 2 m 16-60, 2 f, 1 m ch, 2 f ch + negroes
d. 1 Sep 1704, NYC, bur. Trinity Churchyard, NYC
1705- widow Marguerite Peyret, of Béarn, was granted £12 as the widow of a minister and mother of 2 ch; Béarn is a former province of FR , located in s.w. FR, its southern border is the n. border of Spain
CHILDREN:
Pierre[2], m. Mary Bryan, d/o Samuel & Martha (Whiting) Bryan of Milford, CT; d. a. 16 Jun 1718, adm, New Haven, CT; ch. **Peter**[3], **Margaret**[3]
Magdalene[2], b. FR; m/1, 26 Jan 1702, NY, Bartholomew Feurt (he d. a. 23 Sep 1713, NYC), m/2, c. 1717/8, Thomas Hickel; she d. Elizabethtown, NJ
CHILDREN, m/1:
Margaret[3], b. 12 Nov 1702
Pierre/Peter[3], b. 27 Nov 1703
Bartholomew[3], bp. 18 Feb 1704
Francis[3], b. 6 Mar 1707; m. Mary X
Magdalena[3], bp. 8 Feb 1710
Susanne[2], b. 18 Nov, bp. 28 Nov 1690, FR Ch, NYC
Gabriel[2], b. 30 Jan, bp. 14 Feb 1693/4, FR Ch, NYC
Françoise[2], b. 1 Mar, bp. 15 Mar 1695/6, FR Ch, NYC
Elizabeth[2], b. 22 Dec, bp. 29 Dec 1700, FR Ch, NYC

REF: MYERS, Samuel M., *The French Connection, History of Some of the Ancestors & Descendants of Samuel Mortimer Myers II in America 1635-1973* (Stillwater, OK, 1973); BAIRD, Charles W., *History of the Huguenot Emigration to America* (Baltimore, 1973); WITTMEYER, Rev. Alfred V., *Registers of the Église Françoise à Nouvelle York 1688-1804* (Baltimore, 1968); GANNON, Peter Steven, editor, *Huguenot Refugees in the Settling of Colonial America* (New York, 1987); BUTLER, Jon, *The Huguenots in America A Refugee People in New World Society* (Cambridge, MA, 1983).

PEMBERTON/PA(I)MBRETON, Richard

m/1, Elizabeth X; liv. King William Parish (Manakintown), VA
m/2, 1 Sep 1757, Manakintown, Frances Bradley
d. a. 24 Jul 1769, wp, Cumberland Co, VA
CHILDREN (named in father's will, last 3 or 4 ch *prob.* from m/2):
Michael[2], b. 14 Jan 1745
William[2], b. 30 Jan 1748/9; m/1, 12 May 1771, Manakintown, Joanna Howard, m/2, Nancy Sherwood; he
    d. a. 20 Dec 1814, wp, Washington Co, VA; **issue**
Martha[2], b. 17 Oct 1752
James[2]
Richard[2]
George[2]
Mary[2]
Magdalane[2]

REF: *The Huguenot* #29 (1979-81), #35 (1991-93); wills of Richard and William Pemberton; JONES, W. Mac, editor, *The Douglas Register* (Baltimore, 1985); BROCK, R.A., *Huguenot Emigration to VA* (Baltimore, 1966); MEADE, Bishop, *Old Churches, Ministers & Families of VA*, Vol. I (Philadelphia, 1910).

PÉPIN, Alexandre

early settler to SC
m. Madeleine Garillion, d/o Israel & Susanne (Saunier) Garillion
d. 1688, Charleston, SC
CHILDREN:
Paul[2], m. p. 1696, Marianne X; he d. by 18 Dec 1699, intestate
    CHILD:
      Judith-Marianne[3], d. poss. p. 8 Dec 1712
Madeleine[2], m. Jean Potell/Potell, s/o Nicolas & Marie (Brugnet) Potell

REF: *Transactions of the Huguenot Society of SC*, #91 (1986), #93 (1988)

PÉRON/PERRON dit Suire, Daniel

b. 25 Nov 1638, prob. La Rochelle, FR; bp. 26 Dec 1638, Château de Dampierre et Bourgneuf en Aunis,
    natural s/o François Péron & Jeanne Suire, Protestants from La Rochelle; Jeanne evidently later
    m. a Jacques Laurens and she d. p. 1 Mar 1656, wd; Bourgneuf is n. of Rochefort, now Charente-
    Maritime Dépt, Poitou-Charentes
18 Apr 1657 - from La Rochelle in *Le Taureau*, sent to New France by his father to represent his business
    interests; arr. Québec, 22 Jun 1657; settled Québec
6 Dec 1663 - Québec City, abjuration of the Protestant faith by Daniel – it was next to impossible to do
    business or anything else in Québec unless you were Catholic, so the "conversion" may have been a
    matter of convenience; he was bap in a Protestant ch, his mother was Protestant and remained
    so until her death; he was disowned by his father after this
m. 26 Feb 1664, Château-Richer, Québec, Louise Gargotin (1637/8, Thairé, FR-7 Feb/20 May 1704, L'Ange
    Gardien, Québec), d/o Jacques & Françoise (Bernard) Gargotin; Thairé is a few kms s. of Bourgneuf;
    she m/2, 7 Jan 1679, L'Ange-Gardien, Charles-Louis Alain; Château-Richer & L'Ange- Gardien are
    n.e. of Québec on the St. Lawrence River
name was Peron but the Catholic Society of New France added a second "r" to Peron

apparently a rather contentious man, appearing before the judicial courts many times; enjoyed fighting with words more than tilling the ground; he enjoyed speechifying, debating, protesting, nothing met with his approval

d. p. 11 Feb 1678/9, wd, L'Ange-Gardien, Québec

CHILD (1 of 6):

Antoine[2], b. 29 Nov 1664, L'Ange-Gardien, Québec; m. 15 Jan 1691, Jeanne Tremble (1672, Château-Richer, Québec-23 Jun 1711, Québec City); he d. 26 May 1711, Québec City; Antoine was bap. with the surname **SUIRE**, his paternal grandmother's maiden name

REF: Institut Francophone de Généalogie et d'Historie, La Rochelle, *François Peron*; will of Jeanne Suire, wife of Jacques Laurens, in which she states that she is of the "Reformed religion" & that Daniel is her son; baptismal record of Daniel.

PERONNEAU, Samuel

b. c. 1642, La Rochelle, FR

m. a. 1667, FR, Jeanne Collin

c. 1685 – to SC, settled Charles Town by 1700

18 Feb 1714/5 - act to empower Elder Samuel to sell a tract of land in Berkeley Co, devised to the poor of The FR Ch in Charleston

d. a. 8 Nov 1722, inv, Charles Town, SC

CHILDREN:

Henri/Henry[2], b. 28 May 1667, La Rochelle, FR; to Charleston, Aug 1687, naturalized, 10 Mar 1696/7; m. c. 1700, Desire/Desirée X (1680-30 Dec 1740, bur. Circular Churchyard, Charleston, SC); he d. 31 May 1743, age 76, bur. Circular Churchyard; he was a merchant
    CHILDREN:
    Henri II[3], b. c. 1700; m. 30 Jul 1728, Elizabeth Hall; d. 30 Jan 1754; merchant in Charleston; **11 ch**
    Elizabeth[3], b. 1704; m. 19 Jan 1723, Isaac Holmes (1702-25 Nov 1751); she d. 1773; **7 ch**
    Alexander[3], b. early 1700's; m/1, 7 Jun 1733, Mary Pollock (1709-6 Feb 1741/2) – **5 ch**, m/2, 20 Dec 1744, Margaret Hext – **8 ch**; he d. 22 Apr 1774, bur. Circular Churchyard
    Samuel[3], b. c. 1711; m. 19 Jun 1743, Elizabeth Cochran; he d. 15 Jan 1756; **3 ch**
    Charles[3], b. c. 1712; d. 19 Oct 1740, unmarr.; merchant in Charleston
    Sarah[3], b. 16 Jan 1715/6; m. 17 Jul 1740, William Webb; she d. 30 Sep 1749; **2 ch**
    Martha[3], m/1, 11 Aug 1743, John Witherston – **1 dau**, m/2, William Lloyd – **4 ch**; she d. Jan 1771

Isaac[2], m. a. 17 Aug 1743, Mary/Marianne Fitch (d. p. 21 Oct 1772, wd); family lived St. James Goose Creek
    CHILDREN:
    Mary Ann[3], m/1, X Duguay, m/2, X Peronneau; **Mary**[3] m. George Lewis; **Ann**[3] m. X Parker

Marie[2], b. c. 1685, at sea, en route to SC; m. 1716, as his 2nd wife Pierre Bacot; she d. 1778 (aged 93)
    CHILD: **Samuel**[3]

Elizabeth[2], m. 19 Apr 1734, Paul Marion (d. a. 27 Jan 1737/8, wp), s/o Benjamin & Mary (X) Marion; **2 sons**

REF: *Transactions of the Huguenot Society of SC,* #77 (1972); BAIRD, C.W., *History of the Huguenot Emigration to America,* Vol. 1; HIRSCH, A.H., *The Huguenots of Colonial SC;* Special Collection, SC Historical Society; HUTTON, Michael Jenkins, "Perinneau of SC" in *Transactions of the Huguenot Society of SC,* #89 (1984), #79 (1974), #77 (1972), #5 (1897).

PÉROT/PERROW/PERROULT, Jacques

fled La Rochelle, FR

m. 1698, NY or Bermuda, Marie Cousson

d. c. 1735
CHILD:
Jacques/James[2], b. 20 May NY, bp. May 26 1712, FR Ch, NYC; m. Bermuda, Frances Mallory (d. 1 Mar
      1790); he d. 29 Feb 1780
    CHILDREN:
    Martha[3]
    Mary[3]
    Elliston[3], b. 16 Mar 1747, Bermuda; named for an uncle Robert Elliston; he went to NY to
        be educated by his uncle Robert who was at that time, the Comptroller of the Customs;
        Robert placed Elliston in the school kept by Pasteur Strouppe, in New Rochelle; upon
        his uncle's death, he returned to Bermuda; he conducted business in Dominica, St. Kitts
        & St. Eustatius; back to the U.S. in 1784, where he and his bro John were in business
        together as merchants in Philadelphia; in 1786, he was admitted a member of the Society
        of Friends; m. 1787, Sarah Sansom (d. 33 Aug 1808), d/o Samuel & Hannah (X) Sansom;
        he d. 28 Nov 1834, Philadelphia; **5 ch**
    John[3]
    James[3]
    William[3], had son **William B.**[4] of Parlaville, Hamilton, Bermuda, who d. 1871 - **issue**
    Frances[3]
    Angelina[3]

REF: BAIRD, Charles W., *History of the Huguenot Emigration to America* (Baltimore, 1973); MOON, Robert C., *Genealogy of the Morris Family* (1898).

PERRAULT/PERROW/PERO, Charles

    b. Bordeaux, Guienne, FR, now Gironde Dépt, Aquitaine
    1700 - in Stafford Co, VA; poss sailed on the *Peter and Anthony*; later to Manakintown
    m. Marguerite X; she m/2, c. 1719, Antoine Rapine (d. bet 10 Apr-15 Nov 1737) – dau **Mariane**; she d.
        a. 26 Jan 1756, wp, Cumberland Co, VA
    1705 - on the Henrico tax records w/ wife, 1 son, 2 (?) daus
    20 May 1709 - elected to the office of vestry in King William Parish, a job he held until his death
    d. a. 26 Aug 1717, wp, Henrico Co, VA
    CHILDREN:
Daniel[2], b. c. 1702; m. Marie X; **4 ch**, incl. son **Charles**[3] who m. a. 3 Aug 1750, Françoise Guérrant, d/o
    Daniel & Françoise (L'Orange) Guérrant, & dau **Mary**[3] who m. 25 Nov 1756, Pierre Guérrant, s/o
    Pierre & Magdelaine (Trabue) Guérrant/Guérin; he d. c. 1789, Buckingham Co, VA
unnamed dau[2], c. 1704/5; alive in 1714, prob. d. young
Anne[2], b. 1708; m. by 1731, William Epperson/Apperson; she d. a. 8 Mar 1755; at least **1 son**
Marie/Mary[2], b. c. 1710; m. c. 1731, Étienne Farcy/Forsee, s/o Jean Farcy; **10 ch**; dau **Jane**[3] m. James
    Briant, Jr., s/o Jacques & Elizabeth (LeFèvre) Brian, son **Étienne**[3] m. Frances Brian, d/o
    Jacques & Clare (X) Brian, & son **William**[3] m. Mary Ann Smith, d/o Rev. George & Judith
    (Guérrant) Smith

REF: ALLEN, Cameron, "Preliminary Notes on the Perrault-Perrow Family of Roi Guillaume" in *The VA Genealogist*, Vol. 8 #2 (Apr-Jun, 1964), #3 (Jul-Sep, 1964), #4 (Oct-Dec, 1964); *The Huguenot*, #5 (1931).

PERRIN(E)/PAREYN, Daniel

b. c. 1641, FR, s/o Pierre who was b. or at least liv. in La Rochelle, FR where he was a silk manufacturer & merchant of Norman heritage; 1685, he joined his son Daniel in NY where he d. 1698, Staten Island; Pierre is said to have emig. with another son Henry, whose son Daniel went to Ocean Co, NJ

29 Jul 1665 –arr. NYC, from the Isle of Jersey on the *Philip* w/ (Philip) Carteret Group; went to NJ

m/1, 18 Feb 1666, Elizabethtown, NJ, Marie Thorel of Rouen who had traveled to America on the same ship as Daniel; she d. a. 1687, Staten Island, NY

m/2, c. 1688, Elizabeth X (d. p. 6 Sep 1719)

d. p. 6 Sep 1719 (witness at bap. of his grsons Willem & Daniel Stilwell, sons of his dau Sara)

CHILDREN:

Peter[2], b. 1667; m. 16 Oct 1704, Ann(e) Holmes of Gravesend, LI (b. 20 Dec 1670), d/o Samuel & Alice (Stilwell) Holmes; Alice Holmes, d/o Lt. Nicholas & Anne (X) Stilwell; he d. p. 28 May 1740, New Dorp, Staten Island; **5 sons**

Henry[2], b. 1669, Staten Island; m. Marie X of Staten Is. (d. 1765); he d. p. 1 Nov 1711, Somerset Co, NJ; **3 ch**

James[2], b. 1670, Staten Island; m. XX; d. Staten Island; had **2 sons**

Daniel[2], b. 1672, Staten Island; m. XX, 1699; d. 1745, Staten Island; **4 sons**

William[2], b. 1673; d. p. 1741?

Francyntje[2], m/1, Abraham Egbertson of Staten Island - **3 ch**, m/2, Henry Janzsen/Johnson of Staten Island – **3 ch**

CHILDREN, m/2:

Sara[2], m/1, William Stillwell of Cape May, NJ - posthumous **twin sons**, m/2, c. 1727, James Boster/Bosler of Staten Island - **3 ch**; Sara & her sister Elizabeth m. brothers Willem & Jan Stilwell. Wm. & Jan were grs/o Lt. Nicholas & Anne X) Stilwell mentioned above.

Elizabeth[2], m. Jan/John Stillwell of Cape May, NJ - **1 son**

Maria/Mary[2], m. Johannes Sweem of Staten Island - **1 dau**

REF: PERRINE, Howland Delano, *Daniel Perrin "The Huguenot" and His Descendants in America, 1665-1910* (S. Orange, NJ, 1910); TURK, Marion G., *The Quiet Adventurers in America* (1975); Records of the Dutch Reformed Ch, Port Richard, Staten Island, NY; *Proceedings of the Huguenot Society of PA*, Vol. XXVII (Philadelphia, PA, 1955); BOYER, Carl 3rd, *Ship Passenger Lists, NY & NJ 1600-1825* (Newhall, CA, 1978).

PERRIN, Jean

Perrin family was in Paris by 1450

b. c. 1550, FR

1570 - fled Paris to ENG

1575 - fellow of St. John's College, Oxford University; King's professor of Greek

m. Anne Bruneau, d/o Jean Bruneau

1580 - they were members of St. Dunstan's Parish, London, an Anglican church

1596- Canon of Christ's Ch; one of the King James' translators of the Bible

d. 1615, ENG

CHILD:

unnamed son[2]

    CHILD:

    Jean[3], b, 1614, Chelmsford, Essex, ENG; m. Anna Hubert (bur. 11 Mar 1688/9, Rehoboth, MA), d/o Richard Hubert of Normandie, poss. Canisy, s.w. of St.-Lô; he is *poss.* the John Perryn, age 21, who sailed c. 10 Aug 1635, from Gravesend in the *Safety* for "Virginea"; arr. Boston, 10 Aug 1635; was in Rehoboth, by 4 Jun 1643; d. 13 Sep 1674, Rehoboth, MA; 23 Nov 1674, wp - names wife Anna, sons John & Abraham, daus Anna & Mary; inv presented, 23 Nov 1674, Marshfield - £230 real estate, total of £375, 5 sh, 3 p

    CHILDREN:

Mary[4], b. 22 Feb 1640/1, Braintree, MA; d. young

John[4], b. c. 1643, Rehoboth, MA; m. c. 1667, Mary Polley (bp. 2 Jun 1650, Roxbury), d/o John & Susannah (Bacon) Polley; he d. 1692/3, Roxbury, MA; **10 ch**

Hannah/Anna[4], b. 12 Jul 1645, Rehoboth, MA; m. 16 Jun 1675, Ensign Thomas Read (20 Nov 1641, Braintree-6 Feb 1695/6, Rehoboth), s/o John & Sarah (X) Read as his 2nd wife; she d. 28 Mar 1710; **5 ch**

Abraham[4], b. 1 Mar 1647, Rehoboth, MA; m. 27 Dec 1677, Sarah Walker (Feb 1657, Rehoboth-bur. 2 Aug 1693, Rehoboth), d/o Philip & Jane (Metcalf) Walker; he was bur 15 May 1694, Rehoboth, MA; **8 ch**

Mary[4], b. 2 Feb 1649; m/1, 2 Dec 1670, Rehoboth, Jacob Ormsby (6 Mar 1647/8, Salisbury, MA –bur. 1 Mar 1677), s/o Richard & Sarah (X) Ormsby, m/2, 27 Dec 1677, Rehoboth, Nicholas Ide (Nov 1654, Rehoboth-25 Jun 1723, Attleboro, MA), s/o Nicholas & Martha (Bliss) Ide; she was bur. 9 Sep 1690, Rehoboth, MA

REF: PERIN, Stanley Ernest, *The John Perrin Family of Rehoboth, MA* (Baltimore, 1974); LAPHAM, William B., "The Perrin Family" in *NEHGS Register* (Apr 1878); Vital Records, Rehoboth, MA.

PERSHING/PFÖRSCHING, Frédéric/Frederick/Friedrich

b. 1724, Alsace, FR, liv. Kehl, GER, across the Rhine River from Strasbourg

left Amsterdam for England, then to PA – oath of allegiance, 2 Oct 1749, in Philadelphia; naturalized in Philadelphia, 1765, called resident of York Co.

m. 29 Apr 1750, prob. York Co, PA, Maria Elizabeth Weygandt (1729-1824)

d. 18 Nov 1794, Westmoreland Co, PA; he was a weaver by trade but also a wheelwright and carpenter

CHILDREN:

Christian[2], b. 1751, York Co, PA; m. c. 1777, Anna Maria Brewer (1751-1826); he d. 1825 - **6 ch**

poss. an infant[2], b. and d. 1753/54

Elizabeth[2], b. 1757, York Co, PA

Peter Frederick[2], b. 1759, York Co, PA; m/1, 1791, Elizabeth Ulery (1760-1801), m/2, 1804 Mary Ann McGee who m/2 Hugh Galbraith – they went to St. Joseph Co, IN, where they had 2 ch., John & Eliza; Peter Frederick d. 19 Jul 1822, of typhoid fever, in Indiana Co, PA; the part of Westmoreland Co. where the Pershings lived, became Indiana Co. in 1803.

CHILDREN, m/1 (b. Westmorland Co, PA):

Jacob[3], b. 1793, d. young

Elizabeth[3], (1795-24 Apr 1856) m. 1816, Hugh Cameron (d. 1869) - **9 ch**

John[3], (10 May 1801-15 Nov 1854, prob. Holmes Co, OH), m/1, 1824, Sarah Johns (10 Sep 1809-1832) – 1 son **Robert**[4], m/2, 1833, Elizabeth Shoop (1803- d. p. 1880 census, prob. Owen Co, IN) – **5 ch**, incl. **Eli**[4] (23 Nov 1834, PA-22 Dec 1912, Coal City, IN) m. 9 Mar 1863 Mary E. Fry (20 Aug 1843, OH-1915, prob. Owen Co, IN); as a young man, John went to Pittsburgh, where he was a hatter

CHILDREN, m/2 (b. Indiana Co, PA):

Daniel[3], **James**[3], **Margaret**[3], **Sarah**[3], **Samuel K.**[3], **William**[3], **Jonathan**[3], **Joseph**[3], **Henry B.**[3], **Hezekiah**[3]

Christena[2], b. 1762, York Co, PA

Conrad[2], b. 27 May 1767, York Co, PA

REF: STRASSBURGER Ralph Beaver, *Pennsylvania German Pioneers* (Baltimore, 1975); PERSHING, Edgar J., *The Pershing Family in America* (Philadelphia, 1924); *Publications of the Huguenot Society of London*, Vol XXIV (Manchester, 1921).

PEYSTER, Josse de

b. prob. Ghent, Flanders eldest s/o Josse (d. a. 7 Sep 1587) & Elizabeth (Danckaerts, d. a. 21 Aug 1596) de Peyster; originally a FR family who left FR to escape religious persecution of Charles IX (reigned 1560-1574); took refuge in the United Provinces, aka the Dutch Republic, c. 1572

m. Joanne van de Voorde, d/o Pierre & Joosyne (de Caluwe) van de Voorde

CHILDREN:

Josse[2], of Ghent, Amsterdam and Middelburg

Johannes[2], b. c. 1600, Haarlem, HOL; went from Ghent to Amsterdam, then Haarlem, by 1621, where he was a burgher; m. Jossine Martens; he d. 1648, Haarlem; **4 ch** including **Johannes**[3]

CHILD:

Johannes[3], b. c, 1620, Haarlem, HOL; in New Amsterdam, by Jul 1649; m. 17 Dec 1651, NYC, Cornelia Lubberts (b. Haarlem-d. p. 19 Sep 1699 ,wd-a. 25 Sep 1725, wp); Johannes was a merchant & a very influential man, held a variety of civic offices & was one of the wealthiest citizens in the province; he d. 1689, NY

CHILDREN (all bp in the Old Dutch Ch, NYC):

Johannes[4], bp. Aug 1653; d. in infancy

Johannes[4], bp. 7 Oct 1654; d. young

Abraham[4], bp. 8 Jul 1657; d. 8 Aug 1728, NYC; referred to as *Der Heer Abraham de Peyster*; very illustrious man; m. 5 Apr 1684, Amsterdam, HOL, his cousin Catharina de Peyster*; he was the chief justice; 1692-94, the mayor of NYC; he d. 8 Aug 1728; **13 ch**

Maria[4], b. 5 Sep 1659; m/1, 11 May 1686, Paulus Schrick, s/o Paulus Schrick & Maria Varleth, who d. 11 Oct 1685 – **no issue**; m/2, 26 Aug 1687, John Spratt of Scotland – **1 son, 3 daus**, m/3, 28 Jan 1698/9, David Provoost, II (b. c. 30 Sep 1645), s/o David Prévost/Prevoost & Margaretta Ten Waert – **no issue**; she d. 3 May 1701

Isaac[4], bp. 16 Apr 1662; m. 27 Dec 1687, Maria Van Baal/Van Balen, d/o Jan Hendrickse Van Baal & Helena Teller of Albany; member of the provincial legislature; **10 ch**

Jacob[4], bp. 23 Dec 1663; **no issue**

Johannes[4], bp. 21 Sep 1665; m. 10 Oct 1688, Albany, Anna Bancker, d/o Gerrit Bancker & Elizabeth Direkse Van Eps; 1698-99, he was mayor of NYC, an office that his father had refused as his English was not good; he d. 23 Sep 1711; **12 ch**

Cornelis[4], bp. 4 Oct 1673; m/1, 19 Sep 1694, Maria Bancker, prob. d/o Evert Bancker & Elizabeth Abeel – **7 ch;** m/2, 21 Jul 1711, Cornelia (Dissinton) Stewart, widow of Alexander Stewart**; 1st chamberlain of the City of NY + other public offices - **5 daus**

Cornelia[4], bp. 4 Dec 1678; m. 18 Aug 1699 Alexander Stewart**; **no issue**

*same person; **same person

Jacques[2], 1639, was liv. Rouen; m. Catherine de Lavoye; he d. 1676, Rouen; **8 ch**; was the grf/o Catharina de Peyster* who m. Abraham de Peyster of America

Lievin[2], of Ghent, Haarlem and Amsterdam

Jonas[2], of Ghent and London

Marie[2], m. Jacques de Key of Haarlem

REF: LEACH, Josiah Granville, *History of the Bringhurst Family with Notes on the Clarkson, DePeyster & Baude Families* (Philadelphia, 1901); *Proceedings of the Huguenot Society of PA*, Vol. 29 (1957), p. 107; ALLABEN, Frank, *John Watts de Peyster*, Vol. I; PURPLE, Edwin R., "Contributions to the History of the Ancient Families of NY" in the *NYGBR*, Vol. IX (1878).

PIATT/PYATT, René, aka FLEURISSON, Renatus; also LaFLEUR/FLOWER, Thomas

b. c. 1650, Dauphiné, FR; original name said to be Renatus Fleurisson

*25 Mar 1688 - date on denizations list in London for René Fleurisson; this date must have been entered

later (see date of arr); the denizations listed happened during the reign of Charles II, who d. 1685; René was in America long before that; on a list written in Latin, name is *Rene ffleury,* there is also a *Petro ffleurisson,* a few names further down

a. 1677 arr America via HOL & ENG*

1675-80 - listed as a purchaser of land in Piscataway, NJ, during that time period

m. 13 Dec 1677, LI, NY, Elizabeth Sheffield of Flushing, Long Island, NY

27 Jan 1679/80 - deed re purchase of 55 acres in Piscataway; name given *Reni Piat, alias Laflower* of Woodbridge

c. 1680 - settled Piscataway, NJ

10 Jan 1683/4 – deed re purchase of 55 acres in Piscataway Twp on the Raritan River, name given as *Laflour, alias Reni Piat* of New Piscataway

30 Nov 1687 - deed for 200 acres in Piscataway, name given *La Flower alias Renipiatt*

23 Dec 1690 - *La Flower alias Reni-Piat* sale of 55 acres

1 Mar 1693/4 - deed for 250 acres in Pisacataway, name given *Renne Peeat, alias Le Floaer*

16 Jul 1700 - *Laflower alias Rene Peat*

20 Aug 1701 - release by *Laflooer alias Renne Pecat* of Piscataway of 250 acres for non-payment

d. a. 16 Oct 1705, letters of administration granted to widow Elizabeth; file named *Reyneer (Regnier) Peatt, alias LeFlure*; 18 Oct 1705, inv - £156.1, personal estate incl, £70 2 Indians, 1 Negro + 2 ch

CHILDREN:

Jacob[2], 31 Oct 1678, Woodbridge, NJ; m. 7 Jun 1703, Mary Hull (b.4 Feb 1681, Middlesex Co, NJ), d/o Samuel & Mary (Manning) Hull; he d. p. 1750; at least **8 ch**

René[2], b. 1679; d. 1680

Thomas[2], b. 11 May 1681, Piscataway; m. 1 Feb 1699/00, Mercy Hull (22 Jan 1683, Piscataway-21 Dec 1746, Piscataway), d/o Samuel & Mary (Manning) Hull, she m/2 Rev. Benjamin Stelle); Thomas d. 1706/7 - **4 ch**

James[2], b. c. 1683; 170,1 apprenticed to James Many, mariner; m. Elizabeth X; at least **1 dau**

Francis[2], c. c. 1685; d. p. 1701

Samuel[2], b. c. 1687

prob. others, given the 8 yr. gap

Joan/Jane[2], b. 15 Sep 1695; m. 15 Aug 1714, Piscataway, Rev. Jonathan Dunham (b. 4 Mar 1692/3-11 Jun 1777), s/o Edmund & Mary (Bonham) Dunham; she d. 15 Sep 1779, Piscataway; **8 ch**

NOTE: Despite the fact that their father seemed to change his name frequently, his ch consistently used **PYATT** or **PIATT**.

REF: Oliver B. Leonard Papers from NJ Historical Society; LEONARD, O. B. "Pioneer Planters of Piscataway, NJ ...." in *NYGBR,* Vol. 29 (Jan, 1898); *NJ Archives, 1st Series - NJ Colonial Documents*; *Publications of the Huguenot Society of London,* Vol. XVIII (1911); MONNETTE, Ora E., *First Settlers of Piscataway & Woodbridge,* Parts 4, 5, 6; WHITE, Eleanore M., *The Piatt Family Newsletter,* Vol. 1 (Rockledge, FL, 1986).

PICON/PICKENS/PICKINS, Robert (aka André)

b. c. 1644, FR, s/o André Picon

held a diplomatic post at the court of Henri IV of FR

m. c. 1665, FR, Ester Jane (Benoit) Bonneau, (parents unk), widow of X Bonneau

p. 1685- family left FR via La Rochelle, FR; went to SCOT where he joined the Presbyterian Ch, then to N. IRE

d. c. 1700 IRE, prob. Limerick; bur IRE

CHILDREN:

Andrew[2], b. FR

John[2], b. FR

Robert[2], b. FR

William[2], b. c. 1670, FR; m. 1692, IRE, Margaret Pike (c. 1672-p. 1740, Augusta, VA); to America, settled Bucks Co, PA c. 1720/22; to Lancaster (now Dauphin) Co; he prob. d. 1730-40, Lancaster Co, PA
  CHILDREN (b. IRE, order not certain):
  Israel[3], b. 1693; m/1, Martha Davis? – **3 ch**, m/2, Martha Ann? Nisbit – **4 ch**; a. 1740, to Orange Co, VA; he d. 1749, Lunenburg Co, VA; Martha m/2, John Clark
  Robert[3], b.c.1697; m. c. 1729, MD, Miriam Davis (d. 1793, Pendleton Co, SC); **5 ch**
  Andrew[3], c. 1699; m. a. 1737, Lancaster Co, PA, Anne "Nancy" Davis* (b. IRE, d. c. 1733 PA); he d. c. 1756/7, Anson Co, NC; **6 ch**; * some recs. says Nancy Ann Scott
      Andrew II[4] (b. 19 Sep 1739 d. 11 Aug 1817) m. 19 Mar 1765, Rebecca Calhoun (b. 18 Mar 1745)
  Lucy[3], b. 1702; m/1, 2 Sep 1722, Montgomery Co, PA, Matthew Gillespie (d. 1728) – **2 ch**, m/2, 1730, John Kerr as his 2nd wife; moved to Orange Co, VA; d. Montgomery Co, VA
  William[3], b. c. 1705; m/1 Elizabeth X – **2 ch**, m/2 Ann (Oliver) Scott, d/o Aaron Oliver, widow of Samuel Scott - **3 ch**; he d. p. 1783, Montgomery Co, VA
  John[3], b.c.1710; m. Eleanor X; he d.1769/73, Abbeville Dist, SC; **8 ch**
  Gabriel[3], b. c. 1715; m. c. 1744, Augusta Co, VA, Zerubiah Smith; he d.1775-80, Abbeville Dist, SC; **4 ch**
  Margaret[3], b. c. 1719; m. X Ramsey

REF: The Huguenot, #13 (1945-47); NIX, Lois K. & SNELL, Mary Kay, *Thomas Boone Pickens (1828 -   )His Ancestors Being the Lives of His Pickens, Boone, Calhoun & Molonson Forefathers with Allied Families*; ROBBINS, Mary Donaghey, *The Pickens Family* – The Huguenot #21 (1964-66); WARING, Alice Noble, *Pickens Genealogy Southern Branch* – Transactions of the Huguenot Society of SC, #71 (1966); SHARP, E.M., *Pickens Families of the South* (Memphis, 1966); PICKENS, Monroe, rev. DAY, Kate Pickens, *Cousin Monroe's History of the Pickens Family* (Easley, SC, 1951).

PILLEAU, Alexis (Rev.)

  m. Anne Vigneux (d. by Dec 1671), d/o Jean & Judie (Bouchevreau)Vigneux, he was the minister of the Protestant Ch. at Le Mans
  CHILDREN:
  Anne[2], b. c. 1629; m. c. 10 Oct 1673, Samuel Huet
  Marie[2], b. 1636; m. 27 Dec 1671, Charles Piozet
  Jean[2]
  Jacques[2], m. Marthe Cabaret; d. a. 9 Feb 1694, FR
  Michelle[2], m. Joseph le Magoules/de Magoulais (d. a. Jan 1685); Michelle was in London by that date
  Catherine[2]
  Jean[2], m. Marie Blondeau; d. a. 16 Nov 1683; he was a goldsmith
      CHILD:
      Alexis[3], b. c. 1658, b. FR; m. 1683, Madeleine Pezé, d/o Marin & Marie (Boureau) Pezé of Le Mans; 1688 family joined FR Ch, Threadneedle St, London; he d. p. 23 Sep 1730, wd; a goldsmith and maker of artificial teeth; he lived at the corner of Newport St. & St. Martin's Lane, a few blocks from his business
          CHILDREN:
          Alexis Pierre[4], bp. 13 Mar 1692, FR Ch, Threadneedle St.; d. young
          (Alexis) Pezé[4], b. 23 Jan 1696, bp. Le Carré; m. c. 1724, Parish of St. Martin's in the Fields, London, Henriette Chartier; he d. p. 26 Nov 1762, wd; he was a goldsmith, silversmith and maker of artificial teeth – his business was called the "Golden Cup" on Shandois St. (prob. what is now Chandos St., in the Trafalgar Sq. area)
              CHILDREN (all rec. in the Castle St. Parish Register):
              Alexis Pezé[5], b. 21 Sep , bp. 3 Oct 1725
              Jean[5], b. 22 Mar, bp. 3 Apr 1727

Jean Pezé[5], b. 15 Feb, bp. 9 Mar 1729
Alexis[5], b. 27 Sep, bp. 15 Oct 1731
Isaac[5], b. 19 Feb, bp 28 Feb 1733/4; m. Jane Crispin/Crespin; he d. 6 Feb 1812,
      Newington Place, prob. in London
Henriette Marguerite[5], b. 25 Sep, bp. 30 Sep 1736
Susanne[5], b. 27 Dec, bp. 31 Dec 1738
François[5], b. 6 Feb, bp. 14 Feb 1748
René[4], d. 23 Sep 1730, leaving a wife & a **dau**
Madeleine Louise[4], bp. 14 Dec 1693, Le Carré; d. a. 1730

REF: CLAY, Charles Travis, "Notes on the Ancestors & Descendants of Pezé Pilleau, The London Goldsmith";
Huguenot Society Proceedings.

PINEAU/PINEO/PENAUD, Jacques

b. c. 1667, Lyon, FR; Waldense family; parents *may* have been Jacques Pinneau & Jeanne Lecouve -
    not proven
5 Jan 1688 - naturalized ENG; he was a weaver
c. 1700 - to Plymouth, MA
m. 9 May 1706, Bristol, RI, Dorothy Babcock b. 19 Jan 1684, Bristol, RI, d/o Return & Sarah (Denison)
    Babcock
22 Jul 1717 - bought land in Lebanon, CT
d. c. 1725, prob. Lebanon, CT
CHILDREN:
James[2], b. 19 Apr 1707, Bristol; d. young
James[2], b. 1708; m. 16 Jun 1731, Lebanon, Priscilla Newcomb, d/o Joseph & Joyce (Butler) Newcomb; he
    d. 18 Apr 1789, Lebanon; **9 ch,** 6 of whom b. Lebanon
Elizabeth[2], b. c. 1709; m/1, Solomon Curtice – **issue**, m/2, Noah Carpenter – **issue**; she d. 1764
Sarah[2], b. 19 Dec 1712; m. Joseph Porter - **issue**
Submit[2], b. 19 Oct 1717, Lebanon; m. 5 Mar 1739, Silas Newcomb (2 Sep 1717, Lebanon, CT-24 May
    1773), s/o Hezekiah & Jerusha (Bradford) Newcomb; Jerusha was the grgrdau of William Brad-ford of
    the *Mayflower*; she d. 12 Feb 1804, Lebanon; **12 ch**
Daniel[2], b. 10 Sep 1715, Lebanon; d. young
Joseph[2], b. 14 Jun 1720, Lebanon; m. Hannah Hill; d. 5 Jan 1743, Lebanon
Peter[2], b. 4 May 1723, Lebanon; m. 20 Dec 1743, Lebanon, Elizabeth Samson, d/o David & Mary
    Chaffin/Chapin Samson (grd/o Henry Samson of the *Mayflower*); from CT to NH; 1763, went to
    Cornwallis, Nova Scotia; **7 ch**
Dorothy[2], b. 6 Dec 1725, Lebanon; m. 30 Dec 1746, John Reed; she d. 4 May 1770, Taunton, MA; **issue**

REF: BAIRD, Charles W., *The History of the Huguenot Emigration to American,* Vol. II; LITTLE, George Thomas,
Genealogical & Family History of the State of Maine (NY, 1909); COOPER, Wm. Durrand, *List of Foreign Protest-
ants & Aliens Resident in England, 1618-1688;* NEWCOMB, Bethuel Merritt, *Andrew Newcomb 1618-1686 His
Descendants* (New Haven, 1923); Vital records, Lebanon, CT.

PINGAR, Jacques

native of Paris, FR
m. 22 Jun 1639, FR Ch, Threadneedle St, London, ENG , Magdelaine Despiné, d/o David
    Despiné, a native of Rouen
CHILD:
*****Marie**[2], m. 6 Dec 1663, Fr Ch, London, Benjamin Aidelo/Aydelott, s/o David and Marie (Sochon)
    Aydelott, native of London

*Magdelaine[2], bp. 28 Mar 1641, FR Ch, London
Jacques, bp. 5 Nov 1642, FR Ch, London
*may be the same person; bap rec says Magdelaine, marr rec says Marie

REF: *"Register of the French Church of Threadneedle St, London, 1637-1685"*; *Publications of the Huguenot Society of London,* Vol. 13 (1899).

PINTARD, Antoine/Anthony

b. c. 1665, La Rochelle, FR
Nov 1683 – Antoine named as 1 of 54 French Huguenots of the Antilles who came to NY to settle
1687- settled in Shrewsbury, NJ, and later, NYC, where he was a merchant; Elder of the FR Ch of NYC & was the treasurer of the Poor Fund until 1729
1691 - petitioned for denization "being a Native of the Kingdome of France, was severely used by that prince toward those of the Reformed Churches obliged to depart that Relme"
m. 4 May 1692, prob. NY (license granted there), Catherine Stelle (c. 1673 Lorières*, FR-a. 1729), sis/o Poncet Stelle; *town not found – see Stelle entry for other options
d. a. 11 May 1732, wp, Shrewsbury, Monmouth Co, NJ; will names sons Anthony, John Lewis & Samuel, daus Margaret, Florinda, Frances, Magdalen Hutchins, Catherine Searles, Isabella VanDam
CHILDREN:
Anthony[2], b. c. 1694; m. c. 1725, Abigail Halstead; 1738, he was a vestryman of the Episcopal Ch, Shrewsbury, NJ; he d. a. Jun 1755
John Lewis[2], b. c. 1695; m/1, Lydia Browne (b. c. 1698), m/2, Catherine Carré, d/o Louis & Prégéante (Fleuriau) Carré
Samuel[2], b. c. 1699; m. c. 1732, Ann Glencross; 1738, was a vestryman, Episcopal Ch, Shrewsbury, NJ
Magdalena[2], b. c. 1701; m. a. 1727, James Hutchins
Catherine[2], b. c. 1703; m/1, c. 1731, John Searle(s), m/2, Rev. Robert Jenney
Margaret[2], b. c. 1706; m. 18 Mar 1733, Pierre Le Conte, s/o Guillaume & Margaret (Mahault) Le Conte; she d. 2 Feb 1735; **no known issue**
Isabella[2], b. c. 1708; m. a. 1731, Isaac Van Dam
Florinda[2], b. c. 1710; m. George Spencer
Anna Frances[2], b. c. 1712; m. Moses Gombaud

REF: CROSBY, Temple Finn, *Pintard, Stelle Chronology includes Van Vorst, Marselis, Hutchins* (Baton Rouge, 2000); SEACORD, Morgan H., *Biographical Sketches & Index of the Huguenot Settlers of New Rochelle,1687-1776* (New Rochelle, 1941); BAIRD, Charles W., *History of the Huguenot Emigration to America* (Baltimore, 1973); KOEHLER, Albert F., *The Huguenot or the Early French in NJ* (Baltimore); WITTMEYER, Rev. Albert V., *Register of L'Église Françoise à la Nouvelle York from 1688 to 1804* (Baltimore, 1968).

POINSET, Pierre

of Soubise, Saintonge, now in Charente-Maritime Dépt, Poitou-Charentes, just s.w. of Rochefort
m. Marie X
CHILDREN:
Jean/John[2], b. Soubise, Saintonge, FR; fled w/ bro Pierre to ENG, 1681; 1685, to Charleston, SC; by 1690, to New Egypt, NJ; m. Elizabeth Murrow; he d. a. 22 Nov 1739, Burlington, NJ
CHILDREN:
Susannah/Elizabeth[3], m. 6 Mar 1733, Richard Fordham
John[3], b. c. 1700, Burlington Co, NJ; m/1, 2 Jan 1721, Philadelphia ,Jane Esselby, m/2, Susannah Jackson Cross; he d. 1762
Pierre II[2], b. 1650, Soubise; m. 1674/5, La Rochelle, Sara Fouchereau; 13 Dec 1681, Pierre (called an anchor smith), wife, 4 ch were in London where they rec. their 1st grant from the FR Ch, Thread-

needle St.-the family rec. assistance for several months; 1685, Pierre & son Peter were on the *Margaret* en route to SC; 30 Mar 1695, on "St. Julien Liste" – family members applied for naturalization – Pierre II, Pierre III & wife Anne, Abraham Le Sueur & wife Catherine Poinset, Élie Bisset & wife Jeanne Poinset which was granted 10 Mar 1696/7; Pierre II was granted lot #37 in Charles Town; he d. 25 Oct 1699, Charleston, SC; he was a smith; Sara d. c. 1710

CHILDREN:

Pierre/Peter III[3], m. Anne Gobard; 1696, a coppersmith on the Santee River, SC; d. a. 12 Jun 1700, SC; **no issue**

Catherine[3], m/1, 22 Jun 1687, Threadneedle St. FR Ch, London, Jean Chevalier, m/2, a. 1696, Abraham LeSueur, s/o Isaac & Marie (de Sanee) LeSueur; Abraham was a joiner, b. Harfleur, Normandie, who was bur. 31 Aug 1740, Charleston; she was bur. 9 Jan 1742/3, Charleston; **no known issue**

Jeanne[3], m/1 Élie Bisset, b. St.-Jean-d'Angély, s/o Abraham & Marie (Bitheur) Bisset, a draper who d. by 3 Apr 1719 – **3 daus**, b. SC: **Catherine**[4], m/1, George Martin, m/2, 6 Oct 1729 James Dalton (**issue**), she was bur. 20 Jun 1753; **Anne**[4], m. Francis Garcia; **Mary**[4], m. William Carwithen; Jeanne[3], m/2, p. 3 Apr 1719, Michael Pacquent, she was bur. Sep 1732, Charleston

Joel[3], b. c. 1676, FR; m/1, c. 1699, ENG, Susannah Martineau – **2 daus**, m/2, a. 1710, Susannah Varin, d/o James & Susannah (DuBois) Varin – **2 sons, 2 daus**; he was a vintner and a weaver & d. bet. 26 Jan 1743-11 Apr 1745, bur. FR Huguenot Ch, Charleston, SC

REF: *Transactions of the Huguenot Society of SC*, #85 (1980), #86 (1981); OLIVEROS, Elizabeth LaRoche Christie, "Poinsett Family of SC" in *Transactions of the Huguenot Society of SC,* #104 (2000) – in the same issue is an article re the Poinsett Taven in Charleston originally owned by Joel[3] & then by his son Elisha[4]; RAVENEL, Daniel, *Liste de François et Suisses refugiez en Caroline* (1868, reprint 1968); RIPPY, J.F., *Joel Poinsett, Versatile American*; BAIRD, Charles W., *Huguenot Emigration to America* (Baltimore, 1966).

POITEVIN/POITEVENT, Antoine/Anthony

b. Oisement, Somme Dépt, Picardie, FR, s.w. of Abbeville, s/o Jacques & Jeanne (Modemen) Poitevin
m. Gabrielle (Berou) Maulard, d/o Eutrope & Andrée (LeProu) Berou, widow of Lubin Maulard (dau Suzanne Maulard m. Daniel Trezevant, s/o Théodore & Suzanne (Menou) Trezevant)
a merchant in Maintenon, Eure-et-Loir Dépt, Centre, FR, n.e. of Chartres; fled to ENG
8 Mar 1682 Antoine, Gabrielle, 3 ch naturalized ENG
a. 6 Oct 1685- arr. SC
10 Mar 1696/7, naturalized, SC
d. a. 1703 Orange Quarter, SC

CHILDREN:

Antoine/Anthony II[2], b. Maintenon; m. Marguerite (de Bourdeaux) de Veaux, d/o Jacques & Madeleine (Garilian) de Bourdeaux of Grenoble, widow of André de Veaux; he rec. 400 acres in Berkeley Co, SC, 15 Sep 1705; he d. c. 1708

CHILDREN :

Anthony[3], d. 1731; **no issue**

Magdalen[3], m. X Garner

Marguerite[3], m. 29 Nov 1709 Jean Potell II s/o Jean & Madeleine (Pépin) Potell ; **4 ch**

Pierre[2], b. FR; m. Susannah X; 15 Sep 1705, rec. 1000 acres in Berkeley Co, SC; d. a. 1742; had sons **James**[3] & **Anthony**[3] who had **issue**

Ann[2], b. Maintenon; m. Pierre Dutarte, s/o Daniel & Anne (Renault) Dutarte, who was at Canterbury, 31 Dec 1782; **issue**

REF: *Transactions of the Huguenot Society of SC,* #91 (1986) & #93 (1988); RAVENEL, Daniel, *French & Swiss Protestants* (Baltimore); BARKSDALE, Isabel, "Antoine Poitevent & Some Others" in *Transactions of the Huguenot Society of SC,* #87 (1982), #91 (1986), #88 (1983); MAYNARD, Isabel Thomas Barksdale, *Poitevent Genealogy* (Birmingham, AL, 1867).

PORCHER, Isaac

of Ste-Sévère in Berry, FR, s/o Isaac & Susanne (Ferré) Porcher; now Ste-Sévère-sur-Indre, Indre Dépt, Centre Région, n.e. Guéret

m. 19 Oct 1681, Claude de Cherigny (10 Apr 1661-10 Sep 1726, SC) of La Roche-Posay, Touraine, now in Vienne Dépt, Poitou-Charentes, s.e. of Châtellerault

he was a doctor, graduate of the University of Paris

fled FR, went to ENG; rec. in the FR Ch Threadneedle St, London 18 Apr 1683, based on *témoignage* given at Pruilly, Touraine, now Preuilly-sur-Claise, Indre-et-Loire Dépt, Centre, n.e. La Roche-Posay; his widowed mother went w/ Isaac to ENG

by 1687 - were in SC – a deed recorded

1696 - obtained grant for 150 acres of land in St. James Parish, Goose Creek, c. 20 mi from Charleston

d. 14 Apr 1727, SC; wp, 19 Apr 1727 names ch Isaac, Peter, Elizabeth, Marianne, Susanna

CHILDREN, b. ENG, SC

Isaac II[2], b. 1682, FR/ENG; m. 1712, Rachel Du Pré (d. 1 Sep 1748), d/o Josias & Martha (X) Du Pré; he d. a. 7 Mar 1742/3, appraisal-25 Apr 1743, inv SC; **4 sons, 2 daus**

Marie[2], bp. 2 Sep 1683, Threadneedle St. Ch; d. a. Sep 1695

Elizabeth[2], bp. 12 Aug 1685, London; m. 23 Apr 1713, St. James Santee, SC, Theodore Verdity

Madeleine[2], b. a. Jun 1695; not in father's will of 1726

Claude[2], b. a. Jun 1695; not in father's will of 1726

Pierre/Peter[2], b. 5 Sep 1695, SC; m. 19 Jul 1720, Charlotte Marianna (Gendron) Pasquereau (21 Feb 1694/5, Maran, FR-10 Oct 1769, SC), d/o Philip & Magdelaine (Cardon) Gendron - widow of Louis Pasquereau; Pierre d. 20 Jun 1753; **1 son, 3 daus**

Marianne[2], b. p. 1695; m. Francis Cordes

Susanne[2], b. p. 1695; m/1, Charles Colleton (d. 11 Jul 1728), m/2, James Singleton

REF: PORCHER, Catherine Cordes Porcher, "Porcher, A Huguenot Family of Ancient Lineage" in *Transactions of the Huguenot Society of SC,* #81 (1976); *Publications of the Huguenot Society of London* – "Register of the FR Ch of Threadneedle St, London, Vol. XIII, #7 (1899), "Témoignages de L'Église de Threadneedle St. 1669-1789, Vol. XXI (1909); HIRSCH, Arthur Henry, *The Huguenots of Colonial SC,* (Durham, NC, 1928).

POSHET/POSEY

(2 brothers, parents unknown, *poss.* Marteyn & Anne (de Colnet) Poshet)

Marteyn/Martin[2], m/1, 29 May 1626, Susanna (Desmarets) Conseyn, widow of Jonas Conseyn, m/2, Julienne Boucle

François/Francis[2], b. 1615, Voyaux, nr. Cambrai, FR, Nord Dépt, Pas-de-Calais

1636 - came to VA from London; settled in St. Mary's Co, MD, in 1640

1640-1650 – was a representative of St. Clement's 100 in the MD Lower House of the Assembly

m. c. 1643/5, Elizabeth (Humphrey?), St. Mary's Co, MD; Eliz. m/2, c. 1654, John Belaine, m/3, c. 1664, Alex Smith

2 Jan 1646 - swore an oath of fealty; 3 Feb 1646, was made a sheriff

6 Jul 1650 - owned land on the Potomac River, called Swan Point

d. a. 24 May 1654, at the head of Wicomico Creek, St. Mary's Co, MD

CHILDREN:

Anne[3], m. c. 1669, John Mould

Benjamin[3], b. c. 1648; m/1 XX – no known issue; m/2, 1688, MD, Mary (X) Belaine, widow of
Nicholas Belaine – some recs says Mary Bayne but one of their children is name Belaine;
d. c. 1715; land in St. Charles Co, MD; **6 ch**

John[3], b. 20 Jul 1652, Charles Co, MD; m. c. 1679, Susanna X; d. a. 25 May 1689, Charles Co,
MD; **6 ch**; Susanna m/2, c. 1689, Thomas Austin

REF: JORDAN, Wilford, *Colonial & Revolutionary Families of PA*, Vol. IV (NY, 1932); *The History of the Posey Family in Europe and the US*; POSEY, Lloyd Franklin & Betty Sue Drake, *The Posey Family in America* (Hattiesburg, MS, 1971); *Posey, Wade, Harrison & Other Family Connections.*

POTEL/POTELL, Jean

b. c. 1660, Dieppe, now in Seine-Maritime Dépt, Haute-Normandie, FR, on the English Channel, s/o
Nicolas & Marie (Brugnet) Potell

m. c. 1684, Madeleine Pépin, d/o Alexander & Madelaine (Garillion) Pépin

1686 – from FR to ENG, then to SC, c. 1693; although there is some thought that they were in St.
Kitts, West Indies, for a time prior to arr in SC

12 Jun 1693 - Jean rec. a warrant for 1 town lot by indenture

15 May 1694 - Jean rec. a warrant for lots #177, #178 on Broad St. in Charleston

30 Mar 1696 - petitioned for naturalization in SC w/ his wife, 4 ch & mother; residents of Santee

17 Jan 1710/1 - rec. warrant for 600 acres in Berkeley Co.

d. a. 16 Oct 1729 (date of burial), Charleston, SC, St. Philip's Parish

CHILDREN:

Jean/John[2], b. 1686, SC; m. Hannah Green; he d. 1744/45; called John Sr. or John Potell of Berkeley; **4
sons, 2 daus**

Pierre[2], b. c. 1688, SC; d. 1731, **no issue**

Jacques/James[2], m. Judith X; he d. a. 1757; called James of Berkeley; **3 sons, 2 daus**

Jean, Jr.[2], b. c. 1694; m. a. 1725, Marguerite Poitevin, d/o Antoine & Marguerite (de Bourdeaux) Poitevin;
he d. a. 9 Jun 1737, wp, Charleston Co (written in FR); **2 sons, 1 dau , poss. 1 other ch**

REF: *Transactions of the Huguenot Society of SC*, #93 (1988); HIRSCH, Arthur Henry, *The Huguenots of Colonial SC* (Durham, NC, 1928); POSTELLE, Francis Boeing, *The Postel-Postell-Posello Family in America* (not pub, not Dated); POSTELL William Dosite, "Notes on the Postell Family" in *SC Genealogies*, Vol. 3.

POYAS, Jean Louis

b. FR, perhaps in the Piedmont (Alps in eastern FR), as he was referred to a "Piedmontois" (*Piémontois*)

fled FR to ENG, then to SC; obtained land grant of 350 acres & a town lot, 13 Jul 1737, in return for his
agreeing to teach the settlers there the silk industry; 11 Mar 1737/8, the SC General Assembly passed
"an act for encouraging the manufacture of silk in this Province under the direction of Mr. John Louis
Poyas for 7 yrs."

m/1, XX

m/2, Susanne X; bur 2 Apr 1754?

m/3, Marie/Mary Jourdain who poss. m/2, 14 Oct 1756, Veiruis Lochon

d. a. 30 Apr 1756, wp, SC; will mentions wife Marie, all ch (except Sarah), son-in-law Jean Dodd

CHILDREN, m/2:

Jean/John Ernest[2], b. 1730, FR; m/1, Elizabeth Grant, m/2, 20 May 1755, Rachel Bourget, d/o Daniel
& Suzanne (X) Bourget – **5 ch**, m/3, Nov 1776 (Mrs.) Mary Magdalen Schwartzkoff – **1 dau**; (all 3
marr in St. Philip's Parish, Charleston); Rev. War service; he d. 29 Apr 1786, Charleston, SC, bur
French Churchyard, next to 2nd wife

Jacques/James[2], m. 7 Feb 1755, St. Philip's Parish, Elizabeth Portal; d. Jun 1799, Bath, ENG

Maria Louisa[2], m. a. 1756, Jean Dodd
Susanne[2]
Sarah[2], b. 1 Sep 1738; not in father's will, must have d. young; record says she was d/o of Jean Louis
    & Susannah, St. Philip's Parish
CHILD prob. m/3:
Jean Louis[2], b. 1755 ?; m. Susanna X; d. 1808

REF: PELAYO, Myrtle Kersham, "*Poyas Descendants*" in the LA Genealogical Register, Vol. 1, #4 (1946);
LICHLITER, Assélia Strobhar, *Pioneering with the Beville & Related Families in SC, GA & FL* (1982); HIRSCH,
Arthur Henry, *The Huguenots of Colonial SC* (Durham, NC, 1928); will of Jean Louis Poyas (1765); HOLCOMB,
Brent H., *SC Marriages, 1688-1799* (Baltimore); TOWNSEND, J.M., Sr., *Poyas Family* (1993, not pub.).

PRAA/PRAT, Pieter

    b. Dieppe, Picardie, FR
    m/1, c. 1642, Marie Philippe
    fled FR, went to HOL - in Vlissingen (Flushing) a. going to Leiden
    m/2, a. 1658, Catherine Laitié/Lethie/Lothie/Lettie, d/o Abraham Lothie; she m/2, a. 10 Jun 1663,
        Brooklyn, Joost Casperse Springsteen
    12 Mar 1659 - membership list of the Walloon Ch, Leiden, states the Pierre & his wife have left Leiden
        with letters from the ch - *témoignages*
    25 Apr 1659 - arr New Amsterdam on the *De Moesman*
    Apr 1661- joined Brooklyn Reformed Dutch Ch – "Pieter Prae from Diepe & Catherine Lettie (his wife)
        with letters from Middlewout"
    d. 6 Mar 1663?, Brooklyn, NY
    CHILDREN, m/1(bap Walloon Ch, Leiden):
Pierre[2], bp. 3 May 1643; d. young
Pierre[2], bp. 17 May 1646; d. young
Samuel[2], bp. 9 Jun 1647
Marie[2], bp. 30 May 1648
Catharine[2], bp. 23 Jun 1650
Anne/Annetje Pieterse[2], bp. 4 Feb 1652; m/1, Andries Juriaens (d. Mar 1681), s/o Juriaen Andries &
    Jannetje Jans, m/2, 11 Jun 1682, Brooklyn, Jan Janse Staats (b. c. 1654), s/o Jan Pietersz Staats &
    Grietje Jans; she d. p. 30 Oct 1692, Brooklyn, NY
        CHILDREN, m/1: **Jannetje**[3], bp. 26 Jan 1678, Brooklyn; **Andries**[3], bp. 3 Oct 1680, Brooklyn;
            Juriaen Andriesse[3]; **Lambert Andriessen**[3]; **Lysbeth Anderiesse**[3]
        CHILDREN, m/2: **Jan**[3], bp. 16 Mar 1684, Brooklyn; **Neeltje**[3], bp. 17 Apr 1687, Brooklyn;
            Anneke[3], bp. 9 Sep 1688, Flatbush; **Aeltje**[3], bp. 30 Oct 1692, Brooklyn
    CHILDREN, m/2:
Pieter[2], bp. 17 Mar 1658; to America; m. p. 15 Mar 1684 (date of banns), Maria Hay (bp. 4 Jun 1651,
    NY), d/o Jacob Hay & Christina Cappoens, as her 3rd husband; he d. a. 5 Sep 1740, wp, Kings
    Co, NY; **5 daus**
Adam[2], bp. 6 Feb 1660/1, Brooklyn, NY; d. 8 Feb 1660/1, Brooklyn
Abraham[2], bp. 5 Mar 1662, Brooklyn; no more info

REF: TOTTEN, John Reynolds, "Praa-Bennet Family Notes" in the *NYGBR*, Vol. LXV (NYC, Oct 1934) **&**
Vol. LXVI (NYC, Jan 1935); BURTON, Paul Gibson, "Praa" in the *NYGBR*, Vol. LXIX (NYC, Oct1938) –
additions/corrections to the previous articles citing ch recs from Leiden.

PRÉVOL/PRÉVÔT/PRÉVO(S)T/PREVAT(T), Pierre

b. c. 1673, Guînes, Pas-de-Calais Dépt, Nord Pas-de-Calais, FR, s. of Calais

1700 - to VA on the *Peter & Anthony*

m. XX, prob. VA

d. Manakintown, VA

CHILD:

Peter[2], b. 1718, Manakintown; m. Elizabeth X; 1739, to Craven Co, NC; 6 Dec 1746, bought 400 acres in Johnston Co., on the Neuse River; he d. p. 26 Oct 1767, Johnston Co, NC; surname **PREVAT/TE**

CHILDREN:

Peter[3], alive 26 Oct 1767, Johnston Co, NC

Elizabeth[3], m. 1764, New Bern, Craven Co, NC, Moses Taylor, Sr. (1729-1819, Warren Co, KY); she d. 1833, Warren Co, KY

CHILDREN:

Joseph[4], m. 1785, Mary Slade

Moses[4], m. 1788, Sidney Marshall

James[4], m. 1795, Chloe Marshall (sis/o Sidney)

Thomas (Alfred)[4], m. 1808, Elizabeth Taylor

Redding[2], m. 1801, Polly Macksay

John Prevatte[4], m. 1803, Hughanna Carr

Absolum[4], m. 1818, Polly Robinson

Elizabeth[4], m. 1784, William Beasley

Sina[4], m. Samuel Biggers

Sally/Sarah[4], m. 1784, Robert Dougherty

Nancy[4], m. 1786, Daniel Dougherty (bro/o Robert)

Polly (Ann)[4], m. 1810, Peter Taylor, Jr. – marr. bond says James

REF: BROCK, Robert A., *Huguenot Emigration to VA* (Baltimore, 1966); HOFMANN, Margaret M., *Colony of NC 1735-1764* (Vol. 1) & *Colony of NC 1765-1775* (Vol. 2), *Abstracts of Land Patents*; TAYLOR, L. Rhea, *Pioneers Moses Taylor & Elizabeth Prevatte Taylor* (Bowling Green, KY, 1968, not pub.); *The Huguenot,* #29 (1979-81).

PRIEST/PREST/PRESS, Robert de

b. 1664 FR?; Nicholas Deprize was *poss.* his father or his bro; same for Thomas Depres who came with Nicholas to VA by 1671; Robert may have been b. in VA

m/1, c. 1686, Elizabeth X (d. 27 Sep 1689, St. Peter's Par., New Kent Co, VA)

by 1689 to VA – on Quit Rent Roll

m/2, c. 1690, Mary X

1704 - on Rent Roll of VA – 350 acres

d. 1708/11, VA

CHILD: m/1 (bp. St. Peter's):

Guillaume/William[2], b. 25 Sep, bp. 24 Oct 1689; m. c. 1725, VA, Judith X (c. 1705-d. p. 1755) who m/2, bet Aug 1749-Dec 1750, John Hodges; Wm. d. a. 2 Mar 1738, VA, adm, Goochland Co, VA

CHILDREN:

unknown[3], prob. d. young

Randolph[3], b. c. 1728, Hanover Co, VA; m. 1751, Goochland Co., Mary Mims

William[3], b. c. 1733, Hanover Co; m. 6 Apr 1758, Goochland Co., Tabitha Tony (3 Apr 1729, Goochland-p. 1790, Henry Co, VA), d/o Charles & Elizabeth (Harris) Toney; he d. 13 Mar 1768, Annapolis, MD; **6 ch**

Naomi[3], b. c. 1729, Hanover Co; m. 6 Jun 1759, Goochland Co., John Salmons (d. 1791, Bedford Co, VA); she d. p. 24 Jan 1791

Mary[3], b. c. 1731, Hanover Co; m. c. 1755, George Southerland/Sutherlin III (c. 1725-1804

Pittsylvania Co, VA); Mary d. p. Aug 1768

John[3], b. c. 1738, Goochland Co; m. 6 Jun 1759, Goochland Co., Elizabeth Rice; he d. p.17 Aug
1799, wd-a. 14 Oct 1799, wp, Campbell Co, VA; **8 ch**

Robert[3], b. c. 1738, Goochland Co; m. 15 Oct 1766, Goochland Co., Martha Bailey

CHILDREN, m/2 (daus bp. St. Peter's):

Mary[2], bp. 9 Nov 1690

Sarah[2], bp. 4 Sep 1698

Elizabeth[2], bp. 19 Jul 1702

John[2]

?Robert/Robin[2], m. 1740 X Snead; d. p. 19 Nov 1759, 1785?, Hanover Co; **3 daus**

REF: *The Huguenot*, #25 (1971-73), #35 (1991-93); CHAMBERLAYNE, C.G., editor *Vestry Book & Register St. Peter's Parish New Kent & James City Co, VA, 1684-1786*; DePRIEST, Rev. Dr. Travis T, various articles.

PRIOLEAU, Élias/Élie (Rev.)

b. 1659 Saintonge, FR s/o Samuel & Jeanne (Merlat) Prioleau; Samuel was pastor at Jonzac in 1637, at
Niort in 1642 and at Pons in 1650; when Samuel d. 16 Feb 1683, Élie succeeded him; Élie, grs/o Élisée
Prioleau, Sieur de la Viennerie, pastor at Jonzac & Niort (1639-1650), both reformed churches in
Poitou; Samuel's older bro Élisée was the pastor at Exoudun, 1649-1663

studied theology at the Academy of Geneva, SWI

m. Jeanne Burgeaud, b. Île de Ré, FR

10 May 1683 - became the Huguenot pastor in Pons

1685 - to ENG

15 Apr 1687 – denization, London w/ wife Jane, 2 ch Jane & Élias

1687 – arr. SC; was chosen as the pastor of the ch. in Charleston

14 Jul 1697 - naturalized in SC; had a plantation on the Black River, a branch of the Cooper River, nr. the
Ch. of St. Denis, c. 15 mi from Charleston, which he called Midway/Medway

d. 1699, Medway, SC

CHILDREN:

Jeanne[2], b. St.-Jean-d'Angély, Charente Maritime, Poitou-Charentes, n.e. Saintes

Élias[2], b. FR; prob. d. a. emigration to SC

Samuel[2], b. c. 1690, SC; m. Mary Magdelen Gendron, d/o Philippe & Ma(g)deleine (Chardon) Pasquereau
(widow Louis Pasquereau) Gendron; he d. SC (see Fauconnier, Pierre)
CHILDREN:
Samuel[3], b. 25 Aug 1742; m. 19 Oct 1766, Catherine Cordes; he d. a. 1 Mar 1813, wp; 3 sons –
John Cordes[4], **Philip Gendron**[4], **Elias**[4], 5 daus – **Catherine**[4] m. X Ravenel, **Mary M.**[4] m.
X Ford, **Elizabeth**[4], **Caroline**[4] m. X Dawson, **Martha**[4]
Philip[3], m. Alice Edith Homeyard; **issue**
Hext[3], Lt. of Light Infantry in 1776; **issue**
Ann[3]
Mary Magdeleine[3], m. Thomas Grimball, Jr.
Martha[3]
Elizabeth[3]

Marie[2]

Esther[2]

2 other ch[2], b. SC, rec. on the 1697 list

REF: BRIDGES, Anne Baker Leland & WILLIAMS, Roy III, *St. James Santee Plantation Parish, 1685-1925*
(Spartanburg, SC, 1997); "The Prioleau Family in America" in *Transactions of the Huguenot Society of SC*, #71
(Charleston, 1966); HIRSCH, Arthur Henry, *The Huguenots of Colonial SC*; BAIRD, Charles W., *Huguenot
Emigration to America*, Vol. I, II (Baltimore, 1966).

PROU, Cyprian

b. c. 1663 FR, poss. La Sauoye, FR – not found, poss. La Saussaye, Eure Dépt, Haute-Normandie, s. Rouen <u>or</u> Sauvoy, Meuse Dépt, Lorraine, s.w. Toul

fled FR, went to ENG where he was a *tailleur*, tailor

30 May-11 Jul 1682- rec. aid from the Threadneedle St. Ch – 5 grants for a total of £1.2.0

m. 16 Jul 1683, St. Katherine by the Tower, London, ENG, Margaret Vensauden (c. 1660-a. 1712)

3 Oct 1683- his *témoignage* from "La Sauoye" rec. in the Threadneedle St. Ch

22-28 Aug 1684 - on a list of people apprenticed in Middlesex to serve Richard Bray in VA – Cyprian, age 21 w/ wife Margaret, age 24, in exchange for 4-yr term as indentured servants "but not to work in the fields"; does not mention infant dau Marie – did she d. young and there was another dau named Mary? Judging from Cyprian's will Mary was the eldest dau & the executrix of his will

24 Apr 1704 - naturalized VA by petition

d. a. 5 Nov 1712, wp, Richmond Co, VA; mentions daus Mary, Elizabeth, Margaret, Susan & Frances; son-in-law William Paine – husband of Mary or Elizabeth??

CHILDREN:

Marie/Mary[2], bp. 8 Jun 1684, FR Ch, Threadneedle St, London

Frances[2], m. c. 1713, Richmond Co, VA, Robert Benson (c. 1685, King Geo. Co-c. 1757, Hanover Parish, King Geo. Co), s/o Thomas & Dorothy (Sutton) Benson; she d. a. 1756; **6 sons, 1 dau**

Margaret[2], m. Feb 1712/3, Richmond Co, VA, Mark Rymer, Jr. who d. a. 3 Apr 1737, inv, Richmond Co – **1 son, 1dau**; Margaret survived him, became "concubine" of Rev. John Prince, minister of Hanover Parish – had son called "**John**[3] Prince alias Rymer" and a dau **Thomasin**[3]

Elizabeth[2]

Susanna[2], m. a. 5 Apr 1715, King George Co, VA, Walter Anderson (he d. 1733, King George Co, VA)

REF: COLDHAM, Peter Wilson, *The Complete Book of Emigrants, 1607-1776* (Baltimore, 1990); JACKSON-LAUFER, Guida M., *VA Diaspora* (Bowie, MD); HANDS, A.P. & SCOULOUDI, Irene, *French Protestant Refugees Relieved through the Threadneedle St. Church, London, 1681-1687* (Huguenot Society of London, Quarto Series, Vol. XLIX (London, 1971); marr. rec. from St. Katherine's; MINET, William & Susan, *Livres des Temoignages de l'Église de Threadneedle Street, 1669-1789* (Huguenot Society of London, MCMIX); *The Huguenot*, #29 (1979-81); HEADLEY, Robert K., Jr., *Wills of Richmond Co, VA 1699-1800*; KING, George Harrison Sanford, *Marriages of Richmond Co, VA 1668-1853* (Fredericksburg, VA, 1964, not. pub.).

PROVOST/PROVOOST, Guillaume/Gutielmus/Wilhelmus

b. c. 1545, FR; a family document says he was a resident of Paris in 1572, a person of distinction & eminence among the Protestants of Paris; a man of education; surname was prob. *Prévôt* which means "provost" in French

1572 - escaped from FR, went to HOL, where he became Wilhelmus Provoost; said to have been a wine-dealer in the Heeren Market

m. 1574, HOL, XX, said to have been b. in Paris, FR

CHILDREN:

Johannes[2], b. 1576 Amsterdam; m. 1601, Elizabeth X

  CHILDREN:

  Elias[3], b. 1602; to America bet 1635-40 settled Ft. Orange (Albany); he became clerk to several courts of the colony; had son **Johannes**[4]

  Johannes[3], b. 1605

  David[3], b. 10 Aug 1608 Amsterdam, HOL; 1624 – 1st went to New Netherlands; 1626, ret. to HOL; m. c. 1630, Amsterdam, Margaretta/Grietje Ten Waert, d/o Jillis Ten Waert* & Barbara Schut; 1634, ret to New Netherlands;1639, he was an original grantee of a parcel of land on the present west side of Pearl St nr. Fulton St. where he resided for some time; he built several houses on the "Princess Graft" now Broad St.; he was a merchant and had government service as an employee of the Dutch West Indies Company; Apr 1642, he was in charge of Fort Good

Hope at Hartford, CT; returned to New Amsterdam, Jun 1647; he was schoolmaster, an attorney, a soldier, a sheriff ; 2 Feb 1652, he was Head of the "Nine Men", a group that decided municipal matters & disputed the autocratic power of the Governor – they said they were the chosen representatives of the people; he d. 12 May 1657, or at least by 16 May 1657, NY, when a record in the Orphans Court of New Amsterdam reported that he was d.; Margaretta d. over 70 yrs. later than their marr date
of 1630
CHILDREN (all but William bap. New Amsterdam Dutch Ch):

William[4], b. c. 1635; in Gravesend, in 1656

Margaret[4], bp. 24 Feb 1641; m. 26 Nov 1661, Pieter Janszen Scholt; **4 ch**

David II[4], b. 20 Nov 1642, Hartford, CT, bp. 31(*sic*) Sep 1645, NY; m/1, 29 Jul 1668, Tryntje (Catherine) Laurens; **issue**, incl. son **David III**[5] (1670-1725); m/2 Marie (de Peyster) Spratt, d/o Johannes & Cornelia (Lubberts) de Peyster & widow of John Spratt

Benjamin[4] (twin), bp. 17 Jun 1646, Hartford, CT; m/1, Sara Barents – **1 son**, m/2, 5 Nov 1671, NY, Elsje Alberts, d/o Teunes Eliasz Alberts & Gerritie Gerritz - at least **3 sons, 8 daus**, poss. 15 ch **7 sons, 8 daus**; son **David**[5], (m/2) was the mayor of NYC, 1699-1700

Elias[4] (twin), bp. 17 Jun 1646; m. 3 Nov 1672, Cornelia Roos, d/o Gerrit Jans Roos; he d. 22 Nov 1692; **7 ch**

Barbara[4], bp. 15 Aug 1647; d. young

Samuel[4], b. Hartford, CT, bp. 22 Nov 1648; prob. d. young without issue

Jonathan[4], bp. 26 Mar 1651; m. Catherine Van der Mealen/Van der Veen, d/o Corneliszen Vanderveen & Elsje Tymens; **8 ch**

Barbara[4], bp. 30 Nov 1653; m. 29 Jul 1673, Jan Aukersze Nuys; she d. a. 4 Apr 1680; **2 ch**

Gillis[4], bp. 26 Mar 1656; m. 9 Jun 1680, Marie/Mary Hibon, prob. d/o Jan Hibon & Geertruyd Barents; he d. a. Jul 1709 ,wp – no ch named in will

Margareta[3]
Sarah[3]
Elizabeth[3]
David[2], b. 1578
Wilhelmus[2], b. 1580
Elias[2], b. 1582
Benjamin[2], b. 1584

*NOTE: Gillis/Jillis Ten Waert was a prominent, wealthy merchant; another dau Agnietje, m/2, 1647, Jean de la Montagne.

REF: PROVOST, Andrew J., Jr., "History of the Provoost Family of New Amsterdam & Colonial NY from 1545 to 1724" in the *NYGBR*, Vol. LXXXIX, #4 (Oct 1958) & Vol. XC, #1 (Jan, 1959); PURPLE, Edwin R., "Biographical & Genealogical Sketch of David Provoost of New Amsterdam & Some of His Descendants" in the *NYGBR*. Vol. VI, #1 (Jan 1875); "Records of the Reformed Dutch Ch in NY" in the *NYGBR*, Vol. V, #2 (Apr 1874), #4 (Oct 1875); "Provoost Lineage of Dr. Samuel Outwater" in the *NYGBR*, Vol LX, #4 (Oct, 1924); PROVOST, Andrew J., *Biographical & Genealogical Notes of the Provost Family 1545-1895* (NY, 1895).

PURVIANCE, Jacques

b. FR, s/o or grs/o Jean/Jon who d. bet 1620-30, Royan, then Saintonge, FR, now in Charente-Maritime Dépt, Poitou Charentes; Royan is located at the mouth of the Gironde River, s.w. of Saintes

Oct 1685 - fled Royan, FR to Lisburn, Co. Antrim, to Castle Finn, then in Ulster Prov., N. IRE, w. of Strabane

d. Castle Finn, (now Castlefinn), now in Co. Donegal, N. IRE; had cousins in Donegal, descendants of a

       Jean/John who settled there in 1613

CHILDREN:

Jacques II[2], b. c. 1680/83, Royan, FR; d. Castle Finn, IRE; **8 ch**

    CHILDREN (6 of 8):

    Jacques III[3], remained in IRE

        CHILDREN:

        ?Samuel[4], b. c. 1660 Royan, FR

        John[4]

    Samuel[3], b. 1701, Castle Finn; m. 2 Apr 1725, Castle Finn, Lettice Dinsmore – **8 sons, 3 daus**;

        4 of the sons went to America – Samuel, William & Robert went 1st, John followed later

        CHILDREN (4 of 11):

        Samuel[4], b. 24 Sep 1728; settled 1st in Philadelphia; 1768, joined Robert [4] in Baltimore

        William[4], b. 4 Sep 1740; went to NC, settled down as a planter on the "Sound", c. 14

            mi. from Wilmington; **issue**

        Robert[4], b. 2 Jun 1734; went to Baltimore, MD; m. IRE, Frances Young (1739-3 Mar

            1821), d/o James Young of Co. Donegal; Rev. War Service; he d. 10 Oct 1806; **7

            sons, 4 daus**

        John[4,] b. 30 Nov 1742, IRE; went to w. PA; m/1, Susannah Purviance, d/o Samuel Purvi-

            ance/Purveyance – **no** issue, m/2, Elizabeth Thompson – **6 sons, 2 daus**; Rev. War

            service; he d. 1821 PA

    David[3], b. 1708, IRE; m. Margaretha X; to Dauphin Co, PA; d. 1743; **3 sons, 1 dau**

        CHILD (1 of 4):

        James[4], b. 1743; m. Elizabeth White (28 Feb 1749, W. Caln, Chester, PA-10 Oct 1816,

            Chester Co, PA); he d. 13 Sep 1813, Fayette Co, PA – **10 sons, 2 daus**

    John[3], b. 1712, Castle Finn (5th s/o Jacques); m/1, IRE, Margaret McKnight (d. c. 1760) – **4 sons,

        daus**, m/2, PA, Janet X – **1 son, 1 dau**; c. 1749, to Lancaster Co, PA, where he d. a. 12

        Jan 1749, wp; **4 sons, 1 dau**

        CHILDREN (4 of 5):

        James[4], b. Jan 1733; m. 1764, KY, Sarah Wasson (b. 15 Jan 1745), d/o Archibald &

            Elizabeth (Woods) Wasson; Rev. War service-Capt, NC; he d. 26 Apr 1806,

            Bourbon Co, KY – **6 sons, 6 daus**

        David[4], b. 1739, IRE; m. 1759, Margaret Stevenson; to Rowan Co., NC, later Cabarrus

            Co., where he d. 1763; **9 ch**, incl **John**[5], b. 19 Jun 1760, Lancaster Co., PA, m/1,10 Jul

            1783, Mecklenburg Co., NC, Nancy Ferguson – **6 ch**, m/2, 27 Dec 1798, Cabarrus Co.,

            NC, Elizabeth Lisenby – **4 ch**; Rev. War service he d. 27 Sep 1833, Sangamon Co., IL

        John[4], b. 7 Jun 1743; m. 2 Aug 1764, Rowan Co., NC Jane Wasson (1742 PA-26 Apr

            1806 Wilson Co., TN), sis/o Sarah above; Rev. War service; d. Aug 1823, Wilson

            Co., TN; Rev. War service – **3 sons, 8 daus**

        Mary[4], m. X Snodgrass; one son **Benjamin**[5]

    Jacques[3], remained in IRE

    William[3], emig. to NC

Lewis[2], m. XX; d. 1698 Princess Anne Co., VA; used surname PURVINE; **5 sons, 1 dau**

?Thomas[2]

NOTE: Another family with varying accounts. Additional proof would be welcome.

REF: KENNEDY, Mary Selden, *Seldens of VA*, Vol. I (NYC, 1911); *Soldiers of the American Revolution in IL*; *NSDAR Patriot Index*, Vol. III (Baltimore, MD, 2003); PURVINES, Stuart Hoyle, *The Purviance Family* (1986); BONE, Robert Gehlmann, *History of the Bone Family of America* (Normal, IL, 1972) & *The Gehlmann Family in America* (Oct 1757); STAPLETON, Rev. A., *Memorials of the Huguenots in America* (Baltimore, MD, 1969).

Q

QUINTARD, Isaac

b. a. 1670, Lusignan, Poitou, FR, s/o Pierre & Marie (X) Quintard; Lusignan is now in the Vienne Dépt, Poitou-Charentes, s.w. of Poitiers

bet 1690-93 - from Bretagne to ENG; joined the Huguenot Colony at Bristol; emig. w/ his fa who was a manufacturer of serge cloth

m. 26 Nov 1693, Chapel of the Gaunt, Bristol, ENG, Jeanne Fumé, (b. Meschers, Saintonge-d. Stamford, CT), d/o David & Esther (Herault) Fumé; at his marr Isaac was called an *"ouvrier en laine"* – a wool-worker; Meschers is now Meschers-sur-Gironde in Charente-Maritime, Poitou-Charentes, s.e. of Royan

1697 - to NY; joined FR Ch on Wall St; he was a merchant in NYC

1 Oct 1708 - purchased land in Stamford, CT

d. a. 15 Jan 1714/5, wp, Stamford, CT; estate valued at £1742

CHILDREN:

Marie Anne[2], bp. 13 Jan 1694/5, Bristol; m. Capt. Samuel Morin (19 Jan 1691/2-19 Jun 1739, Stamford), s/o Jean & Elizabeth (Viconte) Morin; she d. p. 1739; 1 son who d. young

Isaac[2], b. 12 Dec, bp. 13 Dec 1696, Bristol; m. 16 Jul 1716, Stamford, Hannah Knapp (10/15 Mar 1699/00, Stamford-1790), d/o John & Hannah (Ferris) Knapp; he d. 28 Feb 1738/9, Stamford

   CHILDREN:

   twin sons[3] who d. young

   Mary[3], b. 21 Oct 1722; m. 18 May 1742, Nathaniel Hubbard (1702-1772), s/o William & Hannah (Mead) Hubbard – **issue**

   Hannah[3], b. 28 Jun 1724

   Isaac[3], b. 29 Dec 1727, Stamford; m. 10 Oct 1754, New Haven, CT, Lucretia Burroughs (6 Jul 1732-10 Sep 1796), d/o Joseph & Lydia (Munson) Burroughs; Rev. War service; he d. 16 Sep 1794, Stamford; **5 ch**

   Peter[3], b. 29 Oct 1730, Stamford; m. 14 Sep 1761, Elizabeth DeMille (29 Jul 1742-2 Apr 1837), d/o Peter & Abigail (Banks) DeMille; Rev. War service; he d. a. 13 Jul 1817, wp; **5 ch**

Abraham[2], bp. 25 Sep 1698, NYC; d. young

Pierre[2], bp. 28 Jan 1699/00, NYC; settled Norwalk, CT

REF: BOYER, Frederic Quintard & POOLE, Herbert Armstrong, "The Quintard Family in America" in the *NEHGR*, Vol. CIX (Jul 1955), CX (Oct 1955); BAIRD, Charles W., *Huguenot Emigration to America*; *Commemorative Biographical Record of Fairfield Co, CT* (Chicago, 1899).

R

RAMBERT/REMBERT, André

b. 15 Apr 1661, Pont-en-Royans, then Dauphiné, now Rhône-Alpes, s.w. of Grenoble, s/o François &
    Judith (Courand) Rambert; ch. records in Pont-en-Royans use Rambert spelling

m/1, c. 1685, Anne Bressan, d/o Jean & Louise (X) Bressau/Bressan

1697- SC, petitioned for naturalization; settled Santee Colony, SC

1706- rec. property in Jamestown, SC – lot #21; 11 Nov 1709, bought 758 acres on the s. side of the
    Santee; got another 1400 acres on the n. side of the Santee on 24 May 1734

m/2, p. 14 Sep 1733, Madeleine (X) Courège Michau, widow of François Courège **&** of <u>Abraham
    Michau</u>; she d. St. James Santee Parish, Craven Co., SC, a. 21 Mar 1734, wp; she wrote the distribution
    of her estate on 14 Sep 1733 when she was still a widow – law at the time did
    not allow a married woman to make a will – André signed the document – she wanted to leave
    her possessions to her heirs & names dau Madeleine, son Abraham & 6 grch

d. p. 4 Mar 1736/7, wd- c. 16 Mar 1736, St. James Santee Parish, Craven Co., SC; will names dau Anne, gr
    dau Anne (wife of John Heverick), grdau Madeline (wife of <u>Pierre DuBose</u>), dau Marguerite, 8
    grch (ch of Marguerite) Elizabeth, Anne, Elisha, Margaret, André, Pierre, Madelaine & Lydia

CHILDREN, m/1 (b. SC):

Anne[2], d. p. Mar 1736/7

André II[2], b. a. 1695/6; m. Judith X; he was a shoemaker; d. bet. 29 May 1717-8 Apr 1721; 3 ch –
    Andrew[3], **Jane**[3], **Caleb**[3]

Gérosme[2], b. c. 1689; d. a. Mar 1736/7 (not in father's will)

Pierre[2], b. c. 1691; m. Jeanne X; d. p. Mar 1736/7; had 5 ch – **Pierre**[3], **James**[3], **Andrew**[3], **Isaac**[3], **Anne**[3]
    m. Daniel DuBose, s/o <u>Isaac & Susanne (Couillandeau) DuBose</u> – one dau **Anne**[4] m. 31 May 1759,
    Daniel Jaudon, grs/o <u>Élie & Sara (Bertonneau) Jaudon</u>

Susanne[2], d. a. Mar 1736/7 (not in father's will)

Jeanne/Jane[2], m. Jean-Jacques Guerri (d. a. 4 Feb 1734/5, wp, Charleston, SC), s/o <u>Pierre & Jeanne
    (Broussard) Guerri</u>; she d. a. Mar 1736/7 (not in father's will); 3 ch – **Jean**[3], **Jacques**[3], **Jane**[3]

Jean[2], m. Marie Lamar; he d. a. Mar 1736/7; dau **Marie**[3]

Madelaine[2], m. Isaac DuBose, s/o <u>Isaac & Susanne (Couillandeau) DuBose</u>; d. a. Mar 1736/7 (not in
    father's will); 2 ch – **Isaac**[3], **Madelaine**[3]

Marguerite[2], b. c. 1700; m/1 1722, Pierre Guerri (d. a. 5 Apr 1737 Charleston, SC), s/o <u>Pierre & Jeanne
    (Broussard) Guerri</u> – 8 ch – **Elizabeth**[3], **Anne**[3], **Elisha**[3], **Margaret**[3], m. X Chicken, **André**[3],
    Pierre[3], **Lydia**[3], (b. 1729) m/1, 1746, John Steele, m/2, Stephen June, poss. grs/o <u>George &
    Suzanne (LeRiche) Juin/June</u>, **Madelaine**[3], prob. m. Peter DuBose, s/o <u>Isaac & Susanne
    (Couillandeau) DuBose</u>; Marguerite[2] m/2, Rev. Peter Duplessis who d. a. 3 Dec 1740 or 1744; she
    d. p. 3 Dec 1740 or 1744

REF: WILSON, Rev. Robert, "Pedigree Tables of the Guerry, Rembert, Michau, DuPont, Cromwell Families" in
the *Transactions of the Huguenot Society of SC*, #75 (1970); "Will of Madelaine Rembert" in *Transactions of the
Huguenot Society of SC* (#28, 1923); DUNAWAY, Sarah Jean Owen, *Rembert, Brown, Rucker, Ham, Mann & King
Families* (Atlanta, GA, 1993); ch records from L'Église Reformée de Pont-en-Royans; André I's will.

RAME/RAHM, Charles/Karl

1st of the name who is known was Eberhard Ram (b. 1560), a member of the Reformed congregation at
    Bergzabern in 1605; now known as Bad Bergzabern, c. 8 km. n.e. of Wissembourg, Alsace, FR

b. 1754/5, Heiligenmoschel, Rhineland, *Pfalz*, GER, n. of Kaiserslautern, s/o Jean Georges/Johann
    Georg & Maria Katharina (Leppla) Rahm

m. Katharina Lutz (c. 1760, Heiligenmoschel-7 Jan 1814 ,Heiligenmoschel), d/o Philip & Anna Katharina
    (Leppla/Leplat) Lutz

d. 19 Jul 1814, Heiligenmoschel

CHILD:

Johan Georg Philip[2], b. 11 Sep 1800, Heiligenmoschel; m. 27 Jun 1824, Heiligenmoschel, Maria Katharina Leppla (3 Dec 1804, Heiligenmoschel-14 Dec 1874, Buffalo, NY), d/o Peter & Maria Elisabetha (Leplat) Leppla; he d. 11 Dec 1875, Buffalo, NY

    CHILDREN:

    George[3], b. 12 Aug 1835, GER; m. 1 Oct 1863 ,Buffalo Eva Groh from Göttendorf, Bavaria, GER (s.w. of Zwickau); he d. 11 Sep 1917, Buffalo, NY - **issue**

    Philip[3], b. c. 1840, GER; liv. Buffalo, 1870 NY census; unmarr.; carpenter

    Helena[3], b. c. 1845 GER; liv. Buffalo, 1870 NY census; unmarr., tailoress

    Elisabeth[3], b. c. 1850 GER; liv. Buffalo, 1870 NY census; unmarr., tailoress

REF: Vital Records – Heiligenmoschel, GER – some in French, some in German from the Landesarchiv, Speyer, GER; Records of the Reformed FR Ch, Heiligenmoschel (estab. c. 1705); GROH, Raymond Philip, Jr., *The Heritage of the Humboldt Parkway Grohs* (Mt. Clemens, MI, Jul 1982, not pub.).

RANC, Jean (Rev.)

b. 1641, Paris, FR, poss. of a family from Languedoc

m. XX, FR

a Huguenot minister, fled w/ son to Strasbourg, FR, then to Mannheim, GER, 1685

d. 1712, Mannheim

CHILD (surname became **RANCK**):

Hans Valentine[2], b. 1668, Paris; m. Mannheim, Margaretha Philippes; he d. 1710, Mannheim

    CHILDREN:

    Ann Barbara[3], b. 1699

    John Michael[3], b. c. 1701; m. Mannheim, Anna Barbara Schwab; sailed from Rotterdam, arr 24 Aug 1728, Philadelphia, on the *Mortonhouse* w/ wife & ch; allotted a tract of land in Earl Twp, Lancaster Co of 700-800 acres, naturalized 3 Apr 1743 Philadelphia; he d. 28 Jul 1778, E. Earl, PA; **5 sons, 4 daus**

    John Phillip[3], b. c. 1704; m. Anna Barbara Schumacher; arr 19 Aug 1729 on the *Mortonhouse*; he rec. 243 acres just east of his bro's land in Lancaster Co; he d. 1785, bur nr. Fetterville, PA (e. of New Holland); **8 sons, 3 daus**

    Rosine Katharine[2], b. 1705; d. 1712

    Susanna Margaretha[3], b. c. 1707; m. 26 Feb 1725, Johann Valentin Weinkraus

    Johann Valentine[3], b. c. 1710; d. 1712

REF: STAPLETON, A., *Memorials of the Huguenots in America* (Baltimore, 1969); GIUSEPPI, M.S., *Natualizations of Foreign Protestants in the American & West Indian Colonies* (Baltimore, 1969); RANCK, J. Allan, *The Ranks of the Rancks* (Lebanon, PA, 1978); RANCK, Harriet M. & Ezra H., *The Ranks of the Rancks*, Vol. II (1980).

RAPAREILLIET, Georges/RAPALJE, Joris Janszen (de)

bp. 28 Apr 1604, St. Nicolas Parish, Valenciennes (now FR), illegitimate s/o Jean Rapareilliet; Jean had 9 ch, only Georges listed as "illegitimate"; Joris is the Dutch form of George and Jansen = son of Jan/Jean; Valenciennes in 1604 was in Hainaut, part of Spanish Netherlands, thus all baptisms had to be in the Catholic Ch. At times the priests, knowing a family had Protestant "leanings" would call a ch. illegitimate.

1623- Joris was recruited to go as a colonist for the West Indies Company venture in America along w/ other families, most of whom were Walloon; had to be marr. to go

m. 21 Jan 1624, Dutch Reformed Ch, Amsterdam, HOL, Catelyntje Trico (1606 Pry, Walslant/Wa(a)lsland

(Walloonsland), now in Namur Prov, BEL, s. of Charleroi -11 Sep 1689), d/o Jeronimus Trico & Michele Sauvagie & ½ sis/o Mary Flamegh/Flamen, wife of Philippe de la Fontaine/de Fonteijn; Joris was a was a *boratwercker* – a weaver of "*bure*" a brown woolen material; 25 Jan 1624, set sail on the *Eendracht (Unity)*; arr New Netherland, late Mar/early Apr ,went to Ft. Orange (Albany); 1626, to New Amsterdam; nr. the present Navy Yard, in a sm. bay or cove known the *Waale-Boght* – now Wallabout Bay – on the w. side of the cove is the site of Joris' 1st house on Long Island, c. 1637; he farmed for a while & then opened the 1st tavern in Manhattan on Pearl St

1654 - moved to the Brooklyn farm

d. 1662/3, Brooklyn, NY; Catalina still alive 14 Feb 1684/5 when she gave a deposition re her arrival in New Netherland, aged c. 4 score yrs (80)

CHILDREN:

Sara[2], b. 9 Jun 1625; m/1, c. 1639, Hans Hansen Bergen (d. a. May 1654) – **8 ch**, m/2, Teunis Gysbert Bogaert – **8 ch**; she d. a. 11 Nov 1687; Sara was the 1st female b. NY of European parentage

Maria[2], b. 11 Mar 1627; m. 18 Nov 1640, Michael Pauluszen Van der Voort/Vanderford; **9 ch**

Jannetje[2], b. 18 Aug 1628; m. Rem Jansen Van der Brock/Beeck; **16 ch**

Judith[2], b. 5 Jul 1635; m. Pieter Van Nest

Jan[2], b. 28 Aug 1637; m. Maria Frederickse Lumbertson; d. 1662, **no issue**

Jacob[2], b. 28 May 1639, killed by Indians, 25 Jun 1642

Catalynte[2], b. 28 Mar 1641; m. Jeremias Jansen Van Westerhout

Jeromus[2], b. 27 Jun 1643; m. Anna Teunise Denyse, d/o Teunis Denyse & Femmetje Seals; **9 ch**

Annetje[2], b. 8 Feb 1646; m/1, 14 May 1663, Martin Ryerson – **11 ch**; m/2, Joost Fransz

Lysbeth/Elizabeth[2], b. 28 Mar 1648; m. Dirck Cornelise Hooglandt; **9 ch**

Daniel[2], b. 29 Dec 1650, bp. 1 Jan 1651, NY Dutch Ref. Ch; m. Sarah Klock, d/o Abraham Klock; d. 26 Dec 1725, Brooklyn; **issue**

NOTE: Some want to assign a coat of arms for Joris. There is a de Rapalje coat of arms but it is for descendants of Gaspard Colet de Rapalje (b. 1505). Gaspard had a grson or grgrson Joris but he and the Joris in this entry were **not** the same man.

REF: LAW, Hugh T., *How to Trace Your Ancestors to Europe* (Salt Lake City, 1987); STRYKER-RODDA, Harriet, *Colonial Tavernkeepers*, Vol. II (1977); McCRACKEN, George E., "Catalyntje Trico Rapalje" in *TAG*, Vol. 35, #4 (Oct, 1959); *New Netherland Connections*, Vol. 1, #3 (Jul-Sep, 1996) – various articles re the Trico Family, pp. 56-63, Vol. 1, #4 – pp. 89-93.

RAVENEL, René

b. 25 Sep, bp. 29 Sep 1656, Vitré, Bretagne, FR, s/o Daniel, Sieur de Cohigné, & Marie (Guerineau) Ravenel; Vitré is now in Deux-Sèvres Dépt, Poitou-Charentes Région, s.e. of Niort

c. 1685/6 - emigrated from Vitré to SC

m. 24 Oct 1687, Pompion Hall Plantation, SC (on the w. branch of the Cooper River, nr. Charleston) Charlotte de St. Julian (bp. 17 May 1668, Vitré), d/o Pierre de St. Julien, Sieur de Malacare, & Jeanne LeFèbvre

c. 1696, family was naturalized, SC

they d. Charleston, SC

CHILDREN:

Jeanne Charlotte[2], b. 1690, SC; m. 20 Feb 1709/10, John Corneille of Cork, IRE

Daniel[2], b. 1692 m. Elizabeth Damaris de St. Julien (17 Dec 1690 Charleston-1781), d/o Pierre & Damaris Elizabeth (Le Serrurier) de St. Julien; he d. 1774

René Louis[2], b. 1694; m. Susanne (LeNoble) de Chastignier, d/o Henry & Catherine (X) Le Noble; he d. at Pooshee, in Berkeley Co., on Lake Moultrie

CHILDREN:

René[3]

Henry[3], b. 25 Jun 1729; m. 13 Sep 1750, Mary de St. Julian (d. 16 Apr 1779), d/o Paul & Mary
Amey (Ravenel) de St. Julian; he d. 5 Apr 1785; at least **6 ch**

James[3]

Elizabeth[3]

Susanne[3]

Daniel[3]

Mary Amey[2], m. Paul de St. Julian, s/o Pierre & Damaris Elizabeth (LeSerrurier) de St. Julien

Paul Francis[2], did not marry

REF: Records from Vitré; RAVENEL, Henry Edmund, *Ravenel Records* (Atlanta, GA, 1898); RAVENEL, William Jervey, *Ravenel Records, A Supplement* (Charleston, SC, 1964); RAVENEL, Daniel, *Ravenel Records by Henry E. Ravenel, New Edition* (Dunwoody, GA, 1971).

RE(G)NAULT/REGNAUT/RE(Y)NAUD/REYNAUT, Pierre

m. Anne Jupille

d. a. 27 Jan 1687 – said to be deceased in the marr. record of dau Susanne

CHILDREN:

Pierre[2], bp. Sunday, 20 (month unclear) 1665, Reformed Ch, Issoudun, FR

Jeanne[2], bp. 6 Jan 1666, Reformed Ch, Issoudun, FR; parents said to be of St. Amand, poss. the
St. Amand-Montrond, 52 km. s. e. of Issoudun

Susanne[2], b. 24 Sep 1667; bp. 6 Oct 1667, Reformed Ch, Issoudun, FR; m. Pierre Chastain

REF: ALLEN, Cameron, "Susanne Regnaud/Reynault (1667-ca. 1701), First Wife of Pierre[1] Chastain (1659-1728) of Manakintown, Virginia, in *TAG*, Vol. 85, #1 (Jan, 2011, published Nov, 2011).

REGNIER, Pierre

b. La Tremblade, Saintonge, FR, s/o Pierre & Elizabeth (Benoist) Regnier

m. 12 Oct 1687, FR Ch, Threadneedle St, London, Rachel Hurtin, d/o Jean & Elizabeth (Rocheteau) Hurtin

a. 1690 arr in NYC; settled Burlington, NJ; later to Philadelphia

d. 1719 Philadelphia, PA

CHILD:

Pierre/Peter[2], b. PA; m. 6 Aug 1709, Philadelphia, Elinor Wells

REF: "Register of the French Ch Threadneedle St, London" in *Quatro Publication Huguenot Society of London*, Vol. 16; Records of the 1st Presbyterian Ch, Philadelphia; GANNON, Peter Steven, *Huguenot Refugees in the Settling of Colonial America* (NYC, 1987).

RÉMI/RÉMY/REMEY/REAMY, de RÉMI(S), Abram/Abraham

b. 1662 FR, poss. Montauban, Tarn-et-Garonne Dépt, Midi-Pyrénées

m. Mary Elizabeth "Bess" X (D'Aubry?), who d. a. 6 Jun 1720, wp, Henrico Co, VA

20 Sep 1700 - he & his wife arr Jamestown, on the *Peter & Anthony*; his uncle Jacques/Jacob (b. 1630
Picardie, FR), settled Westmoreland Co, VA in 1665 – **see entry below**

Feb 1700/01 - on the list to receive 1 bushel of Indian meal monthly

12 May 1705 – naturalized, VA

2 Sep 1707 - elected to the Vestry of King William Parish, 1 of the founders of Manakintown Ch

by 1714 - on the *Liste Générale* – himself, wife, 1 son, 2 daus; 1714 was the last tithing list on which
his name appeared; no male ch of Abram's appears on any tithing lists, so it is assumed that

they were not in the area at the age of 16

23 Mar 1715- rec. patent #899, for 85 acres on the s. side of the James River in Henrico, now Chesterfield, Co. & patent #906, of 85 acres on the s side of the James River in Henrico, now Chesterfield Co; both patents were transferred by estate to his daus Elizabeth & Margaret, so Abram had d.; his wife would have had lifetime rights – this may have been Abram's way of ensuring that his daus would get the land

d. p. 28 Nov 1715, wd, VA-a. 6 Feb 1715/6, wp; he left everything to his 2 daus; there are accts. of more ch, but his will would indicate that his son was dead and he had only the 2 daus; if his son were alive, even if he didn't leave him anything, surely, he would have been mentioned

CHILDREN:

Elizabeth[2], d. a. 2 Oct 1732 when her share of patent #906 was sold to Anthony Trabue by her sis

Margaret Ann(a)[2], b. 1698; m/1, John Leviston/Livingston – **1 dau** , m/2, John Neal – **1 dau**, m/3, 1731 William Hatchett - **7 ch**; 2 Dec 1734, she is referred to as the only surviving dau of Abraham; she d. 1790

Jean[2], b. a. 1714; must have d. young, although some accounts say he went to SC, c. 1735

REF: BROCK, R. A., *Huguenot Emigration to VA* (Baltimore, 1979); CABELL, Priscilla Harriss, *Turff & Twigg*, Vol. I *The French Lands* (Richmond, VA, 1988); RHAMY, Bonnelle William, *The Remy Family in America, 1650-1742* (Ft. Wayne, IN, 1942); *The Huguenot*, #3 (1927).

RÉMY/REMEY/RAMEY, Jacques/Jacob

b. c. 1630, Picardie, poss. Ivors, Oise Dépt. s. e. Compiègne, s/o Pierre Rémy of Ivoy, Ardennes Dépt. - not found, there is an Ivoy-le-Pré, Cher Dépt., Centre, s.e. Gien

1650/51 - his father d. & Jacques escaped to ENG; some of his bros went to Alsace, then part of GER – some of the German branch went to PA much later

m/1, FR, Françoise Haldat d/o Antoine II & Madelaine (Marchand) Haldat; Antoine was the Seigneur de Bonnet

1654 - to VA as an indentured servant to Nicholas Spencer, Sec. of the Colony of VA; his wife traveled on another ship; she was bound to Roger Drayton but apparently did not survive the trip

1661- he was a chain bearer when he surveyed land for Spencer

21 Jul 1671 - acquired 400 acres of land in Cople Parish, Westmoreland Co, VA

m/2, 1671, Mary X, d/o Marmaduke & Jane (X) Miles <u>or</u> the d/o Nicholas Spencer

29 Sep 1680 – naturalized, Westmoreland Co, VA

d. a. 5 Dec 1721, wp; will names wife Mary, sons William & Jacob

CHILDREN, m/2:

William[2], b. 1672; m. c. 1693, Catherine Asbury, d/o Henry & Mary (X) Asbury; he d. a. 30 May 1738, wp, Westmoreland Co which mentions son **William**[3], heirs of **Jacob**[3] Ramey, **Asbury**[3], daus **Mary**[3] Saunders & **Catherine**[3] Wormeth; sons **John**[3], **James**[3], **Daniel**[3], wife Catherine

Jacob[2], b. c. 1675, Westmoreland Co; m. c. 1699, Ann Sanford, d/o Robert & Ann (X) Sanford; d. p. 23 Feb 1726, wd, Westmoreland Co. – names wife Ann, sons **John**[3], **William**[3], **Joseph**[3], **Jacob**[3] **Benjamin**[3]; had total of **6 sons, 1 dau**; wife Ann, m/2, X Omohundro, she d. a. 13 Sep 1763, wp, Loudon Co, VA

REF: RHAMY, Bonnelle William, *The Remy Family in America, 1650-1942* (Ft. Wayne, IN, 1942); CROZIER, William Armstrong, *VA County Record Publications*, Vol. I, Westmoreland Co. (Hasbrouck Hgts, NJ, 1913); various Wills; HAMLIN, Charles Hughes, "The Reamey Family" in *The* Huguenot, Publication #21 (1964-66).

RENAUDET, Jacques/James

b. 29 Jun 1681, Jonzac, FR, then Guienne, now in Charente-Maritime Dépt, Poitou-Charentes, s.e. of Pons
1700 - fled FR; went to London
1710 - arr NY
m. 1714, NYC, Belitia Hoogland (20 Aug 1697-13 Jan 1768), d/o Adrian Hoogland/Hooglan(d)t & Anna
      Beyvanck
d. 1753
CHILDREN:

Adrian[2], b, 28 Oct 1715, NYC; d. 1785, Philadelphia, PA, unmarr.
Jane[2], b. 1 Apr 1717; m. 5 Dec 1735, Christ Ch, NYC, George Lucas Osborn, of Antigua; **issue**
Ann[2], b. 20 Sep 1718; m. 13 Jun 1741, Christ Ch, NYC, Townsend White, of Wiltshire, ENG; she d. 2 Mar
      1777; **issue**
John[2], b. 7 Mar 1720; d. 19 Aug 1720
Elizabeth[2], b. 1 Jun 1721; m. 9 Dec 1770, Christ Ch, NYC, John Beekman (d. 1774); she d. 29 Jun 1790;
      issue
Peter[2], b. 28 Feb 1723, NYC; became a doctor, wrote the account mentioned below; d. p. 1795, Hot-
      wells, a district 1 mi. w. of the city center of Bristol, ENG; his will makes bequests to nieces, friends, a
      nephew, so evidently   d. without issue, perhaps never marr.
Mary[2], b. 20 Jun 1725; d. 6 Aug 1727
Jas./James[2], b. 7 Jun 1727; d. 3 Sep 1727
John[2] (twin), b. 18 Aug 1728; d. 29 Nov 1733, Philadelphia, PA
James[2] (twin), b. 18 Aug 1728; went to sea, bound for St. Croix in 1753 – never heard from again
Mary[2], b. 6 Apr 1732 NY; m. 16 May 1759, Christ Ch, NYC, Peter Chevalier of Philadelphia, PA; **issue**

REF: "A Genealogical Account of the Families of Renaudet & Hooglant, as Taken from Dr. Renaudet's Book, Aug[t] 6th 1788, Philadelphia. Revised March, 1796" in *Genealogies of PA Families, from The PA Genealogical Magazine*, Vol. III (Baltimore, 1982).

RENEAU/RENO, Louis/Lewis de

b. 1600, a native of the Bordeaux region
he was a soldier, in the service of the Duc de Crequy; rose to the rank of General
m. c. 1630, Frances d'Hamel de Douvrin
d. a. 1665
CHILDREN:

Lewis[2], b. c. 1630/40, said to have been of Angoumois; m. Anne X; Sep/Nov 1687, fled FR, went to
      London, where they were granted Bounty & "Necessarier" by King James II; he was granted
      denization, 25 Mar 1688, to be effective as of 31 Mar 1688; they were still in ENG as late as 22
      Sep 1695, when Lewis & Anne witnessed a baptism in Canterbury; prob. did not emigrate
      CHILDREN (4 of 8):
      Francis[3]
      Lewis[3], b. 1676/7 FR; naturalized w/ parents; to VA by 1700; 12 Feb 1700, purchased land in
            Stafford Co; m. Sarah X; he d. a. 27 Jan 1755, wp, Prince William Co – will presented in
            court by sons Lewis and Thomas; a division of Lewis'[3] land, by sons Lewis & Francis,
            was recorded 26 May 1761, Prince William Co, VA
            CHILDREN:
            Thomas[4], b. c. 1702/03; m. Jane (French?, d/o James & Elizabeth (X) French); he d. 24
                Dec 1777, Prince William Co, VA; **6 ch**
            Lewis[4], b. c. 1710, Stafford Co, VA; m. Elizabeth Whitledge, d/o Thomas & Sybel
                (Harrison) Whitledge; went to KY; **5 ch**
            Judith[4], b/ c 1711; m. Henry Halley, Sr.; **5 ch**
            Francis[4], b. 1713; m. Elizabeth (prob. Bayliss); d. a. 2 Oct 1797, wp, Prince William Co,

> > VA; **5 sons, 7 daus**
> > **John**[4], b. 13 Apr 1715; m. 17 Nov 1737, Susannah Thorn (1716-29 Aug 1773), d/o
> > > William & Mary (Orear) Thorne; he d. p. 14 Jun 1806, wd, Carter Co, TN; **12 ch**
> > **Mary**[4], m. X Davis
> > **Margaret**[4], m. X Anderton
> > **Sarah**[4]
> **Mary**[3]
> **Sara**[3]
?Benjamin[2], b. c. 1630/40; m. Mary (Cartier?); went to Currituck, NC, where he d. 1711; he, his wife
> & 2 daus are listed next to Lewis & Anne on a list of those going to the West Indies, dated Sep-
> Nov 1687
> CHILDREN (known):
> **Marianne**[4]
> **Mary**[4]
> **Moses**[4]

NOTE: There is so much misinformation re this family, getting it right is a challenge! Additionally, about 15 different spellings of the surname have been found. Birth dates & order of Lewis[3]'s children vary with each source. Many accounts name Peter as a s/o Louis & Frances, that has since been proven to be an error. Additional proof would be welcomed. Reynaud/Reynauld have been used for this family but, according to family members that form is incorrect.

REF: RENO, William L., Jr. "Some Forebears & Descendants of Lewis Reno, Huguenot Immigrant to VA", Part I in *The Detroit Society for Genealogical Research Magazine*, Vol. XXXVI, #1 (Fall , 1972), Part II (#2, Winter, 1972), Part III (#3, Spring, 1973), Part IV (#4, Summer, 1973); Rennau Bible Records; SHAW, W.A., *Letters of Denization & Acts of Naturalization for Aliens in England & Ireland* (1911); BODDIE, John Bennett, *Historical Southern Families*, Vol. XX, (Baltimore, 1975); "British Mercantile Claims, 1775-1803" in *The VA Genealogist*, Vol. 8, #3 (Jul-Sep 1964); Francis[4]'s will.

RENOLLET/RENOLL/REINHOLLE, Paul

> b. 5 Nov 1676, Ludweiler, Saarland, s/o Jean Renollet/Johann Reinholle, a smith who was a refugee from
> > FR, poss. Bretagne; in Ludweiler by 1664, where there was a Huguenot settlement; now Ludweiler-
> > Warndt, w. of Saarbrücken, c. 10 km. from FR border
> m. Susanne Desgranges (2 Apr 1703, Ludweiler-11 Mar 1772, Ludweiler)
> d. 18 Jan 1743, Ludweiler
> CHILD:
> **Jean Pierre**[2], b. 30 Jul 1740, Ludweiler; m. 2 Jul 1765, Ludweiler, Anne Susanne Henri/Henry (10 Jun
> > 1743, Ludweiler-9 Feb 1784, Ludweiler), d/o Jean & Judith (Duchene) Henri; he d. 23 Mar 1796,
> > Ludweiler
> > CHILD:
> > **Jean Daniel**[3], b. 1 Dec, bp 6 Dec 1769, Ludweiler; m. 2 Jun 1795, Ludweiler, Anne Caterine Laval
> > > (10 Aug 1774, Ludweiler-12 Aug 1840, Ludweiler), d/o Jean Louis & Anne Sophie (Mollet)
> > > Laval; he d. 21 Feb 1810, Ludweiler
> > > CHILD:
> > > **Paul**[4], b. 17 May, bp. 19 May 1804, Ludweiler; m. 17 Mar 1829, Ludweiler, Marie
> > > > Elisabeth Odon (b. 28 Feb 1808, Ludweiler-d. Edgarton, OH), d/o Philippe &
> > > > Caterine (Duchesne) Odon; he sailed to NY, spring/early summer, 1838; he d. 26
> > > > Sep 1875, Paulding Co, OH
> > > > CHILDREN:
> > > > **Daniel**[5], b. 16 Sep, bp. 21 Sep 1834, Ludweiler; d. young
> > > > **Sophie**[5], b. 3 Apr, bp. 8 Apr 1837, Ludweiler; ch rec says she emigrated
> > > > **Daniel**[5], b. 18 Mar 1848, Henry Co, OH; m. 7 Nov 1872, Barbara Brown; he d.

17 Feb 1924; **issue**

REF: *Taufregister der Evangel. Kirchengemeinde Ludweiler-Warndt* – church birth, marr. records are written mostly in French with some German; letter and family info from Otto Treinen, Ludweiler-Warndt; visa for Paul Renollet, 1838; FELTEN, Joseph Maria, *Die Hugenottensidelung – Ludweiler-Warndt,* Landesarchiv, Inv. Nr 685 (1947); RUG, Karl, *Ludweiler Hugenotten Familien vor dem Zahre 1720* – Saarlandische Familien Kunde, Band 1 (1971).

REQUIER/REQUA/L'ESCUYER/L'ÉQUIER, Gabriel

b. c. 1678, nr. La Rochelle, FR, prob. La Tremblade, s/o Claude
family liv in Paris just prior to leaving for ENG; 12 families fled Paris & went to La Rochelle
a. Mar 1682 - emigrated w/ his parents to ENG; Claude was naturalized, 8 Mar 1682, as was his bro
    Jean/John; several records in London for this family
1689 - to America; parents d. during this voyage; Claude's bro Jean/John was also aboard but evidently
    arr. in NY, in chains; records of the FR Ch, NYC note the death of Jean (John) Équier, mariner, native
    of Tremblade, FR, who d. in the harbor, on a ship from London, 23 Dec 1689; a Mary
    Lescuye/l'Escuier, of Bushwyck, m. 23 Sep 1693, Dutch Ch, NY, Jan Sevenhoven – *poss.* a sis
    to Gabriel
m. NY, Jeanne X, who was on board the same ship, in 1689
d. date not known, prob. did not live past early manhood
CHILD:
Glode[2], b. c. 1700 New Rochelle, NY; m. XX; d. Tarrytown, NY; Glode is a form of Claude
    CHILDREN:
    Susan[3], b. 1721; m. Wolfert Acker of Newburgh, later Tarrytown; she d. 1767
    Mary[3], m. 1723; m/ X McFarlin of Tarrytown
    Margaret[3], b. 1725; m. Samuel Husted of Hempstead, LI, NY
    Glode[3], b, 4 May 1727; m. Amy Dean; served in Rev. War; he d. 9 Dec 1806; **issue**
    James[3], b. 1729; m/1, Maritie Acker, m/2, Rebecca Conklin (1735-1811); he served in the
        French & Indian War & the Rev. War; he d. 1817
    John[3], b. 1731; m. Olive Acker; he served in the Rev. War; he d. 1812
    Jannitie/Jeanette[3], b. 1733; m. 10 Apr 1751 Jacob Stymets
    Daniel[3], b. 1735; m. Mary Martling; he d. 1801

REF: REQUA, Rev. Amos C., *The Family of Requa, 1678-1898* (Peekskill, NY, 1898); BAIRD, Charles W., *Huguenot Emigration to America* (Baltimore, 1966).

RESSIGUE/ RESSEGUIE/de RES(S)EGUIER, Alexandre

said to have been a native of Toulouse, then in Languedoc, now Haute-Garonne Dépt, Midi-Pyrénées
c. 1685 - was in ENG, having fled FR, 1st to SWI; evidently arr ENG with only 1 son, no info re his
    wife or if there were other ch
1696 - was a principal silk merchant employed by the *"compagnie royale des lustrez"* in London; had fled
    from FR, a refugee from Trescléoux, then in Dauphiné, now Hautes-Alpes Dépt, Provence-Alpes-
    Côte d'Azur, n.w. Sisteron; prob. remained in ENG
CHILD:
Alexander II[2], m. 19 Oct 1709, Norwalk, CT, Sara Bontecou (d. May 1757), d/o <u>Pierre & Marguerite</u>
    <u>(Collinot) Bontecou</u>; 8 Jan 1710, he was appt. guardian of James Fountain's 2 young daus; he. d.
    p. 3 Oct 1752, wd, - a. 27 Oct 1752, prob. Norwalk, CT, when 3 men, who had witnessed his will,
    said he had d.; wp, 19 Dec 1752 Fairfield, CT; will mentions wife, 4 sons – Alexander, Abraham,
    Isaac, Jacob
    CHILDREN:

Alexander III[3], b. 27 Aug 1710, Norwalk; m. 16 Feb 1737/8, Thankful Belden (b. 5 Oct 1718, Wethersfield, CT), d/o William & Margaret (Hawkes) Belden; both d. p. 1793; **5 sons, 3 daus**

Peter[3], b. 19 Dec 1711, Norwalk; he was educated to return to FR with the hope that he could reclaim family possessions & titles; however, as he was about to sail from NY, he d. of smallpox, prob. unmarr.

James[3], b. 6 Nov 1713, Norwalk; m. c. 1743, XX; soldier in the Provincial Army – d. 1761, lost his life in the FR War, during the invasion of Canada – assume this means the Seven Years' War (1756-63) aka King George's War (begun under Geo. II, ended during reign of Geo. III); **2 sons, 1 dau**

Abraham[3], b. 27 Jul 1715, Norwalk; m. Jane X (d. 31 Jul 1797); he d. a. 31 Jul 1797; **1 son, 4 daus**

Isaac[3], b. 24 May 1717, Norwalk; liv. 3 Oct 1752

Jacob[3], b. 14 Aug 1719, Norwalk; m. Mary Curtis of Stratford, CT; he d. 27 Dec 1801

Sarah[3], b. 12 Jul 1721, Norwalk; d. 25 May 1753 - not in father's will

REF: BAIRD, Charles W., *Huguenot Emigration to America* (Baltimore, 1966); "Fugitives of the King in America" in *The Journal of American History* (1910): MORRIS, John E., *The Resseguie Family* (Hartford, CT, 1888); Vital Records, Norwalk, CT; STILES, Henry R , *The History of Wethersfield, CT*, Vol. II, *Généalogies & Biographies* (NY, 1904).

RETIEF, François

b. 2 Feb 1663 Blois, FR, Loir-et-Cher Dépt, Centre Région

fled FR, went to HOL

1698 - Huguenot settlers to S. Africa w/ the Dutch; settled Drakensberg area of the Cape (s.e. part of S. Africa); named his farm "Le Paris"

m. 2 May 1700, Maria Mouis (15 May 1685, Capetown, S. Africa-21 Sep 1758, Capetown)

d. 23 Sep 1721, S. Africa

CHILDREN (all b. S. Africa):

Maria[2], b. 16 May 1702; m. Pieter Rousseau; she d. 10 Apr 1729

Anna[2], b. 29 Oct 1704; m. Pieter Hugo

Jacques[2], b. 16 Oct 1706

François[2], b. 7 Apr 1709; m. Anna Marais

Paulus[2], b. 27 May 1714; m. 10 Feb 1743 Dorothea Melius

REF: RETIEF, Dr. P. J. Deur, *Die Retief-Familie in Suid-Afrika* (Pretoria, S. Africa, Jun 1971); BOTHA, Colin Graham, *The French Refugees at the Cape* (1919).

RETTEAU/RETTEW/RATTUE/RATEW, William

b. 1658, FR; went to ENG

c. 1685 - arr America

1698 – purchased 119 acres in Chester Co, PA

m. 1698, PA, Mary X

1726 - purchased warrant for land in Delaware Co, PA

d. 1730, Aston Twp, Delaware Co, PA

CHILDREN:

Ann/ Mary[2], m. 14 Nov 1729 Anthony Arnold

Thomas[2], m. Mary X; **no issue**

John[2], b. 1703, Delaware Co, PA; m. Eleanor X; d. 3 Nov 1780, bur. Concordville, Delaware, PA; at

least 2 sons **John**[3] who m. Esther X, according to his wp, 10 Mar 1810, Delaware Co, he had **John**[4],
Eleanor[4], grson **James Beau Clark Heath**[5]; <u>and</u> **Thomas**[3], b. c. 1755, who m. 29 May 1780, Lancaster
Co, PA, Elizabeth Dougherty – **4 ch**

William[2], b. 7 Jul 1719, Delaware Co, PA; m. 15 Jul 1742, Rebecca Jones; he d. 26 Feb 1791

Aaron[2], b. 1721; m. XX; d. p. 27 Jul 1787, wd

 CHILD:

 Aaron[3] (b. 1753) <u>m/1</u>, 1777, Rebecca Aston, <u>m/2</u>, Elizabeth X, he d. 2 Oct 1811, prob. Caernarvon
  Twp, Berks Co, PA, adm of estate granted on that date

  CHILDREN, not clear by which marr.:

  William[4] (m. Ann X), **John**[4], **James**[4], **David**[4], dau **Rebecca**[4] (who m. John Buckhanon
   of Honeybrook Twp, Chester Co.)

REF: RETTEW, Rae Edna, *The Rettew's Genealogy* (1986); Berks Co. Deed Book #35 & Administration Book #7, Vol.
190; DUNAWAY, Wayland Fuller, "The French Racial Strain in Colonial PA" in *The PA Magazine of History &
Biography*, Vol. LIII (Philadelphia, 1929); *Proceedings of the Huguenot Society of PA*, Vol. XXIX (Philadelphia, 1957);
John[3]' will; *Collections of the Genealogical Society of PA* –" Descendants of Aaron Rettew".

REVIÈRE, Abraham de

 b. poss. Rivière, Namur, a province in s. BEL; he was of a Walloon family from the French-speaking
  prov. of Namur

 to Island of Casant, Gouda Parish, S.HOL, aka Cadzand in Zeeland

 m. XX

 1676/7 - to America; prob. settled Brooklyn; poss. later to Staten Island

 1697 - an original elder in the Tarrytown Dutch Reformed Ch at Sleepy Hollow

 d. bet 1700-05, Philipsbourgh Manor, NY

 CHILDREN:

 Abraham[2], b. Island of Casant; <u>m/1</u>, 30 Oct 1698, Philipsburg, Rachgel Van Weert (d. by 1705), d/o
  Joachim Van Weert; <u>m/2</u>, 6 Nov 1705, Phillipsburg, Wyntje Kranckeyt, d/o Theunis
  Kranckeyt Herrickson; he d. by Jun 1716

  CHILDREN, m/1:

  Hannah/Annatie[3], m. 31 Jan 1719, Philipsburg ,Jeremias Kenniff; 1 son bp there – **David**[4]

  Mary/Maria[3], m . 22 Jan 1721, John Nicholas; 3 ch bp Philipsburg – **Rachel**[4], **John**[4], **Hester**[4]

  CHILDREN, m/2:

  Jacobus[3], bp. 16 Jun 1707, Philipsburg; d. young

  Rachel[3], bp. 1 Jun 1708, Philipsburg; m. 11 Jun 1726, Philipsburg, Jan Storm; 5 ch bp Philipsburg – **Abram**[4], **Engeltie**[4], **Gregorus**[4], **Joannis**[4], **David**[4]

  Sophia/Zophya[3], bp. 29 Jun 1709, Tappan; m. a. Apr 1730, Elbert Aertse; **no known issue**

  Johannis[3], bp. 4 Feb 1711, NY Dutch Ch; m. 17 May 1740, Philipsburg, Catharina Van Thexel,
   prob. d/o Cornelis & Wyntie Van Thexel; 9 ch – **Abraham**[4], **Johannis**[4], **Sofya/Sophia**[4],
   Jacobus[4], **Hendricks**[4], **Isaac**[4], **Jacob**[4], **Cornelis**[4], **Catrina**[4]

  Janitje[3], bp. 5 Mar 1712, Philipsburg; m. 27 Jul 1734/5, Adreannis Buys; 5 ch bp Philipsburg –
   Petrus[4], **Abraham**[4], **Wynte**[4], **Johannis**[4], **Jacob**[4]

REF: DEVINE, Donn, "The Family of Abraham de Reviere of Philipsburg Manor" in the NYGBR, Vol. 112 #1
Jan. 1981, Vol. 112 #2 (Apr 1981).

REZEAU, René

 m. 22 Jun 1660 St. Martin, Île de Ré, FR, Anne Coursier

 1685 - fled FR; orig. intended to go to the Carolinas

 1689 - to NYC; settled Staten Island

d. a. 3 Oct 1720, wp, NY (wd, 18 Feb 1719)
CHILDREN (1st 6 all b. St. Martin, Île de Ré):
René[2], bp. 9 Oct 1671
Abraham[2], bp. 6 Nov 1672
Susanne[2], bp. 14 Oct 1674; m. 24 Oct 1697, FR Ch, NYC, <u>Jean Blanchard</u>, as his 3rd wife
Pierre/Peter[2], bp. 27 Dec 1676; m. Dorcas Guilbert (d. p. 14 Sep 1723); he d. a. 8 Aug 1724, wp,
    Richmond Co, NY; will mentions wife Dorcas, sons Peter, Jacob, James, does not mention dau
    Susanna
    CHILDREN:
    Peter[3], d. 1733, unmarr.
    Jacob[3]
    Susanna[3], m. c. 1735/6, Staten Island, John Brown; **8 sons, 3 daus**
    James[3]
Anne[2], bp. 2 Oct 1678; m. 25 Dec 1696, FR Ch, NYC Jean Perlier
    CHILDREN, bp. FR Ch:
    Marie[3], b. 12 Feb, bp. 25 Feb 1699/00
    Anne[3], b. 11 Sep, bp. 21 Sep 1701
    Jean[3], b. 5 Sep, bp. 19 Sep 1703
Marie[2], bp. 14 Mar 1683
Esther b. 22 Dec, bp. 1 Jan 1688/9 FR Ch, NYC

NOTE: Name may have been more like Rousseau, Roseaux at one time. There was a Jacques Rezeau of St. Martin, Île de Ré, who m. 10 Mar 1704/5, FR Ch, NYC, Marie Contess(e) of Dublin – René Rezeau was a witness at the wedding - would seem to indicate a relationship but not certain what it was – a Pierre Rezeau was also there – René's son?

REF: WITTMEYER, Alfred V., *Register of Births, Marriages & Deaths of the Église Françoise à la Nouvelle York from 1688 to 1804* (1886); BAIRD, Charles W., *History of the Huguenot Emigration to America*; LABAW, Rev. George Warne, *A Genealogy of the Warne Family in America* (not dated); letter from Archives de la Charente-Maritime, La Rochelle, 3 Oct 1975; letter from Niort, Dépt. des Deux Sèvres, Centre Départemental de Documentation, 20 Aug 1976; Peter[2]'s will, dated 14 Sep1723.

RIBLET(TE), Christian

    b. c. 1706, prob. GER (based on age on the passenger list, 27 Y); said to have been the s/o of a man (b. c.
        1670) who escaped FR and went to the *Pfalz* in GER after the Revocation; family poss. from
        Charonne which is now part of Paris; there is a short street called Rue Riblette, s.e. St. Germain
        de Charonne Ch & cemetery, just e. of the Cimetière du Père Lachaise, w. of Boulevard Davout
    m. GER?, XX
    28 Aug 1733, arr Philadelphia, on the *Hope of London*
    d. PA, prob. Northampton Co, where he settled
    CHILD:
Bartholomew[2], b. c. 1729, GER; liv. 60 Y, in Northampton Co, PA; c. 1789, moved to Hagerstown, MD,
    later to Bedford Co; m. Catherine Livegood (1734, GER-1814), d/o Philip Livegood/Livengood; he d.
    1794, Bedford Co; known as Bartley Riblet
    CHILDREN:
    Margaret[2], b. c. 1754; m. Michael Kelchiner; **3 sons, 2 daus**
    John[2], b. 1756; m. Catherine Keiper; 1802, settled w/ family in Erie Co, PA; d. 6 Aug 1835; **issue**
    Reuben[2], b. 1758 – taken prisoner at the Battle of Long Island; d. on prison ship, 1776
    Peter[2], Rev. War service; d. a. 1794?
    Casper[2], Rev. War service; d. a. 1794?
    Christian[2], b. 18 Aug 1761; m. Nov 1783, Christiana Magdalene Shull (18 Aug 1763, Lynn Twp,

Northampton Co, PA-9 Nov 1852, Galion, OH), d/o John David & Christina (Ehro) Shull; c. 1802, moved to Union Co, PA; went to Richland Co, OH; he d. 6 Apr 1844, Richland Co, OH, bur. in the Riblet Cemetery; Rev. War service; **2 sons, 2 daus**

Henry[2], b. c. 1763, PA; descendants found in Mercer Co, PA, Youngstown, OH; d. Jan 1839, PA; seems to have had more than 1 wife, 1 was named Mary; **issue**

Regena[2], b. c. 1765; m. Robert Smith; **issue**

Mary Ann/Polly[2], b. 13 Feb 1767; m. 5 May 1789, John Zuck (12 Jan 1767-11 Aug 1812) of Erie Co, PA; she d. 24 Jul 1863; **8 ch**

Abraham[2], b. 26 Jul 1773; m. Catherine Long; descendants in & nr Johnstown, PA; **10 ch**

Elizabeth[2], b. 20 Mar 1775; m. Henry Swartz, Wayne Co, OH

Daniel[2], b. c. 1777 d. young

Michael[2], b. c. 1779; d. a. 1794?

There were **4 ch**[2], not mentioned in the settlement of their father's estate; the conjecture is that they were Peter, Casper, Michael and, of course, Reuben. Daniel had definitely d. a. 1794. The name Jacob has been mentioned. Some discrepancies exist between the accounts of Bartholomew's ch – wife said she had 13 ch.

NOTE: 3 other German Riblets – Jacob, Peter, Abraham – arr 1749, went to Lancaster Co, PA; progenitors of NY and WV Riblets; no relationship has been <u>proven</u> between them and Christian.

REF: SHULL, David Franklin & Laura H., *Descendants of Christian Riblet* (Philadelphia, PA, 1925); Richland Co. Chapter, Ohio Genealogical Society, *Richland County, OH Cemetery Records*; SCHOLL, John William, *Scholl-Sholl-Shull Genealogy* (NY); RIBLET, Clarence E., *Ancestral History & Character Sketches of the Riblets* (Denver, CO, 1953).

RICHEBOURG, Claude Philippe de (Rev.)

b. c. 1670, Sainte-Sévère-sur-Indre, Berry, FR, s.w. of Châteaumeillant

a. 1690 - went to ENG

m. c. 1699, Anne Chastain (b. c. 1682), who m/2, <u>Isaac Porcher</u> II, of Berkeley Co, SC

1700 - sailed from ENG on the *Mary Ann* to Manakin, VA, reaching the James River, on 20 Oct 1700

1712 - to NC; liv. on the Trent River where Indians attacked and killed 111 settlers; the de Richebourgs left and went to SC where they settled on the Santee River

d. p. 15 Jan 1719, wd, SC; a Huguenot minister

CHILDREN (order is correct, dates are iffy):

Charles[2], b. p. 1700; 1719, planter in Berkeley Co; d. a. 2 Nov 1743; d. unmarr.; **no issue**

René[2], m. Elizabeth Catherine Peyre, d/o David & Judith (Boisseau) Peyre; d. Apr 1744 Craven Co, SC; **5 ch**

John[2], 1719 planter in Berkeley Co; d. a. 27 Dec 1743 wp; d. single; **no issue**

James[2], b. c. 1710; d. SC

Claudius[2], b. c. 1715, Berkeley Co, SC (3 yrs at father's d); <u>m/1</u>, c.1736, Elizabeth St. Julien?* – **Henry**[3] (1737-1810) m. Martha Cantey; <u>m/2</u>, c. 1740, Unity Fox, d/o Henry III & Mary (Goodwyn) Fox; a planter on the Santee, Craven Co - **6 ch**; he d. 10 Feb 1788, Jack's Creek, St. Mark's Par, Craven Co; area later became Clarendon Co, SC

*there is some conflicting info – many agree that Claudius m. twice with Unity being wife #2, as she is in his will; some agree that the 1st wife's name was Elizabeth and others say she was Elizabeth St. Julien – no real <u>proof</u>

Elizabeth[2], b. c. 1716; d. p. 1743

REF: DIETRICH, Bobbie M, "Claude Phillipe de Richebourge: A Sense of Noblesse Oblige" in the *NSDAR Magazine* (Nov 1979); SIMPSON, William C., Jr., *Richbourgs/Richburgs* (NC 1998); ERVIN, Sam J., Jr., "The Richbourg Family of SC in the *Transactions of the Huguenot Society of SC*, #78 (1973); CLARK, Chovine R., "John Richbourg & the

American Revolution" in the *Transactions of the Huguenot Society of SC*, #82 (1977); *Transactions of the Huguenot Society of SC*, #81 (1976).

RISTEAU, Jean

b. prob. Ste Foy, Guienne, FR
m. Magdeleine X
25 Mar 1688 - naturalized ENG
d. p. 27 Jun 1700, prob. ENG
CHILD:
Jacques[2], b. c. 1675, Ste. Foy, Agenois*; d. 1695 "succumbed to the persecution"
Mary[2]
Jean/John[2], b. c. 1680, Ste. Foy; naturalized ENG, 1707; to MD, by 1716; m. Catherine (Ogg) Talbot, d/o George & Elizabeth (X) Ogg, widow of William Talbot – she d. a. 22 Feb 1762, wp; he owned a lot of land in Baltimore Co. & was a prominent merchant; he d. a. 12 May 1760, wp, Baltimore, MD
CHILDREN:
Talbot[3], m/1, 20 Jun 1745, Mary Stokes, m/2, by 24 Sep 1751, Susannah Smith; he d. 23 Nov 1753, Baltimore, MD; **issue;** both wives may have been widows - Mary was the administratrix of Humphrey Wells Stokes & Susannah was the administratrix of Winston Smith
Isaac[3], b. 14 Nov 1724; m. 21 Feb 1748, Elizabeth Raven, d/o Abraham Raven; he d. 1764; **5 sons, 5 daus**
Catherine[3], m. 31 Mar 1746, Rev. Thomas Craddock (b. 1718, Staffordshire, ENG)
George[3], m. 17 Aug 1757, Frances Todd, d/o Thomas & Eleanore (Dorsey) Todd; he d. a. 14 Apr 1792, wp, Baltimore Co.; **1 son, 4 daus**
David[3], owned land in Hebron, Wicomico Co, MD
?Mary[3], m. 20 Apr 1747, Isaac Sampson
Isaac[2]
Elias[2]
Suzanne[2]
Margaret[2]

NOTE: Agenois/Agenais is a former province in the area of Guienne; there are at least 5 towns named Ste. Foy in the area & several more nearby, so it is impossible to say which one was the correct one for this family.

REF: BARNES, Robert W., *British Roots of Maryland Families* (Baltimore); BARNES, Robert W., *Baltimore Co. Families, 1659-1759* (Baltimore); STEFFEN, Charles G., *From Gentlemen to Townsmen The Gentry of Baltimore Co, MD, 1660-1776* (Univ. Press of KY).

RIVERS/RIVES, Pierre

b. c. 1678 Niort, FR
1685 - to ENG, poss. Devonshire
m. c. 1700, ENG, Jeanne X
spring 1700 - sailed from Southampton on the *Peter & Anthony* w/ 167 Huguenot immigrants to VA
arr Sep 1700 - liv. Manakintown for less than a yr, went to Brunswick Co, VA
c. 1700/1 - was 1 of 35 people to sign a "supplication" to Francis Nicholson, His Majesty's Lieutenant & Governor General of VA, on behalf of the French refugees – it contained a series of 9 "articles" that they wished to have granted (the document is in R.A. Brock's book)
d. 1750 Brunswick Co, VA

CHILDREN:

Claude[2]

Robert[2], b. 1703; m. Hannah X of Nottoway Co, VA; he d. a. 1771; **3 sons, dau Mary**[3] m/1, c. 1738,
William Collier, as his 2nd wife, m/2, a. Aug 1749 ,William Terrell (**8 ch**, 4 by each husband)

Thomas[2]

REF: ROSS, Robbie Lee Gillis, *Your Inheritance* (Matthews, NC, 1972; "Collier & Christian" in the *VA Genealogist*
(1990); BROCK, Robert A., *Huguenot Emigration to VA*; "Early Rivers Notes".

RIVOIRE/REVERE, Jean de

b. c. 1634/5, s/o Jean (b. c. 1610) & Sarra (Fraissineau) Rivoire, who m. 21 Nov 1632, in Saint-André-de-
Capbeauze Parish (just w. of Sainte-Foy & called Saint-André et Appelles, today); Jean & Sarra
had 5 ch – **Suzanne**, m/1, Apollos Brun, a master apothecary, m/2 , François Fauré, a surgeon;
Daniel, m. Jeanne Barathon -**10 ch**; **Sara,** m. Simon Malapougne; **Jean**; **Mathias,** m. Isabeau Luy
m. c. 1652, Magdeleine Malapo(u)gne

he was a merchant on the Grand Rue in Sainte-Foy (then Sainte-Foy-en-Agenais, now Sainte-Foy-la
Grande) on the Dordogne River 60 km. e. of Bordeaux and 20 km. w. of Bergerac

CHILDREN (baptisms in the *Registre de baptêmes protestants, Sainte-Foy et alentours*):

Jean[2], b/bp May, 1653; m. 1696, Anne Maumont; they were m. by a Protestant pastor which led the
Catholic officials to declare their marriage null and void in 1696; they continued to live together
-the result of the action is not known, they may finally have been mar. by a Catholic priest but
there is no record of that; he d. 1716/7; **1 son**

Jeanne[2], b/bp Jan 1655

Simon[2], b. Dec 1656, bp 15 Jan 1656/7, Riocaud, FR, Gironde Dépt, Aquitaine (e. of Bordeaux, 10 km. s. of
Sainte-Foy-la Grande); fled to HOL, then to Isle of Guernsey; **or** it could be his bro Simon b. 1664
(below) who was the one to go to HOL & Guernsey – it is not perfectly clear; name of his wife is not
known

CHILDREN:

(Simon) Peter[3], c. 1686, was in Lancaster Co, VA; m. a. 1714, Ann [Burke?]; he is referred to as
Peter in 1714 & 1725 deeds; liv. St. Mary's White Chapel Parish, Lancaster Co, in 1725;
at least 3 sons **Peter Jr**[4], **John**[4] (d. a. 18 Jan 1787, wp, Lancaster Co**), William**[4]

William[3]

Appolus[3]

Suzanne[2], b. Dec 1657, bp. 15 Jan 1656/7

Isaac[2], b. b/bp Jul 1660, Riocard; m. 23 Nov 1694, Saint-Pierre d'Eynesse Ch, Serène Lambert (b. c. 1678),
of Eynesse in a Catholic ceremony; he d. c. 1731; 8 ch (5 sons, 3 daus, according to Serène),
although 1 dau Marguerite (her bp is in the records) apparently d. young & is not included in that
number

CHILDREN:

Jean[3] m. Marie Guibert; son **Jean**[4]* m. his 1st cousin Magdeleine Merveilhaud, d/o Pierre &
Suzanne[2] (de Rivoire) Merveilhaud

Marguerite[3], bp. 1697; d. young

Apollos/Paul[3], b. 20 Nov 1702; went to Guernsey , 1715, to his uncle Simon[2] ,who sent him, 15 Nov
1715, to Boston to apprentice w/ John Coney, a goldsmith; m. 19 Jun 1729, Boston, Deborah
Hitchbourn (25 Jan 1703/4, Boston-23 May 1777, Boston), d/o Thomas & Frances (Pattishall)
Hitchbourn; he d. 22 Jul 1754, Boston, bur. Granary; 7 of his 12 ch bap New Brick Ch
Congregational); Surname **REVERE**, although birth recs of Deborah, Paul & Frances have the
name as Rivoire

CHILDREN:

John[4], d. Dec 1730, Boston

        Deborah[4], b. 21 Feb 1731, Boston; m. c. 22 Feb 1759 (date of int.), Boston, Thomas Metcalf

        Paul[4], b. 21 Dec 1734, Boston; <u>m/1</u>, 4 Aug 1757, Boston, Sarah Orne (d. 3 May 1733, age 37, bur. Granary) – **8 ch**, <u>m/2</u>, 23 Sep 1773, Boston, Rachel Walker (d. 26 Jun 1813, age 63, bur. Granary) – **8 ch**- he was the famous silversmith and "midnight rider" in Apr 1775, he d. 10 May 1818, Boston, bur. Granary; wanting to know more about his ancestors he corresponded with a Mathias Rivoire who was the grgrson of Daniel[2] above

        Frances[4]. b. 11 Jul 1736, Boston; m. Edward Calleteau - **twin sons** who d. young; Eliz. d. by Mar 1763, Boston, when Edward remarr.; Edward d. by 31 Dec 1763, adm of his estate, Boston

        unnamed twins[4], d. young, prob. at birth

        Thomas[4], d. young

        Thomas[4] m. Mary X

        John[4], <u>m/1</u>, 26 Jun 1764, Boston, Anna Clemens (d. 12 Nov 1784, Boston), <u>m/2</u>, 21 Aug 1785, Boston, Silence (Swift) Ingerfield, wid/o Paul Ingerfield; he d. 13 Mar 1786, Boston

        Mary[4] (twin), <u>m/1</u>, 21 Mar 1765, Boston, Edward Rose, <u>m/2</u>, 6 Mar 1791, Boston, Alexander Baker; she d. 27 Dec 1801, age 59, Alex. d. 22 May 1801, age 72, both bur. Copp's Hill Cem., Boston

        Elizabeth[4] (twin), d. 20 Jul 1743, Boston

        Elizabeth[4], chr. 20 Jan 1745, Boston; m. 29 May 1776, Medway, MA, David Colson Moseley (17 Dec 1752, Boston- 15 Jun 1812, Boston), s/o Unite & Elizabeth (Colson) Moseley; David was a silversmith apprenticed to Eliz's father; she d. 8 Jan 1811, Boston – **3 ch**

    Suzanne[3], b. c. 1710; m. Pierre Merveilhaud; d. c. 1770; son **Simon**[4] who was his uncle Pierre Simon's heir; dau **Magdeleine**[4], m. her cousin Jean[4]

    Isaac[3]– he left Riocaud, went to Saint-Domingue on the Island of Hispaniola, the half that is Haiti today; he marr., XX, 1737; called himself *Jean*; liv Cape François and was a planter; his bro Simon-Pierre (below) joined him there

    Anne[3] – remained in Riocaud, unmarr.; d. p. 1754

    Simon[3], b. c. 1705; d. Feb 1782, apparently unmarr., aka Pierre-Simon

    Magdeleine[3], bp. 1710; liv, unmarr. in 1754

    Simon-Pierre[3], b. c. 1717; left Riocaud; d. 5 Nov 1743, Hispaniola

Apollos[2], b/bp Nov 1661

Isabeau[2], bp. 1663

Simon[2], b. 8 Oct/bp ? Oct 1664 (yes, they had 2 sons named Simon!)

REF: LABATUT, André, "Some New Information about the Ancestry of Paul Revere" in the *NEHGR*, Vol. CXLIII (Jul 1989); NIELSEN, Donald M., "The Revere Family" in the *NEHGR*, Vol. CXLV (Oct 1991); LABATUT, André J. & Pamela, "Paul Revere's Paternal Ancestry: The Rivoires: A Huguenot Family of Some Account" in the *NEHGR*, Vol. CL (Jul 1996) (contains VR from Sainte-Foy & other FR records); FORBES, Allan & CADMAN, Paul F., *The Boston French* (Cottonport, LA, 1971); VR-Boston.

ROBERDEAU/ROBERDIEU, Isaac

1685 from La Rochelle, FR to St. Christopher's (St. Kitt's) Island, West Indies

m/1, c. 1723, St. Kitt's, Mary Cunnynham/Cunningham (4 Apr 1699, St. Kitt's-13 Mar 1771, Philadelphia), d/o Robert & Judith Elizabeth (X) Cunyngham, supposed to have descended from Scottish Earls of Glencairn, she m/2, p. 1748, PA, X Keighley

c. 1740- emigrated to Philadelphia

d. c. 1743

CHILDREN, m/1:

Elizabeth[2], b. c. 1724, St. Kitt's; d. 31 Mar 1799, Philadelphia; d. unmarr.

Ann Judith[2], b. 1725/6, St. Kitt's; m. 19 Jan 1742, Philadelphia, William Clymer; she d. 1782, Berks Co, PA; **issue**

Daniel[2], b. 1727, St. Kitt's; m/1, 3 Oct 1761, Mary Bostwick (1741-15 Feb 1777), d/o Rev. David & Mary (Hinman) Bostwick, m/2, 3 Dec 1778, Philadelphia, Jane Milligan; he was a member of the PA Assembly, brigadier general, delegate to the Continental Congress; 1785, moved to Alexandria, VA; he d. 5 Jan 1795, Winchester, VA

CHILDREN, m/1:

Isaac[3], b. 11 Sep 1763

Mary[3], b. 24 Aug 1765, Philadelphia; d. 13 Oct 1769

Ann[3], b. 3 Dec 1767, bp. 27 Mar 1768, Philadelphia; m. 24 Sep 1785, Jonathan Swift (d. 22 Aug 1824, Alexandria); she d. 16 Jan 1833, Madison Court House; **11 ch**

David Bostwick[3], b. 22 Aug 1770; d. 14 Sep 1770

unnamed dau[2], b. Aug 1771

Philadelphia[3], b. Jul 1772; d. young

Mary[3], b. 6 May 1774, Philadelphia; m. 14 Nov 1793, Alexandria, Thomas Patten (b. 22 Jul 1769, Roxbury, MA), s/o Thomas & Anna (X) Patten; she d. 31 Oct 1808; **8 ch**

Selina[3], b. 9 Nov 1775, Philadelphia; m. Aug 1793, Scudamore Nickolls; she d. 10 Oct 1837, Richmond, VA; **4 ch**

stillborn dau[3], b. 15 Feb 1777, Lancaster, PA – bur w/ her mother

CHILDREN, m/2:

Jeany[3], b. 17 Jul, bp. 5 Aug 1781, Philadelphia; d. young

Jane[3], b. 22 Jan, bp. 30 Mar 1782, Philadelphia; m. 1803, Winchester, VA, Dr. Daniel Annan; she d. 5 Nov 1842, Winchester; **7 ch**

James Milligan[3], b. 12 Apr 1785, Alexandria, VA; m/1, 8 Jan 1818, Fairfax Co, VA, Mildred Lancaster Denny who d. c. 1821 – **3 ch**, m/2, 20 Jun 1822, Martha Lane Triplett, d/o James Lane & Martha (Jennings) Triplett – **7 ch**; he d. 10 Mar 1832

Heriot[3], b. 1788, Alexandria; m. 16 Feb 1809, Dr. Edward Conrad (d. 25 Dec 1821); she d. 17 Apr 1867

REF: ROCHE, O. J. A., *The Days of the Upright* (NY); GREENE, Katherine Glass, *Winchester, VA, & Its Beginnings* (1926); REMAN, G. Elmore, *The Trail of the Huguenots* (Toronto, CAN); FOSDICK, Lucian J., *The French Blood in America* (Baltimore, 1973); BUCHANAN, Roberdeau, *Genealogy of the Roberdeau Family* (Washington, 1876); McNULTY, Irene McPHERSON, *Roberdeau Family Genealogy, 1876-1979* (Columbia, SC, 1979).

ROBERT, Daniel

b. 1625 Montagne du Droit, Parish of St. Imier, SWI, s/o Pierre & Judith (Sagne) Robert; *poss.* b. 1630, Aberystwyth, Wales. There is some thought that earlier Robert ancestors went from FR to Wales, then back to FR, then to SWI – coat of arms suggests the Welsh connection; a s/o William Robert; emig to FR, m. FR Huguenot Marie X; fam. left Wales, p. 1598, when the Edict of Nantes was proclaimed – all speculative, needs proof

m. 1 Apr 1651, Sonvilier, Marie Pétremand, d/o Pierre Pétremand of Sonvilier

d. a. 11 May 1698, Montagne du Droit

CHILD:

Pierre I[2], b. 30 Dec 1655, St. Imier, SWI. c. 7 mi. e. of border of FR/SWI ; bp 3 Feb 1655/6, St. Imier; m. 1674, Bâle/Basel, SWI, Jeanne Brayé (1660, Basel-1717, Santee, SC), d/o Jéhu & Susanne (X) Brayé; 13 Jan 1674, graduated at St. Étienne as a physician*; 1682, attended the Univ. of Basel; ordained as a minister, 19 Feb 1682/3; he was the pastor of a Waldensian ch. in the Piedmont Valley in SWI; 1686, immigrated to SC w/ Capt. Philippe Gendron & settled St. James Parish; he

was the 1ˢᵗ rector of the FR congregation, FR Santee; 1706, he founded 1ˢᵗ Huguenot Ch in
Charleston; d. 1715 FR Santee, Charleston, SC

*The Rev. Pierre Robert Assoc. says this has not been proven. He was referred as "Doctor" but
the Assoc. feels it may have been an ecclesiastical title. This could be one of those "facts"
that has been repeated so often, it has become accepted as truth.

CHILDREN:

Pierre/Pierre II[3], bp. 9 May 1675, St. Imier Parish, Basel; m/1, 10 Sep 1701, Anne Marie Louise
LeGrand, d/o Louis & Anne (de Magneville) LeGrand, m/2, c. 26 Feb 1709, Charleston,
Judith de Bourdeaux (b. Grenoble, FR), d/o Jacques & Margaret (Garillond) de Bourdeaux; he
d. a. 19 Apr 1731, wp, Santee

CHILD, m/1:

 Pierre/Peter III[4], b. 1704, SC; m. 1728, Mary Lynch; **5 ch**

CHILDREN, m/2:

 Jacques/James[4], b. 3 Apr 1711, Santee; m. 26 Aug 1735, Sarah Jaudon (24 Sep 1710-26
Apr 1779), d/o Daniel & Elizabeth (X) Jaudon; he d. Nov 1774, bur. Stoney
Creek Churchyard, nr. Yamasee/Yemassee, SC, n.w. of Beaufort; **7 ch**

 Elizabeth[4], m. Elias Jaudon, bro/o Sarah above; **5 ch**

 Madelaine, b. 28 Sep 1719, Santee; m/1, Archibald Hamilton – **2ch**, m/2, 7 Mar 1749,
William Gough – **3 ch**

Jean/John[3], b. p. 1686, SC; m. Margaret X; at least **1** son; used surname **ROBERTS** or **ROBARTS**

Elias[3], b. SC; surname **ROBERTS**

REF: MILLER, Annie Elizabeth, *Our Family Circle* (Hilton Head, SC, 1987); LAWTON, Thomas O., Jr.,
"Pasteur Pierre Robert's Swiss Ancestry" in *Transactions of the Huguenot Society of SC*, #90 (Charleston, 1985);
STAFFORD, George Mason Graham, *Three Pioneer Rapides Families* (Baton Rouge, LA, 1968, 1981); BOARDMAN,
Hollis, "The French Huguenots" in *Transactions of the Huguenot Society of SC*, Vol 80 (1975).

ROBERT, Daniel

m. Susanne LaTour

c. 1685- from La Rochelle, FR to the Island of Martinique

3 Jul 1705 – denezized, London

c. end of 17ᵗʰ century - to NY; he had left a considerable estate in FR; it is said that after arr. in America,
he rec. legal notices requiring him to show cause why his lands in NY should not be confiscated
and conveyed to the members of his family who remained in La Rochelle

REF: BAIRD, Charles W., *Huguenot Emigration to America*, Vol. 1, pp. 286-87 (Baltimore, 1966).

ROGER, Jean

b. c. 1719, from Bordeaux, FR; a devout Lutheran

m. FR, Anne L'Espine (d. p. 17 Feb 1776, wd-a. 6 May 1800, wp; will names ch Peter, Jeremiah, Mary;
Pierre "Rocmore" (below) was a witness to her will in 1776

c. 13 Aug 1763 - fled FR, from the port of Royan, to Plymouth, ENG; said to have hidden out in the
mountains for 2 yrs before escaping from FR with his family & his FR Bible

25 Jan 1764 - sailed for America but had to return to Plymouth; sailed again 17 Feb 1764 & arr. Charleston
(Port Royal), SC, 12 Apr 1764; by the 14ᵗʰ, the group was lodged in barracks there

18 Apr 1764 - took Oath of Allegiance w/ his sons; he was appt 1ˢᵗ Justice of the Peace and proceeded to
Hillsborough Twp to take up his duties, leaving his family in Charleston

d. c. 10 Oct 1764, SC; he was returning to Charleston when he became ill and d.; his family went to
Bordeaux (Hillsborough Twp), SC, now in McCormick Co.; family became Presbyterian

CHILDREN:

Pierre/Peter[2], b. c. 1740, nr. Bordeaux, FR m. Anna Béraude, d/o Matthew & Elizabeth (Gregorie) Béraude; he d. a. 7 Oct 1801, wp, 7 Feb 1803, adm, Abbeville Dist, SC; will mentions wife Anna Berraud & his ch but not by name – his wife was d. by then but evidently he never changed his wd, 9 Nov 1789; liv. Hillsborough Twp, Abbeville; he was a Lt. in the Rev. War and was in the "Siege of 96", Sep 1775, & other battles

CHILDREN:

Peter Bayard[3], b. 24 Jun 1775; m/1, 18 Mar 1802, Marie Moragne (31 Mar 1776-18 Jan 1810), d/o Pierre & Susannah (David) Moragne – at least **4 ch**, m/2, 6 Nov 1816, Mary Jane Palmer (5 Apr 1797, VA-25 Mar 1835, SC) – **6 ch**; he was a Capt. in the War of 1812; he d. Feb 1839

Paul[3], b. 7 Aug 1785; m/1, X Moragne – **2 ch**, m/2, Mary Ann Colvin (30 Jan 179x-19 Jul 1879) – **4 ch**; he d. 20 Mar 1862

William[3]

Anna[3]

Jeremiah[2], m. XX

CHILDREN:

Mary[3], m. Jacob M. Devall

John[3], m. XX – **5 ch**

Sarah[3]

Rebecca[3]

Marie/Mary[2], d. unmarr.

REF: WILLIE, Pauline Young, *Abstracts of Old 96 & Abbeville District Wills & Bonds*, (Vidalia, GA, 1669); wills of Peter & Ann; ROGERS, Marion, *Jean Roger, FR Huguenot & His Descendants* (Pelham, GA, 1969, unpub); family Bible records.

RÖHRER/ROEHRER, Hans Michael

b. c. 1665, Alsace, FR

m/1, 6 Jun 1688, Markirch, Alsace, Katherina Schwägler-in; Markirch is now Ste.-Marie-aux-Mines, Haut-Rhin Dépt, Alsace, n.w. Colmar

m/2, XX

c. 1729 - to America

CHILDREN, m/1, from ch recs of *"der Deutsch-reformierten Kirche van Markirch von 1688"*:

Hans Jakob[2], bp. 15 May 1689, Markirch

Hans Michael[2], bp. 15 Apr 1691, Markirch

Verena[2], b. 10 May 1693, Markirch

Johannes/John[2], bp. 13 May 1696, Alsace, FR; he became separated from his family, was imprisoned; p. 1710, went to ENG, where he studied veterinary surgery; went to Lancaster Co, PA; m. 1732, PA, Maria Souder (24 Feb 1716, Mannheim, GER-11 May 1769), d/o Jacob & Ann (X) Souder; he d. 23 Nov 1771; **4 sons, 4 daus**

Anna Maria[2], b. 4 May 1698; d. 25 Sep 1701

Johannes[2], b. 1 Nov 1701

David[2], b. 10 Feb 1704

CHILDREN, m/2:

Frederick[2]

Jacob[2], m. Fronica Igle; he d. a.12 Jan 1758, wp, Frederick Co, MD; **issue**

Samuel[2], *poss.* the Samuel Rohrer who arr on the *Restoration*, 9 Oct 1747; settled Frederick Co, MD, c. 12 mi s. of Hagerstown; m. X Henson; d. a. 12 Aug 1788, Washington Co, MD; **issue**

Martin[2], m. Agnes X; he d. 8 Aug 1786, Washington Co, MD

Christian[2]

REF: ROHRER, Albert L., *John Rohrer of Lancaster Co, PA* (Maplewood, NJ, 1941); WHITLEY, Edythe, *Rhorer Family Notes* (Nashville, TN, 1939, un pub.); Church Records; wills.

RONGNION/RUNYON/RUNYAN, Vincent

b. 1645, FR
c. 1665 -fled from Poitiers, FR, to the Isle of Jersey; in a grant in Elizabethtown, he is referred to as "Vincent Rongnion, mariner of Poitou"
a. 1668 - to Elizabethtown, NJ
m. 17 Jul 1668, NJ, Ann Martha Boutcher (c. 1650-c.1723-25), d/o John Boutcher/Bouchierre of Hertfordshire, ENG; some discussion as to his wife/wives; marriage record say her name was Ann; a wife named Martha – same person? - was the executrix of his estate; there is no definitive evidence either way.
20 Mar 1671/2 - purchased land in Elizabethtown; the strong Puritan element of Elizabethtown was not to his liking so he went to the Baptist community at Pisacataway
spring 1677- purchased a farm of 154½ acres on the Raritan River
d. Nov 1713; bur. Piscataway; he was a carpenter in NJ
CHILDREN (the # of ch attributed each ch varies – sources do not agree).
John[2], b. c. 1669; m. 20 Jul 1692, Hunterdon Co, NJ, Ann Elizabeth Dunn (b. 19 Mar 1676), d/o Hugh & Elizabeth (Drake) Dunn; he d. Nov 1745, Rocky Hill, Somerset Co, NJ; **11 ch**
Vincent[2], b. 1671; m. 2 Dec 1691, Mary Hull (b. 10 Aug 1670), d/o Hopewell & Mary (Martin) Hull; he d. Mar 1723/4; **13 ch**
Ann[2], b. 1673; m. Nathaniel Leonard, s/o Henry Leonard of Shrewsbury, NJ; **issue**
Thomas[2], b. 1675; m. c. 1698, Martha Dunn (b. 13 Jul 1681), sis/o Ann Elizabeth above; he d. Apr 1753, Hunterdon Co, NJ; **7 ch**
Mary[2], b. 2 Jul 1677; m. Benjamin Drake
Peter[2], b. 1 Jul 1680; m. 12 Oct 1704, Providence Blackford, d/o Samuel & Ann (Smalley) Blackford; he d. Oct, 1755, Piscataway, NJ; **14 ch**
Jane[2], b. 19 Jan 1683
Sarah[2], b. 30 Oct 1686; m/1, 25 Jan 1702, Richard Sutton (b. 18 Jul 1676), s/o William & Damaris (Bishop) Sutton, m/2, James Campbell; she d. p. 1732

REF: RUNYON, Robert & Amos, *Runyon Genealogy* (Brownsville, TX, 1955); MONNETTE, Orra Eugene, *1st Settlers of Ye Plantations of Piscataway & Woodbridge, Olde East. NJ,* Part 4 (Los Angeles, 1932); KEPHART, Col. Calvin I., "Runyon-Runyan Family (NJ)" in the *National Genealogical Society Quarterly*, Vol. XXIX (1941).

ROQUEMORE/ROQUEMAURE, Pierre

b. 11 Mar 1694, Eymet, Dordogne Dépt, Aquitaine, s.e. of Bergerac, s/o Pierre & Jeanne (Fourneyrol) Roquemore
m. 2 Oct 1725, FR, Susanne Lafon (b. c. 1708); she went to ENG, then SC w/ son Pierre; called "widow" in 1763
d. 1762/3, FR **or** 1763, ENG
CHILDREN: (3 of 16)
Pierre II[2], b. 19 Sep 1731, Eymet, FR; m. 14 Feb 1757, Eymet, Jeanne Séguin (b. 2 Nov 1729), d/o Jacques & Marie (Meuze) Séguin; mar. rec. in the *registre protestant*; 9 Aug 1763- left FR, w/ Rev. Jean Louis Gibert, Rev. Pierre Boutiton & 428 Huguenot refugees; 25 Aug 1763- arr. Plymouth, ENG, from FR; 22 Nov 1763- list of names included Pierre (22 Y, *bonnetier* – hosier, age was really **32**) his wife, dau Marie (4 Y), Pré Roquemore (18 Y, stockingmaker), & Jean Roquemore* (36 Y, tanner) – relationship of Pré & Jean to Pierre, if any, is unclear, Susanne Lafone (55 Y), Jeanne Séguin (30 Y); c. 1763 - another list names the 212 Huguenots destined for the Abbeville Dist., SC – Peter, Jeanne (Jane), ch Maria, Anne, Peter + Susan Roquemore, widow, & her

unnamed dau (it was Marie Jeanne); 2 Jan 1764- boarded the *Friendship*, arr. Charleston, SC, 12 Apr 1764; 1st went to Fort Lyttleton (nr. Port Royal) for a few months; to the New Bordeaux Settlement, then in the Abbeville Dist, SC, nr. the Savannah River; family rec. multiple land grants which included land for vineyards; 18 Apr 1764 - took Oath of Allegiance; rec. land nr. Long Cane Creek, Hillsborough Twp, New Settlement; remained there until 17 Feb 1776; 1776-1781 - went down the Savannah River to GA; * Pierre had a bro Jacques, b. 20 Jul 1727, who would have been 36 in 1763 – Jacques not Jean?

CHILDREN:

Marie[3], b. 11 Aug 1760, Eymet, bp., 12 Aug 1760, Sainte-Foy-la Grande, Protestant Ch; d. 28 Oct 1820, New Bordeaux, SC

Anne[3], m. as his 1st wife, Lazarus Covin, one of the Gibert-Boutiton group; she d. 1818, New Bordeaux, SC; **2 sons, 1 dau**

Pierre III/Peter[3], said to have been a lt. or capt. during the Rev. War (not in NSDAR Ancestor Database*); rec. 350 acres of land in Washington Co, GA; m. Abigail Van Zant? *all that means that no one has joined DAR as a descendant of Peter; it is possible that Peter's father Pierre/Peter had service, or that the service attributed to his son was actually his, but that is impossible to determine without more information

Pierre Jacques/James[2], b. 27 Aug 1742, Eymet; m. 1777, Elizabeth (Bazemore?,1735, FR-1829, Putnam Co., GA); he d. p. 30 Aug 1803, adm, Warren Co, GA; rec. bounty lands there; patriotic service, Rev. War – **6 ch**: his will, dated 30 Apr 1803 – names wife Elizabeth, sons Peter, James, Jr., Thomas, John, daus Polly Pearson, Elizabeth

Marie Jeanne/Mary Jane[2], b.12 Jul 1745, Eymet, FR; m. 16 Dec 1766, New Bordeaux, André Guillebeau (18 Aug 1738, SC-21 Feb 1815, SC), they had a dau **Susannah**[3] (15 Jan 1776, SC-12 Sep 1814, SC) who m/1, 19 Mar 1798, Joseph James Bouchillon (1777-3 Jan 1803), m/2, Francis Moragne; son **Pierre**[3] (20 Oct 1779, Bordeaux-2 Dec 1854, Bordeaux) m. 20 Dec 1797, Bordeaux, Mary Jane Bellot, d/o Peter Elijah & Jane (Langel) Bellot – their dau **Ann Margaret**[4] (3 Jul 1810-22 Oct 1860) m. 11 Feb 1852, Philip LeRoy, II (11 May 1795-18 Mar 1869)

REF: HUFTAKER, Josephine Costello, *The Roquemore Report of 1967*; NASH, Letitia Roquemore, "One Family's Odyssey from the French Village of Eymet to New Bordeaux" in the *Transactions of the Huguenot Society of SC*, #93 (1988) which cites ch records from Sainte-Foy-la Grande, Gironde Dépt, Aquitaine, e. of Bordeaux where the church records of Eymet are located; DAVIS, Nora Marshall, "The Settlement at New Bordeaux" in the *Transactions of the Huguenot Society of SC*, #56 (1951); GILBERT, Anne C., *Pierre Gilbert, Esq., The Devoted Huguenot* (1976); James[2]'s will, dated 1803.

ROSSET, Louis de

b. 1645, s/o Louis (doctor of laws) & Lady Catherine (de Möynier) de Rosset

m. 10 Feb 1671, Uzès, FR, Lady Gabrielle de Gondin, grdau/o Antoine de Fontfroide, Treasurer of King's Domain in the Sénéchausée de Nîmes

a Captain under the Duke of Schomberg who served King William of Orange; commissioned, 18 Feb 1684, as an officer in the FR army

1685 - left FR, went to HOL

1708 - naturalized in ENG

d. 1725, London

CHILD:

Armand Jean[2], b. c. 1695, prob. Narbonne, Languedoc (s.w. of Béziers); m/1, Basel, SWI, Madeleine of the noble house of Uzès (Ucetia), she d. 1746; 3 Dec 1720, rec. medical degree with honors from the Univ. of Basel; returned to FR, then to London; m/2, 13 Apr 1751, Elizabeth Catherine Bridgen, native of Bristol, d/o Samuel Bridgen of Ludlow Castle – **no issue**; 1735, went to NC; he d. a. 9 Nov 1759, inv, New Hanover Co, NC

CHILDREN, m/1:

Gabrielle de Gondin[3], b. 1722, Montpellier, FR; m. 1741, John duBois; she d. 29 Mar 1755; **issue**

    Louis Henry[3], b. 1724, Montpellier; m. 1755, Margaret Waller (1733-1785); King's Councillor
        for the Prov. of NC, held the rank of Lt. General; he was a merchant, planter and a
        Tory; left NC, 1778; d. 22 Feb 1786, London; **no issue**

    Moses John[3], b. 27 Dec 1726, London; physician; m. 1759, Wilmington, NC, Mary Ivy; was
        mayor of Wilmington, was an officer in the regt. of Col. James Innes during Fr & Ind
        Wars; d. 25 Dec 1767, bur. St. John's Churchyard

        CHILDREN:

        Magdalene Mary[4], b. 2 Feb 1762; m. Henry Toomer; she d. 1799

        Armand John[4], b. 17 Nov 1767, Wilmington, NC; served in Rev. War; graduated 1787,
            Princeton; 1790, rec. M.D. from the Univ. of PA; m/1, 6 Oct 1791, Mary Fullerton of
            Charleston, SC, d/o John Fullerton, she d. Nov 1797 – **1 son**; m/2, 1 Aug 1799,
            Catherine Fullerton (1771-9 Mar 1837), Mary's sis – **2 ch**

REF: STRONG, Ludlow Peter, *Supplement to the Annals of the de Rossets*; *NC Historical & Genealogical Register*, Vol. 11 #1 (Jan 1901); MEARES, Catherine DeRosset, *Annals of the DeRosset Family*; WALKER, Alexander M., *New Hanover Co. Court Minutes, 1738-1769* (Bethesda, MD, 1958).

ROUSSEAU, Théodore de

    arr 1700 – Manakintown, VA, on the *Peter & Anthony*, listed by himself; rec. 1 bushel of Indian meal
        monthly beginning Feb 17001/01

    CHILD:

    Hillaire[2], b. 1675/80, FR; m. 1715, VA, Elizabeth Lynton (1695/6-26 Mar 1751), d/o William &
        Johanna (Lewis) Lynton; Hillaire d. 30 Jun 1720, Stafford Co, VA; Eliz. m/2, Surles Lewis (d. 1736);
        Elizabeth's wp, 26 Mar 1751, Westmoreland Co, VA - names sons Hillaire &, William Rousseau, James
        & John Lewis, son-in-law ? Lewis, John s/o Katherine Garroth, Benjamin Wootten

        CHILDREN:

        Hillaire II[3], b. c. 1715; executor of his mother's will, prob. eldest son

        Elizabeth[3], b. 1716; m. c. 1747, Benjamin Wootten; she d. 1764; **issue**

        David[3], b. 2 Nov 1717 St. Paul's Parish, Stafford Co, VA; m. Ann Harrison who m/2 Samuel
            Dogan; David d. 1748 Culpeper Co, VA - son **James**[3], b. 10 Mar 1746-d. 12 Jun 1824

        William[3], m. 27 Oct 1743 Priscilla Mauzy; he d. Fauquier Co, VA p. 19 Jul 1792 wd (wp 23 Jul 179-);
            issue

REF: BROCK, R.A., *Huguenot Emigration to VA* (Baltimore, 1979); *The Huguenot* #16 (1951-53); wills of William Lynton (wp 26 Mar 1734 Westmoreland Co, VA), Eliz. Lynton Rousseau Lewis, William Rousseau; NICKLIN, John Bailey Calvert, *St. Paul's Parish Register, Stafford-King George, Co, VA, 1715-1798*, p. 53 ; *Wm. & Mary Quarterly*, Vol. 27, p. 104.

ROUTTES/ROOTE(S)/ROOT, Thomas

    there is a town called Routes n. of Yvetot, Seine-Maritime Dépt, Haute-Normandie; surname believed to
        have been Norman

    b. c. 1555, Badby, Northampstonshire, ENG, prob. the s/o FR immigrants

    m/1, c. 1575, Badby, Ann Burrell (1559-1578)

    m/2, c. 1579, Frances Russell

    [1598 - there is a John Rootes & his wife Mary listed as "aliens in London", liv. Nettmakers Alley –
        Vol. 10, Part 3, publication of The Huguenot Society of London]

    prob. was the Thomas Roote who d. 5 Apr 1609, Badby

    CHILD, m/1:

    John I[2], b. 24 Jun 1576, Badby, Northants, ENG; m. 23 Jul 1600, Badby, Mary/Ann Russell (b. 18 Apr
        1574, Badby); not clear if he emigrated or not – records in Badby of this family end in 1609; where

they went is unknown; would have been in his 60's when his sons emigrated – inscription on John II's gravestone has his parents' names but there is no evidence that they are bur there as well – John II prob. wanted their names known; family oral history says that John I d. when his ch were young & that, at least John II, went to live w/ an uncle (his father's bro) who wanted John to join the army but as John had an aversion to war, he decided to emigrate

CHILDREN:

Marie[3], b. 21 Dec 1600, Badby

Susannah[3], b. 18 Oct 1603, Badby

Thomas[3], b. 16 Jan 1604/5, Badby; to America, c. 1637, went to Hartford, CT; m. XX; 1654, moved to Northampton, MA; he d. 17 Jul 1694, Northampton; **6 sons, 1 dau, Joseph**[4] b. 1640, **Thomas**[4] b. 1644, **John**[4] b. 1646, **Jonathan**[4], **Hezekiah**[4], **Jacob**[4], **Sarah**[4].

John II[3], bp. 26 Feb 1608/9, Badby; to America, c. 1640; m. c. 1640, Farmington, Hartford, CT, Mary Kilborne (12 May 1619, Woodditton, Cambridgeshire, ENG-1697, Farmington, CT), d/o Thomas & Frances (Moody) Kilborne; he d. 16 Aug 1684, Farmington, CT, & is bur. in the N. Cemetery, Somers, Tolland, CT – his tombstone reads "Descendants of the Huguenot Routtes who fled from France to England"; he left an estate valued at £819

CHILDREN:

John III[4], b. c. 1642, Farmington; m. 18 Oct 1664, Springfield, MA, Mary Ashley (6 Feb 1644/5, Springfield-9 Mar 1702/3, Westfield, MA), d/o Robert & Mary (X) Ashley; he d. 24 Sep 1687, Westfield, MA; **3 sons, 5 daus**

Samuel[4], b. c. 1644, Farmington; m. Mary Orton (b. 16 May 1650, Windsor, CT), d/o Thomas & Margaret (Pell) Orton; he d. 27 Nov 1711, Westfield, MA; **no issue**

Thomas[4], b. a. 1648 Farmington; m/1, 1670, Mary Gridley – **2 ch**, m/2, 7 Oct 167, Mary Spencer – **6 ch**, m/3, 25 Jan 1692, Sarah (Dumbleton) Leonard – **2 twin daus;** perhaps m. again p. 1694, when Sarah d., but no info

Mary[4], b. c. 1650, Farmington; m. a. 1669. Isaac Bronson; **9 ch**

Stephen[4], b. c. 1652, Farmington; m. Sarah Wadsworth; he d. 6 Jan 1717/8; **5 ch**

Susannah[4], b. c. 1654. Farmington; m. 1 Oct 1683, Farmington, Joseph Langdon, s/o Jean/John Langdon; she d. 5 Dec 1712, Farmington; **9 ch**

Joseph[4], b. c. 1656, Farmington; m/1, 17 Sep 1691, Elizabeth Warner – **1 son**, m/2, 3 May 1727 – **1 dau**

Caleb[4], b. c. 1658, Farmington; m/1, 9 Aug 1693, Westfield, MA Elizabeth Salmon – **5 ch** m/2, a.. 1712, X Gillette; he d. 10 Jun 1712, Farmington

REF: Cemetery Records, Somers, CT; ROOT, James Pierce, *Root Genealogical Records 1600-1870* (NYC, 1870); Vital records – Farmington, CT, Westfield, MA.

ROY, Marie – see **JAUDON**, Daniel

ROZIER, John (Rev.)

b. 30 Sep 1604, London, ENG, s/o Robert Rosier, waterman, grs/o Jean/John (b. FR) who, according to a document, came for "religion & is of the Frenche churche"

educated at Cambridge Univ.; Episcopal/Ch of England minister

by 1637/9 - in VA

m. a. 12 Oct 1637, VA, Elizabeth (Jane) Hillier (c. 1603, ENG-p. 25 Feb 1659, VA), d/o John Hillier

by Mar 1642 - on Eastern Shore, MD

d. a. 15 Dec 1660, wp, Westmoreland Co, VA

CHILD:

John II[2], b. p. 1638, VA; m. a. 1668, VA, Mary Williamson (11 Nov 1662, VA-c. 1715, VA), d/o James and Ann (Underwood) Williamson of Isle of Wight Co, VA; he d. p. 28 Sep 1705, wd-a. 31 Oct 1705, wp, Washington Parish, Westmoreland Co., VA

CHILDREN:

David[3] b. c. 1668, VA; m. by 24 Nov 1688, Sarah Sherwood, d/o Phillip of Rappahannock Co., VA; he d. c. 1748, VA

CHILD:

David II[4], b. 1690, VA; <u>m/1</u>, by 1710, Eleanor Field d/o Abraham II, <u>m/2</u>, Anne Merritt, d/o Mary (X) Merritt; he d. a. Jun 1760, wp, Halifax Co., VA; **5 ch**?

Elizabeth[3] m. by 1705, X Leftwich; d. p. 21 Sep 1759, wd - a. Jun 1760, wp, Halifax Co., VA; **4 ch**

Bridges[3] m. Elizabeth F.

John III[3], d. a. 1702

Williamson[3] (f) d. a. 1702

REF: Wills, John I & II; PERRY, JR, *The Formation of a Society on VA's Eastern Shore, 1615-1655*(Chapel Hill, NC, 1990); BROCK, RA, *Documents Relating to Huguenot Emigration,* Baltimore, 1962; SCHNABEL, R.D, *VA-NC Roziers.*; *A Bridge to France* (Documentary Records, 1571-1787); BIGGS, Kate Britt, *Musselwhites & Allied Families* (1962), Records from *Allens in London* – St. Andrew's, Hubbard's Parish, Billingsgate Ward; Church Recs – Huguenot Society of London.

RUCKER, Peter

b. c. 1670. prob. GER or Alsace Lorraine area of FR, name prob. Rücker/Rücher - **all speculation – no proof**; Rucker is not "very" French, Rucher would have been a poss. FR spelling

bet 1690-1700 - to Essex Co, VA; he paid "tythes" in 1704, on 500 acres of land, c. 30 mi s.e. of Fredericksburg

m. Elizabeth (Fielding**?**), she d. c. 1752, Orange Co, VA

24 Apr 1704 - petitioned for naturalization; on the list with French Refugees; he was a Protestant & supported the Anglican Ch; naturalization granted, 8 May 1704; name used was *Peter Ruckes*

d. p. 18 Jan 1742/3, wd - a. 23 Feb 1743/4, wp, Orange Co, VA; will mentions wife, dau Margaret & her husband Isaac Tinsley, son Ephraim, dau Ann Cook & her husband Shem Cook, sons Thomas, William, James, dau Elizabeth Pearce, dau Mary Offell – son John must have d. a. 18 Jan 1742/3

CHILDREN:

John[2], b. c. 1701, Essex Co, VA; m. Susannah (**prob.**) Phillips (d. c. 1790, Amherst Co, VA), d/o William& Susannah (Lloyd) Phillips; liv Spotsylvania/Orange Co, VA; he d. p. 11 Jan 1742/3, wd - a. 28 Jan 1742/3, wp Orange Co, VA; **12 ch**

Peter[2], b. c. 1703, Essex Co, VA; prob. d. young, no mention p. 1707/8

Thomas[2], b. c. 1705, Essex Co, VA; m. by 1732, VA, Elizabeth Reynolds (1714, Essex Co, VA-c. 1788, Culpeper Co, VA), d/o Cornelius & Martha (X) Reynolds; he d. p. 11 Jun 1763, wd - a. 20 Oct 1763, wp, Bromfield Parish, Culpeper Co, VA; **13 ch**

Elizabeth[2], b. Essex Co, VA; m. James Pierce/Pearce (d. 1778); lived Orange Co, VA; **6 ch**

Margaret[2], b. Essex Co, VA; m. c. 1728, Isaac Tinsley (c. 1704/06, Essex Co, VA-p. 13 Mar 1776, wd- -a. 28 Aug 1777, appraisal, Amelia Co, VA), s/o Thomas III and Sarah (Jackson) Tinsley; lived in what was Orange, later Culpeper, now Madison Co, VA; she d. p. 1771 **son**

William[2], b. Essex Co, VA; m. Honor/Honar X; he d. c. 1794, Amelia Co, VA; **8 ch**

Mary[2], b. Essex Co, VA; m. a. 6 Feb 1730, William Offill/Offall; Wm. patented land in Orange, Rockingham and Page Counties, VA; **5 ch**

James[2], b. Essex Co, VA; m. Margaret X; he d. c. 1804, in what is now Greenbrier Co, WV; at least **3 ch**

Ephraim[2], b. Essex Co, VA; m. c. 1738, Margaret Vawter of Essex Co, VA, d/o John and Margaret (Noel) Vawter; he d. p. 24 Sep 1796, wd - a. 28 Dec 1796, wp, Madison Co, VA; **8 ch**

Ann[2], b. Essex Co, VA; m. Shem Cook; moved to Amelia Co, VA, 1758, on land next to sister

Margaret Tinsley.

REF: WHITLEY, Edythe Johns Rucker - *History of the Rucker Family and Their Descendants* (Nashville, TN, 1927); "Naturalizations of French Refugees" in *The Huguenot*, Publication #29 (1979-81) - *Legislative Journals of the Council of Colonial VA* ed. by H. R. McIlwaine (1918, Richmond, VA), Vol. I, p. 390; ALLEN, Alice Rucker - *Rucker Heritage* (Austin, TX); Will Books of Culpeper, Madison & Orange Counties, VA; WOOD, Sudie Rucker - *The Rucker Family Genealogy* (Richmond, VA, 1932), pp. 1-3, 174-78; HUTTON, Mary Louise Marshall, *Seventeenth Century Colonial Ancestors* (Baltimore, 1983).

RULON/ROULAN(D)/ROUILLON/RULONG, Ruel Pierre

b. Bordeaux, FR; he was Huguenot but his brothers were Catholic; it is said that his bros assisted him in his escape by hiding him in a wine cask and putting it on board a ship bound for America
arr c. 1685- prob. NY, poss. went to Huntington, LI
1704- in Monmouth Co, NJ
m. XX, NJ
d. 1710, Monmouth Co, NJ
CHILDREN (poss. 1 more son; birth order uncertain, David said to have been the youngest son):
Peter[2]
Jesse[2]
Jonathan[2]
Joseph[2]
Luke[2]
David[2], b. c. 1704; m. 1725, Exercise Allen (b. 13 Aug 1705), d/o Henry & Hannah (Corlies) Allen (a Quaker family); settled Barnegat (then in Monmouth Co, now in Ocean Co.); he d. 15 3rd mo 1778, Burlington Co, NJ; he was a weaver
CHILDREN (7 of 12):
    Catherine[3], b. 7th mo 1726 ,m. 10 9th mo 1743, Shrewsbury, NJ, Benjamin Swain – **1 dau**
    Hannah[3], b. 5 2nd mo 1728, m/1, p. 13 Apr 1748 (date of marr. lic.), Jonathan Browne of Burlington, s/o Jebulon & Martha (X) Browne, m/2, X Hepburn – **2 daus**
    Mary[3], b. 5 5th mo 1730, m. William Cubberley (1720-1774), s/o James & Mary (X) Cubberley – **6 ch**
    David[3] m. Esther Camburn
    Henry[3], b. 5 6th mo 1732, m. Theodosa Robbins (b. 15 12mo 1742), he d. 1792– **10 ch**
    Lydia[3], b. 15 12th mo 1737, m. John Cubberley, bro/o William
    Rachel[3], m. Jesse Camburn, bro/of Esther
Harriet[2]

REF: RULON, John C., *The Rulon Family & Their Descendants* (Philadelphia, 1870); REYNOLDS, Mrs. Marion, *Rulon (Rouillon) Family History* (Oct 1969); KOEHLER, Albert F., *The Huguenots or The Early French in NJ*; WEST, Joseph H., *The Hutchinson Family* (Trenton, NJ, 1885).

RUT(T)AN, Abraham

bp. 10 Jun 1658, Metz, Lorraine, FR, s/o David and Anne (de Bize) Rutan
m. by Oct 1683, Marie Petilion (d. p. 19 Feb 1712/3, wd-a. 19 May 1713, wp, New Barbados, NJ)
fled the Palatinate; prob. arr America w/ the Abraham Hasbrouck party from Mannheim, 1 of the founders of New Paltz
1 Sep 1687 – oath of naturalization, Ulster Co, NY
d. p. 10 Sep 1712, wd-a. 19 May 1713, wp, New Barbados, NJ
CHILDREN:
Daniel[2], bp. 23 Sep 1684, New Paltz; m. 1710, Armtie Hanse Spier

Pouel /Paul[2], bp. 20 Mar 1685/6, New Paltz; m/1, Sleepy Hollow Ch, Engeltie/Angelica Davids (who
    d. c. 1716), m/2, 31 Jan 1719, Sleepy Hollow Ch, Eliezabet/Elizabeth Fosuur/ Foshay, bp. 2
    Aug 1698, Philipsburgh, Westchester Co, NY; he d. p. 1740

David[2], bp. 17 Apr 1688, New Paltz; d. 1775, Morristown, NJ, unmarr.

Esther[2], bp. 14 May 1690; d. 5 Aug 1690, New Paltz

Pieter/Peter[2], bp. 24 Oct 1691, New Paltz; m/1, 1713, Geertury Vanderhoef, m/2, Elizabeth (X) Sickles,
    widow/o Abraham Sickles, Sr.

Hester[2], bp. 1694, Kingston, NY

Mary[2], bp. 1701, Kingston, NY; m. 1721, Hackensack, NJ, Thomas Spier

Abraham[2], b. 1702

Susanna[2], m. by 1724, Second River, NJ, Johannes Spier; in mother's will

Sara[2], bp. 1703; m. by 1726, Charles Morgan, Jr. of Staten Island

Samuel[2], bp. 1710; m. 1733, Second River, NJ, Maria Stoutenburgh

NOTE: Name is consistently Rutan, Ruttan, NOT Rutemps

REF: Baptismal Record from Reformed Church of Metz; Calendar of Wills, 1670-1730, NJ Archives, Vol. I; *First
Record Book of the Old Dutch Church of Sleepy Hollow, Organized in 1697 and now The Reformed Church of Tarrytown,
NY,* 5th Division/Book; BAIRD, Charles W., *History of the Huguenot Emigration to America* (Baltimore, 1966);
VEERSTEEG, Dingman, *Records of the Reformed Dutch Ch of New Paltz, NY* (Baltimore, 1977).

S

St. JULIEN/JULIEN/JULIAN, Pierre de, Sieur de Malacare

had sis Marie who m. John Aldercron; she d. a. 24 Apr 1707, wp, Dublin, IRE

m. Vitré, Bretagne, FR, now in Ille-et-Vilaine Dépt, Bretagne, Jeanne LeFèvre, d/o Daniel LeFèvre & his 2nd wife Marie Bozault

c. 1685- to ENG – liv. in St. Anne's Westminster Parish in 1704

d. a. 4 Dec 1705, wp, London; will mentions sis Marie, sons Lewis, Paul & Peter, daus Jane Renata, Emilia, Margaret and Carolina, gr dau Jane Carolina Ravenal (called Jeanne Charlotte in her aunt Aldercron's will)

CHILDREN:

Aimée[2], b. 7 Mar 1667; d. 22 Jan 1705/6

Charlotte/Carolina[2], b. 15 May 1668, Vitré; m. 24 Oct 1687, Pompion Hill Plantation, on the w. branch of the Cooper River, SC (nr. Charleston), <u>René Ravenel</u>, Sieur de la Massais/La Haute Massais (b. 26 Sep 1656 Vitré); both d. Charleston, SC; **issue**

Pierre[2], b. 4 Jul 1669, Vitré; m. 1687, Damaris Elizabeth LeSerrurier (she d. 1737), d/o <u>Jacques & Elizabeth (Léger) LeSerrurier</u>; naturalized London, Apr 1693; to SC, where he was naturalized in 1696; he d. 1719, SC

CHILDREN (b. SC):

Pierre[3], b. 1696; m. 1 Jun 1727, Sarah Godin; d. 1742/3; **issue**

Jacques/James[3], b. 1698; d. 1746; **no issue**

Paul[3], b. a. 1700; <u>m/1</u>, London his 1st cousin <u>Mary Amey Ravenel</u>, m/2, Mary Verditty – **issue**; settled 1714/16, Hanover Co, SC; d. a. Dec 1741, wp; wife m/2, 1744, Thomas Monck

Henry[3], b. 1698; d. 1768, wp, 6 Jan 1769; **no issue**

Joseph[3], m. 1724, Elizabeth Mayrant; d. 1746

Alexander[3]

Daniel[3]

Elizabeth Damaris[3], b. 17 Dec 1690, Charleston, SC; m. a. 1729, Daniel Ravenel, s/o <u>René & Charlotte (de St. Julian) Ravenel</u>; he d. 1781

Jeanne Marie[3]. b. 1704; m. 9 Dec 1728, Isaac Mazyck; she d. 1764

Louis[2], b. 5 Aug 1670; naturalized SC, 1696

Marguerite/Margaret[2], b. 19 Dec 1671; she d. a. 13 Oct 1705; **no issue**

Paul[2], b. 4 Dec 1673

Émilie/Emilia[2], b. 30 Jan 1675; m. Peter Dufoussat

Jeanne Renée/Jane Renata[2], b. 6 May 1678; m. X d'Arabin; **issue**

Marie Ester[2], b. 4 Dec 1679; not in father's will, prob. d. young

?Henri[2]

REF: BAIRD, Charles W., *History of Huguenot Emigration to America*; WHITE, Rebecca D., *The Julian Family In Bohemia Manor, Cecil Co, MD* (July, 1945); MANLEY, Elizabeth C., *The Julians & Allied Families* (Cleveland, TN 1972); JULIAN, Paul R., "A Genealogy of the de St. Julian Family of SC" in *Transactions of the Huguenot Society of SC*, Vol. 105 (2001); BOCKSTRUCK, Lloyd D., *Denizations & Naturalizations in the British Colonies in America, 1607-1775*, p. 251 (Baltimore, 2005); NORTH, Dorothy, *Huguenot Wills & Administrations in England & Ireland, 1617-1849* (London, ENG, 2007).

St. JULIEN/JULIEN/JULIAN, René de

b. c. 1668, FR, *poss.* 4 Jul 1669. Vitré, Bretagne, e. of Rennes; some sources say he was b. in Paris, orphaned young; he enlisted in the army at an early age; the name evolved from de St. Julien to just Julien/Julian

by 1688 - was in ENG where he was in the army of King James II during the English Revolution

1690 - fought for the English in the Battle of Boyne in IRE; described as a very big man, with red hair & a quick temper; a staunch Presbyterian; for his services King William gave him a land grant in America, prob. in the James River District in what is now MD

during a stopover in Bermuda, on his way to America, he m. c. 1695, Mary Bullock (1677-1760), *poss.* d/o Stephen & Mary (X) Bullock, Quakers

c. 1700 - arr America; went to SC

1 Sep 1706 - deed mentions land owned by René Julien in Berkeley Co, SC; there was a Pierre Julien there, *poss.* an older bro of René's, but that has **not** been proven

c. 1712? - went to Cecil Co, MD on the e. shore of the Chesapeake; believed the deaths of 2 sons were due to the climate in SC; may have been more like 1720, when there is a land lease by him in Bohemia Manor, dated, 1 May 1720; but he was in MD by 1716, when son Isaac was b.

c. 15 May 1737 - moved to Frederick Co, VA w/ 5 of his sons

p. 1744, René & his wife d. Frederick Co, VA; bur. Opequon Presbyterian Ch, nr. Winchester

CHILDREN:

2 sons[2], b. & d. young. SC

Stephen[2], b. 1704, SC; m/1, Aletha Bouchelle (bur. 6 Apr 1743) – **3 ch**, m/2, 4 Jul 1743, Ann Hedges, d/o or widow/o William Hedges – **1 son**; the # of ch by each wife "varies " – all that can be said is that he had at least **4 sons**; liv. Prince George's Co, MD

George[2], b. 1706, prob. SC, to VA w/ parents; m. Martha X; 1766, bought land in Mecklenburg Co, NC, which later became part of York Co, SC; Tory during the Rev. War and suffered mortal wounds in a battle at the Fort of Dorchester & d. 1781, at the Creek Meeting House on the Ashley River below Dorchester

John[2], prob. unmarried; went to VA w/parents; 1762, rec. a land grant for 200 acres on Bush Creek, Orange Co, NC; bur. Trogdon Graveyard, nr. Randleman, Randolph Co, NC; **no descendants**

Peter[2], b. c. 1712/4; to VA, w/parents; Regulator for Orange Co, NC; said to have m. 4 times; **1** son by a wife named Mary X, **3 sons** by Susannah Hedges; d. 1806

Mary[2], m. 19 Sep 1734, St. Stephen's Parish, Cecil Co, MD, John Thompson; at least 1 son **Samuel**[3]

Isaac[2], b. 30 Nov 1716, St. Ann's Parish, Annapolis, MD; m. 10 Sep 1741, Frederick Co, VA, Barbara White, d/o Dr. Robert & Maragaret (Hoge) White, from Paisley, SCOT; he d. 8 Jul 1778, Randolph Co, NC, when he was bitten by a rattlesnake; bur. Trogdon Graveyard

CHILDREN, b. Winchester Co, VA:

Martha[3], b, 1744; m. c. 1762, Nehemiah Odell, Regulator; d. 10 May 1824, Randolph Co, NC, both bur. Gray's Chapel/Trogdon Cemetery, Randolph Co, NC; **issue**

Margaret[3], m. John Alred

Catherine[3], m. X Long (*prob.* Solomon a Methodist minister, br/o Tobias, below)

Rebecca[3], b. 17 Mar 1748; m. May 1771, Guilford Co, NC, Samuel Frazier, Delegate to 1st Constitutional Convention of TN (1796), a Quaker, Gov. and Senator; she d. 23 Aug 1828, Knox Co, TN

Isaac[3], b. 1751; m. Randolph Co, NC, Sarah Long (1759, PA [now MD]-1845, Wayne Co, IN), d/o Tobias Long, s/o Edward Langue (d. a. 10 Jun 1735, wp, Cecil Co, MD) & wife Sisley; Isaac d. 17 Feb 1831, Wayne Co, IN; **10 ch**

René[3], b. 1756; m. Randolph Co, NC, Catherine Madon; to Knox Co, TN; descendants to MO

Abigail[3], m. Randolph Co, NC, Samuel Trogdon; **8 ch**

René[2], b. p. 1716; to VA w/ parents, then to GA w/ Gen. Oglethorpe; **issue**

Jacob[2], m. 2 Feb 1743, Catherine Hedges, d/o Joseph Hedges; d. a. 30 Aug 1751, wp, Pr. George 's Co, MD; **2 ch** who left no descendants

Catherine[2], m. 11 Sep 1747, Joseph Wood III; remained in Frederick Co, MD; **issue**

poss another dau, Ruth?

REF: BAIRD, Charles W., *History of Huguenot Emigration to America*; WHITE, Rebecca Downey., *The Julian Family in Bohemia Manor, Cecil Co, MD* (July, 1945); MANLEY, Elizabeth Cate., *The Julians & Allied Families* (Cleveland, TN 1972); HINE, Frances Julian, *The Julian Family* (Winston-Salem, NC, Sep 1974); ROUTH, Lawrence W., *The Rouths of Randolph, NC* (not dated, not pub.); O'DELL, Cecil, *Pioneers of Old Frederick Co, VA* (burial records, Winchester, VA;

KERNS, Wilmer L., *Frederick Co, VA: Settlement & Some 1ˢᵗ Families of Back Creek Valley* (Baltimore, 1995); gravestone pictures, Trogdon Cemetery.

SALLÉ(E)/SALLEY, Abraham

b. 22 Feb, bp. 25 Feb 1673/4, St. Martin-de- Ré, Île de Ré, FR, s/o Jean & Marie (Martin) Sallé; Jean (bp. 23 Mar 1624/5, Courteil, Mougon Parish, Poitou), was a *maître cordonnier* (master shoemaker) in the Île de Ré; Marie was Jean's 2ⁿᵈ wife, 1ˢᵗ wife was Claudia Martin, Marie's sis, both d/o Jacques & Judith (Fortier) Martin

m. 1699, St.-Catherine's-by-the-Tower Ch, London, ENG, Olive (middle name Olympia?) Perrault, prob. d/o or sis/o Daniel Perrault/Perreau, commander of the *Peter & Anthony,* that brought FR refugees to VA in 1700; she d. a. 1714, VA, when Abraham was listed w/ 5 sons, 1 dau, no wife

1700 - NY petitioned governor & council for denization

by 10 Nov 1701 - was in Manakintown, VA, where he was a merchant, Clerk of King William Parish, Capt. of the militia, Justice of Henrico Co.

9 Aug 1718 – wrote his will

d. a. Mar 1719/20, wp, Henrico Co, VA; will names sons Abraham, Jacob, Isaac, William, Peter, dau Olive Magdaleine, mentions that they are entitled to any estate remaining in FR & ENG + his "title" in FR

CHILDREN:

Abraham², b. 3 Sep, bp 17 Nov 1700, FR Church, NYC; m. c. 1720, Magdelaine Amonet (d. 1756 Chesterfield Co, VA), d/o Jacob Amonet; he d. 15 Feb 1731, Henrico Co, VA; **6 ch**

Jacob², b. 28 Jul, bp. 6 Aug 1701, FR CH, NYC; d. 1720, unmarr., soon after the d. of his father

Isaac², b. 1703/04 Manakin, VA; d. bet. 21 Feb 1729/30-3 Feb 173/31, intestate

Guillaume/ William², b. 1706/7, VA; m/1, 1727, Elizabeth Gévaudan (d. 27 Jul 1739), d/o Antoine Gévaudan, m/2, c. 1740, Magdelaine Chastain, d/o Pierre Chastain; he d.15 Feb 1789, Buckingham Co, VA

CHILDREN, m/1:

Elizabeth³, b. 4 Jul 1728; d. young

Elizabeth³, b. 21 Feb 1729/30

William³, b. 17 Apr 1732; d. young

William³, b. 8 May 1734; m. c. 1755, Nancy X; d. c. 1816/20, Washington Co, KY; **9 sons, 7 daus**

Isaac³, b. 27 Jul 1739; d. young

CHILDREN, m/2:

Isaac³, b. 22 Apr 1741; m. Frances Eden?

Pierre/Peter³, b. 13 Jul 1743; m. XX; d. c. 1820, TN; **issue**

Jean/John³, b. 2 Nov 1745

Oliver³, b. 5 Nov 1749 (some sources say Olive, but the birth record says a son); m. Sarah Johnston, d/o William & Anne (Brumfield) Johnston; he d. c. 1832, Pulaski Co, KY; **4 sons, 2 daus**

Pierre/Peter², b. by 1708/9, Manakin, VA; m. 12 Jun 1733, Françoise Bondurant (1715-1779, Powhatan Co, VA), d/o Jean Pierre & Anne (X) Bondurant; he d. a. 27 Nov 1752, wp, Cumberland Co, VA; **6 ch**

Olive Magdaline², b. 1710/11, Manakin, VA; m. 1728 Étienne Malet

REF: BAIRD, Charles W., *History of the Huguenot Emigration to America*; REDDING, Lois H., *Family History of Harris, Patterson, Poer & Collateral Lines* (1975); JONES, W. Mac, *The Douglas Register* (Baltimore, 1966); Abraham Sallé's Will (9 Aug 1718); BAILEY, Jack D., *The Family History of the French Huguenot Abraham Salle and His Descendants* (Harrodsburg, KY, 1992); BODDIE, John Bennett, *Historical Southern* Families, Vol. I; CABELL, Priscilla Harriss, *Turff & Twigg*, Vol. 1 (Richmond, VA, 1988); SALLEE, Richard P., editor of *The Sallé Story* (Spring 1982).

SANXAY, Jacques (Rev.)

b. c. 1650, prob. Taillebourg, FR, n. Saintes, then in Saintonge, now Charente-Maritime Dépt,
    Poitou-Charentes, s/o Josué & Marie (Vivier) Sanxay

1677 – Huguenot pastor at St. Jean d'Angle, s. of Rochefort, Charente-Maritime Dépt, Poitou-Charentes

m. 28 Apr 1678, Taillebourg, Marie Moreau (d. p. 1717)

1683 – pastor at Tonnay-Boutonne, e. Rochefort, then Saintonge, now Charente-Maritime Dépt,
    Poitou-Charentes

by 1685 - a refugee in ENG

1686-1693 – pastor, St. Olave's Ch, Devon

d. c. 1693, Exeter, Devon, ENG

CHILDREN:

2 ch[2], b. FR, d. young

Daniel[2], b. c. 1679, FR; graduate of Oxford Univ; m. 24 Nov 1711, Jane Antrobus (c. 1683-31 Mar 1767),
    d/o Edmund Antrobus of Astbury, Cheshire (s. Manchester); he d. 24 Mar 1739, Cheam, Surrey, ENG;
    both bur. Cheam, s.w. of London; he was a minister

CHILDREN:

    Jane[3], b. 5 Feb 1712, Cheam; m. 14 Feb 1741, London, Rev. Thomas Smyth (c. 1704-Feb 1790);
        she d. Mar 1797; both bur. Swindon, Wiltshire, ENG; **no issue**

    James[3], b. 12 Apr 1714, Cheam; graduate of Oxford Univ; m. c. 1750, Catherine Firmin of Epsom,
        Surrey (c. 1728-12 Apr 1780); he d. 23 Jul 1766; he was a minister; both bur. Sutton, Surrey; **6
        ch**

    Edmund[3], b. 22 Aug 1715, Cheam; m. 174-, his cousin Maria Antrobus (c. 1719-28 Feb 1777), d/o
        Edmond & Mary (Webb) Antrobus, who was a bro to Edmund[3]'s mother Jane; he d. 20 Oct
        1787; he was a surgeon, Essex St, London; both bur. Cheam; **2 daus**

    Robert[3], bp. 23 Oct 1716; a druggist in the Strand, London; d. 1 Aug 1780, bur. Cheam

    Hannah[3], bp. 5 Jan 1719; m. p. 24 Dec 1748 (date of marr. settlement), her cousin John Antrobus
        (d. 22 Nov 1773), s/o Philip & Annie (Varden) Antrobus; she d. 4 Jun 1772; both bur.
        Astbury Ch, nr. Congleton, Cheshire, ENG (s. Manchester); **2 sons**

    Daniel[3], bp. 19 Feb 1720, Cheam; m. 13 Feb 1753, Susanna Dorothea Brisco; he d. 22 Dec 1769,
        bur. Cheam; **2 sons**

    Richard[3], d. young

    Mary[3], d. young

    Cecil[3], d. young

James[2], b. 2 Nov 1690, Exeter, ENG; graduate of Oxford Univ.; m/1, 22 Apr 1720, St. Martins-in-the-
    Fields, London, Charlotte Mary Gaches who was bur. 19 Sep 1722, Penzance, m/2, 22 Dec
    1731, Anna Badger (c. Sep 1709-3 Jul 1758), d/o Rev. Edward Badger; he d. 2 Apr 1768,
    Tetcott, Devon, ENG – he and Anna both bur. Tetcott (n.w. Launceston)

CHILD, m/1:

    Charlotte[3], bp. 24 Aug 1721, Penzance; m. Benjamin Bradley, a London merchant (c. 1723-c.
        1793); she d. p. Apr 1776, Penzance; **no issue**

CHILDREN, m/2:

    Anna[3], bp. 1 Oct 1733

    James[3], bp. 3 Dec 1735; d. c. 1761

    Frances[3], bp. 2 Jun 1737; d. Nov 1756

    Edward[3], bp. 9 Jun 1740

    Mary[3], bp. 6 Apr 1742; d. Jun 1813

    Claudia[3], bp. 17 Sep 1743; m. John Bradley; d. Aug 1820; **3 ch**

    John[3], bp. 10 Sep 1746; to NY, a. 1773; m. 14 Feb 1775, NY, Sarah Devoe/Devaux (8 Dec 1756-
        18 Feb 1801); he d. 10 Mar 1811, Mt. Pleasant, Westchester Co, NY; **12 ch**

Claudia[2]

Mary[2], b. Exeter; m. 1713, Rev. John Courtail of Exeter (c. 1690-Oct 1759 Exeter); **2 sons**

REF: SANXAY, Theodore F., *The Sanxay Family & Descendants of Rev. Jacques Sanxay, Huguenot Refugee to England in 1685* (privately printed, NY, 1907); CHILD, W. B., "Corrections & Additions to Published Genealogical Works" in the *NYGBR*, Vol. L, #1 (Jan, 1919), pp. 78-82

SAS(S)IN, François

23 Jul 1700 - arr in VA on the *Mary Ann*; Listed on "A List of ye French Refugees That Are Settled att ye Mannachin Town… in ye first Shipp"

he worked for 33 days in the mill kitchen, marking & clearing the Cart Road

Feb 1700/01 - on the list to rec. 1 bushel of Indian meal monthly - no wife or ch mentioned

m. by 1705, VA, Elisabeth X; she is listed as the widow of Francis Sassin in 1722; she m/2, c. 1722/3, John Deker – 1 son

12 May 1705 – naturalized, VA

1707-09 - was to rec. 100 acres for the "importation" of himself and his wife

1710-1714 - on the tithable lists

1714 – on the *Liste Généralle*, he is listed w/ a wife, 1 son, 2 daus

30 Dec 1715 - VA, the 1715 tithable list was dated – he is not on it

15 Jul 1717 – Patent #907 for 104 acres, on the s side of the James, Henrico (now Chesterfield) Co.; date misleading, Francis by estate 104 acres to son Elie c. 1715; also, Francis is not "deceased" in the record

CHILDREN:

Élias/Éli[2], b. c. 1706/7; m. c. 1728, Susanne X; d. bet 28 Feb-5 Dec 1777, Chesterfield Co, VA; deeded Patent #907 – 133 acres - to his son David, 6 Sep 1765

CHILDREN:

Pierre[3], b. 21 Dec 1729; said to have served in the Rev. War in the 5th & 9th VA Regt. of the Continental Line

Jean[3], b. 4 Oct 1732; d. young

Louis/Louy[3], b. 11 Apr 1735; d. young

David[3], b. 31 Aug 1740, King William's Parish; m. 10 Dec 1768, Elizabeth Parish; he d. a. 9 Jul 1810, letter of adm., Chesterfield Co, VA; **2 sons, 1 dau**

Richard[3], b. 1742; said to have served in the Rev. War

Alexander[3], b. c. 1744; m. 1767, Sarah/Sally Banton; he d. p. 5 Nov 1777, wd, Chesterfield Co, VA; **2 sons, 2 daus**

Olive[3], b. c. 1746; m. 18 Sep 1766, John Short; **issue**

Elizabeth[2], b. c. 1709; m. 1725, Étienne Monford

CHILDREN:

John[3], b. 29 Oct 1726

Jacob[3], b. 4 May 1729

Mary/Marie[2], b. c. 1712

REF: ALLEN, Cameron, "François Sasin/Sassin of Manakin Town: The First 6 Generations of the Sasin/Sasseen Family in America" in the *VA Genealogist,* Vol. 37 #1 (Jan/Mar 1993), Vol. 37, #2 (Apr/Jun 1993) Vol. 37 #3 (Jul/Sep 1993); *The Huguenot*, #29 (1979-1981), p. 135 (Henrico Co. Orders, 1707-09, p. 34); CABELL, Priscilla Harriss, *Turff & Twigg* (Richmond, VA, 1988).

SCHWING, Jean Martin

s/o Hans Martin Schwing, keeper of a restaurant called "Zur Blume" in Strasbourg

m. 4 May 1716, Salomée Schmidt (19 Jan 1698, Bischwiller-12 Oct 1737, Bischwiller); Bischwiller, Bas-Rhin Dépt, Alsace, FR, n.e. Strasbourg

he was a butcher

CHILDREN, surname became SWYNG/SWING:

Marie Salomé[2], b. 1 Apr 1717; d. 9 Feb 1719

Judith[2], b. 20 Apr 1718; d. 28 Nov 1719

Pierre[2], b. 18 Jan 1726; prob. d. 1761

Marie Magdeleine[2], b. 13 Nov 1717; d. 29 Aug 1729

Abraham[2], b. 6 Jan 1735; m. 20 Oct 1763, Marguerite Gutig (b. 1740); he immigrated to America; had dau
    Anna Margareta[3], b. 7 Jan 1764

Daniel[2], b. 26 May 1737; d. 25 Jul 1737

Anne Marie[2], b. 3 Dec 1719; moved to Grunnstedt or Grünnstadt

Michel[2], b. 1722, Bischwiller; to America on the *Marlborough*, arr Philadelphia, 23 Sep 1741, from
    Rotterdam, via Cowes; he must have ret. to FR, as he is on the list of the *Brotherhood,* from
    Rotterdam via Cowes, arr Philadelphia, 3 Nov 1750, when he took the Oath of Allegiance; m.
    Anna Margaretta Paris; he d. 1782 York Co, PA; 7 ch – 1st 2 bap. Lutheran Ch of St. Michael &
    Zion in Philadelphia, the others b. York , PA – **4 sons, 3 daus**

Salomé[2], b. 27 Nov 1729; to America, 1749; m. X Gump of York Co, PA; she d. 20 Sep 1793

Samuel[2], b. 6 Jun 1732; to America

REF: Church records, Bischwiller; RUPP, Rev. Israel Daniel, *A Collection of Upwards of 30,000 Names of German,
Swiss, Dutch, French Immigrants in PA from 1727-1776* (Baltimore, 1965); SWING, Albert H. & Harry P., *The First
5 Generations of the Swing Family in America* (not dated).

SÉJOURNÉ/SIGOURNEY, André

    b. 1638; family poss from Poitou where there is a town called Sigournais (now in the Vendée Dépt,
        Pays de la Loire), n.e. of La Roche-sur-Yon

    m. Charlotte Pairan; said to have d. in Oxford, MA, & bur. FR burying ground there

    winter 1681 - fled La Rochelle, went to ENG; some accounts give their "escape" from FR as being
        in 1685 at the time of the Revocation; however, that does not account for son Barthélemy
        being bap. 1682, in London

    c. 1686 - arr in Boston

    went w/ pastor Pierre Daillé and others to form a settlement at Oxford, MA; André was constable
        of "the French Plantation" (1694) & perhaps its most influential resident

    1696 - back to Boston after a massacre by Indians

    d. 16 Apr 1727, Boston, bur. Granary Burying Ground, 89 Y

    CHILDREN (one more son – no info):

    André/Andrew II[2], b. 1673, FR; m. 1700, Mary Germaine (1680, FR-20 Mar 1763/4), d/o Capt. X
        Jermon/Germaine who left La Rochelle for ENG, then to Boston, c. 1686; Andrew d. a 7 Jul 1748,
        wp, Suffolk Co, MA; he was a distiller in Boston
        CHILDREN:
        Andrew[3], b. 30 Jan 1702, Boston; m. 7 Oct 1731, Boston, Mary Ronchon, d/o John Ronchon;
            Mary d. 28 Feb 1772; he d. 4 Nov 1762; **12 ch**
        Susannah[3], b. 27 Dec 1704, Boston; m. 24 Oct 1726, Boston, Martin Brimmer (b. 1697, Osten,
            GER); she d. 18 Feb 1793
        Peter[3], b. 1 Mar 1706, Boston; m. Elizabeth Green; d. a. 14 Dec 1738, adm
        Mary[3], b. 1 Aug 1709, Boston; m 20 Feb 1734, Boston, John Baker who d. 27 Sep 1774
        Charles[3], b. 27 Apr 1711, Boston; d. 8 Dec 1731, unmarr.
        Anthony[3], b. 17 Aug 1713; m/1, 10 Apr 1740, Boston, Mary Waters of Salem – **2 daus, 1 son**,
            m/2,widow Elizabeth (Whittemore) Breed- **2 sons**, she d. 18 May 1804, Oxford, 88 Y; he
            d. a. 2 Oct 1761, wp, Suffolk Co, MA
        Daniel[3], b. 17 Nov 1715, Boston; m/1, 1735, Mary Varney (b. 14 Jan 1711), d/o James & Jane
            (Tudor) Varney, m/2, c. 1746, Joanna Tileston (d. 19 Sep 1770, Boston), m/3, 13 Feb 1780,
            Rebecca Tileston (d. 14 Jan 1807, Walden, 88 Y), poss. sis/o Joanna
        Rachel[3], b. 5 Mar 1717/8, Boston; d. 20 Sep 1719

Hannah[3], b. 27 Feb 1719, Boston; m. 23 Jun 1748, Boston, Samuel Dexter, s/o Rev. Samuel
      Dexter of Dedham (b. 16 Mar 1726); she d. 6 Nov 1784
Susanne/Susan[2], m/1, John Johnson who was killed by Indians, 25 Aug 1696, Oxford w/ his 3 ch, m/2,
      18 Apr 1700, her cousin Daniel Johonnot of Boston (1668 FR-1748 Boston, 80 Y) - **issue**
Mary[2], m. a. 1712, Boston, Antoine Olivier
Barthélemy[2], bp. 16 Apr 1682, FR Ch, Threadneedle St, London

REF: SIGOURNEY, Henry H. W., *Genealogy of the Sigourney Family* (Boston, 1857); BAIRD, Charles W., *The Huguenot Emigration to America,* (Baltimore, 1966); Daniels, George F., *History of the Town of Oxford, MA with Genealogies & Notes on Persons & Estates* (Oxford, MA, 1892; FREELAND, Mary de Witt, *The Records of Oxford, MA* (Albany, NY, 1894); Vital Records, Boston.

SELLAIRE/SALLIÈRE/CELLIER/ZELLER, Jacques de

b. 1658-60, Zurich, SWI, s/o Jean Henri Sellaire/Von Zeller
Jacques said to have been a preacher, an evangelist, who left Zurich to travel down the Rhine
m. 1683, Zwiebrücken/Deux Ponts, Clothilde de Valois (1660's, FR-2 Jan 1749, what is now Lebanon Co,
      PA)
1709 - family was in London, part of the Palatinate emigration
d. c. 1709 - in London, or at sea en route to America (embarked 25 Dec 1709) in 1710
14 Jun 1710 - family arr NY – no mention of Jacques; fam. went up the Hudson to Livingston Manor;
      son Johann Heinrich and his bro Johannes were volunteers for the Canadian Expedition of 1711
      during Queen Anne's War; they went to the Schoharie Valley in NY, 1713; bet 1723-30, to PA
there is a Fort Zeller Memorial (dedicated 14 Jun 1941) nr. Newmanstown, Lebanon Co, which states that
      "Lady Clothilde de Valois Zeller, widow of Jacques Zeller (Sallière) of Deux Ponts, France, with her
      sons Jean Henri and Jean Zeller, citizens of Great Britain, born in France Settled here June 14, 1723,
      and built a block house for the protection of the settlers on this frontier of Philadelphia and Chester
      Counties. Present stone Fort erected 1745." This fort is PA's oldest existing fort.
CHILDREN:
Jean Henri/Johann/Hans/ Heinrich[2], b. 1684, FR; m. Anna Maria Briegal (1749-a. 12 Jan 1737/8, wp,
      Lancaster Co, PA), d/o James Briegal/Von Bruegal of HOL; 2 Jun 1707 - he was said to be 23, single, a
      cooper & brewer, Lutheran; he settled Tulpehocken Twp, Lancaster Co, (now Berks), PA; d. a. 20 Jan
      1756, wp
      CHILDREN (prob. all b. Schoharie):
      Johann George[3]
      Johann Henrich[3], b. c. 1717; d. p. 1754; (called "simple" in father's will)
      Johann David[3], b. c. 1719; d. p. 1754; (called "simple" in father's will)
      Hartman[3],
      Anna Maria[3], b. 29 Dec 1715; m. c. 1728, Andreas Saltzgeber/Saltgerber; she d. p. 1776
      Barbara Elizabeth[3], m. Jonas Laure/Lerew/LaRue, Jr.
      Anna Catharina[3], b. 1717; m. 14 Jan 1743, Tulpehocken Twp., Johannes/John Pontius (18
          Aug 1717, Berglangenbach, GER-16 Jun 1792, Buffalo Twp.), s/o Hans Peter & Rosina
          Catharina (Hauch) Pontius; she d. p. 1770 Buffalo Twp, Northumberland (now Union),
          PA; **7 sons, 3 daus**; all 7 sons served in the Rev. War
      Anna Elizabeth[3], m/1, 1745, John Adam Batdorf/Battorf, s/o Johannes Martinus & Maria
          Elisabetha (Walborn) Batdorf – at least **6 ch**, m/2, 12 Nov 1758, Leonard Schwartz (d.
          1803)
      unnamed dau[3], m. Leonard Anspach; she d. a. 1748
Johannes/Jean/John George[2], b. 1686, FR; m. Anna Catharina X (d. 10 Mar 1748/9); wd, 3 Sep 1737,
      written in GER, wp, 12 Jan 1737/8, Philadelphia
      CHILDREN:
      Catherina Elisabeth[3], b. c. 1714; m. a. 1745, John George Reith (4 Jun 1714-23 Jun 1791), s/o

Johann Leonard Reith; she d. bet 1759-5 Oct 1787

Margredalis[3], b. 1715, Schoharie; m. Tobias Bickel; bur. 9 Jun 1748; **1 son, 1 dau**, poss. a 2nd son

John Henry[3], b. c. 1716; m. c. 1740, Anna/Maria Margaretta Reith (c. 1721-c. 1807), d/o Johann Leonard Reith; he d. 1789; **10 ch**

David Peter[3], b. c. 1722; m. 15 Mar 1748, Lancaster Co, PA, Maria Christina Hoerner (d. p. 1764); he d. p. 1782; **5 ch**

Peter[3], b. c. 1728; m. a. 1754, Hannah Bassler; he d. a. 17 Jul 1804; **4 ch**

Anna Maria[3]

Anna Amelia[3], m. 3 Dec 1751, Frederick Weiser, s/o Conrad Weiser

REF: EGLE, William Henry, *Notes & Queries Historical, Biographical & Genealogical, Annual Volume 1900* (Baltimore, 1970); *History of Zeller & Urich Families*; ZELLERS, John A., *A Brief History of the Zeller Family* (1945); VALENTINE, John F., "Zeller Family Reunion" in *The Pennsylvania Genealogical Magazine,* Vol. 27, #2 (1971); ALTHOUSE, Miranda Zeller donated *History of the Zeller and Urich Families* to the NHS in 1920 – she may have been the author; wills of John Henry Zeller, John Pontius; cemetery pix.

SELOIVRE/SELOVER/SELOOVER, Isaac I

b. c. 1634, FR

m. c. 1656, Susanna Sohier, b. 1638

25 Apr 1670 - Isaac was called "a coach builder & alderman of Breskens"

23 May 1673 - sold his "materials" for 1000 Carolus guilders to Jan Carton and he rented his house in Breskens to Jan; finally sells the house to Jan, on 26 Jan 1679

8 Oct 1673- joined FR Walloon Ch of Middelburg by témoignage from the Ch. in Groede; now residents of Middelburg

15 May 1681 - in a testament Isaac & Susanna say that Isaac is lying ill in bed in Schoondijke, a town 5 mi. s. of Breskens; Issac II was a schoolteacher in Schoondijke

d. a. 25 Apr 1682 wp

CHILDREN:

Isaac II[2], b. 1657, Groede or Breskens, Zeeland, HOL; Groede and Breskens n.e. of Brugge, BEL, Groede is 5 km. n. of Oostburg, HOL & Breskens is a few km. n.w. of Groede, both in Zeeland Prov; m/1, HOL, Hester Van Leuvenigh; c. 1683, to America; settled New Castle, DE – on tax rolls of Newcastle, until 1687; by 1695 in NY; a schoolteacher & reader in the New Amsterdam Reformed Dutch Ch; m/2, 23 Jan 1695, Jannekan Van Wilkenhof (Thyssen), widow of Jan Thyssen, m/3, 26 Dec 1699, NY, Judith Waldron (bp. 22 Dec 1675, Harlem, NY-1760), d/o Daniel & Sarah (Rutgers) Waldron; he d. p. 1715, prob. New Amersfoort, NY (Brooklyn)

CHILDREN, m/1:

Susanna[3], b. HOL; m. a. 1696, MD, Peter King (d. Dec 1713); she d. Jan 1714

Sarah[3], b. New Castle, DE; m. 27 Jan 1707, Herman Bussing (d. 29 Jul 1762); she d. 21 Dec 1752

CHILDREN, m/2:

Jacqyemyntie[3], bp. 27 Mar 1696

Abraham[3], bp. 29 Aug 1697; m. c. 1725, Sophia Schermerhorn (b. 9 Nov 1702), d/o Lucas Schermerhorn & Elizabeth Damen; he d. a.1749; **4 ch**

Jannetie[3], b. 29 Aug 1699

CHILDREN, m/3:

Daniel[3], bp. 14 Aug 1700; d. young

Maria[3], bp. 31 Aug 1701, NYC; m. c. 1722, Alexander Filchett

Anna/Annetze[3], bp. 21 Jul 1703, Flatlands, LI, NY; m. 1 Dec 1723, Dutch Reformed Ch New Amsterdam, Bragon Coevert/Covert (29 Mar 1696, Brooklyn, NY-1750, Millstone, Somerset, NJ), s/o Han Teunise Covert & Jannitze Brokaw (who was the d/o Bourgeon Broucard & Catherine LeFèvre); she d. Somerset Co, NJ; **10 ch**

Daniel[3], b. 12 Oct, bp 18 Oct 1704, NYC; m. 3 Sep 1726, NJ, Helena Schermerhorn (b.18 Aug

1708), sis/o Sophia who m. Abraham[3]; he d. 12 Nov 1759, NYC; **6 ch**

    Isaac[3], b. c. 1706, prob. Flatbush; m. c. 1731, Syche Pittenger/Peppenger; he d. c. 1731, Middlesex Co, NJ

    Jacob[3], b. c. 1708, NYC; m. Sarah Vanderlinde; he d. c. 1733

    Judith[3], b. c. 1710, NYC; d. 26 Jul 1743, single

    Saartje[3], b. c. 1712, NYC; m. Cornelius Hulsaert

Susanna[2], m. Jan Dermont

Sara[2], m/1, 4 Aug 1670, Meyndrick Antheuniss Fioen, m/2, Michiel Jans Faro

Abraham[2]

Elysabeth[2], m. Andries de Jonge

NOTE: Surname evolved further in America. **SLOVER** was a common form.

REF: Records from several sources in Zeeland & Leiden; FISCHER, Carl W., COVERT, William V. & PATTERSON, Maurice L., *The Covert Family* (Interlaken, NY, 1989); *Marriages from 1673 to 1801 in the Reformed Dutch Ch New Amsterdam-NYC*, Vol. IX (NY, 1940); HADLER, Mabel Jacques, *Selover-Slover Family 1641-1941*(Egeland, ND, 1941) & *Selover-Slover Family 1641-1968,* 2nd Edition (Long Beach, CA, 1968) – both self-published.

SICARD/SICORD/SEACORD, Ambroise

b. 1631, FR

m. Jeanne X (d. a. the 1698 NY census)

p. 1685- fled Mornac-sur-Seudre, Charente Maritime Dépt, Poitou-Charentes, s.e. Marennes; to ENG w/ his wife, 6 ch; he was in the salt trade, a *saunier* – Marennes is located on the salt marshes

a. 1688 - to NY; 1692, to New Rochelle, NY where he bought 95 acres

1695 - letters of denization to him & 3 sons

1698 – on census; Ambroise, Daniel & wife Catherine, Jeanne

28 Mar 1701, wd - mentions ch Ambroise, Daniel, Jacques, Marie & her husband Guillaume Landrin, Silvie & her husband François Coquillet; Daniel's wife Anne one of the signers (Ambroise had his ch sign his will as proof of their approbation.)

d. p. 9 May 1710 – real estate transaction

CHILDREN:

Jacques[2], b. FR; d. young

Ambroise II[2], b. 1666, FR; m/1, a. 4 Nov 1688, Jeanne Perron – **3 sons, 4 daus**, m/2, Jennie Sarcot?; he d. 1733, New Rochelle

Daniel[2], b. 1672, FR; m. Catherine Voertman/Woertman (b. c. 1677); he d. 1742/3; **6 sons, 3 daus**, CHILDREN (4 of 9):

    Jacques/James[3] (1699, New Rochelle-8 Nov 1773, New Rochelle) who m. Jeanne/Jane Bonnet (9 Apr 1703, New Rochelle-p. 1757, New Rochelle), d/o Daniel & Jeanne Courturier) Bonnet – **9 sons, 3 daus**, incl. **James**[4] (25 Jul 1729-a. 1771) m. 1st cousin Catherine Bertine (14 Oct 1735- a. 1790), d/o Pierre & Catherine (Sicard) Bertine – **1 son, 3 daus**; **Catherine**[4] (b. 18 Dec 1733) m. Benjamin Giraud/Gerow (b. 1739); **Mary**[4] (7 May 1742-1788) m. John Renaud (1743-1837) – **2 daus**; **Israel**[4] (1748-1819) m. Jane Coutant (26 Mar 1746-1 Sep 1794), d/o Jacques & Jeanne (Renaud) Coutant – **issue**. **Catherine**[3] who m. Daniel Giraud, s/o Daniel & Jeanne (X) Giraud/Gerow **Marie**[3] (b. 1712), m. Daniel Chadayne, s/o Jean & Judith (Tilliou) Chad(e)ayne **Isaac**[3] (1715-1759) m. Catherine LeConte (c. 1725-a.1771), d/o Josias II & Esther (Bertine) LeConte

Jacques/James[2], b. 1675, FR; m. 10 Apr 1700, FR Ch, NYC, Anne Terrier; he d. p. 1743; **5 sons, 5 daus**

CHILDREN (4 of 9):

    Jacques/James[3], b. bet. 1701/07, New Rochelle; m. Marianna Reveux/Revaux; he. d. 8 Nov

> 1773, Scarsdale, NY; **7 sons, 3 daus**
>> **Ester**[3], b. 1706, New Rochelle; m. Louis Angevine (b. 1702), grs/o <u>Louis & Marguerite (Chalons)</u>
>>> <u>Angevine</u>; she d. 1792, Scarsdale, NY; **3 sons, 5 daus**
>> **Catherine**[3], b. 1707; m. Pierre/Peter Bertine, s/o <u>Pierre & Anne (Barron) Bertine</u>; **3 sons, 6 daus**
>> **Jean/John**[3], b. 8 Jun 1712; m. Maria <u>Giraud/Gerow</u> (b. c. 1727/8), sis/o Benjamin (b. 1739) above
> (prob.) **Jeanne**[2], b. c. 1675/6; not in father's will
> **Marie**[2], b. 1677 FR; m. Guillaume/William Landrin(e) (1666-p. 1732); **1 son, 2 daus**
> **Silvie**[2], b. FR; m. <u>François Coquillet</u>; dau **Silvie**[3] m. Abraham Mabie, grgrgrs/o <u>Pierre Mabille</u> - **5 ch**

REF: GRAY, Henry David, "*Early History of the Sicard-Secor Family*" in the *NYGBR*, Vol. LXVIII, #4 (Oct, 1937); SEACORD, Morgan H., *Biographical Sketches & Index of the Huguenot Settlers of New Rochelle 1687-1776* (New Rochelle, 1941); FORBES, Jeanne A., *Records of the Town of New Rochelle 1699-1828* (New Rochelle, 1916) ; FROST, Josephine C., *Ancestors of Evelyn Wood Keeler, Wife of Willard Underhill Taylor* (1939); record from Charente-Maritime Archives

SILLE, Nicasius de

> b. 23 Sep 1610, Arnheim, HOL, s/o Laurens de Sille & Wallburga Everwijn
> m/1, Amsterdam, c. 1638/9, Cornelia Meulmans, d/o Peter Meulmans & Anna Marschalk
> summer 1653 - arr New Amsterdam; commissioned as the 1st Councillor to Dir. Gen. Peter
>> Stuyvesant; he was well versed in the law and military affairs; serv in this office until
>> 1660; he was a widower w/ 5 ch; a doctor of law
> bet 1654-56 - held a variety of civic offices
> m/2, 26 May 1655, Tryntje/Catherine Creiger/Crougers, d/o Capt. Martin Krieger – **no issue**
> 1657 – he built the 1st stone house in New Utrecht, L.I.; one of the original proprietors
> served as Atty General of the Province as well as Chancellor & Sheriff
> 1668- he and Tryntje separated; a committee was appt by the Gov. to attempt a reconciliation which
>> did not happen
> d. a. 1674
> CHILDREN, m/1:
> **Walburga**[2], b. 30 Nov 1639, Maastricht (capital of Limburg Prov, extreme s.e. HOL very close to BEL
>> & GER); <u>m/1</u>, 29 Feb 1660, Frans Cregier, br/o her stepmother Tryntje -**1 dau**; <u>m/2</u>, 13 May 1669,
>> Wilhelm/William Bogardus as his 2nd wife; William was the s/o Rev. Everardus & Anneke (Webber)
>> Bogardus; Wm. had div his 1st wife a month earlier – **7 ch**
> **Anna**[2], b. 6 Nov 1640, Maastricht; <u>m/1</u>, 29 Feb 1660, Hendrick Kip, Jr; <u>m/2</u>, Francoys de Bruyenne/de
>> Bruyn
> **Gerardina/Gerdientje**[2], b. 10 Feb 1642, Amsterdam; m. Jan Gerretse Van Couvenhoven
> **Laurens**[2], b. 2 Oct 1643, Wyt, nr. Maastricht; <u>m/1</u>, X Creiger, d/o Capt. Martin Creiger & sis/o his
>> stepmother Tryntje; went to HOL, <u>m/2</u>, XX who d. 27 Aug 1704, Waalwyt; **no issue in America**
> **Petrus**[2], b. 6 Jan 16--,Maastricht; d. 8 Dec 1663, Nieuw Amstel in the Zuyd (South) River; unmarr.

REF: KIP, Frederick E., *The Kip Family* (1928); KOEHLER, Sara Morton, *Register of Ancestors of the Hugue-not Society of NJ* (1965); BERGEN, Teunis G., *Register of the Early Settlers of Kings Co;* GANNON, Peter S., editor, *Huguenot Refugees in the Settling of Colonial America* (NY);l MATTHEWS, Catherine T.V., "The DeSille Family of Holland" in *NYGBR* (Jan 1903).

SIMONS/SIMONDS, Benjamin

> b. 1672, La Rochelle, FR; orphaned early, adopted by Martha, wife of Josias DuPré, a Huguenot
>> minister; Martha has been said to have been his aunt
> 1685 - from FR to Middelburg, HOL w/ the DuPré family; later to ENG, then to Carolina
> by 1686 - was liv. in the Orange Quarter on the s. bank of the east branch of the Cooper River

m. 1692 - Mary Esther DuPré, d/o Josias I & Martha (X) DuPré; Mary d. 1737

became an extensive landowner in Berkeley Co., SC

d. 1717, SC

CHILDREN:

Peter[2], b. 1693; m. 1716, Magdalen (Cordes) Harris, a widow; he was a Capt of the Militia & Justice of the Peace in St. Thomas & St. Denis Parish; killed 1724, while making an arrest; **3 ch**

male child[2], b & d 1695

Samuel Du Pré[2], b. 1696; d. 1759

Francis[2], b. 1697; d. 1731

Ann[2], b. 1699

Mary[2], b. 1701

Elizabeth[2], b. 1705; m. 1728, James Paul Cordes

Martha[2], b. 1706; m. 1726, Archibald Young; **issue**

Benjamin[2], b. 1708; d. 1709

Esther[2], b. 1710

Judith[2], b. 1712; m. 1751, Alexander Swinton; d. 1781; **issue**

Benjamin II[2], b. 1713; m/1, 1736, Ann Keating (b. 1718, d. 1754) – **11 ch**, m/2, 1755, widow Ann (Dymes) Dewick (d. 1776) – **5 ch**; he had a counting house in Charleston, was a prosperous rice planter, he was Commissary General (1766-71), member of the Commons House of Assembly, (1760-69), Justice of the Peace (1761); he d. 1772

Thomas[2], b. 1715; d. 1716

Catherine[2], b. 1717; d. 1731

REF: SIMONS, Robert Bentham, *Thomas Grange Simons III, His Forebears & Relations* (Charleston, 1954); Transactions of the Huguenot Society of SC, #75 (1970), p. 87.

SOBLET/SUBLET(TE), Jean

b. c. 1617/8, native of Beaumont; *notaire royal*, royal notary; there are several places named Beaumont, he was *poss.* from what is now Beaumont-en-Argonne, s. of Mouzon and s.e. of Sedan, in the Ardennes Dépt. of Champagne

m. Judith Lombard, of Sedan (in the Ardennes Dépt, very near the BEL border)

bur. 10 Feb 1674, Sedan, FR, age 56Y

CHILDREN (all baptized Sedan):

Jean[2], bp. 11 Dec 1644; m. 24 Nov 1675, Marie Martinet (25 yrs. old), d/o Nicolas & Jeanne (Buisset) Martinet of Sedan; by 1683, they were in Mannheim; many Huguenots in Mannheim were imprisoned in Vincennes (just e. of Paris), c. 1688, by the troops of Louis XIV; others, fled to Magdeburg (s.w. of Berlin) and elsewhere; no further records on him; he was called a *mr. écrivain*, a master scrivener, 31 yrs, liv in Sedan, at the time of his marr.

CHILDREN:

Jean[3], bp. 29 Apr 1677 Sedan, FR

Abraham[3], bp. 24 Aug 1679 Sedan, FR

Anne[3], bp. 30 Aug 1681, Sedan, FR

Antoine[3], b. 24 Oct, bp. 28 Oct 1685. Mannheim, GER

Isaac[3], b. 15 Sep, bp. 20 Sep 1685. Mannheim, GER

Louise Christine[3], b. 4 Nov, bp. 12 Nov 1687, Mannheim, GER

Élisabeth[2], b. 16 Jul 1647; prob. d. young

Abraham[2], b. 4 Dec, bp. 6 Dec 1648; m. 31 Mar 1675, Sedan Susanne Briant, d/o Jacques & Susanne (Gérard) Brian(t); Abraham was 26, liv. Sedan Torcy; he was in 1675, an *ouvrier en tabac* (a tobacco worker), in 1678, a *monteur* (setter or mounter of jewels), in 1680, a *md.*(prob. a merchant) *à St. Menges* (n.w. of Sedan),; 1681, fled to Mannheim (now in Baden-Württemberg), GER, and went to Wesel in Westphalia, c. 1688, thus avoiding imprisonment in Vincennes; then to HOL, ENG; May

1698, Abraham, his wife and 4 ch were on the Royal Bounty Rolls, rec. £1.15.0; arr 12 Jul 1700, Jamestowne, VA on the *Mary Ann*, with sons Abraham and Jacques (some accounts say that Pierre was 1 of those 2 sons but he would have been 5 yrs. old, so not likely); wife arr 20 Sep 1700, on the *Peter and Anthony* with the other ch; Abraham assumed a fairly prominent position in the settlement from the beginning; she d. a. 1714; he d. p. 30 Dec 1715, Manakintown, VA

CHLDREN:

Anne[3], bp. 22 Oct 1675, Sedan, FR, godparents were Philbert Soblet & wife Anne Godin; m. Pierre Chastain as his 2nd wife; she d. 3 Apr 1723

Jean[3], bp. 29 Apr 1677, Sedan, FR; bur 7 Aug 1678, Sedan

Jacob[3], bp. 14 Sep 1678, Sedan, FR

*Abraham[3], b. a. 1680, Sedan, FR; m. a. 1714, Mary X; d. a. 6 Jun 1720, Powhatan Co, VA; **no heirs**

Jean[3], bp. 10 Mar 1680, Sedan, FR; bur. 17 Oct 1680, Sedan

Agnes[3], bp. 17 Aug 1681, Mannheim, GER

*Jacques/James[3], b. prob. Mannheim; m. c. 1711, Martha X; he d. a. 16 Mar 1741/2, wp, Goochland Co, VA; at least **1 son (1 dau**?)

Marie[3], b. 30 Sep 1688; bp 2 Oct 1688, Mannheim, GER

François[3], b. 15 Jan, bp. 19 Jan 1694, Wesel, GER

Pierre Louis[3], b.15 Aug, bp. 19 Aug 1695, Wesel, GER; m/1, XX – **1 son**, m/2, Marthe Martain, d/o Jérémie & Marie (Archambeau) Martain – **5 sons, 1 dau**; he d. a. 27 Jan 1755, wp, Cumberland Co, VA

Robert[3], b. 20 Apr 1698; bp 1 May 1698, Church of LaPatente, London (Berwick St, Soho); d. young

*these 2 sons are not in the bap. records but are said to be his sons; placement in the birth order is somewhat arbitrary; there are "gaps" between 1681-1687 and 1688--1693 – they may both have been born then, which means they were b. in GER, not FR. Since they both accompanied their father to VA, they would had to have been of a reasonable age, say 16-20; Jacob must have d. young or was not strong enough

Catherine[2], b. 21 Jun, bp. 23 Jun 1652; d. young

Judit[2], b. 7 May, bp. 9 May 1655; m. 4 Jun 1679, Sedan, Hubert Toussaint (bp. 17 Jan 1655, Sedan), s/o Jean & Suzanne (LeRoy) Toussaint; at least 2 ch: **Jean**[3], bp. 29 Sep 1680, bur 12 Oct 1682, Sedan, **David**[3], bp. 8 Feb 1682, bur 8 Nov 1682, Sedan

Élisabeth[2], bp. 2 Jan 1658; m. 3 Aug 1681, Sedan, Daniel Renard, age 35, a *bourgeois* liv. Sedan

Catherine[2], bp. 19 Aug 1662

Marie[2], b. 26 Oct, bp. 30 Oct 1663

Simon[2], bp. c. 1670; bur. 28 Sep 1677, Sedan, age 7Y, "son of the deceased Jean Soblet"

NOTE: With the publishing of the Sedan ch records, children were added and the birth order changed; other corrections were made as well.

REF: ALLEN, Cameron, "The Soblets of the European Refuge, Ancestral to the Soblet-Sublette Family of Manakintown, VA" – *TAG*, Vol. 75, #2 (April 2000) – ch records from Sedan, Mannheim, Wesel. Soho; ALLEN, Cameron, *The Sublett (Soblet) Family of Manakintown, VA* (The Detroit Society for Genealogical Research, 1991); SUBLETT, Samuel S., *A Partial History of the French Huguenots by Name Soblets Who Emigrated to America in 1700 and Settled at Manakin in Powhatan Co, VA* (Richmond, 1896); SUBLETT, Nancy Louise, *Generations Remembered Sublette Family 1700-1850*; BROCK, R. A., *Huguenot Emigration to VA*; NUNIS, Doyce B., Jr., "The Sublettes; A Study of a Refugee Family in the Eighteenth Century" in the *VA Magazine*; CABELL, Priscilla Harriss, *Turff & Twigg*, Vol One, The French Lands (Richmond, VA, 1988).

SOBLET, Philbert/Philibert

related to Jean (1617/8-1674) above, but what the relationship was, is not certain

from Beaumont (prob. what is now Beaumont-en-Ardennes, in Ardennes Dépt, Champagne-Ardennes, s.e. of Sedan) to Sedan, FR; s/o Élie & Susanna (Renaudin) Saublet/Soblet

m. 16 Apr 1643, Anne Godin, d/o Antoine & Bastienne (L'Escot) Godin

CHILDREN (all bap. Sedan, FR):

Henri[2], bp. 29 Apr 1645; d. young; sponsor Jean Soblet

Henri[2], bp. 8 Mar 1648; bur. 18 Feb 1661, Sedan

Anne[2], bp. 14 Apr 1649; m. 11 Feb 1670, Sedan, Jacques deVillett, *mr. orfèvre* (master goldsmith), 24 Y, s/o Jacques & Élisabeth (Robinet) de Villett

> CHILDREN:
>
> **Jacques**[3], bur. 20 Feb 1672, age 4 mo; **Philbert**[3], b. 2 Jan 1674, m. 28 Dec 1710, La Haye, Anna Adrienne Lucrese; **Elizabeth**[3], bp. 3 Jun 1676, bur. 25 Aug 1678, age 3 mo; **Marie**[3], bp. 30 Jan 1678, prob. d. young; **Daniel**[3], bp. 24 Sep 1679; **Marie**[3], bp. 8 Dec 1680, bur. 20 Dec 1680, Sedan, age 10 d; **Abraham**[3], bp. 15 Feb 1682, bur. 25 Feb 1682, Sedan, age 12 d; **Elizabeth**[3], bp. 13 Dec 1691, La Haye (several towns names La Haye, no idea which one! or it could refer to The Hague)

Jean[2], bp. 10 Sep 1651; bur. 15 Oct 1651, Sedan, age 5 mo

Marie[2], bp. 16 Nov 1651; bur. 11 Nov 1653, Sedan, age 1 Y

Jean[2], bp. 20 Oct 1654

Jeanne[2], bp. 23 Jan 1656; bur. 17 Apr 1656, Sedan, age 3 mo.

Jacques[2], bp. 7 Mar 1657; m. Aug 1678, Sedan; m. Marie Boulande, d/o Guillaume & Élisabeth (Chevillet) Boulande; Jacques d. 7 Feb 1705, Emmerich, GER (e. of Nijmegen, NETH), he was a *chant-lecteur de l'église* (precentor – one who leads the singing in a church) & *tapissier et graisser* (tapestry-maker)

> CHILDREN:
>
> **Philbert**[3], bp. 25 Jun 1679, Maastrict, NETH (n.e. Liège, BEL); **Guillaume**[3], bp. 9 Mar 1681, Sedan, d. 27 Jan 1752, age 72 Y; **Daniel**[3], bp. 9 Aug 1687, Amsterdam; **Jean**[3], bp. 19 Jun 1689, Amsterdam; **Rachel Marie**[3], b. 10 Dec 1695, d. next day, Emmerich; **Judith**[3], b. 12 Mar, bp. 17 Mar 1697, Emmerich

Élisabeth[2], bp. 28 Jul 1658; bur. 5 May 1659, Sedan, age 9 mo

Judit[2], bp. 26 Aug 1660

Rachel[2], bp. 8 Jan 1662; m. 12 May 1680, Sedan, Jacques Benoit, age 22, s/o Pierre & Suzanna (Colin) Benoit; Jacques was a *maître horlogeur* (master clockmaker) Rachel d. 11 Jan 1702, Sedan, he d. 11 Jul 1703; at least **3 ch – Anna**[3], b. 15 Aug 1687, Emmerich; **Jacques**[3], b. 19 Sep 1696, d. 22 Sep 1696; **Daniel**[3], b. 30 Jan, bp. 8 Jul 1700

Jean[2], bp. 30 Aug 1664; sponsors Jean Soblet & Judith Lombard

Élisabet[2], bp. 20 Dec 1665; bur. 16 Apr 1666, Sedan, age 4 mo

REF: ALLEN, Cameron, *"The Soblets of the European Refuge Ancestral to the Soblet-Sublette Family of Manakintown, VA"* – TAG, Vol. 75, #2 (April 2000) – ch records from Sedan, Emmerich, Maastricht, Amsterdam, Cleves – all churches were FR churches.

SOLLERS/SALLERS, John

lineage of Huguenot origin, line can be traced back to a FR nobleman Guilbert de Solario

from nr. Gloucester, ENG, prob. Worcestershire; a kinsman Anthony Salway who went from Worcester, ENG to MD where he had 1 of the 1st grants on the Patapsco River in Anne Arundel Co. ; Anthony left John 50 acres of land - 23 Aug 1672, wp, Anne Arundel Co.

16 Mar 1668 - 1st mention of John in MD in the will of Thomas Martin

1670 - settled Anne Arundel Co, MD;

1675 - one of the commissioners to build a court house in Anne Arundel Co. for the purpose of preserving the records of the county; he was a member of the board of commissioners in Londontown which was an old port

m. Anne X, who survived him & she m/2, William Dalrymple, executor of John's will

1679, 1680, 1685-86 - he was a justice in Anne Arundel Co.

later went to Calvert Co. and settled on the Upper Cliffs

shortly after moving to Calvert Co, he was cosignatory to an address from the Protestants of the county
to the King of England

7 Feb 1692 - one of the Commissioners appt. for the laying out of the Established Ch

d. p. 15 Feb 1699, wd; mentions wife Ann, sons Robert, Sabrett, daus Vallinda, Mary, Elizabeth, son-in-
law Samuel Lyle, dau Ann Lyle; son Robert and William Dorrumple (*sic*) executors; uses the
surname **SALLERS**; states that Sabrett, daus Vallinda, Mary & Elizabeth are not yet 18; estate was
not settled until 1708

CHILDREN:

Robert[2], m/1, 1698, Prince Georges Co., Mary Selby, d/o William & Mary (X) Selby, m/2, Elizabeth (X)
Bourne, widow/o Thomas Bourne of Calvert Co, m/3, Dorothy X; d. 18 Nov 1749, Calvert Co;
Wd, 29 Jan 1749/50, names wife Dorothy, son Bennet, dau Althea; Dorothy's wd, 12 Jan 1774 –
mentions **10 ch**

Ann[2], m. Samuel Lyle; **issue**

Vallinda[2], m. 14 Sep 1714, John Claggett

Mary[2], unmarr., Feb 1699

Elizabeth[2], unmarr., Feb 1699

Sabritt[2], b. c. 1681; m. Mary Heighe, d/o James Heighe; he d. 1760; he left lands in Baltimore Co. to
his son Thomas in his will, dated, 3 Feb 1760, wp, 9 Mar 1760; will mentions wife Mary, sons
Sabritt, Heighe, Thomas

CHILDREN:

Sabrett II[3]

Heighe[3],

Thomas[3]

REF: SILVERSON, Katherine T., *Taney & Allied Families* (NY, 1935); STEIN, Charles Francis, *A History of
Calvert Co, MD* (1960).

SOUILLÉ/SOUILLET, Jean

prob. the Jean Souillé, chr 23 Oct 1664, Pézanas, Hérault Dépt, Languedoc-Roussillon, n.e. of Béziers

m. c. 1694, prob. FR, Susanne des Jardins (she d. p. 1714, VA when she was on the *Liste Générale* as a
widow)

a. 1695- to London

c. 1700 - to Manakintown on the *Nasseau* w/ wife, 3 ch

d. a. 1714 - Manakintown, not on the 1714 list of refugees

CHILDREN:

Nicolas[2], chr. 24 Feb 1695, Huguenot Ch (Église de St. Jean), Spitalfields, Stepney, London; m/1, a. 1728,
Manakintown, XX (she d. c. 1728, Manakintown), m/2, fall, 1728, Françoise (L'Orange) Guérrant,
d/o Jean Velas & Françoise (X) L'Orange, widow of Daniel Guérrant II; he rec. patent #782 for 133
acres in the FR lands, 31 Oct 1716; d. p. 19 Jun 1735, wd-a. Jul 1753, wp, Goochland Co, VA (wife
called a widow on that date); his will mentions wife, son Stephen, dau-in-law Ann Jennings
(must be wife of one of Frances' sons from her 1st marr), dau Ann; name became **SWILLE/
SWILLEY**

CHILD, m/1:

Stephen[3], b. 12 Oct 1728, Manakintown, VA; m. c. 1746, prob. NC, Hanaple Parker (she d. p. 12
Jun 1756); he d. p. 7 Jan 1756, wd – a. May 1756, wp, Craven Co, NC; his will mentions
wife Hanaple, all 6 sons, appoints Hanaple's bros Zenas & John Parker as executors

CHILDREN (all mentioned in his will):

Nicholas[4], b. c. 1747

Senous/Zenas[4], b. c. 1748

John[4], b. c. 1749; went to Washington Co, GA w/ his bro Samuel; land became part of

Montgomery Co, 1793, later into Tattnall Co.

Stephen[4], b. c. 1750

Samuel[4], b. c. 1751; m. Sarah X; 1781-82, served in Rev. War from SC; went to Washington Co, GA on the Ohoopee River, where he had 156 acres, c. 1798-1800 to Liberty Co, GA where he d. 1817; widow drew land as the widow of a Rev. War soldier in the 1827 GA Land Lottery; she d. c. 1830; **6 ch**

Solomon[4], b. c. 1752

CHILD, m/2:

Nanni/Ann[4], b. 19 Jun 1735; m. 13 Feb 1757, Will Durham

2 unnamed daus[2], prob. d. young VA

REF: Church records, FR and London; *Nasseau* records; Nicholas' will; Stephen's will; BROCK, R.A., editor & compiler, *Documents Chiefly Unpublished Relating to the Huguenot Emigration to Virginia and to the Settlement at Manakintown*; CABELL, Priscilla Harris, *Turff & Twigg* (Richmond, VA, 1988); DRAKE, Charles E.F., *The Souillés of Manakintown* (unpub, 2006); HUXFORD, Folks, *Pioneers of Wiregrass, GA*, Vol. VII.

SOUPLIÉ/SUPPLÉE/SOUPLIS, André/Andrew

b. 1634, FR, Picardie? Alsace?; an officer in the FR Army

m/1, Anneke X; there is a document dated 26 Apr 1692, signed by Andris Souplis & Annekie Souplis – they were witnesses at the marr of Henry Frey & Anna Catherine Levering

1682- fled to GER

1684- left w/ a group of GER immigrants to go to America

1685 – arr. NYC

7 May 1691- naturalized, Germantown, PA where he was the sheriff

m/2, p. 26 Apr 1692, PA, Gertrude (Stressinger?) Enochsson (b. 1642) as her 3rd (or 4th) husband; she d. a. 20 Nov 1738, wp, Philadelphia Co.

1700 - called a Burgher of NY

d. p. 5 Mar 1724, wd- a. 20 Mar 1726, wp, Philadelphia Co., age 92 Y; he was a weaver, liv. Kingsessing; bur. Old Swede's, Wicaco; will names his 5 ch, wife Gertra

CHILDREN, m/1:

Bartholomew[2], m/1, Rebecca X (d. 14 Jan 1718), m/2, Mary Magdaniels; settled on a farm in Blockley Twp, which is now in the city of Philadelphia, his house stood where the Cathedral Cem. is now; **6 ch**, incl . son **Jacob**[3], who m. Elizabeth Enoch, dau/o his stepmother

Margaret[2], , b. c. 1682; m. 4 Sep 1700, Peter Keyser (26 Nov 1676- 12 Sep 1724), s/o Dirck Keyser & Elizabeth ter Himpel; **11 ch**

Andrew[2], b. 1685/8, PA; m/1, Anna Stackhouse, d/o Thomas Stackhouse, – **1 son** , m/2, Deborah Thomas - **3 sons, 1 dau**; 1712, he purchased a farm in Upper Merion, now Montgomery Co, nr. Matsunk; he d. 1747 at 59 yrs.; bur. Norris City Cemetery, 2 mi. n. of Norristown

Ann[2], m. c. 1704, Philadelphia Charles Yocum; his wp, 11 Apr 1741, her wp, 21 Jun 1760 ,both in Philadelphia Co; at least **1 son, 1 dau**

Jacob[2], m. 11 Jun 1720, Elizabeth (Van Zandt) Enoch (1698-1 Jan 1749/0); Eliz. m/1, John Enochsson, Jr., grs/o of his stepmother Gertrude; he d. Oct 1749; at least **3 ch**

NOTE: There is confusion re André's wives. Some say that Gertrude, aka Goetra/Gerta, was his only wife, others say she was his 2nd wife and that Anneke was the mother of all his ch. Another speculation is that he m/1, GER, a Gertrude Stressinger/Strittzinger, m/2, PA, Anneke (Keyser?), m/3, Gerturde Enochs. Anneke was still alive in 1692, so it would seem that she was the mother of all his children. Dr. Peter Craig in the *Swedish Colonial Society Quarterly* states that Anneke was Andris' 1st wife and the mother of all of his ch.

REF: JOHNSON, Ralph Linwood, *Genealogical Studies of some Providence Families* (1934); WRIGHT, Helen Martha, *The deHaven Family of Early Philadelphia Co, PA* (1936) – manuscript in NY Public Library; CONARD,

Irene D. S., *History of the Suplée-DeHaven Family* (manuscript); ANDERSON, Bart, editor, *The Sharple-Sharpless Family,* Vol. I, II (West Chester, PA, 1966); André's will; ROBERTS, Ellwood, *Biographical Annals, Montgomery Co., PA* (1904).

STELLE, Poncet

b. bet 1635-50, St. Martin, Île de Ré, FR, or Laurière, Poitou; had sis Catherine who also emigrated

"A French gentleman" per passport to MA Bay Colony, by way of HOL and St. Christopher, W. Indies

m. a. 1680, Eugénie Légereau, b. St. Martin or Loriers/Lorières– not found – *perhaps* Laurière, Haute-Vienne Dépt, Limousin, n.e. of Limoges – would have been in Poitou at that time, an area that was one of the strongest citadels of the Huguenots

by 1682 - in Boston

c. 1685 - to Staten Island

29 Apr 1686 - deed of sale for "Ponsett Stelle De Laurier...Victualler" for property in NYC

by 1693 - when he was licensed in Monmouth Co, NJ to keep a "public house of entertainment"

d. p. 1700, NJ; Poncet and Eugénie both bur Monmouth Co.

CHIILDREN:

Peter[2], bp. 22 Jul 1682, Boston, MA

Benjamin[2], b. 1683/4, prob. NYC; m/1, 1708, Mercy, *prob.* Hull (22 Jan 1683/4- 21 Dec 1746), d/o Samuel & Mary (Manning) Hull, m/2, 14 Aug 1752, Lydia Shotwell, d/o John Shotwell; he d. 22 Jan 1759, bur. Piscataway; **6 ch**, m/1

Gabriel[2], b. 2 Feb 1685, NYC; m/1, Elizabeth Woolley (she d. 29 Jul 1723), m/2, Anna X (she d. 29 Mar 1729), m/3, Margaret (Gordon) Carré (d. 1782), widow of Louis Carré, d/o Thomas Gordon of Pitloche; he d. 25 Nov 1738, Perth Amboy, NJ

Ambrose[2], b. 1687, NYC, m. Rebecca X?; d. 1728/9, NJ

Madelaine[2], b. 17 Mar 1689, NYC

Isaac[2], b. 8 Dec 1690, NYC; m. Rachel X; d. a. 10 Sep 1741, wp

Jean/John[2], b. 8 Oct 1693, NYC; d. young

Eugene[2], b. 1695

REF: MORRIS, Maud Barr, "Four Generations in America of the Huguenot Family of Stelle*"* in the *NYGBR*, Vol. XLIV (Apr 1913); FITZ RANDOLPH, Howard Stelle, "Who Was Mercy, the First Wife of Rev. Benjamin Stelle?" in *Genealogical Magazine of NJ,* Vol. I (1925-6); LEONARD, Oliver B., *Outline Sketches of the Pioneer Progenitors of the Piscataway Pioneers 1666-1716* (NY, 1890).

STRE(I)NG/STRANG/STRANGE, Daniel

b. c. 1654/6, Gien, Loiret Dépt., Centre, s.e. of Orléans, formerly in the Province of Orléanais, s/o Henri & Marie (Babault) D'Estreng/Streng who m. 23 Sep 1650

29 Jul 1672 – matriculated at the Protestant Academy of Geneva, SWI, as a student of philosophy

3 Aug 1680 – date of marr. contract which says Daniel's parents are residents of Gien

m. 21 Aug 1680, Orléans, Charlotte Le Maistre/Maître (Mar 1668, FR-a. 31 Jan 1723/4, wp, prob. Rye, NY); Charlotte's will mentions son Daniel, grdaus Luisan & Charlotte David, d/o deceased dau Luisan, marr. daus Clorinda, Charlotte, Mary, Prudence, grson Henry

1685 – fled FR, prob. Paris, to ENG w/wife; he obtained a commission in the guards of James, Duke of York, who became James II, King of ENG

25 Mar 1688 – denizenized in ENG – Daniel, Carlotte, Peter, Matthew, Mary, Ann

c. 1688 – in NY, he participated in the layout of the Davenport Neck area of New Rochelle

21 May 1688 – naturalized in London, shortly after he left for NY

to Westchester Co., where he liv. in New Rochelle; became a man of importance; was a Lt. of the Infantry in the Colonial Militia, Justice of the Peace + other positions.

1693 – an elder in the FR Ch, New Rochelle

30 Mar 1695 – was a freeman of NYC; a keeper of an alehouse

a. 1704 – moved to Rye, NY; purchased property on Post Road where he operated a tavern which his wife and descendants continued to run until the 1840's

d. a. 11 Feb 1707, wp, Rye; named only his wife Charlotte; wd 16 Dec 1706; he was bur. Grace Churchyard

CHILDREN:

poss. a son[2], b. c. 1683, FR; reportedly left behind with Charlotte's sister – <u>not proven</u>

Louisan/Lucy[2], b. a. 1684, Paris; <u>m/1</u>, by 1698, Jean David II, s/o <u>Jean David I</u> – **2 sons**, <u>m/2</u>, a. 1722, X Fragée; Forgée; she d. 20 Oct 1722

Clorinda "Penelope"[2], b. 13 Jan 1687/8, rec. Boston; m. 19 Apr 1709, as his 3rd wife, Samuel Purdy (1 May 1685-4 Mar 1753), s/o Joseph & Elizabeth (Ogden) Purdy; she d. 6 Dec. 1726, Yorktown, NY; **5 sons, 3 daus**

Daniel[2], b. 5 Sep 1691, New Rochelle; m. 1714, Phebe Purdy (c. 1693, Rye, NY-1761, White Plains, NY), d/o Joseph & Elizabeth (Ogden) Purdy; he d. 1747, Cortlandt Manor, Westchester, NY; he was a cooper; **6 sons, 2daus**

Charlotte[2], b. 6 Jun 1692, New Rochelle; m. p. 1711, Roger Park; **2 sons, 4 daus**

Gabriel[2], b. 7 May 1696, Rye, NY; <u>m/1</u>, London, Charlotte X, <u>m/2</u>, XX – **1 son**

Mary Prudence[2], b. 1698/1700, New Rochelle; m. John Budd, s/o John & Sarah (X) Budd of Rye

Henry[2], b. 27 Feb 1703/4, New Rochelle; m. 9 Oct 1726, St. George Episcopal Ch, Hempstead, LI, NY, Elizabeth Kissam (d. a. 27 Jul 1748), d/o Daniel Kissam; he d. a. 1743; **1 son, 3 daus**

NOTE: It has been said that the original name was L'Étrange/L'Estrange/D'Étrange/D'Estrange, but no <u>proof</u> has been presented.

REF: Charlotte's will in *Collections of the New York Historical Society* (NY, 1892), Daniel's will in the same publication (1893); SEACORD, Morgan H., *Biographical Sketches & Index of the Huguenot Settlers of New Rochelle, 1687-1776* (New Rochelle, 1941); STRANGE, Charles Alfred, "The Strangs of Westchester" in the *NYGBR*, Vol. XCVIII, #4 (Oct 1967), Vol. XCIX, #1 (Jan 1968), #3 (Jul 1968), Vol. C (100), #1 (Jan 1969) #3 (Jul 1969), Vol. 101, #1 (Jan 1970), Vol. 102 (1971), Vol. 117, #4 (Oct 1986); BAIRD, Charles W., *Huguenot Emigration to America*; records from FR; *Strang Family Newsletter*, Vol. II, #1 (Jan 1980).

SUMMER, John George

b. 23 Apr 1721, Freystadt, Alsace, FR, aka Freistroff, now in Moselle Dépt, Lorraine, n.e. of Metz

by 1743 - in America; settled Warren Co, NJ

m. Barbara Longstreet

he was an Ensign from NJ, in the Rev. War

d. 8 Aug 1785, Greenwich, Warren, NJ

CHILDREN:

Mary[2], m. Ernest Mann (d. 1813); **issue**

Catherine[2], m. Andrew Banghart

Elizabeth[2], m. Richard Knowles

REF: Sussex Co, NJ Deed; STRYKER, Katherine N., "Records of St. James Lutheran ("Straw") Ch, Greenwich, Warren Co" in *The Genealogical Magazine of NJ,* Vol. 9, #1 (1934).

SY/SIE/SEE/CY, Nicolaus

b. c. 1570, HOL

m. XX

there is a village of Sy w. of the n. part of the Argonne Forest in Champagne, now Ardennes Dépt. – family is said to have left that village and to the area then known as Vermandois, now in

Picardie; fam. then went to the Calais area

by 1600 - in Nord-Pas-de-Calais, FR

CHILDREN:

Jacob[2], b. c. 1595, Amsterdam; m. 18 May 1617, Hanau, GER, Catheline Grand-Martin (b. c. 1660 Malmédy, then a Walloon area, now in Liège Province, BEL, nr. GER border), d/o Coirin Grand-Martin - **3 sons**

CHILD (2 of 3):

Isaac[3], b. c. 1625; m/1, a. 1649 XX – **2 ch**, m/2, 9 Oct 1656, Frankenthal, n.w. of Mannheim, Marie Gertier/Gorlier/Gortier (b. c. 1635) – **4 or 5 ch**

CHILDREN, m/1:

Abraham[4], b. 1649, Calais, Flandern, Nord Frankreich; 1668, from Calais to the *Pfalz;* m. a. 1671, Frankenthal, *Pfalz,* Élisabeth LeConte/Le Com(p)te (1656, Calais or Friesenheim-6 Mar 1710, Bergholz); 1687, to Bergholz, Prussia, GER; he d. 20 Nov 1701, Bergholz; **5 sons, 4 daus**

CHILDREN (7 of 9 – 2 d. young):

Abraham[5], b. 1 Sep 1671, Frankenthal; m. 9 Sep 1696, Battin, Marie Du Fresne/Du Frène (1676, Mutterstadt, *Pfalz*-4 Jun 1736, Wallmow, GER, s.w. of Stettin), d/o Clement & Marie (Le Jeune) Du Frène; he d. 22 Aug 1735, Wallmow, Uckermark; **7 sons, 2 daus**

Jeanne[5], b. c. 1676, Friesenheim; m.14 Apr 1706, David Le Maître (b. 1676, Friesenheim), s/o Gédéon & Jeanne (Cottonie) Le Maître; **2 sons, 1 dau**

Pierre[5], b. 13 Sep 1676, Frankenthal, d. 23 Feb 1742, Bagemühl, GER; m. Joanne Desjardin; dau **Marie**[6] m/1, David Sénéchar, m/2, Jacques Logé, s/o Charles Antoine & Élisabeth (Desombre) Logé

Susanne[5], c. 1681, Mannheim, d. 31 Jan 1731, Berlin, m. 24 Mar 1701, Battin, GER, Abraham Tancre (1667, Steinweiler, *Pfalz*-19 Nov 1744, Battin); **5 ch**

Isaac[5], b. c. 1683, Friesenheim; m. 28 Jun 1710, Bergholz, Judith Hurtienne (Apr 1684, Friesenheim-20 Dec 1762, Bergholz), d/o Jean & Marie (de la Porte) Hurtienne; he d. 12 Apr 1751, Bergholz; **4 sons, 3 daus**; grgrson **Daniel**[8] went to NY

Jacob[5], b. 28 Jul 1689, Bergholz, m/1, 26 Jan 1716, Zerrenthin, Bergholz, Esther Herpin (3 Mar 1692, Zerrenthin-1 Apr 1744, Battin), d/o Antoine & Catherine (Pionnie) Herpin - **2 daus**; m/2, 1745, Esther Dummée; m/3, Susanne Cupper

Elisabeth[5], b. 13 Apr 1694, Bergholz; m. 29 Oct 1712, Bergholz Isaac Desjardins (b. 3 Apr 1690, Rossow, GER), s/o Jacques & Marie Jeanne (Boccard) Desjardins

Marie[4], b. c. 1650, Calais, Flandern; m. Jean Gourdin (b. c. 1650); **1 dau**

CHILDREN, m/2 :

Jeanne[4], b. 1657, Mutterstadt ; m. X Ledoux ; she d. 18 Jun 1734, Strasburg, GER n.w. of Stettin/Szczecin – at least **1 dau**

Magdalaine[4]; **Pierre**[4] ; **Abraham**[4]; **Isaac**[4]

Jacob[3], b. c. 1635; m. Catherine Corneille (1650-14 Dec 1716), d/o Jean & Marie (X) Corneiile' **1 son, 4 daus**

Jean[2], b. c. 1600 Nielles-lès-Ardres, Pas-de-Calais Dépt, Nord-Pas-de-Calais, s.w. Ardres; m. 7 Jan 1617, Leiden, Marie Des Pré; by 1655, his family was in Mutterstadt, GER; early 1657, in Friesenheim; the surname Sie is on a list of German Huguenots; Mutterstadt is s.w. of Mannheim

CHILDREN (2 of 4):

Isaac[3], b. c. 1630; m. 11 Dec 1657, FR Ch, Mannheim, GER, cousin Esther Sy[3], d/o Pierre Sy[2]; fled FR to Mannheim, then to ENG; 22 Oct 1674, arr NY on the *Diamond* w/ Gov. Edmund Andros; settled Harlem; 1676, Staten Island, where he had a tract of 94 acres; 1677, obtained patents for 2 farms of 194 acres; by 1697, to Philipse Manor in Westchester

Co, NY; he and Esther are on the membership roll of the Old Dutch Ch in Sleepy Hollow, N. Tarry town, NY, in 1697; both were sponsors at a bap. 25 Jan 1707; Isaac's son Peter was made administrator of his estate, 4 Nov 1719

CHILDREN:

Peter[4], b. 1668, Mannheim; m. Petronella de la Montagne (b. 1671), d/o <u>Jean/Jan de la Montagne & Maria Vermilye</u>; he d. New Castle, DE; **3 sons, 1 dau**

Jacobus/James[4],b. 16 Oct, 23 Oct 1670, FR Ch, Mannheim; m. a. 17 Apr 1699, Catherine X (DePue?); he d. p. 30 Aug 1735; **6 sons, 3 daus;** dau **Maritie**[5], m. 19 May 1719, Old Sleepy Hollow Ch, Tarrytown, NY, David Ackerman (b. c. 1694), s/o Lodowyck Ackerman & Jannetje Bleyck, grs/o <u>David Ackerman & Elizabeth Bellier</u>

Susanna[4], b. 29 Apr, bp. 1 May 1672, FR Ch, Mannheim; prob. d. young

Esther[4], b. 23 Apr, bp. 27 Apr 1673, FR Ch, Mannheim; m. c. 1694, David Storm; **10 ch** (9 daus, 1 son), incl. **Esther**[5] (b. c. 1696, Tarrytown), **Maritie**[5] (b. 1698, Phillipsburg, NY), **David**[5] (bp. 10 Feb 1717, NYC) who m. Catherine Lent - **issue**

Simon[4], chr. 16 May 1679, Flatbush, NY; d. young

Isaac II[4], b. c. 1681, Flatbush; m. Antje X; **issue**

Marie[3], <u>m/1</u>, Jacques Petilion (d. by 1667), <u>m/2,</u> 10 Jul 1667, FR Ch, Mannheim, <u>Nicolas de Vaux</u> as his 2nd wife; to America w/ Gov. Andros, arr 22 Oct 1674

Pierre[2], b. c. 1605; m. XX, Mannheim

CHILDREN:

Esther[3], b. c. 1635; m. 11 Dec 1657, Mannheim Isaac[3] Sy, her 1st cousin (above)

Abraham[3], b. c. 1636, Calais; m. Sara Descombre, d/o Abraham & Jeanne (Reparlier) Descombre; he d. c. 1676, Mannheim; **1 son, 2 daus**

Marie[3], m. Jacques Despierre (d. c. 1692); she d. c. 1691; **1 son, 2 daus**

NOTE: There are several Friesenheims; the one where this family lived was *prob.* the Friesenheim on the w. bank of the Rhine, w. of Mannheim. Bagemühl, Battin, Bergholz, Plöwen, Schmölln, Zerrenthin are all east or n.e. of Prenzlau in the Uckermark . The Uckermark is an historical region in n.e. GER; it currently straddles the Uckermark Dist. Of Brandenburg & the Uecker-Rankow Dist. of Mecklenburg-Vorpommern. The traditional capital is Prenzlau. There is a Uecker River (a tributary of the Oder) there running from c. Prenzlau north to the Stettin Lagoon; all the towns listed above are on current maps of Germany in that area - west of Stettin/Szczecin. Several people surnamed SY arr in NY, 16 Aug 1845 from Prussia on the *Barque Rainbow* – descendants? This entry combines 2 previous entries for Abraham and (b. 1649) and Isaac (b. 1630) now that a common ancestor has been identified. However, the origins of Nicolaus (b. 1570) are not known. He *prob.* was a Huguenot since his ch were but that is not <u>proven</u>.

REF : Church records of the French Reformed Parish in Bergholz; *Founding of the French Reformed (Huguenot) Church of Bergholz, Kreis Prenzlau, Brandenburg in 1687* by M. Cordier; *Index of Huguenot Immigration to Germany* on microfilm; *Sy-Hugenotten* by Johanna Oqueka and Hans Wendt (Berlin,1978); HILL, Glenna See, "See-DeVeaux Ancestry" in the *NYGBR* (Apr, 1979) – records from the FR Ch at Mannheim, GER, "The See Family of Calais, FR & the Manor of Philipsburgh" in the NYGBR, Vol. 114, #2 (Apr 1983), Vol. 114, #3 (Jul, 1983); DeVOE, Cort R., "Additional Information on the Origins of the Devoe/De Vaux Family of NY" in the *NYGBR*, Vol. 128, #1 (Jan 1997); RIKER, James, *Revised History of Harlem Its Origins & Early Annals* (NY, 1904); COOK, Lewis D., "Corrected Genealogy of Ralph Hunt" in *TAG*, Vol. XXVI, #1 (Jan, 1950); HILL, Eleanor M., *The See Family as I See it* (Salt Lake City, 1984)' ch recs – Old Sleepy Hollow Ch, Tarrytown, NY.

T

TARGER, Marie

b. 22 Feb, bp. 2 Mar 1642, Huguenot Ch, La Rochelle, FR, d/o Daniel & Louise (Martin) Targer; Daniel
   was a mariner; she was evidently Huguenot but prob. converted when she went to Québec as
   it was almost impossible to remain Protestant there at that time; records of children's births
   are from Catholic ch. records

m. 22 Nov 1663, Québec, CAN, Jean Royer

d. p. 1675, Québec

CHILDREN, all b. Québec: Surname **ROYER**

Jean[2], b. 28 Sep 1664; d. 1666

Marie-Ann[2], b. 21 Aug 1665; m. 1681, René Alarie

Madaleine[2], b. 19 Oct 1666; d. 1667

Pierre[2], b. 6 Nov, bp. 7 Nov 1667; d. 17 Mar 1677

Elizabeth[2], b. 14 Sep 1669; m. 1689, Pierre Blais

Jean[2], b. 6 Nov 1671; m. 19 Oct 1694, Catherine Dumont

Thérèse[2], b. 21 Feb, bp 23 Feb 1675; d. 4 Mar 1675

REF: JETTÉ, René, *Dictionnaire généalogique des familles du Québec des origines à 1730* (Montréal, 1983).

THELABALL, James

b. FR; surname was originally LaBalle

m. Elizabeth Mason, d/o Lt. Francis & Alice (X) Mason; d. p. 12 May 1702, wd – a. 15 15 Mar 1707, wp,
   Elizabeth River Parish, Lower Norfolk Co, VA

15 Jul 1660 - took "oath of allegiance" in VA

28 Nov 1683 - naturalized, Lower Norfolk Co, VA; original name of La Balle was miswritten in the court
   records: James The La Ball in 1649, then Ja: The La Ball, James The La Balle

d. p. 9 Apr 1691, wd – a. 15 Sep 1693, Elizabeth River Parish, Lower Norfolk Co, VA; will mentions his
   wife & sons Lemuel (deceased), Francis, James, daus Margaret Langley, Elizabeth Langley,
   Mary Chichester & listed all his possession including his "French books"

CHILDREN:

Lemuel[2], m. Joyce Langley, d/o William & Joyce (X) Langley; he d. a. 9 Apr 1691

Francis[2], m/1, a. 10 Oct 1690, Sarah X, m/2, Margery X; he d.p.12 Dec 1702, wd- a. 15 Mar 1704/5, wp,
   Norfolk, VA; **4 ch**

James[2], m. Ann X ; he d. p. 24 Dec 1707, wd-18 Jan 1711/2, wp Norfolk, VA; **5 ch**

Margaret[2], m. William Langley, s/o William & Joyce (X) Langley; d. by 1702; **9 ch**

Elizabeth[2], m. Thomas Langley, s/o William & Joyce (X) Langley; **3 sons**

Mary[2], m/1, William Chichester – **5 ch**, m/2, her cousin Lemuel Mason, s/o Lemuel & Ann (Seawell/
   Sewell) Mason – **1 dau**; he d. a. 18 Jan 1711/2, appraisal of his estate

REF: JESTER, Annie Lash, *Adventurers of Purse and Person VA 1607-1625* (1964); MEYER, Virginia M. &
DORMAN, John Frederick, *Adventurers of Purse & Person VA 1607-1624/5,* revised (1987); JAMES, Edward Wilson,
   Lower Norfolk Co, VA Antiquary (NY, 1951); TURNER, F.K., *Gateway to the New World A History of Princess
Anne Co, VA 1607-1824*; WALTER, A.G., *Lower Norfolk Co, VA, 2 Nov 1649-15 Jan 1651/2, Book B* (1978); *William &
Mary College Quarterly Historical Magazine*, Vol. 19 #3 (Jan, 1911), pp. 194-99; McINTOSH,
Charles Fleming, *Brief Abstracts of Lower Norfolk County & Norfolk County Wills 1637-1710* (Baltimore, MD, 1998)

THOREL, Marie, see PERRIN(E), Pierre

TIBAULT, Anne, see FAURÉ, Daniel Isaac

TILLOU/TILYOU/TILSON, Pierre

b. c. 1650/55, nr. St. Nazaire, FR - at the mouth of the Loire River, Loire-Atlantique, Pays de la Loire

m. c. 1670, FR, Jeanne Bouguet

c. 1681 - fled from St. Nazaire, FR; went to ENG

21 Mar 1682 - they were naturalized in ENG; some sources say they went to HOL but that doesn't account for the naturalization in ENG, unless their 1st stop was HOL

1691 - petition names Pierre as a FR Protestant along w/ others, who wanted to be made burghers & citizens

d. c. 1705, New Rochelle, NY

CHILDREN:

Vincent[2], b. a. 1671, FR; m. c. 1702, Elizabeth Vigneau, d/o Jean & Elizabeth (Guion/Guyon) Vigneau; naturalized, 3 Jul 1701, America; d. a. 28 May 1709; Elizabeth d. a. 27 Sep 1709, wp, NYC

    CHILDREN:

    Vincent[3], b. c. 1702; m. 10 Jul 1720, Dutch Reformed Ch, NYC, Sarah Mesier (she m/2, 2 Mar 1728, John Hendricks); he d. a. Mar 1728; at least 1 son Vincent[2], bp. 14 Oct 1722

    Jean/John[3], b. 1692, NYC; m. 15 Jun 1718, Mary Van Gelder (b. 20 Dec 1696); he d. p. 1741; he apprenticed in 1707 as a joiner, also was a cabinet maker; 10 ch

    Ann[3], b. 30 Sep, bp. 21 Oct 1702, FR Ch, NYC; m. Charles Louchard; she d. p. 1725

    Peter[3], b. 21 Aug, bp. 16 Sep 1705, FR Ch, NYC; m. Hester/Esther Pelletreau (b. 3 Oct, bp. 5 Oct 1707, FR Ch, NYC), d/o Jean & Madeleine (Vincent) Pelletreau; he d. a. 22 Mar 1791, wp: he was a chairmaker; 7 ch

    Elizabeth[3], b. c. 1707 NYC; d. p. 1725

    Judith[3], b. c. 1708, NYC; m. Jean Chadaine

Guillaume/William[2], m. Margaret Bridon (?) of Staten Island, NY; at least 1 son Peter[3], b. 1716 NY, d. 1791; Wm. d. c. Feb 1739, NYC

?Elizabeth[2]

NOTE: There was a Pierre Tillou who arr, 23 Jul 1700, VA, on the *Mary Ann* – listed as a single man. No information re a possible connection with the Pierre Tillou who went to NY.

REF: FORBES, William A., *Forbes, An Ancestry Notebook* (1983); *A Genealogy of A Cooley Family of Hunterdon County, NJ & A Tilliou Family of French Huguenots* – TILLOU, Juliette, "The Tillou Family" (NSDAR manuscript, 1937): BOYER, Carl, 3rd, *Huguenots in NJ* (Newhall, CA, 1978).

TONNELIER/TUNNELL, Guillaume/William

b. c. 1675, FR

m. FR, XX

c. 1703 - to ENG; settled North Riding, Yorkshire; N. Riding was 1 of 3 historic subdivisions of Yorkshire, situated n. of the city of York

d. ENG, prob. Yorkshire

CHILDREN:

William[2], b. 1702/3, FR; m. ENG, Lady Ann Howard of Yorkshire (d. 18 Feb 1814, nr. Robertsville, Anderson, TN, said to have been 104 Y); c. 1736, to America, settled nr. Fredericksburg, VA; he d. 28 Dec 1787, prob. Loudon Co, bur. Fairfax Co, VA

    CHILDREN (prob. others):

    Robert[3], b. 1747, Fredericksburg; m. XX; went to NC; he was a minister

William[3], b. 1751, Spotsylvania Co, VA; m. 9 Dec 1771, Fairfax Co, VA, Mary Maysey (d. 6 Apr 1814 nr. Robertsville, TN); he d. 16 Aug 1814, Anderson Co, TN; he was a private from VA in the Rev. War; he was a Baptist minister; **13 ch**

Stephen[3], b. 1753, Spotsylvania Co, VA; m. 1776, Georgetown, MD, Kezia Money (d. 1836, Morgan Co, IL); he d. 1828, Tompkinsville, KY; he was a Methodist minister; served in the Rev. War; **11 ch**

John[3], b. 1755, Fredericksburg; d. Jun 1790, Sweet Springs, VA (now WV); unmarr.; he was a minister

John[2], b. ENG; went to Accomack Co, VA; m. "Lady Scarbrough"; d. early days of the American Revolution in DE

James[2], b. ENG; d. NC

REF: ARMSTRONG, Zella, *Notable Southern Families*, Vol. III (Chattanooga, TN, 1926).

TOURGÉE/TOURJÉE/TORGÉ, Pierre

prob. s/o Pierre Tourgée, from Bretagne
fled FR, w/ his brothers; went to the Channel Islands, Isle of Guernsey
1686 - to America; brothers as well
went to the FR settlement at Narragansett, RI; wife *poss.* Ann Jolin
CHILDREN:
Pierre/Peter[2], b. 21 Mar 1689, RI; m. 5 Apr 1722, N. Kingston, RI, Mary Smith, d/o William & Abigail (X) Smith; said to be from Prudence Island in marr. record; Prudence Is. in Narragansett Bay, s.w. of Bristol; d. a. 1756
CHILDREN, b. N. Kingston, RI:
Thomas[3], b. 13 Dec 1722; m. c. 1774, Mary/Amey X; **4 ch**
Philip[3], b. 20 Oct 1724; m. by 1750, Patience Thomas, d/o Peleg & Mehitable (X) Thomas; he d. a. 1776; **6 ch**
Elizabeth[3], b. 18 Nov 1728; m. John Place
Peter[3], b. 5 Feb 1733; m/1, c. 1757, Freelove X, m/2 Bridget Hill
John[3], b. 23 Dec 1735; m. 5 Nov 1761, Priscilla Smith, d/o Jeremiah Smith; he d. 7 Apr 1812; **7 ch**
Mary[3], b. 8 May 1739; m. Benjamin Whitford
John[2]
Phillip[2]

NOTE: Many spellings of the name but one of them is NOT Targé – the latter is an entirely different family.

REF: MAURO, Nancy Tourjée, *Descendants of Piere Tourjée, A French Huguenot Family*(1987); Vital Records, N. Kingston, RI; TURK, Marion G., *The Quiet Adventurers in America*; BAIRD, Charles W., *Huguenot Emigration to America*, Vol. II (Baltimore, 1966); POTTER, Elisha R., *French Settlements in RI* (Baltimore, 1968).

TOURNEUR/TURNEUR, Daniel

b. 1626, Amiens, Picardie, FR
m. 5 Sep 1650, Leiden, HOL, Jacqueline de Parisis; she d. a. 22 Aug 1700, inv
p. 30 Jul 1651 - to Harlem, New Netherland
c. 7 Apr 1654 - was made corporal of a company formed for protection against marauders
granted a corner lot in New Amsterdam but there was not enough timber available to build a house
11 Apr 1657 - he renewed his request to build a house but that was evidently denied
31 May 1660 - bought a lot on the Prince's Graft where he built his house
16 Aug 1660 - was appt. magistrate for Harlem

he was a deacon, delegate to the General Assembly (1664), deputy sheriff
d. 1673, Harlem, NY
CHILDREN:
Daniel[2], bp. 30 Jul 1651, Walloon Ch, Leiden; m. Ann Woodhull; d. fall 1690; **3 ch**
Madeline[2], m. 15 Jun 1673, John Dyckman; **6 ch**
Maria[2], b. Flatbush, bp. 4 Mar 1654; d. young
Esther[2], m. 24 Jun 1677, Frederick deVaux of Westchester Co, NY; **13 ch**
Jacques[2], b. Harlem, NY; m/1, 7 Jun 1683, Aefie Kortright, d/o Michael Kortright – **7 ch**, m/2, 29 May
      1714, Engeltie Thomas, wid/o Gregorie Storm
Marretje[2], bp. 4 Sep 1661
Thomas[2], b.1665, Harlem; m. 5 Apr 1692, Maria Oblenis, d/o Joost Van Oblenis/Oblinus & Maria Sammis
      (she m/2, Sigfredus Alrics); he d. 1710, New Castle, DE, his will of 25 Jul 1709, was proven 28 Mar
      1716 – he signed it *Tomas Tournier* – will mentions wife Mary, eldest son Daniel, other ch Jacob,
      Peter, Frederick Devow; **7 ch** according to records of New Castle Orphan's Court; family name became
      TURNER

REF: Thomas' will; RIKER, James, *History of Harlem*; BAIRD, Charles W., *Huguenot Emigration to America*, Vol.
1 (Baltimore, 1966).

TOURTELLOT, Abraham

  b. c. 1655, Bordeaux, FR
  m/1, FR, Angeline Martinique??; 3 sons Jacques-Thomas, Jacques-Moritz, Jean; 3 sons are mentioned in
      a couple sources, just one gives the 1st wife a name – not really proven; the 2nd son's name given
      as Jacquesions in a couple places
  arr. 1687 - Boston on the *Friendship* from London w/ his bro Benjamin (d. 25 Sep 1687, during the
      voyage); settled Roxbury
  5 Jan 1688 - letters patent of denization for Abraham, sons James, Moses & John, but it is not clear if they
      arr. Boston w/ Abraham; apparently the 3 sons from his 1st marr had anglicized their names
  m/2, c. 1693, Marie Bernon, d/o Gabriel & Esther (LeRoy) Bernon of La Rochelle, FR (she d. Gloucester,
      RI)
  1697 - to Newport, RI
  d. a. 1704, lost at sea, en route to Newport; he was a merchant & mariner
  CHILDREN, m/2:
Gabriel[2], b. 24 Sep 1694, Roxbury; d. w/ father a. 1704
Esther[2], b. 12 Jun 1696, Roxbury; m. 19 Jan 1716, Israel Harding, s/o John & Sarah (Butcher) Harding
Abraham[2], b. 1697, Newport, RI; m/1, Lydia Ballard, d/o Isaac & Dorothy (Herndon) Ballard – **7 ch**, m/2,
      29 Jan 1743, Hannah (Case) Corpe, d/o William & Elizabeth (Stafford) Case, wid/o Jeremiah
      Corpe – **5 ch**, m/3, Welthian (Sheldon) Williams, d/o Nehemiah & Rachel (Mann) Sheldon, wid/o
      John Williams – **no issue** (she m/3, 27 May 1770, Samuel Thurber); he was a joiner; he d. 23 Nov
      1762

REF: AUSTIN, John Osborne, *The Genealogical Dictionary of RI* (Albany, NY, 1887); *Representative Men & Old
Families of RI*, Vol. III (Chicago, 1908); Vital Records, Roxbury & RI.

TRABUC/TRABUE, Guillaume

  "merchant middleman" of Montauban, Guienne, now in Tarn-et-Garonne Dépt, Midi-Pyrénées, FR
  m. 5 Jun 1583, civil, 19 Jun 1583, rel., Montauban, Anne Azam, d/o Jean & Maude (de Marty)Azam, a
      weaver in Montauban
  d. a. 1615
  CHILDREN (all bap. Protestant Ch, Montauban):

Anne[2], bp. 4 Mar 1584

Antoine[2], bp. 27 Mar 1585

Pierre[2], bp. 18 Jan 1587

Marthe[2], bp. 13 Mar 1588

David[2], bp. 29 Oct 1589; d. young

David[2], bp. 31 Dec 1590; butcher of pork in Montauban; m. 19 Jul 1615, civil, 23 Aug 1615, rel, Galharde d'Andrailh, d/o Arnaud & Lizette (de Gascon) d'Andrailh, a plowman of the Moreaux
CHILDREN:

Arnaud[3], bp. 13 May 1618

Jean[3], b. 31 Dec, bp. 7 Jan 1623/4

Antoine[3], b. 10 Feb 1629, bp 18 Feb 1629; he was a master butcher of pork and master tanner of Montauban; m. 14 Jan 1646, civil, 4 Feb 1646, religious, Bernarde Chivalie/Chilbailhe (b. 1 Feb, bp. 18 Feb 1629 Prot. Ch, Montauban), d/o Jean & Marie (Mariette) Chilbailhe; *poss.* m/2, 28 Mar 1676, Montauban, Jeanne Trémolières; he prob. converted to Catholicism, bet 1658-63 to protect his family & business – no mention of Protestantism in the Catholic baptisms
CHILDREN, b. Montauban (1st 6 ch bap. Protestant Ch, excluding the 2 in brackets, last 2 were bap Cathedral of St. Jacques, a Catholic Ch):

David[4], b. 9 Dec, bp. 25 Dec 1646

Jean[4], b. 11 Aug, bp. 22 Aug 1649

Marie[4], b. 19 Sep, bp. 5 Dec 1652; d. young

André[4], b. 5 May, bp. 8 May 1654

[?Marie[4], b. 10 Sep, bp. 1656 (not on all lists)]

Anne[4], b. 20 Dec 1658; d. young

[?Marthe[4], b. 23 Jan 1661 (not on all lists)]

Anne[4], b. 25 Dec 1663; d. 8 Apr 1669 (rec. says fa Catholic, mo Protestant)

Marguerite[4], b. 13 Aug , bp. 25 Aug 1667 Cathedral of St. Jacques

Antoine[4], b. 21 Sep, bp. 28 Sep 1669 Cathedral of St. Jacques; **the immigrant to America**; 15 Sep 1687, to Lausanne, SWI, Apr 1688, to HOL; may have been m. before, m. c. 1699, HOL, Madelaine Verreuil (bp. 28 Jan 1685, FR Ch The Hague), d/o Moyse & Madelaine (Prodon) Verreuil; went to ENG; arr 1700, VA; 12 May 1705, naturalized; he d. 29 Jan 1723/4, Manakintown, VA (wp, May 1724), widow m/2 Pierre Chastain; name in America became **STRABO(O)**
CHILDREN (all b. Henrico Co, VA):

Jacob[5], b. c. 1705; m. 1731/2, Marie/Mary Wooldridge, d/o John & Martha (X) Wooldridge; **9 ch**

Anthony[5], b. c. 1708/9; m. Clark/Claire X; **2 ch**

Magdalene[5], b. 31 Aug 1715; m/1, Peter Guérrant, s/o Daniel Guérrant, - **3 sons, 4 daus**, m/2, p. 1750, Thomas Smith (d. a. 16 Nov 1786, wp, Powhatan Co), as his 3rd wife – **2 ch**

Judith[5], b. 1717/8, m. Stephen Watkins; **issue**

John James[5], b. 1722; m. 1744, Olympia Dupuy, d/o James & Susanne (La Villain) Dupuy; d. 10 Oct/21 Oct 1755, Chesterfield Co, VA; **15 ch**

REF: TRABUE, James D., *The Ancestry of Anthony Trabue (Antoine Trabuc)* (1992, not. pub.); HARPER, Lillie DuPuy Van Culin, *Colonial Men & Times* (Philadelphia, 1915); BROCK, R.A., *Huguenot Emigration to VA* (Baltimore, 1966); YATES, Julie Trabue & TRABUE, Charles C., IV, *The Trabue Family in America 1700-1983*(Baltimore, 1983).

TREGEAU/TREGO, Pierre/Peter

b. 1655, FR
m. Judith X
1682/3 - to America; settled in Delaware Co, PA
d. 1730, Chester Co, PA
CHILDREN:
Jacob[2], b. 8 mo 7d 1687; m. Mary Cartledge; he d. 4 mo 10d 1720
James[2], b. 4 mo 26d 1690; m. Elizabeth X
William[2], b. 5 Aug 1693, Chester Co, PA; m. 26 Jun 1717, Margaret Moore, d/o John Moore; he d. 1770, Goshen Twp, Chester Co, PA; **10 ch**
John[2], b. 12 mo 15d 1696
Peter[2], m. 11 mo 5 d 1726, Ann Whitaker

REF: DAVIS, William W. H., *History of Bucks Co, PA* (NY, 1905); SHERTZER, Trego, *History of the Trego Family*; STAPLETON, Rev. A., *Memorials of the Huguenots in America* (Carlisle, PA, 1901).

TREMAU/SIPPY, Joseph

b. 1764, s/o X & X (Scipio) Tremau; said to be from Le Croisic, Loire-Atlantique Dépt, Pays de la Loire, w. of St. Nazaire - it has been thought to have been his birthplace but Bordeaux was his birthplace according to his son Stephen
enlisted as a 14 yr old seaman on a FR vessel *La Blanche*; the fleet sailed 13 Apr 1778, to America; he was at the Siege of Yorktown, VA, until the surrender of Cornwallis; Joseph fought in the FR army at Yorktown and was wounded in the foot; at the close of the war, all FR soldiers were to return to FR but Joseph was sick and being cared for at a farm house – the fleet sailed without him; he took his mother's maiden name (Scipio) which became **SIPPY**
m. 20 Feb 1787, Martinsburg, WV, Lucretia Johnson (20 Jun 1769-15 Oct 1857), d/o John & Elizabeth (Lenneham) Johnson; she m/2, Samuel Lane; she is bur Citizen's Cemetery in Akron, Fulton, IN; at the time of her death, she had 117 grch living & 92 grgrch
d. 22 Jan 1819, Beaver Co, PA, bur. Old Westfield Meeting House Cemetery, nr. Mt. Jackson; 12 Feb 1819, wp, Beaver Co. – mentions wife Lucretia, 10 sons, 3 marr daus, 3 youngest daus – son William not mentioned
CHILDREN:
John[2], b. 27 Mar 1787; m. XX; d. 6 Sep 1857, Madison Co, IL; may have marr. 2x, at least **3 ch**
Elizabeth[2], b. 25 May 1788; m. Christofer Shaffer; d. 6 Sep 1857, Beaver Co, PA; **12 ch**
Mary[2], b. 27 Sep 1789; d. 26 Sep 1790
Joseph[2], b. 7 Mar 1791; m. 17 Feb 1813, Beaver Co, PA, Martha Cogswell, d/o William & Cloe (Gates) Cogswell; served in the War of 1812; he was a doctor; he d. 11 Sep 1870, Richard Co, WI; **10/12 ch**
Anna Joanna[2], b. 23 Dec 1792; m. 12 Sep 1816, William Whittenberger; d. 11 May 1884, Akron, IN; **11 ch**
Mary[2], b. 16 Apr 1794; m. Abraham Reagle; d. 15 Oct 1882, Summit Co, OH; **10 ch**
Rebecca[2], b. 31 Oct 1794; m. X Sample; at least **1 dau**
William[2], b. 18 Jan 1797; d. prob. a. 1819 – not in father's will
Abraham[2], b. 15 Feb 1799; m/1, 10 Dec 1817, Sally Miller - **no issue**, m/2, Sarah Smedley – **5ch**, m/3, Jemima Newell (11 Dec 1802-19 Jul 1851), m/4, Nov 1851, Mary Morgan; he d. 27 Sep 1867, Madison Co, IL
Isaac[2], b. 22 Sep 1802; m. Marcy Ball; d. 29 Mar 1874, Akron, IN; at least **2 ch**
Jacob[2], b. 22 Sep 1802; m. 12 Jun 1823, Martha Lane, d/o Samuel Lane, his mother's 2nd husband; he d. 29 Mar 1874, Akron, IN; at least **5ch**
Thomas[2], b. 12 Mar 1804; m. w/ **2 sons** in 1840
Eli[2], b. 12 Feb 1805

Nicholas[2], b. 17 Nov 1807; m. 21 May 1829, Abigail McGill; he served in the Civil War; d. 13 May 1863, St. Louis, MO; **9 ch**

Stephen[2], b. 7 Nov 1807; m/1, 8 Mar 1835, Medina Co, OH, Emily Warden (19 Apr 1811-6 Aug 1863) – **11 ch**, m/2, 12 Dec 1863, Fulton Co, IN, Mary Ball, m/3, 7 Apr 1871, Richland Center, WI, Amity Brian, m/4, 2 Jul 1884, Fulton Co., IN, Susanna Groves; he d. 18 Oct 1896, Bourbon, Marshall, IN

Louisa[2], b. 17 Nov 1812; m. Jesse Hughes (1806-1902); d. 12 Nov 1879, Aledo, IL – **10 ch**

Levi[2], b. 20 Nov 1814

Lucinda[2], b. 29 Jun 1817; m/1, 15 Sep 1833, Sterling Crosby, m/2, X Hershey; d. 7 Oct 1912, Chadron, Dawes, NE

REF: *Les Combattants Français de la Guerre Américaine, 1778-1783*; marr. record Berkeley Co, WV; WILLARD, Shirley, editor, *Fulton Co. Folks*, Vol. 2 (Rochester, IN, 1981); SIPPY, D.K., editor, *Sippy News Letter*, Vol. #1 – includes Joseph's will, Vol. I, #2.

TREZEVANT, Daniel

b. Authon-du Perche, now Eure-et-Loire Dépt, Centre, s.e. of Nogent-le-Rotrou, s/o Théodore & Susanne (Menou) Trezevant; Susanne of Châtcaudun, FR

m. FR, Susanne Maulard, d/o Lubin & Gabrielle (Berou) Maulard

he was a merchant in Maintenon, FR

c. 1684 – Daniel & Susanne, fled FR, went to London and were listed at the FR Ch, Threadneedle St., on 6 Jul 1684, w/their 3 ch – Daniel, Matthew, Susanna; Matthew & Susanna must have stayed or d. in ENG as they do not appear on any records in SC

1694/5- settled at Charleston, SC & at the Orange Quarter; on the list of FR & Swiss refugees

10 Mar 1696/7 – naturalized, SC

d. 1726, SC; 3 Jan 1726/7, wp, Berkeley Co, SC – mentions wife Susannah, sons Isaac, Théodore, daus Marian & Madalane; liv. in the parish of St. Thomas & St. Denis in Berkeley Co.

CHILDREN (1st 3 b. a. 6 Jul 1684, FR):

Daniel[2], b. FR; naturalized w/ parents; he was a weaver; d. c. 1706, SC

Matthew[2], b. FR; nothing further – d. young?

Susanne[2], prob. b. FR; nothing further – d. young?

Isaac[2], m. Susannah X; at least 1 son **Daniel**[3]

Théodore[2], m. 24 Feb 1720/1, Martha (Bremer) Screven (d. 3 May 1732), widow of Saville Screven; he d. 23 Jan 1735

CHILDREN:

Theodore[3], b. 20 Apr 1722; m/1, 11 May 1749 Elizabeth Wells (d. 4 Jun 1752), *poss.* d/o Egdezar & Sidney (X) Wells– **1 son**, m/2, 24 Apr 1753, Catherine Timothy (17 Jan 1735-bur. 25 Feb 1764), d/o Lewis & Elizabeth (X) Timothy – **7 ch**, m/3, 20 Apr 1766, Catherine Crouch (b. 20 Feb 1736-22 Sep 1820), d/o Abraham & Ann (X) Crouch – **5 ch**; he d. 14 May 1801

Martha[3], b. 25 Aug 1724; m/1, 22 Jun 1749, Peter Bostock – they divorced – **1 dau**, m/2, Samuel Parsons

Daniel[3], b. 6 Jun 1726

Susannah[3], b. 1727; m. 21 May 1748, William Hall of Charleston (1723-11 Apr 1768); she d. 23 May 1790; William's wp, 22 Apr 1768 – names wife & all 8 ch – **3 sons**, **5 daus**

Elizabeth[3], m. 14 Feb 1765, Joseph Clowney (she was *prob.* d/o Theodore and Martha)

Marian[2], in father's will – no more info

Madalane[2], in father's will – no more info

REF: BARKSDALE, Israel, "Antoine Poitevent, & Some Others" in *Transactions of the Huguenot Society of SC*, #87 (1982); TREZEVANT, John Timothée, *The Trezevant Familly in the U.S.* (Columbia, SC, 1914); SALLEY, A.S., Jr., "Daniel Trezevant, Huguenot, & Some of His Descendants" in *The SC Historical & Genealogical Magazine* Vol. III, #1 (Jan, 1902).

TURQUE/TUR(C)K/TÜRK, Jacob de

grs/o Hugo & Margat (de Privas) Le Turk – they had 4 sons: Michael, Harman, Robert and Sancred – one of them was Jacob's fa

by 30 Jul 1609- fled FR, went to Frankenthal in the *Pfalz*

m/1, c. 1608, prob. FR, Jacquemine Verrisel (d. c. 1614)

m/2, 7 Nov 1615, Frankenthal, Jacquemine Richenbosche/Rickenbasche, d/o Henrick Rickenbosche

d. a. 29 May 1633 – remar. of widow

CHILDREN, m/1 (ch records):

Jacob[2], b. 30 Jul 1609, Frankenthal

Isaac[2], bp. 19 Jan 1612, Frankenthal

Abraham[2], b. 23 Oct 1612, Frankenthal

CHILDREN, m/2 (ch records):

Elizabeth[2], b. 10 Nov 1616, Frankenthal

Johannes[2], b. 1 Nov 1618, Frankenthal; m. Geertrint/Gertrude de Brier

    CHILDREN (ch records):

    Susanna[3], bp. 28 Aug 1644, Frankenthaal

    Janneken[3], bp. 23 Sep 1647, Frankenthal

    Johannes/Hans[3], bp. 30 Jul 1650, l'Église Reformée Néerlandaise de Frankenthal au Palatinat; m. Hester Kip (bp. 28 Apr 1656, Frankenthal), d/o Hans Pieter & Rachel (DuFour) Kip

    CHILDREN:

    John Pieter[4], bp. 1 Mar 1671, Frankenthal

    Jacomina[4], bp. 18 Dec 1677, Frankenthal

    Sarah[4], bp. 8 Jan 1680

    Maria Elisabeth[4], bp. 21 Feb 1684

    Isaac[4], bp. 17 Jan 1685, Frankenthal; m. Maria (de Harcourt) Weimer, a widow, d/o Jean de Harcourt; he went to London where he joined the company of Rev. Joshua Kocherthal which landed in NY 31 Dec 1708 on the *Globe*; Maria (37 Y)and her 2 yr old dau Catherine were also on the ship; 21 Aug 1708, the emigrants were issued a letter of denization by Queen Anne; Isaac and Maria, m. c. 1709, & they settled Esopus, NY, later went to Oley, now Berks Co, PA; he d. a. 1 Apr 1727, wp

    CHILDREN:

    Esther[5], bp. 29 Apr 1712, l'Église Françoise, NYC; m. 1736, Abraham Bertolet, s/o Jean & Susanne (de Harcourt) Bertolet; she d. 1798

        John[5], b. 23 Sep 1713, Oley; m. 13 May 1740, Deborah Hoch, d/o John Hoch; he d. Feb 1781

    Esther Cornelia[4], bp. 17 Aug 1687, Frankenthal

Dina[2], b. 5 Dec 1620, Frankenthal

Susanna[2], b. 30 Mar 1623, Frankenthal

Henrich[2], b. 2 Jul 1625, Frankenthal

REF: DeTURK, Eugene P. , *History & Genealogy of the DeTurk DeTurck Family* (1914); STAPLETON, Rev. A., *Memorials of the Huguenots in America* (Carlisle, PA 1901); CROLL, Rev. P.C., *Annals of the Oley Valley in Berks Co, PA* (Reading, PA 1926).

U

USILIE/UZILLE/UZIEL(L)E/UZZELL/ZIELE/SEELEY, David

b. c. 1645, Calais, FR

c. 1658, m. Marie Casier (b. c. 1640), d/o <u>Philippe & Marie (Taine) Casier</u>

fled Calais, FR to Mannheim, GER

26 Apr 1660 - sailed from Texel (an island in the W. Frisian Is., HOL), arr New Amsterdam on the *Gilded Otter*, a. 25 Aug 1660; settled Staten Island

went to Esopus/Kingston, NY

CHILDREN:

Pierre/Pieter/Peter[2], b. 14 Jan 1660, Mannheim; m. 6 Apr 1686, NYC, Cornelia Damen (b. c. 1666), d/o Jan Corneliszen Damen; liv. Staten Island, Bushwyck; settled Esopus/Kingston; signed his name Pieter Uzielle; he d. p. 1714, Kingston

    CHILDREN:

    Maria[3], b. c. 1688, m. 28 Sep 1703, Old Dutch Ch, Kingston, NY, <u>Leonard Treny LeRoy</u>/Jonar Lar(a)way (bp. 18 Sep 1674, Québec-p. 1750), s/o Siméon & Claude/Blandina (DesChâlets) LeRoy; went to Poughkeepsie, 1714, to Albany, to Schoharie, bet 1725-29

        CHILDREN:

        Petrus[4], bp. 3 Sep 1704, Kingston, uncle Pieter and wife Cornelia as witnesses/sponsors; m. Maria Van Alstyne; **issue**

        Blandina[4], bp. 1708; m. 19 Oct 1732, Schoharie, Adam Vroman

        Cornelia[4], bp. 1709 Kingston; prob. m. Martinus Van Alstyne

        Simeon[4], bp. 1711, Kingston; <u>m/1</u>, Jannetje Van der Volge(n) - **issue**, <u>m/2</u>, Jannetje Valkenburg

        Jonas[4], bp. 1714, Albany; d. young

        Jonas[4], bp. 1716, Albany; no more info

        Jan/John[4], b. Rensselaerwyck, bp. 1718, Albany; m. 20 Jul 1743, Schoharie, Maria Hagedorn; **issue**

        Maria[4], b. "Nisketha" – poss. Niskayuna, n.w. of Albany, bp. 1721, Albany; m. 3 May 1740, Schoharie, Martinus Vroman; **issue**

        David[4], b. Rensselaerwyck, bp. 1723, Albany; m. Marytje Hoogdale

    Jan[3], bp. 28 Sep 1688, Brooklyn; no more info

    Sophia[3], bp. 3 or 5 May 1691, Brooklyn; m. 24 Feb 1712, Storm Bra(d)t; she d. p. 1756, Albany; **issue**

    Cornelia[3], bp. 2 Apr 1693, Brooklyn; m. 15 Oct 1714, Albany, Johannes Becker of Albany; she d. a. 1750; **issue**

    Helena[3], bp 27 Mar 1699, Brooklyn; m. 9 Nov 1716, Albany, Willem Hooghteling; **issue**

    Peter[3], bp. 5 Feb 1698/9, Brooklyn; m. 4 Jun 1724, Albany, Anna Ackerson; d. 1 May 1762, Schoharie; **issue**

    Lysbet[3], bp. 1 May 1701, Brooklyn

    David[3], bp. 1 Feb 1707/8, Esopus; m. a. 1733, Engeltie Vrooman; **issue**

Maria Magdalena[2], bp. 3 Dec 1662, Reformed Dutch Ch, New Amsterdam; m. 1684, Staten Island, <u>Abraham LeRoux</u> as his 1st wife; she d. 1690, Kingston

NOTE: There was a Thomas Uzzell in N. Ireland, then in Isle of Wight Co, VA; his son Thomas went to NC – <u>no</u> connection to the NY family has been found.

REF: HOES, Roswell Randall, editor, *Baptismal & Marriage Registers of the Old Dutch Church of Kingston* (NY, 1891); BERGEN, Teunis G., *Register of the Early Settlers of Kings Co, Long Island, NY*; BECKER, Alfred LeRoy, "The Life & Family of Simeon LeRoy" in the *NYGBR*, Vol. LXIV (Jan, 1933); *New Netherland Connections*, Vol. 1, #2 (1996), Vol. 4, #2 (1999).

V

VAIRIN, Jacques

of Chervey, FR (marr. record), Aube Dept, Champagne-Ardennes, s.e. of Troyes

m. 7 Mar 1672, Landreville, s.w. of Chervey, same area, Louise Mellot of Viviers-sur-Artaut, bet.
Chervey & Landreville; on a list of Protestant marriages; there is a Jean Vairin from Chervey,
who m. Landreville, 7 Jul 1672, Marie Dacorat of Chesne – brother?

family members left FR at the time of the Revocation, went to GER and Russia; some members returned to
FR during the reign of Napoleon I; at the restoration of the Bourbons, some went to America

CHILD:

Jean Jacques[2], m. 29 April 1700, Homburg, GER, Louyse Melot (d. 7 Oct 1759, Homburg, GER, n.e. of
Saarbrücken); he was a merchant; **12 ch**; Homburg is c. 200 km. n.e. of Chervey

CHILDREN (ch. recs., Homburg):

Jean Louis[3], b. 8 Apr 1703; d. 4 May 1708

Élie[3], b. 1 Sep 1704

Marguerithe Louyse[3], b. 23 Sep 1705

Élie[3], b. 18 Feb 1708

Jean Jaques[3], b. 26 Apr 1709

Jaques[3], b. 14 May 1711

Pierre Élie[3], b. 15 Oct 1713

Jean Pierre[3], b. 2 Oct 1715; d. May 1716

Susanne Ester[3], b. 18 Jul 1720

Anne Caterine[3], b. 23 Feb 1723; d. 20 Aug 1725

Pierre Jaques[3], b. 22 Feb 1728, 12th ch (& last ch) of Jacques & Louise (Mellot) Vairin; m/1, 30
Nov 1752, Homburg, GER, Elizabeth Schultz (c. 1730, Homburg- 22 Oct 1759,
Homburg), d/o William Schultz – **3 sons, 1 dau**, m/2, 1 Oct 1760, Homburg, Anne Hahn (d. 28
Sep 1803, Homburg) – **4 sons, 3 daus**, births all recorded in the FR Reformed Ch in
Homburg; he d. 10 Feb 1796, Homburg, age 68 yrs. "and some days" – he was a merchant;
Homburg/Hombourg is also n.w. of Zweibrücken (Deux Ponts); some accounts say Charles
was the fa/ of Nicholas, Jean Pierre and Charles, but the b. records say their fa was Pierre
Jacques – Nicholas is not in the Homburg ch. recs but Jean Pierre and Charles are; according to
the Homburg ch. recs. the 1st ch (& only son older than Jean Pierre) of Pierre Jacques &
Elizabeth was Jean Chrisphle (*sic*), b. 28 Sep 1753 – change of name??

CHILDREN, m/1:

Nicholas[4], was a jeweler and engraver; left Homburg, went to St. Petersburg, Russia;
he and bro Charles encouraged Jean Pierre to go to St. Petersburg; he left St.
Petersburg about the same time as Jean Pierre & went to Moscow

Jean Pierre/ John Peter[4], b. 9 Oct 1757, Homburg; c. 1799, went to St. Petersburg, Russia
where he m. c. 1790, Marguerite Pauline (Piede?) de le Garde (c.1764-May 1827); Jean
was a prof of mathematics at the Polytechnic School there and later, the Chair of
mathematics of the Imperial Polytechnic Inst.; Marguerite was in the household of
Mme. la Duchesse de Pon who had been banished from the court of Louis XIV;
Catherine II "the Great" of Russia ruled that all foreigners must declare allegiance to
Russia or leave; they went to Metz where they lived for 4 yrs, then to Charleville,
Ardennes Dépt, where Jean Pierre was appt. head of the Central School of Ardennes
Dépt which was situated in Mezières; 1810, he was appt. Surveyor General of the Dept
& City of Homburg; both Juste and Auguste fought in the Napoleonic Wars and held
commissions in their regiments; with the defeat of Napoleon in 1815, JP was ruined
and decided to go to America; his credentials as an engineer helped him to find work in
NY; he had letters of introduction to DeWitt Clinton; he was asked to survey the
territory that would become the Albany & Buffalo/Erie Canal and superintend the

project – he declined & headed west; 1815/6, he was in the area of Vevay, Switzerland Co, IN, where he purchased a piece of Louis Gex Oboussier's farm (aka David Louis Gex), on 15 Jun 1816; Juste and Auguste came to NY, 1 Jul 1816, and were in IN by autumn; Jean Pierre d. 29 Aug 1817, of malaria, in Vevay, IN

CHILDREN:

Justine[5], b. & d. Russia

Cécile[5], b. Russia; d. 1798, Metz

Juste Nicolas/Justus[5], b. 19 May 1795, Metz, FR; m/1, 12 Dec 1817, Victoire Helvetia Gex, d/o David Louis Gex – 1 son **John Peter**[6], m/2, 9 Oct 1824, Vevay, IN, Sarah Wright (3 Jul 1803-2 Apr 1839, Orleans Par., LA) -her father was a banker in London – **2 sons, 4 daus** – his sons were businessmen in New Orleans, his daus resided in Owensboro, KY; fam. went to Cincinnati, OH, then to New Orleans, LA, later to Owensboro, KY; he was a merchant; his sons were Justus, Julius; he d. 10 May 1872;

Juste had been one of Napoleon's bodyguards

CHILD, m/2 (1 of 6):

    Julius[6], b. 2 Feb 1833, Cincinnati; m. 10 Feb 1859, New Orleans, Amelia Thomson Nugent (1 Jan 1839, Opelousas, LA-4 Mar 1908, Orleans Par., New Orleans), d/o John Pratt & Anne Lavinia (Lewis) Nugent; he d. 5 May 1899, New Orleans; **6 ch**

Cécile[5], d. 1798, Metz

Auguste/Augustus[5], b. 1799, Charleville, FR; m. 5 Oct 1818, Susan S. Pernet – went to New Orleans ,where he d. – 1 son **Augustus**

Jules/Julius[5], b. 1801; went to New Orleans; became a successful businessman; left his fortune to his bro Justus – perhaps did not marry or have issue

Charles Louis[4] b. 8 Jun 1766, Homburg, was a military surgeon; left Homburg, went to St. Petersburg, Russia; he joined the Russian Army and served in the Crimea; went to Moscow, m. the d/o of a rich druggist

Elizabeth[4], liv. 1837, Homburg

Therèse[4], liv. 1837, Homburg

REF: VAIRIN, Aphra Nugent, *A History of William Lewis Family Descendants* (1912-13, not pub.) – includes obit for Julius; deed, Switzerland Co, IN; DUFOUR, *Indiana Historical Collections*, Vol. XIII, *Swiss Settlement of Switzerland County*; BALDWIN, Sarah Vairin (Mrs. H.F.), *Jeanne Pierre and Marguerite* (Pascagoula, MS, 1935, not pub.); church records, l'Église Françoise de Hombourg, Ev. Erlöserkirchengemende, Bad Homburg; FRANZ, *Reform. Kirchenbuch Homburg und Dornholzhausen, 1686-1825, Kleins franz. Reform. Kirchenbuch Homburg, Taufen, 1750-1807*; ; CHRISTY, Mrs. Beverly Vairin Morris, *Revised History of the Vairin Family Using Up-dated Research, 26.4.1993.*

VALLEAU, Esaïe

b. c. 1608, Île de Ré; called Sieur de la Prée

m/1, Michelle Parcot

m/2, Île de Ré, Marie Sorré, of Loix, now Charente-Maritime Dépt, Poitou-Charente, n.w. of La Rochelle

d. a. 1674

CHILDREN, m/1:

Esaïe/Isaiah[2], b. 1638; m. FR, Suzanne Descard (c. 1636-a. 9 Oct 1710), d/o Jean & Marie (Dumas) Descard; she d. p. 1690; he was a merchant at St. Martin de Ré, at the time of the Revocation; c. 1685, to NY, settled in New Rochelle; 6 Feb 1696, letters of denization; he d. a. 13 May 1713, wp, New Rochelle, 75Y; his will mentions son Peter, dau Borrim's ch, eldest son's ch, FR Ch of New Rochelle

CHILDREN:

Isaiah[3], b. 1661 Île de Ré, FR; m. XX – son **Isaiah**[3]; he was a merchant at St. Thomas

Susanne[3], b. 1665; m. 29 Sep 1689, FR Ch, NYC, Aman Bonnin of Poitiers, FR; d. bet
        1701-03; **6 ch**; Aman m/2, 28 Dec 1705, Mary Prudence de Neufville

Peter[3], b. 1664/7; m/1, Jeanne (Neufville?), m/2, Suzanne X, m/3, Madeleine Fauconnier (bp. 13 May
    1685, London-a. 24 Jun 1755, wp), d/o Pierre & Madeline (Pasquereau) Fauconnier; he d. a. 10 Apr
    1745– **3 sons, 3 daus**, m/3

Jean[3], b. 28 Feb, bp. 4 Mar 1688, St. Martin, Île de Ré

Marie[3], b. 18 Sep, bp. 6 Oct 1669, St. Martin, Île de Ré; she d. 29 Oct 1670

Étienne[3], b. 25 Jan 1671

Paul[3], b. 9 Jun, bp. 12 Jun 1672

Étienne[2], m/1, Esther Villier, m/2, Mary X; 1682, fled from Île de Ré, to ENG; went w/ a group of Huguenots,
    arr. Nov 1686, in NYC, from the Islands of St. Christopher & Martinique, W. Indies; naturalized, NYC,
    27 Sep 1687

CHILDREN (prob. several more):

Gabriel[3], b. 1657; m. 19 Nov 1680, Marthe Distillemau, d/o David & Élisabeth (Baudry)
        Distillemau; **dau**[4], who was b. and d. the same day

Pierre[3], b. 1659; m. 21 Aug 1684, Élisabeth Sallé, d/o Jean & Claude (Martin) Sallé

Étienne II[3], m. Marie Gallais; he was a cooper; 1 least **1 dau**

Arnaud[3]

Sarah[3]

Mary[3]

Anne[2], m. Étienne Bernard; she d. at the age of 28, bur. 4 Jun 1672, St. Martin de Ré

Jean[2],

Marie

Magdelaine

Pierre

CHILDREN, m/2:

Charles[2], m. Anne Brigaud; left FR at the same time as his ½ bro Esaïe; went to Dublin, IRE, where she
        d.; dau **Anne**[3], b. 7 May 1673, m. 24 Aug 1692, FR Ch, NYC Élie Chardavoine – **6 ch**

Marie[2]

REF: HELFFENSTEIN, Abraham Ernest, *Pierre Fauconnier & His Descendants* (Philadelphia, 1911); EARLE,
Mary E. & Elinor E., *Valleau Genealogy* (not dated, not pub.).

VALLIANT, John

    b. c. 1670, FR?, s/o (Jean?) & Mary (X) Valliant; mother's maiden name *poss.* Devallock, but more likely she
        remar & that was the name of her husband in 1685; lived in the Elephant & Castle, Picadilly (*sic*),
        London according to the document below (Elephant & Castle & Piccadilly are on opposite sides of the
        Thames – Elephant & Castle is in Southwark, it was considered "the Piccadilly of South London")

    16 Oct 1685- document recorded in London says that John, w/ the consent of his mother, Mary Devallock,
        bound himself as an apprentice to Samuel Phillips of Lymas*, Co. Middlesex; Phillips was a mariner
        and John was to serve in MD for 4 years; document also mentions an uncle X Valliant of Lincoln's Inn
        Fields, servant to John De la Fontain, Esq. *prob. means Limehouse, a London parish, 3 mi. e. of St.
        Paul's

    m/1, a. 1702, Mary (Frith?) who d. p. 16 Nov 1702, when she & John witnessed a land transaction

    [some say there was another marr between Mary & Judith to Mary (O'Malley) Dawson – not proven]

    m/2, a. 18 Mar 1713, widow Judith X, when she & John witnessed a land transaction - **no issue**; Judith m.
        a 3rd time after John's death; Judith was perhaps the widow of Thomas Bennett

    d. p. 13 Jan 1721, wd - a. 28 May 1722, wp, Treadhaven Creek, Talbot Co, MD; mentions wife Judith, ch
        Mary, wife/o John Weymouth, Dorothy, wife/o Caleb Esgate, John, James, Joseph, Susanah;

Treadhaven Creek is prob. in the area of Easton – today there are a couple places called Tred Avon there

CHILDREN, m/1:

John[2]

James[2], d. p. 25 Oct 1732, wd - a. 8 Nov 1732, wp, Talbot Co, MD; was a carpenter; apparently had **no direct descendants**; his will mentions sisters Elizabeth Spry, Mary Wainoth, Dorothy Esgate, Susaney Clift, bros John, Joseph

Joseph[2]

Elizabeth[2], m. Thomas Spry (d. p. 13 Jan 1741, wd - a. 18 Apr 1746, wp, Talbot Co, MD); will mentions wife Elizabeth, sons Thomas, Christopher, dau Elizabeth

CHILDREN

Thomas[3]

Elizabeth[3], m. Josiah Massey (1757-1789, Kent Co, MD), s/o Peter & Notley (Wright) Massey; at least **2 sons**

Christopher[3], m. Mary X; a planter; d. p. 8 Feb 1766, wd - a. 16 Jun 1767, wp, Talbot Co, MD; will mentions wife Mary, sons Thomas, Christopher, John, Francis (in that order – Christopher & Francis not of age), daus Elizabeth, Sarah, Mary, Rebecca, Eve, Lucrecia

CHILDREN:

Thomas[4]; **John**[4]; **Elizabeth**[4], m. Josiah Massey (b. 1757 d. p. 16 Dec 1789, wd Kent Co, MD; will mentions wife Elizabeth, son **James Maynard**[5] & an unborn ch)   ;
Sarah[4]; **Mary**[4]; **Rebecca**[4]; **Eve**[4]; **Christopher**[4]; **Francis**[4]; **Lucrecia**[4]

Mary[2], m. John Weymouth/Wainoth

Dorothy[2], m. Caleb Esgate (d. a. 26 May 1732, wp, Talbot Co, MD – wife not in will, must have d. a. 3 May 1732 when the will was written); **issue**

Susanah[2], m. X Clift

REF: LEONARD, R.B. *Talbot County Maryland Land Records*, Book 4, p. 7, Book 5, p. 4; *The Maryland Calendar of Wills, 1720-1726,* Vol. V (1968), p. 103, *1726-1732,* Vol. VI (1968), p. 242 , 1744-1749, Vol. 9, p. 70, 1764-1767, Vol. 13, p. 186; *Lord Mayor's (London) Waiting Books,* Vol. 14, p. 432, 16 Oct 1685; MASSEY, Frank A., *Massey Genealogy Addendum* (Ft. Worth, TX).

VAN METRE/VAN METEREN, Jan Joosten

m. Macyken Hendricksen of Meppelen (now Meppel), Drenthe Prov., NETH

from Tielerwaard, Gelderland, NETH, an area in which the town of Tiel is located; the town of Meteren is
 c. 8 km s.w. of Tiel; Van Meteren = of Meteren

12 Apr 1662 - arr New Netherland on *d'Vos* (the Fox); emigrated w/ wife + 5 ch, aged 15, 12, 9, 6, 2 ½ yrs.

summer? of 1662 - moved to Wyltwik (Kingston)

7 Jun 1663 – Macyken + 2 of her ch (one being Joost Jans) were carried away during an Indian raid
 all were later rescued

bet 21-26 Oct 1664 - took Oath of Allegiance

became a prominent citizen & *schepen*, elder of the Reformed Dutch Ch, magistrate

30 Mar 1671 - had a deed for a lot in Marbletown; rec. confirmation of a 30 acre lot, on 11 Oct 1671

1 Sep 1689 - Ulster Co, swore allegiance to the English king

c. 1695 - was in E. Jersey where he & his son-in-law Jan/John Hamel purchased 500 acres at Lassa Point
 (now the site of the city of Burlington) on the Delaware River in Burlington Co, c. 20 mi n.e. of
 Philadelphia

5 Jun 1696 – seems to have returned to Ulster Co, NY; but he & John Hamel owned the land at Lassa Pt
 until 1 May 1699, when Jan deeded to Hamel

13 Sep 1700 - purchased parcels of land in Somerset Co, NJ on the South Branch of the Raritan River nr.
 Somerville, totaling 1835 acres

d. a. 13 Jun 1706, inv., Burlington Co, NJ

CHILDREN:

Lysbeth², d. a. 16 Dec 1681; **issue**

Catharine²

Geertje², m. Jan/John Hamel

Joost Jans², b. c. 1656, Gelderland, NETH; m. 12 Dec 1682, New Paltz, NY Sarah du Bois (bp. 14 Sep 1662-1726), d/o Louis & Catherine (Blanchan) du Bois; d. a. 1706, prob. Raritan, (now Somerville) NJ
CHILDREN:

    Jan/John³, bp. 14 Oct 1683; m/1, c. 1705, Sarah Bodine/Berdine, d/o Jean & Marie (Crocheron) Bodine – **1 son, 2 daus,** m/2, a. 1711, Margaret Mollenauer (1687-1709, Somerset Co, NJ), d/o Hendrick Mollenauer – **4 sons, 4 daus;** he d. 3 Sep 1745, wp, Winchester, VA

    Rebekka³, bp. 26 Apr 1686, Marbletown; m. p. 3 Sep 1704 (date of 1st banns), Kingston, Cornelis Elten/Elting (bp. 29 Dec 1681-1754, Frederick Co, MD), s/o Jan Elten & Jacomyntje Slecht; she d. 1755; **10 ch**

    Lysbeth/Elizabeth³, b. 3 Mar 1689

    Rachel³, b. c. 1692

    Hendrix/Henry³, b. 1 Sep 1695, Marbletown; went to Salem Co, NJ

    Abraham³, b. c. 1700

    Isaac³, b. c. 1702; went to NJ; m/1, Catalina? X, widow of Molenaer Hendrickse, m/2, c. 1725, Annetje Wyncoop, d/o Gerritt Wyncoop; **8 ch**

    ?Jacob³, b. c. 1705

Gysbert Janse², b. c. 1660

REF: SMYTH, Samuel Gordon, *A Genealogy of the Duke-Sheperd-Van Metre Family* (Lancaster, PA, 1909); SMYTH, Samuel Gordon, *The Origin & Descent of an American Van Metre Family* (Lancaster, PA, 1923); HEID-GERD, William, compiler, *The American Descendants of Chrétien du Bois of Wicres, FR*, Part 1 (New Paltz, NY, 1968).

VARIN/VEREEN, Jacques/James

b. 1650, FR; father *poss.* named Jérémie Varin; was from Rouen according to the list of the passengers on the *Richmond*

m. FR, or London, ENG, Susanne Horry (b. 1659 Neufchâtel, SWI-1725), d/o Samuel & Jeanne (DuBois) Horry; she was naturalized in SC in 1696 w/ her ch Susanne and Jacob

29 Apr 1680 – arr, SC on the *Richmond* w/ wife & son; Jacques now called James; on his arr., rec. a warrant for 210 acres for him, his wife & son – assuming that Jean Jacques was the Jacob who was naturalized w/ his mother, Isaac must have d. young in ENG

25 Feb 1683/4 - warrant for 210 acres in Tranquil Hill

1686 - purchased Lot #27 in Charleston on the Great St. leading from the sea to the market place

he was a member of the FR Ch in the Orange Quarter

d. 1690, Orange Quarter, SC; he was a joiner

CHILDREN:

Isaac², bp. 21 Jun 1674, FR Ch, Threadneedle St, London, ENG; prob. d. young ENG

Susanne², bp. 25 Jul 1675, FR Ch, Threadneedle St.; d. young

Jean Jacques², bp. 13 Aug 1676, FR Ch, Threadneedle St; became Jacob in SC??

Susanne², bp. 26 May 1678, FR Ch, Threadneedle St.; m. 1695, Joel Poinsett, s/o Pierre II & Sara (Fouchereau) Poinset; **5 ch**

Jérémie², b. c. 1680, SC; m. Jane Evens, aka Jane Avant, who m/2, 10 Feb 1712, Moses Plumer; on a list dated 1696/7, he was listed as a FR settler rec. grant in the Orange Quarter; he rec. 360 acres in 1711; went from Charleston to Parish of St. Thomas & St. Denis in Berkeley Co; he d. 1710, Berkeley Co, SC
CHILDREN:

    Jeremiah³, b. 6 Jan 1706, SC; m/1, Mary X (17101-27 Jul 1733), m/2, Mary X (Coachman?) (1727-1832); moved to a plantation on the Santee nr. his uncle Samuel; also had property in Horry Co which belonged to his 2nd wife; he d. 1768

CHILDREN, m/1:

William[4], b. 23 Nov 1729; m. 20 Nov 1754, Elizabeth Lewis (30 Nov 1734-7 Jun 1779), d/o Charles & Martha (X) Lewis, Rev. War service, d. 20 Sep 1789, Horry Strand – **8 ch**

Elisabeth[4], b. 14 Nov 1731; m. John Sullivant

poss. **Ann**[4], who m. X Jenkins

Sarah[4], who m. X Lewis

CHILDREN, m/2:

Jeremiah[4]; **Ebenezer**[4], **Rebecca**[4], **Hannah**[4], **Rachel**[4], **Jean**[4], **Martha**[4]

Mary[3], b. 23 Jun 1709, SC

Samuel[2], b. 1683, SC; m. XX; liv. on the n. side of the Santee River-his plantation was along the present Georgetown-Williamsburg Co. line; wd, 1 Nov 1744; he d. 1745

CHILDREN:

James[3], d. age 1 Y

Anne[3], m. Francis Harbin

unnamed dau[3], m. X Crousy; **2 daus**

REF: ANDREA, Leonardo, *The Vereens of Horry* (1957); *SC Historical & Genealogical Magazine*, Vol. XVIII, pp. 109, 114, Vol. XX, pp. 48, 49; *New World Immigrants*, Vol. 1, pp. 222-23; BOCKSTRUCK, Lloyd D., *Denizations & Naturalizations in the British Colonies in America, 1607-1775* (Baltimore, 2005), p. 140.

VASSAL(L), Jean

b. Normandie, FR; birthplace "called Rinart by Cany" [Rinart does not exist and Cany is prob. Caen in Basse-Normandie]; sent his son Jean[2] to ENG because of the unsettled conditions in FR at that time – this information given in a "Visitation of London" in 1643; the family was originally from Rignac in the former province of Périgord* – the Rignac in Lot Dépt, Midi-Pyrénées, n.e. of Cahors or, according to one source, the Rignac in the Aveyron Dépt, Midi-Pyrénées, n.e. of Villefranche-de-Rouergue; surname was prob. spelled Vassal in FR

CHILD:

Jean/John[2], b. Normandie, FR; m/1, 25 Sep 1569, Anne Hewes, m/2, 4 Sep 1580, Anna Russell (bur. 4 May 1593), m/3, 27 Mar 1594, Judith (Aborough) Scott, d/o Stephen & Johanna (Overye) Aborough/Borough, widow of Thomas Scott (she d. Jan 1638/39) – all 3 marr. were at St. Dunstan's, Stepney; Jean was a mariner, captain and owner of 2 ships, the *Little Toby* & the *Samuel*, in the fleet against the Armada (1588); he liv. in Ratcliffe, Stepney Parish, from 1589-1602, then he moved to Cockseyhurst, Eastwood, Co. Essex, n. of Southend-on-Sea; he d. of the plague a. 16 Sep 1625, wp; his will names his wife Judith, dau Judith, widow of John Freeborne, sons Samuel, William; dau Anne Jones; dau Rachel, wife of Peter Andrewes (*sic*); sons Stephen & Thomas; dau Mary, wife of Edward West; dau Elizabeth, wife of Henry Church

CHILD, m/1:

?Andrew[3], bur. from St. Dunstan's 17 Apr 1575 – *may* have been the s/o John and Anne

CHILDREN, m/2, bp. Stepney Parish, London, ENG:

Judith[3], bp. 25 Mar 1582; m. p. 26 Jul 1598, John Freeborne of Prittlewell, Co. Essex who d. a. 17 Feb 1617, wp; **5 ch**

John[3], bp. 1 Apr 1584; bur. 3 Oct 1585, Stepney Parish

Samuel[3], bp. 5 Jun 1586; m. Frances Cartwright (d. by 17 Nov 1660), d/o Abraham & Joan (Wade) Cartwright; he d. a. 24 Sep 1667 (adm) abroad; he was an incorporator of the MA Bay Company in 1628 but there is no proof that he ever went to New England; **8 sons, 2 daus**

John[3], b. 14 Mar 1589 or 24 Mar 1590/91; bur. 20 or 30 Aug 1591

William[3], bp. 27 Aug 1592; m. p. 9 Jun 1613 (date of marr. lic.), Anna King, d/o George King(e)

of Cold Norton, Co. Essex; 1629, emigrated on the *Lion* but ret. to ENG; 1635, emigrated to MA, on the *Blessing*, went to Roxbury; 1636, in Scituate; back to ENG in 1646, 1648 to Barbados where he d. a. 7 Aug 1655, wp; **2 sons, 6 daus**

CHILDREN, m/3:

Anne[3], bp. 10 Jan 1594/5, Stepney; m. John Jones; bur. 24 Jun or Jul 1640 St. Nicholas Acons, where her husband was the rector; her will was proven 27 Jul 1640; **8 sons** named in her will

Rachel[3], m. Peter Andrews, merchant of London who d. a. 3 Oct 1650, wp; **2 daus**

Stephen[3], b. c. 1598; attended Pembroke College, Cambridge, rec. a B.A. & M.A.; m/1, Mary Bromley (d. 20 Jan 1632/3) – **1 dau, 2 sons**, m/2, Mary Grubbe (b. 2 Jan 1614) d/o John Grubbe of St. Albans, Hertfordshire; he d. 1643, Rayleigh, Co. Essex, where he was rector; **1 son, 2 daus**

Thomas[3], b. 2 Apr 1602; m. 25 Jun 1625, St. Nicholas Acons, Anne Dickenson; d. p. 1650; he was a draper

Mary[3], m. a. 1633, Edward West of Ratcliffe, a mariner

?Jane[3], bur. 11 Aug 1603, St. George's Southwark, Co. Surrey

Joan[3], m. 28 Feb 1619, St. Nicholas Acons, Robert Salmon, a mariner

Elizabeth[3], b. c. 1608; m. 20 Jan 1624/5, St. Nicholas Acons, Henry Church, of Wapping

***NOTE:** Périgord was a province located in what are now the départements of Dordogne (now in Aquitaine) & part of Lot

REF: McCRACKEN, George E., "The Vassalls of London and Jamaica" in *Studies in Genealogy & Family History in Tribute to Charles Evans on the Occasion of His Eightieth Birthday*, edited by Lindsay L. Brook (Salt Lake City, 1989); CALDER, Charles M., "Alderman John Vassall & His Descendants" in the *NEHG Register* (Apr 1955); "Genealogical Gleanings in England" in the *NEHG Register* (Apr 1897); "The Vassalls of New England" in the *NEHG Register*, Vol. XVII (Jan, 1863); MEYER, Virginia M. & DORMAN, John Frederick, *Adventurers of Purse & Person, 1607-1624/5* (Richmond, VA, 1987); COOPER, William Durrant, *Lists of Foreign Protestants & Aliens, Resident in England 1618-1688* (1862).

VAUTRIN/VOTRIN/WOTRING, Abraham

family said to have left FR, by 1600, went to Kirrberg* which they helped found w/ other exiles; they settled Kirrberg (now Bas-Rhin Dépt, Alsace, FR), s. of Sarre-Union

bp. 11 Jul 1700, s/o Abraham & Katherina (Brodt) Vautrin of Lixheim* (now Moselle Dépt, Lorraine, FR), n.w. of Sarrebourg; he was a miller at Fénétrange, now Moselle Dépt, Lorraine, n.w. Kirrberg

m. 19 Mar 1723, Anna Margaretha Mertz, d/o Peter Mertz of Lutzelbourg* (now Vosges Dépt, Lorraine, FR) *all 3 towns are within a few km. of each other, as is Hirschland

28 Sep 1733 - arr Philadelphia on the *Richard & Elizabeth* from Rotterdam, via Plymouth, ENG; settled Berks Co, PA; his bro Samuel & his 1st cousin John also emigrated – Samuel arr 15 Sep 1749, on the *Phoenix*, at Philadelphia, John arr Philadelphia, 3 Sep 1739

d. 28 Nov 1752, at which time only 8 of his 16 ch were living

CHILDREN (9 of 16):

Hans/John Peter[2], b. 5 Mar 1724, Fénétrange,; m/1, c. 1748, Anna Margaret X – **3 sons, 1 dau**, m/2, c. 1759, Elizabeth X – **2 daus**, m/3, c. 1765, Catherine X – **1 son, 2 daus**; d. a. 20 Sep 1758, adm, Easton, PA

Anna Margaretha[2], b. 20 Oct 1725, Fénétrange; m. John Schneider; d. 8 Oct 1763 – Margaret & John + 2 of their daus were killed, 8 Oct 1763, Whitehall, PA, by Indians; **7 daus**

Maria Magdalena[2], bp. 16 Mar 1728, Hirschland, Bas-Rhin Dépt Alsace, FR, s.e. Sarre-Union; m. c. 1749, prob. N. Whitehall Twp, Lehigh Co, PA, Paulus Bailliet, grs/o Jacob Baillet; she d. 1802; **5 sons, 4 daus**

Anna Elizabeth[2], d. p. 28 Nov 1730, Hirschland; m. Martin Andreas; **5 sons, 2 daus**

John Jacob[2], b. 3 Aug 1732, Hirschland; d. young

John William[2], b. c. 1738; m. a. Jan 1766, Christina Kocher; d. 3 Jul 1778, Wyoming Massacre, Luzerne
  Co, PA; **5 sons, 2 daus**

Anna Barbara[2], bp. 22 Mar 1739, Egypt Reformed Ch, Lehigh Co, PA; m. Adam Ochs; d. p. 28 Nov
  1752; at least **2 sons, 2 daus**

Abraham[2], b. 1744; m. c. 1766, Mary Margaret Troxell; d. 1809, Aurora, Preston, WV; **7 sons, 2 daus**

Eva[2], b. bet 1748-52; m. David Hahn; went to KY; **5 sons, 2 daus**

REF: BALLIET, Stephen, *The Balliet, Balliett, Balliette, Balyeat, Bolyard & Allied Families* (1968); BELL, Ray-
Mond Martin & GRANQUIST, Mabel Ghering, *The Wotring-Woodring Family of PA* (Washington, PA, 1953 & 3rd
Edition, 1968); ROBERTS, Charles Rhoads, *The First Huguenot Settlers in the Lehigh Valley* (Allentown, PA, 1918)

VAUX/VEAUX/DEVOE, Nicolas de

m. FR, Susanna François

CHILDREN:

Nicolas[2], b. c. 1644, Festubert, Artois, FR, n.e. of Béthune; fled FR, went to Mannheim, GER; m/1, 10 Jul
  1667, FR Reformed Ch, Mannheim, Marie (Sy) Petilion, widow of Jacques Petilion, d/o Jean Sy;
  went to ENG; by 1674 - on the *Diamond* to NYC; later settled in the Huguenot settlement in
  Hackensack, NJ; m/2, 20 Apr 1706, Margaret (Sans/Jans) Batton, widow of Jacques Batton; he
  d. a. 1717, Hackensack, NJ

 CHILDREN, m/1:

 Abraham[3], b. 11 Jun, bp. 14 Jun 1668, FR Reformed Ch, Mannheim; m. 1688, Meyna/Mynno/
   Jemina (Jurckse) Hoppe, d/o Paulus & Christina/Styntie Jurckse, widow of Willem Hoppe;
   deacon & elder of 1st Reformed Ch of Tarrytown; **8 ch**

 John[3], b. 1669

 Hester[2], b. 1671; m. 5 Nov 1698, Dutch Ch, Hackensack, Uldrick Brouwer; she d. 19 May 1710,
   Bergen, NJ

 Susannah[3], b. 1673; d. young

 Maritie[3], b. 1675, Harlem, NY; m. 29 Sep 1710, Jacob Buys of Bergen

 Susanna[3], bp. 11 Oct 1680, Hackensack; m/1, 17 Jul 1697, Dutch Ch, Hackensack, Thomas
   Brickers; m/2, 25 Jun 1706, Dutch Ch, Hackensack, Jacobus Everse Van Gelder - **ch**

 CHILD, m/2:

 Ester[3], bp. 29 Jul 1711, Hackensack

Frédéric/Frederick[2], b. c. 1645, Festubert, Artois, FR, n.e. of Béthune, now in Pas-de-Calais Dépt, Nord-
  Pas-de-Calais; fled FR to Mannheim; m/1, 12 Feb 1668, FR Ch, Mannheim, Marguerite Bonde;
  went to ENG; 1675 - to NY; m/2, 24 Jun 1677, Ester/Hester Tourneur, d/o Daniel & Jacqueline
  (deParisis) Tourneur; he d. 1742, New Rochelle, NY; 8 Dec 1743, wp, Westchester Co, NY; will
  does not mention a wife; mentions eldest son Frederick, sons Joseph, Abel; daus Judith, Rachel,
  Susannah, Esther, Leah, Dinah (dec), Mary; 11 gr ch; sons Frederick and Daniel were executors

 CHILDREN, m/1:

 Susanne[3], bp. 20 Dec 1668, FR Ch, Mannheim

 Frederich[3], bp. 16 Feb 1670, FR Ch, Mannheim

 CHILDREN, m/2:

 Jacob[3] (twin), b. 1 May 1678; d. young

 Rachel[3] (twin), b. 1 May 1678; m. Johannes Dyckman

 Esther[3], b. 8 May 1680; m. Laury Vincent

 Susannah[3], b. 2 Jul 1682; m. Andrew Naudain, s/o André & Marguerite (X) Naud(a)in

 Frederick[3], b. 1684; m/1, Hester Dykman; m/2, 1721, Mary Odell

 Daniel[3]

 Abel[3], b. c. 1688; m. c. 1717, Magdalena Hunt; d. 1774

 Mary[3], m/1, Evert Brown – at least 5 ch; m/2, Joshua Bishop

Leah[3], m. Nathaniel Bayley

Dinah[3], m. Tobias Conkling; d. a. 23 Jan 1741 (date of father's will); at least **5 ch**

Joseph[3]

Judith[3], m. Johannes Barhite

Abigail[3]

REF: BAIRD, Charles W., *Huguenot Emigration to America*; DeVOE, Thomas F., *Genealogy of the DeVeaux Family* 1985); SEACORD, Morgan H., *Biographical Sketches & Index of Huguenot Settlers of New Rochelle, 1678-1776;* RIKER, James, *History of Harlem* (1904); Frederick's will; MACKENZIE, Grenville C., *Families of the Colonial Town of Philipsburgh* (Tarrytown, NY 1976); HILL, Glenna See, "New Information on the See & de Vaux Families" – *NY Genealogical & Biographical Record*, Vol. 110 #2 (Apr 1979); NELSON, William, *NJ Marriage Records, 1665-1800*; RIKER, James, *Revised History of Harlem Its Origin & Early Annals* (NY 1904); DURIE, Haward I., "Some Lesser Known Huguenots on the Hackensack" – *Bergen Co. History* (1971); HEIDGERD, Ruth P., *Mannheim: Records of the French Congregation, 1651-1710.*

VERMEILLE/VERMILYE/VERMILYEA, Jean/Johannes

m/1, Marie Roubley; there was a Marie Vermeille who m. Jean Dimanche – was it this Marie or was there a dau Marie?

c. 1599 - fled Flanders; to London, a. 1612; c. 1613, to HOL

CHILDREN:

Rachel[2], admitted to church in London, 15 Jul 1613; m. 25 Apr 1615, Leiden, HOL, Jacques Bardelo, a Walloon of Valenciennes, FR

Isaac[2], b. 1601, bp. Walloon Ch, London; m. 1627, Leiden, Jacomina Jacobs (b. HOL); emigrated 1662, on *The Brindled Cow*, arr. New Amstel on the Delaware River; 1663, to Harlem, NY; d. 1676, Harlem, NY

CHILDREN, b. Leiden:

Marie[3], bp. 2 Aug 1629, Leiden, HOL; m/1, 10 Jun 1663, John de La Montagne, m/2, Isaac Kip

Johannes[3], b. 1632, bp. Leiden; m. 27 Aug 1670, NY, Aeltie Waldron, d/ Resolved & Rebecca (Hendricks) Waldron – **10 ch**; emig. w/ parents, in 1662; he was appt. to command a military company in NY, 1663, served 2 terms as a magistrate; son **Joost**[4], m. 16 Jan 1707, Josyntie Houpeleine, d/o Joost Houpeleine/Oblinus & Marie Sammis – **3 sons, 5 daus**, Joost d. a. 5 Mar 1767, wp

Abraham[3], **no issue**

Rachel[3], bp. 1637; m/1, John Terbosch, m/2, Derick Wessels

Jean[2], m/1, XX – **ch** b. London, c. 1633, m/2, 1647, Leiden, XX

Rebecca[2], b. 1609, London

REF: RIKER, James, *Harlem Its Origin & Early Annals* (NY, 1881), *Revised History of Harlem (1904)*; BENTON, John H., *Benton Genealogy* (not dated, not pub.); PAGE, Marion Reed & SYMONDS, David, *Ancestors of Charles A. Stymus & His Wife Ella C. Smith 1620-1989* (self-published, 1989).

VERUE(I)L, Moyse/Moïses

b. 22 Sep 1651, Rouen; bp 24 Sep 1651, Rouen-Quevilly, s/o Jean & Magdelaine (DuFay) Veruel who m. 16 Jan 1633, Rouen-Quevilly; he was a merchant in Rouen; Quevilly an area n.w. of Rouen

m/1, a. 1677, XX (d. a. Dec 1677)

m/2, 9 Dec 1677, The Hague, Ma(g)delaine Prudon/Prudhomme (bp. 27 Jun 1658, The Hague), d/o Nicolaas Louis & Magdalena (Teveningh) Prudon/Prudhomme who m. 21 Aug 1653, The Hague; she m/2, 13 Dec 1703, Henrico Co, VA, Jacob Flournoy

c. 12 Sep 1700 - went to VA on the *Peter and Anthony* – list has Moïse, Madelaine + 5 ch so another ch must have d.

d. p. 4 Feb 1700/1- a. Dec 1703, VA

CHILDREN, m/2 (all bap The Hague):

Magdelaine, bp 24 Sep 1679; d. young

Nikolaus, bp 4 Apr 1681

Jean, bp. 28 Jan 1682

Madelaine, bp. 28 Jan 1685, The Hague; m/1, c. 1703/4, Antoine Trabue/Trabac (as his 2nd wife) – **5 ch**, m/2, 1725/6, Pierre Chastain (as his 3rd wife) – **no issue**

Judith, bp 8 Sep 1686; d. young

David, bp. 21 Apr 1688

Jacques, bp 10 Nov 1689

Judith, bp 9 Sep 1694

REF: "Antoine Trabuc/Trabue…. & His Two Wives…" by ALLEN, Cameron, *TAG*, Vol. 83, #3 (Jan/Apr 2009); YATES, Julie Trabue & TRABUE, Charles C.., IV. *The Trabue Family in America 1700-1983* (Baltimore, 1983); BROCK, Robert A., *Huguenot Emigration to VA* (Baltimore, 1979).

VESQUEAU, Jean Philip

b. c. 1700, Alsace-Lorraine area, FR

m. prob. FR, XX

went to HOL

1 Oct 1754 - arr Philadelphia, PA on the *Phoenix* w/ son François; went to Upper Milford Twp., Lehigh Co, PA

d. 8 Oct 1790, Upper Milford Twp, age 90Y

CHILD:

François[2], b. c. 1730, Alsace, FR; naturalized Philadelphia, 23 Mar 1761; m. Eva Margaret Christman; was called Frantz Wesco; d. a. 26 Apr 1809, wp

CHILDREN: Surname became **WESCO/WESCOE** (there is a town called Wescosville, s.w. of Allentown)

Matthias[3], m. Susanna X; **3 sons, 3 daus**

Elizabeth[3], m. 12 Oct 1779, Rudolph Laros (b. Alsace-Lorraine-d. 29 Aug 1806, nr. Millerstown, PA); she d. 15 Feb 1785 – **3 sons, 1 dau**; he m/2, Susanna Breinard who d. 7 Sep 1803 – 3 sons, 4 daus

Rosina[3]

Susanna[3], b. 3 Sep 1753; m. Nicholas Hittel (22 Jan 1748-10 May 1725); she d. 6 Jul 1834; **11 ch**

Philip[3], b. 17 Apr 1763; m. Anna Margaret Stahler (19 Jan 1767-10 Mar 1845); he d. 6 May 1844, Macungie Twp, Lehigh Co, PA; **11 ch**

John[3], bp. 20 Jun 1765; d. young

REF: ROBERTS, Charles Rhoads, *The First Huguenot Settlers in the Lehigh Valley* (Allentown, PA, 1918); *Proceedings of the Huguenot Society of PA* (1919); *History of Lehigh County, P*; STAPLETON, Rev. A., *Memorials of the Huguenots* (1901), p. 84.

VIA/VIAS/VIET, Pierre Amer

b. 1660. FR

by 1677- to VA

m. a. 1688, VA, Margaret X (d. c. 24 Nov 1711, New Kent Co, VA)

by 1698 - in Manakintown, VA

on tithing lists 1710, 1711

d. a. 17 Nov 1711/12, VA, when wife is listed as landowner

CHILDREN:

Nohome[2], d. 26 Mar 1688, St. Peter's Parish, New Kent Co, VA

Judith[2], bp. 11 Apr 1699, St. Peter's Parish, New Kent Co, VA; m. Henry Wade (b. 1690)

Margaret[2], bp. 3 Aug 1701, St. Peter's Parish, d. 1789; m. 1719, VA, Daniel Maupin, s/o Gabriel &
       Mary (Hersent) Maupin; **10 ch**

Mary[2], bp. 27 Feb 1703/4, St. Peter's Parish

Robert[2], b. c. 1687/88, Hanover Co, VA; m. XX; he d. p. 1764 Hanover Co, VA

      CHILD:

        Robert[3], b. c. 1730, Hanover Co, VA; m. Hanover Co, VA, Fanny Ann Ingram, d/o James (she
            d. p. 30 Nov 1795, wd - a. 28 Apr 1796, wp Patrick Co, VA); he d. p. 18 Aug 1788,
            Hanover Co, VA at least **5 ch**

        CHILDREN:

          Robert, Jr.[4], d. p. 19 Aug 1788, prob. a. 30 Nov 1795 - not in mother's will

          William[4], d. p. 30 Nov 1795

          James[4], d. p. 30 Nov 1795

          Anne[4], d. p. 30 Nov 1795

          Sarah[4], d. p. 30 Nov 1795

William[2], b. c. 1698/1700; d. 1783 Albemarle Co, VA; at least 1 son, poss. a dau Sarah

      CHILD:

        William, Jr.[3], b. c. 1730; m. Sarah Burnette?; d. by 1783 - father's will names Wm.'s children

REF: BAIRD, Charles W., *Huguenot Emigration to VA; The Parish Registers of St. Peter's Parish, 1680-1787, New Kent Co, VA; Vestry Book of King William Parish, Huguenot District, Powhatan Co, VA;* SHERMAN, Nell W., *The Maupin Family* (Peoria, IL, 1962); BROCK, *Huguenot Emigration,* p. 75; Records from The Huguenot Society of the Founders of Manakin in the Colony of VA.

VIDEAU, Pierre

     b. a. 1668, La Rochelle, FR, s/o Pierre & Madelaine (Burgaud) Videau(l)

     m. 6 Mar 1685, St. Martin-de-Ré, Île de Ré, FR Jeanne Elizabeth Mauzé, d/o Joseph & Renée (Mercier)
          Mauzé; Pierre was a merchant from La Rochelle according to the ch marr record

     10 Mar 1696/7 – SC, he, Jeanne & dau Jeanne Elizabeth were naturalized

     d. French Santee, SC

CHILDREN:

Jeanne Elizabeth[2], bp. 18 Nov 1685, Threadneedle FR Ch, London, ENG; m. p. 24 Sep 1702 (date of the
        espousal), Antoine Bonneau, s/o Jean & Catherine (Roi) Bonneau; she d. a. Feb 1742 - **5 sons, 6 daus**

Pierre Nicholas[2], b. SC

Jane/Jeanne[2], b. SC; m. Jacob Bonneau, s/o of Jean & Catherine (Roi) Bonneau

Henry Joseph[2], m. Ann Cordes; he was bur. 19 Apr 1773, Pompion Hill, SC; their dau **Mary Esther**[3] m.
        20 Apr 1786, Gen. Francis Marion, "the Swamp Fox" – **no issue**

Marianne[2], b. SC; m. Nicholas Bochet

Judith[2], b. SC

Madelaine[2], b. SC

Marthe Ester[2], b. SC; m. Thomas Young Simons

NOTE: An Elizabeth Videau m. Daniel Jaudon, s/o Élie & Sara (Bertonneau) Jaudon. She *may* have been one of the daus of Pierre – Marthe, Ester, Judith or Madelaine *could* have had Elizabeth as a 2nd name. Needs proof.

REF: BAIRD, Charles W., *History of the Huguenot Emigration to America,* Vol. I (Baltimore, MD, 1966); *Transactions of the Huguenot Society of SC,* #82 (1977), pp. 125-27.

VIGNEAU, Elizabeth – see **TILLOU**, Pierre

VILLEPONTEUX/VILLEPONTOUX, Pierre

b.   1643, Bergerac, Guienne, now in Dordogne Dépt, Aquitaine, s/o Zacharie & Marie (Lentilhac)
c.   Villepontoux
m. Jeanne Rivaison (b. 9 Jan 1655/6, Bergerac)
fled FR to ENG
5 Mar 1690/1 – naturalized in ENG – he, Jeanne, Peter, Marie & Jane
13 Apr 1692 – made a freeman in NYC; served as an attorney while in NY
1694 – purchased land in SC, Goose Creek, St. James Parish, nr. Charleston
1695, 1696 – Elder, FR Ch, NYC
1698 – Oath of Allegiance, New Rochelle, NY
a. 1701, a landowner in NY
1701 – went to SC
d. 1711, Goose Creek, St. James Parish, SC
CHILDREN.
Marie[2], b. 1683, Bergerac; m. 20 Oct 1710, SC, Gidéon Faucheraud (b. 1650, Port, Calvados, Basse-Norm.
     1 son, 3 daus
Peter[2], b. 27 Jul 1684, Bergerac; m. 1725, SC, Frances L'Escot (b. 1705), d/o Rev. Paul L/Escot(t)?; **4
     sons, 2 daus**
Jane[2], b. 14 Jul 1686
Isabel[2], b. 1691, prob. ENG
Suannah[2], b. 1694, NY
Rachel[2], b. 1696, New Rochelle; m/1, 1724, SC, John Moore – son **John**[3], b. 4 Jul 1726, m/2, 24 Nov
     1737, SC, Abijah Russ (b. 12 May 1706, SC), m/3, 1764, Bartholomew Homeli
Zachariah[2], b. 1698, New Rochelle; m. Amariah Perkins; **3 sons, 2 daus**

REF: PECK, I. Howard, "The Villeponteux Family of SC" in *SC Historical Genealogical Magazine*, Vol. 50.

VIVIAN/VIVION, John

b. c. 1655, prob. ENG; surname Vivian on a list of Huguenots naturalized Great Britain & IRE, bet 1681-1712
to VA, settled Middlesex Co.
m/1, c. 1679, Margaret Smith (c. 1660-by 1704), d/o John & Margaret (X) Smith
4 Apr 1681- appt. constable, Middlesex Co, VA
1687- was in the Middlesex Co. Militia, on list dated 23 Nov 1687, of men "Capable to Serve as footmen
     & to finde themselves with Armes"
m/2, 23 Feb 1704, Christ Ch, Middlesex Co., Christian (X) Petty Briscoe, widow/o Maximillian Petty
     & William Briscoe
d. a. 4 Jun 1705, wp, Middlesex Co, VA; will mentions ch Charles, John, Margaret Daniel, Diana, Thomas,
     wife's grdau Anne Smith, wife Christian, bro Thomas Smith
CHILDREN, m/1:
Charles[2,], b. Middlesex Co, VA; m. XX; no further info and was left only 20 sh by his father
John II[2], bp. 28 Apr 1681; m. 19 Jun 1711, Christ Ch, Middlesex Co., Elizabeth Thacker (3 Dec 1694-12
     Jan 1732), d/o Henry & Elizabeth (X) Thacker; he d. 12 Feb 1721/2, wp - 3 Jul 1722; **2 daus, 1 son**
Margaret[2], bp. 2 Apr 1684, Christ Ch, Middlesex Co; m. 27 Jan 1704, Christ Ch, Middlesex Co., James
     Daniell; d. 1750; **5 sons, 4 daus**
Diana[2], b. Middlesex Co, VA; m. 17 Oct 1706, Middlesex Co, VA, Garrett Minor; d. 16 Apr 1718; **issue**
Thomas[2], b. Middlesex Co, VA; m/1, 2 Jan 1717, Frances Thacker (d. 16 Aug 1724), sis/o Elizabeth

(above), <u>m/2</u>, 3 Oct 1727, Mary (X) Paise, widow of Thomas Paise, <u>m/3</u>, Jane X; he d. a. 23 Apr 1761, wp, Westmoreland Co, VA; total of **2 sons, 5 daus**

NOTE: There are several spurious accounts of this family. Some say he was the s/o a Royalist General, Thomas Vivion – there is no proof of that nor that that Thomas Vivion was the one who d. in Isle of Wight Co, VA. Nor is there proof that he had bros William, Joel & Robert. Also, it is not proven that he was involved with Nathaniel Bacon (Bacon's Rebellion, 1675) or that he m. Diana Cummings, niece of Gov. Berkeley of VA. He is said to have been a captain & acted as an emissary of King Charles II to inquire into the situation between Berkeley & Bacon – would seem to have been a bit young for that - again, no proof.

REF: RUBEY, Ann Todd, *The Tod[d]s of Caroline County, VA & Their Kin* (Columbia, MO, 1960); O'HART, John, *Irish Pedigrees* (Baltimore, 1976); HOLLOWAK, Thomas L., indexer, *Genealogies of VA Families from the VA Magazine of History & Biography*, Vol. V (Baltimore, 1981); *Parish Register of Christ Church, Middlesex Co, VA 1653-1812* (Baltimore, 1975); CROZIER, William Armstrong, editor, *Virginia County Records*, Vol. II (Baltimore, 1973); *VA County Court Records, Order Book Abstracts Middlesex Co, VA 1686-1690* (1994); *VA Magazine of History & Biography,* Vol. XXXIV (1926); XLVI (1938), Vol. *Genealogies of VA Families from the William & Mary Quarterly,* Vol. IV (Baltimore, 1982); HEINEMANN, Charles Brunk, "The Vivion Family of VA".

W

WILLEME/WILLAN/WILLIAM, Aventure

family in Calais area, a. 1649

1652 - in St.-Pierre-les-Calais

m. Marie du May (d. 31 Jan 1682)

liv. nr. Calais; appeared in records of the Reformed Ch in Guînes, s.e. Calais, Pas-de-Calais Dépt, Nord-Pas-de-Calais

d. a. 1668; widow + 3 ch fled Calais, went to GER, via HOL, in the winter of 1684/5, then to the *Pfalz,* nr. Mannheim

CHILDREN:

Marie[2], b. c. 1649; m. 24 Jul 1673, Guînes, Abraham du Vinage, s/o Arnoult Jeanne (Petit)du Vinage; Marie d. 10 Aug 1683, St. Pierre-lès-Calais; **4 ch**

Jean[2], b. c. 1656, St. Pierre-lès-Calais; m/1, 20 Feb 1678, Guînes, Marie Watté (d. 3 Jan 1682, St. Pierre), d/o Jean & Marie (Verdure) Watté – **no issue**, m/2, 31 Jan 1683, Guînes, Françoise Tourbier (b. c. 1659, Sainghin-en-Weppes, Artois-d. 1 Dec 1732, Prenzlau), d/o Pasquier & & Claire (de Hennin) Tourbier – **4 sons, 5 daus**; c. 1684/5, fled to GER; spent c. 2 yrs. in the Mannheim area, then to Mark Brandenburg, c. 1687; he d. 9 Apr 1720, Zerrinthin

Daniel[?]

REF: TOPEL, Traugott H., *Meine Hugenottischen vorfahen* (My Huguenot Ancestors) (Duesseldorf, GER, 1974).

X

XAVIER/SEVIER, Jean/John

[descended from a noble family who liv. in Xavier/Xavero Castle, located at the foot of the Pyrenees, nr. Sanguesa, also a castle nr. Pampelonne, Tarn Dépt, Midi-Pyrénées, n.e. of Albi; María de Azpilicueta y Xavier (sole heiress of 2 noble houses of Navarra), m. Don Juan de Costa/Juan de Jasso, a Spaniard – ch were Philip, Miguel, Juan, Valentine, Francisco, Magdalene. Francisco (7 Apr 1506-3 Dec 1552) became St. Francis de Xavier – at that time, Spanish ch could choose their surname, he chose his mother's]

b. 1668, FR, *poss.* the s/o the Valentine who was said to have arr in ENG later

fled Paris to London

m. 6 Aug 1708, St. Aske Hospital Chapel, Hoxton, Mary Smith; Hoxton is an area n. of Shoreditch in London, the hospital is located on the w. side of Kingsland Rd; then in the Parish of St. Giles, Cripplegate

CHILDREN:

Valentine[2], b. 1 Jan, bp 14 Feb 1712/3, St. Giles, Cripplegate, London, bap rec gives birthdate & says he was s/o John, a wheelwright, and Mary; family tradition says that Valentine & his bro William sailed for America, c. 1740, & landed in Baltimore; Valentine m/1, Joanna Goade/Goode (1 Nov 1723, Richmond, VA-c. Aug 1773, prob. Rockingham Co, VA), d/o John & Catherine (X) Goad, m/2, Jemima X; settled Augusta Co, VA (the part that is now Rockingham Co.); he became a lg. landowner, merchant, miller, served in the colonial militia; 27 Aug 1778, he took the Oath of Allegiance; he d. 30 Dec 1803, Carter Co, TN, nr. the Watauga Settlement, said to have been 101

> CHILDREN, m/1:
>
> **John**[3], b. 23 Sep 1745, Augusta Co, VA; m/1, c. 1762, Sarah Hawkins, d/o Joseph Hawkins- **5 sons, 5 daus**, m/2, 14 Aug 1780, Catherine Sherrill, d/o Samuel Sherrill – **8 ch**; he was an invincible Indian fighter, colonel in Rev. War, the Gov. of TN; d. 24 Sep 1815, nr. Ft. Decatur, AL
>
> **Valentine**[3], b. 1747, Rockingham Co, VA; served in the Rev. War, was a sgt. at the Battle of Pt. Pleasant, was a colonel of the militia, a sheriff, justice of the Peace; d. 23 Feb 1800, Clarksville, TN; **5 sons, 2 daus**
>
> **Robert**[3], b. 1749, Rockingham Co, VA; a captain; m. Keziah Robertson, d/o Charles Robertson; d. 16 Oct 1780, after being wounded in the Battle of King's Mountain; had **2 sons**
>
> **Joseph**[3], b. c. 1751 or 1764, Rockingham Co, VA; d. 18 Jun 1826, Overton Co, TN
>
> **Mary/Polly**[3], b. c. 1753, Rockingham Co, VA; m. William Matlock
>
> **Catherine**[3], b. c. 1757, Rockingham Co, VA; m. c. 1784, William Matlock; d. 6 Sep 1824, TN
>
> **Charles**[3], b. c. 1758
>
> **Bethenia**[3], c. 1759; m. James Hawkins; went to TN
>
> **Abraham**[3], b. 14 Feb 1760, Frederick (now Shenandoah) Co, VA; m. Mary Little; d. 18 Jun 1841, Overton (now Clay) Co, TN
>
> **Elizabeth**[3], c. 1762; m. William Matlock, as his 1st wife
>
> **Sophia**[3], b. c. 1765; m. William Peters, s/o Henry Peters; remained in VA

William[2], m. X O'Neil; had at least **1 son**

NOTE: There has been much confusion re birthdates and the name of Valentine's father. According to the baptismal record from London, Valentine was bp. 14 Feb 1712/3, son of John and Mary. There is also a marriage record for John Sevier and Mary Smith dated 1708. These dates are later than the dates usually given, but the records are primary documentation and hard to ignore, particularly given the coincidences of names. There *may* have been another son named Valentine b. earlier, who d. young. The Valentine who came to America was said to have been 101 at his death; he was more like 90.

REF: Marr Record, St. Giles, City of London files; TURNER, Francis M., *Life of General John Sevier* (1909?); FOSDICK, Lucian J., *The French Blood in America*; ARMSTRONG, Zella, *Notable Southern Families*, Vol. I-II (Baltimore, MD, 1974), Vol. IV (1926); SEVIER, Cora Bales & MADDEN, Nancy S., *Sevier Family History* (Washington, DC, 1961).

Index
by
Nancy Wright Brennan

A name may appear more than once on the same page. Please read introduction for indexing guidelines. **All caps bold** indicates ancestor. **Lowercase bold** indicates descendant of ancestor. Check both names with and without space, i.e. Le (space) Roy and LeRoy (no space), Du Bois and DuBois, etc.

(

(Coquefaire), Leah/Seal, 122
(Coquefaire), Mary, 122

,

-, Abigail, 98, 255, 311, 351
-, Abigail M, 98
-, Aellone, 190
-, Agnes, 154, 217, 424
-, Aimée, 61
-, Akra, 306
-, Alce/Alice, 94
-, Alice, 86, 106, 209, 288
-, Angell, 382
-, Ann, 90, 99, 106, 117, 134, 197, 214, 230, 254, 277, 305, 317, 334, 344, 373, 374, 380, 416, 451
-, Anna, 159, 447
-, Anna Apollonia, 59
-, Anna Barbara, 314
-, Anna Catharina, 438
-, Anna Catherina, 362
-, Anna Elizabetha, 59
-, Anna Katharina, 314
-, Anna Margaret, 283, 466
-, Anna Margarete, 314
-, Anna Maria, 370
-, Anna Maria Catherine, 291
-, Anna/Susanna, 266
-, Anne, **50**, 76, 99, 120, 130, 155, 234, 282, 327, 351, 412, 444
-, Anneke, 446
-, Antje, 450
-, Ariaantje, 177
-, Avis, **35**
-, Barbara, 40, 170, 242, 245, 283, 370
-, Barbertje, 48
-, Bety, 93
-, Cataleyn, 78
-, Catalina, 464
-, Catherine, 18, 19, 38, 45, 96, 116, 162, 241, 283, 285, 360, 362, 370, 466
-, Catrijntje, 305
-, Charity, 122, 225
-, Charlotte, 233, 328, 448
-, Christina, 204, 250
-, Christina Anne, 206
-, Clark/Claire, 455

-, Cornelia, 152, 158
-, Desire/Desirée, 388
-, Diane, 17
-, Dorothy, 383, 445
-, Edith, 22
-, Eleanor, 25, 32, 99, 276, 394, 415
-, Eleanore Philippina, 249
-, Elisabeth, 436
-, Elisabetha, 140, 245
-, Elizabeth, 21, 23, **36, 41**, 54, 61, 101, 104, 119, 156, 173, 180, 183, 202, 203, 208, 209, 213, 220, 249, 254, 259, 266, 295, 305, 310, 312, 321, 323, 326, 342, 345, 347, 354, 370, 374, 387, 390, 393, 394, 401, 403, 416, 456, 466
-, Elizabeth F, 429
-, Elizabeth/Betsy, 147
-, Eloise, 350
-, Emma, 33
-, Ester, 128
-, Esther, 59, 74, 234, 242, 247, 416
-, Eve, 229
-, Éve, 31
-, Fannie, 163
-, Frances, 81, 147, 188, 268, 275, 349
-, Françoise, 26, 329
-, Freelove, 453
-, Fytie, 105
-, Geneviève, 76
-, Gertrude, 15
-, Grace, 202
-, Hannah, 119, 172, 232, *420*
-, Harmekie, 315
-, Hester, 273
-, Honor/Honar, 429
-, Isabelle, 295
-, Isabelle/Sabella, 24
-, Jacquemine, 145
-, Jane, 64, 76, 94, 166, 211, 284, 299, 415
-, Jane/Jeanne, 74, 196
-, Janet, 405
-, Jannetie, 175
-, Jannetje, 78, 305, 315
-, Jean, 163
-, Jeanne, 219, 225, 337, 407, 414, *419*, 440
-, Jemima, 474
-, Joanna, 202
-, Johan/Joan, 209
-, Johanna, 252

-, Joyce, 203
-, Judith, 116, 126, 203, 303, 373, 380, 383, 399, 401, 407, 456, 462
-, Katherine, 123, 130, 183, 250
-, Katheryne, 353
-, Kezia(h), 347
-, Keziah, 380
-, Kunigarde, 59
-, Lena, 48
-, Lucy, 60
-, Lydia, 156, 360
-, Madelaine/Magdelene, 156
-, Madeleine, 186
-, Madlenor, 61
-, Magdalena, 283
-, Magdeleine, *419*
-, Margaret, 74, 76, 104, 150, 159, 206, 223, 233, 250, 283, 351, 370, **423**, 429, 469
-, Margaretha, 139, 405
-, Margery, 209, 451
-, Marguerite, 224, 389
-, Marguerite/Margaret, 374
-, Maria, 305
-, Maria Barbara, 30
-, Maria Eva, 115
-, Marianne, 193, 387
-, Marie, 130, 232, 310, 341, 389, 390, 422
-, Marie Catherine, 284
-, Marretje, 78
-, Martha, 33, 154, 158, 163, 216, 340, 369, 372, 384, 433, 443
-, Marthe, 113
-, Martia Elisabeth, 59
-, Mary, 25, **35, 41**, 65, 75, 95, 99, 120, 152, 164, 166, 172, 178, 196, 200, 202, 216, 225, 255, 258, 269, 275, 295, 321, 323, 325, 328, 347, 348, 351, 367, 370, 371, 374, 379, 401, 415, 421, 433, 443, 462, 463, 464
-, Mary Ann, 16
-, Mary Catherine, 184
-, Mary Margaret, 325
-, Mary/Amey, 453
-, May, 349
-, Mehitable, 336
-, Mercy, 163
-, Molly, 23
-, Nancy, 91, 229, 254, 327, 434
-, Naomi, 44

-, Ottillia, 376
-, Peggy, **37**
-, Phebe, 48, 106, 163
-, Priscilla, 224
-, Rachel, 161, 162, 276, 341, 347, 350, 447
-, Rebecca, 91, 180, 229, 265, 446, 447
-, Rebeckah, 244
-, Ruth, 146, 200
-, Sabina, 151
-, Sally, 339
-, Salome, 101
-, Sarah, 24, 34, 65, 94, 106, 146, 158, 214, 272, 294, 306, 336, 350, 360, 362, 372, 377, 412, 446, 451
-, Susan C, 201
-, Susanna, 21, 323, 399, 469
-, Susannah, 144, 166, 178, 185, 253, 276, 397
-, Susanne, **47**, 61, 96, 127, 128, 155, 203, 210, 287, 399, 436
-, Susanne Madeleine, 186
-, Suzanne, 100, 462
-, Temperance, 190
-, Winifred, 25, 122

A

A(r)mand, Elizabeth, 189
A(r)mand, Elizabeth (Washington), 189
A(r)mand, Girard Commander, 189
Aaken, Mariuns Van, 169
Abeel, Elizabeth, 392
Abelin, Jean, 78
Abernathy, David, 191
Abernathy, John, 191
Abernathy, Nancy, 191
Abney, Dannett, 50
Abney, Mary, 50
Abney, Mary (Lee Abney), 50
Abney, Paul, 50
Aborough/Borough, Johanna (Overye), 465
Aborough/Borough, Stephen, 465
Abrahamse, Maritje, 177
Acar/Acart, Philippe, 189
Acar/Acart, Sarah, 189
Achon, Louise, 141
Ackeman, Lysbeth/Elisabeth A., 150
Acker, Maritie, 414
Acker, Olive, 414
Acker, Wolfert, 414
Ackerman, Abraham, 45
Ackerman, Abraham Davidse, 150
Ackerman, Albartus, 45
Ackerman, Anneke Abramse, 150
Ackerman, Anneken/Annetje/Annetie, 45
Ackerman, David, 44, 45, 150, 296, 353, 450
Ackerman, Egbert, 45

Ackerman, Elizabeth, 45
Ackerman, Elysabeth, 45
Ackerman, Janitie, 353
Ackerman, Johannes, 45
Ackerman, Lodewyck, 45
Ackerman, Lodowyck, 450
Ackerman, Louwerans/Laurens, 45
Ackerman, Lysbeth, 45
Ackerman, Marite, 45
Ackerson, Anna, 459
Adams, George, 266
Adams, Randal, 145
Adams, Samuel, 222
Adams, William, 321
Adee, Dame Elizabeth, 264
Adkins, Martin, 383
Adriaens, Barbara, 296
Adrianse, Anneken, 44
Adriens, Janneken, 359
Aelberts, Elsje, 106
Aerden, Pieter van, 333
Aertse, Elbert, 416
Aertson/Arentsen, Jan, 164
Aertszen. Simon, 305
Agache, Nicholas, 144
Agache, Nicolas, 186
Agé, Antoine, 13
Agé, Judith (Chastain), 13
Agé/Agee, Judith (Chastain), 332
Agé/Agee, Mathieu, 332
Age/Agee/Oage, Anthony, 13
Age/Agee/Oage, Isaac, 13
Age/Agee/Oage, James, 13
Age/Agee/Oage, Judith, 13
AGÉ/AGEE/OAGE, Mathieu, 13
Agée, Elizabeth, 187
Agee, Isaac, 332
AGNE Johann Jacob, 19
Agne, Anna Magdalena, 19
AGNE, Johann Heinrich, 19
AGNE, Johann Jacob, 19
AGNE, Johann Theobold, 19
AGNE, Johannes, 18
Agne, Theobald, 19
Aidelo/Aydelott, Benjamin, 395
Ainsworth, Alice, 267
Aitkins, Jenet, 118
Akkerman, Johannes, 44
Alarie, Rene, 451
Albert, Elizabeth (van Houte), 97
Albert, Pierre, 97
Alberti, Andrea, 335
Alberti, Pietro Caesre, 335
Alberti, Veronica (X), 335
Alberts, Elsje, 404
Alberts, Teunes Eliasz, 404
Albertse, Willem, 316
Albertus, Aert/Arthur, 336
Albertus, Elizabeth (Scudder), 229
Albertus, Francyntje, 336
Albertus, Jan/John, 335

Albertus, Marles/Martha, 336
Albertus, Marritje/Marie/ Mary, 336
Albertus, Samuel, 229
Albertus, William, 336
Albrecht, Contwig Nickel, 19
Alburtis/Albertus, Elizabeth, 229
Alden, John, 139, 287
Alden, Priscilla (Mullins), 139, 287
Alden, Rebecca, 139, 287
Aldercron, John, 432
Aldrich, unknown, 246
Alexander, James, 182
Alexander, Rebecca, 91
Alger, Jeunetze, 15
Aliee, Elizabeth, 15
Aliee, Rachel, 15
Aline, Mary, 382
Aline, Rebecca (Clark), 382
Aline, William, 382
Allain, Abraham D', 230
Allain, Susan D', 229
Allaire, Alexander, 14, 205
Allaire, Alexandre, 31
ALLAIRE, Alexandre, 13
Allaire, André/Andrew, 14, 32
Allaire, Anthony, 14
Allaire, Antoine, 13
Allaire, Benjamin, 14
Allaire, Catherine, 13, 14, 31
Allaire, Elizabeth, 14
Allaire, Esther, 14
Allaire, Henriette, 14
Allaire, Jean, 13, 14, 52
Allaire, Jeanne, 13, 205
Allaire, Jeanne (Brochelide), 14
Allaire, Jeanne (Doens), 31
Allaire, Jeanne (Doens/Docus), 205
Allaire, Jeanne (Godeffroy/Godefroi), 13
Allaire, Louis, 13
Allaire, Mary, 14
Allaire, Peter, 14
Allaire, Philippe, 14
Allaire, Pierre, 13, 14
Allaire, Pierre/Peter, 14
Allaire, Sarah, 14
Allaire, Simon, 14
Allaire, Susan, 13
Allaire, Uytendaele, 14
Allée, Jan, 316
Allée, Nicolas, 316
ALLÉE/ALLEY/ALIÉE/ALYER/ALYEA/d'AIL LY, Nicolas, 14
Allee/Alley/Alliee/Alyer/Alyea/d'Ailly, Jan/John, 14
Allee/Alley/Alliee/Alyer/Alyea/d'Ailly, Rachel, 15
Allegné, Anne, 284
Allegre(e)/ Allaigre, Daniel, 16
Allegre(e)/ Allaigre, Giles, 16
Allegre(e)/ Allaigre, Martha/Polley, 16
Allegre(e)/ Allaigre, William, 16

ALLEGRÉ(E)/ALLAIGRE, Giles (Dr.), 15
Allegre(e)/Allaigre, Judith, 16
Allegre(e)/Allaigre, Matthew, 16
Alleman, Anna Maria (Balliet), 30
Alleman, Jacob, 30
Alleman, Susanna, 30
Allemand, Jacob, 30
Allen, Eleanor (X), 99
Allen, Elizabeth, 298
Allen, Esther, 201
Allen, Exercise, 430
Allen, Hannah (Corlies), 430
Allen, Henry, 125, 430
Allen, Jane, 99
Allen, Jonathan, 125
Allen, Martha (Newberry) Davenport, 146
Allen, Mary, 291
Allen, Mary (X) Stevenson, 86
Allen, William, 99, 265
Allen/Alewyn, John, 336
Almond, unknown, 146
Alred, John, 433
Alrics, Sigfredus, 454
Alston, John, 167
Alstyne, Maria Van, 459
Alstyne, Martinus Van, 459
Altman, Catherine, 261
Alvin/Alvyn, Giles, 209
Always, unknown, 377
Alyea, Abraham, 15
Alyea, Hannah/Ann, 15
Alyea, Jacobus/Jacob, 15
Alyea, Jannetje/Jane, 15
Alyea, Johannes/John, 15
Alyea, John, 15
Alyea, John, Jr, 15
Alyea, Jonathan, 15
Alyea, Maritie/Mary, 15
Alyea, Mary, 15
Alyea, Pieter/Peter, 15
Alyea, Rebecca, 15
Alyea, Sabrah, 15
Alyea, Susanna, 15
Ames, Ezra, 212
Ames, Hannah, 212
Amiot, Charles, 141
Amiot, Marie Catherine, 141
Amiot, Rosalie (Duquet), 141
Ammonet, André/Andrew, 16, 17
Ammonet, Andrew, 369
Ammonet, Charles, 17
Ammonet, Charles, Jr., 17
Ammonet, Elizabeth, 17
Ammonet, François, 16
Ammonet, Jacob, 16, 369
AMMONET, JACOB, 16
Ammonet, Jacob, II, 16
Ammonet, Jane, 17
Ammonet, Jean André/John, 16
Ammonet, Jean/John, 17
Ammonet, John Jr., 17

Ammonet, Judith, 16
Ammonet, Magdalene, 17
Ammonet, Mary Ann, 16
Ammonet, Rebecca, 17
Ammonet, William, 16
Ammonet. Magdalene, 17
Amonet, Charlotte Judith, 115
Amonet, Jacob, 434
Amonet, Magdelaine, 434
Amos, unknown, 178
Andeer, François Paul, 379
Andelot, Marquis d' Lt.Gen., 121
Anderson, Ann, 81
Anderson, David, 21
Anderson, Elizabeth, 22
Anderson, Elizabeth (Calvert), 253
Anderson, Francina, 345
Anderson, George, 22
Anderson, Henry, 114
Anderson, Mathew, 22
Anderson, unknown, 268
Anderson, Walter, 403
Anderton, unknown, 413
Andrailh, Arnaud d', 455
Andrailh, Galharde d', 455
Andrailh, Lizette (de Gascon) d', 455
André, John Maj., 154
André/Andrew, Susanna, 375
Andrea, Martin, 466
Andrew, Abigail (Treat), 172
Andrew, Jane, 172
Andrew, Samuel, 172
Andrews, Peter, 466
Andries, Juriaen, 400
Andriesse, Tanneke, 82
Andrieszen, Andries, 297
Andros, Edmund Gov., 307, 449
Andros, Gov., 450
Andross, Gov., **36**
Androvette, Elizabeth, 293
ANGEVIN(E)/L'ANGEVIN, Louis, 17
Angevin(e)/L'Angevin, Daniel, 18
Angevin(e)/L'Angevin, Daniel Jr, 18
Angevin(e)/L'Angevin, Eli, 18
Angevin(e)/L'Angevin, Elizabeth, 18
Angevin(e)/L'Angevin, Ester, 17
Angevin(e)/L'Angevin, Esther, 18
Angevin(e)/L'Angevin, Jean/John, 17, 18
Angevin(e)/L'Angevin, Louis, 18
Angevin(e)/L'Angevin, Margaret, 18
Angevin(e)/L'Angevin, Marguerite/Margaret, 17
Angevin(e)/L'Angevin, Marianne/Mary Ann, 18
Angevin(e)/L'Angevin, Marie, 18
Angevin(e)/L'Angevin, Marie/Mary, 17
Angevin(e)/L'Angevin, Pierre II/Peter, 18
Angevin(e)/L'Angevin, Pierre, II, 18
Angevin(e)/L'Angevin, Pierre/Peter, 18
Angevin(e)/L'Angevin, Susanna, 18
Angevin(e)/L'Angevin, Zachariah, 18

Angevin(e)/L'Angevin, Zacharie/Zachariah, 17
Angevin, Louis, 17, 74
Angevin, Marie (X), 17, 74
Angevin, Pierre/Peter, 74
Angevin, Zacharie, 374
Angevine, Charlotte (Guinere), 17
Angevine, David, 340
Angevine, Elizabeth, 128
Angevine, Esther, 340
Angevine, François, 17, 238
Angevine, Henri, 17, 238
Angevine, John, 303, 340
Angevine, Louis, 238, 441
Angevine, Marguerite (Chalons), 441
Angevine, Marie (Naudin), 128
Angevine, Marie (X), 238
Angevine, Mary, 303
Angevine, Peter, 340
Angevine, Pierre/Peter, 238
Angevine, Zachariah, 340
Angevine, Zacharie, 128
Anguenet/Agne/Ankeny, Agnes, 20
Anguenet/Agne/Ankeny, Anna Catharina, 18
Anguenet/Agne/Ankeny, Anna Eva, 19
Anguenet/Agne/Ankeny, Johann Heinrich, 19
Anguenet/Agne/Ankeny, Johann Nicolaus, 19
Anguenet/Agne/Ankeny, Maria Catharina, 18
ANGUENET/AGNE/ANKENY, Pierre/Peter, 18
Anguenot, Abel, 18
Anguenot, Angelica (Vinan/Vinet), 18
Ankeny, Anna Maria, 19
Ankeny, Catherine, 19
Ankeny, Catherine (X), 72
Ankeny, Christian, 19
Ankeny, David, 19
Ankeny, Dewalt, 19, 72
Ankeny, Elizabeth, 19
Ankeny, Elizabeth J., 249
Ankeny, Georg, 19
Ankeny, Henry, 19
Ankeny, Jakob, 19
Ankeny, John/Johann Georg, 19
Ankeny, Margaret, 19
Ankeny, Peter, 19, 72, 249
Ankeny, Rebecca, 19
Ankeny, Rosanna (Bonnet), 249
Ankrum, Mary, 267
Anna Margaretta, Paris, 437
Anna, Sille, 441
Annan, Daniel, Dr., 422
Anne of Austria, 239
Anneraud, Martha, 269
Annis, Curmac, 211
Annis, Deliverance, 211
Annis, Mary (Chase), 211

Annonier, Marie, 253
Ansley, Frances, 108
Anspach, Leonard, 438
Anthony, John Lt. Col., **51**
Antoine, Barbe, 380
Antrobus, Annie (Varden), 435
Antrobus, Edmond, 435
Antrobus, Edmund, 435
Antrobus, Jane, 435
Antrobus, John, 435
Antrobus, Marie, 435
Antrobus, Mary (Webb), 435
Antrobus, Philip, 435
Antwerpen, Daniel Janse Van, 273
Antwerpen, Maritje Van, 273
Antwerpen, Rebecca Van, 273
Appeby, Benjamin, 93
Appeby, Françoise, 93
Appeby, Rebeca, 93
Arabin d', unknown, 432
Archambault, Françoise (Tourault), 109
Archambault, Jacques, 109
Archambault, Jacquette, 109
Archbishop of Canterbury, 51
Archer, Elizabeth, 113
Archer, Judith, 113
Archer, Mildred (Middy), 115
Archimbaud, Jean, 194
Archimbaud, Pierre, 194
Archimbaud, Timothée, 64
Arents, Tryntje, 296
Arentse, Claes Nicholas, 130
Armistead, Hannah, 133
Armistead, John, 133
Armistead, Mary Marot, 351
Armistead, Robert Booth, 351
Armistead, Sarah, 133
Arnard, Moïse, 342
Arnau(l)d, Anne, 111
Arnau(l)d, Élie, 111
Arnau(l)d, Magdalen (DeValau), 111
Arnaud, André, 112
ARNAUD, André, 20
Arnaud, Anne (Moguen), 20
Arnaud, Jael, 374
Arnaud, Jeanne, 20
Arnaud, Marie, 20, 112
Arnaud, Marie (X), 112
Arnaud, Peter, 20
Arnaud, Samuel, 20
Arnaud, Stephen, 20
Arnaud/Arnaux, Madeleine, 342
Arnauld, John, 271
Arnauld/Arnaud, Anne, 20
Arnauld/Arnaud, Elias, 21
ARNAULD/ARNAUD, Élie/Elias, 20
Arnauld/Arnaud, John, 20
Arnauld/Arnaud, Mary Magdalen, 21
Arnauld/Arnaud, Susanna, 21
Arnold, Anthony, 415
Arnold, Benedict Gen., 154

Arnold, Elizabeth, 171
Arriné, Anne, 233
Arroman, Nicolas d', 66
Artman, unknown, 204
Asbury, Catherine, 411
Asbury, Henry, 411
Asbury, Mary, 411
Ascough, Elizabeth (Ingo), 24
Ascough, Thomas, 24
Ashby, Ann, 343
Ashby, Constantis (Broughton), 343
Ashby, John, 312, 343
Ashby, Mary, 312
Ashby, Thomas, 312
Ashley, Mary, 428
Ashley, Mary (X), 428
Ashley, Robert, 428
Ashton, Susanna, 145
Ashurst, Robert, 195
Ashwood, Jane, 209
Asseton, Robert, 186
Aston, Rebecca, 416
Atchinson, Matthew, 227
Athis, Cécilia d', 147
Athis, Nicolas d', 147
Atkins, unknown, 380
Atkinson, Median, 166
Attoway, unknown, 236
Atwood, Stephen, 62
Auber, Judith, 166
Auber, Marie, 165
Aubert, Charles, 107
Aubigné, Catherine (L'Etange/L'Estang), 21
Aubigné, Jean d', 21
Aubigne/Aubigney/Dabney, Agrippa Théodore d', 21
Aubigne/Aubigney/Dabney, Ann d', 22
Aubigne/Aubigney/Dabney, Benjamin d', 22
Aubigne/Aubigney/Dabney, Charles d', 22
Aubigne/Aubigney/Dabney, Constant/Constance d', 21
Aubigne/Aubigney/Dabney, Cornelius d', 21
Aubigne/Aubigney/Dabney, Cornelius, II d', 22
Aubigne/Aubigney/Dabney, Dorothy d', 22
Aubigne/Aubigney/Dabney, Elizabeth d', 21, 22
Aubigne/Aubigney/Dabney, Fannie d', 22
Aubigne/Aubigney/Dabney, Françoise d', 22
Aubigne/Aubigney/Dabney, George d', 22
Aubigne/Aubigney/Dabney, James d', 22
Aubigne/Aubigney/Dabney, John d', 21
Aubigne/Aubigney/Dabney, Judith d', 22

Aubigne/Aubigney/Dabney, Louise Art(h)émise d', 21
Aubigne/Aubigney/Dabney, Marie d', 22
Aubigne/Aubigney/Dabney, Mary d', 21, 22
Aubigne/Aubigney/Dabney, Mary Elizabeth d', 22
Aubigne/Aubigney/Dabney, Nathan d', 22
Aubigne/Aubigney/Dabney, Nelthan d', 22
Aubigne/Aubigney/Dabney, Sarah d', 22
Aubigne/Aubigney/Dabney, Susannah d', 22
AUBIGNÉ/AUBIGNEY/DABNEY, Théodore Agrippa d', 21
Aubigne/Aubigney/Dabney, Théodulfe d', 21
Aubigne/Aubigney/Dabney, William d', 22
Aubrey, Francis Jr., 133
Aubrey, XX, 16
Aubry, Françoise, *143*
Aubry, Françoise (Sibot), *143*
Aubry, Jean, *143*
Aubuchon, Joseph, 134
Aubussargues, Jacques Vergeze d', 145
Aubussargues, Magdelaine Vergeze d', 145
Aucouturier, Marie, 265
Audebert, Marie, 136
Auge/Dauge/Dozier, Angelosa d', 24
Auge/Dauge/Dozier, Ann d', 24
Auge/Dauge/Dozier, Dennis d', 24
Auge/Dauge/Dozier, Elizabeth d', 23, 24
Auge/Dauge/Dozier, Frances d', 24
Auge/Dauge/Dozier, Hannah d', 23
Auge/Dauge/Dozier, Jacqueline d', 23
Auge/Dauge/Dozier, Jacquelinner d', 24
Auge/Dauge/Dozier, Jacques/James d', 23
Auge/Dauge/Dozier, James d', 23
Auge/Dauge/Dozier, James Ingo d', 24
Auge/Dauge/Dozier, John d', 23, 24
AUGE/DAUGE/DOZIER, Léonard d', 23
Auge/Dauge/Dozier, Leonard II d', 24
Auge/Dauge/Dozier, Leonard III d', 24
Auge/Dauge/Dozier, Macina d', 23
Auge/Dauge/Dozier, Margaret Ann d', 23
Auge/Dauge/Dozier, Margaret/Peggy d', 24
Auge/Dauge/Dozier, Martha d', 23
Auge/Dauge/Dozier, Mary d', 23, 24
Auge/Dauge/Dozier, Nowdina d', 23
Auge/Dauge/Dozier, Peter d', 24
Auge/Dauge/Dozier, Peter/Pierre, Pierre/Peter d', 23
Auge/Dauge/Dozier, Rhoda d', 24
Auge/Dauge/Dozier, Richard d', 23
Auge/Dauge/Dozier, Richard, Jr. d', 23

Auge/Dauge/Dozier, Sarah d', 23, 24
Auge/Dauge/Dozier, Susanna d', 24
Auge/Dauge/Dozier, Thomas d', 23, 24
Auge/Dauge/Dozier, Tull/Tully d', 24
Auge/Dauge/Dozier, William d', 23
Auge/Dauge/Dozier, Willoughby d', 24
Augé/Dugué II, Jacques d', 193
Auge/Dugue, Marianne d', 193
Auguenet/Agne/Ankeny, Anna
    Elisabeth, 19
Auguenet/Agne/Ankeny, Peter, 20
Auguenet/Agne/Ankeny, Susanne, 19
AUGUSTINE, Jean, 24, 255
Austin, James, 383
Austin, Noah, 13
Austin, Thomas, 399
Auter, Abraham, 93
Avant, Jane, 464
AYDELOT(TE)/AIDELOT, David, 24
Aydelot(te)/Aidelot, Benjamin, 25
Aydelot(te)/Aidelot, Benjamin, Jr, 25
Aydelot(te)/Aidelot, Caleb, 25
Aydelot(te)/Aidelot, Catherine, 25
Aydelot(te)/Aidelot, David, 25
Aydelot(te)/Aidelot, Elizabeth, 25
Aydelot(te)/Aidelot, Isaac, 25
Aydelot(te)/Aidelot, Janey, 25
Aydelot(te)/Aidelot, John, 25
Aydelot(te)/Aidelot, Madelayne, 25
Aydelot(te)/Aidelot, Marie, 25
Aydelot(te)/Aidelot, Mary, 25
Aydelot(te)/Aidelot, Ruben, 25
Aydelot(te)/Aidelot, Ruth, 25
Aydelot(te)/Aidelot, Salomon, 25
Aydelot(te)/Aidelot, Samuel, 25
Aydelot(te)/Aidelot, Sara, 25
Aydelot(te)/Aidelot, Sarah, 25
Aydelot(te)/Aidelot, William, 25
Aydelot, Marie (Sochon), 147
Aydelot, Benjamin, 147
Aydelot, David, 147
Aydelott, David, 395
Aydelott, Marie (Sochon), 395
Ayer, Joseph, 124
Aymar/Eymar, Daniel, 337
Aymar/Eymar, Françoise (Belon), 336
Aymar/Eymar, Jean, 336
Ayrault, Anthony, 26, 27
Ayrault, Daniel, 26
Ayrault, Easter/Esther, 25
Ayrault, Elias, 26
Ayrault, Elizabeth, 26
Ayrault, Frances, 27
Ayrault, James, 26
Ayrault, Jane, 26
Ayrault, Judeth, 27
Ayrault, Judith, 27
Ayrault, Lydia, 26
Ayrault, Marian, 26
Ayrault, Marianna, 25
Ayrault, Mary, 26

Ayrault, Mary/Marian, 25
Ayrault, Nicholas, 26
AYRAULT, Nicolas (Dr.), 25
Ayrault, Peter, 25, 26
AYRAULT, Pierre (Dr.), 26
Ayrault, Pierre/Peter, 26
Ayrault, Samuel, 27
Ayrault, Stephen, 25, 26
Ayrault, Susannah, 27
Ayres, Benjamin, 130
Ayries, Sarah, 46
Azam, Anne, 454
Azam, Jean, 454
Azam, Maude (de Marty), 454

B

Baal, Jan Hendrickse Van, 392
Baal/Balen, Maria Van, 392
Babcock, Dorothy, 395
Babcock, Return, 395
Babcock, Sarah (Denison), 395
Babie, Jacques, 134
Babineau, Marguerite, 294
Bachiler, Ann (X), 123
Bachiler, Stephen, 123
Bächlein, Jackob, 19
Bachmann, Catherine, 96
Bachmann, Henry Lt., 96
Backar, Anna Maria, 292
Backer, Nicolas, 293
Bacon, Elizabeth, 323
Bacon, Nathaniel, 472
Bacot, Abraham, 28
Bacot, Anne, 29
Bacot, Antoine, 28
Bacot, Daniel, 28
Bacot, David, 28
Bacot, Elizabeth, 28
Bacot, Esaï, 28
Bacot, Estienne, 29
Bacot, François, 28, 29
BACOT, François, 28
Bacot, François II, 28
Bacot, François III, 28
Bacot, Jean, 29
Bacot, Jean-Christophe, 29
Bacot, Jeanne, 28
Bacot, Madeleine, 28, 29
Bacot, Marthe, 28, 29
Bacot, Mary, 28
Bacot, Paul, 29
Bacot, Peter, 28
Bacot, Pierre, 193, 388
Bacot, Pierre I, 28
Bacot, Pierre II, 28
Bacot, Pierre III, 28
Bacot, Pierre IV/Peter, 28
Bacot, René, 28
Bacot, Samuel, 28, 388
Badeau, Catherine, 29

Badeau, Claude, 29
Badeau, David, 29
Badeau, Elias, 29
Badeau, Élie, 29
BADEAU, Élie, 29
Badeau, Isaac, 29
Badeau, Isaiah, 29
Badeau, Jacob, 29
Badeau, James, 29
Badeau, Jean, 110
Badeau, Jean/John, 29
Badeau, John, 29
Badeau, Magdaline, 29
Badeau, Marie (Triau), 29
Badeau, Peter, 29, 128
Badeau, Pierre, 29
Badeau, William, 29
Badger, Anna, 435
Badger, Edward Rev., 435
Badgett, Elizabeth, 16
Badye, Thomas, 48
Baerdan/Berdan, Jan, 151
Bailey, John, 128
Bailey, Judith, 266
Bailey, Martha, 402
Baillet, Jacob, 466
Baillet/Balliet/Bailette, Abraham, 30
Baillet/Balliet/Bailette, Anna, 30
Baillet/Balliet/Bailette, Anna Elisabetha, 30
Baillet/Balliet/Bailette, Anna Maria, 30
Baillet/Balliet/Bailette, Barbara, 30
Baillet/Balliet/Bailette, Daniel, 30
Baillet/Balliet/Bailette, Jacob, 30
BAILLET/BALLIET/BAILETTE, Jacob, 30
Baillet/Balliet/Bailette, Johan
    Nicholas/Hans Nickle, 30
Baillet/Balliet/Bailette, Johan/John
    Nicholas, 30
Baillet/Balliet/Bailette, Johannes, 30
Baillet/Balliet/Bailette, Joseph, 30
Baillet/Balliet/Bailette, Katherine, 30
Baillet/Balliet/Bailette, Leonard, 30
Baillet/Balliet/Bailette, Magdalena, 30
Baillet/Balliet/Bailette, Maria, 30
Baillet/Balliet/Bailette, Maria Catharina, 30
Baillet/Balliet/Bailette, Maria Magdalen, 30
Baillet/Balliet/Bailette, Paulus, 30
Baillet/Balliet/Bailette, Stefan/Steven, 30
Baillet/Balliet/Bailette, Stephen, 30
Baillet/Balliet/Bailette, Susanna, 30
Bailliet, Paulus, 466
Bailliote, Isaac, 30
Baker, Alexander, 421
Baker, Isaac, 45
Baker, Jane, 369
Baker, John, 437
Baker, Peter, 193

Baker, Rachel, 341
Baker, Samuel, 24
Baker, Thomas, 369
Baker, William, 96, 341
Baker/Baber, Rachel, 275
Balch, Mary, 26
Balck, Dominick, 291
Baldwin, Anna, 295
Baldwin, David Major, 340
Baldwin, Elizabeth (Rogers), 340
Baldwin, Nathan, 340
Ball, Anne (Taylor), 327
Ball, James Maj., 56
Ball, Mary, 456, 457
Ball, Mary Conway, 56
Ball, Rachel, 17
Ball, Samuel, 327
Ball, Sarah, 56
Ball, Susanna, 327
Ball, unknown, 17
Ball, Virginia, 83
Ball, William, 56
Ballard, Dorothy (Herndon), 454
Ballard, Isaac, 454
Ballard, Lydia, 454
Ballard, William, 117
Ballendine, Hannah, 56
Ballendine, William, 56
Ballendine/Balantyne, Fanny, 56
Ballendine/Balantyne, John, 56
Ballew, Gille, 115
Bally, Catherine, 55
Bally, Peter, 55
Balough/Bollough, William, 90
Baltimore, Cecilius Lord, 178
Baluet, Judith, 348
Balwin, Isaac, 295
Balwin, Susannah, 295
Balzac, Honoré de, 327
Banbury, James, 81, 343
Banbury, Judith (Manigault), 81
Banbury, Mary, 81
Bancker, Anna, 392
Bancker, Evert, 392
Bancker, Gerrit, 392
Bancker, Maria, 392
Bancker/Bankert, Aaltje (Storm), 280
Bandt, John Pietersen, 336
Banghart, Andrew, 448
Bankert, Frederick, 280
Banks, Benjamin, 264
Banks, Rebecca, 211
Bant, Jan Peters, 333
Banta, Antie, 324
Banta, Cornelius, 172
Banta, Dirck Epse, 324
Banta, Epke, 172
Banta, Jeanne (DePré), 172
Bantegnie, Paquette/Pasques, 151
Banton, Sarah/Sally, 436
Banvard, Catherine Elizabeth, 31

Banvard, Daniel, 31
Banvard, David, 31
BANVARD, David, 31
Banvard, Francoise (Jean-Perin), 31
Banvard, Jean Dauphine, 31
Banvard, Jeanne, 31
Banvard, Maria Catherine, 31
Banvard, Maria Marguerite, 31
Banvard, Marie Elizabeth, 31
Banvard, Pierre, 31
Banyer, Martha, 318
Baptiste, Anastasia, 17
Bara, Giles, 188
Bara, Jeanne (Snellart), 188
Barathon, Jeanne, 420
Baraud, Elisabeth (Grégoire), 77
Baraud, Matthew, 77
Baraud/Barreau, Jeanne, 78
Barber, Elizabeth, 236
Barber, Jane (Coggin), 222
Barber, Luke, 236
Barber, Margaret, **35**
Barber, Margaret (Martin), **35**
Barber, Mary, 222
Barber, Thomas, 222
Barber, William, **35**
Barberie, Elizabeth, 14, 32
Barberie, Frances, 31
Barberie, Jean, 13, 32
Barberie, Jean Pierre, 32
BARBERIE, Jean/John, 31
Barberie, John, 31
Barberie, Marie Anne, 32
Barberie, Pierre, 13, 14, 31
Barberie, Susanne, 31
Barberie, Susanne (Lambert), 14
Barbier, Anne, 140
BARBIER, Anne, 32
Barbour, Susanna (Brush), 272
Barclift, Ann (Durant), 277
Barclift, Mariam, 277
Barclift, William, 277
Bardelo, Jacques, 468
Barden, unknown, 338
Baremore, James, 295
Barents, Geertruyd, 404
Barents, Sara, 404
Barheit, John, 54
Barhite, Johannes, 468
Barjon, Pastor Guillaume, 67
Barkelo/Barkald, Willem Willemse, 126
Barksdale, Thomas, 306
Barner, John, **50**
Barnes, Sarah, 181
Barnett, Elizabeth, 51
Barnett, John Jr., 51
Barnett, Sarah (McCann), 51
Barnett, Stephen, 55
Barr, David, 32
Barr, Isaac, 32
Barr, Margaret, 32

Barrau, Susanna de, 290
Barré, Pierre, 32
BARRÉ, Pierre/Peter, 32
Barré, X (Bonnomeau), 32
Barrett, Anne, 22
Barrett, Elizabeth (Lewis), 22
Barrett, Robert, 22
Barrett, Tobias, 209
BARRETTE, Barbara de, 32
Barrette, Isaac de, 32
Barrette, Peter de, 32
Barrilliet, Michel, 194
Barrineau, Daniel, 33
Barrineau, Emma (X), 33
Barrineau, Isaac, 33
Barrineau, Levi, 33
Barrineau/Barrino, Arthur, 33
Barrineau/Barrino, Daniel, 33
Barrineau/Barrino, Eleanor, 33
Barrineau/Barrino, Eliza E, 34
Barrineau/Barrino, George, 33
Barrineau/Barrino, Hester C., 34
BARRINEAU/BARRINO, Isaac, 33
Barrineau/Barrino, Isaac III, 34
Barrineau/Barrino, Isaac, Jr, 33
Barrineau/Barrino, Jesse, 33
Barrineau/Barrino, Julian Jane, 34
Barrineau/Barrino, Levi, 34
Barrineau/Barrino, Leviniah, 33
Barrineau/Barrino, Manuel/Mandewell, 34
Barrineau/Barrino, Margaret, 33
Barrineau/Barrino, Margaret Hester, 33
Barrineau/Barrino, Martha M, 34
Barrineau/Barrino, Mary Jane, 33
Barrineau/Barrino, Mary K, 33
Barrineau/Barrino, Nancy/Ann, 33
Barrineau/Barrino, Sarah Eleanor, 34
Barrineau/Barrino, Susan(nah), 33
Barrineau/Barrino, Thomas, 33
Barrineau/Barrino, William, 33
Barron, Priscilla, 312
Barron, Robert, 312
Bart/D'Ibert/Dilbert/LeBere/Diver, Wilhelm de, 34
BART/D'IBERT/DIBERT/LeBÈRE/DIVER, Charles Frédéric de, 34
Bart/D'Ibert/Dibert/LeBere/Diver, David de, 34
Bart/D'Ibert/Dibert/LeBere/Diver, Henry de, 34
Bart/D'Ibert/Dibert/LeBere/Diver, John I de, 34
Bart/D'Ibert/Dibert/LeBere/Diver, John II de, 34
Bart/D'Ibert/Dibert/LeBere/Diver, Mary de, 34
Bart/D'Ibert/Dilbert/LeBere/Diver, Charles Christopher, 34
Bart/D'Ibert/Dilbert/LeBere/Diver, Thomas de, 34

Barthes, Elizabeth de, 214
Bartlett, Deborah, 222
Bartlett, Hannah, 139
Bartlett, Joseph, 298
Bartlett, Lydia, 298
Bartlett, Lydia (Griswold), 298
Bartlett, Sarah, 298
Barton, Caleb, 111, 267
Barton, Hannah (Bridges), 111
Barton, John, 69
Barton,Samuel, 111
Barzet, Christopher, 103
Barzet, Marie, 103
Bascom(e), Abigail, 35
Bascom(e), Adelaide, 34
Bascom(e), Boniface, 35
Bascom(e), Elizabeth, 35
Bascom(e), Françoise, 35
Bascom(e), George, 35
Bascom(e), Guillaume, 34
Bascom(e), Guillaume/William, 35
Bascom(e), Hannah, 35
Bascom(e), Hepzibah, 35
Bascom(e), Jean, 34
Bascom(e), Jean/John, 35
Bascom(e), Joseph, 35
Bascom(e), Marie, 34
Bascom(e), Phillip, 35
BASCOM(E), Robert, 34
Bascom(e), Suzanne, 34, 35
Bascom(e), Thomas, 35
Bascome, Jean, **34**
Bascome, Susanne (Barbey), **34**
Bass, Nathaniel, **36**
Bass, Nathaniel Capt., **35**
Bass, Samuel, **36**
Bassano, Amelia, 286
Bassano, Anthony, 285
Bassano, Baptista, 286
Bassano, Lucretia, 285
Basse, Abigail, 36
Basse, Abraham, 36
Basse, Barnaby, 36
Basse, Hannah, 36
Basse, Hester, 36
Basse, Humphrey, 35, 76
BASSE, Humphrey, 35
Basse, John, 36
Basse, Luke, 36
Basse, Lydia, 36
Basse, Mary, 36
Basse, Nathaniel, 35
Basse, Richard, 36
Basse, Samuel, 36
Basse, Sarah, 36
Basse, Thomas, 36
Basse, William, **35**, **36**
Bassett, Francis, 75
Bassler, Hannah, 439
Basting, Johanna/Jana/Jeanne, 97
Basting, Josias, 97

Basting, Martha (Zonnevylle/Zonneyville), 97
Batcheller, Nathaniel, 123
Batdorf, Johannes Martinus, 438
Batdorf, Maria Elisabetha (Walborn), 438
Batdorf/Battorf, John Adam, 438
Batton, Jacques, 467
Batton, Margaret (Sans/Jans), 467
Bauda, Pierre, 380
Baudoin, Elizabeth (Bureau), 37
Baudoin, Pierre, **36**, 37
Baudoin/ Bowdoin, Mary, 37
Baudoin/Beaudoine, Marguerite, 124
Baudoin/Bowdoin, Chloy, 37
Baudoin/Bowdoin, Elias, 37
Baudoin/Bowdoin, Elizabeth, 37
Baudoin/Bowdoin, Frances, 37
Baudoin/Bowdoin, Hannah, 37
Baudoin/Bowdoin, James II, 37
Baudoin/Bowdoin, Jean/John I, 37
Baudoin/Bowdoin, John, 37
Baudoin/Bowdoin, John II, 37
Baudoin/Bowdoin, John III, 37
Baudoin/Bowdoin, Judith, 37
Baudoin/Bowdoin, Mary, 37
Baudoin/Bowdoin, Peter, 37
BAUDOIN/BOWDOIN, Pierre, 36
Baudoin/Bowdoin, Rhody, 37
Baudoin/Bowdoin, Samuel, 37
Baudoin/Bowdoin, Sarah, 37
Baudoin/Bowdoin, Susannah, 37
Baudoin/Bowdoin, Thomas, 37
Baudoin/Bowdoin, William, 37
Baudouin, Christophe, 28
Baudouin, Jeanne (Gendron), 28
Baudouin, Marguerite, 28
Baugh, Mary, 195
Baugier, Jean, 239
Baugier, Suzanne (Levèsque), 239
Baujot, Jérémie, 380
Baumgardner, John, 261
BaumgardnerFrederich, 261
Baumgartner, Henry, 97
Baun/Bane/Baen/Bain/Beaune, Catarina/Catherine de, 38
Baun/Bane/Baen/Bain/Beaune, Cristeyan/Christian de, 38
Baun/Bane/Baen/Bain/Beaune, Jacobus/James de, 38
BAUN/BANE/BAEN/BAIN/BEAUNE, Joost/Joseph de, 38
Baun/Bane/Baen/Bain/Beaune, Karel/Charles de, 38
Baun/Bane/Baen/Bain/Beaune, Margrietje/Marie de, 38
Baun/Bane/Baen/Bain/Beaune, Matie/Mayke/Martha de, 38
Baun/Bane/Baen/Beaune, Christina de, 38
Bayard, Balthazar, 39
Bayard, Balthazor, **37**

Bayard, Catherine, 39
Bayard, Judith, 39
Bayard, Lazare, 38
Bayard, Nicholas, 39
BAYARD, Nicolas, 38
Bayard, Petrus, 39
Bayard, Richard, 39
Bayard, Samuel, 39, 75, 278
Bayard, Sarah, 39
Bayeux, Abigail, 39
Bayeux, Anne, 39
Bayeux, Élisabeth, 39
Bayeux, Henry, 39
Bayeux, Jean, 39
Bayeux, Jean/John, 39
Bayeux, Jeanne, 39
Bayeux, Magdelaine, 39
Bayeux, Marianne, 39
Bayeux, Marie, 39
Bayeux, Sara (Cuyler), 323
Bayeux, Susanna, 39
Bayeux, Susanne, 39
Bayeux, Thomas, 39, 79, 323
BAYEUX, Thomas, 39
Bayle, Cécile, 368
Bayle, Jean, 368
Bayle, Marie (Seyral), 368
Bayley, Nathaniel, 468
Bayley, Richard, 304
Bayley, William, 304
Bayliss, Elizabeth, 412
Bazemore, Elizabeth, 426
Beal, John, 62
Bean, Hester Elizabeth (Gourdin), 155
Bean, John, 155
Bean, Ralph, 160
Beard, William, 92
Beasley, William, 401
Beattie, unknown, 319
Beau, Marie, 325
BEAU, Marie, 40
Beau/Bueau, Daniel, 279
Beaucham, Marie (Malherbe), 40
Beaucham, Samuel, 40
Beauchamp, Adam, 40
Beauchamp, Isaac, 40
BEAUCHAMP, Jean, 40
Beauchamp, Jean/John, 40
Beauchamp, Katherine, 40
Beauchamp, Margaret, 40
Beauchamp, Marie/Mary, 40
Beauchamp, Mary Ann/Marian, 40
Beauchamp, Peter, 40
Beauchamp, Susanna, 40
Beaudoin, Jacques, 357
Beauford/Beaufort/Buford, Ambrose, 41
Beauford/Beaufort/Buford, Elizabeth, 41
Beauford/Beaufort/Buford, John, 41
BEAUFORD/BEAUFORT/BUFORD, Richard, 40

Beauford/Beaufort/Buford, Susannah, 41
Beauford/Beaufort/Buford, Thomas, 41
Beaumont, Jane, **35**
Beaumont, Thomas, **35**
BEBOUT, John Sr., 41
Bebout, Pieter, 41
Bebout/Bebou/Bebau, Jacob, 41
Bebout/Bibou/Bibau, Ebenezer, 41
Bebout/Bibou/Bibau, Jan II/John, 41
BEBOUT/BIBOU/BIBAU, Jan Pietersz, 41
Bebout/Bibou/Bibau, John, 41
Bebout/Bibou/Bibau, Marytje, 41
Bebout/Bibou/Bibau, Mertien, 41
Bebout/Bibou/Bibau, Peter, 41
Bec/Beck, Alexandre, **42**
Bec/Beck, Anna Marie, **42**
Bec/Beck, Catharina Susanne, **42**
Bec/Beck, Catherine, **42**
BEC/BECK, Daniel, **42**
Bec/Beck, Geoffroi/Cha(u)ffré, **42**
Bec/Beck, Guillaume, **42**
Bec/Beck, Isaac, **42**
Bec/Beck, Jacques, **42**
Bec/Beck, Jacques Guillaume, **42**
Bec/Beck, Jean Daniel, **42**
Bec/Beck, Marie, **42**
Bec/Beck, Pierre, **42**
Beck, Hermann, **42**
Beck, Stephan Alexander, **42**
Becker, Fredrich, 18
Becker, Johannes, 459
Becker, John Jacob, 259
Becker, Philip, 18
Beckwith, Margaret, 300
Becton, Sarah, 275
Bedat, Jean, 211
Bedat, Jeanne, 211
Bedat, Petronille (Léger), 211
Bedell, Stephen, 293
Bedlo/Bedloe/Bedlow,
    Catalina/Catharina, 43
Bedlo/Bedloe/Bedlow, François, 43
Bedlo/Bedloe/Bedlow, Isaac, 43
BEDLO/BEDLOE/BEDLOW, Isaac, 43
Bedlo/Bedloe/Bedlow, Maria, 43
Bedlo/Bedloe/Bedlow, Pieter, 43
Bedlow, Isaac, 287
Beech, George, 352
Beech, Isabella (X), 352
Beekman, Bernard, 320
Beekman, John, 412
Beekman, Martin Henricksen, 41
Beekman, Matye, 159
Beekman, Neeltje, 48
Begend/Begond, Judith, **38**
Beighley, Catherine/Cassie, 97
Beighley, Conrad, 96
Beighley, Daniel, 97
Beighley, Elizabeth, 97
Beighley, Elizabeth/Betsy, 97

Beighley, George, 97
Beighley, Henry, 97
Beighley, Jacob, 97
Beighley, John Adam, 97
Beighley, John/Johannis, 96
Beighley, Mary/Polly, 97
Beighley, Peter, 97
Beighley, Susan/ Shusey, 96
Beighley, William, 97
Beiren/Berrin/Binn(i)on/Binyon, Nancy
    Jane, 13
Beiren/Berrin/Binnon, Rosa Frances, 13
Belaine, John, 398
Belaine, Mary (X), 399
Belaine, Nicholas, 399
Belcher, Francis, 99
Belcher, unknown, 99
Belden, Margaret (Hawkes), 415
Belden, Thankful, 415
Belden, William, 415
Belfield, Joseph Dr., 23
Belfield/Bellefield, Joseph, Jr., 23
Belin, James, 208
Belin, Sarah, 208
Belin, Sarah (Torquet), 208
Bellamy, Timothy, 306
Bellangée, Ives, 289
Bellangee/Bellanger/Bellinger, Elizabeth
    de, 43
Bellangee/Bellanger/Bellinger, Évi/Jué
    de, 44
Bellangee/Bellanger/Bellinger, Isaac de,
    43
BELLANGÉE/BELLANGER/BELLINGER,
    Ives/Éves/Évi de, 43
Bellangee/Bellanger/Bellinger, James
    de, 44
Bellangee/Bellanger/Bellinger, Joshua
    (Sr.) de, 44
Bellangee/Bellanger/Bellinger,
    Michel/Michael de, 44
Bellangee/Bellanger/Bellinger, Nicholas
    de, 44
Bellangee/Bellanger/Bellinger, Samuel
    de, 44
Bellangee/Bellanger/Bellinger,
    Susannah de, 43
Bellemain, Marie, 349
Belleville, Jean, 44
Belleville, Susanne (Arnaud), 44
Belleville/Belville, Hester, 44
Belleville/Belville, Jean II, 44
BELLEVILLE/BELVILLE,
    Jean/Jan/Johannes/John, 44
Belleville/Belville, Mary, 44
Belleville/Belville, Philip, 44
Bellier, Catherine (Herque), 44
Bellier, Elisabeth, 150
Bellier, Elizabeth, 296, 353, 450
BELLIER, Elizabeth/Lysbeth, 44
Bellier, Jean, 44

Bellin, Élie, 79
Bellin, Janice, 79
Bellin, Pierre, 79
Belliveau, Charles, 294
Belliveau, Jean, 294
Belliveau, Jean Antoine, 294
Bellon, François, 249
Bellon, Isabeau, 248
Bellon, Jean, 249
Bellot, Jane (Langel), 426
Bellot, John, 284
Bellot, Lydia (Gogul), 284
Bellot, Mary Jane, 426
Bellot, Peter Elijah, 284, 426
Bellot, Susan, 319
Bellune, Daniel, 45
Bellune, Elizabeth, 45, 46
Bellune, John, 45
Bellune, Martha, 45, 46
Bellune, Mary, 45
Bellune, Michael, 45
BELLUNE, Michael, 45
Bellune, Sarah, 45
Bellune, Sooanne, 45
Bellune, William, 45
Belon, Françoise, 182
Belville/Belleville, Jean/John, 105
BEN(N)ET, Willem Adriaense, 48
Benet, Adrien, 48
BÉNÉZET, (Louis) Jean, 46
Benezet, Ant(h)oin, 46
Benezet, Antoine, 46
Benezet, Chilepior, 47
Benezet, Cirus/Cyrus, 47
Benezet, Claude, 46
Benezet, Daniel, 46
Benezet, Elizabeth, 47
Benezet, Étienne, 46
Benezet, Gertrude, 47
Benezet, Jacque(s)/James, 46
Benezet, Jacques, 47
Benezet, Jean, 47
Benezet, Jean Baptiste, 46
Benezet, Jean Étienne, 46
Benezet, Jean Ja(c)ques, 47
Benezet, Madelaine, 46
Benezet, Madelaine Marguerite, 47
Benezet, Marianne, 46
Benezet, Marie Judith Madelaine, 46
Benezet, Milizior, 47
Benezet, Philip(p)e, 46
Benezet, Pierre, 46, 47
Benezet, Pierre Testart, 47
Benezet, Susanne, 46
Benin(g), Antoine, 257
Benin, Ann (de Bonnet), 175
Benin, Anne, 47
Benin, Anne (deBonnette), 257
Benin, Anthony, 175
Benin, Barbara, 47
Benin, François, 72, 257

Benin/ Benning, Elizabeth, 47
Benin/Benning, Antoine/Anthony, 47
Benin/Benning, Constance, 47
BENIN/BENNING, François/Francis, 47
Benin/Benning, Isaac, 47
Benin/Benning, James, 47
Benin/Benning, Jean/John, 47
Benin/Benning, Joseph, 47
Benin/Benning, Judith, 47
Benin/Benning, Lucy, 47
Benin/Benning, Perkins, 47
Benin/Benning, William, 47
Bennet, Abraham, 48
Bennet, Adriaen/Arie, 48
Bennet, Angnietje, 48
Bennet, Antje, 48
Bennet, Arie, 48
Bennet, Catharina, 48
Bennet, Christian, 48
Bennet, Cornelis, 48
Bennet, Engletje, 48
Bennet, Femmetje, 48
Bennet, Gertruyd, 48
Bennet, Heyltie, 48
Bennet, Isaac, 48
Bennet, Jacob, 48, 302
Bennet, Jan, 48
Bennet, Jan/John, 48
Bennet, Maria, 48
Bennet, Marritje, 48
Bennet, Marytje/Maria, 48
Bennet, Willem, 48
Bennet, Willem/William, 48
Bennett, Bethia, 340
Bennett, Elizabeth, 100
Bennett, Elizabeth (Peyton), 100
Bennett, Gideon, 340
Bennett, Jacob, 302
Bennett, James, 100
Bennett, Martha, 209
Bennett, Thomas, 462
Benneville, George Dr. de, 55
Benoit, Anna, 444
Benoit, Daniel, 444
Benoit, Gabrielle (Mercier), 371
Benoit, Jacques, 371, 444
Benoit, Jacques II, 371
Benoit, Messaline, 250
Benoit, Pierre, 444
Benoit, Suzanna (Colin), 444
Benoit/Benoy, Geurt, 49
Benoit/Benoy, Hendrickie, 49
Benoit/Benoy, Jacob, 49
Benoit/Benoy, Margarita, 49
Benoit/Benoy, Marie, 49
Benoit/Benoy, Martha, 49
Benoit/Benoy, Pierre, 49
BENOIT/BENOY, Pierre, 49
Benskin(e), Elizabeth (X), 181
Benskin(e), Jeremiah, 181
Benskin, Mary, 181

Benson, Dorothy (Sutton), 403
Benson, Elizabeth (Briggs), 297
Benson, John, 297
Benson, Martha, 297
Benson, Mrs., 264
Benson, Robert, 403
Benson, Thomas, 403
Bentyn, Jacques, 48
Bentyn, Pierronne, 153
Béraude, Anna, 424
Beraude, Elizabeth (Gregorie), 424
Beraude, Matthew, 424
Berdan, Annetje, 316
Berdan, Marretie, 151
Berdule, Beatris, 186
Berdule, Jacob, 186
Bergen, Hans Hansen, 409
Berger, (Mary) Catherine Charity, 199
Berger, Andreas, 199
Bergeron, Anne, 49
Bergeron, Éli/Elias, 49
BERGERON, Jacques/James, 49
Bergeron, JeanJohn, 49
Bergeron, Jeanne, 49
Bergeron, Judith, 49
Bergeron, Marguerite/Margaret, 49
Bergeron, Pierre, 49
Bergh, Ingenatia Van den, 317
Bergner/Bergman, Maria, 191
Berkeley, Edward, 352
Berkeley, Gov., 472
Berkeley, Jane (X), 352
Berkeley, Sir William, 334
Bernard, Abner, 51
Bernard, Allen, 51
Bernard, Anne, 142
Bernard, Charlotte, 51
Bernard, David, 141, 142
Bernard, Elizabeth, 51
Bernard, Étienne, 462
Bernard, Francis, 142
Bernard, Jesse B, 51
Bernard, Joanna, 51
Bernard, John, 50, 51, 141
Bernard, Joseph, 51
Bernard, Judith, 141
Bernard, Judith (X), 210
Bernard, Madeleine, 379
Bernard, Mary, 51
Bernard, Peter, 51
Bernard, Pierre, 142
Bernard, Pierre Count, 50
BERNARD, Pierre/Peter, 50
Bernard, Rebekah, 141
Bernard, Samuel, 210
Bernard, Thomas, 210
Bernard, Valentine, 51
Bernard, William, 51
Bernard/Barnar, Ann, 50
Bernard/Barnar, Anne, 50
Bernard/Barnar, Anthony, 50

Bernard/Barnar, Benjamin, 50
Bernard/Barnar, David, 50
BERNARD/BARNAR, David, 50
Bernard/Barnar, David, Jr, 50
Bernard/Barnar, François/Francis, 50
Bernard/Barnar, Jacob, 50
Bernard/Barnar, Jean/John, 50
Bernard/Barnar, John, 50
Bernard/Barnar, Judith, 50
Bernard/Barnar, Magdelaine, 50
Bernard/Barnar, Marie, 50
Bernard/Barnar, Mary Ann, 50
Bernard/Barnar, Mary Magdelen, 50
Bernard/Barnar, Pierre, 50
Bernard/Barnar, Rebekah, 50
Bernard/Barnar, William, 50
Bernardin, Jeanne, 379
Bernheisel, Martin, 116
Berniere, Catherine de, 52
Berniere, Elinor de, 51
Berniere, Henry A. C. de, 51
Bernière, Jean, 51
BERNIÈRE, Jean Antoine de/John Anthony, 51
Berniere, John Anthony de, 51
Berniere, John Henry de, 51
Bernière, Lamelett/Lancelott, 51
Berniere, Louis Crommelin de, 51
Berniere, Louise de, 51
Berniere, Madeleine de, 51
Berniere, Mary Anne de, 51
Bernon, André, 52, 317
Bernon, Esther, 52
Bernon, Esther (LeRoy), 454
Bernon, Eve, 53, 317
Bernon, Éve, 52
Bernon, Gabriel, 13, 52, 53, 317, 454
BERNON, Gabriel, 52
Bernon, Jacques, 52
Bernon, Jean, 52
Bernon, Jeanne, 13
Bernon, Jeanne/Jane, 52
Bernon, Jeanneton, 52
Bernon, Marie, 52, 184, 454
Bernon, Marie/Mary, 52
Bernon, Mary, 53
Bernon, Samuel, 52
Bernon, Sarah, 52
Bernon, Susanne, 53
Bernon, Suzanne, 52
Bernon, Suzanne (Guillemard), 317
Bernon, Suzanne (Guillemard/Guélemard), 52
Beron, André, 184
Beron, Suzanne (Guillemard), 184
Berou, Andrée (LeProu), 397
Berou, Eutrope, 397
Berrien, Agnes/Angenietje, 53
Berrien, Claes, 53
Berrien, Claus/Nicholas Cornelise, 53
Berrien, Cornelis Cornelise, 53

BERRIEN, Cornelis Jansen, 53
Berrien, Jacob Cornelise, 53
Berrien, Jan Claes, 53
Berrien, Jan Cornelise/John, 53
Berrien, John, 53
Berrien, P(i)eter Cornelise, 53
Berrien, Tryntie/Catherine Cornelise, 53
Berry, Elizabeth Jansen, 342
Berry, Nancy, 64
Berryman, Dr., 108
Bert, Adam, 235
Berthet, Pierre, 28
Bertin(e)/Bertain/Bartain/Berton/Bretin, Catherine, 54
BERTIN(E)/BERTAIN/BARTAIN/BERTON/BRETIN, dit Laronde, Pierre, 54
Bertin(e)/Bertain/Bartain/Berton/Bretin, John, 54
Bertin(e)/Bertain/Bartain/Berton/Bretin, Marie, 54
Bertin(e)/Bertain/Bartain/Berton/Bretin, Mary, 54
Bertin(e)/Bertain/Bartain/Berton/Bretin, Pierre II, 54
Bertin(e)/Bertain/Bartain/Berton/Bretin, Pierre III/Peter, 54
Bertin(e)/Bertain/Bartain/Berton/Bretin, Susanne, 54
Bertin(e)/Bertain/Bartain/Breton/Bretin, Esther, 54
Bertin(e)/Bertain/Bartain/Breton/Bretin, Jeanne, 54
Bertin(e)/Bertain/Bartain/Breton/Bretin, Judith, 54
Bertin(e)/Bertain/Bartain/Breton/Bretin, Marianne, 54
Bertin(e)/Bertain/Bartain/Breton/Bretin, Susanne Madelaine, 54
Bertin, Nicolas, 160
Bertine, Anne, 441
Bertine, Anne (Barron), 441
Bertine, Anne (Borron), 303
Bertine, Catherine, 440
Bertine, Catherine (Sicard), 440
Bertine, Esther, 303
Bertine, John, 14
Bertine, Peter, 303
Bertine, Pierre, 14, 303, 317, 440
Bertine, Pierre/Peter, 333, 441
Bertine, Susanna, 303, 333
Bertolet, Abraham, 55, 458
Bertolet, Elizabeth (X), 73
Bertolet, Esther, 55, 73
Bertolet, Frederick, 55
Bertolet, Jean, 73, 206, 241, 458
Bertolet, Jean/John, 55
BERTOLET, Jean/John, 54
Bertolet, Jonathan Dr., 73
Bertolet, Maria, 55
Bertolet, Peter, 54, 55, 73
Bertolet, Susanna, 55, 206

Bertolet, Susanna (Harcourt), 206
Bertolet, Susanne (de Harcourt), 458
Bertonneau, Élisabeth (X), 360
Bertonneau, Elizabeth (X), 255
Bertonneau, Jacques, 255, 360
Bertonneau, Sara, 255
BERTONNEAU, Sara, 55
Bertonneau/Bertomeau, Elisabeth (X), 55
Bertonneau/Bertomeau, Jacques, 55
BERTRAND, Jean/John (Rev.), 55
Bertrand, Mary Ann, 56
Bertrand, Paul, 56
BERTRAND, Paul (Rev.), 56
Bertrand, William, 56, 200
Beshearer/Bescherer, Jacob, 330
Besl(e)y, Diane, 56
Besl(e)y, Isaac, 57
Besl(e)y, James, 57
Besl(e)y, Judith, 56
Besl(e)y, Mary, 57
Besl(e)y, Oliver, Jr, 57
BESL(E)Y, Olivier/Oliver, 56
Besl(e)y, Susanna Mary, 57
Besl(e)y, Thauvet/Tovat, 57
Besley, Diane (Fouquet), 56
Besley, Jacques, 56
Besselieu, Philip Anthony, 57
Bessellieu, Lewis, 57
BESSELLIEU, Mark Anthony, 57
Bessellieu, Mark Anthony III, 57
Bessellieu, Mark Anthony, II, 57
Bessellieu, Mary, 57
Bessellieu, Philip Anthony, 57
Bessellieu, Susanna, 57
Bessonet, Claude, 58
Bessonet, Elizabeth, 107
Bessonet/Bessonett/Besonette, Anne, 58
Bessonet/Bessonett/Besonette, Catherine, 58
Bessonet/Bessonett/Besonette, Charles, 58
BESSONET/BESSONETT/BESONETTE, Charles, 57
Bessonet/Bessonett/Besonette, Daniel, 58
Bessonet/Bessonett/Besonette, Elizabeth, 58
Bessonet/Bessonett/Besonette, James, 58
Bessonet/Bessonett/Besonette, John, 58
Bessonet/Bessonett/Besonette, Margaret, 58
Bessonet/Bessonett/Besonette, Martha, 58
Bessonet/Bessonett/Besonette, Mary, 58
Bessonet/Bessonett/Besonette, Sarah, 58
Bessonnet, Spectable, 107
Best, Katherine, 69

Bethune, George, 184
Bettison, Sarah, 244
Betts, James, 86
Beuchler, unknown, 34
Bevier, Abraham, 59, 308
Bevier, André/Andries, 59
Bevier, Elizabeth, 59
Bevier, Esther, 59
Bevier, Hester, 242
Bevier, Isaac, 59
Bevier, Jean, 59
Bevier, Johannah, 59
Bevier, Johannes, 308
Bevier, Louis, 242
BEVIER, Louis, 58
Bevier, Louis II, 59
Bevier, Louis III, 59
Bevier, Magdalene (Blanshan, 307
Bevier, Magdelene (Blanshan), 308
Bevier, Margaret, 307
Bevier, Maria, 308
Bevier, Marie, 59
Bevier, Marie (Le Blanc), 242
Bevier, Marie (Vernooy), 308
Bevier, Samuel, 59, 307, 308
Bevier, Solomon, 59
Bevoor, Joris, 159
Beyer, Johann Christoph, 59
BEYER/BOYER, 59
Beyer/Boyer, Abraham, 60
Beyer/Boyer, Anna Barbara, 59
Beyer/Boyer, Anna Elizabeth, 60
Beyer/Boyer, Anna Margaretha, 59
Beyer/Boyer, Catherine, 60
Beyer/Boyer, Clara Elisabeth, 59
Beyer/Boyer, Elizabeth, 59
Beyer/Boyer, Eva Catherine, 60
Beyer/Boyer, Eva Elisabeth, 60
Beyer/Boyer, Georg Jakob, 59
Beyer/Boyer, Jacob, 60
Beyer/Boyer, Johann Andreas, 59
Beyer/Boyer, Johann Martin, 60
Beyer/Boyer, Johann Nicolus, 59
Beyer/Boyer, Johann Philipp, 59
Beyer/Boyer, Johann Wendell, 59
Beyer/Boyer, John Christopher, 60
Beyer/Boyer, John Philip, 60
Beyer/Boyer, Maria Magdalena, 59
Beyer/Boyer, Maria Margaret, 59
Beyer/Boyer, Mary Ann, 60
Beyer/Boyer, Mary Margaret, 60
Beyer/Boyer, Michael, 60
Beyer/Boyer, Phillip, 60
Beyer/Boyer, Susan, 59
Beyer/Boyer, Thomas, 59
Beyvanck, Anna, 412
Bezanson, Marie Catherine, 284
Bibau, Symoen, 41
Bibeau, François, 110
Bickel, Mary Elizabeth, 261
Bickel, Tobias, 439

Bickford, Aaron, 246
Bickley/Biélet/Biclet, Mary Dorothy, 72
Biddlecombe, James, 89
Bidwell, Anna, 244
Bidwell, Richard, 244
Biehlen, Peter, 358
Bienaime, Anne (Beraud), 221
Bienaime, Peter, 221
Bienaime, Ysabeau/Elizabeth, 221
Bigelow, unknown, 45
Biggers, Samuel, 401
Biggers, William, 334
Bigham, unknown, 376
Bijeu, Anthoine, 151
Bilbaud, John Peter, 16
Bilbaud, Susannah, 16
Bilbo, Jean, 60
Bilbo, John Peter, 61
Biljow, Jeanq, 61
Billebeau/Bilbaut/Bilbo(u), Elizabeth, *61*
Billebeau/Bilbaut/Bilbo(u), Jacques, 61
BILLEBEAU/BILBAUT/BILBO(U), Jacques, 60
Billebeau/Bilbaut/Bilbo(u), Jean Pierre, 61
Billebeau/Bilbaut/Bilbo(u), Jean/John, *61*
Billebeau/Bilbaut/Bilbo(u), Marie, *61*
Billebeau/Billebaud, Jeanne, 233
Billiou, Chrétienne/Christin, 349
Billiou, François (DuBois), 290
Billiou, Françoise, 120, 130, 290
Billiou, Françoise (DuBois), 74, 273, 349
Billiou, Jacob, 120, 130, 290
Billiou, Margaret (Larzelère), 130
Billiou, Marie, 101
Billiou, Pierre, 74, 152, 273, 290, 349
Billiou/Bilyeu/Balliou/Barlow, Abigail, 62
Billiou/Bilyeu/Balliou/Barlow, Anne, 62
Billiou/Bilyeu/Balliou/Barlow, Ariantie, 62
Billiou/Bilyeu/Balliou/Barlow, Chrétienne/Christina, 62
Billiou/Bilyeu/Balliou/Barlow, Francina, 62
Billiou/Bilyeu/Balliou/Barlow, Françoise, 62
Billiou/Bilyeu/Balliou/Barlow, Françoise/Frances, 61
Billiou/Bilyeu/Balliou/Barlow, Isaac, 62
Billiou/Bilyeu/Balliou/Barlow, Jacob, 62
Billiou/Bilyeu/Balliou/Barlow, Jean, 61
Billiou/Bilyeu/Balliou/Barlow, John, 62
Billiou/Bilyeu/Balliou/Barlow, Marie, 61
Billiou/Bilyeu/Balliou/Barlow, Martha, 61
Billiou/Bilyeu/Balliou/Barlow, Mary, 62
Billiou/Bilyeu/Balliou/Barlow, Peter, 61, 62

Billiou/Bilyeu/Balliou/Barlow, Pierre/Peter, 61
BILLIOU/BILYEU/BALLIOU/BARLOW, Thomas, 61
Billon, Marguerite, 40
Billon, Marye/Marie, 127
Bills, Sylvester, 96
Binford, Betsy Kinsey, 383
Binford, Elizabeth (X), 383
Binford, Thomas, 383
Bingley, Joseph, 185
Bishop of London, 113
Bishop, Abigail (Wetmore), 282
Bishop, Hannah, 282
Bishop, Jane, 376
Bishop, Joshua, 467
Bishop, Samuel, 282
Bishop, Sarah, 282
Bishop, Stephen, 282
Bishop, Tabitha (Wilkinson), 282
Bisk, Elizabeth, 253
Bissell, Abigail, 244
Bissell, Abigail (Holcombe), 244
Bissell, Samuel, 244
Bisset, Abraham, 397
Bisset, Anne, 397
Bisset, Catherine, 397
Bisset, Élie, 397
Bisset, Marie (Bitheur), 397
Bisset, Mary, 397
Bist, Martin Vander, 123
Bistel, Anna Catherine, 235
Bixler, Elizabeth, 97
Blackford, Ann (Smalley), 425
Blackford, Providence, 425
Blackford, Samuel, 425
Blackshear, Mary, 288
Blackston/Blakiston, John, 236
Blackwell, Mary Downing Hudnall, 266
Blackwell, Samuel, 266
Blackwell, unknown, 96
Blackwell/Blackley, Lucy, 266
Blagge, Martha, 198
Blaine, Jean de, 380
Blair, Hannah, 246
Blais, Pierre, 451
Blake, Mary (X), 119
Blake, unknown, 119
Blake, William, 119
Blakiston, Elizabeth (Gerard), 236
Blakiston, Nehemiah, 236
Blanc, Suzanne, 71
Blanchamp/Blanchan, Isabeau (Le Roy), 63
Blanchamp/Blanchan, Leonin, 63
Blanchan, Catherine, 152
Blanchan, Elizabeth, 103
Blanchan, Madeleine Joiré, 129
Blanchan, Magdaleine (Joiré), 152
Blanchan, Magdalena, 59

Blanchan, Margaret (Van Schoonhover), 59
Blanchan, Margriet (VanSchoenven), 103
Blanchan, Marie, 129
Blanchan, Marrys, 106
Blanchan, Matthew, 152
Blanchan, Matthieu, 129
Blanchan, Matthys, 103
Blanchan, Matthys, Jr., 59
Blanchan, Mattys/Matthew, 307
Blanchan/Blanshan/Blancon, Antoine, 63
Blanchan/Blanshan/Blancon, Catherine/Katryn, 63
Blanchan/Blanshan/Blancon, Elizabeth, 63
Blanchan/Blanshan/Blancon, Magdelaine, 63
Blanchan/Blanshan/Blancon, Maria, 63
BLANCHAN/BLANSHAN/BLANCON, Mathieu/Matthys/Matthew, 63
Blanchan/Blanshan/Blancon, Maximilianus, 63
Blanchan/Blanshan/Blandon, Mathieu/Matthew, 63
Blanchard, Anna, 64
Blanchard, Elizabeth, 64
Blanchard, Francis, 167
Blanchard, Isaac, 64
Blanchard, Jean, 257, 417
BLANCHARD, Jean/John, 63
Blanchard, Jean/John II, 64
Blanchard, Jeanne, 64
Blanchard, Mary, 64
Blanchard, Peter, 64
Blanchard, Susannah, 64
Blanchard, unknown, 123
Bland, Elizabeth (Fendin), 135
Bland, Richard, 135
Blanford/Beven, Martha, 276
Blanjean, Mattys, 308
Blankenship, Elizabeth, 369
Blanshan, Catherine, 308
Blanshan, Cornelia, 307
Blanshan, Matthew, 308
Blarcom, Catherine Van, 306
Blauvelt, Herman Hendrickse, 170
Bleyck, Jacob, 45
Bleyck, Jannetje, 450
Bleyck,Jannetie, 45
Blinn, Maria Catharina, 19
Blinn, Philip Henrich, 19
Blizzard, George, 25
Blizzard, John, 25
Blodgett, Daniel, 341
Bloedel, Guillaume, 252
Bloedel, Jeanne (Beauprez), 252
Bloedel/Bloedil, Corinne, 252
Blondeau, Claud(in)e (Fume), 29
Blondeau, François, 29
Blondeau, Marie, 394
Blosser, Susanna, 370

Blosset, Paul de, 145
Blouet(t), Mary, 385
Bloys/DuBliss, Catherine de, 68
Blume, unknown, 292
Blundy, Charles, 270
Bly, Jonathan, 255
BO(E)YER, Alexander/Sander, 87
Bo(e)yer, Catherine, 87
Bo(e)yer, Daniel, 87
Bo(e)yer, Elisabeth, 87
Bo(e)yer, Helena, 87
Bo(e)yer, Jan, 87
Bo(e)yer, Josine/Joseyn, 87
Bo(e)yer, P(i)eter, 87
Bo(e)yer, Samuel, 87
Bobo/Baubeau/Beaubeau/ Bodeau,
   Spencer, 64
Bobo/Baubeau/Beaubeau/Bodeau,
   Absalom, 64
Bobo/Baubeau/Beaubeau/Bodeau,
   Gabriel, 64
BOBO/BAUBEAU/BEAUBEAU/BODEAU,
   Gabriel, 64
Bobo/Baubeau/Beaubeau/Bodeau,
   Lewis, 64
Bobo/Baubeau/Beaubeau/Bodeau,
   Mary Elizabeth, 64
Bobo/Baubeau/Beaubeau/Bodeau,
   Nancy, 64
Bobo/Baubeau/Beaubeau/Bodeau,
   Sampson, 64
Bobo/Baubeau/Beaubeau/Bodeau,
   Spencer, Jr., 64
Bochet, Marianne (Videau), 373
Bochet, Nicholas, 68, 470
Bochet, Nicolas, 373
Bochet, Susannah Elizabeth, 373
Bochett, Frances, 373
Bodine, Heyltje (Smith), 357
Bodine, James, 58
Bodine, Jean, 120, 130, 464
Bodine, Judith, 130
Bodine, Marie (Crocheron), 130, 464
Bodine, Mr. unknown, 58
Bodine, Vincent, 130, 357
Bodine/Berdine, Sarah, 464
Boehm, Anna Margaretha, 151
Boeman, Sarah E., 120
Boer de, unknown, 210
Boerman, Altie, 125
Boerum, Willem Jacobse Van, 169
Bogaert, Aertje, 174
Bogard, Catherine Teunis, 95
Bogardus, Anneke (Webber), 441
Bogardus, Everardus Rev., 441
Bogardus, Wilhelm/William, 441
Bogart, Abigail Uyten, 296
Bogart, Frans Van de, 384
Bogart, Helena Van de, 384
Bogart, Myndert Van de, 384
Bogert, Angenitie, 172

Bogert, Anneke, 302
Bogert, Belitje, 302
Bogert, Catherine, 78
Bogert, Cornelia, 302
Bogert, Elizabeth, 302
Bogert, Henry, 313
Bogert, Jan Louwe, 384
Bogert, Johannes, 302
Bogert, John, 172
Bogert, Margrietje, 302
Bogert, Maria (Bertholf), 172
Bogert, Nicholas/Claes Janse, 302
Bogert, Petrus, 302
Boggess, Thomas, 133
Bohannan, Duncan, 180
Bohannan, Joseph Capt., 270
Bohannon, John, 270
Bohun, Elizabeth, 224
Boice/Boyce, Rachel, 14
Boigard, Mathurin,, 234
Bonyot, 304
Boileau, Charles, 145
Boileau, Marie Madeleine (Collot
   d'Escury), 145
Boisseau, Benjamin, 65
Boisseau, Charles Cantey, 66
Boisseau, David, 66
Boisseau, Elizabeth, 65
Boisseau, Jacques, 65
BOISSEAU, Jacques/James (Rev.), 65
Boisseau, James, 65, 66
Boisseau, James II, 65
Boisseau, Jean, 68
BOISSEAU, Jean, 65
Boisseau, John, 65
Boisseau, Joseph Ehyrr, 65
Boisseau, Judith, 65
Boisseau, Marie (LaCourt), 65
Boisseau, Mary (Jermain/Germain), 68
Boisseau, Molly Holt, 65
Boisseau, René, 65
Boisseau, Samuel Peyre, 66
Boisseau, Sarah, 65
Boisseau, Susanna, 65
Boissevain, Jacques, 66
Boissevain, Lucas, 66
Boissevain, Pierette, 66
Boissevain,Jean, 66
BOISSEVAIN/BOISSAVI/ BOSSAVIN dit
   BOU(Y)SSAVY, Lucas, 66
Boissevain/Boissavi/Bossavin, Isaac, 66
Boissevain/Boissavi/Bossavin, Jérémie,
   66
Boissevain/Boissavi/Bossavin, Marthe
   Anne, 66
Boissière, unknown, 45
Bolen, Rachel Van, 39
Boles, Agnes, 292
Bolin, Sarah, 117
Bolinger, unknown, 279
Bollinger, Joseph, 279

Bolt, Mary, 213
Bommel, Deborah (Davids) Van, 149
Bommel, Margaret Van, 149
Bommel, Peter Van, 149
BommelHendrick van, 177
Bonavas, Jean, 248
Bonavas, unknown, 248
Bond, Elizabeth, 293
Bonde, Marguerite, 467
Bonderick, Jannetje, 306
Bondurant, Ann, 13
Bondurant, Ann (Fauré), 187
Bondurant, Anne, 187
Bondurant, Anne (Fauré), 434
Bondurant, Françoise, 434
Bondurant, Gabrielle (Barjon), 67
Bondurant, Jean Pierre, 13, 67, 187, 434
BONDURANT, Jean Pierre/John Peter, 67
Bonhoste, Catherine (Allaire), 28
Bonhoste, Elizabeth, 28
Bonhoste, Jonas, 28
Bonhôtal, Anne Catherine (Pochard), 228
Bonhôtal, David, 67
Bonhôtal, Elisabeth (Goux), 67
Bonhôtal, Elizabeth (Bourguin), 228
Bonhôtal, Jacques Christophe, 228
BONHÔTAL, Jacques Christophe, 67
Bonhotal, Jean Georges, 68
Bonhôtal, Jean Goerge, 228
Bonhotal, Julie, 68
Bonhôtal, Julie, 228
Bonneau, Ant(h)oine, 68
Bonneau, Anthony, 66, 68, 245
Bonneau, Antoine, 68, 245, 470
Bonneau, Benjamin, 68
Bonneau, Catherine, 68
Bonneau, Catherine (Roi), 470
Bonneau, Elias, 371
Bonneau, Elizabeth, 68
Bonneau, Elizabeth (Videau), 66
Bonneau, Ester, 68
Bonneau, Ester Jane (Benoit), 393
Bonneau, Floride, 68
Bonneau, Henry, 68
Bonneau, Jacob, 68, 233, 371, 373, 470
Bonneau, Jane (Videau), 233, 371
Bonneau, Jane [Videau], 373
BONNEAU, Jean, 68
Bonneau, Jean Henri, 68
Bonneau, Jeanne Elizabeth (Videau), 245
Bonneau, Judith, 68
Bonneau, Magdalene, 233, 373
Bonneau, Mary, 68
Bonneau, Peter, 68
Bonneau, Samuel, 66, 68
Bonneau. Elias, 68
Bonneau. Jacob, 68
Bonneau. Magdalene, 68
Bonnefous, Martha, 25
Bonnefoy, Catherine, 128
Bonnefoy, David, 128, 303

Bonnel(l), Abigail, 69
Bonnel(l), Abraham, 70
Bonnel(l), Anthony, 69
Bonnel(l), Benjamin, 70
Bonnel(l), Daniel, 69
BONNEL(L), Daniel, 69
Bonnel(l), David, 69
Bonnel(l), Ebenezer, 70
Bonnel(l), Elizabeth, 69, 70
Bonnel(l), Hannah, 69
Bonnel(l), Hester, 69
Bonnel(l), Honora, 69
Bonnel(l), Isaac, 70
Bonnel(l), John, 69, 70
Bonnel(l), Judith, 70
Bonnel(l), Judye, 70
Bonnel(l), Katherine, 69
Bonnel(l), Lydia, 70
Bonnel(l), Mary, 70
Bonnel(l), Nathaniel, 70
Bonnel(l), Rebecca, 69
Bonnel(l), Samuel, 69
Bonnel(l), Sarah, 69
Bonnel(l), Susan, 69, 70
Bonnel(l), Susannah Mary, 69
Bonnel(l), Susanne, 69
Bonnel(l), Thomas, 70
BONNEL(L), Thomas, 69
Bonnel(l), William, 70
Bonnel, Jean, 69
Bonner, Elizabeth (Betsey), 247
BONNET(T), Jean Jacques, 71
Bonnet(t), Ann, 72
Bonnet(t), Barbara, 72
Bonnet(t), Christine, 72
Bonnet(t), Daniel, 71, 72
Bonnet(t), Daniel II, 73
Bonnet(t), David, 71
BONNET(T), David, 70
Bonnet(t), Elizabeth, 72, 73
Bonnet(t), Estienne, 71
Bonnet(t), Heinrich Carl, 71
Bonnet(t), Jean, 70, 71
Bonnet(t), Jean Anthoine, 71
Bonnet(t), Jean Jacques, 73
Bonnet(t), Jean Pierre, 71
Bonnet(t), Jeanne, 71
Bonnet(t), Jeanne/Jane, 73
Bonnet(t), Jehanne/Johanne, 70
Bonnet(t), Johann Adam Isaac/John, 72
Bonnet(t), Johann Ludwig, 71
Bonnet(t), Johann Martin Simon/John, 72
Bonnet(t), Lewis, 72
BONNET(T), Louis, 72
Bonnet(t), Marguerite, 71
Bonnet(t), Marguerite/Margaret Catherine, 72
Bonnet(t), Marie, 71, 73
Bonnet(t), Mary, 72
Bonnet(t), Pierre, 71, 73

Bonnet(t), Rosina, 72
Bonnet(t), Samuel, 72
Bonnet(t), Susanna Magdelena, 72
Bonnet(t), Susannah, 72
Bonnet(t), Suzanne, 71
Bonnet(te), Barbara de, 175
Bonnet, Christine (Cousine), 71
Bonnet, Daniel, 225, 440
Bonnet, Daniel De, 175
Bonnet, Jean/John Martin, 19
Bonnet, Jeanne (Courturier/Couterrie/Coliver) De, 175
Bonnet, Jeanne (Couturier), 225, 440
Bonnet, Jeanne/Jane, 440
Bonnet, Mary Dorothy (Bickley), 19
Bonneterre, Jean, 208
Bonnetheau/Bonnetheau, Charles, 82
Bonnett, Rosina/Rosana, 19
Bonnette, Anne de, 47
Bonnette, Daniel de, 47
Bonnette, Jeanne (Courturier), 47
Bonneville, George de, 55
Bonneville, Marie (Granville) de, 55
Bonneville/Benneville, Daniel de, 73
Bonneville/Benneville, Esther de, 73
Bonneville/Benneville, George de, 73
BONNEVILLE/BENNEVILLE, Georges de, 73
Bonneville/Benneville, Marie de, 73
Bonneville/Benneville, Sarah de, 73
Bonneville/Benneville, Susanna de, 73
Bonney, Mary, 23
Bonney, Richard, 23
Bonnin, Aman, 462
Bonrepos Ester (X) de, 18
Bonrepos, Alexander de, 74
BONREPOS, Alexandre de (Rev.), 74
Bonrepos, Anne Marguerite de, 74
Bonrepos, Blanche de, 74, 109
Bonrepos, David de, 74
Bonrepos, Elias de, 74
Bonrepos, Élias/Élie de, 74
Bonrepos, Elie de, 18
Bonrepos, Élie de, 109
Bonrepos, Hester/Esther de, 74
Bonrepos, Jane (X) de, 109
Bonrepos, Jean de, 74
Bonrepos, John de, 74
Bonrepos, Marguerite de, 18
Bonrepos, Marguerite/Margaret de, 74
Bonrepos, Marian de, 74
Bonrepos, Martha de, 74
Bonrepos, Mary de, 74
Bontecou, Daniel, 75
Bontecou, David, 75
Bontecou, James, 75
Bontecou, Marguerite, 75
Bontecou, Marguerite (Collinot), 414
Bontecou, Marie, 75
Bontecou, Peter, 75
Bontecou, Pierre, 414

BONTECOU, Pierre, 75
Bontecou, Rachel, 75
Bontecou, Sara, 75, 414
Bontecou, Susanne, 75
Bontecou, Timothée/Timothy, 75
Bontecou, Timothy, 75
Bonum, Philpot, 133
Bonum, Rose (Neale), 133
Bonviver, Denis, 380
Bonyot/Boignyot, Esther, 304
Bonyot/Boignyot, Ezekiel, 304
Bonyot/Boignyot, Marianne, 304
Booker, Edward, 351
Booker, Mary (Goode), 351
Booker, Richard, 351
Boone, Samuel, 289
Booth, Ebenezer, 340
Booth, Elizabeth, 183, 326
Booth, Mary, 340
Booth, Mary (Clark), 340
Bootle, Marie, 268
Boquet, Anne (Torion), 158
Boquet, Annetje, 158
Boquet, Jérôme, 158
Boradgate, Christian, 214
Borel, Jean, 71
Borel, Marie Elizabeth   Borel, 71
Bornstra, Geertruyt van, 198
Bornstra, Gertrude, 198
Bornstra, Margareta, 198
Bornstra, Wybrant-Andres, 198
Bornstra, Wybrant-Andresz, 198
Borron/Barron, Anne, 54
Borsboom, Anna Pieterse, 333
Borsboom, Pieter Jacobse, 333
Bos, Tryntje Tysen, 129
Bosch, Albertzen, 45
Bosch, Hillegond, 45
Bosch, Lambert Janszen, 366
Bosman, Blandina (Risdon), 202
Bosman, John, 202
Bosman, Mary, 202
Bosquet, unknown, 230
Bossard, Ann Judith, 127
Bossard, Henry, 127
Bossu, Catherine, 131
Bossu, Elizabeth, 309
Boster/Bosler, James, 390
Bostock, Peter, 457
Bostwick, David, 422
Bostwick, Mary, 422
Bostwick, Mary (Hinman), 422
Bosworth, Squire Dr., 83
Boteler, Edward, 267
Bott, Jacob, 249
BOU(Y)SSAVY, Lucas, 66
Boubeau, Françoise (Letard), 110
Bouc(h)elle, Susanna, 39
Boucelle, Anna Margarette (Conde/Couda) de, 39
Boucelle, Liege de, 39

488

Bouchaeous, Mathias, 328
Bouchelle, Aletha, 433
Bouchelle, Elizabeth de, 75
BOUCHELLE, Legé de, 75
Bouchelle, Magdalena de, 75
Bouchelle, Petrus de, 75
Bouchelle, Samuel de, 75
Bouchelle, Susanna de, 75
Boucher, John, 76
BOUCHER, Matthew, 76
Boucher, Peter (Sr.), 76
Boucherie/Bourchier, Jean, 109
Boucherie/Bourchier, Maarie (Barjeau), 109
Boucherie/Bourchier, Marie, 109
Bouchet, Antoine, 380
Bouchet, Gerard, 380
Bouchier/Buscier/Busher, Abraham, 76
Bouchier/Buscier/Busher, Constantine, 76
BOUCHIER/BUSCIER/BUSHER, Dominic/Dominico, 76
Bouchier/Buscier/Busher, Jane, 76
Bouchier/Buscier/Busher, Jeremy, 76
Bouchier/Buscier/Busher, John, 76
Bouchier/Buscier/Busher, Mary, 76
Bouchier/Buscier/Busher, Nathaniel, 76
Bouchillon, Andre, 319
Bouchillon, Elizabeth, 77
Bouchillon, Jean, 319, 368
BOUCHILLON, Jean/John, 77
Bouchillon, Jenny, 77
Bouchillon, John, 77
Bouchillon, Joseph, 77
Bouchillon, Joseph Capt., 319
Bouchillon, Joseph James, 77, 319, 368, 426
Bouchillon, Joseph Leonard, 77
Bouchillon, Marie (Majinett), 319
Bouchillon, Mary Ann (LeRoy), 368
Bouchillon, Mary Jane (Roquemore), 319
Bouchillon, Susannah, 319
Bouchillon, Susannah (Guillebeau), 368
Bouchon, Isabeau, 342
Boucle, Julienne, 398
Boudin/Baudoin/Bodine, Abraham, 78
Boudin/Baudoin/Bodine, Eleazer, 78
Boudin/Baudoin/Bodine, Esther, 78
Boudin/Baudoin/Bodine, Francis, 78
Boudin/Baudoin/Bodine, Isaac, 78
Boudin/Baudoin/Bodine, Jacob, 78
Boudin/Baudoin/Bodine, Jean, 77
BOUDIN/BAUDOIN/BODINE, Jean, 77
Boudin/Baudoin/Bodine, Jean/John, 78
Boudin/Baudoin/Bodine, Judith, 78
Boudin/Baudoin/Bodine, Marianna, 78
Boudin/Baudoin/Bodine, Peter, 78
Boudin/Baudoin/Bodine, Vincent, 78
Boudinot, Abraham, 79
Boudinot, Benjamin, 79
Boudinot, David, 79

Boudinot, Elias III, 79
Boudinot, Élie, 39
Boudinot, Elie I, 104
Boudinot, Elie II, 104
BOUDINOT, Élie/Elias, 78
Boudinot, Élie/Elias II, 79
Boudinot, Jean, 79
Boudinot, Jean/John, 79
Boudinot, Jeannee (Baraud/Barreau), 104
Boudinot, Madelaine, 79
Boudinot, Madeline, 39, 79
Boudinot, Marie, 79
Boudinot, Marie/Mary, 79
Boudinot, Mary, 79
Boudinot, Pierre/Peter, 79
Boudinot, Susanne, 79
Boudinot, Susanne (Papin), 39
Boudrot, Abraham, 294
Boudrot, Alexandre, 294
Bougrand/Bongrand, Louis, 80
BOUGRAND/BONGRAND, Louis, 80
Douguel, Jeanne, 452
Boulande, Élisabeth (Chevillet), 444
Boulande, Guillaume, 444
Boulande, Marie, 444
Boulet, Benjamin de, 80
Boulet/Bullitt, Benjamin, 80
Boulet/Bullitt, Cuthbert, 80
Boulet/Bullitt, Elizabeth, 81
Boulet/Bullitt, Elizabeth/Seth, 80
Boulet/Bullitt, Joseph, 80
BOULET/BULLITT, Joseph, 80
Boulet/Bullitt, Thomas, 80
Boulet/Bullitt, William, 81
Boulier, Maria, 295
Boulier/Bulyea, Hendrick/Henry, 81
Boulier/Bulyea, Jan, 81
BOULIER/BULYEA, Louis, 81
Boulier/Bulyea, Marytie, 81
Boulier/Bulyea, Rachel, 81
Boulier/Bulyer, Catharina, 81
Boulier/Bulyer, Helena, 81
Boulier/Bulyer, Jacob, 81
Boulier/Bulyer, Jan/John, 81
Boulier/Bulyer, John, 81
Boulier/Bulyer, Robben, 81
Boulnois, Marie, 249
Bounetheau/Bonnetheau, Ann, 82
Bounetheau/Bonnetheau, Anne, 81
Bounetheau/Bonnetheau, Danbury Grimball, 82
Bounetheau/Bonnetheau, Daniel, 82
Bounetheau/Bonnetheau, Edward Weyman, 82
Bounetheau/Bonnetheau, Eliza Bond, 82
Bounetheau/Bonnetheau, Gabriel, 82
Bounetheau/Bonnetheau, Gabriel Manigault, 82
Bounetheau/Bonnetheau, Harold DuPré, 82

Bounetheau/Bonnetheau, Henry Breintnall, 82
Bounetheau/Bonnetheau, Henry DuPré, 82
Bounetheau/Bonnetheau, James, 82
BOUNETHEAU/BONNETHEAU, Jean/John, 81
Bounetheau/Bonnetheau, John, 81, 82
Bounetheau/Bonnetheau, Judith, 82
Bounetheau/Bonnetheau, Lewison, 82
Bounetheau/Bonnetheau, Peter, 81, 82
Bounetheau/Bonnetheau, Rebecca, 82
Bounetheau/Bonnetheau, Robert, 82
Bounetheau/Bonnetheau, Thomas, 82
Bounetheau/Bonnetheau, William Danbury, 82
Bouquet, François, 234
Bouquet, unknown, 270
BOUQUET/BOCKE(Y)/BUCKEY, Abraham, 83
Bouquet/Bocke(y)/Buckey, Andreas, 83
Bouquet/Bocke(y)/Buckey, Catherine, 83
Bouquet/Bocke(y)/Buckey, Frantz, 83
Bouquet/Bocke(y)/Buckey, George, 83
Bouquet/Bocke(y)/Buckey, Jacob, 83
Bouquet/Bocke(y)/Buckey, Johann Peter, 83
Bouquet/Bocke(y)/Buckey, Johannes, 83
Bouquet/Bocke(y)/Buckey, John, 83
Bouquet/Bocke(y)/Buckey, Margaret D, 83
Bouquet/Bocke(y)/Buckey, Maria Anna, 83
Bouquet/Bocke(y)/Buckey, Maria Johanetta, 83
Bouquet/Bocke(y)/Buckey, Matheus, 83
Bouquet/Bocke(y)/Buckey, Mathias, 83
Bouquet/Bocke(y)/Buckey, Peter, 83
Bouquet/Bocke(y)/Buckey, Rachel, 83
Bouquet/Bocke(y)/Buckey, Rosina Barbara, 83
Bouquet/Bocke(y)/Buckey, Sara, 83
Bouquet/Bocke(y)/Buckey, Valentine, 83
Bouquet/Boucquet, Abraham, 82
Bouquet/Boucquet, Annetje, 82
Bouquet/Boucquet, Francytje, 82
Bouquet/Boucquet, Jammatje/Jeronemus, 82
BOUQUET/BOUCQUET, Jérôme, 82
Bouquet/Boucquet, Marie, 82
Bourbeau, Claudine, 110
Bourbeau, Simon, 110
Bourbon, Jacques, 218
Bourchard, John, 326
Bourdeaux, Antoine De, 373
Bourdeaux, Catherine (Fresne) de, 84
Bourdeaux, Évrimond/Évremond de, 84
Bourdeaux, Jacques de, 167, 397, 423
Bourdeaux, Madeleine (Garilian) de, 397
Bourdeaux, Madeleine (Garillon) de, 167

Bourdeaux, Margaret (Garillond) de, 423
Bourdeaux, Marianne/Marianna De, 373
Bourdeaux,Judith de, 423
Bourdeaux/Bordeaux, Ant(h)oine/Anthony, 84
Bourdeaux/Bordeaux, Anthony, 84
Bourdeaux/Bordeaux, Daniel, 84
Bourdeaux/Bordeaux, Israel, 84
BOURDEAUX/BORDEAUX, Jacques de/James, 84
Bourdeaux/Bordeaux, Jacques II, 84
Bourdeaux/Bordeaux, James, 84
Bourdeaux/Bordeaux, Jane(t), 84
Bourdeaux/Bordeaux, Judith, 84
Bourdeaux/Bordeaux, Madeleine/Magdalen, 84
Bourdeaux/Bordeaux, Marguerite/Margaret, 84
Bourdieu, Jean de, 157
Bourdin, François, 85
Bourdin, Isaac, 85
Bourdin, Marc, 85
Bourdin, Rachel (Bouchet), 85
Bourdin/Burdine, Pierre, 85
Bourdin/Burdine, Richard, 85
BOURDIN/BURDINE, Samuel, 85
Bourg, Françoise, 294
Bourg, Marie Anne, 294
Bourg, Michel, 294
Bourget, Daniel, 399
Bourget, Rachel, 399
Bourget, Suzanne (X), 399
Bourgnet, Jean, 13
Bourguin, Henri François, 248
Bourne, Elizabeth (X), 445
Bourne, Martha, 326
Bourne, Thomas, 445
Bourquin, Elisabeth, 68
Bourquin, Elisabeth (Maillard), 68
Bourquin, Marie, 248
Bourquin, Pierre, 68
Bours, Ann, 26
Bours, Ann (Fairchild), 26
Bours, Peter, 26
Boursiquot, Aaron, 271
Boursiquot, Anne Élisabeth, 271
Boursiquot, Jeanne (Guillot), 271
Boussens, Amblard, 194
Boussens, Élisabeth (Le Noir), 194
Boussens, Elizabeth, 194
Bout(h)enot, Catherine, 285
Boutcher, Ann Martha, 425
Boutcher/Bouchierre, John, 425
Boutineau, James, 37, 184
Boutineau, Stephen, 37
Boutiton, Pierre Rev., 221, 425
Bouton, Abigail, 86
Bouton, Abraham, 86
Bouton, Bastien, 86
Bouton, Bridget, 86
Bouton, Catherine (X), 86

Bouton, David, 86
Bouton, Esdras, 86
Bouton, Esther, 86
Bouton, Hannah, 86
Bouton, Hermann, 86
Bouton, Jachin, 86
Bouton, Jacob, 86
Bouton, Jean, 87
Bouton, Jean Daniel, 86
Bouton, Jean/John, 86
Bouton, John, 86
Bouton, Joseph, 86
Bouton, Judith, 87
Bouton, Marie, 87
Bouton, Mary, 86
Bouton, Matthew, 86
Bouton, Rachel, 86
Bouton, Richard, 86
Bouton, Ruth, 86
Bouton, Susanne, 87
BOUTON, Théodore, 86
Bouton, Thomas, 86
Bouvet, Elizabeth (Bourgeois), 265
Bouvet, Henri, 265
Bowdoin, Elizabeth (Erving), 37
Bowdoin, James II, 37
Bowdoin, James III, 37
Bowdoin, Sarah, 37
Bowes, Francis, 299
Bowyess, Barbara, 138
Boybellaud/Boisebeleau, Jean, 157
Boyd, Elizabeth, 320
Boyd, John, 304
Boyd, Robert Capt., 320
Bozault, Marie, 432
Bra(d)t, Storm, 459
Brabant, Daniel, 165, 167
Brabant, Daniel Dr., 84
Brabant, Jeanne, 167
Brabant, Magdalen (de Bordeaux), 165, 167
Braconie, Aeltje, 48
Bradford, David, 298
Bradford, Elizabeth (Finney), 298
Bradford, John, 351
Bradford, Samuel, 298
Bradford, Sarah (Gray), 298
Bradford, William, 395
Bradford, William Dr., 298
Brading, unknown, 19
Bradley, Augustine, 327
Bradley, Augustine Capt., 327
Bradley, Benjamin, 435
Bradley, Elizabeth (Lillard), 327
Bradley, Frances, 387
Bradley, John, 435
Bradley, Keziah, 327
Bradley, Lawrence, 327
Bradshaw, Enoch, 33
Bradshaw, Jacob C, 33
Bradshaw, James, 33

Bradshaw,William, 33
Bradt, Eva Albertson, 279
Bragaw, Mary, 95
Bragg, Joseph, 24
Brammell, William, 111
Brammell/Bramwell, Ann, 111
Branch, Benjamin, 246
Branch, Daniel, 176
Branch, Edward, 383
Branch, Eliza Rebecca Bolling, 383
Branch, Matthew, 383
Branch, Pleasant, 203
Brand, Anne, 284
Brandt, Bartha, 363
Brandt, Elizabeth, 80
Brandt, Mary (X), 80
Brandt, Randolph Capt., 80
Branford, Ann/Nancy, 245
Branford, Elizabeth, 245
Branford, Elizabeth (Savage), 245
Branford, William S., 245
Bransford, John, 16
Bransford, Mary (Kingsford), 16
Brassaard, Jeanne (Quelvé), 110
Brassard, Jean, 110
Brassard, Marie-Madeleine, 110
Brasseur, Benois, 88
Brasseur, Benois/Benjamin, 88
Brasseur, Robert I, 88
Brasseur, Thomas, 88
Brasseur/Brashear, Benois, 178
Brasseur/Brashear, Marie, 178
Brasseur/Brashier/Brashear, Ann, 88
Brasseur/Brashier/Brashear, Benjamin, 88
Brasseur/Brashier/Brashear, Benois(t)/Benjamin, 88
Brasseur/Brashier/Brashear, Elizabeth, 88
Brasseur/Brashier/Brashear, John, 88
Brasseur/Brashier/Brashear, Katherine, 88
Brasseur/Brashier/Brashear, Margaret, 89
Brasseur/Brashier/Brashear, Martha, 88
Brasseur/Brashier/Brashear, Mary, 88, 89
Brasseur/Brashier/Brashear, Persi(d)e, 88
BRASSEUR/BRASHIER/BRASHEAR, Robert II, 88
Brasseur/Brashier/Brashear, Robert III, 88
Brasseur/Brashier/Brashear, Robert IV, 88
Brasseur/Brashier/Brashear, Susanna, 88
Brasseur/Brashier/Brashear, Thomas, 88
Brasswell, unknown, 95
Brauld/Brand, Jeanne, 100
Bray, John, 24

Bray, M, 148
BRAY, Rachel de, 89
Brayé, Jeanne, 422
Braye, Jéhu, 422
Brayé, Susanne (X), 422
BRE(T)TON/BRITTON, François/Francis, 89
Brechbiel/Breckbill, John Nicholas, 150
Brecht, David, 104
Brecount/Bricount, Daniel, 93
Brecount/Bricount, David, 93
Brecount/Bricount, David, Jr, 93
Brecount/Bricount, Effa, 93
Brecount/Bricount, Elizabeth, 93
Brecount/Bricount, Mary, 93
Brecount/Bricount, Ruth, 93
Brecount/Bricount, Salomon, 93
Brecount/Bricount, Sarah, 93
Breed, Elizabeth (Whittemore), 437
Breestede, Tryntje, 172
Breestede, Tryntje Jans Van, 150
Breinard, Susanna, 469
Brelsford, Abraham, 58
Brelsford, Joyce (X), 58
Brelsford, Parthena, 58
Breman, Jean, 252
Brengle, George Daniel, 85
Bressan, Anne, 407
BRESSAN/BRESSAU, Anne, 89
Bressau/Bressan, Jean, 407
Bressau/Bressan,Louise (X), 407
Brestede, Jan Jansen, 62
Brestede, Marie, 62
Bret(t)on/Britton, Ann, 90
Bret(t)on/Britton, Benjamin, 90
Bret(t)on/Britton, Daniel, 90
Bret(t)on/Britton, Daniel Laine, 90
Bret(t)on/Britton, Daniel, Jr., 90
Bret(t)on/Britton, David, 90
Bret(t)on/Britton, Elizabeth, 90
Bret(t)on/Britton, Francis II, 90
Bret(t)on/Britton, Francis III, 90
Bret(t)on/Britton, Hannah, 90
Bret(t)on/Britton, Henry, 90
Bret(t)on/Britton, John/Jean, 90
Bret(t)on/Britton, Joseph, 90
Bret(t)on/Britton, Martha, 90
Bret(t)on/Britton, Martin, 90
Bret(t)on/Britton, Mary, 90
Bret(t)on/Britton, Moses, 90
Bret(t)on/Britton, Philip, 90
Bret(t)on/Britton, Rebecca, 90
Bret(t)on/Britton, Sarah, 90
Bret(t)on/Britton, Timothy, 90
Bret(t)on/Britton, William, 90
Breto(u)n, Marianne, 25
Brett, Agnietie, 246
Brevard, Adam, 90, 91
Brevard, Alexander, 91
Brevard, Ann, 92
Brevard, Asenath, 91

Brevard, Benjamin, 91
Brevard, Charlotte, 91
Brevard, David, 92
Brevard, Elizabeth, 91, 92
Brevard, Ephraim, 91
Brevard, Esther, 90
Brevard, Hugh, 91
Brevard, James, 92
Brevard, Jane, 91, 92
BRÉVARD, Jean, 90
Brevard, Joel, 91
Brevard, John, 90, 91
Brevard, Joseph, 91
Brevard, Lydia, 91
Brevard, Margaret, 91
Brevard, Martha, 91
Brevard, Mary, 91
Brevard, Nancy, 91
Brevard, Prudence, 91
Brevard, Rebecca, 91
Brevard, Rhoda, 92
Brevard, Robert, 91
Brevard, Sarah, 91, 92
Brevard, Thomas, 92
Brevard, Zebulon, 91, 92
Brewer, Anna Maria, 391
Brewer, James, 96
Brian(t), Cornelia, 92
Brian(t), Daniel, 92
Brian(t), Élisabeth, 92
Brian(t), Jacques, 92, 442
BRIAN(T), Pierre, 92
Brian(t), Susanne, 92
Brian(t), Susanne (Gérard), 442
Brian(t), Ysaac, 92
Brian, Amity, 457
Brian, Clare (X), 185, 389
Brian, Elizabeth (LeFèvre), 185
Brian, Frances, 389
Brian, Guillaume, 92
Brian, Jacques, 185, 232, 309, 323, 389
Brian/Bryant, Martha, 323
Briant, James Jr., 389
Briant, Susanne, 442
Brice, Elizabeth, 196
Bricker, Frances, 103
Brickers, Thomas, 467
Bricou, Marianne, 93
Bricou, Marie, 93
Bricou/Bricon, Daniel, 93
BRICOU/BRICON, Salomon, 93
Bricou/Bricon, Salomon/Solomon, 93
Brideau, Marie, 250
Brideau, Samuel, 250
Bridgen, Elizabeth Catherine, 426
Bridgen, Samuel, 426
Bridon, Esther, 77
Bridon, Francis, 78
Bridon, François, 77
Bridon, Margaret, 452
Bridon, Susanne (X), 77

Briegal, Anna Maria, 438
Briegal/Von Bruegal, James, 438
Brier, Geertrint/Gertrude de, 458
Brière, Guillemette, 165
Brière, Guillemine, 165
Brière, Jehanne (Guerry), 165
Brière, Robert II, 165
Bries, Jemyme, 299
Brigaud, Anne, 462
Brigaud, Moise, 127
Bright, Sarah, 196
Bright, Simon, 196
Brimmer, Martin, 437
Brina(t), Jeanne, 92
Brinckerhoff, Abraham Jorise, 366
Brinckerhoff, Ida Joris, 366
Brink, Lambert, 324
Brinkerhoff, Abraham, 53
Brinkerhoff, Sarah, 53
Brinley,William, 125
Brinqueman, François, 31
Brinqueman, Marie (Minvielle), 31
Brique/Bricquet/Brickey, Anne de, 94
Brique/Bricquet/Brickey, Betty de, 94
Brique/Bricquet/Brickey, Dorcas de, 94
Brique/Bricquet/Brickey, Elizabeth de, 94
Brique/Bricquet/Brickey, Jarad de, 94
BRIQUE/BRICQUET/BRICKEY, Jean de /John, 94
Brique/Bricquet/Brickey, Jean/John de, 94
Brique/Bricquet/Brickey, Jincy de, 94
Brique/Bricquet/Brickey, John de, 94
Brique/Bricquet/Brickey, Mary de, 94
Brique/Bricquet/Brickey, Nancy de, 94
Brique/Bricquet/Brickey, Peter de, 94
Brique/Bricquet/Brickey, Sarah de, 94
Brique/Bricquet/Brickey, William de, 94
Brique/Bricquet/Brickey, Winifred de, 94
Brique/Briquet/Brichey, Peter de, 94
Brique/Briquet/Brickey, Temperance de, 94
Brisay, Jacques de, 145
Brisco, Susanna Dorothea, 435
Briscoe, Christian (X) Petty, 471
Briscoe, Edward, 111
Briscoe, John Dr., 276
Briscoe, Rachel, 111
Briscoe, Samuel, 111
Briscoe, William, 471
Brissac de, unknown, 47
Brisset, Jacques, 134
Brisset, Jeanne (Fétis), 134
Bristol, Henry, 102
Bristol, Lydia (Brown), 102
Bristol, Rebecca, 102
Britt, Susanna Langel, 319
Britton, Elizabeth (Lake), 44
Britton, Mary (Owen), 219

Britton, Nathaniel, 210
Britton, Nathaniel II, 44
Britton, Nathaniel III, 44
Britton, Sarah, 44, 210
Britton, William, 219
Britton/Brittain, Elizabeth, 219
Brizendine, William, 166
BRO(U)SSARD, Jeanne, 95
Broadhead, Mary, 103
Brochelide, Ester, 14
Brock, John Louis, 319
Brock/BeeckRem Jansen Van der, 409
Brodaway, Ann, 161
Broeck, Sarah Ten, 308
Brokaw, Jannitze, 439
Brokaw, Peter, 131
Bromfield, Edward, 164
Bromfield, Sarah, 164
Bromley, Mary, 466
Bronson, Isaac, 428
Brooks, Joseph, 277
Broome, Samuel, 293
Broret, Rachel, 370
Brosseau, Julian, 110
Broucard, Bourgeon, 131, 439
Broucard, Catherine (LeFèvre), 131
Broucard/Brokaw/Bragaw, Abraham, 95
BROUCARD/BROKAW/BRAGAW,
Bourgeon, 94
Broucard/Brokaw/Bragaw, Catherine, 95
Broucard/Brokaw/Bragaw, Cathrina, 95
Broucard/Brokaw/Bragaw, Isaac, 95
Broucard/Brokaw/Bragaw, Jacob, 95
Broucard/Brokaw/Bragaw, Jan/John, 95
Broucard/Brokaw/Bragaw,
Jannitze/Jeanne/Jane, 95
Broucard/Brokaw/Bragaw, Marie, 94
Broucard/Brokaw/Bragaw, Peter, 95
Broughton, Thomas, 320
Broussard, Jeanne, 234
Broussard, Judith (Broussard), 234
Broussard, Louis, 234
Brousse/Brice, Ann (X), 196
Brousse/Brice, William, 196
BROUSSE/BRUCE/BRURÈ, Jacques, 95
Brousse/Bruce/Brure, Peter, 95
Brousseaux, unknown, 272
Brouwer, Maria, 177
Brouwer, Uldrick, 467
Brouwer, William, 177
Brown, Azubah, 233
Brown, Barbara, 413
Brown, Benjamin, 22
Brown, Daniel, 296
Brown, Elizabeth, 353
Brown, Evert, 467
Brown, Hannah, 133
Brown, John, 202, 417
Brown, Lois, 268
Brown, Margaret, 182
Brown, Mary, 268

Brown, Nathaniel, 52
Brown, Original, 158
Brown, Peter, 222
Brown, Renee, 372
Brown, unknown, 45, 246
Brown, William, 168
Brown/Braun, Jacob, 73
Brown/Braun, Mary, 374
Browne, Elizabeth, 255
Browne, Esther (Makepeace), 255
Browne, Jebulon, 430
Browne, John, 255
Browne, Jonathan, 430
Browne, Lydia, 396
Browne, Martha (X), 430
Bruce, Alice, 95
Bruce, Ann, 95
Bruce, David, 46
Bruce, Elizabeth, 95
Bruce, Jean, 95
Bruce, Sarah, 95
Bruckner, Catherine, 357
Brudnell, Col., **51**
Bruff, Thomas, 300
Brugh/Brugge, Maria Van, 365
Brugière, Isaac de, 290
BrugièreAnna de, 290
Brumeau, Jean, 371
Brun, Apollos, 420
Bruneau, Ann (Peirre), 92
Bruneau, Anne, 390
Bruneau, Claude, 92
Bruneau, Henry, 208
Bruneau, Jean, 390
Bruneau, Marianne (X), 208
Bruneau, Rachel, 92
Brunson, Daniel, 338
Brunson, Mary, 338
Brunt, Cornelis Rutgers Van, 48
Brunt, Nicholas Rutgersz Van, 126
Bruyere/Bruere, Ele(a)nor, 96
BRUYÈRE/BRUÈRE, Jacque, 96
Bruyere/Bruere, Jacques, 96
Bruyere/Bruere, Jean, 96
Bruyere/Bruere, Jeanne, 96
Bruyere/Bruere, Johannes, 96
Bruyere/Bruere, Mary, 96
Bruyere/Bruere, Pierre, 96
Bruyere/Bruere, Pierre/Peter, 96
Bruyere/Bruere, Susanne, 96
Bruyere/Bruere, Suzanne, 96
Bryan, Anne, 277
Bryan, Christiana (X), 277
Bryan, Edward, 277
Bryan, Elizabeth, 171, 277
Bryan, Jesse, 277
Bryan, John, 277
Bryan, Lewis, 277
Bryan, Martha (Whiting), 386
Bryan, Mary, 386
Bryan, Mary (Wilmot), 171

Bryan, Richard, 171
Bryan, Samuel, 386
Bryan, William, 277
Bryant, Frances, 185
Bryant, James Jr., 185, 232
BUART, Mariane, 96
Buart, Marianne, 176
Buchle, Heinrich, 97
Buchle, Jacob, 96
Buchle, Leonard, 96
Buchle, Peter, 97
BUCHLE/BÜCHLI/BUEHL, Johan, 96
Buchle/Buchli/Buehl, Johannis Conrad,
96
Buckey/Bockey, Christine, 83
Buckey/Bockey, Daniel, 83
Buckey/Bockey, Eunice, 83
Buckey/Bockey, George, 83
Buckey/Bockey, Hannah, 83
Buckey/Bockey, John, 83
Buckey/Bockey, Marteny, 83
Buckey/Bockey, Mary, 83
Buckey/Bockey, William, 83
Buckhanon, John, 416
Budd, John, 448
Budd, Josephine, 125
Bueau, Daniel, 153
Bueau, Ester (Gaillard), 153
Bueau, Rene, 153
Buehl, John, 96
Buffington, Ruth, 193
Buffington, Ruth (Cope), 193
Buffington, Thomas, 193
Buffington, William, 192
Bufkin, Dorothy (Newby), 89
Bufkin, Levin, 89
Buford, Emma Cooper, 236
Buford, Frances June, 236
Buford, William, 236
Bullis, Silas, 295
Bullock, Mary, 433
Bullock, Mary (X), 433
Bullock, Stephen, 433
Bullpaine, John, 209
Bunn, Rebecca, 251
Bunsen/Bulsing/Boolsan, Cornelus, 123
Bunsen/Bulsing/Boolsan, Neeltje, 123
Bunsen/Sulsing/Boolsan, Johanna, 123
Burce, Peter, 95
Burdell, Jacob, 104
Burden, Benjamin, 138
Burditt, Benoni, 81
Burditt, Burwell, 81
Burditt, George, 81
Burditt, John, 81
Burditt, Parmanus, 81
Bureau, Anna (X), 184
Bureau, Anne, 184
Bureau, Elizabeth, **36**
Bureau, François, 184
Bureau, Jean, **36**

Burel, David, 97
Burel, Jeanne (Planchar), 97
Burel/Burell, Francis, 97
Burel/Burell, Marie, 97
Burel/Burrell, Jeanne Elizabeth, 97
Burel/Burrell, Pierre, 97
BUREL/BURRELL, Pierre, 97
Buren, Hillegond Willemsz Van, 130
Buren, Jan Roosa Van, 130
Burgaart, Coenraadt Hendrickse, 274
Burgaart, Marytje, 274
Burge, Abraham van, 300
Burgeaud, Jeanne, 402
Burger, Anne, 225
Burger, Catharina, 43
Burger, Claes, 43
Burgh, Elizabeth, 89
Burgh, Margaret, 89
Burgh, William, 89
Burke, Ann, 420
Burkhalter, Elizabeth Barbara, 364
Burkhalter, Ulrich, 364
Burlamacchi, Renee, 21
Burnette, Sarah, 470
Burnley, Ann, 268
Burnley, Thomas, 268
Burr, Mary, 263
Burr, Nathaniel, 263
Burr, Sarah (Ward), 263
Burrell, Ann, 427
Burroughs, Joseph, 406
Burroughs, Lucretia, 406
Burroughs, Lydia (Munson), 406
Bursum, Mary Van, 80
Burt, Jonathan, 282
Burton, Ann, 137
Burton, John, 383
Burton, Joseph, 200
Burton, Magdaline, 157
Burton, Martha, 158, 383
Burton, Mary, 86, 272
Burton, Mary Ann (David), 181
Burton, Phoebe (X), 92
Burton, Robert, 272
Burton, Sarah, 200
Burton, William, 137
Burwick, Lysbet, 349
Buscier, Dominic, **35**
Buscier, Geneviève (X), **35**
Buscier, Mary, **35**
Bush, Agnes, 234
Bush, Grace, 297
Bushnell, John, 255
Bussing, Arent Harmanse, 313
Bussing, Herman, 439
Butcher, Thomas, 58
Butin, Abraham, 98
Butin, Athonis Herny, 98
Butin, Élisabeth (Tancre), 97
Butin, Jacob J, 98
Butin, Jannes, 97

Butin, Johanna, 98
Butin, John Anthonis, 98
Butin, Josias, 97
Butin, Mariah, 98
Butin, Nicolas, 97
Butin, Peter Isaac Josias, 98
BUTIN, Pierre, 97
Butin, Susanna, 98
Butler, Abigail (X), 385
Butler, Christopher, 385
Butler, Henrietta, 385
Butler, Mary, 111
Butler, Valentine, 111, 268
Buys, Abraham, 416
Buys, Adreannis, 416
Buys, Jacob, 416, 467
Buys, Johannis, 416
Buys, Petrus, 416
Buys, Tryntje, 384
Buys, Wynte, 416
Bygote, Jaque Marie/Jaquemaine, 69
Byrd, William, 350
Byrd, William II, 113
Byrdine, Barbara, 85
Byrdine, Hannah, 85
Byrdine, John, 85
Byrdine, Nathaniel, 85
Byrdine, Reginall/Reginald, 85
Byrdine, Samuel, 85
Byrdine, Susannah, 85

C

Cabanis, Amy Clay, 99
Cabanis, Ann, 99
Cabanis, Anne (Soulière), 99
Cabanis, Charles, 99
Cabanis, Elijah, 99
Cabanis, Elizabeth, 99
Cabanis, George, 99
Cabanis, Hannah, 99
CABANIS, Henri, 99
Cabanis, Henri II, 99
Cabanis, Henry, 99
Cabanis, John, 99
Cabanis, Mary, 99
Cabanis, Matthew, 99
Cabanis, Matthew, Jr, 99
Cabanis, Phoebe, 99
Cabanis, Pierre, 99
Cabanis/Chabanas, Isaac, 99
Cabaret, Marthe, 394
Cable, Elizabeth, 171
Cadet Young, Anne, 100
Cadet Young, Bennett, 100
Cadet Young, Francis, 100
Cadet Young, James, 100
Cadet Young, Le Gros, 100
Cadet Young, Michael II, 100
Cadet Young, Thomas, 100
Cadet Young, Thomas Michael, 100

Cadet, Benjamin, 100
Cadet, Francis, 100
CADET, François/Francis, 100
Cadet, Jacques, 100
Cadet, John, 100
Cadet, Marie, 100
Cadet, Martha, 100
Cadet, Michael, 100
Cadet, Pierre, 100
Caer, Anna/Hannah, 112
Caer, Annetje, 112
Caer, Anthony, 112
Cahmois/Shumway, Dorcas, 111
Cahoon, Charles, 15
Cahoon, Elizabeth, 15
Cahoon, Jean, 15
Cahoon, Mark, 15
Cahoon, Nancy, 15
Cahoon, Rachel, 15
Cahoon, Thomas, 15
Cahoon, William, 15
Cahoon. William, 15
Cail, Toussaint, 243
Cail,Josine (Pellerin), 243
Caillaud, Isaac, 81
Caille, Isabelle Jeanne, 243
Caille, Theophilus, 186
Caine, Margaret Blanton, 368
Caldwell, Jemima, 94
Calhoun, John Ewing, 68
Calhoun, Mary, 331
Calhoun, Rebecca, 394
Call, Nathan, 246
Calleteau, Edward, 421
Calvert, John, 253
Calvet, Isabeau (Pagés), 100
Calvet, Pierre, 100
Calvet/Calvit/Calver, Anne, 100, 101
Calvet/Calvit/Calver, Antoine/Anthony, 101
Calvet/Calvit/Calver, Étienne/Stephen, 101
Calvet/Calvit/Calver, Frederick, 101
Calvet/Calvit/Calver, Jean II, 100
CALVET/CALVIT/CALVER, Jean/John (Rev.), 100
Calvet/Calvit/Calver, Joseph, 101
Calvet/Calvit/Calver, Pierre/Peter, 101
Calvet/Calvit/Calver, Sara, 100
Calvet/Calvit/Calver, Suzanne, 101
Calvet/Calvit/Calver, Thomas, 101
Calvet/Calvit/Calver, William, 101
Calvet/Calvit/Calvit, Guillaume/William, 101
Camburn, Esther, 430
Camburn, Jesse, 430
Cameron, Hugh, 391
Cammock, Margaret, 364
Cammock, Margaret (Williams?) Thatcher, 364
Cammock, Warwick, 364

Camp, Altje de, 101
Camp, Arent de, 101
Camp, Christina de, 101
Camp, Christyntje/Christina, 101
Camp, Gideon de, 101
Camp, Hendrik/Henry de, 101
Camp, Jean de, 101
Camp, Joannes de, 101
Camp, Johanis de, 101
Camp, Laurens Jansen de, 342
CAMP, Laurents de/Laurens/Lourens
    Jansen, 101
Camp, Lucy, 99
Camp, Martha de, 101
Camp, Styntje de, 101
Camp, Weraichie/Maritje de, 101
Campbell, James, 425
Campbell, Sarah, 37, 90
Canadel, Moïse, 195
Canadelle, Frédéric, 195
Canadelo, Fedirigo, 195
Canby, James, 269
Canby, Mary, 269
Candee/de Cande/Conde, Abigail, 102
Candee/de Cande/Conde, Caleb, 102
Candee/de Cande/Conde, Desire, 102
Candee/de Cande/Conde, Gideon, 102
Candee/de Cande/Conde, Hannah, 102
Candee/de Cande/Conde, Isaac, 102
CANDÉE/de CANDÉ/CONDÉ, Jean/John,
    102
Candee/de Cande/Conde, Lois, 102
Candee/de Cande/Conde, Mary, 102
Candee/de Cande/Conde, Rebecca, 102
Candee/de Cande/Conde, Samuel, 102
Candee/de Cande/Conde, Sarah, 102
Candee/de Cande/Conde, Thankful, 102
Candee/de Cande/Conde, Theophilus,
    102
Candee/de Cande/Conde, Timothy, 102
Candee/de Cande/Conde, Zaccheus, 102
Candee/de Cande/Conde,
    Zaccheus/Zachariah, 102
Canniff, Anatje (Woelffs), 38
Canniff, Anatje/Anna, 38
Canniff, Jeremiah, 38
Cannon, Abraham, 293
Cannon, Ann, 118
Cannon, Ann (X), 118
Cannon, Edward, 118
Cannon, Thomas, 23
Cannon, William, 114
Canon, Catherine, 159
Cantein(e)/Kantyn, Peter, 103
Cantey, Christiana, 321
Cantey, Martha, *418*
Cantey, Martha (Brown), 321
Cantey, Samuel, 321
Cantine, Catrina, 308
Cantine, Elizabeth (Blanchan), 308
Cantine, Elizabeth (Deyo), 308

Cantine, Moise, 308
Cantine, Moses, 149, 307
Cantine, Peter, 308
CANTINE/CANTAIN/KANTYN/QUANTIN,
    Moïse/Moyse/Moses, 102
Cantine/Cantain/Kantyn/Quantin, Peter,
    103
Cantor, Anna Christina, 19
Cantor, Johannes, 19
Capon, Anne (X), 154
Capon, Jacob, 144
Capon, Jeanne, 154
Capon, Marie, 155
Capon, Nicolas, 154
Cappoens, Christina, 400
Caquelin, Nicolas, 103
Caquelin/Coquelin/Cocklin, Cathrina,
    104
Caquelin/Coquelin/Cocklin, D(i)etrich,
    103
Caquelin/Coquelin/Cocklin, Jean
    Jacques/Jacob, 104
Caquelin/Coquelin/Cocklin, Jean/John,
    103
Caquelin/Coquelin/Cocklin, John, 103
Caquelin/Coquelin/Cocklin, Marie, 104
Caquelin/Coquelin/Cocklin, Sara, 104
Caquelin/Coquelin/Cocklin, Sebastian II,
    103
CAQUELIN/COQUELIN/COCKLIN/GAGLIN
    , Sébastien I, 103
Cardillac, Jeanne de, 21
Cardwell, Richard, 311
Care, Jan, 122
Care, Johannes, 122
Care, Marytje, 122
Care, Richard, 122
Carey, Anne, 211
Carion, Moïse, 255
Carion, Moise II, 361
Carle, George, 150
Carlie, Philippe, 86
Carlie, Sara (X), 86
Carlie/Carlier, Sarah, 86
Carlier, Vincentine/Sentyne, 144
Carlile, John, 227
Carlin, Catherine-Elizabeth (Lovy), 31
Carman, Phebe, 315
Carmiere, Nöe, 300
Carney, Mary, 277
Carney, Mary (X), 277
Caron, Marguerite, 141
Caron, Marguerite (Gagnon), 141
Caron, Vital, 141
Carpenter, Adam, 138
Carpenter, Barbara, 192
Carpenter, Catherine (Lein), 192
Carpenter, Emmanuel, 193
Carpenter, Henry, 192
Carpenter, John, 138
Carpenter, Mary, 15, 192

Carpenter, Noah, 395
Carpenter, Salome (Rufenu), 192
Carpenter, Susannah, 192
Carr, Hughanna, 401
Carr, Rachel, 302
Carr, Thomas Maj., 22
Carraway, unknown, 277
Carraway, William, 277
Carré, Catherine, 396
Carre, Elizabeth, 104
Carre, Jane, 104
Carré, Jean, 104
Carre, Louis, 104
Carré, Louis, 79, 396, 447
CARRÉ, Louis, 104
Carré, M., 40
Carré, Margaret (Gordon), 447
Carre, Marie Catherine, 104
Carré, Marie Catherine, 79
Carre, Pierre, 104
Carre, Prégéante (Fleuriau), 79, 396
Carriere, Deborah, 105
Carriere, Elizabeth, 104
Carrière, Jean, 104
CARRIÈRE, Jean, 104
Carriere, Joanna, 105
Carriere, John, 104
Carriere, Martha, 105
Carriere, Susannah, 104
Carstand, Isaac, 122
Carstang, Catharine, 122
Carstang, Gideon, 122
Carstang, Jan, 122
Carstang, Jannetje, 122
Carstang, Judith, 122
Carstang, Maria, 122
Carstang, Martha, 122
Carstang, Peter, 122
Carter, Judith, 220
Carter, Keltie (X), 306
Carter, unknown, 83, 99
Carter, Zebulon Capt., 306
Cartier, Jacques, 194
Cartier, Mary, 413
Cartier, unknown, 198
Cartledge, Mary, 456
Carton, Jan, 439
Cartwright, Abraham, 465
Cartwright, Frances, 465
Cartwright, Joan (Wade), 465
Carwithen, William, 397
Cary, Thomas, 123
Case, Anna, 295
Case, Elizabeth (Sheldon), 454
Case, William, 454
Casier, Hester, 44, 105
Casier, Jacques, 105
Casier, Jean/Jan, 105
Casier, Marie, 105, 459
Casier, Marie (Taine), 44, 152
Casier, Philip, 246

Casier, Philippe, 44, 105, 152
CASIER, Philippe, 105
Casier, Sarah, 105
Cassel, Arnold, 289
Cassel, Elizabeth, 289
Castelnau, Simon Boileau de, 145
Catalin/Catterlin/Casterline, Abraham, 106
Catalin/Catterlin/Casterline, Amariah, 106
Catalin/Catterlin/Casterline, Ann, 106
Catalin/Catterlin/Casterline, Barneet/Bernard, 106
Catalin/Catterlin/Casterline, Benjamin, 106
Catalin/Catterlin/Casterline, Francis, 106
Catalin/Catterlin/Casterline, François, 106
CATALIN/CATTERLIN/CASTERLINE, François, 105
Catalin/Catterlin/Casterline, Jacob, 106
Catalin/Catterlin/Casterline, James, 106
Catalin/Catterlin/Casterline, Jonathan, 106
Catalin/Catterlin/Casterline, Joseph, 106
Catalin/Catterlin/Casterline, Mary, 106
Catalin/Catterlin/Casterline, Nathaniel, 106
Catalin/Catterlin/Casterline, Phebe, 106
Catalin/Catterlin/Casterline, Samuel, 106
Catalin/Catterlin/Casterline, Stephen, 106
Catalin/Catterlin/Casterline, John, 106
Cater, Elizabeth, 349
Cater, William, 349
Catherine de Medici, 249
Catherine II, 460
Catherine, Laitié/Lethie/Lothie/Lettie, 400
Catherine, Voertman/Woertman, 440
Cathiel, Josiah Walker, 310
Catlett, Elizabeth (Thompson), 88
Catlett, Mrs., 264
Catlett, Peter, 264
Catlett, Robert, 264
Catlett, William, 88
Cats/Cott, Janike Van, 302
Catterlin, Joseph, 93
Caudebec, Jacques, 237
Caudebec/Codebec/Cuddeback/Koddeb ek Maria, 106
Caudebec/Codebec/Cuddeback/Koddeb ek, Benjamin, 106
Caudebec/Codebec/Cuddeback/Koddeb ek, Dina, 106
Caudebec/Codebec/Cuddeback/Koddeb ek, Elsje, 106
Caudebec/Codebec/Cuddeback/Koddeb ek, Jacobus/Jacob, 106

CAUDEBEC/CODEBEC/CUDDEBACK/KOD DEBEK, Jacques/Jacob, 106
Caudebec/Codebec/Cuddeback/Koddeb ek, James, 106
Caudebec/Codebec/Cuddeback/Koddeb ek, Magdalena/Eleanor, 106
Caudebec/Codebec/Cuddeback/Koddeb ek, William, 106
Caudebec/Codebec/Cuddleback/Koddeb ek, Abraham, 107
Caudebec/Codebec/Cuddleback/Koddeb ek, Naomy, 107
Caumond, Josué de, 22
Caumont, Pierre de, 180
CAUMONT, Pierre de (Rev.), 107
Caumont, Sara de, 107, 180
Cavalier, Louis, 246
Cavalier, Mary, 246
Cavelier, Pieter, 299
Caviness, Amos, 99
Caviness, Frederick, 99
Caviness, Henry, 99
Caviness, Matthew, 99
Caviness, Richard, 99
Caviness, Thomas, 99
Caviness, William, 99
Cayran, Peter, 143
Cazalede, Marguerite, 140
Cazenove, Ann Maria, 108
Cazenove, Ann Paulina, 108
Cazenove, Antoine Charles, 107
Cazenove, Antoinette, 107
Cazenove, Charles, 107, 108
Cazenove, Charles-John, 108
Cazenove, Charlotte, 108
Cazenove, Charlotte Busti, 108
Cazenove, David, 108
Cazenove, Eleuthera du Pont, 108
Cazenove, Eliza Frances, 108
Cazenove, Frances Ann, 108
Cazenove, Harriet, 108
Cazenove, Henriette, 108
Cazenove, Jacob, 107
Cazenove, Jean, 107
Cazenove, Jean-Antoine, 107
Cazenove, Jean-Pierre, 107
Cazenove, Kitty, 107
Cazenove, Louis-Albert, 108
Cazenove, Louis-Albert, Jr, 108
Cazenove, Madeleine, 107
Cazenove, Marie, 107, 108
Cazenove, Marie Charlotte, 107
Cazenove, Octavius-Anthony, 108
Cazenove, Paul, 107
Cazenove, Paul-Charles, 108
Cazenove, Philippe, 108
Cazenove, Philippe-Jean, 108
Cazenove, Pierre, 107
CAZENOVE, Pierre, 107
Cazenove, Sara, 108

Cazenove, Suzanne, 107
Cazenove, Theophile, 108
Cazenove, William Gardner, 108
Cazneau/Casno, Isaac, 108
Cazneau/Casno, Mary, 108
CAZNEAU/CASNO, Paix, 108
Cazneau/Casno, Peace, 109
Cazneau/Casno, Susanna, 108
Centurier, Antoine, 342
Centurier, Catherine, 342
Chabanel, J. H., 317
Chaboussant, Catherine (Bellet), 216
Chaboussant, Jean, 216
Chaboussant, Jeanne, 216
Chaboussant, Louise, 216
Chackelford, Richard, 127
Chad(e)ayne, Jean, 440
Chad(e)ayne, Judith (Tilliou), 440
Chadaine, Jean, 452
Chadaine, Marie, 357
Chadaine/Chad(e)ayne, Élisabeth/Elizabeth, 109
Chadaine/Chad(e)ayne, Henri/Henry, 109
Chadaine/Chad(e)ayne, Jean/John, 109
CHADAINE/CHAD(E)AYNE, Jean/John, 109
Chadaine/Chad(e)ayne, Marie I, 109
Chadaine/Chad(e)ayne, Marie II, 109
Chadaine/Chad(e)ayne, Marthe/Martha, 109
Chadaine/Chad(e)ayne, Pierre, 109
Chadaine/Chadeayne, unknown, 357
Chadayne, Daniel, 440
Chadeayne, Elizabeth, 128
Chadeayne, Jean, 128, 357
Chadeayne, Marie (Boucherie), 128
Chadeayne, Marie (Boucherie/Bourchier), 357
Chadeayne, Marie (Renaud), 109
Chadeayne, Henri, 109
Chaden, Henry, 74
Chadeu, Henry, 74
Chadwell, Mary, 266
Chaillon, Marie, 270
Chalifou(r)/Chalifoux, Anne, 110
Chalifou(r)/Chalifoux, Étienne, 110
Chalifou(r)/Chalifoux, Françoise, 110
Chalifou(r)/Chalifoux, Jean Baptiste, 110
Chalifou(r)/Chalifoux, Jeanne, 110
Chalifou(r)/Chalifoux, Louise, 110
Chalifou(r)/Chalifoux, Marguerite, 110
Chalifou(r)/Chalifoux, Marie, 109
Chalifou(r)/Chalifoux, Marie Madeleine, 110
CHALIFOU(R)/CHALIFOUX, Paul, 109
Chalifou(r)/Chalifoux, Paul François, 110
Chalifou(r)/Chalifoux, Pierre, 110
Chalifou(r)/Chalifoux, Simone, 110
Chalifou, Marie (Gaborit), 109
Chalifou, Paul, 109

Chalivou(r)/Chalifoux, Claude, 110
Challié, Anne (Tavernier), 263
Challié, Elizabeth, 263
Challié, Michel, 263
Chalôns, Marguerite, 17
Chamberlain, Ann, 224
Chamberlain, Job, 224
Chamberlain, Ruth, 341
Chamberlain, Sarah (Norman), 224
Chambers, David, 218
Chambers, Keziah, 383
Chambert, Marthe/Martha, 335
Chambon, Gideon, 144
CHAMOIS, Pierre, 267
Chamois/Shumway, Amos, 111
Chamois/Shumway, David, 111
Chamois/Shumway, Hepsibah, 111
Chamois/Shumway, Jacob, 111
Chamois/Shumway, Jeremiah, 110
Chamois/Shumway, John, 111
Chamois/Shumway, Joseph, 111
Chamois/Shumway, Mary, 111
Chamois/Shumway, Oliver, 110
Chamois/Shumway, Peter, 110
CHAMOIS/SHUMWAY, Pierre/Peter, 110
Chamois/Shumway, Samuel, 111
Chamois/Shumway,Samuel, 111
Chandler, Elizabeth, 310
Chandler, Judith (X), 310
Chandler, William, 310
Chap(p)elier/Chappelie/Chappelear, Arnaud, 111
Chap(p)elier/Chappelie/Chappelear, É(s)tienne, 111
Chap(p)elier/Chappelie/Chappelear, Elias Arnold, 111
CHAP(P)ELIER/CHAPPELIÉ/CHAPPELEAR, Isaac (Dr.), 111
Chap(p)elier/Chappelie/Chappelear, Isaac, Jr.
Chap(p)elier/Chappelie/Chappelear, James, 111
Chap(p)elier/Chappelie/Chappelear, Louis, 111
Chap(p)elier/Chappelie/Chappelear, Marienne, 111
Chapell, Jean, 251
Chaperon, Pierre, 280
Chapman, Bethia, 163
Chapman, Jebediah, 153
Chapman, Jedediah Rev., 304
Chapman, Robert Hett, 153
Chapman, William Smith, 153
Chappelier, Isaac, 20
Chappelier, Louis, 111
Chappelier, Simone (Rons), 111
Chardavoine, Anne, 112
Chardavoine, Anthony, 112
Chardavoine, Elie, 136, 462
CHARDAVOINE, Élie, 112
Chardavoine, Élie III, 112

Chardavoine, Élie/Elias II, 112
Chardavoine, Estienne, 112
Chardavoine, Isaac, 112
Chardavoine, Jean, 112
Chardavoine, Jérémie, 20, 112
Chardavoine, Susanne, 112
Chardavoine/Chadaine, Anne (Valleau), 20
Chardavoine/Chadaine, Elie, 20
Chardon, Madeleine, 186
Chardovaine, Elie II, 170
Charlé, Marie Jeanne, 263
Charles I, 145
Charles II, 135, 231, 393
Charles III, 218
Charles IX, 392
Charles, Anne, 251
Charlton, Richard Rev., 39
Charneau(x)/Charroneau, Pierre, 85
Charneau(x)/Charroneau, Rachel (Roy), 85
Charneau, Marthe, 85
Charoussin, D'hiller, 97
Charoussin, Elizabeth, 97
Charoussin, Marie (Aubineau), 97
Charoy, Marguerite, 172
Charpentier, Antoine, 250
Charpentier, ELeanore, 250
Charpentier, Jean, 252
Charpentier, Marguerite (Dijon), 250
Charpentier, Susanne, 159
Chartier, Henriette, 394
Chartier/Cartier, Magdalene Margaret, 34
Chastain, (Marie) Magdelaine, 115
Chastain, Anna (Soblet), 220
Chastain, Anne, 114, 418
Chastain, Anne (Soblet), 220, 323
Chastain, Arthuze/Aréthuse, 115
CHASTAIN, É(s)tienne/Stephen, 113
Chastain, Elizabeth, 115, 323
Chastain, Estienne, 114, 185
Chastain, Étienne, 114
Chastain, Étienne/Stephen, 168
Chastain, Françoise Jeanne (Reno/Regnault/Renaut), 13
Chastain, Jacques, 114
Chastain, Janne, 115
Chastain, Jean Adam/John, 115
Chastain, Jean François, 13
Chastain, Jean/John, 115
Chastain, Jeanne (Audet), 114
Chastain, Jeanne (Laurent), 114
Chastain, Jeanne Françoise, 115
Chastain, Judith, 115
Chastain, Magdalene, 220
Chastain, Magdelaine, 434
Chastain, Magdelene, 220
Chastain, Marie Magdelaine, 113
Chastain, Marie Susanne, 115
Chastain, Mary, 115

Chastain, Mildred (Archer), 220
Chastain, Pauline Elizabeth, 115
Chastain, Pierre, 195, 220, 323, 410, 434, 443, 455, 469
CHASTAIN, Pierre, 114
Chastain, Pierre II, 115
Chastain, Pierre Samuel, 115
Chastain, Pierre/Peter, 115
Chastain, René, 115, 352
Chastain, René,, 220
Chastain, Susanna, 115
Chastain, Susanne, 115
Chastain,Pierre, 220
Chastignier, Susanne (LeNoble) de, 409
Chateau/ Shatto, John Anthony, 116
Chateau/Shatto, Anna Barbara, 115
Chateau/Shatto, Anna Christina Margaretha, 116
Chateau/Shatto, Catharina, 115
Chateau/Shatto, Henrich/Fridich, *116*
CHÂTEAU/SHATTO, Jean Nichol(as), 115
Chateau/Shatto, Johannes, 116
Chateau/Shatto, Nicholas, 115
Chateau/Shatto, Ursula, 116
Chatfield, Cornelius, 297
Chatfield, Elizabeth (Johnson), 171
Chatfield, John, 171
Chatfield, Martha, 297
Chatfield, Martha (Kelsey), 297
Chatfield, Sarah, 171
Chaudoin/Chadouin, Andrew, 116
Chaudoin/Chadouin, David, 116
Chaudoin/Chadouin, Francis, Jr, 116
CHAUDOIN/CHADOUIN, François/Francis, 116
Chaudoin/Chadouin, John (SHADDEN), 116
Chaudoin/Chadouin, Lewis, 116
Chaudoin/Chadouin, Reuben, 116
Chaudoin/Chadouin, William, 116
Chauvel, Marthe, 228
Chauvin, Damaris, 163
Chauvin, Isaac, 163
Chayer, Jacqueline, 22
Cheinel, Marie (Latour), 343
Cheinel, Marie Madeleine, 343
Cheinel, Pierre, 343
Cheneau/Chenault, Benjamin, 117
Cheneau/Chenault, Elizabeth, 117
CHENEAU/CHENAULT, Étienne, 117
Cheneau/Chenault, Howlett/Hugo, 117
Cheneau/Chenault, John, 117
Cheneau/Chenault, Mary, 117
Cheneau/Chenault, Stephen, Jr., 117
Cheneau/Chenault, William, 117
Chenward, John Michael, 40
Cherf, Peter de, 375
Cherigny, Claude de, 398
Chevalier, Jean, 397
Chevalier, Peter, 412
Chevallier, Jean, 299

Chevallier, Jeanne (de Creguy), 299
Chevron, François, 117
Chevron, Nicole (Fèbre), 117
Chevron/Cheuvront/Cheauvant, Aaron, 117
Chevron/Cheuvront/Cheauvant, Amos, 117
Chevron/Cheuvront/Cheauvant, Caleb, 117
Chevron/Cheuvront/Cheauvant, Casandra, 117
Chevron/Cheuvront/Cheauvant, Catharine, 117
Chevron/Cheuvront/Cheauvant, David, 117
Chevron/Cheuvront/Cheauvant, Enoch, 117
Chevron/Cheuvront/Cheauvant, Gideon, 117
Chevron/Cheuvront/Cheauvant, James Liteford, 117
Chevron/Cheuvront/Cheauvant, Joseph, 117
CHEVRON/CHEUVRONT/CHEAUVANT, Joseph Louis, 117
Chevron/Cheuvront/Cheauvant, Mary Elizabeth, 117
Chevron/Cheuvront/Cheauvant, Moses, 117
Chevron/Cheuvront/Cheauvant, Priscilla, 117
Chevron/Cheuvront/Cheauvant, Simeon, 117
Chevron/Cheuvront/Cheauvant, Thomas, 117
Chibailhe/Chivalier/Chivalie, Anne, 118
Chibailhe/Chivalier/Chivalie, Bernarde, 118
Chibailhe/Chivalier/Chivalie, Guilliamette, 118
Chibailhe/Chivalier/Chivalie, Jean, 118
Chibailhe/Chivalier/Chivalie, Marye, 118
Chibailhe/Chivalier/Chivalie, Pierre, 118
CHIBAILHE/CHIVALIER/CHIVALIE, Pierre, 118
Chibailhe/Chivalier/Chivalie, Ramond, 118
Chicet/Chichet/Cheché, Martha, 57
Chichester, William, 451
Chichet, Jeanne (X), 57
Chicken, unknown, 407
Chiel/Dashiell, George de.
CHIEL/DASHIELL, Jacques de, 118
Chiel/Dashiell, James de, 118
Chiel/Dashiell, Jane de, 119
Chiel/Dashiell, Katherine de, 119
Chiel/Dashiell, Robert, 119
Chiel/Dashiell, Thomas de, 118
Chilbailhe, Jean, 455
Chilbailhe, Marie (Mariette), 455
Chivalie/Chilbailhe, Bernarde, 455

Chorpinning/Corpenning, John, 19
Chrisman, George, 138
Chrisman, Hannah (McDowell), 138
Chrisman, Margaret, 138
Christian, Charles Jr., 268
Christian, Judith, 268
Christman, Eva Margaret, 469
Christopher, Christoffel, 101
Christopher, Susanna, 293
Chuno, Nicolas, 92
Chupret, Madeleine, 370
Church, Henry, 466
Churchill, Hannah (Pontus), 287
Churchill, John, 139, 287
Churchill, Sarah, 298
Cisneau, Anna, 210
Claerhout, Belitje, 299
Claes, Elisabeth, 151
Claggett, John, 445
Claiborne , William IV, 178
Claiborne, Daniel, 355
Claiborne, Lucy, 178
Claig, unknown, 361
Clapper, Margaret, 60
Clare, Mark, 88
Clarisse, Catherine, 119, 155
Clarisse, Jean, 155
CLARISSE, Jean/Jehan, 119
Clarisse, Jeanne (X), 119
Clarisse, Marie, 119
Clarisse, Mathieu, 119
Clarisse, Samuel, 119
Clarisse, Sara (LeConte), 155
Clark, Ann, 334
Clark, Barbara, 223
Clark, Daniel Capt., 179
Clark, Elizabeth, 139
Clark, Elizabeth (Ijams), 179
Clark, Frances, 162
Clark, George Rogers, 226
Clark, James, 158
Clark, John, 341, 394
Clark, Martha (Nash), 139
Clark, Rhoda, 93
Clark, Ruth, 158
Clark, Susanna, 158
Clark, unknown, 99, 223
Clark, William, 139
Clarke, Abraham, 179
Clarke, John, 183
Clatworthy, Anna (Luerson), 14
Clatworthy, Hester/Esther, 14
Clatworthy, John, 14
Claude/Claud, Elizabeth, 119
Claude/Claud, John, 119
Claude/Claud, Joseph, 119
Claude/Claud, Joshua, 119
Claude/Claud, Lidia, 119
Claude/Claud, Mary, 119
Claude/Claud, Phebe, 119
CLAUDE/CLAUD, Philippe, 119

Claude/Claud, Phillip, 119
Claude/Claud, William, 119
Claughton, Magdeleine, 133
Clauss, George, 120
Claussé, Jeanne (Famelart), 129
Claussé, Pierre, 129
Claussé/Clossé, Rachel, 129
Clavell/Clewell, Abraham, 120
Clavell/Clewell, Anna Catherine, 120
Clavell/Clewell, Anna Dorothea, 120
Clavell/Clewell, Anna Maria, 120
Clavell/Clewell, Catherine, 120
Clavell/Clewell, Christian, 120
Clavell/Clewell, Christina, 120
Clavell/Clewell, Daniel, 120
Clavell/Clewell, Elizabeth, 120
Clavell/Clewell, Francis, 120
CLAVELL/CLEWELL, François, 120
Clavell/Clewell, George, 120
Clavell/Clewell, George Craft, 120
Clavell/Clewell, Jacob, 120
Clavell/Clewell, Johannes Franz/John Francis, 120
Clavell/Clewell, John, 120
Clavell/Clewell, Joseph, 120
Clavell/Clewell, Julianna, 120
Clavell/Clewell, Maria Magdelena, 120
Clavell/Clewell, Nathaniel, 120
Clavell/Clewell, Rosina, 120
Clavell/Clewell, Saloma, 120
Clavell/Clewell, Saloma Maria, 120
Clavelle, Martha, 379
Clay, Hannah, 99
Clay, Thomas Col., 99
Clayton, Lambert, 91
Clayton, Thomas, 277
Clearwater, Elsie, 149
Clearwater, Jacob, 149
Clearwater, Teunis Jacobsz, 149
Clemens, Anna, 421
Clement, Jean Michel, **42**
Clements, Hannah, 280
Clements, John Dr., 291
Clercq, Jean de, 313
Cleve, Jane Van, 345
Clift, unknown, 463
Clifton, John, 119
Clinquement, Marie, 160
Clinton, DeWitt, 460
Close, Hannah, 305
Close, Sarah (X), 305
Close, Thomas, 305
Cloutsome, Thomas, 377
Clowney, Joseph, 457
Clute, Anne Barber, 273
Clute/Cloet, Frederic, 273
Clute/Cloet, Frederick, 164
Clymer, William, 422
Coachman, Mary (X), 464
Coates, Dr., 73
Coates, Elizabeth (X), 73

Cobb(s), Samuel, 350
Cobb, Henry, 62
Cobb, Mary, 62, 139, 347
Cobb, Patience (Hurst), 62
Cobb, Sarah, 47
Cobbs, Mary, 350
Cobbs, Samuel, 385
Cobbs, William, 350
Cobreath, John, 88
Cochelin, Tobias, 238
Cocheron, Adrianna, 120
Cocheron, Anthony, 120
Cocheron, Jannetje, 121
COCHERON, Jean, 120
Cocheron, Jean/John, 120
Cocheron, Katherine, 120
Cocheron, Margaret, 121
Cocheron, Marie, 120
Cocheron, Nicholas, 120
Cochran, Elizabeth, 388
Cochran, Thomas, 320
Cock, Hannah, 289
Cock, James, 289
Cock, Sarah (X), 289
Cocke, Chastain, 113
Cocke, Elizabeth Chastain, 114
Cocke, James, 113
Cocke, James Powell, 113
Cocke, Martha, 114
Cocke, Martha (Herbert), 113
Cocke, Mary, 88
Cocke, Sarah, 202
Cocke, Stephen, 114
Cocke,William, 202
Coddington, Governor William, 53
Coddington, Nathaniel, 53
Coddington, Susannah (Hutchinson), 53
Coddington, William Col., 52
Coden, Francis, 78
Coehorn, Christian, 357
Coerten, Geertje Harmens, 125
Coevert/Covert, Bragon, 439
Cogswell, Cloe (Gates), 456
Cogswell, Martha, 456
Cogswell, William, 456
Colden, Elizabeth, 281
Cole, James, 328
Cole, Peter, 293
Cole, Spencer, 256
Cole, William, 106
Coleman, Anna, 98
Coleman, Asa, 98
Coleman, Hannah (X), 98
Coleman, Jacob, 33
Coleman, Margaret, 33
Coleman, Olive, 98
Coleman, Rebecca, 98
Coleman, Susannah (X), 33
Coligny, Admiral Gaspard de, 333
Coligny, Annietta de, 189
Coligny, Gaspard de, 102, 121, 189

COLIGNY, Gaspard de, Comte de
   Châtillon, Admiral of France, 121
Colin, Henry, 86
Colin, Judith, 86
Collet, Hannah, 286
Colleton, Charles, 398
Collier, William, *420*
Collin, Jean, 122
COLLIN, Jean, 122
Collin, Jeanne, 388
Collin, John, 122
Collin, Judith, 122
Collin, Marthe, 122
Collin, Paul, 122
Collin, Pierre, 122
Collinot, Marguerite, 75
Collins, Catherine, 264
Collins, Eleanor, 328
Collins, Eleanor (Oliver), 328
Collins, James, 300
Collins, John, 328
Collins, Margaret (X), 146
Collins, Thomas, 146, 265
Colliver/Couturier, Jeanne, 72
Collums, Jacques, 381
Cologny, Béatrice/Béatrix de, 121
Cologny, Charles de, 121
Cologny, François de, 121
Cologny, Gaspard de, 121
Cologny, Henri, 121
Cologny, Louise de, 121
Cologny, Odet de, 121
Cologny, Renée de, 121
Colombe, Nicolas, 141
Colvett, John II, 275
Colvin, Mary Ann, 424
Combeau, Marguerite, 294
Combs, Cuthbert, 80
Combs, Elizabeth, 264
Combs, John, 80
Commeni, Marie, 189
Commennus, John Amos, 189
Commennus, Marie (X), 189
Comparet, Jean Antoine, 195
Comparet, Jeanne Françoise, 195
Comparet, Sarah (Mallet), 195
Compton, Amy, 94
Concelye, Annetje, 302
Conchilier, Jan de, 301
Condé/Condi, Blandina, **38**
Conelly, Françoise, 93
Coney, John, 420
Conklin, Casper, 353
Conklin, Elizabeth, 132
Conklin, Hannah, 280
Conklin, Hester, 353
Conklin, Mary, 326
Conklin, Mary (Thompkins), 280
Conklin, Rebecca, 414
Conklin, Timothy, 280
Conkling, Tobias, 468

Connalee, Edmond, 377
Conner, Frances (Williams), 173
Conner, Francis, 173
Conner, Sarah (X), 173
Conner, unknown, 173
Conner, William, 173
Connett, William, 93
Connyer, William, 356
Connyers, Elizabeth, 356
Connyers, Henry, 356
Connyers, Hester, 356
Conrad, Edward Dr., 422
Consalis-Duk, Manuel, 301
Consalis-Duk, Marytje (Davids), 301
Consalis-Duk, Rebecca, 301
Conselyea, Peter, 305
Conseyn, Jonas, 398
Conseyn, Susanna (Desmarets), 398
Conte, Abraham, 71
Conte, Ansonius, 75
Conte, Margaretha (Ules), 75
Conte/Couda, Margaretha, 75
Conway, Peter, 266
Conway, Thomas, 356
Cook, George, 19
Cook, Shem, 429
Cook, unknown, 277
Cooke, Bentley, 128, 155
Cooke, Elizabeth, 337
Cooke, Francis, 139, 286, 337
Cooke, Hester, 337
Cooke, Jacob, 337
Cooke, Jane, 337
Cooke, John, 337
Cooke, Mary, 337
Cooksey, John, 312
Cool, Marytje, 106
Coole/Coel, Jacques, 328
Coon, Mary Elizabeth, 127
Cooper, Dorothy, 320
Cooper, Rosanna, 218
Copeland, Ann, 193
Copeland, Mary, 193
Coppet, Marie, 148
Coppet, Marie (Scabelle), 148
Coppet, Oliver, 148
Coquefaire/Cockefair/Cockever,
   Alexander, 123
COQUEFAIRE/COCKEFAIR/COCKEVER,
   Alexandre, 122
Coquefaire/Cockefair/Cockever,
   Cataline/Caroline, 122
Coquefaire/Cockefair/Cockever,
   Catherina/Trinche/Tryntje, 122
Coquefaire/Cockefair/Cockever,
   Dara(c)k^2, 123
Coquefaire/Cockefair/Cockever,
   Elizabeth, 123
Coquefaire/Cockefair/Cockever,
   Helena/Lena, 123

498

Coquefaire/Cockefair/Cockever, Jan/Johannes, 123
Coquefaire/Cockefair/Cockever, Jan/John, 122
Coquefaire/Cockefair/Cockever, Jannetje/Jane, 123
Coquefaire/Cockefair/Cockever, Judith, 123
Coquefaire/Cockefair/Cockever, Marytje/Mari, 122
Coquefaire/Cockefair/Cockever, Sander/Alexander, 123
Coquefaire/Cockefair/Cockever, Stineche/Christina, 122
Coquefaire/Cockefair/Cockever, Tryntje, 123
Coquiel dit le Mercier, Jean/Jan de, 123
Coquiel, Antoinette, 123
COQUIEL, Jehan de, 123
Coquiel, Renaud, 123
Coquillet, Francis, 333
Coquillet, François, 124
COQUILLET, François, 124
Coquillet, Silvia, 333
Coquillet, Silvia (Sicard), 333
Coquillet, Silvie, 441
Coquillet, Sylvie, 124
Corbeau, Jean, 71
Corbee/Corbin, unknown, 282
Cordea, Mark, 300
Cordeary, Ann (X), 43
Cordeary, William, 43
Cordes, Ann, 470
Cordes, Anthony Dr., 348
Cordes, Catherine, 402
Cordes, Eleanor (X), 248
Cordes, Esther, 348
Cordes, Esther Madeline (Baluet), 348
Cordes, Francis, 398
Cordes, Isaac, 248
Cordes, James Paul, 442
Cordes, Mary, 248
Cordier, Françoise (Martinet), 147
Cordier, Louis, 147
Cordier, Marie, 147
Cordonne, Nicola, 337
Corenll, Daniel, 122
Corleis/Curlies/Curlis(s), Benjamin, 125
Corleis/Curlies/Curlis(s), Deborah, 125
Corleis/Curlies/Curlis(s), Dinah, 125
Corleis/Curlies/Curlis(s), Elizabeth, 125
Corleis/Curlies/Curlis(s), George, 125
Corleis/Curlies/Curlis(s), Hannah, 125
Corleis/Curlies/Curlis(s), Jacob, 125
Corleis/Curlies/Curlis(s), John, 125
Corleis/Curlies/Curlis(s), Joseph, 125
Corleis/Curlies/Curlis(s), Mary, 125
Corleis/Curlies/Curlis(s), Thomas, 125
Corleis/Curlies/Curlis(s), Timothy, 125
Corleis/Curlies/Curlis(s), William, 125
Corlies/Corliss, Ann, 124

Corlies/Corliss, Deborah, 124
Corlies/Corliss, Huldah, 124
Corlies/Corliss, Joanna, 124
Corlies/Corliss, John, 124
Corlies/Corliss, Martha, 124
Corlies/Corliss, Mary, 124
Corlies/Corliss, Sarah, 124
Corliez, Antoine, 124
CORLIEZ, Antoine, 124
Corliez, George, 124
Corliez, Henriette (Auger), 124
Corliez, Jane, 124
Corliez, Jean, 124
Corliez, Louis, 125
Corliez, Marie, 124
Corliez, Nicholas, 124
Corliez, Nicol, 125
Corliez, William, 124
Corneille, Catherine, 449
Corneille, John, 409
Cornel. Albert, 316
Cornelis, Annetie, 365
Cornelis, Annetje, 59
Cornelis, Geertie, 305
Cornelis,Tryntgen, 377
Cornelissen, Gerrit, 130
Cornelissen, Neeltje, 126
Cornell, Hannah, 318
Corpe, Hannah (Case), 454
Corpe, Jeremiah, 454
Corpening, Mary, 191
Corsen, Jacob, 357
Corsen, Mary, 357
Corssen, Teunis, 246
Cortelyou, Anetje, 302, 305
Cortelyou, Cornelis, 305
Cortelyou, Elsken (Hendricks), 125
Cortelyou, Jacques, 125
Cortelyou/Corteljou, Annetje, 125
Cortelyou/Corteljou, Cornelis, 126
Cortelyou/Corteljou, Helena, 126
CORTELYOU/CORTELJOU, Ja(c)ques, 125
Cortelyou/Corteljou, Jaques, 125
Cortelyou/Corteljou, Maria, 126
Cortelyou/Corteljou, Pieter, 126
Cortelyou/Corteljou, Willem/William, 126
Cortlandt, Anne Van, 281
Cortlandt, Stephanus Van, 281
Corvets/Goverts, Belje, 174
Corwin, Sarah, 326
Cossaart/Cozart, Rachelle, 126
Cossart, George/Joris Dr., 126
Cossart, Jacques, 165
Cossart, Jan, 126
Cossart, Marguerite (Toustain), 165
Cossart, Marie, 165
Cossart, Pierre, 185
Cossart/Cozart, Anthony, 126
Cossart/Cozart, David, 126
Cossart/Cozart, Jacques, 126

COSSART/COZART, Jacques, 126
Cossart/Cozart, Jannetje, 126
Cossart/Cozart, Lea, 126
Cossart/Cozart, Rachel, 126
Cossart/Cozart, Susanne, 126
Cossou, Esther, 78
Cossou, Jelan, 78
Costa, Don Juan de, 474
Costa/Jasso, Francisco de, 474
Costa/Jasso, Magdalene de, 474
Costa/Jasso, Miguel de, 474
Costa/Jasso, Philip de, 474
Costa/Jasso, Valentine de, 474
Costebadie, Jean de Rev., 157
Costebadie, Marie de, 157
Cothonneau, Élisabeth (Nombret), 127
Cothonneau, Germain, 127
Cothonneau/Cuttino, Ester Marthe.
Cothonneau/Cuttino, Germain, 127
COTHONNEAU/CUTTINO, Jérémie, 127
Cothonneau/Cuttino, Pierre, 127
Cott, Janetje Van, 305
Cott, Johannes Van, 302
Cott, Tunis Van, 302
Cottigny, Anne de, 160
Cottin, Jean, 63, 152
Cottman, Joseph, 216
Cotton, Anna, 190
Cotton, Robert Bruce, 190
Cotts, unknown, 358
Cou(s)tant, Catherine, 128
COu(s)tant, Daniel, 128
Cou(s)tant, Elizabeth, 128
Cou(s)tant, Guillaume/William, 128
Cou(s)tant, Henry, 128
Cou(s)tant, Isaac, 128
Cou(s)tant, Jacob, 128
COU(S)TANT, Jean I, 128
Cou(s)tant, Jean II, 128
Cou(s)tant, Jeanne/Jane, 128
Cou(s)tant, Madeleine, 128
Cou(s)tant, Marie, 128
Cou(s)tant, Susanne, 128
Cou(s)tant, Zacharie, 128
Couant, Jean, 18
Couck,William, 333
Coudret, Daniel, 277
Couillandeau, Marie (Fougeraut), 127
Couillandeau, Pierre, 127, 155
COUILLANDEAU, Pierre, 127
Couillandeau, Pierrot, 128
Couillandeau, Susanne, 128
Couillandeau, Suzanne, 155
Couillandeau, Suzanne (X), 155
Count of Nassau, 328
Courault, Anne (Marchant), 21
Courault, Jean, 21
Courège Michau, Madeleine (X), 407
Courège, Charlotte, 360
Courège, Francois, 360, 407
Courège, Madeleine, 360

Courège, Madeleine (X), 360
Courège, Manassah, 360
Coursier, Anne, 416
Coursier, Anne (Perrot[e]au), 258
Coursier, Jehan, 258
Coursier, Marie, 258
Courtail, John, 435
Courtald, Samuel, 379
Courtney, Letitia, 347
Courts, Mary H., 144
Cousseau, Marie, 184
Cousson, Marie, 388
Coutant, Catherine Bonnefois, 29
Coutant, Elizabeth, 225
Coutant, Elizabeth (Angevine), 20, 109, 225
Coutant, Henry, 109
Coutant, Jacob, 20
Coutant, Jacques, 440
Coutant, Jane, 440
Coutant, Jane (Renoud), 29
Coutant, Jean, 20, 109, 225
Coutant, Jeanne (Renaud), 440
Coutant, John, 18, 29
Coutant, Susanna (Gouin), 18
Couvain, Lazare, 319
Couvenhoven, Jan Gerretse Van, 441
Couvers, Marritye Tennis, 358
Couvert, Elizabeth, 216
Couwenhoven, Willem Gerritse van, 366
Covell, John, 178
Covert, Elizabeth, 280
Covert, Han Teunise, 439
Covert, Isaac, 280
Covert, Johannes (Hans Theunis), 95
Covert, Theunis Jans(en), 95
Covin, Lazarus, 77, 319, 426
Covin/Couvain, Elizabeth, 319
Covin/Couvain, Louis, 319
Covin/Couvain, Mary Anne, 319
Covin/Couvain, Susan, 319
Cox, Antjie, 353
Cox, John, 187
Cox, Judith, 15
Cox, Margaret (Dalbo), 170
Cox, Peter, 170
Cox, Philip, 377
Cox, Vincent, 133
Cozens, William Dr., 376
Crabtree, James, 162
Crabtree, Jane (X), 162
Crabtree, William, 162
Craddock, Thomas Rev., *419*
Craig, Peter Dr., 446
Craig, Sarah, 91
Craik, James, 56
Cranston, Ann Mercy (Newberry), 27
Cranston, James, 26
Cranston, John Col., 27
Cranston, Mary (Hart), 26
Cranston, Samuel, 26

Cranston, Walter, 27
Crats, unknown, 95
Crawford, Gideon, 53
Crawford, Joseph, 53
Crawford, Sarah (Whipple), 53
Crawford, William, 53
Creas, Thomas, 354
Cregier, Frans, 441
Creiger, Hannah, 92
Creiger, Martin Capt., 441
Creiger, unknown, 441
Creiger/Crougers, Tryntje/Catherine, 441
Creison (Cresson?), Marie, 77
Crespin, Anne, 22
Cresson, Alche/Olive (Gerritsen), 315
Cresson, Christina, 129
Cresson, Élie/Elias/Elizacus, 129
Cresson, Élisabet (Vuilesme), 129
Cresson, Elizabeth, 315
Cresson, Jacques, 129
Cresson, Joshua, 129, 315
Cresson, Pierre, 129, *142*, 288, 315
CRESSON, Pierre, 129
Cresson, Rachel, 129, *142*, 172
Cresson, Rachel (Clausee), 315
Cresson, Rachel (Clausse), *142*
Cresson, Rachel (Claussé), 288
Cresson, Susanna, 288
Cresson, Susannah, 129
Cretin/Carten, Jeanne, 358
Creuzé, Catherine, 379
Creuzé, Elizabeth (X), 379
Creuzé, Francis, 379
Cricket, Daniel, 337
CRISPEL(L)/CRÉPEL, Antoine, 129
Crispel(l)/Crepel, Jan, 129, 130
Crispel(l)/Crepel, Jannetie, 130
Crispel(l)/Crepel, Jean, 130
Crispel(l)/Crepel, Lysbet, 130
Crispel(l)/Crepel, Maria Magdalene, 129
Crispel(l)/Crepel, Pieter, 129, 130
Crispel(l)/Crepel, Sara, 130
Crispell, Antoine, 63
Crispin/Crespin, Jane, 395
Crocheron, Adrianna, 130
Crocheron, Anthony, 130
Crocheron, Jannetje, 130
Crocheron, Jean, 77, 153, 290
CROCHERON, Jean, 130
Crocheron, John, 130
Crocheron, Katherine, 130
Crocheron, Margaret, 131
Crocheron, Marie, 77, 130
Crocheron, Marie (X), 153, 290
Crocheron, Mary (X), 77
Crocheron, Nicholas, 130
Crocheron, Sarah (Dupuy), 58
Crocketagné, Gabriel Gustave de, 131
CROCKETAGNÉ/CROCKETT, Antoine Desasure/Desasurre Perronette de, 131

Crockett, Davy, 131
Crockett, Gabriel Gustave, 131
Crockett, James, 131
Crockett, Joseph Louis, 131
Crockett, Louise Desaix, 131
Crockett, Mary Frances, 131
Crockett, Robert Watkins, 131
Crockett, Sarah Elizabeth, 131
Croft, unknown, 150
Crofts, George, 310
Crokatt, Charles, 208
Crokatt, James, 208
Crom, Elizabeth, 274
Crommelin, Anne, 132
Crommelin, Anne (Crommelin), 51
Crommelin, Charles, 132
Crommelin, Daniel, 132
CROMMELIN, Daniel, 131
Crommelin, Elisabeth, 132
Crommelin, Isaac, 132
Crommelin, Jean, 46
Crommelin, Jeanne, 16
Crommelin, Judith, 132
Crommelin, Louis, 51
Crommelin, Marie, 132
Crommelin, Marie Anne, 132
Crommelin, Marie Madeleine, **47, 51**
Crommelin, Martin, 16
Crommelin, Rachel, 131
Crommelin, Robert, 132
Crommelin, Susanne (Doublet), 16
Crommelin/Crommelinck, Jean, 131
Cromwell, Oliver, 360, 361
Croom, Daniel, 362
Crosby, George, 356
Crosby, John, 385
Crosby, Mark, 385
Crosby, Samuel, 385
Crosby, Sara (X), 385
Crosby, Sterling, 457
Crosier, Mary Jane, 226
Cross, André de, 194
Cross, Jeanne (Ferra) de, 194
Cross, Marie de, 194
Cross, Susannah Jackson, 396
Crosse, Joan, 209
Crosse, William, 253
Crossley, unknown, 350
Crossman, Robert, 207
Crouch, Abraham, 457
Crouch, Ann (X), 457
Crouch, Catherine, 457
Crousy, unknown, 465
Crow, William, 331
Cruger, David, 234
Crump, Benjamin, 266
Crump, Mary Barbour (Price), 266
Crump, Susanna, 266
Crutcher, Lucy, 201
Crutcher, Sally, 201
Cubberley, John, 430

Cubberley, Mary (X), 430
Cubberley, William, 430
Cubberley,James, 430
Cuelen, Matthys Jansz Van, 63
Culmann, Maria Elizabeth, 199
Culver, Elizabeth (Ford), 70
Cummings, Alexander, 372
Cummings, Archibald Dr., 186
Cummings, Diana, 472
Cummings, William, 372
Cunningham, Alexander, 362
Cunningham, Elizabeth Ann, 355
Cunnynham/Cunningham, Mary, 421
Cunyngham, Elizabeth (X), 421
Cunyngham, Robert, 421
Cupper, Susanne, 449
Currier, Seth, 246
Curtice, Solomon, 395
Curtis, Mary, 415
Curtis,Richard, 61
Cushman, Elkanah, 298
Cushman, Lydia (Bradford), 298
Cuthbert, John, 320
Cutler, Mary, 184
Cutler, Timothy Dr., 184
Cuttino, Ann Judith, 127
Cuttino, Benjamin Thomas, 127
Cuttino, David William, 127
Cuttino, Elizabeth, 127
Cuttino, Henry, 127
Cuttino, Jacob, 127
Cuttino, Jeremiah, 127
Cuttino, Mary, 127
Cuttino, Peter, 127
Cuttino, Sarah, 127
Cuttino, Thomas I, 127
Cuttino, Thomas II, 127
Cuttino, William, 127
CUVELLIER, Adrienne, 132
Cuvellier/Cuvilje, Adrienne/Ariantje, 296
Cuvellier/Cuvilje, Jean, 296
Cuyler, Catherine, 318

D

D'Aubigne/Dabney, Cornelius, 354
D'Aubry, Mary Elizabeth "Bess", 410
d'Entremont, Marie Martuerite-Muis, 294
d'Entremont, Philippe, 294
D'oyle, Christina, 376
Dabney, John, 21
Dabney, Susanna, 21
Dacorat, Marie, 460
Dagorne, Marie, 165
Daigneau, Simon, 188
Daillé, Pierre, 437
Daleu/Dallou, Marthe, 28
Dalrymple, Anne, 88
Dalrymple, William, 444
Dalrymple, William Jr., 88

Dalton, James, 397
Dam, Isaac Van, 396
Damen, Celetje/Celia, 320
Damen, Cornelia, 459
Damen, Cornelissen, 320
Damen, Elizabeth, 105, 439
Damen, Jan, 105
Damen, Jan Corneliszen, 384, 459
Damen, Jan Jantzen, 296
Damen, Neeltje Janse, 384
Dames, Maria, 204
Damouv(r)el/Damourville/DeMourvell, Elizabeth, 133
Damouv(r)el/Damourville/DeMourvell, Hannah, 133
Damouv(r)el/Damourville/DeMourvell, Magdaline, 133
DAMOUV(R)EL/DAMOURVILLE/DeMOU RVELL, Samuel, 133
Damouv(r)el/Damourville/DeMourvell, Samuel Lewis, 133
Dana, Joseph, 267
Dana, Mary, 110, 111, 267
Dana, Mary (Wood), 267
Dandonneau, Élisabeth, 134
Dandonneau, Étiennette, 134
Dandonneau, Françoise-Marguerite, 134
Dandonneau, Françoise-Pétronille, 134
Dandonneau, Jacques, 134
DANDONNEAU, Jacques, 133
Dandonneau, Jeanne, 134
Dandonneau, Louis, 134
Dandonneau, Marguerite, 134
Dandonneau, Marie-Louise, 134
Dandonneau, Marie-Renée, 134
Dandonneau, Pierre, 133
Dandridge, John, 334
Dane/Doyne/Hyde, Jane, 33
Dangerfield, John, 56
Daniau, Pierre, *142*
Daniel, Antoine, 252
Daniel, Dean, 165
Daniel, James, 471
Daniel, Jeanne, 252
Danielsson, Brigitta, 250
Danke, John Frederick, 120
Danner, Dieter/Peter, 243
Danner, unknown, 83
Darby, Bernard, 198
Darby, Mary, 68
Darling, Sarah, 41
Darrell, Margaret, 367
Dasher, Casper, 261
Dashwood, unknown, 132
Daubert, Margaret, 34
Daucet, Marie, 188
Dauge, Capt., 23
Dausey, Pierre, 188
Davant, Jean, 134
Davant, Louis, 134
Davant, Marie (Hardilly), 134

Davant/Davan, Charles, 135
Davant/Davan, Isaac, 134
Davant/Davan, James, 135
Davant/Davan, Jean/John, 134, 135
DAVANT/DAVAN, Jean/John, 134
Davant/Davan, John, 134
Davant/Davan, Julie, 134
Davant/Davan, Mary, 135
Davant/Davan, Sarah, 134
Davenport, Addington Rev., 184
Davenport, Anne, 146
Davenport, Charity, 280
Davenport, Elizabeth (Leggett), 280
Davenport, Elles, 81
Davenport, John, 49
Davenport, Peter/Petrus, 49
Davenport, Rachel, 81
Davenport, Samuel, 81
Davenport, Thomas, 280
David(s), Angelica, 136
David(s), Anne, 136
David(s), Carel, 136
David(s), Daniel, 135, 136
David(s), Ezachiel/Ezéchiel, 136
David(s), Jacques, 136
David(s), Jean, 135, 136
DAVID(S), Jean, 135
David(s), Jean II, 135
David(s), John, 136
David(s), Josué, 136
DAVID(S), Josué, 136
David(s), Madeleine, 135
David(s), Marguerite/Margaret, 135
David(s), Marie, 136
David(s), Pierre, 136
David(s), Susanne, 136
David, Abraham, 137
DAVID, Abraham, 137
David, Ann, 181
David, Anne, 137, 170
David, Anne (DeBray), 176
David, Anne (Dutertre), 181, 369
David, Charlotte, 447
David, Elizabeth, 137, 318
David, Esaye, 137
David, Esther (Vincent), 112, 170
David, Henriette, 138
David, Isaac, 137
David, Jean, 112, 170
David, Jean I, 448
David, Jean II, 448
David, Jeney, 137
David, Jude, 137
David, Judith, 138
David, Luisan, 447
David, Magdalene, 137
David, Marianne, 115
David, Marie, 138
David, Mary, 116, 137
David, Maryan, 137
David, Nancy, 137

David, **Peter**, 137, 170, 181
David, **Phebe**, 137
David, **Pierre**, 137, 176, 181, 323, 369
DAVID, **Pierre**, 136
David, **Pierre/Peter**, 137
David, Pierre/Peter the Younger, 137
David, **Rachel**, 138
David, Susannah, 368
David, Susanne, 112, 170
Davids, Engeltie/Angelica, 431
Davids, Harman, 81
Davids, **Helena**, 81
Davids, Isaac, 95
Davids, Maritje/Mary, 95
Davidson, Ephraim, 91
Davidson, George, 91
Davidson, John Judge, 91
Davidson, John Maj., 91
Davidson, Rebecca, 91
Davidson, Robert, 91
Davidson, Sarah, 91
Davidson, William Lee Gen., 91
Davis, Anne"Nancy", 394
Davis, Clementius, 276
Davis, Henry Winter, 108
Davis, James, 265
Davis, Joanna, 124
Davis, John, 345
Davis, Martha, 394
Davis, Miriam, 394
Davis, Richard, 192
Davis, Robert, 24
Davis, Sallie (X), 193
Davis, Susannah (Jacobus), 24
Davis, unknown, 89, 413
Davison, Grace, 382
Davison, John, 382
Davison, Sarah (Babcock), 382
Dawson, Elizabeth, 200, 277
Dawson, Elizabeth (Bryan), 277
Dawson, Francis, 277
Dawson, John, 200
Dawson, Mary (O'Malley), 462
Dawson, Sarah, 200
Dawson, Thomas, 201
Dawson, unknown, 277, 350, 402
de Bruyenne/de Bruyn, Francoys, 441
De la Noye/Delano, Mary, 62
De Vries, Johanns, 274
De Vries, Margarieta (Costers), 274
Dean, Amy, 414
Dean, Elizabeth, 319
Dean, Mary, 101
Dean, William, 101
Deane, Mary, 291
Deane, Richard, 76
Dearborn, Henry Gen., **37**
Dearling, Mary, 56
Debaun, Christian, 172
Debaun, Judith (Demarest), 172
deBonrepos, Élie, 18

deBonrepos, Ester (X), 18
DeCamp, Lydia, 93
Dechezeau, Adam, 108
Decker, Christopher, 106
Decker, Neeltje, 106
Defrenne, Abraham, 263
Defrenne, Esther (Rebour), 263
Defrenne, Marie, 263
DeGrave, Maritje, 14
DeGroot, William, 293
Deininger, John Adam, 149
Deininger, Leonard, 150
Deininger, Margaret (X), 150
Deitzler, Anna Maria, 235
Deker, John, 436
Delacque/Des Planq/Delplanque, Marie, 144
Delage, Jean, 110
Delage, Michelle (de la Mazerolle), 110
Delamar, Isaac, 276
DELAMAR/LAMAR, **Francois**, 276
Delamater, Abraham, 324
Delameter, Elizabeth, 103
Delameter, Geertje, 103
Delancey, Etienne, 205
DeLancey, Marguerite (Bertrand), 280
Delancey, Stephen, 280
Delancque/Des Planq/Delplanque, Jacques, 144
DeLancy, Jacques, 280
Delano, Esther, 287
Delano, Hester (Dewsbury), 62
Delano, Jane, 287
Delano, John, 287
Delano, Jonathan, 287
Delano, Mary, 286
Delano, Philip, 62, 287
Delano, Rebecca, 287
Delano, Samuel, 287
Delano, Thomas, 287
DELANO/De la NOYE, Marie Louisa, 138
Delano/deLannoy/de La Noye, Hester/Esther, 139
Delano/deLannoy/de la Noye, Isaïe/Isaiah, 139
DELANO/deLANNOY/de la Noye, Jan/Jean, 139
Delano/deLannoy/de la Noye, Jane, 139
Delano/deLannoy/de la Noye, Jeanne, 139
Delano/deLannoy/de la Noye, John, 139
Delano/deLannoy/de la Noye, Jonathan, 139
Delano/deLannoy/de la Noye, Mary, 139
Delano/deLannoy/de la Noye, Philip, 139
Delano/deLannoy/de la Noye, Philippe/Philip, 139
Delano/deLannoy/de la Noye, Rebecca, 139

Delano/deLannoy/de la Noye, Samuel, 139
Delano/deLannoy/de la Noye, Thomas, 139
Delaplaine, Elizabeth (Shoemaker), 192
Delaplaine, James, 192
Delaplaine, Sarah, 192
DeLASHMOTT, Catherine, 266
Delashmutt, Catherine, 350
DeLASHMUTT/DeLASHMET, John, 266
DeLASMUTT, Mary, 266
Delatre/DeLatre/Delautre/Delauter, Absalom, 140
Delatre/DeLatre/Delautre/Delauter, Anna Barbara, 140
Delatre/DeLatre/Delautre/Delauter, Anna Maria, 140
Delatre/DeLatre/Delautre/Delauter, Anthoni, 140
Delatre/DeLatre/Delautre/Delauter, Barbara, 140
Delatre/DeLatre/Delautre/Delauter, Catharina, 140
Delatre/DeLatre/Delautre/Delauter, Catherine, 140
Delatre/DeLatre/Delautre/Delauter, Charlotte, 140
Delatre/DeLatre/Delautre/Delauter, Christina, 140
Delatre/DeLatre/Delautre/Delauter, David, 140
DELATRE/DeLATRE/DELAUTRE/DELAUTER, David, 139
Delatre/DeLatre/Delautre/Delauter, George, 140
Delatre/DeLatre/Delautre/Delauter, George William, 140
Delatre/DeLatre/Delautre/Delauter, Heinrich/ Henry, 140
Delatre/DeLatre/Delautre/Delauter, Jacob, 140
Delatre/DeLatre/Delautre/Delauter, Johann Heinrich, 140
Delatre/DeLatre/Delautre/Delauter, Johann Jacob, 140
Delatre/DeLatre/Delautre/Delauter, Johann Nicholaus, 140
Delatre/DeLatre/Delautre/Delauter, Johannes, 140
Delatre/DeLatre/Delautre/Delauter, Judith, 140
Delatre/DeLatre/Delautre/Delauter, Madelina, 140
Delatre/DeLatre/Delautre/Delauter, Margaretha, 140
Delatre/DeLatre/Delautre/Delauter, Maria Catharina, 140
Delatre/DeLatre/Delautre/Delauter, Maria Elisabeth, 140
Delatre/DeLatre/Delautre/Delauter, Marie Jeanne, 140

Delatre/DeLatre/Delautre/Delauter, Philip Lorenz, 140
Delatre/DeLatre/Delautre/Delauter, Solomon, 140
Delaunay, Anne, 141
DELAUNAY, Claude, 140
Delaunay, Jeanne, 141
Delaunay, Louis, 140
Dell, Richard, 146
Delpish, Anne, **50**, 141
Delpish, Francis, **50**, 166
DELPISH, Francis, 141
Delpish, Judith, 141
Delpish, Marie/Mary, 141
Delpish, Mary (Dupré), **50**
Delpish, Peter, 142
Delpreuch, Isabeau, 157
Demarest, David, 38, 315
Demarest, David Jr., 129, 172
Demarest, Judith, 38
Demarest, Maria (DeRuine), 172
Demarest, Maria (Druen), 38
Demarest, Marie (Schier), 38, 129
Demarest, Samuel, 38, 172
Demarets/Demarest/des Marets/des Marest, Daniel, *142*
Demarets/Demarest/des Marets/des Marest, David, *142*
DEMARÊTS/DEMAREST/des MARÊTS/des MAREST, David, 142
Demarets/Demarest/des Marets/des Marest, Jean, *142*
Demarets/Demarest/des Marets/des Marest, Marie, *142*
Demarets/Demarest/des Marets/des Marest, Samuel, *142*
Demere, Catherine, *143*
Demere, Margaret, *143*
Demere, Paul, *143*
Demere, Raymond, *143*
Demere/Demeray, Catherine, *142*
Demere/Demeray, Françoise, *143*
Demere/Demeray, Isaac, *143*
Demere/Demeray, Jacob, *143*
Demere/Demeray, Jean, *143*
DEMÉRÉ/DEMÉRAY, Louis, *142*
Demere/Demeray, Louis II, *143*
Demere/Demeray, Louis III, *143*
Demere/Demeray, Louis IV, *143*
Demere/Demeray, Marguerite, *143*
Demere/Demeray, Samuel, *143*
DeMil, Anthonis Laurense, 365
DeMil, Grietgen (Pieters/Plovier), 365
DeMoss, Louis Count, 162
Demovell, Hannah, 133
Denman, John, 210
Denman, Martha, 231
Dennis, Martha, 312
Denny, Mildred Lancaster, 422
Dent, Elizabeth, 111
Dent, John, 111

Denyse, Anna Teunise, 409
Denyse, Teunis, 409
Dep(e), Jean, 143
Deplancque, Jacques, 186
Deplancque/Des Planq/Delplanque, Anne, 144
DEPLANCQUE/DES PLANQ/DELPLANQUE, Guillaume, 144
Deplancque/Des Planq/Delplanque, Josse, 144
Deplancque/Des Planq/Delplanque, Rachelle, 144
Deplancque/Des Planq/Delplanque, Sara, 144
Depp, Peter, 382
Deppe/Depp, Ann, 144
Deppe/Depp, Elenor, 144
Deppe/Depp, John, 144
Deppe/Depp, Peter, 144
Deppe/Depp, Peter II, 144
DEPPE/DEPP, Pierre, 143
Deppe/Depp, Thomas, 144
Deppe/Depp, William, 144
Depres, Thomas, 401
Deprize, Nicholas, 401
DePue, Catherine, 450
Der Cuyl, Annatje Cornelis Van, 153
der Heul, Abraham Janszen Van, 262
der Hoven, Cornelis Van, 159
der Hoven, Susanne Van, 159
der Linde, Pieter van, 335
Dermont, Jan, 440
Derstraaten, Magdalena Van, *142*
Des Brisay/Du Brisay/De Brise, Bonne, 145
Des Brisay/Du Brisay/De Brise, Elizabeth, 145
Des Brisay/Du Brisay/De Brise, Henry Rev., 145
Des Brisay/Du Brisay/De Brise, James Lt Col., 145
Des Brisay/Du Brisay/De Brise, Jasper General, 145
Des Brisay/Du Brisay/De Brise, Madeleine Elizabeth, 145
Des Brisay/Du Brisay/De Brise, Magdalaine Marie de la Cour, 145
Des Brisay/Du Brisay/De Brise, Paul Lt Col., 145
Des Brisay/Du Brisay/De Brise, Samuel Théophile/Theophilus de la Cour, 145
DES BRISAY/DU BRISAY/DE BRISÉ, Théophile de la Cour, 145
Des Brisay/Du Brisay/De Brise, Theophilus Lt Col., 145
Des Brisay/Du Brisay/De Brise, Thomas de la Cour, 145
Des Châlets, Claude, 319
Des Châlets, Magdeleine, 320
Des Cou(x)/DeCou/Decow, Abraham, 146

Des Cou(x)/DeCou/Decow, Daniel, 146
Des Cou(x)/DeCou/Decow, Elizabeth, 146
Des Cou(x)/DeCou/Decow, Emanuel, 146
Des Cou(x)/DeCou/Decow, Hannah, 146
Des Cou(x)/DeCou/Decow, Isaac, 145, 146
Des Cou(x)/DeCou/Decow, Jacob, 146
Des Cou(x)/DeCou/Decow, John, 146
DES COU(X)/DECOU/DECOW, Leure, 145
Des Cou(x)/DeCou/Decow, Mary, 146
Des Cou(x)/DeCou/Decow, Susanna, 146
Des Cou(x)/DeCou/Decow, Susanne, 146
des Hommets, Löyse, 165
des Jardins, Susanne, 445
Des Jong/De Jonque, Eleazer, 154
des Marêts, Jean, 142
des Marêts, Marguerite (de Herville), 142
Des Meaux, Guillaume, 146
Des Meaux, Sara (Evynard), 146
Des Meaux/ Dismukes, Sarah, 146
Des Meaux/Dismukes, Ann, 146
Des Meaux/Dismukes, Anna, 147
Des Meaux/Dismukes, Benjamin, 146
Des Meaux/Dismukes, Elisha, 147
Des Meaux/Dismukes, Elizabeth, 146
Des Meaux/Dismukes, Evynard, 147
DES MEAUX/DISMUKES, Guillaume/William, 146
Des Meaux/Dismukes, James, 146, 147
Des Meaux/Dismukes, John, 147
Des Meaux/Dismukes, Lucy, 146
Des Meaux/Dismukes, Mary, 146
Des Meaux/Dismukes, Millie, 146
Des Meaux/Dismukes, Reuben, 146
Des Meaux/Dismukes, William, 146
des Plancque, Jacques, 366
des Plancque, Sara (Fauconnier), 366
Des Pré, Marie, 449
DES PREZ/DU PREZ/DU PRÉ, Hércule/Hercules, 147
Des Prez/Du Prez/DuPre, Elizabeth, 147
Des Prez/Du Prez/DuPre, François-Jean, 147
Des Prez/Du Prez/DuPre, Hercules, 147
Des Prez/Du Prez/DuPre, Jacquemine, 148
Des Prez/Du Prez/DuPre, Marie-Jeanne, 147
Des Prez/Du Prez/DuPre, Philippe, 148
Descamps, Salmon, 189
Descard, Jean, 461
Descard, Marie (Dumas), 461
Descard, Suzanne, 461
Descombre, Abraham, 450
Descombre, Jeanne (Reparlier), 450
Descombre, Sara, 450
Desgranges, Susanne, 413
Deshler, David Dr., 307
Desjardin, Joanne, 449
Desjardins, Isaac, 449

Desjardins, Jacques, 449
Desjardins, Jean, 148
Desjardins, Jeanne (Deluran), 148
Desjardins, Judith, 148
Desjardins, Marie-Jeanne (Boccard), 449
Desjarrie, Lucretia, 271
Desmaret, Charl., 148
Desmarets, Adrian, 148
Desmarets, Elisabeth, 148
Desmarets, Susanne (Collier/Collié), 148
Desmoulins, Jacques, 141
Desmoulins, Pierre, 141
Desmuille/Desmullie/Desmulle, Jeanne,
   154
Desombre, Elizabeth, 329
Desombre, Jean, 329
Desombre, Magdeleine (Parent), 329
Despierre, Jacques, 450
Despiné, David, 395
DESPINÉ, David, 147
Despine, Ma(g)deleine, 147
Despiné, Magdelaine, 395
Despré, Ester, 92
Despré, Jacques, 92
Despré, Marie (Roger), 92
Desreux, Abraham, 71
Desreux, Anne Marie, 71
Desreux, Judith (Guerit), 71
Desrivières, Peter, 291
Desrosiers, Jean, 134
Dessenex, Peter, 234
Dessenex, Susannah (Bouquet), 233
Destouché, Catherine, 148
Detouche, Jean, 329
Detouche, Louise (Vaquier), 329
Detouche, Maria, 329
Deudon, Philipotte, 151
Deursen, Abraham Pieter Van, 177
Deusen, Isaac Jr. Van, 316
DeValau/Devallaud, Madeline, 20
Devall, Jocob M., 424
Devallock, Mary, 462
Devantier/Devantie, Abraham, 148
Devantier/Devantie, David, 148
Devantier/Devantie, Elizabeth, 148
Devantier/Devantie, Ester, 148
Devantier/Devantie, Isaac, 148
Devantier/Devantie, Jacob, 148
Devantier/Devantie, Jacques, 148
Devantier/Devantie, Jeanne, 148
Devantier/Devantie, Jehan, 148
Devantier/Devantie, Judith, 148
Devantier/Devantie, Marie, 148
Devantier/Devantie, Pierre, 148
DEVANTIER/DEVANTIÉ, Pierre, 148
Devantier/Devantie, Suzanne, 148
Deveaux, Andrew, 224
Devoe, Daniel, 353
Devoe/Devaux,Sarah, 435
Devoor, Andiaen, 159
Devoor, David, 159

Devoor, Glaude, 159
Devoor, Peter/Pieter, 159
Devoor, Teunis/Anthony, 159
DeVos, Judith, **38**
DeVries, Annatie, 274
Dewar, Charles, 28
Dewick, Ann (Dymes), 442
DeWitt, Bowdewyn, 103
Dewitt, Charity, 237
DeWitt, Marytje (DeBois), 103
Dewsbury, Hester, 139, 286
Dexter, Samuel, 438
Dexter, Samuel Rev., 438
Dey, Dick, 64
Dey, James, 78
Dey, Maria, 78
Dey, Mary (Mulliner), 78
Deyo, Abraham, 242
Deyo, Agatha (Nichol), 301
Deyo, Anna, 242
Deyo, Chrétien, 103, 152, 242, 290, 307
Deyo, Christian, 301
Deyo, Diana, 307
Deyo, Elizabeth, 258
Deyo, Elizabeth/Lysbet, 307
Deyo, Elsie (Clearwater), 242
Deyo, Jeanne (Verbeau), 152, 242, 290,
   307
Deyo, Margaret, 152
Deyo, Maria, 242
Deyo, Pierre, 301
Deyo, Wyntje, 242
Deyo.Deyoe/De Joux, Abraham, 149
Deyo/ Deyoe/De Joux, Elizabeth, 149
Deyo/Deyoe/De Joux, Anna, 149
DEYO/DEYOE/DE JOUX,
   Chrétien/Christian, 149
Deyo/Deyoe/De Joux, Christian, 149
Deyo/Deyoe/De Joux, Hendricus, 149
Deyo/Deyoe/De Joux, Madeline, 149
Deyo/Deyoe/De Joux, Margaret, 149
Deyo/Deyoe/De Joux, Marie, 149
Deyo/Deyoe/De Joux, Mary, 149
Deyo/Deyoe/De Joux, Pierre, 149
Deytet, Isabeau, 157
Dibble, Eben, 244
Dibble, Mary, 244
Dibble, Mary (Wakefield), 244
Dibble, Miriam, 222
Dibble, Thomas, 222
Dibrell, Anthony, 158
Dibrell, Charles, 158
Dibrell, Judith, 158
Dibrell, Lee Ann/Leanna, 158
Dicken, Elizabeth "Betty", 85
Dickenson, Anne, 466
Dickinson, Frances (Foote), 222
Dickinson, Hannah, 222
Dickinson, John, 222
Dickinson, Nathaniel, 222
Diez, Barbara, 243

Digges, John, 173, 174
Digges, Nancy, 174
Dijon, Joseph, 250
Dill(i)er, Benjamin, 150
DILL(I)ER, Caspar Élias, 149
Dill(i)er, Casper, 150
Dill(i)er, Catharine, 150
Dill(i)er, Christina, 150
Dill(i)er, David, 150
Dill(i)er, Eleanor, 150
Dill(i)er, Elizabeth, 150
Dill(i)er, George, 150
Dill(i)er, Jean/Hans Martin, 149
Dill(i)er, John, 149, 150
Dill(i)er, Juliana, 150
Dill(i)er, Margaret, 150
Dill(i)er, Martin, 150
Dill(i)er, Mary Magdalena, 150
Dill(i)er, Philip Adam, 149
Dill(i)er, Rosina, 149
Dill(i)er, Solomon, 150
Dill(i)er. Adam, 149
Dillahunt(y), Ann(a), 275
Dillahunt(y), Daniel, 275
Dillahunt(y), Hannah, 275
Dillahunt(y), John, 275
Dillahunt(y), Mary Ann, 275
Dillahunt(y), Rachel, 275
Dillahunt(y), Samuel, 275
Dillahunt(y), Thomas, 275
Dillahunt(y), William, 275
Dilley, Redigon, **35**
Dimanche, Jean, 468
Dinsmore, Lettice, 405
Dircks, Rachel, 304
Dircks, Volkert, 126
Dircks/Dircksen, Artiantje, 296
Dircks/Dircksen, Christina, 296
Dircks/Dircksen, Grietje/Margaret, 296
Dircks/Dircksen, Jacob, 296
Dircks/Dircksen, Jannetje, 297
Dircks/Dircksen, Magdalena, 296
Dircks/Dircksen, Nicholas, 297
Dircks/Dircksen, Philip, 297
Dircks/Dircksen, Rachel, 296
Dircks/Dircksen, Sara, 296
Dircks/Dircksen, Volkert, 296
Dirckse, Geertruy, 302
Dirckse, Margaret/Grietje, 301
Dirckse, Rachel, 174
Disler, John, 104
Distillemau, David, 462
Distillemau, Elisabeth (Baudry), 462
Distillemau, Marthe, 462
Ditmar, Barbara, 250
Ditsler, Jacob, 104
Dixon, Anne, 64
Dixon, Frances, 183
Dixon, James, 218
Dixon, William, 64, 258
Doatloan/Dottando, Ester, 300

Dobbs, Elizabeth, 182
Dochett, Frances, 233
Dodd, Jean, 400
Dodd, John, 188
Dodson, Abraham, 266
Dodson, Barbara (Russell), 266
Dodson, Mary, 266
Dodson, Tabitha, 266
Doens/Docus, Jeanne, 13
Dogan,Samuel, 427
Doggitt, Richard, 24
Dolbere, Mary (Michell), 222
Dolbere, Rawkey, 222
Dolbere/Dolbiar, Mary, 222
Dollinger, Susanna, 348
Dolliver, John, 348
Dolliver, Mary (Elwell), 348
Dolliver, Samuel, 348
Dolmans, Thomas Sir, 231
Donaldson, Benjamin Chapman, 167
Donaldson, Mary, 167
Dongan, Gov., 280
Donlevy, Henry, **51**
Donnaman/Downmann, Meelin, 201
Donnelly, Isabel (X), 272
Donnelly, James, 272
Donnelly, Martha, 272
Donnelson, William, 152
Donnmann, William, 201
Doolittle, Thomas, 239
Dooren, Jacobus, 48
Doremus, Cornelis, 45, 150
DOREMUS, Cornelius, 150
Doremus, Hendrick, 151
Doremus, Janneke, 150
Doremus, Jannetje, 150
Doremus, Johannes, 150
Doremus, Joris, 151
Doremus, Maijke, 150
Doremus, Thomas, 150
Doriot, Jean Nicolas, 359
Doriot, Jeanne (Ponssot), 359
Doriot, Marie Françoise, 359
Dorman, Edmund, 70
Dormer/Domar, Mary Jane, 19
Dornand, Jacques, 253
Dornand, Madelaine, 253
Dornant, Anatole, **35**
Dornant, Françoise (duPré), **35**
Dornant, Marie, **35**
Dornblesser, unknown, 204
Dorselle, Elizabeth, 134
Dorsey, Dr. X, 108
Dorsey, Maria Ridgeley, 108
Douay, Adrien, 151
Douay, Jehanne (Telier), 151
Douay/Duey/ Duy, Nicholas de, 151
Douay/Duey/Duy, Amand de, 151
Douay/Duey/Duy, Catherine de, 151
Douay/Duey/Duy, Claudine de, 151
DOUAY/DUEY/DUY, Jacques de, 151

Douay/Duey/Duy, Johan Conrad de, 151
Douay/Duey/Duy, Pierre de, 151
Douay/Duey/Duy, Simonne de, 151
Douay/Duey/Duy, Thomas de, 151
Doublet, Elizabeth, 212
Doublet, Jean, 212
Doublet, Marie (X), 212
Doucinet, Susanne Marie, 357
Dougherty, Daniel, 401
Dougherty, Elizabeth, 416
Dougherty, Robert, 401
Douslet, Louise, 96
Douvrin, Frances d'Hamel, 412
Dow, Isaac, 17
Downes, Richard, 312
Downing, Ferriby/Pherebe (X), 33
Downing, Renates, 33
Dowsing, William, 355
Doyé, Antoine, 243
Doyé, Jeanne, 243
Doyé, Rose (Dugardin), 243
Drabbe, Elisabeth, 38
Dragaud/ Dragoo, Margrietza, 152
Dragaud/Dragoo, Jean, 151
Dragaud/Dragoo, Jean/John, 151, 152
Dragaud/Dragoo, Marie/Mary, 151
Dragaud/Dragoo, Peter IV, 152
DRAGAUD/DRAGOO, Pierre, 151
Dragaud/Dragoo, Pierre II, 151
Dragaud/Dragoo, Pierre/Peter III, 151
Drageau, Pierre, 105
Drake, Abraham, 330
Drake, Benjamin, 425
Drake, Deliverence (Wooden), 330
Drake, Elizabeth, 330
Draughton, Simon, 15
Drayton, Charlotte, 343
Drayton, Roger, 411
Drommeau, Jeanne, 313
Druine, Simon, *142*
Du Bois, Auguste, 154
du Bois, Catherine (Blanchan), 131
Du Bois, Catherine (Blanchan), 149
Du Bois, Catherine (Clarisse), 313
du Bois, Charles, 152
Du Bois, Charles, 154
du Bois, Daniel, 308
Du Bois, Esther/Hester, 313
du Bois, Isaac, 152, 308
du Bois, Jean, 152
du Bois, Louis, 131
Du Bois, Louis, 149, 154
Du BOIS, Louis, 154
du Bois, Madeleine (de Croix), 152
Du Bois, Margaret, 154
du Bois, Maria (Hasbrouck), 308
Du Bois, Mary, 154
du Bois, Pierre, 152
du Bois, Sarah, 464
du Bois, Simon, 308
du Bois, Solomon, 152

du Bois, Wallerand, 152
Du Bois,Pierre, 313
du Bonrepos, David, 61
Du Bosc, Françoise (Olivier/Olliver de
   Lienville), 155
Du Bosc, Pierre, 155
Du Bosc/Du Bose, Andrew, 156
Du Bosc/Du Bose, Anne, 156
Du Bosc/Du Bose, Antoine, 155
Du Bosc/Du Bose, Beersheba, 155
Du Bosc/Du Bose, Daniel, 156
Du Bosc/Du Bose, Elizabeth, 156
Du Bosc/Du Bose, Esther, 155
Du Bosc/Du Bose, Isaac, 155
Du Bosc/Du Bose, Jeptha, 155
Du Bosc/Du Bose, John, 156
Du Bosc/Du Bose, Jonathan, 155
Du Bosc/Du Bose, Joshua, 155
Du BOSC/Du BOSE, Louis, 155
Du Bosc/Du Bose, Stephen, 156
Du Bosc/Du Bose, Susannah, 155
Du Bosc/DuBose, Madelaine, 155
Du Bourdieu, Andrée LeValet, 157
Du Bourdieu, Armand, 157
Du Bourdieu, Charlotte, 157
Du Bourdieu, Elizabeth, 156
Du Bourdieu, Ester, 157
Du Bourdieu, Isaac, 157
Du Bourdieu, James Lord, 157
Du Bourdieu, Jean, 156, 157
Du Bourdieu, Jean Armand, 157
Du Bourdieu, Louis-Philippe, 156
Du Bourdieu, Mathieu, 157
Du Bourdieu, Olivier, 156
Du Bourdieu, Pierre, 156
Du BOURDIEU, Pierre, 156
Du Bourdieu, Pierre Gov., 156
Du Bourdieu, Renée, 157
Du Bourdieu, Samuel, 156
Du Bourdieu, Saumerez, 157
du Brois, Jean, 317
Du Can, Magariete, 197
du Chesne, Anne (Fabri), 177
du Chesne, Gédéon, 66
du Chesne, Marie (Boissonet), 66
du Chesne, Marie -Charlotte, 66
du Chesne, Pierre, 177
du Chesne, Susanna, 177
du Chesne, Valentine, 130
du Cloisy, unknown, 376
du Cloux, Magdeleine, 197
du Cloux, Marie, 197
du Cloux, Marie (Aubertin), 197
du Cloux, Nicaise, 197
du Fau, Jacques, 144
du Four, Catherine, 229
Du Four, Jean, 315
Du Frène, Clement, 449
Du Frène, Marie (Le Jeune), 449
Du Fresne/Du Frène, Marie, 449
du Gaure, Oliver, 301

du Joue, Pierre, 149
Du Maurier, unknown, 51
du May, Marie, 94, 473
du Pont, Abraham, 234
du Pont, Anne (Faucheraud), 234
du Pont, Eleuthère Irénée, 108
du Portal, Isabelle, 249
Du Pré, Josias, 398
Du Pré, Martha (X), 398
Du Pré, Rachel, 398
du Sauchoy, Madeleine, 241
du Sauchoy, Marc(us), 241
du Sauchoy,Elizabeth (Rossingnol), 241
du Trieu, Jaspar/Gaspard, 177
du Trieux, Philippe, 198
du Trieux, Susanna (du Chesne), 198
du Truchot, unknown, 92
du Vigneau, Jean-Isaac, 215
du Vigneau, Marie-Henriette-Suzanne,
   215
du Vinage, Abraham, 473
du Vinage, Arnoult, 473
du Vinge, Jeanne (Petit), 473
Dubblin/D'Aubin, Elizabeth, 21
Dubé, Charles, 379
Dubé/Dubois, Francis, 379
Dubé/Dubois, Marie (Barbey), 379
Duberdeaux, Ann (X) Mrs., 373
DuBois, Abraham, 149, 152, 155, 192,
   290
DuBois, Anne, 152, 155
DuBois, Benjamin, 152
DuBois, Blanche, 74, 153
DuBois, Catherin, 152
Dubois, Catherine (Blanchan), 290
DuBois, Catherine (Blanchan), 192, 242
DuBois, Chrétien, 61, 63, 154
DuBOIS, Chrétien, 152
DuBois, Daniel, 308
DuBois, David, 153
DuBois, Eleazer, 155
DuBois, Elisabeth, 155
DuBois, Élisabeth, 155
DuBois, Elizabeth, 356
DuBois, Esther, 59, 155, 379
Dubois, Esther (Guérin), 233
DuBois, Françoise, 61, 152
DuBois, George, 155
DuBois, Gertrude (Bruyn), 308
DuBois, Isaac, 152, 155, 242
DuBois, Jacob, 153, 155
DuBois, Jacques, 153, 154, 155
DuBOIS, Jacques/James, 153
Dubois, James, 233
DuBois, James, 373
DuBois, Jean, 124, 141, 155, 178
DuBois, Jeane, 211
DuBois, Jeanne, 154, 155
DuBois, Jeanne (Desmuille), 119
DuBois, Joel, 152
duBois, John, 426

DuBois, Jonathan, 307
DuBois, Judith, 154, 155
DuBois, Laurent/Laurens, 155
DuBois, Leah, 149, 192
DuBois, Leya/Leah, 152
Dubois, Louis, 230
DuBois, Louis, 63, 152, 153, 192, 230,
   242, 290, 307
DuBois, Magdalen, 153
duBois, Magdalena, 131
Dubois, Margaret (Deyo), 192
DuBois, Margaret (Deyo), 290
DuBois, Marie, 124, 155
DuBois, Marie (Deyaget), 178
DuBois, Martin, 152
Dubois, Mary, 68
DuBois, Mary, 152
DuBois, Mary LeFèvre, 308
DuBois, Marye, 155
DuBois, Mattheus, 153
DuBois, Michel, 155
DuBois, Nathaniel, 308
DuBois, Noah, 152
DuBois, Philadelphia, 178
DuBois, Philip, 59
DuBois, Pierre, 119, 155
DuBOIS, Pierre I, 154
DuBois, Pierre II, 119, 155
DuBois, Rachel, 152, 153, 155, 308
DuBois, Rachel (Hasbrouck), 307
DuBois, Rebecca, 153
DuBois, Salomon, 153
DuBois, Sara, 153
DuBois, Sarah, 152
DuBois, Simon, 308
DuBois/DuBroix, Jean, 317
DuBose, Anne, 128, 255, 407
DuBose, Anne (Rembert), 255
DuBose, Daniel, 255, 407
DuBose, Isaac, 128, 407
DuBose, Louis, 128
DuBose, Madelaine, 407
DuBose, Peter, 407
DuBose, Susanne (Couillandeau), 407
DuBreuil, Christoffe, 176
DuBREUIL/DUBRIL/DIBRELL,
   Christophe/Christoffe/Christophe,
   157
DuBreuil/Dubril/Dibrell, Jean Antoine,
   157
DuBuse/Busc, Marie, 165
DuChemin/Dishman, Anne, 158
DuChemin/Dishman, David, 158
DuChemin/Dishman, Elizabeth, 158
DuChemin/Dishman, Isaac, 158
DuChemin/Dishman, James, 158
DuChemin/Dishman, John, 158
DuChemin/Dishman, Mary, 158
DuChemin/Dishman, Peter, 158
DuChemin/Dishman, Samuel, 158
DuCHEMIN/DISHMAN, Samuel, 158

DuChesne, Ann, 159
DuChesne, Anna, 159
Duchesne, Anthony, 82
DuCHESNE, Anthony, 158
DuChesne, Francytje, 159
DuChesne, Gerret, 159
DuChesne, Isaac, 159
DuChesne, Jannetje, 159
DuChesne, Jerome, 159
DuChesne, Michael, 159
Dudevant, Françoise, **35**
Dudevant, Jacques, **35**
Dudevant, Marie, 125
Duero, (Olimp?), 203
Duero, James, 203
Duffield, Elizabeth, 227
Duffield, Priscilla (Farnsead), 227
Duffield, William, 227
Dufour(s)/DuFour/DeFord, Abraham,
   160
Dufour(s)/DuFour/DeFord, Aurélie, 160
Dufour(s)/DuFour/DeFord, Claud, 160
Dufour(s)/DuFour/DeFord, Délie
   Corneille, 160
Dufour(s)/DuFour/DeFord, Émilie, 160
Dufour(s)/DuFour/DeFord, Félix, 160
Dufour(s)/DuFour/DeFord, Hyacinthe,
   160
Dufour(s)/DuFour/DeFord, Isaac, 160
Dufour(s)/DuFour/DeFord, Jacques, 160
Dufour(s)/DuFour/DeFord, Jean, 160
DUFOUR(S)/DuFOUR/DeFORD, Jean, 159
Dufour(s)/DuFour/DeFord, Joseph, 160
Dufour(s)/DuFour/DeFord, Marie, 160
Dufour(s)/DuFour/DeFord, Pierre I, 160
Dufour(s)/DuFour/DeFord, Pierre II, 160
Dufour(s)/DuFour/DeFord, Richard, 160
Dufour(s)/DuFour/DeFord, Sara, 160
Dufour(s)/DuFour/DeFord, Théodore,
   160
Dufour(s)/DuFour/DeFord, William, 160
DuFour, David, 105
Dufour, Jean, 159
DuFour, Jean/Jan, 159
Dufour, Jehan, 159
Dufour, Matilde (Beaudoin), 159
Dufoussat, Peter, 432
DuFrêne, Madeleine, 244
Dugardin, Alard, 243
Dugardin, Jeanne (Roger), 243
Dugas, Abraham, 294
Dugas, Marguerite Louise (Doucet), 294
Dugas, Marie, 294
Duguay, unknown, 388
Dugue, Elizabeth, 161
Dugue, Isaac, 161
Dugué, Jacques, 193
DuGué, Jacques, 28
DUGUÉ, Jacques, 160
Dugue, Jacques/James, 161
DuGue, Marianne (Fleury de la Plaine), 28

Dugue, Pierre, 161
DuGué/Dugué, Judith, 156
DuHamel, Alfred, 161
DuHamel, Ann, 161
DuHamel, Anne, 161
DuHamel, Benjamin, 161
DuHAMEL, Isaac, 161
DuHamel, James, 161
DuHamel, Jane, 161
DuHamel, John, 161
DuHamel, Peter, 161
DuHamel, Rachel, 161
DuHamel, Samuel, 161
DuHamel, William, 161
Duke of Devonshire, 157
Dumas, Benjamin, 162
Dumas, David, 162
Dumas, Frances, 162
Dumas, Jeremiah, 162
Dumas, Jérémie, 162
DUMAS, Jérôme/Jeremiah, 162
Dumas, Mathen, 162
Dumas, Sarah, 162
Dumas, Susanna (Fauré), 162
Dumas, Temperance, 162
Dumas/DeMos(s), Catherine, 162
Dumas/DeMos(s), Charles, 162, 163
Dumas/DeMos(s), James, 163
Dumas/DeMos(s), Jane, 163
Dumas/DeMos(s), John, 162
DUMAS/DeMOS(S), Louis II, 162
Dumas/DeMos(s), Louis/Lewis III, 162
Dumas/DeMos(s), Peter, 162
Dumas/DeMos(s), Pine/Ping, 163
Dumas/DeMos(s), Thomas, 163
Dumas/DeMos(s), William, 162
DuMay, Elizabeth Martha, 163
DUMAY, Étienn, 163
Dumay, Étienne, 235
DuMay, Joseph, 163
DuMay, Mary Jane, 163
DuMay, Peter, 163
DuMay, Stephen, 163
Dumbauld, Abraham, 60
Dummée, Esther, 449
DuMond/LeMan, Petronella, 129
DUMONT, ?Jean, 163
Dumont, Abraham, 164
Dumont, Catelyntje, 164
Dumont, Catherine, 451
Dumont, Elizabeth, 163, 258
Dumont, Francyntie, 164
Dumont, Francyntj, 273
Dumont, Jan Baptist, 164
Dumont, Jannetje, 164
Dumont, John, 164
Dumont, Margaret, 163, 164, 377
Dumont, Peter, 164
Dumont, Wallerand, 163, 258, 273
Dumont, Walran, 164
Dunbar, Goutier, 372

Dunbar, Stephen, 372
Dunbar, Susan, 226
Dunham, Abigail, 62
Dunham, Abigail (Barlow), 286
Dunham, Benajah, 62
Dunham, Benjamin, 62
Dunham, Daniel, 62
Dunham, Edmund, 393
Dunham, Hannah, 62
Dunham, Humility, 62
Dunham, John, 62, 286
Dunham, Jonathan, 139, 286
Dunham, Jonathan Rev., 393
Dunham, Jonathan/John, 62
Dunham, Joseph, 62
Dunham, Mary (Bonham), 393
Dunham, Persis, 62
Dunham, Samuel, 62
Dunham, Sarah, 330
Dunham, Thomas, 62
Dunn, Ann Elizabeth, 425
Dunn, Elinor Purcell, 346
Dunn, Elizabeth (Drake), 425
Dunn, Hugh, 425
Dunn, Martha, 425
Dunnom, unknown, 127
Duntzfelt, Cécile Olivia, 215
DuPay, Elizabeth, 103
DuPEUX/DuPOUX/DuPUS/DuPEE, Élie, 164
DuPeux/DuPoux/DuPus/DuPee, Charles, 164
DuPeux/DuPoux/DuPus/DuPee, Daniel, 164
DuPeux/DuPoux/DuPus/Dupee, Elias, 164
DuPeux/DuPoux/DuPus/DuPee, Elias, 164
DuPeux/DuPoux/DuPus/DuPee, Isaac, 164
DuPeux/DuPoux/DuPus/DuPee, Jean/John, 164
DuPeux/DuPoux/DuPus/DuPee, John, 164
DuPeux/DuPoux/DuPus/DuPee, Mary, 164
DuPeux/DuPoux/DuPus/DuPee, Susanna, 164
Duplessis, Peter Rev., 407
duPont de Nemours, Pierre Samuel, 166
DuPONT, Jehan, 165
DuPont, Abraham, 165, 167
duPont, Alexander, 234
DuPont, Alexander, 165
DuPont, Ann, 165
DuPont, Charles, 165
DuPont, Cornelius, 165
DuPont, Esther, 165, 166
DuPont, Eustace, 166
DuPont, Gideon, 165
DuPont, Jane, 165

DuPont, Jean, 165
DuPont, John, 165
DuPont, Jonas, 165
DuPont, Josiah, 165
DuPont, Judith, 166
DuPont, Margariete, 186
DuPont, Marie, 165, 166, 184
DuPont, Mary Anne/Marie, 165
duPont, Paul, 52
DuPont, Pierre, 165
DuPont, Samuel, 166
Duprat, Emilie, 159
Duprat, Émilie (X), 159
Duprat, Pierre, 159
DuPre(e)/ DuPray, Haley, 167
DuPre(e)/DuPray, Elizabeth, 166
DuPre(e)/DuPray, James, 167
DuPre(e)/DuPray, Jane, 166
DuPRE(E)/DuPRAY, Jean, 166
DuPre(e)/DuPray, John, 166
DuPre(e)/DuPray, Joseph, 166
DuPre(e)/DuPray, Lewis, 166
DuPre(e)/DuPray, Louis/Lewis, 167
DuPRE(E)/DuPRAY, Louis/Lewis, 166
DuPre(e)/DuPray, Margaret, 166
DuPre(e)/DuPray, Mary, 166
DuPre(e)/DuPray, Nancy, 166
DuPre(e)/DuPray, Thomas, 166, 167
DuPRE(E)/DuPRAY, Thomas, 166
DuPre(e)/DuPray, William, 166
DuPré, Ann (Blake), 373
DuPre, Cornelius, 167
DuPré, Cornelius, 165, 322
DuPre, Elizabeth, 167
DuPre, James, 167
Dupré, Jane (X), 50
DuPré, Jane Elizabeth, 165
Dupré, Jean, 50
DuPré, Jeanne (Brabant), 165, 322
DuPre, Jeanne Elizabeth, 167
Dupré, Jeanne/Jane, 203
DuPré, John, 141
DuPré, John, 203
DuPré, Josias, 90, 441
DuPRÉ, Josias, 167
DuPré, Josias Blake, 373
DuPré, Josias Garnier, 373
DuPre, Josias II, 167
DuPré, Julia, 82
DuPré, Julia C., 82
DuPre, Martha, 167
DuPré, Martha, 441
Dupré, Mary, 141
DuPré, Mary, 203
DuPre, Mary Esther, 167
DuPré, Mary Esther, 442
DuPré, Mary Magdalen, 322
DuPre, Mary Magdalen, 167
DuPre, Rachel, 167
DuPre, Sarah, 167
DuPré, Sarah, 90

DuPré, Sarah, (Garnier), 90
DuPré, Thomas, 181
Dupuis/Dupee, Martha, 256
DuPuy, Abigail, 302
DuPuy, André, 230
DuPUY, André, 167
DuPuy, Andrew, 168
DuPuy, Anne, 112
DuPuy, Anne (St.Heyer), 168
DuPuy, Antoine, 168
DuPUY, Bartholomé/Barthélémy/Bartholomew, 168
Dupuy, Bartholomew, 309
DuPuy, Bartholomew, 113, 326
DuPuy, Catherine, 168
DuPuy, Daniel, 170
Dupuy, Élizabet, 160
DuPuy, Elizabeth, 168
DuPuy, Francis, 170
DuPuy, Hester, 168, 170
DuPuy, Isabel, 170
Dupuy, James, 455
Dupuy, Jane, 230
DuPuy, Jane, 168
DuPuy, Jane/Jeanne, 170
DuPuy, Jean, 168
DuPuy, Jean Cochon, 317
DuPuy, Jean Dr., 136
Dupuy, Jean Jacques/John James, 232
DuPuy, Jean Jacques/John James, 326
DuPuy, Jean/John, 112
DuPUY, Jean/John, 170
DuPuy, Jean-Jacques/John James, 168
DuPuy, Jeanne, 168
DuPuy, Jeanne (Archambaud), 230
DuPuy, Jean-Pierre, 168
DuPuy, John, 170
Dupuy, John Bartholomew, 232
DuPuy, Marianne, 168
DuPuy, Marie (Gardié), 113, 326
Dupuy, Marie (Gardier), 309
DuPuy, Marthe, 113, 168
DuPuy, Nicholas, 302
DuPuy, Olimpe/Olymphia, 326
Dupuy, Olympia, 455
DuPuy, Paul, 170
DuPuy, Philippa, 168, 326
Dupuy, Pierre, 309
DuPuy, Pierre/Peter, 168
Dupuy, Susanne (LaVillain), 455
Dupuy, Susanne (LeVillian), 232
DuPuy, Thomas, 170
DuPuy/DuPui(s)/ DePew, Nicholas, 170
DuPuy/DuPui(s)/DePew, Aaron, 169
DuPUY/DuPUI(S)/DePEW, François, 169
DuPuy/DuPui(s)/DePew, Geertje, 170
DuPuy/DuPui(s)/DePew, Grietje/Margaret, 170
DuPuy/DuPui(s)/DePew, Jannetje/Jane, 170

DuPuy/DuPui(s)/DePew, Jean/John, 170
DuPuy/DuPui(s)/DePew, John, 169
DuPuy/DuPui(s)/DePew, Joseph, 169
DuPuy/DuPui(s)/DePew, Magdalena, 169
DuPuy/DuPui(s)/DePew, Marie, 170
DuPuy/DuPui(s)/DePew, Mary, 170
DuPuy/DuPui(s)/DePew, Moses, 169
DuPuy/DuPui(s)/DePew, Nicholaes/Nicholas, 169
DuPuy/DuPui(s)/DePew, Nicolas, 169
DuPUY/DuPUI(S)/DePEW, Nicolas/Nicolaes, 169
DuPuy/DuPui(s)/DePew, Paulus, 169
DuPuy/DuPui(s)/DePew, Sara, 170
DuPuy/DuPui(s)/DePew, Susanna, 169
DuPuy/DuPui(s)/DePew, Willem, 170
Durand, Abigail, 172
Durand, Alexandre, 171
Durand, Andrew, 172
Durand, Anna, 171
Durand, Anne (Moran(d)/Meraud/Moraud), 171
Durand, Charles, 171
Durand, Charles Emmanuel, 171
Durand, Charlotte, 171
Durand, Ebenezer, 172
Durand, Eleazor, 171
Durand, Elizabeth, 172
DURAND, François Josèphe/Francis Joseph, 171
Durand, George, 171
Durand, Je(h)an, 171
DURAND, Jean/John, 171
Durand, John, 171
Durand, Joseph, 171, 172
Durand, Joseph Francis, 171
Durand, Louis, 171
Durand, Margaretha, 30
Durand, Marie, 171
Durand, Mary, 172
Durand, Mary/Polly, 171
Durand, Mathieu, 30
Durand, Merari, 171
Durand, Noah, 171, 172
Durand, Samuel, 172
Durand, Simeon, 171
Durant, Henry Fowle, 108
Duret, Antonia (X) de, 173
Duret, Paul Parrain de, 173
Durham, Will, 446
Durié, Jan, *142*
Durie, Jean, 129
Durier/Durie/Duree/Duryea, Catherine, 172
Durier/Durie/Duree/Duryea, Jean, 172
Durier/Durie/Duree/Duryea, Jean/Jan, 172
Durier/Durie/Duree/Duryea, Jeanne, 172

Durier/Durie/Duree/Duryea, Jeanne/Janeken, 172
Durier/Durie/Duree/Duryea, Marguerite, 172
DURIER/DURIÉ/DURÉE/DURYEA, Pierre, 172
Durier/Durie/Duree/Duryea, Pierre/Pieter, 172
DuRieu, Adrienne (Rau/Roul), 174
DuRieu, Simon, 174
Durje, unknown, 358
DURRETT(E), François/Francis Parrain de, 173
Durrett, Ann/Nancy, 173
Durrett, Benjamin, 174
Durrett, James, 174
Durrett, Marshall, 173
Durrett, Mary, 173
Durrett, Mildred, 173
Durrett, Richard, 173
DURRETT, Richard, 173
Durrett, Robert, 173
Durrett, Sarah/Sally, 174
Durrett, William, 173
Duryea, Antoinette, 305
Duryea, Deborah (Blake), 302
Duryea, Joost, 305
Duryea, Madeline (Le Fèvre), 305
Duryea, Peter, 302
Duryea, Phoebe, 302
Duryee/Duryea/DuRieu/Durie, Abraham, 174
Duryee/Duryea/DuRieu/Durie, Antoinette, 174
Duryee/Duryea/DuRieu/Durie, Charles, 174
Duryee/Duryea/DuRieu/Durie, Elizabeth, 174
Duryee/Duryea/DuRieu/Durie, Françoise, 174
Duryee/Duryea/DuRieu/Durie, Jacob, 174
Duryee/Duryea/DuRieu/Durie, Jacques, 174
Duryee/Duryea/DuRieu/Durie, Jacques/Jean, 174
DURYÉE/DURYEA/DuRIEU/DURIE, Joost/George, 174
Duryee/Duryea/DuRieu/Durie, Joost/Justin, 174
Duryee/Duryea/DuRieu/Durie, Magdalena, 174
Duryee/Duryea/DuRieu/Durie, Magdeleine, 174
Duryee/Duryea/DuRieu/Durie, Marie, 174
Duryee/Duryea/DuRieu/Durie, Peter, 174
Duryee/Duryea/DuRieu/Durie, Philip, 174

Duryee/Duryea/DuRieu/Durie, Simon, 174

DuSAUCHOY/DISOWAY/du (de) SOISON, Marc, 175

DuSauchoy/Disoway/Du(de)Soison, Janneties, 175

DuSauchoy/Disoway/Du(de)Soison, Jean, 175

DuSauchoy/Disoway/du(de)Soison, Madeleine/Magdaleentie, 175

DuSauchoy/Disoway/du(de)Soison, Marcus, 175

DuSauchoy/Disoway/Du(de)Soison, Maria, 175

Dusjean, Gerret, 280

Dutarque, Ann, 373

Dutarque, Lewis, 373

Dutarque, Louis, 360

Dutarque, Martha, 372

Dutarte, Anne (Renault), 397

Dutarte, Daniel, 397

Dutarte, Pierre, 397

Duteau, Catherine, 134

Duteau, Charles, 134

Duteau, Jeanne (Rivaud), 134

Dutertre, Anne, 137, 176

Dutertre, Louis, 137

DUTERTRE, Louis, 176

Dutertre, Mariane (Buart), 137

DuToi(s)/DuToy/DuToit, Elizabeth, 176

DuToi(s)/DuToy/DuToit, Isaac, 176

DuToi(s)/DuToy/DuToit, Mary Ann, 176

DuTOI(S)/DuTOY/DuTOIT, Pierre/Peter, 175

Dutoi, Barbara (de Bonnette/Bonnet), 332

Dutoi, Maryann, 332

Dutoi, Peter, 60

Dutois, Pierre, 332

Dutois/Dutoit, Pierre, 72

Dutoit, Barbara (de Bonnette), 157

Dutoit, Marianne, 157

DuToit, Marie (Frossard [de Saugy]), 175

Dutoit, Pierre, 157

DuToit, Pierre, 175

Dutoit/Dutois, Pierre, 47

DuTrieu(x)/DeTruye/Truax, Abraham, 177

DuTrieu(x)/DeTruye/Truax, Isaac, 177

DuTrieu(x)/DeTruye/Truax, Jacob. See DuTrieu(x)/DeTruye/Truax, Madeleine, 177

DuTrieu(x)/DeTruye/Truax, Maria, 177

DuTrieu(x)/DeTruye/Truax, Marie, 177

DuTrieu(x)/DeTruye/Truax, Philippe, 177

DuTRIEU(X)/DeTRUYE/TRUAX, Philippe I, 176

DuTrieu(x)/DeTruye/Truax, Philippe II/Philip, 177

DuTrieu(x)/DeTruye/Truax, Rachel, 177

DuTrieu(x)/DeTruye/Truax, Rebecca, 177

DuTrieu(x)/DeTruye/Truax, Sara, 177

DuTrieu(x)/DeTruye/Truax, Susanna, 177

duTrieux, Sarah, 198

DuVAL, DUVAL(L), Marin/Mareen, 178

DuVal/Duval, Benjamin, 178, 179

DuVal/Duval, Catherine, 179

DuVal/Duval, Daniel, 178

DuVAL/DUVAL, Daniel, 178

DuVal/Duval, Eleanor, 179

DuVal/Duval, Elizabeth, 179

DuVal/Duval, Johanna, 179

DuVal/Duval, John, 178

DuVal/Duval, Lewis, 178

DuVal/Duval, Mareen (the Elder), 178

DuVal/Duval, Mareen (the Younger), 179

DuVal/Duval, Mary, 179

Duval/Duval, Mary/Polly, 178

DuVal/Duval, Samuel, 178, 179

DuVal/Duval, Susannah, 179

DuVal/Duval, William, 178

Duvall, Mareen, 88

Duvall, Nicola (Stagard), 178

Duvall, Thomas, 178

Duycking, Evert, 287

Duyn, Cornelius Garrit Van, 125

Duyn, Neeltje Van, 125

Duyster, Cornelis de, 279

D'Val/Darnall/Danvall, Charles, 79

Dyck, Angnietje Jan Van, 48

Dyck, Catherine/Trynje Van, 154

Dyck, Jacob Van, 154

Dyck, Jans Thomasze Van, 48

Dyckman, Johannes, 467

Dyckman, John, 454

Dye/Dey, Sarah, 58

Dyer, Anna (Small), 348

Dyer, Elizabeth, 212

Dyer, Henry, 348

Dyer, James, 348

Dyer, Jonathan, 348

Dyer, Micah, 348

Dyer, Susanna (Brown), 348

Dyke, Nicholas Van, 15

Dykman, Hester, 467

Dylander, Eleanor (Cox), 170

Dylander, John Rev., 170

DyPont, Jehan, 166

E

Earhardt, Abram, 191

Earle, Archibald, 83

Easley, Ann (Parker), 166

Easley, Daniel, 137

Easley, John, 137

Easley, Margaret, 166

Easley, Mary (Benskin), 137

Easley, Mary (Pyrant), 137

Easley, Miller Woodson, 181

Easley, Robert, 166

Easley, Stephen, 137

Easley, William, 137

Eastman, Thomas, 124

Eaton, Joanna (Wardell), 53, 304

Eaton, John, 53, 304

Eaton, Margaret, 53

Eaton, Valeria, 304

Eberly, Magdalena, 103

Echols, Elizabeth, 137

Echols, William, 137

Eckert/A(c)kard, Jacob, 292

EDDENS/ED(D)INS/EDDINGS, John, 180

Eddens/Ed(d)ins/Eddings, William, 180

Eddings, Abraham, 180

Eddings, Anne, 180

Eddings, Benjamin, 180

Eddings, Elizabeth, 180

Eddings, Isaac, 180

Eddings, Jacob, 180

Eddings, John, 180

Eddings, Joseph, 180

Eddings, Mary, 180

Eddings, Rebecca, 180

Eddings, Theophelus, 180

Eddings, William, 180

Eden, Frances, 434

Edgar, Catherine, 211

Edmiston, David, 92

Edmiston, Isabelle, 92

Edmond, Rachel, 137

Edsall, Elizabeth, 53

Edsall, Maria, 287

Edsall, Ruth, 53

Edsall, Samuel, 53

Edwards, Abiah, 125

Edwards, Elizabeth (X), 125

Edwards, John, 15

Edwards,Naomi,, 125

Effard, Élisabeth (Perrin), 107, 180

Effard, Elizabeth, 180

Effard, Jean, 107, 180

Effard, Jean/John, 180

Effard, Jeanne, 181

Effard, Judith, 180

Effard, Marie, 181

Effard, Martha, 180

Effard, Nicholas, Jr, 181

EFFARD, Nicolas, 180

Effard, Nicolas Rev., 107

Effard, Pierre/Peter, 181

Effard, Sara, 180

Effard, Susanna, 181

Egbartsz, Egbert, 159

Egberts, Geertie, 45

Egbertson, Abraham, 390

Eggens, Christine, 195

Eggleston, Betty, 114

Eggleston, Hester (Williams), 244

Eggleston, Jane Segar, 114

Eggleston, Janes, 244
Eggleston, Mary (Chubb), 114
Eggleston, Richard, 114
Egmont, Cornelis, 101
Eichacker, Peter, 19
Eichaker, Anna Barbara, 18
Eldertsen, Jacob, 105
Ellemaker, unknown, 192
Ellens, Charles, 101
Ellens, Johannes, 101
Ellesby, Lurana, 166
Elliche, Isabella, 264
Elliott, Elliott, 377
Elliott, Mary, 234
Elliott, William, 234
Ellis, Bastian, 101
Ellis, Christopher, 88
Ellis, Henrietta, 101
Ellis, Mary, 146
Ellis, Sarah (X), 101
Ellis, unknown, 265, 306
Elliston, Frances, 170
Elliston, Robert, 389
Ellmaker, Leonard, 149
Ellmaker, Mary Magdalena, 149
Ellrod, Anna Margaretha, 243
Elsasser, Eva Maria, 370
Elsasser, Melchoir, 370
Elsten, Annie, 169
Elsworth, Elizabeth, 117
Elsworth, George, 358
Elsworth, Moses, 117
Elten, Jan, 464
Elten/Elting, Cornelis, 464
Elting, Jacomyntjen/Jemima, 106
Elting, Jan, 152, 237
Elting, Roelof, 152
Elting, Roeloff, 106
Elting, William, 324
Elting/Eltinge, Elizabeth, 192
Elwell, David, 348
Elwell, Isaac, 348
Elwell, Mehitabel (Millet), 348
Emerson, Elizabeth, 251
Emott, John, 79
England, Nathan, 83
England, Thomas, 146
English, Susanna, 44
Ennis, Thomas, 324
Ennis, William, 324
Enoch, Elizabeth, 446
Enoch, Elizabeth (Van Zandt), 446
Enochs, Gertrude, 446
Enochsson, John, 446
EnochssonGertrude (Stressinger), 446
Entremont, Comtesse d', 121
Epperson, Anne (Perrow), 185
Epperson/Apperson, William, 389
Eps, Elizabeth Direkse Van, 392
Équier, Jean (John), 414
Erikson, Michael, 124

Erné, Susanne, 241
Erving, Elizabeth, **37**
Erving, John, **37**
Eschâlets, Francois d', 319
Eschâlets, Jacquette (Chevallereau) d', 319
Escuyer, Jan, 296
Esdell, Mary, 298
Esgate, Caleb, 463
Eshuysen, Marietje, 45
ESLE/ES(E)LY/d'ESLEY/EASLEY, Robert, 181
Esle/Es(e)ly/Esley/Easley, Daniel, 181
Esle/Es(e)ly/Esley/Easley, Elizabeth, 181
Esle/Es(e)ly/Esley/Easley, John, 181
Esle/Es(e)ly/Esley/Easley, Judith (Judah), 181
Esle/Es(e)ly/Esley/Easley, Margaret, 181
Esle/Es(e)ly/Esley/Easley, Peter, 181
Esle/Es(e)ly/Esley/Easley, Robert, 181
Esle/Es(e)ly/Esley/Easley, Sarah, 181
Esle/Es(e)ly/Esley/Easley, Stephen, 181
Esle/Es(e)ly/Esley/Easley, Susanah Francey (Frances), 181
Esle/Es(e)ly/Esley/Easley, Thomas, 181
Esle/Es(e)ly/Esley/Easley, Warham, 181
Esle/Es(e)ly/Esley/Easley, William, 181
Esle/Es(e)ly/Esley/Easley, Worham, 181
Esselby, Jane, 396
Essels/Hesselse, Annatie, 151
Esther, Elizabeth (Ehbrurzen), 194
Esther, Jean, 194
Esther, Jean Henri, 194
Esther/Ester, Jane, 230
Estreng/Streng, Henri D', 447
Estreng/Streng, Marie (Babault) D', 447
Etheridge, James, 24
Etheridge, John, 24
Étienne, Remard, 54
Evans, Elizabeth, 377
Evans, Mary Ann, 279
Evans, Reese, 377
Eveland, John, 330
Evens, Jane, 464
Everett, Mrs. Mary, 256
Everitt, Anne (Nancy), 336
Everitt, Esther (Butterfield), 336
Everitt, Robert, 336
Everleigh, Ann (Simmons), 236
Everleigh, Harriet Ann, 236
Everleigh, Thomas, 236
Ewell, Bertand Maj., 56
Ewell, Bertrand, 56
Ewell, Charles, 56
Ewell, Charlotte, 56
Ewell, Frances, 56
Ewell, James, 56
Ewell, Jesse, 56
Ewell, Marianne, 56
Ewell, Mary, 56
Ewell, Mary Ann, 56

Ewell, Sarah, 56
Ewell, Solomon, 56
Eymar, Madeleine, 336
Eymar/Aymar(d)/Aima, Charlotte, 182
Eymar/Aymar(d)/Aima, Daniel, 182
Eymar/Aymar(d)/Aima, Jean, 182
EYMAR/AYMAR(D)/AIMA, Jean, 182
Eymar/Aymar(d)/Aima, Jean Jacques, 182
Eymar/Aymar(d)/Aima, Jeanne, 182
Eymar/Aymar(d)/Aima, Judith, 182
Eymar/Aymar(d)/Aima, Lucrèce, 182
Eymar/Aymar(d)/Aima, Marie, 182
Eynard, Jean-Pierre, 107
Eyraud, Gaspard, 195
Eyraud, Julie, 195
Eyraud, Rachel (Legris), 195
Eyre, Jane, 202
Eyre, Joseph, 202
Eyre, Margaret (Humphreys), 202

F

Faget, Jean, 135
Fain, Isabella, 133
FAIN, Isabella, 183
Fairfax, Lady, 133
Fairly, Thomas, 229
Faison/Fayson, Ann, 183
Faison/Fayson, Elias, 183
Faison/Fayson, Elizabeth, 183
FAISON/FAYSON, Henri von Doverage/Henryk van Doveracke, 183
Faison/Fayson, Henry, 183
Faison/Fayson, James, 183
Faison/Fayson, Rebecca, 183
Faison/Fayson, Sarah, 183
Falconer, André, 186
Falconer, Anne Madeleine, 186
Falconer, Étienne, 186
Falconer, Jeanne Élisabeth, 186
Falconer, John, 186
Falconer, Pierre, 186
Falconer, Susanne Madeleine, 186
Falconer, Théodore/Theodorus, 186
Falconer, William, 186
Fall, Elizabeth, 381
Fall/Fahl, Anna Margaretha (X), 381
Fall/Fahl, Dietrich, 381
Fallowell, Martha (Beal), 62
Fallowell, William, 62
Faneuil, André/Andrew, 184
Faneuil, Anne, 184
Faneuil, Anne (Bureau), **37**
Faneuil, Benjamin, **37**, 52, 184, 205
FANEUIL, Benjamin, 184
Faneuil, Esther, 184
Faneuil, François/Francis, 184
Faneuil, Jean, 184
Faneuil, Jean/John, 184
Faneuil, Jeanne Catherine, 184

Faneuil, Jeanne/Jane, 185
Faneuil, Marianne/Mary Ann, 184
Faneuil, Marie, 184
Faneuil, Marie/Mary, 184
Faneuil, Mary, 184
Faneuil, Peter, 184
Faneuil, Pierre, 184
Faneuil, Susannah, **37**
Faneuil, Susanne, 184
Faneuil, Suzanne, 184, 185
Faneuil, Suzanne (L'Epine), **37**
Fanis, Francis, 190
Fanton, Elizabeth, 212
Fanton, Rachel, 212
Fanueil, Peter, 190
Farcy, Jean, 389
Farcy/Farci/Farcee/Forsee, Anne, 185
Farcy/Farci/Farcee/Forsee, Charles, 185
Farcy/Farci/Farcee/Forsee, Elizabeth, 185
Farcy/Farci/Farcee/Forsee, Estienne/Stephen I, 185
Farcy/Farci/Farcee/Forsee, Estienne/Stephen II, 185
Farcy/Farci/Farcee/Forsee, Francis, 185
Farcy/Farci/Farcee/Forsee, Jane, 185
FARCY/FARCI/FARCEE/FORSEE, Jean/John, 185
Farcy/Farci/Farcee/Forsee, Jean-François, 185
Farcy/Farci/Farcee/Forsee, John, 185
Farcy/Farci/Farcee/Forsee, Judith, 185
Farcy/Farci/Farcee/Forsee, Mariane, 185
Farcy/Farci/Farcee/Forsee, Marie, 185
Farcy/Farci/Farcee/Forsee, Pierre, 185
Farcy/Farci/Farcee/Forsee, William, 185
Farcy/Forsee, Étienne, 389
Farcy/Forsee, Jane, 389
Farcy/Forsee, William, 389
Farmer, Daniel, 201
Farmer, Elizabeth, 33
Farmer, Thomas, 122
Faro, Michiel Jans, 440
Farqhar, Nancy, 253
Farquhar, Alexander, 253
Farquhar, Margaret (Leitsche), 253
Farrand, Daniel, 286
Farrar, Ann, 369
Farrar, Benjamin, 226
Farrar, John, 114
Farrar, Judith, 114
Farrar, Mary, 114
Farrar, Peter, 113
Farrar, Rebecca, 114
Farrar, Samuel, 114
Farrar, Sarah (X), 268
Farrar, William, 268
Farrel, Mary, 374
Farres/Farrar/Ferrar, Perrin, 268
Faucheraud, Anne, 165
Faucheraud, Anne (Vignaud), 165

Faucheraud, Charles, 165
Faucheraud, Gideon, 471
Fauconnier, Anne, 186
Fauconnier, Anne (de la Forcade), 186
Fauconnier, Madeleine, 462
Fauconnier, Madeline (Pasquereau), 462
Fauconnier, Margariete (DuPont), 144
Fauconnier, Matthieu, 186
Fauconnier, Pierre, 144, 402, 462
FAUCONNIER, Pierre, 186
Fauconnier, Pierre I, 186
FAUCONNIER, Pierre II, 186
Fauconnier, Sara, 186
Fauconnier, Saua, 144
Fauguion, Marie, 316
Faulkner, Thomas, 192
Fauntleroy, Ann Bushrod, 201
Fauntleroy, Bushrod Capt., 201
Fauntleroy, Griffin, 201
Fauntleroy, Katherine (Griffin), 364
Fauntleroy, Moore, 364
Fauntleroy, William, 364
Fauré, Ann, 67
Fauré, Anne (Tibault), 369
Faure, Daniel, 187
Fauré, Daniel, 369
FAURÉ, Daniel Isaac, 187
Faure, Elizabeth, 187
Fauré, Elizabeth, 369
Faure, François, 420
Faure, Jacques/James, 187
Faure, Jean/John, 187
Faure, John, 187
Faure, Joseph, 187
Faure, Judith, 187
Fauré, Marie, 202
Faure, Mary, 187
Faure, Peter, 187
Faure, Pierre, 187
Fauré, Pierre, 13
Fauré/Ford, Judith, 202
Fauré/Ford, Pierre/Peter, 202
Fayen, Abraham, 160
Fayen, Anne, 160
Fayen, Pierre de, 160
FAYSSOUX/FOISSEAU, Daniel, 188
Fayssoux/Foisseau, Mary Ann, 188
Fayssoux/Foisseau, Peter, 188
Fearn, John, 272
Fearn, Leeanna (Lee), 272
Fearn, Thomas, 272
Felgate, Roger Capt., 352
Felgate, Sybilla (X), 352
Fell, Katherine, 323
Fender, Anna Maria, 314
Fenelon, Elizabeth, 189
Fenelon, Marquis Bertrand, 189
Fenne, Otto, 190
Fenne, Rebecca, 69
Fennel, Tobias, 190
Feree, Marie (de la Warenbuer), 307

Feree/Fierre, Abraham, 192
Feret, Givonne Marie, 92
Feret/Ferre/Ferry, Antoine, 189
Feret/Ferre/Ferry, Charles, 188
Feret/Ferre/Ferry, Christophe, 189
FERET/FERRÉ/FERRY, Christophle/Christophe, 188
Feret/Ferre/Ferry, Elizabeth, 189
Feret/Ferre/Ferry, Jacques, 189
Feret/Ferre/Ferry, Jean, 189
Feret/Ferre/Ferry, Jean/John, 188
Feret/Ferre/Ferry, Jeanne, 189
Feret/Ferre/Ferry, Marguerite, 188
Feret/Ferre/Ferry, Marie, 188
Feret/Ferre/Ferry, Nicolas, 189
Feret/Ferre/Ferry, Pierre, 188
Feret/Ferre/Ferry, Samuel, 189
Feret/Ferre/Ferry, Sara, 188
Feret/Ferre/Ferry, Vincent, 189
Ferguson, Nancy, 405
Fernald, Edward, 190
Fernald, Elizabeth, 190
Fernald, Henry, 190
Fernald, John, 190
Fernald, Joseph, 190
Fernald, Mary, 190
Fernald, Renald/Reginald, 189
Fernald, Robert, 190
Fernald, Samuel, 190
Fernald, Sarah, 190
Fernald, Strong/Strongue, 190
Fernald, Temperance, 190
Fernald, Thomas, 190
Fernald, William, 190
Fernalius, Nicholas, 190
Fernand, Mousse, 379
Fernel, Jean, 189
Fernel, Magdalene (Luillier), 189
Fernel/Fernald, Ann, 190
Fernel/Fernald, Francis, 190
FERNEL/FERNALD, François Junius (Rev., 189
Fernel/Fernald, Jean, 189
Fernel/Fernald, Magdalen, 190
Fernel/Fernald, Margaret, 190
Fernel/Fernald, Maria, 190
Fernel/Fernald, William, 189
Fernelion, Bertrand, 190
Fernell, Henriette Catherine, 190
FERNEY/FERNAY/FORNEY/FARNEY (Pierre, Chevalier de), 191
Ferney/Fernay/Forney/Farney, Jacob, 191
Ferrabosco, Alphonse, 286
Ferrée, Anna Maria (Leininger) Ferree, 307
Ferree, Anna Marie (Leininger), 192
Ferrée, Daniel, 149, 152, 307
Ferrée, Daniel II, 192
Ferree, Elisabeth[3], 192
Ferrée, Elizabeth, 192, 307

Ferree, Jacob, 192
Ferrée, Jacob, 193
Ferrée, Joel, 192
Ferree, Leah (DuBois), 192
Ferrée, Lydia, 192, 307
Ferrée, Marie (de la Warenbuer), 149, 152
Ferrée, Mary (Copeland), 192
Ferrée, Philip, 149, 152
Ferree, Philip[2], 192
Ferrée, Rachel, 192
Ferrée, Susan (Green), 193
FERRÉE/ Fier(r)e, Daniel, 191
Ferree/Fierre, Andrew, 192
Ferree/Fierre, Catherine, 192
Ferree/Fierre, Daniel II, 192
Ferree/Fierre, Daniel III, 192
Ferree/Fierre, Elisabeth, 192
Ferree/Fierre, Elizabeth, 192
Ferree/Fierre, Isaac, 192
Ferree/Fierre, Jacob, 192
Ferree/Fierre, Jane, 192
Ferree/Fierre, Joel, 193
Ferree/Fierre, John, 192, 193
Ferree/Fierre, Joseph, 192
Ferree/Fierre, Leah, 193
Ferree/Fierre, Lydia, 192
Ferree/Fierre, Magdalena, 192
Ferree/Fierre, Marie/Mary, 192
Ferree/Fierre, Philip, 192, 193
Ferree/Fierre, Rachel, 193
Ferrée/Fuehre, Catherine, 307
Ferri, Marguerite, 151
Ferris, John, 225
Feurt, Bartholomew, 386
Feurt, Francis, 386
Feurt, Magdalena, 386
Feurt, Margaret, 386
Feurt, Pierre/Peter, 386
Fickling, Samuell, 104
Field, Abraham II, 429
Field, Ambrose, 146
Field, Eleanor, 429
Field, Elizabeth Mrs., 212
Field, John, 231
Field, Molly, 327
Fielding, Elizabeth, 429
Fields, Samuel, 197
Fields, Sarah, 197
Fiery, Catherine, 19
Filchett, Alexander, 439
Fillelen, Joannen, 190
Filley, Margaret (X), 222
Filley, William, 222
Filley,Samuel, 222
Fine, Hannah, 302
Fine, Mercy, 302
Finley, Ann (O/Neill), 331
Finley, Michael, 331
Fioen, Meyndrick Antheuniss, 440
Firmin, Catherine, 435

Fiscus, Anna Cunigunda, 243
Fish, Samuel, 53
Fishback, Elizabeth (Heimback), 351
Fishback, Philip, 351
Fisher, Eleanor (Archibald), 284
Fisher, John, 376
Fisher, Samuel, 284
Fisher, William, 284
Fiske, unknown, 282
Fitch, Marianne, 193
Fitch, Mary/Marianne, 388
Fitch, Tobias, 193
Fitch, William D., 51
FitzRandolph, Benjamin, 345
FitzRandolph, Nathaniel, 345
FitzRandolph, Sarah (Dennis), 345
Flaesbeek, Fiammetia/Phebe van, 198
Flamegh/Flamen, Mary, 409
Flamen, Abraham, 119
Flamen, Antoine, 119
Flanders, William, 339
Flandreau, Adam, 304
Flandreau, Peter, 304
Fleming, Catherine, 310
Fleming, Charles, 89
Fleming, Elizabeth, 89, 133
Fleming, Susanna (Tarlton), 89
Fleming, William Col., 327
Fletcher, Elizabeth, 213
Fletcher, Mary, 85
Fleuriau, Daniel, 104
Fleuriau, Marie (X), 104
Fleuriau, Marquise, 104, 298
Fleuriau, Pierre, 104
Fleuriau, Prégéante/Bridget, 104
FLEURISSON, Renatus, 392
Fleury, (**Damaris) Marianne**, 193
Fleury, Abraham, 28, 161
FLEURY, Abraham, Sieur de la Plaine, 193
Fleury, Charles, 193
Fleury, Isaac, 193
Fleury, Louis, 157
Fleury, Louis Rev., 157
Fleury, Madeleine (Soupzmain/Soubmain), 193
Fleury, Marianne, 161
Fleury, Pierre, 157
Flick, Catherine, 249
Flocquet, Simon, 204
Flourney/Flournoy, André, 195
Flourney/Flournoy, Anne, 196
Flourney/Flournoy, Anne-Gabrielle, 195
Flourney/Flournoy, Claude, 193
Flourney/Flournoy, David, 195
Flourney/Flournoy, Délie, 194
Flourney/Flournoy, Élisabeth, 194, 195
Flourney/Flournoy, Esaïe, 195, 196
Flourney/Flournoy, Esther, 194
Flourney/Flournoy, Francis, 195
Flourney/Flournoy, Françoise, 195

Flourney/Flournoy, Gabriel, 195
Flourney/Flournoy, Gédéon, 194, 195
Flourney/Flournoy, Henry, 195
Flourney/Flournoy, Jacob, 195
Flourney/Flournoy, Jacques, 194, 195
Flourney/Flournoy, Jean, 194
Flourney/Flournoy, Jean Jacques/John James, 195
Flourney/Flournoy, Jeanne, 194
Flourney/Flournoy, Jeanne-Françoise, 195
Flourney/Flournoy, Jeanne-Marie, 194, 195
Flourney/Flournoy, Judith, 195
Flourney/Flournoy, Julie, 195
FLOURNEY/FLOURNOY, Laurent, 193
Flourney/Flournoy, Magdalene, 195
Flourney/Flournoy, Marguerite, 195
Flourney/Flournoy, Marie, 194, 195
Flourney/Flournoy, Michel, 194
Flourney/Flournoy, Mie, 194
Flourney/Flournoy, Nicolas, 193
Flourney/Flournoy, Rachel, 195
Flourney/Flournoy, Sara, 194
Flourney/Flournoy, Susanna, 196
Flournoy, Jacob, 468
Flournoy, unknown, **50**
Flucker, Thomas, **37**
Focken, Gerrit Cornelissen, 153
Focken, Tryntje Gerritsen, 153
Fogg, Anna (Hanscom), 348
Fogg, Betsy, 339
Fogg, Daniel, 348
Fogg, Polly, 339
Fogg, Ruth (Lane), 339
Fogg, Samuel, 339, 348
Foissen, Marie, 372
Foissin, Élie/Elias, 28
Foissin, Louise (Frisselle), 28
Foissin, Rebecca, 28
Foix, Gaston IX de, 217
Foix, Jean/Gion de, 217
Folkers, Jannetje, 48
Folkers, Johannes, 48
Fongallon, Anna Elizabeth, 292
Fonnereau, Françoise Élisabeth, **47**
Fontaine, Aaron, 271
Fontaine, Anne, 271
Fontaine, Anne Élisabeth (Boursiquot), 355
Fontaine, Elizabeth, 271, 272
Fontaine, Esther, 271
Fontaine, Francis, 271, 272
Fontaine, Jacques II, 270
Fontaine, Jacques/James III, 271
Fontaine, James, 131, 271, 355
Fontaine, Jane, 271
Fontaine, John, 271
Fontaine, Judith, 271
Fontaine, Marie de, 160
Fontaine, Marie/Mary, 271

Fontaine, Mary Anne, 271
Fontaine, Moses, 272
Fontaine, Peter, 271
Fontaine, Susanne, 271
Fontfroide, Antoine de, 426
Fonvielle, Jean, 196
Fonvielle, Marguerite (Nouvel), 196
FONVIELLE/FONVEILLE /FONVILLE, Jean/John, 196
Fonvielle/Fonveille/Fonville, Anne, 197
Fonvielle/Fonveille/Fonville, Cornelius, 197
Fonvielle/Fonveille/Fonville, David, 197
Fonvielle/Fonveille/Fonville, Elizabeth, 196
Fonvielle/Fonveille/Fonville, Esther, 197
Fonvielle/Fonveille/Fonville, Francis Marion, 196
Fonvielle/Fonveille/Fonville, Frederick, 196
Fonvielle/Fonveille/Fonville, Isaac, 197
Fonvielle/Fonveille/Fonville, Jeremiah, 197
Fonvielle/Fonveille/Fonville, John, 196
Fonvielle/Fonveille/Fonville, Mary, 196
Fonvielle/Fonveille/Fonville, Peter, 197
Fonvielle/Fonveille/Fonville, Priscilla, 197
Fonvielle/Fonveille/Fonville, Stephen, 196
Fonvielle/Fonveille/Fonville, Thomas, 197
Fonvielle/Fonveille/Fonville, William Brice, 196
Fooks, Sarah, 25
Foquan, Eva Jeanne, 151
Forbush, Elizabeth, 192
Force, Hannah, 377
Forche, Théophite, 54
Forcuron, Moses, 351
Ford, Daniel, 187
Ford, Martha, 254
Ford, Mary, 202
Ford, Pierre, 187
Ford, Sarah, 244
Ford, unknown, 402
Ford/Fauré, Mary/Marie (Elizabeth ?), 13
Ford/Foure, James/Jacques, 13
Fordham, Abraham, 288
Fordham, Annie, 288
Fordham, Benjamin, 288
Fordham, Benjamin, Jr, 288
Fordham, Martha, 288
Fordham, Richard, 396
Fore/Foree, Peter, 187
Foree, Joseph, 220
Forest, Barent de, 57
Forest, Catalina (Sarley) de, 57
Forest, Catharine de, 57
Forest, Cornelia de, 57
Forest, Elizabeth (Ver Duyn), 57

Forest, Henri de, 198
Forest, Isaac de, 177
Forest, Jesse de, 177
Forest, Marie (du Cloux) de, 177
Forest, Marie (X) de, 198
Forest, Michel de, 198
Forestier, Janette, 271
Forestier, Peter Rev., 271
Forestier/Forestière, T(h)omasa, 238
Forêt, Catherine (Du Fosset) de, 197
Forêt, Melchoir II de, 197
FORÊT/FOREST, Jean/Jehan de, 197
Foret/Forest, Anne de, 198
Foret/Forest, Crispin de, 198
Foret/Forest, David de, 198
Foret/Forest, Elizabeth de, 198
Foret/Forest, Gérard de, 198
Foret/Forest, Henri de, 198
Foret/Forest, Henry/Hendrick de, 198
Foret/Forest, Isaac de, 198
Foret/Forest, Israel de, 198
Foret/Forest, Jean, 197
Foret/Forest, Jean de, 197
Foret/Forest, Jeanne de, 198
Foret/Forest, Jesse, 197
Foret/Forest, Jesse de, 198
Forêt/Forest, Jesse de, 278
Forêt/Forest, Marie (du Cloux) de, 278
Foret/Forest, Marie de, 197
Forêt/Forest, Marie de, 278
Foret/Forest, Michel/Melchior de, 198
Foret/Forest, Nicaise de, 198
Foret/Forest, Philippe de, 198
Foret/Forest, Rachel de, 198
Forêt/Forest, Rachel de, 278
Forge, Abeltje de, 322
Forman, Eleanor, 206
Forney, Abram, 191
Forney, Catherine, 191
Forney, Christina, 191
Forney, Elizabeth, 191, 279
Forney, Elizabeth (Sherz), 279
Forney, Eve, 191
Forney, Hannah, 279
Forney, Jacob, 191
Forney, Peter, 191
Forney, Philip, 279
Forney, Susannah/Susan, 191
Forreau, Elizabeth, 271
Fort, Anna, 49
Fortineux, Jean Henri, 199
Fortineux, Jean Henry, 199
Fortineux, Jean Jacob, 199
FORTINEUX, Jonas, 199
Fortineux, Jonas Peter, 199
Fortineux, Marie Margarite, 199
Fortineux, Marie Rosine, 199
Fortney, (John) Hendrick/Henry, 199
Fortney, Charity (Charlotte), 199
Fortney, Christina, 199
Fortney, Daniel, 199

Fortney, David, 199
Fortney, Peter, 199
Fortney, Susanna (Catherine) Catarina, 199
Fosdick, Margaret, 341
Fosler, George, 150
Foster, John, 62
Foster, Judith/Juda, 64
Foster, Peter/Pierre, 62
Foster, Stephen, 62
Fosuur/Foshay, Eliezabet/Elizabeth, 431
Foüace, Charles, 200
Fouace, Jean, 200
Fouace, Jeanne (X), 200
Foüace, Stephen, 200
FOUACE/FOUASSE, Gabriel, 200
Fouace/Fouasse, Sarah, 200
Foucault, Hector, 28
FOUCHÉ (E)/FAUCHÉ/FOUSHEE, Jean/John, 201
Fouche(e)/Fauche/Foushee, Benjamin, 201
Fouche(e)/Fauche/Foushee, Charles, 201
Fouche(e)/Fauche/Foushee, Elijah, 201
Fouche(e)/Fauche/Foushee, Elizabeth, 201
Fouche(e)/Fauche/Foushee, George, 201
Fouche(e)/Fauche/Foushee, Hannah, 201
Fouche(e)/Fauche/Foushee, Jeminah, 201
Fouche(e)/Fauche/Foushee, John.
Fouche(e)/Fauche/Foushee, Joseph, 201
Fouche(e)/Fauche/Foushee, Nathaniel, 201
Fouche(e)/Fauche/Foushee, Thornton, 201
Fouche(e)/Fauche/Foushee, William, 201
FOUCHÉ(E)/FOUSHEE, Jacques/James, 200
Fouche(e)/Foushee, Charlotte, 200, 201
Fouche(e)/Foushee, Elizabeth, 201
Fouche(e)/Foushee, John, 200
Fouche(e)/Foushee, Mary, 201
Fouche(e)/Foushee, Susannah, 200
Fouche(e)/Foushee, William, 201
Fouchereau, Sara, 396
Fougère, Isabeau, 295
Fouke, Eleanor, 210
Fountain, James, 414
Fountain, John, 95
Fountaine, Andrew, 202
Fountaine, Anne, 202
Fountaine, Bridget, 202
Fountaine, Collier, 202
Fountaine, Dennis (Denise), 202
Fountaine, John, 202
Fountaine, Mary, 202
Fountaine, Mercy, 202
Fountaine, Mercy/Marcy, 202

Fountaine, Nicholas, 202
FOUNTAINE, Nicolas (alias WICART), 202
Fountaine, Prudence, 202
Fountaine, Samuel, 202
Fountaine, Stephen, 202
Fountaine, William, 202
Fouquet/Fuqua(y), Giles, 202
FOUQUET/FUQUA(Y), Guillaume, 202
Fouquet/Fuqua(y), Joseph, 202
Fouquet/Fuqua(y), Ralph, 203
Fouquet/Fuqua(y), William, 202
Four/Fore, John, 351
Fourgéaud, Genevieve, 265
Fourgéaud, Joseph, 265
Fourni, Sieur de, 290
Fournier, Anne, 160
Fourqueran, Jean, 166
Fourqueran/Forqueraan(d)/Forcuron, Peter, 203
Fourqueran/Forqueran(d)/ Forcuron, Elizabeth/Betty, 203
Fourqueran/Forqueran(d)/Forcuron, Elizabeth, 203
Fourqueran/Forqueran(d)/Forcuron, Janne, 203
Fourqueran/Forqueran(d)/Forcuron, Jean/John, 203
FOURQUERAN/FORQUERAN(D)/FORCURON, Jean/John, 203
Fourqueran/Forqueran(d)/Forcuron, John, 203
Fourqueran/Forqueran(d)/Forcuron, Moses, 203
Fourqueran/Forqueran(d)/Forcuron, Peter, 203
Foushee, James, 200
Foushee, Susan, 201
Fowle, John Lt. Col., 108
Fowle, Paulina Adelina, 108
Fox, Henry, 300
Fox, Henry III, 418
Fox, Mary (Goodwyn), 418
Fox, Unity, 418
Foxe, Thomas, 286
Frache, Louisa, 120
Fragée;Forgée, unknown, 448
Fraissinet, David, 107
France, François de, 315
France, Louis de, 315
Frances, Jeanne, 159
Franchimont, Marie de, 214
Francis, Mary, 25
François I, 270
François II, 270
François, Catharina, 369
François, Jean, 369
François, Susanna, 467
Françoise, 96, 171, 257, 299, 417
Frank, Anne, 239
Frans, Jannetje, 159
Fransz, Joost, 409

Frantz, Angelica, 151
Frantz, Barbary, 204
Frantz, Catarina, 204
Frantz, Elizabeth, 204
Frantz, Jacob, 204
Frantz, Johann Jacob, 204
Frantz, Johann Paulus/Paul Jr, 204
Frantz, John, 204
Frantz, John George, 204
Frantz, John K, 204
Frantz, Ludwig, 204
Frantz, Madland, 204
Frantz, Mary, 204
Frantz, Michael, 204
Frantz, Nancy, 204
Frantz, Nicholas, 204
Frantz, Paulus, 204
FRANTZ, Paulus/Paul, 204
Frantz, Philip, 204
Frantz, Sarah, 204
Frantz, Susanna, 204
Frantz, Tobias, 204
Frasey/Frazee, Joseph, 366
Frazier, Samuel, 433
Frederick, Jeremiah, 320
Frederick, Margaret (Becker), 19
Frederick, Mary, 320
Frederick, Noah, 19
Freeborne, John, 465
Freeman, unknown, 366
Freer, Abraham, 301
Freer, Abram, 301
Freer, Catrina, 308
Freer, Hugo, 308, 319
Freer, Marie (Haye), 320
Freer, Marie (Le Roy), 308
Freer, Marit/Maritjen, 308
Freer/Frere, Abraham, 205
Freer/Frere, Blandina, 205
Freer/Frere, Catrina, 205
Freer/Frere, Elizabeth, 205
Freer/Frere, Hester, 205
Freer/Frere, Hugo, 205
FREER/FRÈRE, Hugo/Hugues, 204
Freer/Frere, Hugues/Hugo, 205
Freer/Frere, Isaac, 205
Freer/Frere, Jacob, 205
Freer/Frere, Jannetie, 205
Freer/Frere, Jean/John, 205
Freer/Frere, Jonas, 205
Freer/Frere, Joseph, 205
Freer/Frere, Marie, 205
Freer/Frere, Rachel, 205
Freer/Frere, Rebecca, 205
Freer/Frere, Sara, 205
Freer/Frere, Sarah, 205
Freer/Frere, Simon, 205
Freer/Frere,Marie/Mary, 205
Freesers, George, 259
Freest, David De, 198
Freest, Gerrit De, 198

Freest, Hendrick De, 198
Freest, Isaac De, 198
Freest, Jesse De, 198
Freest, John De, 198
Freest, Maria De, 198
Freest, Marie De, 198
Freest, Michael De, 198
Freest, Philip De, 198
Freest, Susannah De, 198
Fremeau, Marie (Jery), 314
Fremor, Isaac, 315
Fremor/Fremeau/Fourmeau, Jeanne (Du Four), 315
French, Abigail (Hubbell), 340
French, Elizabeth (X), 70, 412
French, Francis, 70
French, Gamakill, 340
French, James, 412
French, Jane, 412
French, Rhoda, 340
French, Samuel, 340
French, Sarah, 340
French, William, 70
Freneau, Philip Morin, 205
Frere/Frere, Maria, 205
Fresneau, Andre, 13, 368
Fresneau, André, 206
FRESNEAU, André, 205
Fresneau, François, 206
Fresneau, Jacques, 205
Fresneau, Jean, 205
Fresneau, Marguerite, 206
Fresneau, Marie, 206
Fresneau, Philip P., 205
Fresneau, Pierre, 206
Fresneau, Thomas Louis, 206
Frey, Abraham, 206
Frey, Amelia Elizabeth, 206
Frey, Anna (Hirtzeller), 206
Frey, Anna Catherine (Levering), 55
Frey, Anna Veronica (Merkle), 55
Frey, Benjamin, 206
Frey, Elizabeth, 206
Frey, George, 206
Frey, Heinrich, 55
FREY, Heinrich, 206
Frey, Henry, 206, 446
Frey, Jacob, 55, 206
Frey, John, 206
Frey, Rebecca, 206
Frey, William, 55, 206
Frink, Samuel, 46
Frith, Mary, 462
Fritz, Henrich, 30
Frost, Thomas, 312
Froumi, Jean, 92
Fruibeau, Anna, 30
Fry, Joshua Col., 364
Fry, Mary E., 391
Frye, John C., 138
Fuller, Sarah, 352

514

Fuller, Thomas, 255
Fuller, William Capt., 352
Fullerton, Catherine, 427
Fullerton, John, 427
Fullerton, Mary, 427
Fumé, Daniel, 29
Fumé, David, 406
Fumé, Ester (Herault), 29
Fumé, Esther (Herault), 406
Fumé, Jeanne, 406
Fuqua, Elizabeth (X), 187
Fuqua, William, 187
Furkerin (Fourqueran), Peter, 166
Furnas, Alexander, 190
Furnieu, Daniel, 190
Furnival, Joanna, 190
Furnival, Thomas, 190

G

G'Fellern/Gefaeller, Johannes, 120
Ga(i)neau/Geneau/Gano, Daniel, 210
GA(I)NEAU/GENEAU/GANO, Étienne, 210
Ga(i)neau/Geneau/Gano, Francis, 210
Ga(i)neau/Geneau/Gano, James, 210
Ga(i)neau/Geneau/Gano, Lidie Marie, 210
Ga(i)neau/Geneau/Gano, Louis, 210
Ga(i)neau/Geneau/Gano, Marie Madeleine/Mary, 210
Ga(i)neau/Geneau/Gano, Sarah, 210
Ga(i)neau/Geneau/Gano, Stephen Jr., 210
Ga(i)neau/Geneau/Gano, Susanna, 210
GABEAU, Anthon, 207
Gabeau, Anthony, 207
Gabeau, Benjamin, 207
Gabeau, Daniel, 207
Gabeau, Elizabeth, 207
Gabeau, James, 207
Gabeau, John, 207
Gabeau, Mary Hannah, 207
Gabeau, Pierre Antoine, 207
Gabeau, Samuel, 207
Gabeau, Simon, 207
Gabeau, Susannah, 207
Gabourel, Joshua, 237
Gabriel, Rachel, 191
Gaches, Charlotte Mary, 435
Gachet/Gashet, Abigail, 207
Gachet/Gashet, Daniel, 207
Gachet/Gashet, David, 207
Gachet/Gashet, Elizabeth, 208
Gachet/Gashet, Hannah, 207
GACHET/GASHET, Henri/Henry, 207
Gachet/Gashet, Isaac, 208
Gachet/Gashet, Martha, 207
Gachet/Gashet, Mercy, 207
Gachet/Gashet, Sarah, 207
Gachet/Gashet, Susannah, 208

Gachot, Étienne, 271
Gagné, Joachim, 141
Gagné, Louise (Marcoux), 141
Gaier, Angelica, 81
Gaillard, Alcimus, 208
Gaillard, Bartholomew, 208
Gaillard, Elizabeth, 208, 322
Gaillard, Elizabeth Mary/Eliza, 127
Gaillard, Ester, 279
Gaillard, Esther, 208, 322
Gaillard, Frederick, 208
Gaillard, Hélène/Eleanor, 208
Gaillard, Jean, 208, 321
GAILLARD, Jean/Jehan, 208
Gaillard, Jean/John, 208
Gaillard, Joachim, 208, 321
Gaillard, John, 208, 322
Gaillard, Marguerite, 208
Gaillard, Marie, 208
Gaillard, Pierre, 208
Gaillard, Pierre/Pierre, 208
Gaillard, Simond, 208
Gaillard, Susanne, 208, 322
Gaillard, Tacitus, 208
Gaillard, Theodore, 208
GAILLARD/GAYLORD, Nic(h)olas II, 209
Gaillardy, Louis de, 156
Gaillare, Esther (Peperel/Paparel), 321
Gaineau, Étienne, 210
Gaines, unknown, 181
Galbraith, Hugh, 391
Galiard, Nicolas I, 209
Gallahue/Gallahough, Darby, 56
Gallais, Marie, 462
Gallaudet, David, 211
Gallaudet, Elisha, 211
Gallaudet, Hester, 211
Gallaudet, Jean, 211
Gallaudet, Joshua, 211
Gallaudet, Leah, 211
Gallaudet, Margaret (Prioleau), 211
Gallaudet, Paul, 211
Gallaudet, Peter, 211
GALLAUDET, Pierre Elisée, 211
Gallaudet, Susanna, 211
Gallaudet, Thomas, 211
Galliardello, Anthony, 286
Galliardello, Frances, 286
Galliardello, Margerie (Galliardello), 286
Gallihaut, Marie, 20
Gallois, Comte, 246
Gallois, Marie, 246
Galman, unknown, 199
Gando, Barthelémie (Morel), 194
Gando, Étienne, 194
Gando, Marie, 194
Gando, Sibois, 194
Gandovin, Ann (Pleasant), 13
Gandovin, Isaac, 13
Gannugh, Jeremiah, 210
Gano, Mary, 210

Gar(r)ard, Anthony, 213
Gar(r)ard, Daniel, 213
Gar(r)ard, Eleanor, 213
Gar(r)ard, Henry, 213
Gar(r)ard, James, 213
Gar(r)ard, Mary Anne, 213
GAR(R)ARD, Pierre/Peter, 213
Gar(r)ard, Robert, 213
Gar(r)ard, William, 213
Garcelon, Daniel, 212
Garcelon, James, 211, 212
Garcelon, Louise, 211
Garcelon, Lucy, 212
Garcelon, Mark, 212
Garcelon, Peter, 212
GARCELON, Pierre, 211
Garcelon, Sally, 212
Garcelon, William, 212
Garcia, Francis, 397
Garden, Alexander, 232
Gardié/Gardier, Marie, 168
Gardiner, Sarah, 386
Gardner, Anne Eliza, 108
Gardner, Charles, 108
Gardner, Constance Tabor, 108
Gardner, William Collins, 108
Gardner, William Fowler, 108
Gargotin, Françoise (Bernard), 387
Gargotin, Jacques, 387
Gargotin, Louise, 387
Garillion, Isreal, 84, 387
Garillion, Madeleine, 387
Garillion, Susanne (Saunier), 387
Garland, Marie/Mary, 14
Garland, Nathaniel, 23
Garlard, Joan/Jane, 209
Garlington, Christopher, 201
Garlington, Elizabeth (Conway), 201
Garner, Elizabeth, 64
Garner, Joseph, 64
Garner, unknown, 397
Garnier, Anne, 212, 213
Garnier, Daniel, 167, 212, 245
GARNIER, Daniel, 212
Garnier, Elizabeth, 212, 213, 245
Garnier, Elizabeth (Fanton), 167
Garnier, Étienne/Stephen, 212
Garnier, François, 213
Garnier, Isaac, 212, 213
GARNIER, Isaac, 212
Garnier, Jean, 213
Garnier, Louis, 213
Garnier, Marguerite, 212
Garnier, Marie, 212
Garnier, Marie (Chevallier), 212
Garnier, Rachel, 212
Garnier, Sarah, 167
Garnier, Susanne, 213
Garnier/Garnié/Garnée, Jeanne, 151
Garrett, Rachel, 327
Garrett, unknown, 327

Garrett/Garrott, John, 17
Garrigues, Abraham, 214
Garrigues, Anne, 215
Garrigues, Antoine, 215
Garrigues, Antoine-Henri, 215
Garrigues, Charles-George-Ferdinand, 215
Garrigues, Charlotte- Frédéric, 215
Garrigues, Dauphine, 215
Garrigues, Elizabeth, 214, 215
Garrigues, Étienne, 215
Garrigues, Francis, 214
Garrigues, François, 214
Garrigues, François Philippe, 214
Garrigues, Guillaume, 215
Garrigues, Hannah, 214
Garrigues, Isaac, 214
Garrigues, Jacob, 214
Garrigues, Jacques, 215
GARRIGUES, Jacques, 214
Garrigues, Jacques-Louis, 215
Garrigues, Jean, 214, 215
Garrigues, Jean-Antoine-Henri, 215
Garrigues, Jean-Claude, 215
Garrigues, Jean-Frédéric, 215
Garrigues, Jeanne, 215
Garrigues, John, 214
Garrigues, Judith, 215
Garrigues, Justine-Élisabeth, 215
Garrigues, Justine-Marguerite, 215
Garrigues, Margaret Jeanne, 214
Garrigues, Marie, 215
Garrigues, Marthe, 215
Garrigues, Mary, 214
Garrigues, Mathurin, 214
Garrigues, Matthew, 214
Garrigues, Moyse, 214, 215
Garrigues, Pierre, 214
Garrigues, Rachel, 214
Garrigues, Samuel, 214
Garrigues, Sarah, 214
Garrigues, Susanna, 214
Garrillion, Susanne (Saunier), 84
Garris, Susannah, 167
Garrison, Beverly/Bavil, 216
Garrison, Catherine (de Romagnac), 215
Garrison, David, 216
Garrison, Isaac, 215, 216
GARRISON, Isaac, 215
Garrison, James, 216
Garrison, Jan Gerrits, 129
Garrison, Joseph, 215
Garrison, Moses, 216
Garrison, Oliver, 216
Garrison, Richard Major, 225
Gasherie, Mary,, 379
Gaspard, Admiral, 189
Gaspard, Pierre, 333
Gasque, Marguerite de, 252
Gasset, Élisabeth (Coustardeur), 230
Gastineau, Elizabeth, 216, 379

Gastineau, George Lewis, 216
Gastineau, Jane, 216
Gastineau, Jean, 216
Gastineau, Job, 216
Gastineau, Louis Salomon, 216
Gastineau, Magdeleine, 216
Gastineau, Marguerite, 216
Gastineau, Marie, 216
Gastineau, Mary, 216
Gastineau, Matharin, 216
Gastineau, Olivier, 216
Gastineau, Pierre, 216
GASTINEAU, Pierre, 216
Gastineau, Tabitha, 216
Gaston, Alexander, 217, 218
Gaston, Ann, 218
Gaston, Elizabeth, 217
Gaston, Hugh, 217, 218
Gaston, James, 217, 218
Gaston, Jane, 217
GASTON, Jean, 217
Gaston, Jean/John, 217
Gaston, Jennet/Janet/Jinny, 217
Gaston, John, 217, 218
Gaston, Joseph, 217, 218
Gaston, Margaret, 218
Gaston, Martha, 217, 218
Gaston, Mary, 217
Gaston, Matthew, 217
Gaston, Purcilla, 218
Gaston, Robert, 217, 218
Gaston, William, 217, 218
Gaulthier, Amata, 244
GAURY/GUERRI/GOREE/GORY, Jean/John, 219
Gause, Elizabeth (Hankin), 45
Gause, Martha (Frink), 45
Gause, Mary, 45
Gause, unknown, 45
Gause, William Bacot, 45
Gautier, Elizabeth, 64
Gautier, Jeanne, 63
Gauvain, Charlotte, 379
Gauwin, Marie, 187
Gaylard, Agnes, 209
Gaylard, Alice, 209
Gaylard, Alice/Alis, 209
Gaylard, Antis, 209
Gaylard, Catherine, 209
Gaylard, Christopher, 209
Gaylard, Ede/Edith, 209
Gaylard, Edmund, 209
Gaylard, Elizabeth, 209
Gaylard, George, 209
Gaylard, Honor, 210
Gaylard, Hugh, 209
Gaylard, Joan, 209
Gaylard, John, 209
Gaylard, Mary, 209
Gaylard, Richard, 209
Gaylard, Robert, 210

Gaylard, Valentine, 210
Gaylard, William, 209
Gayle, Ann, 24
Gaylord, Luce, 209
Gayneau, Étienne, 210
Gazeau, Catherine, 160
Gazeau, Jean, 160
Geiselman, Eva, 370
Geiselman, Margaret (X), 370
Geiselman, Michael, 370
Gelder, Jacobus Everse Van, 467
Gelder, Mary Van, 452
Gelton, Rachel(le), 126
Gendron, Elizabeth, 208, 247
Gendron, Elizabeth (Mazyck), 208
Gendron, John, 208
Gendron, Ma(g)deleine (Chardon) Pasquereau, 402
Gendron, Magdalen (X), 248
Gendron, Magdelaine (Cardon), 398
Gendron, Mary Magdelen, 186, 402
Gendron, Philip, 248, 398
Gendron, Philippe, 186, 402
Gendron, Philippe Capt., 422
Geneau, Marie, 210
Gennes, Marguerite de, 156
Gennes, Marie de, 156
Gentle, Isaac Perrot, 345
Gentle, Judith Marie (Jacob), 345
George, Joseph, 266
Ger(r)ard, Jacob, 214
Ger(r)ard, John, 213
Gérard, Jean, 92, 380
Gérard, Susanne, 92
Gerard, Thomas, 236
Gérard. Jeanne (d'Orleans), 92
Gerber/Tanner, Robert, 85
Gerin, Judith, 233
Geringer, Anna Elisabetha, 140
Geringer, Jacob, 140
Geringer, Susanna (Glatt), 140
Germaine, Margaret, 108
Germaine, Mary, 437
Germon, Marie, 122
Germon/Germaine, Jean, 108
Gerneau, Étienne, 210
Gerneau, Francis, 210
Gerneau, Jeremiah, 210
Gerneau, Mary, 210
Gernes, Jacques, 92
GEROULD, see JERAULD, 219
Gerow, Benjamin, 226
Gerow, Daniel, 226
Gerow, Jannetie, 226
Gerow, Lea, 226
Gerow, Maria, 226
Gerow, Tryntie, 226
Gerow/Giraud, Daniel III, 128
Gerri/Gerry, James, 234
Gerrits, Annatjie Hoogland, 205
Gerrits, Chieltie, 153

Gerrits, Lysbeth, 150
Gerritsen, Alche/Olive, 129
Gerritsen, Gysbert, 122
Gerritsen, Lubbert, 105
Gerritsen, Willem, 122
Gerritszen, Barent, 296
Gerritz, Gerritie, 404
Gertier/Gorlier/Gortier, Marie, 449
Geste, Jan Janse Van, 15
Gévaudan, Antoine, 434
Gévaudan, Elizabeth, 434
Gévaudan, Thomas, 352
Gevaudan/Givaudan, Ann, 220
GÉVAUDAN/GIVAUDAN, Antoine, 219
Gevaudan/Givaudan, Elizabeth, 220
Gevaudan/Givaudan, Jean/John, 220
Gevaudan/Givaudan, John, 220
Gevaudan/Givaudan, Joseph, 220
Gevaudan/Givaudan, Thomas, 220
Gevedon/Gévaudan, Judith (Martain), 115
Gevedon/Gévaudan, Thomas, 115
Gex, David Louis, 461
Gex, Victoire Helvetia, 461
Ghieslin, William, 220
GHISELIN, César, 220
Ghiselin, Hannah, 220
Ghiselin, Jean, 220
Ghiselin, Mary Catherine, 220
Ghiselin, Nicholas, 220
Ghiselin, Reverdy, 220
Ghiselin, Septima, 220
Ghiselin, William, 220
Ghiselin,William, 220
Ghislein, Nicholas, 220
Gibbs, Daniel Capt., 211
Gibbs, Joseph, 234
Gibert, Jean Louis Rev., 368, 425
Gibert, Pierre, 221
GIBERT, Pierre/Peter, 221
Gibson, Mary, 195
Gidding, Bartholomew, 210
Giddins, unknown, 49
Giger, Jacob, 259
Gignilliant, Jean François, 208
Gignilliat, Abraham, 321, 322
GIGNILLIAT, Abraham, 221
Gignilliat, Benjamin, 222
Gignilliat, Étienne, 222
Gignilliat, François/Francis, 322
Gignilliat, Gaspard, 221
Gignilliat, Henri/Henry, 321
Gignilliat, Henry, 348
Gignilliat, James, 65, 167, 322
Gignilliat, Jean François, 167, 222, 321, 348
Gignilliat, Jean Louis, 222
Gignilliat, Madeleine, 222
Gignilliat, Marie (de Ville), 321
Gignilliat, Marie Elizabeth/Mary, 321
Gignilliat, Pierre/Peter, 321

Gignilliat, Stephe (Seigneux), 221
Gignilliat, Susanne, 322
Gignilliat, Susanne (Le Serrurier), 167
Gignilliat, Susanne (leSerrurier), 348
Gignon, Jean, 155
Gignon, Marie, 155
Giguilliat, Judith, 222
Giguilliat, Susanne (LeSerrurier), 208
Gilbert, Clement, 221
Gilbert, Elijah, 221
Gilbert, Elizabeth, 221
Gilbert, Étienne Rev., 221
Gilbert, Harriet, 221
Gilbert, Jean Louis, 207
Gilbert, Jean Louis Rev., 221
Gilbert, John Louis, 221
Gilbert, Joseph Bienaime, 221
Gilbert, Lucy, 221
Gilbert, Marie (Mizel), 221
Gilbert, Mary, 221
Gilbert, Peter, 221
Gilbert, Stephen, 221
Gilbert, Susan, 221
Gille/Usillie, Magdalen, 315
Gillebeau, Ann Margaret, 426
Gillebeau, Pierre, 426
Gilles, René, 29
Gillespie, Matthew, 394
Gillet(t)/Gyllet, Abigail, 222
Gillet(t)/Gyllet, Anna/Hannah, 222
Gillet(t)/Gyllet, Cornelius, 222
Gillet(t)/Gyllet, Habiah/Abiah, 223
Gillet(t)/Gyllet, Jeremiah, 222, 223
Gillet(t)/Gyllet, John, 222
Gillet(t)/Gyllet, Jonathan, 222
Gillet(t)/Gyllet, Joseph, 222
Gillet(t)/Gyllet, Josiah, 222
Gillet(t)/Gyllet, Mary, 222, 223
Gillet(t)/Gyllet, Nathan, 223
Gillet(t)/Gyllet, Samuel, 222
Gillet(t)/Gyllet, Silas/Elias, 223
Gillet(t)/Gyllet, Thomas, 223
Gillet(t)/Gyllet, William, 223
GILLET(T)/GYLLET, William (Rev.), 222
Gillett, Sarah, 295
Gillette, unknown, 428
Gilliland, unknown, 223
Gilmer, Geroge Dr., 385
Giltner, Johannes Frantz/John Frank, 60
Gindra, Abraham, 223
Gindrat, Abraham, 223
GINDRAT, Abraham, 223
Gindrat, Abraham Henry, 223
Gindrat, Catherine, 223
Gindrat, Daniel Henry, 223
Gindrat, Dorcas, 223
Gindrat, Eve (Droz), 223
Gindrat, Henrietta, 223
Gindrat, John, 223
Gindrat, Louis, 223
Gindrat, Marguerite, 223

Gindrat, Mary, 223
Gindrat, Mary Magdalena, 223
Gindrat, Pierre, 223
Gindrat, Rhoda, 223
Gindrat, Susan, 223
Gir(e)ault, Jean, 226
Gir(e)ault, Perinne (X), 226
Girard, Elizabeth Damaris, 377
Girard, Isaac, 377
Girardeau, Catherine (Lareine), 224
Girardeau, Isaac, 224
Girardeau, James, 224
GIRARDEAU, Jean, 224
Girardeau, John, 224
Girardeau, Peter, 224
Girardeau, Pierre, 224
Girardeau, Richard, 224
Girardin, Anne, 224
Girardin, David, 224
Girardin, Henry, 224
GIRARDIN, Jean Henri, 224
Girardin, Louis, 224
Giraud, André, 225
Giraud, André/Andrew, 226
Giraud, Anne/Annie, 226
Giraud, Catherine, 225
Giraud, Catherine (Sicard), 128
Giraud, Comfort, 225
Giraud, Daniel, 225, 440
Giraud, Daniel II, 128
Giraud, Frederick, 225
Giraud, Jeanne, 225
Giraud, Marie Elizabeth, 226
Giraud, Mary, 225
Giraud, Peter, 225
Giraud, Pierre/Peter, 225
Giraud, William, 225
Giraud/Gerow, André, 225
Giraud/Gerow, André/Andrew, 225
Giraud/Gerow, Benjamin, 225, 440
Giraud/Gerow, Daniel, 225, 440
GIRAUD/GEROW, Daniel, 225
Giraud/Gerow, Isaac, 225
Giraud/Gerow, Jeanne, 225
Giraud/Gerow, Jeanne (X), 440
Giraud/Gerow, Maria, 441
Giraud/Gerow, Marie, 225
Giraud/Gerrow, Benjamin, 226
Girault, Ann Mary, 226
Girault, Clara Scott, 227
Girault, Francis Spain, 226
Girault, George Rogers Clark, 227
Girault, Helen Perina, 226
Girault, Isaac Farrar, 226
Girault, James Augustus, 226
GIRAULT, Jean/John, 226
Girault, John Ruffin, 226
Girault, Martha Cordelia, 227
Girault, Mary, 226
Girault, Perina, 226
Girault, Thomas Richard, 227

Giron, Jean, 320
Gissendanner, John, 57
Giubert/Guybert, Rebecka, 236
Givens, Elixabeth Anne, 331
Givens, Samuel, 331
Givens, Sarah (Cathey), 331
Givens, William, 92
Glas, Maria Elizabeth, 199
Glass, James, 139, 286
Glass, John/Jehu, 23
Glass, Mary (Pontus), 139, 286
Glen, Martha, 82
Glen, Martha (X), 82
Glen, William, 82
Glencross, Ann, 396
Glenisson, John, 272
Glenisson, Marie, 272
Go(u)don, Abraham, 227
Go(u)don, Caterynne/Catherine, 227
Go(u)don, Elisabeth, 227
Go(u)don, Ester, 227
Go(u)don, Gabriel, 227
Go(u)don, Isaac, 227
GO(U)DON, Jaco, 227
Go(u)don, Jan, 227
Go(u)don, Peter, 227
Go(u)don, Rachel, 227
Go(u)don, Samuel, 227
Goad, Catherine (X), 474
Goad, John, 474
Goade/Goode, Joanna, 474
Gobert, Marie, 198
Goddard, Francis, 90
Goddard, Jane, 90
Goddard, Mary, 90
Godde, Benjamin, 370
Godeffroy, Jeanne, 14
Godefrin, Judith, 86
Godfrey, Alice, 207
Godfrey, Mary (Richmond), 207
Godfrey, Richard, 207
Godin, Anne, 443, 444
Godin, Antoine, 444
Godin, Bastienne (L'Escot), 444
Godin, Benjamin, 232
Godin, Marianne, 232
Godin, Sarah, 432
Godowne, Abraham, 227
Godowne, Elizabeth, 227
Godowne, Jacob, 227
Godowne, Joseph, 227
Godowne, Mary, 227
Godsey, Thomas Jr., 268
Godwin, Susannah (Preeson), **37**
Godwin/Gaudovin, Ann, 13
Goelet, Francis, 126
Goelet, Jacobus, 126
Goff, David, 83
Goff/ Goss, James, 332
Goheen, Anna (X), 58
Goheen, John, 58

Goheen, Richard, 58
Golders, Abraham, 159
Golillot Marie (Marchant), 68
GOLILLOT, Antoine, 228
Golillot, Auguste, 68, 228
Golillot, Michel, 68, 228
Gombaud, Moses, 396
Gombert, Jacques, 148
Gombert, Margaret (Salomé), 148
Gombert, Marguerite, 148
Gondin, Lady Gabrielle de, 426
Gooch, William Col., 216
Good, Eve Moser, 370
Good, Jacob, 370
Goodbee, Anne, 165
Goode, William, 369
Goodloe, Elizabeth, 173
Goodrich, David Col., 75
Goodrich, Mary, 75
Goodrich, Prudence (Churchill), 75
Goodrich, William, 25
Goodridge, Mary, 164
Goodwin, Ann (Pleasant), 187
Goodwin, Benjamin, 298
Goodwin, George, 246
Goodwin, Isaac, 187
Goodwin, John C. Dr., 57
Goodwin, Judith, 187
Goodwin, Nathaniel, 298
Goodwin, Robertson/Robison, 191
Goodwyn, Martha, 65
Gooris, Sarra/Sarah, 228
Gooris, Solomon/Samuel, 228
Gorden, Alberts/Gysbert Van, 106
Gorden, Harmanus Van, 106
Gordon, John, 369
Gordon, Susan, 75
Gordon, Thomas, 447
Goris, David, 186
Gorry, Isaac, 219
Gorry, Jean, 219
Gorsaline/Gorsline, Jacob, 229
Gorsaline/Gorsline, James, 229
Gorsaline/Gorsline, John, 229
Gorsaline/Gorsline, Josse/Joseph, 229
Gorsaline/Gorsline, Judith, 229
Gorsaline/Gorsline, Marie Madeleine, 229
Gorsaline/Gorsline, Mary/Mary Madeleine, 229
Gorsaline/Gorsline, Samuel, 229
Gorton, Freelove, 256
Gory, Claude/Glaude, 219
Gory, Daniel, 219
Gory, Jean, 219
Gory, Pierre/Peter, 219
Goss, Elizabeth, 176
Goss, John, 157
Goss/Goff, Benjamin, 176
Goss/Goff, David, 176
Goss/Goff, Elizabeth, 176

Goss/Goff, James, 176
Goss/Goff, Sara Bonne, 176
Gosselin/Gorsline, Claude, 228
Gosselin/Gorsline, Étienne, 229
Gosselin/Gorsline, Guillaume, 228
Gosselin/Gorsline, Jacob I, 228
GOSSELIN/GORSLINE, Jacob II, 228
Gosselin/Gorsline, Jacob III, 228
Gosselin/Gorsline, Jacob IV, 228
Gosselin/Gorsline, Jan, 228
Gosselin/Gorsline, Jean, 228
Gosselin/Gorsline, Marie, 228
Gosselin/Gorsline, Philippe, 228
Gosselin/Gorsline, Sarah, 228
Gosset, Abraham, 229, 230
Gosset, Gideon, 230
Gosset, Isaac, 230
Gosset, Isaac Rev. Dr., 230
Gosset, Jacob, 229
Gosset, Jane, 230
GOSSET, Jean, 229
Gosset, John, 229
Gosset, Mary, 229
Gosset, Matthew, 230
Gosset, Matthias, 229
Gosset, Peter, 229
Gosset, William, 229
Gotley, Marie, **35**
Gough, William, 423
Gouin, Abraham, 167
Gouin, Jeanne (Archambaud), 167
Gouin, Susanna, 128
Gould, Frances, 267
Gould, Phebe (Deacon), 267
Gould, Zaccheus, 267
Goulding, George, 26
Gourdin, Charlotte, 260
Gourdin, Jean, 449
Gourdin, Louis, 155
Gourdin, Theodore, 260
Goury/Gory/Gaury/Garry, Claude, 228
Goury/Gory/Gaury/Garry, Isaac, 228
GOURY/GORY/GAURY/GARRY, Jean, 228
Goury/Gory/Gaury/Garry, John, 228
Goury/Gory/Gaury/Garry, Peter, 228
Goy, Jacqueline, 194
Goy, unknown, 194
Graaf, Moses de, 149
Grae, Michael de, 273
Graff, Abraham De, 384
Graff, Hester (LeMaître) LeConte de, 149
Graff, Maria de, 149
Graffenried, Metcalfe de, 355
Graffenried, Sara (Rust) Lowery de, 355
Graffenried, Tscharner de, 355
Grafton, Phrisdiswith, 286
Graham, unknown, 34
Grandin, Jean, 154
Grand-Martin, Catheline, 449
Grand-Martin, Coirin, 449
Granger, Ann, 357

Granger, Marie Anne, 294
Grant, Elizabeth, 399
Granville, Marie, 73
Grasset, André, 231
Grasset, Auguste, 154, 168, 230, 231, 366
GRASSET, Auguste, 230
Grasset, Ester, 230
Grasset, Ester/Hester, 154, 230
Grasset, Jacques, 230
Grasset, Marianne, 231, 366
Grasset, Marie (Pele), 168, 366
Grasset, Marie (Pelé), 154
Grasset, Marthe, 230
Grasset, Pierre, 230
Grasset, Samuel, 168, 230
Gratel/Grutel, Marie, 316
Graves, Anne, 196
Graves, Hannah, 196
Graves, Nancy, 201
Graves, Sarah (Turner), 196
Graves, Thomas, 196
Graw/Graau, Walter de, 287
Gray, Ann, 23
Gray, Charity (Sawyer), 23
Gray, Griffith, 23
Gray,unknown, 47
Grayson, Benjamin, 346
Grayson, Elizabeth Osborne (Neale), 346
Green, Anne (Coleman), 346
Green, Eleanor C., 346
Green, Elizabeth, 437
Green, Hannah, 399
Green, Joseph, 345
Green, Ruth, 295
Green, Susan, 192
Green, unknown, 295
Green, William, 196
Green, William Col., 346
Greene, Mary, 275
Greene, Rachel, 295
Greene, Timonthy, 295
Greening, Margaret (Haynsworth), 338
Greenleaf, Samuel, 108
Greenleaf, Sarah, 108
Grégord/Gregory, Augilloce/Angelica, 23
Gregory, Luke, 23
Gregory, Mary, 86
Gregory, Minnie, 266
Gregory, Sarah (Wilkie), 23
Grellier, François, 379
Gremjon/Grangen/Grançon/Granson,
    Maria/Marie, 289
Grey, Susannah, 171
Gridley. Mary, 428
Griffin, Leroy, 56
Griffith, Jane, 328
Griffith, Kessiah, 268
Griffith, Ro(w)land, 328
Griffith, Sarah (Maccubin), 179
Griffith, Sophia, 179
Griffith, Thomas, 289

Griffith, William, 179
Grift, Johannes Van der, 126
Grigsby, Thomas, 158
Grim, Anna Catharina (X), 358
Grim, Catherine, 358
Grim, Elizabeth, 358
Grim, Johan Egidius, 358
Grimball, John, 104, 134
Grimball, Paul, 104
Grimball, Thomas, Jr., 402
Grissom/Gresham, Betty, 85
Grissom/Gresham, Hannah, 85
Grissom/Gresham, John, 85
Grissom/Gresham, John Sr., 85
Grissom/Gresham, Katy, 85
Grissom/Gresham, Molly, 85
Grissom/Gresham, Susannah, 85
Griswold, Simeon, 25
Groenendahl, Hermina, 43
Groesbeck, John, 39
Groh, Eva, 408
Gronbal, Anna, 244
Groom, Martha, 230
Groot, Dirk Jansen de, 177
Groot, Maria, 273
Groot, Simon Symonse, 177
Groot, Symon Symonse, 273
Grosch, Capt., 83
Grosch, Christian (Roemer), 83
Grove, unknown, 204
Grubbe, John, 466
Grubbe, Mary, 466
Gruendyck, Peter, 287
Gu(e)tilius/Gutelius, Frederick Adam,
    235
GU(E)TILIUS/GUTELIUS, Jean
    Pierre/Johann Peter/John Peter, 235
Gu(e)tilius/Gutelius, John Peter, 235
Gu(e)tilius/Gutelius, Mary, 235
Guenon/Genen/Genung, Saertje, 231
Guenon/Genon/Genung, Grietje, 231
Guenon/Genon/Genung,
    Hannah/Annetje, 231
GUENON/GENON/GENUNG, Jean/Jan,
    231
Guenon/Genon/Genung, Jeremias, 231
Guenon/Genon/Genung, John/Jan, 231
Guenon/Genon/Genung, Susanna, 231
Guérard, Jacob, 104
Guerard/Guerrard, Benjamin, 232
Guerard/Guerrard, David, 232
Guerard/Guerrard, Isaac, 232
GUÉRARD/GUÉRRARD, Jacques/Jacob,
    231
Guerard/Guerrard, Jean, 232
Guerard/Guerrard, John, 232
Guerard/Guerrard, Margaret, 232
Guerard/Guerrard, Martha, 232
Guerard/Guerrard, Pierre Jacques/Peter
    Jacob, 232
Guerin, Andrew, 233

Guerin, Charlotte, 233
Guerin, Elizabeth, 233, 234
Guerin, Epemetus, 233
Guerin, Esther, 233, 373
Guerin, Frances, 233, 234
Guerin, Francis, 234
Guerin, François/Francis, 233
Guerin, Henry, 233, 373
Guérin, Henry, 68
Guerin, Isaac, 233, 373
Guérin, Isaac, 373
Guerin, Isaac, Jr., 233
Guérin, Issac, 68
Guerin, James, 233, 234
Guerin, James Bileau, 233
Guérin, Jeanne, 315
Guerin, Jemima, 233
Guerin, John, 233, 234
Guerin, John Vincent, 233
Guérin, John Vincent, 233
Guerin, Joseph, 233
Guerin, Joshua, 233
Guérin, Jucith (X), 373
Guerin, Judith, 233
Guerin, Levi, 233
Guerin, Lewis, 233, 373
Guerin, Marian, 233
Guerin, Martha, 233
Guérin, Martha (Mouzon), 68
Guerin, Mary Johnson, 233
Guerin, Mary/Manon, 234
Guerin, Mathurin I, 233
Guerin, Mathurin II, 234
Guerin, Mathurin III, 234
Guerin, Mehetible, 233
Guerin, Moses, 233
Guerin, Nathan, 233
Guerin, Peter, 233
GUÉRIN, Pierre, 233
Guerin, Pierre/Peter, 233
Guerin, Robert, 233, 373
Guerin, Samuel, 233, 373
Guerin, Sarah, 233
Guerin, Susannah, 233, 234
Guerin, Susannah Elizabeth, 233
Guerin, Susannah Isabella, 233
Guerin, Thomas, 233, 234
Guerin, Vincent, 233
Guérin, Vincent, 373
Guerin, William, 234
Guerin/Guerrant, Daniel, 232
GUÉRIN/GUÉRRANT, Daniel, 232
Guerin/Guerrant, Esther, 232
Guerin/Guerrant, Jane, 232
Guerin/Guerrant, Jean/John, 232
Guerin/Guerrant, John, 232
Guerin/Guerrant, Judith, 232
Guerin/Guerrant, Magdelaine, 232
Guerin/Guerrant, Peter, Jr., 232
Guerin/Guerrant, Pierre/Peter, 232
Guerineau, John, 304

Guerineau, Peter, 304
Guering, Jehanne, 315
Guérrant II, Daniel, 445
Guerrant, Daniel, 116
Guérrant, Daniel, 330, 389, 455
Guerrant, Frances/Françoise (L'Orange), 116
Guérrant, Françoise, 389
Guerrant, Françoise (L'Orange), 445
Guérrant, Françoise (L'Orange), 389
Guerrant, Nicolas, 116
Guérrant, Peter, 455
Guérrant, Pierre, 389
Guérrant/Guérin, Magdelaine (Trabue), 389
Guérrant/Guérin, Pierre, 389
Guerri, André, 407
Guerri, Anne, 407
Guerri, Anne (X), 234
Guerri, Elisha, 407
Guerri, Elizabeth, 407
Guerri, Jacques, 234, 407
Guerri, James, 234
Guerri, Jane, 407
Guerri, Jean, 407
Guerri, Jean Jacques, 361
Guerri, Jean-Jacques, 407
Guerri, Jeanne (Broussard), 219, 407
Guerri, Jeanne (Rembert), 234
Guerri, Jeanne/Jane, 234
Guerri, Lydia, 407
Guerri, Madelaine, 407
Guerri, Margaret, 407
Guerri, Marguerite (Rembert), 260
Guerri, Pierre, 156, 219, 260, 407
Guerri/Guerry, André, 234
Guerri/Guerry, Anne, 234
Guerri/Guerry, Elisha, 234
Guerri/Guerry, Elizabeth, 234
Guerri/Guerry, Esther, 234
Guerri/Guerry, François, 234
Guerri/Guerry, Jane, 234
Guerri/Guerry, Jean, 234
Guerri/Guerry, Jean-Jacques, 234
Guerri/Guerry, Jeanne Elizabeth, 235
Guerri/Guerry, John, 234
Guerri/Guerry, Lydia, 234
Guerri/Guerry, Made-leine, 234
Guerri/Guerry, Margaret, 234
Guerri/Guerry, Mary, 235
Guerri/Guerry, Peter, 234
GUERRI/GUERRY, Pierre, 234
Guerri/Guerry, Pierre II, 234
Guerri/Guerry, Stephen, 234
Guerry, Anne, 165
Guerry, Elizabeth, 208
Guerry, Jane/Jeanne Elizabeth, 163
Guerry, Jeanne (Broussard), 163
Guerry, Marguerite (Rembert), 165
Guerry, Peter, 165
Guerry, Pierre, 163

Guerst, Juliana, 358
Guespin, Marie, 269
Guibert, Anna Maria Catherine, 235
GUIBERT, François/Franz, 235
Guibert, Franz, 235
Guibert, Johann George, 235
Guibert, Marie, 420
Guibert/Guybert, Anne, 236
Guibert/Guybert, Elizabeth, 236
Guibert/Guybert, Joshua, 236
GUIBERT/GUYBERT, Josué/Joshua, 236
Guibert/Guybert, Mary, 236
Guibert/Guybert, Matthew, 236
Guibert/Guybert, Susanna, 236
Guibert/Guybert, Thomas, 236
Guichenet, Marie Catherine, 79
Guidon, Marthe, 239
Guidon, Oliver, 239
Guiennot, unknown, 271
Guiermand, Moïse, 42
Guignard, Anna, 236
Guignard, Anna Magdalen/Nancy, 236
Guignard, Frances, 236
GUIGNARD, Gabriel, 236
Guignard, John Gabriel, 236
Guignard, Margaret, 236
Guignilliat, Jean François de, 165
Guignilliat, Suzanne (LeSerrurier) de, 165
Guilbert, Dorcas, 417
Guillabeau, Anne, 319
Guillardit, Jean, 380
Guillaume, Démange, 86
Guillaume, Élisabeth, 86
Guillebeau, André, 368, 426
Guillebeau, Mary Jane (Bellot), 319
Guillebeau, Mary Jane (Roquemore), 77, 368
Guillebeau, Pierre, 319
Guillebeau, Susannah, 77, 319, 426
Guillelmon, Abraham, 71
Guillelmon, Marie, 71
Guillelmon/Guillaumont, Etienne, 71
Guillet, Charles Willliam, 237
Guillet, Daniel, 237
Guillet, Elizabeth, 237
Guillet, George, 237
Guillet, Jacques, 237
GUILLET, Jacques, 237
Guillet, Jacques Louis, 237
Guillet, James Charles, 237
Guillet, James Louis, 237
Guillet, Jean, 237
Guillet, Marie Ann, 237
Guillet, Mary Ann, 237
Guillet, Moyes, 237
Guillet, Sally Ann, 237
Guillet, Thomas, 237
Guimar, Pierre/Peter, 106
Guimar/Guymard, Anna, 237
Guimar/Guymard, Elizabeth, 237
Guimar/Guymard, Hester, 237

Guimar/Guymard, Mary, 237
Guimar/Guymard, Pierre, 237
GUIMAR/GUYMARD, Pierre, 237
Guimar/Guymard, Rachel, 237
Guincestre, Jean, 194
Guincestre, Marie (St. Amour de), 194
Guinere, Charlotte, 238
GUINÈRE, Louis, 238
Guion, Abraham, 128
Guion, Aman/Louis Amon, 238
Guion, Anne (Vigneau/Vincent), 152
Guion, Deborah, 18, 238
Guion, Isaac, 73, 238
Guion, Jacques, 105
Guion, Jacques I, 152
Guion, Jacques II, 152
Guion, Jacques/James, 238
Guion, Jeanne (Guion), 128
Guion, Louis I, 238
GUION, Louis II, 238
Guion, Louis III, 238
Guion, Marie (Malherbe), 73
Guion, Mary, 73
Guion, Sarah (Casier), 152
Guion, Susannah, 238
Guisbert, Anne, 317
Guise, François de, 121
Guit(t)eau/Guitaut/ Guyteau, Ruth, 239
Guit(t)eau/Guitaut/Guyteau, Ebenezer, 239
Guit(t)eau/Guitaut/Guyteau, Ephraim, 239
Guit(t)eau/Guitaut/Guyteau, Francis IV, 239
GUIT(T)EAU/GUITAUT/GUYTEAU, François I, 239
Guit(t)eau/Guitaut/Guyteau, François II, 239
Guit(t)eau/Guitaut/Guyteau, François Théophile, 239
Guit(t)eau/Guitaut/Guyteau, François Théophile/Francis Theophilus, 239
Guit(t)eau/Guitaut/Guyteau, François/Francis III, 239
Guit(t)eau/Guitaut/Guyteau, Joshua, 239
Guit(t)eau/Guitaut/Guyteau, Josué/Joshua, 240
Guit(t)eau/Guitaut/Guyteau, Louis-Olivier, 239
Guit(t)eau/Guitaut/Guyteau, Marc, 239
Guit(t)eau/Guitaut/Guyteau, Martha, 239
Guit(t)eau/Guitaut/Guyteau, Mary, 239
Guit(t)eau/Guitaut/Guyteau, Moïse-Louis, 239
Guit(t)eau/Guitaut/Guyteau, Phebe, 239
Guit(t)eau/Guitaut/Guyteau, Philippe, 239
Guit(t)eau/Guitaut/Guyteau, Susanne, 240

Guit(t)eau/Guitaut/Guyteau, Theophilus, 239
Guitaut, Moïse de, 239
Guitaut, Philippe (Bellin) de, 239
Guiton, 238
Gump, unknown, 437
Gurlandt, John, 296
Gushee, David, 207
GUSTIN, Jean/John, 240, 255
Guthry, Mary, 203
Gutig, Marguerite, 437
Gutilius, Adam Frederick, 235
Guy, Thomas, **41**
Guyon/Guion, Elizabeth/Lysbeth, 151
Gwaltney, Philadelphia, 22
Gylett, Jacques de Rev., 222
Gysbert, Teunis, 409
Gysbertszen, Frederick, 287

H

Haayar, Pierre, 242
Hache, Martine, 189
Hache, Pontue, 189
Hack, Peter Spencer, 201
Hack, Sarah Ann (Garlington), 200
Hackett, Ann, 161
Haes, Mary de, 254
Haes, Roeloff, De, 253
Haes, Sarah De, 253
Haes, Sarah Williamsen(Neering) de, 253
Haes, Roeloff de, 253
Haes/Haas, Jan Gerrits de, 129
Haft, Margaret, 174
Hafte, Hendrick Henricke, 126
Hagedorn, Maria, 459
Hahn, Anne, 460
Hahn, Catherina, 30
Hahn, David, 467
Hahn, Jacob, 30
Halbert, Martha, 85
Haldet, Antoine II, 411
Haldet, Françoise, 411
Haldet, Madelaine (Marchand), 411
Hale, Elizabeth, 137
Hall, Caleb, 203
Hall, Elizabeth, 388
Hall, Elnathan, 376
Hall, Grace, 203
Hall, Hannah (Bishop, 376
Hall, Henry Rev., 179
Hall, John, 91, 188
Hall, Mary, 306
Hall, Millasant, 254
Hall, Phebe, 17
Hall, Sarah, 254, 276
Hall, Talmadge Lt., 376
Hall, William, 457
Halley, Henry Sr., 412
Hallock, Margaret, 282
Halstead, Abigail, 396

Halstead, John, 64
Hamel, Jan/John, 464
Hamilton, Archibald, 423
Hamilton, Elizabeth, 176
Hamilton, unknown, 87
Hammer, unknown, 26
Hammett, Abraham, 298
Hammett, Lucy (Howland), 298
Hance, Deborah, 125
Hance, Elizabeth (Hanson), 125
Hance, John, 125
Hanchet, Thomas, 282
Hancock, Jeremiah, 383
Hankin, Dennis, 45
Hankin, Martha (Masters), 45
Hannum, John, 282
Hanot, unknown, 249
Hanrot, Jonas, 379
Hanrot, Marianne, 379
Hanrot, Marianne (Bocquet/Boquet), 379
Hanscom, Abigail, 348
Hansen, Marretje, 149
Harbin, Francis, 465
Harbison, James, 217
Harbison, Jane, 217
Harcourt, Jean, 54
Harcourt, Jean de, 458
Harcourt, Judith (leSeuer) de, 54
Harcourt, Susanna, 54
Harcourt/Haraucourt/Herancourt/Heraucourt, Anna Marie de, 241
Harcourt/Haraucourt/Herancourt/Heraucourt, Esther de, 241
HARCOURT/HARAUCOURT/HERANCOURT/HÉRAUCOURT, Jean de, 241
Harcourt/Haraucourt/Herancourt/Heraucourt, Paul de, 241
Harcourt/Haraucourt/Herancourt/Heraucourt, Pierre/Peter de, 241
Harcourt/Haraucourt/Herancourt/Heraucourt, Susanne de, 241
Harcourt/Haraucourt/Herancourt/Heraucourt, Tochter de, 241
Harcum, Elizabeth, 271
Hardain/Harding, William, 272
Harden, Abijah (Bouquet), 152
Harden, Jacques, 152
Harden, Jean, 152
Hardenbergh, Johannes, 308
Hardenbergh, Maria (DuBois), 308
Hardin, unknown, 351
Hardin/Hardouin/Hardewyn, Abraham, 241
Hardin/Hardouin/Hardewyn, Elizabeth/Lysbeth, 241
Hardin/Hardouin/Hardewyn, Isaac, 241
Hardin/Hardouin/Hardewyn, Jacob, 241
Hardin/Hardouin/Hardewyn, Marcus/Mark, 241
Hardin/Hardouin/Hardewyn, Martin, 241

HARDIN/HARDOUIN/HARDEWYN, Martin, 241
Harding, Giles, 272
Harding, Isreal, 454
Harding, John, 454
Harding, Mary (Giles), 272
Harding, Sarah (Butcher), 454
Harding, Thomas, 272
Harding, William, 272, 276
Hardwin, Christenah, 138
Hardwyn/Hardin, Martin, 175
Haring, Jane, 38
Haring, Jannetje Van, 106
Haring, Margaret (Bogart), 38
Haring, Peter, 38
Harlie, Marie de, 155
Harmanson, Adah, **37**
Harmanson, Kendall, **37**
Harmanson, Susannah (Kendall), **37**
Harmon, Daniel, 307
Harmon, Elizabeth (X), 188
Harmon, John, 188
Harmon, Sarah, 188
Harper, Sarah/Sally, 91
Harramond, Elizabeth, 28
Harramond, Henry, 28
Harriette, Benjamin d', 79
Harriette, Susanne (Papin) d', 79
Harriette, Susanne d', 79
Harris, Ann, 22
Harris, Benjamin, 162
Harris, Christopher, 22
Harris, Elnathan (Tew), 52
Harris, James, 16, 203
Harris, John, 17
Harris, Magdalen (Cordes), 442
Harris, Maria, 212
Harris, Martha, 385
Harris, Mary, 52
Harris, Mourning (Glenn), 22
Harris, Robert, 22
Harris, Temperance (Overton), 162
Harris, Thomas, 52
Harris, William, 162
Harrison, Ann, 427
Harrison, Elizabeth, 80, 311
Harrison, George, 99
Harrison, Magdalane, 99
Harrison, Palatea, 99
Harrison, Sarah (X), 80
Harrison, Thomas, 80
Harrison, unknown, **50**, 133
Harrison, William, 133
Harshman, Jacob, 140
Harshman, Elizabeth (Kline), 140
Hart, Annetje de, 305
Hart, Daniel, 83
Hart, Elizabeth, 83
Hart, Mary, 200
Hartley, Hannah, 133
Hartmann, Anna Katharina, 19

Hartwell, Mary, 335
Hartzell, unknown, 204
Harvey, Sir John, 352
Hasbrouck, Abraham, 149, 153, 430
Hasbrouck, Anna (Deyo), 59, 152, 237
Hasbrouck, Elizabeth, 59
Hasbrouck, Hester, 237
Hasbrouck, Jacob, 59
Hasbrouck, Jean, 59, 149, 152, 237
Hasbrouck, Joseph, 307
Hasbrouck, Maria, 152
Hasbrouck, Maria (Deyo), 153
Hasbrouck, Petronella, 307
Hasbrouck, Rachel, 153
Hasbroucq/Haesbroug,
    Christophe/Christoffel, 144
Hasbroucq/Haesbroug, Maria, 144
Hasbroucq/Hasbrouck, Abraham, 242
Hasbroucq/Hasbrouck, Andries, 242
Hasbroucq/Hasbrouck, Anna, 242
Hasbroucq/Hasbrouck, Benjamin, 242
Hasbroucq/Hasbrouck, Daniel, 242
Hasbroucq/Hasbrouck, Elizabeth/Lysbet,
    242
Hasbroucq/Hasbrouck, Hester, 242
Hasbroucq/Hasbrouck, Isaac, 242
Hasbroucq/Hasbrouck, Jacob, 242
Hasbroucq/Hasbrouck, Jean, 242
HASBROUCQ/HASBROUCK, Jean, 242
Hasbroucq/Hasbrouck, Jonas, 242
Hasbroucq/Hasbrouck, Joseph, 242
Hasbroucq/Hasbrouck, Maria, 242
Hasbroucq/Hasbrouck, Peter, 242
Hasbroucq/Hasbrouck, Rachel, 242
Hasbroucq/Hasbrouck, Salomon, 242
Hasbroucq/Hasbrouck,Elizabeth, 242
Hasell, Ann, 46
Haseur, Esther (X), 86
Haseur, Mathis, 86
Haseur, Rachel, 86
Haskins/Hoskins, Sarah, 207
Haskins/Hoskins, Sarah (Caswell), 207
Haskins/Hoskins, William, 207
Hassel, Priscilla, 24
Haste, Sarah, 119
Hasting, Lord Henry, 352
Hastler, Thomas, **36**
Hatch, John, 196
Hatch, Lemuel Sr., 196
Hatch, Mary, 196
Hatchett, William, 411
Hatfield, Matthias, 360
Hathaway, Anne Elizabeth, 199
Hatock, Catherine, 128
Hauck, Barthel, 329
Hauck, Maria Magdalena, 329
Hauser, Daniel, 243
Hauser, Georg Peter, 243
Hauser, Hans George, 243
Hauser, Jacob, 243
Hauser, Johann Georg/Hans, 243

Hauser, Martin, 243
HAUSER, Martin I, 243
Hauser, Martin II, 243
Hauser, Michael, 243
Hauser, Susanna (Burckhardt), 243
Hawie, Robert, 320
Hawkins, Abraham, 15
Hawkins, Arnal, 15
Hawkins, Damaris (Wooster), 172
Hawkins, Ebenezer, 172
Hawkins, Hannah, 89
Hawkins, James, 474
Hawkins, John, 15, 88
Hawkins, Joseph, 474
Hawkins, Sarah, 474
Hawkins, Susanna, 15
Hawkins, Thomas, 15, 89
Hawks, Eliza (X), 222
Hawks, Elizabeth, 222
Hawks, John, 222
Hay, Jacob, 400
Hay, Maria, 358, 400
Hayes, John Champion, 284
Hayes, Mary, 86
Haynes, Edmund, 281
Haynes, Hannah (X), 281
Haynes, Laura Josephine, 82
Haynsworth, Rachel, 338
Hayward, John, 62
Hayward, Mehitable, 62
Hazard, Anna, 211
Heap(e), Elizabeth, 224
Heath, Henry, Dr., 346
Heath, James, 346
Heath, James Beau Clark, 416
Heath, Laetitia, 346
Heathcote, Anne, 281
Heck, unknown, 59
Heckendorn, Johannes, 120
Hedger, Joseph, 231
Hedges, Ann, 433
Hedges, Catherine, 433
Hedges, Joseph, 433
Hedges, Susannah, 433
Hedges, William, 433
Hedgman, Peter, 356
Heereman, Jannetje/Jane, 353
Heermance, Jan Foockens, 63
Heighe, James, 445
Heighe, Mary, 445
Heiliger, Anna Margaretha, 330
Heiliger, Joris, 330
Hek, Elizabeth, 353
Helling, Hendrick Teunisz, 315
Helm, William, 264
Hemphill, James, 319
Henderson, Annie Elbertina Van Ness,
    108
Henderson, Archibald Gen., 108
Henderson, Charles Alexander, 108
Henderson, Charlotte Shepard, 108

Henderson, Elizabeth, 226
Henderson, Elizabeth Gardner, 108
Henderson, Jacob Rev., 178
Henderson, Octavius Cazenove, 108
Henderson, Richard Henry, 108
Hendicksen, Maeyken, 153
Hendrick, Ezekial, 220
Hendrick, Leah, 220
Hendricke Helling, Thomas/Theunis, 14
Hendricks, Altje/Elise, 101
Hendricks, Conrad, 175
Hendricks, Elise, 342
Hendricks, Gerhard, 206
Hendricks, Grietje/Margaret, 164
Hendricks, Margaret, 273
Hendricks, Susanne (LeRoux/LaRue), 14
Hendricks, Thomas, 316
Hendricks, Trintje, 365
Hendricks, Wybregh, 315
Hendrickse, Molenaer, 464
Hendricksen, Cornelis, 296
Hendricksen, Macyken, 463
Hendrickson, Arfje, 48
Henley, Cornelius, 23
Henley, Cornelius II, 23
Henley, Elizabeth, 23
Henley, Elizabeth Brinkley, 207
Henley, James, 23
Henley, Kezia, 23
Henley, Mary, 23
Henley, Thomas, 207
Henne, Jacques de, 243
Henne, Jeanne (Doye) de, 243
Henneman, Catherine WIlhelmine, 71
Henno(t)/Henne/de Henne/En(n)o,
    Jacques/James, 244
Henno(t)/Henne/de Henne/En(n)o,
    James, 244
HENNO(T)/HENNE/de HENNE/EN(N)O,
    Jean/John, 243
Henno(t)/Henne/de Henne/En(n)o,
    John, 244
Henno(t)/Henne/de Henne/En(n)o,
    Sarah, 244
Henno, Collard, 243
Henno, Jacques, 243
Henri de Navarre, 78
Henri II, 270, 285
Henri IV, 21, 156, 239, 250
Henri IV of FR, 393
Henri of Navarre, King of France, 218
Henri of Navarre, 250
Henri, 3rd Duc de Guise, 121
Henri, Jean, 413
Henri, Judith (Duchene), 413
Henri/Henry, Anne Susanne, 413
Henry of Navarre, 21
Henry, Elizabeth, 299
Henry, Robert, 60
Henson, unknown, 424
Hepburn, unknown, 430

Herbert, Walter III, 125
Herbert/Herbaire, Elizabeth, 216
Herdin, Johannes, 43
Herdin, Thomas, 43
Hergert, Magdalena/Mary, 381
Herny, Johanna, 97
Herpel, Anna Dorothea, 71
Herpin, Antoine, 449
Herpin, Catherine (Pionnie), 449
Herpin, Esther, 449
Herr, Christian, 307
Herr, Mary, 307
Hersent, Mary, 354
Hersent/Erssen, Louis, 354
Hersent/Erssen, Marie (Pillon), 354
Hershey, unknown, 457
Hersulier or Gautier, Jeanne, 172
Herter, Anna Maria, 204
Herter, Johann Bartholomaus, 204
Hess, Anna Barbara (Kelli), 140
Hess, Jacob, 140
Hessels, Pieter, 150
Het, Marie/Mary, 154
Het, René, 153, 205
HET, René, 244
Het, Sarah, 153
Hetzel, Susanna, 250
Hetzel, William, 250
Heul, Abraham Janszen Ven der, 365
Heul, Marie Van der, 365
Heverick, John, 407
Hewes, Anne, 465
Hext, Margaret, 388
Hezall, Mary, 75
Hibon, Jan, 404
Hibon, Marie/Mary, 404
Hickel, Thomas, 386
Hickle, Anne, 183
Higdon, Daniel, 101
Hildebrand, Jannatie, 324
Hilden, David, 292
Hill, Anna Christina, 358
Hill, Bridget, 453
Hill, Catherine, 230
Hill, Charles, 232
Hill, Elizabeth, 232
Hill, Elizabeth (Perry), 344
Hill, Hannah, 395
Hill, Harmon, 328
Hill, Johann Jacob, 358
Hill, John, 269
Hill, Jonathan, 344
Hill, Joseph, 253
Hill, Leonard, 364
Hill, Mary, 276
Hill, Susanna, 344
Hill, William, 328
Hillhouse, Joseph, 221
Hillier, Elizabeth (Jane), 428
Hillier, John, 428
Hilton, Stephen, 339

Himpel, Elizabeth, 446
Hind, Peter, 285
Hinds, James, 254
Hinkle, Asa, 93
Hinson/Henson, James, 33
Hitchbourn, Deborah, 420
Hitchbourn, Frances (Pattishall), 420
Hitchbourn, Thomas, 420
Hittel, Nicholas, 469
Hix/Hicks, Prewid, 162
Hoar, Esther, 267
Hobbs, Rose, 201
Hobson, Thomas, **36**
Hoch, Deborah, 458
Hoch, John, 458
Hodeson, Sarah, 377
Hodges, John, 401
Hodsden, Joseph Bridger, 385
Hoerner, Maria Christina, 439
Hoff, Lewis, 199
Hoff, Pieter, 95
Hottman, Anna Maria, 83
Hoffman, Barbara, 266
Hoffman, Hans Georg, 83
Hoffman, Jacob, 308
Hoffman, John, 266
Hoffman, Lorenz, 83
Hoffman, Martinus, 130
Hoffman, Nicolas, 130
Hoffmann, Goersdorf Dorothee, 261
Hoffmann, Mary Elizabeth, 266
Hoffmann, Peter, 261
Hofmann, Elizabeth X, 83
Hogan, Anne, 107
Hogan, Edward, 107
Hogan, Mary, 107
Hogencamp, Myndert Hendrickse, 170
Hohn, Anna Elizabeth, 199
Hohn, Casper, 199
Hohn, Christina (Porth), 199
Holcomb, Benajah, 244
Hol-comb, Elizabeth (X), 244
Holcomb, Timothy, 244
Holden, Davis, 266
Hole, Antoinette de, 380
Holland, Ann, 334
Holland, Edward, 39
Holland, Frankie, 268
Holland, Nehemiah, 25
Holland, Susannah, 334
Holmes, Alice (Stilwell), 390
Holmes, Anne(e), 390
Holmes, Isaac, 388
Holmes, Jane, 101
Holmes, Joseph, 105
Holmes, Mary, 105
Holmes, Samuel, 390
Holmes, Sarah, 255
Holst, Johanne Christiane Augusta, 363
Holt, John, 64
Holt, Joseph Rev., 65

Homeli, Bartholomew, 471
Homeyard, Edith, 402
Homs, Jan, 130
Homsted, Reuben, 339
Honnie, Simon, 195
Hood, Martha, 382
Hoodt, Casper, 289
Hoogdale, Marytje, 459
Hooges, Anthony de, 279
Hooges, Elenora de, 279
Hooghteling, Willem, 459
Hoogland, Belitia, 412
Hoogland/Hooglan(d)t, Adrian, 412
Hooglandt, Dirck Cornelise, 409
Hooper, Matilda, 116
Hooper, Stephen, 349
Hoornbeck, Cornelius Judge, 107
Hoornbeck, Evert, 106
Hoornbeek, Lodewych, 107
Hoover, Christina, 97
Hopkins, Stephen, 337
Hopkins, Damaris, 337
Hoppe, Willem, 467
Hormish, Christly, 370
Horn, Christian Cornelius Van, 172
Horn, Joseph, 339
Horn, Margaret Van, 172
Horne, Joris Janses Van, 126
Horne, Styntje Joris Van, 126
Horner, Abraham, 59
Hornish, Elizabeth Moser, 370
Horns, Janetye, 358
Horry, Claudius, 244
Horry, Daniel, 212, 244, 245
Horry, Elias, 68
Horry, Élias, 247
Horry, Elias II, 244
Horry, Elias III, 245
Horry, Élie/Élias, 244
Horry, Elizabeth Mary, 212
Horry, James, 245
Horry, Jeanne (DuBois), 464
Horry, John, 245
Horry, Lidie, 212
Horry, Magdalen, 245
Horry, Margaret (Huger), 68
Horry, Margaret Henrietta, 245
Horry, Margeret Henriette, 68
Horry, Mary, 212
Horry, Peter, 236, 245
Horry, Richard Alexander, 244
Horry, Samuel, 464
Horry, Susanne, 464
Horry, Thomas, 245
HORRY/HORRŸ, Jean, 244
Horsful, James, 96
Horsful, Ruth (Rogers), 96
Horsful, Sarah, 96
Horton, David, 102
Horton, Mary, 336

Hottel/Hodel/Hoed(e)l/Hoddle/Huddle, **Anna**, 245

Hottel/Hodel/Hoed(e)l/Hoddle/Huddle, **Anna Barbara/ Anna**, 245

Hottel/Hodel/Hoed(e)l/Hoddle/Huddle, **Barbara**, 245

Hottel/Hodel/Hoed(e)l/Hoddle/Huddle, **Catharina Elizabetha**, 245

Hottel/Hodel/Hoed(e)l/Hoddle/Huddle, **Daniel**, 245

Hottel/Hodel/Hoed(e)l/Hoddle/Huddle, **Elizabeth**, 245

Hottel/Hodel/Hoed(e)l/Hoddle/Huddle, **Jacob**, 245

HOTTEL/HODEL/HOED(E)L/HODDLE/HUDDLE, Jean/Johannes/John, 245

Hottel/Hodel/Hoed(e)l/Hoddle/Huddle, **Joahnn Georg/**George, 245

Hottel/Hodel/Hoed(e)l/Hoddle/Huddle, **Johann Carl/Charles**, 245

Hottel/Hodel/Hoed(e)l/Hoddle/Huddle, **John**, 245

Hottel/Hodel/Hoed(e)l/Hoddle/Huddle, **Joseph**, 245

Hottel/Hodel/Hoed(e)l/Hoddle/Huddle, **Magdalene**, 245

Hottel/Hodel/Hoed(e)l/Hoddle/Huddle, **Mary**, 245

Hottel/Hodel/Hoed(e)l/Hoddle/Huddle, **Solomon**, 245

Hottel/Hodel/Hoed(e)l/Hoddle/Huddle, **Susannah**, 245

Houblon, Peter, 123

Houblon, Sarah (X), 123

Houd(e) lette, Mary, 246

Houd(e) lette, Sally, 246

Houd(e)lette, Anne Catherine, 246

Houd(e)lette, Charles, 246

HOUD(E)LETTE, Charles Étienne, 246

Houd(e)lette, Dorothy, 246

Houd(e)lette, Elizabeth, 246

Houd(e)lette, Francis, 246

Houd(e)lette, George, 246

Houd(e)lette, James, 246

Houd(e)lette, Jane, 246

Houd(e)lette, Louis, 246

Houd(e)lette, Lucy, 246

Houd(e)lette, Marthe, 246

Houd(e)lette, Mary, 246

Houd(e)lette, Philip, 246

Houghton, Thomas, 344

Houpeleine, Josyntie, 468

HOUPELEINE/(VAN) OBLINUS, Juste/Joost, 246

Houpeleine/Oblinus, Joost, 468

Houpeleine/Van Oblinus, Hendrick, 246

Houpeleine/Van Oblinus, John, 246

Houpeleine/Van Oblinus, Josyntie/Jossynthea, 246

Houpeleine/Van Oblinus, Maria, 246

Houpeleine/Van Oblinus, Peter, 246

Houpeleine/Van Oblinus Josina, 246

House, Anna (X), 226

House, Elizabeth, 226

House, Reinhard, 226

Houston, James, 91

How, Robert, 233

Howard, Ann Lady, 452

Howard, Ann(a), 260

Howard, Janes, 144

Howard, Joanna, 387

Howard, William, 16

Howell, Freelove, 326

Howell, Joseph, 326

Howell, Lydia (Stocking), 326

Howland, Consider, 298

Howland, Jeremiah, 295

Howland, Martha, 298

Howland, Ruth (Bryant), 298

Howlett, Elizabeth, 117

Hubbard, Hannah, 360

Hubbard, Hannah (Mead), 406

Hubbard, Nathaniel, 406

Hubbard, William, 406

Hubert, Anne, 390

HUBERT, Benjamin B, 247

Hubert, David, 247

Hubert, Eldred, 247

Hubert, Fanny, 247

Hubert, Gabriel, 247

Hubert, Hester, 247

Hubert, Jean, 314

Hubert, Mary/Polly, 247

Hubert, Matthew, 247

Hubert, Richard, 390

Hubert, William, 247

Hubertary, Elisabeth, 22

Huddleston, Benjamin, 383

Hudson, Adam Brevard, 90

Hudson, Benjamin, 90

Hudson, Bryan, 23

Hudson, Elizabeth, 268

Hudson, Elizabeth (X), 187

Hudson, Jonathan, 326

Hudson, Mary, 326

Hudson, Mary (X), 23

Hudson, Samuel, 326

Hudson, Sarah (X), 326

Hudson, unknown, 90

Hudson/Hogsdon, Elizabeth, 23

Huet, Samuel, 394

Huett, unknown, 95

Hufron, Élisabeth, 129

Huger, Anne, 248

Huger, Daniel, 244, 247, 312

Huger, Daniel I, 247

Huger, Daniel II, 247

Huger, Jean, 248

HUGER, Jean, 247

Huger, Magdaleine, 248

Huger, Magdalen/Madeleine, 247

Huger, Margaret, 244

Huger, Margaret (Perdriau), 244

Huger, Margaret/Marguerite, 247

Huger, Marie, 248

Huger, Marie (Bichet), 247

Huggins, James Jr., 91

Huggins, John, 91

Hughes, Jesse, 457

Hugo, Pieter, 415

Huguenin, Jeanne Antoinette/Jane Antonia, 311

Huguenin, Jeanne Marguerite, 248

Huguenin/Hugenin/Hugenor/Hugony, Abraham, 248

Huguenin/Hugenin/Hugenor/Hugony, Anne Marie, 248

Huguenin/Hugenin/Hugenor/Hugony, Daniel, 248

Huguenin/Hugenin/Hugenor/Hugony, David, 248

HUGUENIN/HUGENIN/HUGENOR/HUGONY, David, 248

Huguenin/Hugenin/Hugenor/Hugony, Jean Jacques, 248

Huguenin/Hugenin/Hugenor/Hugony, Jeanne Marguerite, 248

Huguenin/Hugenin/Hugenor/Hugony, Jeanne Marie, 248

Huguenin/Hugenin/Hugenor/Hugony, Rose Marie, 248

Huguenin/Hugenin/Hugenor/Hugony,Susanne, 248

Hugues, John, 19

Hugues, Margaretta (Shupe), 19

Hugues/Hugus, Catherine Margaretta, 249

Hugues/Hugus, David, 249

Hugues/Hugus, Guillaume, 249

Hugues/Hugus, Henry, 249

Hugues/Hugus, Jacob, 249

HUGUES/HUGUS, Jacques/Jacob, 248

Hugues/Hugus, Jean/John, 249

Hugues/Hugus, John J., 249

Hugues/Hugus, Magdalena, 249

Hugues/Hugus, Michael, 249

Hugues/Hugus, Paul, 249

Hugues/Hugus, Peter, 249

Hugues/Hugus, Pierre, 249

Hugues/Hugus, Sarah, 249

Hugues/Hugus, Suzanne, 249

Hugues/Hugus, Wilhelm/William, 249

Hugues/Hugus, William, 249

Hugus/Hugues, Michael, 19

Hulder, Ann, 101

Huling, Abraham, 250

Huling, Dinah, 250

Huling, Israel, 250

Huling, Joseph, 250

Huling, Lars/Laurens, 250

Huling, Laurens, 250

Huling, Laurens II, 250

Huling, Laurens III, 250

Huling, Laurens IV, 250
Huling, Marcus, 250
Huling, Marcus I, 250
Huling, Marcus II, 250
Huling, Michael, 250
HULINGUES/HULINGS, Jean Paul
   Frederick, Marquis de, 249
Hulingues/Hulings, Lars/Laurens, 250
Hull, Hopewell, 425
Hull, Mary, 393, 425
Hull, Mary (Manning), 393, 447
Hull, Mary (Martin), 425
Hull, Mercy, 393, 447
Hull, Samuel, 393, 447
Hulsaert, Cornelius, 440
Humberdroz, Abraham, 148
Humbert, Adam, 251
Humbert, Antoine, 250
Humbert, Antoine/Anthony, 250
Humbert, Charles, 251
Humbert, Charlotte, 251
Humbert, Frederick, 250
Humbert, Jacques, 250
Humbert, Jean, 251
Humbert, Johannes George, 251
Humbert, Joseph, 251
Humbert, Judith (X), 250
Humbert, Marguerite/Margaret, 339
Humbert, Nicolas, 250
HUMBERT, Noël, 250
Humbert, Peter, 251
Humbert, Philip Jacob, 250
Humbert, Wilhelm, 250
Humphrey, Elizabeth, 398
Humphrey, Michael, 239
Humphrey, Phebe, 239
Humphreys, David Rev., 221
Humphreys, William, 202
Hunt, Anne, 335
Hunt, Hannah, 241
Hunt, Magdalena, 467
Hunt, Tabitha (Underwood), 335
Hunt, William III, 335
Hunter, Alexander, 221
Hunter, George Heriot Dr., 226
Hunter, Gov., 230
Hunter, James, 188
Hunter, Mary, 226
Hupman, Anna Barbara (X), 279
Hupman, Barbara, 279
Hupman, Jacob, 279
Huppé, Catherine, 110
Huppé, Madeleine (Roussin), 110
Huppé, Michel, 110
Hurtienne, Jean, 449
Hurtienne, Judith, 449
Hurtienne, Marie (de la Porte), 449
Hurtin, Elizabeth (Rocheteau), 410
Hurtin, Jean, 410
Hurtin, Rachel, 410
Hussey, Sampson, 76

Husted, Ebenezer, 294
Husted, Mary, 294
Husted, Samuel, 414
Husted, Sarah (Holmes), 295
Huston, Abigail, 138
Huston, Archibald, 138
Huston, Mary (Stephenson), 138
Hutcheson/Hutchinson, Daniel, 182
Hutcheson/Hutchinson, Elizabeth, 182
Hutching, Judith (X), 116
Hutching, Lawrence, 116
Hutchins, James, 396
Hutchins, Joseph, 124
Hutchinson, Martha, 319
Hutchinson, Thomas, 127
Huyke, Annetje, 112
Huyken, Macktelje, 125
Huysen, Maritje, 136
Huyten/Wit Wytes, Weiske, 297
Hyrne, Ann, 90
Hyrne, Edward Col., 90
Hyrne, Elizabeth, 90

I

Ide, Martha (Bliss), 391
Ide, Nicholas, 391
Iffandt/Evelan, Maria/Mary, 330
Igle, Fronica, 424
Ijams, Elizabeth (Cheney), 179
Ijams, William, 179
Imbert, Isaac, 208
Imbert, Isabeau, 208
Imbert, Isabeau (Carquet), 208
Imboden, Johann Schwenckhard, 150
Imbroech, Gysbert Dr. Van, 278
Ingerfield, Paul, 421
Ingerfield, Silence (Swift), 421
Inglis, James, 351
Inglis, Margaret, 118
Ingo, John, Sr., 24
Ingo, Mary, 24
Ingram, Fanny Ann, 470
Innes, James Col., 427
Isselsteyn, Jannetje/Jeanne van, 159
Isselsteyn, Willimtje (Jans) Van, 159
Ivy, Mary, 427
Izambent, Marie, 69
Izard, Mary, 343

J

Ja(c)ques/Jack, Guillaume, 252
Ja(c)ques/Jack, Jacob, 253
JA(C)QUES/JACK, Jacobus/Jean, 252
Ja(c)ques/Jack, Jean, 252
Ja(c)ques/Jack, Margaret, 253
Ja(c)ques/Jack, Patrick, 253
Ja(c)ques/Jack, Thomas, 253
Jackson, Alice (Spriggs) Mrs., 88
Jackson, Christopher Dominick, 133

Jackson, Christopher Maccabeus, 133
Jackson, Julius, 133
Jackson, Magdalen, 133
Jackson, Mary, 125
Jackson, Thaddeus, 133
Jackson, Thomas, 88
Jacob, 30, 33, 48, 50, 104, 145, 188, 191,
   197, 205, 206, 228, 229, 231, 232, 233,
   247, 290, 292, 295, 325, 330, 347, 357,
   358, 371, 374, 375, 391, 400, 410, 411,
   414, 424, 434, 443, 464, 466, 467, 470
Jacob, Abraham, 252
Jacob, Agnes, 252
Jacob, Anna, 252
Jacob, Anna Catharina, 252
Jacob, Anna Catharina Margaretha, 252
Jacob, David, 345
Jacob, Elizabeth, 179
Jacob, Hans Christoffel, 252
Jacob, Hans Wolff, 252
Jacob, Johanna, 252
Jacob, John Capt., 179
Jacob, Susanna, 252
Jacob, Veronica, 252
Jacobs, Cornelius, 374
Jacobs, Jacomina, 468
Jacobs, Mary, 267
Jacobs, Trientje, *142*
Jacobus, Angell, 24
Jacobus, Elizabeth (Clark), 24
Jacot, Daniel, 248
Jacot, Susanne, 248
JACQUEMIN(E)/JACOB, Abraham, 252
Jacques, Roger, 252
Jacquet, Mary, 253
Jafford, John, 236
Jafford, unknown, 236
Jamain, Étienne, 368
Jamain, Gérard, 182
Jamain, Marie, 368
Jamain, Marie (Billard), 368
James I, 328
James II, 186
James II, King of ENG, 447
James, Duke of York, 447
Jane, 472
Jans, Aeltje, 353
Jans, Grietje, 231, 400
Jans, Gysbert, 95
Jans, Hilletje, 95
Jans, Hubrechtje, 150
Jans, Jannetje, 45, 400
Jans, Judith, 122
Jans, Magdelena, 130
Jans, Stynje, 365
Jans, Susanna, 41
Janse, Adriantje, 78
Jansen, Elizabeth, 159
Jansen, Hendricus, 103
Jansen, Jan Mattys, 63
Janszen Van St. Obyn, Jan, 262

Janszen, Jan, 261
Janvier, Philippe, 253
Janvier, Suzanne (Mousnier), 253
Janvier, Thomas, 253
Janvier/Jauvier/January, Benjamin, 254
Janvier/Jauvier/January, Francis, 253
Janvier/Jauvier/January, Isaac, 253
Janvier/Jauvier/January, John, 254
Janvier/Jauvier/January, Mary, 253
Janvier/Jauvier/January, Philip, 253
Janvier/Jauvier/January, Sarah, 254
Janvier/Jauvier/January, Susannah, 254
JANVIER/JAUVIER/JANUARY, Thomas, 253
Janvier/Jauvier/January, Thomas II, 253
Janzsen/Johnson, Henry, 390
Jaques, Jacob, 252
Jaques, Sara (Van Haestrecht), 252
Jarnat/Jarnette, Ann Rebecca/Annaka de, 254
Jarnat/Jarnette, Daniel de, 254
Jarnat/Jarnette, Elias de, 254
Jarnat/Jarnette, Elizabeth de, 254
Jarnat/Jarnette, Ellenor de, 254
JARNAT/JARNETTE, Jean de, 254
Jarnat/Jarnette, John de, 254
Jarnat/Jarnette, John Thomas de, 254
Jarnat/Jarnette, Joseph de, 254
Jarnat/Jarnette, Mary de, 254
Jarnat/Jarnette, Marymiah de, 254
Jarnat/Jarnette, Thomas de, 254
Jarvis, Ellen/Elizabeth, 253
Jasso, Juan de, 474
Jaudon, Daniel, 55, 152, 156, 407, 423, 470
Jaudon, Elias, 423
Jaudon, Élie, 407, 470
Jaudon, Elizabeth (Videau), 156
Jaudon, Elizabeth (X), 423
Jaudon, Esther, 360
Jaudon, François, 255
Jaudon, Marie (Roy), 255
Jaudon, Paul, 233, 255
Jaudon, Sara (Bertonneau), 360, 407, 470
Jaudon, Sarah, 423
Jaudon/Jodon, Elie, 360
Jaudon/Jodon/Jeudon, Daniel, 255
JAUDON/JODON/JEUDON, Daniel, 255
Jaudon/Jodon/Jeudon, David, 255
Jaudon/Jodon/Jeudon, Elias, 255
Jaudon/Jodon/Jeudon, Élie/Elias, 255
Jaudon/Jodon/Jeudon, Elisha, 255
Jaudon/Jodon/Jeudon, Esther, 255
Jaudon/Jodon/Jeudon, Matthew, 255
Jaudon/Jodon/Jeudon, Noah, 255
Jaudon/Jodon/Jeudon, Paul, 255
Jaudon/Jodon/Jeudon, Sarah, 255
Jaudon/Jodon/Jeudon, Susannah Elizabeth, 255
Jay, Auguste, 205
Jean, Abigail, 255

JEAN, Augustine, 255
Jean, David, 255
Jean, Ebenezer, 255
Jean, Edmond, 255
Jean, Elizabeth, 255
Jean, Esther (le Rossignol), 255
Jean, John, 255
Jean, Mary, 255
Jean, Samuel, 255
Jean, Sarah, 255
Jean, Thomas, 255
Jean, William, 255
Jeannet, Claude, 109
Jeannet, Jeanne (Mallebault), 109
Jeannet, Marie, 109
Jefferson, Thomas, **37**
Jeffords, Ann, 371
Jeffords, John, 371
Jeffords, Margaret (X), 371
Jehou, Mary (X), 349
Jenkins, James, 90
Jenkins, John, 90
Jenkins, Jonas, 94
Jenkins, Samuel, 90
Jenkins, unknown, 339, 465
Jenney, Robert Rev., 186, 396
Jennings, Ann, 445
Jennings, Catherine (Lunford), 21
Jennings, Charles, 22
Jennings, John, 276
Jennings, Mary, 361
Jennings, Peter, 21
Jennings, Sarah, 21, 22
Jennings, Stephen, 222
Jerauld, Dutees (Dupee?), 256
Jerauld, Gamaliel, 256
JERAULD, Jacques/James, 256
Jerauld, James, 256
Jerauld, Johanna/Hannah, 256
Jerauld, Mary, 256
Jerauld, Stephen, 256
Jerauld, Susanna, 256
Jerauld,Martha, 256
Jerian, Antoinette, 192
Jerman, Edward, 66
Jerman/Gemain, Mary, 66
Jermon/Germaine, Capt., 437
Jess, George, 382
Jeter, George, 24
Jetton, John, 91
Jetton, Sarah Sharpe, 92
Jewell, Sarah, 41
Jobin, Françoise, 133
Jobin, Jacques, 133
Jobin, Marguerite (Roy), 133
Jodon/Jaudon, Elie, 55
Johannes, Philip, 261
Johns, Sarah, 391
Johnson, Abner, 172
Johnson, Anne (Belcher), 108
Johnson, Anne (Brumfield), 434

Johnson, Aquilla, 173
Johnson, Elizabeth (Lenneham), 456
Johnson, Elizabeth Roberta, 233
Johnson, Hannah, 108, 172
Johnson, Isaac Capt., 283
Johnson, Jeremiah, 172
Johnson, John, 438, 456
Johnson, Joseph, 108, 172
Johnson, Joseph E. Col., 275
Johnson, Lucretia, 456
Johnson, Lydia, 248
Johnson, Mary, 268
Johnson, Mary (X), 248
Johnson, Richard, 58
Johnson, Robert, 248
Johnson, Samuel, 58, 172
Johnson, Sarah, 58, 434
Johnson, Sarah (X), 268
Johnson, Tabitha, 260
Johnson, unknown, 123, 293
Johnson, William, 22
Johnston, Ann (Smith), 188
Johnston, Jacob, 197
Johnston, Jane, 193
Johnston, John, 146
Johnston, Judith, 100
Johnston, Mary, 197
Johnston, Robert, 100
Johnston, William, 144, 434
JohnstonWilliam, 188
Johonnot, Daniel, 438
Joire, Jacoba (LeBlan/c), 63
Joiré, Ma(g)deleine, 63
JOIRÉ, Magdalen, 256
Joiré, Magdalena, 106
Joiré, Petrus/Pierre, 63
Jolie, Charlotte de, 55
Jolin(e), Marie/Mary, 64
Jolin(e)/Jaulin, André, 257
JOLIN(E)/JAULIN, André, 257
Jolin(e)/Jaulin, Anne Madelaine, 257
Jolin(e)/Jaulin, David, 257
Jolin(e)/Jaulin, Jean, 257
Jolin(e)/Jaulin, Jeanne, 257
Jolin(e)/Jaulin, Marie/Mary, 257
Jolin, Ann, 453
Jolin/Jaulin, André, 64
Jolin/Jaulin, Madeleine (Poupin), 64
Joly, Suzanne, 362
Jones, Aertse/Orser, 81
Jones, Ann (X), 306
Jones, Anne, **51**
Jones, Edward S., 108
Jones, Elizabeth, 178
Jones, Elizabeth (Williams), 195
Jones, Frances, 334
Jones, Frank Cazenove, 108
Jones, John, 184, 257, 466
Jones, Lane, 334
Jones, Margaret, 250, 327
Jones, Margaret (X), 119

Jones, Mary, 266
Jones, Michael, 158
Jones, Orlando, 334
Jones, Rebecca, 416
Jones, Rowland, 334
Jones, Samuel, 91
Jones, Susanna, 291
Jones, Susannah, 19
Jones, Thomas, 24, 306
Jones, unknown, 91, 207
Jones, William, 119, 178, 291
Jonge, Andries de, 440
Joor, George, 236
Joosten, Magdalena, 151
Joquen, Jeanne, 314
Jordan, Benjamin, 89
Jordan, James, 89
Jordan, John, 89
Jordan, Joseph, 89
Jordan, Joshua, 89
Jordan, Mary, **36**
Jordan, Mathew, 89
Jordan, Richard, 89
Jordan, Robert, 89
Jordan, Samuel, 89
Jordan, Thomas, 89
Jordan, Thomas Jordan, 89
Joris, Jannetje, 150
Jorisse, Magdalena Brissen, 63
Joseph, Sarah Elizabeth, 117
Jouany, Elizabeth, 47
Jouany, Esther (LaFuitte/Fitte), 47
Jouany, Jean, 47
Jouany/Joannis/Jones, Elizabeth, 257
Jouany/Joannis/Jones, Hester/Esther, 257
Jouany/Joannis/Jones, Isaac, 257
Jouany/Joannis/Jones, Jean, 257
JOUANY/JOANNIS/JONES, Jean/John, 257
Joüet, Daniel I, 258
Joüet, Elisabeth, 258
Jouet/Jouett/ Jewett, Élizabeth, 258
JOÜET/JOUETT/JEWETT, Daniel II, 258
Jouet/Jouett/Jewett, Daniel III, 258
Jouet/Jouett/Jewett, Ézéchiel, 258
Jouet/Jouett/Jewett, Jean, 258
Jouet/Jouett/Jewett, Marie/Mary, 258
Jouet/Jouett/Jewett, Pierre/Peter, 258
Jouet/Jouett/Jewett/, Anne, 258
Jour, Eleanor, 306
Jourdain, John Dr., 253
Jourdain, Marie/Mary, 399
Jourdain, Mary (Tayne), 253
Jourdain, Sarah, 253
Jourlis, Christine, 241
Jourlis, Jakob, 241
Journeay, Meynard, 163
Journee/Journeay, Ann, 258
Journee/Journeay, Audrey, 258
Journee/Journeay, Catherine, 258

Journee/Journeay, Elizabeth, 258
Journee/Journeay, James, 258
Journee/Journeay, John, 258
Journee/Journeay, Joseph, 258
JOURNÉE/JOURNEAY, Meynard/Moilliart/Meyndert/Malliard, 258
Journee/Journeay, Peter, 258
Jouvenal, Marguerite, **42**
Jouy/Jouis/Jue/Schue/Schwe/Shuey, Johannes, 259
Jouy/Jouis/Jue/Schui/Schwe/Shuey, Abraham, 259
Jouy/Jouis/Jue/Schui/Schwe/Shuey, Anna Margaretha, 259
Jouy/Jouis/Jue/Schui/Schwe/Shuey, Barbara, 259
Jouy/Jouis/Jue/Schui/Schwe/Shuey, Catherine, 259
Jouy/Jouis/Jue/Schui/Schwe/Shuey, Charles, 259
Jouy/Jouis/Jue/Schui/Schwe/Shuey, Daniel, 259
JOUY/JOUIS/JUE/SCHUI/SCHWE/SHUEY, Daniel, 259
Jouy/Jouis/Jue/Schui/Schwe/Shuey, David, 259
Jouy/Jouis/Jue/Schui/Schwe/Shuey, David/Daniel, 259
Jouy/Jouis/Jue/Schui/Schwe/Shuey, Elizabeth, 259
Jouy/Jouis/Jue/Schui/Schwe/Shuey, Johann Peter, 259
Jouy/Jouis/Jue/Schui/Schwe/Shuey, John, 259
Jouy/Jouis/Jue/Schui/Schwe/Shuey, Maria Magdalena, 259
Jouy/Jouis/Jue/Schui/Schwe/Shuey, Martin, 259
Jouy/Jouis/Jue/Schui/Schwe/Shuey, Peter, 259
Jouy/Jouis/Jue/Schui/Schwe/Shuey, Salomon, 259
Jouy/Jouis/Jue/Schui/Schwe/Shuey, Susanne, 259
Joyeulx, Pierre, 303
Judd, Esther, 239
Judson, Damaris (Sherman), 344
Judson, Elizabeth/Betty, 344
Judson, Jerusha, 239
Judson, Nathan, 344
Juhan, Jean-Jacques/John James, 382
Juhan, Jean-Marc, 382
Juhan, Suzanne-Marguerite (Guesler), 382
Juin(g)/June, Anna, 260
Juin(g)/June, Catherine, 260
Juin(g)/June, Edward, 260
Juin(g)/June, Elizabeth, 260
Juin(g)/June, Frances, 260
JUIN(G)/JUNE, George, 259

Juin(g)/June, George II, 260
Juin(g)/June, Jean/John I, 260
Juin(g)/June, John II, 260
Juin(g)/June, John III, 260
Juin(g)/June, Lydia, 260
Juin(g)/June, Nancy, 260
Juin(g)/June, Peter, 260
Juin(g)/June, Solomon, 260
Juin(g)/June, Stephen, 260
Juin(g)/June, Susanna, 260
Juin, Elizabeth, 259
Juin, Jean, 259
Juin, Judithe (Pie), 259
Juin, Louis, 259
Juin, René, 259
Juin/June, George, 407
Juin/June, Suzanne (LeRiche), 407
Julian, Abraham, 379
Julien, Pierre, 433
Julion, Philippine Barbe, 249
June, Solomon, 260
June, Stephen, 407
Jung, Anna Maria (Dietz), 86
Jung, Maria Margarete, 86
Jung, Wilhelm, 86
Jupille, Anne, 410
Jurckse, Christina/Styntie, 467
Jurckse, Paulus, 467
Juriaens, Andries, 400
Juriaens, Jannetje, 400
Juriaens, Juriaen Andriesse, 400
Juriaens, Lambert Andriessen, 400
Juriaens, Lysbeth Anderiesse, 400
Jurriaens, Eva, 273

K

Kaempf, Anna (Fouerfauch), 192
Kaempf, John, 192
Kantein/Contein, Abraham, 103
Kantein/Contein, Catrina, 103
Kantein/Contein, Cornelia, 103
Kantein/Contein, Elisabeth, 103
Kantein/Contein, Johannis/John, 103
Kantein/Contein, Margrietjen, 103
Kantein/Contein, Maria, 103
Kantein/Contein, Mattheus/Matthew, 103
Kantein/Contein, Moses, 103
Kantein/Contein, Nathaniel/Daniel, 103
Kantein/Contein, Peter/Petrus, 103
Karns, unknown, 59
Kay, Ann, 178
Kay, Robert, 178
Kearney, Thomas Major, 206
Kearsley, John Dr., 186
Keating, Ann, 442
Keating, Ann (X), 137
Keaton, William, 85
KEEFER, Andrew, 261
KEEFER, Catherine, 261

KEEFER, Elizabeth, 261
KEEFER, Eve, 261
KEEFER, Frederich, 261
KEEFER, George, 261
KEEFER, Jacob, 261
KEEFER, John, 261
KEEFER, Sarah, 261
Keighley, unknown, 421
Keim, John, 73
Keinadt, Conrad, 150
Keinadt/Keiner, Michael, 150
Keiper, Catherine, 417
Keisler/Keyser, Maria, 206
Keith, John Capt., 40
Kelchiner, Michael, 417
Kelchner, Eva, 357
Keller, Anna, 245
Keller, Barbara, 245
Keller, Bernardus, 330
Keller, Elizabeth, 245
Keller, George, 245
Keller, Henry, 245
Keller, Jacob, 245
Keller, John, 245
Keller, Margaret, 245
Keller, Mary, 245
Kelli, Johannes Georg, 140
Kellogg, Daniel, 86
Kellogg, Martin, 87
Kellogg, Prudence (Bird), 87
Kelsey, Mary, 222
Kelsey, Prescilla, 222
Kelsey, William, 222
Kelshaw, Elizabeth, 383
Kelshaw, John, 383
Kemerer, Eliabeth, 345
Kemerer, Ludwick, 345
Kemp, Christian, 192
Kemp, M., 226
Kemp,, James, 226
Kendall, Joanna, 246
Kendall, John, **37**
Kendall, Peter, 256
Kendall, Susannah (Savage), **37**
Kendig, Martin, 192
Kennedy, Benjamin, 221
Kennel, Lucretia/Lucy, 260
Kenner, Frances, 56
Kenner, Mary, 346
Kenner, Richard, 56
Kenniff, David, 416
Kenniff, Jeremias, 416
Kennoy, Sarah, 248
Kenny/Kinney, Edward, 266
Kent, Henry Jr., 88
Ker, Elizabeth, 218
Kerr, Elizabeth, 99
Kerr, John, 394
Kerr, Mary Catherine, 307
Kershaw, Ely Capt., 91
Kershaw, Rebecca, 91

Kessler, Jean Daniel, 215
Kessler, Susanna Maria, 243
Kettle, Anna, 253
Keuren, Matthys Matthyssen Van, 153
Keuren, Sara Matthyseen Van, 153
Key, Jacques de, 392
Keyser, Anna Catherine, 285
Keyser, Dirck, 446
Keyser, Peter, 446
Kibble, Abraham, 196
Kibble, Lucy, 196
Kief(f)er, Andres/Andrew, 261
Kief(f)er, Hans Georg, 261
KIEF(F)ER, Johan Jacob, 261
Kiefer, Catharina (Schnepp) Kieffer, 261
Kiefer, Johann Melchoir, 261
Kieft, Gov., 359
Kieft, Governor, 335
Kieft, Willem, 335
Kierson, Kier Woullters, 45
Kierstade, Hans Dr., **39**
Kierstade, Sarah (Roelofs), **39**
Kierstede, Blandina, **39**
Kierstede, Lucus, 315
Kilborn, Abigail, 26
Kilborn, Hezekiah, 26
Kilborne, Mary, 428
Kilborne, Thomas, 428
Kilborne,Frances (Moody), 428
Killen, Elizabeth, 15
Killen, Mary, 15
Killen, Rebecca, 15
Killen, William, 15
Kimberly, Hannah (Downs), 102
Kimberly, Nathaniel, 102
Kimberly,Nathaniel, 102
Kinder, Bridget (X), 119
Kinder, John, 119
Kindt, Johanna, 123
King Charles II, 216, 472
King Charles VIII, 189
King François I, 270
King George, 112
King Henri II, 189
King Henri IV, 78
King James II, 265, 432
King Louis XII, 217
King Louis XIII, 238
King Louis XIV, 239, 339
King Louis XV, 73
King of England, 445
King of Spain, 171
King William, 238, 433
King(e), George, 465
King, Anna, 465
King, Peter, 439
King, Pierre/Peter Michel, 318
King, Salome, 369
King/Kern, Adam, 369
Kingbury, Samuel, 124
Kingcart, Thomas, 351

Kinloch, James, 208
Kinney, Mary, 124
Kip, Abraham, 261, 287
Kip, Annatje, 182, 337
Kip, Beertjen/Baertje, 261
Kip, Femmetje, 262
Kip, Hans Pieter, 458
Kip, Hendrick, 164, 441
Kip, Hendrick Hendrickszen, 262, 279
Kip, Hester, 458
Kip, Isaac, 278, 365
Kip, Isaac Hendickszen, 261
Kip, Issac, 468
Kip, Jacob Hendrickszen, 262, 279
Kip, Jacobus, 296
Kip, Rachel (DuFour), 458
Kip, Tryntie, 198
Kip, Tryntje, 262
Kirkpatrick, Andrew, 218
Kirkpatrick, Catherine (X), 218
Kirkpatrick, Jennett, 218
Kirkpatrick, William, 218
Kirns, Dr. William, 351
Kirtland, Elizabeth, 305
Kissam, Daniel, 448
Kissam, Elizabeth, 448
Kleeck, Baltus Van, 384
Kleeck, Barent Van, 384
Kleeck, Sara Van, 384
Klein, Anna Johanna, 120
Klein, Elizabeth, 120
Klein, Susanna, 120
Kleyn, Elizabeth Huygens de, 39
Klock, Abraham, 409
Klock, Sarah, 53, 409
Klyne, Leonard Huygens de, 323
Klyne/Kleyn, Elizabeth Huygens de, 323
Knapp, Hannah, 406
Knapp, Hannah (Ferris), 406
Knapp, John, 406
Knauss, Anna Johanna, 120
Knauss, Magdalena, 120
Knowles, Mary, 214
Knowles, Richard, 448
Knox, John, 217
Kobel, Huldah, 303
Koch, Johannes, 30
Kocher, Christina, 467
Kocherthal, Joshua Rev., 458
Kockhuyt, Joost Capt., 305
Koehler, Leonard, 120
Konig, Margaret, 251
Konig/Koneg, Abraham, 251
Konnick, Antje, 81
Koonce, George, 288
Koonce, Jacob, 288
Kooser, Mary, 19
Korten, Myndert, 306
Korten, Wyntje, 306
Kortright, Aefie, 454
Kortright, Michael, 454

Kötter, Bernhard, 330
Kraftt, Johannes, 252
Kramer, Johann Frederick, 358
Kranckeyt Herrickson, Theunis, 416
Kranckeyt, Wyntje, 416
Kreider, Maria R., 120
Kreiger/Creager, Susan, 83
Kreuser, Conrad, 120
Krieg, Marie Magdalene, 71
Küchleine/Kuechle, Anna Maria, 120
Küchleine/Kuechle, Seloma/Salome, 120
Kuechle(y), Johannes, 120
Kuiper, Annetje, 226
Kuiper, Jan Claessen, 226
Kype, Ruloff de, 261
Kype/Kip, Hendrick de, 261
Kype/Kip, Hendrick Hendickszen de, 261
KYPE/KIP, Ruloff de, 261

L

L/Escot(t), Rev. Paul, 471
L'Agache, Anna, 82
L'AMOUREUX/LAMOUREUX, André, 279
L'Avenant, Judith, 259
L'Écuyer, Guillaume, 304
L'Écuyer, Jean, 174, 304
L'ÉCUYER/L'ESCUYER/L'ESQUIER/LEQU(I)ER, Jean/Jan, 304
L'Écuyer/Laquer, Abraham, 174
L'ÉGARÉ/LÉGARÉ, François, 305
L'Escot, Frances, 471
L'ESPENARD/LISPENARD, Antoine, 322
L'Espine, Anne, 423
l'Espine/l'Épine, Suzanne de, 184
L'Esquier, Jean, 296
L'ESTRANGE, 323
L'Estrange, George, 145
L'Hommeau, unknown, 271
L'HOMMEDIEU, Benjamin, 326
L'Hommedieu, Martha (Peron), 326
L'Hommedieu, Pierre, 326
l'Obel, Jean de, 328
L'OBEL/LOBEL, Mathias/Mathieu de, 328
L'Orange, Jean Velas, 445
L'ORANGE, Jean Velas, 329
La Barrare, John, 116
la Barre, Abraham de, 263
la BARRE, Abraham de, 263
la Barre, Ferdinand Louis de, 263
la Barre, François de, 263
la Barre, Johann Carl de, 263
la Calmes, Ann de, 264
la Calmes, Elizabeth de, 264
la Calmes, Isabella de, 264
la Calmes, Marquis (II) de, 264
la Calmes, Marquis (III) de, 264
la CALMES, Marquis de, 264
la Calmes, William de, 264
la Calmes, William Waller de, 264
la CHAIR, Jan de/CHAIRS, John, 264

la Chair/Chairs, Benjamin de, 265
la Chair/Chairs, Hannah de, 265
la Chair/Chairs, James de, 265
la Chair/Chairs, John de, 264
la Chair/Chairs, Joseph de, 265
la Chair/Chairs, Nathaniel de, 265
la Chair/Chairs, Thomas de, 265
La Chapelle, Marie, *143*
la Chaumete, Bailey de, 266
la Chaumette, Alice de, 265
la Chaumette, Amos de, 267
la Chaumette, Anne de, 266
la Chaumette, Antoine de, 265
la CHAUMETTE, Arnoul/Arnell de; SHUMATE/SHUMWAY, Arnoul, 265
la Chaumette, Benjamin de, 266
la Chaumette, Blackwell/ Blackley de, 266
la Chaumette, Daniel de, 265, 266
la Chaumette, Daniel II de, 266
la Chaumette, David de, 267
la Chaumette, Deveril de, 266
la Chaumette, Dorcas de, 268
la Chaumette, Frances de, 265
la Chaumette, Hepzibah de, 267
la Chaumette, Jacob de, 267
la Chaumette, James de, 266
la Chaumette, Jane de, 265
la CHAUMETTE, Jean de, 265
la Chaumette, Jemima de, 266
la Chaumette, Jeremiah de, 267
la Chaumette, John de, 266, 267
la Chaumette, John III de, 266
la Chaumette, John, Jr. de, 266
la Chaumette, Joseph de, 268
la Chaumette, Joshua de, 266
la Chaumette, Lettice de, 266
la Chaumette, Lydia de, 266
la Chaumette, Margaret/ Peggy de, 266
la Chaumette, Margery de, 265
la Chaumette, Marie (Aucouturier) de, 266
la Chaumette, Mark Hardin de, 266
la Chaumette, Mary de, 266, 267
la Chaumette, Moise/Moses de, 265
la Chaumette, Moses de, 266
la Chaumette, Nancy de, 266
la Chaumette, Oliver de, 267
la Chaumette, Peter de, 267
la Chaumette, Pierre de, 265, 350
la CHAUMETTE, Pierre de, 267
La CHAUMETTE, Pierre de, 266
la Chaumette, Richard de, 266
la Chaumette, Samuel de, 266, 267, 268
la Chaumette, Sarah de, 265
la Chaumette, Strother de, 266
la Chaumette, Susanna de, 266
la Chaumette, Thomas de, 266
la Chaumette, William de, 266
la Chaumette, Winifred de, 266
La Comte/Le Count/de Graaf, Moses, 313

la Coussaye, Philippe Brouard de, 322
la Coussaye, Susanna de, 321
la Croix/Delacroix, Abraham de, 185
La esiliere/Larzalere, Jacques, 152
La esiliere/Larzalere, Marie (Grangen), 152
La Fayette,General, 294
La FON, Nicholas, 270
la Fontain, John De, 462
la Fontaine, Abraham de, 272
la Fontaine, Jacques/James I de, 270
la FONTAINE, Jean de, 270
la Fontaine/de Fonteijn, Philippe de, 409
La Force, Agnes, 272
La Force, Ann, 272
La Force, Judith, 272
La Force, Monsire, 272
La Force, Rachel, 272
La Force, René, 272
La FORCE, René, 272
La Force, Robert, 272
La Force, Sarah, 272
La FORGE/LeFORTE/LAFORT/LaFORD (alias Liberté), Jean/Johannes/Jan/John, 273
La Forge/LeForte/Lafort/LaFord, Adrian II, 273
La Forge/LeForte/Lafort/LaFord, Adriean I/Abraham, 273
La Forge/LeForte/Lafort/LaFord, Aeltje, 273
La Forge/LeForte/Lafort/LaFord, Annatje/Anna, 274
La Forge/LeForte/Lafort/LaFord, Catherine, 273
La Forge/LeForte/Lafort/LaFord, Charles, 273
La Forge/LeForte/Lafort/LaFord, Daniel, 273
La Forge/LeForte/Lafort/LaFord, David, 273
La Forge/LeForte/Lafort/LaFord, Isaac, 273
La Forge/LeForte/Lafort/LaFord, Jacob, 273
La Forge/LeForte/Lafort/LaFord, Jane, 273
La Forge/LeForte/Lafort/LaFord, Johannes, 273
La Forge/LeForte/Lafort/LaFord, Johannes/John, 273
La Forge/LeForte/Lafort/LaFord, John, 273
La Forge/LeForte/Lafort/LaFord, Maria/Mary, 274
La Forge/LeForte/Lafort/LaFord, Marie/Mary, 273
La Forge/LeForte/Lafort/LaFord, Nicholas, 273
La Forge/LeForte/Lafort/LaFord, Nicolaas, 273

La Forge/LeForte/Lafort/LaFord, Peter, 273
la Grange, Agnes de, 198
La Grange, Annetje, 274
La Grange, Arnoldus, 274
La Grange, Christiana, 274
la Grange, Crispin de, 198
la Grange, Hester de, 198
La Grange, Isaac, 274
La Grange, Jacobus, 274
La GRANGE, Jean/John (Omie) de, 274
La Grange, Jean/John/Omie, 274
La Grange, Jellis, 274
La Grange, Johannes, 274
La Grange, Joost, 274
La Grange, Margaretta, 274
La Grange, Omie, 274
la Hunte/Dillahunt(y), Abraham de, 275
la HUNTÉ/DILLAHUNT(Y), Daniel de, 275
la Hunte/Dillahunt(y), Edmond de, 275
la Hunte/Dillahunt(y), Isaac de, 275
la Hunte/Dillahunt(y), John de, 275
la Hunte/Dillahunt(y), Mary de, 275
La Jeunesse, Pierre, 133
la Malière, Jacques de, 155
La Mare, Ann de, 277
La Mare, Anne de, 277
La Mare, Francis de, 277
La Mare, Francis II de, 276
La Mare, Francis III de, 277
La Mare, Francis IV de, 277
La MARE, François de, 276
La Mare, Isaac de, 277
La Mare, John de, 277
La Mare, Mary de, 277
La Mare, Rhesa de, 277
La Mare, Sarah de, 277
La Mare, Smith de, 277
La Mare, Stephen de, 277
La Mare, Susannah de, 277
La Mare, Thomas de, 277
la Marlière, Jeanne de, 155
la Mejanelle, Judith (Lienrard) de, 46
la Méjanelle, Judith de, 46
la Méjanelle, Leon de, 46
La Monta(i)gne, Gillis de, 279
La MONTA(I)GNE, Jean Mousnier de/Johannes, 278
La Monta(i)gne, Jean/Jan/John de, 278
La Monta(i)gne, Jesse de, 278, 279
La Monta(i)gne, Johannes de, 279
La Monta(i)gne, Jolant de, 278
La Monta(i)gne, Maria de, 279
La Monta(i)gne, Rachel de, 278
La Monta(i)gne, Willem/William de, 279
la Montagne, Abram de, 159
la Montagne, Eleanora (deHooges) de, 59
la Montagne, Jannetie de, 159
la Montagne, Jean de, 159, 261, 262, 404
la Montagne, Jean/Johannes de, 198
La Montagne, John de, 468

la Montagne, Maria de, 262
la Montagne, Marie (Vermilye) de, 159
la Montagne, Petronella de, 450
la Montagne, Rachel (de Foret) de, 262
la Montagne, Rebecca (Van Huyse) de, 159
la Montagne, William de, 59
la MontagneJean/Jan de, 450
La Pierre, Charles de, 287
La PIERRE, Jean de/John (Rev.), 287
La Pierre, Jeanne de, 288
La Pierre, Martha de, 288
la Pla, Oliver, 287
La Plaine, Carel de, 289
la Plaine, Crejanne/Christian de, 43
La Plaine, Crejanne/Christiana de, 289
La Plaine, Elisabeth de, 289
La Plaine, Isaac de, 289
la Plaine, Jacques de, 288
La Plaine, James de, 289
La Plaine, Jean de, 289
La Plaine, Judith de, 289
la Plaine, Marie de, 299
La Plaine, Marie de, 129, 289
La Plaine, Nicholas de, 289
la Plaine, Nicolas de, 43, 299
La PLAINE, Nicolas de, 288
La Plaine, Rachel de, 289
la Plaine, Susanna (Cresson) de, 299
La Plaine, Susanna de, 289
la PlaineSusanna (Cresson) de, 43
la Porte, Marie de, 165
la Porte, Pierre de, 165
La Resilière, Jacques, 62
La Resilière, Maria (Grangen), 62
La Resiliere/Larzalere, Marie, 152
la Roche, Jan de, 337
la Ruelle, Guillaume de, 370
la Ruelle, Jeanne de, 370
la Ruelle, Rachel (Loret), 370
la Tour, Jacques de, 294
La Tour/LaTur/Latture, Anna Margaretha, 292
La Tour/LaTur/Latture, Elisabetha, 292
La Tour/LaTur/Latture, Georgius Michael, 292
La Tour/LaTur/Latture, Johannes Hermannus/Herman, 292
La TOUR/LaTÜR/LATTURE, Thomas, 291
La Tour/LaTur/Latture,JohannesThomas, 292
La Tourette, Jean, 357
La Tourette, Marie (Mercereau), 357
La Tourette, Pierre, 357
La Tourette/LaTourrette/Latourette, Ann, 293
La Tourette/LaTourrette/Latourette, Cathrin, 293
La Tourette/LaTourrette/Latourette, Daniel, 293

La Tourette/LaTourrette/Latourette, David, 293
La Tourette/LaTourrette/Latourette, Elizabeth, 293
La Tourette/LaTourrette/Latourette, Esther, 293
La Tourette/LaTourrette/Latourette, Fanny, 293
La Tourette/LaTourrette/Latourette, Henricus, 293
La Tourette/LaTourrette/Latourette, Henry, 293
La Tourette/LaTourrette/Latourette, Jacques/James, 293
La Tourette/LaTourrette/Latourette, James, 293
La TOURETTE/LaTOURRETTE/LATOURETTE, Jean, 292
La Tourette/LaTourrette/Latourette, Jean/John, 293
La Tourette/LaTourrette/Latourette, John, 293
La Tourette/LaTourrette/Latourette, Marie, 293
La Tourette/LaTourrette/Latourette, Marie Susanne, 293
La Tourette/LaTourrette/Latourette, Marie/Mary, 293
La Tourette/LaTourrette/Latourette, Mary, 293
La Tourette/LaTourrette/Latourette, nJohn, 293
La Tourette/LaTourrette/Latourette, Paul, 293
La Tourette/LaTourrette/Latourette, Peter, 293
La Tourette/LaTourrette/Latourette, Pierre/Peter, 293
La Tourette/LaTourrette/Latourette, Susanne, 293
La Valade, Count de, 157
la Verdure, Charles, 294
la Verdure, John, 294
La VERDURE, Pierre, 294
la Vergne, Benjamin de, 295
la Vergne, Ebenezer de, 295
la Vergne, Elizabeth de, 295
la Vergne, Frances de, 295
la Vergne, Giles de, 295
la Vergne, Hannah de, 295
la Vergne, James Henry de, 295
la Vergne, Joseph de, 295
la Vergne, Louis de, 295
la Vergne, Mary de, 295
la Vergne, Nicholas de, 295
la VERGNE, Nicolas de, 294
la Vergne, Sarah de, 295
la Vergne, Susanna de, 295
la Vergne, Walter de, 295
La Vigne, Abraham, 297

La Vigne, Abraham & Sara, 297
la Vigne, Amos de, 295
la Vigne, Ariantje (Cuvellier), 45
la Vigne, Christina de, 301, 304
la VIGNE, Étienne de/ LeVINESS, Stephen, 295
la Vigne, Guleyn, 45
la VIGNE, Guleyn/Guillaume de/ VIGNÉ, Ghislain, 296
La Vigne, Jan/Jean/John, 297
la Vigne, Jean de, 296
La Vigne, Kristyn/Christina, 296
la Vigne, Maria de, 296
La Vigne, Rachel, 297
La Vigne, Rachel de, 296
la Vigne, Stephen de, 295
La Vigueur, Jean, 110
la Warenbuer/Warembur, Marie de, 191
Labauve, Marie, 148
Laboissière, Anne De, 28
Laborie, Ann, 264
Laboric, Anthony, 263
LABORIE, Jacques/James (Rev.), 263
Laborie, James, 264
Laborie, Jeanne, 264
Laborie, John, 264
Laborie, Mary, 264
Laborie, Susanne, 264
Labyt, Isaac, 97
Labyt, Magdeline/Madeleine (Albert), 97
Lacey, Keziah, 332
Lacy, William, 268
Lacy/Lacey/Dela(n)cy, Agnes, 268
Lacy/Lacey/Dela(n)cy, Benjamin, 268
Lacy/Lacey/Dela(n)cy, Charles, 268
Lacy/Lacey/Dela(n)cy, Drury, 268
Lacy/Lacey/Dela(n)cy, Elijah, 268
Lacy/Lacey/Dela(n)cy, Elkanah, 268
Lacy/Lacey/Dela(n)cy, Elliott, 268
Lacy/Lacey/Dela(n)cy, Henry, 268
Lacy/Lacey/Dela(n)cy, Jesse, 268
Lacy/Lacey/Dela(n)cy, Johnson, 268
Lacy/Lacey/Dela(n)cy, Keziah, 268
Lacy/Lacey/Dela(n)cy, Lucy, 268
Lacy/Lacey/Dela(n)cy, Mary, 268
Lacy/Lacey/Dela(n)cy, Matthew, 268
Lacy/Lacey/Dela(n)cy, Nathaniel, 268
Lacy/Lacey/Dela(n)cy, Noah, 268
Lacy/Lacey/Dela(n)cy, Phoebe, 268
Lacy/Lacey/Dela(n)cy, Sarah, 268
Lacy/Lacey/Dela(n)cy, Stephen, 268
Lacy/Lacey/Dela(n)cy, Thomas, 268
LACY/LACEY/DELA(N)CY, Thomas, 268
Lacy/Lacey/Dela(n)cy, Thomas II, 268
Lacy/Lacey/Dela(n)cy, Thomas III, 268
Lacy/Lacey/Dela(n)cy, William, 268
Ladd, Samuel, 124
Ladnor, Absalom, 258
Ladou(e)/Ladoux/Ladue, Ambrose/Andrew, 269
Ladou(e)/Ladoux/Ladue, Daniel, 269

Ladou(e)/Ladoux/Ladue, Elizabeth/Betty, 269
Ladou(e)/Ladoux/Ladue, Étienne/Stephen, 269
Ladou(e)/Ladoux/Ladue, Jeanne/Jane, 269
Ladou(e)/Ladoux/Ladue, Judith, 269
Ladou(e)/Ladoux/Ladue, Magdalaine, 269
Ladou(e)/Ladoux/Ladue, Marie/Mary, 269
Ladou(e)/Ladoux/Ladue, Martha, 269
Ladou(e)/Ladoux/Ladue, Peter, 269
LADOU(E)/LADOUX/LADUE, Pierre, 269
Laer, Adrian Van, 45, 296
Laer, Aeltie Van, 45
Laer, Aeltje Van, 150
Laer, Gerrit Stoffelsen Van, 296
Lafeit/Lafitte, Ester, 341
Lafeit/Lafitte, Tobias, 341
Lafitte, David, 270
Lafitte, Jane, 270
Lafitte, Peter, 270
LAFITTE, Peter, 269
LaFLEUR/FLOWER, Thomas, 392
LaFon, Elizabeth, 270
LaFon, Hannah, 270
LaFon, Richard, 270
Lafon, Susanne, 425
LaForge, Adriean/Abraham, 349
LaForge/LaFort, John, 349
LaFuitte, Esther, 257
LaFuitte, Tobias, 257
LaFuitte/LaFite/LaFete, François, 257
LaFuitte/LaFite/LaFête, Joanne (X), 257
LAGAMET, Peter II, 266
Lagier, Ester, 42
Lagier, Jaque, 42
Lagier, Norade, 42
LAGRO, John, 311
Laican, Helena (Lom), 250
Laican, Michael, 250
Laican/Lycon, Catharine, 250
Laignel, Jean, 154
Laignel/Laigneil, Elizabeth, 154
Lake, Sarah, 130
Lakeman, Anne (de Sanchoy), 130
Lakerman, Abraham, 120, 130, 290
Lakerman, Catherine (Crocheron), 290
Lakerman, Hester, 290
Lakerman, Louis, 130
Lakerman, Maria (Wouters/Walters), 290
Lalon, Marie, 69
Lamar, Alexander, 276
Lamar, Ann, 275, 276
Lamar, Charlotte, 108
Lamar, Elizabeth, 276
Lamar, Gazaway Buggs, 108
Lamar, Gazaway DeRosselt, 108
Lamar, Harriet Cazenove, 108
Lamar, James, 276

Lamar, John, 276
Lamar, Mareen, 276
Lamar, Margaret, 275
Lamar, Marie, 407
Lamar, Mary, 275, 276
Lamar, Pierre/Peter, 275
Lamar, Priscilla, 276
Lamar, Rachel, 276
Lamar, Richard, 276
Lamar, Robert, 276
Lamar, Samuel, 276
Lamar, Susanna, 276
Lamar, Thomas, 275, 276
LAMAR/LAMORE/LEMAR, 275
Lamars, Maria de, 101
LaMasson, Anne Marguerite, 382
Lambert, Anne, 240
LAMBERT, Daniel, 277
Lambert, Denis, 31
Lambert, Frances, 278
Lambert, Françoise (Drinqueman), 31
Lambert, Jan/John, 123
Lambert, Judith, 123
Lambert, Mary, 123
Lambert, Nicholas, 123
Lambert, Serène, 420
Lambert, Simeon, 123
Lambert, Stineche/Tryntje, 123
Lambert, Susanne, 31
Lamberts, Aeltje, 296
Lambrail/Lombrail, Barnarde de, 118
Lambremont, David de, 197
Lamkin, George, 133
Lamkin, Hannah (Cox), 133
Lamkin, James, 133
Lamkin, Peter, 133
Lamkin, Samuel, 133
LaMotte/Lamott, Abram, 279
LaMotte/Lamott, Daniel, 279
LaMotte/Lamott, Francis, 279
LaMotte/Lamott, Henry, 279
LaMOTTE/LAMOTT, Jean Henri/Johannes Heinrich, 279
LaMotte/Lamott, John Henry, 279
Lamoureux, André, 279
L'Amoureux/Lamoureux, André/Andrew, 280
L'Amoureux/Lamoureux, Daniel, 280
L'Amoureux/Lamoureux, Elizabeth, 280
L'Amoureux/Lamoureux, Isaac, 280
L'Amoureux/Lamoureux, Jacques, 280
L'Amoureux/Lamoureux, Jacques/James, 280
L'Amoureux/Lamoureux, Jean/John, 280
L'Amoureux/Lamoureux, Josué/Joshua, 280
L'Amoureux/Lamoureux, Judith, 280
L'Amoureux/Lamoureux, Pierre/Peter, 280
L'Amoureux/Lamoureux, Susanne, 280
LaMude, Annette, 143

L'Amy, Françoise, 196
Lancey, James de Lt. Gov. NY, 182
Lançois, Anne, 305
Lancy/Lancey/Delancey, Anne, 281
LANCY/LANCEY/DELANCEY, Étienne de/Stephen, 280
Lancy/Lancey/Delancey, Étienne/Stephen, 281
Lancy/Lancey/Delancey, Jacques/James, 281
Lancy/Lancey/Delancey, Jean/John, 281
Lancy/Lancey/Delancey, Olivier/Oliver, 281
Lancy/Lancey/Delancey, Pierre/Peter, 281
Lancy/Lancey/Delancey, Susannah, 281
Landers/Landen, Ellen, 145
Landis, Christian, 370
LANDON/LANGDON, Jacques Morin de, 281
Landon/Langdon, Ann de, 282
Landon/Langdon, Benjamin de, 283
Landon/Langdon, Daniel de, 282
Landon/Langdon, David de, 282
Landon/Langdon, Deliverance de, 282
Landon/Langdon, Elizabeth de, 282
Landon/Langdon, Ester/Hester de, 282
Landon/Langdon, George(s) de, 281
Landon/Langdon, Hannah de, 282
Landon/Langdon, Jacques Nathaniel de, 281
Landon/Langdon, James de, 282
Landon/Langdon, Jean/John de, 282
Landon/Langdon, John de, 282
Landon/Langdon, Joseph de, 282
Landon/Langdon, Lydia de, 282
Landon/Langdon, Mary de, 282
Landon/Langdon, Nathan de, 282
Landon/Langdon, Nathaniel de, 282
Landon/Langdon, Rachel de, 282
Landon/Langdon, Samuel de, 282
Landrin(e), Guillaume/William, 441
Landrin, Maria, 333
Landrine, Guillaume, 333
Landrine, Marie (Sicard), 333
Landry, Jan Baptiste, 294
Landzine, Mary, 20
Lane, Catrina, 293
Lane, George, 202
Lane, Henry, 43, 44
Lane, Isaac, 102
Lane, Martha, 456
Lane, Samuel, 456
Lane, Sarah, 102
Lang, Anna Veronika, 283
Lang, Christian (X), 150
Lang, Julianna, 150
LANG, Peter, 283
Lang, Urban, 150
Langdon, Elizabeth, 190
Langdon, Joseph, 428

Lange, Alida de, 239
Lange, Anna Marthe, **42**
Lange, Jannetje De, 242
Langel, Elizabeth, 284
LANGEL, Jacques/James, 284
Langel, Susannah, 284
Langelan, Annetje Phillipse, 296
Langelan, Phillip, 296
Langham/Langhorn, Margaret, 209
Langille, Anne, 284
Langille, Catherine, 284
Langille, Catherine Margaret, 285
Langille, Catherine-Elizabeth, 285
Langille, Daniel, 284
LANGILLE, Daniel, 284
Langille, David, 284, 285
Langille, Françoise, 285
Langille, Frederick, 285
Langille, Jacques, 285
Langille, James, 284
Langille, Jean Jacques/John James, 284
Langille, John David, 285
Langille, John Frederick, 285
Langille, John George, 285
Langille, John Nicholas, 284
Langille, Léonard, 285
Langille, Léopold Frédéric, 285
Langille, Lewis, 285
Langille, Margaret, 285
Langille, Margaretta, 284
Langille, Marie Catherine, 285
Langille, Marie Elizabeth, 285
Langille, Marie Magdalena, 284
Langille, Mathieu/Matthew, 285
Langille, Susanne Catherine, 285
Langley, Joyce, 451
Langley, Joyce (X), 451
Langley, Thomas, 451
Langley, William, 451
Langlois, Germain, 110
Langlois, Jehanne, 166
Langue, Edward, 433
Lanier, Alphonse, 286
Lanier, Andrea, 286
Lanier, Clement, 286
Lanier, Ellen, 286
Lanier, Frances, 286
Lanier, Innocent, 286
Lanier, Jerome, 286
Lanier, John, 286
Lanier, Katherine, 286
Lanier, Mark, 286
Lanier, Mary, 286
LANIER, Nicolas, 285
Lankford, William, 383
Lannoy, Jan de, 337
Lannoy, Jean de, 286
Lannoy, Jeanne (de Ligne, Dame de Barbançon) de, 286
Lannoy, Jeanne de, 313
Lano, Gysbert (de), 139

Lanois/Lannoy/Launoy/La Noy/Delano, Abraham, 287
Lanois/Lannoy/Launoy/La Noy/Delano, Antoinette, 287
Lanois/Lannoy/Launoy/La Noy/Delano, Catalyntje, 287
Lanois/Lannoy/Launoy/La Noy/Delano, Cornelia, 287
Lanois/Lannoy/Launoy/La Noy/Delano, Esaie/Isaiah, 286
LANOIS/LANNOY/LAUNOY/La NOY/DELANO, Gysbert/Gilbert de, 286
Lanois/Lannoy/Launoy/La Noy/Delano, Henri Martin, 287
Lanois/Lannoy/Launoy/La Noy/Delano, Jacques, 287
Lanois/Lannoy/Launoy/La Noy/Delano, Jean/Jan, 286
Lanois/Lannoy/Launoy/La Noy/Delano, Margriete, 287
Lanois/Lannoy/Launoy/La Noy/Delano, Maria, 287
Lanois/Lannoy/Launoy/La Noy/Delano, Marie, 287
Lanois/Lannoy/Launoy/La Noy/Delano, Pieter/Peter, 287
Lanois/Lanoy/Launoy/La Noy/Delano, Jenne, 286
Lanois/Lanoy/Launoy/La Noy/Delano, Philippe/Philip, 286
Lansdon/Langsdon, William, 257
Lansing, John, 274
LaQuir, Antaletta, 302
Lar(a)way, Jonar, 459
LARAWAY, Jonar/Jonas, 320
Lardan, Jacques, 289
Lardan, Marie (Poullard), 289
LARDENT/LARDANT/LARDAN(S), Jacques I, 289
Lardent/Lardant/Lardan(s), Jacques II[2], 289
Lardent/Lardant/Lardan(s), Martha, 289
LaResiliere, Anthony, 290
LaResiliere, Benjamin, 290
LaResiliere, Catherine, 290
LaResiliere, Elizabeth, 290
LaRESILIÈRE, Jacques/Jacob, 289
LaResiliere, James, 290
LaResiliere, Magdalen, 290
LaResiliere, Margaret, 290
LaResiliere, Mary/Marij/Maria, 290
LaResiliere, Marya/Marie, 290
LaResiliere, Michael, 290
LaResiliere, Nicholas, 290
LaResilière, Nicholas, 289
LaResiliere, Peter, 290
LARGOE, Freeborn, 311
Laroche, John, 212
Laroe, Jacques, 172
LAROE, James, 315

Laroe, Wybrech (Hendrickse), 172
Laronde, Pierre, 54
Laros, Rudolph, 469
Larzelère, Hester (Lakerman), 58
Larzelere, Jacques, 290
Larzelère, Jacques, 61
Larzelère, Margaret, 120, 290
Larzelère, Maria (Grangen), 61
Larzelere, Marie, 290
Larzelere, Nicholas, 61
Larzelère, Nicholas, 58, 61, 290
Larzelère/La Resilière, Margaret, 62
Lashamast/DeLashmutt, Ann, 267
Lashamast/DeLashmutt, Basil, 267
LASHAMAST/DeLASHMUTT, Elias, 267
Lashamast/DeLashmutt, Elizabeth, 267
Lashamast/DeLashmutt, Lindsay, 267
LaSHAMET, Anna, 266
Lasie/Lacy, William, 269
Lasie/Lacy, Wm. II, 269
Lataile, unknown, 40
Latane, Anna, 291
Latane, Catherine, 291
Latane, Charlotte, 291
Latane, Henri, 291
Latane, Henrietta, 291
Latane, Henry, 291
Latane, Isaac, 291
Latane, John, 291
Latane, Joseph, 290, 291
Latane, Lewis, 291
Latane, Maryanne/Marian, 291
Latane, Phebe, 291
Latane, Pierre, 291
LATANÉ, Pierre (Rev.), 290
Latane, Susanna, 291
Latane, William, 291
Lathbery/Leatherbury, Mary, 25
Lathrop, unknown, 75
Latour, Elizabeth, 381
LaTourette, David, 292
LaTourette, Jacob, 292
LaTourette, Jean, 357
LaTourette, John, 357
LaTourette, Magdeleine (X), 292
LaTourette, Marie, 292
Latre, Christine Marie (Bentz) de, 263
Latre, Dorothie Christine Anna de, 263
Latre, Jean de, 263
Latture, Elisabeth, 292
Latture, Elizabeth, 292
Latture, George Michael[3], 292
Latture, Harmon/Herman, 292
Latture, Jacob, 292
Latture, James, 292
Latture, Nancy, 292
Latture, Nicklaus, 292
Latture, Susanna Margaretha, 292
Latture, Susannah, 292
Latture, Thomas, 292
Lâty, Anne Martha, 303

Lâty/Lâtys, Catherine, 303
Lâty/Lâtys, Jacques, 303
Laub, Anna Maria, 370
Lauff, Catharine Margaretha, 252
Lauff, Christoph, 252
Lauffer, Gottlieb, 199
Laure/Lerew/LaRue, Jonas Jr., 438
Laurens, Jacques, 387
Laurens, Jean Samuel, 230
Laurens, Marie, 301
Laurens, Tryntje (Catherine), 404
Laval, Anne Caterine, 413
Laval, Anne Sophie (Mollet), 413
Laval, Antoinette (de Daillon) de, 121
Laval, Charlotte de, 121
Laval, Guy de, 121
Laval, Jean Louis, 413
Lavandier, Ann (Dufour), 303
Lavandier, Josias, 303
LaVillon/Villain, Susanne Comtesse, 168
Lavoye, Catherine de, 392
Lawter/Laffer/Lauffer, Christian, 249
Lawrence, Augustine Hicks, 305
Lawrence, Elizabeth, 304
Lawrence, John Capt., 40
Lawrence, Rebecca, 256
Lawton, William Capt., 104
Lazey, Susanne de, 21
Le CHEVALLIER/CHEVALIER, Jean/John, 299
Le SER(R)URIER, Jacques/James, 321
Le Baron, Bartlett, 298
Le Baron, David, 297
Le Baron, Elizabeth, 298
Le Baron, Francis, 297, 298
Le BARON, François/Francis, 297
Le Baron, Hannah, 298
Le Baron, Isaac, 298
Le Baron, James, 297
Le Baron, John, 297
Le Baron, Joseph, 298
Le Baron, Joshua, 297
Le Baron, Lazarus, 298
Le Baron, Lemuel, 298
Le Baron, Lydia, 298
Le Baron, Margaret, 298
Le Baron, Martha, 297
Le Baron, Mary, 297
Le Baron, Priscilla, 298
Le Baron, Theresa, 298
Le Baron, William, 298
Le Blanck, Maria, 301
Le Boiteux/Boyteaux/Boyteulx, Benjamin, 299
Le Boiteux/Boyteaux/Boyteulx, Catherine, 299
Le Boiteux/Boyteaux/Boyteulx, Elizabeth, 299
Le Boiteux/Boyteaux/Boyteulx, Gabriel, 299

Le BOITEUX/BOYTEAUX/BOYTEULX, Gabriel, 298
Le Boiteux/Boyteaux/Boyteulx, Jantien, 299
Le Boiteux/Boyteaux/Boyteulx, Jeanne, 299
Le Boiteux/Boyteaux/Boyteulx, Marie, 298
Le Boiteux/Boyteaux/Boyteulx, Marquise, 299
Le Boiteux/Boyteaux/Boyteulx, Mary, 299
Le Boiteux/Boyteaux/Boyteulx, Paul, 299
Le Boiteux/Boyteaux/Boyteulx, Peter, 299
Le Boiteux/Boyteaux/Boyteulx, Suzanne, 299
Le Boylteux, Gabriel, 374
Le Chamois, Jacob, 267
Le Chamois, Marie (Lenain), 267
Le Chevalier, Ester (Dallain), 84
Le Chevalier, Jean, 129, 289
Le Chevalier, Pierre, 84
Le Chevalier, Roland, 84
Le Chevallier/Chevalier, Catherine, 299
Le Chevallier/Chevalier, Daniel, 299
Le Chevallier/Chevalier, Élisabeth, 299
Le Chevallier/Chevalier, Elizabeth, 299
Le Chevallier/Chevalier, Ester, 299
Le Chevallier/Chevalier, Helena, 299
Le Chevallier/Chevalier, Henricus, 299
Le Chevallier/Chevalier, Jean/John, 299
Le Chevallier/Chevalier, Jeanne, 299
Le Chevallier/Chevalier, Johannes, 299
Le Chevallier/Chevalier, Judith, 299
Le Chevallier/Chevalier, Marie, 299
Le Chevallier/Chevalier, Peter, 299
Le Chevallier/Chevalier, Rachel, 299
Le Chevallier/Chevalier, Susanne, 299
Le CLERC, Jeanne, 300
Le Co(u)nte, Pierre, 62
Le Compte, Anthony, 300
Le COMPTE, Anthony, 300
Le Compte, Esther/Hester, 300
Le Compte, John, 300
Le Compte, Katherine, 300
Le Compte, Moses, 300
Le Compte, Philip, 300
Le COMTE, Michel, 300
Le Comte, Abraham, 301
Le Comte, Boudewyn, 301
Le Comte, Charles, 301
Le Comte, Élisabeth, 300
Le Comte, Esther, 301
Le Comte, Jacqueline, 301
Le Comte, Jacques, 300
Le Comte, Jan, 301
Le Comte, Jannetje, 301
Le Comte, Jean, 301
Le Comte, Margaret, 301

Le Comte, Marguerite, 300
Le Comte, Maria, 301
Le Comte, Marie, 301
Le Comte, Michel, 301
Le Comte, Moses, 301
Le Comte, Rachel, 301
Le Comte, Samuel, 301
Le Comte, Susanna, 301
Le Comte/Le Conte, Anne, 304
Le Comte/Le Conte, Esther, 304
Le COMTE/Le CONTE, Guillaume, 303
Le Comte/Le Conte, Guillaume/Willam, 304
Le Comte/Le Conte, HesterEsther, 304
Le Comte/Le Conte, John Eaton, 304
Le Comte/Le Conte, Margaret(ta), 304
Le Comte/Le Conte, Marianne, 304
Le Comte/Le Conte, Peter, 304
Le Comte/Le Conte, Susanne, 304
Le Comte/Le Conte, Thomas, 304
Le Comte/Le Conte, William, 304
Le Comte/Le Conte. Pierre, 304
Le Conseille(r)/de
    Conchilier/Conselye(a)/Conselje,
    Annaken/Annetje, 302
Le Conseille(r)/de
    Conchilier/Conselye(a)/Conselje,
    Barbara, 302
Le Conseille(r)/de
    Conchilier/Conselye(a)/Conselje,
    Jean/Jan II, 301
Le CONSEILLE(R)/de
    CONCHILIER/CONSELYE(A)/CONSELJE,
    Jean/Jan/John, 301
Le Conseille(r)/de
    Conchilier/Conselye(a)/Conselje,
    John, 302
Le Conseille(r)/de
    Conchilier/Conselye(a)/Conselje,
    Lysbet, 301
Le Conseille(r)/de
    Conchilier/Conselye(a)/Conselje,
    Magaret/Grietje, 302
Le Conseille(r)/de
    Conchilier/Consulye(a)/Conselje,
    Antje, 302
Le Conseille(r)/de
    Conchilier/Consulye(a)/Conselje,
    Pieter/Peter, 302
Le Conseille(r)/de
    Conchilier/Consulye(a)/Consulje,
    Andries, 302
Le Conseille(r)/de
    Conchilier/Consulye(a)/Consulje,
    Arie, 302
Le Conseille(r)/de
    Conchilier/Consulye(a)/Consulje,
    Barbara/Barratje, 302
Le Conseille(r)/de
    Conchilier/Consulye(a)/Consulje,
    Barent, 302

Le Conseille(r)/de
    Conchilier/Consulye(a)/Consulje,
    Elizabeth, 302
Le Conseille(r)/de
    Conchilier/Consulye(a)/Consulje, Jan,
    302
Le Conseille(r)/de
    Conchilier/Consulye(a)/Consulje,
    John, 302
Le Conseille(r)/de
    Conchilier/Consulye(a)/Consulje,
    Mary, 302
Le Conseille(r)/de
    Conchilier/Consulye(a)/Consulje,
    Peter, 302
Le Conseille(r)/de
    Conchilier/Consulye(a)/Consulje,
    Petrus, 302
Le Conseille(r)/de
    Conchilier/Consulye(a)/Consulje,
    Pieter, 302
Le Conseille(r)/de
    Conchilier/Consulye(a)/Consulje,
    Sarah, 302
Le Conseille(r)/de
    Conchilier/Consulye(a)/Consulje,
    Willem, 302
Le Conseille(r)/de
    Conchilier/Consulye(a)/Consulje,
    William, 302
Le Conseille(r)/de
    Condhilier/Consulye(a)/Conselje,
    Sarah, 302
Le Conte, Anne, 303
Le Conte, Catherine, 303
Le Conte, Catherine (Sicard), 303
Le Conte, Estienne, 146
Le Conte, Francis, 303
Le Conte, François, 303
Le CONTE, François, 303
Le Conte, Guillaume, 396
Le Conte, Josias I, 303
Le Conte, Josias II, 303
Le Conte, Judith, 303
Le Conte, Madeleine, 303
Le Conte, Margaret (Mahault), 396
Le Conte, Marie (Amon), 303
Le Conte, Pierre, 396
Le Count, Hester, 74
Le Faulx, Anne, 166
Le Faulx, Guillaume, 166
Le Faulx, Rachel, 166
Le Fèvre, Antoine, 174
Le FÈVRE, Isaac, 309
Le Fèvre, Jean, 198
le Fèvre, Marie, 156
Le Gaigneur, Jehanne, 165
le Garde, Marguerite Pauline (Piede) de,
    460
Le Gendre, Louis, 354
Le Grand, Abraham, 310

Le Grand, Alexander, 311
Le Grand, Anne, 310
Le Grand, Anne (Bruneau), 208
Le Grand, Daniel, 310
Le Grand, Elizabeth, 310
Le Grand, Isaac, 208, 310
Le Grand, Jacques/James, 310
Le Grand, James, 311
Le Grand, Jane Magdalene, 310
Le Grand, Jean Pierre/John Peter, 310,
    361
Le Grand, Jean/John, 310
Le Grand, John, 310
Le Grand, Judith, 310
Le Grand, Judith (Vreil), 361
Le Grand, Peter, 311
Le Grand, Pierre, 361
Le GRAND, Pierre, 310
Le Grand, Susanna, 311
Le JAU, François/Francis (Rev.), 311
le Magoules/de Magoulais, Joseph, 394
le Maistre, Marguerite, 313
Le Maistre/Maître, Charlotte, 447
Le Maître, Claude, 155
Le Maître, David, 449
Le Maitre, Gédéon, 449
Le Maître, Jean, 312
Le Maitre, Jeanne (Cottonie), 449
Le Maître, Sarah (X), 312
Le MAÎTRE/ Le MAISTRE/ DELAMATER,
    Claude/ Glaude, 313
Le Maître/Delamater, Claude, 301
Le Maître/Delamater, Hester/Ester
    (DuBois), 301
Le Maitre/Le Maistre/Delamater,
    Abraham, 313
Le Maitre/Le Maistre/Delamater, Isaac,
    313
Le Maitre/Le Maistre/Delamater,
    Johannes/Jan, 313
Le Maitre/Le Maistre/Delamater, Mary,
    313
Le Maitre/Le Maistre/Delamater,
    Susanna, 313
Le Maitre/Le Maistre/Delamater,
    Susanne, 313
Le MAÎTRE/Le MASTER, Abraham, 312
Le Maitre/Le Master, Anne, 312
Le Maitre/Le Master, Eleanor, 312
Le Maitre/Le Master, Issac, 312
Le Maitre/Le Master, John, 312
Le Maitre/Le Master, Mary, 312
Le Maitre/Le Master, Richard, 312
Le Maitre/Le Master, Sarah, 312
Le Maitre/LeMaistre/Delamater,
    Esther/Hester, 313
Le Maitre/LeMaistre/Delamater,
    Jacobus, 313
Le MERCIER, Jean, 313
le Mercier, Jehan, 123
Le Mercier, Renee, 316

Le Mesureur, Antoinette, 151
Le MOINE/Le MOYNE, Moïse/Moses, 313
Le Moyne, Rachel, 156
Le Myre, Louis, 328
Le Myre, Mathyas, 328
Le Noble, Catherine (X), 409
Le Noble, Henry, 409
Le PLAT/LEPPLA, Daniel, 314
le Riche, Anne (Ferment), 260
le Riche, Jean, 260
le Riche, Suzanne, 260
Le Roux/ La Rue/Larew, Rachel, 316
Le Roux/La Rue/Larew, Abraham, 315, 316
Le Roux/La Rue/Larew, Angentie, 316
Le Roux/La Rue/Larew, Anne, 316
Le Roux/La Rue/Larew, Antie, 316
Le ROUX/La RUE/LAREW, Antoine, 314
Le Roux/La Rue/Larew, Daniel, 315
Le Roux/La Rue/Larew, David, 315, 316
Le Roux/La Rue/Larew, Elizabeth, 316
Le Roux/La Rue/Larew, Hendrick, 316
Le Roux/La Rue/Larew, Isaac, 315
Le Roux/La Rue/Larew, Jacques, 315
Le Roux/La Rue/Larew, Jannetie, 315
Le Roux/La Rue/Larew, Jeanne, 315
Le Roux/La Rue/Larew, Johannes, 316
Le Roux/La Rue/Larew, Margaret, 316
Le Roux/La Rue/Larew, Maria, 316
Le Roux/La Rue/Larew, Marie, 316
Le Roux/La Rue/Larew, Peter, 315
Le Roux/La Rue/Larew, Pierre, 315
LE ROUX/LA RUE/LAREW, Pierre, 315
Le Roux/La Rue/Larew, Pieter, 316
Le Roux/La Rue/Larew, Samuel, 316
Le Roux/La Rue/Larew, Susanna, 316
Le Roux/La Rue/Larew, Susanne, 316
Le Roy, Amatheur, 317
Le ROY, Ant(h)oine, 316
Le Roy, Benjamin, 317
Le Roy, Catherine, 317
Le Roy, Charles Louis, 318, 319
Le Roy, Daniel, 317, 318
Le Roy, David, 316
Le Roy, Elizabeth, 318, 319
Le Roy, Ester, 317
Le Roy, Esther, 316
Le Roy, Étienne, 317
Le Roy, Ezekiel, 316
Le Roy, François, 316
Le Roy, Gaspard, 54, 317
Le Roy, Gilette (Jacquet), 319
Le Roy, Guernarie, 317
Le Roy, Henri, 317
Le Roy, Henriette, 317
Le Roy, Herman, 318
Le Roy, Ingenatia, 318
Le Roy, Isaac, 317, 319
Le Roy, Jacob, 317, 318
Le Roy, Jacques, 316, 318

Le Roy, Jean Philippe, 318
Le Roy, Jeanne, 319
Le Roy, John, 319
Le Roy, Jonathan, 319
Le Roy, Judith, 54, 317
Le Roy, Louis, 316
Le Roy, Madeleine, 317
Le Roy, Maria Ann, 317, 318
Le Roy, Maria Anna, 317
Le Roy, Marianne, 317
Le Roy, Marie, 317
Le Roy, Marie (Sanceau), 54
Le Roy, Marie Anne, 319
Le Roy, Marie Magdeleine, 317
Le Roy, Mary, 319
Le Roy, Peter Charles, 319
Le Roy, Philip II, 319
Le Roy, Pierre, 317
Le Roy, Pierre Antoine, 318
Le ROY, Pierre Michel, 318
Le Roy, Pierre/Philippe I, 318
Le Roy, Richard, 319
Le Roy, Robert, 318
Le Roy, Siméon, 316
Le ROY, Siméon, 319
Le Roy, Susan Anne, 319
Le Roy, Théodore, 317
Le Roy, Veronique, 318
Le Ser(r)urier, Catherine, 322
Le Ser(r)urier, Damaris Elizabeth, 322
Le Ser(r)urier, Marianne, 322
le Ser(r)urier, Susanne, 222
Le Ser(r)urier, Susanne, 321
Le Serrurier, Elizabeth (Léger), 165
Le Serrurier, Jacques, 165
Le Serurier, Jacques, 321
Le Serurier, Marie (Le Compte), 321
le Seure/Feure, Judith, 241
Le Soigue, Maria Susanne, 199
Le Sueur, Catherine, 323, 324
Le Sueur, Chastain, 323
Le Sueur, David, 323
Le SUEUR, David, 323
Le Sueur, Elizabeth, 323
Le Sueur, Esther, 323
Le Sueur, Esther (Buire), 323
Le Sueur, Fell, 323
Le Sueur, Jacques/James, 323, 324
Le Sueur, John, 323
Le Sueur, Marie, 323
Le Sueur, Marie Anne, 324
Le Sueur, Martell, 323
Le Sueur, Peter, 323
Le Sueur, Pierre, 323
Le Sueur, Samuel, 323, 324
Le Turk, Harman, 458
Le Turk, Hugo, 458
Le Turk, Margat (de Privas), 458
Le Turk, Michael, 458
Le Turk, Robert, 458
Le Turk, Sancred, 458

Le Van, Abraham, 55
Le Van, Catherine (Von Weimer), 55
Le Van, Daniel, 55
Le VAN, Daniel, 325
Le Van, Marie (Beau), 55
Le Vasseur, Marie, 166
Le Villian, Antoine, 326
Le Villian, Elizabeth, 326
Le Villian, Jean, 326
Le VILLIAN, Jean II, 325
Le Villian, Jean/John, Jr./John Peter, 326
Le Villian, Mary, 326
Le VIllian, Samuel, 326
Le Villian, Susanne, 326
Le/La Grove/Le Grou, Hannah, 311
Le/La GROVE/Le GROU, Nicholas, 311
Le/La Grove/Le Grou, Peter, 311
Le/La Grove/Le Grou, Susannah, 311
Le/La Grove/LeGrou, Nicholas, 311
Leake, John, 187
Learned, Experience, 110, 267
Learned, Isaac, 111, 267
Learned, Sarah, 111, 267
Learned, Sarah (How), 267
LearnedSarah (How), 111
Leau, Éve, 284
Leau/Lowe, Eve (X), 284
Leau/Lowe, George, 284
LeBlanc, Marie, 58
LeBrun, Agnes Constance, 298
LeBrun, Jean Philippe, 318
LeBrun, Marie Michelle, 318
LeBrun, Moise, 298
LeCaze, James, 351
LeCaze, Margaret (Coop), 351
Lechier, Hillebrant, 313
Lechten, Lammetie (X) Van, 130
LeClerc, Arnould, 123
LeClerc, Jeanne (Lippenson), 123
LeClerc, Jeanne/Janne, 123
LeClercq, Marguerite, 151
Leclercq/LeClercq, Jacques, 148
LeConte, Antoine, 119
LeConte, Catherine, 440
LeConte, Catherine (Levandier), 54
LeConte, Esther (Bertine), 440
LeConte, François, 54
LeConte, Jean, 105
LeConte, Josias, 54
LeConte, Josias II, 440
LeConte, Martha, 74
LeConte, Peter, 74
LeConte, Pierre, 290
LeConte, Sara, 119, 155
LeConte, Susannah, 105
LeConte/Le Com(p)te, Elisabeth, 449
Lecouve, Jeanne, 395
L'Ecuyer/L'Escuyer/L/Esquier/Lequ(i)er, Christina, 305
L'Ecuyer/L'Escuyer/L'Esquier/Lequ(i)er, Annetje, 305

L'Ecuyer/L'Escuyer/L'Esquier/Lequ(i)er, Antonette, 305
L'Ecuyer/L'Escuyer/L'Esquier/Lequ(i)er, Catherine, 305
L'Ecuyer/L'Escuyer/L'Esquier/Lequ(i)er, Gerardus, 305
L'Ecuyer/L'Escuyer/L'Esquier/Lequ(i)er, Guilliam/William, 305
L'Ecuyer/L'Escuyer/L'Esquier/Lequ(i)er, Isaac, 305
L'Ecuyer/L'Escuyer/L'Esquier/Lequ(i)er, Jan/Johannes, 305
L'Ecuyer/L'Escuyer/L'Esquier/Lequ(i)er, John, 305
L'Ecuyer/L'Escuyer/L'Esquier/Lequ(i)er, Maria/Mary, 305
L'Ecuyer/L'Escuyer/L'Esquier/Lequ(i)er, Nicholas, 305
L'Ecuyer/L'Escuyer/L'Esquier/Lequ(i)er, Pieter, 305
L'Ecuyer/L'Escuyer/L'Esquier/Lequ(i)er, Ragel/Rachel, 305
Ledoux, unknown, 449
leDuc, Marie, 180
leDuc, Nicholas, 180
Lee, Cassius F., 108
Lee, Elizabeth, 157
Lee, Lydia, 338
Lee, Stephen, 221
Lee, Thomas, 157
LeFanu, William, 32
LeFebre, Abraham, 306
LeFEBRE, Isaac, 306
LeFebre, Maria, 306
LeFebre, Myndert, 306
LeFebvre, Anne, 141
LeFebvre, Geneviève (Pelletier), 141
LeFèbvre, Jeanne, 409
LeFebvre, Thomas, 141
LeFÈVRE, 307
LeFevre, Abraham, 192, 307, 308
LeFèvre, Abraham, 192
LeFevre, André, 307
LeFevre, Andries, 307
LeFèvre, Andries, 308
LeFevre, Andries/Andrew, 308
LeFevre, Antoinette (Vilain), 174
LeFèvre, Catherine, 439
LeFèvre, Catherine (Blanshan), 308
LeFèvre, Catherine (Ferrée)[2], 192
LeFevre, Catrina/Catherine, 308
LeFèvre, Cornelia (Blanchan), 308
LeFèvre, Cornelia (Blanshan), 308
LeFevre, Daniel, 307, 308
LeFèvre, Daniel, 103
LeFèvre, David, 147
LeFevre, Elisabeth, 308
LeFevre, Élisabeth, 307
LeFevre, Elizabeth, 309
LeFèvre, Elizabeth (Deyo), 103
LeFèvre, Elizabeth (LeBleu), 147

LeFevre, Esther, 307
LeFevre, Isaac, 307, 308
LeFèvre, Isaac, 168, 185, 192
LeFèvre, Jan, 308
LeFevre, Jan/John, 308
LeFevre, Johannes, 308
LeFevre, Judith, 309
LeFèvre, Judith, 168
LeFèvre, Madeleine (Parenteau), 185
LeFèvre, Magdalena, 103
LeFevre, Magdalene, 308
LeFevre, Magdelaine, 309
LeFèvre, Magdelaine (Parenteau), 168
LeFèvre, Magdeleine, 174
LeFevre, Margaret, 308
LeFevre, Margrietje/Margaret, 308
LeFèvre, Marie, 147, 308
LeFevre, Maritjen/Marie, 308
LeFevre, Mary, 307, 308
LeFevre, Mary/Maritje, 308
LeFevre, Matheus/Matthew, 307
LeFèvre, Nathaniel, 308
LeFèvre, Nathaniel, 308
LeFevre, Petrus/Peter, 308
LeFevre, Philip, 307
LeFevre, Rachel, 308
LeFevre, Samuel, 192, 307
LeFèvre, Samuel, 192
LeFevre, Simon, 307, 308
LeFèvre, Simon, 103, 149
LeFevre, Zara/Sarah, 308
LeFèvre. Catrina/Catherine, 308
LeFèvre/Febre, Catherine, 94
Leftwich, unknown, 429
LeGard, Elijah, 319
Légare, Laurent, 194
L'Egare/Legare, Daniel, 306
L'Egare/Legare, Daniel James, 306
L'Egare/Legare, François Solomon, 306
L'Egare/Legare, Hannah, 306
L'Egare/Legare, John, 306
L'Egare/Legare, Mary, 306
L'Egare/Legare, Sarah, 306
L'Egare/Legare, Solomon, 306
L'Egare/Legare, Stephen John, 306
L'Egare/Legare, Thomas, 306
Leger, Elizabeth, 309
Léger, Elizabeth, 321
LÉGER, Jacques, 309
Leger, Peter, 310
Leger, Sara, 310
LEGEREAU, Eugénie, 310
Légereau, Eugenie, 447
Legoux, Henriette, **36**
LeGrand, Ann François, 208
LeGrand, Anna, 208
LeGrand, Anne (de Magneville), 423
LeGrand, Anne Marie Louise, 423
LeGrand, Elisabeth (Dieu), 234
LeGrand, Isaac, 234
LeGrand, Jacques de Lomboy, 208

LeGrand, Louis, 423
LeGrand, Mary Ann, 234
LeGros, Marie Marthe, 100
Leinbach, Anna Maria, 120
Leinback, Frederick, 206
Leininger, Anna Maria, 192
LeJau, Ann, 248, 312
LeJau, Catherine, 312
LeJau, Dorothy, 312
LeJau, Elizabeth, 312
LeJau, Francis, 248, 312
LeJau, Francis Thomas, 312
LeJau, George, 312
LeJau, Mary (Ashby), 248
Lem(m)on, Mary/Olivet, 217
LeMaître/LeMaistre, Hester, 301
Lemaster, unknown, 267
LeMoine/LeMoyne, Françoise, 314
LeMoine/LeMoyne, Mary, 314
LeMoine/LeMoyne, Moyse, 314
LeMoine/LeMoyne, Peter, 314
Lemonier, James/Jacques, 156
Lemonier, Susannah, 156
LeMoyne, Marguerite (X), 156
LeMoyne, Pierre, 156
Lenhart, Sarah, 97
LeNoble, Henry, 322
LeNoir, Jean, 134
LeNoir, Jeanne (Jacob), 134
LeNoir, Jeanne-Marguerite, 134
LeNoir, Magdeleine, 287
Lent, Abraham, 170
Lent, Catherine, 450
Lenud, Henry Capt., 310
LeNud, Nicholas, 255
LeNud, Nicholas II, 360
Leonard, Ann (X), 53
Leonard, Henry, 425
Leonard, Mary, 53
Leonard, Nathaniel, 425
Leonard, Samuel Capt., 53
Leonard, Sarah, 298
Leonard, Sarah (Dumbleton), 428
LePlat/Leppla, Anna Katherine, 314
LePlat/Leppla, Jacob, 314
LePlat/Leppla, Jean Jacques Henri/Johann Jacob Heinrich, 314
LePlat/Leppla, Jean Pierre, 314
LePlat/Leppla, Jean/Johan Daniel, 314
LePlat/Leppla, Johann/Hans Georg, 314
Leppla, Maria Elisabetha (Leplat), 408
Leppla, Maria Katharina, 408
Leppla, Peter, 408
LeQueux, Lea, 155
LeQuie, Jan, 304
Lequier, Antonette, 302
Lequier, Isaac, 302
Lerber/Herbert, Anna Barbara, 362
LeRoi/Roy, Jean, 105
LeRoo, Susannah, 79
LeRoux, Abraham, 459

LeRoux, Alida (Vryman), 375
LeRoux, Jeanne (Guerin), 14
LeRoux, Lydia/Alida, 375
LeRoux, Peter, 375
LeRoux, Pierre, 14
LeRoy, Adrien, 318
LeRoy, Blandina, 459
LeRoy, Claude (Deschâlets), 205
LeRoy, Claude/Blandina (DesChâlets), 459
LeRoy, Cornelia, 459
LeRoy, David, 459
LeRoy, Ester, 52
LeRoy, Ester (Mocquay), 52
LeRoy, François, 52
LeRoy, François/Frans, 320
LeRoy, Jan/John, 459
LeRoy, Jean, 319
LeRoy, Jerôme, 160
LeRoy, Jonas, 459
LeRoy, Leonard Treny, 320, 459
LeRoy, Maria, 459
LeRoy, Maria Anne, 205
LeRoy, Marie, 319
LeRoy, Marie (Labrun), 77
LeRoy, Marie Anne, 319
LeRoy, Marie Joseph (Blass), 318
LeRoy, Mary Ann, 77
LeRoy, Olivier, 319
LeRoy, Peter Michel, 318
LeRoy, Petrus, 459
LeRoy, Philip II, 426
LeRoy, Pierre Michel, 77
LeRoy, Sara, 320
LeRoy, Simeon, 459
LeRoy, Siméon, 205, 459
LeSade, Ann, 224
LeSade, Ann (Gornier), 224
LeSade, Pierre, 224
LeSage, Anne, 134
LeSage, Pierre, 134
Lescuye/l'Escuier, Mary, 414
L'Escuyer/L'Escuyer/L'Esquier/Lequ(i)er,
    Abraham, 305
LeSerrurier, Damaris Elizabeth, 432
LeSerrurier, Elizabeth (Leger), 208
LeSerrurier, Elizabeth (Léger), 432
LeSerrurier, Jacques, 432
LeSerrurier, James, 208
LESESNE (Le SENS ?), Isaac, 320
Lesesne, Ann, 320
Lesesne, Anne, 320
Lesesne, Charles Frederick, 321
Lesesne, Daniel, 320, 321
Lesesne, Elizabeth, 320
Lesesne, Esther/Hester, 320
Lesesne, Francis, 321
Lesesne, Francis II, 321
Lesesne, Henry James, 320
Lesesne, Isaac, 373
Lesesne, Isaac II, 320
Lesesne, Isaac Walker, 320

Lesesne, James, 320
Lesesne, James Henry, 321
Lesesne, John, 320
Lesesne, Martha, 321
Lesesne, Mary, 321
Lesesne, Peter George, 321
Lesesne, Sarah, 320, 321
Lesesne, Susannah, 320
Lesesne, Thomas, 320
Lesesne, William, 320
LeSeurrier, Jacques, 309
Lespau, Jean De, 189
Lespau, Salomon De, 189
L'Espenard/Lispenard, Abeltje/Abigail,
    323
L'Espenard/Lispenard, Anthony, 323
L'Espenard/Lispenard, Cornelia, 323
L'Espenard/Lispenard, David, 323
L'Espenard/Lispenard, Johannes, 323
L'Espenard/Lispenard, John, 323
L'Espenard/Lispenard, Margarita, 322,
    323
L'Espenard/Lispenard, Mary, 323
Lespinasse, Jean, 141
Lespineu, Jeanne, 151
Lessese, John, 321
Lester, Jacob, 80
Lester, Jane, 143, 144
LeStevenon, Gurtruydt, 196
Lestre, Anne de, 165
LeSueur, Abraham, 397
LeSueur, Catherine (Fell), 115
LeSueur, David, 115, 137
LeSueur, Isaac, 397
LeSueur, Marie (de Sanee), 397
LeSueur/Lechier/Lozier, Eustache, 324
LeSUEUR/LECHIER/LOZIER, François, 324
LeSueur/Lechier/Lozier, Hildebrand, 324
LeSueur/Lechier/Lozier, Jacob, 324
LeSueur/Lechier/Lozier, Jannatie, 324
LeSUEUR/LECHIER/LOZIER,
    Jeanne/Jannetie, 324
LeSueur/Lechier/Lozier, Nicholas, 324
LeSueur/Lechier/Lozier. John, 324
Letelier, Jean, 129
LeTellier, Marie, 237
LeTour/Latour, Suzanne, 279
Lettice, Thomas, 337
Leuvenigh, Hester Van, 439
LeValet/LaValade, unknown, 157
LeVan, Abraham, 325
LeVan, Anna Elisabeth, 325
LeVan, Daniel, 325
LeVan, Esther, 55
LeVan, Isaac, 325
LeVan, Jacob, 325
LeVan, Joseph, 325
Levasseur, Noël, 141
Levereau, Moses, 310
Levering, Anna Catherine, 206, 446
Levering, Joseph, 120

Levering, Magdalena (Boker), 206
Levering, Wigard, 206
Levèsque, Catherine (Fraigneau), 239
Levèsque, Louis, 239
Levesque, Marie, 14
LeVil(l)ain, Elizabeth, 168
LeVil(l)ain, Jean-Jacques, 168
LeVil(l)ain, Jean-Pierre/John Jr., 168
LeVil(l)ain, Olympe (X), 168
LeVil(l)ain, Olympe,(X), 168
LeVil(l)ain, Susanne, 168
LeVillain, Josias, 269
LeVillian, Jean, 325
Leviston/Livingston, John, 411
Lewis, Charles, 212, 465
Lewis, Elizabeth, 293, 465
Lewis, Elizabeth (Christopher), 201
Lewis, George, 388
Lewis, James, 427
Lewis, John, 372, 427
Lewis, John II, 201
Lewis, John III, 201
Lewis, Jonathan, 293
Lewis, Martha (X), 465
Lewis, Mary, 213
Lewis, Surles,, 427
Lewis, unknown, 132, 465
Lewis/Lomax, Lunsford, 364
Lezai, Ambroise de, 21
L'Hommedieu, Benjamin, 326
L'Hommedieu, Grissell, 326
L'Hommedieu, Hosea, 326
L'Hommedieu, John, 326
L'Hommedieu, Osée (Hosea), 326
L'Hommedieu, Peter, 326
L'Hommedieu, Susannah, 326
L'Hommedieu, Sylvester, 326
Liart, Jenne, 301
Liesseline, Frances de, 236
Liesseline, Jean, 236
Liesseline, Magdelen (Bruneau) de, 236
Liferage, John, 33
Liferage/Lifrage, William, 33
Lifrage, Margaret (Barrineau), 33
Lifrage, William, 33
Liggett, Phoebe, 128
Lightfoot, Elizabeth, 327
Lightfoot, William, 327
Ligon, unknown, 380
Lillard, Benjamin, 327
Lillard, Elizabeth, 327
Lillard, James, 327
Lillard, Jasper, 327
LILLARD, Jean, 327
Lillard, John, 327
Lillard, Mary/Polly, 327
Lillard, Moses, 327
Lillard, Nancy, 327
Lillard, Sarah, 327
Lillard, Sarah/Sally, 327
Lillard, Thomas, 327

Lillard, **William**, 327
Lillard, X (Isaacs), 327
Lillard/Lillart, Lilli (Balssa), 327
Lillard/Lillart, Moise, 327
Lillie, Mehitable, **37**
Lillie, Mehitable (Frary), **37**
Lillie, Samuel, **37**
Lilly, Edmund Fleming, 162
Linington, John, 73
Linn, Abigail, 340
Linn, Margaret, 218
Linn, Margaret X, 218
Liphorst, Elizabeth van der, 365
Liphorst, Pieter Lucaszoon Van der, 365
Lipscomb, Ann, 85
Lirion, Joanna, 340
Liron, Lewis, 340
Lis, John, 78
Lischy, Jacob, 46
Lisenby, Elizabeth, 405
Lispenard, Anthony, 14, 39
Lispenard, Marie (Uytendaele), 14
Lispenard, Mary, 39
Litch, John, 79
Liter, Barbara Ann, 60
Liter, Catherine (X), 60
Liter, Henry, 60
Liter, John, 60
Little, Lucy, 166
Little, Mary, 474
Little, Robert, 166
Littlejohn, Martha (X), 327
Littler, Mary (X), 229
Littler, Samuel, 152
Livegood, Catherine, 417
Livegood/Livengood, Philip, 417
Liverau, Moses, 166
Livereau, Moses, 203
Livingston, John, 318
Livingston, Robert, 318
Lloyd, **Abigail (Delatre)**, 140
Lloyd, William, 388
Loach, Ann de, 328
Loach, Francis de, 328
Loach, Martha de, 328
Loach, Michael de, 328
LOACH, Michael de, 327
Loach, Samuel de, 328
Loach, Thomas de, 328
Loach, William de, 328
Lobdell, Ann, 283
Lobdell, Jane (Stowers), 227
Lobel, Mestre Matias de, 328
L'Obel/Lobel, Anne de, 328
L'Obel/Lobel, Faldoe de, 328
L'Obel/Lobel, Katherine de, 328
L'Obel/Lobel, Louise/Lucy de, 328
L'Obel/Lobel, Mary de, 328
Loches, Brig. General Solomon de, 145
Lochon, Veiruis, 399
Lockwood, Richard, 25

Lodisoir/Laudesoir, Catherine, 188
Loen, Bowen/Boudewyn, 365
Logan, Margaret, 217
Loge, August Ferdinand, 329
Logé, Charles Antoine, 449
Logé, Elisabeth (Descombre), 449
Logé, Jacques, 449
Loge, Pierre, 329
Loge, Wilhemine Christine, 329
LOGÉ/ LOGIER, Pierre/Peter, 329
Loge/Loger/Loger/Logez, Jacques, 329
Loge/Loger/Loget, Jacques, 329
Loge/Logier, Charles, 329
Loge/Logier, Jean, 329
Loge/Logier, Pierre, 329
Loger/Loge, Charles Antoine, 329
Loije/Lozier, Jannetje/Jane, 273
Lombard, Judith, 442, 444
Long, Catherine, 418
Long, Edward, 15
Long, Hester/Esther, 134
Long, Sarah, 433
Long, Tobias, 433
Long, unknown, 433
Long, William, 331
Longley, Elizabeth, 51
Longstreet, Barbara, 448
Longuemare, Frances de, 68
Loon, Elsie Van, 274
Loon, John Van, 274
Looyse/Luce, Jacobus, 301
Looyse/Luce, Maria, 301
Loper, Jacob, 360
L'Orange, Françoise, 232, 330
L'Orange, Françoise (X), 232, 445
L'Orange, Jean Velas, 232
Lorentz, Mary Elizabeth, 72
Lorentz/Laurents, Ablonia/Anna Apollonia, 330
Lorentz/Laurents, Anaelizabeth/ Anna Elisabetha/Anna Lys/Anna Elizabeth, 330
Lorentz/Laurents, Barwer/Anna Barbara, 330
LORENTZ/LAURENTS, Johannes/Jean, 330
Lorentz/Laurents, Madlen/Magdalena, 330
Lorentz/Lourents, Anna Margaretha, 330
Lorentz/Lourents, Daniel, 330
Lorentz/Lourents, Johann Jacob, 330
Lorentz/Lourents, Johannes Peter, 330
Lorentz/Lourents, Susanna, 330
Lorentz/Lourentz, Alexander, 330
Lormeiasse, Isabeau, 380
Lorne, Lorena, 93
Losee/Lozier, Jans Corneliszen, 273
Lothie, Abraham, 400
Lothrop, Ansel, 298
Lothrop, Mary (Thomas), 298
Lott, Engelbert, 287

Louchard, Charles, 452
Louis XII, 218
Louis XIII, 121
Louis XIV, 22, 43, 78, 131, 168, 218, 460
Louis, Jean, 331
Louis/Lewis, Alice, 331
Louis/Lewis, Andrew, 331
Louis/Lewis, Anne, 331
Louis/Lewis, Charles, 331
LOUIS/LEWIS, Guillaume/William, 331
Louis/Lewis, Jean/John, 331
Louis/Lewis, John, 331
Louis/Lewis, Margaret, 331
Louis/Lewis, Samuel, 331
Louis/Lewis, Thomas, 331
Louis/Lewis, William, 331
Louw, Abraham, 106
Louw, Pieter Cornelisen, 63
Louw, Tys/Matthys, 106
Louys, Marie, 199
Louys, Philippe, 199
Love, Elias, 183
Love, Mary, 183
Love, Sarah (X), 183
Loverage, Temperance, 360
Loveredge,William, 164
Loverser/Louereer/Lowery, unknown, 231
Lowle/Towle, James, 255
Loyse, Cornelis, 301
Lozier, Hildebrandt, 38
Lozier, Jane, 349
Lubberts, Cornelia, 392
Lubberts, Geertje, 273
Lubberts, Maritie, 287
Lubberts, Tryntje, 261, 279
Lubetze, Elizabeth, 78
Luc, Antoine De, 194
Luc, Susanne De, 194
Lucadoo, John, 157
Lucadou, Elizabeth (X), 13
Lucadou, Mary Ann, 13
Lucadou, Peter Anthony, 13
Lucadou/Loucado/Lookadoe, John, 176
Lucadou/Loucado/Lookadoe, William, 176
Lucadou/Loucado/Luckado/Lookadoo, Elizabeth, 332
Lucadou/Loucado/Luckado/Lookadoo, Guillaume/William, 332
Lucadou/Loucado/Luckado/Lookadoo, Isaac, 332
Lucadou/Loucado/Luckado/Lookadoo, James, 332
Lucadou/Loucado/Luckado/Lookadoo, Jean/John, 332
LUCADOU/LOUCADO/LUCKADO/LOOKADOO, Jean/John, 332
Lucadou/Loucado/Luckado/Lookadoo, John, 332

Lucadou/Loucado/Luckado/Lookadoo, Judith, 332
Lucadou/Loucado/Luckado/Lookadoo, Marianne/Mary Ann, 332
Lucadou/Loucado/Luckado/Lookadoo, Pierre Antoine/Peter Anthony, 332
Lucadou/Loucado/Luckado/Lookadoo, Rebecca, 332
Lucadou/Loucado/Luckado/Lookadoo, William, 332
Lucas, Barbara, 95
Lucas, Elizabeth, 40
Lucas, Winifred, 94
Lucrese, Anna Adrienne, 444
Luddon, Hugh, 209
Ludlow, Daniel, 132
Ludlow, Gabriel, 132
Ludlow, Robert Crommelin, 132
Ludlow, Sarah (Hammer), 132
Ludwig, Elector Karl, 329
Luillier, Jean, 189
Lum, Jonathan, 171
Lum, Sarah, 171
Lum, Sarah (Riggs), 171
Lumbertson, Maria Frederickse, 409
Lumkin, unknown, 99
Lundy, unknown, 119
Lunny, unknown, 332
Lusby, Naomi, 220
Lutin, Hester (Donrinees), 120, 130
Lutin, Walraven, 120
Lutin,Walraven, 130
Lutine, Hester, 120
Lutines, Hester, 130
Lutz, Anna Katharina (Leppla/Leplat), 407
Lutz, Katharina, 407
Lutz, Philip, 407
Lutz, Philipp, 314
Luy, Isabeau, 420
Luyster, Marretje/Maria Pieters, 366
lw Chaumette, Charlotte de, 266
Lyde, Allen, 190
Lyde/Lloyd, Elizabeth (Moore), 335
Lyle, Samuel, 445
Lyman, David, 239
Lynch, Jonathan, 244
Lynch, Margaret, 244
Lynch, Mary, 423
Lynch, Susannah Margaret (Schulf), 244
Lynn, Margaret, 331
Lynn, William, 331
Lynton, Elizabeth, 427
Lynton, Johanna (Lewis), 427
Lynton, William, 427
Lyon, Christian (Harmon), 181
Lyon, James, 181
Lyon, Mary, 181
Lyon, Samuel, 51
Lyon, Susannah, 106

M

M(e)yer, Elizabeth, 243
M'Ghie, Mary, 253
Mabie, Abraham, 441
Mabie, Elizabeth (Schuerman), 54
Mabie, John, 54
Mabie, Pieter, 333
MABILLE de NEVI/MABIE, Pierre, 333
Mabille de Nevi/Mabie, Abraham, 333
Mabille de Nevi/Mabie, Casper, 333
Mabille de Nevi/Mabie, Casper Pieterson, 333
Mabille de Nevi/Mabie, Elizabeth, 333
Mabille de Nevi/Mabie, Engeltie/Angelica, 333
Mabille de Nevi/Mabie, Jan/John, 333
Mabille de Nevi/Mabie, Johannes/John, 333
Mabille de Nevi/Mabie, Marritje/Martha, 333
Mabille de Nevi/Mabie, Metje/Mary, 333
Mabille de Nevi/Mabie, Pieter, 333
Mabille de Nevi/Mabie, Sara, 333
Mabille de Nevi/Mabie, Simon, 333
Mabille de Nevi/Mabie, Tryntie/Catherine, 333
Mabille, Pierre, 54, 124
Mabille,Pierre, 441
Mabille/Mabie, Abraham, 124
Mabille/Mabie, Casper, 124
Mabille/Mabie, Elizabeth (Schuerman), 124
Mabry, Hannah, 332
Machet, Jean, 75, 336
Machet, Jeanne, 336
Machet, Jeanne (Thomas), 336
Machet, Mariane, 75
Machet, Marianne, 336
Machet, Pierre/Peter, 336
Machfiedt/Machfet/Manswell/Maxwell, Marie, 213
MacIntosh, Lachlan, 321
Mackall, unknown, 367
Macksay, Polly, 401
Macky, Anna, 239
Macon, Ann(e), 334
Macon, Gideon, 334
Macon, James, 335
Macon, John, 335
Macon, Martha, 334
Macon, Mary, 334
Macon, William, 335
MAÇON/MACON, Gidéon, 333
Maçon/Mason, Susanna, 57
Madison, James, 327
Madison, unknown, 331
Madon, Catherine, 433
Magdaniels, Mary, 446
Maginier/Majinnet, Marie, 77

Magnan, Ambroise (Doight), 110
Magnan, Anne, 110
Magnan, Jacques, 110
MAGNE /MANJE/ MAINJE, Jean/Jan/John, 335
Magne/Manje/Mainje, Judith Janse, 335
Magnon, Jean, 29
Magny, Anna Magdalena, 337
Magny, Anna Magdelene, 182
Magny, François, 182
Magny, Jeremias, 337
Magny, Jérémie, 337
Magny, Marguerite (Vincent), 337
Magny/Man(n)y, (John) Wines, 336
Magny/Man(n)y, Barnabas, 336
Magny/Man(n)y, Elizabeth, 336
Magny/Man(n)y, Francis, 336
Magny/Man(n)y, François/Francis, 336
Magny/Man(n)y, Gabriel, 336
Magny/Man(n)y, Jacques/James, 336
MAGNY/MAN(N)Y, Jacques/James, 336
Magny/Man(n)y, James, 336
Magny/Man(n)y, Jean/John, 336
MAGNY/MAN(N)Y, Jean/John, 336
Magny/Man(n)y, Jeanne Magdeleine, 336
Magny/Man(n)y, John, 336
Magny/Man(n)y, Vincent, 336
Magny/Many, Anne (Vincent), 182
Magny/Many, François, 182
Magny/Many, Françoise, 182
Magny/Many, Jacques, 182
Magruder, Alexander, 276
Mahault, Margaret/Marguerite, 303
Mahieu, Antoinette/Antonette, 338
Mahieu, Françoise, 337
Mahieu, Hester, 139, 286, 337
Mahieu, Jacques, 139, 286
MAHIEU, Jacques, 337
Mahieu, Jeanne (X), 139, 286
Mahieu, Jeanne/Jenne, 337
Mahieu, Marie, 139, 286, 337
Mahn, Catherine, 140
Mahoult, Anna, 63
Maillard, Jacques, 359
Maillard, Louise Françoise, 379
Mailliet, Elizabeth (LeClerc), 338
Mailliet, Jean, 338
Mailliet/Jailhet/Mellett(e)/Melet, Milton J, 338
Mailliet/Mailhet/Mellett(e)/Melet, Ann, 338
Mailliet/Mailhet/Mellett(e)/Melet, Gideon, 338
Mailliet/Mailhet/Mellett(e)/Melet, James, 338
Mailliet/Mailhet/Mellett(e)/Melet, John, 338
Mailliet/Mailhet/Mellett(e)/Melet, Margaret, 338

Mailliet/Mailhet/Mellett(e)/Melet, Martha, 338
Mailliet/Mailhet/Mellett(e)/Melet, Mary, 338
Mailliet/Mailhet/Mellett(e)/Melet, Peter, 338
MAILLIET/MAILHET/MELLETT(E)/MELET, Pierre, 338
Mailliet/Mailhet/Mellett(e)/Melet, Rebecca, 338
Mailliet/Mailhet/Mellett(e)/Melet, Richard, 338
Mailliet/Mailhet/Mellett(e)/Melet, Sarah, 338
Mailloux, Anne, 141
Mailloux, Jacques, 141
Mailloux, Jean-Baptiste, 141
Mailloux, Jeanne, 141
Mailloux, Joseph, 141
Mailloux, Marie, 141
Mailloux, Noël, 141
Mailloux, Pierre, 141
Mailloux, Suzanne (Arnaud), 141
Mailly, Frédéric de, 121
Major, Ann, 344
Major, Lavina/Lovea/Lovey, 347
Major, Thomas, 347
MaKorry/Cory/Quorry, Kellan, 170
Malapougne, Simon, 420
Malbon, Betsy, 339
Malbon, Betsy/Elizabeth, 339
Malbon, Daniel, 339
MALBON, Daniel, 339
Malbon, James, 339
Malbon, Joanna, 339
Malbon, Lucy, 339
Malbon, Nancy, 339
Malbon, Nathaniel, 339
Malbon, Peter, 339
Malbon, Polly, 339
Malbon, Rachel, 339
Malbon, Sally, 339
Malbone, Pater, 23
Malet, Étienne, 434
Malet, Jacob, 341
Malet, Madeleine (Aidolet), 341
Malett, Étienne, 25
Malett, Jacob, 25
Malherbe, Marie, 238
Malherbe, Nicolas, 238
Mallet(t), David, 18
Mallet(t)/Malet/Mallott/Malle, Elizabeth, 341
Mallet(t)/Malet/Mallott/Malle, Ester, 341
Mallet(t)/Malet/Mallott/Malle, Etienne/Stephen, 341
MALLET(T)/MALET/MALLOTT/MALLE, Étienne/Stephen, 341
Mallet(t)/Malet/Mallott/Malle, Guillaume/William, 341

Mallet(t)/Malet/Mallott/Malle, Judith, 341
Mallet(t)/Malet/Mallott/Malle, Marie, 341
Mallet(t)/Malet/Mallott/Malle, Marie Magdeleine, 341
Mallet(t)/Malet/Mallott/Malle, Susanne, 341
Mallet, Andrew, 341
Mallet, Avis, 340
Mallet, David, 340
Mallet, Elizabeth, 341
Mallet, Esther, 340
Mallet, Estienne, 350
Mallet, Étienne/Stephen, 350
Mallet, Eunice, 340
Mallet, Hannah, 340
Mallet, Jean/John, 340
Mallet, Joanna, 340
Mallet, John, 340
Mallet, Joseph, 340
Mallet, Lewis, 340
Mallet, Louis/Lewis, 341
Mallet, Marie, 350
Mallet, Mary, 341
Mallet, Matthew, 340
Mallet, Peter, 340
Mallet, Suzanne, 350
Mallet/Mellett, Joanna/Johannah, 18
MALLETT(E), David, 339
Mallett(e), Jean/John, 339
Mallett, Jean, 18
Mallett, Johanna (Liron), 18
Mallett, Johanna (Liron/Lyon), 18
Mallory, Abigail (Trowbridge), 102
Mallory, Daniel, 102
Mallory, Frances, 389
Mallory, Lois, 102
Mallory, Mary (Preston), 70
Mallory, Peter, 70
Mallory, Rebecca, 70
Mallot, Catherine, 350
Mallot, Elizabeth, 350
Mallot, Joseph, 350
Mallot, Mary, 350
Mallot, Peter, 350
Mallot, Ruth, 350
Mallott, Théophile, 350
Malone, Mary, 23
Malot, Theodotius, 350
Mambru/Membru/Manbrut/Membrut, Élie, 210
Mambru/Membru/Manbrut/Membrut, Étienne, 210
Mambru/Membru/Manbrut/Membrut, François, 210
Mambru/Membru/Manbrut/Membrut, Jean, 210
Mambru/Membru/Manbrut/Membrut, Lidie, 210

Mambru/Membru/Manbrut/Membrut, Sarra, 210
Mambru/MembruManbrut/Membrut, Ezéchiel, 210
Manchet, Jane, 336
Mandeville, Aeltje/Elsie de, 342
Mandeville, David de, 342
Mandeville, Elsie/Altje de, 101
Mandeville, Gerretje de, 342
Mandeville, Giles Jansen de, 101
MANDEVILLE, Giles Jansen/Yellis de, 342
Mandeville, Greitie de, 342
Mandeville, Hendricks de, 342
Mandeville, Jan de, 342
Mandeville, Tyntje/Catherine de, 342
Mandeville, William de, 342
Maneval, Charles Daniel, 342, 343
Maneval, Elisabet/Isabeau, 343
Maneval, Elizabeth, 381
Maneval, Isaac, 342, 343
Maneval, Jean, 342
Maneval, Jeremi, 343
Maneval, Jérémie, 342
Maneval, Judit, 342
Maneval, Lucrèce, 342
Maneval, Marie Madeleine, 343
Maneval, Mathieu, 342
Maneval, Pierre, 342, 381
MANEVAL, Pierre, 342
Maneval, Salomon, 343
Maneval, Suzanne, 343
Maney, Jacques/James, 336
Mangeot, Susan, 364
Manigault, Gabriel, 343
Manigault, Marie (Dubartet), 343
Manigault/Manigaud, Gabriel, 343
Manigault/Manigaud, Joseph, 343
Manigault/Manigaud, Judith, 343
Manigault/Manigaud, Peter, 343
MANIGAULT/MANIGAUD, Pierre, 343
Manley, unknown, 209
Mann, Ernest, 448
Mann, Jerusha, 256
Mann, Mary, 182
MANNEVILLE, Jean de, 344
Manneville, John de, 344
Mannoo, Robert, 286
Manoo, Robert, 139, 337
Mansfield, Andrew, 288
Manvill/Manvel/Manviel, Adrian, 344
Manvill/Manvel/Manviel, Daniel, 344
Manvill/Manvel/Manviel, David, 344
Manvill/Manvel/Manviel, James, 344
Manvill/Manvel/Manviel, John, 344
Manvill/Manvel/Manviel, Mary, 344
Manvill/Manvel/Manviel, Nicholas, 344
MANVILLE, John, 344
Manzelius, Jean Frédéric, 215
Maple, Benjamin, 350
Maple, Catherine, 350
Maple, Elizabeth (Lee), 350

Marais, Anna, 415
Marcet, Antoine, 194
Marcet, Jean, 194
Marchand, Abraham, 346
Marchand, Adam, 345
Marchand, Catherine, 345
Marchand, Catherine (Lavandier), 303
Marchand, Daniel, 303, 345
Marchand, David, 345
Marchand, Elizabeth, 345
Marchand, Esther, 345
Marchand, Frederick, 345
MARCHAND, Henri, 344
Marchand, Henri II, 344
Marchand, Jacob, 345
MARCHAND, Jacob, 345
Marchand, Jehan, 345
Marchand, Judith, 345
Marchand, Lewis, 345
Marchand, Marie Magdeleine, 346
Marchand, Marie Marguerite, 345
Marchand, Samuel, 239
Marchand, Susanna, 345
Marchant, Jean-Claude, 228
Marchant, Marie, 228
Marchant, Marie (Dubois), 228
Marconnier, Antoine, 215
Mareen, Alexander, 347
Margare, Eleonore/Lenora, 243
Margot, Pierre, 379
Marie, 109, 127, 136, 141, 145, 147, 151,
    152, 153, 155, 157, 159, 160, 166, 172,
    177, 182, 184, 185, 187, 199, 212, 237,
    246, 247, 250, 255, 263, 277, 294, 301,
    309, 319, 320, 321, 324, 329, 333, 341,
    343, 345, 346, 349, 357, 369, 385, 396,
    406, 437, 462, 468,473
Marie Anne (Druart) LeBrun, 318
Marie, Boulon/Boulen/Boulyn, 159
Marie, Jacques, 346
Marie, Susanna (Morisse), 346
MARIE/MARYE, Jacques/James (Rev.),
    346
Marie/Marye, James, 346
Marie/Marye, Lucy Mary, 346
Marie/Marye, Peter, 346
Marie/Marye, Susanna, 346
Marie/Marye, William C., 346
Mariette, Jean, 118
Mariette, Marie, 118
Marin, Alexandre, 347
Marin, X (Milleson), 347
Marin/Marine/Mareen, Alexander de,
    347
Marin/Marine/Mareen, Charles de, *347*
Marin/Marine/Mareen, James de, *347*
Marin/Marine/Mareen, John de, *347*
Marin/Marine/Mareen, Jonathan de,
    347
Marin/Marine/Mareen, Major de, *347*

MARIN/MARINE/MAREEN, Milleson de,
    347
Marin/Marine/Mareen, Thomas de, *347*
Marin/Marine/Mareen, William de, *347*
Mariner, Benjamin, 348
Mariner, Elizabeth, 348
Mariner, Hannah, 348
MARINER, Jean/John, 347
Mariner, John, 347, 348
Mariner, Joseph, 348
Mariner, Martha, 348
Mariner, Mary, 348
Mariner, Rachel, 348
Mariner, Sarah, 348
Mariner, Susanna, 348
Marion, Anne, 349
Marion, Benjamin, 321, 388
MARION, Benjamin, 348
Marion, Elizabeth, 349
Marion, Esther, 321, 348
Marion, Francis, 348
Marion, Francis Gen., 244
Marion, Francis General, 338
Marion, Gabriel, 348
Marion, Gen. Francis, 470
Marion, James, 349
Marion, Jean, 348
Marion, John, 349
Marion, Judith, 349
Marion, Judith (Balluet), 321
Marion, Mary, 349
Marion, Mary (X), 388
Marion, Paul, 349, 388
Marion, Perrine (Boutignon), 348
Marion, Peter, 349
Markham, John, 356
Markham, William, 356
Markle, Anna Veronica, 206
Marlett, Abraham, 273
Marlett, Christina (Billiou), 273
Marlett, Frances, 273
Marley, Anthony, **51**
Marley, Bishop George, **51**
Marley, Elinor, **51**
Marley, Elizabeth (Morgan), **51**
Marlitt/Merlet/Malott, Abraham, 349
Marlitt/Merlet/Malott, Anne, 350
Marlitt/Merlet/Malott, Esechias, 349
Marlitt/Merlet/Malott, Frances, 349
Marlitt/Merlet/Malott, Gédéon, 350
**MARLITT/MERLET/MALOTT,
    Gédéon/Gideon**, 349
Marlitt/Merlet/Malott, Henry, 350
Marlitt/Merlet/Malott, Isaac, 349
Marlitt/Merlet/Malott, Jacob, 349
**Marlitt/Merlet/Malott,
    Jannetje/Janneken**, 349
**Marlitt/Merlet/Malott, Jean Pierre/John
    Peter**, 349
Marlitt/Merlet/Malott, Jeanne, 350

**Marlitt/Merlet/Malott, Josias/Josué
    /Joseph**, 349
Marlitt/Merlet/Malott, Margaret, 349
Marlitt/Merlet/Malott, Marie, 349
Marlitt/Merlet/Malott, Nöe, 350
MARLITT/MERLET/MALOTT, Paul, 350
Marlitt/Merlet/Malott, Paulas/Paul, 349
Marlot, Anne, 351
Marlot, Edith, 350
MARLOT, Jean, 350
Marlot, Rachel, 351
Marmen, Keziah, 167
Marneil, Margaret de, 261
Marolles, Marie de, 92
Marques, Deborah de, 266
Marr, Christopher, 351
Marr, Daniel, 351
Marr, John, 351
MARR, John, 351
Marriott, Joyce, 46
Marriott, Mary (X), 46
Marriott, Samuel, 46
Marschalk, Anna, 441
Marsden, James S., 346
Marseveen, Pieter Janz Van, 147
Marsh, John, 377
Marsh, Sarah, 377
Marshall, Chloe, 401
Marshall, Elizabeth (Williams), 173
Marshall, Hannah, 146
Marshall, John, 87
Marshall, Mungo Rev., 346
Marshall, Sarah, 173, 276
Marshall, Sidney, 401
Marshall, Wm., 173
Marshall/Marchant, John, 70
Martain, Jean, 115, 220
Martain, Jérémie, 443
Martain, John, 187
Martain, Margaret (X), 115
Martain, Marie (Archambeau), 443
Martain, Marthe, 443
Martain, Mary (Scott), 187
Martain/Martin, Jacques/James, 351
Martain/Martin, Jane, 352
MARTAIN/MARTIN, Jean/John, 351
Martain/Martin, John, 351
Martain/Martin, Judith, 352
Martain/Martin, Pierre/Peter, 351
Martel, Isabeau, 214
Marteline/Martling, Peter, 353
Martens, Jossine, 392
Martens, Sophia, 320
Martense, Sophia, 384
Martiau, Elizabeth, 352
Martiau, Mary, 352
Martiau, Nicolas, 352
MARTIAU, Nicolas, 352
Martiau, Sarah, 352
Martijn/Martin, Marguerite Marie, 349
Martiline/Martling, Abraham, 353

Martiline/Martling, Adaline, 353
Martiline/Martling, Barent, 353
Martiline/Martling, Daniel, 353
Martiline/Martling, Hendrick, 353
Martiline/Martling, Isaac, 353
MARTILINE/MARTLING, Jean/Johannes, 353
Martiline/Martling, Johannis, 353
Martiline/Martling, Myno, 353
Martiline/Martling, Peter, 353
Martin, Ann, 225
Martin, Austin, 185
Martin, Catherine, **42**
Martin, Claudia, 434
Martin, George, 397
Martin, Jacques, 434
Martin, James, 270
Martin, Jeanne Elizabeth, 107
Martin, Joachim, 110
Martin, John, 15, 226
Martin, Judith, 220
Martin, Judith (Fortier), 434
Martin, Matthew, 16
Martin, Thomas, 444
Martin, William, 16
Martineau, Susannah, 397
Martinet, Jeanne (Buisset), 442
Martinet, Marie, 442
Martinet, Nicolas, 442
Martinique, Angeline, 454
Martling, Mary, 414
Marvin, Abigail, 86
Marvin, Elizabeth (X), 86
Marvin, Matthew, 86
Mason, Alice (X), 451
Mason, Ann (Seawell/Sewell), 451
Mason, Elizabeth, 451
Mason, Francis Lt., 451
Mason, Lemuel, 451
Mason, unknown, 236
Masse, Elizabeth (Mersereau), 280
Massé, Jeanne, 280
Massé, Pierre, 280, 357
Massey, Charlotte, 157
Massey, Josiah, 463
Massey, Notley (Wright), 463
Massey, Peter, 463
Massie, Anne, 334
Massie, Cecilia, 334
Massie, Charles, 334
Massie, David, 334
Massie, Elizabeth, 334
Massie, Gideon, 334
Massie, Gordon, 334
Massie, James, 334
Massie, Mary, 334
Massie, Nathaniel, 334
Massie, Peter, 334
Massie, Thomas, 334
Massie, unknown, 108
Masson, Suzanne, *142*

Massu, Susanne, 300
Mastin, Edward, 203
Mathenay/Metteneye/Matheny, Charles, 354
Mathenay/Metteneye/Matheny, Daniel, 354
MATHENAY/METTENEYE/MATHENY, Jean/John, 353
Mathenay/Metteneye/Matheny, Michael, 354
Mathenay/Metteneye/Matheny, William, 354
Mathews, Maurice, 232
Mathurin, unknown, 214
Matlock, William, 474
Matterr, Jean, 18
Matthews, Sarah (Moore), 116
Matthews, unknown, 116
Matthyssen, Joris, 150
Matton, Philippe, 300
Mauhr, Anna, 375
Mauhr, Barbara, 375
Mauhr, Nickel, 375
Maulard, Gabrielle (Berou), 397, 457
Maulard, Lubin, 397, 457
Maulard, Susanne, 457
Maulard, Suzanne, 397
Mauldin, Balaam, 85
Maulevault, Michelle, 156
Maumont, Anne, 420
Maupin, Claude, 354
Maupin, Daniel, 22, 354, 470
Maupin, Gabriel, 355, 385, 470
MAUPIN, GABRIEL, 354
Maupin, John, 22
Maupin, Magdeleine, 354
Maupin, Margaret (Via), 22
Maupin, Marie, 301
Maupin, Marie (Hersent), 385
Maupin, Marie/Mary, 354
Maupin, Mary (Hersent), 470
Maupin, Sara Catherine, 354
Maur, Diebolt, 376
Maur, Otillia (Junt), 376
Maury, Abraham, 355
Maury, Abram, 271, 355
Maury, Elizabeth, 355
Maury, James, 355
Maury, Marie (Feauguereau), 271
Maury, Martha, 355
Maury, Mary, 355
Maury, Mary Anne, 355
Maury, Matthew, 131, 271, 355
MAURY, Matthew, 355
Maury, Philip Poindexter, 355
Maury, Susanna, 355
Maus, Mathew Dr., 376
Mauvau, Suzanne Catherine, 359
Mauzé, Jeanne Elizabeth, 470
Mauzé, Joseph, 470
Mauze, Renée (Mercier), 470

Mauze/Moze/Mauzy, Elizabeth, 356
Mauze/Moze/Mauzy, George, 356
Mauze/Moze/Mauzy, Isabel, 356
Mauze/Moze/Mauzy, John, 356
Mauze/Moze/Mauzy, Margaret, 356
Mauze/Moze/Mauzy, Michael, 356
MAUZÉ/MOZÉ/MAUZY, Michel/Michael, 356
Mauze/Moze/Mauzy, Peter, 356
Mauzy, Priscilla, 427
Maxey, John, 185
Maxfield/Maxwell, Mary, 311
May, John Rodolph de, 165
May, Mary, 223
May, Mary Elizabeth (de Guignilliat) de, 165
May, Peter Rodolph de, 165
May, Rodolphus, 321
Maybank, Joseph, 168
Mayer, George, 246
Mayer, Philip, 246
Maynard, Anne, 373
Mayo, Edward Sr., 276
Mayrant, Elizabeth, 432
Mayrant, James Nicholas/Nicholson, 322
Mayrant, James Nicholson, 208
Maysey, Mary, 453
Mazel, Marie, 108
Mazel, Pierre, 108
Mazyck, Isaac, 322, 432
McBee, John, 351
McCain, Daniel, 218
McCaleb, Henrietta, 227
McCall, John Hart, 320
McClellan, Esther Susanna, 373
McClelland, Mary, 331
McClendon, Martha, 162
McClure, James, 217
McConnell, Julius C., 227
McConnico, William, 180
McDavid, Annie, 266
McDavid, Jane, 266
McDonald, Adam, 321
McDonald, Binkey, 321
McDonald, Daniel, 321
McDonald, James, 321
McDonald, Mary, 321
McDonald, Mary (Lewis), 321
McDonald, Susannah (Lee), 321
McElvain, Saphira, 25
McEvers, Julian, 318
McFarland, Daniel, 253
McFarlin, unknown, 414
McFee, William, 92
McGee, Mary Ann, 391
McGehee, Ann (Bastrop), 254
McGehee, Edward, 254
McGehee, Jacob, 254
McGehee, Thomas, 254
McGill, Abigail, 457
McKnight, Margaret, 405

McKnight, Mary (X), 34
McKnight, unknown, 34
McKnitt, Katherine, 90
McKnitt, Mary, 90
McLean, Alexander, 91
McLean, Allan, 40
McLendon, Jamima, 162
McMillan, Nancy, 253
McMurtry, Elizabeth, 233
McRae, Susanne Margaret, 246
McWhorter, Alexander, Dr., 90
McWhorter, Jane/Jean, 90
Mead, Elizabeth, 31
Mead, John, 64
Mead/Meare, Edward, 209
Médici, Catherine de Queen Mother, 121
Meet, John, 342
Meet, Pieter, 342
Melanson, Ambroise, 294
Melanson, Cécile, 294
Melanson, Charles, 294
Melanson, Claude, 294
Melanson, Françoise, 294
Melanson, Isabelle, 294
Melanson, Jean, 294
Melanson, Madeleine, 294
Melanson, Marguerite, 294
Melanson, Marie, 294
Melanson, Marie Anne, 294
Melanson, Pierre, 294
Melanson/Mellison, Priscilla, 294
Melius, Dorothea, 415
Mellett, Thomas, 341
Mellin, Antoine, 194
Mellin, Gabrielle, 194
Mellot, Louise, 460
Mellott, John, 350
Mellott, Peter, 350
Melot, Hannah, 349
Melot, Jean Pierre/Peter, 350
Melot, Louyse, 460
Melot, Madeline, 350
Melot, Marie, 349
Melot, Theodores, 350
Melyn, Abraham, 360
Melyn, André, 359
Melyn, Cornelia, 360
Melyn, Cornelis, 360
MELYN, Cornielle/Cornelis, 359
Melyn, Isaac, 360
Melyn, Jacob, 360
Melyn, Johannes, 360
Melyn, Magdalen, 360
Melyn, Marie (Ghuedinx-Botens), 359
Melyn, Mariken, 360
Melyn, Susanna, 360
Menago, Susan Catherine, 285
Menessier, Abraham, 28
Menessier, Jacquine (Phelipeaux), 28
Menessier/Mercier, Jacquine, 28
Menton, Sara, 199

Mercer, Anne, 123
Mercer, Daniel, 123
Mercer, Elizabeth, 123
Mercer, Francis, 123
Mercer, Hester, 123
Mercer, Hester/Esther, 123
Mercer, Jane, 123
Mercer, Judith, 123
Mercer, Marie/Mary, 123
Mercer, Paul, 123
Mercer, Philippe, 123
Mercer, Pierre/Peter, 123
Mercer, Samuel, 123
Mercer, Thomas, 123
Mercereau, Abigail, 293
Mercereau, Abigail (Broome), 293
Mercereau, Daniel, 293, 357
Mercereau, Elizabeth (DuBois), 109, 292
Mercereau, Jean, 109, 292
Mercereau, Josué, 293
Mercereau, Josué/Joshua, 109
Mercereau, Marianne, 293
Mercereau, Marie, 292, 293
Mercereau, Marie (Chadaine), 293
Mercereau, Paul, 78, 293
Mercereau, Pierre, 134
Mercereau, Susanna (Doucinet), 293
Mercereau, Susanne Marie (Doucinet), 357
Mercereau/Mersereau, Daniel, 357
Mercereau/Mersereau, David, 357
Mercereau/Mersereau, Elizabeth, 357
Mercereau/Mersereau, Jean, 357
MERCEREAU/MERSEREAU, Jean, 356
Mercereau/Mersereau, Josué/Joshua, 356
Mercereau/Mersereau, Marianne, 357
Mercereau/Mersereau, Marie, 357
Mercereau/Mersereau, Marthe/Martha, 357
Mercereau/Mersereau, Paul, 357
Mercereau/Mersereau, Susanne Marie, 357
Mercier, Bartholomew, 303
Mercier, Isaac, 57, 304
Mercier, Marianne, 304
Mercier, Susan, 57
Mercier, Susannah (X), 57
Mercier, Susanne (X), 304
Méré, Jean Poltrot de, 121
Merkel, Pierre, 357
Merkel, Sophia Maria (Beaudoin), 357
Merkel/Merklen/Markle, Anna Catharina, 358
Merkel/Merklen/Markle, Anna Helena, 358
Merkel/Merklen/Markle, Anna Maria, 358
Merkel/Merklen/Markle, Casper/Gaspard, 358

Merkel/Merklen/Markle, Christian, 357, 358
Merkel/Merklen/Markle, Francianna, 358
Merkel/Merklen/Markle, George, 358
Merkel/Merklen/Markle, Hans, 357
Merkel/Merklen/Markle, Jacob, 358
Merkel/Merklen/Markle, Johan Christian, 357
Merkel/Merklen/Markle, John, 358
Merkel/Merklen/Markle, Maria Apollonia, 358
Merkel/Merklen/Markle, Peter, 358
MERKEL/MERKLEN/MARKLE, Pierre/Peter, 357
Merlet, Abraham, 62
Merlet, Frances, 62
Merlet, Gidéon, 62
Merlet, Isaac, 62
Merlet, Jacob, 62
Merlet, Margaret, 62
Merlet, Marie (Martin), 62
Merlin, Rev., 271
Merrill, Sarah, 293
Merritt, Anne, 429
Merritt, Mary, 336
Merritt, Mary (X), 429
Mershon, Andrew, 345
Mershon, Ann, 345
Mershon, Elizabeth, 345
Mershon, Henry, 344
Mershon, Houghton, 345
Mershon, Mary, 344
Mershon, Peter, 345
Mershon, Rebeckah, 345
Mershon, Sarah, 345
Mershon, Thomas, 345
Mertens, Catherine, 375
Mertens, Johann, 375
Mertz, Anna Margaretha, 466
MERTZ, Anna Margaretha, 358
Mertz, Peter, 466
Merveilhaud, Magdeleine, 420, 421
Merveilhaud, Pierre, 420, 421
Merveilhaud, Simon, 421
Merveilhaud, Suzanne[2] (de Rivoire), 420
Merwin, Hannah, 122
Merwin, Hannah (Platt), 122
Merwin, Mary, 340
Merwin, Mary (Trowbridge), 340
Merwin, Miles, 340
Merwin, John, 122
Merzeau, Isaac, 379
Mesier, Jannetie, 279
Mesier, Sarah, 452
Mesnard, Daniel, 153
Mesnard, Élisabeth (Vincent), 153
Mesnard, Estienne, 153
Messervy, Catherine (Lemprière), 180
Messervy, Clément, 180
Messick, Nehemiah, 216

Messmer, Eugénie, 215
Mestereau, Lydie, 210
Mesurol(l)e/Mesuroll/Meseroll, Cornelius, 358
Mesurol(l)e/Mesuroll/Meseroll, Deborah, 358
Mesurol(l)e/Mesuroll/Meseroll, Jane, 358
MESUROL(L)E/MESUROLL/MESEROLL, Jean, 358
Mesurol(l)e/Mesuroll/Meseroll, Jean II, 358
Mesurol(l)e/Mesuroll/Meseroll, John, 358
Mesurol(l)e/Mesuroll/Meseroll, Margaret, 358
Metcalf, Eliazur, 108
Metcalf, Melitiah (Fisher), 108
Metcalf, Timothy, 108
Metern, Jan Joosten Van, 153
Metern, Joost Jansen Van, 153
Metselaer, Barent Egbert, 274
Metteneye, Richard, 353
Mettetal, Catherine Marguerite, 359
Mettetal, David, 359
Mettetal, Frédéric, 359
Mettetal, Jean Christophe, 359
METTETAL, Jean Georges, 359
Mettetal, Louise, 359
Mettetal, Peter, 359
Mettetal, Pierre Christophe, 359
Meulmans, Cornelia, 441
Meulmans, Peter, 441
Mew, James, 35
Meyer, Eva Magdalena, 149
Meyers, Margrieje, 95
Meyna/Mynno, Jemina (Jurckse) Hoppe, 467
Mich(e)aux/Missheux, Abraham, 362
MICH(E)AUX/MISSHEUX, Abraham, 361
Mich(e)aux/Missheux, Ann Madelin/Agnes, 362
Mich(e)aux/Missheux, Anne/Nannie, 361
Mich(e)aux/Missheux, Elizabeth, 362
Mich(e)aux/Missheux, Esther Mary, 362
Mich(e)aux/Missheux, Isaac, 362
Mich(e)aux/Missheux, Jacob, 361
Mich(e)aux/Missheux, Jacques/James, 362
Mich(e)aux/Missheux, Jean/John, 362
Mich(e)aux/Missheux, Jeanne/Jane Magdalin, 361
Mich(e)aux/Missheux, John Paul, 362
Mich(e)aux/Missheux, Olive Judith/Judi, 362
Mich(e)aux/Missheux, Susanne, 362
Michau(d), Abraham, 55, 255
Michau(d), Charlotte, 255
Michau(d), Esther, 255
Michau(d), Jeanne, 255

Michau(d), Madeleine, 255
Michau(d), Pierre, 55, 255
Michau, Abraham, 407
Michau/Michaud, Abraham I, 360
Michau/Michaud, Abraham II, 360
Michau/Michaud, Abraham III, 360
Michau/Michaud, Charlotte, 361
Michau/Michaud, Daniel, 361
Michau/Michaud, Hester, 361
Michau/Michaud, Hester/Esther, 361
MICHAU/MICHAUD, Jean, 360
Michau/Michaud, Jeanne, 361
Michau/Michaud, Julienne, 360
Michau/Michaud, Lydia, 361
Michau/Michaud, Noah, 361
Michau/Michaud, Paul, 361
Michau/Michaud, Peter, 361
Michau/Michaud, Pierre, 360
Michau/Michaud, William, 361
Michaud, Catherine (X), 55
Michaud, Jean, 55
Michaux, Abraham, 310
Michaux, Anne (Severin/Sauvin), 361
Michaux, Jacob, 361
Michaux, Jane Magdalen, 310
Michaux, Susanne (Rochet), 310
Michel, Anna Barbara, 362
Michel, Anna Maria, 362
Michel, Christoph/Christopher, 362
Michel, Christopher, 362
Michel, David, 362
MICHEL, Francis Louis/Franz Ludwig, 362
Michel, George, 362
Michel, Ludwig, 362
Michel, Petter, 362
Michel, Ursula (Fels), 362
Michelet, Barbé, 364
Michelet, Carl/Charles Jules, 363
Michelet, Christian Frederick, 363
Michelet, Hans, 363
Michelet, Jacques, 363
MICHELET, Jacques, 362
Michelet, Jacques/Jacob, 363
Michelet, Jakob Post, 363
Michelet, Jean Jacques/John Jacob, 364
Michelet, Johan Wilhelm, 363
Michelet, John, 363
Michelet, Louis, 364
MICHELET, Louis (Rev.), 364
Michelet, Madeline, 363
Michelet, Marie, 364
Michelet, Michel, 363
Michelet, Paul, 363
Michelet, Peter, 363
Michelet, Pierre, 363, 364
Michelet, Rachel, 363
Michelet, Suzanne, 363
Michelsdatter, Karen, 363
Michelsz, Philip Houze, 155
Mico, Ann(e), 339
Micou, Clara, 364

Micou, Elizabeth, 364
Micou, Henry, 364
Micou, James, 364
Micou, John, 364
Micou, Judith, 364
Micou, Margaret, 364
Micou, Mary, 364
Micou, Paul, 364
MICOU, Paul, 364
Middaugh, Sara, 305
Middlebrook, Jerusha, 340
Middlesward, Jan Teunis, 95
Middlesward, Sarah Teunis Van, 95
Middleswart, Femmetje/Fannie Teunise Van, 164
Middleton, Benjamin, 133
Middleton, Elizabeth, 133
Middleton, Henrietta, 343
Middleton, John, 133
Middleton, Mary, 133
Mil/Milt/Mill/Mille, Anna de, 365
Mil/Milt/Mill/Mille, Anthony de, 365
Mil/Milt/Mill/Mille, Hannah de, 365
MIL/MILT/MILL/MILLE, Isaac Anthonis de, 365
Mil/Milt/Mill/Mille, Maria de, 365
Mil/Milt/Mill/Mille, Mary de, 365
Mil/Milt/Mill/Mille, Peter de, 365
Mil/Milt/Mill/Mille, Pieter/Petrus de, 365
Mil/Milt/Mill/Mille, Sarah de, 365
Mil/Milt/Mill/Mille. Isaac de, 365
Miles, Jane (X), 411
Miles, Marmaduke, 411
Millbanks, Katherine, 212
Mille, Abigail (Banks) De, 406
Mille, Elizabeth De, 406
Mille, Peter De, 406
Miller, Alice, 356
Miller, Jacob, 372
Miller, John, 306
Miller, Magdalene, 371
Miller, Mary, 41, 68, 371
Miller, Moses, 371
Miller, Ruth, 218
Miller, Samuel, 372
Miller, Sarah, 302
Miller, Simon, 356
Miller, Susannah, 68, 371
Miller, Willem, 302
Miller, William, 372
Milligan, Jane, 422
Millington, Mary, 58
Milliron, Catherine, 97
Milliron, Nicholas, 96
Milliron, Susan, 97
Mills, Mary Ann, 69
Mims, Elizabeth (Woodson), 220
Mims, Kitty/Catherine/Katurah, 116
Mims, Mary, 220, 401
Mims, Shadrach, 220

Ming(e), Eleanor, 371
Mingael, Thomas Janse, 177
Minor, Charles, 108
Minor, Frances (X), 133
Minor, Garrett, 471
Minvielle, David, 79
Minvielle, Élie, 79
Minvielle, Françoise, 79
Minvielle, Gabriel, 31
Minvielle, Jacques, 79
Minvielle, Jean Jacques, 79
Minvielle, Paul la Coze, 79
Minvielle, Pierre, 79
Minvielle, Susanne, 79
Minvielle, Thomas, 79
Miranda, Mary, 336
Mitchell, Ann, 51
Mitchell, Elizabeth, 118, 337
Mitchell, Experience, 337
Mitchell, George, 118
Mitchell, Henry L., 58
Mitchell, Isabel, 118
Mitchell, Isabel (Higgins), 118
Mitchell, Priscilla, 118
Mitchell, Sarah, 58
Mitchell, Thomas, 337
Mius d'Entremont, Madeleine (Helie),
    294
Mix, John, 102
Mixon, Michael, 90
Mock, unknown, 72
Mocquay, Élie, 317
Mocquay, Esther, 317
Mocquay, Marie (de la Coste), 317
Moffat, William, 218
Moffit, John, 182
Mohr/Moore, Johannes, 330
Mol, Jan Jansen, 333
Molenaar, Ari, 274
Molenaar, Jannetje Adrianse, 274
Molenaer, Cornelia, 302
Molenaer/Miller, Geertie (X), 302
Molenaer/Miller. William, 302
Molenear, Joost Arriansen, 274
Mollenauer, Hendrick, 464
Mollenauer, Margaret, 464
Mollison, Gilbert, 293
Mollison, Ruth (Black-Ford), 293
Mollissen, Christine, 41
Molllissen, John, 41
MON(T)FORT/MON(T)FOORT, Jean/Jan,
    366
Mon(t)fort/Mon(t)foort, Jan/John, 366
Mon(t)fort/Mon(t)foort, Jannetje, 366
Mon(t)fort/Mon(t)foort,
    Pierre/Pieter/Peter, 366
Mon(t)fort/Mon(t)foort, Pieter, 366
Mon(t)fort/Mon(t)foort, Sara, 366
Monceau, Jean de, 189
Monck, Thomas, 432
Money, Henry de, 186, 230, 231

Money, Kezia, 453
Money, Marianne (Grasset) de, 186
Money/Monye, Albert de, 366
Money/Monye, Anne de, 366
Money/Monye, Auguste/Augustus de,
    366
Money/Monye, Ester de, 366
MONEY/MONYE, Henri de, 366
Money/Monye, Henry de, 366
Money/Monye, Jean/John de, 366
Money/Monye, Maria/Mary de, 366
Money/Monye, Peter de, 366
Money/Monye, Susanne de, 366
MONEY/MOONEY, James, 367
MoneyAnne de, 186
Monfoort, Peter, 174
Monford, Étienne, 436
Monnet, Aaron, 367
Monnet, Abraham, 367
Monnet, Ann, 367
Monnet, Catherine, 367
Monnet, Elizabeth, 367
Monnet, Isaac, 367
Monnet, Jean, 367
Monnet, John, 367
Monnet, Mary, 367
Monnet, Pierre, 367
MONNET, Pierre, 367
Monnet, Robert, 367
Monnet, Sarah, 367
Monnet, Susanne, 367
Monnet, Susanne (Chastain?), 367
Monnet, Thomas, 367
Monnet, William, 367
Monpensier, Aurélie (Hocart), 160
Monpensier,Richard, 160
Montagne, Catherine, 59
Montague, Abraham, 291
Montague, Mary, 270
Montague, Samuel, 270
Montaudon, Jacques, 248
Montbel, Jacqueline de, 121
Montchanin, Anne Alexandrine de, 166
Montfoor/Montfoort, Pieter, 144
Montgomery, Ann, 331
Montgomery, Martha, 131
Montgomery, Thomas, 131
Montjoy, John Col., 213
Montmorency, Louise de, 121
Montras/Montross, Angelique, 135
Montras/Montross, Hendrick, 135
Montras/Montross, Margriet, 135
Montras/Montross, Pierre, 135
Moody, Carter, 383
Moody, John, 116
Moody, Lucy, 116
Moody, Robert, 212
Moody,Susannah (X), 116
Moore, Anna Eliza, 226
Moore, Anne, 278
Moore, Augustine, 335

Moore, Carson, 23
Moore, Charles, 278
Moore, Daniel I, 278
Moore, Daniel II, 278
Moore, Daniel III, 278
Moore, Elizabeth, 326
Moore, Frances, 278
Moore, Francis Col., 327
Moore, John, 278, 456, 471
Moore, John Col., 278
Moore, Lambert, 278
Moore, Margaret, 456
Moore, Peter I, 278
Moore, Peter II, 278
Moore, Rebecca, 278
Moore, Rebecca (Axtell), 278
Moore, Richard, 278
Moore, Robert, 116
Moore, Samuel, 282
Moore, Stephen, 278
Moore, Susanna, 278
Moore, Susanna (X), 116
Moore, Susanna II, 278
Moore, Thomas I, 278
Moore, Thomas II, 278
Moore, William, 278
Moorman, Sarah, 162
Moragne, Cécile (Bayle), 77
Moragne, Francis, 77, 319, 426
Moragne, Jennie, 221
Moragne, Marie, 424
Moragne, Marie (Paris), 368
Moragne, Pierre, 77, 368, 424
MORAGNE, Pierre, 368
Moragne, Pierre II, 368
Moragne, Susannah (David), 424
Moragne, unknown, 424
Morange, Francis, 368
Morange, Isaac, 368
Morange, John, 368
Morange, Marie, 368
More, Jane, 133
Moreau, Elizabeth, 350
Moreau, Esaïe, 28
Moreau, Jacqueline, 366
Moreau, Jeanne, 28
Moreau, Marguerite (Corbeau), 28
Moreau, Marie, 435
Moreau, Marie Charlotte, 141
Moreau, Marie-Madeleine (Lemire), 141
Moreau, Marthe, 289
Moreau, Pierre, 141
Morehouse, Lemuel, 86
Morel, Louis, 195
Morel, Marguerite (Forel), 195
Morel, Marthe, 195
Morel, Mathieu, 381
Morel, Rachel, 137
Morel, unknown, 223
Morell, Elizabeth, 137, 323
Morell, Louis, 137

Morell, Susanna, 137
Morgan, Ann (X), 161
Morgan, Anthony, 362
Morgan, Charles, 61
Morgan, Charles, Jr., 431
Morgan, Elizabeth, 293
Morgan, Frances (Bellin), 121, 130
Morgan, John, 61, 121, 130, 290
Morgan, Mary, 121, 130
Morgan, Morgan Rev., 229
Morin, Elizabeth (Viconte), 406
Morin, Estienne, 368
Morin, Jean, 93, 406
Morin, Judith, 369
Morin, Marguerite, 368
Morin, Marie, 205, 238, 368
Morin, Marie (Jamain), 205, 368
Morin, Marie Anne, 369
Morin, Moïse, 93
Morin, Philip, 206
Morin, Pierre, 205, 368, 369
MORIN, Pierre, 368
Morin, Samuel Capt., 406
Morris, Amidia/Amy, 272
Morris, Elizabeth (Brooks), 277
Morris, John, 183, 277
Morris, Martha, 341
Morriset(te), Daniel Fauré, 369
Morriset(te), David, 369
Morriset(te), Elizabeth, 369
Morriset(te), Jeanne/Jane, 369
Morriset(te), John, 369
Morriset(te), Judith, 369
Morriset(te), Katherine, 369
Morriset(te), Margaret, 369
Morriset(te), Mary, 369
MORRISET(TE), Pierre/Peter, 369
Morriset(te), William, 369
Morriset, Elizabeth, 137
Morriset, Elizabeth (Faure), 16
Morriset, Elizabeth (Fauré), 137
Morriset, Jeanne/Jane, 16
Morriset, Pierre, 16, 137, 187
Morrison, Asher, 138
Morrye, Jacques, 152
Morrye, Jeanne (Blondel), 152
Morrye, Susanne, 152
Morton, Lydia (Cooper), 62
Morton, Mercy, 62
Morton, Nathaniel, 62
Mosby, Littleberry Sr., 361
Moschel/Marshall, John, 170
Moseby, Agnes, 272
Moseley, Benjamin, 88
Moseley, David, 421
Moseley, David Colson, 421
Moseley, Edward, 88
Moseley, Elizabeth, 88
Moseley, Elizabeth (Colson), 421
Moseley, Martha, 89
Moseley, Robert, 88, 232

Moseley, Unite, 421
Moseley, William, 89
Moseley, William Capt., 88
Mosely, Samuel, 283
Moser, Hans, 369
Moser, Henry, 259
Moser/Mosier/Musser, Anna Maria, 369
Moser/Mosier/Musser, Johann Michael, 370
Moser/Mosier/Musser, Johann Peter, 369
Moser/Mosier/Musser, Maria Elizabeth, 370
Moser/Mosier/Musser, Maria Esther, 369
Moser/Mosier/Musser, Samuel, 369
MOSER/MOSIER/MUSSER, Samuel, 369
Moser/Mossier/Musser, Abraham, 370
Moser/Mossier/Musser, Anna Maria, 370
Moser/Mossier/Musser, Aron, 370
Moser/Mossier/Musser, Daniel, 370
Moser/Mossier/Musser, Hans Michael, 370
Moser/Mossier/Musser, Hans Peter, 370
Moser/Mossier/Musser, Johann Peter, 370
Moser/Mossier/Musser, Johann/Hans Michael, 370
Moser/Mossier/Musser, John, 370
Moser/Mossier/Musser, John Jacob, 370
Moser/Mossier/Musser, Samuel, 370
Mosher, Samuel, 295
Mosher, Sarah, 295
Mosnard, François de, **34**
Mosnard, Raimond de, **34**
Moss, Elizabeth, 213
Moss, John, 334
Moss, unknown, 137
Moucheron, Catherine de, 157
Mouis, Maria, 415
Mould, John, 399
Moulin, Marie de, 227
MOULIN/des MOULINS/MULLEN, Abraham, 370
Moulin/des/Moulins/Mullen, Jacob, 371
Moulin/desMoulins/Mullen, Abraham, 370, 371
Moulin/desMoulins/Mullen, Isaac, 371
Moulin/desMoulins/Mullen, Jean, 371
Moulin/desMoulins/Mullen, Marie, 371
Moulin/desMoulins/Mullen, Paul, 370
Moulinars, Jean, 371
MOULINARS, Jean Josèphe Brumeau de (Rev.), 371
Moulinars, Susanne Hélène, 371
Moullu, Juanvre, 28
Moullu, Marguerite (Drouyn), 28
Moullu/Moullins, Anne, 28
Moulton, Mary (Cook), 311
Moulton, Robert, 311

Mounier, Elizabeth (Martineaux), 371
Mounier, Étienne/Stephen, 372
Mounier, John, 372
Mounier, Louis, 371
Mounier, Moïse/Moses, 371
MOUNIER, Pierre, 371
Mounier, Sarah, 371
Mountjoy, Edward, 356
Mountjoy, Elizabeth, 213
Mountjoy, Mary (Crosby), 356
Mouton/Mutton, Elizabeth, 372
Mouton/Mutton, Frances, 372
MOUTON/MUTTON, Jean/John, 372
Mouton/Mutton, John, 372
Mouton/Mutton, Sarah, 372
Mouzon, Ann, 373
Mouzon, Charles, 373
Mouzon, Eleona, 373
Mouzon, Elizabeth, 373
Mouzon, Esther, 373
Mouzon, Henry, 373
Mouzon, Henry II, 373
Mouzon, Isaac Anthony, 373
Mouzon, James, 373
Mouzon, Judith, 373
Mouzon, Lewis, 373
Mouzon, Louis, 68, 233
Mouzon, Louis/Lewis, 373
MOUZON, Louis/Lewis, 372
Mouzon, Martha, 233
Mouzon, Martha Esther, 373
Mouzon, Mary, 373
Mouzon, Mary Ann, 373
Mouzon, Peter, 373
Mouzon, Samuel, 373
Mouzon, Sarah Jane, 373
Mouzon, Susanna, 373
Mouzon, Susanna Elizabeth, 373
Mouzon, Susannah Mary, 373
Moyenden, Christine, 224
Moynot, Peter, 18
Mucot, André, 79
Mueller/Müller, Elizabeth, 252
Mule, Anne Christensdatter, 363
Mulheym, Gertruyd Van, 48
Müller, Abraham, 19
Muller, Johannes Dr., 206
Müller, Reinhard, 19
Müller, Tobias, 252
Mumford, Edward, 254
Mumford, Mary, 254
Mumford, Mary (Watkins), 254
Mundell, unknown, 119
Munden, Millicent, 24
Murdock, Phoebe, **37**
Murphy, Elizabeth, 386
Murray, Daniel, 344
Murray, Gertrude, 107
Murray, Mary (Sperry), 344
Murray, Mary/Molly, 344
Murray, Sarah, 331

Murrow, Elizabeth, 396
Muse, Daniel, 23
Musgrave, John, 193
Musgrave, Mary, 193
Musgrave, Mary (Hastings), 193
Mussard, Anne (Le Grand), 194
Mussard, Françoise, 194
Mussard, Simon, 194
Muthel, John, 342
Myers, Annie, 97

N

Naarden, Pieter Casparre Mabie, 333
Naerden, Aechtje/Agatha Jans Van, 333
Naerden/Norden, John Van, 333
Nagel, Jan, 296
Nagel, Sebastian, 150
Namen, Anna Van, 353
Namen, Deliante Van, 353
Namen, Jochem Engelbert Van, 353
Napier, Alex, 206
Nash, John, Sr. Col., 311
Nash, Lucy, 311
Nash, Thomas Capt., 376
Naud(a)in, Andre, 467
Naud(a)in, André, 17
Naud(a)in, Arnauld, 375
Naud(a)in, Élias, 375
NAUD(A)IN, Élias/Élie, 374
Naud(a)in, Françoise, 375
Naud(a)in, Margaret (X), 17
Naud(a)in, Marguerite (X), 467
Naud(a)in, Mary, 375
Naudain, Andrew, 467
Naudin, Marie, 17
NAUDIN/NAUDAIN, André, 374
Naudin/Naudain, André II, 374
Naudin/Naudain, Louis, 374
Naudin/Naudain, Marie, 374
Naughty,Mary, 213
Neal, Anna (Farrell), 275
Neal, Francis, 275
Neal, Hannah, 275
Neal, John, 411
Neal, Mary, 275
Neale, Ann (Osborne), 346
Neale, Christopher, 346
Neale, Dorcas (Spence), 133
Neale, Richard, 133
Neargrass, Susannah, 26
Needham, Robert Capt., 43
Neef, Anna Margaretha, 375
Neegken, Anna Margaretha, 86
Neegken, Catharina (Keidten), 86
Neegken, Johannes, 86
Neeley, Mary, 138
Neely, Elizabeth, 138
Neely, William, 138
Neff, William, 124
Nei/Ney, Margaret, 34

Nelson, Elizabeth, 267
Nelson, Hasty (X), 277
Nelson, Jane (X), 266
Nelson, John, 266
Nelson, Sarah, 266
Ness, Cornelia Evertse Van, 313
Ness, Grietje Van, 367
Ness, Judith (Raplaje) Van, 131
Ness, Judith Van, 131
Ness, Peter Van, 121, 131, 153
Nessepolt, Jasper, 322
Nest, Judith Van, 95
Nest, Peter Peterson Van, 95
Nest, Pieter Van, 409
Netherton, Frances, 320
Nettle, unknown, 351
Neufville, Abraham de, 375
Neufville, Anna Maria de, 375
Neufville, David de, 375
Neufville, Jeanne, 462
Neufville, Mary Prodence de, 462
Neufville, Peter de, 375
Neufville, Robert, 375
Neufville, Sébastien de, 375
NEUFVILLE, Sébastien de, 375
Neumann, Anna Barbara, 19
Neumann, Jacob, 19
Neuparz, Andreas, 376
Neuparz, Dorothea, 376
NEUPARZ, Georg/Jörg, 375
Neuparz, George, 376
Neuparz, Hans Michael, 376
Neuparz, Margaret, 376
Neuparz, Peter, 376
Neveu, Adrien, 134
Neville, George, 264
Neville, Lucy, 264
Neville, Mary (Gibbs), 264
Newbold, Elizabeth (Powell), 146
Newbold, James, 146
Newby, John, 203
Newby, Rachel, 146
Newcomb, Hezekiah, 395
Newcomb, Jerusha (Bradford), 395
Newcomb, Joseph, 395
Newcomb, Joyce (Butler), 395
Newcomb, Priscilla, 395
Newcomb,Silas, 395
Newkirk, Neeltje Gerritsen, 130
Newkirt, Dorothy, 103
Newman, Jonathan, 138
Newman, Samuel, 260
Newsome, Margaret, 298
Newton, Abigail (Briscoe), 340
Newton, Eunice, 340
Newton, Ezekial, 340
Nichol, Agatha, 149
Nicholas, Hester, 416
Nicholas, John, 416
Nicholas, Margaret, 235
Nicholas, Marie, 233

Nicholas, Rachel, 416
Nicholls, Susannah, 181
Nichols, Agatha/Agnes, 310
Nichols, Annie, 330
Nichols, John, 310
Nichols, Joshua, 330
Nichols, Mary (X), 310
Nichols, William, 88
Nicholson, Francis, *419*
Nicholson, Nathaniel, 371
Nicholson, Sarah, 371
Nicholson, unknown, 68
Nickless, John, 372
Nickolls, Scudamore, 422
Nicola, Charles, 376
Nicola, Daniel, 376
NICOLA, Jean/John, 376
Nicola, Louis/Lewis, 376
Nicola, Susan (Malengin), 376
Nicola/Nicholas, Ann, 376
Nicola/Nicholas, Charlotte, 376
Nicola/Nicholas, Jane, 376
Nicola/Nicholas, John, 376
Nicola/Nicholas, Lewis, 376
Nicola/Nicholas, Margaret, 376
Nicola/Nicholas, Mary, 376
Nicola/Nicholas, Sarah, 376
Nicolas, Andre, 233
Nicolas, Françoise (Dunot), 233
Nicolas, Jean, 215
Nicolas, Marguerite, 215
Nicque, Agnietje, 174
Nieukerk, Chieltje (Slecht) Van, 130
Nieuwkirk, Gerit Cornelissen Van, 153
Nieuwkirk, Gerretje Gerritsen Van, 153
Nisbit, Martha Ann, 394
Nison, Charel de, 358
Noailles, Adrien-Maurice de, 22
Noarth, Hannah, 320
Noarth, William Capt., 320
Noch, Wolfe Dorothy, 60
Nodine, Andrew, 374
Nodine, Ann, 374
Nodine, Elizabeth, 374
Nodine, Judith, 374
Nodine, Lewis, 374
Nodine, Peter, 374
Noé, Isaac, 148
Nöe, Margaret (Dumont), 258
Noë, Pierre, 163
Nöe, Stephen, 312
NOÉ/NOË/NOUE/NIU/NEVE/NUEE, Pierre, 377
Noe/Noue/Niu/Neve/Nuee, Damaris, 377
Noe/Noue/Niu/Neve/Nuee, Daniel, 377
Noe/Noue/Niu/Neve/Nuee, Isaac, 377
Noe/Noue/Niu/Neve/Nuee, Jean/John, 377
Noe/Noue/Niu/Neve/Nuee, John, 377

Noe/Noue/Niu/Neve/Nuee, Magdalene, 377

Noe/Noue/Niu/Neve/Nuee, Marguerite/Margaret, 377

Noe/Noue/Niu/Neve/Nuee, Mary, 377

Noe/Noue/Niu/Neve/Nuee, Peter, 377

Noel, Boudewyn, 378

Noel, Cornelis, 377

Noel, Cornelius, 377

Noel, Daniel, 377

Noel, Elizabeth, 377

Noël, Elizabeth (DeNault), 377

NOËL, JACOB, 377

Noel, James, 377

Noel, Jan/John, 378

Noel, Margaret, 377

Noel, Mary, 377

Noël, Pierre, 377

Noel, Siburgh, 378

Noell, Sally, 332

Noget/Nazette, Marie Anne, 382

Noiret, Arnould, 176

Noiret, Barbe (du Chesne), 176

Noiret, Jacquemine, 176

Noiret, Jeanne, 177

Nolin, Jacques, 110

Norden, Andries Van, 316

Norieux, Elisabeth, *143*

Norieux, Françoise (Villamoine), *143*

Norieux, Noé, *143*

Norman, Barshaba, 80

Norman, Mary Ann, 233

Normand, Jean, 110

Normand, Philippe, 259

North, Elizabeth, 46

Northrup, Anna, 239

Norton, George Capt., 222

Nottingham, Cathrina, 103

Nourse, Eliza (Gregory), 200

Nourse, John, 200

Nugent, Amelia Thomson, 461

Nugent, Anne Lavinia (Lewis), 461

Nugent, John Pratt, 461

Nutterwell, Elizabeth, 216

Nuys, Jan Aukersze, 404

Nuyse Van, unknown, 174

O

O'Bryan, Martha (Seth), 161

O'Hare, Mary, 275

O'Neil, unknown, 474

O'Neill, Peter, 275

O'Rouk, Mary, 210

Oblenis, Maria, 454

Oblenis/Oblinus, Joost Van, 454

Oblinus, Joost, 246

Oblinus, Martina (X), 246

Oboussier, Louis Gex, 461

Ochs, Adam, 467

Odell, Mary, 467

Odell, Nehemiah, 433

Odier, M, 107

Odingsell, Charles, 289

Odingsell, Mary (Wilkins), 289

Odon, Caterine (Duchesne), 413

Odon, Marie Elisabeth, 413

Odon, Philippe, 413

Offley, Araminta, 161

Ogden, Elizabeth, 280

Ogden, Sarah, 218

Ogg, Elizabeth (X), *419*

Ogg, George, *419*

Ogier, Abraham, 379

Ogier, André, 379

Ogier, Daniel, 379

Ogier, Elizabeth, 379

Ogier, François, 379

Ogier, Françoise Catherine, 379

Ogier, Jean, 379

Ogier, Jeanne, 379

Ogier, Louis, 379

Ogier, Louise, 379

Ogier, Marie, 379

Ogier, Marie Renée, 379

Ogier, Moïse, 379

Ogier, Pierre, 379

OGIER, Pierre, 379

Ogier, Pierre Abraham, 379

Ogier, Thomas Abraham, 379

Oglethorpe, Gen., 433

Oissard, unknown, 271

Okie, Jan, 174

Oldfield, John, 230

Oldfield, Joseph, 230

Oldfield, Sara (X), 230

Oldsdatter, Gregine, 363

Oliver, Aaron, 394

Oliver, Elizabeth, 277

Oliver, James Capt., 283

Oliver, John, 277

Oliver, Mary (Shine), 277

Oliver, Reuben, 211

Olivier, Antoine, 438

Omohundro, unknown, 411

Ongars, Martin, 240

Oosterhout, Maritje, 273

Orange, Elizabeth, 380

Orange, John, 380

Orange, Judith, 380

Orange, Lewis, 380

ORANGE, Louis, 379

Orange, Magdalin, 380

Orange, Mary, 380

Orange, Peter, 380

Oremus, Hendrik D', 150

Orleans, Anne d', 380

Orleans, Ester d', 380

Orleans, Jacques d', 380

Orleans, Janne/Jeanne d', 380

ORLÉANS, Jean d', 380

Orleans, Judit d', 380

Orleans, Marie d', 380

Orléans, Marie d', 217

Orléans, Philippe d', 218

Orleans, Suzanne d', 380

Ormsby, Jacob, 391

Ormsby, Richard, 391

Ormsby, Sarah (X), 391

Orne, Sarah, 421

Orrick, James, 179

Orrick, William, 179

Orrick,Mary (Slade), 179

Orser, Albert, 81

Orser, Jan, 81

Orton, Margaret (Pell), 428

Orton, Mary, 428

Orton, Thomas, 428

Orvin, George, 371

Osborn, George Lucas, 412

Osborn, Valinda, 276

Osborne, Samuel, 130

Osbourne, Audrey, 258

Osmon, Prudence, 282

Otto, John Frederick, 46

Oudewater, Thomas Franzen, 150

Oudtwater, Frans, 150

Ourlet, Elisabeth, 92

Outwater, Thomas Frans, 172

Owen, Brackett Col., 311

Owen, Elizabeth (Brooks), 203

Owen, Elizabeth (McGehee), 311

Owen, Jane, 210

Owen, Priscilla, 203

Owen, Thomas, 203

Owen, William, 311

Oxford, Margaret (Strother), 266

Oxford, Roger, 266

Oxford, Winifred, 266

Ozias, Antoine, 343, 381

OZIAS, Antoine, 380

Ozias, Catherine, 343

Ozias, Catherine Lucrèce, 381

Ozias, Charles Daniel, 381

Ozias, Étienne/Stephen, 343, 381

Ozias, Henry/Heinrich, 381

Ozias, Isabeau (Lormeiasse), 343

Ozias, Jean/John, 381

Ozias, Jeanne, 381

Ozias, Jeanne Marie, 381

Ozias, John, 343

Ozias, Lucresse/Lucrèce, 381

Ozias, Madeleine, 381

Ozias, Peter, 343

Ozias, Pierre/Peter, 381

P

Pa(l)mer, Anna, 74

Pace, Charlotte/Charity, 140

Pace, Drury Capt., 140

Pacque, Pierre, 227

Pacquent, Michael, 397

Page, Abram, 246
Page, Elizabeth, 377
Page, Lydia, 135
Page, Mary Esther, 208
Page, Thomas, 377
Pages, Isaac, 215
Pages, John, 104
Paillet, Jeanne, 379
Paillet, Pierre, 379
Pain, Charles, 141, 166
Paine, William, 403
Painter, Thomas, 102
Pairan, Charlotte, 437
Paisant/Paysant, Anne, 382
Paisant/Paysant, Jacques, 382
Paisant/Paysant, Jean Louis, 382
Paisant/Paysant, Jean/John, 382
Paisant/Paysant, Lisette, 382
Paisant/Paysant, Louis, 382
PAISANT/PAYSANT, Louis Philippe, 382
Paisant/Paysant, Marie, 382
Paisant/Paysant, Marie/Mary, 382
Paisant/Paysant, Philippe/Philip, 382
Paisant/Paysant, Suzanne, 382
Paise, Mary (X), 472
Paise, Thomas, 472
Palasy, Clovis Pastor, 265
Palasy. Anne, 265
Palmatier, Elizabeth, 301
Palmer, Anne(deBonrepos), 18
Palmer, Esther/Hester, 18
Palmer, Joseph, 208
Palmer, Martha, 254
Palmer, Mary (Drake?), 74
Palmer, Mary Jane, 424
Palmer, Obadiah, 74
Palmer, Robert, 254
Palmer, Samuel, 74
Palmer, Thomas, 254
Palmié, Marie Dorothea (Nannette), 215
Pamerton, John, 169
Panetier/Panetie/Panit(o)ur/Pankey, Dorothy, 383
Panetier/Panetie/Panit(o)ur/Pankey, Edward, 383
Panetier/Panetie/Panit(o)ur/Pankey, Elizabeth, 383
Panetier/Panetie/Panit(o)ur/Pankey, Étienne/Stephen, 383
Panetier/Panetie/Panit(o)ur/Pankey, Jean Pierre/John Peter, 383
PANETIER/PANETIÉ/PANIT(O)UR/PANKEY, Jean/John, 382
Panetier/Panetie/Panit(o)ur/Pankey, John, 383
Panetier/Panetie/Panit(o)ur/Pankey, Loring Young, 383
Panetier/Panetie/Panit(o)ur/Pankey, Mary Ann, 383
Panetier/Panetie/Panit(o)ur/Pankey, Samuel, 383

Panetier/Panetie/Panit(o)ur/Pankey, Sarah, 383
Panetier/Panetie/Panit(o)ur/Pankey, Stephen, 383
Panhuysen, Johannes, 198
Panitour/Pankey, John Peter, 144
Paparel, André, 208
Paparel, Catherine (Bollioud), 208
Paparel, Esther, 208
Paparel. Jean, 208
Papin, Georges, 317
Papin, Marie, 317
Papin, Marie (Brunet), 317
Paradijs, Claes Allertsen, 360
Parandier, Marie, 70
Parcot, Françoise, (Gendron), 29
Parcot, James, 73
Parcot, Michelle, 461
Parcot, Pierre, 29
Pardo, Charles, 171
Parenteau, Madeline, 309
Paris, John, 304
Parish, Elizabeth, 436
Parisis, Jacqueline de, 453
Park, Mary (Botsford), 127
Park, Roger, 448
Park, Susan Parnice, 127
Park, Thomas Dr., 127
Parker, Alice, 44
Parker, Ann, 181
Parker, Ann (Well), 181
Parker, Hanaple, 445
Parker, Jacob, 295
Parker, John, 85, 445
Parker, Martin, 266
Parker, Polly, 212
Parker, Ruth, 111, 267
Parker, unknown, 388
Parker, William, 181, 297
Parker, William S., 320
Parker, Zenas, 445
Parmentier, Antointette, 384
Parmentier, Damen Michaelse, 384
Parmentier, Jan Michaelse, 384
Parmentier, Jean, 383
Parmentier, Jeanne (Fouré), 383
Parmentier, Joanna, 384
Parmentier, Lysbet, 384
Parmentier, Michael, 384
Parmentier, Michael Pieterse, 384
Parmentier, Neelje, 384
PARMENTIER, Pierre/Peter, 383
Parmentier, Pieter Michaelse, 384
Parmentier, Sophia, 384
Parquot/Parcot, Madeline, 29
Parrain, unknown, 299
Parrish, Joel, 355
Parrot, Abraham, 285
Parry, John, 312
Parsons, Samuel, 457
Partridge, John, 190

Pase/Pare, Elizabeth, 209
Pasquereau, Charlotte Marianna (Gendron), 398
Pasquereau, Isaac, 186
Pasquereau, Louis, 398, 402
Pasquereau, Louis II, 186
Pasquereau, Madeleine, 186
Pasquereau, Madeleine (Houssaye), 186
Pasquereau, Peter, 186
Pasquereau, Pierre, 186
Pasquereau,Louis, 186
Pasteur, Ann, 350
Pasteur, Anne, 385
Pasteur, Annie Mckinnie, 384
Pasteur, Blouvet, 385
Pasteur, Charles, 384, 385
PASTEUR, Charles, 384
Pasteur, Elizabeth, 385
Pasteur, Francis, 384
Pasteur, James, 384
Pasteur, James Blouvet, 385
Pasteur, Jean, 355
PASTEUR, Jean, 385
Pasteur, John, 384, 385
Pasteur, John II, 385
Pasteur, John James, 384
Pasteur, Judith, 355, 385
Pasteur, Lucretia, 385
Pasteur, Magdalene, 385
Pasteur, Martha, 385
Pasteur, Martha Jane, 384
Pasteur, Mary, 385
Pasteur, Mary (Blouet), 355
Pasteur, Mary Gilmour, 384
Pasteur, Mary/Polly, 385
Pasteur, Solomon W, 385
Pasteur, William, 385
Pastre, Marie Susanne, 343
Patch, Benjamin, 311
Pateu-Jeanz, Jean, 155
Patmore, Cliffy, 293
Patrick, Anna, 65
Patten, Anna (X), 422
Patten, Thomas, 422
Patterson, Beulah, 344
Patterson, Hannah (Hubbell), 344
Patterson, Lucy, 158
Patterson, Samuel, 344
Patterson, unknown, 218
Patteson, David Jr., 158
Patton, Margaret, 331
Pauer, David, 101
Paul, Abraham, 329
Paul, Judith (Hurtienne), 329
Paul, Maria Margaretha, 252
Paul, Marie, 329
Paulus, Hendrickje, 130
Paus, Georg Jacob, 252
Pawley, Percival, 361
Payari, Étienne, 194
Payari, Hortense (Puerari), 194

Payari, Judith, 194
Peachey, Phebe (Slaughter), 291
Peachey, Samuel, 89
Peachey, William, 291
Peacock, Mary, 234
Pearson, Polly Roquemore, 426
Pechin, Anne-Judith (Hauser), 285
Pechin, unknown, 285
Peck, Eleazer, 70
Peck, Henry, 70
Peck, Joan (X), 70
Peeck, Jan, 177
Peeck, John, 279
Pegues, Claudius, 386
PEGUES, Claudius, 385
Pegues, Harriet, 386
Pegues, Henriette, 386
Pegues, William, 386
Peiret, Pierre Rev., 292
Peiret/Peyret, Elizabeth, 386
Peiret/Peyret, Françoise, 386
Peiret/Peyret, Gabriel, 386
Peiret/Peyret, Magdalene, 386
Peiret/Peyret, Margaret, 386
Peiret/Peyret, Peter, 386
Peiret/Peyret, Pierre, 386
PEIRET/PEYRET, Pierre (Rev.), 386
Peiret/Peyret, Susanne, 386
Pekok/Peacock, Elizabeth (Denis), 301
Pekok/Peacock, Maria, 301
Pekok/Peacock, Robert, 301
Pelé, Marie, 230
Pelé, Marie (Gautier), 230
Pelé, Pierre, 230
Péletan(t), Judith, 49
Pelissari, Claire, 22
Pelletreau, Benjamin, 336
Pelletreau, Eli, 17
Pelletreau, Elie, 336
Pelletreau, Hester/Esther, 452
Pelletreau, Jean, 452
Pelletreau, Madeleine (Vincent), 452
Pels, Hendrich, 384
Pels, Sarah, 205
Pelt, Anthony Teunissen Van, 151
Pelt, Hendrick Thys Lanen Van, 48
Pelt, Jan Van, 293
Pelt, Johannes Van, 320
Pelt, Teunis Van, 151
Peltrau, Hester, 135
Pemberton, Mary, 254
Pemberton/Pa(i)mbreton, George, 387
Pemberton/Pa(i)mbreton, James, 387
Pemberton/Pa(i)mbreton, Magdalane, 387
Pemberton/Pa(i)mbreton, Martha, 387
Pemberton/Pa(i)mbreton, Mary, 387
Pemberton/Pa(i)mbreton, Michael, 387
Pemberton/Pa(i)mbreton, Richard, 387
PEMBERTON/PA(I)MBRETON, Richard, 387

Pemberton/Pa(i)mbreton, William, 387
Penn, William, 192
Pépin, Alexander, 399
Pépin, Alexandre, 84
PÉPIN, Alexandre, 387
Pepin, Judith-Marianne, 387
Pépin, Madelaine (Garillion), 399
Pepin, Madeleine, 387
Pépin, Madeleine, 399
Pépin, Madeleine
    (Garillion/Garillond/Gaillard), 84
Pepin, Paul, 387
Péquigny, Marguerite d'Ailly de, 121
Perdiau, Étienne/Stephen, 75
Perdiau, John, 234
Perdiau, Marguerite, 75
Perdiau, Ozée/Hosea, 75
Perdiguer, Claude, 208
Perdrian, Margaret (Gourvin), 247
Perdrian, Orie, 247
Perdrian/Perdriau, Margaret/Marguerite, 247
Perin, Elizabeth, 380
Perine, Elizabeth, 357
Perkins, Amariah, 471
Perkins, Luch Ann, 47
Perkins, Lucy (Watlins), 47
Perkins, Lydia, 378
Perkins, Mary, 330, 378
Perkins, Nicholas, 378
Perkins, Willian, 47
Perlier, Anne, 417
Perlier, Anne (Rezeau), 293
Perlier, Jean, 293, 417
Perlier, Marie, 417
Perlier, Susanne, 293
Pernet, Susan S., 461
Pero/Pierrot, Jan, 333
Peroe, 322
Peron, François, 387
Peron/Perron, Antoine, 388
PÉRON/PERRON, Daniel, 387
Peronneau, Alexander, 388
Peronneau, Ann, 388
Peronneau, Charles, 388
Peronneau, Elizabeth, 349, 388
Peronneau, Henri II, 388
Peronneau, Henri/Henry, 388
Peronneau, Isaac, 388
Peronneau, Jeanne (Collin), 28, 349
Peronneau, Marie, 28, 388
Peronneau, Martha, 388
Peronneau, Mary, 388
Peronneau, Mary Ann, 388
Peronneau, Sameul, 349
Peronneau, Samuel, 28, 388
PERONNEAU, Samuel, 388
Peronneau, Sarah, 388
Peronneau, unknown, 388
Perot/Parrott, Elizabeth, **41**
Perot/Perrow.Perroult, John, 389

Perot/Perrow/Perroult, Angelina, 389
Perot/Perrow/Perroult, Elliston, 389
Perot/Perrow/Perroult, Frances, 389
PÉROT/PERROW/PERROULT, Jacques, 388
Perot/Perrow/Perroult, Jacques/James, 389
Perot/Perrow/Perroult, James, 389
Perot/Perrow/Perroult, Martha, 389
Perot/Perrow/Perroult, Mary, 389
Perot/Perrow/Perroult, William, 389
Perot/Perrow/Perroult, William B, 389
Perrault, Olive, 434
Perrault/ Perrow, Charles, 185
Perrault/Perreau, Daniel, 434
Perrault/Perrow/Pero, Anne, 389
Perrault/Perrow/Pero, Charles, 389
PERRAULT/PERROW/PERO, Charles, 389
Perrault/Perrow/Pero, Daniel, 389
Perrault/Perrow/Pero, Mariane, 389
Perrault/Perrow/Pero, Marie/Mary, 389
Perreault, Charles, 232
Perreault/Perrow, Mary, 232
Perrenon, Catherine, 359
Perrenon, François, 359
Perrenon, Françoise (Pourchot), 359
Perrenot, Françoise, 284
Perret, Catherine (Bouteiller), 68
Perret, Catherine Elisabeth, 68
Perret, Jean Georges, 68
Perriman, John, 338
Perriman, Mary (Snipes), 338
Perrin(e)/Pareyn, Daniel, 390
PERRIN(E)/PAREYN, Daniel, 390
Perrin(e)/Pareyn, Elizabeth, 390
Perrin(e)/Pareyn, Francyntje, 390
Perrin(e)/Pareyn, Henry, 390
Perrin(e)/Pareyn, James, 390
Perrin(e)/Pareyn, Maria/Mary, 390
Perrin(e)/Pareyn, Peter, 390
Perrin(e)/Pareyn, Pierre, 390
Perrin(e)/Pareyn, Sara, 390
Perrin(e)/Pareyn, William, 390
Perrin, Abraham, 263, 391
Perrin, Catherine Louisa, 285
Perrin, Christopher, 285
Perrin, Edmund, 180
Perrin, Elizabeth, 263
Perrin, Hannah/Anna, 391
Perrin, Jean, 390
PERRIN, Jean, 390
Perrin, John, 391
Perrin, Marie (LeJeune), 263
Perrin, Marie Catherin, 285
Perrin, Marie Catherine (Dauphiné), 285
Perrin, Mary, 391
Perron, Jeanne, 440
Perrot, Margaret (X), **41**
Perrot, Richard Sr, **41**
Perrow, Anne, 323
Perrow, Marie, 185

Perry, John, 207
Perry, Joyce, 286
Perry, unknown, 207, 360
Perryn, John, 390
Pershing/Pforsching, Christena, 391
Pershing/Pforsching, Christian, 391
Pershing/Pforsching, Conrad, 391
Pershing/Pforsching, Daniel, 391
Pershing/Pforsching, Eli, 391
Pershing/Pforsching, Elizabeth, 391
PERSHING/PFÖRSCHING, Frédéric/Frederick/Friedrich, 391
Pershing/Pforsching, Henry B., 391
Pershing/Pforsching, Hezekiah, 391
Pershing/Pforsching, Jacob, 391
Pershing/Pforsching, James, 391
Pershing/Pforsching, John, 391
Pershing/Pforsching, Jonathan, 391
Pershing/Pforsching, Joseph, 391
Pershing/Pforsching, Margaret, 391
Pershing/Pforsching, Peter Frederick, 391
Pershing/Pforsching, Robert, 391
Pershing/Pforsching, Samuel K., 391
Pershing/Pforsching, Sarah, 391
Pershing/Pforsching, William, 391
Pesquier, Nicholas, 243
Pesquier, unknown, 243
Pesyn/Pesin, Jean, 286
Petilion, Jacques, 450, 467
Petilion, Marie, 430
Petilion, Marie (Sy), 467
Petit, M. René, 231
Petitot, Madeleine, 294
Petre, Jacquemin, 363
Pétremand, Marie, 422
Pétremand, Pierre, 422
Petry, Marie, 300
Pettigrew, Sarah B., 221
Pettingill, Jeannette, 212
Pettremond, Daniel, 345
Pettremond, Marie Eve, 345
Pettus, Dabney, 22
Pettus, Pettus, 22
Petty, Maximillian, 471
Peugeot, Benôit, 285
Peyer, Judith (Boisseau), 208
Peyre, Ann, 320
Peyre, David, 65, 208, 418
Peyre, Elizabeth Catherine, 418
Peyre, Jane, 65
Peyre, Judith (Boisseau), 418
Peyre, Lydia, 208
Peyrolet, Jacques, 166
Peyster, Abraham de, 392
Peyster, Catharina de, 392
Peyster, Cornelia (Lubberts) de, 404
Peyster, Cornelia de, 392
Peyster, Cornelis de, 392
Peyster, Elizabeth de, 392
Peyster, Isaac de, 392

Peyster, Jacob de, 392
Peyster, Jacques de, 392
Peyster, Johannes de, 392, 404
Peyster, Jonas de, 392
Peyster, Josse de, 392
PEYSTER, Josse de, 392
Peyster, Lievin de, 392
Peyster, Maria de, 392
Peyster, Marie de, 392
Pez, Jean, **42**
Pezé, Madeleine, 394
Pezé, Marie (Boureau), 394
Pezé, Martin, 394
Phelps, Samuel, 244
Philippe, Marie, 400
Philippeau, Claude, 110, 141
Philippeau, Jeanne, 110
Philippeau, Jeanne (Énard), 110, 141
Philippeau, Louise, 141
Philippes, Margaretha, 408
Philipse, Adolphe, 43
Phillips, Gillam, 184
Phillips, Samuel, 462
Phillips, Susannah, 429
Phillips, Susannah (Lloyd), 429
Phillips, William, 429
Phippard, William, 236
PIATT/PYATT, René,, 392
Pichler, Christophel, 342
Pickenpaugh, Anna Barbara (X), 199
Pickenpaugh, Barbara, 199
Pickenpaugh, Peter, 199
Pickens, Ezekial, 68
Pickens, Isreal, 254
Picon, André, 393
Picon/Pickens/Pickins, Andrew, 393
Picon/Pickens/Pickins, Andrew II, 394
Picon/Pickens/Pickins, Gabriel, 394
Picon/Pickens/Pickins, Israel, 394
Picon/Pickens/Pickins, John, 393
Picon/Pickens/Pickins, Lucy, 394
Picon/Pickens/Pickins, Margaret, 394
PICON/PICKENS/PICKINS, Robert (aka André), 393
Picon/Pickens/Pickins, William, 394
Pierce, Sarah, 23
Pierce, William, 23
Pierce/Pearce, James, 429
Pierre, Jean del, 144
Pieters, Geertje, 366
Pieterse(n), Rachel, 150
Pieterse, Hesssel, 151
Pieterse, Matje, 172
Pietersen, Hildebrand, 324
Pieterson, Casper, 54
Pieterszen, Nathaniel/Daniel, 45
Pike, Margaret, 394
Pikes, Jan, 278
Pikes/Pyckes, Peternella, 278
Pilleau, Alexis, 394, 395
PILLEAU, Alexis (Rev., 394

Pilleau, Alexis Pezé, 394
Pilleau, Alexis Pierre, 394
Pilleau, Anne, 394
Pilleau, Catherine, 394
Pilleau, François, 395
Pilleau, Henriette Marguerite, 395
Pilleau, Isaac, 395
Pilleau, Jacques, 394
Pilleau, Jean, 394
Pilleau, Jean Pezé, 395
Pilleau, Madeleine Louise, 395
Pilleau, Marie, 394
Pilleau, Michelle, 394
Pilleau, René, 395
Pilleau, Susanne, 395
Pillon, Anne, 363
Pillon, Josué, 363
Pillot, Catherine, 367
Pillot, Isreal, 367
Pillot, Jeanne (Goudry), 367
Pinckney, Isreal, 374
Pinckney, William Henry, 128
Pineau/Pineo/Penaud, Daniel, 395
Pineau/Pineo/Penaud, Dorothy, 395
Pineau/Pineo/Penaud, Elizabeth, 395
PINEAU/PINEO/PENAUD, Jacques, 395
Pineau/Pineo/Penaud, James, 395
Pineau/Pineo/Penaud, Joseph, 395
Pineau/Pineo/Penaud, Peter, 395
Pineau/Pineo/Penaud, Sarah, 395
Pineau/Pineo/Penaud, Submit, 395
Pingar, Jacques, 25, 147, 396
PINGAR, Jacques, 395
Pingar, Ma(g)deleine, 147
Pingar, Madeline (Despine), 25
Pingar, Magdelaine, 396
Pingar, Marie, 25, 147, 395
Pinion, Abigail, 102
Pinion, Mercy (X), 102
Pinion, Thomas, 102
Pinneau, Jacques, 395
Pinson, Jean, 177
Pintard, Anna Frances, 396
Pintard, Anthony, 396
Pintard, Antoine, 304
PINTARD, Antoine/Anthony, 396
Pintard, Catherine, 396
Pintard, Catherine (Stelle), 304
Pintard, Florinda, 396
Pintard, Isabella, 396
Pintard, John Lewis, 396
Pintard, Magdalena, 396
Pintard, Margaret, 304, 396
Pintard, Samuel, 396
Piozet, Charles, 394
Pitre, Geneviève, 22
Pitt, Mary, 88
Pittenger/Peppenger, Syche, 440
Pitts, James, **37**
Pitts, unknown, 207
Place, John, 453

Planck, Sara de, 366
Platt, Mercy, 86
Pleasanton, Mary, 161
Plosch, Hans, 376
Plouvier, Françoise (X), 183
Plouvier, Pierre II, 183
Plouvier, Pierre/Peter, 183
Plouvier, Rebecca, 183
Plovier, Pieter, 365
Pluck, Andries Canon, 77
Pluck, Jan, 77
Pluck, Jannetje, 77
Plumer, Moses, 464
Poachin/Pouchin, Jacob, 155
Poachin/Pouchin, Marie, 155
Pochard, Anne Catherine, 67
Pochard, Charles Jean, 246
Pochard, Jean, 339
Pochard, Jeanne (Mounier), 339
Pochard, Peter, 339
Pochard, Pierre Emanuel, 339
Pococke, Mary, 209
Poel, Melgert Wynantse Van der, 296
Poel, Tryntje (Melgers) Van der, 296
Poel, Wynant Van der, 296
Poilet/Pellet, Arnold, 188
Poilet/Pellet, Marguerite, 188
Poillon, Adrianna (Crocheron), 159
Poillon, Catherine, 130, 293
Poillon, Catherine (LeConte), 293
Poillon, Jacques, 62, 78, 120, 130, 159, 293, 357
Poillon, Jean Crocheron, 130
Poillon, Marie, 130, 159
Poindexter, Elizabeth (X), 355
Poindexter, George, 181
Poindexter, Jacob, 180
Poindexter, Philip, 180
Poindexter, Phillip, 355
Poindexter, Rachel, 181
Poindexter, Susanna, 355
Poindexter, Thomas, 180
Poingdestre, Edouard, 180
Poingdestre, Marguerite (Messervy), 180
Poinset, Catherine, 397
Poinset, Jean/John, 396
Poinset, Jeanne, 397
Poinset, Joel, 397
Poinset, John, 396
Poinset, Pierre, 396
POINSET, Pierre, 396
Poinset, Pierre II, 396, 464
Poinset, Pierre/Peter III, 397
Poinset, Sara (Fouchereau), 464
Poinset, Susannah/Elizabeth, 396
Poinsett, Joel, 464
Poissonier, Marie Jeanne, 97
Poitevin II, Antoine, 84
Poitevin, Antoine, 399
Poitevin, Gabrielle (Berou), 84
Poitevin, Jacques, 397

Poitevin, Jeanne (Modemen), 397
Poitevin, Marguerite, 399
Poitevin, Marguerite (de Bourdeaux), 399
Poitevin/Poitevent, Ann, 397
Poitevin/Poitevent, Anthony, 397
POITEVIN/POITEVENT, Antoine/Anthony, 397
Poitevin/Poitevent, Antoine/Anthony II, 397
Poitevin/Poitevent, James, 397
Poitevin/Poitevent, Magdalen, 397
Poitevin/Poitevent, Marguerite, 397
Poitevin/Poitevent, Pierre, 397
Polhemus, Adriana, 62
Polhemus, Adrianna, 299
Polhemus, Catrina, 174
Polhemus, Elizabeth, 126, 174
Polhemus, Theodorus, 174
Polk, Thomas Gen., 91
Polk, unknown, 91
Pollard, Mary, 164
Pollinger, Abraham, 150
Pollock, Mary, 388
Pon, Duchesse de, 460
Pons, Pons, 71
Ponsin, Nicholas, 93
Ponsin, Pierre, 93
Pontius, Hans Peter, 438
Pontius, Johannes/John, 438
Pontius, Nicholas, 259
Pontius, Rosina Catharina (Hauch), 438
Pontus, William, 139, 286
Pontus, Wybra (Hanson), 139, 286
Poole, Richard, 179
Poor, Enoch, 91
Poore, George, 85
Poore, William, 85
Pope, Richard, 276
Porcher, Claude, 398
Porcher, Elizabeth, 398
Porcher, Isaac, 167, 398
PORCHER, Isaac, 398
Porcher, Isaac II, 167, 398, 418
Porcher, Madeleine, 398
Porcher, Marianne, 398
Porcher, Marie, 398
Porcher, Paul, 167
Porcher, Pierre/Peter, 398
Porcher, Rachel (DuPré), 167
Porcher, Susanne, 398
Porcher, Susanne (Ferré), 398
Portage, Hannah, **37**
Portal, Elizabeth, 399
Porter, Anne, 176
Porter, Dutoy, 176
Porter, Elizabeth, 232
Porter, Elizabeth Barbara, 176
Porter, John, 176
Porter, Joseph, 395
Porter, Josiah, **50**
Porter, Mary, 232

Porter, Mary (Kemp), 176
Porter, Rebecca, 340
Porter, Seth, 340
Porter, Thomas, 176
Porter, William, **50**
Porterfield, Robert, 114
Poshet, Anne (de Colnet), 398
Poshet, Marteyn, 398
Poshet/Posey, Anne, 399
Poshet/Posey, Benjamin, 399
POSHET/POSEY, François/Francis, 398
Poshet/Posey, John, 399
POSHET/POSEY, Marteyn/Martin, 398
Post, Agnietje (Bonen), 177
Post, Hester (Hyde), 70
Post, John, 70
Post, Lodewyck, 177
Post, Lysbeth, 177
Postel(l), Marie, 65
Postell, Mary, 224
Postmael/Post, Jan Jansen, 324
Postre, Madeleine (Perrot), 343
Postre, Pierre, 343
Potel/Potell, Jacques/James, 399
POTEL/POTELL, Jean, 399
Potel/Potell, Jean, Jr, 399
Potel/Potell, Jean/John, 399
Potel/Potell, Pierre, 399
Potell, Jean, 397
Potell, Jean II, 397
Potell, Madeleine (Pépin), 397
Potell/Postell, Jean, 387
Potot, Rose Élisabeth, 228
Potter, Elisabeth/Lysbeth de, 43
Potter, Elizabeth de, 287
Pottinger, Anna, 276
Pouillon, Judith (Bodine), 357
Poupart, Jeanne (Decorby), 92
Poupart, Marie, 92
Poupart, Mathias, 92
Poupin, Martha, 230
Poupin/Pepin, Madeleine, 257
Powe, William, 386
Powell, Adam, 52
Powell, Betty, 383
Powell, Mary (McKnitt), 90
Powell, Mary (X), 383
Powell, Prudence, 146
Powell, Robert, 146
Powell, Sarah, 214
Powell, Thomas, 90
Powell, unknown, **37**
Powell, William, 383
Poyas, Jacques/James, 399
Poyas, Jean Louis, 400
POYAS, Jean Louis, 399
Poyas, Jean/John Ernest, 399
Poyas, Maria Louisa, 400
Poyas, Sarah, 400
Poyas, Susanne, 400
Poytevin, Jeanne de, 157

Praa, Lysbeth, 358
Praa, Pieter, 358
Praa/Prat, Abraham, 400
Praa/Prat, Adam, 400
Praa/Prat, Catharine, 400
Praa/Prat, Marie, 400
Praa/Prat, Pierre, 400
Praa/Prat, Pieter, 400
PRAA/PRAT, Pieter, 400
Praa/Prat, Samuel, 400
Praal, Arendt, 101
Praal, Maria (Christopher), 101
Praal, Mary, 101
Praal, Pieter, 101
Prall, Isaac, 154
Prall/Praal/Prael, Arendt Jansen, 61
Pratt, Benajah, 62
Pratt, Sarah, 110, 267
Pratter/Pretter, Anna Barbara, 149
Praul, Ann, 315
Préduin, Mary, 224
Pree, Pieternelletjen/Peternelje De, 169
Pressy, Charles, 76
Prevat/te, Elizabeth, 401
Prevat/te, Peter, 401
Prévo(s)t, Charles, 148
Prévo(s)t, Elisabeth, 148
Prévo(s)t, Marie (LeFevre), 148
Prevol/Prevot/Prevo(s)t, Peter, 401
PRÉVOL/PRÉVÔT/PRÉVO(S)T/PREVAT(T)
, Pierre, 401
Prévost/Prevoost, David, 392
Price, Edward, 96
Price, Elinor, 96
Price, Mary, 96
Price, unknown, 185
Priest, William, 41
Priest/Prest/Press, Elizabeth de, 402
Priest/Prest/Press, Guillaume/William
de, 401
Priest/Prest/Press, John de, 402
Priest/Prest/Press, Mary de, 401
Priest/Prest/Press, Naomi de, 401
Priest/Prest/Press, Randolph de, 401
Priest/Prest/Press, Robert de, 402
PRIEST/PREST/PRESS, Robert de, 401
Priest/Prest/Press, Robert/Robin de,
402
Priest/Prest/Press, Sarah de, 402
Priest/Prest/Press, William de, 401
Priester/Beisasse, Maria Elizabeth, 71
Prince of Orange, 189, 328
Prince, John, 403
Prince, John Rev., 403
Prince, Thomasin, 403
Printz, Johan Lt. Col., 87
Prioleau, Ann, 402
Prioleau, Caroline, 402
Prioleau, Catherine, 402
Prioleau, Elias, 402
Prioleau, Élias, 402

PRIOLEAU, Élias/Élie (Rev.), 402
Prioleau, Élisée, 211, 402
Prioleau, Elizabeth, 402
Prioleau, Esther, 402
Prioleau, Hext, 402
Prioleau, Jeanne, 402
Prioleau, Jeanne (Merlat), 402
Prioleau, John Cordes, 402
Prioleau, Marie, 402
Prioleau, Martha, 402
Prioleau, Mary M, 402
Prioleau, Mary Magdeleine, 402
Prioleau, Philip, 402
Prioleau, Philip Gendron, 402
Prioleau, Samuel, 186, 402
Pritchard, Margaret (Sawyer), 24
Pritchett, Nathaniel, 282
PROU, Cyprian, 403
Prou, Elizabeth, 403
Prou, Frances, 403
Prou, Margaret, 403
Prou, Marie/Mary, 403
Prou, Susanna, 403
Prout, John, 75
Prout, Susanna, 75
Provoost, David, 392
Provoost, Helen, 206
Provoost, Wilhelmus, 403
Provost, Benjamin, 106
Provost, David, 278
Provost, Margaretta, 106
Provost/ Provoost, Wilhelmus, 404
Provost/Provoost, Barbara, 404
Provost/Provoost, Benjamin, 404
Provost/Provoost, David, 403, 404
Provost/Provoost, David II, 404
Provost/Provoost, David III, 404
Provost/Provoost, Elias, 403, 404
Provost/Provoost, Elizabeth, 404
Provost/Provoost, Gillis, 404
PROVOST/PROVOOST,
Guillaume/Gutielmus/Wilhelmus, 403
Provost/Provoost, Johannes, 403
Provost/Provoost, Jonathan, 404
Provost/Provoost, Margaret, 404
Provost/Provoost, Margareta, 404
Provost/Provoost, Samuel, 404
Provost/Provoost, Sarah, 404
Provost/Provoost, William, 404
Prudon/Prudhomme, Ma(g)delaine, 468
Prudon/Prudhomme, Magdalena
(Teveningh, 468
Prudon/Prudhomme, Nicolaas Louis, 468
Pryaulx, Pierre/Peter, 123
Pue, William de, 302
Puerari, Daniel, 194
Puerari, Giuditta/Judith, 194
Puerari, Jeanne (Marcet), 194
Purdy, Elizabeth (Ogden), 448
Purdy, Joseph, 448
Purdy, Joshua, 225

Purdy, Phebe, 448
Purdy, Phoebe, 186
Purdy, Phoebe (Ketchum), 186
Purdy, Samuel, 448
Purdy, Seth, 186
Pursell, Thomas, 88
Purviance, David, 405
Purviance, Jacques, 405
PURVIANCE, Jacques, 404
Purviance, Jacques II, 405
Purviance, Jacques III, 405
Purviance, James, 405
Purviance, Jean/Jon, 404
Purviance, John, 405
Purviance, Mary, 405
Purviance, Robert, 405
Purviance, Samuel, 405
Purviance, Susannah, 405
Purviance, Thomas, 405
Purviance, William, 405
Purviance/Purveyance, Samuel, 405
Purvine, Lewis, 405
Pury, Jean Pierre de, 223
Puten, Sarah, 45
Putter, Fytje Van, 95
Puy, Susanne, 42
Pyatt/Piatt, Francis, 393
Pyatt/Piatt, Jacob, 393
Pyatt/Piatt, James, 393
Pyatt/Piatt, Joan/Jane, 393
Pyatt/Piatt, René, 393
Pyatt/Piatt, Samuel, 393
Pyatt/Piatt, Thomas, 393
Pyrlaeus, John Christopher, 46

Q

Queen Anne, 73, 192, 458
Quenet/Duguenois, Marguerite de, 214
Quennell, Anthoine, 313
Quennell, Louise, 313
Quilling, unknown, 275
Quinn, John, 362
Quintard, Abraham, 406
Quintard, Hannah, 406
Quintard, Isaac, 406
QUINTARD, Isaac, 406
Quintard, Marie (X), 406
Quintard, Marie Anne, 406
Quintard, Mary, 406
Quintard, Peter, 406
Quintard, Pierre, 406

R

R------, Frances, 110
Rabaud, Catherine, 379
Rabeau, unknown, 342
Raboteau, Henriette, 32
Raboteau, unknown, 32
Rader, John, 138

Raganar/Regeinor, Jeanne, 215
Ragsdale, John, 100
Ragsdale, Lucy, 100
Rahm, Jean Georges/Johann Georg, 407
Rahm, Maria Katharina (Leppla), 407
Raley, Thomas, 89
Ram, Everhard, 407
Rambert, André, 155
Rambert, Anna (Bressau), 155
Rambert, François, 407
Rambert, Judith (Courand), 407
RAMBERT/REMBERT, André, 407
Rambert/Rembert, André II, 407
Rambert/Rembert, Andrew, 407
Rambert/Rembert, Anne, 407
Rambert/Rembert, Caleb, 407
Rambert/Rembert, Gérosme, 407
Rambert/Rembert, Isaac, 407
Rambert/Rembert, James, 407
Rambert/Rembert, Jane, 407
Rambert/Rembert, Jean, 407
Rambert/Rembert, Jeanne/Jane, 407
Rambert/Rembert, Madelaine, 407
Rambert/Rembert, Marguerite, 407
Rambert/Rembert, Marie, 407
Rambert/Rembert, Pierre, 407
Rambert/Rembert, Susanne, 407
RAME/RAHM, Charles/K, 407
Rame/Rahm, Elisabeth, 408
Rame/Rahm, George, 408
Rame/Rahm, Helena, 408
Rame/Rahm, Johan Georg Philip, 408
Rame/Rahm, Philip, 408
Ramsay, Major General, 145
Ramsey, Margaret, 162
Ramsey, Susan(nah), 162
Ramsey, unknown, 394
RANC, Jean (Rev.), 408
Ranchon, John Dr., 40
Ranck, Ann Barbara, 408
Ranck, Hans Valentine, 408
Ranck, Johann Valentine, 408
Ranck, John Michael, 408
Ranck, John Phillip, 408
Ranck, Rosine Katharine, 408
Ranck, Susanna Margaretha, 408
Randolph, Thomas, 325
Rankin, Christian, 135
Rantowle, Jerusa, 224
Rapalie, Jeronimus Jorise, 164
Rapalje, Catalyntje (Trico), 53, 131
Rapalje, Daniel, 53
Rapalje, Fermetje, 48
Rapalje, Joris, 53
Rapalje, Joris Jansen, 131
RAPALJE, Joris Janszen (de), 408
Rapalje, Joris Lt., 53
Rapalyea, Catelyntje, 164
RAPAREILLIET, Georges, 408
Rapareilliet, Jean, 408
Rapareilliet/Rapalje, Annetje, 409

Rapareilliet/Rapalje, Catalynte, 409
Rapareilliet/Rapalje, Daniel, 409
Rapareilliet/Rapalje, Jacob, 409
Rapareilliet/Rapalje, Jan, 409
Rapareilliet/Rapalje, Jannetje, 409
Rapareilliet/Rapalje, Jeromus, 409
Rapareilliet/Rapalje, Judith, 409
Rapareilliet/Rapalje, Lysbeth/Elizabeth,
   409
Rapareilliet/Rapalje, Maria, 409
Rapareilliet/Rapalje, Sara, 409
Rapelje, Jacob, 53
Rapelje, Jannetje, 53
Rapin, Anthony, 351
Rapine, Antoine, 389
Rapine, Margaret (X), 351
Rapine, Mary Ann, 351
Rassin/Rufin, Antoine, 247
Rassin/Rufin, Marie (Rou), 247
Ratier, Jacob, 374
Rattcliff, Rebecca, 89
Rau, Rev. Louis, 298
Raveau, Daniel, 182
Raveau, Jeanne, 182
Raven, Abraham, *419*
Raven, Elizabeth, *419*
Raven, Marie (Raven), 182
Ravenel, Abraham, 379
Ravenel, Charlotte (de St. Julian), 432
Ravenel, Daniel, 409, 410, 432
Ravenel, Elizabeth, 410
Ravenel, Henry, 410
Ravenel, James, 410
Ravenel, Jeanne Charlotte, 409
Ravenel, Marie (Guerineau), 409
Ravenel, Mary Amey, 410, 432
Ravenel, Paul Francis, 410
Ravenel, Pierre, 379
Ravenel, René, 410, 432
RAVENEL, René, 409
Ravenel, René Louis, 409
Ravenel, Susanne, 410
Ravenel, unknown, 402
Rawles, Francis, 253
Ray, Mary, 33
Ray, William, 90
Raymond, Mary, 15
Raynal, Esther, 214
Rayne, Richard, 119
Re(g)nault/Regnaut/Re(y)naud/
   Reynaut, Pierre, 410
Re(g)nault/Regnaut/Re(y)naud/Reynaut
   , Jeanne, 410
RE(G)NAULT/REGNAUT/RE(Y)NAUD/REY
   NAUT, Pierre, 410
Re(g)nault/Regnaut/Re(y)naud/Reynaut
   , Susanne, 410
Read, John, 391
Read, Sarah (X), 391
Read, Thomas Ensign, 391
Reade, Elizabeth, 352

Reade, George Col., 352
Reade, Lady Mildred (Windebank), 352
Reade, Mildred, 352
Reade, Naemoe, 211
Reade, Robert, 352
Reagle, Abraham, 456
Reason, Ann, 343
Reau/Réaud, unknown, 270
Rebe, Christian (Beck), **42**
Rebe, Hermann, **42**
Rebe, Louise Christina, **42**
Rector, Elizabeth (Fishback), 351
Rector, John Jacob, 351
Redd, Allen, 80
Redd, Joseph, 80
Redd, Joseph Bullett, 80
Redd, Permercis, 80
Redd, Philip, 80
Redd, Priscilla, 80
Redd, Susannah, 80
Redinbow, Frederick, 60
Reed, John, 395
Reed, Mary, 192
Reed, Susanna, 246
Reeder, John, 229
Reese, James Polk, 91
Reeves, Elizabeth (X), 88
Reeves, James, 88
Reeves, Martha, 88
Regnault/Renaud/Reynaud, Anne
   (Jupille), 114
Regnault/Renaud/Reynaud, Pierre, 114
Regnier, Elizabeth (Benoist), 410
Regnier, Pierre, 410
REGNIER, Pierre, 410
Regnier, Pierre/Peter, 410
Reid, Hannah, 167
Reid, James, 289
Reimer, Isaac de, 198
Reimer, Peter de, 198
Reinholle, Johann, 413
Reipel, Anna Maria, 140
Reipel, Jacob, 140
Reiss, Anna Marie, 151
Reith, Anna/Maria Margaretta, 439
Reith, Johann Leonard, 439
Reith, John Goerge, 438
Rembert, Andre, 361
Rembert, André, 234
Rembert, Anne, 156
Rembert, Anne (Bressau), 234
Rembert, Isaac, 255
Rembert, Isaac Sr., 208
Rembert, Jacques, 54
Rembert, Jeanne, 234
Rembert, Jeanne (X), 156
Rembert, Madelaine, 155
Rembert, Madeleine, 255
Rembert, Marguerite, 156, 234
Rembert, Mary Jane, 234
Rembert, Pierre, 156

Remeyn, Luyda, 316
RÉMI/RÉMY/REMEY/REAMY, de RÉMI(S), Abram/Abraham, 410
Remi/Remy/Remey/Reamy, Elizabeth, 411
Remi/Remy/Remey/Reamy, Jean, 411
Remi/Remy/Remey/Reamy, Margaret Ann(a), 411
Remsen, Jeronimus/Jeremiah, 53
Remsperger, Charlotte, 83
Rémy, Pierre, 411
Remy/Remey/Ramey, Asbury, 411
Remy/Remey/Ramey, Benjamin, 411
Remy/Remey/Ramey, Daniel, 411
Remy/Remey/Ramey, Jacob, 411
RÉMY/REMEY/RAMEY, Jacques/Jacob, 411
Remy/Remey/Ramey, James, 411
Remy/Remey/Ramey, John, 411
Remy/Remey/Ramey, Joseph, 411
Remy/Remey/Ramey, William, 411
Ren(n)o, Stephen, 187
Ren(n)o/Regnault, Anne, 187
Rénard, Catherine (Oliver), 315
Renard, Daniel, 443
Renard, Madeline (X), 54
Renard/de Vos, Catharina, 169
Renaud, Corcas (Marie), 54
Renaud, Jérémie, 66
Renaud, John, 440
Renaud, unknown, 109
Renaud/Arnaud, Jeanne, 128
Renaudet, Adrian, 412
Renaudet, Ann, 412
Renaudet, Elizabeth, 412
RENAUDET, Jacques/James, 412
Renaudet, James, 412
Renaudet, Jane, 412
Renaudet, Jas./James, 412
Renaudet, John, 412
Renaudet, Mary, 412
Renaudet, Peter, 412
Renaut, Charles, 13
Reneau/Reno, Benjamin de, 413
Reneau/Reno, Francis de, 412
Reneau/Reno, John de, 413
Reneau/Reno, Judith de, 412
Reneau/Reno, Lewis de, 412
RENEAU/RENO, Louis/Lewis de, 412
Reneau/Reno, Margaret de, 413
Reneau/Reno, Marianne de, 413
Reneau/Reno, Mary de, 413
Reneau/Reno, Moses de, 413
Reneau/Reno, Sara de, 413
Reneau/Reno, Sarah de, 413
Reneau/Reno, Thomas de, 412
Renollet, Jean, 413
Renollet/Renoll/Reinholle, Daniel, 413
Renollet/Renoll/Reinholle, Jean Daniel, 413

Renollet/Renoll/Reinholle, Jean Pierre, 413
Renollet/Renoll/Reinholle, Paul, 413
RENOLLET/RENOLL/REINHOLLE, Paul, 413
Renollet/Renoll/Reinholle, Sophie, 413
Renquyre, Guillaume de, 338
Requier, Claude, 414
Requier, Jean/John, 414
REQUIER/REQUA/L'ESCUYER/L'EQUIER, Gabriel, 414
Requier/Requa/L'Escuyer/L'Equier, Daniel, 414
Requier/Requa/L'Escuyer/L'Equier, Glode, 414
Requier/Requa/L'Escuyer/L'Equier, James, 414
Requier/Requa/L'Escuyer/L'Equier, Jannitie/Jeanette, 414
Requier/Requa/L'Escuyer/L'Equier, John, 414
Requier/Requa/L'Escuyer/L'Equier, Margaret, 414
Requier/Requa/L'Escuyer/L'Equier, Mary, 414
Requier/Requa/L'Escuyer/L'Equier, Susan, 414
Resseguie, Alexander, 75
Resseguire/Ressiguier/Resseguie, Jeanne, 263
RESSIGUE/ RESSEGUIE/de RES(S)EGUIER, Alexandre, 414
Ressigue/Resseguie/de Res(s)eguier, Abraham, 415
Ressigue/Resseguie/de Res(s)eguier, Alexander II, 414
Ressigue/Resseguie/de Res(s)eguier, Alexander III, 415
Ressigue/Resseguie/de Res(s)eguier, Isaac, 415
Ressigue/Resseguie/de Res(s)eguier, Jacob, 415
Ressigue/Resseguie/de Res(s)eguier, James, 415
Ressigue/Resseguie/de Res(s)eguier, Peter, 415
Ressigue/Resseguie/de Res(s)eguier, Sarah, 415
Retief, Anna, 415
Retief, François, 415
RETIEF, François, 415
Retief, Jacques, 415
Retief, Maria, 415
Retief, Paulus, 415
Retteau/Rettew/Rattue/Ratew, Aaron, 416
Retteau/Rettew/Rattue/Ratew, Ann/Mary, 415
Retteau/Rettew/Rattue/Ratew, David, 416

Retteau/Rettew/Rattue/Ratew, Eleanor, 416
Retteau/Rettew/Rattue/Ratew, James, 416
Retteau/Rettew/Rattue/Ratew, John, 415
Retteau/Rettew/Rattue/Ratew, Rebecca, 416
Retteau/Rettew/Rattue/Ratew, Thomas, 415, 416
Retteau/Rettew/Rattue/Ratew, William, 416
RETTEAU/RETTEW/RATTUE/RATEW, William, 415
Reverday, Katherine, 220
Reverday, Pierre, 220
Revere, Elizabeth, 421
Revere, John, 420, 421
Revere, Mary, 421
Revere, Thomas, 421
Reveux/Revaux, Mariana, 440
Reviere, Abraham de, 416
REVIÈRE, Abraham de, 416
Reviere, Catrina de, 416
Reviere, Cornelis de, 416
Reviere, Hannah/Annatie de, 416
Reviere, Hendricks de, 416
Reviere, Isaac de, 416
Reviere, Jacob de, 416
Reviere, Jacobus de, 416
Reviere, Janitje de, 416
Reviere, Johannis de, 416
Reviere, Mary/Maria de, 416
Reviere, Rachel de, 416
Reviere, Sofya/Sophia de, 416
Reviere, Sophia/Zophya de, 416
Revout/Ravot, François Gabriel, 248
Rey, Florence, 88
Rey, Guillelme, 70
Rey, Jean, 70
Rey, Jeanne, 70
Rey, Madelene, 70
Rey, Peter, 88
Reyly, Sara, 273
Reynard, Marie, 129
Reynaud, Susanne, 114
Reynolds, Cornelius, 429
Reynolds, Elizabeth, 429
Reynolds, John, 270
Reynolds, Martha (X), 429
Reyster, Richard, 135
Rezeau, Abraham, 417
Rezeau, Anne, 417
Rezeau, Anne (Coursier), 63
Rezeau, Esther, 417
Rezeau, Jacob, 417
Rezeau, James, 417
Rezeau, Marie, 417
Rezeau, Peter, 417
Rezeau, Pierre/Peter, 417
Rezeau, René, 63, 417

REZEAU, René, 416
Rezeau, Susanna, 417
Rezeau, Susanne, 63, 417
Rezon, Sarah, 105
Rhinewald, Casper, 245
Rhinewald, Johann Heinrich, 245
Rhinewald, Maria Maargaretha (Steph), 245
Rhode, Maria, 358
Rhodes, Elizabeth, 197
Rhodes, Henry, 197
Riant, Marie de, 189
Riblet(te), Abraham, 418
Riblet(te), Bartholomew, 417
Riblet(te), Casper, 417
Riblet(te), Christian, 417
RIBLET(TE), Christian, 417
Riblet(te), Daniel, 418
Riblet(te), Elizabeth, 418
Riblet(te), Henry, 418
Riblet(te), John, 417
Riblet(te), Margaret, 417
Riblet(te), Mary Ann/Polly, 418
Riblet(te), Michael, 418
Riblet(te), Peter, 417
Riblet(te), Regena, 418
Riblet(te), Reuben, 417
Riblet, Bartley, 417
Rice, Elizabeth, 268, 402
Rice, Elizabeth (House), 268
Rice, James, 268
Rice, Phebe, 268
Rice, Thomas, 268
Richard, Jacques, 141
Richard, Louise (DesPrez), 141
Richard, Suzanne, 141
Richards, Abner, 308
Richardson, Edward, 236
Richardson, Elizabeth (X), 236
Richardson, Joseph, 264
Richardson, Sarah (Thomas), 264
Richardson, William, 236, 264
Richardson, William Guignard, 236
Richebourg, Charles de, *418*
RICHEBOURG, Claude Philippe de (Rev.), 418
Richebourg, Claude Philippe de Rev., 34
Richebourg, Claudius de, *418*
Richebourg, Elizabeth de, *418*
Richebourg, Henry de, *418*
Richebourg, James de, *418*
Richebourg, John de, *418*
Richebourg, René de, *418*
Richelieu, Cardinal, 238
Richenbosche/Rickenbasche, Jacquemine, 458
Richford, Marie/Mary, 88
Richmond, Mary, 297
Rickards, Giles, 62
Rickenbosche, Henrick, 458
Rider, Lydia, 164

Ridgaile, John, 377
Ridgely, Henry, 178
Ridgely, Martha, 178
Ridgely, Martha (X), 178
Ridgely, Robert, 178
Riemer, Peter de, 198
Rife, Christopher, 138
Riggs, Abigail, 172
Righter, Abraham, 150
Riley, Ashbel, 26
Riley, Lydia, 33
Rinckhout, Jan, 273, 322
Rinckhout, Marguerite/Margriet, 273
Rineur, Jacques, 20
Rineurs, Magdalen/Madeleine, 20
Riroire/Revere, Peter Jr de, 420
Risteau, Catherine, *419*
Risteau, David, *419*
Risteau, Elias, *419*
Risteau, George, *419*
Risteau, Isaac, *419*
Risteau, Jacques, *419*
RISTEAU, Jean, *419*
Risteau, Jean/John, *419*
Risteau, Margaret, *419*
Risteau, Mary, *419*
Risteau, Suzanne, *419*
Risteau, Talbot, *419*
Rittal, Francis, 246
Ritter, Eliza, 19
Rivaison, Jeanne, 471
Rivers, Mary, 84
Rivers/Rives, Claude, *420*
Rivers/Rives, Mary, *420*
RIVERS/RIVES, Pierre, *419*
Rivers/Rives, Robert, *420*
Rivers/Rives, Thomas, *420*
Rivoire, Daniel, 420
Rivoire, Deborah, 421
Rivoire, Frances, 421
Rivoire, Jean, 420
Rivoire, Mathias, 420, 421
Rivoire, Paul, 421
Rivoire, Sara, 420
Rivoire, Sarra (Fraissineau), 420
Rivoire, Suzanne, 420
Rivoire/Revere, (**Simon**) **Peter de**, 420
Rivoire/Revere, Anne de, 421
Rivoire/Revere, Apollos de, 421
Rivoire/Revere, Apollos/Paul de, 420
Rivoire/Revere, Appolus de, 420
Rivoire/Revere, Isaac de, 420, 421
Rivoire/Revere, Isabeau de, 421
Rivoire/Revere, Jean de, 420
RIVOIRE/REVERE, Jean de, 420
Rivoire/Revere, Jeanne de, 420
Rivoire/Revere, John de, 420
Rivoire/Revere, Magdeleine de, 421
Rivoire/Revere, Marguerite de, 420
Rivoire/Revere, Simon de, 420, 421
Rivoire/Revere, Simon-Pierre de, 421

Rivoire/Revere, Suzanne de, 420, 421
Rivoire/Revere, William de, 420
Roadarmel/Rothermel, Maria/Mary, 358
Robb, John Capt., 32
Robbins, Ammi Ruhamah Rev., 298
Robbins, Nathaniel, 88
Robbins, Theodosa, 430
Roberdeau/Roberdieu, Ann, 422
Roberdeau/Roberdieu, Ann Judith, 422
Roberdeau/Roberdieu, Daniel, 422
Roberdeau/Roberdieu, David Bostwick, 422
Roberdeau/Roberdieu, Elizabeth, 422
Roberdeau/Roberdieu, Heriot, 422
Roberdeau/Roberdieu, Isaac, 422
ROBERDEAU/ROBERDIEU, Isaac, 421
Roberdeau/Roberdieu, James Milligan, 422
Roberdeau/Roberdieu, Jane, 422
Roberdeau/Roberdieu, Jeany, 422
Roberdeau/Roberdieu, Mary, 422
Roberdeau/Roberdieu, Philadelphia, 422
Roberdeau/Roberdieu, Selina, 422
Roberson, Maria, 174
Robert II, Pierre, 84
ROBERT, Daniel, 422, 423
Robert, Elizabeth, 104, 423
Robert, Jacques de Bourdeaux, 104
Robert, Jacques/James, 423
Robert, Jean/John, **423**
Robert, Jeanne (Brayé), 84
Robert, Judith (Sagne), 422
Robert, Madelaine, **423**
Robert, Pierre, 84, 422
Robert, Pierre I, 422
Robert, Pierre/Peter III, 423
Robert, Pierre/Pierre II, 423
Robert, Sarah (Jaudon), 104
Robert, William, 422
Roberts, Anne, 245
Roberts, Ebenezer, 348
Roberts, Eleanor, 73
Roberts, Elias, **423**
Roberts, John, 73, 179
Roberts, Jonah, 235
Roberts, Mary (Lynch), 245
Roberts, Peter Capt., 245
Roberts, Sarah, 348
Roberts, Sarah (Elwell), 348
Robertson, Charles, 474
Robertson, Keziah, 474
Robeson, Andrew, 266
Robeson, Samuel, 266
Robesoune, Elizabeth, 118
Robichaud, Alexandre, 294
Robie, John, 124
Robin, Marie, 160
Robineau, Étienne, 26
Robineau, Judith (Pare), 26
Robineau, Marie, 26
Robinet, Jean, 380
Robinet, Louis, 371

Robinet, Louise, 371
Robinet, Thevenin, 380
Robins, Thomas, **37**
Robins, unknown, **37**
Robinson, James, 115
Robinson, Polly, 401
Roche(t), Suzanna, 214
Rochet, Isaac, 361
Rochet, Jeanne (Dufray), 361
Rochet, Susanne, 361
Rodman, William, 323
Roe, Susanna, 384
Roehrig, Anna Catherina, 120
Roemer, Amilia (Hartranft), 83
Roemer, John Michael, 83
Roger, Anna, 424
ROGER, Jean, 423
Roger, Jeremiah, 424
Roger, John, 424
Roger, Marie/Mary, 424
Roger, Paul, 424
Roger, Peter Bayard, 368, 424
Roger, Pierre/Peter, 424
Roger, Rebecca, 424
Roger, Sarah, 424
Roger, William, 424
Rogers, Bathsheba, 17
Rohde, Rebecca (Starr) (Tyler), 75
Rohrer/Roehrer, Anna Maria, 424
Rohrer/Roehrer, Christian, 424
Rohrer/Roehrer, David, 424
Rohrer/Roehrer, Frederick, 424
Rohrer/Roehrer, Hans Jakob, 424
Rohrer/Roehrer, Hans Michael, 424
RÖHRER/ROEHRER, Hans Michael, 424
Rohrer/Roehrer, Jacob, 424
Rohrer/Roehrer, Johannes, 424
Rohrer/Roehrer, Martin, 424
Rohrer/Roehrer, Samuel, 424
Rohrer/Roehrer, Verena, 424
Roi, Catherine, 68
Roland, Marie, 92
Romain, Theodore, 38
Römer, Adam, 18
Romeyn, Elizabeth, 172
Romsey, Martha, 245
Ronchon, John, 437
Ronchon, Mary, 437
Ronde, Henri de, 252
Ronde, Marguerite de, 252
Rongnion/Runyon, Ann (Boutcher), 377
Rongnion/Runyon, Vincent, 377
Rongnion/Runyon/Runyan, Ann, 425
Rongnion/Runyon/Runyan, Jane, 425
Rongnion/Runyon/Runyan, Mary, 425
Rongnion/Runyon/Runyan, Peter, 425
Rongnion/Runyon/Runyan, Sarah, 425
Rongnion/Runyon/Runyan, Thomas, 425
Rongnion/Runyon/Runyan, Vincent, 425
RONGNION/RUNYON/RUNYAN, Vincent, 425

Rongnion/Runyou/Runyan, John, 425
Roome, John, 299
Roome, Marie, 302
Roos, Cornelia, 404
Roos, Gerrit Jans, 404
Roos, Gerrit Janses, 296
Roos, Jan, 296
Roosa, Geertje Jans, 130
Roosevelt/Croesvert, Eytje, 274
Root, John, 282
Root, Mary (Kilborne), 282
Root, Susannah, 282
Roque, Jeanne, 288
Roquemore, Jeanne (Fourneyrol), 425
Roquemore, Pierre, 425
Roquemore/Roquemaure, Anne, 426
Roquemore/Roquemaure, Elizabeth, 426
Roquemore/Roquemaure, James Jr., 426
Roquemore/Roquemaure, John, 426
Roquemore/Roquemaure, Marie, 426
Roquemore/Roquemaure, Marie Jeanne/Mary Jane, 426
Roquemore/Roquemaure, Peter, 426
ROQUEMORE/ROQUEMAURE, Pierre, 425
Roquemore/Roquemaure, Pierre II, 425
Roquemore/Roquemaure, Pierre III/Peter, 426
Roquemore/Roquemaure, Pierre Jacques/James, 426
Roquemore/Roquemaure, Thomas, 426
Rosamond, Robert, 191
Rosborough, Alexander, 217
Rose, Edward, 421
Rose, Lurana, 344
Rosecrans, Harmen Hendricksen, 296
Rosenkrans, Rachael, 106
Rosier, Robert, 428
Rosiljon, Lysbeth, 175
Rosset, Armand Jean de, 426
Rosset, Armand John de, 427
Rosset, Gabrielle de Gondin de, 426
Rosset, Lady Catherine (de Moynier) de, 426
Rosset, Louis de, 426
ROSSET, Louis de, 426
Rosset, Louis Henry de, 427
Rosset, Magdalene Mary de, 427
Rosset, Moses John de, 427
Rossignol, Elisabeth, 175
Roth, Christina, 279
Rothwell, Henry, 15
Roubley, Marie, 468
Rougeon, Pierre, 182
Roulain, Abraham, 233
Roumas, Pierre Marchays de, 66
Rouse, Johathan, 109
Rouse, Martha (X), 109
ROUSSEAU, Théodore de, 427
Rousseau, David de, 427
Rousseau, Elizabeth de, 427

Rousseau, Hillaire de, 427
Rousseau, Hillaire II de, 427
Rousseau, James de, 427
Rousseau, Jan de, 287
Rousseau, Pieter, 415
Rousseau, William de, 427
Routtes/Roote(s)/Root, Caleb, 428
Routtes/Roote(s)/Root, Hezekiah, 428
Routtes/Roote(s)/Root, Jacob, 428
Routtes/Roote(s)/Root, John, 428
Routtes/Roote(s)/Root, John I, 427
Routtes/Roote(s)/Root, John II, 428
Routtes/Roote(s)/Root, John III, 428
Routtes/Roote(s)/Root, Jonathan, 428
Routtes/Roote(s)/Root, Joseph, 428
Routtes/Roote(s)/Root, Marie, 428
Routtes/Roote(s)/Root, Mary, 428
Routtes/Roote(s)/Root, Samuel, 428
Routtes/Roote(s)/Root, Sarah, 428
Routtes/Roote(s)/Root, Stephen, 428
Routtes/Roote(s)/Root, Susannah, 428
Routtes/Roote(s)/Root, Thomas, 428
ROUTTES/ROOTE(S)/ROOT, Thomas, 427
Roux, Anne, 66
Roux, Marthe, 66
Rowe, Mary/Polly, 60
Rowland, Harriet C., 108
Rowland, John A., 108
Roy, Jean, 225
ROY, Marie, **428**
Royer, Anna (X), 245
Royer, Elizabeth, 451
Royer, Jean, 451
Royer, John, 245
Royer, Judith (Giton), 343
Royer, Madaleine, 451
Royer, Marie-Ann, 451
Royer, Noë, 343
Royer, Pierre, 451
Royer, Thérèse, 451
Rozier, Bridges, 429
Rozier, David, 429
Rozier, David II, 429
Rozier, Elizabeth, 429
ROZIER, John (Rev.), 428
Rozier, John II, 429
Rozier, John III, 429
Rozier, Williamson, 429
Rucker, Ann, 429
Rucker, Elizabeth, 429
Rucker, Ephraim, 429
Rucker, James, 429
Rucker, John, 429
Rucker, Margaret, 429
Rucker, Mary, 429
Rucker, Peter, 429
RUCKER, Peter, 429
Rucker, Thomas, 429
Rucker, William, 429
Rue, Mary, 219, 228
Rufin/Rassin, Anne, 247

Rugh/Ruch, Michael, 358
Ruine, Jacomina de, *142*
Ruine, Marie de, *142*
Rulon.Roulan(d)/Rouillon/Rulong, **Harriet**, 430
Rulon/Roulan(d), Rouillon/Rulong, Peter, 430
Rulon/Roulan(d)/ Rouillon/Rulong, Jesse, 430
Rulon/Roulan(d)/ Rouillon/Rulong, Joseph, 430
Rulon/Roulan(d)/Rouillon/Rulong, Catherine, 430
Rulon/Roulan(d)/Rouillon/Rulong, David, 430
Rulon/Roulan(d)/Rouillon/Rulong, Hannah, 430
Rulon/Roulan(d)/Rouillon/Rulong, Henry, 430
Rulon/Roulan(d)/Rouillon/Rulong, Jonathan, 430
Rulon/Roulan(d)/Rouillon/Rulong, Luke, 430
Rulon/Roulan(d)/Rouillon/Rulong, Lydia, 430
Rulon/Roulan(d)/Rouillon/Rulong, Mary, 430
Rulon/Roulan(d)/Rouillon/Rulong, Rachel, 430
RULON/ROULAN(D)/ROUILLON/RULON G, Ruel Pierre, 430
Runnels, Dudley Capt., 247
Runnels, Harmon Col., 247
Runner, Henry, 199
Runyon, Joseph, 377
Runyou, Thomas, 377
Rush, Benjamin Dr., 188
Russ, Abijah, 471
Russell, Anna, 465
Russell, Caleb, 128
Russell, Frances, 427
Russell, John, 216
Russell, unknown, 17
Russell. Mary/Ann, 427
Rust, Ann, 133
Rust, Benjamin, 133
Rust, George, 133
Rust, Hannah, 133
Rust, Jeremiah, 133
Rust, John, 133
Rust, Martha, 133
Rust, Martha (X), 133
Rust, Matthew, 133
Rust, Peter, 133
Rust, Samuel, 133
Rust, William, 133
Rut(t)an, Abraham, 431
RUT(T)AN, Abraham, 430
Rut(t)an, Daniel, 430
Rut(t)an, David, 431
Rut(t)an, Esther, 431

Rut(t)an, Hester, 431
Rut(t)an, Mary, 431
Rut(t)an, Pieter/Peter, 431
Rut(t)an, Pouel /Paul, 431
Rut(t)an, Samuel, 431
Rut(t)an, Sara, 431
Rut(t)an, Susanna, 431
Rutan, Anne (deBize), 430
Rutan, David, 430
Rutgers, Catherine, 317
Rutgers, Cornelia, 317
Rutgers, Herman III, 317
Rutgers, Maria, 126
Rutgersz, Cornelius, 154
Rutherford, John Col., 247
Rutherford, Susanna, 268
Rutherford, unknown, 158
Ruton, Paul, 136
Rutsen, Sara, 103
Ryerson, Martin, 409
Rykert, Matthew, 109
Rykert, Peter, 109
Rymer, John, 403
Rymer, Mark, 403
Rymer, Ralph, 236

S

Sabatier, John, 271
Sabatier, Mary Magdalen, 271
Sabourin, François, 195
Sabourin, Pierre, 195
Sachet, Marie, **42**
Sack, August Friedrich Wilhelm Pastor, 215
Sadler, Temperance, 100
Safre, Catherine de, 329
Sagathy, Peter, 163
Saix, Louise de, 131
Salle(e)/ Salley, Jean/John, 434
Salle(e)/Salley, Abraham, 434
SALLÉ(E)/SALLEY, Abraham, 434
Salle(e)/Salley, Elizabeth, 434
Salle(e)/Salley, Guillaume/ William, 434
Salle(e)/Salley, Isaac, 434
Salle(e)/Salley, Jacob, 434
Salle(e)/Salley, Olive Magdaline, 434
Salle(e)/Salley, Oliver, 434
Salle(e)/Salley, Pierre/Peter, 434
Salle(e)/Salley, William, 434
Sallé, Abraham, 17, 220, 341
Sallé, Elisabeth, 462
Sallé, Elizabeth, 100
Salle, Elizabeth (Gévaudan), 100
Sallé, Guillaume, 100, 115
Sallé, Jean, 434
Sallé, Marie (Martin), 434
Sallé, Olive (Perrault), 17, 220, 341
Sallé, Olive Magdeleine, 341
Sallers, Althea, 445
Sallers, Ann, 445

Sallers, Bennet, 445
Sallers, Elizabeth, 445
Sallers, Heighe, 445
Sallers, Mary, 445
Sallers, Robert, 445
Sallers, Sabrett II, 445
Sallers, Thomas, 445
Sallers, Vallinda, 445
Sallows, Freeborn (Woolfe), 311
Sallows, Hannah, 311
Sallows, Robert, 311
Salmon, Edward Capt., 83
Salmon, Elizabeth, 428
Salmon, Mary, 83
Salmon, Robert, 466
Salmons, John, 401
Saltzgeber/Saltgerber, Andreas, 438
Salway, Anthony, 444
Sammis, Maria, 246
Sammis, Marie, 454, 468
Sample, Margaret, 87
Sample, unknown, 456
Sample, William, 87
Sampson Esther (Nash), 287
Sampson, Abraham, 287
Sampson, Ann, 85
Sampson, Anna, 202
Sampson, Bridget, 202
Sampson, Charles, 176
Sampson, Elizabeth, 287
Sampson, Francis, 202
Sampson, Samuel, 139
Samson, David, 395
Samson, Dorothea, 360
Samson, Elizabeth, 238, 395
Samson, Henry, 395
Samson, Mary Chaffin/Chapin, 395
Samuel, Elder, 388
Samuels, Grietie, 315
Sanbourne, Daniel, 89
Sanbourne, Elizabeth, 89
Sanbourne, Sarah (X), 89
Sanceau, Marie, 317
Sanceau, Marie (Cholet), 317
Sanceau, Pierre, 52, 317
Sanders, Elizabeth, 236
Sanders, James, 236
Sanders, Mary, 234
Sanders, Sarah, 233, 373
Sanders, Sarah (Slann), 236
Sandert, Bloemert, 261
Sandford, Catherine, 279
Sandiford, Elizabeth, 234
Sandoz, Jacques, 285
Sandoz, Madeleine (Amez), 285
Sandoz, Marguerite, 285
Sanford, Ann, 411
Sanford, Ann (X), 411
Sanford, Frances, 158
Sanford, Richard Capt., 158
Sanford, Robert, 411

Sanford, Susannah (Franklin), 158
Sansom, Hannah (X), 389
Sansom, Samuel, 389
Sansom, Sarah, 389
SANXAY, Jacques (Rev.), 435
Sanxay, Anna, 435
Sanxay, Cecil, 435
Sanxay, Charlotte, 435
Sanxay, Claudia, 435
Sanxay, Daniel, 435
Sanxay, Edmund, 435
Sanxay, Edward, 435
Sanxay, Frances, 435
Sanxay, Hannah, 435
Sanxay, James, 435
Sanxay, Jane, 435
Sanxay, John, 435
Sanxay, Josué, 435
Sanxay, Marie (Vivier), 435
Sanxay, Mary, 435
Sanxay, Richard, 435
Sanxay, Robert, 435
Sarcot, Jeannie, 440
Sargent, Lydia, 298
Sas(s)in, Alexander, 436
Sas(s)in, David, 436
Sas(s)in, Élias/Éli, 436
Sas(s)in, Elizabeth, 436
SAS(S)IN, François, 436
Sas(s)in, Jean, 436
Sas(s)in, Louis/Louy, 436
Sas(s)in, Mary/Marie, 436
Sas(s)in, Olive, 436
Sas(s)in, Pierre, 436
Sas(s)in, Richard, 436
Sassin, Francis, 436
Sassyar/Sise, Sarah Joost Van, 365
Satchell, unknown, **37**
Saublet/Soblet, Élie, 443
Saublet/Soblet, Susanna (Renaudin), 443
Sauchoy, Marcus de, 231
Sauerbronn, Friedrich, 19
Saunders, George, 386
Saunders, Hannah (Gibson), 386
Saunders, Jesse, 326
Saunders, Marcia, 386
Saunders, Mary (X), 355
Saunders, Mary Remy, 411
Saunders, Robert, 355
Saussure, Mathilde H.S. De, 65
Sautreau, Isaac, 271
Sauvage, Marie, 380
Sauvagie, Michele, 409
Sauzeau, Marennes Blanche, 153
Savage, John, 21
Savage, Thomas Major, 283
Savell/Savil, Anne, **36**
Savineau, Esther, 84
Sawyer, James, 347
Sawyer, Margaret, 24
Sawyer, Sarah, 347

Sawyer, Sarah (Bray), 347
Sawyer, Thomas, 24
Sax, Michael, 59
Sayer, Rachel, 69
Sayer, Thomas, 69
Sayre, John Sr., 299
Sayre, Mary, 299
Sca(r)sbrooke, Mary, 352
Scadding, Richard, 209
Scarborough, Ann (Mayo) Pope, 276
Scarborough, unknown, 276
Scarron, Paul, 22
Schaefer, Johann Michel, 243
Schaefer, Margaretha, 243
Schaefer, Maria Barbara (Geiger), 243
Schaers, Johannes Christoffel, 48
Schäfer, Anna Appolonia (X), 83
Schäfer, Anna Maria, 83
Schäfer, Christoph, 83
Schaick, Margaret Van, 279
Schall, Anna Maria, 204
Schardt, Catherine Elizabeth, 381
Schellinger, Jacob, 360
Schenck, Cornelia, 174
Schepmoes, Jan Jansen, 333
Schepmoes, Johannes, 130
Schermerhorn, Lucas, 439
Schermerhorn, Helena, 384, 439
Schermerhorn, Sophia, 439
Schilling, Maria Martha, 259
Schmidt, Salomée, 436
Schmitt, Dirck Ensign, 304
Schmitt, Dorothy, 362
Schneider, Anna Maria, 86
Schneider, John, 466
Schneider, Margaret, 358
Scholl, Annetje Pieterse, 342
Scholt, Pieter Janszen, 404
Schomberg, Duke of, 426
Schomp, Cornelia (Monfoort), 174
Schomp, Joost, 174
Schon/Sochon, Marie, 25
Schonnon, Margarethe Bird, 19
Schoohoven, Hennrikje Van, 49
Schoonhoven, Margreitje Claes Van, 63
Schoonhoven, Margrietje Claasse Van, 307, 308
Schoonmaker, Elsje, 242, 307
Schoonmaker, Joachim, 242
Schoonmaker, Petronella (Sleght), 242
Schreck, Elizabeth, 97
Schrick, Paulus, 392
Schrieber, Jacob Capt., 188
Schuerman, Elizabeth, 333
Schuerman, Frederick, 333
Schultz, Elizabeth, 460
Schultz, William, 460
Schumacher, Anna Barbara, 408
Schuren, Elena Van der, 15
Schut, Barbara, 403
Schut, Jan Harmensen, 296

Schuyler, David Pieterse, 296
Schuyler, Gertruj Van, 281
Schuyler, Jeremiah, 39
Schuyler, Peter, Col., 322
Schuyler, Pieter, 281
Schwab, Anna Barbara, 408
Schwägler, Katherina, 424
Schwartz, Isaac Abraham, 215
Schwartz, Leonard, 438
Schwartzkoff, Mary Magdalen, 399
Schweitzer, Maria Ketharina, 30
Schweitzer, Nicholas, 30
Schwing, Hans Matin, 436
SCHWING, Jean Martin, 436
Scott, Ann (Oliver), 394
Scott, Helen, 80
Scott, James, 80, 364
Scott, Joseph, 320
Scott, Judith (Aborough), 465
Scott, Nancy Ann, 394
Scott, Samuel, 394
Scott, Sarah (Brown), 80
Scott, Thomas, 465
Scott, Ursula (Goode), 187
Scott, Walter, 187
Scramverier, Marie, 136
Screven, Martha (Bremer), 457
Screven, Saville, 457
Scruggs, William, 187
Scudder, Elizabeth, 335
Scutt, Elizabeth (Spencer), 109
Scutt, James, 109
Scutt, Mary, 109
Se(a)venhoven, Jan/John, 305
Seabrook, Mary (X), 306
Sealey, Rachel, 90
Seals, Femmetje, 409
Sealy, Elizabeth, 89
Sealy, John, 209
Sealy, Joseph, 89
Sealy, Mary (X), 89
Searing, Peninah, 106
Searing, Peninah (Burnet), 106
Searing, William, 106
Searle(s), John, 396
Searsbrook/Scarbrook, John Col., 352
Seaworth, Mary, 34
Sebring, Daniel, 299
Sebring, Jan Roeloffsen, 299
Sebring, Rudolph, 298
Secor/Sicor, Jean/John, 226
Seeu, Cornelis Jansen de, 342
Séguin, Elizabeth, 134
Séguin, Jacques, 425
Séguin, Jeanne, 425
Séguin, Marie (Meuze), 425
SÉJOURNÉ/SIGOURNEY, André, 437
Sejourne/Sigourney, André/Andrew II, 437
Sejourne/Sigourney, Andrew, 437
Sejourne/Sigourney, Anthony, 437

Sejourne/Sigourney, Barthélemy, 438
Sejourne/Sigourney, Charles, 437
Sejourne/Sigourney, Daniel, 437
Sejourne/Sigourney, Hannah, 438
Sejourne/Sigourney, Mary, 437, 438
Sejourne/Sigourney, Peter, 437
Sejourne/Sigourney, Rachel, 437
Sejourne/Sigourney, Susannah, 437
Sejourne/Sigourney, Susanne/Susan, 438
Selby, Mary, 445
Selby, Mary (X), 445
Selby, William, 445
Sellaire/Salliere/Cellier/Zeller, Anna Amelia, 439
Sellaire/Salliere/Cellier/Zeller, Anna Catharina de, 438
Sellaire/Salliere/Cellier/Zeller, Anna Elizabeth de, 438
Sellaire/Salliere/Cellier/Zeller, Anna Maria, 439
Sellaire/Salliere/Cellier/Zeller, Anna Maria de, 438
Sellaire/Salliere/Cellier/Zeller, Barbara Elizabeth de, 438
Sellaire/Salliere/Cellier/Zeller, Catherina Elisabeth de, 438
Sellaire/Salliere/Cellier/Zeller, David Peter de, 439
Sellaire/Salliere/Cellier/Zeller, Hartman de, 438
SELLAIRE/SALLIÈRE/CELLIER/ZELLER, Jacques de, 438
Sellaire/Salliere/Cellier/Zeller, Jean Henri/Johann/Hans/Heinrich de, 438
Sellaire/Salliere/Cellier/Zeller, Johann David de, 438
Sellaire/Salliere/Cellier/Zeller, Johann George de, 438
Sellaire/Salliere/Cellier/Zeller, Johann Henrich de, 438
Sellaire/Salliere/Cellier/Zeller, Johannes/Jean/John George de, 438
Sellaire/Salliere/Cellier/Zeller, John Henry de, 439
Sellaire/Salliere/Cellier/Zeller, Margredalis de, 439
Sellaire/Salliere/Cellier/Zeller, Peter de, 439
Sellaire/Von Zeller, 438
Sellman, John, 88
Seloivre/Selover/Seloover, Abraham, 439, 440
Seloivre/Selover/Seloover, Anna/Annetze, 439
Seloivre/Selover/Seloover, Daniel, 439
Seloivre/Selover/Seloover, Elysabeth, 440
Seloivre/Selover/Seloover, Isaac, 440
SELOIVRE/SELOVER/SELOOVER, Isaac I, 439

Seloivre/Selover/Seloover, Isaac II, 439
Seloivre/Selover/Seloover, Jacob, 440
Seloivre/Selover/Seloover, Jacqyemyntie, 439
Seloivre/Selover/Seloover, Jannetie, 439
Seloivre/Selover/Seloover, Judith, 440
Seloivre/Selover/Seloover, Maria, 439
Seloivre/Selover/Seloover, Sara, 440
Seloivre/Selover/Seloover, Sarah, 439
Seloivre/Selover/Seloover, Susanna, 439
Semmes, Cleoborn, 312
Senéchar, David, 329
Sénéchar, David, 449
Senéchar, Marie (Sy), 329
Sensabach, unknown, 150
Serdow, Ruth, 162
Serré, Catherine (Challion), 208
Serré, Elizabeth, 208
Serré, Noe, 208
Serres, Guillaume, 215
Serres, Marie (Barabon), 215
Serres, Wilhemine-Henriette, 215
Servant, Susanne, 239
Seth, William C., 161
Seubering, Lambertje, 53
Seuberingh, Ida, 62
Seuberingh, Jan Roel, 62
Sevenhoven, Jan, 414
Sevenhoven, Marie Van, 317
Sevenhoven, Theodore van, 317
Shaffer, Christofer, 456
Shaffer, George, 19
Shaffer, Mary Anna, 370
Sharpe, Francis, 350
Sharpe, Margaret, 218
Shattuck, Exercise, 124
Shatuck, William, 124
Shaver/Shaffer, Elizabeth, 19
Shaw, John, 226
Shaw, Jonathan, 62
Shay, Sophia, 124
Shead, George, 220
Sheffield, Elizabeth, 393
Sheldon, Nehemiah, 454
Sheldon, Rachel (Mann), 454
Shepard, Gertrude Murray, 108
Shepard, unknown, 40
Shepard, William B., 108
Sherman, Hannah, 344
Sherman, John, 171
Sherrill, Catherine, 474
Sherrill, Samuel, 474
Sherwood, Nancy, 387
Sherwood, Phillip, 429
Sherwood, Sarah, 429
Shields, Ann (Bray), 351
Shields, James, 350
Shields, Matthew, 385
Shields, Mingo, 351
Shine, Sally, 277
Shoop, Elizabeth, 391

Short, John, 436
Short, Samuel, 323
Short, Young, 61
Shotwell, John, 85, 447
Shotwell, Lydia, 447
Shotwell, Robert V., 85
Shotwell, Sarah (Woodley), 85
Shuey, Ludwig Heinrich/Lewis Henry, 259
Shull, Christiana Magdalene, 417
Shull, Christina (Ehro), 418
Shull, John David, 418
SHUMATE/SHUMWAY, John, 265
SHUMWAY, Peter, 267
Shupe, Margaretta, 249
Shurtleff, Abiel, 297
Shurtleff, Bethia (Lucas), 297
Shurtleff, David, 297
Shurtleff, Elizabeth (Lettice), 337
Shut(t), Frytje/Phebe, 301
Shut(t), Hermanse, 301
Shut(t), Jan Sgt., 301
Shut, Barbara, 278
Sicard, Ambroise, 124, 225
Sicard, Anna, 213
Sicard, Anne (Terrier), 18, 213, 226, 303
Sicard, Anne Terrier, 54
Sicard, Catherine, 54, 225, 226
Sicard, Catherine (Woertman), 73
Sicard, Daniel, 73
Sicard, Ester, 18
Sicard, Isaac, 303
Sicard, Jacques, 18, 54, 213, 226, 303
Sicard, Jacques/James, 54, 73, 225
Sicard, James, 54
Sicard, Jane (Bonnet), 226
Sicard, Jean/Jacques, 128
Sicard, Jeanne/Jane (Bonnet), 54, 128, 225
Sicard, Silvie, 124
Sicard/Seacord, Isreal, 128
SICARD/SICORD/SEACORD, Ambroise, 440
Sicard/Sicord/Seacord, Ambroise II, 440
Sicard/Sicord/Seacord, Catherine, 440, 441
Sicard/Sicord/Seacord, Daniel, 440
Sicard/Sicord/Seacord, Ester, 441
Sicard/Sicord/Seacord, Isaac, 440
Sicard/Sicord/Seacord, Israel, 440
Sicard/Sicord/Seacord, Jacques, 440
Sicard/Sicord/Seacord, Jacques/James, 440
Sicard/Sicord/Seacord, Jean/John, 441
Sicard/Sicord/Seacord, Jeanne, 441
Sicard/Sicord/Seacord, Marie, 440, 441
Sicard/Sicord/Seacord, Mary, 440
Sicard/Sicord/Seacord, Silvie, 441
Sicklen, Eve, 151
Sickles, Abraham Sr., 431
Sickles, Elizabeth (X), 431

Sicord, Catherine, 225
Sicord, Catherine (Woertman), 225
Sicord, Daniel, 225
Sie, Jacobus, 45
Sie, Maritie, 45, 353
Siegfried, Elizabeth, 325
Siegfried, Johannes, 325
Siegfried, Susanna, 325
Sille, Anna de, 262
Sille, Cornelia (Muelmans) de, 262
Sille, Gerardina/Gerdientje, 441
Sille, Laurend de, 441
Sille, Laurens, 441
Sille, Nicasius de, 262
SILLE, Nicasius de, 441
Sille, Petrus, 441
Sille, Walburga, 441
Silsbe, Mary, 253
Silsbe, Samuel, 253
Silver, Matthias, 140
Simmons, William Glasgow, 24
Simons, Ann (Keating), 321
Simons, Benjamin, 167, 321
Simons, Martha (X), 167
Simons, Mary, 321
Simons, Samuel, 68
Simons, Thomas Young, 470
Simons/Simonds, Ann, 442
Simons/Simonds, Benjamin, 442
SIMONS/SIMONDS, Benjamin, 441
Simons/Simonds, Benjamin II, 442
Simons/Simonds, Catherine, 442
Simons/Simonds, Elizabeth, 442
Simons/Simonds, Esther, 442
Simons/Simonds, Francis, 442
Simons/Simonds, Judith, 442
Simons/Simonds, Martha, 442
Simons/Simonds, Mary, 442
Simons/Simonds, Peter, 442
Simons/Simonds, Samuel Du Pré, 442
Simons/Simonds, Thomas, 442
Simonson, Mary, 293
Simonton, Ann, 217
Simpson, Joseph Green, 64
Simpson, Sarah/Salley Mary, 64
Sims, Amy, 64
Sims, Thomas, 64
Sinclair, Anna, 132
Sinclair, Elizabeth, 156, 373
Sinclair, George, 156
Sinclair, James, 373
Sinclair, Jane (Guerard), 373
Sinclair/Sinclaer, Maria/Marritie
    (Duyckinck), 132
Sinclair/Sinclaer, Robert, 132
Singletary, Thomas, 233
Singleton, James, 398
Singleton, Richard, 165
Sinkler, Daniel, 373
Sinkler, John, 90
Sinkler, Peter Capt., 66

Sinkler/Sinclair, Peter, 373
Sint Merty, Guillaume de, 338
Sippy, Abraham, 456
Sippy, Anna Joanna, 456
Sippy, Eli, 456
Sippy, Elizabeth, 456
Sippy, Isaac, 456
Sippy, Jacob, 456
Sippy, John, 456
Sippy, Joseph, 456
Sippy, Levi, 457
Sippy, Louisa, 457
Sippy, Lucinda, 457
Sippy, Mary, 456
Sippy, Nicholas, 457
Sippy, Rebecca, 456
Sippy, Stephen, 457
Sippy, Thomas, 456
Sippy, William, 456
Sire, Jean, 294
Sise/Sysen, Joost Carelszen van, 365
Siths, Magdalena, 19
Six/Sickes/Sykes, Conrad, 72
Skillman, John, 302
Skillman, Joseph, 302
Skillman, Mercy/Mary, 302
Skillman, Sarah (Meserole), 302
Skinner, Mary, 300
Skinner, Thomas, 300
Skinner, William, 300
Skrine, Jonathan, 208
Slade, Mary, 401
Slaughter, Elizabeth, 201
Slaughter, Francis, 201
Slaughter, Sarah (Coleman), 201
Slecht, Jacomyntie, 152
Slecht, Jacomyntje, 464
Slecht, Jacomyntje Cornelise, 153
Sleght, Cornelis Barentsen, 129
Sleght, Mattys Cornelis, 129
Sleght, Petru, 103
Slegt, Maria, 103
Slot, Marretje (van Winckle), *142*
Slot, Peter Jansen, *142*
Slote, Peter, 324
Slote, Tryntie, 324
Slought, unknown, 204
Sluys, Emmentje Goosens Van der, 297
Sluyter, Elizabeth, **39**
Sluyter, Peter, **39**
Sluyter, Petrus, 75
Smack, Marretje Hendricks, 125
Smack/Smock, Hendrick Matthyse, 125
Smedes, Rachel, 324
Smidt, Catryntje, 316
Smidt, Lambert Andreaesen, 316
Smidt, Marritie Lammerse, 316
Smith, Abigail (X), 453
Smith, Alathea (Dalton), 44
Smith, Alex, 398
Smith, Andrew, 345

Smith, Bailey, 339
Smith, Blanche, 153
Smith, Caroline Mathilda (X), 383
Smith, Elizabeth, 164
Smith, Frances, 162
Smith, George, 232
Smith, George Rev., 389
Smith, Henry Wells, 108
Smith, Hester/Ester (Caswell), 207
Smith, Heyltje, 78
Smith, Jacques/James, 322
Smith, James, 383
Smith, Jasiel, 207
Smith, Jeremiah, 453
Smith, John, 94, 102, 471
Smith, John Capt., 190
Smith, Joshua Het, 154
Smith, Judith (Guérrant), 389
Smith, Lucy, 113
Smith, Margaret, 471
Smith, Margaret (X), 471
Smith, Margery, 44
Smith, Maria, 267
Smith, Mariah, 110
Smith, Martha, 229
Smith, Mary, 453, 474
Smith, Mary (French), 110
Smith, Mary Ann, 383, 389
Smith, Mehitabel, 102
Smith, Mehitable (Talmadge), 102
Smith, Nancy, 94
Smith, Pierre, 322
Smith, Priscilla, 453
Smith, Robert, 43, 418
Smith, Samuel, 207
Smith, Sarah, 102, 153, 339
Smith, Savage, 127
Smith, Susannah, *419*
Smith, Thomas, 44, 154, 455
Smith, Trueworthy, 339
Smith, Unity, 162
Smith, unknown, 86, 322
Smith, William, 188, 214, 453
Smith, William Capt., 153
Smith, William Esq., 154
Smith, Winston, *419*
Smith, Zerubiah, 394
Smith,, Robert, 110
Smock, Elizabeth, 299
Smyth, Thomas Rev., 435
Snap, Margaret, 266
Snead, unknown, 402
Sneden, Jan, 231
Sneden, Margreta/Grietie, 231
Snipes, Thomas, 338
Snodgrass, Benjamin, 405
Snodgrass, unknown, 405
Snyder, Catalina de Suyers/Hendricks,
    365
Snyers/Snyder/de Suyers, Catalyntje
    Hendrick, 261

561

Soblet, Abraham, 92
Soblet, Anne, 444
Soblet, Daniel, 444
Soblet, Élisabet, 444
Soblet, Élisabeth, 444
Soblet, Guillaume, 444
Soblet, Henri, 444
Soblet, Jacques, 444
Soblet, Jean, 444
Soblet, Jeanne, 444
Soblet, Judit, 444
Soblet, Judith, 444
Soblet, Marie, 444
Soblet, Philbert, 443, 444
SOBLET, Philbert/Philibert, 443
Soblet, Rachel, 444
Soblet, Rachel Marie, 444
Soblet/Sublet(te), Abraham, 442
Soblet/Sublet(te), Agnes, 443
Soblet/Sublet(te), Anne, 442, 443
Soblet/Sublet(te), Antoine, 442
Soblet/Sublet(te), Catherine, 443
Soblet/Sublet(te), Élisabeth, 442, 443
Soblet/Sublet(te), François, 443
Soblet/Sublet(te), Isaac, 442
Soblet/Sublet(te), Jacob, 443
Soblet/Sublet(te), Jacques/James, 443
Soblet/Sublet(te), Jean, 442
SOBLET/SUBLET(TE), Jean, 442
Soblet/Sublet(te), Judit, 443
Soblet/Sublet(te), Louise Christine, 442
Soblet/Sublet(te), Marie, 443
Soblet/Sublet(te), Pierre Louis, 443
Soblet/Sublet(te), Robert, 443
Soblet/Sublet(te), Simon, 443
Sobriche, Gaspard, 175
Sobrish, Jeanne, 175
Sohier, François, 142
Sohier, Margarieta (X), 142
Sohier, Marie, 142
Sohier, Susanna, 439
Solario, Guilbert de, 444
SOLLERS/SALLERS, John, 444
Solomon, Sarah, 64
Solt, Johannes, 30
Solt, Johannes Nicholas, 30
Sommer, Maria Magdelene, 235
Sommer, Maria Margaret (Wolf), 235
Sommer, Philip, 235
Sorey, Ann, 23
Sorey, Francis, 23
Sorey, Ledey, 23
Sorey, Peter, 24
Sorré, Marie, 461
Souder, Ann (X), 424
Souder, Jacob, 424
Souder, Maria, 424
SOUILLÉ/SOUILLET, Jean, 445
Souille/Souillet, Nicolas, 445
Souillie, Daniel, 116
Souillie, Marie (X) (Guerrant), 116

Souillié, Nicolas, 233, 330
Soule, John, 139
Soulice, Jean, 73
Soulice, John, 303
Soulice, Mary (X), 303
Soulice, Susanna, 303
SOUPLIÉ/SUPPLÉE/SOUPLIS, André/Andrew, 446
Souplie/Supplee/Souplis, Andrew, 446
Souplie/Supplee/Souplis, Ann, 446
Souplie/Supplee/Souplis, Bartholomew, 446
Souplie/Supplee/Souplis, Jacob, 446
Souplie/Supplee/Souplis, Margaret, 446
Soupzmain, Judith, 160
Southerland/Sutherlin, George III, 401
Spain, Mary, 226
Spalden, Susannah, 332
Spann, Rebecca A., 338
Spare, Francynatje Van, 159
Spare, Jan Claason Van, 159
Sparks, Mary, 64
Sparks, William, 87
Sparrow, Thomas, 277
Spaulding, Ann (Cleveland), 256
Spaulding, Azariah, 256
Spaulding, Charles, 256
Spaulding, Daniel, 256
Spaulding, Hannah, 256
Spaulding, Hesther, 256
Spaulding, Magdalen, 256
Spaulding, Martha, 256
Spaulding, Molle, 256
Spaulding, Molly, 256
Spaulding, Phillip, 256
Spaulding, Rufus, 256
Spaulding, Susannah, 256
Spaulding, Zilpha, 256
Spears, Henry, 138
Spears, Margaret Graefenreid (Henlopin), 138
Spears, Peter Abram, 138
Spears/Speyers, Catherine, 138
Spears/Speyers, Daniel, 138
Spears/Speyers, David, 138
Spears/Speyers, Elizabeth, 138
Spears/Speyers, George F, 138
Spears/Speyers, George Frederick, 138
Spears/Speyers, Hannah, 138
Spears/Speyers, Jacob, 138
Spears/Speyers, John, 138
Spears/Speyers, Mary Agnes, 138
Spears/Speyers, Michael Christopher, 138
Spears/Speyers, Sarah, 138
Spencer, George, 396
Spencer, Mary, 428
Spencer, Nicholas, 411
Spencer, Thomas, 64
Sperry, Elizabeth (Post), 70
Sperry, John, 70

Spicler, Catherine Barbara, 292
Spiegelaer, Gerritje (Lamberts), 61
Spiegelaer, Jan, 61
Spier, Armtie Hanse, 430
Spier, Hans Hendricks, 333
Spier, Johannes, 431
Spier, Thomas, 431
Spinney, Hannah, 190
Spinney, Mary, 190
Spo(h)n, Renarde/Renata, 199
Spoe, Elizabeth, 201
Spohn, Susanne Rosina "Rosa", 199
Spönhauer, Maria Elizabeth, 243
Spooner, Elizabeth Ingraham, 127
Spratt, John, 392, 404
Spratt, Marie (de Peyster), 404
Springsteen, Ann Maria, 126
Springsteen, Casper, 302
Springsteen, Catherine, 216
Springsteen, Gertruyt, 302
Springsteen, Johannes Caspers, 126
Springsteen, Joost Casperse, 400
Sprong(h)/Sprungh, Gabriel, 302
Sprong, David, 305
Sprong, Gabriel Janse, 302
Sprung, Annetje, 174
Spry, Christopher, 463
Spry, Elizabeth, 463
Spry, Eve, 463
Spry, Francis, 463
Spry, James Maynard, 463
Spry, John, 463
Spry, Lucrecia, 463
Spry, Mary, 463
Spry, Rebecca, 463
Spry, Sarah, 463
Spry, Thomas, 463
St Julien/Julien/Julian, Pierre de, 432
St. Croix, Joshua de, 211
St. John/Sension, Matthias, 86
St. Julian, Amey (Ravenel) de, 410
St. Julian, Charlotte de, 409
St. Julian, Mary de, 410
St. Julian, Paul de, 410
St. Julian, Pierre de, 322
St. Julien, Damaris Elizabeth (Le Serrurier) de, 409
St. Julien, Elizabeth, *418*
St. Julien, Elizabeth Damaris de, 409
St. Julien, Marie de, 432
St. Julien, Pierre de, 409
St. Julien/Julien/Julian, Abigail de, 433
St. Julien/Julien/Julian, Aimée de, 432
St. Julien/Julien/Julian, Alexander de, 432
St. Julien/Julien/Julian, Catherine de, 433
St. Julien/Julien/Julian, Charlotte/Carolina de, 432
St. Julien/Julien/Julian, Daniel de, 432

St. Julien/Julien/Julian, Elizabeth Damaris de, 432
St. Julien/Julien/Julian, Émilie/Emilia de, 432
St. Julien/Julien/Julian, George de, 433
St. Julien/Julien/Julian, Henri de, 432
St. Julien/Julien/Julian, Henry de, 432
St. Julien/Julien/Julian, Isaac de, 433
St. Julien/Julien/Julian, Jacob de, 433
St. Julien/Julien/Julian, Jacques/James de, 432
St. Julien/Julien/Julian, Jeanne Marie de, 432
St. Julien/Julien/Julian, Jeanne Renée/Jane Renata de, 432
St. Julien/Julien/Julian, John de, 433
St. Julien/Julien/Julian, Joseph de, 432
St. Julien/Julien/Julian, Louis de, 432
St. Julien/Julien/Julian, Margaret de, 433
St. Julien/Julien/Julian, Marguerite/Margaret de, 432
St. Julien/Julien/Julian, Marie Ester de, 432
St. Julien/Julien/Julian, Martha de, 433
St. Julien/Julien/Julian, Mary de, 433
St. Julien/Julien/Julian, Paul de, 432
St. Julien/Julien/Julian, Peter de, 433
St. JULIEN/JULIEN/JULIAN, Pierre de, Sieur de Malacare, 432
St. Julien/Julien/Julian, Rebecca de, 433
St. Julien/Julien/Julian, René de, 433
St. JULIEN/JULIEN/JULIAN, René de, 432
St. Julien/Julien/Julian, Ruth de, 433
St. Julien/Julien/Julian, Stephen de, 433
St. Léger, Madelaine Boisrone de, 145
St. Léger, Samuel Boisrond de, 145
St. Paul, Marie, 239
St. Seine, Madeleine, 294
Staats, Aeltje, 400
Staats, Anneke, 400
Staats, Jan, 400
Staats, Jan Janse, 400
Staats, Jan Pietersz, 400
Staats, Neeltje, 400
Stackhouse, Anna, 446
Stackhouse, Thomas, 446
Stafford, Eleanor, 201
Stafford, William, 223
Staggers, David Martin, 33
Stahl, Anna Christina (X), 116
Stahl, George, 116
Stahl, Maria Catherine, 116
Stahle, Anna Margaret, 469
Staige, Laetitia Maria Anne, 346
Staige, William Rev., 346
Stallard, Sarah, 377
Stalliard, Randolph, 80
Stallings, Sarah, 223
Stam, Arent Corssen, 278
Stamp, Ann, 24

Stanard, Mary Elizabeth, 108
Standish, Alexander, 139, 287
Standish, Elizabeth, 139, 287
Standish, Sarah (Alden), 287
Stanford, David, 203
Stanley, Anna, 260
Stanley, Edward, 260
Staples, Elizabeth, 24
Staples, James, 348
Staples, Mary (Tetherly), 348
Staples, Samuel, 348
Starkey, Benjamin, 204
Starkey, Joseph, 326
Starr, Joseph, 75
Starr, Sarah (Southmayd), 75
Stauch, Nikolaus, 18
Stauch, Peter, 18
Stautenberger, Barbara, 192
Stealard (Stalliard?), Mary, 80
Stealard, Joseph Bullett, 80
Steele, John, 107
Steele, Lydia (Guerri), 260
Steindam, Abraham, 291
Steindam, Margaret, 291
Steiner, Johan Jakob, 241
Stelle, Ambrose, 447
Stelle, Benjamin, 393, 447
Stelle, Catherine, 396
Stelle, Eugene, 447
Stelle, Gabriel, 447
Stelle, Isaac, 447
Stelle, Jean/John, 447
Stelle, Madelaine, 447
Stelle, Peter, 447
Stelle, Poncet, 396
STELLE, Poncet, 447
Steph, Johannes, 245
Stephens, James, 239
Sterling, Anne, 88
Sterling, Thomas, 88
Sternberger, Elisabeth, 18
Sternberger, Elisabeth (Fischer), 18
Sternberger, Hans, 18
Stevens, Ensign Thomas, 256
Stevens, Ruth, 256
Stevens, Ruth (Hall), 256
Stevenson, Margaret, 405
Stewart, Alexander, 392
Stewart, Ann, 201
Stewart, Cornelia (Dissinton), 392
Stewart, Elizabeth, 116
Stewart, Hezekiah, 72
Stewart/Stuart, Sarah, 131
Stiel, Matthew, 226
Stillwell, Ann (X), 61
Stillwell, Jan/John, 390
Stillwell, Martha (Billiou), 130
Stillwell, Martha (Billou), 74
Stillwell, Nicholas, 61, 74
Stillwell, Sarah, 350
Stillwell, Thomas, 74, 130

Stillwell, Thomas Lt., 61
Stillwell, William, 390
Stilphen, Lucy, 246
Stilwell, Anne (X), 390
Stilwell, Daniel, 390
Stilwell, Jan, 390
Stilwell, Nicholas Lt., 390
Stilwell, Willem, 390
Stith, Elizabeth, 385
Stith, William, 385
Stock, Mary/Amy, 306
Stockett, Frances, 178
Stockett, Mary (Wells), 178
Stockett, Thomas, 178
Stocking, Daniel, 26
Stocking, Jane, 26
Stocking, Jane (Mould), 26
Stockley, Isaac, 277
Stockley, Joseph, 277
Stockley, Mary, 277
Stockley, Susannah, 37
Stockley/Stoakley, Joseph, 277
Stockton, Susannah, 345
Stoever, Johann Casper, 358
Stokes, David Sr., 166
Stokes, Humphrey Wells, 419
Stokes, Mary, 419
Stone, Daniel, 311
Stone, David, 311
Stone, Hannah (Woodbury), 311
Stone, John, 104
Stone, Mary, 104
Stone, Mary (X), 375
Stone, Thomas, 234, 375
Stonne, Adouin de, 380
Storm, Abram, 416
Storm, Catharina, 81
Storm, Catherine, 353
Storm, David, 416, 450
Storm, Engeltie, 416
Storm, Esther, 450
Storm, Gregorus, 416
Storm, Gregory, 280
Storm, Jan, 416
Storm, Joannis, 416
Storm, Maritie, 450
Stout, Mary, 370
Stoutenburgh, Maria, 431
Strabo(o), Anthony, 455
Strabo(o), Jacob, 455
Strabo(o), John James, 455
Strabo(o), Judith, 455
Strabo(o), Magdalene, 455
Stratmaker, Trinitie, 226
Stre(i)ng/Strang/Strange, Charlotte, 448
Stre(i)ng/Strang/Strange, Clorinda "Penelope", 448
Stre(i)ng/Strang/Strange, Daniel, 448
STRE(I)NG/STRANG/STRANGE, Daniel, 447
Stre(i)ng/Strang/Strange, Gabriel, 448

Stre(i)ng/Strang/Strange, Henry, 448
Stre(i)ng/Strang/Strange, Louisan/Lucy, 448
Stre(i)nge/Strang/Strange, Mary Prudence, 448
Streing, Charlotte (LeMaître), 135
Streing, Daniel, 135
Streing, Louise, 135
Streshly, Elizabeth, 270
Stressinger/Strittzinger, Gertrude, 446
Stroad, unknown, 123
Strong, Charles, 217
Strong, Elijah Frink, 34
Strother, Francis, 21
Strother, Jane, 331
Strother, William, 331
Strother, Wm., Jr., 22
Strouppe, Pasteur, 389
Stryker, Aeltie, 53
Stryker, Jan, 53
Stryker, Jannetje, 53
Stuart, Harriott Turberville, 108
Stukey, unknown, 103
Sturm, Anna Barbara, 283
Sturm, Anna Maria (Ruester), 283
Stuteck, Anna Maria, 263
Stuyvesant, Anneke/Ann, **39**
Stuyvesant, Balthazar, **39**
Stuyvesant, Gov., 129
Stuyvesant, Peter, 87, 359
Stuyvesant, Peter Dir. Gen., 441
Stuyvestant, Margaretta (Hardenstein), **39**
Stuyvestant, Peter Gov., **39**
Stymets, Jacob, 414
Suber, unknown, 315
SUIRE, Antoine, 388
Suire, Daniel, 387
Suire, Jeanne, 387
Suire, Margaret, 238
Sullivan, Timothy, 350
Sullivant, John, 465
Summer, Catherine, 448
Summer, Elizabeth, 448
SUMMER, John George, 448
Summer, Mary, 448
Summers, David, 340
Sumner, Elizabeth, 356
Sumner, Joseph, 356
Sumwald, Johann Andreas, 252
Süss, Bartholomew, 235
Süss, Catherine Salome (X), 235
Sutton, Constant (X), 361
Sutton, Damaris (Bishop), 425
Sutton, Elizabeth, 371
Sutton, Richard, 425
Sutton, William, 425
Suylandt, Huybert, 129, 130
Swaim/Sweem, William, 290
Swain, Benjamin, 430
Swart, Maritie, 205

Swart, Neeltje, 205
Swartout, James Jacobsen, 237
Swartout, Samuel, 237
Swartwout, Esther, 107
Swartwout, James Maj., 107
Swartz, Elizabeth, 249
Swartz, Henry, 418
Swartz, Susanna, 249
Swearingen, Elizabeth Van, 33
Swearingen, Gerret/Gerritt Van, 32
Swearingen, Jane Van, 33
Swearingen, John Van, 33
Swearingen, Samuel Van, 33
Swearingen, Thomas Van, 33
Swearingen, Van Van, 33
Swearingen, Zacharias Van, 33
Sweem, Anthony, 41
Sweem, Barent, 44, 169
Sweem, Johannes, 390
Sweem, Mary, 41
Sweem, Petronella/Petroneltje, 169
Sweiger, unknown, 150
Swift, Jonathan, 422
Swille/Swilley, John, 445
Swille/Swilley, Nanni/Ann, 446
Swille/Swilley, Nicholas, 445
Swille/Swilley, Samuel, 446
Swille/Swilley, Senous/Zenas, 445
Swille/Swilley, Solomon, 446
Swille/Swilley, Stephen, 445, 446
Swin/Sweem, Johannes, 273
Swinton, Alexander, 442
Swyng/Swing, Abraham, 437
Swyng/Swing, Anna Margareta, 437
Swyng/Swing, Anne Marie, 437
Swyng/Swing, Daniel, 437
Swyng/Swing, Judith, 437
Swyng/Swing, Marie Magdeleine, 437
Swyng/Swing, Marie Salomé, 437
Swyng/Swing, Michel, 437
Swyng/Swing, Pierre, 437
Swyng/Swing, Salomé, 437
Swyng/Swing, Samuel, 437
Sy, Esther, 449
Sy, Issac, 450
Sy, Jean, 467
Sy, Jeanne (Dujardin), 329
Sy, Nicolas, 45, 353
Sy, Pierre, 329, 449
Sy/Sie/See/Cy, Abraham, 449, 450
Sy/Sie/See/Cy, Elisabeth, 449
Sy/Sie/See/Cy, Esther, 450
Sy/Sie/See/Cy, Isaac, 449
Sy/Sie/See/Cy, Isaac II, 450
Sy/Sie/See/Cy, Jacob, 449
Sy/Sie/See/Cy, Jacobus/James, 450
Sy/Sie/See/Cy, Jean, 449
Sy/Sie/See/Cy, Jeanne, 449
Sy/Sie/See/Cy, Magdalaine, 449
Sy/Sie/See/Cy, Marie, 449, 450
Sy/Sie/See/Cy, Maritie, 450

SY/SIE/SEE/CY, Nicolaus, 448
Sy/Sie/See/Cy, Peter, 450
Sy/Sie/See/Cy, Pierre, 449, 450
Sy/Sie/See/Cy, Simon, 450
Sy/Sie/See/Cy, Susanna, 450
Sy/Sie/See/Cy, Susanne, 449
Sylvester, Grissell (Brinley), 326
Sylvester, Nathaniel, 326
Sylvester, Patience, 326
Synnott, Elizabeth, 124
Synnott, James, 124

T

Tabb, Frances/Euphany, 355
Taboy, unknown, 369
Tacquelet, Guillaume, 132
Tacquelet, Rachel, 46, 131
Tailler/Taylor, Thomas, 135
Taine, Isaac, 105
Taine, Marie, 105
Taintor, Elizabeth (Rose), 223
Taintor, Joanna, 222
Taintor, Michael, 223
Talbort, Susannah, 15
Talbot, Catherine (Ogg), *419*
Talbot, William, *419*
Taliaferro, Elizabeth, 266
Taliaferro, John, 266
Taliaferro, Sarah (Smith), 266
Tallet, Abraham, 223
Tallet, Mary Ann/Marianne, 223
Tallet, Susanne Marguerite, 223
Tancre, Abraham, 449
Tancré, Abraham, 148
Tancré, Anne, 148
Tancré, Chretienne (Gombert), 148
Tancré, Esther, 148
Tanner, Ann, 67
Tanner, Catherine, 85
Tanner, Christopher, 85
Tanner, Dorothea, 85
Tanner, Elizabeth (Oehler), 85
Tanner, Reginald, 85
Taplady, Charles, 328
Tappan, Elsie, 324
Tappan, Elsje, 313
Tappan, Julien, 324
Tappan, Jurian, 313
Targer, Daniel, 451
Targer, Louise (Martin), 451
TARGER, Marie, 451
Tate, William, 91
Tattrie, George, 285
Tavaud, Elizabeth, 151
Tavaud, Marie (Goubeilla), 151
Tavaud, Pierre, 151
Taylor, Absolum, 401
Taylor, Allen, 108
Taylor, Ann (Plowden), 373
Taylor, Elizabeth, 401

Taylor, Eve (Ball), 56
Taylor, George, 88
Taylor, James, 401
Taylor, John, 370
Taylor, John Prevatte, 401
Taylor, Joseph, 401
Taylor, Mary, 332
Taylor, Mary Moser, 370
Taylor, Moses, 401
Taylor, Moses Sr., 401
Taylor, Nancy, 401
Taylor, Peter Jr., 401
Taylor, Polly (Ann), 401
Taylor, Rebecca (Delatre), 140
Taylor, Redding, 401
Taylor, Sally/Sarah, 401
Taylor, Samuel, 373
Taylor, Sina, 401
Taylor, Susanna, 373
Taylor, Thomas, 56
Taylor, Thomas (Alfred), 401
Tayne/Tine, Isaac, 253
Tébaux, Marie, 277
Tebbs, Daniel, 200
Téligny, Charles de, 121
Teller, Helena, 392
Tellor, Elizabeth W., 296
Temple, James III, 37
Temple, John, **37**
Temple, Sir Thomas, 294
Templeton, Ann, 91
Templeton, Thomas, 23
TenBrouck, Wessel Capt., 242
Tennison, Christian, 312
Tennison, John, 312
Terbosch, Catrina, 164
Terbosch, John, 468
Terhuyse/Terhune, Albert, 14
Terpenning, Dick, 301
Terpenning, Theunis, 301
Terrell, Abigail, 173
Terrell, Henry, 173
Terrell, Sarah (Woodson), 173
Terrell, William, *420*
Terrier, Anne, 440
Terrin, Antoinette, 384
Terry, Jane, 221
Terry, Jeremiah Stephen Capt., 221
Terry, Susanna (Carothers), 221
Tescard, Léon, 271
Testart, Anne, 131
Testart, Isaac, **47**
Testart, Marie Madelaine, 46
Testart, Pierre, 131
Testart, Pierre Dr., 46
Testart, Rachel (Crommelin), 46
Testart,Cyrus, **47**
Teunissen, Denyse, 126
Teunissen, Ian, 164
Thacker, Elizabeth, 471
Thacker, Frances, 471

Thatcher, Sylvester, 364
Thauvet/Thevett, Marie, 56
Thayer, Abigail, 255
Thelaball, Elizabeth, 451
Thelaball, Francis, 451
Thelaball, James, 451
THELABALL, James, 451
Thelaball, Lemuel, 451
Thelaball, Margaret, 451
Thelaball, Mary, 451
Thelin, Collignion de, 380
Theobald, Mary, 246
Theobald, Nancy, 246
Therond, Jacques, 147
Thexel, Catharina Van, 416
Thexel, Cornelis Van, 416
Thexel, Wyntie Van, 416
Thomas, Anna Catharina, 283
Thomas, Anna Margaretha (X), 283
Thomas, Anne (Moore), 327
Thomas, Christian, 283
Thomas, Christoph, 283
Thomas, David, 332
Thomas, Deborah, 446
Thomas, Elizabeth, 332
Thomas, Esther, 316
Thomas, Frances, 306
Thomas, Gabriel, 283
Thomas, Hans Michel, 283
Thomas, Jehiel, 75
Thomas, Johann Michel, 283
Thomas, Johann Valentin, 283
Thomas, Johannes, 283
Thomas, Maria Catharina, 283
Thomas, Mary (X), 75
Thomas, Mehitable (X), 453
Thomas, Patience, 453
Thomas, Peleg, 453
Thomas, Philipp Henrich, 283
Thomas, Rebecca, 332
Thomas, Robert Capt., 327
Thomas, Susanna, 75
Thomas, Thomas, 332
Thomas, unknown, 83, 277
Thomas,Christian, 283
Thomegeux/Thomegay, Jean, 195
Thompson, Alexander Rev., 218
Thompson, Ann, 147
Thompson, Elizabeth, 270, 405
Thompson, Hannah, 91
Thompson, Henry, 178
Thompson, Janet, 218
Thompson, John, 337, 433
Thompson, Mary, 157, 178
Thompson, Mary (X), 218
Thompson, Robert, 323
Thompson, Samuel, 433
Thompson, Susanna, 178
Thompson, unknown, 22
Thomson, James Rev., 217
Thomson, Mary, 217

Thoreau, Henry David, 237
Thoreau, Jean, 237
Thoreau, Marie, 237
Thoreau, Marie Anne (Tantin), 237
Thorel, Marie, 390
THOREL, Marie, 451
Thorn, Susannah, 413
Thorne, Mary (Orear), 413
Thorne, William, 413
Thornton, Alice (Savage), 22
Thornton, Aphia, 201
Thornton, Elizabeth, 146
Thornton, Francis, 22, 146
Thornton, Margaret, 22
Thornton, Mark, 24
Thornton, Mary, 24
Thorpe, Robert, 145
Thorpe, unknown, **36**
Thoury, Louise, 156
Threadcraft, George, 320
Threadcraft, George, Jr, 320
Threadcraft, Jammie, 321
Threadcraft, Sarah, 321
Throckmorton,Rebecca, 163
Thurber, Samuel, 454
Thurman, Mary, 41
Thurman, Pleasant, 17
Thurmond, Eleanor (Delatre), 140
Thyssen, Jan, 439
Tibault, Anne, 187
TIBAULT, Anne, 452
Tibout, Andries, 14, 15
Tibout, Jan, 313
Tibout, Jannetie, 246
Tice, Elizabeth, 280
Tienhoven, Cornelius Van, 297
Tiertsoort, Helena, 384
Tietsoort, Maria, 384
Tietsorte/Titsoort, Aagien/Aeche Willem, 205
Tiffield, Philippe, 76
Tilba/D'Elba, Antoine, 324
Tilburg, Catherina Van, 302
Tilburg, Jan Van, 302
Tilburg, Johannes Van, 302
Tileston, Joanna, 437
Tileston, Rebecca, 437
Tillinghast, Mary, 314
Tillinghast, Mary (Keech), 314
Tillinghast, Mercy, 314
Tillinghast, Pardon, 314
Tillinghast, Philip Pardon, 27
Tillou, Elizabeth (Vigneau), 109
Tillou, Judith, 109
Tillou, Vincent, 109
Tillou/Tilyou/Tilson, Ann, 452
Tillou/Tilyou/Tilson, Elizabeth, 452
Tillou/Tilyou/Tilson, Guillaume/William, 452
Tillou/Tilyou/Tilson, Jean/John, 452
Tillou/Tilyou/Tilson, Judith, 452

Tillou/Tilyou/Tilson, Peter, 452
TILLOU/TILYOU/TILSON, Pierre, 452
Tillou/Tilyou/Tilson, Vincent, 452
Tilson, Edmond, 62
Tilson, Elizabeth, 62
Tilson, Mary, 62
Tilton, Sabrah, 15
Tilton, Thomas, 15
Timothy, Catherine, 457
Timothy, Elizabeth (X), 457
Timothy, Lewis, 457
Timson, William, 196
Tinsley, Isaac, 429
Tinsley, Sarah (Jackson), 429
Tinsley, Thomas III, 429
Tisdale, Ephraim, 208
Tisdale, unknown, 34
Tisort/Tietsoort, Jacob, 151
Titis, Cornelia, 305
Titsoort, Willem, 205
Titus, unknown, 344
Toche, Richard, 352
Todd, Eleanore (Dorsey), 419
Todd, Frances, 419
Todd, Thomas, 419
Toll, Cornelia, 287
Tomkins, Jan, 227
Tomlinson, Ann, 172
Tomlinson, Isaac, 172
Tomlinson, John, 226
Tomlinson, Patience (X), 172
Tompkins, unknown, 362
Toney, Charles, 401
Toney, Elizabeth (Harris), 401
TONNELIER/TUNNELL,
  Guillaume/William, 452
Tonnelier/Tunnell, James, 453
Tonnelier/Tunnell, John, 453
Tonnelier/Tunnell, Robert, 452
Tonnelier/Tunnell, Stephen, 453
Tonnelier/Tunnell, William, 452, 453
Tony, Tabitha, 401
Tooker, unknown, 377
Toomer, Henry, 427
Toomer, Joshua, 68
Torin, Daniel, 272
Torion, Anne, 82
Toulouse, Guillaume, 71
Tourbier, Claire (de Hennin), 473
Tourbier, Françoise, 473
Tourbier, Pasquier, 473
Tourgée, Pierre, 453
Tourgee/Tourjee/Torge, Elizabeth, 453
Tourgee/Tourjee/Torge, John, 453
Tourgee/Tourjee/Torge, Peter, 453
Tourgee/Tourjee/Torge, Philip, 453
Tourgee/Tourjee/Torge, Phillip, 453
TOURGÉE/TOURJÉE/TORGÉ, Pierre, 453
Tourgee/Tourjee/Torge, Pierre/Peter, 453
Tourgee/Tourjee/Torge, Thomas, 453

Tourneur, Daniel, 467
Tourneur, Ester/Hester, 467
Tourneur, Jacqueline (deParisis), 467
Tourneur, Thomas, 246
Tourneur/Turneur, Daniel, 454
TOURNEUR/TURNEUR, Daniel, 453
Tourneur/Turneur, Esther, 454
Tourneur/Turneur, Jacques, 454
Tourneur/Turneur, Madeline, 454
Tourneur/Turneur, Maria, 454
Tourneur/Turneur, Marretje, 454
Tourneur/Turneur, Thomas, 454
Tourtellot, Abraham, 52, 454
TOURTELLOT, Abraham, 454
Tourtellot, Benjamin, 454
Tourtellot, Esther, 454
Tourtellot, Gabriel, 454
Tourtellot, Jacques-Moritz, 454
Tourtellot, Jacques-Thomas, 454
Tourtellot, James, 454
Tourtellot, Jean, 454
Tourtellot, John, 454
Tourtellot, Moses, 454
Toussaint, David, 443
Toussaint, Hubert, 443
Toussaint, Jean, 443
Toussaint, Suzanne (LeRoy), 443
Townsend, Daniel, 104
Trabuc/Trabue, André, 455
Trabuc/Trabue, Anne, 455
Trabuc/Trabue, Antoine, 118, 455
Trabuc/Trabue, Arnaud, 455
Trabuc/Trabue, David, 455
TRABUC/TRABUE, Guillaume, 454
Trabuc/Trabue, Jean, 455
Trabuc/Trabue, Marguerite, 455
Trabuc/Trabue, Marie, 455
Trabuc/Trabue, Marthe, 455
Trabuc/Trabue, Pierre, 455
Trabue, Anthony, 114, 232, 411
Trabue, Anthony Sir, 195
Trabue, Antoine, 326
Trabue, Jean Jacques/Jacob, 326
Trabue, Magdelaine (Verreuil), 114
Trabue, Magdeleine, 232
Trabue, Magdeleine (Verreuil), 326
Trabue/Trabac, Antoine, 469
Tracy, Sarah, 350
Tranchepain, Jeanne, 165
Trapier, Elizabeth (DuGue), 245
Trapier, Paul, 245
Trautmaenin, Catherine, 140
Trautmann, Anna Elisabeth (Romer), 18
Trautmann, Georg, 18
Trautmann, Nickel, 252
Trautmann, Ottilie, 18
Travis, Daniel, 276
Travis, Susannah (X), 276
Tregeau/Trego, Jacob, 456
Tregeau/Trego, James, 456
Tregeau/Trego, John, 456

Tregeau/Trego, Peter, 456
TREGEAU/TREGO, Pierre/Peter, 456
Tregeau/Trego, William, 456
Tremau, unknown, 456
Tremau, X (Scipio), 456
TREMAU/SIPPY, Josep, 456
Tremble, Jean Jacques, 377
Tremble, Jeanne, 388
Trembly, Ann/Hannah, 377
Trembly, Elizabeth (Rachel), 377
Trembly, Jean/John, 377
Trembly, John, 377
Trembly, Margaret, 377
Trembly, Mary, 377
Trembly, Peter, 377
Trembly, Sarah, 377
Tremellius, Emanuel, 189
Tremellius, Rachel (X), 189
Tremellius, Rebecca, 189
Trémolières, Jeanne, 455
Trépanier, Angelique, 141
Trépanier, Charles, 141
Trépanier, Marguerit (Jacquereau), 141
Trezevant, Daniel, 397, 457
TREZEVANT, Daniel, 457
Trezevant, Elizabeth, 457
Trézévant, Elizabeth, 320
Trezevant, Isaac, 457
Trezevant, Madalane, 457
Trezevant, Marian, 457
Trézévant, Marianne, 84
Trezevant, Martha, 457
Trezevant, Matthew, 457
Trezevant, Susannah, 457
Trezevant, Susanne, 457
Trezevant, Susanne (Menou), 457
Trezevant, Suzanne (Menou), 397
Trezevant, Théodore, 397, 457
Tribout, Jan, 155
Trice, James, 22
Trico, Catelyntje, 408
Trico, Jeronimus, 409
Trimm, Peter, 18
Triplett, James, 422
Triplett, Martha (Jennings), 422
Triplett, Martha Lane, 422
Trogdon, Samuel, 433
Trott/Treat, Richard, 209
Trotter, Mary, 257
Troutte, Elizabeth, 92
Troxell, Mary Margaret, 467
Tucker, Samuel, 133
Tull, Bridget, 202
Tulle/Tully, Benjamin, 23
Tuller/Teller/Deller/Diller, Johannes, 30
Tullier, Jean, 142
Tullier, Magdalena (Laurens), 142
Tully, Jane, 23
Tunnis, Christina, 206
Turck, Esther De, 55
Turck, Isaac de, 55

Turck, Jacob de, 55
Tureman, John, 201
Turk, Hester (Kip) de, 241
Türk, Isaac de, 241
Turk, Johannes de, 241
Turner, Charlotte, 119
Turner, Daniel, 454
Turner, Elizabeth (Copley), 282
Turner, Elizabeth (Morse), 297
Turner, Frederick Devow, 454
Turner, Hannah, 297
Turner, Jacob, 454
Turner, Japhet, 297
Turner, John, 119
Turner, Martha, 347
Turner, Mary, 454
Turner, Peter, 454
Turner, Praisever, 282
Turner, Thomas, 236
Turner, unknown, 380
Turner, William, 367
Turney, Benjamin, 86
Turney, Mary (X), 86
Turney, Ruth, 86
Turquand, Marthe, 379
Turquand, René, 379
Turque/Tur(c)k/Turk, Abraham de, 458
Turque/Tur(c)k/Turk, Dina de, 458
Turque/Tur(c)k/Turk, Elizabeth de, 458
Turque/Tur(c)k/Turk, Esther Cornelia de, 458
Turque/Tur(c)k/Turk, Esther de, 458
Turque/Tur(c)k/Turk, Henrich de, 458
Turque/Tur(c)k/Turk, Isaac de, 458
Turque/Tur(c)k/Turk, Jacob de, 458
TURQUE/TUR(C)K/TÜRK, Jacob de, 458
Turque/Tur(c)k/Turk, Jacomina de, 458
Turque/Tur(c)k/Turk, Johannes de, 458
Turque/Tur(c)k/Turk, Johannes/Hans de, 458
Turque/Tur(c)k/Turk, John de, 458
Turque/Tur(c)k/Turk, John Pieter, 458
Turque/Tur(c)k/Turk, Maria Elisabeth de, 458
Turque/Tur(c)k/Turk, Sarah de, 458
Turque/Tur(c)k/Turk, Susanna de, 458
Turville, Susan, 227
Tuthill, Bethia, 282
Tuthill, Bethia (Horton), 326
Tuthill, Henry, 326
Tuthill, Jonathan, 326
Tuttle, Joseph, 344
Tuxen, Sophie Amalie, 363
Twiller, Wouter Van, 198
Tybout, Capt. James, 15
Tybout/Tiebout, unknown, 14
Tyler, Joan (X), 179
Tyler, John III, 351
Tyler, Mary, 239
Tyler, Mary (Lathrop), 239
Tyler, President John, 351

Tyler, Robert, 179
Tyler, William, 239
Tylor, Mary(X), 276
Tylor, Robert, 276
Tylor, Susanna, 276
Tysen, Elizabeth (Sweem), 169

U

Ulery, Elizabeth, 391
Ulin/Ean, Elias, 130
Urquhuart, Martha, 276
Usilie/Uzille/Uziel(l)e/Uzzell/Ziele/Seeley, Cornelia, 459
Usilie/Uzille/Uziel(l)e/Uzzell/Ziele/Seeley, David, 459
USILIE/UZILLE/UZIEL(L)E/UZZELL/ZIELE/SEELEY, David, 459
Usilie/Uzille/Uziel(l)e/Uzzell/Ziele/Seeley, Helena, 459
Usilie/Uzille/Uziel(l)e/Uzzell/Ziele/Seeley, Jan, 459
Usilie/Uzille/Uziel(l)e/Uzzell/Ziele/Seeley, Lysbet, 459
Usilie/Uzille/Uziel(l)e/Uzzell/Ziele/Seeley, Maria, 459
Usilie/Uzille/Uziel(l)e/Uzzell/Ziele/Seeley, Maria Magdalena, 459
Usilie/Uzille/Uziel(l)e/Uzzell/Ziele/Seeley, Peter, 459
Usilie/Uzille/Uziel(l)e/Uzzell/Ziele/Seeley, Pierre/Pieter/Peter, 459
Usilie/Uzille/Uziel(l)e/Uzzell/Ziele/Seeley, Sophia, 459
Usille, David, 320
Usille, Maria Oeycke, 320
Usille, Marie (Casier), 320
Usillie, David, 315
Usillie, Marie (Casier), 315
Uytendaele, Johannes, 14
Uytendaele, Maria (leBreton), 14
Uzès (Ucetia), Madeleine, 426
Uzielle, Pieter, 459
Uzile, David, 105
Uzzell, Thomas, 459

V

V(e)sleton, Francis I, 210
V(e)sleton, Susannah, 210
Vachan, Jean, 157
Vail, Grace (Braddick/Burgess), 282
Vail, John, 282
Vail, Mary, 282
Vairin, Anne Caterine, 460
Vairin, Auguste/Augustus, 461
Vairin, Augustus, 461
Vairin, Cécile, 461
Vairin, Charles Louis, 461
Vairin, Élie, 460
Vairin, Elizabeth, 461

VAIRIN, Jacques, 460
Vairin, Jaques, 460
Vairin, Jean, 460
Vairin, Jean Jacques, 460
Vairin, Jean Louis, 460
Vairin, Jean Pierre, 460
Vairin, Jean Pierre/ John Peter, 460
Vairin, John Peter, 461
Vairin, Jules/Julius, 461
Vairin, Julius, 461
Vairin, Justine, 461
Vairin, Marguerithe Louyse, 460
Vairin, Nicholas, 460
Vairin, Pierre Élie, 460
Vairin, Pierre Jaques, 460
Vairin, Susanne Ester, 460
Vairin, Therèse, 461
Valentine, DuChesne, 159
Valentine, Jan Tymensen, 126
Valentine, Tymensen, 126
Valkenburg, Jannetje, 459
Valkenburg, Thomas van, 98
Valle, Hester, 321
Valleau, Anne, 112, 462
Valleau, Anne (Brigaud), 112
Valleau, Arnaud, 462
Valleau, Charles, 112, 462
Valleau, Esaïe, 112
VALLEAU, Esaïe, 461
Valleau, Esaïe/Isaiah, 186, 461
Valleau, Étienne, 112, 462
Valleau, Étienne II, 462
Valleau, Gabriel, 462
Valleau, Isaiah, 462
Valleau, Jean, 462
Valleau, Judith, 122
Valleau, Magdelaine, 462
Valleau, Marguerite (Plondreau), 122
Valleau, Marguerite de, 303
Valleau, Marie, 112, 462
Valleau, Mary, 462
Valleau, Nicolas, 122
Valleau, Paul, 462
Valleau, Peter, 186, 462
Valleau, Pierre, 462
Valleau, Sarah, 462
Valleau, Susanne, 462
Valleau, Suzanne (Descard), 186
Valliant, Dorothy, 463
Valliant, Elizabeth, 463
Valliant, James, 463
Valliant, Jean, 462
Valliant, John, 463
VALLIANT, John, 462
Valliant, Joseph, 463
Valliant, Mary, 463
Valliant, Susanah, 463
Valliant,Mary (X), 462
Valois Zeller, Clothilde de Lady, 438
Valois, Benjamin de, 21
Valois, Clothilde de, 438

Van de Water, Alburtus, 48
Van Der Hoeven, Cornelis, 41
Van Der Hoeven, Metje/Mattie
 (Beekman), 41
van Hoose, Rebecca, 33
**VAN METRE/VAN METEREN, Jan
 Joosten**, 463
Van Metre/Van Meteren, Abraham, 464
Van Metre/Van Meteren, Catharine, 464
Van Metre/Van Meteren, Geertje, 464
Van Metre/Van Meteren, Gysbert Janse,
 464
**Van Metre/Van Meteren,
 Hendrix/Henry**, 464
Van Metre/Van Meteren, Isaac, 464
Van Metre/Van Meteren, Jacob, 464
Van Metre/Van Meteren, Jan/John, 464
Van Metre/Van Meteren, Joost Jans, 464
Van Metre/Van Meteren, Lysbeth, 464
**Van Metre/Van Meteren,
 Lysbeth/Elizabeth**, 464
Van Metre/Van Meteren, Rachel, 464
Van Metre/Van Meteren, Rebekka, 464
Vandandaigne, Joseph, 110
Vander Beeck, Poulus, 48
Vander Linde/Vanderlinda, Roeloff, *142*
Vanderbeck, Rem Jansen, 53
Vanderburgh, Hendrick, 365
Vanderburgh, Lucus Dirckszen, 365
Vanderhoef, Geertury, 431
Vanderlinde, Roelof, 129
Vanderlinde, Sarah, 440
Vanderspiegel, Elizabeth/Lysbet, 198
Vanderwoort, Abraham, 302
Vandewater, Adriaentje, 48
Vangasco, John, 15
Vanguer (Vegneur), Stephen, 223
Vansant, Rebeckah, 315
Varin, James, 397
Varin, Jérémie, 464
Varin, Susannah, 397
Varin, Susannah (DuBois), 397
Varin/ Vereen, Anne, 465
Varin/Vereen, Ann, 465
Varin/Vereen, Ebenezer, 465
Varin/Vereen, Elisabeth, 465
Varin/Vereen, Hannah, 465
Varin/Vereen, Isaac, 464
VARIN/VEREEN, Jacques/James, 464
Varin/Vereen, James, 465
Varin/Vereen, Jean, 465
Varin/Vereen, Jean Jacques, 464
Varin/Vereen, Jeremiah, 464, 465
Varin/Vereen, Jérémie, 464
Varin/Vereen, Martha, 465
Varin/Vereen, Mary, 465
Varin/Vereen, Rachel, 465
Varin/Vereen, Rebecca, 465
Varin/Vereen, Samuel, 465
Varin/Vereen, Sarah, 465
Varin/Vereen, Susanne, 464

Varin/Vereen, William, 465
Varleth, Maria, 392
Varney, James, 437
Varney, Jane (Tudor), 437
Varney, Mary, 437
Varnor, Henry, 208
Varnoye, Lysbeth, 153
Varrel, Thomas, 348
Vassal(l), Andrew, 465
Vassal(l), Anne, 466
Vassal(l), Elizabeth, 466
Vassal(l), Jane, 466
VASSAL(L), Jean, 465
Vassal(l), Jean/John, 465
Vassal(l), Joan, 466
Vassal(l), John, 465
Vassal(l), Judith, 465
Vassal(l), Mary, 466
Vassal(l), Rachel, 466
Vassal(l), Samuel, 465
Vassal(l), Stephen, 466
Vassal(l), Thomas, 466
Vassal(l), William, 465
Vasset, Jérôme, 92
Vaughan, James, 137
Vaughan, Susannah (X), 137
Vaulx, Robert, 346
Vaulx, Sarah, 346
Vaulx, Sarah (Elliot), 346
Vautrin, Abraham, 30, 466
Vautrin, Anna Margaretha, 30
Vautrin, Katherina (Brodt), 466
Vautrin/Votrin/Wotring, Abraham, 467
VAUTRIN/VOTRIN/WOTRING, Abraham,
 466
Vautrin/Votrin/Wotring, Anna Barbara,
 467
Vautrin/Votrin/Wotring, Anna Elizabeth,
 466
**Vautrin/Votrin/Wotring, Anna
 Margaretha**, 466
**Vautrin/Votrin/Wotring, Hans/John
 Peter**, 466
Vautrin/Votrin/Wotring, John Jacob, 466
Vautrin/Votrin/Wotring, John William,
 467
**Vautrin/Votrin/Wotring, Maria
 Magdalena**, 466
Vautrin/Votrin/Wotring, Samuel, 466
Vautrin/Wotring, Maria Magdalena, 30
Vaux, Esther (Tourneur) De, 374
Vaux, Frédéric De, 374
Vaux, Frederick de, 454
Vaux, Margaret, **40**
Vaux, Nicolas de, 450
Vaux, Susanna De, 374
Vaux/Vaus, Jean, **40**
Vaux/Veaux/Devoe, Abel de, 467
Vaux/Veaux/Devoe, Abigail de, 468
Vaux/Veaux/Devoe, Abraham de, 467
Vaux/Veaux/Devoe, Daniel de, 467

Vaux/Veaux/Devoe, Dinah de, 468
Vaux/Veaux/Devoe, Ester de, 467
Vaux/Veaux/Devoe, Esther de, 467
**Vaux/Veaux/Devoe, Frédéric/Frederick
 de**, 467
Vaux/Veaux/Devoe, Frederich de, 467
Vaux/Veaux/Devoe, Frederick de, 467
Vaux/Veaux/Devoe, Hester de, 467
Vaux/Veaux/Devoe, Jacob de, 467
Vaux/Veaux/Devoe, John de, 467
Vaux/Veaux/Devoe, Joseph de, 468
Vaux/Veaux/Devoe, Judith de, 468
Vaux/Veaux/Devoe, Leah de, 468
Vaux/Veaux/Devoe, Maritie de, 467
Vaux/Veaux/Devoe, Mary de, 467
Vaux/Veaux/Devoe, Nicolas de, 467
VAUX/VEAUX/DEVOE, Nicolas de, 467
Vaux/Veaux/Devoe, Rachel de, 467
Vaux/Veaux/Devoe, Susanna de, 467
Vaux/Veaux/Devoe, Susannah de, 467
Vaux/Veaux/Devoe, Susanne de, 467
VaWie, Geezie Hendrickse, 274
Vawter, John, 429
Vawter, Margaret, 429
Vawter, Margaret (Noel), 429
Veaux, Andre de, 84
Veaux, André de, 397
Veaux, Dinah de, 238
Veaux, Frederick De, 238
Veaux, Marguerite (de Bourdeaux) de,
 397
Veaux, Rachel De, 353
Veaux/Voe, Abraham De, 353
Veaux/Voe, Mynno (Yerkes) De, 353
Vechten, Gerret Klaasz, 121, 130
Vechten, Hendrick Claesen, 164
Vechten, Lummetje, 130
Vechten/Veghte, Janetie, 164
Vedder, Johannes/John, 274
Veeder, Engeltie, 274
Veeder, Johannas, 274
Veelham, Margaret, 353
Vegten, Michael Van, 164
Vegten, Neeltje Cornelus Van, 164
Velck, Isaac Van, 287
Vensauden, Margaret, 403
Ver Planck, Abigail, 296
Ver Planck, Ariaentje, 296
Ver Planck, Catalyna, 296
Ver Planck, Guleyn, 296
Ver Planck, Hillegond, 45, 296
Ver Planck, Isaac, 296
Ver Planck, Isaaczen, 296
Ver Planck, Jacomyntje, 296
Ver Planck, Susanna, 296
Ver Plancken, Abigail, 45
Verbeau/Wibau, Jeanne, 149
Verdier, Andre, 270
Verdier, Jane (X), 270
Verdier, Mary, 270
Verditty, Mary, 432

Verdity, Theodore, 398
Verdon, Barbara, 48
Verdon, Jacob, 48
Verdon, Mary, 48
Verdon, Mary Thomas (Badye), 48
Vergereau, Pierre/Peter, 79
Verhulst, Jacob, 48
Verkindere, Maria, 41
Verlet, Susannah, 198
Vermeille, Marie, 468
Vermeille/Vermilye, Issac, 278
Vermeille/Vermilye, Jacomina (Jacobs), 278
Vermeille/Vermilye/Vermilyea, Abraham, 468
Vermeille/Vermilye/Vermilyea, Isaac, 468
Vermeille/Vermilye/Vermilyea, Jean, 468
VERMEILLE/VERMILYE/VERMILYEA, Joan/Johannes, 468
Vermeille/Vermilye/Vermilyea, Johannes, 468
Vermeille/Vermilye/Vermilyea, Joost, 468
Vermeille/Vermilye/Vermilyea, Marie, 468
Vermeille/Vermilye/Vermilyea, Rachel, 468
Vermeille/Vermilye/Vermilyea, Rebecca, 468
Vermeulen, Marie, 197
Vermilye, Isaac, 246
Vermilye, Johannes, 246
Vermilye, Maria, 261
Vermilye, Marie, 278, 450
Vermuyden, Cornelius, 145
Vernooy, Coenrad, 308
Vernooy, Cornelis, 308
Vernooy, Cornelis C., 59
Vernooy, Elizabeth, 308
Vernooy, Rachel, 59
Vernooy, Sarah, 308
Vernoy, Celeste/Selitje, 313
Vernoy, Cornelius, 313
Vernoye, Cornelia, 153
Vernoye, Cornelis Cornelissen, 153
Verplanck, Abram Isaacs, 45
Verplanck, Daniel, 132
Verplanck, Guillaume/Gulian, 132
Verplanck, Gulian, 132
Verplanck, Samuel, 132
Verreuil, Madelaine, 455
Verreuil, Madelaine (Prodon), 455
Verreuil, Madeleine (Prudhomme), 114
Verreuil, Madeline/Magdaleine (Prodham/Prudhomme), 195
Verreuil, Moise, 195
Verreuil, Moïse, 114
Verreuil, Moyse, 455
Verrisel, Jacquemine, 458

Verschuer, Magdalena/Helena/Lena, 174
Verschuer, Wouter Gysbertsen, 174
Verton, Marie de, 166
Verton, Salomon de, 166
VERUE(I)L, Moyse/Moïses, 468
Verue(i)l, David, 469
Verue(i)l, Jacques, 469
Verue(i)l, Jean, 469
Verue(i)l, Judith, 469
Verue(i)l, Madelaine, 469
Verue(i)l, Magdelaine, 469
Verue(i)l, Nikolaus, 469
Veruel, Jean, 468
Veruel, Magdelaine (DuFay), 468
VerVeeler, Gideon, 301
Vesqueau, François, 469
VESQUEAU, Jean Philip, 469
Vetter, Jacob, 54
Via, Amer, 354
Via, Margaret, 354
Via/Vias/Viet, Anne, 470
Via/Vias/Viet, James, 470
Via/Vias/Viet, Judith, 470
Via/Vias/Viet, Margaret, 470
Via/Vias/Viet, Mary, 470
Via/Vias/Viet, Nohome, 470
VIA/VIAS/VIET, Pierre Amer, 469
Via/Vias/Viet, Robert, 470
Via/Vias/Viet, Robert, Jr., 470
Via/Vias/Viet, Sarah, 470
Via/Vias/Viet, William, 470
Via/Vias/Viet, William, Jr., 470
Vial, Alexander, **42**
Vial, Jean, **42**
Vial, Susanne (Turquais), **42**
Viaux, Daniel, 341
Vidar, Jean, *143*
Videau, Ann (Cordes), 349
Videau, Elizabeth, 68, 255, 470
Videau, Elizabeth (Mauze), 68
Videau, Henry Joseph, 470
Videau, Jane, 68
Videau, Jane/Jeanne, 470
Videau, Jeanne (Mauzé), 373
Videau, Jeanne Elizabeth, 470
Videau, Jeanne Elizabeth (Mauzé, 373
Videau, Joseph Henry, 349
Videau, Judith, 470
Videau, Madelaine, 470
Videau, Madelaine (Burgaud), 470
Videau, Marianne, 470
Videau, Marthe Ester, 470
Videau, Mary Esther, 349, 470
Videau, Pierre, 68, 373, 470
VIDEAU, Pierre, 470
Videau, Pierre Nicholas, 470
Viele, Jacomyntje/Joan, 273
Viele, Lewis, 273
Viele, Sara, 273
Viervant, Cornelia, 324
Viervant, Cornelis Arentsen, 324

Vigne, Josephine, 189
Vigne, Marguerine de, 189
Vigne, Maria, 45
Vigneau, Elizabeth, 452
VIGNEAU, Elizabeth, 471
Vigneau, Elizabeth (Guion/Guyon), 452
Vigneau, Jean, 452
Vigneaux, Judie (Bouchevreau), 394
Vigneux, Anne, 394
Vigneux, Jean, 394
Vignoles, Charlotte De, 376
Vigreaux, Éloi, 380
Ville, Claudia Antoinia (de Rovereaz), 221
Ville, Georges de, 221
Ville, Marie de, 221
Villeau, Anne, 462
VILLEPONTEUX/VILLEPONTOUX, Pierre, 471
Villeponteux/Villepontoux, Isabel, 471
Villeponteux/Villepontoux, Jane, 471
Villeponteux/Villepontoux, Marie, 471
Villeponteux/Villepontoux, Peter, 471
Villeponteux/Villepontoux, Rachel, 471
Villeponteux/Villepontoux, Zachariah, 471
Villepontoux, Zacharie, 471
VillepontouxMarie (Lentilhac), 471
Villett, Abraham de, 444
Villett, Daniel de, 444
Villett, Élisabeth (Robinet) de, 444
Villett, Elizabeth de, 444
Villett, Jacques, 444
Villett, Jacques de, 444
Villett, Marie de, 444
Villett, Philbert de, 444
Villier, Esther, 462
Villiers, Jean, 28
Villiers, Madeleine, 28
Villiers, Marguerite (Maubon), 28
Villion, Cornelia (Campenar), 147
Villion, François, 147
Villion/Viljeon, Cornelia, 147
Vinage, Susanne De, 329
Vincens, Joachim, 208
Vincens, Marie, 208
Vincent, Abigail (Fowler), 39
Vincent, Anne, 336
Vincent, Elijah, 39
Vincent, Ester/Hester, 135
Vincent, François, 135
Vincent, Hester, 57
Vincent, Jane (Rouse), 109
Vincent, Jean, 135, 336
Vincent, Laury, 467
Vincent, Lewis, 39
Vincent, Mary, 54
Vincent, Susanne (Nuquerque/Newkirk), 336
Vincon, Jacques, **42**
Viriat, Suzanne, 363
Vivian, John, 173

Vivian/ Vivion, Diana, 471
Vivian/Vivion, Charles, 471
Vivian/Vivion, Joel, 472
VIVIAN/VIVION, John, 471
Vivian/Vivion, John II, 471
Vivian/Vivion, Margaret, 471
Vivian/Vivion, Robert, 472
Vivian/Vivion, Thomas, 471
Vivian/Vivion, William, 472
Vivien, Marie, 165
Vivier, Abraham, 148
Vivion, General Thomas, 472
Volckers, Neeltje, 126
Volckerszen, Dirck, 301
Volckertsen, Cornelius, 177
Volckertszen, Dirck, 304
Volge(n), Jannetje Van der, 459
Volgen, Claus Lourens Vander, 205
Volgen, Clausen Vander, 205
Volkerse, Neeltje, 305
Volkertszen, Dirck, 296
Volque, Jacques, 63
Volque, Martine, 63
von Fölkling, Countess X, 314
von Fölkling, Johann Hermann, 314
von Opeynen, Anna Cock, 375
Von Valkenburgh, Christina, 248
Von Wart, John, 353
Von Wart/Work, Maria, 353
Vondel/Fondel, Josse/Justus, 190
Voorde, Joanne van de, 392
Voorde, Pierre van de, 392
Voorhees, Albert Stevense Van, 15
Voorhees, Margrietje Albertse Van, 15
Voorhees, Steven Albertse Van, 15
Voort/Vanderford, Michael Pauluszen Van der, 409
Vosqun, Noël, 250
Vosqun/Vosguin, Marie, 250
Voysine, Margaret, 157
Vreil/Vryl, Judith, 310
Vries, Johannis De, 226
Vroman, Adam, 459
Vroman, Martinus, 459
Vrooman, Engeltie, 459

W

Waal, Jeronimus de, 82
Waddell, Rev. Mr., 365
Wade, Elizabeth, 311
Wade, Hampton, 311
Wade, Henry, 470
Wade, Jane (Ellis), 311
Wade, Joseph, 271
Wade, Robert, 311
Wade. Sarah, 271
Wadsworth, Sarah, 428
Waert, Angenietie Gillis Ten, 278
Waert, Gillis Ten, 278
Waert, Gillis/Jillis Ten, 404

Waert, Jillis Ten, 403
Waert, Margaretta Ten, 392
Waert, Margaretta/Grietje Ten, 278, 403
Wagenen, Jacob Van, 205
Wagenen, Sara Van, 242
Wagener/Van Wagenen, Rebecca, 205
Waggoner, Anna Elizabeth, 72
Wagnen, Jacob Aertsen Van, 242
Wagnen, Sara (Pels) Van, 242
Waite, Return, 297
Wald, Henry, 350
Walde(r)n, Naomi, 164
Walden, Samuel Sr., 147
Waldern, Dorcas (Rice), 164
Waldern, John, 164
Waldron, Aeltie, 246, 468
Waldron, Cornelia, 246
Waldron, Daniel, 439
Waldron, Judith, 439
Waldron, Marytje, 225
Waldron, Rebecca (Hendricks), 468
Waldron, Resolved, 246, 313, 468
Waldron, Ruth, 313
Walker, Ann, 61
Walker, Catherine, 364
Walker, Elizabeth, 33, 320
Walker, Hannah, 207
Walker, James, 364
Walker, Jane (Metcalf), 391
Walker, Judith (Baker), 311
Walker, Lucy, 311
Walker, Martha, 111, 267
Walker, Mary, 355
Walker, Nathaniel, 62
Walker, Obadiah, 267
Walker, Obadiah/Kosick, 111
Walker, Philip, 391
Walker, Rachel, 421
Walker, Sarah, 320, 391
Walker, Thomas, 115, 217
Walker, William, 311
Wall, Judith, 328
Wall, Lucy, 328
Wall, Richard, 328
Wallace, Benjamin, 91
Wallace, Martha, 247
Wallace, Rachel, 99
Wallace, Robert, 247
Wallace, unknown, 90
Waller, Elizabeth, 264
Waller, Elizabeth (Allen), 356
Waller, George, 356
Waller, Jane/Jenny, 356
Waller, Margaret, 427
Waller, William, 264
Waller, Winnifred, 264
Wallin, Jane, 209
Walter, John, 19
Walter, Mary, 209
Walter, Michael, 19
Walter, Thomas, 320

Walters, Jacob, 33
Walters, Priscilla, 33
Walters, unknown, 236
Walthall, Luke, 36
Walthall, Mary, 36
Walthall, William, 36
Wandelier, Sara de, 273
Wanshaer, Jan, 262
Warburton, Joanna, 189
Warburton, John Sir, 189
Warburton, Mary (X), 189
Ward, Jan, 170
Ward, John, 310
Ward, Richard, 255
Warden, Emily, 457
Warfield, unknown, 267
Waring, Edmund, 86
Warner, Dr. Benjamin, 294
Warner, Elizabeth, 428
Warner, Frances, 294
Warren, Elizabeth (X), 337
Warren, Mercy, 139, 287
Warren, Nathaniel, 139, 287
Warren, Peter Sir, 281
Warren, Richard, 337
Warren, Sarah, 337
Warren, Sarah (Walker), 139, 287
Warthen, Rebecca, 114
Washburn, John II, 337
Washburn, unknown, 223
Washington, Augustine Col., 352
Washington, Gen., 80
Washington, Geo., 327
Washington, George, 352
Washington, Martha (Dandridge) Custis, 334
Washington, Samuel, 190
Wasson, Archibald, 405
Wasson, Elizabeth (Woods), 405
Wasson, Jane, 405
Wasson, Sarah, 405
Waterhouse, Richard, 190
Waterman, Abraham, 256
Waterman, Anna (Brown), 256
Waters, Higail, 94
Waters, Mary, 118, 437
Watkins, Elizabeth, 334
Watkins, John, 47
Watkins, Mary, 383
Watkins, Rachel, 131
Watkins, Stephen, 455
Watkins, Thomas, 383
Watson, Agnes, 206
Watson, David, 206
Watson, Elizabeth (Coats/Coatesworth), 85
Watson, Isabella (X), 134
Watson, James, 158, 166, 181
Watson, Joseph, 134
Watson, Sarah (X), 62
Watson, Thomas, 85

Watson, Wilmuth, 158
Watson, X, 16
Watté, Jean, 473
Watté, Marie, 473
Watté, Marie (Verdure), 473
Waugh, Esther, 217
Waugh, Joseph, 356
Waugh, Robert, 239
Way, Elizabeth, 336
Weaver, Daniel, 330
Weaver, Samuel, 116, 233, 330
Weaver, Sarah, 116
Webb, Jacob, 376
Webb, William, 388
Weckman, Maria Elisabeth, 199
Weed, Alice (Clark), 344
Weed, Elizabeth, 344
Weed, John, 344
Weed, Patience, 171
Weedon, John, 158
Weedon, Mary, 158
Weedon, Sarah, 158
Weert, Joachim Van, 416
Weert, Rachgel Van, 416
Weidtmann, Andreas, 252
Weidtmann, Catharina Elisabeth, 252
Weigner, unknown, 34
Weimar, Anne Marie (Harcourt), 325
Weimar, Catherine, 325
Weimer, Anna Maria (Harcourt), 55
Weimer, Maria (de Harcourt), 458
Weinkraus, Johann Valentin, 408
Weinland, Anna E.E., 120
Weinland, Christina, 120
Weisbach, Magdeline, 250
Weiser, Conrad, 439
Weiser, Frederick, 439
Weiss, Catherine, 369
Weiss, Hans Michael, 369
Weisz, Mary, 283
Welch, John, 253
Welch, Rebecca, 253
Wells, Egdezar,, 457
Wells, Elinor, 410
Wells, Elizabeth, 457
Wells, Richard, 338
Wells, Sidney (X), 457
Wemple, Susanna, 274
Wendell, Evert Jansen, 177
Wentworth, Sarah, 354
Wentworth, Thomas, 354
Werckhoven, Cornelis van, 125
Wesco/Wescoe, Elizabeth, 469
Wesco/Wescoe, John, 469
Wesco/Wescoe, Matthias, 469
Wesco/Wescoe, Philip, 469
Wesco/Wescoe, Rosina, 469
Wesco/Wescoe, Susanna, 469
Wessels, Derick, 468
Wessels, Hendrickje, 296
Wessels, Jannetje, 53

Wessels, Metje, 296
West, Edward, 466
West, George, 275
West, Jane (Wing), 125
West, Jerusha, 125
West, John, 125
West, Nathaniel, 334
West, Sarah, 125
Westaway, Mary (X), 237
Westbrook, Jannettje, 106
WesterhoutJeremias Jansen Van, 409
Westfall, Jurian, 106
Weston, Edmund, 139, 287
Weston, Jane (Delano), 287
Weston, Mary, 139, 287
Westphael, Johannes Juriaans, 106
Wetherburn, Henry, 351
Wetzel, John Capt., 72
Wetzel, Nicholas, 72
Weurtz, Jemima, 357
Weyen, Antje Van, 205
Weyen, Hendrick Van, 205
Weygandt, Maria Elizabeth, 391
Weyman, Edward, 81
Weyman, Elizabeth, 81
Weyman, Rebecca (Breintnall), 81
Weymouth/Wainoth, John, 463
Whalley, Elizabeth, 171
Wheeler, "the widow", 239
Wheeler, Aaron, 256
Wheeler, John, 340
Wheeler, Moses, 86, 256
Wheeler, Obadiah, 344
Whilden, John, 156
Whilden, Jonathan, 156
Whilden, Mary, 156
Whipple, Benjamin, 52
Whipple, Ruth (Matthewson), 52
Whiston, Bathsheba, 62
White, Barbara, 433
White, Britton, 125
White, Celia (Page), 137
White, Chapman, 355
White, Charles, 135
White, Elizabeth, 137, 170, 405
White, Elizabeth (Spencer), 64
White, Elizabeth (X), 135
White, Hannah, 172
White, Henry, 137
White, Honora, 69
White, Isaac, 56
White, Jane, 229
White, John, 57, 64
White, Katherine, 282
White, Maragaret (Hoge), 433
White, Mildred/Nilly, 137
White, Robert Dr., 433
White, Sarah, 125
White, Townsend, 412
Whitecotton, Harris, 266
Whitehead, Isaac, 70

Whitehead, Jane, 233
Whitehead, John, 141
Whitehead, Susannah, 70
Whitehurst, unknown, 23
Whitford, Benjamin, 453
Whitledge, Elizabeth, 412
Whitledge, Sybel (Harrison), 412
Whitledge, Thomas, 412
Whitlock, Thomas, 166
Whitney, Samuel, 264
Whitten, Rebecca, 145
Whittenberger, William, 456
Whittingham, Henry, 268
Wibau, Jannetje/Jeanine/Jeanne, 204
Wibau, Toussaint, 204
Wicks, Anne, 225
Wiemer, unknown, 241
Wilcox, Damsel, 161
Wilcox, Daniel, 161
Wilcox, Margaret, 161
Wilder, Edward, 297
Wilder, Elizabeth (Eames), 297
Wilder, James, 338
Wilder, Mary, 297
Wilder, Sarah (Yopp), 338
Wilder, Spencer Capt., 338
Wiles, George, 96
Wiles, Margaretta, 96
Wilford, Mary, 124
Wilkenhof (Thyssen), Jannekan Van, 439
Wilkins, Elizabeth (Woodward), 289
Wilkins, John, 49
Wilkins, William, 289
Wilkinson, Sarah, 116
Willams, Jannetje, 48
WILLEME/WILLAN/WILLIAM, Aventure, 473
Willeme/Willan/William, Daniel, 473
Willeme/Willan/William, Jean, 473
Willeme/Willan/William, Marie, 473
Willems, Aeche, 301
Willems, Geertje, 169
Willems/Villeman, Lea/Lydia, 126
Willemse, Annetje, 225
Willemse, Frederick, 225
William III of England, 16
William of Orange, 16, 303, 426
William Prince of Orange, 121
William the Silent, 328
William, Offill/Offall, 429
Williams, Anna (Richardson), 79
Williams, Anne, 225
Williams, Anne (Whitley), 265
Williams, Arthur, 79
Williams, Catherine, 79
Williams, Catherine Read, 368
Williams, Dorcas (Stafford), 223
Williams, Dorothy, 24
Williams, Elizabeth, 24, 367
Williams, Helena, 81
Williams, Henry, 93

Williams, John, 265, 454
Williams, Lucy, 26
Williams, Ludwick, 24
Williams, Mary, 334
Williams, Mary (X), 247
Williams, Paul, 247
Williams, Phebe, 302
Williams, Polly (Young), 340
Williams, Roger, 52
Williams, Sarah (X), 367
Williams, Susan, 323
Williams, Tabitha, 134
Williams, unknown, 223
Williams, Welthian (Sheldon), 454
Williams, William, 276, 367
Williams, Winifred, 200
Williamson, Ann (Underwood), 429
Williamson, James, 429
Williamson, Mary, 429
Williamson, unknown, 119
Williamzen, Abraham, 333
Williford, Elizabeth, 286
Willingham, Amy, 166
Willis, Elizabeth, 302
Willis, George, 302
Willis, James, 277
Willis, Jane, 248
Willis, unknown, 380
Wilmont, Ann (X), 70
Wilmore, Judith, 362
Wilmot, Ann, 70
Wilmot, Benjamin, 70
Wilmot, Mary (Brown), 282
Wilsea, Mary, 353
Wilson, Algernon, 188
Wilson, Elias, 88
Wilson, Elizabeth, 88
Wilson, Henay, 23
Wilson, Honour, 385
Wilson, James, 23
Wilson, Joseph, 276
Wilson, Mary, 218
Wilson, Richard, 147
Wilson, Sarah, 23, 188, 276
Wilson, William, 92
Wilson, Winfred, 23
Wiltse, Hendrick Martensen, 170
Wiltsee, Hendrick, 95
Wiltsee, Martensen, 95
Wiltsee, Myndert, 95
Wiltsie, Jannetje, 170
Winans, John, 360
Winborn, Susannah, 104
Winborn, Thomas, 104
WINCART, Nicolas, 202
Winckell, Jacob Wallings Van, *142*
Windham, Patience, 69
Windham, William, 196
Wines, Ann, 336
Wing, Sarah, 125
Winkle, Jacob Van, 15

Winkle, John Van, 15
Winkle, Simon Jacobson Van, 15
Winkle, Simon Van, 15
Winkle, SusannahVan, 15
Winn, John, 266
Winslow, Mary, 91
Winsmore, Ann, 300
Winsmore, Robert Dr., 300
Winston, Isaac, 22
Winston, Isaac Sr., 21
Winston, Lucy, 22
Winston, William, 21
Winter, Deborah (Golt), 311
Winter, Edward, 311
Winter, Hannah, 311
Winter, Obadias, 169
Wise, Magdalen (Acton), 79
Witherston, John, 388
Witt, Deborah/Diewertje De, 126
Witt, Emerentje De, 130
Witt, Taatje De, 153
Witter, Thomas, 343
Woert, Marten Van, 296
Woglum, Mary Van, 159
Woglum, Peter Van Capt., 159
Wolf, Elizabeth Deitrich, 60
Wolfertsen, Peter, 177
Wood, Elizabeth (Merriam), 267
Wood, Isaac, 267
Wood, John, 24
Wood, Joseph III, 433
Wood, Judith, 229
Wood, Phoebe, 280
Wood, Sarah (Lane), 293
Wood, Stephen, 293
Wood, Susanna, 57
Wood, unknown, 366
Woodbury, Hannah (Haskell), 311
Woodbury, William, 311
Woodhull, Ann, 454
Woodhull, Ruth, 53
Woodmansee, Margaret, 125
Woodroof, Dorothy (Digges), 173
Woodroof, Wiatt, 173
Woodson, Ann, 181
Woodson, Ann (Smith), 361
Woodson, John, 181
Woodson, Judith, 361
Woodson, Mary, 311
Woodson, Mary (Miller), 181
Woodson, Matthew, 326
Woodson, Richard, 361, 362
Woodson, Sally, 335
Woodson, Sanborn, 362
Woodward, Martha, 334
Woodward, William, 334
Wooldridge, John, 455
Wooldridge, Marie/Mary, 455
Wooldridge, Martha (X), 455
Woolley, Elizabeth, 447
Woortman, Catherine, 302

Woortman, Teunis, 302
Wootten, Benjamin, 427
Worley, Christian, 13
Wormall, Hester, 62
Wormeth, Catherine Remy, 411
Wornall, Joseph, 62
Worsham, Martha Branch, 355
Wortman, Dennis, 182
Wortman, Margaret, 370
Wragg, Elizabeth, 343
Wragg, Joseph, 343, 373
Wragg, Judith (Rothmahler), 373
Wragg, Samuel, 373
Wright, John, 221
Wright, Richard, 337
Wright, Sarah, 461
Wright, William, 294
Wulff, Christine Louise, 329
Wulff, Friedrich, 329
Wulff, Sophie (Ziethen), 329
Wyatt, John, 266
Wyckoff, Claes Pieterse, 366
Wyckoff, Pieter Claesen, 366
Wynants, Antje, 48
Wyncoop, Annetje, 464
Wyncoop, Cornelius, 169
Wyncoop, Gerritt, 464
Wyncoop, Maria, 169
Wyncoop, Maria (Langedyck), 169
Wyngaart, Elizabeth, 136
Wyngaart, Johannes, 136

X

Xavier, Maria de Azpilicueta y, 474
Xavier, St. Francis de, 474
Xavier/ Sevier, Charles, 474
Xavier/ Sevier, Valentine, 474
Xavier/Sevier, Abraham, 474
Xavier/Sevier, Bethenia, 474
Xavier/Sevier, Catherine, 474
Xavier/Sevier, Elizabeth, 474
XAVIER/SEVIER, Jean/John, 474
Xavier/Sevier, John, 474
Xavier/Sevier, Joseph, 474
Xavier/Sevier, Mary/Polly, 474
Xavier/Sevier, Robert, 474
Xavier/Sevier, Sophia, 474
Xavier/Sevier, Valentine, 474
Xavier/Sevier, William, 474

Y

Yancey, Robert, 162
Yarbrough, Henry, 146
Yarbrough, James, 146
Yard, Mary, 344
Yard, Mary (X), 344
Yard, William, 344
Yates, Marshall, 174
Yeager, Barbara, 249

Yerion, Christine, 19
Yerkes, Adaline, 353
Yerxa, Engeltie (Storm), 81
Yeverdon, Judith d', 222
Yocum, Charles, 446
Young, Archibald, 442
Young, Benjamin, 91
Young, Elizabeth, 57
Young, Frances, 405
Young, Gary E., 112
Young, James, 405
Young, Jane, 91
Young, John, 191

Young, Lucy (Ragsdale), 100
Young, unknown, 326
Youngs, John Rev., 282
Youngs, Martha, 282
Youst, Mary Anna, 60
Ysselsteyn, Geertje, 313
Ysselsteyn/Esselsteyn, Martin Cornelisz, 313

Z

Zabriskie, Albert, 172
Zabriskie, John, 172

Zabriskie, Machtelt (Vanderlinda), 172
Zant, Abigail Van, 426
Zebry, Marie de, 160
Zeller (Sallière), Jacques, 438
Ziegenfuss, Adam, 204
Ziegenfuss, Catherine, 204
Ziegenfuss, Catherine (X), 204
Zimmerman, Jacob, 140
Zimmerman, Sebastian, 325
Zuck, John, 418
Zwilt/Gwilt, unknown, 385

CPSIA information can be obtained
at www.ICGtesting.com
Printed in the USA
BVHW07s0919190918
527933BV00024B/1121/P